GARDNER'S
ART through the AGES

GARDNER'S

Volume II

ART through the AGES

THE WESTERN PERSPECTIVE

FRED S. KLEINER

FOURTEENTH EDITION

WADSWORTH
CENGAGE Learning

Australia • Brazil • Japan • Korea • Mexico • Singapore • Spain • United Kingdom • United States

WADSWORTH
CENGAGE Learning

Gardner's Art through the Ages:
The Western Perspective, Fourteenth Edition, Volume II
Fred S. Kleiner

Publisher: Clark Baxter

Senior Development Editor: Sharon Adams Poore

Assistant Editor: Ashley Bargende

Editorial Assistant: Marsha Kaplan

Brand Manager: Lydia LeStar

Executive Marketing Communications Manager:
Jason LaChapelle

Senior Content Project Manager: Lianne Ames

Senior Art Director: Cate Rickard Barr

Print Buyer: Sandee Milewski

Senior Rights Acquisition Specialist: Mandy Groszko

Production Service & Layout: Joan Keyes, Dovetail
Publishing Services

Text and Cover Designer: tani hasegawa

Cover Image: SANDRO BOTTICELLI, *Primavera,* ca. 1482. Tempera
on wood, 6′ 8″ × 10′ 4″. Galleria degli Uffizi, Florence, Italy.
Credit: © Scala/Art Resource, NY

Compositor: Thompson Type

For product information and technology assistance, contact us at
Cengage Learning Customer & Sales Support, 1-800-354-9706

For permission to use material from this text or product,
submit all requests online at **www.cengage.com/permissions.**
Further permissions questions can be emailed to
permissionrequest@cengage.com.

Library of Congress Control Number: 2012942247

Student Edition, Volume II:
ISBN-13: 978-1-133-95480-4
ISBN-10: 1-133-95480-4

Wadsworth
20 Channel Center Street
Boston, MA 02210
USA

Cengage Learning is a leading provider of customized learning
solutions with office locations around the globe, including Singapore,
the United Kingdom, Australia, Mexico, Brazil and Japan. Locate your
local office at **international.cengage.com/region**

Cengage Learning products are represented in Canada by Nelson
Education, Ltd.

For your course and learning solutions, visit **www.cengage.com.**
Purchase any of our products at your local college store or at our
preferred online store **www.cengagebrain.com.**

Instructors: Please visit **login.cengage.com** and log in to access
instructor-specific resources.

Printed in the United States of America
1 2 3 4 5 6 7 16 15 14 13 12

SANDRO BOTTICELLI, *Primavera*, ca. 1482. Tempera on wood, 6′ 8″ × 10′ 4″. Galleria degli Uffizi, Florence, Italy.

The Medici of Florence have become synonymous with the extraordinary cultural phenomenon called the Italian Renaissance. The work of one of their favorite painters, SANDRO BOTTICELLI (1444–1510), is a testament to the intense interest that the Medici had in the art, literature, and mythology of the Greco-Roman world.

Botticelli painted *Primavera* (*Spring*) for Lorenzo di Pierfrancesco de' Medici (1463–1503). Venus, the goddess of love, stands just to the right of center with her son Cupid hovering above her head. To the left are the dancing Three Graces. Although based closely on ancient prototypes, they are clothed instead of nude, albeit in thin, transparent garments. At the right, the blue ice-cold Zephyrus, the west wind, is about to carry off and marry the nymph Chloris, whom he transforms into Flora, goddess of spring, appropriately shown wearing a rich floral gown. At the far left, Mercury reaches up, perhaps to dispel storm clouds. The sensuality of the representation, the appearance of Venus in springtime, and the abduction and marriage of Chloris all suggest the occasion for the painting was Lorenzo's wedding in May 1482. But the painting also sums up the Renaissance view that earthly love is compatible with Christian theology: Venus as the source of love provokes desire through Cupid. Desire can lead either to lust and violence (Zephyr) or, through reason and faith (Mercury), to the love of God.

That we know Botticelli's name and details of his career is not surprising, because it was during the Renaissance that the modern notion of individual artistic genius took root. But in many periods of the history of art, artists toiled in anonymity to fulfill the wishes of their patrons, whether Egyptian pharaohs, Roman emperors, or medieval monks. *Art through the Ages: The Western Perspective* surveys the art of all periods of Western art from prehistory to the present and examines how artworks of all kinds have always reflected the historical contexts in which they were created.

BRIEF CONTENTS

CONTENTS

ix

PREFACE

THE GARDNER LEGACY IN THE 21ST CENTURY

I take great pleasure in introducing the extensively revised and expanded 14th edition of *Gardner's Art through the Ages: The Western Perspective*, which, like the enhanced 13th edition, is a hybrid art history textbook—the first, and still the only, introductory survey of the history of art of its kind. This innovative new kind of "Gardner" retains all of the best features of traditional books on paper while harnessing 21st-century technology to increase by 25% the number of works examined—without increasing the size or weight of the book itself and at very low additional cost to students compared to a larger book.

When Helen Gardner published the first edition of *Art through the Ages* in 1926, she could not have imagined that more than 85 years later instructors all over the world would still be using her textbook in their classrooms. Indeed, if she were alive today, she would not recognize the book that, even in its traditional form, long ago became—and remains—the most widely read introduction to the history of art and architecture in the English language. During the past half-century, successive authors have constantly reinvented Helen Gardner's groundbreaking survey, always keeping it fresh and current, and setting an ever-higher standard with each new edition. I am deeply gratified that both professors and students seem to agree that the 13th edition, released in 2008, lived up to that venerable tradition, for they made it the number-one choice for art history survey courses. I hope they will find the 14th edition of this best-selling book exceeds their high expectations.

In addition to the host of new features (enumerated below) in the book proper, the 14th edition follows the enhanced 13th edition in incorporating an innovative new online component. All new copies of the 14th edition are packaged with an access code to a web site with *Bonus Essays* and *Bonus Images* (with zoom capability) of more than 250 additional important paintings, sculptures, buildings, and other art forms of all eras, from prehistory to the present. The selection includes virtually all of the works professors have told me they wished had been in the 13th edition, but were not included for lack of space. I am extremely grateful to Cengage Learning/Wadsworth for the considerable investment of time and resources that has made this remarkable hybrid textbook possible.

In contrast to the enhanced 13th edition, the online component is now fully integrated into the 14th edition. Every one of the more than 250 bonus images is cited in the text of the traditional book and a thumbnail image of each work, with abbreviated caption, is inset into the text column where the work is mentioned. The integration extends also to the maps, index, glossary, and chapter summaries, which seamlessly merge the printed and online information. The 14th edition is in every way a unified, comprehensive history of art and architecture, even though the text is divided into paper and digital components.

KEY FEATURES OF THE 14TH EDITION

In this new edition, I have added several important features while retaining the basic format and scope of the previous edition. Once again, the hybrid Gardner boasts roughly 1,400 photographs, plans, and drawings, nearly all in color and reproduced according to the highest standards of clarity and color fidelity, including hundreds of new images. Among them is a new series of superb photos taken by Jonathan Poore exclusively for *Art through the Ages* during three photographic campaigns in France and Italy in 2009, 2010, and 2011. The online component also includes custom videos made at each site by Sharon Adams Poore. This extraordinary new archive of visual material ranges from ancient Roman ruins in southern France to Romanesque and Gothic churches in France and Tuscany to Le Corbusier's modernist chapel at Ronchamp and the postmodern Pompidou Center and the Louvre Pyramid in Paris. The 14th edition also features the highly acclaimed architectural drawings of John Burge. Together, these exclusive photographs, videos, and drawings provide readers with a visual feast unavailable anywhere else.

The captions accompanying those illustrations contain, as before, a wealth of information, including the name of the artist or architect, if known; the formal title (printed in italics), if assigned, description of the work, or name of the building; the provenance or place of production of the object or location of the building; the date; the material(s) used; the size; and the present location if the work is in a museum or private collection. Scales accompany not only all architectural plans, as is the norm, but also appear next to each photograph of a painting, statue, or other artwork—another unique feature of the Gardner text. The works discussed in the 14th edition of *Art through the Ages* vary enormously in size, from colossal sculptures carved into mountain cliffs and paintings covering entire walls or ceilings to tiny figurines, coins, and jewelry that one can hold in the hand. Although the captions contain the pertinent dimensions, it is difficult for students who have never seen the paintings or statues in person to translate those dimensions into an appreciation of the real size of the objects. The scales provide an effective and direct way to visualize how big or how small a given artwork is and its relative size compared with other works in the same chapter and throughout the book.

Also retained in this edition are the *Quick-Review Captions* introduced in the 13th edition. Students have overwhelmingly reported that they found these brief synopses of the most significant aspects of each artwork or building illustrated invaluable when preparing for examinations. These extended captions accompany not only every image in the printed book but also all the digital images in the online supplement. Another popular tool introduced in the 13th edition to aid students in reviewing and mastering the material reappears in the 14th edition. Each chapter ends with a full-page feature called *The Big Picture*, which sets forth in bullet-point format the most important characteristics of each period or artistic movement discussed in the chapter. Small illustrations of characteristic works accompany the summary of major points. The 14th edition, however, introduces two new features in every chapter: a *Timeline* summarizing the major developments during the era treated (again in bullet-point format for easy review) and a chapter-opening essay on a characteristic painting, sculpture, or building. Called *Framing the Era*, these in-depth essays are accompanied by a general view and four enlarged details of the work discussed.

The 14th edition of *Art through the Ages* is available in several different traditional paper formats—a single hardcover volume; two paperback volumes designed for use in the fall and spring semesters of a yearlong survey course; a four-volume "backpack" set; and an interactive e-book version. Another pedagogical tool not found in any other introductory art history textbook is the *Before 1300* section that appears at the beginning of the second volume of the paperbound version of the book and at the beginning of Book D of the backpack edition. Because many students taking the second half of a survey course will not have access to Volume I or to Books A and B, I have provided a special set of concise primers on architectural terminology and construction methods in the ancient and medieval eras, and on mythology and religion—information that is essential for understanding the history of Western art after 1300. The subjects of these special boxes are Greco-Roman Temple Design and the Classical Orders; Arches and Vaults; Basilican Churches; Central-Plan Churches; The Gods and Goddesses of Mount Olympus; and The Life of Jesus in Art.

Boxed essays once again appear throughout the book as well. This popular feature first appeared in the 11th edition of *Art through the Ages,* which in 2001 won both the Texty and McGuffey Prizes of the Text and Academic Authors Association for a college textbook in the humanities and social sciences. In this edition the essays are more closely tied to the main text than ever before. Consistent with that greater integration, almost all boxes now incorporate photographs of important artworks discussed in the text proper that also illustrate the theme treated in the boxed essays. These essays fall under six broad categories:

Architectural Basics boxes provide students with a sound foundation for the understanding of architecture. These discussions are concise explanations, with drawings and diagrams, of the major aspects of design and construction. The information included is essential to an understanding of architectural technology and terminology. The boxes address questions of how and why various forms developed, the problems architects confronted, and the solutions they used to resolve them. Topics discussed include how the Egyptians built the pyramids; the orders of classical architecture; Roman concrete construction; and the design and terminology of mosques and Gothic cathedrals.

Materials and Techniques essays explain the various media artists employed from prehistoric to modern times. Since materials and techniques often influence the character of artworks, these discussions contain essential information on why many monuments appear as they do. Hollow-casting bronze statues; fresco painting; Islamic tilework; embroidery and tapestry; engraving, etching, and lithography; and daguerreotype and calotype photography are among the many subjects treated.

Religion and Mythology boxes introduce students to the principal elements of the world's great religions, past and present, and to the representation of religious and mythological themes in painting and sculpture of all periods and places. These discussions of belief systems and iconography give readers a richer understanding of some of the greatest artworks ever created. The topics include the gods and goddesses of Egypt, Mesopotamia, Greece, and Rome; the life of Jesus in art; Muhammad and Islam; and medieval monasteries and Benedictine rule.

Art and Society essays treat the historical, social, political, cultural, and religious context of art and architecture. In some instances, specific monuments are the basis for a discussion of broader themes, as when the Hegeso stele serves as the springboard for an exploration of the role of women in ancient Greek society. Another essay discusses how people's evaluation today of artworks can differ from those of the society that produced them by examining the problems created by the contemporary market for undocumented archaeological finds. Other subjects include Egyptian mummification; Etruscan women; Byzantine icons and iconoclasm; artistic training in Renaissance Italy; 19th-century academic salons and independent art exhibitions; primitivism and colonialism; and public funding of controversial art.

Written Sources present and discuss key historical documents illuminating important monuments of art and architecture throughout the world. The passages quoted permit voices from the past to speak directly to the reader, providing vivid and unique insights into the creation of artworks in all media. Examples include Bernard of Clairvaux's treatise on sculpture in medieval churches; Giovanni Pietro Bellori's biographies of Annibale Carracci and Caravaggio; Jean François Marmontel's account of 18th-century salon culture; as well as texts that bring the past to life, such as eyewitness accounts of the volcanic eruption that buried Roman Pompeii and of the fire that destroyed Canterbury Cathedral in medieval England.

Finally, in the *Artists on Art* boxes, artists and architects throughout history discuss both their theories and individual works. Examples include Sinan the Great discussing the mosque he designed for Selim II; Leonardo da Vinci and Michelangelo debating the relative merits of painting and sculpture; Artemisia Gentileschi talking about the special problems she confronted as a woman artist; Jacques-Louis David on Neoclassicism; Gustave Courbet on Realism; Henri Matisse on color; Pablo Picasso on Cubism; Diego Rivera on art for the people; and Judy Chicago on her seminal work *The Dinner Party.*

In every new edition of *Art through the Ages,* I also reevaluate the basic organization of the book. In the 14th edition, the treatment of the art of the later 20th century and the opening decade of the 21st century has been significantly reconfigured. There are now separate chapters on the art and architecture of the period from 1945 to 1980 and from 1980 to the present. Moreover, the second chapter (Chapter 26, "Contemporary Art Worldwide") is no longer confined to Western art but presents the art and architecture of the past three decades as a multifaceted global phenomenon. Furthermore, some chapters now appear in more than one of the paperbound versions of the book in order to provide enhanced flexibility to instructors who divide the global history of art into two or three semester-long courses. Chapter 14—on Italian art from 1200 to 1400—appears in both Volumes I and II and in backpack Books B and D.

Rounding out the features in the book itself is a greatly expanded Bibliography of books in English with several hundred new entries, including both general works and a chapter-by-chapter list of more focused studies; a Glossary containing definitions of all italicized terms introduced in both the printed and online texts; and, for the first time, a complete museum index listing all illustrated artworks by their present location.

The 14th edition of *Art through the Ages* also features a host of state-of-the-art online resources (enumerated on page xxi).

WRITING AND TEACHING THE HISTORY OF ART

Nonetheless, some things have not changed in this new edition, including the fundamental belief that guided Helen Gardner so many years ago—that the primary goal of an introductory art history textbook should be to foster an appreciation and understanding of historically significant works of art of all kinds from all periods. Because of the longevity and diversity of the history of art, it is tempting to assign responsibility for telling its story to a large team of specialists. The original publisher of *Art through the Ages* took this approach for the first edition prepared after Helen Gardner's death, and it has now become the norm for introductory art history surveys. But students overwhelmingly say the very complexity of the history of art makes it all the more important for the story to be told with a consistent voice if they are to master so much diverse material. I think Helen Gardner would be pleased to know that *Art through the Ages* once again has a single storyteller—aided in no small part by invaluable advice from more than a hundred reviewers and other consultants whose assistance I gladly acknowledge at the end of this Preface.

I continue to believe that the most effective way to tell the story of art through the ages, especially to anyone studying art history for the first time, is to organize the vast array of artistic monuments according to the civilizations that produced them and to consider each work in roughly chronological order. This approach has not merely stood the test of time. It is the most appropriate way to narrate the *history* of art. The principle underlying my approach to every period of art history is that the enormous variation in the form and meaning of the paintings, sculptures, buildings, and other artworks men and women have produced over the past 30,000 years is largely the result of the constantly changing contexts in which artists and architects worked. A historically based narrative is therefore best suited for a comprehensive history of Western art because it enables the author to situate each work discussed in its historical, social, economic, religious, and cultural context. That is, after all, what distinguishes art history from art appreciation.

In the 1926 edition of *Art through the Ages,* Helen Gardner discussed Henri Matisse and Pablo Picasso in a chapter entitled "Contemporary Art in Europe and America." Since then many other artists have emerged on the international scene, and the story of art through the ages has grown longer and even more complex. As already noted, that is reflected in the addition of a new chapter at the end of the book on contemporary art in which developments on all continents are treated together for the first time. Perhaps even more important than the new directions artists and architects have taken during the past several decades is that the discipline of art history has also changed markedly—and so too has Helen Gardner's book. The 14th edition fully reflects the latest art historical research emphases while maintaining the traditional strengths that have made previous editions of *Art through the Ages* so popular. While sustaining attention to style, chronology, iconography, and technique, I also ensure that issues of patronage, function, and context loom large in every chapter. I treat artworks not as isolated objects in sterile 21st-century museum settings but with a view toward their purpose and meaning in the society that produced them at the time they were produced. I examine not only the role of the artist or architect in the creation of a work of art or a building, but also the role of the individuals or groups who paid the artists and influenced the shape the monuments took. Further, in this expanded hybrid edition, I devote more space than ever before to the role of women and women artists in Western societies over time. In every chapter, I have tried to choose artworks and buildings that reflect the increasingly wide range of interests of scholars today, while not rejecting the traditional list of "great" works or the very notion of a "canon." Indeed, the expanded hybrid nature of the 14th edition has made it possible to illustrate and discuss scores of works not traditionally treated in art history survey texts without reducing the space devoted to canonical works.

CHAPTER-BY-CHAPTER CHANGES IN THE 14TH EDITION

All chapters feature many new photographs, revised maps, revised Big Picture chapter-ending summaries, and changes to the text reflecting new research and discoveries.

Introduction: What is Art History? New painting by Ogata Korin added.

14: Late Medieval Italy. New Framing the Era essay "Late Medieval or Proto-Renaissance?" and new timeline. New series of photos of architecture and sculpture in Florence, Orvieto, Pisa, and Siena. Andrea Pisano Baptistery doors added.

15: Late Medieval and Early Renaissance Northern Europe. New Framing the Era essay "The Virgin in a Flemish Home" and new timeline. New section of the *Nuremberg Chronicle* illustrated. Diptych of Martin van Nieuwenhove added.

16: The Renaissance in Quattrocento Italy. New Framing the Era essay "Medici Patronage and Classical Learning" and new timeline. Expanded discussion of Botticelli and Neo-Platonism. Revised boxes on linear and atmospheric perspective and on Cennino Cennini. Tomb of Leonardo Bruni and *Resurrection* by Piero della Francesca added.

17: Renaissance and Mannerism in Cinquecento Italy. New Framing the Era essay "Michelangelo in the Service of Julius II" and new timeline. Michelangelo's late *Pietà* and Parmigianino's self-portrait added. Revised box on "Palma il Giovane and Titian." Series of new photos of Florence, Rome, and Venice.

18: High Renaissance and Mannerism in Northern Europe and Spain. New Framing the Era essay "Earthly Delights in the Netherlands" and new timeline. Dürer's self-portrait and *Melencolia I* and El Greco's *View of Toledo* added.

19: The Baroque in Italy and Spain. New Framing the Era essay "Baroque Art and Spectacle" and new timeline. Bernini's Four Rivers Fountain and Gentileschi's self-portrait added.

20: The Baroque in Northern Europe. New Framing the Era essay "Still-Life Painting in the Dutch Republic" and new timeline. Expanded discussion of Dutch mercantilism. Vermeer's *Woman Holding a Balance* added.

21: Rococo to Neoclassicism: The 18th Century in Europe and America. New Framing the Era essay "Art and Science in the Era of Enlightenment" and new timeline. Expanded discussion of Diderot as art critic. Adelaide Labille-Guiard added.

22: Romanticism, Realism, Photography: Europe & America, 1800 to 1870. New Framing the Era essay "Napoleon at Jaffa" and new timeline. Friedrich's *Wanderer above a Sea of Mist* and Altes Museum, Berlin, added.

23: Impressionism, Post-Impressionism, Symbolism: Europe and America, 1870 to 1900. New Framing the Era essay "Impressions of Modern Life" and new timeline. New discussion of Manet and Monet. Rodin's *Gates of Hell* and James Ensor added.

24: Modernism in Europe and America, 1900 to 1945. New Framing the Era essay "Global War, Anarchy, and Dada" and new timeline. New box on "Walter Gropius and the Bauhaus." Grosz's *Eclipse of the Sun,* de Chirico's *Song of Love,* Arthur Dove, Egon Schiele, Adolf Loos, and Margaret Bourke-White added.

25: Modernism and Postmodernism in Europe and America, 1945 to 1980. Former 1945–Present chapter significantly expanded and divided into two chapters. New Framing the Era essay "Art and Consumer Culture" and new timeline. Arshile Gorky, Lee Krasner, Franz Kline, Robert Motherwell, Joan Mitchell, Bridget Riley, Isamu Noguchi, George Segal, Niki de Saint-Phalle, Lucian Freud, Diane Arbus, Minor White, and Vanna Venturi house added.

26: Contemporary Art Worldwide. Former 1945–Present chapter significantly expanded and divided into two chapters. This chapter also now includes contemporary non-Western art. New Framing the Era essay "Art as Socio-Political Message" and new timeline. Robert Mapplethorpe, Shahzia Sikander, Carrie Mae Weems, Jean-Michel Basquiat, Kehinde Wiley, Shirin Neshat, Edward Burtynksy, Wu Guanzhong, Emily Kame Kngwarreye, Tara Donovan, Jenny Saville, Marisol, Rachel Whiteread, Andy Goldsworthy, Keith Haring, Andreas Gursky, Zaha Hadid, I.M. Pei, Daniel Libeskind, and green architecture added.

Go to the online instructor companion site or PowerLecture for a more detailed list of chapter-by-chapter changes and the Image Transition Guide.

ACKNOWLEDGMENTS

A work as extensive as a history of Western art and architecture from prehistory to the present could not be undertaken or completed without the counsel of experts in all eras. As with previous editions, Cengage Learning/Wadsworth has enlisted more than a hundred art historians to review every chapter of *Art through the Ages* in order to ensure that the text lives up to the Gardner reputation for accuracy as well as readability. I take great pleasure in acknowledging here the important contributions to the 14th edition made by the following: Michael Jay Adamek, Ozarks Technical Community College; Charles M. Adelman, University of Northern Iowa; Christine Zitrides Atiyeh, Kutztown University; Gisele Atterberry, Joliet Junior College; Roann Barris, Radford University; Philip Betancourt, Temple University; Karen Blough, SUNY Plattsburgh; Elena N. Boeck, DePaul University; Betty Ann Brown, California State University Northridge; Alexandra A. Carpino, Northern Arizona University; Anne Walke Cassidy, Carthage College; Harold D. Cole, Baldwin Wallace College; Sarah Cormack, Webster University, Vienna; Jodi Cranston, Boston University; Nancy de Grummond, Florida State University; Kelley Helmstutler Di Dio, University of Vermont; Owen Doonan, California State University Northridge; Marilyn Dunn, Loyola University Chicago; Tom Estlack, Pittsburgh Cultural Trust; Lois Fichner-Rathus, The College of New Jersey; Arne R. Flaten, Coastal Carolina University; Ken Friedman, Swinburne University of Technology; Rosemary Gallick, Northern Virginia Community College; William V. Ganis, Wells College; Marc Gerstein, University of Toledo; Clive F. Getty, Miami University; Michael Grillo, University of Maine; Amanda Hamilton, Northwest Nazarene University; Martina Hesser, Grossmont College; Heather Jensen, Brigham Young University; Mark Johnson, Brigham Young University; Jacqueline E. Jung, Yale University; John F. Kenfield, Rutgers University; Asen Kirin, University of Georgia; Joanne Klein, Boise State University; Yu Bong Ko, Tappan Zee High School; Rob Leith, Buckingham Browne & Nichols School; Adele H. Lewis, Arizona State University; Kate Alexandra Lingley, University of Hawaii–Manoa; Ellen Longsworth, Merrimack College; Matthew Looper, California State University–Chico; Nuria Lledó Tarradell, Universidad Complutense, Madrid; Anne McClanan, Portland State University; Mark Magleby, Brigham Young University; Gina Miceli-Hoffman, Moraine Valley Community College; William Mierse, University of Vermont; Amy Morris, Southeastern Louisiana University; Charles R. Morscheck, Drexel University; Johanna D. Movassat, San Jose State University; Carola Naumer, Truckee Meadows Community College; Irene Nero, Southeastern Louisiana University; Robin O'Bryan, Harrisburg Area Community College; Laurent Odde, Kutztown University of Pennsylvania; E. Suzanne Owens, Lorain County Community College; Catherine Pagani, The University of Alabama; Martha Peacock, Brigham Young University; Mabi Ponce de Leon, Bexley High School; Curtis Runnels, Boston University; Malia E. F. Serrano, Grossmont College; Molly Skjei, Normandale Community College; James Swensen, Brigham Young University; John Szostak, University of Hawaii–Manoa; Fred T. Smith, Kent State University; Thomas F. Strasser, Providence College; Katherine H. Tachau, University of Iowa; Debra Thompson, Glendale Community College; Alice Y. Tseng, Boston University; Carol Ventura, Tennessee Technological University; Marc Vincent, Baldwin Wallace College; Deborah Waite, University of Hawaii–Manoa; Lawrence Waldron, Saint John's University; Victoria Weaver, Millersville University; and Margaret Ann Zaho, University of Central Florida.

I am especially indebted to the following for creating the instructor and student materials for the 14th edition: William J. Allen, Arkansas State University; Ivy Cooper, Southern Illinois University Edwardsville; Patricia D. Cosper, The University of Alabama at Birmingham; Anne McClanan, Portland State University; and Amy M. Morris, Southeastern Louisiana University. I also thank the members of the Wadsworth Media Advisory Board for their input: Frances Altvater, University of Hartford; Roann Barris, Radford University; Bill Christy, Ohio University-Zanesville; Annette Cohen, Great Bay Community College; Jeff Davis, The Art Institute of Pittsburgh–Online Division; Owen Doonan, California State University-Northridge; Arne R. Flaten, Coastal Carolina University; Carol Heft, Muhlenberg College; William Mierse, University of Vermont; Eleanor F. Moseman, Colorado State University; and Malia E. F. Serrano, Grossmont College.

I am also happy to have this opportunity to express my gratitude to the extraordinary group of people at Cengage Learning/Wadsworth involved with the editing, production, and distribution of *Art through the Ages*. Some of them I have now worked with on various projects for nearly two decades and feel privileged to count among my friends. The success of the Gardner series in all of its various permutations depends in no small part on the expertise and unflagging commitment of these dedicated professionals, especially Clark Baxter, publisher; Sharon Adams Poore, senior development editor (as well as videographer extraordinaire); Lianne Ames, senior content project manager; Mandy Groszko, rights acquisitions specialist; Robert White, product manager; Ashley Bargende, assistant editor; Marsha Kaplan, editorial assistant; Amy Bither and Jessica Jackson, editorial interns; Cate Rickard Barr, senior art director; Lydia LeStar, brand manager; Jason LaChapelle, executive marketing communications manager; and the incomparable group of local sales representatives who have passed on to me the welcome advice offered by the hundreds of instructors they speak to daily during their visits to college campuses throughout North America.

I am also deeply grateful to the following out-of-house contributors to the 14th edition: the peerless and tireless Joan Keyes, Dovetail Publishing Services; Helen Triller-Yambert, development editor; Ida May Norton, copy editor; Do Mi Stauber, indexer; Susan Gall, proofreader; tani hasegawa, designer; Catherine Schnurr, Mary-Lise Nazaire, Lauren McFalls, and Corey Geissler, PreMediaGlobal, photo researchers; Alma Bell, Scott Paul, John Pierce, and Lori Shranko, Thompson Type; Jay and John Crowley, Jay's Publishing Services; Mary Ann Lidrbauch, for all her help; Kim Meyer, image consulting; and, of course, Jonathan Poore and John Burge, for their superb photos and architectural drawings respectively.

Finally, I owe thanks to my former co-author, Christin J. Mamiya of the University of Nebraska–Lincoln, for her friendship and advice, especially with regard to the expanded contemporary art section of the 14th edition, as well as to my colleagues at Boston University and to the thousands of students and the scores of teaching fellows in my art history courses since I began teaching in 1975. From them I have learned much that has helped determine the form and content of *Art through the Ages* and made it a much better book than it otherwise might have been.

Fred S. Kleiner

FRED S. KLEINER (Ph.D., Columbia University) is the author or co-author of the 1st, 2nd, and 3rd editions of *Art through the Ages: A Concise History,* as well as the 10th, 11th, 12th, 13th, and 14th editions of *Art through the Ages,* and more than a hundred publications on Greek and Roman art and architecture, including *A History of Roman Art,* also published by Wadsworth, a part of Cengage Learning. He has taught the art history survey course for more than three decades, first at the University of Virginia and, since 1978, at Boston University, where he is currently Professor of Art History and Archaeology and Chair of the Department of History of Art and Architecture. From 1985 to 1998, he was Editor-in-Chief of the *American Journal of Archaeology.* Long acclaimed for his inspiring lectures and dedication to students, Professor Kleiner won Boston University's Metcalf Award for Excellence in Teaching as well as the College Prize for Undergraduate Advising in the Humanities in 2002, and he is a two-time winner of the Distinguished Teaching Prize in the College of Arts and Sciences Honors Program. In 2007, he was elected a Fellow of the Society of Antiquaries of London, and, in 2009, in recognition of lifetime achievement in publication and teaching, a Fellow of the Text and Academic Authors Association.

Also by Fred Kleiner: *A History of Roman Art, Enhanced Edition* (Wadsworth/Cengage Learning 2010; ISBN 9780495909873), winner of the 2007 Texty Prize for a new college textbook in the humanities and social sciences. In this authoritative and lavishly illustrated volume, Professor Kleiner traces the development of Roman art and architecture from Romulus's foundation of Rome in the eighth century BCE to the death of Constantine in the fourth century CE, with special chapters devoted to Pompeii and Herculaneum, Ostia, funerary and provincial art and architecture, and the earliest Christian art. The enhanced edition also includes a new introductory chapter on the art and architecture of the Etruscans and of the Greeks of South Italy and Sicily.

RESOURCES

FOR FACULTY

PowerLecture with Digital Image Library

This flashdrive is an all-in-one lecture and class presentation tool that makes it easy to assemble, edit, and present customized lectures for your course using Microsoft® PowerPoint®. The Digital Image Library provides high-resolution images (maps, diagrams, and most of the fine art images from the text, including the over 300 new images) for lecture presentations, either in PowerPoint format, or in individual file formats compatible with other image-viewing software. A zoom feature allows you to magnify selected portions of an image for more detailed display in class, or you can display images side by side for comparison. You can easily add your own images to those from the text. The Google Earth™ application allows you to zoom in on an entire city, as well as key monuments and buildings. There are links to specific figures for every chapter in the book. PowerLecture also includes an Image Transition Guide, an electronic Instructor's Manual and a Test Bank with multiple-choice, matching, short-answer, and essay questions in ExamView® computerized format. The text-specific Microsoft® PowerPoint® slides are created for use with JoinIn™, software for classroom personal response systems (clickers).

WebTutor™ with eBook on WebCT® and Blackboard®

WebTutor™ enables you to assign preformatted, text-specific content that is available as soon as you log on. You can also customize the WebTutor™ environment in any way you choose. Content includes the Interactive ebook, Test Bank, Practice Quizzes, Video Study Tools, and CourseMate™.

To order, contact your Cengage Learning representative.

FOR STUDENTS

CourseMate™ with eBook

Make the most of your study time by accessing everything you need to succeed in one place. Open the interactive eBook, take notes, review image and audio flashcards, watch videos, and take practice quizzes online with CourseMate™. You will find hundreds of zoomable, high-resolution bonus images (represented by thumbnail images in the text) along with discussion of the images, videos created specifically to enhanced your reading comprehension, audio chapter summaries, compare-and-contrast activities, Guide to Studying, and more.

Slide Guide

The Slide Guide is a lecture companion that allows you to take notes alongside thumbnails of the same art images that are shown in class. The Slide Guide is available as a downloadable Word® document in CourseMate™.

GARDNER'S
ART through the AGES

BEFORE 1300

Students enrolled in the second semester of a yearlong introductory survey of the history of art may not have access to paperback Volume I. Therefore, Volume II of *Art through the Ages: A Western Perspective* opens with a special set of concise primers on Greco-Roman and medieval architectural terminology and construction methods and on Greco-Roman iconography—information that is essential for understanding the history of art and architecture after 1300 in the West.

CONTENTS

ARCHITECTURAL BASICS

Greco-Roman Temple Design and the Classical Orders

The gable-roofed columnar stone temples of the Greeks and Romans have had more influence on the later history of architecture in the Western world than any other building type ever devised. Many of the elements of classical temple architecture are present in buildings from the Renaissance to the present day.

The basic design principles of Greek and Roman temples and the most important components of the classical orders can be summarized as follows.

▌ **Temple design** The core of a Greco-Roman temple was the *cella*, a room with no windows that usually housed the statue of the god or goddess to whom the shrine was dedicated. Generally, only the priests, priestesses, and chosen few would enter the cella. Worshipers gathered in front of the building, where sacrifices occurred at open-air altars. In most Greek temples, for example, the temple erected in honor of Hera or Apollo at Paestum, a *colonnade* was erected all around the cella to form a *peristyle*.

In contrast, Roman temples, for example, the Temple of Portunus in Rome, usually have freestanding columns only in a porch at the front of the building. Sometimes, as in the Portunus temple, *engaged* (attached) half-columns adorn three sides of the cella to give the building the appearance of a *peripteral* temple. Architectural historians call this a *pseudoperipteral* design. The Greeks and Romans also built round temples (called *tholos* temples), a building type that also had a long afterlife in Western architecture.

▌ **Classical orders** The Greeks developed two basic architectural orders, or design systems: the *Doric* and the *Ionic*. The forms of the columns and *entablature* (superstructure) generally differentiate the orders. Classical columns have two or three parts, depending on the order: the shaft, which is usually marked with vertical channels (*flutes*); the *capital*; and, in the Ionic order, the *base*. The Doric capital consists of a round *echinus* beneath a square abacus block. Spiral *volutes* constitute the distinctive feature of the Ionic capital. Classical entablatures have three parts: the *architrave*, the *frieze*, and the triangular *pediment* of the gabled roof, framed by the *cornice*. In the Doric order, the frieze is subdivided into *triglyphs* and *metopes*, whereas in the Ionic, the frieze is left open.

The *Corinthian capital*, a later Greek invention very popular in Roman times, is more ornate than either the Doric or Ionic. It consists of a double row of acanthus leaves, from which tendrils and flowers emerge. Although this capital often is cited as the distinguishing element of the Corinthian order, in strict terms no Corinthian order exists. Architects simply substituted the new capital type for the volute capital in the Ionic order, as in the Roman temple probably dedicated to Vesta at Tivoli.

Sculpture played a major role on the exterior of classical temples, partly to embellish the deity's shrine and partly to tell something about the deity to those gathered outside. Sculptural ornament was concentrated on the upper part of the building, in the pediment and frieze.

Doric and Ionic orders

Greek Doric peripteral temple (Temple of Hera or Apollo, Paestum, Italy, ca. 460 BCE)

Roman Ionic pseudoperipteral temple
(Temple of Portunus, Rome, Italy, ca. 75 BCE)

Roman Corinthian tholos temple
(Temple of Vesta, Tivoli, Italy, early first century BCE)

Arches and Vaults

Although earlier architects used both arches and vaults, the Romans employed them more extensively and effectively than any other ancient civilization. The Roman forms became staples of architectural design from the Middle Ages until today.

▌ *Arch* The arch is one of several ways of spanning a passageway. The Romans preferred it to the *post-and-lintel* (column-and-architrave) system used in the Greek orders. Builders construct arches using wedge-shaped stone blocks called *voussoirs*. The central voussoir is the arch's *keystone*.

▌ *Barrel vault* Also called the *tunnel vault,* the barrel vault is an extension of a simple arch, creating a semicylindrical ceiling over parallel walls.

▌ *Groin vault* The groin vault, or *cross vault,* is formed by the intersection at right angles of two barrel vaults of equal size. When a series of groin vaults covers an interior hall, the open lateral arches of the vaults function as windows admitting light to the building.

▌ *Dome* The hemispherical dome may be described as a round arch rotated around the full circumference of a circle, usually resting on a cylindrical *drum.* The Romans normally constructed domes using *concrete,* a mix of lime mortar, volcanic sand, water, and small stones, instead of with large stone blocks. Concrete dries to form a solid mass of great strength, which enabled the Romans to puncture the apex of a concrete dome with an *oculus* (eye), so that much-needed light could reach the interior of the building.

Barrel vaults, as noted, resemble tunnels, and groin vaults are usually found in a series covering a similar *longitudinally* oriented interior space. Domes, in contrast, crown *centrally* planned buildings, so named because the structure's parts are of equal or almost equal dimensions around the center.

Arch

Barrel vault

Groin vault

Hemispherical dome with oculus

Roman arch (Arch of Titus, Rome, Italy, ca. 81)

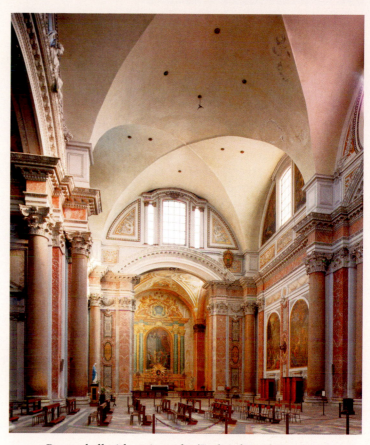

Roman hall with groin vaults (Baths of Diocletian, now
Santa Maria degli Angeli, Rome, Italy, ca. 298–306)

Medieval barrel-vaulted church
(Saint-Savin, Saint-Savin-sur-Gartempe, France, ca. 1100)

Roman dome with oculus (Pantheon, Rome, Italy, 118–125)

Basilican Churches

Church design during the Middle Ages set the stage for ecclesiastical architecture from the Renaissance to the present. Both the longitudinal- and central-plan building types of antiquity had a long postclassical history.

In Western Christendom, the typical medieval church had a *basilican* plan, which evolved from the Roman columnar hall, or basilica. The great European cathedrals of the Gothic age, which were the immediate predecessors of the churches of the Renaissance and Baroque eras, shared many elements with the earliest basilican churches constructed during the fourth century, including a wide central *nave* flanked by *aisles* and ending in an *apse*. Some basilican churches also have a *transept,* an area perpendicular to the nave. The nave and transept intersect at the *crossing.* Gothic churches, however, have many additional features. The key components of Gothic design are labeled in the drawing of a typical French Gothic cathedral, which can be compared to the interior view of Amiens Cathedral and the plan of Chartres Cathedral.

Gothic architects frequently extended the aisles around the apse to form an *ambulatory,* onto which opened *radiating chapels* housing sacred relics. Groin vaults formed the ceiling of the nave, aisles, ambulatory, and transept alike, replacing the timber roof of the typical Early Christian basilica. These vaults rested on *diagonal* and *transverse ribs* in the form of pointed arches. On the exterior, *flying buttresses* held the nave vaults in place. These masonry struts transferred the thrust of the nave vaults across the roofs of the aisles to tall piers frequently capped by pointed ornamental *pinnacles.* This structural system made it possible to open up the walls above the *nave arcade* with huge *stained-glass* windows in the nave *clerestory.*

Cutaway view of a typical French Gothic cathedral

(1) pinnacle, (2) flying buttress, (3) vaulting web, (4) diagonal rib,
(5) transverse rib, (6) springing, (7) clerestory, (8) oculus, (9) lancet,
(10) triforium, (11) nave arcade, (12) compound pier with responds

Nave of Amiens Cathedral, France, begun 1220

In the later Middle Ages, especially in the great cathedrals of the Gothic age, church facades featured extensive sculptural ornamentation, primarily in the portals beneath the stained-glass *rose windows* (circular windows with *tracery* resembling floral petals). The major sculpted areas were the *tympanum* above the doorway (akin to a Greco-Roman temple pediment), the *trumeau* (central post), and the *jambs*.

Plan of Chartres Cathedral, Chartres, France, rebuilt after 1194

West facade of Amiens Cathedral, Amiens, France, begun 1220

Diagram of medieval portal sculpture

Central portal, west facade, Chartres Cathedral, ca. 1145–1155

Central-Plan Churches

The domed central plan of classical antiquity dominated the architecture of the Byzantine Empire but with important modifications. Because the dome covered the crossing of a Byzantine church, architects had to find a way to erect domes on square bases instead of on the circular bases (cylindrical drums) of Roman buildings. The solution was *pendentive* construction in which the dome rests on what is in effect a second, larger dome. The top portion and four segments around the rim of the larger dome are omitted, creating four curved triangles, or pendentives. The pendentives join to form a ring and four arches whose planes bound a square. The first use of pendentives on a grand scale occurred in the sixth-century church of Hagia Sophia (Holy Wisdom) in Constantinople.

The interiors of Byzantine churches differed from those of basilican churches in the West not only in plan and the use of domes but also in the manner in which they were adorned. The original mosaic decoration of Hagia Sophia is lost, but at Saint Mark's in Venice, some 40,000 square feet of mosaics cover all the walls, arches, vaults, and domes.

Hagia Sophia, Constantinople (Istanbul), Turkey, 532–537

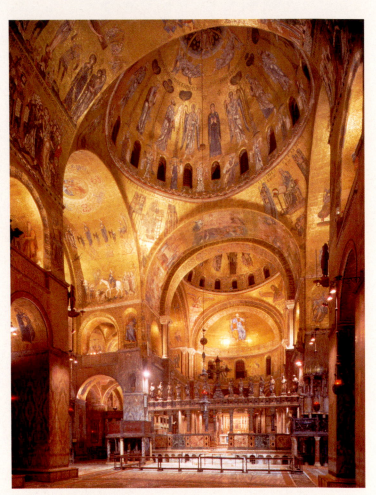

Saint Mark's, Venice, Italy, begun 1063

☐ Pendentives

Dome on pendentives

The Gods and Goddesses of Mount Olympus

The chief deities of the Greeks ruled the world from their home on Mount Olympus, Greece's highest peak. They figure prominently not only in Greek, Etruscan, and Roman art but also in art from the Renaissance to the present.

The 12 Olympian gods (and their Roman equivalents) were:

- *Zeus* (*Jupiter*) King of the gods, Zeus ruled the sky and allotted the sea to his brother Poseidon and the Underworld to his other brother, Hades. His weapon was the thunderbolt. Jupiter was also the chief god of the Romans.

- *Hera* (*Juno*) Wife and sister of Zeus, Hera was the goddess of marriage.

- *Poseidon* (*Neptune*) Poseidon was lord of the sea. He controlled waves, storms, and earthquakes with his three-pronged pitchfork (*trident*).

- *Hestia* (*Vesta*) Sister of Zeus, Poseidon, and Hera, Hestia was goddess of the hearth.

- *Demeter* (*Ceres*) Third sister of Zeus, Demeter was the goddess of grain and agriculture.

- *Ares* (*Mars*) God of war, Ares was the son of Zeus and Hera and the lover of Aphrodite. His Roman counterpart, Mars, was the father of the twin founders of Rome, Romulus and Remus.

- *Athena* (*Minerva*) Goddess of wisdom and warfare, Athena was a virgin born from the head of her father, Zeus.

- *Hephaistos* (*Vulcan*) God of fire and of metalworking, Hephaistos was the son of Zeus and Hera. Born lame and, uncharacteristically for a god, ugly, he married Aphrodite, who was unfaithful to him.

- *Apollo* (*Apollo*) God of light and music and son of Zeus, the young, beautiful Apollo was an expert archer, sometimes identified with the sun (*Helios/Sol*).

- *Artemis* (*Diana*) Sister of Apollo, Artemis was goddess of the hunt. She was occasionally equated with the moon (*Selene/Luna*).

- *Aphrodite* (*Venus*) Daughter of Zeus and a *nymph* (goddess of springs and woods), Aphrodite was the goddess of love and beauty.

- *Hermes* (*Mercury*) Son of Zeus and another nymph, Hermes was the fleet-footed messenger of the gods and possessed winged sandals. He carried the *caduceus*, a magical herald's rod.

Other important Greek gods and goddesses were:

- *Hades* (*Pluto*), lord of the Underworld and god of the dead. Although the brother of Zeus and Poseidon, Hades never resided on Mount Olympus.

- *Dionysos* (*Bacchus*), god of wine, another of Zeus's sons.

- *Eros* (*Amor* or *Cupid*), the winged child-god of love, son of Aphrodite and Ares.

- *Asklepios* (*Aesculapius*), god of healing, son of Apollo. His serpent-entwined staff is the emblem of modern medicine.

Zeus, from Cape Artemision,
ca. 460–450 BCE

Athena, by Phidias,
ca. 438 BCE

Aphrodite (*Venus de Milo*),
by Alexandros, ca. 150–125 BCE

Hermes and infant Dionysos,
by the Phiale Painter,
ca. 440–435 BCE

The Life of Jesus in Art

Christians believe Jesus of Nazareth is the son of God, the *Messiah* (Savior, Christ) of the Jews prophesied in Hebrew scripture. His life—his miraculous birth from the womb of a virgin mother, his preaching and miracle working, his execution by the Romans and subsequent ascent to Heaven—has been the subject of countless artworks from Roman times through the present day.

INCARNATION AND CHILDHOOD

The first "cycle" of the life of Jesus consists of the events of his conception (incarnation), birth, infancy, and childhood.

▌ *Annunciation to Mary* The archangel Gabriel announces to the Virgin Mary that she will miraculously conceive and give birth to God's son, Jesus.

▌ *Visitation* The pregnant Mary visits her cousin Elizabeth, who is pregnant with John the Baptist. Elizabeth is the first to recognize that the baby Mary is bearing is the Son of God.

▌ *Nativity*, *Annunciation to the Shepherds*, and *Adoration of the Shepherds* Jesus is born at night in Bethlehem and placed in a basket. Mary and her husband, Joseph, marvel at the newborn, while an angel announces the birth of the Savior to shepherds in the field, who rush to adore the infant Jesus.

▌ *Adoration of the Magi* A bright star alerts three wise men (*magi*) in the East that the King of the Jews has been born. They travel 12 days to present precious gifts to the infant Jesus.

▌ *Presentation in the Temple* In accordance with Jewish tradition, Mary and Joseph bring their firstborn son to the temple in Jerusalem, where the aged Simeon recognizes Jesus as the prophesied savior of humankind.

▌ *Massacre of the Innocents* and *Flight into Egypt* King Herod, fearful a rival king has been born, orders the massacre of all infants, but the holy family escapes to Egypt.

▌ *Dispute in the Temple* Joseph and Mary travel to Jerusalem for the feast of Passover. Jesus, only a boy, debates the astonished Jewish scholars in the temple, foretelling his ministry.

PUBLIC MINISTRY

The public-ministry cycle comprises the teachings of Jesus and the miracles he performed.

▌ *Baptism* Jesus's public ministry begins with his baptism at age 30 by John the Baptist in the Jordan River. God's voice is heard proclaiming Jesus as his son.

▌ *Calling of Matthew* Jesus summons Matthew, a tax collector, to follow him, and Matthew becomes one of his 12 disciples, or *apostles* (from the Greek for "messenger").

▌ *Miracles* Jesus performs many miracles, revealing his divine nature. These include acts of healing and raising the dead, turning water into wine, walking on water and calming storms, and creating wondrous quantities of food.

▌ *Delivery of the Keys to Peter* Jesus chooses the fisherman Peter (whose name means "rock") as his successor. He declares Peter

Annunciation, Byzantine icon, Ohrid, Macedonia, early 14th century

Baptism of Jesus, baptismal font, Liège, Belgium, 1118

is the rock on which his church will be built and symbolically delivers to Peter the keys to the kingdom of Heaven.

- *Transfiguration* Jesus scales a mountain and, in the presence of Peter and two other disciples, is transformed into radiant light. God, speaking from a cloud, discloses Jesus is his son.

- *Cleansing of the Temple* Jesus returns to Jerusalem, where he finds money changers and merchants conducting business in the temple. He rebukes them and drives them out.

PASSION

The passion (Latin *passio*, "suffering") cycle includes the events leading to Jesus's trial, death, resurrection, and ascent to Heaven.

- *Entry into Jerusalem* On the Sunday before his crucifixion (Palm Sunday), Jesus rides into Jerusalem on a donkey.

- *Last Supper* In Jerusalem, Jesus celebrates Passover with his disciples. During this last supper, Jesus foretells his imminent betrayal, arrest, and death and invites the disciples to remember him when they eat bread (symbol of his body) and drink wine (his blood). This ritual became the celebration of *Mass* (*Eucharist*).

- *Agony in the Garden* Jesus goes to the Mount of Olives in the Garden of Gethsemane, where he struggles to overcome his human fear of death by praying for divine strength.

- *Betrayal* and *Arrest* The disciple Judas Iscariot betrays Jesus to the Jewish authorities for 30 pieces of silver. Judas identifies Jesus to the soldiers by kissing him, and Jesus is arrested.

- *Trials of Jesus* The soldiers bring Jesus before Caiaphas, the Jewish high priest, who interrogates Jesus about his claim to be the Messiah. Jesus is then brought before the Roman governor of Judaea, Pontius Pilate, on the charge of treason because he had proclaimed himself king of the Jews. Pilate asks the crowd to choose between freeing Jesus or Barabbas, a murderer. The people choose Barabbas, and the judge condemns Jesus to death.

- *Flagellation* The Roman soldiers who hold Jesus captive whip (flagellate) him and mock him by dressing him as king of the Jews and placing a crown of thorns on his head.

- *Carrying of the Cross, Raising of the Cross*, and *Crucifixion* The Romans force Jesus to carry the cross on which he will be crucified

from Jerusalem to Mount Calvary. Soldiers erect the cross and nail Jesus's hands and feet to it. Jesus's mother, John the Evangelist, and Mary Magdalene mourn at the foot of the cross, while the soldiers torment Jesus. One of them stabs Jesus in the side with a spear. After suffering great pain, Jesus dies on Good Friday.

- *Deposition*, *Lamentation*, and *Entombment* Two disciples, Joseph of Arimathea and Nicodemus, remove Jesus's body from the cross (deposition) and take him to his tomb. Joseph, Nicodemus, the Virgin Mary, John the Evangelist, and Mary Magdalene mourn over the dead Jesus (lamentation). (When in art the isolated figure of the Virgin Mary cradles her dead son in her lap, it is called a *Pietà*—Italian for "pity.") Then his followers lower Jesus into a sarcophagus in the tomb (entombment).

- *Resurrection* and *Three Marys at the Tomb* On the third day (Easter Sunday), Christ rises from the dead and leaves the tomb. The Virgin Mary, Mary Magdalene, and Mary, the mother of James, visit the tomb but find it empty. An angel informs them Christ has been resurrected.

- *Noli Me Tangere, Supper at Emmaus,* and *Doubting of Thomas* During the 40 days between Christ's resurrection and his ascent to Heaven, he appears on several occasions to his followers. Christ warns Mary Magdalene, weeping at his tomb, with the words "Don't touch me" (*Noli me tangere* in Latin). At Emmaus he eats supper with two astonished disciples. Later, Christ invites Thomas, who cannot believe Christ has risen, to touch the wound in his side inflicted at his crucifixion.

- *Ascension* On the 40th day, on the Mount of Olives, with his mother and apostles as witnesses, Christ gloriously ascends to Heaven in a cloud.

Crucifixion, Church of the Dormition, Daphni, Greece, ca. 1090–1100

Entry into Jerusalem, Sarchophagus of Junius Bassus, Rome, Italy, ca. 359

Why did this Benin kingdom sculptor vary the sizes of the figures? Why is the central equestrian figure much larger than his horse? How did the artist inform the viewer the rider is a king?

Art historians seek to understand not only why individual artworks appear as they do but also why those works exist at all. Who paid this African artist to make this bronze plaque? Why?

Dating and signing artworks are relatively recent practices. How can art historians determine when an unlabeled work such as this one was made, and by whom? Style, technique, and subject are clues.

1 in.

I-1 King on horseback with attendants, from Benin, Nigeria, ca. 1550–1680. Bronze, 1′ 7½″ high. Metropolitan Museum of Art, New York (Michael C. Rockefeller Memorial Collection, gift of Nelson A. Rockefeller).

Introduction

WHAT IS ART HISTORY?

What tools and techniques did the African sculptor employ to transform molten bronze into this plaque representing a king and his attendants projecting in high relief from the background plane?

What is art history? Except when referring to the modern academic discipline, people do not often juxtapose the words *art* and *history*. They tend to think of history as the record and interpretation of past human actions, particularly social and political actions. In contrast, most think of art, quite correctly, as part of the present—as something people can see and touch. Of course, people cannot see or touch history's vanished human events, but a visible, tangible artwork is a kind of persisting event. One or more artists made it at a certain time and in a specific place, even if no one now knows who, when, where, or why. Although created in the past, an artwork continues to exist in the present, long surviving its times. The first painters and sculptors died 30,000 years ago, but their works remain, some of them exhibited in glass cases in museums built only a few years ago.

Modern museum visitors can admire these objects from the remote past—and countless others humankind has produced over the millennia, whether small bronze sculptures from Africa (FIG. **I-1**) or large paintings on canvas by American artists (FIG. I-2)—without any knowledge of the circumstances leading to the creation of those works. The beauty or sheer size of an object can impress people, the artist's virtuosity in the handling of ordinary or costly materials can dazzle them, or the subject depicted can move them emotionally. Viewers can react to what they see, interpret the work in the light of their own experience, and judge it a success or a failure. These are all valid responses to a work of art. But the enjoyment and appreciation of artworks in museum settings are relatively recent phenomena, as is the creation of artworks solely for museum-going audiences to view.

Today, it is common for artists to work in private studios and to create paintings, sculptures, and other objects commercial art galleries will offer for sale. This is what American painter CLYFFORD STILL (1904–1980) did when he created large canvases (FIG. **I-2**) of pure color titled simply with the year of their creation. Usually, someone the artist has never met will purchase the artwork and display it in a setting the artist has never seen. This practice is not a new phenomenon in the history of art—an ancient potter decorating a vase for sale at a village market stall probably did not know who would buy the pot or where it would be housed—but it is not at all typical. In fact, it is exceptional. Throughout history, most artists created paintings, sculptures, and other objects for specific patrons and settings and to fulfill a specific purpose, even if today no one knows the original contexts of those artworks. Museum visitors can appreciate the visual and tactile qualities of these objects, but they cannot understand why they were made or why they appear as they do without knowing the circumstances of their creation. Art *appreciation* does not require knowledge of the historical context of an artwork (or a building). Art *history* does.

1 ft.

I-2 CLYFFORD STILL, *1948-C,* 1948. Oil on canvas, 6′ 8⅞″ × 5′ 8¾″. Hirshhorn Museum and Sculpture Garden, Smithsonian Institution, Washington, D.C. (purchased with funds of Joseph H. Hirshhorn, 1992).

Clyfford Still painted this abstract composition without knowing who would purchase it or where it would be displayed, but throughout history, most artists created works for specific patrons and settings.

Thus, a central aim of art history is to determine the original context of artworks. Art historians seek to achieve a full understanding not only of why these "persisting events" of human history look the way they do but also of why the artistic events happened at all. What unique set of circumstances gave rise to the construction of a particular building or led an individual patron to commission a certain artist to fashion a singular artwork for a specific place? The study of history is therefore vital to art history. And art history is often indispensable for a thorough understanding of history. Art objects and buildings are historical documents that can shed light on the peoples who made them and on the times of their creation in ways other historical documents may not. Furthermore, artists and architects can affect history by reinforcing or challenging cultural values and practices through the objects they create and the structures they build. Thus, the history of art and architecture is inseparable from the study of history, although the two disciplines are not the same.

The following pages introduce some of the distinctive subjects art historians address and the kinds of questions they ask, and explain some of the basic terminology they use when answering these questions. Readers armed with this arsenal of questions and terms will be ready to explore the multifaceted world of art through the ages.

ART HISTORY IN THE 21ST CENTURY

Art historians study the visual and tangible objects humans make and the structures humans build. Scholars traditionally have classified these works as architecture, sculpture, the pictorial arts (painting, drawing, printmaking, and photography), and the craft arts, or arts of design. The craft arts comprise utilitarian objects, such as ceramics, metalwork, textiles, jewelry, and similar accessories of ordinary living. Artists of every age have blurred the boundaries among these categories, but this is especially true today, when multimedia works abound.

Beginning with the earliest Greco-Roman art critics, scholars have studied objects their makers consciously manufactured as "art" and to which the artists assigned formal titles. But today's art historians also study a multitude of objects their creators and owners almost certainly did not consider to be "works of art." Few ancient Romans, for example, would have regarded a coin bearing their emperor's portrait as anything but money. Today, an art museum may exhibit that coin in a locked case in a climate-controlled room, and scholars may subject it to the same kind of art historical analysis as a portrait by an acclaimed Renaissance or modern sculptor or painter.

The range of objects art historians study is constantly expanding and now includes, for example, computer-generated images, whereas in the past almost anything produced using a machine would not have been regarded as art. Most people still consider the performing arts—music, drama, and dance—as outside art history's realm because these arts are fleeting, impermanent media. But during the past few decades, even this distinction between "fine art" and "performance art" has become blurred. Art historians, however, generally ask the same kinds of questions about what they study, whether they employ a restrictive or expansive definition of art.

The Questions Art Historians Ask

HOW OLD IS IT? Before art historians can write a history of art, they must be sure they know the date of each work they study. Thus, an indispensable subject of art historical inquiry is *chronology,* the dating of art objects and buildings. If researchers cannot determine a monument's age, they cannot place the work in its historical context. Art historians have developed many ways to establish, or at least approximate, the date of an artwork.

Physical evidence often reliably indicates an object's age. The material used for a statue or painting—bronze, plastic, or oil-based pigment, to name only a few—may not have been invented before a certain time, indicating the earliest possible date (the *terminus post quem*: Latin "point after which") someone could have fashioned the work. Or artists may have ceased using certain materials—such as specific kinds of inks and papers for drawings—at a known time, providing the latest possible date (the *terminus ante quem*: Latin "point before which") for objects made of those materials. Sometimes the material (or the manufacturing technique) of an object or a building can establish a very precise date of production or construction. The study of tree rings, for instance, usually can determine within a narrow range the date of a wood statue or a timber roof beam.

Documentary evidence can help pinpoint the date of an object or building when a dated written document mentions the work. For example, official records may note when church officials commissioned a new altarpiece—and how much they paid to which artist.

Internal evidence can play a significant role in dating an artwork. A painter might have depicted an identifiable person or a kind of hairstyle, clothing, or furniture fashionable only at a certain time. If so, the art historian can assign a more accurate date to that painting.

Stylistic evidence is also very important. The analysis of *style*—an artist's distinctive manner of producing an object—is the art historian's special sphere. Unfortunately, because it is a subjective assessment, stylistic evidence is by far the most unreliable chronological criterion. Still, art historians find style a very useful tool for establishing chronology.

WHAT IS ITS STYLE? Defining artistic style is one of the key elements of art historical inquiry, although the analysis of artworks solely in terms of style no longer dominates the field the way it once did. Art historians speak of several different kinds of artistic styles.

Period style refers to the characteristic artistic manner of a specific era or span of years, usually within a distinct culture, such as "Archaic Greek" or "High Renaissance." But many periods do not display any stylistic unity at all. How would someone define the artistic style of the second decade of the new millennium in North America? Far too many crosscurrents exist in contemporary art for anyone to describe a period style of the early 21st century—even in a single city such as New York.

Regional style is the term art historians use to describe variations in style tied to geography. Like an object's date, its *provenance*, or place of origin, can significantly determine its character. Very often two artworks from the same place made centuries apart are more similar than contemporaneous works from two different regions. To cite one example, usually only an expert can distinguish between an Egyptian statue carved in 2500 BCE and one made in 500 BCE. But no one would mistake an Egyptian statue of 500 BCE for one of the same date made in Greece or Mexico.

Considerable variations in a given area's style are possible, however, even during a single historical period. In late medieval Europe, French architecture differed significantly from Italian architecture. The interiors of Beauvais Cathedral (FIG. I-3) and the church of Santa Croce (FIG. I-4) in Florence typify the architectural styles of France and Italy, respectively, at the end of the 13th century. The rebuilding of the east end of Beauvais Cathedral began in 1284. Construction commenced on Santa Croce only 10 years later. Both structures employ the *pointed arch* characteristic of this era, yet the two churches differ strikingly. The French church has towering stone ceilings and large expanses of colored windows, whereas the Italian building has a low timber roof and small, widely separated windows. Because the

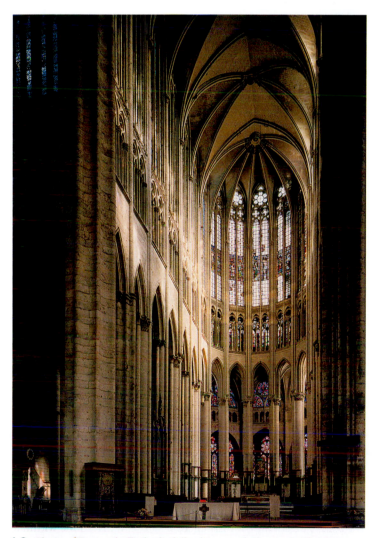

I-3 Choir of Beauvais Cathedral (looking east), Beauvais, France, rebuilt after 1284.

The style of an object or building often varies from region to region. This cathedral has towering stone vaults and large stained-glass windows typical of 13th-century French architecture.

I-4 Interior of Santa Croce (looking east), Florence, Italy, begun 1294.

In contrast to Beauvais Cathedral (FIG. I-3), this contemporaneous Florentine church conforms to the quite different regional style of Italy. The building has a low timber roof and small windows.

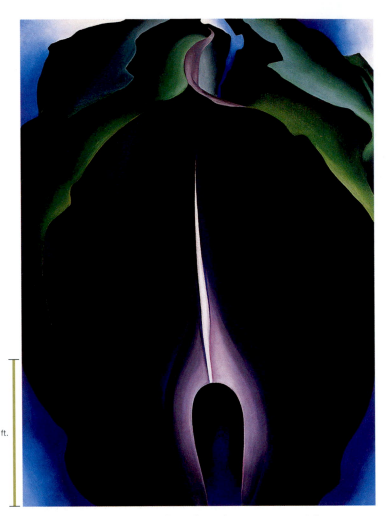

I-5 GEORGIA O'KEEFFE, *Jack-in-the-Pulpit No. 4,* 1930. Oil on canvas, 3' 4" × 2' 6". National Gallery of Art, Washington (Alfred Stieglitz Collection, bequest of Georgia O'Keeffe).

O'Keeffe's paintings feature close-up views of petals and leaves in which the organic forms become powerful abstract compositions. This approach to painting typifies the artist's distinctive personal style.

I-6 BEN SHAHN, *The Passion of Sacco and Vanzetti,* 1931–1932. Tempera on canvas, 7' $\frac{1}{2}$" × 4'. Whitney Museum of American Art, New York (gift of Edith and Milton Lowenthal in memory of Juliana Force).

O'Keeffe's contemporary, Shahn developed a style markedly different from hers. His paintings are often social commentaries on recent events and incorporate readily identifiable people.

two contemporaneous churches served similar purposes, regional style mainly explains their differing appearance.

Personal style, the distinctive manner of individual artists or architects, often decisively explains stylistic discrepancies among monuments of the same time and place. In 1930 the American painter GEORGIA O'KEEFFE (1887–1986) produced a series of paintings of flowering plants. One of them—*Jack-in-the-Pulpit No. 4* (FIG. I-5)—is a sharply focused close-up view of petals and leaves. O'Keeffe captured the growing plant's slow, controlled motion while converting the plant into a powerful abstract composition of lines, forms, and colors (see the discussion of art historical vocabulary in the next section). Only a year later, another American artist, BEN SHAHN (1898–1969), painted *The Passion of Sacco and Vanzetti* (FIG. I-6), a stinging commentary on social injustice inspired by the trial and execution of two Italian anarchists, Nicola Sacco and Bartolomeo Vanzetti. Many people believed Sacco and Vanzetti had been unjustly convicted of killing two men in a robbery in 1920. Shahn's painting compresses time in a symbolic representation of the trial and its aftermath. The two executed men lie in their coffins. Presiding over them are the three members of the commission (headed by a college president wearing academic cap and gown) who declared the original trial fair and cleared the way for the

executions. Behind, on the wall of a stately government building, hangs the framed portrait of the judge who pronounced the initial sentence. Personal style, not period or regional style, sets Shahn's canvas apart from O'Keeffe's. The contrast is extreme here because of the very different subjects the artists chose. But even when two artists depict the same subject, the results can vary widely. The *way* O'Keeffe painted flowers and the *way* Shahn painted faces are distinctive and unlike the styles of their contemporaries. (See the "Who Made It?" discussion on page 6.)

The different kinds of artistic styles are not mutually exclusive. For example, an artist's personal style may change dramatically during a long career. Art historians then must distinguish among

I-7 GISLEBERTUS, The weighing of souls, detail of *Last Judgment* (FIG. 12-1), west tympanum of Saint-Lazare, Autun, France, ca. 1120–1135.

In this high relief portraying the weighing of souls on judgment day, Gislebertus used disproportion and distortion to dehumanize the devilish figure yanking on the scales of justice.

the different period styles of a particular artist, such as the "Rose Period" and the "Cubist Period" of the prolific 20th-century artist Pablo Picasso.

WHAT IS ITS SUBJECT? Another major concern of art historians is, of course, subject matter, encompassing the story, or narrative; the scene presented; the action's time and place; the persons involved; and the environment and its details. Some artworks, such as modern *abstract* paintings (FIG. I-2), have no subject, not even a setting. The "subject" is the artwork itself—its colors, textures, composition, and size. But when artists represent people, places, or actions, viewers must identify these features to achieve complete understanding of the work. Art historians traditionally separate pictorial subjects into various categories, such as religious, historical, mythological, *genre* (daily life), portraiture, *landscape* (a depiction of a place), *still life* (an arrangement of inanimate objects), and their numerous subdivisions and combinations.

Iconography—literally, the "writing of images"—refers both to the content, or subject, of an artwork, and to the study of content in art. By extension, it also includes the study of *symbols,* images that stand for other images or encapsulate ideas. In Christian art, two intersecting lines of unequal length or a simple geometric cross can serve as an emblem of the religion as a whole, symbolizing the cross of Jesus Christ's crucifixion. A symbol also can be a familiar object the artist imbued with greater meaning. A balance or scale, for example, may symbolize justice or the weighing of souls on judgment day (FIG. I-7).

Artists may depict figures with unique *attributes* identifying them. In Christian art, for example, each of the authors of the biblical gospel books, the four evangelists (FIG. I-8), has a distinctive attribute. People can recognize Saint John by the eagle associated with him, Luke by the ox, Mark by the lion, and Matthew by the winged man.

Throughout the history of art, artists have used *personifications*—abstract ideas codified in human form. Worldwide, people visualize Liberty as a robed woman wearing a rayed crown and holding a torch because of the fame of the colossal statue set up in New York City's harbor in 1886.

I-8 The four evangelists, folio 14 verso of the *Aachen Gospels,* ca. 810. Ink and tempera on vellum, $1' \times 9\frac{1}{2}''$. Domschatzkammer, Aachen.

Artists depict figures with attributes in order to identify them for viewers. The authors of the four gospels have distinctive attributes—eagle (John), ox (Luke), lion (Mark), and winged man (Matthew).

1 in.

1 in.

I-9 ALBRECHT DÜRER, *The Four Horsemen of the Apocalypse,* ca. 1498. Woodcut, 1′ 3¼″ × 11″. Metropolitan Museum of Art, New York (gift of Junius S. Morgan, 1919).

Personifications are abstract ideas codified in human form. Here, Albrecht Dürer represented Death, Famine, War, and Pestilence as four men on charging horses, each one carrying an identifying attribute.

The Four Horsemen of the Apocalypse (FIG. I-9) is a terrifying late-15th-century depiction of the fateful day at the end of time when, according to the Bible's last book, Death, Famine, War, and Pestilence will annihilate the human race. German artist ALBRECHT DÜRER (1471–1528) personified Death as an emaciated old man with a pitchfork. Dürer's Famine swings the scales for weighing human souls (compare FIG. I-7), War wields a sword, and Pestilence draws a bow.

Even without considering style and without knowing a work's maker, informed viewers can determine much about the work's period and provenance by iconographical and subject analysis alone. In *The Passion of Sacco and Vanzetti* (FIG. I-6), for example, the two coffins, the trio headed by an academic, and the robed judge in the background are all pictorial clues revealing the painting's subject. The work's date must be after the trial and execution, probably while the event was still newsworthy. And because the two men's deaths caused the greatest outrage in the United States, the painter–social critic was probably American.

WHO MADE IT? If Ben Shahn had not signed his painting of Sacco and Vanzetti, an art historian could still assign, or *attribute* (make an *attribution* of), the work to him based on knowledge of

the artist's personal style. Although signing (and dating) works is quite common (but by no means universal) today, in the history of art countless works exist whose artists remain unknown. Because personal style can play a major role in determining the character of an artwork, art historians often try to attribute anonymous works to known artists. Sometimes they assemble a group of works all thought to be by the same person, even though none of the objects in the group is the known work of an artist with a recorded name. Art historians thus reconstruct the careers of artists such as "the Achilles Painter," the anonymous ancient Greek artist whose masterwork is a depiction of the hero Achilles. Scholars base their attributions on internal evidence, such as the distinctive way an artist draws or carves drapery folds, earlobes, or flowers. It requires a keen, highly trained eye and long experience to become a *connoisseur,* an expert in assigning artworks to "the hand" of one artist rather than another. Attribution is subjective, of course, and ever open to doubt. At present, for example, international debate rages over attributions to the famous 17th-century Dutch painter Rembrandt van Rijn.

Sometimes a group of artists works in the same style at the same time and place. Art historians designate such a group as a *school. School* does not mean an educational institution or art academy. The term connotes only shared chronology, style, and geography. Art historians speak, for example, of the Dutch school of the 17th century and, within it, of subschools such as those of the cities of Haarlem, Utrecht, and Leyden.

WHO PAID FOR IT? The interest many art historians show in attribution reflects their conviction that the identity of an artwork's maker is the major reason the object looks the way it does. For them, personal style is of paramount importance. But in many times and places, artists had little to say about what form their work would take. They toiled in obscurity, doing the bidding of their *patrons,* those who paid them to make individual works or employed them on a continuing basis. The role of patrons in dictating the content and shaping the form of artworks is also an important subject of art historical inquiry.

In the art of portraiture, to name only one category of painting and sculpture, the patron has often played a dominant role in deciding how the artist represented the subject, whether that person was the patron or another individual, such as a spouse, son, or mother. Many Egyptian pharaohs and some Roman emperors, for example, insisted artists depict them with unlined faces and perfect youthful bodies no matter how old they were when portrayed. In these cases, the state employed the sculptors and painters, and the artists had no choice but to portray their patrons in the officially approved manner. This is why Augustus, who lived to age 76, looks so young in his portraits (FIG. I-10). Although Roman emperor for more than 40 years, Augustus demanded artists always represent him as a young, godlike head of state.

All modes of artistic production reveal the impact of patronage. Learned monks provided the themes for the sculptural decoration of medieval church portals (FIG. I-7). Renaissance princes and popes dictated the subject, size, and materials of artworks destined for display in buildings also constructed according to their specifications. An art historian could make a very long list of commissioned works, and it would indicate patrons have had diverse tastes and needs throughout the history of art and consequently have demanded different kinds of art. Whenever a patron contracts an artist or architect to paint, sculpt, or build in a prescribed manner, personal style often becomes a very minor factor in the ultimate

1 in.

I-10 Bust of Augustus wearing the corona civica, early first century CE. Marble, 1′ 5″ high. Glyptothek, Munich.

Patrons frequently dictate the form their portraits will take. The Roman emperor Augustus demanded he always be portrayed as a young, godlike head of state even though he lived to age 76.

painted on a canvas) or in three dimensions (such as a statue carved from a marble block). Two forms may take the same shape but may differ in their color, texture, and other qualities. *Composition* refers to how an artist *composes* (organizes) forms in an artwork, either by placing shapes on a flat surface or by arranging forms in space.

MATERIAL AND TECHNIQUE To create art forms, artists shape materials (pigment, clay, marble, gold, and many more) with tools (pens, brushes, chisels, and so forth). Each of the materials and tools available has its own potentialities and limitations. Part of all artists' creative activity is to select the *medium* and instrument most suitable to the purpose—or to develop new media and tools, such as bronze and concrete in antiquity and cameras and computers in modern times. The processes artists employ, such as applying paint to canvas with a brush, and the distinctive, personal ways they handle materials constitute their *technique*. Form, material, and technique interrelate and are central to analyzing any work of art.

LINE Among the most important elements defining an artwork's shape or form is *line*. A line can be understood as the path of a point moving in space, an invisible line of sight. More commonly, however, artists and architects make a line visible by drawing (or chiseling) it on a *plane,* a flat surface. A line may be very thin, wirelike, and delicate. It may be thick and heavy. Or it may alternate quickly from broad to narrow, the strokes jagged or the outline broken. When a continuous line defines an object's outer shape, art historians call it a *contour line.* All of these line qualities are present in Dürer's *The Four Horsemen of the Apocalypse* (FIG. I-9). Contour lines define the basic shapes of clouds, human and animal limbs, and weapons. Within the forms, series of short broken lines create shadows and textures. An overall pattern of long parallel strokes suggests the dark sky on the frightening day when the world is about to end.

COLOR Light reveals all *colors.* Light in the world of the painter and other artists differs from natural light. Natural light, or sunlight, is whole or *additive light.* As the sum of all the wavelengths composing the visible *spectrum,* it may be disassembled or fragmented into the individual colors of the spectral band. The painter's light in art—the light reflected from pigments and objects—is *subtractive light.* Paint pigments produce their individual colors by reflecting a segment of the spectrum while absorbing all the rest. Green pigment, for example, subtracts or absorbs all the light in the spectrum except that seen as green.

Hue is the property giving a color its name. Although the spectrum colors merge into each other, artists usually conceive of their hues as distinct from one another. Color has two basic variables—the apparent amount of light reflected and the apparent purity. A change in one must produce a change in the other. Some terms for these variables are *value,* or *tonality* (the degree of lightness or darkness), and *intensity,* or *saturation* (the purity of a color, its brightness or dullness).

Artists call the three basic colors—red, yellow, and blue—the *primary colors.* The *secondary colors* result from mixing pairs of primaries: orange (red and yellow), purple (red and blue), and green (yellow and blue). *Complementary colors* represent the pairing of a primary color and the secondary color created from mixing the two other primary colors—red and green, yellow and purple, and blue and orange. They "complement," or complete, each other, one absorbing colors the other reflects.

appearance of the painting, statue, or building. In these cases, the identity of the patron reveals more to art historians than does the identity of the artist or school. The portrait of Augustus illustrated here (FIG. I-10)—showing the emperor wearing a *corona civica,* or civic crown—was the work of a virtuoso sculptor, a master wielder of hammer and chisel. But scores of similar portraits of this Roman emperor also exist today. They differ in quality but not in kind from this one. The patron, not the artist, determined the character of these artworks. Augustus's public image never varied.

The Words Art Historians Use

As in all fields of study, art history has its own specialized vocabulary consisting of hundreds of words, but certain basic terms are indispensable for describing artworks and buildings of any time and place. They make up the essential vocabulary of *formal analysis,* the visual analysis of artistic form. Definitions and discussions of the most important art historical terms follow.

FORM AND COMPOSITION *Form* refers to an object's shape and structure, either in two dimensions (for example, a figure

1 ft.

I-11 JOSEF ALBERS, *Homage to the Square: "Ascending,"* 1953. Oil on composition board, 3′ 7½″ × 3′ 7½″. Whitney Museum of American Art, New York.

Albers painted hundreds of canvases using the same composition but employing variations in hue, saturation, and value in order to reveal the relativity and instability of color perception.

Artists can manipulate the appearance of colors, however. One artist who made a systematic investigation of the formal aspects of art, especially color, was JOSEF ALBERS (1888–1976), a German-born artist who emigrated to the United States in 1933. In connection with his studies, Albers created the series *Homage to the Square*—hundreds of paintings, most of which are color variations on the same composition of concentric squares, as in the illustrated example (FIG. **I-11**). The series reflected Albers's belief that art originates in "the discrepancy between physical fact and psychic effect."[1] Because the composition in most of these paintings remains constant, the works succeed in revealing the relativity and instability of color perception. Albers varied the hue, saturation, and value of each square in the paintings in this series. As a result, the sizes of the squares from painting to painting appear to vary (although they remain the same), and the sensations emanating from the paintings range from clashing dissonance to delicate serenity. Albers explained his motivation for focusing on color juxtapositions:

> They [the colors] are juxtaposed for various and changing visual effects. . . . Such action, reaction, interaction . . . is sought in order to make obvious how colors influence and change each other; that the same color, for instance—with different grounds or neighbors—looks different. . . . Such color deceptions prove that we see colors almost never unrelated to each other.[2]

TEXTURE The term *texture* refers to the quality of a surface, such as rough or shiny. Art historians distinguish between true texture, that is, the tactile quality of the surface, and represented texture, as when painters depict an object as having a certain tex-

ture even though the pigment is the true texture. Sometimes artists combine different materials of different textures on a single surface, juxtaposing paint with pieces of wood, newspaper, fabric, and so forth. Art historians refer to this mixed-media technique as *collage.* Texture is, of course, a key determinant of any sculpture's character. People's first impulse is usually to handle a work of sculpture—even though museum signs often warn "Do not touch!" Sculptors plan for this natural human response, using surfaces varying in texture from rugged coarseness to polished smoothness. Textures are often intrinsic to a material, influencing the type of stone, wood, plastic, clay, or metal sculptors select.

SPACE, MASS, AND VOLUME *Space* is the bounded or boundless "container" of objects. For art historians, space can be the real three-dimensional space occupied by a statue or a vase or contained within a room or courtyard. Or space can be *illusionistic,* as when painters depict an image (or illusion) of the three-dimensional spatial world on a two-dimensional surface.

Mass and *volume* describe three-dimensional objects and space. In both architecture and sculpture, mass is the bulk, density, and weight of matter in space. Yet the mass need not be solid. It can be the exterior form of enclosed space. Mass can apply to a solid Egyptian pyramid or stone statue, to a church, synagogue, or mosque—architectural shells enclosing sometimes vast spaces—and to a hollow metal statue or baked clay pot. Volume is the space that mass organizes, divides, or encloses. It may be a building's interior spaces, the intervals between a structure's masses, or the amount of space occupied by three-dimensional objects such as a statue, pot, or chair. Volume and mass describe both the exterior and interior forms of a work of art—the forms of the matter of which it is composed and the spaces immediately around the work and interacting with it.

PERSPECTIVE AND FORESHORTENING *Perspective* is one of the most important pictorial devices for organizing forms in space. Throughout history, artists have used various types of perspective to create an illusion of depth or space on a two-dimensional surface. The French painter CLAUDE LORRAIN (1600–1682) employed several perspective devices in *Embarkation of the Queen of Sheba* (FIG. **I-12**), a painting of a biblical episode set in a 17th-century European harbor with a Roman ruin in the left foreground. For example, the figures and boats on the shoreline are much larger than those in the distance. Decreasing the size of an object makes it appear farther away. Also, the top and bottom of the port building at the painting's right side are not parallel horizontal lines, as they are in a real building. Instead, the lines converge beyond the structure, leading the viewer's eye toward the hazy, indistinct sun on the horizon. These perspective devices—the reduction of figure size, the convergence of diagonal lines, and the blurring of distant forms—have been familiar features of Western art since the ancient Greeks. But it is important to note at the outset that all kinds of perspective are only pictorial conventions, even when one or more types of perspective may be so common in a given culture that people accept them as "natural" or as "true" means of representing the natural world.

In *Waves at Matsushima* (FIG. **I-13**), a Japanese seascape painting on a six-part folding screen, OGATA KORIN (1658–1716) ignored these Western perspective conventions. A Western viewer might interpret the left half of Korin's composition as depicting the distant horizon, as in Claude's painting, but the sky is a flat, unnatural gold, and in five of the six sections of the composition, waves fill the

I-12 Claude Lorrain, *Embarkation of the Queen of Sheba,* 1648. Oil on canvas, 4′ 10″ × 6′ 4″. National Gallery, London.

To create the illusion of a deep landscape, Claude Lorrain employed perspective, reducing the size of and blurring the most distant forms. Also, all diagonal lines converge on a single point.

1 ft.

full height of the screen. The rocky outcroppings decrease in size with distance, but all are in sharp focus, and there are no shadows. The Japanese artist was less concerned with locating the boulders and waves in space than with composing shapes on a surface, playing the water's swelling curves against the jagged contours of the rocks. Neither the French nor the Japanese painting can be said to project "correctly" what viewers "in fact" see. One painting is not a "better" picture of the world than the other. The European and Asian artists simply approached the problem of picture-making differently.

1 ft.

I-13 Ogata Korin, *Waves at Matsushima,* Edo period, ca. 1700–1716. Six-panel folding screen, ink, color, and gold leaf on paper, 4′ 11⅛″ × 12′ ⅞″. Museum of Fine Arts, Boston (Fenollosa-Weld Collection).

Korin was more concerned with creating an intriguing composition of shapes on a surface than with locating boulders and waves in space. Asian artists rarely employed Western perspective.

Art History in the 21st Century **9**

I-14 PETER PAUL RUBENS, *Lion Hunt*, 1617–1618. Oil on canvas, 8′ 2″ × 12′ 5″. Alte Pinakothek, Munich.

Foreshortening—the representation of a figure or object at an angle to the picture plane—is a common device in Western art for creating the illusion of depth. Foreshortening is a type of perspective.

1 ft.

Artists also represent single figures in space in varying ways. When Flemish artist PETER PAUL RUBENS (1577–1640) painted *Lion Hunt* (FIG. I-14), he used *foreshortening* for all the hunters and animals—that is, he represented their bodies at angles to the picture plane. When in life one views a figure at an angle, the body appears to contract as it extends back in space. Foreshortening is a kind of perspective. It produces the illusion that one part of the body is farther away than another, even though all the forms are on the same surface. Especially noteworthy in *Lion Hunt* are the gray horse at the left, seen from behind with the bottom of its left rear hoof facing viewers and most of its head hidden

I-15 Hesire, relief from his tomb at Saqqara, Egypt, Dynasty III, ca. 2650 BCE. Wood, 3′ 9″ high. Egyptian Museum, Cairo.

Egyptian artists combined frontal and profile views to give a precise picture of the parts of the human body, as opposed to depicting how an individual body appears from a specific viewpoint.

1 ft.

by its rider's shield, and the fallen hunter at the painting's lower right corner, whose barely visible legs and feet recede into the distance.

The artist who carved the portrait of the ancient Egyptian official Hesire (FIG. I-15) did not employ foreshortening. That artist's purpose was to present the various human body parts as clearly as possible, without overlapping. The lower part of Hesire's body is in profile to give the most complete view of the legs, with both the heels and toes of the foot visible. The frontal torso, however, allows viewers to see its full shape, including both shoulders, equal in size, as in nature. (Compare the shoulders of the hunter on the gray horse or those of the fallen hunter in *Lion Hunt*'s left foreground.) The result—an "unnatural" 90-degree twist at the waist—provides a precise picture of human body parts. Rubens and the Egyptian sculptor used very different means of depicting forms in space. Once again, neither is the "correct" manner.

PROPORTION AND SCALE *Proportion* concerns the relationships (in terms of size) of the parts of persons, buildings, or objects. People can judge "correct proportions" intuitively ("that statue's head seems the right size for the body"). Or proportion can be a mathematical relationship between the size of one part of an artwork or building and the other parts within the work. Proportion in art implies using a *module,* or basic unit of measure. When an artist or architect uses a formal system of proportions, all parts of a building, body, or other entity will be fractions or multiples of the module. A module might be a *column*'s diameter, the height of a human head, or any other component whose dimensions can be multiplied or divided to determine the size of the work's other parts.

In certain times and places, artists have devised *canons,* or systems, of "correct" or "ideal" proportions for representing human figures, constituent parts of buildings, and so forth. In ancient Greece, many sculptors formulated canons of proportions so strict and all-encompassing that they calculated the size of every body part in advance, even the fingers and toes, according to mathematical ratios.

Proportional systems can differ sharply from period to period, culture to culture, and artist to artist. Part of the task art history students face is to perceive and adjust to these differences. In fact, many artists have used disproportion and distortion deliberately for expressive effect. In the medieval French depiction of the weighing of souls on judgment day (FIG. I-7), the devilish figure yanking down on the scale has distorted facial features and stretched, lined limbs with animal-like paws for feet. Disproportion and distortion make him appear "inhuman," precisely as the sculptor intended.

In other cases, artists have used disproportion to focus attention on one body part (often the head) or to single out a group member (usually the leader). These intentional "unnatural" discrepancies in proportion constitute what art historians call *hierarchy of scale*, the enlarging of elements considered the most important. On the bronze plaque from Benin, Nigeria, illustrated here (FIG. I-1), the sculptor enlarged all the heads for emphasis and also varied the size of each figure according to the person's social status. Central, largest, and therefore most important is the Benin king, mounted on horseback. The horse has been a symbol of power and wealth in many societies from prehistory to the present. That the Benin king is disproportionately larger than his horse, contrary to nature, further aggrandizes him. Two large attendants fan the king. Other figures of smaller size and status at the Benin court stand on the king's left and right and in the plaque's upper corners. One tiny figure next to the horse is almost hidden from view beneath the king's feet.

One problem students of art history—and professional art historians too—confront when studying illustrations in art history books is that although the relative sizes of figures and objects in a painting or sculpture are easy to discern, it is impossible to determine the absolute size of the work reproduced because they all appear at approximately the same size on the page. Readers of *Art through the Ages: The Western Perspective* can learn the exact size of all artworks from the dimensions given in the captions and, more intuitively, from the scales positioned at the lower left or right corner of each illustration.

I-16 MICHELANGELO BUONARROTI, unfinished statue, 1527–1528. Marble, 8′ 7½″ high. Galleria dell'Accademia, Florence.

Carving a freestanding figure from stone or wood is a subtractive process. Michelangelo thought of sculpture as a process of "liberating" the statue within the block of marble.

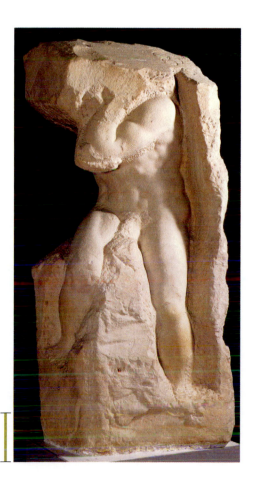

1 ft.

I-17 Head of a warrior, detail of a statue (FIG. 5-35) from the sea off Riace, Italy, ca. 460–450 BCE. Bronze, full statue 6′ 6″ high. Museo Archeologico Nazionale, Reggio Calabria.

The sculptor of this life-size statue of a bearded Greek warrior cast the head, limbs, torso, hands, and feet in separate molds, then welded the pieces together and added the eyes in a different material.

1 in.

CARVING AND CASTING Sculptural technique falls into two basic categories, *subtractive* and *additive. Carving* is a subtractive technique. The final form is a reduction of the original mass of a block of stone, a piece of wood, or another material. Wood statues were once tree trunks, and stone statues began as blocks pried from mountains. The unfinished marble statue illustrated here (FIG. I-16) by renowned Italian artist MICHELANGELO BUONARROTI (1475–1564) clearly reveals the original shape of the stone block. Michelangelo thought of sculpture as a process of "liberating" the statue within the block. All sculptors of stone or wood cut away (subtract) "excess material." When they finish, they "leave behind" the statue—in this example, a twisting nude male form whose head Michelangelo never freed from the stone block.

In additive sculpture, the artist builds up (*models*) the forms, usually in clay around a framework, or *armature*. Or a sculptor may fashion a *mold*, a hollow form for shaping, or *casting*, a fluid substance such as bronze or plaster. The ancient Greek sculptor who made the bronze statue of a warrior found in the sea near Riace, Italy, cast the head (FIG. I-17) as well as the limbs, torso, hands, and feet (FIG. 5-35) in separate molds and then *welded* them together (joined them by heating). Finally, the artist added features, such as the pupils of the eyes (now missing), in other materials. The warrior's teeth are silver, and his lower lip is copper.

RELIEF SCULPTURE *Statues* and *busts* (head, shoulders, and chest) that exist independent of any architectural frame or setting and that viewers can walk around are *freestanding* sculptures, or *sculptures in the round,* whether the artist produced the piece by carving (FIG. I-10) or casting (FIG. I-17). In *relief* sculpture, the subjects project from the background but remain part of it. In *high-relief* sculpture, the images project boldly. In some cases, such as the medieval weighing-of-souls scene (FIG. I-7), the relief is so high the forms not only cast shadows on the background, but some parts are even in the round, which explains why some pieces, for example, the arms of the scales, broke off centuries ago. In *low-relief,* or *bas-relief, sculpture,* such as the portrait of Hesire (FIG. I-15), the projection is slight. Artists can produce relief sculptures, as they do sculptures in the round, either by carving or casting. The plaque from Benin (FIG. I-1) is an example of bronze-casting in high relief.

ARCHITECTURAL DRAWINGS Buildings are groupings of enclosed spaces and enclosing masses. People experience architecture both visually and by moving through and around it, so they perceive architectural space and mass together. These spaces and masses can be represented graphically in several ways, including as plans, sections, elevations, and cutaway drawings.

A *plan,* essentially a map of a floor, shows the placement of a structure's masses and, therefore, the spaces they circumscribe and enclose. A *section,* a kind of vertical plan, depicts the placement of the masses as if someone cut through the building along a plane. Drawings showing a theoretical slice across a structure's width are *lateral sections.* Those cutting through a building's length are *longitudinal sections.* Illustrated here are the plan and lateral section of Beauvais Cathedral (FIG. **I-18**), which readers can compare with the photograph of the church's *choir* (FIG. I-3). The plan shows the choir's shape and the location of the *piers* dividing the *aisles* and supporting the *vaults* above, as well as the pattern of the crisscrossing vault *ribs.* The lateral section shows not only the interior of the choir with its vaults and tall *stained-glass* windows but also the structure of the roof and the form of the exterior *flying buttresses* holding the vaults in place.

Other types of architectural drawings appear throughout this book. An *elevation* drawing is a head-on view of an external or internal wall. A *cutaway* combines in a single drawing an exterior view with an interior view of part of a building.

This overview of the art historian's vocabulary is not exhaustive, nor have artists used only painting, drawing, sculpture, and architecture as media over the millennia. Ceramics, jewelry, textiles, photography, and computer graphics are just some of the numerous other arts. All of them involve highly specialized techniques described in distinct vocabularies. As in this introductory chapter, new terms are in *italics* when they first appear. The comprehensive Glossary at the end of the book contains definitions of all italicized terms.

Art History and Other Disciplines

By its very nature, the work of art historians intersects with the work of others in many fields of knowledge, not only in the humanities but also in the social and natural sciences. Today, art historians must go beyond the boundaries of what the public and even professional art historians of previous generations traditionally considered the specialized discipline of art history. In short, art historical research in the 21st century is typically interdisciplinary in nature. To cite one example, in an effort to unlock the secrets of a particular statue, an art historian might conduct archival research hoping to uncover new documents shedding light on who paid for the work and why, who made it and when, where it originally stood, how its contemporaries viewed it, and a host of other questions. Realizing, however, that the authors of the written documents often were not objective recorders of fact but observers with their own biases and agendas, the art historian may also use methodologies developed in fields such as literary criticism, philosophy, sociology, and gender studies to weigh the evidence the documents provide.

At other times, rather than attempting to master many disciplines at once, art historians band together with other specialists in multidisciplinary inquiries. Art historians might call in chemists

I-18 Plan (*left*) and lateral section (*right*) of Beauvais Cathedral, Beauvais, France, rebuilt after 1284.

Architectural drawings are indispensable aids for the analysis of buildings. Plans are maps of floors, recording the structure's masses. Sections are vertical "slices" across either a building's width or length.

to date an artwork based on the composition of the materials used, or might ask geologists to determine which quarry furnished the stone for a particular statue. X-ray technicians might be enlisted in an attempt to establish whether a painting is a forgery. Of course, art historians often reciprocate by contributing their expertise to the solution of problems in other disciplines. A historian, for example, might ask an art historian to determine—based on style, material, iconography, and other criteria—if any of the portraits of a certain king date after his death. Such information would help establish the ruler's continuing prestige during the reigns of his successors. (Some portraits of Augustus [FIG. I-10], the founder of the Roman Empire, postdate his death by decades, even centuries.)

DIFFERENT WAYS OF SEEING

The history of art can be a history of artists and their works, of styles and stylistic change, of materials and techniques, of images and themes and their meanings, and of contexts and cultures and patrons. The best art historians analyze artworks from many viewpoints. But no art historian (or scholar in any other field), no matter how broad-minded in approach and no matter how experienced, can be truly objective. As were the artists who made the works illustrated and discussed in this book, art historians are members of a society, participants in its culture. How can scholars (and museum visitors and travelers to foreign locales) comprehend cultures unlike their own? They can try to reconstruct the original cultural contexts of artworks, but they are limited by their distance from the thought patterns of the cultures they study and by the obstructions to understanding—the assumptions, presuppositions, and prejudices peculiar to their own culture—their own thought patterns raise. Art historians may reconstruct a distorted picture of the past because of culture-bound blindness.

A single instance underscores how differently people of diverse cultures view the world and how various ways of seeing can result in sharp differences in how artists depict the world. Illustrated here are two contemporaneous portraits of a 19th-century Maori chieftain (FIG. I-19)—one by an Englishman, JOHN HENRY SYLVESTER (active early 19th century), and the other by the New Zealand chieftain himself, TE PEHI KUPE (d. 1829). Both reproduce the chieftain's facial tattooing. The European artist (FIG. I-19, *left*) included the head and shoulders and downplayed the tattooing. The tattoo pattern is one aspect of the likeness among many, no more or less important than the chieftain's European attire. Sylvester also recorded his subject's momentary glance toward the right and the play of light on his hair, fleeting aspects having nothing to do with the figure's identity.

In contrast, Te Pehi Kupe's self-portrait (FIG. I-19, *right*)—made during a trip to Liverpool, England, to obtain European arms to take back to New Zealand—is not a picture of a man situated in space and bathed in light. Rather, it is the chieftain's statement of the supreme importance of the tattoo design announcing his rank among his people. Remarkably, Te Pehi Kupe created the tattoo patterns from memory, without the aid of a mirror. The splendidly composed insignia, presented as a flat design separated from the body and even from the head, is Te Pehi Kupe's image of himself. Only by understanding the cultural context of each portrait can art historians hope to understand why either representation appears as it does.

As noted at the outset, the study of the context of artworks and buildings is one of the central concerns of art historians. *Art through the Ages: The Western Perspective* seeks to present a history of art and architecture that will help readers to understand not only the subjects, styles, and techniques of paintings, sculptures, buildings, and other art forms created in all parts of the world during 30 millennia but also their cultural and historical contexts. That story now begins.

I-19 *Left:* JOHN HENRY SYLVESTER, *Portrait of Te Pehi Kupe,* 1826. Watercolor, 8¼″ × 6¼″. National Library of Australia, Canberra (Rex Nan Kivell Collection). *Right:* TE PEHI KUPE, *Self-Portrait,* 1826. From Leo Frobenius, *The Childhood of Man* (New York: J. B. Lippincott, 1909).

These strikingly different portraits of the same Maori chief reveal the different ways of seeing by a European artist and an Oceanic one. Understanding the cultural context of artworks is vital to art history.

Giotto's cycle of biblical frescoes in the Arena Chapel includes 38 framed panels depicting the lives of the Virgin, her parents, and Jesus. The passion cycle opens with *Entry into Jerusalem*.

Giotto's vision of the *Last Judgment* fills the west wall above the entrance to the Arena Chapel. The Paduan banker Enrico Scrovegni built the chapel to expiate the moneylender's sin of usury.

Giotto was a pioneer in pursuing a naturalistic approach to representation based on observation. In *Betrayal of Jesus,* he revived the classical tradition of depicting some figures from the rear.

14-1 GIOTTO DI BONDONE, interior of the Arena Chapel (Cappella Scrovegni; looking west), Padua, Italy, 1305–1306.

Giotto was also a master of composition. In *Lamentation*, the rocky slope behind the figures leads the viewer's eye toward the heads of Mary and the dead Jesus at the lower left.

LATE MEDIEVAL ITALY

LATE MEDIEVAL OR PROTO-RENAISSANCE?

Art historians debate whether the art of Italy between 1200 and 1400 is the last phase of medieval art or the beginning of the rebirth, or *Renaissance,* of Greco-Roman *naturalism.* All agree, however, the pivotal figure of this age was the Florentine painter GIOTTO DI BONDONE (ca. 1266–1337), whose masterwork was the fresco cycle of the Arena Chapel (FIG. **14-1**) in Padua. A banker, Enrico Scrovegni, built the chapel on a site adjacent to his palace in the hope it would expiate the moneylender's sin of usury. Consecrated in 1305, the chapel takes its name from an ancient Roman arena (*amphitheater*) nearby.

Some scholars have suggested Giotto himself may have been the chapel's architect, because its design so perfectly suits its interior decoration. The rectangular hall has only six windows, all in the south wall, leaving the other walls as almost unbroken and well-illuminated surfaces for painting. In 38 framed panels, Giotto presented the most poignant incidents from the lives of the Virgin and her parents, Joachim and Anna, in the top level, and, in the middle and lower levels, the life and mission (middle), and the passion and resurrection (bottom) of Jesus. The climactic event of the cycle of human salvation, *Last Judgment,* covers most of the west wall above the chapel's entrance.

The *Entry into Jerusalem, Betrayal of Jesus,* and *Lamentation* panels reveal the essentials of Giotto's style. In contrast to the common practice of his day, Giotto based his method of pictorial expression on observation of the natural world—the approach championed by the ancient Greeks and Romans but largely abandoned in the Middle Ages. Subtly scaled to the chapel's space, Giotto's stately and slow-moving half-life-size figures act out the religious dramas convincingly and with great restraint. The biblical actors are sculpturesque, simple, and weighty, often *foreshortened* (seen from an angle) and modeled with light and shading in the classical manner. They convey individual emotions through their postures and gestures. Giotto's naturalism displaced the Byzantine style in Italy (see Chapter 9), inaugurating an age some scholars call "early scientific." By stressing the preeminence of sight for gaining knowledge of the world, Giotto and his successors contributed to the foundation of empirical science. They recognized that the visual world must be observed before it can be analyzed and understood. Praised in his own and later times for his fidelity to nature, Giotto was more than a mere imitator of it. He showed his generation a new way of seeing. With Giotto, Western painters turned away from the spiritual world—the focus of medieval European artists—and once again moved resolutely toward the visible world as the inspiration for their art.

13TH CENTURY

When the Italian humanists of the 16th century condemned the art of the late Middle Ages in northern Europe as *"Gothic"* (see Chapter 13), they did so by comparing it with the contemporaneous art of Italy, which consciously revived *classical** art. Italian artists and scholars regarded medieval artworks as distortions of the noble art of the Greeks and Romans. Interest in the art of classical antiquity was not entirely absent during the medieval period, however, even in France, the center of the Gothic style. For example, on the west front of Reims Cathedral, the 13th-century statues of Christian *saints* and angels (FIG. 13-24) reveal the unmistakable influence of ancient Roman art on French sculptors. However, the classical revival that took root in Italy during the 13th and 14th centuries was much more pervasive and longer-lasting.

Sculpture

Italian admiration for classical art surfaced early on at the court of Frederick II, king of Sicily (r. 1197–1250) and Holy Roman emperor (r. 1220–1250). Frederick's nostalgia for Rome's past grandeur fostered a revival of classical sculpture in Sicily and southern Italy not unlike the classical *renovatio* (renewal) Charlemagne encouraged in Germany and France four centuries earlier (see Chapter 11).

NICOLA PISANO The sculptor Nicola d'Apulia (Nicholas of Apulia), better known as NICOLA PISANO (active ca. 1258–1278) after his adopted city (see "Italian Artists' Names," page 405, and MAP 14-1), received his early training in southern Italy under Frederick's rule. In 1250, Nicola traveled northward and eventually settled in Pisa. Then at the height of its political and economic power, the maritime city was a magnet for artists seeking lucrative commissions. Nicola specialized in carving marble reliefs and ornamentation for large *pulpits* (raised platforms from which priests led church services), completing the first (FIG. 14-2) in 1260 for Pisa's century-old baptistery (FIG. 12-26, *left*). Some elements of the pulpit's design carried on medieval traditions—for example, the *trefoil* (triple-curved) *arches* and the lions supporting some of the *columns*—but Nicola also incorporated classical elements. The large *capitals* with two rows of thick overlapping leaves crowning the columns are a Gothic variation of the *Corinthian capital* (see page 151 and FIG. 5-73, or page xxvi–xxvii in Volume II). The arches are round, as in Roman architecture, rather than pointed (*ogival*), as in Gothic buildings. Also, each of the large rectangular relief panels resembles the sculptured front of a Roman *sarcophagus* (coffin; for example, FIG. 7-70).

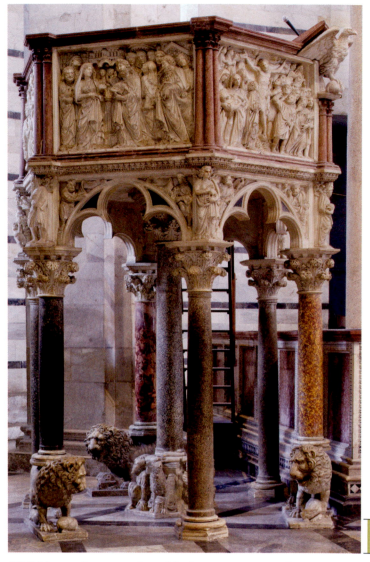

14-2 NICOLA PISANO, pulpit of the baptistery, Pisa, Italy, 1259–1260. Marble, 15′ high. ◼◀

Nicola Pisano's Pisa baptistery pulpit retains many medieval features, for example, the trefoil arches and the lions supporting columns, but the figures derive from ancient Roman sarcophagus reliefs.

*In *Art through the Ages* the adjective "Classical," with uppercase C, refers specifically to the Classical period of ancient Greece, 480–323 BCE. Lowercase "classical" refers to Greco-Roman antiquity in general, that is, the period treated in Chapters 5, 6, and 7.

LATE MEDIEVAL ITALY

1200	1300	1400

- Bonaventura Berlinghieri and Cimabue are the leading painters working in the Italo-Byzantine style, or *maniera greca*
- Nicola and Giovanni Pisano, father and son, represent two contrasting sculptural styles, the classical and the Gothic respectively
- Fresco cycles in Rome and Assisi foreshadow the revolutionary art of Giotto

- In Florence, Giotto, considered the first Renaissance artist, pioneers a naturalistic approach to painting based on observation
- In Siena, Duccio softens the maniera greca and humanizes religious subject matter
- Secular themes emerge as important subjects in civic commissions, as in the frescoes of Siena's Palazzo Pubblico
- Florence, Siena, and Orvieto build new cathedrals that are stylistically closer to Early Christian basilicas than to French Gothic cathedrals

14-3 Nicola Pisano, *Annunciation, Nativity,* and *Adoration of the Shepherds,* relief panel on the baptistery pulpit, Pisa, Italy, 1259–1260. Marble, 2′ 10″ × 3′ 9″. ◼◗

Classical sculpture inspired the faces, beards, coiffures, and draperies, as well as the bulk and weight of Nicola's figures. The *Nativity* Madonna resembles lid figures on Roman sarcophagi.

1 ft.

14-4 Giovanni Pisano, *Annunciation, Nativity,* and *Adoration of the Shepherds,* relief panel on the pulpit of Sant'Andrea, Pistoia, Italy, 1297–1301. Marble, 2′ 10″ × 3′ 4″.

The French Gothic style had a greater influence on Giovanni Pisano, Nicola's son. Giovanni arranged his figures loosely and dynamically. They display a nervous agitation, as if moved by spiritual passion.

1 ft.

The densely packed large-scale figures of the individual panels also seem to derive from the compositions found on Roman sarcophagi. One of these panels (FIG. 14-3) depicts scenes from the infancy cycle of Christ (see "The Life of Jesus in Art," Chapter 8, pages 240–241, or pages xxxiv–xxxv, in Volume II), including *Annunciation* (*top left*), *Nativity* (*center* and *lower half*), and *Adoration of the Shepherds* (*top right*). Mary appears twice, and her size varies. The focus of the composition is the reclining Virgin of *Nativity,* whose posture and drapery are reminiscent of those of the lid figures on Etruscan (FIGS. 6-5 and 6-15) and Roman (FIG. 7-61) sarcophagi. The face types, beards, and coiffures, as well as the bulk and weight of Nicola's figures, also reveal the influence of classical relief sculpture. Art historians have even been able to pinpoint the models of some of the pulpit figures on Roman sarcophagi in Pisa.

GIOVANNI PISANO Nicola's son, Giovanni Pisano (ca. 1250–1320), likewise became a sought-after sculptor of church pulpits. Giovanni's pulpit in Sant'Andrea at Pistoia also has a panel (FIG. 14-4) featuring *Nativity* and related scenes. The son's version of the subject offers a striking contrast to his father's thick carving and placid, almost stolid presentation of the religious narrative. Giovanni arranged the figures loosely and dynamically. They twist and bend in excited animation, and the deep spaces between them suggest their motion. In *Annunciation* (*top left*), the Virgin shrinks from the angel's sudden appearance in a posture of alarm touched with humility. The same spasm of apprehension contracts her supple body as she reclines in *Nativity* (*center*). The drama's principals share in a peculiar nervous agitation, as if spiritual passion suddenly moves all of them. Only the shepherds and the sheep (*right*)

The Great Schism, Mendicant Orders, and Confraternities

In 1305, the College of Cardinals (the collective body of all cardinals) elected a French pope, Clement V (r. 1305–1314), who settled in Avignon. Subsequent French popes remained in Avignon, despite their announced intentions to return to Rome. Understandably, the Italians, who saw Rome as the rightful capital of the universal Church, resented the Avignon papacy. The conflict between the French and Italians resulted in the election in 1378 of two popes—Clement VII, who resided in Avignon (and who does not appear in the Catholic Church's official list of popes), and Urban VI (r. 1378–1389), who remained in Rome. Thus began what became known as the Great Schism. After 40 years, Holy Roman Emperor Sigismund (r. 1410–1437) convened a council that resolved this crisis by electing a new Roman pope, Martin V (r. 1417–1431), who was acceptable to all.

The pope's absence from Italy during much of the 14th century contributed to an increase in prominence of *monastic orders*. The Augustinians, Carmelites, and Servites became very active, ensuring a constant religious presence in the daily life of Italians, but the largest and most influential monastic orders were the *mendicants* (begging friars)—the Franciscans, founded by Francis of Assisi (FIG. 14-5), and the Dominicans, founded by the Spaniard Dominic de Guzman (ca. 1170–1221). These mendicants renounced all worldly goods and committed themselves to spreading God's word, performing good deeds, and ministering to the sick and dying. The Dominicans, in particular, contributed significantly to establishing urban educational institutions. The Franciscans and Dominicans became very popular in Italy because of their devotion to their faith and the more personal relationship with God they encouraged. Although both mendicant orders worked for the glory of God, a degree of rivalry nevertheless existed between the two. For example, in Florence they established their churches on opposite sides of the city—Santa Croce (FIG. I-4), the Franciscan church, on the eastern side, and the Dominicans' Santa Maria Novella (FIG. 14-6A) on the western (MAP 16-1).

14-5 BONAVENTURA BERLINGHIERI, *Saint Francis Altarpiece,* San Francesco, Pescia, Italy, 1235. Tempera on wood, 5′ × 3′ × 6′. ◼◀

Berlinghieri painted this altarpiece in the Italo-Byzantine style, or *maniera greca*, for the mendicant (begging) order of Franciscans. It is the earliest known representation of Saint Francis of Assisi.

Confraternities, organizations consisting of laypersons who dedicated themselves to strict religious observance, also grew in popularity during the 14th and 15th centuries. The mission of confraternities included tending the sick, burying the dead, singing hymns, and performing other good works. The confraternities as well as the mendicant orders continued to play an important role in Italian religious life through the 16th century. The numerous artworks and monastic churches they commissioned have ensured their enduring legacy.

do not yet share in the miraculous event. The swiftly turning, sinuous draperies, the slender figures they enfold, and the general emotionalism of the scene are features not found in Nicola Pisano's interpretation. The father worked in the classical tradition, the son in a style derived from French Gothic. These styles were two of the three most important ingredients in the formation of the distinctive and original art of 14th-century Italy.

Painting and Architecture

The third major stylistic element in late medieval Italian art was the Byzantine tradition (see Chapter 9). Throughout the Middle Ages, the Byzantine style dominated Italian painting, but its influence was especially strong after the fall of Constantinople in 1204, which precipitated a migration of Byzantine artists to Italy.

BONAVENTURA BERLINGHIERI One of the leading painters working in the Italo-Byzantine style, or *maniera greca* (Greek style), was BONAVENTURA BERLINGHIERI (active ca. 1235–1244) of Lucca. His most famous work is the *Saint Francis Altarpiece* (FIG. 14-5) in the church of San Francesco (Saint Francis) in Pescia. Painted in 1235 using *tempera* on wood panel (see "Tempera and Oil Painting," Chapter 15, page 427), the *altarpiece* honors Saint Francis of Assisi (ca. 1181–1226), whose most important shrine (FIG. 14-5A), at Assisi itself, boasts the most extensive cycle of

Italian Artists' Names

In contemporary societies, people have become accustomed to a standardized method of identifying individuals, in part because of the proliferation of official documents such as driver's licenses, passports, and student identification cards. Modern names consist of given names (names selected by the parents) and family names, although the order of the two (or more) names varies from country to country. In China, for example, the family name precedes the given name.

This kind of regularity in names was not, however, the norm in premodern Italy. Many individuals were known by their place of birth or adopted hometown. Nicola Pisano (FIGS. 14-2 and 14-3) was "Nicholas the Pisan," Giulio Romano was "Julius the Roman," and Domenico Veneziano was "the Venetian." Leonardo da Vinci ("Leonard from Vinci") hailed from the small town of Vinci, near Florence (MAP 14-1). Art historians therefore refer to these artists by their given names, not the names of their towns. (The title of Dan Brown's best-selling novel should have been *The Leonardo Code*, not *The Da Vinci Code*.)

Nicknames were also common. Giorgione was "Big George." People usually referred to Tommaso di Cristoforo Fini as Masolino ("Little Thomas") to distinguish him from his more famous pupil, Masaccio ("Brutish Thomas"). Guido di Pietro was called Fra Angelico (the Angelic Friar). Cenni di Pepo is remembered as Cimabue (FIG. 14-6), which means "bull's head."

Names were also impermanent and could be changed at will. This flexibility has resulted in significant challenges for historians, who often must deal with archival documents and records referring to the same artist by different names.

MAP 14-1 Italy around 1400.

---

frescoes from 13th-century Italy. Berlinghieri depicted Francis wearing the costume later adopted by all Franciscan monks: a coarse clerical robe tied at the waist with a rope. The saint displays the *stigmata*—marks resembling Christ's wounds—that miraculously appeared on his hands and feet. Flanking Francis are two angels, whose frontal poses, prominent halos, and lack of modeling reveal the Byzantine roots of Berlinghieri's style. So, too, does the use of *gold leaf* (gold beaten into tissue-paper-thin sheets, then applied to surfaces), which emphasizes the image's flatness and spiritual nature. The narrative scenes along the sides of the panel provide an active contrast to the stiff formality of the large central image of Francis. At the upper left, taking pride of place at the saint's right, Francis receives the stigmata. Directly below, the saint preaches to the birds, a subject that also figures prominently in the fresco program (FIG. 14-5B) of San Francesco at Assisi, the work of a painter art historians call the SAINT FRANCIS MASTER. These and the scenes depicting Francis's

14-5A San Francesco, Assisi, 1228–1253.

14-5B St. Francis Master, *Preaching to the Birds*, ca. 1290–1300.

miracle cures strongly suggest Berlinghieri's source was one or more Byzantine *illuminated manuscripts* (compare FIG. 9-17) with biblical narrative scenes.

Berlinghieri's *Saint Francis Altarpiece* also highlights the increasingly prominent role of religious orders in late medieval Italy (see "The Great Schism, Mendicant Orders, and Confraternities," page 404). Saint Francis's Franciscan order worked diligently to impress on the public the saint's valuable example and to demonstrate the order's commitment to teaching and to alleviating suffering. Berlinghieri's Pescia altarpiece, painted only nine years after Francis's death, is the earliest known signed and dated representation of the saint. Appropriately, Berlinghieri's panel focuses on the aspects of the saint's life the Franciscans wanted to promote, thereby making visible (and thus more credible) the legendary life of this holy man. Saint Francis believed he could get closer to God by rejecting worldly goods, and to achieve this he stripped himself bare in a public square and committed himself to a strict life of fasting, prayer, and meditation. His followers considered the appearance of stigmata on Francis's hands and feet (clearly visible in the saint's frontal image, which resembles a Byzantine *icon*) as God's blessing, and viewed Francis as a second Christ. Fittingly, four of the six narrative scenes on the altarpiece depict miraculous healings, connecting Saint Francis even more emphatically to Christ.

14-6 CIMABUE, *Madonna Enthroned with Angels and Prophets,* from Santa Trinità, Florence, ca. 1280–1290. Tempera and gold leaf on wood, 12′ 7″ × 7′ 4″. Galleria degli Uffizi, Florence. ◼

Cimabue was one of the first artists to break away from the *maniera greca.* Although he relied on Byzantine models, Cimabue depicted the Madonna's massive throne as receding into space.

14-6A Santa Maria Novella, Florence, begun ca. 1246. ◼

CIMABUE One of the first artists to break from the Italo-Byzantine style that dominated 13th-century Italian painting was Cenni di Pepo, better known as CIMABUE (ca. 1240–1302). Cimabue challenged some of the major conventions of late medieval art in pursuit of a new naturalism, the close observation of the natural world—the core of the classical tradition. He painted *Madonna Enthroned with Angels and Prophets* (FIG. **14-6**) for Santa Trinità (Holy Trinity) in Florence, the Benedictine church near the Arno River built between 1258 and 1280, roughly contemporaneous with the Dominican church of Santa Maria Novella (FIG. **14-6A**). The composition and the gold background reveal the painter's reliance on Byzantine models (compare FIG. **9-18**).

Cimabue also used the gold embellishments common to Byzantine art for the folds of the Madonna's robe, but they are no longer merely decorative patterns. In his panel they enhance the three-dimensionality of the drapery. Furthermore, Cimabue constructed a deeper space for the Madonna and the surrounding figures to inhabit than was common in Byzantine art. The Virgin's throne, for example, is a massive structure and Cimabue convincingly depicted it as receding into space. The overlapping bodies of the angels on each side of the throne and the half-length prophets who look outward or upward from beneath it reinforce the sense of depth.

14TH CENTURY

In the 14th century, Italy consisted of numerous independent *city-states,* each corresponding to a geographic region centered on a major city (MAP 14-1). Most of the city-states, such as Venice, Florence, Lucca, and Siena, were republics—constitutional oligarchies governed by executive bodies, advisory councils, and special commissions. Other powerful 14th-century states included the Papal States, the Kingdom of Naples, and the Duchies of Milan, Modena, Ferrara, and Savoy. As their names indicate, these states were politically distinct from the republics, but all the states shared in the prosperity of the period. The sources of wealth varied from state to state. Italy's port cities expanded maritime trade, whereas the economies of other cities depended on banking or the manufacture of arms or textiles.

The outbreak of the Black Death (bubonic plague) in the late 1340s threatened this prosperity, however. Originating in China, the Black Death swept across Europe. The most devastating natural disaster in European history, the plague eliminated between 25 and 50 percent of the Continent's population in about five years. The Black Death devastated Italy's inhabitants. In large Italian cities, where people lived in relatively close proximity, the death tolls climbed as high as 50 to 60 percent of the population. The bubonic plague had a significant effect on art. It stimulated religious bequests and encouraged the commissioning of devotional images. The focus on sickness and death also led to a burgeoning in hospital construction.

Another significant development in 14th-century Italy was the blossoming of a vernacular (commonly spoken) literature, which dramatically affected Italy's intellectual and cultural life. Latin remained the official language of Church liturgy and state documents. However, the creation of an Italian vernacular literature (based on the Tuscan dialect common in Florence) expanded the audience for philosophical and intellectual concepts because of its greater accessibility. Dante Alighieri (1265–1321, author of *The Divine Comedy*), the poet and scholar Francesco Petrarch (1304–1374), and Giovanni Boccaccio (1313–1375, author of *Decameron*) were most responsible for establishing this vernacular literature.

RENAISSANCE HUMANISM The development of a vernacular literature was one important sign that the essentially religious view of the world dominating medieval Europe was about to change dramatically in what historians call the *Renaissance.* Although religion continued to occupy a primary position in the lives of Europeans, a growing concern with the natural world, the individual, and humanity's worldly existence characterized the Renaissance period—the 14th through the 16th centuries. The word *renaissance* in French and English (*rinascità* in Italian) refers to a "rebirth" of art and culture. A revived interest in classical cultures—indeed, the veneration of classical antiquity as a model—was central to this rebirth. The notion of the Renaissance representing the restoration of the glorious past of Greece and Rome gave rise to the concept of the "Middle Ages" as the era falling between antiquity and the Renaissance. The transition from the medieval to the Renaissance, though dramatic, did not come about abruptly, however. In fact, much that is medieval persisted in the Renaissance and in later periods.

Fundamental to the development of the Italian Renaissance was *humanism,* which emerged during the 14th century and became a central component of Italian art and culture in the 15th and 16th centuries. Humanism was more a code of civil conduct, a theory of education, and a scholarly discipline than a philosophical system. As their name suggests, Italian humanists were concerned chiefly with human values and interests as distinct from—but not opposed to—religion's otherworldly values. Humanists pointed to classical cultures as particularly praiseworthy. This enthusiasm for antiquity, represented by the elegant Latin of Cicero (106–43 BCE) and the Augustan age, involved study of Latin literature and a conscious emulation of what proponents believed were the Roman civic virtues. These included self-sacrificing service to the state, participation in government, defense of state institutions (especially the administration of justice), and stoic indifference to personal misfortune in the performance of duty. With the help of a new interest in and knowledge of Greek, the humanists of the late 14th and 15th centuries recovered a large part of Greek as well as Roman literature and philosophy that had been lost, left unnoticed, or cast aside in the Middle Ages. Indeed, classical cultures provided humanists with a model for living in this world, a model primarily of human focus derived not from an authoritative and traditional religious dogma but from reason.

Ideally, humanists sought no material reward for services rendered. The sole reward for heroes of civic virtue was fame, just as the reward for leaders of the holy life was sainthood. For the educated, the lives of heroes and heroines of the past became as edifying as the lives of the saints. Petrarch wrote a book on illustrious men, and his colleague Boccaccio complemented it with 106 biographies of famous women—from Eve to Joanna, queen of Naples (r. 1343–1382). Both Petrarch and Boccaccio were famous in their own day as poets, scholars, and men of letters—their achievements equivalent in honor to those of the heroes of civic virtue. In 1341 in Rome, Petrarch received the laurel wreath crown, the ancient symbol of victory and merit. The humanist cult of fame emphasized the importance of creative individuals and their role in contributing to the renown of the city-state and of all Italy.

Giotto

14-6B CAVALLINI, *Last Judgment,* ca. 1290–1295.

Critics from Giorgio Vasari[†] to the present day have regarded Giotto di Bondone (FIG. 14-1) as the first Renaissance painter. A pioneer in pursuing a naturalistic approach to representation based on observation, he made a much more radical break with the past than did Cimabue, whom Vasari identified as Giotto's teacher. Scholars still debate the sources of Giotto's style, however. One formative influence must have been Cimabue's work,

although Vasari lauded Giotto as having eclipsed his master by abandoning the "crude maniera greca." The 13th-century *murals* of San Francesco at Assisi (FIGS. 14-5A and 14-5B) and those of PIETRO CAVALLINI (ca. 1240–ca. 1340) in Rome (FIG. 14-6B) may also have influenced the young Giotto. French Gothic sculpture (which Giotto may have seen but which was certainly familiar to him from the work of Giovanni Pisano, who had spent time in Paris) and ancient Roman art probably also contributed to Giotto's artistic education. Yet no mere synthesis of these varied influences could have produced the significant shift in artistic approach that has led some scholars to describe Giotto as the father of Western pictorial art. Renowned in his own day, his reputation has never faltered. Regardless of the other influences on his artistic style, his true teacher was nature—the world of visible things.

MADONNA ENTHRONED On nearly the same great scale as Cimabue's enthroned Madonna (FIG. 14-6) is Giotto's panel (FIG. **14-7**) depicting the same subject, painted for the high altar

1 ft.

14-7 GIOTTO DI BONDONE, *Madonna Enthroned,* from the Church of Ognissanti, Florence, ca. 1310. Tempera and gold leaf on wood, 10′ 8″ × 6′ 8″. Galleria degli Uffizi, Florence.

Giotto displaced the Byzantine style in Italian painting and revived classical naturalism. His figures have substance, dimensionality, and bulk, and give the illusion they could throw shadows.

†Giorgio Vasari (1511–1574) was both a painter and an architect. Today, however, people associate him primarily with his landmark book, *Lives of the Most Eminent Painters, Sculptors, and Architects,* first published in 1550. Despite inaccuracies, Vasari's *Lives* is an invaluable research tool. It is the major contemporary source of information about Italian Renaissance art and artists.

Fresco Painting

Fresco painting has a long history, particularly in the Mediterranean region, where the Minoans (FIGS. 4-7 to 4-9B) used it as early as the 17th century BCE. *Fresco* (Italian for "fresh") is a mural-painting technique involving the application of permanent limeproof pigments, diluted in water, on freshly laid lime plaster. Because the surface of the wall absorbs the pigments as the plaster dries, fresco is one of the most durable painting techniques. The stable condition of the ancient Minoan frescoes, as well as those found at Pompeii and other Roman sites (FIGS. 7-17 to 7-26), in San Francesco (FIGS. 14-5A and 14-5B) at Assisi, and in the Arena Chapel (FIGS. 14-1 and 14-8 to 14-8B) at Padua, testify to the longevity of this painting method. The colors have remained vivid (although dirt and soot have necessitated cleaning—most famously in the Vatican's Sistine Chapel; FIG. 17-18B) because of the chemically inert pigments the artists used. In addition to this *buon fresco* (good, that is, true fresco) technique, artists used *fresco secco* (dry fresco). Fresco secco involves painting on dried lime plaster, the method the ancient Egyptians favored (FIGS. 3-28 and 3-29). Although the finished product visually approximates buon fresco, the plaster wall does not absorb the pigments, which simply adhere to the surface, so fresco secco is not as permanent as buon fresco.

The buon fresco process is time-consuming and demanding and requires several layers of plaster. Although buon fresco methods vary, generally the artist prepares the wall with a rough layer of lime plaster called the *arriccio* (brown coat). The artist then transfers the composition to the wall, usually by drawing directly on the arriccio with a burnt-orange pigment called *sinopia* (most popular during the 14th century), or by transferring a *cartoon* (a full-size preparatory drawing). Cartoons increased in usage in the 15th and 16th centuries, largely replacing sinopia underdrawings. Finally, the painter lays the *intonaco* (painting coat) smoothly over the drawing in sections (called *giornate*—Italian for "days") only as large as the artist expects to complete in that session. (In Giotto's *Lamentation*

1 ft.

14-8 GIOTTO DI BONDONE, *Lamentation,* Arena Chapel (Cappella Scrovegni), Padua, Italy, ca. 1305. Fresco, 6' 6¾" × 6' ¾". ◼◣

Giotto painted *Lamentation* in several sections, each corresponding to one painting session. Artists employing the buon fresco technique must complete each section before the plaster dries.

[FIG. 14-8], the giornate are easy to distinguish.) The buon fresco painter must apply the colors quickly, because once the plaster is dry, it will no longer absorb the pigment. Any unpainted areas of the intonaco after a session must be cut away so that fresh plaster can be applied for the next giornata.

In areas of high humidity, such as Venice, fresco was less appropriate because moisture is an obstacle to the drying process. Over the centuries, fresco became less popular, although it did experience a revival in the 1930s with the Mexican muralists (FIGS. 24-73 and 24-74).

of Florence's Church of the Ognissanti (All Saints). Although still portrayed against the traditional gold background, Giotto's Madonna rests within her Gothic throne with the unshakable stability of an ancient marble goddess (compare FIG. 7-30). Giotto replaced Cimabue's slender Virgin, fragile beneath the thin ripplings of her drapery, with a weighty, queenly mother. In Giotto's painting, the Madonna's body is not lost—indeed, it is asserted. Giotto even showed Mary's breasts pressing through the thin fabric of her white undergarment. Gold highlights have disappeared from her heavy robe. Giotto aimed instead to construct a figure with substance, dimensionality, and bulk—qualities suppressed in favor of a spiritual immateriality in Byzantine and Italo-Byzantine art. Works painted in the new style portray statuesque figures projecting into the light and giving the illusion they could throw shadows. Giotto's *Madonna Enthroned* marks the end of medieval painting in Italy and the beginning of a new naturalistic approach to art.

14-8A Giotto, *Entry into Jerusalem*, ca. 1305.

14-8B Giotto, *Betrayal of Jesus*, ca. 1305.

ARENA CHAPEL Projecting on a flat surface the illusion of solid bodies moving through space presents a double challenge. Constructing the illusion of a weighty, three-dimensional body also requires constructing the illusion of a space sufficiently ample to contain that body. In his *fresco* cycles (see "Fresco Painting," page 408), Giotto constantly strove to reconcile these two aspects of illusionistic painting. His murals in Enrico Scrovegni's Arena Chapel (FIG. 14-1) at Padua show his art at its finest. In 38 framed scenes (FIGS. 14-8, 14-8A, and 14-8B), Giotto presented one of the most impressive and complete Christian pictorial cycles ever rendered. The narrative unfolds on the north and south walls in three zones, reading from top to bottom. Below, imitation marble veneer—reminiscent of ancient Roman decoration (FIG. 7-51), which Giotto may have seen—alternates with personified Virtues and Vices painted in *grisaille* (monochrome grays, often used for modeling in paintings) to resemble sculpture. On the west wall above the chapel's entrance is Giotto's dramatic *Last Judgment,* the culminating scene also of Pietro Cavallini's late-13th-century fresco cycle (FIG. 14-6B) in Santa Cecilia in Trastevere in Rome. The chapel's vaulted ceiling is blue, an azure sky dotted with golden stars symbolic of Heaven. Medallions bearing images of Christ, Mary, and various prophets also appear on the vault. Giotto painted the same blue in the backgrounds of the narrative panels on the walls below. The color thereby functions as a unifying agent for the entire decorative scheme.

The panel in the lowest zone of the north wall, *Lamentation* (FIG. 14-8), illustrates particularly well the revolutionary nature of Giotto's style. In the presence of boldly foreshortened angels, seen head-on with their bodies receding into the background and darting about in hysterical grief, a congregation mourns over the dead Savior just before his entombment. Mary cradles her son's body, while Mary Magdalene looks solemnly at the wounds in Christ's feet and Saint John the Evangelist throws his arms back dramatically. Giotto arranged a shallow stage for the figures, bounded by a thick diagonal rock incline defining a horizontal ledge in the foreground. Though narrow, the ledge provides firm visual support for the figures. The rocky setting recalls the landscape of a 12th-century Byzantine mural (FIG. 9-29) at Nerezi in Macedonia. Here, the steep slope leads the viewer's eye toward the picture's dramatic focal point at the lower left. The postures and gestures of Giotto's figures convey a broad spectrum of grief. They range from Mary's almost fierce despair to the passionate outbursts of Mary Magdalene and John to the philosophical resignation of the two disciples at the right and the mute sorrow of the two hooded mourners in the foreground. In *Lamentation,* a single event provokes a host of individual responses in figures that are convincing presences both physically and psychologically. Painters before Giotto rarely attempted, let alone achieved, this combination of naturalistic representation, compositional complexity, and emotional resonance.

The formal design of the *Lamentation* fresco—the way Giotto grouped the figures within the constructed space—is worth close study. Each group has its own definition, and each contributes to the rhythmic order of the composition. The strong diagonal of the rocky ledge, with its single dead tree (the tree of knowledge of good and evil, which withered after Adam and Eve's original sin), concentrates the viewer's attention on the heads of Christ and his mother, which Giotto positioned dynamically off center. The massive bulk of the seated mourner in the painting's left corner arrests and contains all movement beyond Mary and her dead son. The seated mourner to the right establishes a relation with the center figures, who, by gazes and gestures, draw the viewer's attention back to Christ's head. Figures seen from the back, which are frequent in Giotto's compositions (compare FIG. 14-8B), represent an innovation in the development away from the formal Italo-Byzantine style. These figures emphasize the foreground, aiding the visual placement of the intermediate figures farther back in space. This device, the very contradiction of Byzantine frontality, in effect puts viewers behind the "observer figures," who, facing the action as spectators, reinforce the sense of stagecraft as a model for painting.

Giotto's new devices for depicting spatial depth and body mass could not, of course, have been possible without his management of light and shade. He shaded his figures to indicate both the direction of the light illuminating their bodies and the shadows (the diminished light), thereby giving the figures volume. In *Lamentation,* light falls upon the upper surfaces of the figures (especially the two central bending figures) and passes down to dark in their garments, separating the volumes one from the other and pushing one to the fore, the other to the rear. The graded continuum of light and shade, directed by an even, neutral light from a single steady source—not shown in the picture—was the first step toward the development of *chiaroscuro* (the use of contrasts of dark and light to produce modeling) in later Renaissance painting (see Chapter 16).

The stagelike settings made possible by Giotto's innovations in *perspective* (the depiction of three-dimensional objects in space on a two-dimensional surface) and lighting suited perfectly the dramatic narrative the Franciscans emphasized then as a principal method for educating the faithful in their religion. In this new age of humanism, the old stylized presentations of the holy mysteries had evolved into *mystery plays.* Actors extended the drama of the Mass into one- and two-act tableaus and scenes and then into simple narratives offered at church portals and in city squares. (Eventually, confraternities also presented more elaborate religious dramas called *sacre rappresentazioni*—holy representations.) The great increase in popular sermons to huge city audiences prompted a public taste for narrative, recited as dramatically as possible. The arts of illusionistic painting, of drama, and of sermon rhetoric with all their theatrical flourishes developed simultaneously and were mutually influential. Giotto's art masterfully synthesized dramatic narrative, holy lesson, and truth to human experience in a visual idiom of his own invention, accessible to all. Not surprisingly, Giotto's frescoes served as textbooks for generations of Renaissance painters.

Siena

Among 14th-century Italian city-states, the Republics of Siena and Florence were the most powerful. Both were urban centers of bankers and merchants with widespread international contacts and large sums available for the commissioning of artworks (see "Artists' Guilds, Artistic Commissions, and Artists' Contracts," page 410).

Artists' Guilds, Artistic Commissions, and Artists' Contracts

The structured organization of economic activity during the 14th century, when Italy had established a thriving international trade and held a commanding position in the Mediterranean world, extended to many trades and professions. *Guilds* (associations of master craftspeople, apprentices, and tradespeople), which had emerged during the 12th century, became prominent. These associations not only protected members' common economic interests against external pressures, such as taxation, but also provided them with the means to regulate their internal operations (for example, work quality and membership training).

Because of today's international open art market, the notion of an "artists' union" may seem strange. The general public tends to think of art as the creative expression of an individual artist. However, artists did not always enjoy this degree of freedom. Historically, they rarely undertook major artworks without receiving a specific commission. The patron contracting for the artist's services could be a civic group, religious entity, private individual, or even the artists' guild itself. Guilds, although primarily business organizations, contributed to their city's religious and artistic life by subsidizing the building and decoration of numerous churches and hospitals. For example, the wool manufacturers' guild oversaw the start of Florence Cathedral (FIGS. 14-18 and 14-18A) in 1296, and the wool merchants' guild supervised the completion of its dome (FIG. 16-30A). The guild of silk manufacturers and goldsmiths provided the funds to build Florence's foundling hospital, the Ospedale degli Innocenti (FIG. 16-31).

Monastic orders, confraternities, and the popes were also major art patrons. In addition, wealthy families and individuals—for example, the Paduan banker Enrico Scrovegni (FIG. 14-1)—commissioned artworks for a wide variety of reasons. Besides the aesthetic pleasure these patrons derived from art, the images often also served as testaments to the patron's piety, wealth, and stature. Because artworks during this period were the product of service contracts, a patron's needs or wishes played a crucial role in the final form of any painting, sculpture, or building. Some early contracts between patrons and artists still exist. Patrons normally asked artists to submit drawings or models for approval, and they expected the artists they hired to adhere closely to the approved designs. The contracts usually stipulated certain conditions, such as the insistence on the artist's own hand in the production of the work, the quality of pigment and amount of gold or other precious items to be used, completion date, payment terms, and penalties for failure to meet the contract's terms.

A few extant 13th- and 14th-century painting contracts are especially illuminating. Although they may specify the subject to be represented, these binding legal documents always focus on the financial aspects of the commission and the responsibilities of the painter to the patron (and vice versa). In a contract dated November 1, 1301, between Cimabue (FIG. 14-6) and another artist and the Hospital of Santa Chiara in Pisa, the artists agree to supply an altarpiece

> with colonnettes, tabernacles, and predella, painted with histories of the divine majesty of the Blessed Virgin Mary, of the apostles, of the angels, and with other figures and pictures, as shall be seen fit and shall please the said master of or other legitimate persons for the hospital.*

Other terms of the Santa Chiara contract specify the size of the panel and require the artists to use gold and silver gilding for parts of the altarpiece.

The contract for the construction of an altarpiece was usually a separate document, because it necessitated employing the services of a master carpenter. For example, on April 15, 1285, the leading painter of Siena, Duccio di Buoninsegna (FIGS. 14-9 to 14-11), signed a contract with the rectors of the Confraternity of the Laudesi, the lay group associated with the Dominican church of Santa Maria Novella (FIG. 14-6A) in Florence. The contract specified only that Duccio was to provide the painting, not its frame—and it imposed conditions the painter had to meet if he was to be paid.

> [The rectors] promise . . . to pay the same Duccio . . . as the payment and price of the painting of the said panel that is to be painted and done by him in the way described below . . . 150 lire of the small florins. . . . [Duccio, in turn, promises] to paint and embellish the panel with the image of the blessed Virgin Mary and of her omnipotent Son and other figures, according to the wishes and pleasure of the lessors, and to gild [the panel] and do everything that will enhance the beauty of the panel, his being all the expenses and the costs. . . . If the said panel is not beautifully painted and it is not embellished according to the wishes and desires of the same lessors, they are in no way bound to pay him the price or any part of it.†

Sometimes patrons furnished the materials and paid artists by the day instead of a fixed amount. That was the arrangement Duccio made on October 9, 1308, when he agreed to paint the *Maestà* (FIG. 14-9) for the high altar of Siena Cathedral.

> Duccio has promised to paint and make the said panel as well as he can and knows how, and he further agreed not to accept or receive any other work until the said panel is done and completed. . . . [The church officials promise] to pay the said Duccio sixteen solidi of the Sienese denari as his salary for the said work and labor for each day that the said Duccio works with his own hands on the said panel . . . [and] to provide and give everything that will be necessary for working on the said panel so that the said Duccio need contribute nothing to the work save his person and his effort.‡

In all cases, the artists worked for their patrons and could count on being compensated for their talents and efforts only if the work they delivered met the standards of those who ordered it.

*Translated by John White, *Duccio: Tuscan Art and the Medieval Workshop* (London: Thames & Hudson, 1979), 34.
†Translated by James H. Stubblebine, *Duccio di Buoninsegna and His School* (Princeton, N.J.: Princeton University Press, 1979), 1: 192.
‡Stubblebine, *Duccio,* 1: 201.

Duccio derived the formality and symmetry of his composition from Byzantine painting, but relaxed the rigidity and frontality of the figures, softened the drapery, and individualized the faces.

14-10 DUCCIO DI BUONINSEGNA, *Life of Jesus*, 14 panels from the back of the *Maestà* altarpiece, from Siena Cathedral, Siena, Italy, 1308–1311. Tempera and gold leaf on wood, 7′ × 13′. Museo dell'Opera del Duomo, Siena.

On the back of the *Maestà* altarpiece, Duccio painted Jesus' passion in 24 scenes on 14 panels, beginning with *Entry into Jerusalem* (FIG. 14-10A), at the lower left, through *Noli me tangere*, at top right.

DUCCIO The works of DUCCIO DI BUONINSEGNA (active ca. 1278–1318) represent Sienese art at its most supreme. His most famous painting, the immense altarpiece called *Maestà* (*Virgin Enthroned in Majesty;* FIG. 14-9), replaced a much smaller painting of the Virgin Mary on the high altar of Siena Cathedral (FIG. 14-12A). The Sienese believed the Virgin had brought them victory over the Florentines at the battle of Monteperti in 1260, and she was the focus of the religious life of the republic. Duccio and his assistants began work on the prestigious commission in 1308 and completed *Maestà* in 1311, causing the entire city to celebrate. Shops closed and the bishop led a great procession of priests, civic officials, and the populace at large in carrying the altarpiece from Duccio's studio outside the city gate through the Campo (FIG. 14-15) up to its home on Siena's highest hill. So great was Duccio's stature that church officials permitted him to include his name in the dedicatory inscription on the front of the altarpiece on the Virgin's footstool: "Holy Mother of God, be the cause of peace for Siena and of life for Duccio, because he painted you thus."

As originally executed, Duccio's *Maestà* consisted of the seven-foot-high central panel (FIG. 14-9) with the dedicatory inscription,

surmounted by seven *pinnacles* above, and a *predella,* or raised shelf, of panels at the base, altogether some 13 feet high. Painted in tempera front and back (FIG. 14-10), the work unfortunately can no longer be seen in its entirety, because of its dismantling in subsequent centuries. Many of Duccio's panels are on display today as single masterpieces, scattered among the world's museums.

The main panel on the front of the altarpiece represents the Virgin enthroned as queen of Heaven amid choruses of angels and saints. Duccio derived the composition's formality and symmetry, along with the figures and facial types of the principal angels and saints, from Byzantine tradition. But the artist relaxed the strict frontality and rigidity of the figures. They turn to each other in quiet conversation. Further, Duccio individualized the faces of the four saints kneeling in the foreground, who perform their ceremonial gestures without stiffness. Similarly, he softened the usual Byzantine hard body outlines and drapery patterning. The folds of the garments, particularly those of the female saints at both ends of the panel, fall and curve loosely. This is a feature familiar in French Gothic works (FIG. 13-37) and is a mark of the artistic dialogue between Italy and northern Europe in the 14th century.

Despite these changes revealing Duccio's interest in the new naturalism, he respected the age-old requirement that as an altarpiece, *Maestà* would be the focus of worship in Siena's largest and most important church, its *cathedral,* the seat of the bishop of Siena. As such, Duccio knew *Maestà* should be an object holy in itself—a work of splendor to the eyes, precious in its message and its materials. Duccio thus recognized how the function of the altarpiece naturally limited experimentation in depicting narrative action and producing illusionistic effects (such as Giotto's) by modeling forms and adjusting their placement in pictorial space.

Instead, the queen of Heaven panel is a miracle of color composition and texture manipulation, unfortunately not fully revealed in photographs. Close inspection of the original reveals what the Sienese artist learned from other sources. In the 13th and 14th centuries, Italy was the distribution center for the great silk trade from China and the Middle East. After processing the silk in city-states such as Lucca and Florence, the Italians exported the precious fabric throughout Europe to satisfy an immense market for sumptuous dress. (Dante, Petrarch, and many other humanists decried the appetite for luxury in costume, which to them represented a decline in civic and moral virtue.) People throughout Europe (Duccio and other artists among them) prized fabrics from China, Persia, Byzantium, and the Islamic world. In *Maestà,* Duccio created the glistening and shimmering effects of textiles, adapting the motifs and design patterns of exotic materials. Complementing the luxurious fabrics and the (lost) gilded wood frame are the halos of the holy figures, which feature tooled decorative designs in gold leaf (*punchwork*). But Duccio, like Giotto (FIG. 14-7), eliminated almost all the gold patterning of the figures' garments in favor of creating three-dimensional volume. Traces remain only in the Virgin's red dress.

In contrast to the main panel, the predella and the back (FIG. 14-10) of *Maestà* present an extensive series of narrative panels of different sizes and shapes, beginning with *Annunciation* and culminating with Christ's *Resurrection* and other episodes following his *Crucifixion* (see "The Life of Jesus in Art," Chapter 11, pages 240–241, or pages xxxiv–xxxv in Volume II). The section reproduced here, consisting of 24 scenes in 14 panels, relates Christ's passion. Duccio drew the details of his scenes from the accounts in all four Gospels. The viewer reads the pictorial story in zig-zag fashion, beginning with *Entry into Jerusalem* (FIG. 14-10A) at the lower left. *Crucifixion* is at the top center. The narrative ends with

14-10A DUCCIO, *Entry into Jerusalem,* 1308–1311.

14-11 DUCCIO DI BUONINSEGNA, *Betrayal of Jesus,* panel on the back of the *Maestà* altarpiece, from Siena Cathedral, Siena, Italy, 1309–1311. Tempera and gold leaf on wood, 1′ 10½″ × 3′ 4″. Museo dell'Opera del Duomo, Siena.

In this dramatic depiction of Judas's betrayal of Jesus, the actors display a variety of individual emotions. Duccio here took a decisive step toward the humanization of religious subject matter.

Christ's appearance to Mary Magdalene (*Noli me tangere*) at the top right. Duccio consistently dressed Jesus in blue robes in most of the panels, but beginning with *Transfiguration,* he gilded the Savior's garment.

On the front panel, Duccio showed himself as the great master of the formal altarpiece. However, he allowed himself greater latitude for experimentation in the small accompanying panels, front and back. (Worshipers could always view both sides of the altarpiece because the high altar stood at the center of the sanctuary.) *Maestà*'s biblical scenes reveal Duccio's powers as a narrative painter. In *Betrayal of Jesus* (FIG. 14-11; compare FIG. 14-8B), for example, the artist represented several episodes of the event—the betrayal of Jesus by Judas's false kiss, the disciples fleeing in terror, and Peter cutting off the ear of the high priest's servant. Although the background, with its golden sky and rock formations, remains traditional, the style of the figures before it has changed radically. The bodies are not the flat frontal shapes of Italo-Byzantine art. Duccio imbued them with mass, modeled them with a range of tonalities from light to dark, and arranged their draperies around them convincingly. Even more novel and striking is the way the figures seem to react to the central event. Through posture, gesture, and even facial expression, they display a variety of emotions. Duccio carefully differentiated among the anger of Peter, the malice of Judas (echoed in the faces of the throng about Jesus), and the apprehension and timidity of the fleeing disciples. These figures are actors in a religious drama the artist interpreted in terms of thoroughly human actions and reactions. In this and the other narrative panels, for example, Jesus' *Entry into Jerusalem* (FIG. 14-10A), a theme treated also by Giotto in the Arena Chapel (FIG. 14-8A), Duccio took a decisive step toward the humanization of religious subject matter.

ORVIETO CATHEDRAL While Duccio was working on *Maestà* for Siena's most important church, a Sienese architect, LORENZO MAITANI, received the commission to design Orvieto's Cathedral (FIG. 14-12). The Orvieto *facade,* like the earlier facade of Siena Cathedral (FIG. 14-12A), begun by Giovanni Pisano (FIG. 14-4), demonstrates the appeal of the decorative vocabulary of French Gothic architecture in Italy at the end of the 13th and beginning of the 14th century. Characteristically French are the pointed gables over Orvieto Cathedral's three doorways, the *rose window* and

1 ft.

14-12 LORENZO MAITANI, Orvieto Cathedral (looking northeast), Orvieto, Italy, begun 1310. ◼◀

The pointed gables over the doorways, the rose window, and the large pinnacles derive from French Gothic architecture, but the facade of Orvieto Cathedral masks a traditional timber-roofed basilica.

statues in niches in the upper zone, and the four large *pinnacles* dividing the facade into three *bays* (see "The Gothic Cathedral," Chapter 13, page 373, or page xxx in Volume II). The outer pinnacles serve as miniature substitutes for the tall northern European west-front towers. Maitani's facade, however, is a Gothic overlay masking a marble-revetted *basilican* structure in the Tuscan *Romanesque* tradition, as the three-quarter view of the cathedral in FIG. 14-12 reveals. Few Italian architects fully embraced the Gothic style. The Orvieto facade resembles a great altar screen, its single plane covered with carefully placed carved and painted decoration. In principle, Orvieto belongs with Pisa Cathedral (FIG. 12-26) and other earlier Italian buildings, rather than with the French cathedrals at Amiens (FIG. 13-19) and Reims (FIG. 13-23). Inside, Orvieto Cathedral has a timber-roofed *nave* with a two-story *elevation* (columnar *arcade* and *clerestory*) in the Early Christian manner. Both the *chancel arch* framing the *apse* and the nave arcade's arches are round as opposed to pointed.

14-12A Siena Cathedral, begun ca. 1226. ◼◀

SIMONE MARTINI Duccio's successors in the Sienese school also produced innovative works. SIMONE MARTINI (ca. 1285–1344) was a pupil of Duccio's and may have assisted him in painting *Maestà*. Martini was a close friend of Petrarch's, and the poet praised him highly for his portrait of "Laura" (the woman to whom Petrarch dedicated his sonnets). Martini worked for the French kings in Naples and Sicily and, in his last years, produced paintings for the papal court at Avignon, where he came in contact with French painters. By adapting the insubstantial but luxuriant patterns of the Gothic style to Sienese art and, in turn, by acquainting painters north of the Alps with the Sienese style, Martini was instrumental in creating the so-called *International style*. This new style swept Europe during the late 14th and early 15th centuries because it appealed to the aristocratic taste for brilliant colors, lavish costumes, intricate ornamentation, and themes involving splendid processions.

The *Annunciation* altarpiece (FIG. 14-13) Martini created for Siena Cathedral features elegant shapes and radiant color, fluttering line, and weightless figures in a spaceless setting—all hallmarks of the artist's style.

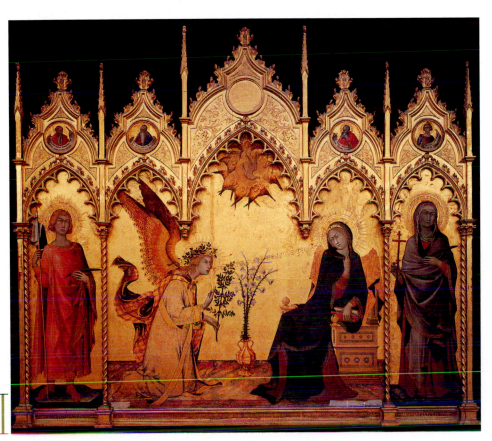

1 ft.

14-13 SIMONE MARTINI and LIPPO MEMMI, *Annunciation* altarpiece, from Siena Cathedral, 1333 (frame reconstructed in the 19th century). Tempera and gold leaf on wood, center panel 10′ 1″ × 8′ 8¾″. Galleria degli Uffizi, Florence.

A pupil of Duccio's, Martini was instrumental in the creation of the International style. Its hallmarks are elegant shapes, radiant color, flowing line, and weightless figures in golden, spaceless settings.

Artistic Training in Renaissance Italy

In Italy during the 14th through 16th centuries, training to become a professional artist capable of earning membership in the appropriate guild (see "Artists' Guilds," page 410) was a laborious and lengthy process. Aspiring artists started their training at an early age, anywhere from age 7 to 15. Their fathers would negotiate an arrangement with a master artist whereby each youth lived with that master for a specified number of years, usually five or six. During that time, the boys served as apprentices to the master of the workshop, learning the trade. (This living arrangement served as a major obstacle for female artists, because it was inappropriate for young girls to live in a male master's household.) The guilds supervised this rigorous training. They wanted not only to ensure their professional reputations by admitting only the most talented members but also to control the number of artists (and thereby limit competition). Toward this end, they frequently tried to regulate the number of apprentices working under a single master.

The skills apprentices learned varied with the type of studio they joined. Those apprenticed to painters learned to grind pigments, draw, prepare wood panels for painting, gild, and lay plaster for fresco. Sculptors in training learned to manipulate different materials—wood, stone, terracotta (baked clay), wax, bronze, or stucco—although many sculpture workshops specialized in only one or two of these materials. For stone carving, apprentices learned their craft by blocking out the master's designs for statues. As their skills developed, apprentices took on increasingly difficult tasks.

Cennino Cennini (ca. 1370–1440) explained the value of this apprenticeship system, and in particular, the advantages for young artists in studying and copying the works of older masters, in an influential book he published in 1400, *Il Libro dell'Arte* (*The Handbook of Art*):

> Having first practiced drawing for a while, . . . take pains and pleasure in constantly copying the best things which you can find done by the hand of great masters. And if you are in a place where many good masters have been, so much the better for you. But I give you this advice: take care to select the best one every time, and the one who has the greatest reputation. And, as you go on from day to day, it will be against nature if you do not get some grasp of his style and of his spirit. For if you undertake to copy after one master today and after another one tomorrow, you will not acquire the style of either one or the other, and you will inevitably, through

enthusiasm, become capricious, because each style will be distracting your mind. You will try to work in this man's way today, and in the other's tomorrow, and so you will not get either of them right. If you follow the course of one man through constant practice, your intelligence would have to be crude indeed for you not to get some nourishment from it. Then you will find, if nature has granted you any imagination at all, that you will eventually acquire a style individual to yourself, and it cannot help being good; because your hand and your mind, being always accustomed to gather flowers, would ill know how to pluck thorns.*

After completing their apprenticeships, artists entered the appropriate guilds. For example, painters, who ground pigments, joined the guild of apothecaries. Sculptors were members of the guild of stoneworkers, and goldsmiths entered the silk guild, because metalworkers often stretched gold into threads wound around silk for weaving. Guild membership served as certification of the artists' competence, but did not mean they were ready to open their own studios. New guild-certified artists usually served as assistants to master artists, because until they established their reputations, they could not expect to receive many commissions, and the cost of establishing their own workshops was high. In any case, this arrangement was not permanent, and workshops were not necessarily static enterprises. Although well-established and respected studios existed, workshops could be organized around individual masters (with no set studio locations) or organized for a specific project, especially an extensive decoration program.

Generally, assistants to painters were responsible for gilding frames and backgrounds, completing decorative work, and, occasionally, rendering architectural settings. Artists regarded figures, especially those central to the represented subject, as the most important and difficult parts of a painting, and the master reserved these for himself. Sometimes assistants painted secondary or marginal figures but only under the master's close supervision. That was probably the case with Simone Martini's *Annunciation* altarpiece (FIG. 14-13), in which the master painted the Virgin and angel, and the flanking saints are probably the work of his assistant, Lippo Memmi.

*Translated by Daniel V. Thompson Jr., *Cennino Cennini, The Craftsman's Handbook* (*Il Libro dell'Arte*) (New York: Dover Publications, 1960; reprint of 1933 ed.), 14–15.

The complex etiquette of the European chivalric courts probably dictated the presentation. The angel Gabriel has just alighted, the breeze of his passage lifting his mantle, his iridescent wings still beating. The gold of his sumptuous gown signals he has descended from Heaven to deliver his message. The Virgin, putting down her book of devotions, shrinks demurely from Gabriel's reverent genuflection—an appropriate act in the presence of royalty. Mary draws about her the deep blue, golden-hemmed mantle, colors befitting the queen of Heaven. Between the two figures is a vase of white lilies, symbolic of the Virgin's purity. Despite Mary's modesty and diffidence and the tremendous import of the angel's message, the scene subordinates drama to court ritual, and structural experimentation to surface splendor. The intricate *tracery* of the richly

tooled (reconstructed) French Gothic–inspired frame and the elaborate punchwork halos (by then a characteristic feature of Sienese panel painting) enhance the tactile magnificence of *Annunciation*.

Simone Martini and his student and assistant, LIPPO MEMMI (active ca. 1317–1350), signed the altarpiece and dated it (1333). The latter's contribution to *Annunciation* is still a matter of debate, but most art historians believe he painted the two lateral saints. These figures, which are reminiscent of the jamb statues of Gothic church portals, have greater solidity and lack the linear elegance of Martini's central pair. Given the nature of medieval and Renaissance workshop practices, it is often difficult to distinguish the master's hand from those of assistants, especially if the master corrected or redid part of the pupil's work (see "Artistic Training in Renaissance Italy," above).

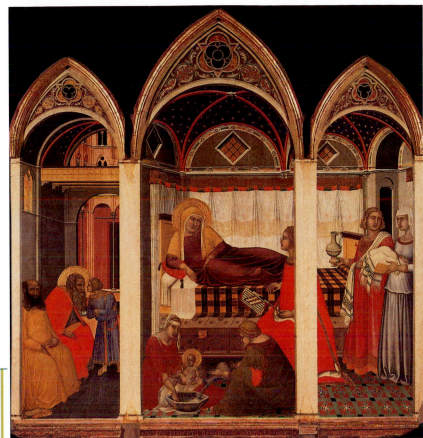

14-14 Pietro Lorenzetti, *Birth of the Virgin,* from the altar of Saint Savinus, Siena Cathedral, Siena, Italy, 1342. Tempera on wood, 6′ 1″ × 5′ 11″. Museo dell'Opera del Duomo, Siena.

In this triptych, Pietro Lorenzetti revived the pictorial illusionism of ancient Roman murals and painted the architectural members dividing the panel as if they extended back into the painted space.

PIETRO LORENZETTI Another of Duccio's students, Pietro Lorenzetti (active 1320–1348), contributed significantly to the general experiments in pictorial realism taking place in 14th-century Italy. Surpassing even his renowned master, Lorenzetti achieved a remarkable degree of spatial illusionism in his *Birth of the Virgin* (FIG. **14-14**), a large *triptych* (three-part panel painting) created for the altar of Saint Savinus in Siena Cathedral. Lorenzetti painted the wooden architectural members dividing the altarpiece into three sections as though they extended back into the painted space. Viewers seem to look through the wooden frame (added later) into a boxlike stage, where the event takes place. That one of the vertical members cuts across a figure, blocking part of it from view, strengthens the illusion. In subsequent centuries, artists exploited this use of architectural elements to enhance the illusion of painted figures acting out a drama a mere few feet away. This kind of pictorial illusionism characterized ancient Roman mural painting (FIGS. 7-18 and 7-19, *right*) but had not been practiced in Italy for a thousand years.

Lorenzetti's setting for his holy subject also represented a marked step in the advance of worldly realism. Saint Anne—who, like Nicola Pisano's Virgin in *Nativity* (FIG. 14-3), resembles a reclining figure on the lid of a Roman sarcophagus (FIG. 7-61)—props herself up wearily as the midwives wash the child and the women bring gifts. She is the center of an episode occurring in an upper-class Italian house of the period. A number of carefully observed domestic details and the scene at the left, where Joachim eagerly awaits news of the delivery, create the illusion that the viewer has opened the walls of Saint Anne's house and peered inside. Lorenzetti's altarpiece is noteworthy both for the painter's innovations in spatial illusionism and for his careful inspection and recording of details of the everyday world.

PALAZZO PUBBLICO Not all Sienese painting of the early 14th century was religious in character. One of the most important fresco cycles of the period (FIGS. 14-16 and 14-17) was a civic commission for Siena's Palazzo Pubblico ("public palace" or city hall). Siena was a proud commercial and political rival of Florence. The secular center of the community, the civic meeting hall in the main square (the Campo, or Field), was almost as great an object of civic pride as the city's cathedral (FIG. 14-12A). The Palazzo Pubblico (FIG. **14-15**) has a slightly concave

14-15 Palazzo Pubblico (looking east), Siena, Italy, 1288–1309. ◼◀

Siena's Palazzo Pubblico has a concave facade and a gigantic tower visible for miles around. The tower served as both a defensive lookout over the countryside and a symbol of the city-state's power.

14-16 AMBROGIO LORENZETTI, *Peaceful City,* detail from *Effects of Good Government in the City and in the Country,* east wall, Sala della Pace, Palazzo Pubblico, Siena, Italy, 1338–1339. Fresco. ◼️◀

In the Hall of Peace (FIG. 14-16A) of Siena's city hall (FIG. 14-15), Ambrogio Lorenzetti painted an illusionistic panorama of the bustling city. The fresco served as an allegory of good government in the Sienese republic.

facade (to conform to the irregular shape of the Campo) and a gigantic tower visible from miles around (compare FIGS. 13-29 and 14-18B). The imposing building and tower must have earned the admiration of Siena's citizens as well as of visitors to the city, inspiring in them respect for the republic's power and success. The tower served as a lookout over the city and the countryside around it and as a bell tower (*campanile*) for ringing signals of all kinds to the populace. Siena, as other Italian city-states, had to defend itself against neighboring cities and often against kings and emperors. In addition, it had to secure itself against internal upheavals common in the history of the Italian city-republics. Class struggle, feuds among rich and powerful families, and even uprisings of the whole populace against the city governors were constant threats in medieval Italy. The heavy walls and *battlements* (fortified *parapets*) of the Sienese town hall eloquently express how frequently the city governors needed to defend themselves against their own citizens. The Palazzo Pubblico tower, out of reach of most missiles, incorporates *machicolated galleries* (galleries with holes in their floors to enable defenders to dump stones or hot liquids on attackers below) built out on *corbels* (projecting supporting architectural members) for defense of the tower's base.

AMBROGIO LORENZETTI The painter entrusted with the major fresco program in the Palazzo Pubblico was Pietro Loren-

14-16A Sala della Pace, Siena, 1338–1339.

zetti's brother AMBROGIO LORENZETTI (active 1319–1348). In the frescoes Ambrogio produced for the Sala della Pace (Hall of Peace; FIG. 14-16A), he elaborated his brother's advances in illusionistic representation in spectacular fashion while giving visual form to Sienese civic concerns. The subjects of Ambrogio's murals are *Allegory of Good Government, Bad Government and the Effects of Bad Government in the City,* and *Effects of Good Government in the City and in the Country.* The turbulent politics of the

Italian cities—the violent party struggles, the overthrow and reinstatement of governments—called for solemn reminders of fair and just administration, and the city hall was just the place to display these allegorical paintings. Indeed, the leaders of the Sienese government who commissioned this fresco series had undertaken the "ordering and reformation of the whole city and countryside of Siena."

In *Effects of Good Government in the City and in the Country,* Ambrogio depicted the urban and rural effects of good government. *Peaceful City* (FIG. **14-16**) is a panoramic view of Siena, with its clustering palaces, markets, towers, churches, streets, and walls, reminiscent of the townscapes of ancient Roman murals (FIG. 7-19, *left*). The city's traffic moves peacefully, guild members ply their trades and crafts, and radiant maidens, clustered hand in hand, perform a graceful circling dance. Dancers were regular features of festive springtime rituals. Here, their presence also serves as a metaphor for a peaceful commonwealth. The artist fondly observed the life of his city, and its architecture gave him an opportunity to apply Sienese artists' rapidly growing knowledge of perspective.

As the viewer's eye passes through the city gate to the countryside beyond its walls, Ambrogio's *Peaceful Country* (FIG. **14-17**) presents a bird's-eye view of the undulating Tuscan terrain with its villas, castles, plowed farmlands, and peasants going about their occupations at different seasons of the year. Although it is an allegory, not a mimetic picture of the Sienese countryside on a specific day, Lorenzetti particularized the view of Tuscany—as well as the city view—by careful observation and endowed the painting with the character of a portrait of a specific place and environment. *Peaceful Country* represents one of the first appearances of *landscape* in Western art since antiquity (FIG. 7-20).

An allegorical figure of Security hovers above the hills and fields, unfurling a scroll promising safety to all who live under the rule of law. But Siena could not protect its citizens from the plague sweeping through Europe in the mid-14th century. The Black Death (see page 406) killed thousands of Sienese and may have ended the careers of both Lorenzettis. They disappear from historical records in 1348.

14-17 AMBROGIO LORENZETTI, *Peaceful Country,* detail from *Effects of Good Government in the City and in the Country,* east wall, Sala della Pace (FIG. 14-16A), Palazzo Pubblico (FIG. 14-15), Siena, Italy, 1338–1339. Fresco. ◼◀

This sweeping view of the countryside is one of the first instances of landscape painting in Western art since antiquity. The winged figure of Security promises safety to all who live under Sienese law.

Florence

Like Siena, the Republic of Florence was a dominant city-state during the 14th century. The historian Giovanni Villani (ca. 1270–1348), for example, described Florence as "the daughter and the creature of Rome," suggesting a preeminence inherited from the Roman Empire. Florentines were fiercely proud of what they perceived as their economic and cultural superiority. Florence controlled the textile industry in Italy, and the republic's gold *florin* was the standard coin of exchange everywhere in Europe.

FLORENCE CATHEDRAL Florentines translated their pride in their predominance into such landmark buildings as Santa Maria del Fiore (FIGS. **14-18** and **14-18A**), Florence's cathedral, the center for the most important religious observances in the city. ARNOLFO DI CAMBIO (ca. 1245–1302) began work on the cathedral (*Duomo* in Italian) in 1296, three years before he received

14-18A Nave, Florence Cathedral, begun 1296.

the commission to build the city's town hall, the Palazzo della Signoria (FIG. **14-18B**). Intended as the "most beautiful and honorable church in Tuscany," the cathedral reveals the competitiveness Florentines felt with cities such as Siena (FIG. 14-12A) and Pisa (FIG. 12-26). Church authorities planned for the

14-18B Palazzo della Signoria, Florence, 1299–1310.

14-18 ARNOLFO DI CAMBIO and others, aerial view of Santa Maria del Fiore (and the Baptistery of San Giovanni; looking northeast), Florence, Italy, begun 1296. Campanile designed by GIOTTO DI BONDONE, 1334. ◼◀

The Florentine Duomo's marble revetment carries on the Tuscan Romanesque architectural tradition, linking this basilican church more closely to Early Christian Italy than to Gothic France.

Duomo to hold the city's entire population, and although its capacity is only about 30,000 (Florence's population at the time was slightly less than 100,000), the building seemed so large even the noted architect Leon Battista Alberti (see Chapter 16) commented it seemed to cover "all of Tuscany with its shade." The builders ornamented the cathedral's surfaces, in the old Tuscan fashion, with marble-encrusted geometric designs, matching the *revetment* (decorative wall paneling) to that of the facing 11th-century Romanesque baptistery of San Giovanni (FIGS. 12-27 and 14-18, *left*).

The vast gulf separating Santa Maria del Fiore from its northern European counterparts becomes evident in a comparison between the Florentine church and the High Gothic cathedrals of Amiens (FIG. 13-19), Reims (FIG. 13-23), and Cologne (FIG. 13-52). Gothic architects' emphatic stress on the vertical produced an awe-inspiring upward rush of unmatched vigor and intensity. The French and German buildings express organic growth shooting heavenward, as the pierced, translucent stone tracery of the spires merges with the atmosphere. Florence Cathedral, in contrast, clings to the ground and has no aspirations to flight. All emphasis is on the horizontal elements of the design, and the building rests firmly and massively on the ground. The clearly defined simple geometric volumes of the cathedral show no tendency to merge either into each other or into the sky.

Giotto di Bondone designed the Duomo's campanile in 1334. In keeping with Italian tradition (FIGS. 12-21 and 12-26), it stands apart from the church. In fact, it is essentially self-sufficient and could stand anywhere else in the city without looking out of place. The same cannot be said of the towers of Amiens, Reims, and Cologne cathedrals. They are essential elements of the structures behind them, and it would be unthinkable to detach one of them and place it somewhere else. No individual element of Gothic churches seems capable of an independent existence. One form merges into the next in a series of rising movements pulling the eye upward and never permitting it to rest until it reaches the sky. The Florentine campanile is entirely different. Neatly subdivided into cubic sections, Giotto's tower is the sum of its component parts. Not only could this tower be removed from the building without adverse effects, but also each of the parts—cleanly separated from each other by continuous moldings—seems capable of existing independently as an object of considerable aesthetic appeal. This compartmentalization is reminiscent of the Romanesque style, but it also forecasts the ideals of Renaissance architecture. Artists hoped to express structure in the clear, logical relationships of the component parts and to produce self-sufficient works that could exist in complete independence. Compared with northern European towers, Giotto's campanile has a cool and rational quality more appealing to the intellect than to the emotions.

1 ft.

14-19 ANDREA PISANO, south doors of the Baptistery of San Giovanni (FIG. 12-27), Florence, Italy, 1330–1336. Gilded bronze, doors 16′ × 9′ 2″; individual panels 1′ 7¼″ × 1′ 5″. (The door frames date to the mid-15th century.)

Andrea Pisano's bronze doors have 28 panels with figural reliefs in French Gothic quatrefoil frames. The lower eight depict Christian virtues. The rest represent the life of Saint John the Baptist.

The facade of Florence Cathedral was not completed until the 19th century, and then in a form much altered from its original design. In fact, until the 17th century, Italian builders exhibited little concern for the facades of their churches, and dozens remain unfinished to this day. One reason for this may be that Italian architects did not conceive the facades as integral parts of the structures but rather, as in the case of Orvieto Cathedral (FIG. 14-12), as screens that could be added to the church exterior at any time.

A generation after work began on Florence's church, the citizens decided also to beautify their 11th-century baptistery (FIGS. 12-27 and 14-18, *left*) with a set of bronze doors (FIG. **14-19**) for the south entrance to the building. The sponsors were the members of

Florence's guild of wool importers, who competed for business and prestige with the wool manufacturers' association, an important sponsor of the cathedral building campaign. The wool-importers' guild hired ANDREA PISANO (ca. 1290–1348), a native of Pontedera in the territory of Pisa—unrelated to Nicola and Giovanni Pisano (see "Italian Artists' Names," page 405)—to create the doors. Andrea designed 28 bronze panels for the doors, each cast separately, of which 20 depict episodes from the life of Saint John the Baptist, to whom the Florentines dedicated their baptistery. Eight panels (at the bottom) represent personified Christian virtues. The *quatrefoil* (four-lobed, cloverlike) frames are of the type used earlier for reliefs flanking the doorways of Amiens Cathedral (FIG. 13-19), suggesting French Gothic sculpture was one source of Andrea's style. The gilded figures stand on projecting ledges in each quatrefoil. Their proportions and flowing robes also reveal a debt to French sculpture, but the compositions, both in general conception (small groups of figures in stagelike settings) and in some details, owe a great deal to Giotto, for whom Andrea had earlier executed reliefs for the cathedral's campanile, perhaps according to Giotto's designs.

The wool importers' patronage of the baptistery did not end with this project. In the following century, the guild paid for the even more prestigious east doors (FIGS. 21-9 and 21-10), directly across from the cathedral's west facade, and also for a statue of Saint John the Baptist on the facade of Or San Michele, a multipurpose building housing a 14th-century tabernacle (FIG. **14-19A**) by ANDREA ORCAGNA (active ca. 1343–1368) featuring the painting *Madonna and Child Enthroned with Saints* by BERNARDO DADDI (active ca. 1312–1348).

14-19A ORCAGNA, Or San Michele tabernacle, 1355–1359.

Pisa

Siena and Florence were inland centers of commerce. Pisa was one of Italy's port cities, which, with Genoa and Venice (MAP 14-1), controlled the rapidly growing maritime avenues connecting western Europe with the lands of Islam, with Byzantium and Russia, and with China. As prosperous as Pisa was as a major shipping power, however, it was not immune from the disruption the Black Death wreaked across all of Italy and Europe in the late 1340s. Concern with death, a significant theme in art even before the onset of the plague, became more prominent in the years after midcentury.

CAMPOSANTO *Triumph of Death* is a tour de force of death imagery (FIG. **14-20**). The creator of this large-scale (over 18 by 49 feet) fresco remains disputed. Some art historians attribute the work to FRANCESCO TRAINI (active ca. 1321–1363), while others argue for BUONAMICO BUFFALMACCO (active 1320–1336). Painted on the wall of the Camposanto (Holy Field), the enclosed burial ground adjacent to Pisa's cathedral (FIG. 12-26), the fresco captures the horrors of death and forces viewers to confront their mortality. The painter rendered each scene with naturalism and emotive power. In the left foreground (FIG. 14-20, *top*), young aristocrats, mounted in a stylish cavalcade, encounter three coffin-encased corpses in differing stages of decomposition. As the horror of the confrontation with death strikes them, the ladies turn away with delicate disgust, while a gentleman holds his nose. (The animals, horses and dogs, sniff excitely.) At the far left, the hermit Saint Macarius unrolls a scroll bearing an inscription commenting on the folly of pleasure and

1 ft.

1 ft.

14-20 FRANCESCO TRAINI or BUONAMICO BUFFALMACCO, two details of *Triumph of Death*, 1330s. Full fresco, 18′ 6″ × 49′ 2″. Camposanto, Pisa. ◼️

Befitting its location on a wall in Pisa's Camposanto, the enclosed burial ground adjacent to the cathedral, this fresco captures the horrors of death and forces viewers to confront their mortality.

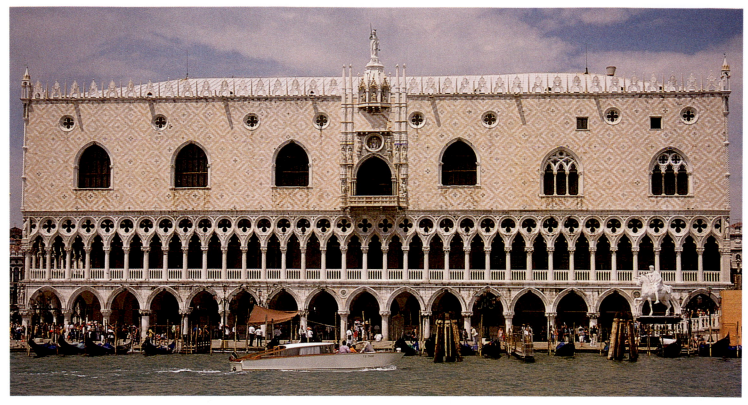

14-21 Doge's Palace, Venice, Italy, begun ca. 1340–1345; expanded and remodeled, 1424–1438.

The delicate patterning in cream- and rose-colored marbles, the pointed and ogee arches, and the quatrefoil medallions of the Doge's Palace constitute a Venetian variation of northern Gothic architecture.

the inevitability of death. On the far right, ladies and gentlemen ignore dreadful realities, occupying themselves in an orange grove with music and amusements while above them (FIG. 14-20, *bottom*) angels and demons struggle for the souls of the corpses heaped in the foreground.

In addition to these direct and straightforward scenes, the mural contains details conveying more subtle messages. For example, the painter depicted those who appear unprepared for death—and thus unlikely to achieve salvation—as wealthy and reveling in luxury. Given that the Dominicans—an order committed to a life of poverty (see "Mendicant Orders," page 404)—participated in the design for this fresco program, this imagery surely was a warning against greed and lust.

Venice

One of the wealthiest cities of late medieval Italy—and of Europe—was Venice, renowned for its streets of water. Situated on a lagoon on the northeastern coast of Italy, Venice was secure from land attack and could rely on a powerful navy for protection against invasion from the sea. Internally, Venice was a tight corporation of

ruling families that, for centuries, provided stable rule and fostered economic growth.

DOGE'S PALACE The Venetian republic's seat of government was the Doge's (Duke's) Palace (FIG. **14-21**). Begun around 1340 to 1345 and significantly remodeled after 1424, it was the most ornate public building in medieval Italy. In a stately march, the first level's short and heavy columns support rather severe *pointed arches* that look strong enough to carry the weight of the upper structure. Their rhythm doubles in the upper arcades, where more slender columns carry *ogee arches* (made up of double-curving lines), which terminate in flamelike tips between medallions pierced with quatrefoils. Each story is taller than the one beneath it, the topmost as high as the two lower arcades combined. Yet the building does not look top-heavy. This is due in part to the complete absence of articulation in the top story and in part to the walls' delicate patterning, in cream- and rose-colored marbles, which makes them appear paper-thin. The Doge's Palace represents a delightful and charming variant of Late Gothic architecture. Colorful, decorative, light and airy in appearance, the Venetian palace is ideally suited to this unique Italian city that floats between water and sky.

LATE MEDIEVAL ITALY

13TH CENTURY

Bonaventura Berlinghieri,
Saint Francis Altarpiece, 1235

▌ Diversity of style characterizes the art of 13th-century Italy, with some artists working in the *maniera greca*, or Italo-Byzantine style, some in the mode of Gothic France, and others in the newly revived classical tradition.

▌ The leading painters working in the Italo-Byzantine style were Bonaventura Berlinghieri and Cimabue. Both drew inspiration from Byzantine icons and illuminated manuscripts. Berlinghieri's *Saint Francis Altarpiece* is the earliest dated portrayal of Saint Francis of Assisi, who died in 1226.

▌ Trained in southern Italy in the court style of Frederick II (r. 1197–1250), Nicola Pisano was a master sculptor who settled in Pisa and carved pulpits incorporating marble panels that, both stylistically and in individual motifs, derive from ancient Roman sarcophagi. Nicola's son, Giovanni Pisano, also was a sculptor of church pulpits, but his work more closely reflects the Gothic sculpture of France.

Nicola Pisano, Pisa Baptistery
pulpit, 1259–1260

▌ At the end of the century, in Rome and Assisi, Pietro Cavallini and other fresco painters created mural programs foreshadowing the revolutionary art of Giotto.

14TH CENTURY

▌ During the 14th century, Italy suffered the most devastating natural disaster in European history—the Black Death—but it was also the time when Renaissance humanism took root. Although religion continued to occupy a primary position in Italian life, scholars and artists became increasingly concerned with the natural world.

▌ Art historians regard Giotto di Bondone of Florence as the first Renaissance painter. An architect as well, Giotto designed the bell tower of Florence's Cathedral. His masterpiece is the fresco program of the Arena Chapel in Padua, where he established himself as a pioneer in pursuing a naturalistic approach to representation based on observation, which was at the core of the classical tradition in art. The Renaissance marked the rebirth of classical values in art and society.

Giotto, Arena Chapel,
Padua, ca. 1305

▌ The greatest master of the Sienese school of painting was Duccio di Buoninsegna, whose *Maestà* still incorporates many elements of the *maniera greca*. He relaxed the frontality and rigidity of his figures, however, and in the narrative scenes on the back of the gigantic altarpiece in Siena Cathedral took a decisive step toward humanizing religious subject matter by depicting actors displaying individual emotions.

Duccio, *Maestà*, Siena Cathedral,
1308–1311

▌ Secular themes also came to the fore in 14th-century Italy, most notably in Ambrogio Lorenzetti's frescoes for Siena's Palazzo Pubblico. His depictions of the city and its surrounding countryside are among the first landscapes in Western art since antiquity.

▌ The prosperity of the 14th century led to many major building campaigns, including new cathedrals in Florence, Siena, and Orvieto, and new administrative palaces in Florence, Siena, and Venice. Florence's 11th-century baptistery also received new bronze doors by Andrea Pisano.

▌ The 14th-century architecture of Italy underscores the regional character of late medieval art. Orvieto Cathedral's facade, for example, incorporates some elements of the French Gothic vocabulary, but it is a screen masking a timber-roofed structure with round arches in the nave arcade in the Early Christian tradition.

Orvieto Cathedral,
begun 1310

The carefully rendered cityscape seen through the window in the right wing of the *Mérode Altarpiece* confirms the identification of the locale of the biblical event as the Inghelbrechts' home.

Campin was the leading painter of Tournai. In the *Mérode Altarpiece,* he set *Annunciation* in a Flemish merchant's home in which the objects represented have symbolic significance.

In the altarpiece's left wing, Campin depicted his patrons, Peter Inghelbrecht and Margarete Scrynmakers, as kneeling witnesses to the announcement of the Virgin's miraculous pregnancy.

1 ft.

15-1 ROBERT CAMPIN (MASTER OF FLÉMALLE), *Mérode Altarpiece* (open), ca. 1425–1428. Oil on wood, center panel 2′ 1⅜″ × 2′ ⅞″, each wing 2′ 1⅜″ × 10⅞″. Metropolitan Museum of Art, New York (The Cloisters Collection, 1956). ◼◂

Joseph, in his workshop and unaware of the angel's arrival, has constructed two mousetraps, symbols of the theological concept that Christ is bait set in the trap of the world to catch the Devil.

15

LATE MEDIEVAL AND EARLY RENAISSANCE NORTHERN EUROPE

FRAMING THE ERA

THE VIRGIN IN A FLEMISH HOME

In 15th-century Flanders—a region corresponding to what is today Belgium, the Netherlands, Luxembourg, and part of northern France—lay patrons far outnumbered the clergy in the commissioning of religious artworks. Especially popular were small altarpieces for household prayer, such as the *Mérode Altarpiece* (FIG. **15-1**), the most famous work by the "MASTER OF FLÉMALLE," whom many scholars identify as ROBERT CAMPIN (ca. 1378–1444), the leading painter of Tournai. Perhaps the most striking feature of these private devotional images is the integration of religious and secular concerns. For example, artists often presented biblical scenes as taking place in a Flemish home. Religion was such an integral part of Flemish life that separating the sacred from the secular was almost impossible—and undesirable. Moreover, the presentation in religious art of familiar settings and objects no doubt strengthened the direct bond the patron or viewer felt with biblical figures.

The *Annunciation* theme, as prophesied in Isaiah 7:14, occupies the Mérode triptych's central panel. The archangel Gabriel approaches Mary, who sits reading inside a well-kept home. The view through the window in the right wing and the depicted accessories, furniture, and utensils confirm the locale as Flanders. However, the objects represented are not merely decorative. They also function as symbols. The book, extinguished candle, and lilies on the table, the copper basin in the corner niche, the towels, fire screen, and bench all symbolize the Virgin's purity and her divine mission.

In the right panel, Joseph, apparently unaware of the angel's arrival, has constructed two mousetraps, symbolic of the theological concept that Christ is bait set in the trap of the world to catch the Devil. The ax, saw, and rod Campin painted in the foreground of Joseph's workshop not only are tools of the carpenter's trade but also are mentioned in Isaiah 10:15. In the left panel, the closed garden is symbolic of Mary's purity, and the flowers Campin included relate to Mary's virtues, especially humility.

The altarpiece's donor, Peter Inghelbrecht, a wealthy merchant, and his wife, Margarete Scrynmakers, kneel in the garden and witness the momentous event through an open door. *Donor portraits*—portraits of the individual(s) who commissioned (or "donated") the work—became very popular in the 15th century. In this instance, in addition to asking to be represented in their altarpiece, the Inghelbrechts probably specified the subject. Inghelbrecht means "angel bringer," a reference to the *Annunciation* theme of the central panel. Scrynmakers means "cabinet- or shrine-makers," referring to the workshop scene in the right panel.

NORTHERN EUROPE IN THE 15TH CENTURY

As the 15th century opened, Rome and Avignon were still the official seats of two competing popes (see "The Great Schism," Chapter 14, page 404), and the Hundred Years' War (1337–1453) between France and England still raged. The general European movement toward centralized royal governments, begun in the 12th century, continued apace, but the corresponding waning of *feudalism* brought social turmoil. Nonetheless, despite widespread conflict and unrest, a new economic system emerged—the early stage of European capitalism. In response to the financial requirements of trade, new credit and exchange systems created an economic network of enterprising European cities. Trade in money accompanied trade in commodities, and the former financed industry. Both were in the hands of international trading companies, such as those of Jacques Coeur in Bourges (see Chapter 13) and the Medici in Florence (see Chapter 16). In 1460, Flemish entrepreneurs established the first international commercial stock exchange in Antwerp. In fact, the French word for stock market (*bourse*) comes from the name of the van der Beurse family of Bruges, the wealthiest city in 15th-century Flanders.

Art also thrived in northern Europe during this time under royal, ducal, church, and private patronage. Two developments in particular were of special significance: the adoption of oil-based pigment as the leading medium for painting, and the blossoming of printmaking as a major art form, which followed the invention of moveable type. These new media had a dramatic influence on artistic production worldwide.

BURGUNDY AND FLANDERS

In the 15th century, Flanders (MAP 15-1) was not an independent state but a region under the control of the duke of Burgundy, the ruler of the fertile east-central region of France still famous for its

MAP 15-1 France, the duchy of Burgundy, and the Holy Roman Empire in 1477.

LATE MEDIEVAL AND EARLY RENAISSANCE NORTHERN EUROPE

1385	1425	1450	1475	1500
▌ Claus Sluter carves life-size statues of biblical figures with portraitlike features for Philip the Bold, duke of Burgundy ▌ The Limbourg brothers expand the illusionistic capabilities of manuscript illumination for Jean, duke of Berry	▌ Robert Campin, Jan van Eyck, and Rogier van der Weyden popularize the use of oil paints in Flanders to record the exact surface appearance of objects, fabrics, faces, and landscapes ▌ Flemish painters establish portraiture as a major art form ▌ German graphic artists pioneer woodcut printing, making art affordable to the masses	▌ The second generation of Flemish master painters—Petrus Christus, Dirk Bouts, and Hugo van der Goes—continue to use oil paints for altarpieces featuring naturalistic representations of religious themes ▌ In Germany, Johannes Gutenberg invents moveable type and prints the first Bibles on a letterpress	▌ In Flanders, Hans Memling specializes in portraiture and paintings of the Madonna and Child ▌ The Late Gothic style lingers in Germany in the large wooden altarpieces carved by Veit Stoss and Tilman Riemenschneider ▌ Martin Schongauer becomes the first northern European master of metal engraving	

wines. Duke Philip the Bold (r. 1363–1404) was one of four sons of King John II (r. 1350–1364) of France. In 1369, Philip married Margaret de Mâle, the daughter of the count of Flanders, and acquired territory in the Netherlands. Thereafter, the major source of Burgundian wealth was Bruges, the city that made Burgundy a dangerous rival of France, which then, as in the Gothic age (see Chapter 13), was a smaller kingdom geographically than the modern nation-state. Bruges initially derived its wealth from the wool trade but soon expanded into banking, becoming the financial clearinghouse for all of northern Europe. Indeed, Bruges so dominated Flanders that the duke of Burgundy eventually chose to make the city his capital and moved his court there from Dijon. Due to the expanded territory and the prosperity of the duchy of Burgundy, Philip the Bold and his successors were probably the most powerful northern European rulers during the first three quarters of the 15th century. Although members of the French royal family, they usually supported England (on which they relied for the raw materials used in their wool industry) during the Hundred Years' War and, at times, controlled much of northern France, including Paris, the seat of the French monarchy. At the height of Burgundian power, the reigning duke's lands stretched from the Rhône River to the North Sea.

Chartreuse de Champmol

The dukes of Burgundy were great patrons of the arts. They fully appreciated that artworks could support their dynastic and political goals as well as adorn their castles and townhouses. Philip the Bold's grandest artistic enterprise was the building of the Chartreuse de Champmol, near Dijon. A *chartreuse* ("charter house" in English) is a Carthusian *monastery*. The Carthusian order, founded by Saint Bruno in the late 11th century at Chartreuse, near Grenoble in southeastern France, consisted of monks who devoted their lives to solitary living and prayer. Unlike monastic orders that earned income from farming and other work, the Carthusians generated no revenues. Philip's generous endowment at Champmol was therefore the sole funding for an ambitious artistic program inspired by Saint-Denis, the royal abbey of France and burial site of the French kings (FIGS. 13-2 to 13-3A). The architect the duke chose was DROUET DE DAMMARTIN, who had worked for Philip's brother, King Charles V (r. 1364–1380), on the Louvre (FIG. 15-16), the French royal palace in Paris. Philip intended the Dijon chartreuse to become a ducal *mausoleum* and serve both as a means of securing salvation in perpetuity for the Burgundian dukes (the monks prayed continuously for the souls of the ducal family) and as a dynastic symbol of Burgundian power.

CLAUS SLUTER In 1389, Philip the Bold placed the Haarlem (Netherlands) sculptor CLAUS SLUTER (active ca. 1380–1406) in charge of the sculptural program (FIGS. 15-2 and 15-2A) for the Chartreuse de Champmol. For the portal (FIG. 15-2A) of the monastery's chapel, Sluter's workshop produced statues of the duke and his wife kneeling before the Virgin and Child. For the cloister, Sluter designed a large sculptural fountain located in a well (FIG. 15-2). The well served as a water source for the monastery, but water

15-2A SLUTER, Chartreuse de Champmol portal, 1385–1393. ◼

probably did not spout from the fountain because the Carthusian commitment to silence and prayer would have precluded anything that produced sound.

Sluter's *Well of Moses* features statues of Moses and five other prophets (David, Daniel, Isaiah, Jeremiah, and Zachariah) surrounding a base that once supported a 25-foot-tall group of Christ on the cross, the Virgin Mary, John the Evangelist, and Mary Magdalene. The Carthusians called the

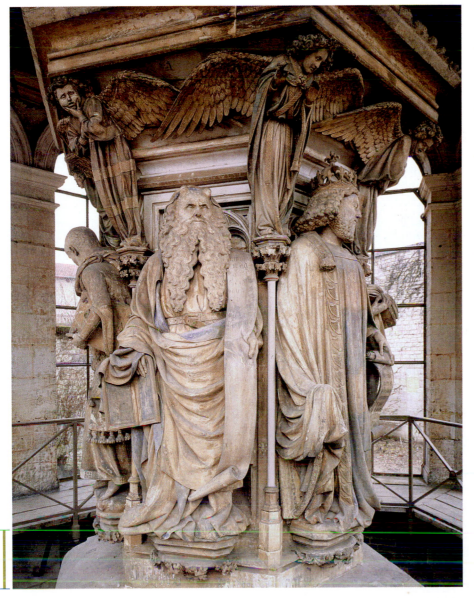

1 ft.

15-2 CLAUS SLUTER, *Well of Moses*, Chartreuse de Champmol, Dijon, France, 1395–1406. Limestone, painted and gilded by JEAN MALOUEL, Moses 6′ high. ◼

The *Well of Moses*, a symbolic fountain of life made for the duke of Burgundy, originally supported a *Crucifixion* group. Sluter's figures recall French Gothic jamb statues but are far more realistic.

Well of Moses a *fons vitae*, a fountain of everlasting life. The blood of the crucified Christ symbolically flowed down over the grieving angels and Old Testament prophets, spilling into the well below, washing over Christ's prophetic predecessors and redeeming anyone who would drink water from the well. Whereas the models for the Dijon chapel statues were the sculptured portals of French Gothic cathedrals, the inspiration for the *Well of Moses* may have come in part from contemporaneous *mystery plays* in which actors portraying prophets frequently delivered commentaries on events in Christ's life.

The six figures are much more realistically rendered than Gothic jamb statues (FIGS. 13-18 and 13-18A), and the prophets have almost portraitlike features and distinct individual personalities and costumes. David is an elegantly garbed Gothic king, Moses an elderly horned prophet (compare FIG. 12-35) with a waist-length beard. Sluter's intense observation of natural appearance provided him with the information necessary to sculpt the prophets in minute detail. Heavy draperies with voluminous folds swathe the life-size figures. The artist succeeded in making their difficult, complex surfaces seem remarkably naturalistic. He enhanced this effect by skillfully differentiating textures, from coarse drapery to smooth flesh and silky hair. Originally, paint, much of which has flaked off, further augmented the naturalism of the figures. (The painter was JEAN MALOUEL [ca. 1365–1415], another Netherlandish master.) This fascination with the specific and tangible in the visible world became one of the chief characteristics of 15th-century Flemish art.

MELCHIOR BROEDERLAM Philip the Bold also commissioned a major altarpiece for the main altar in the chapel of the Chartreuse. A collaborative project between two Flemish artists, this altarpiece consisted of a large sculptured shrine by Jacques de Baerze (active ca. 1384–1399) and a pair of painted exterior panels (FIG. **15-3**) by MELCHIOR BROEDERLAM (active ca. 1387–1409).

Altarpieces were a major art form north of the Alps in the late 14th and 15th centuries. From their position behind the altar, they served as backdrops for the Mass. The Mass represents a ritual celebration of the Holy *Eucharist*. At the Last Supper, Christ commanded his apostles to repeat in memory of him the communion credo that he is tendering them his body to eat and his blood to drink, as reenacted in the Eucharist (see "The Life of Jesus in Art," Chapter 8, pages 240–241, or xxxiv–xxxv in Volume II). This act serves as the nucleus of the Mass, which involves this reenactment as well as prayer and contemplation of the Word of God. Because the Mass involves not only a memorial rite but complex Christian doctrinal tenets as well, art has traditionally played an important role in giving visual form to these often complex theological concepts for the Christian faithful. Like sculpted medieval church *tympana*, these altarpieces had a didactic role, especially for the illiterate. They also reinforced Church doctrines for viewers and stimulated devotion.

Given their function as backdrops to the Mass, it is not surprising many altarpieces depict scenes directly related to Christ's sacrifice. The Champmol altarpiece, or *retable*, for example, features sculpted passion scenes on the interior. These public altarpieces most often took the form of *polyptychs*—hinged multipaneled paintings or multiple carved relief panels. The hinges enabled the clergy to close the polyptych's side wings over the central panel(s). Artists decorated both the exterior and interior of the altarpieces. This multi-image format provided the opportunity to construct narratives through a sequence of images, somewhat as in manuscript illustration. Although concrete information is lacking about

when the clergy opened and closed these altarpieces, the wings probably remained closed on regular days and open on Sundays and feast days. On this schedule, viewers could have seen both the interior and exterior—diverse imagery at various times according to the liturgical calendar.

The painted wings (FIG. 15-3) of the *Retable de Champmol* depict *Annunciation* and *Visitation* on the left panel and *Presentation into the Temple* and *Flight into Egypt* on the right panel. Dealing with Christ's birth and infancy, Broederlam's painted images on the altarpiece's exterior set the stage for de Baerze's interior sculpted passion scenes (not illustrated). The exterior panels are an unusual amalgam of different styles, locales, and religious symbolism. The two paintings include both landscape and interior scenes. Broederlam depicted the buildings in both Romanesque and Gothic styles (see Chapters 12 and 13). Scholars have suggested the juxtaposition of different architectural styles in the left panel is symbolic. The *rotunda* (round building, usually with a dome) refers to the Old Testament, whereas the Gothic porch relates to the New Testament. In the right panel, a statue of a Greco-Roman god falls from the top of a column as the holy family approaches. These and other details symbolically announce the coming of the new order under Christ. Stylistically, Broederlam's panels are a mixture of three-dimensional rendition of the landscape and buildings with a solid gold background and flat golden halos for the holy figures, regardless of the positions of their heads. Despite these lingering medieval pictorial conventions, the altarpiece is an early example of many of the artistic developments that preoccupied European artists throughout the 15th century, especially the illusionistic depiction of three-dimensional objects and the naturalistic representation of landscape.

Jan van Eyck

The *Retable de Champmol* also foreshadowed another significant development in 15th-century art—the widespread adoption of *oil paints* (see "Tempera and Oil Painting," page 427). Oil paints facilitated the exactitude in rendering details so characteristic of northern European painting. Although the Italian biographer Giorgio Vasari (1511–1574) and other 16th-century commentators credited Jan van Eyck (FIGS. 15-4 to 15-7) with the invention of oil painting, recent evidence has revealed oil paints had been known for some time, well before Melchior Broederlam used oils for Philip the Bold's Dijon altarpiece and Robert Campin painted the *Mérode Altarpiece* (FIG. 15-1) for Peter Inghelbrecht. Flemish painters built up their pictures by superimposing translucent paint layers on a layer of underpainting, which in turn had been built up from a carefully planned drawing made on a panel prepared with a white ground. With the oil medium, artists could create richer colors than previously possible, giving their paintings an intense tonality, the illusion of glowing light, and enamel-like surfaces. These traits differed significantly from the high-keyed color, sharp light, and rather *matte* (dull) surface of *tempera*. The brilliant and versatile oil medium suited perfectly the formal intentions of the generation of Flemish painters after Broederlam, including Campin (FIG. 15-1) and van Eyck, who aimed for sharply focused clarity of detail in their representation of objects ranging in scale from large to almost invisible.

GHENT ALTARPIECE The first Netherlandish painter to achieve international fame was JAN VAN EYCK (ca. 1390–1441), who in 1425 became the court painter of Philip the Good, duke of Burgundy (r. 1419–1467). In 1432, he moved his studio to Bruges, where the duke maintained his official residence. That same

Tempera and Oil Painting

The generic words *paint* and *pigment* encompass a wide range of substances artists have used through the ages. Fresco aside (see "Fresco Painting," Chapter 14, page 408), during the 14th century, egg *tempera* was the material of choice for most painters, both in Italy and northern Europe. Tempera consists of egg combined with a wet paste of ground pigment. In his influential guidebook *Il libro dell'arte (The Artist's Handbook,* 1437), Cennino Cennini (ca. 1370–ca. 1440) noted that artists mixed only the egg yolk with the ground pigment, but analyses of paintings from this period have revealed some artists chose to use the entire egg. Images painted with tempera have a velvety sheen. Artists usually applied tempera to the painting surface with a light touch because thick application of the pigment mixture results in premature cracking and flaking.

Some artists used oil paints as far back as the eighth century, but not until the early 1400s did oil painting become widespread. Melchior Broederlam (FIG. 15-3) and other Flemish artists were among the first to employ oils extensively (often mixing them with tempera), and Italian painters quickly followed suit. The discovery of better drying components in the early 15th century enhanced the setting capabilities of oils. Rather than apply these oils in the light, flecked brushstrokes tempera encouraged, artists laid down the oils in transparent layers, or *glazes,* over opaque or semiopaque underlayers. In this manner, painters could build up deep tones through repeated glazing. Unlike works in tempera, whose surface dries quickly due to water evaporation, oils dry more uniformly and slowly, giving the artist time to rework areas. This flexibility must have been particularly appealing to artists who worked very deliberately, such as the Flemish masters discussed in this chapter, as well as the Italian Leonardo da Vinci (see Chapter 17). Leonardo also preferred oil paint because its gradual drying process and consistency enabled him to blend the pigments, thereby creating the impressive *sfumato* (smoky) effect that contributed to his fame.

Both tempera and oils can be applied to various surfaces. Through the early 16th century, wood panels served as the foundation for most paintings. Italians painted on poplar. Northern European artists used oak, lime, beech, chestnut, cherry, pine, and silver fir. Availability of these timbers determined the choice of wood. Linen canvas became increasingly popular in the late 16th century. Although evidence suggests artists did not intend permanency for their early images on canvas, the material proved particularly useful in areas such as Venice where high humidity warped wood panels and made fresco unfeasible. Further, until artists began to use wooden bars to stretch the canvas to form a taut surface, canvas paintings were more portable than wood panels.

1 ft.

15-3 MELCHIOR BROEDERLAM, *Retable de Champmol,* from the chapel of the Chartreuse de Champmol, Dijon, France, installed 1399. Oil on wood, each wing 5' 5¾" × 4' 1¼". Musée des Beaux-Arts, Dijon.

This early example of oil painting attempts to represent the three-dimensional world on a two-dimensional surface, but the gold background and flat halos recall medieval pictorial conventions.

year, he completed the *Ghent Altarpiece* (FIGS. **15-4** and **15-5**), which, according to an inscription, his older brother HUBERT VAN EYCK (ca. 1366–1426) had begun. This retable is one of the largest (nearly 12 feet tall) of the 15th century. Jodocus Vyd, diplomat-retainer of Philip the Good, and his wife, Isabel Borluut, commissioned this polyptych as the centerpiece of the chapel Vyd built in the church originally dedicated to Saint John the Baptist (since 1540, Saint Bavo Cathedral). Vyd's largesse and the political and social connections the *Ghent Altarpiece* revealed to its audience contributed to Vyd's appointment as burgomeister (chief magistrate) of Ghent shortly after the unveiling of the work. Two of the exterior panels (FIG. 15-4) depict the donors. The husband and wife, painted in illusionistically rendered niches, kneel with their hands clasped in prayer. They gaze piously at illusionistic stone sculptures of Ghent's patron saints, Saint John the Baptist and Saint John the Evangelist (who was probably also Vyd's patron saint). The *Annunciation* appears on the upper register, with a careful representation of a Flemish town outside the painted window of the center panel. In the uppermost arched panels, van Eyck depicted the Old Testament prophets Zachariah and Micah, along with *sibyls,* Greco-Roman mythological female prophets whose writings the Christian Church interpreted as prophecies of Christ.

15-4 HUBERT and JAN VAN EYCK, *Ghent Altarpiece* (closed), Saint Bavo Cathedral, Ghent, Belgium, completed 1432. Oil on wood, 11′ 5″ × 7′ 6″. ◼◀

Monumental painted altarpieces were popular in Flemish churches. Artists decorated both the interiors and exteriors of these polyptychs, which often, as here, included donor portraits.

15-5A VAN EYCK, *Madonna in a Church,* ca. 1425–1430.

When opened (FIG. 15-5), the altarpiece reveals a sumptuous, superbly colored painting of humanity's redemption through Christ. In the upper register, God the Father—wearing the pope's triple tiara, with a worldly crown at his feet, and resplendent in a deep-scarlet mantle—presides in majesty. To God's right is the Virgin, represented, as in the Gothic age and in an earlier van Eyck *diptych* (two-paneled painting; FIG. **15-5A**), as the queen of Heaven, with a crown of 12 stars upon her head. Saint John the Baptist sits to God's left. To either side is a choir of angels, with an angel playing an organ on the right. Adam and Eve appear in the far panels. The inscriptions in the arches above Mary and Saint John extol the Virgin's virtue and purity and Saint John's greatness as the forerunner of Christ. The inscription above the Lord's head translates as "This is God, all-powerful in his divine majesty; of all the best, by the gentleness of his goodness; the most liberal giver, because of his infinite generosity." The step behind the crown at the Lord's feet bears the inscription, "On his head, life without death. On his brow, youth without age. On his right, joy without sadness. On his left, security without fear." The entire altarpiece amplifies the central theme of salvation. Even though humans, symbolized by Adam and Eve, are sinful, they will be saved because God, in his infinite love, will sacrifice his own son for this purpose.

The panels of the lower register extend the symbolism of the upper. In the central panel, the community of saints comes from the four corners of the earth through an opulent, flower-spangled landscape. They proceed toward the altar of the lamb and the octagonal fountain of life (compare FIG. 15-2). The book of Revelation passage recounting the *Adoration of the Lamb* is the main reading on All Saints' Day (November 1). The lamb symbolizes the sacrificed son of God, whose heart bleeds into a chalice, while into the fountain spills the "pure river of water of life, clear as crystal, pro-

ceeding out of the throne of God and of the Lamb" (Rev. 22:1). On the right, the 12 apostles and a group of martyrs in red robes advance. On the left appear prophets. In the right background come the virgin martyrs, and in the left background the holy confessors approach. On the lower wings, hermits, pilgrims, knights, and judges approach from left and right. They symbolize the four cardinal virtues: Temperance, Prudence, Fortitude, and Justice, respectively. The altarpiece celebrates the whole Christian cycle from the fall of man to the redemption, presenting the Church triumphant in heavenly Jerusalem.

Van Eyck used oil paints to render the entire altarpiece in a shimmering splendor of color that defies reproduction. No small detail escaped the painter. With pristine specificity, he revealed the beauty of the most insignificant object as if it were a work of piety as much as a work of art. He depicted the soft texture of hair, the glitter of gold in the heavy brocades, the luster of pearls, and the flashing of gems, all with loving fidelity to appearance. This kind of meticulous attention to recording the exact surface appearance of humans, animals, objects, and landscapes, already evident in

15-5 Hubert and Jan van Eyck, *Ghent Altarpiece* (open), Saint Bavo Cathedral, Ghent, Belgium, completed 1432. Oil on wood, 11′ 5″ × 15′ 1″. ◼◀

In this sumptuous painting of salvation from the original sin of Adam and Eve, God the Father presides in majesty. Van Eyck used oil paints to render every detail with loving fidelity to appearance.

the *Mérode Altarpiece* (FIG. 15-1), became the hallmark of Flemish panel painting in the 15th century.

GIOVANNI ARNOLFINI Emerging capitalism led to an urban prosperity that fueled the growing bourgeois market for art objects, particularly in Bruges, Antwerp, and, later, Amsterdam. This prosperity contributed to a growing interest in secular art in addition to religious artworks. Both the *Mérode Altarpiece* and the *Ghent Altarpiece* include painted portraits of their donors. These paintings marked a significant revival of portraiture, a genre that had languished since antiquity.

A purely secular portrait, but one with religious overtones, is Jan van Eyck's oil painting of *Giovanni Arnolfini and His Wife* (FIG. **15-6**). Van Eyck depicted the Lucca financier (who had established himself in Bruges as an agent of the Medici family) in his home, a setting that is simultaneously mundane yet charged with the spiritual. Arnolfini holds the hand of his second wife, whose name is not known. According to the traditional interpretation of the painting, van Eyck recorded the couple taking their marriage

vows. As in the *Mérode Altarpiece* (FIG. 15-1), almost every object portrayed carries meaning. The cast-aside clogs indicate this event is taking place on holy ground. The little dog symbolizes fidelity (the common canine name *Fido* originated from the Latin *fidere*, "to trust"). Behind the pair, the curtains of the marriage bed have been opened. The bedpost's *finial* (crowning ornament) is a tiny statue of Saint Margaret, patron saint of childbirth. (The bride is not yet pregnant, although the fashionable costume she wears makes her appear so.) From the finial hangs a whisk broom, symbolic of domestic care. The oranges on the chest below the window may refer to fertility. The single candle burning in the left rear holder of the ornate chandelier and the mirror, in which the viewer sees the entire room reflected, symbolize the all-seeing eye of God. The small medallions set into the mirror frame show tiny scenes from the passion of Christ and represent God's promise of salvation for the figures reflected on the mirror's convex surface. Viewers of the period would have been familiar with many of the objects included in the painting because of traditional Flemish customs. Husbands customarily presented brides with clogs, and the solitary lit candle

15-6 JAN VAN EYCK, *Giovanni Arnolfini and His Wife*, 1434. Oil on wood, 2′ 9″ × 1′ 10½″. National Gallery, London. ◼◀

Van Eyck played a major role in establishing portraiture as an important Flemish art form. In this portrait of an Italian financier and his wife, he also portrayed himself in the mirror.

1 ft.

in the chandelier was part of Flemish marriage practices. Van Eyck's placement of the two figures suggests conventional gender roles—the woman stands near the bed and well into the room, whereas the man stands near the open window, symbolic of the outside world.

Van Eyck enhanced the documentary nature of this scene by exquisitely painting each object. He carefully distinguished textures and depicted the light from the window on the left reflecting off various surfaces. He also augmented the scene's credibility by including the convex mirror (complete with its spatial distortion, brilliantly recorded), because viewers can see not only the principals, Arnolfini and his wife, but also two persons who look into the room through the door. (Arnolfini's raised right hand may be a gesture of greeting to the two men.) One of these must be the artist himself, as the florid inscription above the mirror, *Johannes de Eyck fuit hic* ("Jan van Eyck was here"), announces he was present. The picture's purpose, then, would have been to record and sanctify this marriage.

Most scholars now reject this traditional reading of the painting, however. The room is a public reception area, not a bedchamber, and it has been suggested that Arnolfini is conferring legal privileges on his wife to conduct business in his absence. In either case, the artist functions as a witness. The self-portrait of van Eyck in the mirror also underscores the painter's self-consciousness as a professional artist whose role deserves to be recorded and remembered. (Compare the 12th-century monk Eadwine's self-portrait as "prince of scribes" [FIG. 12-36], a very early instance of an artist engaging in "self-promotion.")

MAN IN A RED TURBAN In 15th-century Flanders, artists also painted secular portraits without the layer of religious inter-

pretation present in the Arnolfini double portrait. These private commissions began to multiply as both artists and patrons became interested in the reality (both physical and psychological) portraits could reveal. For various reasons, great patrons embraced the opportunity to have their likenesses painted. They wanted to memorialize themselves in their dynastic lines and to establish their identities, ranks, and stations with images far more concrete than heraldic coats of arms. Portraits also served to represent state officials at events they could not attend. Sometimes, royalty, nobility, and the very rich would send artists to paint the likeness of a prospective bride or groom. For example, when young King Charles VI of France sought a bride, he dispatched a painter to three different royal courts to make portraits of the candidates.

In *Man in a Red Turban* (FIG. 15-7), the man van Eyck portrayed looks directly at the viewer. This is the first known Western painted portrait in a thousand years where the sitter does so. The

Framed Paintings

Until the 20th century, when painters began simply to affix canvas to wooden *stretcher bars* to provide a taut painting surface devoid of ornamentation, artists considered the frame an integral part of the painting. Frames served a number of functions, some visual, others conceptual. For paintings such as large-scale altarpieces that were part of a larger environment, frames often served to integrate the painting with its surroundings. Frames could also be used to reinforce the illusionistic nature of the painted image. For example, the Italian painter Giovanni Bellini, in his *San Zaccaria Altarpiece* (FIG. 17-32), duplicated the carved pilasters of the architectural frame in the painting itself, thereby enhancing the illusion of space and giving the painted figures an enhanced physical presence. In the *Ghent Altarpiece,* the frame seems to cast shadows on the floor between the angel and Mary in the *Annunciation* (FIG. 15-4, *top*.) More commonly, artists used frames specifically to distance the viewer from the (often otherworldly) scene by calling attention to the separation of the image from the viewer's space.

Most 15th- and 16th-century paintings included elaborate frames the artists themselves helped design and construct. Extant contracts reveal the frame could account for as much as half of the cost of an altarpiece. Frequently, the commissions called for painted or gilded frames, adding to the expense. For small works, artists sometimes affixed the frames to the panels before painting, creating an insistent visual presence as they worked. Occasionally, a single piece of wood served as both panel and frame, and the artist carved the painting surface from the wood, leaving the edges as a frame. Larger images with elaborate frames, such as altarpieces, required the services of a woodcarver or stonemason. The painter worked closely with the individual constructing the frame to ensure its appropriateness for the image(s) produced.

Unfortunately, over time, many frames have been removed from their paintings. For instance, in 1566 church officials dismantled the *Ghent Altarpiece* and detached its elaborately carved frame in order to protect the sacred work from Protestant *iconoclasts* (see Chapter 18). As ill luck would have it, when the panels were reinstalled in 1587, no one could find the frame. Sadly, the absence of many of the original frames of old paintings deprives viewers today of the painter's complete artistic vision. Conversely, when the original frames exist, they sometimes provide essential information, such as the subject, name of the painter, and date. For

15-7 JAN VAN EYCK, *Man in a Red Turban,* 1433. Oil on wood, 1' 1⅛" × 10¼". National Gallery, London.

Man in a Red Turban is the first known Western painted portrait in a thousand years in which the sitter looks directly at the viewer. The inscribed frame suggests it is a self-portrait.

example, the inscriptions on the frame of Jan van Eyck's *Man in a Red Turban* (FIG. 15-7) state he painted it on October 21, 1433, and the inclusion of "As I can" and omission of the sitter's name suggest the painting is a self-portrait.

level, composed gaze, directed from a true three-quarter head pose, must have impressed observers deeply. The painter created the illusion that from whatever angle a viewer observes the face, the eyes return that gaze. Van Eyck, with his considerable observational skill and controlled painting style, injected a heightened sense of specificity into this portrait by including beard stubble, veins in the bloodshot left eye, and weathered, aged skin. Although a definitive identification of the sitter has yet to be made, most scholars consider *Man in a Red Turban* a self-portrait, which van Eyck painted by looking at his image in a mirror (as he depicted himself

in the mirror in the Arnolfinis' home). The inscriptions on the frame (see "Framed Paintings," above) reinforce this identification. Across the top, van Eyck wrote "As I can" in Flemish using Greek letters. (One suggestion is this portrait was a demonstration piece intended for prospective clients, who could compare the painting with the painter and judge what he "could do" in terms of recording a faithful likeness. Across the bottom appears the statement (in Latin) "Jan van Eyck made me" and the date. The use of both Greek and Latin suggests the artist's view of himself as a successor to the fabled painters of antiquity.

15-8 Rogier van der Weyden, *Deposition*, center panel of a triptych from Notre-Dame hors-les-murs, Louvain, Belgium, ca. 1435. Oil on wood, 7′ 2⅝″ × 8′ 7⅛″. Museo del Prado, Madrid. ◼◀

Deposition resembles a relief carving in which the biblical figures act out a drama of passionate sorrow as if on a shallow theatrical stage. The painting makes an unforgettable emotional impression.

Rogier van der Weyden

When Jan van Eyck received the commission for the *Ghent Altarpiece*, Rogier van der Weyden (ca. 1400–1464) was an assistant in the workshop of Robert Campin (FIG. 15-1), but the younger painter's fame eventually rivaled van Eyck's. Rogier quickly became renowned for his dynamic compositions stressing human action and drama. He concentrated on Christian themes such as *Deposition* (FIG. 15-8) and other episodes in the life of Jesus that elicited powerful emotions, for example, *Crucifixion* and *Pietà* (the Virgin Mary cradling the dead body of her son), moving observers deeply by vividly portraying the sufferings of Christ. He also painted a dramatic vision of *Last Judgment* (FIG. 15-8A).

15-8A Van der Weyden, *Last Judgment Altarpiece*, ca. 1444–1448. ◼◀

DEPOSITION One of Rogier's early masterworks is his 1435 *Deposition* (FIG. 15-8), the center panel of a triptych commissioned by the archers' guild of Louvain for the church of Notre-Dame hors-les-murs (Notre-Dame "outside the [town] walls"). Rogier acknowledged the patrons of this large painting by incorporating the crossbow (the guild's symbol) into the decorative tracery in the corners. Instead of creating a deep landscape setting, as van Eyck might have, Rogier compressed the figures and action onto a shallow stage with a golden back wall, imitating the large sculptured shrines so popular in the 15th century, especially in the Holy Roman Empire (FIGS. 15-19 and 15-20). The device admirably served his purpose of expressing maximum action within a limited space. The painting, with the artist's crisp drawing and precise modeling of forms, resembles a stratified relief carving. A series of lateral undulating movements gives the group a compositional unity, a formal cohesion Rogier strengthened by depicting the desolating anguish many of the figures share. Present are the Virgin and several of her half-sisters, Joseph of Arimathea, Nicodemus, Saint John the Evangelist, and Mary Magdalene. The similar poses of Christ and his mother further unify the composition and reflect the belief that Mary suffered the same pain at the crucifixion as her son. Their echoing postures also resemble the shape of a crossbow.

Few painters have equaled Rogier van der Weyden in rendering passionate sorrow as it vibrates through a figure or distorts a tearstained face. His depiction of the agony of loss in *Deposition* is

The Artist's Profession in Flanders

As in Italy (see "Artistic Training," Chapter 14, page 414), guilds controlled artistic production in Flanders. To pursue a craft, individuals had to belong to the guild controlling that craft. Painters, for example, sought admission to the Guild of Saint Luke, the patron saint of painters because Luke made a portrait of the Virgin Mary (FIG. 15-9). The path to eventual membership in the guild began, for men, at an early age, when the father apprenticed his son in boyhood to a master, with whom the young aspiring painter lived. The master taught the fundamentals of his craft—how to make implements, prepare panels with *gesso* (plaster mixed with a binding material), and mix colors, oils, and varnishes. Once the youth mastered these procedures and learned to work in the master's traditional manner, he usually spent several years working as a journeyman in various cities, observing and absorbing ideas from other masters. He then was eligible to become a master and could apply for admission to the guild. Fees could be very high, especially if an artist was not a citizen of the same city. Sometimes, an artist seeking admission to a guild would marry the widow of a member. A woman could inherit her husband's workshop but not run it. Guild membership was essential for establishing an artist's reputation and for obtaining commissions. The guild inspected paintings to evaluate workmanship and ensure its members used quality materials. It also secured adequate payment for its artists' labor.

Women had many fewer opportunities than men to train as artists, in large part because of social and moral constraints that forbade women to reside as apprentices in the homes of male masters. Moreover, from the 16th century, when academic training courses supplemented and then replaced guild training, until the 20th century, women would not as a rule expect or be permitted instruction in figure painting, because it involved dissection of cadavers and study of the nude male model. Flemish women interested in pursuing art as a career, for example, Caterina van Hemessen (FIG. 18-18), most often received tutoring from fathers and husbands who were professionals and whom the women assisted in all the technical procedures of the craft. Despite these obstacles, membership records of the art guilds of Bruges and other cities reveal a substantial number of Flemish

15-9 Rogier van der Weyden, *Saint Luke Drawing the Virgin*, ca. 1435–1440. Oil and tempera on wood, 4' 6$\frac{1}{8}$" × 3' 7$\frac{5}{8}$". Museum of Fine Arts, Boston (gift of Mr. and Mrs. Henry Lee Higginson).

Probably commissioned by the painters' guild in Brussels, this painting honors the first Christian artist and the profession of painting. Saint Luke may be a self-portrait of Rogier van der Weyden.

women were able to establish themselves as artists during the 15th century. That they succeeded in negotiating the difficult path to acceptance as professionals is a testament to both their tenacity and their artistic skill.

among the most authentic in religious art and creates an immediate and unforgettable emotional effect on the viewer. It was probably Rogier whom Michelangelo had in mind when, according to the Portuguese painter Francisco de Hollanda (1517–1584), the Italian master observed, "Flemish painting [will] please the devout better than any painting of Italy, which will never cause him to shed a tear, whereas that of Flanders will cause him to shed many."[1]

SAINT LUKE Slightly later in date is Rogier's *Saint Luke Drawing the Virgin* (FIG. **15-9**), probably painted for the Guild of Saint Luke, the artists' guild in Brussels. The panel depicts the patron saint of painters drawing the Virgin Mary using a *silverpoint* (a sharp *stylus* that creates a fine line). The theme paid tribute to the profession of painting in Flanders (see "The Artist's Profession in Flanders," above) by drawing attention to the venerable history of the painter's craft and documenting the preparatory work required before the artist could begin painting the figures and setting. Portrait painting was a major source of income for Flemish artists, and Rogier was one of the best (FIG. 15-9A). In fact, many scholars believe Rogier's Saint Luke is a self-portrait, identifying the Flemish painter with the first Christian artist and underscoring the holy nature of painting. Rogier shared with Campin and van Eyck the aim of recording every detail of a scene with loving fidelity to optical appearance, seen here in the rich fabrics, the floor pattern, and the landscape visible through the window. Also, as his older colleagues did, Rogier imbued much of the representation with symbolic significance. At the right, the ox identifies the figure recording the Virgin's features as Saint Luke (see "The Four Evangelists," Chapter 11, page 314). The carved armrest of the Virgin's bench depicts Adam, Eve, and the serpent, reminding the viewer that Mary is the new Eve and Christ the new Adam who will redeem humanity from original sin.

Later Flemish Painters

Robert Campin, Jan van Eyck, and Rogier van der Weyden were the leading figures of the first generation of "Northern Renaissance" painters. (Art historians usually transfer to northern Europe, with less validity than in its original usage, the term *Renaissance*, coined to describe the conscious revival of classical art in Italy. They also use the uppercase designation *Northern European* as a stylistic term parallel to Italian, as opposed to the geographic designation *northern European*.) The second generation of Flemish masters, active during the latter half of the 15th century, had much in common with their illustrious predecessors, especially a preference for using oil paints to create naturalistic representations, often, although not always, of traditional Christian subjects for installation in churches.

PETRUS CHRISTUS One work of uncertain Christian content is *A Goldsmith in His Shop* (FIG. 15-10) by PETRUS CHRISTUS (ca. 1410–1472), who settled in Bruges in 1444. According to the traditional interpretation, *A Goldsmith in His Shop* portrays Saint Eligius (who was initially a master goldsmith before committing his life to God) sitting in his stall, showing an elegantly attired couple a selection of rings. The bride's betrothal girdle lies on the table as a symbol of chastity, and the woman reaches for the ring the goldsmith weighs. The artist's inclusion of a crystal container for Eucharistic wafers (on the lower shelf to the right of Saint Eligius) and the scales (a reference to the last judgment) supports a religious interpretation of this painting and continues the Flemish tradition of imbuing everyday objects with symbolic significance. A halo once encircled the goldsmith's head, seemingly confirming the religious nature of this scene. Scientists have determined, however, that the halo was a later addition by another artist, and restorers have removed it.

Most scholars now think the painting, although not devoid of religious content, should be seen as a vocational painting of the type often produced for installation in Flemish guild chapels. Although the couple's presence suggests a marriage portrait, the patrons were probably not the couple portrayed but rather the goldsmiths' guild in Bruges. Saint Eligius was the patron saint of gold- and silversmiths, blacksmiths, and metalworkers, all of whom shared a chapel

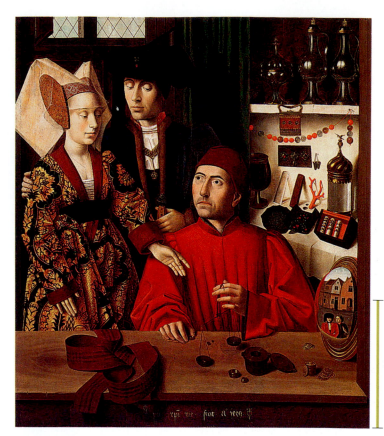

15-10 PETRUS CHRISTUS, *A Goldsmith in His Shop*, 1449. Oil on wood, 3′ 3″ × 2′ 10″. Metropolitan Museum of Art, New York (Robert Lehman Collection, 1975).

Once thought to depict Eligius, the patron saint of goldsmiths, Christus's painting, made for the Bruges goldsmiths guild, is more likely a generic scene of a couple shopping for a wedding ring.

in a building adjacent to their meetinghouse. The reconsecration of this chapel took place in 1449, the same date as the Christus painting. Therefore, it seems probable the artist painted *A Goldsmith in His Shop*, which illustrates an economic transaction and focuses on the goldsmith's profession, specifically for the guild chapel.

Christus went to great lengths to produce a historically credible image. For example, the variety of objects depicted in the painting serves as advertisement for the goldsmiths' guild. Included are the goldsmiths' raw materials (precious stones, beads, crystal, coral, and seed pearls) scattered among finished products (rings, buckles, and brooches). The pewter vessels on the upper shelves are donation pitchers, which town leaders gave to distinguished guests. All these meticulously painted objects not only attest to the centrality and importance of goldsmiths to both the secular and sacred communities but also enhance the naturalism of the painting. The convex mirror in the foreground showing another couple and a street with houses serves to extend the painting's space into the viewer's space, further creating the illusion of reality, as in van Eyck's Arnolfini portrait (FIG. 15-6).

DIRK BOUTS In *Last Supper* (FIG. 15-11), DIRK BOUTS (ca. 1415–1475) of Haarlem chose a different means of suggesting spatial recession. The painting is the central panel of the *Altarpiece of the Holy Sacrament*, which the Confraternity of the Holy Sacrament in Louvain commissioned

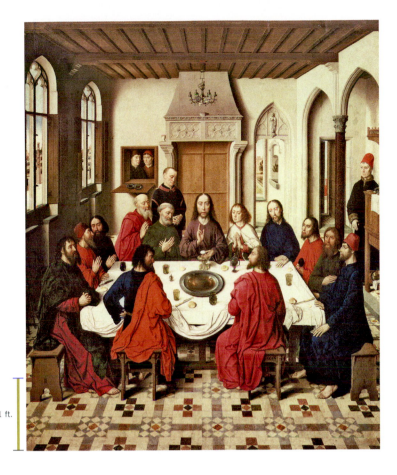

15-11 **DIRK BOUTS,** *Last Supper,* center panel of the *Altarpiece of the Holy Sacrament,* Saint Peter's, Louvain, Belgium, 1464–1468. Oil on wood, 6′ × 5′. ◼◂

One of the earliest Northern European paintings to employ Renaissance linear perspective, this *Last Supper* includes four servants in Flemish attire—portraits of the altarpiece's patrons.

perpendicular to the picture plane) lead to the vanishing point in the center of the mantelpiece above Christ's head. The small side room, however, has its own vanishing point, and neither it nor the vanishing point of the main room falls on the horizon of the landscape seen through the windows, as in Italian Renaissance paintings.

In *Last Supper,* Bouts did not focus on the biblical narrative itself but instead presented Christ in the role of a priest performing a ritual from the liturgy of the Christian Church—the consecration of the Eucharistic wafer. This contrasts strongly with other depictions of the same subject, which often focused on Judas's betrayal or on Christ's comforting of John. The Confraternity of the Holy Sacrament dedicated itself to the worship of the Eucharist, and the smaller panels on the altarpiece's wings depict Old Testament *prefigurations* of the Eucharist. Bouts also added four servants (two in the window and two standing) not mentioned in the biblical account, all dressed in Flemish attire. These are portraits of the four members of the confraternity who contracted Bouts to paint the altarpiece, continuing the Flemish tradition of inserting into representations of biblical events portraits of the painting's patrons, first noted in the *Mérode Altarpiece* (FIG. 15-1).

in 1464, four years before Bouts became the city's official painter and produced a series of panels—*Justice of Otto III* (FIG. **15-11A**)—for Louvain's town hall. Bouts's *Last Supper* is one of the earliest Northern Renaissance paintings to demonstrate the use of a *vanishing point* (see "Linear and Atmospheric Perspective," Chapter 16, page 455) for creating *perspective.* All of the central room's *orthogonals* (converging diagonal lines imagined to be behind and

HUGO VAN DER GOES By the mid-15th century, Flemish art had achieved renown throughout Europe. The *Portinari Altarpiece* (FIG. **15-12**), for example, is a large-scale Flemish work in a family chapel in Florence, Italy. The artist who received the commission was HUGO VAN DER GOES (ca. 1440–1482), the dean of the painters' guild of Ghent from 1468 to 1475. Hugo painted the triptych for Tommaso Portinari, an Italian shipowner and agent for the powerful Medici family of Florence. Portinari appears on the wings

15-12 HUGO VAN DER GOES, *Portinari Altarpiece* (open), from Sant'Egidio, Florence, Italy, ca. 1476. Tempera and oil on wood, center panel 8′ 3½″ × 10′, each wing 8′ 3½″ × 4′ 7½″. Galleria degli Uffizi, Florence.

This altarpiece is a rare instance of the awarding of a major commission in Italy to a Flemish painter. The Florentines admired Hugo's realistic details and brilliant portrayal of human character.

of the altarpiece with his family and their patron saints. The subject of the central panel is *Adoration of the Shepherds*. On this large surface, Hugo displayed a scene of solemn grandeur, muting the high drama of the joyous occasion. The Virgin, Joseph, and the angels seem to brood on the suffering to come rather than to meditate on the miracle of Jesus' birth. Mary kneels, somber and monumental, on a tilted ground, a device the painter used to situate the main actors at the center of the panel. (The compositional device may derive from the tilted stage floors of 15th-century mystery plays.) Three shepherds enter from the right rear. Hugo represented them in attitudes of wonder, piety, and gaping curiosity. Their lined faces, work-worn hands, and uncouth dress and manner seem immediately familiar.

The architecture and a continuous wintry northern European landscape unify the three panels. Symbols surface throughout the altarpiece. Iris and columbine flowers are emblems of the sorrows of the Virgin. The angels represent the 15 joys of Mary. A sheaf of wheat stands for Bethlehem (the "house of bread" in Hebrew), a reference to the Eucharist. The harp of David, emblazoned over the building's portal in the middle distance (just to the right of the Virgin's head), signifies the ancestry of Christ. To stress the meaning and significance of the illustrated event, Hugo revived medieval pictorial devices. Small scenes shown in the background of the altarpiece represent (from left to right) the flight into Egypt, the annunciation to the shepherds, and the arrival of the magi. Hugo's variation in the scale of his figures to differentiate them by their importance to the central event also reflects older traditions. Still,

he put a vigorous, penetrating realism to work in a new direction, characterizing human beings according to their social level while showing their common humanity.

After Portinari placed the altarpiece in his family's chapel in the Florentine church of Sant'Egidio, it created a considerable stir among Italian artists. Although the painting may have seemed unstructured to them, Hugo's masterful technique and what the Florentines deemed incredible realism in representing drapery, flowers, animals, and, above all, human character and emotion made a deep impression on them. At least one Florentine artist, Domenico Ghirlandaio (FIGS. 16-26 and 16-27), paid tribute to the Flemish master by using Hugo's most striking motif, the adoring shepherds, in one of his own *Nativity* paintings.

HANS MEMLING Hugo's contemporary, HANS MEMLING (ca. 1430–1494), became a citizen of Bruges in 1465 and received numerous commissions from the city's wealthy merchants, Flemish and foreign alike. He specialized in portraits of his patrons (one of whom was Tommaso Portinari) and images of the Madonna. Memling's many paintings of the Virgin portray young, slight, pretty princesses, each holding a doll-like infant Christ. The center panel of the *Saint John Altarpiece* depicts the *Virgin with Saints and Angels* (FIG. **15-13**). The patrons of this altarpiece—two brothers and two sisters of the order of the Hospital of Saint John in Bruges—appear on the exterior side panels (not illustrated). In the central panel, two angels, one playing a musical instrument and the other holding a book, flank the Virgin. To the sides of Mary's throne

15-13 HANS MEMLING, *Virgin with Saints and Angels,* center panel of the *Saint John Altarpiece,* Hospitaal Sint Jan, Bruges, Belgium, 1479. Oil on wood, center panel 5′ 7¾″ × 5′ 7¾″, each wing 5′ 7¾″ × 2′ 7⅛″.

Memling specialized in images of the Madonna. His *Saint John Altarpiece* exudes an opulence that results from the sparkling and luminous colors and the realistic depiction of rich tapestries and brocades.

15-14 HANS MEMLING, *Diptych of Martin van Nieuwenhove*, 1487. Oil on wood, each panel 1′ 5⅜″ × 1′ 1″. Memlingmuseum, Bruges.

In this diptych the Virgin and Child pay a visit to the home of 23-year-old Martin van Nieuwenhove. A round convex mirror reflects the three figures and unites the two halves of the diptych spatially.

stand Saint John the Baptist on the left and Saint John the Evangelist on the right, and seated in the foreground are Saints Catherine and Barbara. This gathering celebrates the *mystic marriage* of Saint Catherine of Alexandria, one of many virgin saints believed to have entered into a spiritual marriage with Christ. As one of the most revered virgins of Christ, Saint Catherine provided a model of devotion that resonated with women viewers (especially nuns). The altarpiece exudes an opulence that results from the rich colors, meticulously depicted tapestries and brocades, and the serenity of the figures. The composition is balanced and serene, the color sparkling and luminous, and the execution of the highest technical quality.

Memling combined portraiture and Madonna imagery again in a much less ambitious—and more typical—work (FIG. 15-14) commissioned by Martin van Nieuwenhove, the scion of an important Bruges family that held various posts in the civic government. Martin himself served as burgomeister (mayor) of Bruges in 1497. The painting takes the form of a diptych, with the patron portrayed on the right wing and praying to the Madonna and Child on the left wing. According to inscriptions on the frames, van Nieuwenhove commissioned the work in 1487 when he was 23 years old (he died in 1500).

The format of the van Nieuwenhove diptych follows the pattern Memling used earlier for his wedding triptych of *Tommaso Portinari and Maria Baroncelli* (FIG. 15-14A) but with only a single (male) portrait. The left panel representing the Madonna

and Child is probably similar to the lost central section of the Portinari triptych. Memling's portrayals of the Virgin and Child differ little in his smaller, private devotional works and his larger altarpieces (FIG. 15-13) and consistently feature a tender characterization of the young Virgin and her nude in-

15-14A MEMLING, *Tommaso Portinari and Maria Baroncelli*, ca. 1470.

fant son. Here, however, Memling set both the Madonna and her patron in the interior of a well-appointed Flemish home featuring stained-glass windows. The window to the left of the Virgin's head bears van Nieuwenhove's coat of arms. The window behind the donor depicts his patron saint, Martin of Tours. These precisely recorded details identify the home as van Nieuwenhove's (the Minnewater Bridge in Bruges is visible through the open window), and the Madonna and Child have honored him by coming to his private residence. The conceit is a familiar one in Flemish painting. An early example is the *Annunciation* taking place in the home of Peter Inghelbrecht in Robert Campin's *Mérode Altarpiece* (FIG. 15-1). In the Memling portrait diptych, the Christ Child sits on the same ledge as the donor's open prayer book. Also uniting the two wings of the diptych is the round convex mirror behind the Virgin's right shoulder in which the viewer sees the reflection of the Virgin and van Nieuwenhove as well as the rest of the room (compare FIGS. 15-6 and 15-10).

The sumptuous pictures in *Les Très Riches Heures* depict characteristic activities of each month. The prominence of genre subjects reflects the increasing integration of religious and secular art.

FRANCE

In contrast to the prosperity and peace Flanders enjoyed during the 15th century, in France the Hundred Years' War crippled economic enterprise and prevented political stability. The anarchy of war and the weakness of the kings gave rise to a group of duchies, each with significant power and the resources to commission major artworks. The strongest and wealthiest of these has already been examined—the duchy of Burgundy, which controlled Flanders. But the dukes of Berry, Bourbon, and Nemours as well as members of the French royal court were also important art patrons.

Manuscript Painting

During the 15th century, French artists built on the achievements of Gothic painters (see Chapter 13) and produced exquisitely refined illuminated manuscripts. Among the most significant developments in French manuscript painting was a new conception and presentation of space. Paintings in manuscripts took on more pronounced characteristics as illusionistic scenes. Increased contact with Italy, where Renaissance artists had revived the pictorial principles of classical antiquity, may have influenced French painters' interest in illusionism.

LIMBOURG BROTHERS The most innovative early-15th-century manuscript illuminators were the three LIMBOURG BROTHERS—POL, HERMAN, and JEAN—from Nijmegen in the Netherlands. They were nephews of Jean Malouel, the court artist of Philip the Bold. Following in the footsteps of earlier illustrators such as Jean Pucelle (FIGS. 13-36 and 13-36A), the Limbourg brothers expanded the illusionistic capabilities of illumination. Trained in the Netherlands, the brothers moved to Paris no later than 1402, and between 1405 and their death in 1416, probably from the plague, they worked in Paris and Bourges for Jean, duke of Berry (r. 1360–1416) and brother of King Charles V (r. 1364–1380) of France and of Philip the Bold of Burgundy.

The duke ruled the western French regions of Berry, Poitou, and Auvergne (MAP 15-1). He was an avid art patron and focused on collecting manuscripts, jewels, and rare artifacts. Among the more than 300 manuscripts the duke owned were Pucelle's *Belleville Breviary* (FIG. 13-36) and the *Hours of Jeanne d'Évreux* (FIG. 13-36A) as well as *Les Très Riches Heures du Duc de Berry* (*The Very Sumptuous Hours of the Duke of Berry;* FIGS. 15-15 and 15-16), which he commissioned the Limbourg brothers to produce. A Book of Hours, like a *breviary,* was a book used for reciting prayers (see "Medieval Books," Chapter 11, page 312). As prayer books, they replaced the traditional *psalters* (books of psalms), which were the only liturgical books in private hands until the mid-13th century. The centerpiece of a Book of Hours was the "Office [prayer] of the Blessed Virgin," which contained liturgical passages to be read privately at set times during the day, from *matins* (dawn prayers) to *compline* (the last of the prayers recited daily). An illustrated calendar containing local religious feast days usually preceded the Office of the Blessed Virgin. Penitential psalms, devotional prayers, litanies to the saints, and other prayers, including those of the dead and of the Holy Cross, followed the center-

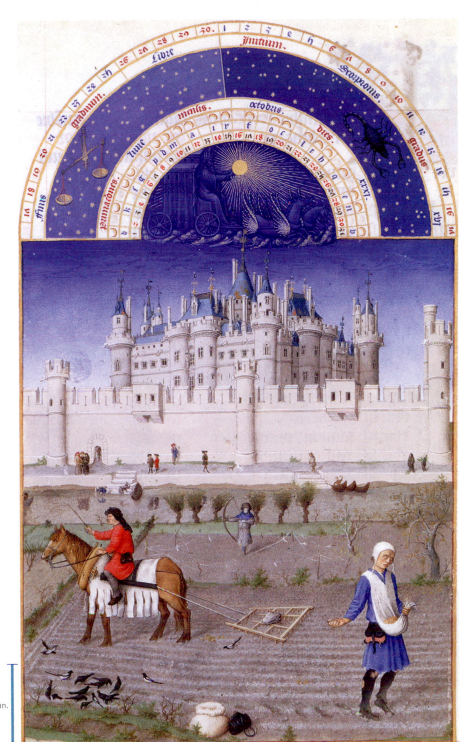

15-16 LIMBOURG BROTHERS (POL, HERMAN, JEAN), *October*, from *Les Très Riches Heures du Duc de Berry*, 1413–1416. Colors and ink on vellum, $8\frac{7}{8}'' \times 5\frac{3}{8}''$. Musée Condé, Chantilly. ◼◀

The Limbourg brothers expanded the illusionistic capabilities of manuscript painting with their care in rendering architectural details and convincing depiction of cast shadows.

1 in.

The full-page calendar pictures of *Les Très Riches Heures* are the most famous in the history of manuscript illumination. They represent the 12 months in terms of the associated seasonal tasks, alternating scenes of nobility and peasantry. Above each picture is a *lunette* in which the Limbourgs depicted the zodiac signs and the chariot of the sun as it makes its yearly cycle through the heavens. Beyond its function as a religious book, *Les Très Riches Heures* also visually captures the power of the duke and his relationship to the peasants. For example, the colorful calendar picture for January (FIG. 15-15) portrays a New Year's reception at court. The duke appears as magnanimous host, his head circled by the fire screen, almost halolike, behind him. His chamberlain stands next to him, urging the guests forward with the words "*aproche, aproche.*" The lavish spread of food on the table and the large tapestry on the back wall augment the richness and extravagance of the setting and the occasion.

In contrast, the illustration for October (FIG. 15-16) focuses on the peasantry. Here, the Limbourg brothers depicted a sower, a harrower on horseback, and washerwomen, along with city dwellers, who promenade in front of the Louvre (the French king's residence at the time, now one of the world's great art museums). The peasants do not appear discontented as they go about their assigned tasks. Surely this imagery flattered the duke's sense of himself as a compassionate master. The growing artistic interest in naturalism is evident here in the careful way the painter recorded the architectural details of the Louvre and in the convincing shadows of the people and objects (such as the archer scarecrow and the horse) in the scene.

As a whole, *Les Très Riches Heures* reinforced the image of the duke of Berry as a devout man, cultured bibliophile, sophisticated art patron, and powerful and magnanimous leader. Further, the expanded range of subject matter, especially the prominence of *genre* subjects in a religious book, reflected the increasing integration of religious and secular concerns in both art and life at the time. Although all three Limbourg brothers worked on *Les Très Riches Heures*, art historians have never been able to ascertain definitively which brother painted which images. Given the common practice of collaboration on artistic projects at this time, however, the determination of specific authorship is not very important.

piece. Books of Hours became favorite possessions of the northern European aristocracy during the 14th and 15th centuries. (Mary, the last duchess of Burgundy, commissioned a Book of Hours in which she was portrayed praying; FIG. **15-16A**. It is the masterpiece of the illuminator known as the MASTER OF MARY OF BURGUNDY, possibly ALEXANDER BENING [ca. 1444–1519].) These sumptuous books eventually became available to affluent burghers and contributed to the decentralization of religious practice that was one factor in the Protestant Reformation in the early 16th century (see Chapter 18).

15-16A *Hours of Mary of Burgundy*, ca. 1480.

Panel Painting

Images for private devotional use were popular in France, as in Flanders, and the preferred medium was oil paint on wood panels.

JEAN FOUQUET Among the French artists whose paintings were in demand was JEAN FOUQUET (ca. 1420–1481), who worked for King Charles VII (r. 1422–1461, the patron and client of Jacques Coeur; FIG. 13-30) and for the duke of Nemours. Fouquet painted a diptych (FIG. **15-17**) for Étienne Chevalier, who, despite his lowly origins, became Charles VII's treasurer in 1452. In the left panel of the *Melun Diptych* (named for its original location in Melun Cathedral), Chevalier appears with his patron saint, Saint Stephen (Étienne in French). Appropriately, Fouquet's donor portrait of Chevalier depicts his prominent patron as devout—kneeling, with hands clasped in prayer. The representation of the pious donor with his standing saint recalls Flemish art, as do the three-quarter stances and the realism of Chevalier's portrait. The artist portrayed Saint Stephen, whose head also has a portraitlike quality, holding the stone of his martyrdom (death by stoning) atop a volume of the holy scriptures, thereby ensuring that viewers properly identify the saint. Fouquet rendered the entire image in meticulous detail and included a highly ornamented architectural setting.

In its original diptych form (the two panels are now in different museums), the viewer would follow the gaze of Chevalier and Saint Stephen over to the right panel, which depicts the Virgin Mary and Christ Child in a most unusual way—with marblelike flesh, surrounded by red and blue *cherubs* (chubby winged child angels). The juxtaposition of these two images enabled the patron to bear witness to the sacred. The integration of sacred and secular (especially the political or personal), prevalent in other northern European artworks, also emerges here, which complicates the reading of this diptych. Agnès Sorel (1421–1450), the mistress of King Charles VII, was Fouquet's model for the Virgin Mary, whose left breast is exposed and who does not look at the viewer. Chevalier commissioned this painting after Sorel's death, probably by poisoning while pregnant with the king's child. Thus, in addition to the religious interpretation of this diptych, there is surely a personal and political narrative here as well.

HOLY ROMAN EMPIRE

Because the Holy Roman Empire (whose core was Germany) did not participate in the drawn-out saga of the Hundred Years' War, its economy remained stable and prosperous. Without a dominant court to commission artworks, wealthy merchants and clergy became the primary German patrons during the 15th century.

Panel Painting

The art of the early Northern Renaissance in the Holy Roman Empire displays a pronounced stylistic diversity. Some artists followed developments in Flemish painting, and large-scale altarpieces featuring naturalistically painted biblical themes were familiar sights in the Holy Roman Empire.

KONRAD WITZ Among the most notable 15th-century German altarpieces is the *Altarpiece of Saint Peter*, painted in 1444 for the chapel of Notre-Dame des Maccabées in the Cathedral of Saint Peter in Geneva, Switzerland. KONRAD WITZ (ca. 1400–1446), whose studio was in Basel, painted one exterior wing of this triptych with a

15-17 JEAN FOUQUET, *Melun Diptych*. Left wing: *Étienne Chevalier and Saint Stephen*, ca. 1450. Oil on wood, 3′ ½″ × 2′ 9½″. Gemäldegalerie, Staatliche Museen zu Berlin, Berlin. Right wing: *Virgin and Child*, ca. 1451. Oil on wood, 3′ 1¼″ × 2′ 9½″. Koninklijk Museum voor Schone Kunsten, Antwerp.

Fouquet's meticulous representation of a pious kneeling donor with a standing patron saint recalls Flemish painting, as do the three-quarter stances and the realism of the portraits.

15-18 KONRAD WITZ, *Miraculous Draught of Fish*, exterior wing of *Altarpiece of Saint Peter*, from the Chapel of Notre-Dame des Maccabées, Cathedral of Saint Peter, Geneva, Switzerland, 1444. Oil on wood, 4′ 3″ × 5′ 1″. Musée d'Art et d'Histoire, Geneva.

Konrad Witz set this biblical story on Lake Geneva. The painting is one of the first 15th-century works depicting a specific locale and is noteworthy for the painter's skill in rendering water effects.

1 ft.

representation of *Miraculous Draught of Fish* (FIG. **15-18**). The other exterior wing (not illustrated) depicts the release of Saint Peter from prison. The central panel is lost. On the interior wings, Witz painted scenes of *Adoration of the Magi* and of Saint Peter's presentation of the donor (Bishop François de Mies) to the Virgin and Child. *Miraculous Draught of Fish* shows Peter, the first pope, unsuccessfully trying to emulate Christ walking on water. Some scholars think the choice of subject is a commentary on the part of Witz's patron, the Swiss cardinal, on the limited power of the pope in Rome.

The painting is particularly significant because of the landscape's prominence. Witz showed precocious skill in the study of water ef-fects—the sky glaze on the slowly moving lake surface, the mirrored reflections of the figures in the boat, and the transparency of the shallow water in the foreground. He observed and represented the landscape so carefully that art historians have been able to determine the exact location shown. Witz presented a view of the shores of Lake Geneva, with the town of Geneva on the right and Le Môle Mountain in the distance behind Christ's head. This painting is one of the first 15th-century works depicting a specific, identifiable site.

The work of other leading German painters of the mid-15th century, for example, STEFAN LOCHNER (ca. 1400–1451), retained medieval features to a much greater degree, as is immediately evident in a comparison between Witz's landscape and Lochner's *Madonna in the Rose Garden* (FIG. **15-18A**).

15-18A LOCHNER, *Madonna in the Rose Garden*, ca. 1440.

Sculpture

In contrast to Flanders, where painted altarpieces were the norm, in the Holy Roman Empire many of the leading 15th-century artists specialized in carving large wooden retables. These grandiose sculpted altarpieces reveal the power of the lingering Late Gothic style.

VEIT STOSS The sculptor VEIT STOSS (1447–1533) trained in the Upper Rhine region but settled in Kraków (in present-day Poland) in 1477. In that year, he began work on a monumental altarpiece (FIG. **15-19**) for the church of Saint Mary in Kraków. In the central boxlike shrine, huge carved and painted figures, some nine feet high,

15-19 VEIT STOSS, *Death and Assumption of the Virgin* (wings open), altar of the Virgin Mary, church of Saint Mary, Kraków, Poland, 1477–1489. Painted and gilded wood, center panel 23′ 9″ high.

In this huge sculptured and painted altarpiece, Stoss used every figural and ornamental element from the vocabulary of Gothic art to heighten the emotion and to glorify the sacred event.

1 ft.

represent Death and Assumption of the Virgin. On the wings, Stoss portrayed scenes from the lives of Christ and Mary. The altar forcefully expresses the intense piety of Gothic culture in its late phase, when artists used every figural and ornamental motif in the repertoire of Gothic art to heighten the emotion and to glorify sacred events. In the Kraków altarpiece, Christ's disciples congregate around the Virgin, who collapses, dying. One of them supports her, while another wrings his hands in grief. Stoss posed others in attitudes of woe and psychic shock, striving for realism in every minute detail. He engulfed the figures in restless, twisting, and curving swaths of drapery whose broken and writhing lines unite the whole tableau in a vision of agitated emotion. The artist's massing of sharp, broken, and pierced forms that dart flamelike through the composition—at once unifying and animating it—recalls the design principles of Late Gothic architecture (FIG. 13-27). Indeed, in the Kraków altarpiece, Stoss merged sculpture and architecture, enhancing their union with paint and gilding.

TILMAN RIEMENSCHNEIDER *Assumption of the Virgin* is also the subject of the center panel (FIG. **15-20**) of the *Creglingen Altarpiece*, created by TILMAN RIEMENSCHNEIDER (ca. 1460–1531) of Würzburg for a parish church in Creglingen, Germany. He incorporated intricate Gothic forms, especially in the altarpiece's elaborate canopy, but unlike Stoss, he did not paint the figures or the background. By employing an endless and restless line running through the garments of the figures, Riemenschneider succeeded in setting the whole design into fluid motion, and no individual element functions without the rest. The draperies float and flow around bodies lost within them, serving not as descriptions but as design elements that tie the figures to one another and to the framework. A look of psychic strain, a facial expression common in Riemenschneider's work, heightens the spirituality of the figures, immaterial and weightless as they appear.

Graphic Arts

A new age blossomed in the 15th century with a sudden technological advance that had widespread effects—the invention by Johannes Gutenberg (ca. 1400–1468) of moveable type around 1450 and the development of the printing press. Printing had been known in China centuries before but had never fostered, as it did in 15th-century Europe, a revolution in written communication and in the generation and management of information. Printing provided new and challenging media for artists, and the earliest form was the *woodcut* (see "Woodcuts, Engravings, and Etchings," page 444). Artists produced inexpensive woodcuts such as the *Buxheim Saint Christopher* (FIG. **15-20A**) before the development of moveable-type printing. But when a rise in literacy and the im-

15-20 TILMAN RIEMENSCHNEIDER, *Assumption of the Virgin,* center panel of *Creglingen Altarpiece,* parish church, Creglingen, Germany, ca. 1495–1499. Lindenwood, 6′ 1″ wide.

Riemenschneider specialized in carving large wood retables. His works feature intricate Gothic tracery and religious figures whose bodies are almost lost within their swirling garments.

15-20A *Buxheim Saint Christopher,* 1423.

proved economy necessitated production of illustrated books on a grand scale, artists met the challenge of bringing the woodcut picture onto the same page as the letterpress.

MICHAEL WOLGEMUT The so-called *Nuremberg Chronicle,* a history of the world produced in Nuremberg by ANTON KOBERGER (ca. 1445–1513) with more than 650 illustrations by the workshop of MICHAEL WOLGEMUT (1434–1519), documents this achievement. The hand-colored illustration (FIG. **15-21**) spread across two facing pages represents *Madeburga* (modern Magdeburg, Germany; see MAP 11-1 and FIG. 11-26). The blunt, simple lines of the woodcut technique give a detailed perspective of the

Berta etas mudi

Berta etas mudi CLXXX

Madeburga

15-21 MICHAEL WOLGEMUT and shop, *Madeburga* page from the *Nuremberg Chronicle*, 1493. Woodcut, 1′ 6⅛″ × 2′ 1⅝″. Printed by ANTON KOBERGER.

The *Nuremberg Chronicle* is an early example of woodcut illustrations in printed books. The more than 650 pictures include detailed views of towns, but they are generic rather than specific portrayals.

city, its harbor and shipping, its walls and towers, its churches and municipal buildings, and a statue-topped columnar monument. Despite the numerous architectural structures, this illustration is not an accurate depiction of the city but the product of the artist's fanciful imagination. Artists often reprinted the same image as illustrations of different cities, and this depiction of Magdeburg is a generic view of a late medieval German town. Regardless, the work is a monument to a new craft, which expanded in concert with the art of the printed book.

MARTIN SCHONGAUER The woodcut medium hardly had matured when the technique of *engraving* (see "Woodcuts, Engravings, and Etchings," page 444), begun in the 1430s and well developed by 1450, proved much more flexible. Predictably, in the second half of the century, engraving began to replace the woodcut process, for making both book illustrations and widely popular single prints.

MARTIN SCHONGAUER (ca. 1430–1491) was the most skilled and subtle 15th-century Northern Renaissance master of metal engraving. His *Saint Anthony Tormented by Demons* (FIG. **15-22**) shows both the versatility of the medium and the artist's mastery

of it. The stoic saint is caught in a revolving thornbush of spiky demons, who claw and tear at him furiously. With unsurpassed skill and subtlety, Schongauer incised lines of varying thickness and density into a metal plate and created marvelous distinctions of tonal values and textures—from smooth skin to rough cloth, from the furry and feathery to the hairy and scaly. The use of *cross-hatching* (sets of engraved lines at right angles) to describe forms, which Schongauer probably developed, became standard among German graphic artists. The Italians preferred *parallel hatching* (FIG. 16-30) and rarely adopted cross-hatching, which, in keeping with the general Northern European approach to art, tends to describe the surfaces of things rather than their underlying structures.

Schongauer probably engraved *Saint Anthony* between 1480 and 1490. By then, the political geography of Europe had changed dramatically. Charles the Bold, who had assumed the title of duke of Burgundy in 1467, died in 1477, bringing to an end the Burgundian dream of forming a strong middle kingdom between France and the Holy Roman Empire. After Charles's death at the battle of Nancy, the French monarchy reabsorbed the southern Burgundian lands, and the Netherlands passed to the Holy Roman Empire

Holy Roman Empire **443**

Woodcuts, Engravings, and Etchings

With the invention of moveable type in the 15th century and the new widespread availability of paper from commercial mills, the art of printmaking developed rapidly in Europe. A *print* is an artwork on paper, usually produced in multiple impressions. The set of prints an artist creates from a single print surface is called an *edition*. As with books manufactured on a press, the printmaking process involves the transfer of ink from a printing surface to paper. This can be accomplished in several ways. During the 15th and 16th centuries, artists most commonly used the *relief* and *intaglio* methods of printmaking.

Artists produce relief prints, the oldest and simplest of the printing methods, by carving into a surface, usually wood. Relief printing requires artists to conceptualize their images negatively— that is, they remove the surface areas around the images using a gouging instrument. Thus, when the printmaker inks the ridges that carry the design, the hollow areas remain dry, and a positive image results when the artist presses the printing block against paper. Because artists produce *woodcuts* through a subtractive process (removing parts of the material), it is difficult to create very thin, fluid, and closely spaced lines. As a result, woodcut prints (for example, FIGS. 15-21 and 15-21A) tend to exhibit stark contrasts and sharp edges.

In contrast to the production of relief prints, the intaglio method involves a positive process. The artist *incises* (cuts) an image on a metal plate, often copper. The image can be created on the plate manually (*engraving* or *drypoint;* for example, FIG. 15-22) using a tool (a *burin* or *stylus*) or chemically (*etching;* for example, FIG. 20-16). In the etching process, an acid bath eats into the exposed parts of the plate where the artist has drawn through an acid-resistant coating. When the artist inks the surface of the intaglio plate and wipes it clean, the ink is forced into the incisions. Then the artist runs the plate and paper through a roller press, and the paper absorbs the remaining ink, creating the print. Because the artist "draws" the image onto the plate, intaglio prints differ in character from relief prints. Engravings, drypoints, and etchings generally present a wider variety of linear effects, as is immediately evident in a comparison of the roughly contemporaneous woodcut of *Madeburga* (FIG. 15-21) by Michael Wolgemut and Martin Schongauer's engraving of *Saint Anthony Tormented by Demons* (FIG. 15-22). Intaglio prints also often reveal to a greater extent evidence of the artist's touch, the result of the hand's changing pressure and shifting directions.

The paper and inks artists use also affect the finished look of the printed image. During the 15th and 16th centuries, European printmakers used papers produced from cotton and linen rags that papermakers mashed with water into a pulp. The papermakers then applied a thin layer of this pulp to a wire screen and allowed it to dry to create the paper. As contact with Asia increased, printmakers made greater use of what was called Japan paper (of mulberry fibers) and China paper. Artists, then as now, could select from a

1 in.

15-22 MARTIN SCHONGAUER, *Saint Anthony Tormented by Demons,* ca. 1480–1490. Engraving, 1' ¼″ × 9″. Fondazione Magnani Rocca, Corte di Mamiano.

Schongauer was the most skilled of the early masters of metal engraving. By using a burin to incise lines in a copper plate, he was able to create a marvelous variety of tonal values and textures.

wide variety of inks. The type and proportion of the ink ingredients affect the consistency, color, and oiliness of inks, which various papers absorb differently.

Paper is lightweight, and the portability of prints has appealed to artists over the years. The opportunity to produce numerous impressions from the same print surface also made printmaking attractive to 15th- and 16th-century artists. In addition, prints can be sold at lower prices than paintings or sculptures. Consequently, prints reached a much wider audience than did one-of-a-kind artworks. The number and quality of existing 15th- and 16th-century European prints attest to the importance of the new print medium.

by virtue of the dynastic marriage of Charles's daughter, Mary of Burgundy (FIG. 15-16A), to Maximilian of Habsburg, inaugurating a new political and artistic era in northern Europe (see Chapter 18). The next two chapters, however, explore Italian developments in painting, sculpture, and architecture during the 15th and 16th centuries.

LATE MEDIEVAL AND EARLY RENAISSANCE NORTHERN EUROPE

BURGUNDY AND FLANDERS

I The most powerful rulers north of the Alps during the first three-quarters of the 15th century were the dukes of Burgundy. They controlled Flanders, which derived its wealth from wool and banking, and were great art patrons.

I Duke Philip the Bold (r. 1363–1404) endowed the Carthusian monastery at Champmol, near Dijon, which became a ducal mausoleum. He employed Claus Sluter, whose *Well of Moses* features innovative statues of prophets with portraitlike features and realistic costumes.

I Flemish painters popularized the use of oil paints on wood panels. By superimposing translucent glazes, they created richer colors than possible using tempera or fresco. One of the earliest examples of oil painting is Melchior Broederlam's *Retable de Champmol* (1339).

I A major art form in churches and private homes alike was the altarpiece with folding wings. In Robert Campin's *Mérode Altarpiece,* the *Annunciation* takes place in a Flemish home. The work's donors, depicted on the left wing, are anachronistically present as witnesses to the sacred event. Typical of "Northern Renaissance" painting, the everyday objects depicted often have symbolic significance.

I Jan van Eyck, Rogier van der Weyden, and others established portraiture as an important art form in 15th-century Flanders. Their subjects were successful businessmen, both Flemish and foreign, for example, the Italian financier Giovanni Arnolfini. Rogier's *Saint Luke Drawing the Virgin,* a celebration of the painter's craft, is probably a self-portrait.

I Among the other major Flemish painters were Petrus Christus and Hans Memling of Bruges, Dirk Bouts of Louvain, and Hugo van der Goes of Ghent, all of whom produced both altarpieces for churches and portraits for the homes of wealthy merchants. Hugo achieved such renown that he won a commission to paint an altarpiece for a church in Florence. The Italians marveled at the Flemish painter's masterful technique and extraordinary realism.

FRANCE

I During the 15th century, the Hundred Years' War crippled the French economy, but dukes and members of the royal court still commissioned some notable artworks.

I The Limbourg brothers expanded the illusionistic capabilities of manuscript illumination in the Book of Hours they produced for Jean, duke of Berry (r. 1360–1416) and brother of King Charles V (r. 1364–1380). Their full-page calendar pictures alternately represent the nobility and the peasantry, always in seasonal, naturalistic settings with realistically painted figures.

I French court art—for example, Jean Fouquet's *Melun Diptych*—owes a large debt to Flemish painting in style and technique as well as in the integration of sacred and secular themes.

HOLY ROMAN EMPIRE

I The Late Gothic style remained popular in 15th-century Germany for large carved wooden retables featuring highly emotive figures amid Gothic tracery.

I The major German innovation of the 15th century was the development of the printing press, which publishers soon used to produce books with woodcut illustrations. Woodcuts are relief prints in which the artist carves out the areas around the lines to be printed.

I German artists were also the earliest masters of engraving. The intaglio technique allows for a wider variety of linear effects because the artist incises the image directly onto a metal plate.

Sluter, *Well of Moses,* 1395-1406

Campin, *Mérode Altarpiece,* ca. 1425–1428

Van Eyck, *Giovanni Arnolfini and His Wife,* 1434

Limbourg brothers, *Les Très Riches Heures du Duc de Berry,* 1413–1416

Wolgemut, *Nuremberg Chronicle,* 1493

Mercury is the most enigmatic figure in Botticelli's lyrical painting celebrating love in springtime, probably a commemoration of the May 1482 wedding of Lorenzo di Pierfrancesco de' Medici.

The dancing Three Graces closely resemble ancient prototypes Botticelli must have studied, but in 15th-century Florence, the Graces are clothed, albeit in thin, transparent garments.

Cupid hovers over Venus, the central figure in this mythological allegory. The sky seen through the opening in the landscape behind Venus forms a kind of halo around the goddess of love's head.

1 ft.

16-1 SANDRO BOTTICELLI, *Primavera*, ca. 1482. Tempera on wood, 6′ 8″ × 10′ 4″. Galleria degli Uffizi, Florence. ◼◀

The blue ice-cold Zephyrus, the west wind, carries off and marries the nymph Chloris, whom he transforms into Flora, goddess of spring, appropriately shown wearing a rich floral gown.

THE RENAISSANCE IN QUATTROCENTO ITALY

MEDICI PATRONAGE AND CLASSICAL LEARNING

The Medici family of Florence has become synonymous with the extraordinary cultural phenomenon called the Italian Renaissance. By early in the 15th century (the '400s, or *Quattrocento* in Italian), the banker Giovanni di Bicci de' Medici (ca. 1360–1429) had established the family fortune. His son Cosimo (1389–1464) became a great patron of art and of learning in the broadest sense. For example, Cosimo provided the equivalent of $20 million to establish the first public library since the ancient world. Cosimo's grandson Lorenzo (1449–1492), called "the Magnificent," was a member of the Platonic Academy of Philosophy and gathered about him a galaxy of artists and gifted men in all fields. He spent lavishly on buildings, paintings, and sculptures. Indeed, scarcely a single great Quattrocento architect, painter, sculptor, philosopher, or humanist scholar failed to enjoy Medici patronage.

Of all the Florentine masters the Medici employed, perhaps the most famous today is SANDRO BOTTICELLI (1444–1510). His work is a testament to the intense interest that the Medici and Quattrocento humanist scholars and artists had in the art, literature, and mythology of the Greco-Roman world—often interpreted by writers, painters, and sculptors alike in terms of Christianity according to the philosophical tenets of Neo-Platonism.

Botticelli painted *Primavera* (*Spring*; FIG. 16-1) for Lorenzo di Pierfrancesco de' Medici (1463–1503), one of Lorenzo the Magnificent's cousins. Venus stands just to the right of center with her son Cupid hovering above her head. Botticelli drew attention to Venus by opening the landscape behind her to reveal a portion of sky that forms a kind of halo around the goddess of love's head. To her right, seemingly the target of Cupid's arrow, are the dancing Three Graces, based closely on ancient prototypes but clothed, albeit in thin, transparent garments. At the right, the blue ice-cold Zephyrus, the west wind, is about to carry off and marry the nymph Chloris, whom he transforms into Flora, goddess of spring, appropriately shown wearing a rich floral gown. At the far left, the enigmatic figure of Mercury turns away from all the others and reaches up with his distinctive staff, the *caduceus,* perhaps to dispel storm clouds. The sensuality of the representation, the appearance of Venus in springtime, and the abduction and marriage of Chloris all suggest the occasion for the painting was young Lorenzo's wedding in May 1482. But the painting also sums up the Neo-Platonists' view that earthly love is compatible with Christian theology. In their reinterpretation of classical mythology, Venus as the source of love provokes desire through Cupid. Desire can lead either to lust and violence (Zephyr) or, through reason and faith (Mercury), to the love of God. *Primavera,* read from right to left, served to urge the newlyweds to seek God through love.

RENAISSANCE HUMANISM

The humanism Petrarch and Boccaccio promoted during the 14th century (see Chapter 14) fully blossomed in the 15th century. Increasingly, Italians in elite circles embraced the tenets underlying humanism—an emphasis on education and on expanding knowledge (especially of classical antiquity), the exploration of individual potential and a desire to excel, and a commitment to civic responsibility and moral duty. Quattrocento Italy also enjoyed an abundance of artistic talent. The fortunate congruence of artistic genius, the spread of humanism, and economic prosperity nourished the Renaissance, forever changing the direction and perception of art in the Western world.

For the Italian humanists, the quest for knowledge began with the legacy of the Greeks and Romans—the writings of Socrates, Plato, Aristotle, Ovid, and others. The development of a literature based on the commonly spoken Tuscan dialect expanded the audience for humanist writings. Further, the invention of moveable metal type in Germany around 1445 (see Chapter 15) facilitated the printing and wide distribution of books. Italians enthusiastically embraced this new printing process. By 1464, Subiaco (near Rome) boasted a press, and by 1469, Venice had established one as well. Among the first books printed in Italy using these new presses was Dante's *Divine Comedy,* his vernacular epic about Heaven, Purgatory, and Hell. The production of editions in Foligno (1472), Mantua (1472), Venice (1472), Naples (1477 and 1478–1479), and Milan (1478) testifies to the widespread popularity of Dante's work.

The humanists also avidly acquired information in a wide range of fields, including botany, geology, geography, optics, medicine, and engineering. Leonardo da Vinci's phenomenal expertise in many fields—from art and architecture to geology, aerodynamics, hydraulics, botany, and military science, among many others—still defines the modern notion of the "Renaissance man." Humanism also fostered a belief in individual potential and encouraged individual achievement, as well as civic responsibility. Whereas people in medieval society accorded great power to divine will in determining the events that affected lives, those in Renaissance Italy adopted a more secular stance. Humanists not only encouraged individual improvement but also rewarded excellence with fame and honor. Achieving and excelling through hard work became moral imperatives.

Quattrocento Italy witnessed constant fluctuations in its political and economic spheres, including shifting power relations among the numerous city-states and the rise of princely courts (see "Italian Princely Courts," page 479). *Condottieri* (military leaders) with large numbers of mercenary troops at their disposal played a major role in the ongoing struggle for power. Princely courts, such as those in Urbino and Mantua, emerged as cultural and artistic centers alongside the great art centers of the 14th century, especially the Republic of Florence. The association of humanism with education and culture appealed to accomplished individuals of high status, and humanism had its greatest impact among the elite and powerful, whether in the republics or the princely courts. These individuals were in the best position to commission art. As a result, humanist ideas came to permeate Italian Renaissance art. The intersection of art with humanist doctrines during the Renaissance is evident in the popularity of subjects selected from classical history or mythology (for example, FIG. 16-1); in the increased concern with developing perspective systems and depicting anatomy accurately; in the revival of portraiture and other self-aggrandizing forms of patronage; and in citizens' extensive participation in civic and religious art commissions.

FLORENCE

Because high-level patronage required significant accumulated wealth, those individuals, whether princes or merchants, who had managed to prosper came to the fore in artistic circles. The best-known Italian Renaissance art patrons were the Medici of the Republic of Florence (see "Medici Patronage and Classical Learning," page 447), yet the earliest important artistic commission in 15th-century Florence (MAP **16-1**) was not a Medici project but rather a competition held by the Cathedral of Santa Maria del Fiore and sponsored by the city's guild of wool merchants.

Sculpture

In 1401, the cathedral's art directors held a competition to make bronze doors for the east portal of the Baptistery of San Giovanni (FIG. 12-27). Artists and public alike considered this commission particularly prestigious because the east entrance to the baptistery faced the cathedral (FIG. 14-18). The competition is historically

THE RENAISSANCE IN QUATTROCENTO ITALY

1400	1425	1450	1475	1500
▌Ghiberti wins the competition to design new doors for Florence's baptistery ▌Nanni di Banco, Donatello, and others create statues for Or San Michele ▌Masaccio carries Giotto's naturalism further in the Brancacci chapel ▌Brunelleschi develops linear perspective and designs the Ospedale degli Innocenti, the first Renaissance building	▌Ghiberti installs the *Gates of Paradise* facing Florence Cathedral ▌Donatello revives freestanding nude male statuary ▌Michelozzo builds the new Medici palace in Florence ▌Alberti publishes his treatise on painting	▌Federico da Montefeltro brings Piero della Francesca to the Urbino court ▌Alberti designs palaces and churches in Florence and Mantua ▌Mantegna creates illusionistic paintings for the Camera Picta in Mantua	▌Botticelli paints Neo-Platonic mythological allegories for the Medici ▌Alberti publishes his treatise on architecture ▌Pope Sixtus IV employs leading painters to decorate the Sistine Chapel ▌Savonarola condemns humanism and the Medici flee Florence	

MAP 16-1 Renaissance Florence.

important not only for the quality of the work submitted by those seeking the commission but also because it already showcased several key elements associated with mature Renaissance art: personal or, in this case, guild patronage as both a civic imperative and a form of self-promotion; the esteem accorded to individual artists; and the development of a new pictorial illusionism.

SACRIFICE OF ISAAC Between 1330 and 1335, Andrea Pisano had designed the south doors (FIG. 14-19) of the baptistery. The jurors of the 1401 competition for the second set of doors required each entrant to submit a relief panel depicting the sacrifice of Isaac in a similar French Gothic quatrefoil frame. This episode from the book of Genesis centers on God's order to Abraham to sacrifice his son Isaac as a demonstration of Abraham's devotion (see "Jewish Subjects in Christian Art," Chapter 8, page 238). As Abraham was about to comply, an angel intervened and stopped him from plunging the knife into his son's throat. Because of the parallel between Abraham's willingness to sacrifice Isaac and God's sacrifice of his son Jesus to redeem humankind, Christians viewed the sacrifice of Isaac as a *prefiguration* (prophetic forerunner) of Jesus' crucifixion. Both refer to *covenants* (binding agreements between God and humans), and given that the sacrament of baptism initiates the newborn or the convert into these covenants, Isaac's sacrifice was an appropriate choice for baptistery doors.

Contemporary developments, however, may also have been an important factor in the selection of this theme. In the late 1390s, Giangaleazzo Visconti, the first duke of Milan (r. 1378–1395), began a military campaign to take over the Italian peninsula. By 1401, when the cathedral's art directors initiated the baptistery doors competition, Visconti's troops had surrounded Florence, and its in-

dependence was in serious jeopardy. Despite dwindling water and food supplies, Florentine officials exhorted the public to defend the city's freedom. For example, the humanist chancellor Coluccio Salutati (1331–1406) urged his fellow citizens to adopt the republican ideal of civil and political liberty associated with ancient Rome and to identify themselves with its spirit. To be a citizen of the Florentine Republic was to be Roman. Freedom was the distinguishing virtue of both societies. The story of Abraham and Isaac, with its theme of sacrifice, paralleled the message Florentine officials had conveyed to rally the public's support. The wool merchants, asserting both their preeminence among Florentine guilds and their civic duty, may have selected the biblical subject with this in mind. The Florentines' reward for their faith and sacrifice came in 1402, when Visconti died suddenly, ending the invasion threat.

BRUNELLESCHI AND GHIBERTI The jury selected seven semifinalists from among the many artists who entered the widely advertised competition. Only the panels of the two finalists, FILIPPO BRUNELLESCHI (1377–1446) and LORENZO GHIBERTI (1378–1455), have survived. As instructed, both artists used the same French-style frames Andrea Pisano had used for the south doors (FIG. 14-19) and depicted the same moment of the narrative—the angel's interruption of the action. Brunelleschi's entry (FIG. **16-2**) is a vigorous interpretation of the theme and recalls the emotional agitation of Giovanni Pisano's relief sculptures (FIG. 14-4). Abraham seems suddenly to have summoned the dreadful courage needed to murder his son at God's command. He lunges forward, robes flying, and exposes Isaac's throat to the knife. Matching Abraham's energy, the saving angel flies in from the left, grabbing Abraham's arm to stop the killing. Brunelleschi's figures demonstrate his

1 in.

1 in.

16-2 Filippo Brunelleschi, *Sacrifice of Isaac*, competition panel for east doors of the Baptistery of San Giovanni, Florence, Italy, 1401–1402. Gilded bronze, 1′ 9″ × 1′ 5½″. Museo Nazionale del Bargello, Florence.

Brunelleschi's entry in the competition to create new bronze doors for the Florentine baptistery shows a frantic angel about to halt an emotional, lunging Abraham clothed in swirling Gothic robes.

16-3 Lorenzo Ghiberti, *Sacrifice of Isaac*, competition panel for east doors of the Baptistery of San Giovanni, Florence, Italy, 1401–1402. Gilded bronze, 1′ 9″ × 1′ 5½″. Museo Nazionale del Bargello, Florence.

In contrast to Brunelleschi's panel (FIG. 16-2), Ghiberti's entry in the baptistery competition features gracefully posed figures that recall classical statuary. Isaac's altar has a Roman acanthus frieze.

ability to represent faithfully and dramatically all the elements in the biblical narrative.

Whereas Brunelleschi imbued his image with violent movement and high emotion, Ghiberti, the youngest artist in the competition, emphasized grace and smoothness. In Ghiberti's panel (FIG. **16-3**), Abraham appears in a typically Gothic pose with outthrust hip (compare FIG. 13-26) and seems to contemplate the act he is about to perform, even as he draws back his arm to strike. The figure of Isaac, beautifully posed and rendered, recalls Greco-Roman statuary and could be regarded as the first classical nude since antiquity. (Compare, for example, the torsion of Isaac's body and the dramatic turn of his head with the posture of the Hellenistic statue of a Gaul plunging a sword into his own chest, FIG. 5-80.) Unlike his medieval predecessors, Ghiberti revealed a genuine appreciation of the nude male form and a deep interest in how the muscular system and skeletal structure move the human body. Even the altar on which Isaac kneels displays Ghiberti's emulation of antique models. Decorating it are acanthus scrolls of a type that commonly adorned Roman temple friezes in Italy and throughout the former Roman Empire (for example, FIG. 7-32). These classical references reflect the influence of humanism in Quattrocento Italy. Ghiberti's entry in the baptistery competition is also noteworthy for the artist's interest in spatial illusion. The rocky landscape seems to emerge from the blank panel toward the viewer, as does the strongly foreshortened angel. Brunelleschi's image, in contrast, emphasizes the planar orientation of the surface.

Ghiberti's training included both painting and metalwork. His careful treatment of the gilded bronze surfaces, with their sharply and accurately incised detail, proves his skill as a goldsmith. That Ghiberti cast his panel in only two pieces (thereby reducing the amount of bronze needed) no doubt also impressed the selection committee. Brunelleschi's panel consists of several cast pieces. Thus, not only would Ghiberti's doors, as proposed, be lighter and more impervious to the elements, but they also represented a significant cost savings. The younger artist's submission clearly had much to recommend it, both stylistically and technically, and the judges awarded the commission to him. Ghiberti's pride in winning the competition is evident in his description of the award, which also reveals the fame and glory increasingly accorded to individual achievement in 15th-century Italy:

> To me was conceded the palm of the victory by all the experts and by all who had competed with me. To me the honor was conceded universally and with no exception. To all it seemed that I had at that time surpassed the others without exception, as was recognized by a great council and an investigation of learned men.... There were thirty-four judges from the city and the other surrounding countries. The testimonial of the victory was given in my favor by all.[1]

OR SAN MICHELE A second major Florentine sculptural project of the early 1400s was the sculptural decoration of the exterior of Or San Michele, an early-14th-century building prominently located on the main street connecting the Palazzo della Signoria

(FIG. 14-18B; seat of the *Signoria,* Florence's governing body) and the cathedral (MAP 16-1). At various times, Or San Michele housed a church, a granary, and the headquarters of Florence's guilds. City officials had assigned niches on the building's four sides to specific guilds, instructing each guild to place a statue of its patron saint in its niche. Nearly a century after completion of Or San Michele, however, the guilds had filled only 5 of the 14 niches. In 1406, the Signoria issued a dictum requiring the guilds to comply with the original plan to embellish their assigned niches. A few years later, Florence was once again under siege, this time by King Ladislaus (r. 1399–1414) of Naples. Ladislaus had marched north, occupied Rome and the Papal States (MAP 14-1) by 1409, and threatened to overrun Florence. As they had done when Visconti was at the republic's doorstep, Florentine officials urged citizens to stand firm and defend their city-state from tyranny. Once again, Florence escaped unscathed. Ladislaus, on the verge of military success in 1414, fortuitously died. The guilds may well have viewed this new threat as an opportunity to perform their civic duty by rallying their fellow Florentines while also promoting their own importance and position in Florentine society. By 1423, statues by Ghiberti and other leading Florentine artists were on display in the nine remaining niches of Or San Michele.

NANNI DI BANCO Among the niches filled during the Neapolitan king's siege was the one assigned to the Florentine guild of stone- and woodworkers. They chose a guild member, the sculptor NANNI DI BANCO (ca. 1380–1421), to create four life-size marble statues of the guild's martyred patron saints. These four Christian sculptors had defied an order from Emperor Diocletian (r. 284–305) to carve a statue of a Roman deity. In response, the emperor ordered them put to death. Because they placed their faith above all else, these saints were perfect role models for the 15th-century Florentines whom city leaders exhorted to stand fast in the face of Ladislaus's armies.

Nanni's sculptural group, *Four Crowned Saints* (FIG. **16-4**), is an early Renaissance attempt to solve the problem of integrating figures and space on a monumental scale. The artist's positioning of the figures, which stand in a niche that is *in* but confers some separation *from* the architecture, furthered the gradual emergence of sculpture from its architectural setting. This process began with works such as the 13th-century statues (FIG. 13-24) on the jambs of the west facade portals of Reims Cathedral. At Or San Michele, the niche's spatial recess presented Nanni di Banco with a dramatic new possibility for the interrelationship of the figures. By placing them in a semicircle within their deep niche and relating them to one another by their postures and gestures, as well as by the arrangement of robes, the Quattrocento sculptor arrived at a unified spatial composition. A remarkable psychological unity also connects these unyielding figures, whose bearing expresses the discipline and integrity necessary to face adversity. As the figure on the right speaks, pointing to his right, the two men opposite listen and the one next to him looks out into space, pondering the meaning of the words and reinforcing the formal cohesion of the figural group with psychological cross-references.

In *Four Crowned Saints,* Nanni also displayed a deep respect for and close study of Roman portrait statues. The emotional intensity of the faces of the two inner saints owes much to the extraordinarily moving portrayals in stone of third-century Roman emperors (FIGS. 7-68 and 7-68A), and the bearded heads of the outer saints reveal a familiarity with second-century imperial portraiture (FIGS. 7-59 and 7-59A). Often, when Renaissance artists sought to

16-4 NANNI DI BANCO, *Four Crowned Saints,* Or San Michele, Florence, Italy, ca. 1410–1416. Marble, figures 6′ high. Modern copy in exterior niche. Original sculpture in museum on second floor of Or San Michele, Florence. ◼◀

Nanni's group representing the four martyred patron saints of Florence's sculptors guild is an early example of Renaissance artists' attempt to liberate statuary from its architectural setting.

portray individual personalities, they turned to ancient Roman models for inspiration, but they did not simply copy them. Rather, they strove to interpret or offer commentary on their classical models in the manner of humanist scholars dealing with classical texts.

DONATELLO Another sculptor who carved statues for Or San Michele's niches was Donato di Niccolo Bardi, called DONATELLO (ca. 1386–1466), who incorporated Greco-Roman sculptural principles in his *Saint Mark* (FIG. **16-5**), executed for the guild of

16-5 Donatello, *Saint Mark,* Or San Michele, Florence, Italy, ca. 1411–1413. Marble, figure 7′ 9″ high. Modern copy in exterior niche. Original sculpture in museum on second floor of Or San Michele, Florence. ■◀

In this statue carved for the guild of linen makers and tailors, Donatello introduced classical contrapposto into Quattrocento sculpture. The drapery falls naturally and moves with the body.

16-6 Donatello, *Saint George,* Or San Michele, Florence, Italy, ca. 1410–1415. Marble, figure 6′ 10″ high. Modern copy in exterior niche. Original statue in Museo Nazionale del Bargello, Florence. ■◀

Donatello's statue for the armorers guild once had a bronze sword and helmet. The warrior saint stands defiantly, ready to spring from his niche to defend Florence, his sword pointed at the spectator.

linen makers and tailors. In this sculpture, Donatello took a fundamental step toward depicting motion in the human figure by recognizing the principle of weight shift, or *contrapposto*. Greek sculptors of the fifth century BCE were the first to grasp that the act of standing requires balancing the position and weight of the different parts of the human body, as they demonstrated in works such as *Kritios Boy* (FIG. 5-34) and *Doryphoros* (FIG. 5-40). In contrast to earlier sculptors, Greek artists recognized the human body is not a rigid mass but a flexible structure that moves by continuously shifting its weight from one supporting leg to the other, its constituent parts moving in consonance. Donatello reintroduced this concept into Renaissance statuary. As the saint's body "moves," his garment "moves" with it, hanging and folding naturally from and around different body parts so that the viewer senses the figure as a nude human wearing clothing, not as a stone statue with arbitrarily incised drapery. Donatello's *Saint Mark* is the first Renaissance statue whose voluminous robe (the pride of the Florentine guild that paid for the statue) does not conceal but

accentuates the movement of the arms, legs, shoulders, and hips. This development further contributed to the sculpted figure's independence from its architectural setting. Saint Mark's stirring limbs, shifting weight, and mobile drapery suggest impending movement out of the niche.

SAINT GEORGE For the Or San Michele niche of the guild of armorers and swordmakers, Donatello made a statue of *Saint George* (FIG. 16-6). The saintly knight stands proudly with his shield in front of him. He once held a bronze sword in his right hand and wore a bronze helmet on his head, both fashioned by the sponsoring guild. The statue continues the Gothic tradition of depicting warrior saints on church facades, as seen in the statue of Saint Theodore (FIG. 13-18) on the westernmost jamb of the south *transept* portal of Chartres Cathedral, but here it has a civic role to play. Saint George stands in a defiant manner—ready to spring from his niche to defend Florence against attack from another Visconti or Ladislaus, his sword jutting out threateningly at all

⌶ 1 in.

passersby. The saint's body is taut, and Donatello gave him a face filled with nervous energy.

Directly below the statue's base is Donatello's marble relief representing *Saint George and the Dragon* (FIG. **16-7**). Commissioned about two years after the sculptor installed his statue in the niche, the relief marks a turning point in Renaissance sculpture. Even the landscapes in the baptistery competition reliefs (FIGS. 16-2 and 16-3) are modeled forms seen against a blank background. In *Saint George and the Dragon,* Donatello created an atmospheric effect by using incised lines. It is impossible to talk about a background plane in this work. The landscape recedes into distant space, and the depth of that space cannot be measured. The sculptor conceived the relief as a window onto an infinite vista.

FEAST OF HEROD Donatello's mastery of relief sculpture is also evident in *Feast of Herod* (FIG. **16-8**), a bronze relief on the baptismal font in Siena Cathedral. Some of the figures, especially the dancing Salome (to the right), derive from classical reliefs, but nothing in Greco-Roman art can match the illusionism of Donatello's rendition of this biblical scene. In Donatello's relief, Salome has already delivered the severed head of John the Baptist, which the kneeling executioner offers to King Herod. The other figures recoil in horror in two groups. At the right, one man covers his face with his hand. At the left, Herod and two terrified children shrink back in dismay. The psychic explosion drives the human elements apart, leaving a gap across which the emotional electricity crackles. This masterful stagecraft obscures another drama Donatello was playing out on the stage itself. His *Feast of Herod* marks the introduction of rationalized perspective in Renaissance art. As in *Saint George and the Dragon* (FIG. 16-7), Donatello opened the space of the action well into the distance. But here he employed the new mathematically based science of linear perspective to depict two arched courtyards and the groups of attendants in the background.

RENAISSANCE PERSPECTIVE In the 14th century, Italian artists, such as Giotto, Duccio, and the Lorenzetti brothers, had used several devices to indicate distance, but with the development of *linear perspective,* Quattrocento artists acquired a way to make the illusion of distance certain and consistent (see "Linear and Atmospheric Perspective," page 455). In effect, they conceived the picture plane as a transparent window through which the observer looks to see the constructed pictorial world. This discovery was enormously important, for it made possible what has

been called the "rationalization of sight." It brought all random and infinitely various visual sensations under a simple rule that could be expressed mathematically. Indeed, Renaissance artists' interest in linear perspective reflects the emergence at this time of modern science itself. Of course, 15th-century artists were not primarily scientists. They simply found perspective an effective way to order and clarify their compositions. Nonetheless, there can be little doubt that linear perspective, with its new mathematical certitude, conferred a kind of aesthetic legitimacy on painting by making the picture measurable and exact. The projection of measurable objects on flat surfaces not only influenced the character of Renaissance paintings but also made possible scale drawings, maps, charts, graphs, and diagrams—means of exact representation that laid the foundation for modern science and technology.

⌶ 1 in.

16-8 DONATELLO, *Feast of Herod,* panel on the baptismal font of Siena Cathedral, Siena, Italy, 1423–1427. Gilded bronze, 1′ 11½″ × 1′ 11½″. ◼◀

Donatello's *Feast of Herod* marked the introduction of rationalized perspective space in Renaissance relief sculpture. Two arched courtyards of diminishing size open the space of the action into the distance.

16-9 LORENZO GHIBERTI, east doors (*Gates of Paradise*), Baptistery of San Giovanni, Florence, Italy, 1425–1452. Gilded bronze, 17′ high. Modern replica, 1990. Original panels in Museo dell'Opera del Duomo, Florence. ◼️◄

In Ghiberti's later doors for the Florentine baptistery, the sculptor abandoned the Gothic quatrefoil frames for the biblical scenes (compare FIG. 16-3) and employed painterly illusionistic devices.

1 ft.

The inventor (or rediscoverer) of linear perspective was Filippo Brunelleschi. In his biography of the Florentine artist, written around 1480, Antonio Manetti (1423–1497) emphasized the importance of the scientific basis of Brunelleschi's system:

> [Filippo Brunelleschi] propounded and re-alized what painters today call perspective, since it forms part of that science which, in effect, consists of setting down properly and rationally the reductions and enlargements of near and distant objects as perceived by the eye of man: buildings, plains, moun-tains, places of every sort and location, with figures and objects in correct proportion to the distance in which they are shown. He originated the rule that is essential to whatever has been accomplished since his time in that area. We do not know whether centuries ago the ancient painters . . . knew about perspective or employed it rationally. If indeed they employed it by rule (I did not previously call it a science without reason) as he did later, . . . [no] records about it have been discovered. . . . Through industry and intelligence [Brunelleschi] either rediscov-ered or invented it.[2]

GATES OF PARADISE Lorenzo Ghib-erti, Brunelleschi's chief rival in the baptis-tery competition, was, with Donatello, among the first artists to embrace Brunelleschi's unified system for representing space. Ghi-berti's enthusiasm for perspective illusion is on display in the new east doors (FIG. **16-9**) for Florence's baptistery (FIG. 12-27), which the cathedral officials commissioned him to make in 1425. Ghiberti's patrons moved his first pair of doors to the north entrance to make room for the new ones they commis-sioned him to make for the prestigious east side. Michelangelo later declared Ghiberti's second doors as "so beautiful that they would do well for the gates of Paradise."[3] In the *Gates of Paradise,* as the doors have been called since then, Ghiberti abandoned the quatre-foil frames of Andrea Pisano's south doors (FIG. 14-19) and his own earlier doors and reduced the number of panels from 28 to 10. Each panel contains a relief set in plain molding and depicts an episode from the Old Testament. The complete gilding of the reliefs creates an effect of great splendor and elegance.

The individual panels, such as *Isaac and His Sons* (FIG. **16-10**), clearly recall painting techniques in their depiction of space as well as in their treatment of the narrative. Some exemplify more fully than painting many of the principles the architect and theorist Leon Battista Alberti formulated in his 1435 treatise, *On Painting.* In his relief, Ghiberti created the illusion of space partly through the use of linear perspective and partly by sculptural means. He

Linear and Atmospheric Perspective

Scholars long have noted the Renaissance fascination with perspective. In essence, portraying perspective involves constructing a convincing illusion of space in two-dimensional imagery while unifying all objects within a single spatial system. Renaissance artists were not the first to focus on depicting illusionistic space. Both the Greeks and the Romans were well versed in perspective rendering. Many frescoes of buildings and colonnades (for example, FIG. 7-19, *right*) using a Renaissance-like system of converging lines adorn the walls of Roman houses. However, the Renaissance rediscovery of and interest in perspective contrasted sharply with the portrayal of space during the Middle Ages, when spiritual concerns superseded the desire to depict objects illusionistically.

Renaissance knowledge of perspective included both *linear perspective* and *atmospheric perspective*.

▍**Linear perspective.** Developed by Filippo Brunelleschi, linear perspective enables artists to determine mathematically the relative size of rendered objects to correlate them with the visual recession into space. The artist first must identify a horizontal line that marks, in the image, the horizon in the distance (hence the

term *horizon line*). The artist then selects a *vanishing point* on that horizon line (often located at the exact center of the line). By drawing *orthogonals* (diagonal lines) from the edges of the picture to the vanishing point, the artist creates a structural grid that organizes the image and determines the size of objects within the image's illusionistic space. Among the works that provide clear examples of linear perspective are Ghiberti's *Isaac and His Sons* (FIGS. 16-10 and 16-11), Masaccio's *Holy Trinity* (FIG. 16-21), and Perugino's *Christ Delivering the Keys of the Kingdom to Saint Peter* (FIG. 16-41).

▍**Atmospheric perspective.** Unlike linear perspective, which relies on a structured mathematical system, atmospheric perspective involves optical phenomena. Artists using atmospheric perspective (sometimes called *aerial perspective*) exploit the principle that the farther back the object is in space, the blurrier, less detailed, and bluer it appears. Further, color saturation and value contrast diminish as the image recedes into the distance. Leonardo da Vinci used atmospheric perspective to great effect in works such as *Madonna of the Rocks* (FIG. 17-2) and *Mona Lisa* (FIG. 17-5).

1 ft.

16-10 LORENZO GHIBERTI, *Isaac and His Sons* (detail of FIG. 16-9), east doors (*Gates of Paradise*), Baptistery of San Giovanni, Florence, Italy, 1425–1452. Gilded bronze, 2′ 7½″ × 2′ 7½″. Museo dell'Opera del Duomo, Florence. ◼◀

In this relief, Ghiberti employed linear perspective to create the illusion of distance, but he also used sculptural aerial perspective, with forms appearing less distinct the deeper they are in space.

1 ft.

16-11 Perspective diagram of FIG. 16-10. ◼◀

All of the orthogonals of the floor tiles in this early example of linear perspective converge on a vanishing point on the central axis of the composition, but the orthogonals of the architecture do not.

represented the pavement on which the figures stand according to a painter's vanishing-point perspective construction (see "Linear and Atmospheric Perspective," above, and FIG. **16-11**), but the figures themselves appear almost fully in the round. In fact, some of their heads stand completely free. As the eye progresses upward,

the relief increasingly flattens, concluding with the architecture in the background, which Ghiberti depicted using barely raised lines. In this manner, the artist created a sort of sculptor's atmospheric perspective, with forms appearing less distinct the deeper they are in space. Regardless of the height of the reliefs, however, the size of each figure decreases in exact correspondence to its distance from the foreground, just as do the dimensions of the floor tiles, as specified in Alberti's treatise.

Ghiberti described the baptistery's east doors as follows:

> I strove to imitate nature as closely as I could, and with all the perspective I could produce [to have] excellent compositions rich with many figures. In some scenes I placed about a hundred figures, in some less, and in some more.... There were ten stories, all [sunk] in frames because the eye from a distance measures and interprets the scenes in such a way that they appear round. The scenes are in the lowest relief and the figures are seen in the planes; those that are near appear large, those in the distance small, as they do in reality. I executed this entire work with these principles.[4]

In the reliefs of the *Gates of Paradise*, Ghiberti achieved a greater sense of depth than had previously seemed possible in sculpture. His principal figures do not occupy the architectural space he created for them. Rather, the artist arranged them along a parallel plane in front of the grandiose architecture. (According to Leon Battista Alberti, in his *On the Art of Building*, the grandeur of the architecture reflects the dignity of the events shown in the foreground.) Ghiberti's figure style mixes a Gothic patterning of rhythmic line, classical poses and motifs, and a new realism in characterization, movement, and surface detail. Ghiberti retained the medieval narrative method of presenting several episodes within a single frame. In *Isaac and His Sons*, the women in the left foreground attend the birth of Esau and Jacob in the left background. In the central foreground, Isaac sends Esau and his dogs to hunt game. In the right foreground, Isaac blesses the kneeling Jacob as Rebecca looks on. Yet viewers experience little confusion because of Ghiberti's careful and subtle placement of each scene. The figures, in varying degrees of projection, gracefully twist and turn, appearing to occupy and move through a convincing stage space, which Ghiberti deepened by showing some figures from behind. The classicism derives from the artist's close study of ancient art. Ghiberti admired and collected classical sculpture, bronzes, and coins. Their influence appears throughout the panel, particularly in the figure of Rebecca, which Ghiberti based on a popular Greco-Roman statuary type. The emerging practice of collecting classical art in the 15th century had much to do with the incorporation of classical motifs and the emulation of classical style in Renaissance art.

DONATELLO, *DAVID* The use of perspective systems in relief sculpture and painting represents only one aspect of the Renaissance revival of classical principles and values in the arts. Another was the revival of the freestanding nude statue. The first Renaissance sculptor to portray the nude male figure in statuary was Donatello. He probably cast his bronze *David* (FIG. **16-12**) sometime between 1440 and 1460 for display in the courtyard (FIG. 16-38) of the Medici palace in Florence. In the Middle Ages, the clergy regarded nude statues as both indecent and idolatrous, and nudity in general appeared only rarely in art—and then only in biblical or moralizing contexts, such as the story of Adam and Eve or depictions of sinners in Hell. With *David*, Donatello reinvented the classical nude. His subject, however, was not a Greco-Roman god, hero, or athlete but the youthful biblical slayer of Goliath who had become the symbol of the Florentine Republic—and therefore an ideal choice of subject for the residence of the most powerful family in Florence. The Medici were aware of Donatello's earlier *David* in Florence's town hall (FIG. 14-18B), which the artist had produced during the threat of invasion by King Ladislaus. Their selection

16-12 DONATELLO, *David*, ca. 1440–1460. Bronze, 5′ 2¼″ high. Museo Nazionale del Bargello, Florence. ◼◄

Donatello's *David* possesses both the relaxed contrapposto and the sensuous beauty of nude Greek gods (FIG. 5-63). The revival of classical statuary style appealed to the sculptor's patrons, the Medici.

of the same subject suggests the Medici identified themselves with Florence or, at the very least, saw themselves as responsible for Florence's prosperity and freedom. The invoking of classical poses and formats also appealed to the Medici as humanists. Donatello's *David* possesses both the relaxed classical contrapposto stance and the proportions and sensuous beauty of the gods (FIG. 5-63) of Praxiteles, a famous Greek sculptor. These qualities were, not surprisingly, absent from medieval figures—and they are also lacking, for different reasons, in Donatello's depiction of the aged Mary Magdalene. The contrast between the sculptor's *David* and his *Penitent Mary Magdalene* (FIG. **16-12A**) demonstrates the extraordinary versatility of this Florentine master.

16-12A DONATELLO, *Penitent Mary Magdalene*, ca. 1455.

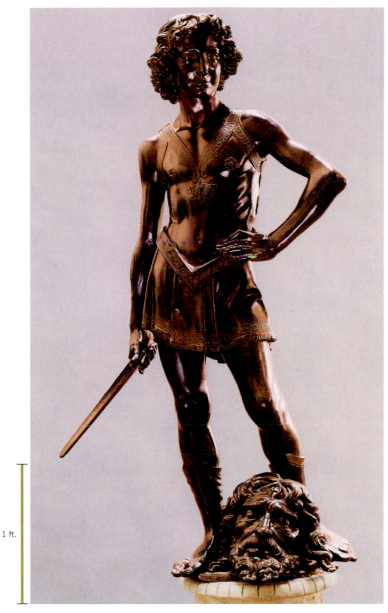

1 ft.

16-13 Andrea del Verrocchio, *David,* ca. 1465–1470. Bronze, 4′ 1½″ high. Museo Nazionale del Bargello, Florence.

Verrocchio's *David,* also made for the Medici, displays a brash confidence. The statue's narrative realism contrasts strongly with the quiet classicism of Donatello's *David* (FIG. 16-12).

1 in.

16-14 Antonio del Pollaiuolo, *Hercules and Antaeus,* ca. 1470–1475. Bronze, 1′ 6″ high with base. Museo Nazionale del Bargello, Florence.

The Renaissance interest in classical culture led to the revival of Greco-Roman mythological themes in art. *Hercules and Antaeus* exhibits the stress and strain of the human figure in violent action.

VERROCCHIO Another *David* (FIG. 16-13), by ANDREA DEL VERROCCHIO (1435–1488), one of the most important sculptors during the second half of the 15th century, reaffirms the Medici family's identification with the heroic biblical king and with Florence. A painter as well as a sculptor, Verrocchio directed a flourishing *bottega* (studio-shop) in Florence that attracted many students, among them Leonardo da Vinci. Verrocchio's *David* contrasts strongly in its narrative realism with the quiet classicism of Donatello's *David.* Verrocchio's hero is a sturdy, wiry young apprentice clad in a leather doublet who stands with a jaunty pride. As in Donatello's version, Goliath's head lies at David's feet. He poses like a hunter with his kill. The easy balance of the weight and the lithe, still thinly adolescent musculature, with prominent veins, show how closely Verrocchio read the biblical text and how clearly he knew the psychology of brash young men. The Medici eventually sold Verrocchio's bronze *David* to the Florentine government

for placement in the Palazzo della Signoria. After the expulsion of the Medici from Florence, civic officials appropriated Donatello's *David* for civic use and moved it to the city hall as well.

POLLAIUOLO As noted in the discussion of Botticelli's *Primavera* (FIG. 16-1), the Renaissance interest in classical culture naturally also led to the revival of Greco-Roman mythological themes in art. The Medici were Florence's leading patrons in this sphere as well. Around 1470, ANTONIO DEL POLLAIUOLO (ca. 1431–1498), who was also an important painter and engraver (FIG. 16-30), received a Medici commission to produce a small-scale sculpture, *Hercules and Antaeus* (FIG. 16-14). The subject matter, derived from Greek mythology, and the emphasis on human anatomy reflect the Medici preference for humanist imagery. Even more specifically, the Florentine seal had featured Hercules since the end of the 13th century. As commissions such as the two *David* sculptures demonstrate, the Medici clearly embraced every opportunity to associate themselves with the glory of the Florentine Republic and claimed much of the credit for its preeminence.

In contrast to the placid presentation of Donatello's *David* (FIG. 16-12), Pollaiuolo's *Hercules and Antaeus* exhibits the stress and strain of the human figure in violent action. This sculpture departs dramatically from the convention of frontality that had dominated statuary during the Middle Ages and the Early Renaissance. Not quite 18 inches high, *Hercules and Antaeus* embodies the ferocity and vitality of elemental physical conflict. The group illustrates the wrestling match between Antaeus (Antaios), a giant and son of the goddess Earth, and Hercules (Herakles), a theme the Greek painter Euphronios had represented on an ancient Greek vase (FIG. 5-23) 2,000 years before. According to the Greek myth, each time Hercules threw him down, Antaeus sprang up again, his strength renewed by contact with the earth. Finally, Hercules held him aloft—so Antaeus could not touch the ground—and strangled him around the waist. Pollaiuolo strove to convey the final excruciating moments of the struggle—the strained sinews of the combatants, the clenched teeth of Hercules, and the kicking and screaming of Antaeus. The figures intertwine and interlock as they fight, and the flickering reflections of light on the dark gouged bronze surface contribute to a fluid play of planes and the effect of agitated movement.

TOMB OF LEONARDO BRUNI Given the increased emphasis on individual achievement and recognition that humanism fostered, it is not surprising portraiture enjoyed a revival in the 15th century. In addition to likenesses of elite individuals made during their lifetime, commemorative portraits of the deceased were common in Quattrocento Italy, as in ancient Rome. Leonardo Bruni (1369–1444) of Arezzo was one of the leading Early Renaissance humanist scholars. Around 1403 he wrote a *laudatio* (essay of praise) in honor of Florence, celebrating the city as the heir of the ancient Roman Republic. His most ambitious work, published in 1429 when he served as Florence's chancellor (1427–1444), was a history of the Florentine Republic. When Bruni died on March 9, 1444, the Signoria ordered a state funeral "according to ancient custom," during which the eminent humanist Giannozzo Manetti (1396–1459) delivered the eulogy and placed a laurel wreath on the head of Bruni's toga-clad corpse. The Florentine government also commissioned BERNARDO ROSSELLINO (1409–1464) to carve a monumental tomb (FIG. 16-15) for the right wall of the nave of Santa Croce (FIG. I-4) honoring the late chancellor. Rossellino was the most prominent member of a family of stonecutters from Settignano, a town near Florence noted for its quarries.

Rossellino's monument in honor of Leonardo Bruni established the wall tomb as a major genre of Italian Renaissance sculpture. (Later examples include Michelangelo's tombs of the Medici [FIG. 17-16] in Florence and of Pope Julius II [FIGS. 17-14 and 17-15] in Rome.) The tomb is rich in color—white, black, and red marbles with selective gilding. Rossellino based his effigy of Bruni on ancient Roman sarcophagi (FIG. 7-61). The chancellor lies on a funerary bier supported by Roman eagles atop a sarcophagus resting on the foreparts of lions. Bruni, dressed in a toga and crowned with a laurel wreath, as during his state funeral, holds one of his books, probably his history of Florence. The realism of Bruni's head has led many scholars to postulate that Rossellino based his portrait on a wax death mask following ancient Roman practice (see "Roman Ancestor Portraits," Chapter 7, page 185). Two winged Victories hold aloft a plaque with a Latin inscription stating that History mourns the death of Leonardus, Eloquence is now si-

1 ft.

16-15 BERNARDO ROSSELLINO, tomb of Leonardo Bruni, Santa Croce, Florence, Italy, ca. 1444–1450. Marble, 23′ 3½″ high. ◼◀

Rossellino's tomb in honor of the humanist scholar and Florentine chancellor Leonardo Bruni combines ancient Roman and Christian motifs. It established the pattern for Renaissance wall tombs.

lenced, and the Greek and Latin muses cannot hold back their tears. Framing the effigy is a round-arched niche with Corinthian pilasters. The base of the tomb is a frieze of *putti* (cupids) carrying garlands, a standard motif on Roman sarcophagi, which also commonly have lions as supports (FIG. 7-70). The classically inspired tomb stands in sharp contrast to the Gothic tomb (FIG. 13-42A) of King Edward II in Gloucester Cathedral. But the Renaissance tomb is a creative variation of classical models, not a copy, and the motifs are a mix of classical and Christian themes. In the lunette beneath

1 ft.

16-16 Donatello, *Gattamelata* (equestrian statue of Erasmo da Narni), Piazza del Santo, Padua, Italy, ca. 1445–1453. Bronze, 12′ 2″ high.

Donatello based his gigantic portrait of a Venetian general on equestrian statues of ancient Roman emperors (FIG. 7-59). Together, man and horse convey an overwhelming image of irresistible strength.

1 ft.

16-17 Andrea del Verrocchio, *Bartolommeo Colleoni* (equestrian statue), Campo dei Santi Giovanni e Paolo, Venice, Italy, ca. 1481–1496. Bronze, 13′ high.

Eager to compete with Donatello's *Gattamelata* (FIG. 16-16), Colleoni provided the funds for his own equestrian statue in his will. The statue stands on a pedestal even taller than Gattamelata's.

the arch is a tondo of the Madonna and Child between praying angels. Above the arch, two putti hold up a wreath circling the lion of the Florentine Republic. A lion's head is also the central motif in the putto-and-garland frieze below the deceased's coffin.

GATTAMELATA The grandest and most costly Quattrocento portraits in the Roman tradition were over-life-size bronze equestrian statues. The supremely versatile Donatello also excelled in this genre. In 1443, he left Florence for northern Italy to accept a rewarding commission from the Republic of Venice to create a commemorative monument in honor of the recently deceased Venetian condottiere Erasmo da Narni, nicknamed Gattamelata ("honeyed cat," a wordplay on his mother's name, Melania Gattelli). Although Gattamelata's family paid for the general's portrait (FIG. 16-16), the Venetian senate formally authorized its placement in the square in front of the church of Sant'Antonio in Padua, the condottiere's birthplace. Equestrian statues occasionally had been set up in Italy in the late Middle Ages, but Donatello's *Gattamelata* was the first since antiquity to rival the grandeur of Roman imperial mounted portraits, such as that of Marcus Aurelius (FIG. 7-59), which the artist must have seen in Rome. Donatello's contemporaries, one of whom described Gattamelata as sitting on his horse "with great magnificence like a triumphant Caesar,"[5] recognized this reference to antiquity. The statue stands on a lofty base, set

apart from its surroundings, celebrating the Renaissance liberation of sculpture from architecture. Massive and majestic, the great horse bears the armored general easily, for, unlike the sculptor of the Marcus Aurelius statue, Donatello did not represent the Venetian commander as superhuman and disproportionately larger than his horse. Gattamelata dominates his mighty steed by force of character rather than sheer size. The Italian rider, his face set in a mask of dauntless resolution and unshakable will, is the very portrait of the Renaissance individualist. Such a man—intelligent, courageous, ambitious, and frequently of humble origin—could, by his own resourcefulness and on his own merits, rise to a commanding position in the world. Together, man and horse convey an overwhelming image of irresistible strength and unlimited power—an impression Donatello reinforced visually by placing the left forefoot of the horse on an orb, reviving a venerable ancient symbol for hegemony over the earth (compare FIG. 11-12). The imperial imagery is all the more remarkable because Erasmo da Narni was not a head of state.

BARTOLOMMEO COLLEONI Verrocchio also received a commission to fashion an equestrian statue of another condottiere who fought for the Venetians, Bartolommeo Colleoni (1400–1475). His portrait (FIG. 16-17) provides a counterpoint to Donatello's statue. Eager to garner the same fame the *Gattamelata* portrait

16-18 GENTILE DA FABRIANO, *Adoration of the Magi*, altarpiece from the Strozzi chapel, Santa Trinità, Florence, Italy, 1423. Tempera on wood, 9′ 11″ × 9′ 3″. Galleria degli Uffizi, Florence.

Gentile was the leading Florentine painter working in the International style. He successfully blended naturalistic details with Late Gothic splendor in color, costume, and framing ornamentation.

achieved, Colleoni provided funds in his will for his own statue. Because both Donatello and Verrocchio executed their statues after the deaths of their subjects, neither artist knew personally the individual he portrayed. The result is a fascinating difference of interpretation (like that between their two *Davids*) as to the demeanor of a professional captain of armies. Verrocchio placed the statue of the bold equestrian general on a pedestal even taller than the one Donatello used for *Gattamelata*, elevating it so viewers could see the dominating, aggressive figure from all approaches to the piazza (the Campo dei Santi Giovanni e Paolo). In contrast with the near repose of *Gattamelata*, the *Colleoni* horse moves in a prancing stride, arching and curving its powerful neck, while the commander seems suddenly to shift his whole weight to the stirrups and rise from the saddle with a violent twist of his body. The artist depicted both horse and rider with an exaggerated tautness—the animal's bulging muscles and the man's fiercely erect and rigid body together convey brute strength. In *Gattamelata,* Donatello created a portrait of grim sagacity. Verrocchio's *Bartolommeo Colleoni* is a portrait of merciless might.

Painting

In Quattrocento Italy, humanism and the celebration of classical artistic values also largely determined the character of panel and mural painting. The new Renaissance style did not, however, immediately displace all vestiges of the Late Gothic style. In particular, the International style, the dominant mode in painting around 1400 (see Chapter 14), persisted well into the 15th century.

Cennino Cennini on Imitation and Emulation in Renaissance Art

Although many of the values championed by Renaissance humanists endure to the present day, the premium that modern Western society places on artistic originality is a fairly recent phenomenon. In contrast, imitation and emulation were among the concepts Renaissance artists most valued. Many 15th- and 16th-century artists, of course, developed unique, recognizable styles, but convention, in terms of both subject matter and representational practices, predominated. In Italian Renaissance art, certain themes, motifs, and compositions appear with great regularity, fostered by training practices that emphasized the importance of tradition for aspiring Renaissance artists.

Imitation The starting point in a young artist's training (see "Artistic Training in Renaissance Italy," Chapter 14, page 414) was imitation. Italian Renaissance artists believed the best way to learn was to copy the works of masters. Accordingly, much of an apprentice's training consisted of copying exemplary artworks. Leonardo da Vinci filled his sketchbooks with drawings of well-known sculptures and frescoes, and Michelangelo spent days sketching artworks in churches around Florence and Rome.

Emulation The next step was emulation, which involved modeling one's art after that of another artist. Although imitation still provided the foundation for this practice, an artist used features of another's art only as a springboard for improvements or innovations. Thus, developing artists went beyond previous artists and attempted to prove their own competence and skill by improving on established and recognized masters. Comparison and a degree of competition were integral to emulation. To evaluate the "improved" artwork, viewers had to be familiar with the original "model."

Renaissance artists believed developing artists would ultimately arrive at their own unique style through this process of imitation and emulation. Cennino Cennini (ca. 1370–1440) explained the value of this training procedure in a book he published around 1400, *Il Libro dell'Arte* (*The Artist's Handbook*), which served as a practical guide to artistic production:

> Having first practiced drawing for a while, . . . take pains and pleasure in constantly copying the best things which you can find done by the hand of great masters. And if you are in a place where many good masters have been, so much the better for you. But I give you this advice: take care to select the best one every time, and the one who has the greatest reputation. And, as you go on from day to day, it will be against nature if you do not get some grasp of his style and of his spirit. For if you undertake to copy after one master today and after another one tomorrow, you will not acquire the style of either one or the other, and you will inevitably, through enthusiasm, become capricious, because each style will be distracting your mind. You will try to work in this man's way today, and in the other's tomorrow, and so you will not get either of them right. If you follow the course of one man through constant practice, your intelligence would have to be crude indeed for you not to get some nourishment from it. Then you will find, if nature has granted you any imagination at all, that you will eventually acquire a style individual to yourself, and it cannot help being good; because your hand and your mind, being always accustomed to gather flowers, would ill know how to pluck thorns.*

*Translated by Daniel V. Thompson Jr., *Cennino Cennini, The Craftsman's Handbook* (*Il Libro dell'Arte*), (New York: Dover Publications, 1960; reprint of 1933 ed.), 14–15.

GENTILE DA FABRIANO The leading Quattrocento master of the International Style was GENTILE DA FABRIANO (ca. 1370–1427), who in 1423 painted *Adoration of the Magi* (FIG. **16-18**) as the altarpiece for the family chapel of Palla Strozzi (1372–1462) in the church of Santa Trinità in Florence. At the beginning of the 15th century, the Strozzi family was the wealthiest in the city. The altarpiece, with its elaborate gilded Gothic frame, is testimony to the patron's lavish tastes. So too is the painting itself, with its gorgeous surface and sumptuously costumed kings, courtiers, captains, and retainers accompanied by a menagerie of exotic animals. Gentile portrayed all these elements in a rainbow of color with extensive use of gold. The painting presents all the pomp and ceremony of chivalric etiquette in a religious scene centered on the Madonna and Child. Although the style is fundamentally International Gothic, Gentile inserted striking naturalistic details. For example, the artist depicted animals from a variety of angles and foreshortened the forms convincingly, most notably the horse at the far right seen in a three-quarter rear view. Gentile did the same with human figures, such as the kneeling man removing the spurs from the standing *magus* in the center foreground. In the left panel of the predella, Gentile painted what may have been the first nighttime *Nativity* scene with the central light source—the radiant Christ Child—introduced into the picture itself. Although predominantly conservative, Gentile demonstrated he was not oblivious to Quattrocento experimental trends and could blend naturalistic and inventive elements skillfully and subtly into a traditional composition without sacrificing Late Gothic splendor in color, costume, and framing ornamentation.

MASACCIO The artist who epitomizes the innovative spirit of early-15th-century Florentine painting was Tommaso di ser Giovanni di Mone Cassai, known as MASACCIO (1401–1428). Although his presumed teacher, Masolino da Panicale (see "Italian Artists' Names," Chapter 14, page 405), had worked in the International Style, Masaccio broke sharply from the normal practice of imitating his master's style (see "Cennino Cennini on Imitation and Emulation in Renaissance Art," above). He moved suddenly, within the short span of six years, into unexplored territory. Most art historians recognize no other painter in history to have contributed so much to the development of a new style in so short a time as Masaccio, whose untimely death at age 27 cut short his brilliant career. Masaccio was the artistic descendant of Giotto (see Chapter 14), whose calm, monumental style he carried further by introducing a whole new repertoire of representational devices that generations of Renaissance painters later studied and developed.

16-19 MASACCIO, *Tribute Money*, Brancacci chapel, Santa Maria del Carmine, Florence, Italy, ca. 1424–1427. Fresco, 8′ 4⅛″ × 19′ 7⅛″. ◼◢

Masaccio's figures recall Giotto's in their simple grandeur, but they convey a greater psychological and physical credibility. He modeled his figures with light coming from a source outside the picture.

BRANCACCI CHAPEL The frescoes Masaccio painted in the family chapel that Felice Brancacci (1382–1447) sponsored in Santa Maria del Carmine in Florence provide excellent examples of his innovations. In *Tribute Money* (FIG. **16-19**), painted shortly before his death, Masaccio depicted an episode from the Gospel of Matthew (17:24–27). As the tax collector confronts Jesus at the entrance to the Roman town of Capernaum, Jesus directs Saint Peter to the shore of Lake Galilee. There, as Jesus foresaw, Peter finds the tribute coin in the mouth of a fish and returns to pay the tax. Masaccio divided the story into three parts within the fresco. In the center, Jesus, surrounded by his disciples, tells Peter to retrieve the coin from the fish, while the tax collector stands in the foreground, his back to spectators and hand extended, awaiting payment. At the left, in the middle distance, Peter extracts the coin from the fish's mouth, and, at the right, he thrusts the coin into the tax collector's hand.

Masaccio's figures recall Giotto's in their simple grandeur, but they convey a greater psychological and physical credibility. Masaccio created the figures' bulk through modeling not with a flat, neutral light lacking an identifiable source but with a light coming from a specific source outside the picture. The light comes from the right and strikes the figures at an angle, illuminating the parts of the solids obstructing its path and leaving the rest in shadow, producing the illusion of deep sculptural relief. Between the extremes of light and dark, the light appears as a constantly active but fluctuating force highlighting the scene in varying degrees. Giotto used light only to model the masses. In Masaccio's works, light has its own nature, and the masses are visible only because of its direction and intensity. The viewer can imagine the light as playing over forms—revealing some and concealing others, as the artist directs it. The figures in *Tribute Money* are solemn and weighty, but they also move freely and reveal body structure, as do Donatello's statues. Masaccio's representations adeptly suggest bones, muscles, and the pressures and tensions of joints. Each figure conveys a maximum of contained energy. *Tribute Money* helps the viewer understand Giorgio Vasari's comment: "[T]he works made before his

[Masaccio's] day can be said to be painted, while his are living, real, and natural."[6]

Masaccio's arrangement of the figures is equally inventive. They do not stand in a line in the foreground. Instead, the artist grouped them in circular depth around Jesus, and he placed the whole group in a spacious landscape, rather than in the confined stage space of earlier frescoes. The group itself generates the foreground space and the architecture on the right amplifies it. Masaccio depicted the building in perspective, locating the vanishing point, where all the orthogonals converge, at Jesus' head. He also diminished the brightness of the colors as the distance increases, an aspect of atmospheric perspective. Although ancient Roman painters used aerial perspective (FIG. 7-20), medieval artists had abandoned it. Thus, it virtually disappeared from art until Masaccio and his contemporaries rediscovered it. They came to realize that the light and air interposed between viewers and what they see are two parts of the visual experience called "distance."

In an awkwardly narrow space at the entrance to the Brancacci chapel, to the left of *Tribute Money*, Masaccio painted *Expulsion of Adam and Eve from Eden* (FIG. **16-20**), another fresco displaying the representational innovations of *Tribute Money*. For example, the sharply slanted light from an outside source creates deep relief, with lights placed alongside darks, and acts as a strong unifying agent. Masaccio also presented the figures with convincing structural accuracy, thereby suggesting substantial body weight. Further, the hazy background specifies no locale but suggests a space around and beyond the figures. Adam's feet, clearly in contact with the ground, mark the human presence on earth, and the cry issuing from Eve's mouth voices her anguish. The angel does not force them physically from Eden. Rather, they stumble on blindly, the angel's will and their own despair driving them. The composition is starkly simple, its message incomparably eloquent.

HOLY TRINITY Masaccio's *Holy Trinity* fresco (FIG. **16-21**) in Santa Maria Novella is another of the young artist's masterworks and

1 ft.

16-20 MASACCIO, *Expulsion of Adam and Eve from Eden*, Brancacci chapel, Santa Maria del Carmine, Florence, Italy, ca. 1424–1427. Fresco, 7′ × 2′ 11″. ◼◀

Adam and Eve, expelled from Eden, stumble on blindly, driven by the angel's will and their own despair. The hazy background specifies no locale but suggests a space around and beyond the figures.

1 ft.

16-21 MASACCIO, *Holy Trinity*, Santa Maria Novella, Florence, Italy, ca. 1424–1427. Fresco, 21′ 10⅝″ × 10′ 4¾″.

Masaccio's pioneering *Holy Trinity* is the premier early-15th-century example of the application of mathematics to the depiction of space according to Brunelleschi's system of perspective.

the premier early-15th-century example of the application of mathematics to the depiction of space. Masaccio painted the composition on two levels of unequal height. Above, in a barrel-vaulted chapel reminiscent of a Roman *triumphal arch* (FIGS. 7-40 and 7-44B; compare FIG. 16-49A), the Virgin Mary and Saint John appear on either side of the crucified Christ. God the Father emerges from behind Christ, supporting the arms of the cross and presenting his son to the worshiper as a devotional object. The dove of the Holy Spirit hovers between God's head and Christ's head. Masaccio also included portraits of the donors of the painting, Lorenzo Lenzi and his wife, who kneel just in front of the *pilasters* framing the chapel's

entrance. Below, the artist painted a tomb containing a skeleton. An inscription in Italian above the skeleton reminds the spectator, "I was once what you are, and what I am you will become."

The illusionism of *Holy Trinity* is breathtaking. In this fresco, Masaccio brilliantly demonstrated the principles and potential of Brunelleschi's new science of perspective. Indeed, some art historians have suggested Brunelleschi may have collaborated with Masaccio. The vanishing point of the composition is at the foot of the cross. With this point at eye level, spectators look up at the Trinity and down at the tomb. About 5 feet above the floor level, the vanishing point pulls the two views together, creating the illusion of a real structure transecting the wall's vertical plane. Whereas the tomb appears to project forward into the church, the chapel recedes visually behind the wall and appears as an extension of the spectator's space. This adjustment of the picture's space to the viewer's position was an important innovation in illusionistic painting that other artists of the Renaissance and the later Baroque period would develop further. Masaccio was so exact in his metrical proportions it is possible to calculate the dimensions of the chapel (for example, the span of the painted vault is 7 feet and the depth of the chapel is 9 feet). Thus, he achieved not only a successful illusion but also a rational measured coherence that is responsible for the unity and harmony of the fresco. *Holy Trinity* is, however, much more than a demonstration of Brunelleschi's perspective or of the painter's ability to represent fully modeled figures bathed in light. In this painting, Masaccio also powerfully conveyed one of the central tenets of Christian faith. The ascending pyramid of figures leads viewers from the despair of death to the hope of resurrection and eternal life through Christ's crucifixion.

FRA ANGELICO As Masaccio's *Holy Trinity* clearly demonstrates, humanism and religion were not mutually exclusive. In fact, for many Quattrocento Italian artists, humanist concerns were not a primary consideration. The art of FRA ANGELICO (ca. 1400–1455) focused on serving the Roman Catholic Church. In the late 1430s, the abbot of the Dominican monastery of San Marco (Saint Mark) in Florence asked Fra Angelico to produce a series of frescoes for the monastery. The Dominicans (see "Mendicant Orders," Chapter 14, page 404) of San Marco had dedicated themselves to lives of prayer and work, and the religious compound was mostly spare and austere to encourage the monks to immerse themselves in their devotional lives. Fra Angelico's *Annunciation* (FIG. **16-22**) appears at the top of the stairs leading to the friars' cells. Appropriately, Fra Angelico presented the scene of the Virgin Mary and the Archangel Gabriel with simplicity and serenity. The two figures appear in a plain *loggia* resembling the *portico* of San Marco's *cloister,* and the artist painted all the fresco elements with a pristine clarity. As an admonition to heed the devotional function of the images, Fra Angelico included a small inscription at the base of the image: "As you venerate, while passing before it, this figure of the intact Virgin, beware lest you omit to say a Hail Mary." Like most of Fra Angelico's paintings, *Annunciation,* with its simplicity and directness, still has an almost universal appeal and fully reflects the artist's simple, humble character.

ANDREA DEL CASTAGNO Fra Angelico's younger contemporary ANDREA DEL CASTAGNO (ca. 1421–1457) also accepted a commission to produce a series of frescoes for a religious establishment. Castagno's *Last Supper* (FIG. **16-23**) in the *refectory* (dining hall) of Sant'Apollonia in Florence, a convent for Benedictine nuns, manifests both a commitment to the biblical narrative and an interest in perspective. The lavishly painted room Jesus and his 12 disciples occupy suggests the artist's absorption with creating the illusion of three-dimensional space. However, closer scrutiny reveals inconsistencies, such as how Renaissance perspective systems make it impossible to see both the ceiling from inside and the roof from outside, as Castagno depicted. The two side walls also do not appear parallel. Castagno chose a conventional compositional format, with the figures seated at a horizontally placed table. He derived the apparent self-absorption of most of the disciples and the malevolent features of Judas (who sits alone on the outside of the table) from the Gospel of Saint John, rather than the more familiar version of the last supper recounted in the Gospel of Saint Luke. Castagno's dramatic and spatially convincing depiction of the event no doubt was a powerful presence for the nuns during their daily meals.

1 ft.

16-22 FRA ANGELICO, *Annunciation,* San Marco, Florence, Italy, ca. 1438–1447. Fresco, 7′ 1″ × 10′ 6″.

Painted for the Dominican monks of San Marco, Fra Angelico's fresco is simple and direct. Its figures and architecture have a pristine clarity befitting the fresco's function as a devotional image.

16-23 ANDREA DEL CASTAGNO, *Last Supper,* refectory of the convent of Sant'Apollonia, Florence, Italy, 1447. Fresco, 15′ 5″ × 32′. ◼◀

Judas sits isolated in this *Last Supper* based on the Gospel of Saint John. The figures are small compared with the setting, reflecting Castagno's preoccupation with the new science of perspective.

FRA FILIPPO LIPPI Another younger contemporary of Fra Angelico, FRA FILIPPO LIPPI (ca. 1406–1469), was also a friar—but there all resemblance ends. Fra Filippo was unsuited for monastic life. He indulged in misdemeanors ranging from forgery and embezzlement to the abduction of a pretty nun, Lucretia, who became his mistress and the mother of his son, the painter Filippino Lippi (1457–1504). Only the intervention of the Medici on his behalf at the papal court preserved Fra Filippo from severe punishment and total disgrace. An orphan, Fra Filippo spent his youth in a monastery adjacent to the church of Santa Maria del Carmine, and when he was still in his teens, he must have met Masaccio there and witnessed the decoration of the Brancacci chapel. Fra Filippo's early work survives only in fragments, but these show he tried to work with Masaccio's massive forms. Later, probably under the influence of Ghiberti's and Donatello's relief sculptures, he developed a linear style that emphasized the contours of his figures and enabled him to suggest movement through flying and swirling draperies.

In a painting from Fra Filippo's later years, *Madonna and Child with Angels* (FIG. **16-24**), the Virgin sits in prayer at a slight angle to the viewer. Her body casts a shadow on the window frame behind her. But the painter's primary interest was not in space but in line, which unifies the composition and contributes to the precise and smooth delineation of forms. The Carmelite brother interpreted his subject in a surprisingly worldly manner. The Madonna

16-24 FRA FILIPPO LIPPI, *Madonna and Child with Angels,* ca. 1460–1465. Tempera on wood, 2′ 11½″ × 2′ 1″. Galleria degli Uffizi, Florence.

Fra Filippo, a monk guilty of many misdemeanors, represented the Virgin and Christ Child in a distinctly worldly manner, carrying the humanization of the holy family further than any artist before him.

Christ miraculously rises from his tomb while the Roman guards sleep. The viewer sees the framing portico and the soldiers from below, but has a head-on view of the seminude muscular figure of Christ.

1 ft.

is a beautiful young mother, albeit with a transparent halo, in an elegantly furnished Florentine home, and neither she nor the Christ Child, whom two angels hold up, has a solemn expression. One of the angels, in fact, sports the mischievous, puckish grin of a boy refusing to behave for the pious occasion. Significantly, all figures reflect the use of live models (perhaps Lucretia for the Madonna). Fra Filippo plainly relished the charm of youth and beauty as he found it in this world. He preferred the real in landscape also. The background, seen through the window, incorporates recognizable features of the Arno valley. Compared with the earlier Madonnas by Giotto (FIG. 14-7) and Duccio (FIG. 14-9), this work shows how far artists had carried the humanization of the religious theme. Whatever the ideals of spiritual perfection may have meant to artists in past centuries, Renaissance artists realized those ideals in terms of the sensuous beauty of this world.

PIERO DELLA FRANCESCA One of the most renowned painters in 15th-century Italy was PIERO DELLA FRANCESCA (ca. 1420–1492), a native of Borgo San Sepolcro in southeastern Tuscany, who worked for diverse patrons, including the Medici in Florence and Federico de Montefeltro in Urbino (FIG. 16-43). In Tuscany, his commissions included frescoes of Christ's *Resurrection* (FIG. **16-25**) for the town hall of his birthplace and *Legend of the True Cross* (FIG. **16-25A**) for the church of San Francesco at Arezzo. He painted *Resurrection* at the request of the Borgo San Sepolcro civic council on the wall

facing the entrance to its newly remodeled Palazzo Comunale. Normally, the subjects chosen for city halls were scenes of battles, townscapes, or allegories of enlightened governance, as in Siena's Palazzo Pubblico (FIGS. 14-16, 14-16A, and 14-17). But the San Sepolcro council chose instead a religious subject. The town's name—Holy Sepulcher—derived from the legend that two 10th-century saints, Arcanus and Egidius, brought a fragment of Christ's tomb to the town from the Holy Land. Christ's *Resurrection* was also the subject of the central panel of the altarpiece painted between 1346 and 1348 by the Sienese painter Niccolò di Segna for the cathedral of San Sepolcro.

16-25A PIERO DELLA FRANCESCA, *Legend of the True Cross*, ca. 1450–1455.

In Piero's *Resurrection*, the viewer witnesses the miracle of the risen Christ through the Corinthian columns of a classical portico (preserved only in part because the painting was trimmed during its installation in a new location). Piero chose a viewpoint corresponding to the viewer's position and depicted the architectural frame at a sharp angle from below. The Roman soldiers who have fallen asleep when they should be guarding the tomb are also seen from below in a variety of foreshortened poses. (The bareheaded guard second from the left with his head resting on Christ's sarcophagus may be a self-portrait of the artist.) The soldiers form the

16-26 DOMENICO GHIRLANDAIO, *Birth of the Virgin,* Cappella Maggiore, Santa Maria Novella, Florence, Italy, ca. 1485–1490. Fresco, 24′ 4″ × 14′ 9″. ◼◂

Ludovica Tornabuoni holds as prominent a place in Ghirlandaio's fresco as she must have held in Florentine society—evidence of the secularization of sacred themes in 15th-century Italian painting.

base of a compositional triangle culminating at Christ's head. For Christ, Piero violated the perspective of the rest of the fresco and used a head-on view of the resurrected savior, imbuing the figure with an iconic quality. Christ's muscular body has the proportions of Greco-Roman nude statues. His pastel cloak stands out prominently from the darker colors of the soldiers' costumes. Christ holds the banner of his victory over death and displays his wounds. His face has portraitlike features. The tired eyes and somber expression are the only indications of his suffering on the cross.

DOMENICO GHIRLANDAIO Although projects undertaken with church, civic, and Medici patronage were significant sources of income for Florentine artists, other wealthy families also offered attractive commissions. Toward the end of the 15th century, DOMENICO GHIRLANDAIO (1449–1494) received the contract for an important project for Giovanni Tornabuoni, one of the wealthiest Florentines of his day. Tornabuoni asked Ghirlandaio to paint a cycle of frescoes depicting scenes from the lives of the Virgin and Saint John the Baptist for the choir of Santa Maria Novella (FIG. 14-6A), the Dominican church where Masaccio had earlier painted his revolutionary *Holy Trinity* (FIG. 16-21). In *Birth of the Virgin* (FIG. **16-26**), Mary's mother, Saint Anne, reclines in a palatial Renaissance room embellished with fine wood inlay and sculpture, while midwives

prepare the infant's bath. From the left comes a solemn procession of women led by a young Tornabuoni family member, probably Ludovica, Giovanni's only daughter. Ghirlandaio's composition epitomizes the achievements of Quattrocento Florentine painting: clear spatial representation, statuesque figures, and rational order and logical relations among all figures and objects. If any remnant of earlier traits remains here, it is the arrangement of the figures, which still cling somewhat rigidly to layers parallel to the picture plane. New, however, and in striking contrast to the dignity and austerity of Fra Angelico's frescoes (FIG. 16-22) for the Dominican monastery of San Marco, is the dominating presence of the donor's family in the religious tableau. Ludovica holds as prominent a place in the composition (close to the central axis) as she must have held in Florentine society. Her appearance in the painting (a different female member of the house appears in each fresco) is conspicuous evidence of the secularization of sacred themes. Artists depicted living persons of high rank not only as present at biblical dramas (as Masaccio did in *Holy Trinity*) but also even stealing the show from the saints—as here, where the Tornabuoni women upstage the Virgin and Child. The display of patrician elegance tempers the biblical narrative and subordinates the fresco's devotional nature.

Ghirlandaio also painted individual portraits of wealthy Florentines. His 1488 panel painting of an aristocratic young woman is

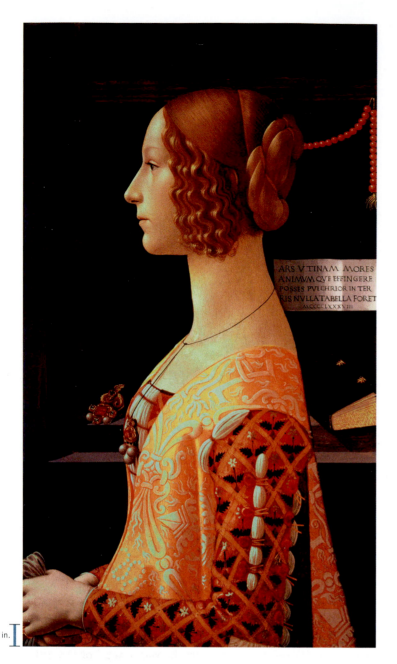

16-27 DOMENICO GHIRLANDAIO, *Giovanna Tornabuoni*(?), 1488. Oil and tempera on wood, 2′ 6″ × 1′ 8″. Museo Thyssen-Bornemisza, Madrid.

Renaissance artists revived the ancient art of portraiture. This portrait reveals the wealth, courtly manners, and humanistic interest in classical literature that lie behind much 15th-century Florentine art.

ARS VTINAM MORES ANIMVM QVE EFFINGERE POSSES PVICHRIOR IN TER RIS NVLLA TABELLA FORET MCCCCLXXXVIII

probably a portrait of Giovanna Tornabuoni (FIG. **16-27**), a member of the powerful Albizzi family and wife of Lorenzo Tornabuoni, one of Lorenzo Medici's cousins. Although artists at this time were beginning to employ three-quarter and full-face views for portraits (FIG. 16-29A) in place of the more traditional profile pose, Ghirlandaio used the older format. This did not prevent him from conveying a character reading of the sitter. His portrait reveals the proud bearing of a sensitive and beautiful young woman. It also tells viewers much about the advanced state of culture in Florence, the value and careful cultivation of beauty in life and art, the breeding of courtly manners, and the great wealth behind it all. In addition, the painting shows the powerful attraction classical literature held for Italian humanists. In the background, an epitaph (Giovanna Tornabuoni died in childbirth in 1488 at age 20) quotes the ancient Roman poet Martial:

> If art could depict character and soul,
> No painting on earth would be more beautiful.[7]

PAOLO UCCELLO A masterpiece of this secular side of Quattrocento art is *Battle of San Romano* (FIG. **16-28**) by PAOLO UCCELLO (1397–1475), a Florentine painter trained in the International Style. The large panel painting is one of three Lorenzo de' Medici acquired for his bedchamber in the palatial Medici residence (FIGS. 16-37 and 16-38) in Florence. There is some controversy about the date of the painting because documents have been discovered suggesting Lorenzo may have purchased at least two of the paintings from a previous owner instead of commissioning the full series himself. The scenes commemorate the Florentine victory over the Sienese in 1432 and must have been painted no earlier than the mid-1430s if not around 1455, the traditional date assigned to the commission. In the panel illustrated, Niccolò da Tolentino (ca. 1350–1435), a friend and supporter of Cosimo de' Medici, leads the charge against the Sienese. Although the painting focuses on Tolentino's military exploits, it also acknowledges the Medici, albeit in symbolic form. The bright orange fruit behind the raised lances on the left are *mela medica* (Italian, "medicinal apples"). Because the name *Medici* means

16-28 PAOLO UCCELLO, *Battle of San Romano*, ca. 1435 or ca. 1455. Tempera on wood, 6′ × 10′ 5″. National Gallery, London.

In this panel once in Lorenzo de' Medici's bedchamber, Niccolò da Tolentino leads the charge against the Sienese. The foreshortened spears and figures reveal Uccello's fascination with perspective.

1 in.

1 ft.

Inspired by an Angelo Poliziano poem and classical Aphrodite statues (FIG. 5-62), Botticelli revived the theme of the female nude in this elegant and romantic representation of Venus born of sea foam.

1 ft.

"doctors," this fruit was a fitting symbol of the family. Orange apples also appear in Botticelli's *Primavera* (FIG. 16-1). Their inclusion here suggests that at least this panel was a Medici commission, if all three were not.

In *Battle of San Romano*, Uccello created a composition that recalls the International style processional splendor of Gentile da Fabriano's *Adoration of the Magi* (FIG. 16-18) yet also reflects Uccello's obsession with perspective. In contrast with Gentile, who emphasized surface decoration, Uccello painted life-size, classically inspired figures arranged in the foreground and, in the background, a receding landscape resembling the low cultivated hillsides between Florence and Lucca. He foreshortened broken spears, lances, and a fallen soldier and carefully placed them along the converging orthogonals of the perspective system to create a base plane akin to a checkerboard, on which he then placed the larger volumes in measured intervals. The rendering of three-dimensional form, used by other painters for representational or expressive purposes, became for Uccello a preoccupation. For him, it had a magic of its own, which he exploited to satisfy his inventive and original imagination.

BOTTICELLI, *BIRTH OF VENUS* Also painted for the Medici and rivaling *Primavera* (FIG. 16-1) in fame is Sandro Botticelli's *Birth of Venus* (FIG. **16-29**). The theme was the subject of a poem by Angelo Poliziano (1454–1494), a leading humanist of the day. In Botticelli's lyrical painting of Poliziano's retelling of the Greek myth, Zephyrus, carrying Chloris, blows Venus, born of the sea foam and carried on a cockle shell, to her sacred island, Cyprus. There, the nymph Pomona runs to meet her with a brocaded mantle. The lightness and bodilessness of the winds move all the figures without effort. Draperies undulate easily in the gentle gusts, perfumed by rose petals that fall on the whitecaps. In this painting, unlike in *Primavera*, Botticelli depicted Venus as nude. As noted earlier, the nude, especially the female nude, was exceedingly rare during the Middle Ages. The artist's use (especially on such a large scale—roughly life-size) of an ancient Venus statue (a Hellenistic variant of Praxiteles' famous *Aphrodite of Knidos*, FIG. 5-62) as a

model could have drawn harsh criticism. But in the more accommodating Renaissance culture and under the protection of the powerful Medici, the depiction went unchallenged, in part because *Birth of Venus*, which has several mythological figures in common with *Primavera*, is susceptible to a Neo-Platonic reading. Marsilio Ficino (1433–1499), for example, made the case in his treatise *On Love* (1469) that those who embrace the contemplative life of reason—including, of course, the humanists in the Medici circle—will immediately contemplate spiritual and divine beauty whenever they behold physical beauty.

Botticelli's style is clearly distinct from the earnest search many other artists pursued to comprehend humanity and the natural world through a rational, empirical order. Indeed, Botticelli's elegant and beautiful linear style (he was a pupil of Fra Filippo Lippi, FIG. 16-24) seems removed from all the scientific knowledge 15th-century artists had gained in the areas of perspective and anatomy. For example, the seascape in *Birth of Venus* is a flat backdrop devoid of atmospheric perspective. Botticelli's style paralleled the Florentine allegorical pageants that were chivalric tournaments structured around allusions to classical mythology. The same trend is evident in the poetry of the 1470s and 1480s. Artists and poets at this time did not directly imitate classical antiquity but used the myths, with delicate perception of their charm, in a way still tinged with medieval romance. Ultimately, Botticelli created a style of visual poetry parallel to the love poetry of Lorenzo de' Medici. His paintings possess a lyricism and courtliness that appealed to cultured Florentine patrons, whether the Medici themselves or associates of the family (FIG. **16-29A**).

16-29A BOTTICELLI, *Young Man Holding a Medal*, ca. 1474–1475. ◼◀

ENGRAVING Although the most prestigious commissions in 15th-century Florence were for large-scale panel paintings and frescoes and for monumental statues and reliefs, some artists also produced important small-scale works, such as Pollaiuolo's

16-30 Antonio del Pollaiuolo, *Battle of Ten Nudes*, ca. 1465. Engraving, 1′ 3⅛″ × 1′ 11¼″. Metropolitan Museum of Art, New York (bequest of Joseph Pulitzer, 1917).

Pollaiuolo was fascinated by how muscles and sinews activate the human skeleton. He delighted in showing nude figures in violent action and from numerous foreshortened viewpoints.

1 in.

Hercules and Antaeus (FIG. 16-14). Pollaiuolo also experimented with the new medium of engraving, which northern European artists had pioneered around the middle of the century. But whereas German graphic artists, such as Martin Schongauer (FIG. 15-22), described their forms with hatching that followed the forms, Italian engravers, such as Pollaiuolo, preferred parallel hatching. The former method was in keeping with the general northern European approach to art, which tended to describe surfaces of forms rather than their underlying structures, whereas the latter better suited the anatomical studies that preoccupied Pollaiuolo and his Italian contemporaries.

Battle of Ten Nudes (FIG. **16-30**), like Pollaiuolo's *Hercules and Antaeus* (FIG. 16-14), reveals the artist's interest in the realistic presentation of human figures in action. Earlier artists, such as Donatello (FIG. 16-12) and Masaccio (FIG. 16-20), had dealt effectively with the problem of rendering human anatomy, but they usually depicted their figures at rest or in restrained motion. As is evident in his engraving as well as in his sculpture, Pollaiuolo took delight in showing violent action. He conceived the body as a powerful machine and liked to display its mechanisms, such as knotted muscles and taut sinews that activate the skeleton as ropes pull levers. To show this to best effect, Pollaiuolo developed a figure so lean and muscular it appears *écorché* (as if without skin), with strongly accentuated delineations at the wrists, elbows, shoulders, and knees. *Battle of Ten Nudes* shows this figure type in a variety of poses and from numerous viewpoints, enabling Pollaiuolo to demonstrate his prowess in rendering the nude male figure. In this, he was a kindred spirit of late-sixth-century Greek vase painters, such as Euthymides (FIG. 5-23), who had experimented with foreshortening for the first time in history. Even though the figures in *Ten Nudes* hack and slash at one another without mercy, they nevertheless seem somewhat stiff and frozen because Pollaiuolo depicted *all* the muscle groups at maximum tension. Not until several decades later did an even greater anatomist, Leonardo da Vinci, observe that only some of the body's muscle groups participate in any one action, while the others remain relaxed.

Architecture

Filippo Brunelleschi's ability to codify a system of linear perspective derived in part from his skill as an architect. Although according to his biographer, Antonio Manetti, Brunelleschi turned to architecture out of disappointment over the loss to Lorenzo Ghiberti of the commission for the baptistery doors (FIGS. 16-2 and 16-3), he continued to work as a sculptor for several years and received commissions for sculpture as late as 1416. It is true, however, that as the 15th century progressed, Brunelleschi's interest turned increasingly toward architecture. Several trips to Rome (the first in 1402,

probably with his friend Donatello), where the ruins of ancient Rome captivated him, heightened his fascination with architecture. His close study of Roman monuments and his effort to make an accurate record of what he saw may have been the catalyst that led Brunelleschi to develop his revolutionary system of geometric linear perspective.

OSPEDALE DEGLI INNOCENTI

At the end of the second decade of the 15th century, Brunelleschi received two important architectural commissions in Florence—to construct a dome (FIG. **16-30A**) for the city's late medieval cathedral (FIG. 14-18), and to design the Ospedale degli Innocenti (Hospital of the Innocents, FIG. **16-31**), a home for Florentine orphans and foundlings. The latter commission came from Florence's guild of silk manufacturers and goldsmiths, of which Brunelleschi, a goldsmith, was a member. The

16-30A Brunelleschi, Florence Cathedral dome, 1420–1436. ■🎥

site chosen for the orphanage, adjacent to the church of the Santissima Annunziata (Most Holy Annunciation), was appropriate. The church housed a miracle-working image of the Annunciation that attracted large numbers of pilgrims. With the construction of the new foundling hospital, the Madonna would now watch over infants as well, assisted by the guild, which supported the orphanage with additional charitable donations.

Most scholars regard Brunelleschi's Ospedale degli Innocenti as the first building to embody the new Renaissance architectural style. As in earlier similar buildings, the facade of the Florentine orphanage is a loggia opening onto the street, a sheltered portico where, in this case, parents could anonymously deliver unwanted children to the care of the foundling hospital. Brunelleschi's arcade consists of a series of round arches on slender Corinthian columns. Each bay is a domed compartment with a *pediment*-capped window above. Both plan and elevation conform to a *module* that embodies the rationality of classical architecture. Each column is 10 *braccia* (approximately 20 feet; 1 braccia, or arm, equals 23 inches) tall. The distance between the columns of the facade and the distance between the columns and the wall are also 10 braccia. Thus, each of the bays is a cubical unit 10 braccia wide, deep, and high. The height of the columns also equals the diameter of the arches (except in the two outermost bays, which are slightly wider and serve as framing elements in the overall design). The color scheme, which would become a Brunelleschi hallmark, is austere: white stucco walls with gray *pietra serena* ("serene stone") columns and moldings. In 1487, Andrea della Robbia (1435–1525), nephew of Luca della Robbia (FIG. 16-36A) and his successor as head of the family workshop, added more color to the loggia in the form of a series of *glazed terracotta roundels,* one above each column, depicting a baby in swaddling clothes (no two are identical)—the only indication on the building's facade of its charitable function.

SANTO SPIRITO Begun around 1446 and completed, with some changes, after Brunelleschi's death, Santo Spirito (FIG. **16-32**) is one of two *basilican* churches the architect built in Florence. (The other is San Lorenzo; FIG. **16-32A**.) Santo Spirito showcases the clarity and classically inspired rationality that characterize Brunelleschi's mature designs. Brunelleschi laid out this *cruciform* building in either multiples or segments of the dome-covered *crossing square.* The aisles, subdivided into small squares

16-32A BRUNELLESCHI, San Lorenzo, ca. 1421–1469. ■◀

covered by shallow, saucer-shaped vaults, run all the way around the flat-roofed central space. They have the visual effect of compressing the longitudinal design into one more comparable to a *central plan,* because the various aspects of the interior resemble one another, no matter where an observer stands. Originally, this centralization effect would have been even stronger. Brunelleschi had planned to extend the aisles across the front of the nave as well, as shown on the plan (FIG. **16-33,** *left*). However, adherence to that design would have de-

16-31 FILIPPO BRUNELLESCHI, Loggia of the Ospedale degli Innocenti (Foundling Hospital; looking northeast), Florence, Italy, begun 1419. ■◀

Often called the first Renaissance building, the loggia of the orphanage sponsored by Florence's silk and goldsmith guild features a classically austere design based on a module of 10 braccia.

16-33 FILIPPO BRUNELLESCHI, early plan (*left*) and plan as constructed (*right*) of Santo Spirito, Florence, Italy, designed 1434–1436; begun 1446.

Santo Spirito displays the classically inspired rationality of Brunelleschi's mature style in its all-encompassing modular scheme based on the dimensions of the dome-covered crossing square.

16-32 FILIPPO BRUNELLESCHI, interior of Santo Spirito (looking northeast), Florence, Italy, designed 1434–1436; begun 1446. ■◀

The austerity of the decor and the mathematical clarity of the interior of Santo Spirito contrast sharply with the soaring drama and spirituality of the nave arcades and vaults of Gothic churches.

Italian Renaissance Family Chapel Endowments

During the 14th through 16th centuries in Italy, wealthy families regularly endowed chapels in or adjacent to major churches. These family chapels were usually on either side of the choir near the altar at the church's east end. Particularly wealthy families sponsored chapels in the form of separate buildings constructed adjacent to churches. For example, the Medici Chapel (Old Sacristy) abuts San Lorenzo in Florence. Other powerful banking families— the Baroncelli, Bardi, and Peruzzi— each sponsored chapels in the Florentine church of Santa Croce. The Pazzi family commissioned a chapel (FIGS. 16-34 to 16-36) adjacent to Santa Croce, and the Brancacci family sponsored the decorative program (FIGS. 16-19 and 16-20) of their chapel in Santa Maria del Carmine.

These families endowed chapels to ensure the well-being of the souls of individual family members and ancestors. The chapels served as burial sites and as spaces for liturgical celebrations and commemorative services. Chapel owners sponsored Masses for the dead, praying to the Virgin Mary and the saints for intercession on behalf of their deceased loved ones.

Changes in Christian doctrine prompted these concerted efforts to enhance donors' chances for eternal salvation. Until the 13th century, most Christians believed that after death, souls went either to Heaven or to Hell. In the late 1100s and early 1200s, the concept of Purgatory—a way station between Heaven and Hell where souls could atone for sins before judgment day—increasingly won favor. Pope Innocent III (1198–1216) officially recognized the existence of such a place in 1215. Because Purgatory represented a chance for the faithful to improve the likelihood of eventually gaining admission to Heaven, Christians eagerly embraced this opportunity.

When the Church extended this idea for believers to improve their prospects while alive, charitable work, good deeds, and devotional practices proliferated. Family chapels provided the space

16-34 FILIPPO BRUNELLESCHI, facade of the Pazzi Chapel, Santa Croce, Florence, Italy, begun 1433. ◼◁

The Pazzi family erected this chapel as a gift to the Franciscan church of Santa Croce. It served as the monks' chapter house and is one of the first independent Renaissance central-plan buildings.

necessary for the performance of devotional rituals. Most chapels included altars, as well as chalices, vestments, candlesticks, and other objects used in the Mass. Most patrons also commissioned decorations, such as painted altarpieces, frescoes on the walls, and sculptural objects. The chapels were therefore not only expressions of piety and devotion but also opportunities for donors to enhance their stature in the larger community.

---

manded four entrances in the facade, instead of the traditional and symbolic three, a feature hotly debated during Brunelleschi's lifetime and changed after his death. Successor builders also modified the appearance of the exterior walls (FIG. 16-33, *right*) by filling in the recesses between the projecting semicircular chapels to convert the original highly sculpted wall surface into a flat one.

The major features of Santo Spirito's interior (FIG. 16-32), however, are much as Brunelleschi designed them. In this modular scheme, as in the loggia of the Ospedale degli Innocenti (FIG. 16-31), a mathematical unit served to determine the dimensions of every aspect of the church. This unit—the crossing bay measuring 20 by 20 braccia—subdivided throughout the plan creates a rhythmic harmony. Fixed ratios also determined the elevation. For example, the nave is twice as high as it is wide, and the arcade and clerestory are of equal height, which means the height of the arcade equals

the nave's width. Astute observers can read the proportional relationships among the interior's parts as a series of mathematical equations. The austerity of the decor enhances the rationality of the design and produces a restful and tranquil atmosphere. Brunelleschi left no space for expansive wall frescoes that would only detract from the clarity of his architectural scheme. The calculated logic of the design echoes that of ancient Roman buildings, such as the Pantheon (FIG. 7-50, *right*). The rationality of Santo Spirito contrasts sharply, however, with the soaring drama and spirituality of the nave arcades and vaults of Gothic churches (for example, FIGS. 13-19 and 13-20). It even deviates from the design of Florence Cathedral's nave (FIG. 14-18A), whose verticality is restrained in comparison to its northern European counterparts. Santo Spirito fully expresses the new Renaissance spirit that placed its faith in reason rather than in the emotions.

16-35 FILIPPO BRUNELLESCHI, plan of the Pazzi Chapel, Santa Croce, Florence, Italy, begun 1433.

Although the Pazzi Chapel is rectangular, rather than square or round, Brunelleschi created a central plan by placing all emphasis on the dome-covered space at the heart of the building.

16-36 FILIPPO BRUNELLESCHI, interior of the Pazzi Chapel (looking southeast), Santa Croce, Florence, Italy, begun 1433. ◼◀

The interior trim of the Pazzi Chapel is gray pietra serena, which stands out against the white stuccoed walls and crisply defines the modular relationships of Brunelleschi's plan and elevation.

PAZZI CHAPEL Brunelleschi's apparent effort to impart a centralized effect to the interior of Santo Spirito suggests that he found intriguing the compact and self-contained qualities of central-plan buildings—for example, the Pantheon (FIGS. 7-49 to 7-51) and the Florentine Baptistery of San Giovanni (FIG. 12-27). He had already explored this interest in his design for the chapel (FIG. 16-34) the Pazzi family donated to the Franciscan church of Santa Croce in Florence (see "Italian Renaissance Family Chapel Endowments," page 472). Brunelleschi began to work on the project around 1423, but construction continued until the 1460s, long after his death. The exterior probably does not reflect Brunelleschi's original design. The loggia, admirable as it is, likely was added as an afterthought, perhaps by the sculptor-architect Giuliano da Maiano (1432–1490). The Pazzi Chapel served as the *chapter house* (meeting hall) of the local chapter of Franciscan monks. Historians have suggested the monks needed the expansion to accommodate more of their brethren.

Behind the loggia stands one of the first independent Renaissance buildings conceived basically as a central-plan structure. Although the Pazzi Chapel's plan (FIG. 16-35) is rectangular, rather than square or round, Brunelleschi placed all emphasis on the central dome-covered space. The short barrel-*vault* sections bracing the dome on two sides appear to be incidental appendages. The interior trim (FIG. 16-36) is Brunelleschi's favorite gray pietra serena, which stands out against the white stuccoed walls and crisply defines the modular relationships of plan and elevation. As he did in his design for the Ospedale degli Innocenti (FIG. 16-31) and later for Santo Spirito (FIG. 16-32), Brunelleschi used a basic unit that enabled him to construct a balanced, harmonious, and regularly proportioned space.

Circular medallions, or *tondi,* in the dome's *pendentives* (see "Pendentives and Squinches," Chapter 9, page 262) consist of glazed terracotta reliefs representing the four evangelists. The technique for manufacturing these baked clay reliefs was of recent invention. Around 1430, LUCA DELLA ROBBIA (1400–1482) perfected the application of vitrified (heat-fused) colored potters' glazes to sculpture (FIG. 16-36A). Inexpensive, durable, and decorative, they became extremely popular and provided the basis for a flourishing family business. Luca's nephew Andrea della Robbia produced roundels for Brunelleschi's loggia of the Ospedale degli Innocenti (FIG. 16-31) in 1487, and Andrea's sons, Giovanni della Robbia (1469–1529) and Girolamo della Robbia (1488–1566), carried on this tradition well into the 16th century. Most of the tondi in the Pazzi Chapel are the work of Luca della Robbia himself. Together with the images of the 12 apostles on the pilaster-framed wall panels, they add striking color accents to the tranquil interior.

16-36A LUCA DELLA ROBBIA, *Madonna and Child,* ca. 1455–1460. ◼◀

PALAZZO MEDICI It seems curious that Brunelleschi, the most renowned architect of his time, did not participate in the upsurge of palace building Florence experienced in the 1430s and 1440s. This proliferation of palazzi testified to the stability of the Florentine economy and to the affluence and confidence of the city's leading citizens. Brunelleschi, however, confined his efforts in this field to work on the Palazzo di Parte Guelfa (headquarters of Florence's then-ruling "party") and to a rejected model for a new palace that Cosimo de' Medici intended to build.

When the Medici returned to Florence in 1434 after a brief exile imposed upon them by other elite families who resented the Medicis' consolidation of power, Cosimo, aware of the importance of public perception, attempted to maintain a lower profile and to wield his power from behind the scenes. In all probability, this attitude accounted for his rejection of Brunelleschi's design for the Medici residence, which he evidently found too imposing and ostentatious to be politically wise. Cosimo eventually awarded the commission to MICHELOZZO DI BARTOLOMMEO (1396–1472), a young architect who had been Donatello's collaborator in several sculptural enterprises. Although Cosimo passed over Brunelleschi, his architectural style nevertheless deeply influenced Michelozzo. To a limited extent, the Palazzo Medici (FIG. **16-37**) reflects Brunelleschian principles.

Later bought by the Riccardi family (hence the name Palazzo Medici-Riccardi), who almost doubled the facade's length in the 18th century, the palace, both in its original and extended form, is a simple, massive structure. Heavy *rustication* (rough, unfinished masonry) on the ground floor accentuates its strength. Michelozzo divided the building block into stories of decreasing height by using long, unbroken *stringcourses* (horizontal bands), which give it coherence. *Dressed* (smooth, finished) masonry on the second level and an even smoother surface on the top story modify the severity of the ground floor and make the building appear progressively lighter as the eye moves upward. The extremely heavy *cornice,* which Michelozzo related not to the top story but to the building as a whole, dramatically reverses this effect. Like the ancient Roman cornices that served as Michelozzo's models (compare FIGS. 7-32, 7-40, and 7-44B), the Palazzo Medici-Riccardi cornice is a very effective lid for the structure, clearly and emphatically defining its proportions. Michelozzo perhaps also was inspired by the many extant examples of Roman rusticated masonry, and Roman precedents even exist for the juxtaposition of rusticated and dressed stone masonry on the same facade (FIG. 7-34). However, nothing in the ancient world precisely compares with Michelozzo's design. The Palazzo Medici exemplifies the simultaneous respect for and independence from the antique—features that characterize the Early Renaissance in Italy. The classicism and fortresslike appearance of the palace stand in vivid contrast to the Late Gothic delicacy of the facade (FIG. **16-37A**) of the so-called Ca d'Oro ("House of Gold"), the roughly contemporaneous palace of the wealthy Venetian merchant Marino Contarini. The comparison underscores the marked regional differences between the art and architecture of Florence and Venice (see Chapter 17).

The heart of the Palazzo Medici is an open colonnaded court (FIG. **16-38**) that clearly shows Michelozzo's debt to Brunelleschi. The round-arched colonnade, although more massive in its proportions, closely resembles Brunelleschi's foundling-hospital loggia (FIG. 16-31) and the nave colonnades of Santo Spirito (FIG. 16-32) and San Lorenzo (FIG. 16-32A). The Palazzo Medici's internal court

16-37A Ca d'Oro, Venice, 1421–1437. ◼◀

16-37 MICHELOZZO DI BARTOLOMMEO, east facade of the Palazzo Medici-Riccardi (looking northwest) Florence, Italy, begun 1445. ◼◀

The Medici palace, with its combination of dressed and rusticated masonry and classical moldings, draws heavily on ancient Roman architecture, but Michelozzo creatively reinterpreted his models.

surrounded by an arcade was the first of its kind and influenced a long line of descendants in Renaissance domestic architecture.

LEON BATTISTA ALBERTI Although he entered the profession of architecture rather late in life, LEON BATTISTA ALBERTI (1404–1472) nevertheless made a remarkable contribution to architectural design. He was the first to study seriously the ancient Roman architectural treatise of Vitruvius (see page 167), and his knowledge of it, combined with his own archaeological investigations, made him the first Renaissance architect to understand classical architecture in depth. Alberti's most influential theoretical work, *On the Art of Building* (written about 1450, published in 1486), although inspired by Vitruvius, contains much original material. Alberti advocated a system of ideal proportions and believed the central plan was the ideal form for churches. He also considered incongruous the combination of column and arch, which had persisted since Roman times and throughout the Middle Ages. For Alberti, the arch was a wall opening that should be supported only by a section of wall (a pier), not by an independent sculptural element (a column), as in Brunelleschi and Michelozzo's buildings.

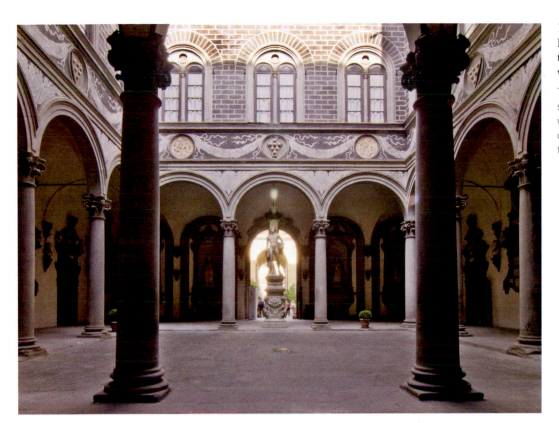

16-38 MICHELOZZO DI BARTOLOMMEO, interior court of the Palazzo Medici-Riccardi (looking west), Florence, Italy, begun 1445. ◼◀

The Medici palace's interior court surrounded by a round-arched colonnade was the first of its kind. The austere design clearly reveals Michelozzo's debt to Brunelleschi (FIG. 16-31).

PALAZZO RUCELLAI Alberti's architectural style represents a scholarly application of classical elements to contemporaneous buildings. He designed the Palazzo Rucellai (FIG. **16-39**) in Florence, although his pupil and collaborator, Bernardo Rossellino (FIG. 16-15), constructed the building using Alberti's plans and sketches. The facade of the palace is much more severe than that of the Palazzo Medici-Riccardi (FIG. 16-37). Pilasters define each story, and a classical cornice crowns the whole. Between the smooth pilasters are subdued and uniform wall surfaces. Alberti created the sense that the structure becomes lighter in weight toward its top by adapting the ancient Roman manner of using different capitals for each story. He chose *Tuscan* (the Etruscan variant of the Greek *Doric order;* FIG. 5-13, *left,* or page xxvi in Volume II) for the ground floor, *Composite* (the Roman combination of *Ionic volutes* with the acanthus leaves of the *Corinthian;* FIG. 5-73) for the second story, and Corinthian for the third floor. Alberti modeled his facade on the most imposing Roman ruin of all, the Colosseum (FIG. 7-37), but he was no slavish copyist. On the Colosseum's facade, the capitals employed are, from the bottom up, Tuscan, Ionic, and Corinthian. Moreover, Alberti adapted the Colosseum's varied surface to a flat facade, which does not allow the deep penetration of the building's mass that is so effective in the Roman structure. By

16-39 LEON BATTISTA ALBERTI and BERNARDO ROSSELLINO, Palazzo Rucellai (looking northwest), Florence, Italy, ca. 1452–1470. ◼◀

Alberti was an ardent student of classical architecture. By adapting the Roman use of different orders for each story, he created the illusion that the Palazzo Rucellai becomes lighter toward its top.

converting his ancient model's *engaged columns* (half-round columns attached to a wall) into shallow pilasters that barely project from the wall, Alberti created a large-meshed linear net. Stretched tightly across the front of his building, it not only unifies the three levels but also emphasizes the wall's flat, two-dimensional qualities.

SANTA MARIA NOVELLA The Rucellai family also commissioned Alberti to design the facade (FIG. **16-40**) of the 13th-century Gothic church of Santa Maria Novella in Florence. Here, Alberti took his cue from a *Romanesque* design—that of the Florentine church of San Miniato al Monte. Following his medieval model, he designed a small, pseudoclassical, pediment-capped temple front for the facade's upper part and supported it with a pilaster-framed arcade incorporating the six tombs and three doorways of the Gothic building. But in the organization of these elements, Alberti applied Renaissance principles. The height of Santa Maria Novella (to the pediment tip) equals its width. Consequently, the entire facade can be inscribed in a square. Throughout the facade, Alberti defined areas and related them to one another in terms of proportions that can be expressed in simple numerical ratios. For example, the upper structure can be encased in a square one-fourth the size of the main square. The cornice separating the two levels divides the major square in half so that the lower portion of the building is a rectangle twice as wide as it is high. In his treatise, Alberti wrote at length about the necessity of employing harmonic proportions to achieve beautiful buildings. Alberti shared this conviction with Brunelleschi, and this fundamental dependence on classically derived mathematics distinguished their architectural work from that of their medieval predecessors. They believed in the eternal and universal validity of numerical ratios as the source of beauty. In this respect, Alberti and Brunelleschi revived the true spirit of the High Classical age of ancient Greece, as epitomized by the architect Iktinos and the sculptor Polykleitos, who produced canons of proportions for the perfect temple and the perfect statue (see "The Perfect Temple," and "Polykleitos's Prescription for the Perfect Statue," Chapter 5, pages 105 and 132). Still, it was not only a desire to emulate Vitruvius and the Greek masters that motivated Alberti to turn to mathematics in his quest for beauty. His contemporary, the Florentine humanist Giannozzo Manetti (1396–1459), had argued that Christianity itself possessed the order and logic of mathematics. In his 1452 treatise, *On the Dignity and Excellence of Man,* Manetti insisted Christian religious truths were as self-evident as mathematical axioms.

The Santa Maria Novella facade was an ingenious solution to a difficult design problem. On one hand, it adequately expressed the organization of the structure attached to it. On the other hand, it subjected preexisting and quintessentially medieval features, such as the large round window on the second level, to a rigid geometrical order that instilled a quality of classical calm and reason. This facade also introduced a feature of great historical consequence—the scrolls that simultaneously unite the broad lower and narrow upper levels and screen the sloping roofs over the aisles. With variations, similar spirals appeared in literally hundreds of church facades throughout the Renaissance and Baroque periods.

GIROLAMO SAVONAROLA In the 1490s, Florence underwent a political, cultural, and religious upheaval. Florentine artists and their fellow citizens responded then not only to humanist ideas but also to the incursion of French armies and especially to the preaching of the Dominican monk Girolamo Savonarola (1452–1498), the reformist priest-dictator who denounced the humanistic secularism of the Medici and their artists, philosophers, and poets. Savonarola exhorted the people of Florence to repent their sins, and when Lorenzo de' Medici died in 1492, the priest prophesied the downfall of the city and of Italy and assumed absolute control of the state. As did a large number of citizens, Savonarola believed the Medici family's political, social, and religious power had corrupted Florence and invited the scourge of foreign invasion. Savonarola encouraged citizens to burn their classical texts, scientific treatises, and philosophical publications. The Medici fled in 1494. Scholars still debate the significance of Savonarola's brief span of power. Apologists for the undoubtedly sincere monk deny his actions played a role in the decline of Florentine culture at the end of the 15th century. But the puritanical spirit that moved Savonarola must have dampened considerably the enthusiasm for classical antiquity of the Florentine Early Renaissance. Certainly, Savonarola's condemnation of humanism as heretical nonsense, and his banishing of the Medici, Tornabuoni, and other wealthy families from Florence, deprived local artists of some of their major patrons, at least in the short term. There were, however, commissions aplenty for artists elsewhere in Italy.

16-40 LEON BATTISTA ALBERTI, west facade of Santa Maria Novella, Florence, Italy, 1456–1470. ◼◀

Alberti's design for the facade of this Gothic church features a pediment-capped temple front and pilaster-framed arcades. Numerical ratios are the basis of the proportions of all parts of the facade.

16-41 PERUGINO, *Christ Delivering the Keys of the Kingdom to Saint Peter*, Sistine Chapel, Vatican, Rome, Italy, 1481–1483. Fresco, 11′ 5½″ × 18′ 8½″.

Painted for the Vatican, this fresco depicts the event on which the papacy bases its authority. The converging lines of the pavement connect the action in the foreground with the background.

THE PRINCELY COURTS

Although Florentine artists led the way in creating the Renaissance in art and architecture, the arts flourished throughout Italy in the 15th century. The princely courts in Rome, Urbino, Mantua, and elsewhere also deserve credit for nurturing Renaissance art (see "Italian Princely Courts and Artistic Patronage," page 479). Whether the "prince" was a duke, condottiere, or pope, the considerable wealth the heads of these courts possessed, coupled with their desire for recognition, fame, and power, resulted in major art commissions.

Rome and the Papal States

Although not a secular ruler, the pope in Rome was the head of a court with enormous wealth at his disposal. In the 16th and 17th centuries, the popes became the major patrons of art and architecture in Italy (see Chapters 17 and 19), but even during the Quattrocento, the papacy was the source of some significant artistic commissions.

PERUGINO Between 1481 and 1483, Pope Sixtus IV (r. 1471–1484) summoned a group of artists to Rome to decorate the walls of the newly completed Sistine Chapel (MAP 17-1 and FIG. 17-1). Among the artists the pope employed were Botticelli, Ghirlandaio, and Pietro Vannucci, known as PERUGINO (ca. 1450–1523) because his birthplace was Perugia in Umbria. The project followed immediately the completion of the new Vatican library, which the pope also or-

dered decorated with frescoes by MELOZZO DA FORLÌ (1438–1494; FIG. **16-41A**) and others. Perugino's contribution to the Sistine Chapel fresco cycle was *Christ Delivering the Keys of the Kingdom to Saint Peter* (FIG. **16-41**). The papacy had, from the beginning, based its claim to infallible and total authority over the Roman Catholic Church on this biblical event, and therefore the subject was one of obvious appeal to Sixtus IV. In Perugino's fresco, Christ

16-41A MELOZZO DA FORLÌ, *Sixtus IV Confirming Platina*, ca. 1477–1481.

hands the keys to Saint Peter, who stands amid an imaginary gathering of the 12 apostles and Renaissance contemporaries. These figures occupy the apron of a great stage space that extends into the distance to a point of convergence in the doorway of a central-plan temple. (Perugino used parallel and converging lines in the pavement to mark off the intervening space; compare FIGS. 16-10 and 16-11.) Figures in the middle distance complement the near group, emphasizing its density and order by their scattered arrangement. At the corners of the great piazza, duplicate triumphal arches serve as the base angles of a distant compositional triangle whose apex is in the central building. Perugino modeled the arches closely on the Arch of Constantine (FIG. 7-75) in Rome. Although an anachronism in a painting depicting a scene from Christ's life, the arches served to underscore the close ties between Saint Peter and Constantine, the first Christian emperor of Rome and builder of the great basilica (FIG. 8-9)

16-42 LUCA SIGNORELLI, *The Damned Cast into Hell,* San Brizio chapel, Orvieto Cathedral, Orvieto, Italy, 1499–1504. Fresco, 23′ wide. 🎥

Few figure compositions of the 15th century have the same psychic impact as Signorelli's fresco of writhing, foreshortened muscular bodies tortured by demons in Hell.

1 ft.

over Saint Peter's tomb. Christ and Peter flank the triangle's central axis, which runs through the temple's doorway, the vanishing point of Perugino's perspective scheme. Brunelleschi's new spatial science allowed the Umbrian artist to organize the action systematically. The composition interlocks both two-dimensional and three-dimensional space, and the placement of central actors emphasizes the axial center.

LUCA SIGNORELLI Another Umbrian painter Sixtus IV employed for the decoration of the Sistine Chapel was LUCA SIGNORELLI (ca. 1445–1523), in whose work the fiery passion of Savonarola's sermons found its pictorial equal. Signorelli further developed Pollaiuolo's interest in the depiction of muscular bodies in violent action in a wide variety of poses and foreshortenings. In the San Brizio chapel in the cathedral of the papal city of Orvieto (MAP 14-1), Signorelli painted for Pope Alexander VI (r. 1492–1503) scenes depicting the end of the world, including *The Damned Cast into Hell* (FIG. **16-42**). Few Quattrocento figure compositions equal Signorelli's in psychic impact. Saint Michael and the hosts of Heaven hurl the damned into Hell, where, in a dense, writhing mass, they are vigorously tortured by demons, some winged. The horrible consequences of a sinful life had not been so graphically depicted since Gislebertus carved his vision of *Last Judgment* (FIG. 12-1) in the west *tympanum* of Saint-Lazare at Autun around 1130. The figures—nude, lean, and muscular—assume every conceivable posture of anguish. Signorelli was a master both of foreshortening the human figure and depicting bodies in violent movement. Although each figure is clearly a study from a model, Signorelli incorporated the individual studies into a convincing and coherent narrative composition. Terror and rage pass like storms through the wrenched and twisted bodies. The fiends, their hair flaming and their bodies the color of putrefying flesh, lunge at their victims in ferocious frenzy.

Urbino

Under the patronage of Federico da Montefeltro (1422–1482), Urbino, southeast of Florence across the Apennines (MAP 14-1), became an important center of Renaissance art and culture. In fact, the humanist writer Paolo Cortese (1465–1540) described Federico as one of the two greatest artistic patrons of the 15th century (the other was Cosimo de' Medici). Federico was a condottiere so renowned for his military expertise that he was in demand by popes and kings, and soldiers came from across Europe to study under his direction.

PIERO DELLA FRANCESCA One of the artists who received several commissions from Federico was Piero della Francesca, who had already established a major reputation in his native Tuscany. At the Urbino court, Piero produced both official portraits and religious works for Federico, among them a double portrait (FIG. **16-43**) of the count and his second wife, Battista Sforza (1446–1472), and the *Brera Altarpiece* (FIG. **16-43A**), in which Federico kneels before the enthroned Madonna and saints.

16-43A PIERO DELLA FRANCESCA, *Brera Altarpiece,* ca. 1472–1474.

Federico de Montefeltro married Battista Sforza in 1460 when she was 14 years old. The daughter of Alessandro Sforza (1409–1473), lord of Pesaro and brother of the duke of Milan, Battista was a well-educated humanist who proved to be an excellent administrator of Federico's territories during his frequent military campaigns. She gave birth to eight daughters in 11 years and finally, on January 25, 1472, to the male heir for which the couple had prayed. When the countess died of pneumonia five months later at age 26, Federico went into mourning for virtually the rest of his life. He never remarried.

Italian Princely Courts and Artistic Patronage

During the Renaissance, the absence of a single sovereign ruling all of Italy and the fragmented nature of the independent city-states (MAP 14-1) provided a fertile breeding ground for the ambitions of power-hungry elites. In the 15th century, princely courts proliferated throughout the peninsula. A prince was in essence the lord of a territory, and, despite this generic title, he could have been a duke, marquis, count, cardinal, pope, or condottiere. At this time, major princely courts emerged in papal Rome (FIGS. 16-41, 16-41A, and 16-42), Milan, Naples, Ferrara, Savoy, Urbino (FIGS. 16-43, 16-43A, and 16-44), and Mantua (FIGS. 16-45 to 16-50). Rather than denoting a specific organizational structure or physical entity, the term *princely court* refers to a power relationship between the prince and the territory's inhabitants based on imperial models. Each prince worked tirelessly to preserve and extend his control and authority, seeking to establish a societal framework of people who looked to him for employment, favors, protection, prestige, and leadership. The importance of these princely courts derived from their role as centers of power and culture.

The efficient functioning of a princely court required a sophisticated administrative structure. Each prince employed an extensive household staff, ranging from counts, nobles, cooks, waiters, stewards, footmen, stable hands, and ladies-in-waiting to dog handlers, leopard keepers, pages, and runners. The duke of Milan had more than 40 chamberlains to attend to his personal needs alone. Each prince also needed an elaborate bureaucracy to oversee political, economic, and military operations and to ensure his continued control. These officials included secretaries, lawyers, captains, ambassadors, and condottieri. Burgeoning international diplomacy and trade made each prince the center of an active and privileged sphere. Their domains extended to the realm of culture, for they saw themselves as more than political, military, and economic leaders. As the wealthiest individuals in their regions, princes possessed the means to commission numerous artworks and buildings. Art functioned in several capacities in the princely courts—as evidence of princely sophistication and culture, as a form of prestige or commemoration, as propaganda, as a demonstration of wealth—in addition to being a source of visual pleasure.

Princes often researched in advance the reputations and styles of the artists and architects they commissioned. Such assurances of excellence were necessary, because the quality of the work reflected not solely on the artist but on the patron as well. Yet despite the importance of individual style, princes sought artists who also were willing, at times, to subordinate their personal styles to work collaboratively on large-scale projects.

Princes bestowed on selected individuals the title of "court artist." Serving as a court artist had its benefits, among them a guaranteed salary (not always forthcoming), living quarters in the palace, liberation from guild restrictions, and, on occasion, status as a member of the prince's inner circle, perhaps even a knighthood. For artists struggling to elevate their profession from the ranks of craftspeople, working for a prince presented a marvelous opportunity. Until the 16th century, artists had limited status, and people considered them in the same class as small shopkeepers and petty merchants. Indeed, at court dinners, artists most often sat with the other members of the salaried household: tailors, cobblers, barbers, and upholsterers. Thus, the possibility of advancement was a powerful and constant incentive.

Princes demanded a great deal from court artists. Artists not only created the frescoes, portraits, and sculptures that have become their legacies but also designed tapestries, seat covers, costumes, masks, and decorations for various court festivities. Because princes constantly received ambassadors and dignitaries and needed to maintain a high profile to reinforce their authority, lavish social functions were the norm. Artists often created gifts for visiting nobles and potentates. Recipients judged these gifts on the quality of both the work and the materials. By using expensive materials—gold leaf, silver leaf, lapis lazuli (a rich azure-blue stone imported from Afghanistan), silk, and velvet brocade—and employing the best artists, princes could impress others with their wealth and good taste.

1 ft.

16-43 PIERO DELLA FRANCESCA, *Battista Sforza and Federico da Montefeltro,* ca. 1472–1474. Oil and tempera on wood in modern frame, each panel 1' 6½" × 1' 1". Galleria degli Uffizi, Florence. 🎞️◀

Piero's portraits of Federico da Montefeltro and his recently deceased wife combine the profile views on Roman coins with the landscape backgrounds of Flemish portraiture (FIG. 15-14).

Federico commissioned Piero della Francesca to paint their double portrait shortly after Battista's death to pay tribute to her and to have a memento of their marriage. The present frame is a 19th-century addition. Originally, the two portraits formed a hinged diptych. The format—two bust-length portraits with a landscape background—follows Flemish models, such as the portraits by Hans Memling (FIGS. 15-14 and 15-14A), as does Piero's use of oil-based pigment (see "Tempera and Oil Painting," Chapter 15, page 427). Piero would have been familiar with northern European developments because Federico employed Flemish painters at his court. But Piero depicted the Urbino count and countess in profile, in part to emulate the profile portraits of Roman rulers on coins (FIG. 7-81, *left*) that Renaissance humanists avidly collected, and in part to conceal the disfigured right side of Federico's face. (He lost his right eye and part of the bridge of his nose in a tournament in 1450.) That injury also explains why Federico is on the right in left profile (compare FIG. 16-43A). Roman coins normally show the emperor in right profile, and Renaissance marriage portraits almost always place the husband at the viewer's left.

Piero probably based Battista's portrait on her death mask, and the pallor of her skin may be a reference to her death. Latin inscriptions on the reverse of the two portraits refer to Federico in the present tense and to Battista in the past tense, confirming the posthumous date of her portrait. The backs of the panels also bear paintings. They represent Federico and Battista in triumphal chariots accompanied by personifications of their respective virtues, including Justice, Prudence, and Fortitude (Federico) and Faith, Charity, and Chastity (Battista). The placement of scenes of triumph on the reverse of profile portraits also emulates ancient Roman coinage.

FLAGELLATION Piero may also have painted his most enigmatic work, *Flagellation* (FIG. 16-44), for Federico da Montefeltro. The setting for the passion drama is the portico of Pontius Pilate's palace in Jerusalem. Curiously, the focus of the composition is not Jesus but the group of three large figures in the foreground, whose identity scholars still debate. Some have described the bearded figure as a Turk and interpreted the painting as a commentary on the capture in 1453 of Christian Constantinople by the Muslims (see Chapter 9). Other scholars, however, identify the three men as biblical figures, including King David, one of whose psalms Christian theologians believed predicted the conspiracy against Jesus. In any case, the three men appear to discuss the event in the background. As Pilate, the seated judge, watches, Jesus, bound to a column topped

16-44 PIERO DELLA FRANCESCA, *Flagellation*, ca. 1455–1465. Oil and tempera on wood, 1′ 11$\frac{1}{8}$″ × 2′ 8$\frac{1}{4}$″. Galleria Nazionale delle Marche, Urbino.

In this enigmatic painting, the three unidentified foreground figures appear to be discussing the biblical tragedy taking place in Pilate's palace, which Piero rendered in perfect perspective.

16-45 LEON BATTISTA ALBERTI, west facade of Sant'Andrea, Mantua, Italy, designed 1470, begun 1472.

Alberti's design for Sant'Andrea reflects his study of ancient Roman architecture. Employing a colossal order, the architect combined a triumphal arch and a Roman temple front with pediment.

16-46 LEON BATTISTA ALBERTI, plan of Sant'Andrea, Mantua, Italy, designed 1470, begun 1472.

In his architectural treatise, Alberti criticized the traditional basilican plan as impractical. He designed Sant'Andrea as a single huge hall with independent chapels branching off at right angles.

16-47 LEON BATTISTA ALBERTI, interior of Sant'Andrea (looking east), Mantua, Italy, designed 1470, begun 1472.

For the nave of Sant'Andrea, Alberti abandoned the medieval columnar arcade. The tremendous vaults suggest that Constantine's Basilica Nova (FIG. 7-78) in Rome may have served as a prototype.

by a classical statue, is about to be whipped. Piero's perspective is so meticulous the floor pattern can be reconstructed perfectly as a central porphyry (purple marble) circle with surrounding squares composed of various geometric shapes. Whatever the solution to the iconographical puzzle of Piero's *Flagellation,* the small wood panel reveals a mind cultivated by mathematics. The careful delineation of architecture suggests an architect's vision, certainly that of a man entirely familiar with compass and ruler. Piero planned his compositions almost entirely by his sense of the exact and lucid structures defined by mathematics. He believed the highest beauty resides in forms that have the clarity and purity of geometric figures. Toward the end of his long career, Piero, a skilled geometrician, wrote the first theoretical treatise on systematic perspective, after having practiced the art with supreme mastery for almost a lifetime. His association with the architect Leon Battista Alberti at Ferrara and at Rimini (FIGS. 16-46 and 16-47) around 1450–1451 probably turned his attention fully to perspective (a science in which Alberti was an influential pioneer; see page 454) and helped determine his later, characteristically architectonic compositions. This approach appealed to Federico, a patron fascinated by architectural space and its depiction.

Mantua

Marquis Ludovico Gonzaga (1412–1478) ruled the court of Mantua in northeastern Italy (MAP 14-1) during the mid-15th century. A famed condottiere like Federico de Montefeltro, Gonzaga established his reputation as a fierce military leader while general of the

Milanese armies. The visit of Pope Pius II (r. 1458–1464) to Mantua in 1459 stimulated the marquis's determination to transform his city into one all Italy would envy.

SANT'ANDREA One of the major projects Gonzaga instituted was the redesign and replacement of the 11th-century church of Sant'Andrea (FIGS. **16-45** to **16-47**). Gonzaga turned to the renowned architect Leon Battista Alberti (FIGS. 16-39 and 16-40) for

16-48 ANDREA MANTEGNA, *interior of the Camera Picta (Painted Chamber), Palazzo Ducale, Mantua, Italy,* 1465–1474. Fresco.

Working for Ludovico Gonzaga, who established Mantua as a great art city, Mantegna produced for the duke's palace the first completely consistent, illusionistic decoration of an entire room.

this important commission. The facade (FIG. 16-45) Alberti designed incorporated two major ancient Roman architectural motifs—the temple front and the triumphal arch. The combination was already a familiar feature of Roman buildings still standing in Italy. For example, many triumphal arches, including an Augustan (late first century BCE) arch at Rimini on Italy's northeast coast, feature a pediment over the arcuated passageway and engaged columns, but there is no close parallel in antiquity for Alberti's eclectic and ingenious design. The Renaissance architect's concern for proportion led him to equalize the vertical and horizontal dimensions of the facade, which left it considerably shorter than the church behind it. Because of the primary importance of visual appeal, many Renaissance architects made this concession not only to the demands of a purely visual proportionality in the facade but also to the facade's relation to the small square in front of it, even at the expense of continuity with the body of the building. Yet structural correspondences to the building do exist in Sant'Andrea's facade. The pilasters are the same height as those on the nave's interior walls, and the large barrel vault over the central portal, with smaller barrel vaults branching off at right angles, introduces on a smaller scale the arrangement of the church's nave and chapels (FIGS. 16-46 and 16-47). The facade pilasters, as part of the wall, run uninterrupted through three stories in an early application of the *colossal* or *giant order* that became a favorite motif of Michelangelo (see Chapter 17).

The tremendous vaults in the interior of Sant'Andrea suggest Alberti's model may have been Constantine's Basilica Nova (FIG. 7-78) in Rome—erroneously thought in the Middle Ages and Renaissance to be a Roman temple. Consistent with his belief that arches should not be used with freestanding columns, Alberti abandoned the medieval columnar arcade Brunelleschi still used in Santo Spirito (FIG. 16-32) and San Lorenzo (FIG. 16-32A). Thick walls alternating with vaulted chapels, interrupted by a massive dome over the *crossing,* support the huge coffered barrel vault. Because FILIPPO JUVARA (1678–1736) added the present dome in the 18th century, the effect may be somewhat different from what Alberti planned. Regardless, the vault calls to mind the vast interior spaces and dense enclosing masses of Roman architecture. In his treatise, Alberti criticized the traditional basilican plan (with continuous aisles flanking the central nave) as impractical because the colonnades conceal the ceremonies from the faithful in the aisles. For this reason, he designed a single huge hall (FIG. 16-47) with independent chapels branching off at right angles (FIG. 16-46). This break with a Christian building tradition that had endured for a thousand years was extremely influential in later Renaissance and Baroque church planning.

ANDREA MANTEGNA Like other princes, Ludovico Gonzaga believed an impressive palace was an important visual expression of his authority. One of the most spectacular rooms in the

1 ft.

16-49 ANDREA MANTEGNA, ceiling of the Camera Picta (Painted Chamber), Palazzo Ducale, Mantua, Italy, 1465–1474. Fresco, 8′ 9″ in diameter. ◼◀

Inside the Camera Picta, the viewer becomes the viewed as figures gaze into the room from a painted oculus opening onto a blue sky. This is the first perspective view of a ceiling from below.

Palazzo Ducale (ducal palace) is the duke's bedchamber and audience hall, the so-called Camera degli Sposi ("Room of the Newlyweds"), originally the Camera Picta ("Painted Room"; FIGS. **16-48** and **16-49**). ANDREA MANTEGNA (ca. 1431–1506) of Padua took almost nine years to complete the extensive fresco program in which he sought to aggrandize Ludovico Gonzaga and his family. The particulars of each scene are still a matter of scholarly debate, but any viewer standing in the Camera Picta surrounded by the spectacle and majesty of courtly life cannot help but be thoroughly impressed by both the commanding presence and elevated status of the patron and the dazzling artistic skills of Mantegna.

In the Camera Picta, Mantegna performed a triumphant feat by producing the first completely consistent illusionistic decoration of an entire room. By integrating real and painted architectural elements, Mantegna illusionistically dissolved the room's walls in a manner foretelling 17th-century Baroque decoration (see Chapter 19). The Camera Picta recalls the efforts of Italian painters more than 15 centuries earlier at Pompeii and elsewhere to merge mural painting and architecture in frescoes of the so-called Second Style of Roman painting (FIGS. 7-18 and 7-19). Mantegna's *trompe l'oeil* (French, "deceives the eye") design, however, went far beyond

anything preserved from ancient Italy. The Renaissance painter's daring experimentalism led him to complete the room's decoration with the first perspective of a ceiling (FIG. 16-49) seen from below (called, in Italian, *di sotto in sù*, "from below upward"). Baroque ceiling decorators later broadly developed this technique. Inside the Camera Picta, the viewer becomes the viewed as figures look down into the room from the painted *oculus* ("eye"). Seen against the convincing illusion of a cloud-filled blue sky, several putti, strongly foreshortened, set the amorous mood of the Room of the Newlyweds, as the painted spectators (who are not identified) smile down on the scene. The prominent peacock, perched precariously as if ready to swoop down into the room, is an attribute of Juno, Jupiter's bride, who oversees lawful marriages. This brilliant feat of illusionism is the climax of decades of experimentation with perspective representation by numerous Quattrocento artists as well as by Mantegna himself—for example, in his frescoes (FIG. **16-49A**) in the Church of the Eremitani in Padua.

16-49A MANTEGNA, *Saint James Led to Martyrdom,* 1454–1457.

1 in.

16-50 ANDREA MANTEGNA, *Foreshortened Christ* (*Lamentation over the Dead Christ*), ca. 1500. Tempera on canvas, 2′ 2¾″ × 2′ 7⅞″. Pinacoteca di Brera, Milan. ◼◀

In this work of overwhelming emotional power, Mantegna presented both a harrowing study of a strongly foreshortened cadaver and an intensely poignant depiction of a biblical tragedy.

FORESHORTENED CHRIST One of Mantegna's later paintings (FIG. **16-50**) is another example of the artist's mastery of perspective. In fact, Mantegna seems to have set up for himself difficult problems in perspective simply for the joy he took in solving them. The painting often called *Lamentation over the Dead Christ,* but recorded under the name *Foreshortened Christ* at the time of Mantegna's death, is a work of overwhelming power. At first glance, as its 16th-century title implies, this painting seems to be a strikingly realistic study in foreshortening. Careful scrutiny, however, reveals Mantegna reduced the size of Christ's feet,

which, as he clearly knew, would cover much of the body if properly represented according to the rules of perspective, in which the closest objects, people, or body parts are the largest. Thus, tempering naturalism with artistic license, Mantegna presented both a harrowing study of a strongly foreshortened cadaver and an intensely poignant depiction of a biblical tragedy. The painter's harsh, sharp line seems to cut the surface as if it were metal and conveys, by its grinding edge, the theme's corrosive emotion. Remarkably, in the supremely gifted hands of Mantegna, all of Quattrocento science here serves the purpose of devotion.

THE RENAISSANCE IN QUATTROCENTO ITALY

FLORENCE

▮ The fortunate congruence of artistic genius, the spread of humanism, and economic prosperity nourished the flowering of the new artistic culture historians call the Renaissance—the rebirth of classical values in art and life. The greatest center of Renaissance art in the 15th century was Florence, home of the powerful Medici, who were among the most ambitious art patrons in history.

▮ Some of the earliest examples of the new Renaissance style in sculpture are the statues Nanni di Banco and Donatello made for Or San Michele. Donatello's *Saint Mark* reintroduced the classical concept of contrapposto into Renaissance statuary. His later *David* was the first nude male statue since antiquity. Donatello was also a pioneer in relief sculpture, the first to incorporate the principles of linear and atmospheric perspective, devices also employed brilliantly by Lorenzo Ghiberti in his *Gates of Paradise* for the Florentine baptistery.

▮ The Renaissance interest in classical culture naturally also led to the revival of Greco-Roman mythological themes in art, for example, Antonio del Pollaiuolo's *Hercules and Antaeus,* and to the revival of equestrian portraits, such as Donatello's *Gattamelata* and Andrea del Verrocchio's *Bartolommeo Colleoni*.

▮ Although some painters continued to work in the Late Gothic International Style, others broke fresh ground by exploring new modes of representation. Masaccio's figures recall Giotto's, but have a greater psychological and physical credibility, and the light shining on Masaccio's figures comes from a source outside the picture. His *Holy Trinity* epitomizes Early Renaissance painting in its convincing illusionism, achieved through Filippo Brunelleschi's new science of linear perspective, yet it remains effective as a devotional painting in a church setting.

▮ The secular side of Quattrocento Italian painting is on display in historical works, such as Paolo Uccello's *Battle of San Romano* and Domenico Ghirlandaio's portrait *Giovanna Tornabuoni*. The humanist love of classical themes comes to the fore in the works of Sandro Botticelli, whose lyrical *Primavera* and *Birth of Venus* were inspired by poetry and Neo-Platonic philosophy.

▮ Italian architects also revived the classical style. Brunelleschi's Ospedale degli Innocenti showcases the clarity and Roman-inspired rationality of 15th-century Florentine architecture. The model for Leon Battista Alberti's influential 1450 treatise *On the Art of Building* was a similar work by the ancient Roman architect Vitruvius.

Donatello, *David,* ca. 1440–1460

Masaccio, *Holy Trinity,* ca. 1424–1427

Brunelleschi, Ospedale degli Innocenti, begun 1419

THE PRINCELY COURTS

▮ Although Florentine artists led the way in creating the Renaissance in art and architecture, the papacy in Rome and the princely courts in Urbino, Mantua, and elsewhere also were major art patrons.

▮ Among the important papal commissions of the Quattrocento was the decoration of the walls of the Sistine Chapel with frescoes, including Perugino's *Christ Delivering the Keys of the Kingdom to Saint Peter,* a prime example of linear perspective.

▮ Under the patronage of Federico da Montefeltro, Urbino became a major center of Renaissance art and culture. The leading painter in Federico's employ was Piero della Francesca, a master of color and light and the author of the first theoretical treatise on perspective.

▮ Mantua became an important art center under Marquis Ludovico Gonzaga, who commissioned Alberti to rebuild the church of Sant'Andrea. Alberti applied the principles he developed in his architectural treatise to the project and freely adapted forms from Roman religious and civic architecture.

▮ Gonzaga hired Andrea Mantegna to decorate the Camera Picta of the ducal palace, in which the painter produced the first completely consistent illusionistic decoration of an entire room.

Piero della Francesca, *Battista Sforza and Federico da Montefeltro,* 1472–1474

Alberti, Sant'Andrea, Mantua, 1470

Michelangelo, the Renaissance genius who was primarily a sculptor, reluctantly spent almost four years painting the ceiling of the Sistine Chapel under commission from Pope Julius II.

Michelangelo's retelling of the biblical narrative often departed from traditional iconography. In one panel he combined *Temptation* and *Expulsion*, suggesting God's swift punishment for original sin.

The fresco cycle illustrates the creation and fall of humankind as related in Genesis. Michelangelo always painted with a sculptor's eye. His heroic figures resemble painted statues.

17-1 Interior of the Sistine Chapel (looking west), Vatican City, Rome, Italy, built 1473; ceiling and altar wall frescoes by MICHELANGELO BUONARROTI, 1508–1512 and 1536–1541, respectively. ◼◂

Michelangelo completed his fresco cycle in the Sistine Chapel for another pope—Paul III—with this terrifying vision of the fate awaiting sinners at the *Last Judgment.* It includes his self-portrait.

17

RENAISSANCE AND MANNERISM IN CINQUECENTO ITALY

MICHELANGELO IN THE SERVICE OF JULIUS II

Michelangelo Buonarroti (1475–1564) was the first artist in history whose prodigious talent and brooding personality matched today's image of the temperamental artistic genius. His self-imposed isolation, creative furies, proud independence, and daring innovations led Italians of his era to speak of the charismatic personality of the man and the expressive character of his works in one word—*terribilità,* the sublime shadowed by the awesome and the fearful. Yet, unlike most modern artists, who create works in their studios and offer them for sale later, Michelangelo and his contemporaries produced most of their paintings and sculptures under contract for wealthy patrons who dictated the content—and sometimes the form—of their artworks.

In Italy in the 1500s—the *Cinquecento*—the greatest art patron was the Catholic Church headed by the pope in Rome. Michelangelo's most famous work today—the ceiling of the Sistine Chapel (FIG. **17-1**) in the Vatican palace (MAPS **17-1** and 19-1)—was, in fact, a commission he did not want. His patron was Julius II (r. 1503–1513), an immensely ambitious man who sought to extend his spiritual authority into the temporal realm, as other medieval and Renaissance popes had done. Julius selected his name to associate himself with Julius Caesar and found inspiration in ancient Rome. His enthusiasm for engaging in battle earned Julius the designation "warrior-pope," but his ten-year papacy was most notable for his patronage of the arts. He understood well the propagandistic value of visual imagery and upon his election immediately commissioned artworks that would present an authoritative image of his rule and reinforce the primacy of the Catholic Church.

When Julius asked Michelangelo to take on the challenge of providing frescoes for the ceiling of the Sistine Chapel, the artist insisted painting was not his profession (a protest that rings hollow after the fact, but Michelangelo's major works until then had been in sculpture). The artist had no choice, however, but to accept the pope's assignment.

In the Sistine Chapel frescoes, as in his sculpture, Michelangelo relentlessly concentrated his expressive purpose on the human figure. To him, the body was beautiful not only in its natural form but also in its spiritual and philosophical significance. The body was the manifestation of the character of the soul. In the *Creation of Adam, Temptation and Expulsion*, and *Last Judgment* frescoes, Michelangelo represented the body in its most elemental aspect—in the nude or simply draped, with no background and no ornamental embellishment. He always painted with a sculptor's eye for how light and shadow reveal volume and surface. It is no coincidence that many of the figures in the Sistine Chapel seem to be painted statues.

HIGH AND LATE RENAISSANCE

The art and architecture of 16th-century Italy built on the foundation of the Early Renaissance of the 15th century, but no single artistic style characterized Italian 16th-century art, and regional differences abounded, especially between central Italy (Florence and Rome) and Venice. The period opened with the brief era art historians call the High Renaissance—the quarter century between 1495 and the deaths of Leonardo da Vinci in 1519 and Raphael in 1520. The Renaissance style and the interest in classical culture, perspective, proportion, and human anatomy dominated the remainder of the 16th century (the Late Renaissance), but a new style, called Mannerism, challenged Renaissance naturalism almost as soon as Raphael had been laid to rest (inside the ancient Roman Pantheon, FIG. 7-51). The one constant in Cinquecento Italy is the astounding quality, both technical and aesthetic, of the art and architecture produced.

Indeed, the modern notion of the "fine arts" and the exaltation of the artist-genius originated in Renaissance Italy. Humanist scholars and art patrons alike eagerly adopted the ancient Greek philosopher Plato's view of the nature of poetry and of artistic creation in general: "All good poets . . . compose their beautiful poems not by art, but because they are inspired and possessed. . . . For not by art does the poet sing, but by power divine."[1] In Cinquecento Italy, the pictorial arts achieved the high status formerly held only by poetry. During the High Renaissance, artists first became international celebrities, none more so than Leonardo da Vinci, Raphael, and Michelangelo.

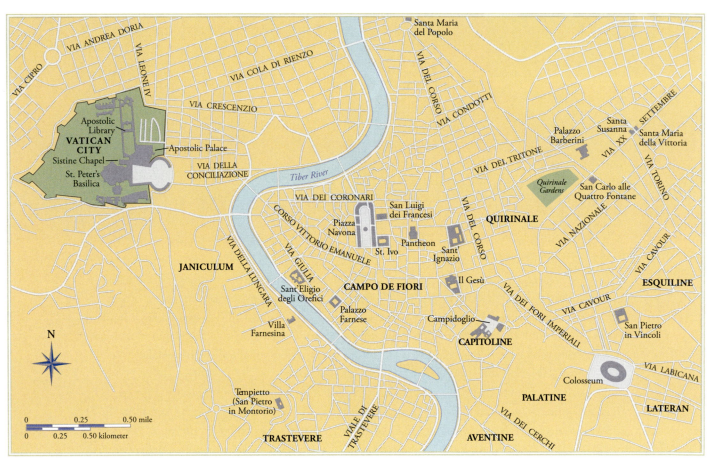

MAP 17-1 Rome with Renaissance and Baroque monuments.

RENAISSANCE AND MANNERISM IN CINQUECENTO ITALY

1495	1520	1550	1575	1600
▍Leonardo da Vinci paints *Last Supper* in Milan and *Mona Lisa* in Florence ▍High Renaissance art emerges in Rome under Pope Julius II ▍Raphael paints *School of Athens* for the papal apartments ▍Michelangelo carves *David* for the Palazzo della Signoria in Florence and paints the ceiling of the Sistine Chapel in Rome	▍Paul III launches the Counter-Reformation ▍Michelangelo paints *Last Judgment* in the Sistine Chapel ▍In Venice, Titian uses rich colors and establishes oil on canvas as the preferred medium of Western painting ▍Mannerism emerges as an alternative to High Renaissance style in the work of Pontormo, Parmigianino, Bronzino, and Giulio Romano	▍Council of Trent defends religious art ▍Andrea Palladio becomes chief architect of the Venetian Republic ▍Giorgio Vasari publishes *Lives of the Most Eminent Painters, Sculptors, and Architects*	▍Tintoretto is the leading Venetian Mannerist painter ▍Veronese creates a huge illusionistic ceiling painting for the Doge's Palace ▍Giovanni da Bologna uses spiral compositions for Mannerist statuary groups ▍Construction of Il Gesù in Rome	

Leonardo da Vinci

Born in the small town of Vinci, near Florence, LEONARDO DA VINCI (1452–1519) trained in the studio of Andrea del Verrocchio (FIGS. 16-13 and 16-17). The quintessential "Renaissance man," Leonardo possessed unequaled talent and an unbridled imagination. Art was but one of his innumerable interests, the scope and depth of which were without precedent. His unquenchable curiosity is evident in the voluminous notes he interspersed with sketches in his notebooks dealing with botany, geology, geography, cartography, zoology, military engineering, animal lore, anatomy, and aspects of physical science, including hydraulics and mechanics. Leonardo stated repeatedly that his scientific investigations made him a better painter. That is undoubtedly the case. For example, Leonardo's in-depth exploration of optics provided him with a thorough understanding of perspective, light, and color. Leonardo was a true artist-scientist. Indeed, his scientific drawings (FIG. 17-6) are themselves artworks.

Leonardo's great ambition in his painting, as well as in his scientific endeavors, was to discover the laws underlying the processes and flux of nature. With this end in mind, he also studied the human body and contributed immeasurably to the fields of physiology and psychology. Leonardo believed reality in an absolute sense is inaccessible and humans can know it only through its changing images. He considered the eyes the most vital organs and sight the most essential function. Better to be deaf than blind, he argued, because through the eyes, individuals can grasp reality most directly and profoundly.

LEONARDO IN MILAN Around 1481, Leonardo left Florence after offering his services to Ludovico Sforza (1451–1508), the son and heir apparent of the ruler of Milan. The political situation in Florence was uncertain, and Leonardo may have felt his particular skills would be in greater demand in Milan, providing him with the opportunity for increased financial security. He devoted most of a letter to Ludovico to advertising his competence and his qualifications as a military engineer, mentioning only at the end his abilities as a painter and sculptor. The letter illustrates the relationship between Renaissance artists and their patrons (see "Michelangelo in the Service of Julius II," page 487) as well as Leonardo's breadth of competence. That he should select expertise in military engineering as his primary attraction for the Sforzas is an index of the period's instability.

> And in short, according to the variety of cases, I can contrive various and endless means of offence and defence. . . . In time of peace I believe I can give perfect satisfaction and to the equal of any other in architecture and the composition of buildings, public and private; and in guiding water from one place to another. . . . I can carry out sculpture in marble, bronze, or clay, and also I can do in painting whatever may be done, as well as any other, be he whom he may.[2]

Ludovico accepted Leonardo's offer, and the Florentine artist remained in Milan for almost 20 years.

MADONNA OF THE ROCKS Shortly after settling in Milan, Leonardo painted *Madonna of the Rocks* (FIG. 17-2) as the central panel of an altarpiece for the chapel of the Confraternity of the Immaculate Conception in San Francesco Grande. The painting builds on Masaccio's understanding and usage of chiaroscuro, the subtle play of light and dark. Modeling with light and shadow and expressing emotional states were, for Leonardo, the heart of painting:

> A good painter has two chief objects to paint—man and the intention of his soul. The former is easy, the latter hard, for it must be

17-2 LEONARDO DA VINCI, *Madonna of the Rocks,* from San Francesco Grande, Milan, Italy, begun 1483. Oil on wood (transferred to canvas), 6′ 6½″ × 4′. Musée du Louvre, Paris. ◼◀

Leonardo used gestures and a pyramidal composition to unite the Virgin, John the Baptist, the Christ Child, and an angel in this work, in which the figures share the same light-infused environment.

expressed by gestures and the movement of the limbs. . . . A painting will only be wonderful for the beholder by making that which is not so appear raised and detached from the wall.[3]

Leonardo presented the figures in *Madonna of the Rocks* in a pyramidal grouping and, more notably, as sharing the same environment. This groundbreaking achievement—the unified representation of objects in an atmospheric setting—was a manifestation of his scientific curiosity about the invisible substance surrounding things. The Madonna, Christ Child, infant John the Baptist, and angel emerge through nuances of light and shade from the half-light of the cavernous visionary landscape. Light simultaneously veils and reveals the forms, immersing them in a layer of atmosphere. Leonardo's effective use of atmospheric perspective is the result in large part of his mastery of the relatively new medium of oil painting, which had previously been used mostly by northern European painters (see "Tempera and Oil Painting," Chapter 15, page 427). The four figures pray, point, and bless, and these acts and

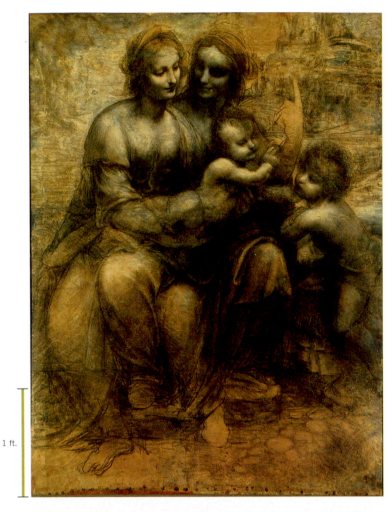

17-3 LEONARDO DA VINCI, cartoon for *Madonna and Child with Saint Anne and the Infant Saint John*, ca. 1505–1507. Charcoal heightened with white on brown paper, 4′ 6″ × 3′ 3″. National Gallery, London. ◼◄

In this cartoon for a painting of the Madonna and Child and two saints, Leonardo drew a scene of tranquil grandeur filled with monumental figures reminiscent of classical statues.

gestures, although their meanings are uncertain, visually unite the individuals portrayed. The angel points to the infant John and, through his outward glance, involves the viewer in the tableau. John prays to the Christ Child, who blesses him in return. The Virgin herself completes the series of interlocking gestures, her left hand reaching toward the Christ Child and her right hand resting protectively on John's shoulder. The melting mood of tenderness, which the caressing light enhances, suffuses the entire composition. By creating an emotionally compelling, visually unified, and spatially convincing image, Leonardo succeeded in expressing "the intention of [man's] soul."

MADONNA AND CHILD **CARTOON** Leonardo's style fully emerges in *Madonna and Child with Saint Anne and the Infant Saint John* (FIG. **17-3**), a preliminary drawing (*cartoon*) for a painting (see "Renaissance Drawings," page 492) he made in 1505 or shortly thereafter. Here, the glowing light falls gently on the majestic forms in a scene of tranquil grandeur and balance. Leonardo ordered every part of his cartoon with an intellectual pictorial logic that results in an appealing visual unity. The figures are robust and monumental, the stately grace of their movements reminiscent of the Greek statues of goddesses (FIG. 5-49) in the pediments of the

17-4 LEONARDO DA VINCI, *Last Supper*, ca. 1495–1498. Oil and tempera on plaster, 13′ 9″ × 29′ 10″. Refectory, Santa Maria delle Grazie, Milan. ◼◄

Christ has just announced that one of his disciples will betray him, and each one reacts. Christ is both the psychological focus of Leonardo's fresco and the focal point of all the converging perspective lines.

Parthenon. Leonardo's infusion of the principles of classical art into his designs, however, cannot be attributed to specific knowledge of Greek monuments. He and his contemporaries never visited Greece. Their acquaintance with classical art extended only to Etruscan and Roman monuments, Roman copies of Greek statues in Italy, and ancient texts describing Greek and Roman works of art and architecture, especially Vitruvius's treatise *On Architecture* (FIG. **17-3A**).

LAST SUPPER For the refectory of the church of Santa Maria delle Grazie in Milan, Leonardo painted *Last Supper* (FIG. **17-4**), which both formally and emotionally is Leonardo's most impressive work. Jesus and his 12 disciples sit at a long table placed parallel to the picture plane in a simple, spacious room. The austere setting amplifies the painting's highly dramatic action. Jesus, with outstretched hands, has just said, "One of you is about to betray me" (Matt. 26:21). A wave of intense excitement passes through the group as each disciple asks himself and, in some cases, his neighbor, "Is it I?" (Matt. 26:22). Leonardo visualized a sophisticated conjunction of the dramatic "One of you is about to betray me" with the initiation of the ancient liturgical ceremony of the Eucharist, when Jesus, blessing bread and wine, said, "This is my body, which is given for you. Do this for a commemoration of me.... This is the chalice, the new testament in my blood, which shall be shed for you" (Luke 22:19–20).

In the center, Jesus appears isolated from the disciples and in perfect repose, the calm eye of the swirling emotion around him. The central window at the back, whose curved pediment arches above his head, frames his figure. The pediment is the only curve in the architectural framework, and it serves here, along with the diffused light, as a halo. Jesus' head is the focal point of all converging perspective lines in the composition. Thus, the still, psychological focus and cause of the action is also the perspective focus, as well as the center of the two-dimensional surface. The two-dimensional, the three-dimensional, and the psychodimensional focuses are the same.

Leonardo presented the agitated disciples in four groups of three, united among and within themselves by the figures' gestures and postures. The artist sacrificed traditional iconography to pictorial and dramatic consistency by placing Judas on the same side of the table as Jesus and the other disciples (compare FIG. 16-23). Judas's face is in shadow (the light source in the painting corresponds to the windows in the Milanese refectory). He clutches a money bag in his right hand as he reaches his left forward to fulfill Jesus' declaration: "But yet behold, the hand of him that betrayeth me is with me on the table" (Luke 22:21). The two disciples at the table ends are quieter than the others, as if to bracket the energy of the composition, which is more intense closer to Jesus, whose serenity both halts and intensifies it. The disciples register a broad range of emotional responses, including fear, doubt, protestation, rage, and love. Leonardo's numerous preparatory studies—using live models—suggest he thought of each figure as carrying a particular charge and type of emotion. Like a stage director, he read the Gospel story carefully, and scrupulously cast his actors as the Bible described their roles. In this work, as in his other religious paintings, Leonardo revealed his extraordinary ability to apply his voluminous knowledge about the observable world to the pictorial representation of a religious scene, resulting in a psychologically complex and compelling painting.

Leonardo's *Last Supper* is unfortunately in poor condition today, even after the completion in 1999 of a cleaning and restoration project lasting more than two decades. In a bold experiment, Leonardo had mixed oil and tempera, applying much of it *a secco* (to dried, rather than wet, plaster) in order to create a mural that more closely approximated oil painting on canvas or wood instead of fresco. But because the wall did not absorb the pigment as in the *buon fresco* technique, the paint quickly began to flake (see "Fresco Painting," Chapter 14, page 408). The humidity of Milan further accelerated the deterioration. The restoration involved extensive scholarly, chemical, and computer analysis. Like similar projects elsewhere, however, most notably in the Sistine Chapel (FIGS. 17-1 and 17-18B), this one was not without controversy. One scholar has claimed 80 percent of what is visible today is the work of the modern restorers, not Leonardo.

MONA LISA Leonardo's *Mona Lisa* (FIG. **17-5**) is probably the world's most famous portrait. The sitter's identity is still the subject of scholarly debate, but in his biography of Leonardo, Giorgio Vasari asserted she was Lisa di Antonio Maria Gherardini, the wife of Francesco del Giocondo, a wealthy Florentine—hence, "Mona

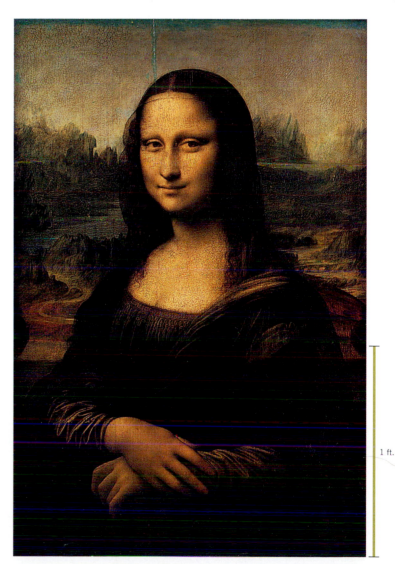

1 ft.

17-5 LEONARDO DA VINCI, *Mona Lisa,* ca. 1503–1505. Oil on wood, 2′ 6¼″ × 1′ 9″. Musée du Louvre, Paris.

Leonardo's skill with chiaroscuro and atmospheric perspective is on display in this new kind of portrait depicting the sitter as an individual personality who engages the viewer psychologically.

Renaissance Drawings

In Cinquecento Italy, drawing (or *disegno*) assumed a position of greater artistic prominence than ever before. Until the late 15th century, the expense of drawing surfaces and their lack of availability limited the production of preparatory sketches. Most artists drew on *parchment* (prepared from the skins of calves, sheep, and goats) or on *vellum* (made from the skins of young animals; FIG. 13-31). Because of the high cost of these materials, drawings in the 14th and 15th centuries tended to be extremely detailed and meticulously executed. Artists often drew using a silverpoint stylus (FIG. 15-9) because of the fine line it produced and the sharp point it maintained. The introduction in the late 15th century of less expensive paper made of fibrous pulp produced for the developing printing industry (see "Woodcuts, Engravings, and Etchings," Chapter 15, page 444) enabled artists to experiment more and to draw with greater freedom. As a result, sketches proliferated. Artists executed these drawings in pen and ink (FIG. 17-6), chalk, charcoal (FIG. 17-3), brush, and graphite or lead.

During the Renaissance, the importance of drawing transcended the mechanical or technical possibilities it afforded artists, however. The term *disegno* referred also to design, an integral component of good art. Design was the foundation of art, and drawing was the fundamental element of design. In his 1607 treatise *L'idea de' pittori, scultori ed architteti*, Federico Zuccari (1542–1609), director of the Accademia di San Luca (Academy of Saint Luke), the Roman painting academy, summed up this philosophy when he stated that drawing is the external physical manifestation (*disegno esterno*) of an internal intellectual idea or design (*disegno interno*).

The design dimension of art production became increasingly important as artists cultivated their own styles. The early stages of artistic training largely focused on imitation and emulation (see "Cennino Cennini on Imitation and Emulation," Chapter 16, page 461), but to achieve widespread recognition, artists had to develop their own styles. Although the artistic community and public

17-6 LEONARDO DA VINCI, *The Fetus and Lining of the Uterus*, ca. 1511–1513. Pen and ink with wash over red chalk and traces of black chalk on paper, $1' \times 8\frac{5}{8}''$. Royal Library, Windsor Castle. ◼◄

The introduction of less expensive paper in the late 15th century enabled artists to draw more frequently. Leonardo's analytical anatomical studies epitomize the scientific spirit of the Renaissance.

1 in.

at large acknowledged technical skill, the conceptualization of the artwork—its theoretical and formal development—was paramount. Disegno, or design in this case, represented an artist's conceptualization and intention. In the literature of the period, the terms often invoked to praise esteemed artists included *invenzione* (invention), *ingegno* (innate talent), *fantasia* (imagination), and *capriccio* (originality).

(an Italian contraction of *ma donna,* "my lady") Lisa." Despite the uncertainty of this identification, Leonardo's portrait is a convincing representation of an individual. Unlike earlier portraits, it does not serve solely as an icon of status. Indeed, Mona Lisa wears no jewelry and holds no attribute associated with wealth. She sits quietly, her hands folded, her mouth forming a gentle smile, and her gaze directed at the viewer. Renaissance etiquette dictated a woman should not look directly into a man's eyes. Leonardo's portrayal of this self-assured young woman without the trappings of power but engaging the audience psychologically is thus quite remarkable.

The enduring appeal of *Mona Lisa* derives in large part from Leonardo's decision to set his subject against the backdrop of a mysterious uninhabited landscape. This setting, with roads and

bridges seemingly leading nowhere, recalls that of his *Madonna of the Rocks* (FIG. 17-2). The composition also resembles Fra Filippo Lippi's *Madonna and Child with Angels* (FIG. 16-24) with figures seated in front of a window through which the viewer glimpses a distant landscape. Originally, the artist represented Mona Lisa in a loggia. A later owner trimmed the painting, eliminating the columns, but partial column bases remain to the left and right of Mona Lisa's shoulders.

The painting is darker today than 500 years ago and the colors are less vivid, but *Mona Lisa* still reveals Leonardo's fascination and skill with chiaroscuro and atmospheric perspective. The portrait is a prime example of the artist's famous smoky *sfumato* (misty haziness)—his subtle adjustment of light and blurring of precise planes.

ANATOMICAL STUDIES *Mona Lisa* is also exceptional because Leonardo completed very few paintings. His perfectionism, relentless experimentation, and far-ranging curiosity diffused his efforts. However, the drawings (see "Renaissance Drawings," page 604) in his notebooks preserve an extensive record of his ideas. His interests focused increasingly on science in his later years, and he embraced knowledge of all facets of the natural world. His investigations in anatomy yielded drawings of great precision and beauty of execution. *The Fetus and Lining of the Uterus* (FIG. **17-6**), although it does not meet 21st-century standards for accuracy (for example, Leonardo regularized the uterus's shape to a sphere, and his characterization of the lining is incorrect), was an astounding achievement in its day. Leonardo's analytical anatomical studies epitomize the scientific spirit of the Renaissance, establishing that era as a prelude to the modern world and setting it in sharp contrast to the preceding Middle Ages. Although Leonardo may not have been the first scientist of the modern world (at least not in today's sense of the term), he did originate the modern method of scientific illustration incorporating *cutaway* views. Scholars have long recognized the importance of his drawings for the development of anatomy as a science, especially in an age predating photographic methods such as X-rays.

17-6A LEONARDO, central-plan church, ca. 1487–1490.

Leonardo also won renown in his time as both architect and sculptor, although no extant buildings or sculptures can be definitively attributed to him. From his many drawings of central-plan structures (FIG. **17-6A**), it is evident he shared the interest of other Renaissance architects in this building type. As for Leonardo's sculptures, numerous drawings of monumental equestrian statues survive, and he made a full-scale model for a monument to Francesco Sforza (1401–1466), Ludovico's father. The French used the statue as a target and shot it to pieces when they occupied Milan in 1499.

Leonardo left Milan at that time and served for a while as a military engineer for Cesare Borgia (1476–1507), who, with the support of his father, Pope Alexander VI (r. 1492–1503), tried to conquer the cities of the Romagna region in north-central Italy and create a Borgia duchy. Leonardo eventually returned to Milan in the service of the French. At the invitation of King Francis I (FIG. 18-12), he then went to France, where he died at the château of Cloux in 1519.

Raphael

Alexander VI's successor was Julius II (see page 487). Among the many projects the ambitious new pope sponsored were a design for a modern Saint Peter's (FIGS. 17-22 and 17-23) to replace the timber-roofed fourth-century basilica (FIG. 8-9), the decoration of the papal apartments (FIG. 17-9), and the construction of his tomb (FIGS. 17-14 and 17-15), in addition to commissioning Michelangelo to paint the Sistine Chapel ceiling (FIGS. 17-1 and 17-17).

In 1508, Julius II called Raffaello Santi (or Sanzio), known as RAPHAEL (1483–1520) in English, to the papal court in Rome (see "Italian Princely Courts," Chapter 16, page 479). Born in a small town in Umbria near Urbino, Raphael probably learned the rudiments of his art from his father, Giovanni Santi (d. 1494), a painter connected with the ducal court of Federico da Montefeltro (FIG. 16-43), before entering the studio of Perugino (FIG. 16-41) in Perugia. Although strongly influenced by Perugino, Leonardo, and others, Raphael developed an individual style exemplifying the ideals of High Renaissance art.

MARRIAGE OF THE VIRGIN Among Raphael's early works is *Marriage of the Virgin* (FIG. **17-7**), which he painted for the chapel of Saint Joseph in the church of San Francesco in Città di Castello, southeast of Florence. The subject was a fitting one for Saint Joseph. According to the *Golden Legend* (a 13th-century collection of stories about the lives of the saints), Joseph competed with other suitors for Mary's hand. The high priest was to give the Virgin to whichever suitor presented to him a rod that had miraculously bloomed. Raphael depicted Joseph with his flowering rod in his left hand. In his right hand, Joseph holds the wedding ring he is about to place on Mary's finger. Other virgins congregate at the left, and the unsuccessful suitors stand on the right. One of them breaks his rod in half over his knee in frustration, giving Raphael an opportunity to demonstrate his mastery of foreshortening. The perspective system he used is the one he learned from Perugino (compare FIG. 16-41). The temple in the background is Raphael's version of a centrally planned building, featuring Brunelleschian arcades (FIG. 16-31).

1 ft.

17-7 RAPHAEL, *Marriage of the Virgin*, from the Chapel of Saint Joseph, San Francesco, Città di Castello, Italy, 1504. Oil on wood, 5′ 7″ × 3′ 10½″. Pinacoteca di Brera, Milan.

In this early work depicting the marriage of the Virgin to Saint Joseph, Raphael demonstrated his mastery of foreshortening and of the perspective system he learned from Perugino (FIG. 16-41).

17-8 RAPHAEL, *Madonna in the Meadow,* 1505–1506. Oil on wood, 3′ 8½″ × 2′ 10¼″ Kunsthistorisches Museum, Vienna.

Emulating Leonardo's pyramidal composition (FIG. 17-2) but rejecting his dusky modeling and mystery, Raphael set his Madonna in a well-lit landscape and imbued her with grace, dignity, and beauty.

MADONNA IN THE MEADOW Raphael spent the four years from 1504 to 1508 in Florence. There, still in his early 20s, he discovered that the painting style he had learned so painstakingly from Perugino was already outmoded (as was Brunelleschi's Early Renaissance architectural style). Florentine crowds flocked to the church of Santissima Annunziata to see Leonardo's recently unveiled cartoon of the Virgin, Christ Child, Saint Anne, and Saint John (probably an earlier version of FIG. 17-3). Under Leonardo's influence, Raphael began to modify the Madonna compositions he had employed in Umbria. In *Madonna in the Meadow* (FIG. **17-8**) of 1505–1506, Raphael adopted Leonardo's pyramidal composition and modeling of faces and figures in subtle chiaroscuro. Yet the Umbrian artist placed the large, substantial figures in a Peruginesque landscape, with his former master's typical feathery trees in the middle ground. Although Raphael experimented with Leonardo's dusky modeling, he tended to return to Perugino's lighter tonalities and blue skies. Raphael preferred clarity to obscurity, not fascinated, as Leonardo was, with

17-8A ANDREA DEL SARTO, *Madonna of the Harpies,* 1517.

mystery. Raphael quickly achieved fame for his Madonnas. His work, as well as Leonardo's, deeply influenced Raphael's slightly younger contemporary, ANDREA DEL SARTO (1486–1530), whose most famous painting is *Madonna of the Harpies* (FIG. **17-8A**).

SCHOOL OF ATHENS Three years after completing *Madonna in the Meadow,* Raphael received one of the most important painting commissions Julius II awarded—the decoration of the papal apartments in the Apostolic Palace of the Vatican (MAP 19-1). Of the suite's several rooms (*stanze*), Raphael painted the Stanza della Segnatura (Room of the Signature—the papal library, where Julius II signed official documents) and the Stanza d'Eliodoro (Room of Heliodorus—the pope's private audience room, named for one of the paintings there). His pupils completed the others, following his sketches. On the four walls of the Stanza della Segnatura, Raphael presented images symbolizing the four branches of human knowledge and wisdom under the headings *Theology,*

Law (*Justice*), *Poetry,* and *Philosophy*—the learning required of a Renaissance pope. Given Julius II's desire for recognition as both a spiritual and temporal leader, it is appropriate the *Theology* and *Philosophy* frescoes face each other. The two images present a balanced picture of the pope—as a cultured, knowledgeable individual and as a wise, divinely ordained religious authority.

In Raphael's *Philosophy* mural (commonly called *School of Athens,* FIG. **17-9**), the setting is not a "school" but a congregation of the great philosophers and scientists of the ancient world. Raphael depicted these luminaries, revered by Renaissance humanists, conversing and explaining their various theories and ideas. The setting is a vast hall covered by massive vaults that recall ancient Roman architecture, especially the much-admired coffered barrel vaults of the Basilica Nova (FIG. 7-78). Colossal statues of Apollo and Athena, patron deities of the arts and of wisdom, oversee the interactions. Plato and Aristotle are the central figures around whom Raphael carefully arranged the others. Plato holds his book *Timaeus* and points to Heaven, the source of his inspiration, while Aristotle carries his book *Nichomachean Ethics* and gestures toward the earth, from which his observations of reality sprang. Appropriately,

17-9 RAPHAEL, *Philosophy* (*School of Athens*), Stanza della Segnatura, Vatican Palace, Rome, Italy, 1509–1511. Fresco, 19′ × 27′. ◼◀

Raphael included himself in this gathering of great philosophers and scientists whose self-assurance conveys calm reason. The setting recalls the massive vaults of the Basilica Nova (FIG. 7-78).

ancient philosophers, men concerned with the ultimate mysteries that transcend this world, stand on Plato's side. On Aristotle's side are the philosophers and scientists concerned with nature and human affairs. At the lower left, Pythagoras writes as a servant holds up the harmonic scale. In the foreground, Heraclitus (probably a portrait of Michelangelo) broods alone. Diogenes sprawls on the steps. At the right, students surround Euclid, who demonstrates a theorem. Euclid may be a portrait of the architect Bramante, whom Julius II had recently commissioned to design the new church (FIGS. 17-22 and 17-23) to replace Constantine's 1,200-year-old Saint Peter's (FIG. 8-9). (The architectural setting of *School of Athens* approximates Bramante's design for the interior of Saint Peter's; compare FIG. 19-5.) At the extreme right, just to the right of the astronomers Zoroaster and Ptolemy, both holding globes, Raphael included his self-portrait.

The groups appear to move easily and clearly, with eloquent poses and gestures that symbolize their doctrines and present an engaging variety of figural positions. The self-assurance and natural dignity of the figures convey calm reason, balance, and measure—those qualities Renaissance thinkers admired as the heart of philosophy. Significantly, Raphael placed himself among the mathematicians and scientists in *School of Athens*. Certainly, the evolution of pictorial science approached perfection in this fresco

in which Raphael convincingly depicted a vast space on a two-dimensional surface.

The artist's psychological insight matured along with his mastery of the problems of perspective representation. All the characters in Raphael's *School of Athens,* like those in Leonardo's *Last Supper* (FIG. 17-4), communicate moods that reflect their beliefs, and the artist's placement of each figure tied these moods together. From the center, where Plato and Aristotle stand, Raphael arranged the groups of figures in an ellipse with a wide opening in the foreground. Moving along the floor's perspective pattern, the viewer's eye penetrates the assembly of philosophers and continues, by way of the reclining Diogenes, up to the here-reconciled leaders of the two great opposing camps of Renaissance philosophy. The vanishing point falls on Plato's left hand, drawing attention to *Timaeus.* In the Stanza della Segnatura, Raphael reconciled and harmonized not only the Platonists and Aristotelians but also classical humanism and Christianity, surely a major factor in the fresco's appeal to Julius II.

LEO X Succeeding Julius II as Raphael's patron was Pope Leo X (r. 1513–1521). By this time, Raphael had achieved renown throughout Italy and moved in the highest circles of the papal court. The new pope entrusted the Umbrian artist with so many projects in

17-10 RAPHAEL, *Pope Leo X with Cardinals Giulio de' Medici and Luigi de' Rossi*, ca. 1517. Oil on wood, 5' ⅝" × 3' 10⅞". Galleria degli Uffizi, Florence.

In this dynastic portrait of the Medici pope and two Medici cardinals, Raphael depicted Leo X as an art collector and man of learning. The meticulous details reveal a debt to Netherlandish painting.

17-11 RAPHAEL, *Galatea*, Sala di Galatea, Villa Farnesina, Rome, Italy, ca. 1513. Fresco, 9' 8" × 7' 5".

Based on a poem by Poliziano, Raphael's fresco depicts Galatea fleeing from Polyphemus. The painting, made for the banker Agostino Chigi's private palace, celebrates human beauty and zestful love.

17-10A RAPHAEL, *Baldassare Castiglione*, ca. 1514.

Rome, including overseeing construction of Saint Peter's, that Raphael became a wealthy man at a young age. Leo himself (Giovanni de' Medici) was a scion of Italy's most famous family. The second son of Lorenzo the Magnificent, he received a princely humanistic education. His election as pope came only a year after the return of the Medici to Florence following nearly two decades of exile (see Chapter 16), and Leo used his position to advance the family's interests. The portrait (FIG. **17-10**) he commissioned Raphael to paint in 1517—a few years after the artist portrayed the famed courtier Baldassare Castiglione (FIG. **17-10A**)—is, in essence, a dynastic portrait. Appropriately, the pope dominates the canvas, seated in his study before a table with an illuminated 14th-century manuscript, the magnifying glass he required because of his myopia, and a bell engraved with classical decorative motifs. Raphael portrayed Leo as he doubtless wished to be represented—as a man of learning and a collector of beautiful objects rather than as a head of state. To the pope's right is his cousin Cardinal Giulio de' Medici, who became Pope Clement VII (r. 1523–1534). Behind Leo's chair is Luigi de' Rossi (1474–1519), his cousin on his mother's side, whom the pope appointed cardinal.

The three men look neither at one another nor at the painter or spectator, but are absorbed in their own thoughts.

Raphael's mastery of the oil technique is evident in every detail. His depiction of the rich satin, wool, velvet, and fur garments the three men wear skillfully conveys their varied textures. His reproduction of the book on the pope's desk is so meticulous that scholars have been able to identify it as the *Hamilton Bible* in the Berlin Staatsbibliothek, open to folio 400 verso, the beginning of the Gospel of Saint John with illustrations of Christ's passion. The light illuminating the scene comes from the right—from a window reflected in the spherical brass finial of the pope's chair, in which the viewer can also see the indistinct form of the painter. In details such as these, Raphael revealed his knowledge and admiration of earlier Netherlandish painting, especially the work of Jan van Eyck (see Chapter 15).

GALATEA As a star at the papal court, Raphael also enjoyed the patronage of other prominent figures in Rome. Agostino Chigi (1465–1520), an immensely wealthy banker who managed the Vatican's financial affairs, commissioned Raphael to decorate his palace on the Tiber River with scenes from classical mythology. Outstanding among the frescoes Raphael painted in the small but splendid Villa Farnesina is *Galatea* (FIG. **17-11**), which he based on

Leonardo and Michelangelo on Painting versus Sculpture

Both Leonardo da Vinci and Michelangelo produced work in a variety of artistic media, earning enviable reputations not just as painters and sculptors but as architects and draftsmen as well. The two disagreed, however, on the relative merits of the different media. In particular, Leonardo, with his intellectual and analytical mind, preferred painting to sculpture, which he denigrated as manual labor. In contrast, Michelangelo, who worked in a more intuitive manner, saw himself primarily as a sculptor. Two excerpts from their writings reveal their positions on the relationship between the two media.

Leonardo da Vinci wrote the following in his so-called *Treatise on Painting*:

> Painting is a matter of greater mental analysis, of greater skill, and more marvelous than sculpture, since necessity compels the mind of the painter to transform itself into the very mind of nature, to become an interpreter between nature and art. Painting justifies by reference to nature the reasons of the pictures which follow its laws: in what ways the images of objects before the eye come together in the pupil of the eye; which, among objects equal in size, looks larger to the eye; which, among equal colors will look more or less dark or more or less bright; which, among things at the same depth, looks more or less low; which, among those objects placed at equal height, will look more or less high, and why, among objects placed at various distances, one will appear less clear than the other.

> This art comprises and includes within itself all visible things such as colors and their diminution, which the poverty of sculpture cannot include. Painting represents transparent objects but the sculptor will show you the shapes of natural objects without artifice. The painter will show you things at different distances with variation of color due to the air lying between the objects and the eye; he shows you mists through which visual images penetrate with difficulty; he shows you rain which discloses within it clouds with mountains and valleys; he shows the dust which discloses within it and beyond it the combatants who stirred it up; he shows streams of greater or lesser density; he shows fish playing between the surface of the water and its bottom; he shows the polished pebbles of various colors lying on the washed sand at the bottom of rivers, surrounded by green plants; he shows the stars at various heights above us, and thus he achieves innumerable effects which sculpture cannot attain.*

As if in response, although decades later, Michelangelo wrote these excerpts in a letter to Benedetto Varchi (1502–1565), a Florentine poet best known for his 16-volume history of Florence:

> I believe that painting is considered excellent in proportion as it approaches the effect of relief, while relief is considered bad in proportion as it approaches the effect of painting.

> I used to consider that sculpture was the lantern of painting and that between the two things there was the same difference as that between the sun and the moon. But . . . I now consider that painting and sculpture are one and the same thing.

> Suffice that, since one and the other (that is to say, both painting and sculpture) proceed from the same faculty, it would be an easy matter to establish harmony between them and to let such disputes alone, for they occupy more time than the execution of the figures themselves. As to that man [Leonardo] who wrote saying that painting was more noble than sculpture, if he had known as much about the other subjects on which he has written, why, my serving-maid would have written better![†]

*Leonardo da Vinci, *Treatise on Painting*, 51. In Robert Klein and Henri Zerner, *Italian Art 1500–1600: Sources and Documents* (Evanston, Ill.: Northwestern University Press, 1966), 7–8.
[†]Michelangelo to Benedetto Varchi, Rome, 1549. In Klein and Zerner, *Italian Art 1500–1600*, 13–14.

Stanzas for the Joust of Giuliano de' Medici by Angelo Poliziano, whose poetry had earlier inspired Botticelli to paint *Birth of Venus* (FIG. 16-29). In Raphael's fresco, Galatea flees on a shell drawn by leaping dolphins to escape her uncouth lover, the cyclops Polyphemus (painted on another wall by a different artist). Sea creatures and playful cupids surround her. The painting is an exultant song in praise of human beauty and zestful love. Compositionally, Raphael enhanced the liveliness of the image by placing the sturdy figures around Galatea in bounding and dashing movements that always return to her as the energetic center. The cupids, skillfully foreshortened, repeat the circling motion. Raphael conceived his figures sculpturally, and Galatea's body—supple, strong, and vigorously in motion—contrasts with Botticelli's delicate, hovering, almost dematerialized Venus while suggesting the spiraling compositions of Hellenistic statuary (FIG. 5-80). In *Galatea*, classical myth presented in monumental form, in vivacious movement, and in a spirit of passionate delight resurrects the naturalistic art and poetry of the Greco-Roman world.

Michelangelo

Although Michelangelo is most famous today as the painter of the Sistine Chapel frescoes (FIG. 17-1), he was also an architect, poet, engineer, and, first and foremost, a sculptor. Michelangelo considered sculpture superior to painting because the sculptor shares in the divine power to "make man" (see "Leonardo and Michelangelo on Painting versus Sculpture," above). Drawing a conceptual parallel to Plato's ideas, Michelangelo believed the image the artist's hand produces must come from the idea in the artist's mind. The idea, then, is the reality the artist's genius has to bring forth. But artists are not the creators of the ideas they conceive. Rather, they find their ideas in the natural world, reflecting the absolute idea, which, for the artist, is beauty. One of Michelangelo's best-known observations about sculpture is that the artist must proceed by finding the idea—the image locked in the stone. By removing the excess stone, the sculptor extricates the idea from the block (FIG. I-16), bringing forth the living form. The artist, Michelangelo felt, works for many

17-12 MICHELANGELO BUONARROTI, *Pietà,* ca. 1498–1500. Marble, 5′ 8½″ high. Saint Peter's, Vatican City, Rome.

Michelangelo's representation of Mary cradling Christ's corpse captures the sadness and beauty of the young Virgin but was controversial because the Madonna seems younger than her son.

1 ft.

years to discover this unceasing process of revelation and "arrives late at novel and lofty things."[4]

Michelangelo did indeed arrive "at novel and lofty things," for he broke sharply from the lessons of his predecessors and contemporaries in one important respect. He mistrusted the application of mathematical methods as guarantees of beauty in proportion. Measure and proportion, he believed, should be "kept in the eyes." Vasari quoted Michelangelo as declaring "it was necessary to have the compasses in the eyes and not in the hand, because the hands work and the eye judges."[5] Thus, Michelangelo set aside Vitruvius, Alberti, Leonardo, and others who tirelessly sought the perfect measure, and insisted the artist's inspired judgment could identify other pleasing proportions. In addition, Michelangelo argued the artist must not be bound, except by the demands made by realizing the idea. This assertion of the artist's authority was typical of Michelangelo and anticipated the modern concept of the right to a self-expression of talent limited only by the artist's own judgment. The artistic license to aspire far beyond the "rules" was, in part, a manifestation of the pursuit of fame and success that humanism fostered. In this context, Michelangelo created works in architecture, sculpture, and painting that departed from High Renaissance regularity. He put in its stead a style of vast, expressive strength conveyed through complex, eccentric, and often titanic forms looming before the viewer in tragic grandeur.

As a youth, Michelangelo was an apprentice in the studio of the painter Domenico Ghirlandaio (FIGS. 16-26 and 16-27), but he left before completing his training. Although Michelangelo later claimed he owed nothing artistically to anyone, he made detailed drawings based on the work of the great Florentines Giotto and Masaccio. Early on, he came to the attention of Lorenzo the Magnificent and studied sculpture under one of Lorenzo's favorite artists, Bertoldo di Giovanni (ca. 1420–1491), a former collaborator of Donatello's. When the Medici fell in 1494, Michelangelo fled Florence for Bologna, where the sculptures of the Sienese artist Jacopo della Quercia (1367–1438) impressed him.

PIETÀ Michelangelo made his first trip to Rome in the summer of 1496, and two years later, still in his early 20s, he produced his first masterpiece there: a *Pietà* (FIG. **17-12**) for the French cardinal Jean de Bilhères Lagraulas (1439–1499). The cardinal commissioned the statue to be placed in the rotunda attached to the south transept of Old Saint Peter's (FIG. 8-9) in which he was to be buried beside other French churchmen. (The work is now on view in the new church [FIG. 19-4] that replaced the fourth-century basilica.) The theme—Mary cradling the dead body of Christ in her lap—was a staple in the repertoire of French and German artists (FIG. 13-50), and Michelangelo's French patron doubtless chose the subject. The Italian, however, rendered the northern European theme in an unforgettable manner. Michelangelo transformed marble into flesh, hair, and fabric with a sensitivity for texture almost without parallel. The polish and luminosity of the exquisite marble surface can be fully appreciated only in the presence of the original. Breathtaking, too, is the tender sadness of the beautiful and youthful Mary as she mourns the death of her son. In fact, her age—seemingly less than that of Christ—was a subject of controversy from the moment the statue was unveiled. Michelangelo explained Mary's ageless beauty as an integral part of her purity and virginity. Beautiful, too, is the son whom she holds. Christ seems less to have died a martyr's crucifixion than to have drifted off into peaceful sleep in Mary's maternal arms. His wounds are barely visible.

DAVID Michelangelo returned to Florence in 1501. In 1495, during the Medici exile, the Florentine Republic had ordered the transfer of Donatello's *David* (FIG. 16-12) from the Medici residence to the Palazzo della Signoria to join Verrocchio's *David* (FIG. 16-13) there. The importance of David as a civic symbol led the Florence Cathedral building committee to invite Michelangelo to work a great block of marble left over from an earlier aborted commission into still another *David* statue for the Signoria. The colossal statue (FIG. **17-13**)—Florentines referred to it as "the Giant"—Michelangelo created from that block forever assured his reputation as an extraordinary talent. Vasari, for example, extolled the work, claiming

> without any doubt [Michelangelo's *David*] has put in the shade every other statue, ancient or modern, Greek or Roman . . . [The statue] was intended as a symbol of liberty [in front of Florence's city hall], signifying that just as David had protected his people and governed them justly, so whoever ruled Florence should vigorously defend the city and govern it with justice.[6]

Despite the traditional association of David with heroic triumph over a fearsome adversary, Michelangelo chose to represent the young biblical warrior not after his victory, with Goliath's head at his feet (as Donatello and Verrocchio had done), but before the encounter, with David sternly watching his approaching foe. *David* exhibits the characteristic representation of energy in reserve that imbues Michelangelo's later figures with the tension of a coiled spring. The anatomy of David's body plays an important part in this prelude to action. His rugged torso, sturdy limbs, and large hands and feet alert viewers to the triumph to come. Each swelling vein and tightening sinew amplifies the psychological energy of David's pose.

Michelangelo doubtless had the classical nude in mind when he conceived his *David*. Like many of his colleagues, he greatly admired Greco-Roman statues, in particular the skillful and precise rendering of heroic physique. Without strictly imitating the antique style, the Renaissance sculptor captured in his portrayal of the biblical hero the tension of Lysippan athletes (FIG. 5-65) and the psychological insight and emotionalism of Hellenistic statuary (FIGS. 5-80, 5-81, and 5-89). His *David* differs from Donatello's and Verrocchio's creations in much the same way later Hellenistic statues departed from their Classical predecessors (see Chapter 5). Michelangelo abandoned the self-contained compositions of the 15th-century *David* statues by abruptly turning the hero's head toward his gigantic adversary. This *David* is compositionally and emotionally connected to an unseen presence beyond the statue, a feature also of Hellenistic sculpture (FIG. 5-86). As early as 1501, then, Michelangelo invested his efforts in presenting towering, pent-up emotion rather than calm, ideal beauty. He transferred his own doubts, frustrations, and passions into the great figures he created or planned.

TOMB OF JULIUS II The formal references to classical antiquity in Michelangelo's *David* surely appealed to Julius II, who associated himself with the humanists and with Roman emperors. Thus, this sculpture and the fame that accrued to Michelangelo on its completion called the artist to the pope's attention, leading shortly thereafter to major papal commissions. The first project Julius II commissioned from Michelangelo was the pontiff's tomb, to be placed in Old Saint Peter's. The sculptor's original 1505 design called for a freestanding, two-story structure with some 28 statues. The proposed monument, of unprecedented size (compare FIG. 16-15), would have given Michelangelo the latitude to sculpt

1 ft.

17-13 MICHELANGELO BUONARROTI, *David*, from Piazza della Signoria, Florence, Italy, 1501–1504. Marble, 17′ high. Galleria dell'Accademia, Florence. ◼◀

In this colossal statue, Michelangelo represented David in heroic classical nudity, capturing the tension of Lysippan athletes (FIG. 5-65) and the emotionalism of Hellenistic statuary (FIGS. 5-80 and 5-81).

numerous human figures while providing Julius II with a grandiose memorial that would associate the Cinquecento pope with the first pope, Peter himself. Shortly after Michelangelo began work on this project, the pope interrupted the commission, possibly because funds had to be diverted to the rebuilding of Saint Peter's. After Julius II's death in 1513, Michelangelo reluctantly reduced the scale of the project step-by-step until, in 1542, a final contract specified a simple wall tomb with fewer than one-third of the originally planned figures. Michelangelo completed the tomb in 1545 and saw it placed in San Pietro in Vincoli (MAP 17-1), where Julius II had served as a cardinal before his accession to the papacy. Given Julius's ambitions, it is safe to say that had he seen the final design of his tomb, or known where it would eventually be located, he would have been bitterly disappointed.

The spirit of the tomb may be summed up in *Moses* (FIG. 17-14), which Michelangelo carved between 1513 and 1515 during one of his sporadic resumptions of work on the project. Meant to be seen from below and to be balanced with seven other massive forms related to it in spirit, *Moses* in its final comparatively paltry setting does not convey the impact originally intended. Michelangelo depicted the Old Testament prophet seated, the Tablets of the Law under one arm and his hands gathering his voluminous beard. The horns on Moses's head were a convention in Christian art (based on a mistranslation of the Hebrew word for "rays") and helped Renaissance viewers identify the prophet (compare FIGS. 12-35 and 15-2). Here, as in his *David*, Michelangelo used the device of the turned head, in this case to concentrate the expression of awful wrath stirring in the prophet's mighty frame and eyes. Moses' muscles

17-14 MICHELANGELO BUONARROTI, *Moses,* from the tomb of Pope Julius II, Rome, Italy, ca. 1513–1515. Marble, 7′ 8½″ high. San Pietro in Vincoli, Rome. ◼◣

Not since Hellenistic times had a sculptor captured as much pent-up energy, both emotional and physical, in a seated statue as Michelangelo did in the over-life-size *Moses* he carved for Julius II's tomb.

17-15 MICHELANGELO BUONARROTI, *Bound Slave* (*Rebellious Slave*), from the tomb of Pope Julius II, Rome, Italy, ca. 1513–1516. Marble, 7′ ⅝″ high. Musée du Louvre, Paris.

For Pope Julius II's grandiose tomb, Michelangelo planned a series of statues of captives or slaves in various attitudes of revolt and exhaustion. This defiant figure exhibits a violent contrapposto.

bulge, his veins swell, and his great legs seem to begin slowly to move. Not since Hellenistic times had a sculptor captured so much pent-up energy—both emotional and physical—in a seated statue (FIGS. 5-86 and 5-89).

Michelangelo also intended to incorporate in the pope's tomb some 20 statues of captives, popularly known as slaves, in various attitudes of revolt and exhaustion. Art historians have traditionally believed *Bound Slave,* or *Rebellious Captive* (FIG. **17-15**), and the unfinished statue shown in FIG. I-16 to be two of those destined for Julius's tomb. Some scholars now doubt this attribution, and some even reject the identification of the statues as "slaves" or "captives." Whatever their identity, these statues, like Michelangelo's *David* and *Moses,* testify to the sculptor's ability to create figures embodying powerful emotional states. In *Bound Slave,* the defiant figure's

violent contrapposto is the image of frantic but impotent struggle. Michelangelo based his whole art on his conviction that whatever can be said greatly through sculpture and painting must be said through the human figure.

TOMB OF GIULIANO DE' MEDICI Following the death of Julius II, Michelangelo, like Raphael, went into the service of Leo X and his successor, Clement VII. These Medici popes chose not to perpetuate a predecessor's fame by permitting Michelangelo to complete Julius's tomb. Instead, they (Pope Leo X and the then-cardinal Giulio de' Medici; FIG. 17-10) commissioned him in 1519 to build a funerary chapel, the New Sacristy, attached to Brunelleschi's San Lorenzo (FIG. 16-32A) in Florence. At opposite sides of the New Sacristy stand Michelangelo's sculpted tombs of Giuliano (1478–1516), duke of Nemours (south of Paris), and Lorenzo (1492–1519), duke of Urbino, son and grandson of Lorenzo the Magnificent. Giuliano's tomb (FIG. **17-16**) is compositionally the twin of Lorenzo's. Michelangelo finished neither tomb. Scholars believe he intended to place pairs of recumbent river gods at the bottom of the sarcophagi, balancing the pairs of figures resting on the sloping sides, but Michelangelo's grand design for the tombs remains a puzzle.

According to the traditional interpretation, the arrangement Michelangelo planned, but never completed, mirrors the soul's ascent through the levels of the Neo-Platonic universe. Neo-Platonism, the school of thought based on Plato's idealistic, spiritualistic philosophy, experienced a renewed popularity in the 16th-century humanist community. The lowest level of the tomb, which the river gods represent, would have signified the Underworld of brute matter, the source of evil. The two statues on the sarcophagi would symbolize the realm of time—the specifically human world of the cycles of dawn, day, evening, and night. Humanity's state in this world of time was one of pain and anxiety, of frustration and exhaustion. At left, the muscular female Night—Michelangelo used male models even for his female figures—and, at right, the male Day appear to be chained into

1 ft.

17-16 MICHELANGELO BUONARROTI, tomb of **Giuliano de' Medici,** New Sacristy (**Medici Chapel**), San Lorenzo, **Florence,** Italy, 1519–1534. Marble, central figure 5′ 11″ high.

Michelangelo's portrait of Giuliano de' Medici in Roman armor depicts the deceased as the model of the active and decisive man. Below are the anguished, twisting figures of Night and Day.

High and Late Renaissance   **501**

never-relaxing tensions. Both exhibit the anguished twisting of the body's masses in contrary directions seen also in Michelangelo's *Bound Slave* (FIG. 17-15; compare FIG. I-16) and in his Sistine Chapel paintings (FIGS. 17-18 and 17-18A). This contortion is a staple of Michelangelo's figural art. Day, with a body the thickness of a great tree and the anatomy of Hercules (or of a reclining Greco-Roman river god that may have inspired Michelangelo's statue), strains his huge limbs against each other, his unfinished visage rising menacingly above his shoulder. Night, the symbol of rest, twists as if in troubled sleep, her posture wrenched and feverish. The artist surrounded her with an owl, poppies, and a hideous mask symbolic of nightmares. Some scholars argue, however, that the Night and Day personifications allude not to humanity's pain but to the life cycle and the passage of time leading ultimately to death.

On their respective tombs, sculptures of Lorenzo and Giuliano appear in niches at the apex of the structures. Transcending worldly existence, they represent the two ideal human types—the contemplative man (Lorenzo) and the active man (Giuliano). Giuliano (FIG. 17-16) sits clad in the armor of a Roman emperor and holds a commander's baton, his head turned alertly as if in council (he looks toward the statue of the Virgin at one end of the chapel). Across the room, Lorenzo appears wrapped in thought, his face in deep shadow. Together, they symbolize the two ways human beings might achieve union with God—through meditation or through the active life fashioned after that of Christ. In this sense, they are not individual portraits. Indeed, Michelangelo declined to sculpt likenesses of Lorenzo and Giuliano. Who, he asked, would care what they looked like in a thousand years? This attitude is consistent with Michelangelo's interests. Throughout his career he demonstrated less concern for facial features and expressions than for the overall human form. The rather generic visages of the two Medici captains of the Church attest to this view. For the artist, the contemplation of what lies beyond the corrosion of time counted more.

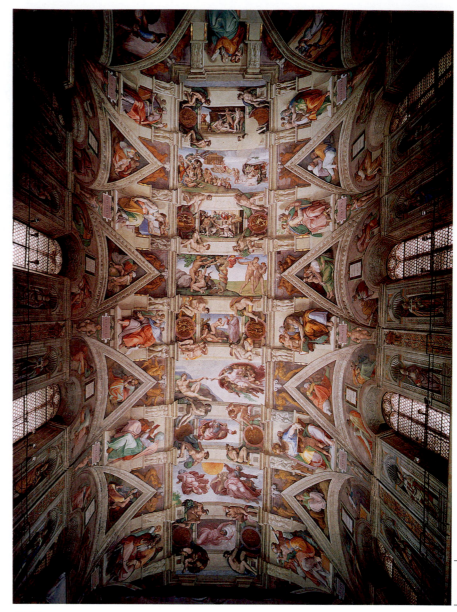

17-17 MICHELANGELO BUONARROTI, ceiling of the Sistine Chapel, Vatican City, Rome, Italy, 1508–1512. Fresco, 128′ × 45′. ◼◀

Michelangelo labored almost four years for Pope Julius II on the frescoes for the ceiling of the Sistine Chapel. He painted more than 300 figures illustrating the creation and fall of humankind.

10 ft.

SISTINE CHAPEL CEILING When Julius II suspended work on his tomb, the pope offered the bitter Michelangelo the commission to paint the ceiling (FIG. **17-17**) of the Sistine Chapel (FIG. 17-1) in 1508. The artist reluctantly assented in the hope the tomb project could be revived. Michelangelo faced enormous difficulties in painting the Sistine ceiling: its dimensions (some 5,800 square feet), its height above the pavement (almost 70 feet), and the complicated perspective problems the vault's height and curve presented, as well as his inexperience in the fresco technique. (Michelangelo had to redo the first section he completed because of faulty preparation of the intonaco; see "Fresco Painting," Chapter 14, page 408.) Yet, in less than four years, Michelangelo produced an extraordinary series of monumental frescoes incorporating his patron's agenda, Church doctrine, and his own interests. In depicting the most august and solemn themes of all, the creation, fall, and redemption of humanity—subjects most likely selected by Julius II with input from Michelangelo and Cardinal Marco Vigerio della Rovere (1446–1516)—Michelangelo spread a colossal compositional scheme across the vast surface. He succeeded in weaving together more than 300 figures in an ultimate grand drama of the human race.

A long sequence of narrative panels describing the creation, as recorded in Genesis, runs along the crown of the vault, from *God's Separation of Light and Darkness* (above the altar) to *Drunkenness of Noah* (nearest the entrance to the chapel). Thus, as viewers enter the chapel, look up, and walk toward the altar, they review, in reverse order, the history of the fall of humankind. The Hebrew prophets and ancient sibyls who foretold the coming of Christ appear seated in large thrones on both sides of the central row of scenes from Genesis, where the vault curves down. In the four corner *pendentives*, Michelangelo placed four Old Testament scenes with David, Judith, Haman, and Moses and the Brazen Serpent. Scores of lesser figures also appear. The ancestors of Christ (FIG. 17-18B) fill the triangular compartments above the windows, nude youths punctuate the corners of the central panels, and small pairs of putti in *grisaille* (monochrome painting using shades of gray to imitate sculpture)

1 ft.

17-18 MICHELANGELO BUONARROTI, *Creation of Adam,* detail of the ceiling of the Sistine Chapel (FIG. 17-17), Vatican City, Rome, Italy, 1511–1512. Fresco, 9′ 2″ ×18′ 8″. ▪◀

Life leaps to Adam like a spark from the extended hand of God in this fresco, which recalls the communication between gods and heroes in the classical myths Renaissance humanists admired so much.

support the painted cornice surrounding the entire central corridor. The overall conceptualization of the ceiling's design and narrative structure not only presents a sweeping chronology of Christianity but also is in keeping with Renaissance ideas about Christian history. These ideas included interest in the conflict between good and evil and between the energy of youth and the wisdom of age. The conception of the entire ceiling was astounding in itself, and the articulation of it in its thousands of details was a superhuman achievement.

Unlike Andrea Mantegna's decoration of the ceiling of the Camera Picta (FIGS. 16-48 and 16-49) in Mantua, the strongly marked unifying architectural framework in the Sistine Chapel does not construct "picture windows" framing illusions within them. Rather, the viewer focuses on figure after figure, each sharply outlined against the neutral tone of the architectural setting or the plain background of the panels.

CREATION OF ADAM The two central panels of Michelangelo's ceiling represent *Creation of Adam* (FIG. **17-18**) and *Fall of Man* (FIG. **17-18A**). In both cases, Michelangelo rejected traditional iconographical convention in favor of bold new interpretations of the momentous events. In *Creation of Adam,* God and Adam confront each other in a primordial unformed landscape of which Adam is still a material part, heavy as

17-18A MICHELANGELO, *Fall of Man,* ca. 1510.

earth. The Lord transcends the earth, wrapped in a billowing cloud of drapery and borne up by his powers. Life leaps to Adam like a spark from the extended and mighty hand of God. The communication between gods and heroes, so familiar in classical myth, is here concrete. This blunt depiction of the Lord as ruler of Heaven in the classical, Olympian sense indicates how easily High Renaissance thought joined classical and Christian traditions. Yet the classical trappings do not obscure the essential Christian message.

Beneath the Lord's sheltering left arm is a woman, apprehensively curious but as yet uncreated. Scholars traditionally believed she represented Eve, but many now think she is the Virgin Mary (with the Christ Child at her knee). If the second identification is correct, it suggests Michelangelo incorporated into his fresco one of the essential tenets of Christian faith—the belief that Adam's original sin eventually led to the sacrifice of Christ, which in turn made possible the redemption of all humankind (see "Jewish Subjects in Christian Art," Chapter 8, page 238).

As God reaches out to Adam, the viewer's eye follows the motion from right to left, but Adam's extended left arm leads the eye back to the right, along the Lord's right arm, shoulders, and left arm to his left forefinger, which points to the Christ Child's face. The focal point of this right-to-left-to-right movement—the fingertips of Adam and the Lord—is dramatically off-center. Michelangelo replaced the straight architectural axes found in Leonardo's compositions with curves and diagonals. For example, the bodies of the two great figures are complementary—the concave body of Adam fitting the convex body and billowing "cloak" of God. Thus, motion directs not only the figures but also the whole composition. The reclining positions of the figures, the heavy musculature, and the twisting poses are all intrinsic parts of Michelangelo's style.

The photographs of the Sistine Chapel reproduced here record the appearance of Michelangelo's frescoes after the completion of a 12-year cleaning project (1977–1989). The painstaking restoration (FIG. **17-18B**) elicited considerable controversy because it revealed vivid colors that initially shocked art historians, producing accusations the restorers were destroying Michelangelo's masterpieces. That reaction, however, was largely attributable to

17-18B Sistine Chapel restoration, 1977–1989.

the fact that for centuries no one had ever seen Michelangelo's frescoes except covered with soot and grime.

17-19 Michelangelo Buonarroti, *Last Judgment,* altar wall of the Sistine Chapel, Vatican City, Rome, Italy, 1536–1541. Fresco, 48′ × 44′. ◼◂

Michelangelo completed his fresco cycle in the Sistine Chapel with this terrifying vision of the fate awaiting sinners. Near the center, he placed his own portrait on the flayed skin Saint Bartholomew holds.

10 ft.

THE COUNTER-REFORMATION

Paul III (r. 1534–1549) succeeded Clement VII as pope in 1534 at a time of widespread dissatisfaction with the leadership and policies of the Roman Catholic Church. Led by clerics such as Martin Luther and John Calvin in the Holy Roman Empire (see Chapter 18), early-16th-century reformers directly challenged papal authority, especially regarding secular issues. Disgruntled Catholics voiced concerns about the sale of *indulgences* (pardons for sins, reducing the time a soul spent in purgatory), nepotism (the appointment of relatives to important positions), and high Church officials pursuing personal wealth. This Reformation movement resulted in the establishment of Protestantism, with sects such as Lutheranism and Calvinism. Central to Protestantism was a belief in personal faith rather than adherence to decreed Church practices and doctrines. Because the Protestants believed the only true religious relationship was the personal relationship between an individual and God, they were, in essence, eliminating the need for Church intercession, which is central to Catholicism.

The Catholic Church, in response, mounted a full-fledged campaign to counteract the defection of its members to Protestantism. Led by Paul III, this response, the Counter-Reformation, consisted of numerous initiatives. The Council of Trent, which met intermittently from 1545 through 1563, was a major component of this effort. Composed of cardinals, archbishops, bishops, abbots, and theologians, the Council of Trent dealt with issues of Church doctrine, including many the Protestants contested. Many papal commissions during this period can be viewed as an integral part of the Counter-Reformation effort. Popes long had been aware of the power of visual imagery to construct and reinforce ideological claims, and 16th-century popes exploited this capability (see "Religious Art in Counter-Reformation Italy," page 505).

LAST JUDGMENT Among Paul III's first papal commissions was an enormous (48 feet tall) fresco for the Sistine Chapel. Michelangelo agreed to paint *Last Judgment* (FIG. **17-19**) on the chapel's altar (west) wall. Here, the artist depicted Christ as the stern judge of the world—a giant who raises his mighty right arm in a gesture of damnation so broad and universal as to suggest he will destroy all creation. The choirs of Heaven surrounding him pulse with anxiety and awe. Crowded into the space below are trumpeting angels, the ascending figures of the just, and the downward-hurtling figures of the damned. On the left, the dead awake and assume flesh. On the right, demons, whose gargoyle masks and burning eyes revive the demons of Romanesque tympana (FIG. 12-1), torment the damned.

Michelangelo's terrifying vision of the fate awaiting sinners goes far beyond even Signorelli's gruesome images (FIG. 16-42). Martyrs who suffered especially agonizing deaths crouch below the judge. One of them, Saint Bartholomew, who was skinned alive, holds the flaying knife and the skin, its face a grotesque self-portrait of Michelangelo. The figures are huge and violently twisted, with small heads and contorted features. Yet while this immense fresco impresses on viewers Christ's wrath on judgment day, it also holds out hope. A group of saved souls—the elect—crowd around Christ, and on the far right appears a figure with a cross, most likely the Good Thief (crucified with Christ) or a saint martyred by crucifixion, such as Saint Andrew.

Religious Art in Counter-Reformation Italy

Both Catholics and Protestants took seriously the role of devotional imagery in religious life. However, their views differed dramatically. Catholics deemed art valuable for cultivating piety. Protestants believed religious imagery encouraged idolatry and distracted the faithful from the goal of developing a personal relationship with God (see Chapter 18). As part of the Counter-Reformation effort, Pope Paul III convened the Council of Trent in 1545 to review controversial Church doctrines. At its conclusion in 1563, the Council issued the following edict:

> The holy council commands all bishops and others who hold the office of teaching and have charge of the *cura animarum* [literally, "cure of souls"—the responsibility of laboring for the salvation of souls], that in accordance with the usage of the Catholic and Apostolic Church, received from the primitive times of the Christian religion, and with the unanimous teaching of the holy Fathers and the decrees of sacred councils, they above all instruct the faithful diligently in matters relating to intercession and invocation of the saints, the veneration of relics, and the legitimate use of images. . . . Moreover, that the images of Christ, of the Virgin Mother of God, and of the other saints are to be placed and retained especially in the churches, and that due honor and veneration is to be given them; . . . because the honor which is shown them is referred to the prototypes which they represent, so that by means of the images which we kiss and before which we uncover the head and prostrate

ourselves, we adore Christ and venerate the saints whose likeness they bear. That is what was defined by the decrees of the councils, especially of the Second Council of Nicaea, against the opponents of images.

> Moreover, let the bishops diligently teach that by means of the stories of the mysteries of our redemption portrayed in paintings and other representations the people are instructed and confirmed in the articles of faith, which ought to be borne in mind and constantly reflected upon; also that great profit is derived from all holy images, not only because the people are thereby reminded of the benefits and gifts bestowed on them by Christ, but also because through the saints the miracles of God and salutary examples are set before the eyes of the faithful, so that they may give God thanks for those things, may fashion their own life and conduct in imitation of the saints and be moved to adore and love God and cultivate piety. . . . That these things may be the more faithfully observed, the holy council decrees that no one is permitted to erect or cause to be erected in any place or church, howsoever exempt, any unusual image unless it has been approved by the bishop.[*]

[*]*Canons and Decrees of the Council of Trent,* December 3–4, 1563. Quoted in Robert Klein and Henri Zerner, *Italian Art 1500–1600: Sources and Documents* (Evanston, Ill.: Northwestern University Press, 1966), 120–121.

UNFINISHED *PIETÀ* Six years after completing the *Last Judgment* fresco and nearly 50 years after carving the *Pietà* (FIG. 17-12) for the burial chapel of Cardinal Jean de Bilhères Lagraulas, Michelangelo, already in his 70s, began work on another *Pietà* (FIG. **17-20**), this one destined for his own tomb in Santa Maria Maggiore in Rome. For this group, the aged master set for himself an unprecedented technical challenge—to surpass the sculptors of the ancient *Laocoön* (FIG. 5-89) and carve four life-size figures from a single marble block. He did not succeed. Christ's now-missing left leg became detached, perhaps because of a flaw in the marble, and in 1555 Michelangelo abandoned the project and began to smash the statue. His assistants intervened, and he eventually permitted one of them, Tiberio Calcagni (1532–1565), to repair some of the damage and finish the work in part.

In composition and tone, this later *Pietà*—actually a *Deposition* group (see "The Life of Jesus in Art," Chapter 8, pages 240–241, or pages xxxiv–xxxv in Volume II)—stands in stark contrast to the work of Michelangelo's youth. The composition is vertical with three figures—the Virgin, Mary Magdalene, and Nicodemus—supporting the lifeless body of Christ, the slumping form of which may have been inspired by a famous Roman copy of Myron's *Discus*

17-20 Michelangelo Buonarroti, *Pietà*, ca. 1547–1555. Marble, 7′ 8″ high. Museo dell'Opera del Duomo, Florence.

Left unfinished, this *Pietà*, begun when Michelangelo was in his 70s and intended for his own tomb, includes a self-portrait of the sculptor as Nicodemus supporting the lifeless body of the Savior.

1 ft.

High and Late Renaissance   **505**

Thrower (FIG. 5-39). The Virgin is now a subsidiary figure, half hidden by her son, whose left leg originally rested on her left thigh, a position suggesting sexual union, which elicited harsh criticism—a possible reason Michelangelo smashed the statue. The undersized Mary Magdalene is in a kneeling position, and her hand does not make contact with Christ's flesh, underscoring the sacred nature of the Savior's body. Forming the apex of the composition is the hooded Nicodemus, a self-portrait of Michelangelo. This late work is therefore very personal in nature. The sculptor placed himself in direct contact with Christ, without the intercession of priests or saints, a heretical concept during the Counter-Reformation and another possible explanation why Michelangelo never completed the statue.

Architecture

Michelangelo was an accomplished architect as well as a sculptor and painter, and his Vatican commissions included designing a new church to replace the basilica Constantine erected over the site of Saint Peter's burial place (Old Saint Peter's, FIG. 8-9). By the 15th century, it was obvious the ancient timber-roofed church was insufficient for the needs and aspirations of the Renaissance papacy. Rebuilding the fourth-century basilica would occupy some of the leading architects of Italy for more than a century.

BRAMANTE The first in the distinguished line of architects of the new Saint Peter's was DONATO D'ANGELO BRAMANTE (1444–1514). Born in Urbino and trained as a painter (perhaps by Piero della Francesca), Bramante went to Milan in 1481 and, as Leonardo did, stayed there until the French arrived in 1499. In Milan, he abandoned painting to become his generation's most renowned architect. Under the influence of Filippo Brunelleschi, Leon Battista Alberti, and perhaps Leonardo, all of whom strongly favored the art and architecture of classical antiquity, Bramante developed the High Renaissance form of the central-plan church.

TEMPIETTO The architectural style Bramante championed was, consistent with the humanistic values of the day, based on ancient Roman models. Bramante's first major work in the classical mode was the small architectural gem known as the Tempietto (FIG. **17-21**) on the Janiculum hill overlooking the Vatican. The building received its name because, to contemporaries, it had the look of a small ancient temple. "Little Temple" is, in fact, a perfect nickname for the structure, because the round temples of Roman Italy (FIG. 7-4) directly inspired Bramante's design. King Ferdinand (r. 1479–1516) and Queen Isabella of Spain commissioned the Tempietto to mark the presumed location of Saint Peter's crucifixion. Bramante undertook the project in 1502, but construction may not have begun until the end of the decade. Today the Tempietto stands inside the rectangular cloister of the church of San Pietro in Montorio, but Bramante planned, although never executed, a circular colonnaded courtyard to frame the "temple." His intent was to coordinate the Tempietto and its surrounding portico by aligning the columns of the two structures.

17-21 DONATO D'ANGELO BRAMANTE, Tempietto, San Pietro in Montorio, Rome, Italy, begun 1502.

Contemporaries celebrated Bramante as the first architect to revive the classical style. Roman temples (FIG. 7-4) inspired his "little temple," but Bramante combined the classical parts in new ways.

The Tempietto's design is severely rational with its sober circular *stylobate* (stepped temple platform) and the austere *Tuscan* style of the colonnade. Bramante achieved a wonderful balance and harmony in the relationship of the parts (dome, drum, and base) to one another and to the whole. Conceived as a tall domed cylinder projecting from the lower, wider cylinder of its colonnade, this small building incorporates all the qualities of a sculptured monument. Bramante's sculptural eye is most evident in the rhythmical play of light and shadow around the columns and balustrade and across the deep-set rectangular windows alternating with shallow shell-capped niches in the *cella* (central room of a temple), walls, and drum. Although the Tempietto, superficially at least, may resemble a Greek *tholos* (a circular shrine; FIG. 5-72), and although antique models provided the inspiration for all its details, the combination of parts and details was new and original. (Classical tholoi, for instance, had neither drum nor balustrade.)

One of the main differences between the Early and High Renaissance styles of architecture is the former's emphasis on detailing flat wall surfaces versus the latter's sculptural handling of architectural masses. Bramante's Tempietto initiated the High Renaissance era in architecture. Andrea Palladio, a brilliant theorist as well as a major later 16th-century architect (FIGS. 17-28 to 17-31), included the Tempietto in his survey of ancient temples because Bramante was "the first to bring back to light the good and beautiful architecture that from antiquity to that time had been hidden."[7] Round in plan and elevated on a base that isolates it from its surroundings, the Tempietto conforms to Alberti's and Palladio's strictest demands for an ideal church.

NEW SAINT PETER'S As noted, Bramante was the architect Julius II selected to design a replacement for the Constantinian basilican church of Old Saint Peter's (FIG. 8-9). The earlier building had fallen into considerable disrepair and, in any event, did not suit this ambitious pope's taste for the colossal. Julius wanted to gain control over all Italy and to make the Rome of the popes the equal of (if not more splendid than) the Rome of the caesars. He intended the new building to serve, as did Constantine's church, as a *martyrium* to mark the apostle's grave, but the pope also hoped to install his own tomb (FIGS. 17-14 and 17-15) in the new Saint Peter's.

Bramante's ambitious design (FIG. **17-22**) for the new church consisted of a cross with arms of equal length, each terminating in an apse. A large dome would have covered the crossing, and smaller domes over subsidiary chapels would have capped the diagonal axes of the roughly square plan. Bramante's design also called for a boldly sculptural treatment of the walls and piers under the dome. The organization of the interior space was complex in the extreme:

nine interlocking crosses, five of them supporting domes. The scale of Bramante's Saint Peter's was titanic. The architect boasted he would place the dome of the Pantheon (FIGS. 7-49 to 7-51) over the Basilica Nova (Basilica of Constantine; FIG. 7-78).

A commemorative medal (FIG. **17-23**) by CRISTOFORO FOPPA CARADOSSO (ca. 1452–1526) shows how Bramante planned to accomplish that feat. As in the Pantheon, Saint Peter's dome would be hemispherical, but Bramante broke up the massive unity of the ancient temple by adding two towers and a medley of domes and porticos. In light of Julius II's interest in the Roman Empire, using the Pantheon as a model was entirely appropriate. That Bramante's design for the new Saint Peter's appeared on a commemorative medal is in itself significant. Such medals proliferated in the 15th century, reviving the ancient Roman practice of placing images of important imperial building projects on the reverse side of coins. Roman coins also bore on the fronts portraits of the emperors who commissioned the buildings. Julius II appears on the front of the Caradosso medal.

MICHELANGELO, SAINT PETER'S During Bramante's lifetime, construction of Saint Peter's did not advance beyond the erection of the crossing piers and the lower choir walls. After his death, the work passed from one architect to another and, in 1546, to Michelangelo. With the Church facing challenges to its supremacy, Pope Paul III surely felt a sense of urgency about the completion of this project. Michelangelo's work on Saint Peter's became a long-term show of dedication, thankless and without pay. Among Michelangelo's difficulties was his struggle to preserve and carry through Bramante's original plan (FIG. 17-22), which he praised and chose to retain as the basis for his own

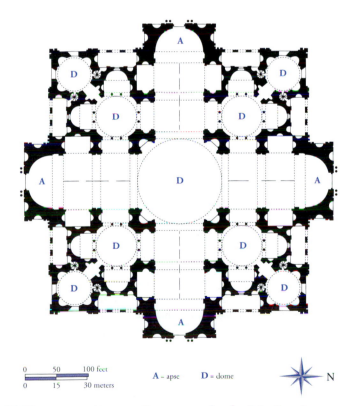

0   50   100 feet
0   15   30 meters

A = apse   D = dome   N

17-22 DONATO D'ANGELO BRAMANTE, plan for Saint Peter's, Vatican City, Rome, Italy, 1505.

Bramante proposed to replace the Constantinian basilica of Saint Peter's (FIG. 8-9) with a central-plan church featuring a cross with arms of equal length, each of which terminated in an apse.

1 in.

17-23 CRISTOFORO FOPPA CARADOSSO, reverse side of a medal showing Bramante's design for Saint Peter's, 1506. Bronze, 2¼″ diameter. British Museum, London.

Bramante's unexecuted 1506 design for Saint Peter's called for a large dome over the crossing, smaller domes over the subsidiary chapels, and a boldly sculptural treatment of the walls and piers.

17-24 MICHELANGELO BUONARROTI, plan for Saint Peter's, Vatican City, Rome, Italy, 1546.

In his modification of Bramante's plan (FIG. 17-22), Michelangelo reduced the central component from a number of interlocking crosses to a compact domed Greek cross inscribed in a square.

0 50 100 feet
0 15 30 meters
D = dome   A = apse   P = portico   N

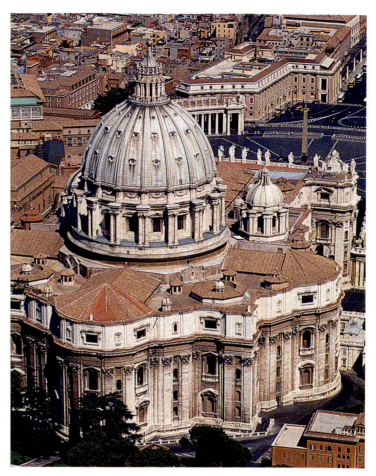

17-25 MICHELANGELO BUONARROTI, Saint Peter's (looking northeast), Vatican City, Rome, Italy, 1546–1564. Dome completed by GIACOMO DELLA PORTA, 1590.

The west end of Saint Peter's offers the best view of Michelangelo's intentions. The giant pilasters of his colossal order march around the undulating wall surfaces of the central-plan building.

design (FIG. **17-24**). Michelangelo shared Bramante's conviction that a central plan was the ideal form for a church. Always a sculptor at heart, Michelangelo carried his obsession with human form over to architecture and reasoned that buildings should follow the form of the human body. This meant organizing their units symmetrically around a central axis, as the arms relate to the body or the eyes to the nose. "For it is an established fact," he wrote, "that the members of architecture resemble the members of man. Whoever neither has been nor is a master at figures, and especially at anatomy, cannot really understand architecture."[8]

In his modification of Bramante's plan, Michelangelo reduced the central component from a number of interlocking crosses to a compact domed *Greek cross* inscribed in a square and fronted with a double-columned portico. Without destroying the centralizing features of Bramante's plan, Michelangelo, with a few strokes of the pen, converted its crystalline complexity into massive, cohesive unity. His treatment of the building's exterior further reveals his interest in creating a unified and cohesive design. Because of later changes to the front of the church, the west (apse) end (FIG. **17-25**) offers the best view of Michelangelo's style and intention. His design incorporated the colossal order, the two-story pilasters first seen in more reserved fashion in Alberti's Mantuan church of Sant'Andrea (FIG. 16-45). The giant pilasters seem to march around the undulating wall surfaces, confining the movement without interrupting it. The architectural sculpturing here extends up from the ground through the attic stories and into the drum and dome, unifying the whole building from base to summit.

The domed west end—as majestic as it is today and as influential as it has been on architecture throughout the centuries—is not quite as Michelangelo intended it. Originally, he had planned a dome with an ogival section, like the one Brunelleschi designed for Florence Cathedral (FIGS. 14-18 and 16-30A). But in his final version, he decided on a hemispherical dome to temper the verticality of the design of the lower stories and to establish a balance between dynamic and static elements. However, when Giacomo della Porta executed the dome (FIGS. 17-25 and 19-4) after Michelangelo's death, he restored the earlier high design, ignoring Michelangelo's later version. Giacomo's reasons were probably the same ones that had impelled Brunelleschi to use an ogival section for the Florentine dome—greater stability and ease of construction. The result is the dome seems to rise from its base, rather than rest firmly on it—an effect Michelangelo might not have approved.

PALAZZO FARNESE Another architectural project Michelangelo took over at the request of Paul III was the construction of the lavish private palace the pope had commissioned when he was still Cardinal Alessandro Farnese. The future pope had selected ANTONIO DA SANGALLO THE YOUNGER (1483–1546) to design the Palazzo Farnese (FIG. **17-26**) in Rome. (At Antonio's death in 1546, Michelangelo assumed control of the building's completion, while also overseeing the reorganization of the Capitoline Hill

17-26 ANTONIO DA SANGALLO THE YOUNGER, Palazzo Farnese (looking southwest), Rome, Italy, 1517–1546; completed by MICHELANGELO BUONARROTI, 1546–1550.

Paul III's construction of a lavish private palace in Rome reflects his ambitions for his papacy. The facade features a rusticated central doorway and alternating triangular and segmental pediments.

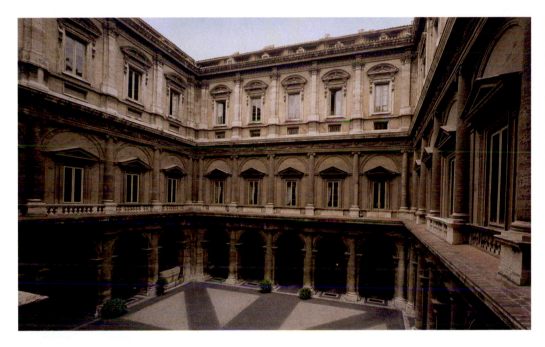

17-27 ANTONIO DA SANGALLO THE YOUNGER, courtyard of the Palazzo Farnese, Rome, Italy, ca. 1517–1546. Third story and attic by MICHELANGELO BUONARROTI, 1546–1550.

The interior courtyard of the Palazzo Farnese set the standard for later Italian palaces. It fully expresses the order, regularity, simplicity, and dignity of the High Renaissance style in architecture.

17-26A MICHELANGELO, Campidoglio, Rome, 1538–1564.

[FIG. **17-26A**] for the pope.) Antonio, the youngest of a family of architects, went to Rome around 1503 and became Bramante's draftsman and assistant. He is the perfect example of the professional architect. Indeed, his family constituted an architectural firm, often planning and drafting for other architects.

The broad, majestic front of the Palazzo Farnese asserts to the public the exalted station of a great family. It is significant that Paul chose to enlarge greatly the original rather modest palace to its present form after his accession to the papacy in 1534, reflecting his ambitions both for his family and for the papacy. Facing a spacious paved square, the facade is the very essence of princely dignity in architecture. The *quoins* (rusticated building corners) and cornice firmly anchor the rectangle of the smooth front, and lines of windows (the central row with alternating triangular and *segmental* [curved] pediments, in Bramante's fashion) mark a majestic march across it. The window frames are not flush with the wall, as in the Palazzo Medici-Riccardi (FIG. 16-37), but project from its surface, so instead of being a flat, thin plane, the facade is a spatially active three-dimensional mass. The rusticated doorway and second-story balcony, surmounted by the Farnese coat of arms, emphasize the central axis and bring the design's horizontal and vertical forces into harmony. This centralizing feature, absent from the palaces of Michelozzo (FIG. 16-37) and Alberti (FIG. 16-39), is the external opening of a central corridor axis running through the entire building and continuing in the garden beyond. Around this axis, Sangallo arranged the rooms with strict regularity.

The interior courtyard (FIG. **17-27**) displays stately column-framed arches on the first two levels, as in the Colosseum (FIG. 7-37). On the third level, Michelangelo incorporated his sophisticated variation on that theme (based in part on the Colosseum's fourth-story Corinthian pilasters), with overlapping pilasters replacing the weighty columns of Sangallo's design. The Palazzo Farnese set the standard for Italian Renaissance palaces and fully expresses the classical order, regularity, simplicity, and dignity of the High Renaissance.

High and Late Renaissance **509**

17-28 ANDREA PALLADIO, Villa Rotonda (formerly Villa Capra; looking southwest), near Vicenza, Italy, ca. 1550–1570.

The Villa Rotonda has four identical facades, each one resembling a Roman temple with a columnar porch. In the center is a great dome-covered rotunda modeled on the Pantheon (FIG. 7-49).

VENICE For centuries a major Mediterranean port, Venice served as the gateway to the Orient. After reaching the height of its commercial and political power during the 15th century, the city saw its fortunes decline in the 16th century. Even so, Venice and the Papal States were the only Italian sovereignties to retain their independence during the century of strife. Either France or Spain dominated all others. Although the discoveries in the New World and the economic shift from Italy to areas such as the Netherlands were largely responsible for the decline of Venice, even more immediate and pressing events drained its wealth and power. After their conquest of Constantinople (see Chapters 9 and 10), the Turks began to vie with the Venetians for control of the eastern Mediterranean. The Ottoman Empire evolved into a constant threat to Venice. Early in the century, the European powers of the League of Cambrai also attacked the Italian port city. Formed and led by Pope Julius II, who coveted Venetian holdings on Italy's mainland, the league included Spain, France, and the Holy Roman Empire, in addition to the Papal States. Despite these challenges, Venice developed a flourishing, independent, and influential school of artists.

ANDREA PALLADIO The chief architect of the Venetian Republic from 1570 until his death a decade later was Andrea di Pietro of Padua, known as ANDREA PALLADIO (1508–1580). (The surname derives from Pallas Athena, Greek goddess of wisdom, an appropriate reference for an architect schooled in the classical tradition of Alberti and Bramante.) Palladio began his career as a stonemason and decorative sculptor in Vicenza. At age 30, however, he turned to architecture, the ancient literature on architecture, engineering, topography, and military science. In order to study the ancient buildings firsthand, Palladio made several trips to Rome. In 1556, he illustrated Daniele Barbaro's edition of Vitruvius's *De architectura* and later wrote his own treatise on architecture, *I quattro libri dell'architettura* (*The Four Books of Architecture*), originally published in 1570. That work had wide-ranging influence on succeeding generations of architects throughout Europe. Palladio's influence outside Italy, most significantly in England and in colonial America (see Chapter 21), was stronger and more lasting than any other architect's.

Palladio accrued his significant reputation from his many designs for villas, built on the Venetian mainland. Nineteen still stand, and they especially influenced later architects. The same spirit that prompted the ancient Romans to build villas in the countryside

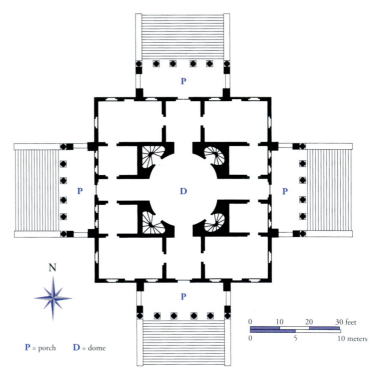

P = porch   D = dome

17-29 ANDREA PALLADIO, plan of the Villa Rotonda (formerly Villa Capra), near Vicenza, Italy, ca. 1550–1570.

Andrea Palladio published an influential treatise on architecture in 1570. Consistent with his design theories, all parts of the Villa Rotonda relate to one another in terms of mathematical ratios.

motivated a similar villa-building boom in 16th-century Venice, which, with its very limited space, was highly congested. But a longing for the countryside was not the only motive. Declining fortunes prompted the Venetians to develop their mainland possessions with new land investment and reclamation projects. Citizens who could afford to do so set themselves up as aristocratic farmers and developed swamps into productive agricultural land. The villas were thus aristocratic farms surrounded by service outbuildings (like the much later American plantations, which emulated many aspects of Palladio's architectural style). Palladio generally arranged the outbuildings in long, low wings branching out from the main building and enclosing a large rectangular court area.

VILLA ROTONDA Palladio's most famous villa, Villa Rotonda (FIG. **17-28**), near Vicenza, is exceptional because the architect did not build it for an aspiring gentleman farmer but for a retired monsignor who wanted a villa for social events. Palladio planned and designed Villa Rotonda, located on a hilltop, as a kind of *belvedere* (literally "beautiful view"; in architecture, a structure with a view of the countryside or the sea), without the usual wings of secondary buildings. It has a central plan (FIG. **17-29**) featuring four identical facades with projecting porches, each of which resembles a Roman Ionic temple. In placing a traditional temple porch in front of a dome-covered unit, Palladio doubtless had the Pantheon (FIG. 7-49) in mind. But, as Bramante did in his Tempietto (FIG. 17-21), Palladio transformed his model into a new design without parallel in antiquity. Each of the villa's four porches is a platform for enjoying a different view of the surrounding landscape. In this design, the central dome-covered rotunda logically functions as a circular reception area from which visitors may turn in any direction for the preferred view. The result is a building with functional parts systematically related to one another in terms of calculated mathematical relationships. Villa Rotonda embodies all the qualities of self-sufficiency and formal completeness most Renaissance architects sought.

SAN GIORGIO MAGGIORE One of the most dramatically placed buildings in Venice is San Giorgio Maggiore (FIG. **17-30**), directly across the Grand Canal from Piazza San Marco. Palladio began work on the church a few years before he succeeded JACOPO SANSOVINO (1486–1570; FIG. **17-30A**) as Venice's official architect. Dissatisfied with earlier solutions to the problem of integrating a high central nave and lower aisles into a unified facade design, Palladio solved it by superimposing a tall and narrow classical porch on a low broad one. This solution reflects the building's interior arrangement (FIG. **17-31**) and in that sense is strictly logical, but the

17-30A SANSOVINO, Mint and Library, Venice, begun 1536.

17-30 ANDREA PALLADIO, San Giorgio Maggiore (looking southeast), Venice, Italy, begun 1566.

Dissatisfied with earlier solutions to the problem of integrating a high central nave and lower aisles into a unified facade, Palladio superimposed a tall and narrow classical porch on a low broad one.

17-31 ANDREA PALLADIO, interior of San Giorgio Maggiore (looking east), Venice, Italy, begun 1566.

In contrast to the somewhat irrational intersection of two temple facades on the exterior of San Giorgio Maggiore, Palladio's interior is strictly logical, consistent with classical architectural theory.

intersection of two temple facades is irrational and ambiguous, consistent with contemporaneous developments in Mannerist architecture (see page 520). Palladio's design also created the illusion of three-dimensional depth, an effect intensified by the strong projection of the central columns and the shadows they cast. The play of shadow across the building's surfaces, its reflection in the water, and its gleaming white against sea and sky create a remarkably colorful effect. The interior of the church lacks the ambiguity of the facade and exhibits strong roots in High Renaissance architectural style. Light floods the interior and crisply defines the contours of the rich wall decorations, all beautifully and "correctly" profiled—the exemplar of what classical architectural theory meant by "rational" organization.

Venetian Painting

In the 16th century, the Venetians developed a painting style distinct from that of Rome and Florence. Artists in the maritime republic showed a special interest in recording the effect of Venice's soft-colored light on figures and landscapes. The leading Venetian master at the turn of the century was Giovanni Bellini, who contributed significantly to creating the High Renaissance painting style in Venice.

GIOVANNI BELLINI Trained in the International Style by his father, Jacopo, a student of Gentile da Fabriano (FIG. 16-18), GIOVANNI BELLINI (ca. 1430–1516) worked in the family shop and did not develop his own style until after his father's death in 1470. His early independent works show the dominant influence of his brother-in-law Andrea Mantegna (FIGS. 16-48 to 16-50). But in the late 1470s, he came into contact with the work of the Sicilian-born painter Antonello da Messina (ca. 1430–1479). Antonello received his early training in Naples, where he must have encountered Flemish painting and mastered using mixed oil (see "Tempera and Oil Painting," Chapter 15, page 427). This more flexible medium is wider in coloristic range than either tempera or fresco. Antonello arrived in Venice in 1475 and during his two-year stay introduced his Venetian colleagues to the possibilities the new oil technique offered. In Saint Francis

17-31A BELLINI, *Saint Francis in the Desert*, ca. 1470–1480.

in the Desert (FIG. **17-31A**), his most famous work of this period, Bellini used a mixture of oil and tempera. As a direct result of Bellini's contact with Antonello, Bellini abandoned Mantegna's harsh linear style and developed a sensuous coloristic manner destined to characterize Venetian painting for a century.

SAN ZACCARIA ALTARPIECE Bellini earned great recognition for his many Madonnas, which he painted both in half-length (with or without accompanying saints) on small devotional panels and in full-length on large, monumental altarpieces of the sacra conversazione (holy conversation) type. In the sacra conversazione, which became a popular theme for religious paintings from the middle of the 15th century on, saints from different epochs occupy the same space and seem to converse either with one another or

17-32 GIOVANNI BELLINI, *Madonna and Child with Saints* (*San Zaccaria Altarpiece*), 1505. Oil on wood transferred to canvas, 16′ 5½″ × 7′ 9″. San Zaccaria, Venice.

In this *sacra conversazione* uniting saints from different eras, Bellini created a feeling of serenity and spiritual calm through the harmonious and balanced presentation of color and light.

with the audience. (Raphael employed much the same conceit in his School of Athens, FIG. 17-9, where he gathered Greek philosophers of different eras.) Bellini carried on the tradition in the *San Zaccaria Altarpiece* (FIG. **17-32**) which he painted in 1505, already in his 70s. The Virgin Mary sits enthroned, holding the Christ Child, with saints flanking her. Bellini placed the group in a carefully painted shrine. Attributes aid the identification of all the saints: Saint Lucy holding a tray with her plucked-out eyes displayed on it; Peter with his key and book; Catherine with the palm of martyrdom and the broken wheel; and Jerome with a book (representing his translation of the Bible into Latin). At the foot of the throne sits an angel playing a viol. The painting radiates a feeling of serenity and spiritual calm. Viewers derive this sense less from the figures (no interaction occurs among them) than from Bellini's harmonious and balanced presentation of color and light. Line is not the chief agent of form, as it generally is in paintings produced in Rome and Florence. Indeed, outlines dissolve in light and shadow. Glowing color produces a soft radiance that envelops the forms with an atmospheric haze and enhances their majestic serenity.

FEAST OF THE GODS Painted a decade later, *Feast of the Gods* (FIG. **17-33**) is one of Bellini's acknowledged masterpieces. By this time, the aged master was already looking to the work of some of his students for inspiration. *Feast of the Gods* draws upon the poetic "Arcadian" landscapes of Giorgione (FIG. 17-34). Derived from Arcadia, a region in southern Greece, the term *Arcadian* referred, by the time of the Renaissance, to an idyllic place of rustic peace and simplicity. After Giorgione's premature death, Bellini embraced his student's interests and, in *Feast of the Gods,* developed a new kind of mythological painting. The duke of Ferrara, Alfonso d'Este (r. 1505–1534), commissioned this work for the Camerino d'Alabastro (Alabaster Room), a private apartment in the Palazzo Ducale complex. Alfonso hired four painters—Bellini, Titian, Raphael, and Fra Bartolommeo (1472–1517) of Florence—to provide four paintings of related mythological subjects for the room, carefully selected for the duke by the humanist scholar Mario Equicola (1470–1515). Both Raphael and Fra Bartolommeo died before fulfilling the commission. Although for his painting Bellini drew some of the figures from the standard repertoire of Greco-Roman art—most notably, the nymph carrying a vase on her head and the sleeping nymph in the lower right corner—the Olympian gods appear as peasants enjoying a picnic in a shady glade. The ancient literary source was the Roman poet Ovid's *Fasti* (1:391–440; 6:319–348), which describes the gods banqueting. Satyrs attend the gods, nymphs bring jugs of wine, and couples engage in love play. At the far right, Priapus lifts the dress of the sleeping nymph with exposed breast. (All four paintings in the Camerino centered on Venus or Bacchus, the Roman gods of love and wine.) The mellow light of a long afternoon glows softly around the gathering, caressing the surfaces of colorful fabrics, smooth flesh, and polished metal. Here, Bellini communicated the delight the Venetian school took in the beauty of texture revealed by the full resources of gently and subtly harmonized color. Behind the warm, lush tones of the figures, a background of cool green tree-filled glades extends into the distance. At the right, a screen of trees creates a verdant shelter. The atmosphere is idyllic, a lush countryside providing a setting for the never-ending pleasure of the immortal gods.

With Bellini, Venetian art became the great complement of the schools of Florence and Rome. The Venetians' instrument was color, that of the Florentines and Romans sculpturesque form. Scholars often distill the contrast between these two approaches down to *colorito* (colored or painted) versus *disegno* (drawing and design). Whereas most central Italian artists emphasized careful design preparation based on preliminary drawing (see "Renaissance Drawings," page 492), Venetian artists focused on color and the process of paint application. In addition, the general thematic focus of their work differed. Venetian artists painted the poetry of the senses and delighted in nature's beauty and the pleasures of humanity. Artists in Florence and Rome gravitated toward more intellectual themes—the epic of humanity, the masculine virtues, the grandeur of the ideal, and the lofty conceptions of religion involving the heroic and sublime. Much of the later history of Western art involves a dialogue between these two traditions.

17-33 GIOVANNI BELLINI, *Feast of the Gods,* from the Camerino d'Alabastro, Palazzo Ducale, Ferrara, Italy, 1514; repainted in part by TITIAN, 1529. Oil on canvas, 5′ 7″ × 6′ 2″. National Gallery of Art, Washington (Widener Collection).

In *Feast of the Gods,* based on Ovid's *Fasti,* Bellini developed a new kind of mythological painting in which the Olympian deities appear as peasants enjoying a picnic in the soft afternoon light.

1 ft.

17-34 Giorgione da Castelfranco, *The Tempest,* ca. 1510. Oil on canvas, 2′ 8¼″ × 2′ 4¾″. Galleria dell'Accademia, Venice.

The subject of this painting set in a lush landscape beneath a stormy sky is uncertain, contributing, perhaps intentionally, to the painting's enigmatic quality and intriguing air.

GIORGIONE Describing Venetian art as "poetic" is particularly appropriate, given the development of *poesia,* or painting meant to operate in a manner similar to poetry. Both classical and Renaissance poetry inspired Venetian artists, and their paintings focused on the lyrical and sensual. Thus, in many Venetian artworks, discerning concrete narratives or subjects is virtually impossible. That is certainly the case with *The Tempest* (FIG. **17-34**), a painting that continues to defy interpretation. It is the greatest work attributed to the short-lived GIORGIONE DA CASTELFRANCO (ca. 1477–1510), the Venetian artist who deserves much of the credit for developing the poetic manner of painting. To an even greater extent than in Bellini's later *Feast of the Gods* (for which Giorgione's work served as inspiration for his teacher, Bellini), a lush landscape fills most of Giorgione's *Tempest.* Stormy skies and lightning in the middle background threaten the tranquility of the pastoral setting, however. Pushed off to both sides are the few human figures depicted—a young woman nursing a baby in the right foreground and a man

17-35 Titian, *Pastoral Symphony,* ca. 1508–1511. Oil on canvas, 3′ 7¼″ × 4′ 6¼″. Musée du Louvre, Paris.

Venetian art conjures poetry. In this painting, Titian so eloquently evoked the pastoral mood that the uncertainty about the picture's meaning is not distressing. The mood and rich color are enough.

carrying a *halberd* (a combination spear and battle-ax—but he is not a soldier) on the left. Much scholarly debate has centered on the painting's subject, fueled by X-rays of the canvas that revealed Giorgione altered many of the details as work progressed. Most notably, a seated nude woman originally occupied the position where Giorgione subsequently placed the standing man. The changes the painter made have led many art historians to believe Giorgione did not intend the painting to have a definitive narrative, which is appropriate for a Venetian poetic rendering. Other scholars have suggested various mythological and biblical narratives. The uncertainty about the subject contributes to the painting's intriguing air.

TITIAN Giorgione's masterful handling of light and color and his interest in landscape, poetry, and music—Vasari reported he was an accomplished lutenist and singer—influenced not only his much older yet constantly inquisitive master, Bellini, but also his younger contemporary, Tiziano Vecelli, called TITIAN (ca. 1490–1576) in English. Indeed, a masterpiece long attributed to Giorgione—*Pastoral Symphony* (FIG. **17-35**)—is now widely believed to be an early work of Titian. Out of dense shadow emerge the soft forms of figures and landscape. Titian, a supreme colorist and master of the oil medium, cast a mood of tranquil reverie and dreaminess over the entire scene, evoking the landscape of a lost but never forgotten paradise. As in Giorgione's *Tempest*, the theme is as enigmatic as the lighting. Two nude women, accompanied by two clothed young men, occupy the bountiful landscape through which a shepherd passes. In the distance, a villa crowns a hill. The artist so eloquently evoked the pastoral mood that the viewer does not find the uncertainty about the picture's precise meaning distressing. The mood is enough. The shepherd symbolizes the poet. The pipes and lute symbolize his poetry. The two women accompanying the young men may be thought of as their invisible inspiration, their muses. One turns to lift water from the sacred well of poetic inspiration. The voluptuous bodies of the women, softly modulated by the smoky shadow, became the standard in Venetian art. The fullness of their figures contributes to their effect as poetic personifications of nature's abundance.

ASSUMPTION OF THE VIRGIN On Bellini's death in 1516, the Republic of Venice appointed Titian as its official painter. Shortly thereafter, the prior of the Franciscan basilica of Santa Maria Gloriosa dei Frari commissioned Titian to paint a monumental altarpiece (nearly 23 feet high) for the high altar of the church. In *Assumption of the Virgin* (FIG. **17-36**), a fitting theme for the shrine of the "glorious Saint Mary," Titian's remarkable coloristic sense and his ability to convey light through color are again on display. The subject is the ascent of the Virgin to Heaven on a great white cloud borne aloft by putti. Above, golden clouds, so luminous they seem to glow and radiate light into the church, envelop the Virgin, whose head is on the vertical axis of the composition. God the Father appears above, slightly off-center, awaiting Mary with open arms. Below, closest to the viewer, over-life-size apostles gesticulate wildly as they witness the glorious event. Through his mastery of the oil medium—fresco was not a good choice for Venetian churches because of the dampness and salinity of this city with saltwater streets—Titian used vibrant color to infuse the image with intensity and amplify the drama.

17-36 TITIAN, *Assumption of the Virgin*, 1515–1518. Oil on wood, 22′ 7½″ × 11′ 10″. Santa Maria Gloriosa dei Frari, Venice.

Titian won renown for his ability to convey light through color. In this dramatic depiction of the Virgin Mary's ascent to Heaven, the golden clouds seem to glow and radiate light into the church.

1 ft.

17-37 TITIAN, *Madonna of the Pesaro Family*, 1519–1526. Oil on canvas, 15' 11" × 8' 10". Pesaro Chapel, Santa Maria Gloriosa dei Frari, Venice.

In this dynamic composition presaging a new kind of pictorial design, Titian placed the figures on a steep diagonal, positioning the Madonna, the focus of the composition, well off the central axis.

1 ft.

PESARO MADONNA A year after installing *Assumption of the Virgin* in the main altar of the Venetian church of the Frari, Titian received a commission to paint *Madonna of the Pesaro Family* (FIG. **17-37**) for the same church. Jacopo Pesaro (d. 1547), bishop of Paphos in Cyprus and commander of the papal fleet, had led a successful expedition in 1502 against the Turks during the Venetian-Turkish war. He dedicated a family chapel in Santa Maria Gloriosa and donated Titian's altarpiece in gratitude. In a stately sunlit setting in what may be the Madonna's palace in Heaven, Mary receives the commander, who kneels dutifully at the foot of her throne. A soldier (Saint George?) behind the commander carries a banner with the *escutcheons* (shields with coats of arms) of the Borgia pope, Alexander VI, and of Pesaro. Behind him is a turbaned Turk, a prisoner of war of the Christian forces. Saint Peter appears on the steps of the throne, and Saint Francis introduces other Pesaro family members (all male—Italian depictions of donors in this era typically excluded women and children), who kneel solemnly in the right foreground. Thus, Titian entwined the human and the heavenly, depicting the Madonna and saints honoring the achievements of a specific man. A quite worldly transaction takes place (albeit beneath a heavenly cloud bearing angels) between a queen and her court and loyal servants, consistent with Renaissance protocol and courtly splendor.

A prime characteristic of High Renaissance painting is the massing of monumental figures, singly and in groups, within a weighty and majestic architecture. But here Titian did not compose a horizontal and symmetrical arrangement, as did Leonardo in *Last Supper* (FIG. 17-4) and Raphael in *School of Athens* (FIG. 17-9). Rather, he placed the figures on a steep diagonal, positioning the Madonna, the focus of the composition, well off the central axis. Titian drew attention to her with the perspective lines, the inclination of the figures, and the directional lines of gaze and gesture. The banner inclining toward the left beautifully brings the design into equilibrium, balancing the rightward and upward tendencies of its main direction. This kind of composition is more dynamic than most High Renaissance examples and presaged a new kind of pictorial design—one built on movement rather than rest.

BACCHUS AND ARIADNE After the deaths of Raphael and Fra Bartolommeo, Titian took over their commissions to paint bacchanalian scenes for Alfonso d'Este's Camerino d'Alabastro in addition to his own assignment. Titian also contributed the landscape background to Bellini's *Feast of the Gods* (FIG. 17-33). Completed in 1523, *Meeting of Bacchus and Ariadne* (FIG. **17-38**), based on an ancient Latin poem by Catullus, is a roughly six-feet-square canvas in which Bacchus, accompanied by a boisterous group, arrives on the island of Naxos in a leopard-drawn chariot to save Ariadne, whom Theseus had abandoned there. Consistent with the mythological subject, Titian looked to classical art for models and derived one of the figures, the snake-entwined satyr, from the recently unearthed

Laocoön (FIG. 5-89), a marble statue that also made an indelible impression on Michelangelo and many others. Titian's rich and luminous colors add greatly to the sensuous appeal of the painting, making it perfect for what Alfonso called his "pleasure chamber."

VENUS OF URBINO In 1538, at the height of his powers, Titian painted the so-called *Venus of Urbino* (FIG. **17-39**) for Guidobaldo II, who became the duke of Urbino the following year (r. 1539–1574). The title (given to the painting later) elevates to the status of classical mythology what is probably a representation of a sensual Italian woman in her bedchamber. Whether the subject is divine or mortal, Titian based his version on an earlier (and pioneering) painting of Venus (not illustrated) by Giorgione. Here, Titian established the compositional elements and the standard for paintings of the reclining female nude, regardless of the many ensuing variations. This "Venus" reclines on the gentle slope of her luxurious pillowed couch. Her softly rounded body contrasts with the sharp vertical edge of the curtain behind her, which serves to direct the viewer's attention to her left hand and pelvis as well as to divide the foreground from the background. At the woman's feet is a slumbering lapdog—where Cupid would be if this were Venus. In the right background, near the window opening onto a landscape, two servants bend over a chest, apparently searching for garments (Renaissance households stored clothing in carved wooden chests

17-38 TITIAN, *Meeting of Bacchus and Ariadne,* from the Camerino d'Alabastro, Palazzo Ducale, Ferrara, Italy, **1522–1523.** Oil on canvas, 5′ 9″ × 6′ 3″. National Gallery, London.

Titian's rich and luminous colors add greatly to the sensuous appeal of this mythological painting in which he based one of the figures on the recently unearthed *Laocoön* (FIG. 5-89).

1 ft.

17-39 TITIAN, *Venus of Urbino,* 1536–1538. Oil on canvas, 3′ 11″ × 5′ 5″. Galleria degli Uffizi, Florence.

Titian established oil color on canvas as the preferred painting medium in Western art. Here, he also set the standard for representations of the reclining female nude, whether divine or mortal.

1 ft.

Women in the Renaissance Art World

The Renaissance art world was decidedly male-dominated. Few women could become professional artists because of the many obstacles they faced. In particular, for centuries, training practices mandating residence in a master's house (see "Artists' Guilds," Chapter 14, page 410) precluded women from acquiring the necessary experience. In addition, social proscriptions, such as those preventing women from drawing from nude models, hampered an aspiring woman artist's advancement through the accepted avenues of artistic training.

17-40A FONTANA, *Portrait of a Noblewoman*, ca. 1580.

Still, some determined Renaissance women surmounted these barriers and produced not only considerable bodies of work but earned enviable reputations as well. One was Sofonisba Anguissola (FIG. 17-47), who was so accomplished she can be considered the first Italian woman to have ascended to the level of international art celebrity. LAVINIA FONTANA (1552–1614; FIG. **17-40A**) also achieved notable success, and her paintings constitute the largest surviving body of work by any woman artist before 1700. Fontana learned her craft from her father, Prospero Fontana (1512–1597), a leading Bolognese painter. (Paternal training was the norm for aspiring women artists.) She was in demand as a portraitist and received commissions from important patrons, including members of the ruling Habsburg family. She even spent time as an official painter to the papal court in Rome.

Perhaps more challenging for women than the road to becoming a professional painter was the mastery of sculpture, made more difficult by the physical demands of the medium. Yet Properzia de' Rossi (ca. 1490–1530) established herself as a professional sculptor and was the only woman artist Giorgio Vasari included in his comprehensive publication, *Lives of the Most Eminent Painters, Sculptors, and Architects*. Active in the early 16th century, she died of the plague in 1530, bringing her promising career to an early end.

Beyond the realm of art production, Renaissance women exerted significant influence as art patrons. Scholars only recently have begun to explore systematically the role of women in commissioning works of art. As a result, current knowledge is sketchy at best but suggests women played a much more extensive role than previously acknowledged. Among the problems researchers face in their quest to clarify women's activities as patrons is that women often wielded their influence and decision-making power behind the scenes. Many of them acquired their positions through marriage. Their power was thus indirect and provisional, based on their husbands' wealth and status. Thus, documentation of the networks within which women patrons operated and of the processes they used to exert power in a society dominated by men is less substantive than for male patrons.

One of the most important Renaissance patrons, male or female, was Isabella d'Este (1474–1539), the marquess of Mantua. The daughter of Ercole d'Este, duke of Ferrara (r. 1471–1505), and brought up in the cultured princely court there, Isabella married Francesco Gonzaga, marquis of Mantua (1466–1519), in 1490. The marriage gave Isabella access to the position and wealth necessary to pursue her interest in becoming a major art patron. An avid collector, she enlisted the aid of agents who scoured Italy for appealing artworks. Isabella

17-40 TITIAN, *Isabella d'Este*, 1534–1536. Oil on canvas, 3′ 4⅛″ × 2′ 1³⁄₁₆″. Kunsthistorisches Museum, Vienna.

Isabella d'Este was one of the most powerful women of the Renaissance era. When, at age 60, she commissioned Titian to paint her portrait, she insisted the artist depict her in her 20s.

did not limit her collection to painting and sculpture but included ceramics, glassware, gems, cameos, medals, classical texts, musical manuscripts, and musical instruments.

Undoubtedly, Isabella was a proud and ambitious woman well aware of how art could boost her fame and reputation. Accordingly, she commissioned several portraits of herself from the most esteemed artists of her day—Leonardo da Vinci, Andrea Mantegna, and Titian (FIG. 17-40). The detail and complexity of many of her contracts with artists reveal her insistence on control over the artworks.

Other Renaissance women positioned themselves as serious art patrons. One was Caterina Sforza (1462–1509), daughter of Galeazzo Maria Sforza (heir to the duchy of Milan), who married Girolamo Riario (1443–1488) in 1484. The death of her husband, lord of Imola and count of Forlì, gave Sforza, who survived him by two decades, access to power denied most women. Another female art patron was Lucrezia Tornabuoni (1425–1482), who married Piero di Cosimo de' Medici (1416–1469), one of many Medici, both men and women, who earned reputations as unparalleled art patrons. Further archival investigation of women's roles in Renaissance Italy undoubtedly will produce more evidence of how women established themselves as patrons and artists and the extent to which they contributed to the flourishing of Renaissance art.

Palma il Giovane on Titian

An important change occurring in Titian's time was the almost universal adoption of canvas, with its rough-textured surface, in place of wood panels for paintings. Titian's works established oil-based pigment on canvas as the typical medium of the Western pictorial tradition thereafter. Palma il Giovane, one of Titian's students, who completed the *Pietà* (FIG. 17-41) Titian intended for his tomb in Santa Maria Gloriosa dei Frari in Venice, wrote a valuable account of his teacher's working methods and of how Titian used the new medium to great advantage:

Titian [employed] a great mass of colors, which served . . . as a base for the compositions. . . . I too have seen some of these, formed with bold strokes made with brushes laden with colors, sometimes of a pure red earth, which he used, so to speak, for a middle tone, and at other times of white lead; and with the same brush tinted with red, black and yellow he formed a highlight; and observing these principles he made the promise of an exceptional figure appear in four brushstrokes. . . . Having constructed these precious foundations he used to turn his pictures to the wall and leave them there without looking at them, sometimes for several months. When he wanted to apply his brush again he would examine them with the utmost rigor . . . to see if he could find any faults. . . . In this way, working on the figures and revising them, he brought them to the most perfect symmetry that the beauty of art and nature can reveal. . . . [T]hus he gradually covered those quintessential forms with living flesh, bringing them

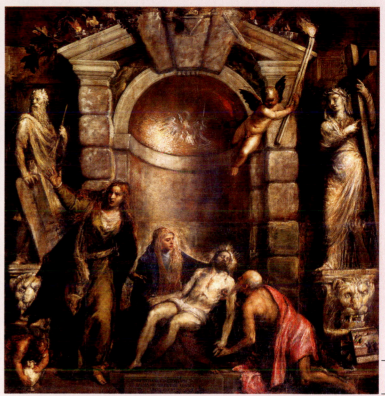

17-41 TITIAN and PALMA IL GIOVANE, *Pietà*, ca. 1570–1576. Oil on canvas, 11′ 6″ × 12′ 9″. Galleria dell'Accademia, Venice.

In this late work characterized by broad brushstrokes and a thick impasto, Titian portrayed himself as the penitent Saint Jerome kneeling before the dead Christ. Titian intended the work for his own tomb.

1 ft.

by many stages to a state in which they lacked only the breath of life. He never painted a figure all at once and . . . in the last stages he painted more with his fingers than his brushes.*

*Quoted in Francesco Valcanover, "An Introduction to Titian," in Valcanover, *Titian: Prince of Painters* (Venice: Marsilio Editori, 1990), 23–24.

---

called *cassoni*) to clothe their reclining nude mistress. Beyond them, a smaller vista opens into a landscape. Titian masterfully constructed the view backward into the room and the division of the space into progressively smaller units.

As in other Venetian paintings, color plays a prominent role in *Venus of Urbino*. The red tones of the matron's skirt and the muted reds of the tapestries against the neutral whites of the matron's sleeves and the kneeling girl's gown echo the deep Venetian reds set off against the pale neutral whites of the linen and the warm ivory gold of the flesh. The viewer must study the picture carefully to realize the subtlety of color planning. For instance, the two deep reds (in the foreground cushions and in the background skirt) play a critical role in the composition as a gauge of distance and as indicators of an implied diagonal opposed to the real one of the reclining figure. Here, Titian used color not simply to record surface appearance but also to organize his placement of forms.

ISABELLA D'ESTE Titian was a highly esteemed portraitist as well and in great demand. More than 50 portraits by his hand survive. One of the best is *Isabella d'Este* (FIG. **17-40**), Titian's portrait of one of the most prominent women of the Renaissance (see "Women in the Renaissance Art World," page 518). Isabella was the sister of Alfonso d'Este, for whom Titian painted three mythological scenes

for the Ferrara ducal palace. At 16, she married Francesco Gonzaga, marquis of Mantua, and through her patronage of art and music was instrumental in developing the Mantuan court into an important cultural center. Portraits by Titian generally emphasize his psychological reading of the subject's head and hands. Thus, Titian sharply highlighted Isabella's face, whereas her black dress fades into the undefined darkness of the background. The unseen light source also illuminates Isabella's hands, and Titian painted her sleeves with incredible detail to further draw viewers' attention to her hands. This portrait reveals not only Titian's skill but the patron's wish too. Painted when Isabella was 60 years old, the portrait depicts her in her 20s—at her specific request. Titian used an earlier likeness of her as his guide, but his portrait is no copy. Rather, it is a distinctive portrayal of his poised and self-assured patron that owes little to its model.

PIETÀ As Michelangelo had done late in his life, Titian began to contemplate death and salvation and around 1570 decided to create a memorial for his tomb. He, too, chose *Pietà* (FIG. **17-41**) as the theme, albeit for a painting, not a statuary group, as in Michelangelo's case (FIG. 17-20). Intended for the altar of his burial chapel in the right aisle of Santa Maria Gloriosa dei Frari in Venice, which housed two of his earlier altarpieces (FIGS. 17-36 and 17-37),

Titian's *Pietà* remained unfinished when he died of the plague in 1576. His assistant, Jacopo Negretti, known as Palma il Giovane (1548–1628)—Palma the Younger—piously completed the painting.

Titian set the scene of grief over Christ's death in a rusticated niche reminiscent of the bays of Sansovino's Mint (FIG. 17-30A, *left*) on the Canale San Marco. The Virgin cradles her son's body, while Mary Magdalene runs forward with her right arm raised in a gesture of extreme distress. (Echoing her form, but in reverse, is the torch-carrying angel added by Palma.) The other penitent mourner is Saint Jerome, seen from behind kneeling at Christ's side. His head has the features of the aged, balding Titian—another parallel with Michelangelo's *Pietà*. Both artists apparently wanted to portray themselves touching Jesus' body, hoping for their salvation.

For this huge (roughly 12 feet square) canvas, Titian employed one of his favorite compositional devices (compare FIG. 17-37), creating a bold diagonal movement beginning at Jerome's feet and leading through Christ, the Virgin, and Mary Magdalene to the statue of Moses with the Ten Commandments at the left. (The other statue represents the Hellespontine Sibyl. The votive painting leaning against its pedestal depicts Titian and his son Orazio, who also died of the plague in 1576, praying before another *Pietà*.) But unlike Titian's early and mature works, in which he used smooth and transparent oil glazes, this *Pietà,* as his other late paintings, features broken brushstrokes and rough, uneven patches of pigment built up like paste (*impasto*) that catch the light. Many Baroque painters, especially Peter Paul Rubens and Rembrandt van Rijn (see Chapter 20), subsequently adopted Titian's innovative and highly expressive manner of applying thick paint to canvas (see "Palma il Giovane on Titian," page 519).

MANNERISM

The Renaissance styles of Rome, Florence, and Venice dominated Italian painting, sculpture, and architecture for most of the 16th century, but already in the 1520s another style—Mannerism—had emerged in reaction to it. *Mannerism* is a term derived from the Italian word *maniera,* meaning "style" or "manner." In the field of art history, the term *style* usually refers to a characteristic or representative mode, especially of an artist or period (for example, Titian's style or Gothic style). *Style* can also refer to an absolute quality of fashion (for example, someone has "style"). Mannerism's style (or representative mode) is characterized by style (being stylish, cultured, elegant).

Painting

Among the features most closely associated with Mannerism is artifice. Of course, all art involves artifice, in the sense that art is not "natural"—it is something humans fashion. But many artists, including High Renaissance painters such as Leonardo and Raphael, chose to conceal that artifice by using devices such as perspective and shading to make their representations of the world look natural. In contrast, Mannerist painters consciously revealed the constructed nature of their art. In other words, Renaissance artists generally strove to create art that appeared natural, whereas Mannerist artists were less inclined to disguise the contrived nature of art production. This is why artifice is a central feature of discussions about Mannerism, and why Mannerist works can seem, appropriately, "mannered." The conscious display of artifice in Mannerism often reveals itself in imbalanced compositions and unusual complexities, both visual and conceptual. Ambiguous space, departures from expected conventions, and unusual presentations of traditional themes also surface frequently in Mannerist art.

1 ft.

17-42 Jacopo da Pontormo, *Entombment of Christ,* Capponi chapel, Santa Felicità, Florence, Italy, 1525–1528. Oil on wood, 10′ 3″ × 6′ 4″. ◼

Mannerist paintings such as this one represent a departure from the compositions of the earlier Renaissance. Instead of concentrating masses in the center of the painting, Pontormo left a void.

PONTORMO *Entombment of Christ* (FIG. **17-42**) by the Florentine painter Jacopo Carucci, known as Jacopo da Pontormo (1494–1557) after his birthplace, exhibits almost all the stylistic features characteristic of Mannerism's early phase in painting—as does *Fall of the Rebel Angels* (FIG. **17-42A**) by Pontormo's older contemporary Domenico Beccafumi (1481–1551). Christ's descent from the cross and subsequent entombment had frequently been depicted in art (see "The Life of Jesus in Art," Chapter 8, pages 240–241, or on pages xxxiv–xxxv in Volume II), and Pontormo exploited the familiarity 16th-century viewers would have had by playing off their expectations. For example, he omitted from the painting both the cross and Christ's tomb, and consequently scholars debate whether he meant to represent *Descent from the Cross* or *Entombment*. Also, instead of presenting the action as tak-

17-42A Beccafumi, *Fall of the Rebel Angels,* ca. 1524.

ing place across the perpendicular picture plane, as artists such as Raphael and Rogier van der Weyden (FIG. 15-8) had done in their paintings of these episodes from Christ's passion, Pontormo rotated the conventional figural groups along a vertical axis. As a result, the Virgin Mary falls back (away from the viewer) as she releases her dead son's hand. Unlike High Renaissance artists, who had concentrated their masses in the center of the painting, Pontormo left a void. This emptiness accentuates the grouping of hands filling that hole, calling attention to the void—symbolic of loss and grief. The artist enhanced the painting's ambiguity with the curiously anxious glances the figures cast in all directions. (The bearded young man at the upper right who gazes at the viewer is probably a self-portrait of Pontormo.) Athletic bending and twisting characterize many of the figures, with distortions (for example, the torso of the foreground figure bends in an anatomically impossible way), elastic elongation of the limbs, and heads rendered as uniformly small and oval. The contrasting colors, primarily light blues and pinks, add to the dynamism and complexity of the work. The painting represents a departure from the balanced, harmoniously structured compositions of the High Renaissance.

PARMIGIANINO Girolamo Francesco Maria Mazzola of Parma, known as PARMIGIANINO (1503–1540), achieved a reputation as a gifted painter while still in his teens. When he was 21, a visit to a barber's shop, where he saw his reflection in a convex mirror, inspired him to paint a self-portrait (FIG. 17-43) of unique format with the intention of presenting it to Pope Clement VII as a demonstration of his virtuosity. According to Vasari, the pope proclaimed the work a "marvel," and Parmigianino, who possessed charm and good looks as well as artistic talent, quickly became the favorite painter of the elite in Rome, the successor to Raphael, who had died just four years before Parmigianino's arrival at the papal court.

To imitate the appearance of a convex mirror, Parmigianino had a carpenter prepare a section of a wooden sphere of the same size and shape as a barber's mirror (about 10 inches in diameter) and used oil glazes to produce a surface luster that heightens the illusion of the viewer looking into a mirror and not at a painting. The viewer in this case is also the painter, whose handsome countenance Vasari described as an angel's, not a man's. The pope remarked that Parmigianino's portrait of himself in his studio was "astonishing" in its success in creating the appearance of someone gazing at his reflection. As in a real convex mirror, the artist's face—at the center of the reflective surface and some distance from it—is free of distortion, but his hand and sleeve are of exaggerated size. The emphasis on the hand no doubt is also a statement on Parmigianino's part about the supreme importance of the painter's hand in fashioning an artwork. That emphasis on artifice as the essence of painting is the core principle of Mannerism.

MADONNA WITH THE LONG NECK Parmigianino's best-known work, however, is *Madonna with the Long Neck* (FIG. **17-44**), which exemplifies the elegant stylishness that was a principal aim

17-44 PARMIGIANINO, *Madonna with the Long Neck*, from the Baiardi chapel, Santa Maria dei Servi, Parma, Italy, 1534–1540. Oil on wood, 7′ 1″ × 4′ 4″. Galleria degli Uffizi, Florence. ▣◀

Parmigianino's Madonna displays the stylish elegance that was a principal aim of Mannerism. Mary has a small oval head, a long slender neck, attenuated hands, and a sinuous body.

1 in.

17-43 PARMIGIANINO, *Self-Portrait in a Convex Mirror*, 1524. Oil on wood, 9⅝″ diameter. Kunsthistorisches Museum, Vienna.

Painted to impress Pope Clement VII with his virtuosity, Parmigianino's self-portrait brilliantly reproduces the young Mannerist's distorted appearance as seen in a barber's convex mirror.

17-45 BRONZINO, *Venus, Cupid, Folly, and Time*, ca. 1546. Oil on wood, 4′ 9½″ × 3′ 9¾″. National Gallery, London.

In this painting of Cupid fondling his mother Venus, Bronzino demonstrated a fondness for learned allegories with lascivious undertones. As in many Mannerist works, the meaning is ambiguous.

BRONZINO *Venus, Cupid, Folly, and Time* (FIG. **17-45**), by Agnolo di Cosimo, called BRONZINO (1503–1572), also displays all the chief features of Mannerist painting. A pupil of Pontormo, Bronzino was a Florentine and painter to the first grand duke of Tuscany, Cosimo I de' Medici (r. 1537–1574). In this painting, which Cosimo commissioned as a gift for King Francis I of France (FIG. 18-12), Bronzino demonstrated the Mannerists' fondness for learned allegories that often had lascivious undertones, a shift from the simple and monumental statements and forms of the High Renaissance. Bronzino depicted Cupid—here an adolescent who has reached puberty, not an infant—fondling his mother, Venus, while Folly prepares to shower them with rose petals. Time, who appears in the upper right corner, draws back the curtain to reveal the playful incest in progress. Other figures in the painting represent other human qualities and emotions, including Envy. The masks, a favorite device of the Mannerists, symbolize deceit. The picture seems to suggest that love—accompanied by envy and plagued by inconstancy—is foolish and that lovers will discover its folly in time. But as in many Mannerist paintings, the meaning here is ambiguous, and interpretations of the painting vary. Compositionally, Bronzino placed the figures around the front plane, and they almost entirely block the space. The contours are strong and sculptural, the surfaces of enamel smoothness. Of special interest are the heads, hands, and feet, for the Mannerists considered the extremities the carriers of grace, and the clever depiction of them as evidence of artistic skill.

ELEANORA OF TOLEDO In 1540, Cosimo I de' Medici married Eleanora of Toledo (1519–1562), daughter of Charles V's viceroy in Naples, and thereby cemented an important alliance with the Spanish court. Several years later Cosimo asked Bronzino to paint Eleanora and their second son, Giovanni (FIG. **17-46**), who then was about three years old. Bronzino painted dozens of portraits of members of the Medici family, but never portrayed Eleanora with any of her daughters (she and Cosimo had three daughters as well as eight sons). This painting therefore should be seen as a formal dynastic portrait intended to present the duke's wife as the mother of one of his heirs.

As in other Bronzino portraits (FIG. **17-46A**), the subjects appear aloof and emotionless. Bronzino idealized both Eleanora and Giovanni, giving both of them perfect features and blemishless skin that glows like alabaster. Eleanora's figure takes up most of the panel's surface, and Bronzino further underscored her primacy by lightening the blue background around her head, creating a halolike frame for her face and perhaps associating the mother and son with the Madonna and Christ Child. Seated with one arm around Giovanni and the other resting on her lap, Eleanora looks out at the viewer with cool detachment. She is richly attired in a brocaded gown and wears a costly pearl necklace and a tiara. The painter reproduced the various tex-

17-46A BRONZINO, *Portrait of a Young Man*, ca. 1530–1545. ◼◣

of Mannerism. In Parmigianino's hands, this traditional, usually sedate, religious subject became a picture of exquisite grace and precious sweetness. The Madonna's small oval head, her long and slender neck, the otherworldly attenuation and delicacy of her hand, and the sinuous, swaying elongation of her frame—all are marks of the aristocratic, sumptuous courtly taste of Mannerist artists and patrons alike. Parmigianino amplified this elegance by expanding the Madonna's form as viewed from head to toe. On the left stands a bevy of angelic creatures, melting with emotions as soft and smooth as their limbs. On the right, the artist included a line of columns without capitals and an enigmatic figure with a scroll, whose distance from the foreground is immeasurable and ambiguous—the antithesis of rational Renaissance perspective diminution of size with distance.

Although the elegance and sophisticated beauty of the painting are due in large part to the Madonna's attenuated limbs, that exaggeration is not solely decorative in purpose. *Madonna with the Long Neck* takes its subject from a simile in medieval hymns comparing the Virgin's neck with a great ivory tower or column, such as the one Parmigianino depicted to the right of the Madonna.

tures of fabric, jewels, hair, and flesh with supreme skill. The boy stands stiffly, staring forward, suppressing all playful thoughts in

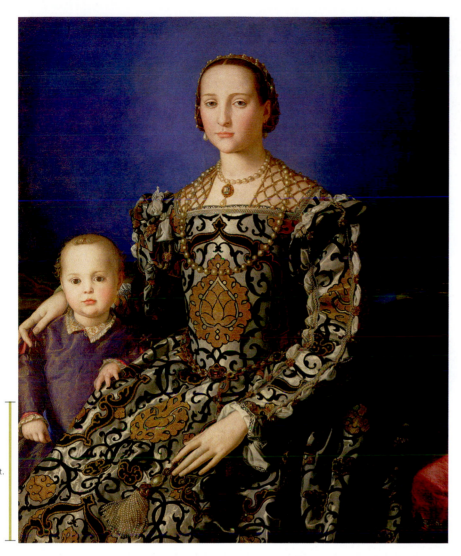

17-46 Bronzino, *Eleanora of Toledo and Giovanni de' Medici*, ca. 1546. Oil on wood, 3' 9¼″ × 3' 1¾″. Galleria degli Uffizi, Florence. ◼◀

Bronzino was the official portraitist of Grand Duke Cosimo de' Medici. His portrayal of Cosimo's Spanish wife and their second son features rich costumes and coolly detached personalities.

order to behave as expected on this formal occasion. Bronzino's portrayal of Eleanora and Giovanni is in some ways less a portrait of a mother and child than of a royal audience.

SOFONISBA ANGUISSOLA The aloof formality of Bronzino's dynastic portrait is much relaxed in the portraiture of Sofonisba Anguissola (ca. 1532–1625) of Cremona in northern Italy. Anguissola introduced a new kind of group portrait of irresistible charm, characterized by an informal intimacy and subjects that are often moving, conversing, or engaged in activities. Like many of the other works she produced before emigrating to Spain in 1559, the portrait illustrated here (FIG. **17-47**) represents members of her family. Against a neutral ground, Anguissola placed her two sisters and brother in an affectionate pose meant not for official display but for private showing. The sisters, wearing matching striped gowns, flank their brother, who caresses a lapdog. The older sister (at the left) summons the dignity required for the occasion, while the boy looks quizzically at the portraitist with an expression of naive curiosity, and the other girl diverts her attention toward something or someone to the painter's left.

Anguissola's use of relaxed poses and expressions, her sympathetic personal presentation, and her graceful treatment of the forms brought her international acclaim (see "Women in the Renaissance Art World," page 518). She received praise from the aged Michelangelo, was court painter to Phillip II (r. 1556–1598) of Spain, and, at the end of her life, gave advice on art to a young admirer of her work, Anthony Van Dyck (FIG. 20-5), the great Flemish master.

17-47 Sofonisba Anguissola, *Portrait of the Artist's Sisters and Brother*, ca. 1555. Oil on wood, 2' 5¼″ × 3' 1½″. Methuen Collection, Corsham Court, Wiltshire.

Anguissola was the leading woman artist of her time. Her contemporaries admired her use of relaxed poses and expressions in intimate and informal group portraits such as this one of her family.

Tintoretto adopted many Mannerist pictorial devices to produce oil paintings imbued with emotional power, depth of spiritual vision, glowing Venetian color schemes, and dramatic lighting.

1 ft.

TINTORETTO Venetian painting of the later 16th century built on established High Renaissance Venetian ideas, but incorporated many elements of the Mannerist style. Jacopo Robusti, known as TINTORETTO (1518–1594), claimed to be a student of Titian and aspired to combine Titian's color with Michelangelo's drawing, but art historians consider Tintoretto the outstanding Venetian representative of Mannerism. He adopted many Mannerist pictorial devices, which he employed to produce works imbued with dramatic power, depth of spiritual vision, and glowing Venetian color schemes.

Toward the end of Tintoretto's life, his art became spiritual, even visionary, as solid forms melted away into swirling clouds of dark shot through with fitful light. In Tintoretto's *Last Supper* (FIG. **17-48**), painted for the right wall next to the high altar in Andrea Palladio's church of San Giorgio Maggiore (FIG. 17-31), the figures appear in a dark interior illuminated by a single light in the upper left of the image. The shimmering halos establish the biblical nature of the scene. The ability of this dramatic scene to engage viewers was fully in keeping with Counter-Reformation ideals

17-49 PAOLO VERONESE, *Christ in the House of Levi,* from the refectory of Santi Giovanni e Paolo, Venice, Italy, 1573. Oil on canvas, 18′ 3″ × 42′. Galleria dell'Accademia, Venice.

Veronese's paintings feature superb color and majestic classical settings. The Catholic Church accused him of impiety for including dogs and dwarfs near Christ in this work originally titled *Last Supper.*

1 ft.

(see "Religious Art in Counter-Reformation Italy," page 505) and the Catholic Church's belief in the didactic nature of religious art.

Tintoretto's *Last Supper* incorporates many Mannerist devices, including an imbalanced composition and visual complexity. In terms of design, the contrast with Leonardo's *Last Supper* (FIG. 17-4) is both extreme and instructive. Leonardo's composition, balanced and symmetrical, parallels the picture plane in a geometrically organized and closed space. The figure of Christ is the tranquil center of the drama and the perspective focus. In Tintoretto's painting, Christ is above and beyond the converging perspective lines racing diagonally away from the picture surface, creating disturbing effects of limitless depth and motion. The viewer locates Tintoretto's Christ via the light flaring, beaconlike, out of darkness. The contrast of the two pictures reflects the direction Renaissance painting took in the 16th century, as it moved away from architectonic clarity of space and neutral lighting toward the dynamic perspectives and dramatic chiaroscuro of the coming Baroque.

VERONESE Among the great Venetian masters was Paolo Caliari of Verona, called PAOLO VERONESE (1528–1588). Whereas Tintoretto gloried in monumental drama and deep perspectives, Veronese specialized in splendid pageantry painted in superb color and set within majestic classical architecture. Like Tintoretto, Veronese painted on a huge scale, with canvases often as large as 20 by 30 feet or more. His usual subjects, painted for the refectories of wealthy monasteries, afforded him an opportunity to display magnificent companies at table.

Veronese painted *Christ in the House of Levi* (FIG. 17-49), originally called *Last Supper,* for the dining hall of Santi Giovanni e Paolo in Venice. In a great open loggia framed by three monumental arches, Christ sits at the center of the splendidly garbed elite of Venice. In the foreground, with a courtly gesture, the very image of gracious grandeur, the chief steward welcomes guests. Robed lords, their colorful retainers, dogs, and dwarfs crowd into the spacious loggia. Painted during the Counter-Reformation, this depiction prompted criticism from the Catholic Church. The Holy Office of the Inquisition accused Veronese of impiety for painting lowly creatures so close to the Lord, and it ordered him to make changes at his own expense. Reluctant to do so, he simply changed the painting's title, converting the subject to a less solemn one. As Palladio looked to the example of classically inspired High Renaissance architecture, so Veronese returned to High Renaissance composition, its symmetrical balance, and its ordered architectonics. His shimmering colors span the whole spectrum, although he avoided solid colors in favor of half shades (light blues, sea greens, lemon yellows, roses, and violets), creating veritable flowerbeds of tone.

10 ft.

17-50 PAOLO VERONESE, *Triumph of Venice,* ca. 1585. Oil on canvas, 29′ 8″ × 19′. Hall of the Grand Council, Doge's Palace, Venice.

Veronese's immense oval ceiling painting presents a tableau of Venice crowned by Fame amid columns, clouds, and personifications. Baroque painters adopted this 45-degree view from the ground.

The Venetian Republic employed both Tintoretto and Veronese to decorate the grand chambers and council rooms of the Doge's Palace (FIG. 14-21). A great and popular decorator, Veronese revealed himself a master of imposing illusionistic ceiling compositions, such as *Triumph of Venice* (FIG. 17-50). Here, within an oval frame, he presented Venice, crowned by Fame, enthroned between two great twisted columns in a balustraded loggia, garlanded with clouds, and attended by figures symbolic of its glories. Unlike Mantegna's *di sotto in sù* (FIG. 16-49) perspective, Veronese's is not a projection directly up from below, but at a 45-degree angle to spectators, a technique used by many later Baroque decorators (see Chapter 19).

17-51 Correggio, *Assumption of the Virgin,* 1526–1530. Fresco, 35′ 10″ × 37′ 11″. Parma Cathedral, Parma.

Working long before Veronese, Correggio, the teacher of Parmigianino, won little fame in his day, but his illusionistic ceiling designs, such as this one in Parma Cathedral, inspired many Baroque painters.

CORREGGIO One painter who developed a unique personal style almost impossible to classify was Antonio Allegri, known as CORREGGIO (ca. 1489–1534) from his birthplace, near Parma. The teacher of Parmigianino, Correggio pulled together many stylistic trends, including those of Leonardo, Raphael, and the Venetians. Working more than a half century before Veronese, Correggio's most enduring contribution was his development of illusionistic ceiling perspectives. In Parma Cathedral, he painted away the entire dome with his *Assumption of the Virgin* (FIG. **17-51**). Opening up the *cupola,* the artist showed worshipers a view of the sky, with concentric rings of clouds where hundreds of soaring figures perform a wildly pirouetting dance in celebration of the Assumption. Versions of these angelic creatures became permanent tenants of numerous Baroque churches in later centuries. Correggio was also an influential painter of religious panels, anticipating in them many other Baroque compositional devices. Correggio's *Assumption of the Virgin* predates Veronese's *Triumph of Venice* by more than a half century, but contemporaries expressed little appreciation for his achievement. Later, during the 17th century, Baroque painters recognized him as a kindred spirit.

Sculpture

Mannerism extended beyond painting. Artists translated its principles into sculpture and architecture as well.

BENVENUTO CELLINI Among those who made their mark as Mannerist sculptors was BENVENUTO CELLINI (1500–1571), the author of a fascinating autobiography. It is difficult to imagine a medieval artist composing an autobiography. Only in the Renaissance, with the birth of the notion of individual artistic genius, could a work such as Cellini's (or Vasari's *Lives*)

17-52 BENVENUTO CELLINI, *Saltcellar of Francis I,* 1540–1543. Gold, enamel, and ebony, $10\frac{1}{4}″ \times 1′ 1\frac{1}{8}″$. Kunsthistorisches Museum, Vienna.

Famed as a master goldsmith, Cellini fashioned this costly saltcellar for the table of Francis I of France. The elongated proportions of the figures clearly reveal Cellini's Mannerist approach to form.

have been conceived and written. Cellini's literary self-portrait presents him not only as a highly accomplished artist but also as a statesman, soldier, and lover, among many other roles. He was, first of all, a goldsmith, but only one of his major works in that medium survives, the saltcellar (FIG. **17-52**) he made for the royal table of Francis I (FIG. 18-12). The king had hired Cellini with a retainer of an annual salary, supplemented by fees for the works he produced, for example, his *Genius of Fontainebleau* (FIG. **17-52A**) for the royal hunting lodge outside Paris. The price Francis paid Cellini for the luxurious gold-and-*enamel* saltcellar illustrated here was almost 50 percent greater than the artist's salary for the year. Neptune and Tellus (or, as Cellini named them, Sea—the source of salt—and Land) recline atop an ebony base decorated with relief figures of Dawn, Day, Twilight, Night, and the four winds—some based on Michelangelo's statues in the Medici Chapel (FIG. 17-16) in San Lorenzo. The boat next to Neptune's right leg contained the salt, and the triumphal arch (compare FIG. 7-75) next to the right leg of the earth goddess held the pepper. The elongated proportions of the figures, especially the slim, small-breasted figure of Tellus, whom ancient artists always represented as a matronly woman (FIG. 7-30), reveal Cellini's Mannerist approach to form.

GIOVANNI DA BOLOGNA The lure of Italy drew a brilliant young Flemish sculptor, Jean de Boulogne, to Italy, where he practiced his art under the equivalent Italian name of GIOVANNI DA BOLOGNA (1529–1608). Giovanni's *Abduction of the Sabine Women* (FIG. **17-53**) exemplifies Mannerist principles of figure composition. Drawn from the legendary history of early Rome, the group of figures received its current title—relating how the Romans abducted wives for themselves from the neighboring Sabines—only after its exhibition. Earlier, it was *Paris Abducting Helen*, among other mythological titles. In fact, Giovanni did not intend to depict any particular subject. He created the group as a demonstration piece. His goal was to achieve a dynamic spiral figural composition involving an old man, a young man, and a woman, all nude in the tradition of ancient statues portraying deities and mythological figures. Although Giovanni would have known Antonio Pollaiuolo's *Hercules and Antaeus* (FIG. 16-14), whose Greek hero lifts his opponent off the ground, he turned directly to ancient sculpture for inspiration, especially to *Laocoön* (FIG. 5-89). *Abduction of the Sabine Women* includes references to that universally admired statue in the crouching old man and in the woman's up-flung arm. The three bodies interlock on a vertical axis, creating an ascending spiral movement.

To appreciate the sculpture fully, the viewer must walk around it, because the work changes radically according to the viewing point. One factor contributing to the shifting imagery is the prominence of open spaces passing through the masses (for example, the space between an arm and a body), which have as great an effect as the solids. This sculpture was the first large-scale group since classical antiquity designed to be seen from multiple viewpoints, in striking contrast to Pollaiuolo's group, which the artist fashioned to be seen from the angle shown in FIG. 16-14. Giovanni's figures do not break out of this spiral vortex but remain as if contained within a cylinder. Nonetheless, they display athletic flexibility and Michelangelesque potential for action.

1 ft.

17-53 GIOVANNI DA BOLOGNA, *Abduction of the Sabine Women*, Loggia dei Lanzi, Piazza della Signoria, Florence, Italy, 1579–1583. Marble, 13′ 5½″ high. ◼►

This sculpture was the first large-scale group since classical antiquity designed to be seen from multiple viewpoints. The three bodies interlock to create a vertical spiral movement.

17-54 GIULIO ROMANO, courtyard of the Palazzo del Tè (looking southeast), Mantua, Italy, 1525–1535.

The Mannerist divergences from architectural convention, for example, the slipping triglyphs, are so pronounced in the Palazzo del Tè that they constitute a parody of Bramante's classical style.

Architecture

Mannerist architects used classical architectural elements in a highly personal and unorthodox manner, rejecting the balance, order, and stability that were the hallmarks of the High Renaissance style, and aiming instead to reveal the contrived nature of architectural design.

GIULIO ROMANO Applying that anticlassical principle was the goal of GIULIO ROMANO (ca. 1499–1546) when he designed the Palazzo del Tè (FIG. **17-54**) in Mantua and, with it, formulated almost the entire architectural vocabulary of Mannerism. Early in his career, Giulio was Raphael's chief assistant in decorating the Vatican stanze. After Raphael's premature death in 1520, Giulio became his master's artistic executor, completing Raphael's unfinished frescoes and panel paintings. In 1524, Giulio went to Mantua, where

17-54A GIULIO ROMANO, *Fall of the Giants*, 1530–1532.

he found a patron in Duke Federigo Gonzaga (r. 1530–1540), for whom he built and decorated (FIG. **17-54A**) the Palazzo del Tè between 1525 and 1535. Gonzaga intended the palace to serve as both suburban summer residence and stud farm for his famous stables. Originally planned as a relatively modest country villa, Giulio's building so pleased his patron that Gonzaga soon commissioned the architect to enlarge the structure. In a second building campaign, Giulio expanded the villa to a palatial scale by adding three wings, which he placed around a square central court. This once-paved court, which functions both as a passage and as the focal point of the design, has a nearly urban character. Its surrounding buildings form a self-enclosed unit with a large garden, flanked by a stable, attached to it on the east side.

Giulio's Mannerist style is on display in the facades facing the palace's courtyard (FIG. 17-54), where the divergences from architectural convention are pronounced. Indeed, the Palazzo del Tè constitutes an enormous parody of Bramante's classical style, a veritable Mannerist manifesto announcing the artifice of archi-

tectural design. In a building laden with structural surprises and contradictions, the courtyard is the most unconventional of all. The *keystones* (central *voussoirs*), for example, either have not fully settled or seem to be slipping from the arches—and, more eccentric still, Giulio even placed voussoirs in the pediments over the rectangular niches, where no arches exist. The massive Tuscan columns flanking these niches carry incongruously narrow *architraves*. That these architraves break midway between the columns stresses their apparent structural insufficiency, and they seem unable to support the weight of the *triglyphs* of the *Doric frieze* above (see "Doric and Ionic Orders," Chapter 5, page 116, or on page xxvi in Volume II), which threaten to crash down on the head of anyone foolish enough to stand beneath them. To be sure, only a highly sophisticated observer can appreciate Giulio's witticism. Recognizing some quite subtle departures from the norm presupposes a thorough familiarity with the established rules of classical architecture. That the duke delighted in Giulio's mannered architectural inventiveness speaks to his cultivated taste.

LAURENTIAN LIBRARY Although he personifies the High Renaissance artist, Michelangelo, like Giulio Romano, also experimented with architectural designs that flouted most of the classical rules of order and stability. The restless nature of Michelangelo's genius is evident in the vestibule (FIG. **17-55**) he designed for the Medici library adjoining the Florentine church of San Lorenzo. The Laurentian Library had two contrasting spaces Michelangelo had to unite: the long horizontal of the library proper and the vertical of the vestibule. The need to place the vestibule windows up high (at the level of the reading room) determined the narrow verticality of the vestibule's elevation and proportions. Much taller than it is wide, the vestibule gives the impression of a vertically compressed, shaftlike space. Anyone schooled exclusively in the classical architecture of Bramante and the High Renaissance would have been appalled by Michelangelo's indifference here to classical norms in proportion and in the application of the rules of the classical orders. For example, he used columns in pairs and sank them into the walls, where they perform no supporting function. Michelangelo also split columns in halves around corners. Elsewhere, he placed scroll *corbels* on the walls beneath columns. They seem to

17-55 Michelangelo Buonarroti, vestibule of the Laurentian Library, Florence, Italy, 1524–1534; staircase, 1558–1559. ◼◢

With his customary independence of spirit, Michelangelo, working in a Mannerist mode in the Laurentian Library vestibule, disposed willfully of almost all the rules of classical architecture.

hang from the moldings, holding up nothing. He arbitrarily broke through pediments as well as through cornices and stringcourses. He sculpted pilasters that taper downward instead of upward. In short, the High Renaissance master, working in a Mannerist mode, disposed willfully and abruptly of classical architecture. Moreover, in the vast, flowing stairway (the latest element of the vestibule) that protrudes tonguelike into the room from the "mouth" of the doorway to the library, Michelangelo foreshadowed the dramatic movement of Baroque architecture (see Chapter 19). With his customary trailblazing independence of spirit, Michelangelo created an interior space that conveyed all the strains and tensions found in his statuary and in his painted figures. Michelangelo's art began in the style of the Quattrocento, developed into the epitome of High Renaissance art, and, at the end, moved toward Mannerism. He was 89 when he died in 1564, still hard at work on Saint Peter's and other projects. Few artists, then or since, could escape his influence.

IL GESÙ Probably the most influential building of the later Cinquecento was the mother church of the Jesuit order. The activity of the Society of Jesus, known as the Jesuits, was an important component of the Counter-Reformation. Ignatius of Loyola (1491–1556), a Spanish nobleman who dedicated his life to the service of God, founded the Jesuit order. He attracted a group of followers, and in 1540 Pope Paul III formally recognized his group as a religious order. The Jesuits were the papacy's invaluable allies in its quest to reassert the supremacy of the Catholic Church. Particularly successful in the field of education, the order established numerous schools. In addition, its members were effective missionaries and carried the message of Catholicism to the Americas, Asia, and Africa.

As a major participant in the Counter-Reformation, the Jesuit order needed a church appropriate to its new prominence. Because Michelangelo was late in providing the designs for their church,

17-56 GIACOMO DELLA PORTA, west facade of Il Gesù, Rome, Italy, ca. 1575–1584.

In Giacomo della Porta's innovative design, the march of pilasters and columns builds to a climax at the central bay. Many Roman Baroque church facades are architectural variations of Il Gesù.

N = nave   **D** = dome   **C** = chapel

| 0 | 25 | 50 feet |
| 0 | 10 | 20 meters |

N

17-57 GIACOMO DA VIGNOLA, plan of Il Gesù, Rome, Italy, 1568.

Giacomo da Vignola's plan for Il Gesù, with its exceptionally wide nave with side chapels instead of aisles—ideal for grand processions—won wide acceptance in the Catholic world.

called Il Gesù, or Church of Jesus, in 1568 the Jesuits turned to GIACOMO DELLA PORTA (ca. 1533–1602), who was responsible for the facade (FIG. **17-56**)—and who later designed the dome of Saint Peter's (FIG. 17-25)—and GIACOMO DA VIGNOLA (1507–1573), who designed the ground plan (FIG. **17-57**).

The plan of Il Gesù reveals a monumental expansion of Alberti's scheme for Sant'Andrea (FIGS. 16-46 and 16-47) in Mantua. Here, the nave takes over the main volume of space, making the structure a great hall with side chapels. A dome emphasizes the approach to the altar. The wide acceptance of the Gesù plan in the Catholic world, even in modern times, speaks to its ritual efficacy. The opening of the church building into a single great hall provides an almost theatrical setting for large promenades and processions (which combined social with priestly functions). Above all, the ample space could accommodate the great crowds that gathered to hear the eloquent preaching of the Jesuits.

The facade of Il Gesù was also not entirely original, but it too had an enormous influence on later church design. The union of the lower and upper stories, achieved by scroll buttresses, harks back to Alberti's Santa Maria Novella (FIG. 16-40). Its classical pediment is familiar in Alberti's work (FIG. 16-45), as well as in that of Palladio (FIGS. 17-28 and 17-30). The paired pilasters appear in Michelangelo's design for Saint Peter's (FIG. 17-25). Giacomo della Porta skillfully synthesized these existing motifs and unified the two stories. The horizontal march of the pilasters and columns builds to a dramatic climax at the central bay, and the bays of the facade snugly fit the nave-chapel system behind them. Many Roman church facades of the 17th century are architectural variations on della Porta's design. Chronologically and stylistically, Il Gesù belongs to the Late Renaissance, but its enormous influence on later churches marks it as one of the significant monuments for the development of Italian Baroque church architecture, discussed in Chapter 19.

RENAISSANCE AND MANNERISM IN CINQUECENTO ITALY

HIGH AND LATE RENAISSANCE 1495–1600

Michelangelo, *David,*
1501–1504

- During the High (1495–1520) and Late (1520–1600) Renaissance periods in Italy, artists, often in the employ of the papacy, further developed the interest in classical cultures, perspective, proportion, and human anatomy that had characterized Quattrocento Italian art.

- The major regional artistic centers were Florence and Rome in central Italy and Venice in the north. Whereas most Florentine and Roman artists emphasized careful design preparation based on preliminary drawing (*disegno*), Venetian artists focused on color and the process of paint application (*colorito*).

- Leonardo da Vinci, the quintessential "Renaissance man," won renown as a painter for his *sfumato* (misty haziness) and for his psychological insight in depicting biblical narrative (*Last Supper*) and contemporary personalities (*Mona Lisa*).

- Raphael favored lighter tonalities than Leonardo and clarity over obscurity. His sculpturesque figures appear in landscapes under blue skies (*Madonna of the Meadows*) or in grandiose architectural settings rendered in perfect perspective (*School of Athens*).

Bramante, Tempietto, Rome,
begun 1502

- Michelangelo was a pioneer in several media, including architecture, but his first love was sculpture. He carved (*David, Moses*) and painted (Sistine Chapel ceiling) emotionally charged figures with heroic physiques, preferring pent-up energy to Raphael's calm, ideal beauty.

- The leading architect of the early 16th century was Bramante, who championed the classical style of the ancients. He based his design for the Tempietto—the first High Renaissance building—on antique models, but the combination of parts was new and original.

- Andrea Palladio, an important theorist as well as architect, carried on Bramante's classical style during the Late Renaissance. Renowned for his villa designs, he had a lasting influence upon later European and American architecture.

Titian, *Meeting of Bacchus
and Ariadne,* 1522–1523

- The greatest master of the Venetian painting school was Titian, famed for his rich surface textures and dazzling display of color in all its nuances. In paintings such as *Meeting of Bacchus and Ariadne,* he established oil color on canvas as the standard medium of the Western pictorial tradition.

MANNERISM 1520–1600

Parmigianino, *Madonna with
the Long Neck,* 1534–1540

- Mannerism emerged in the 1520s in reaction to the High Renaissance style of Leonardo and Raphael. A prime feature of Mannerist art is artifice. Renaissance painters generally strove to create art that appeared natural, whereas Mannerist artists were less inclined to disguise the contrived nature of art production. Ambiguous space, departures from expected conventions, and unusual presentations of traditional themes are hallmarks of Mannerist painting.

- Parmigianino's *Madonna with the Long Neck* epitomizes the elegant stylishness of Mannerist painting. The elongated proportions of the figures, the enigmatic line of columns without capitals, and the ambiguous position of the figure with a scroll are the antithesis of High Renaissance classical proportions, clarity of meaning, and rational perspective.

- Mannerism was also a sculptural style. Benvenuto Cellini created a costly saltcellar for the table of the French king Francis I. The figures, based on antique statuary, have the slim waists and long limbs that appealed to Mannerist taste.

Cellini, *Saltcellar of Francis I,*
1540–1543

- The leading Mannerist architect was Giulio Romano, who rejected the balance, order, and stability of the High Renaissance style. In the Palazzo del Tè in Mantua, which he also decorated with frescoes, the divergences from architectural convention parody Bramante's classical style and include triglyphs that slip out of the Doric frieze.

Garden of Earthly Delights is Bosch's most enigmatic painting, but scholars agree it depicts Paradise in the left and central panels and Hell in the right wing. At the left, God as Christ presents Eve to Adam.

In the inky darkness of Bosch's Hell are unidentifiable objects that are imaginative variations on chemical apparatus of the day. Alchemy is a prominent theme of the work.

In the fantastic sunlit landscape that is Bosch's Paradise, scores of nude people in the prime of life blithely cavort. The oversize fruits are fertility symbols, and the scene celebrates procreation.

1 ft.

18-1 HIERONYMUS BOSCH, *Garden of Earthly Delights*, 1505–1510. Oil on wood, center panel 7′ 2⅝″ × 6′ 4¾″, each wing 7′ 2⅝″ × 3′ 2¼″. Museo del Prado, Madrid. ◼◀

The horrors of Hell include beastly creatures devouring people, and sinners enduring tortures tailored to their conduct while alive. A glutton vomits eternally. A miser defecates gold coins.

HIGH RENAISSANCE AND MANNERISM IN NORTHERN EUROPE AND SPAIN

EARTHLY DELIGHTS IN THE NETHERLANDS

The leading Netherlandish painter of the early 16th century was HIERONYMUS BOSCH (ca. 1450–1516), one of the most fascinating and puzzling artists in history. Bosch's most famous painting, the *Garden of Earthly Delights* (FIG. 18-1), is also his most enigmatic, and no interpretation has ever won universal acceptance. Although the work is a monumental triptych, which would suggest a religious function as an altarpiece, *Garden of Earthly Delights* was on display in the palace of Henry III of Nassau, regent of the Netherlands, no later than seven years after its completion. This suggests the triptych was a secular commission, and some scholars have proposed that given the work's central themes of sex and procreation, the painting may commemorate a wedding. Marriage was a familiar theme in Netherlandish painting (FIGS. 15-6 and 15-10). Any similarity to earlier paintings ends there, however. Whereas Jan van Eyck and Petrus Christus grounded their depictions of betrothed couples in 15th-century life and custom, Bosch's image portrays a visionary world of fantasy and intrigue—a painted world without close parallel until the advent of Surrealism more than 400 years later (see Chapter 24).

In the left panel, God (in the form of Christ) presents Eve to Adam in a landscape, presumably the Garden of Eden. Bosch's wildly imaginative setting includes an odd pink fountainlike structure in a body of water and an array of fanciful and unusual animals, including a giraffe, an elephant, and winged fish.

The central panel is a continuation of Paradise, a sunlit landscape filled with nude people, all in the prime of youth, blithely cavorting amid bizarre creatures and unidentifiable objects. The youths play with abandon. Some stand on their hands or turn somersaults. The numerous fruits and birds (fertility symbols) in the scene suggest procreation, and, indeed, many of the figures pair off as couples.

In contrast to the orgiastic overtones of the central panel is the terrifying image of Hell in the right wing, where viewers must search through the inky darkness to find all of the fascinating though repulsive details Bosch recorded. Beastly creatures devour people, while other condemned souls endure tortures tailored to their conduct while alive. A glutton must vomit eternally. A miser defecates gold coins. A spidery monster fondles a promiscuous woman. Scholars have traditionally interpreted Bosch's triptych as a warning of the fate awaiting the sinful, decadent, and immoral, but as a secular work, *Garden of Earthly Delights* may have been intended for a learned audience fascinated by *alchemy*—the study of seemingly magical chemical changes. Details throughout the triptych are based on chemical apparatus of the day, which Bosch knew well because his in-laws were pharmacists.

NORTHERN EUROPE IN THE 16TH CENTURY

The dissolution of the Burgundian Netherlands in 1477 led in the early 16th century to a realignment in the European geopolitical landscape (MAP 18-1). France and the Holy Roman Empire absorbed the former Burgundian territories and increased their power. But by the end of the century, through calculated marriages, military exploits, and ambitious territorial expansion, Spain was the dominant European state. Throughout the Continent, monarchs increasingly used art and architecture to glorify their reigns and to promote a stronger sense of cultural and political unity among their subjects, thereby laying the foundation for today's European nations. Wealthy merchants also cultivated art as a status symbol, as the commissioning and collecting of artworks became less and less the exclusive province of the aristocracy. Some artists, most notably Albrecht Dürer (FIGS. 18-4 to 18-7), became successful businessmen themselves by selling their works to the public.

These important societal changes occurred against the backdrop of a momentous religious crisis. Concerted attempts to reform Western Christendom led to the Reformation and the establishment of Protestantism (as distinct from Catholicism), which in turn prompted the Catholic Church's response, the Counter-Reformation (see Chapter 17). Ultimately, the Reformation split the Western Church in half and produced a hundred years of civil war between Protestants and Catholics. But the tumultuous religious conflict engulfing 16th-century Europe did not prevent—and may, in fact, have accelerated—the exchange of intellectual and artistic ideas, because artists frequently moved from one area to another in search of religious freedom and lucrative commissions. Catholic Italy and the (mostly) Protestant Holy Roman Empire shared in a lively commerce—economic and cultural—and 16th-century art throughout

MAP 18-1 Europe in the early 16th century.

HIGH RENAISSANCE AND MANNERISM IN NORTHERN EUROPE AND SPAIN

1500	1530	1560	1600

- In Catholic countries, commissions for religious works, such as the *Isenheim Altarpiece*, continue, but, consistent with Reformation values, Protestant patrons prefer secular themes, including portraiture, classical mythology, and the macabre
- Albrecht Dürer, master printmaker, becomes the first international art celebrity outside Italy

- In France under Henry II (r. 1547–1559), architectural designs are a mix of Italian and Northern Renaissance elements
- Netherlandish painters inject moralizing religious messages into seemingly secular genre paintings
- Hans Holbein, Caterina van Hemessen, and Levina Teerlinc achieve renown as portrait painters

- Pieter Bruegel the Elder, the greatest Netherlandish artist of the mid-16th century, produces masterful landscapes that nonetheless focus on human activities
- Greek-born El Greco settles in Toledo and creates paintings that are a uniquely personal mix of Byzantine and Italian Mannerist elements. His hybrid style captured the fervor of Spanish Catholicism

Europe was a major beneficiary of that exchange. Humanism filtered up from Italy and spread throughout northern Europe. Northern humanists, like their southern counterparts, cultivated knowledge of classical cultures and literature, but they focused more on reconciling humanism with Christianity.

Among the most influential of these "Christian humanists" were the Dutch-born Desiderius Erasmus (1466–1536) and the Englishman Thomas More (1478–1535). Erasmus demonstrated his interest in both Italian humanism and religion with his "philosophy of Christ," emphasizing education and scriptural knowledge. Both an ordained priest and avid scholar, Erasmus published his most famous essay, *In Praise of Folly*, in 1509. In this widely read work, he satirized not just the Church but various social classes as well. His ideas were to play an important role in the development of the Reformation, but he consistently declined to join any of the Reformation sects. Equally erudite was Thomas More, who served King Henry VIII (r. 1509–1547). Henry eventually ordered More's execution because of his opposition to England's break with the Catholic Church. In France, François Rabelais (ca. 1494–1553), a former monk who advocated rejecting stagnant religious dogmatism, disseminated the humanist spirit.

The turmoil emerging during the 16th century lasted well into the 17th century and permanently affected the face of Europe. The concerted challenges to established authority and the persistent philosophical inquiry eventually led to the rise of new political systems (for example, the nation-state) and new economic systems (such as capitalism).

HOLY ROMAN EMPIRE

Although at the opening of the 16th century, many in the Holy Roman Empire (MAP 18-1) expressed dissatisfaction with the Church in Rome, Martin Luther had not yet posted the *Ninety-five Theses* that launched the Protestant Reformation. The Catholic clergy in Germany still offered artists important commissions to adorn churches and other religious institutions.

MATTHIAS GRÜNEWALD Matthias Neithardt, known conventionally as MATTHIAS GRÜNEWALD (ca. 1480–1528), worked for the archbishops of Mainz in several capacities, from court painter and decorator to architect, hydraulic engineer, and superintendent of works. Grünewald eventually moved to northern Germany, where he settled at Halle in Saxony. Around 1510, he began work on the *Isenheim Altarpiece* (FIG. **18-2**), a complex and fascinating monument reflecting Catholic beliefs and incorporating several references to Catholic doctrines, such as the lamb (symbol of the son of God), whose wound spurts blood into a chalice in the *Crucifixion* scene (FIG. 18-2, *top*) on the exterior of the altarpiece.

Created for the monastic hospital order of Saint Anthony of Isenheim, the *Isenheim Altarpiece* takes the form of a wooden shrine (carved around 1505 by NIKOLAUS HAGENAUER, active 1493–1538) featuring large gilded and polychromed statues of Saints Anthony Abbot, Augustine, and Jerome in the main zone and smaller statues of Christ and the 12 apostles in the predella (FIG. 18-2, *bottom*). To Hagenauer's centerpiece, Grünewald added two pairs of painted moveable wings that open at the center. Hinged at the sides, one pair stands directly behind the other. Grünewald painted the exterior panels of the first pair (visible when the altarpiece is closed,

FIG. 18-2, *top*) between 1510 and 1515: *Crucifixion* in the center, *Saint Sebastian* on the left, *Saint Anthony Abbot* on the right, and *Lamentation* in the predella. When these exterior wings are open, four additional scenes (not illustrated)—*Annunciation, Angelic Concert, Madonna and Child,* and *Resurrection*—appear. Opening this second pair of wings exposes Hagenauer's interior shrine, flanked by Grünewald's panels depicting *Meeting of Saints Anthony and Paul* and *Temptation of Saint Anthony* (FIG. 18-2, *bottom*).

The placement of this altarpiece in the choir of a church adjacent to the monastery's hospital dictated much of the imagery. Saints associated with the plague and other diseases and with miraculous cures, such as Saints Anthony and Sebastian, appear prominently in the *Isenheim Altarpiece*. Grünewald's panels specifically address the themes of dire illness and miraculous healing and accordingly emphasize the suffering of the order's patron saint, Anthony. The painted images served as warnings, encouraging increased devotion from monks and hospital patients. They also functioned therapeutically by offering some hope to the afflicted. Indeed, Saint Anthony's legend emphasized his dual role as vengeful dispenser of justice (by inflicting disease) and benevolent healer.

One of the most memorable scenes is *Temptation of Saint Anthony* (FIG. 18-2, *bottom right*). It is a terrifying image of the five temptations, depicted as an assortment of ghoulish and bestial creatures in a dark landscape, attacking the saint. In the foreground Grünewald painted a grotesque image of a man, whose oozing boils, withered arm, and distended stomach all suggest a horrible disease. Medical experts have connected these symptoms with ergotism (a disease caused by ergot, a fungus that grows especially on rye). Although doctors did not discover the cause of this disease until about 1600, people lived in fear of its recognizable symptoms (convulsions and gangrene). The public referred to this illness as "Saint Anthony's Fire," and it was one of the major diseases treated at the Isenheim hospital. The gangrene often compelled amputation, and scholars have noted that the two moveable halves of the altarpiece's predella (FIG. 18-2, *top*), if slid apart, make it appear as if Christ's legs have been amputated. The same observation applies to the two main exterior panels. Due to the off-center placement of the cross, opening the left panel "severs" one arm from the crucified figure.

Thus, Grünewald carefully selected and presented his altarpiece's iconography to be particularly meaningful for viewers at this hospital. In the interior shrine, the artist balanced the horrors of the disease and the punishments awaiting those who did not repent with scenes such as *Meeting of Saints Anthony and Paul*, depicting the two saints, healthy and aged, conversing peacefully. Even the exterior panels (the closed altarpiece; FIG. 18-2, *top*) convey these same concerns. *Crucifixion* emphasizes Christ's pain and suffering, but the knowledge that this act redeemed humanity tempers the misery. In addition, Saint Anthony appears in the right wing as a devout follower of Christ who, like Christ and for Christ, endured intense suffering for his faith. Saint Anthony's appearance on the exterior thus reinforces the themes Grünewald intertwined throughout this entire work—themes of pain, illness, and death, as well as those of hope, comfort, and salvation. Grünewald also brilliantly used color to enhance the effect of the painted scenes of the altarpiece. He intensified the contrast of horror and hope by playing subtle tones and soft harmonies against shocking dissonances of color.

18-2 Matthias Grünewald, *Isenheim Altarpiece* (closed, *top*; open, *bottom*), from the chapel of the Hospital of Saint Anthony, Isenheim, Germany, ca. 1510–1515. Oil on wood, center panel 9′ 9½″ × 10′ 9″, each wing 8′ 2½″ × 3′ ½″, predella 2′ 5½″ × 11′ 2″. Shrine carved by Nikolaus Hagenauer, ca. 1505. Painted and gilt limewood, 9′ 9½″ × 10′ 9″. Musée d'Unterlinden, Colmar.

Befitting its setting in a monastic hospital, Matthias Grünewald's *Isenheim Altarpiece* includes painted panels depicting suffering and disease but also miraculous healing, hope, and salvation.

HANS BALDUNG GRIEN The son of a prosperous attorney and the brother of a university professor, HANS BALDUNG GRIEN (ca. 1484–1545) chose to pursue painting and printmaking as a profession rather than the law or letters. He settled in Strasbourg, a center of humanistic learning, where he enjoyed a long and successful career. Baldung produced some religious works, although none on the scale of the *Isenheim Altarpiece*. His reputation rested primarily on his exploration of nontraditional subjects, such as witchcraft.

Witches' Sabbath (FIG. **18-3**) is a *chiaroscuro woodcut,* a recent German innovation. The technique requires the use of two blocks of wood instead of one. The printmaker carves and inks one block in the usual way in order to produce a traditional black-and-white print (see "Woodcuts, Engravings, and Etchings," Chapter 15, page 444). Then the artist cuts a second block consisting of broad highlights to be inked in grays or colors and printed over the first block's impression. Chiaroscuro woodcuts therefore incorporate some of the qualities of painting and feature tonal subtleties absent in traditional woodcuts.

Witchcraft was a counter-religion in the 15th and 16th centuries involving magical rituals, secret potions, and devil worship. Witches prepared brews they inhaled or rubbed into their skin, sending them into hallucinogenic trances in which they allegedly flew through the night sky on broomsticks or goats. The popes condemned all witches, and Church inquisitors vigorously pursued these demonic heretics and subjected them to torture to wrest confessions from them. Witchcraft fascinated Baldung, and he turned to the subject repeatedly. For him and his contemporaries, witches were evil forces in the world, threats to man—as was Eve herself, whom Baldung also frequently depicted as a temptress responsible for original sin.

In *Witches' Sabbath,* Baldung depicted a night scene in a forest featuring a coven of naked witches. Female nudity and macabre scenes were persistent elements in Baldung's art (compare FIG. **18-3A**). These themes were popular with the public, who avidly purchased his relatively inexpensive prints. The coven in this woodcut includes both young seductresses and old hags. They gather around a covered jar from which a fuming concoction escapes into the air. One young witch rides through the night sky on a goat. She sits backward—Baldung's way of suggesting witchcraft is the inversion of the true religion, Christianity.

18-3A BALDUNG GRIEN, *Death and the Maiden,* 1509–1511.

ALBRECHT DÜRER The dominant artist of the early 16th century in the Holy Roman Empire was ALBRECHT DÜRER (1471–1528) of Nuremberg. Dürer was the first artist outside Italy to become an international celebrity. He traveled extensively, visiting and studying in Colmar, Basel, Strasbourg, Venice, Antwerp, and Brussels, among other locales. As a result of these travels, Dürer met many of the leading humanists and artists of his time, including Erasmus of Rotterdam and the Venetian master Giovanni Bellini (FIGS. 17-31A, 17-32, and 17-33). A man of exceptional talents and tremendous energy, Dürer achieved widespread fame in his own time and has enjoyed a lofty reputation ever since.

Fascinated with the classical ideas of the Italian Renaissance, Dürer was among the first Northern Renaissance artists to travel to Italy expressly to study Italian art and its underlying theories at their source. After his first journey in 1494–1495 (the second was in 1505–1506), he incorporated many Italian developments into his art. Art historians have acclaimed Dürer as the first artist north of the Alps to understand fully the basic aims of the Renaissance in Italy. Like Leonardo da Vinci, Dürer wrote theoretical treatises on a variety of subjects, such as perspective, fortification, and the ideal in human proportions. Unlike Leonardo, he both finished and published his writings. Dürer also was the first northern European artist to leave a record of his life and career through his correspondence, a detailed and eminently readable diary, and a series of self-portraits.

SELF-PORTRAITS Dürer's earliest preserved self-portrait—a silverpoint drawing now in the Albertina in Vienna—dates to 1484, when he was only 13, two years before he began his formal education as an apprentice in the workshop of Michel Wolgemut (FIG. 15-21). In 1498, a few years after his first visit to Italy, he painted a likeness of himself in the

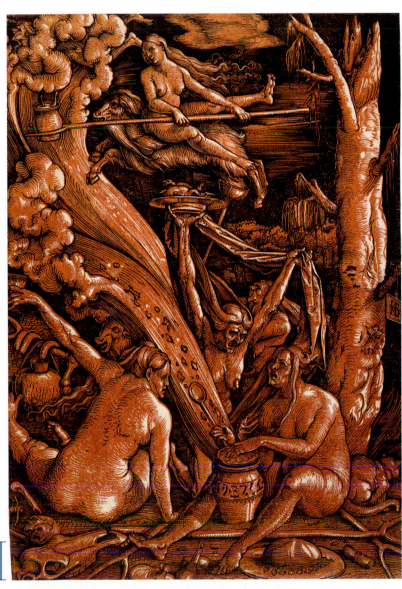

1 in.

18-3 HANS BALDUNG GRIEN, *Witches' Sabbath,* 1510. Chiaroscuro woodcut, 1′ 2⅞″ × 10¼″. British Museum, London.

Baldung's woodcut depicts witches gathered around a cauldron containing a secret potion. One witch flies mounted backward on a goat, suggesting witchcraft is the inversion of Christianity.

18-4 ALBRECHT DÜRER, *Self-Portrait*, 1500. Oil on wood, 2′ 2¼″ × 1′ 7¼″. Alte Pinakothek, Munich.

Dürer here presents himself as a frontal Christlike figure reminiscent of medieval icons. It is an image of the artist as a divinely inspired genius, a concept inconceivable before the Renaissance.

18-4A DÜRER, *Great Piece of Turf*, 1503.

Italian mode—a seated half-length portrait in three-quarter view in front of a window through which the viewer sees a landscape. The *Self-Portrait* reproduced here (FIG. **18-4**), painted just two years later, is markedly different in character. Inscribed with his monogram and the date (*left*) and four lines (*right*) stating the painting depicts him at age 28, the panel portrays the artist in a fur-trimmed coat in a rigid frontal posture against a dark background. Dürer has a short beard and shoulder-length hair, and the portrait intentionally evokes medieval devotional images of Christ. The position of Dürer's right hand resembles but does not duplicate (which would have been blasphemous) Christ's standard gesture of blessing in Byzantine icons (FIG. 9-33). The focus on the hand is also a reference to the artist's hand as a creative instrument. Doubtless deeply affected by the new humanistic view that had emerged in Renaissance Italy of the artist as a divinely inspired genius, Dürer responded by painting himself as a Christlike figure. He also embraced Italian artists' interest in science, as is evident in his botanically accurate 1503 watercolor study *Great Piece of Turf* (FIG. **18-4A**).

FALL OF MAN Dürer's fame in his own day, as today, rested more on his achievements as a printmaker than as a painter. Trained as a goldsmith by his father before he took up painting and printmaking, he developed an extraordinary proficiency in handling the burin, the engraving tool. This technical ability, combined with a feeling for the form-creating possibilities of line, enabled him to produce a body of graphic work few artists have rivaled for quality and number. Dürer created numerous book illustrations. He also circulated and sold prints in single sheets, which people of ordinary means could buy, expanding his audience considerably. Aggressively marketing his prints with the aid of an agent, Dürer became a wealthy man from the sale of these works. His wife, who served as his manager, and his mother also sold his prints at markets. Through his graphic works, he exerted strong influence throughout northern Europe and also in Italy. The lawsuit Dürer brought in 1506 against an Italian artist for copying his prints reveals his business acumen. Scholars generally regard this lawsuit as the first in history over artistic copyright.

One of Dürer's early masterpieces, *Fall of Man* (*Adam and Eve*; FIG. **18-5**), represents the first distillation of his studies of the Vitruvian theory of human proportions (compare FIG. 17-3A), a theory based on arithmetic ratios. Clearly outlined against the dark

18-5 ALBRECHT DÜRER, *Fall of Man* (*Adam and Eve*), 1504. Engraving, 9⅞″ × 7⅝″. Museum of Fine Arts, Boston (centennial gift of Landon T. Clay).

Dürer was the first Northern Renaissance artist to achieve international celebrity. *Fall of Man*, with two figures based on ancient statues, reflects his studies of the Vitruvian theory of human proportions.

18-5A DÜRER, *Knight, Death, and the Devil,* 1513.

background of a northern European forest, the two idealized figures of Adam and Eve stand in poses reminiscent of specific classical statues probably known to Dürer through graphic representations. Preceded by numerous geometric drawings in which the artist attempted to systematize sets of ideal human proportions in balanced contrapposto poses, the final print presents Dürer's concept of the "perfect" male and female figures. Yet he tempered this idealization with naturalism, demonstrating his well-honed observational skills in his rendering of the background foliage and animals (compare FIGS. 18-4A and 18-5A). The gnarled bark of the trees and the feathery leaves authenticate the scene, as do the various creatures skulking underfoot. The animals populating the print are symbolic. The choleric cat, the melancholic elk, the sanguine rabbit, and the phlegmatic ox represent humanity's temperaments based on the "four humors," body fluids that were the basis of theories developed by the ancient Greek physician Hippocrates and practiced in medieval physiology. The tension between cat and mouse in the foreground symbolizes the relation between Adam and Eve at the crucial moment in *Fall of Man*.

MELENCOLIA I Dürer took up the theme of the four humors, specifically melancholy, in one of his most famous engravings, *Melencolia I* (FIG. 18-6), which many scholars regard as a kind of self-portrait of Dürer's artistic psyche as well as a masterful example of the artist's ability to produce a wide range of tonal values and textures. (Erasmus praised Dürer as "the Apelles [the most renowned ancient Greek painter] of black lines,"[1] and the German artist's mastery of all aspects of printmaking is evident also in his woodcuts, for example, FIG. I-9.)

The Italian humanist Marsilio Ficino (1433–1499) had written an influential treatise (*De vita triplici,* 1482–1489) in which he asserted that artists were distinct from the population at large because they were born under the sign of the planet Saturn, named for the ancient Roman god. They shared that deity's melancholic temperament because they had an excess of black bile, one of the four body humors, in their systems. Artists therefore were "saturnine"—eccentric and capable both of inspired artistic frenzy and melancholic depression. Raphael had depicted Michelangelo in the guise of the brooding Heraclitus in his *School of Athens* (FIG. 17-9), and Dürer used a similarly posed female figure for his winged personification of Melancholy in *Melencolia I*. (In 1510, in *De occulta philosophia,* Heinrich Cornelius Agrippa of Nettesheim [1486–1535] identified three levels of melancholy. The first was artistic melancholy, which explains the Roman numeral on the banner carried by the bat—a creature of the dark—in Dürer's engraving.) All around the brooding figure of Melancholy are the tools of the artist and builder (compare FIG. 13-32)—compass, hammer, nails, and saw among them—but they are useless to the frustrated artist while he is suffering from melancholy. Melancholy's face is obscured by shadow, underscoring her state of mind, but Dürer also included a burst of light on the far horizon behind the bat, an optimistic note suggesting artists can overcome their depression and produce works of genius—such as this engraving.

18-6 ALBRECHT DÜRER, *Melencolia I,* 1514. Engraving, $9\frac{3}{8}'' \times 7\frac{1}{2}''$. Victoria & Albert Museum, London.

In this "self-portrait" of his artistic personality, Dürer portrayed Melancholy as a brooding winged woman surrounded by the tools of the artist and builder but incapable of using them.

18-7 ALBRECHT DÜRER, *Four Apostles,* 1526. Oil on wood, each panel 7′ 1″ × 2′ 6″. Alte Pinakothek, Munich. ◼◀

Dürer's support for Lutheranism surfaces in his portraitlike depictions of four saints on two painted panels. Peter, representative of the pope in Rome, plays a secondary role behind John the Evangelist.

1 ft.

FOUR APOSTLES Dürer's major work in the oil medium is *Four Apostles* (FIG. **18-7**), a two-panel oil painting he produced without commission and presented to the city fathers of Nuremberg in 1526 to be hung in the city hall. Saints John and Peter appear on the left panel, Mark and Paul on the right. In addition to showcasing Dürer's mastery of the oil technique, of his brilliant use of color and light and shade, and of his ability to imbue the four saints with individual personalities and portraitlike features, *Four Apostles* documents Dürer's support for the German theologian Martin Luther (1483–1546), who sparked the Protestant Reformation. Dürer conveyed his Lutheran sympathies by his positioning of the figures. He relegated Saint Peter (as representative of the pope in Rome) to a secondary role by placing him behind John the Evangelist. John assumed particular prominence for Luther because of the evangelist's focus on Christ's person in his Gospel. In addition, Peter and John both read from the Bible, the single authoritative source of religious truth, according to Luther. Dürer emphasized the Bible's centrality by depicting it open to the passage "In the beginning was the Word, and the Word was with God, and the Word was God" (John 1:1). At the bottom of the panels, Dürer included quotations from the four apostles' books, using Luther's German translation of the New Testament. The excerpts warn against the coming of perilous times and the preaching of false prophets who will distort God's word.

LUTHER AND THE REFORMATION The Protestant Reformation, which came to fruition in the early 16th century, had its roots in long-term, growing dissatisfaction with Catholic Church leadership. The deteriorating relationship between the faithful and the Church of Rome's hierarchy stood as an obstacle for the millions who sought a meaningful religious experience. Particularly damaging was the perception that the Roman popes concerned themselves more with temporal power and material wealth than with the salvation of Church members. The fact that many 15th-century popes and cardinals came from wealthy families, such as the Medici (FIG. 17-10), intensified this perception. It was not only those at the highest levels who seemed to ignore their spiritual duties. Archbishops, bishops, and abbots began to accumulate numerous offices, thereby increasing their revenues but making it more difficult for them to fulfill all of their responsibilities. By 1517, dissatisfaction with the Church had grown so widespread that Luther felt free to challenge papal authority openly by posting in Wittenberg his *Ninety-five Theses,* in which he enumerated his objections to Church practices, especially the sale of indulgences. *Indulgences* were Church-sanctioned remittances (or reductions) of time Catholics had to spend in Purgatory for confessed sins. The increasing frequency of their sale suggested that those who could afford to purchase indulgences were buying their way into Heaven.

Luther's goal was significant reform and clarification of major spiritual issues, but his ideas ultimately led to the splitting of Christendom. According to Luther, the Catholic Church's extensive ecclesiastical structure needed casting out, for it had no basis in scripture. The Bible and nothing else could serve as the foundation for Christianity. Luther declared the pope the Antichrist (for which the pope excommunicated him), called the Church the "whore of Babylon," and denounced ordained priests. He also rejected most of Catholicism's sacraments other than baptism and communion, decrying them as obstacles to salvation (see "Catholic and Protestant Views of Salvation," page 541, and FIG. **18-8**). Luther maintained that for Christianity to be restored to its original purity, the Church needed cleansing of all the doctrinal impurities that had collected through the ages. Luther advocated the Bible as the source of all religious truth. The Bible—the sole scriptural authority—was the word of God, which did not exist in the Church's councils, law, and rituals. Luther facilitated the lay public's access to biblical truths by producing the first translation of the Bible in a vernacular language.

ART AND THE REFORMATION In addition to doctrinal differences, Catholics and Protestants took divergent stances on the role of visual imagery in religion. Catholics embraced church decoration as an aid to communicating with God (see "Religious Art in Counter-Reformation Italy," Chapter 17, page 505). In contrast, Protestants believed images of Christ, the Virgin, and saints could lead to idolatry and distracted viewers from focusing on the real reason for their presence in church—to communicate directly with God. Because of this belief, Protestant churches were relatively bare, and the extensive church pictorial programs found especially in Italy but also in northern Europe (FIGS. 15-19, 15-20, and 18-2) were not as prominent in Protestant churches.

The Protestant concern over the role of religious imagery at times escalated to outright *iconoclasm*—the objection to and destruction of religious imagery. In encouraging a more personal relationship with God, Protestant leaders spoke out against much of the religious art being produced. In his 1525 tract *Against the*

Catholic and Protestant Views of Salvation

A central concern of the Protestant reformers was the question of how Christians achieve salvation. Rather than perceive salvation as something for which weak and sinful humans must constantly strive through good deeds performed under the watchful eye of a punitive God, Martin Luther argued that faithful individuals attained redemption solely by God's bestowal of his grace. Therefore, people cannot earn salvation. Further, no ecclesiastical machinery with all its miraculous rites and indulgent forgivenesses could save sinners face-to-face with God. Only absolute faith in Christ could redeem sinners and ensure salvation. Redemption by faith alone, with the guidance of scripture, was the fundamental doctrine of Protestantism.

In *Law and Gospel* (FIG. 18-8), a woodcut dated about a dozen years after Luther set the Reformation in motion with his *Ninety-five Theses,* Lucas Cranach the Elder gave visual expression to the doctrinal differences between Protestantism and Catholicism. Cranach contrasted Catholicism (based on Old Testament law, according to Luther) and Protestantism (based on the Gospel belief in God's grace) in two images separated by a centrally placed tree. On the left half, judgment day has arrived, as represented by Christ's appearance at the top of the scene, hovering amid a cloud halo and accompanied by angels and saints. Christ raises his left hand in the traditional gesture of damnation, and, below, a skeleton drives off a terrified person to burn for eternity in Hell. This person tried to live a good and honorable life, but despite his efforts, he fell short. Moses stands to the side, holding the tablets of the law—the Ten Commandments Catholics follow in their attempt to attain salvation. In contrast to this Catholic reliance on good works and clean living, Protestants emphasized God's grace as the source of redemption. Accordingly, God showers the sinner in the right half of the print with grace, as streams of blood flow from the crucified Christ. At the far left are Adam and Eve, whose original sin necessitated Christ's sacrifice. In the lower right corner of the woodcut, Christ emerges from the tomb and promises salvation to all who believe in him.

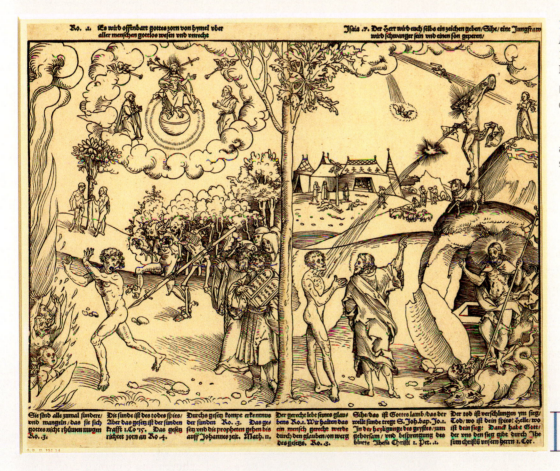

18-8 LUCAS CRANACH THE ELDER, *Law and Gospel,* ca. 1530. Woodcut, $10\frac{5}{8}''$ × $1'\frac{3}{4}''$. British Museum, London.

Lucas Cranach was a close friend of Martin Luther, whose *Ninety-five Theses* launched the Reformation in 1517. This woodcut contrasts Catholic and Protestant views of how to achieve salvation.

1 in.

Heavenly Prophets in the Matter of Images and Sacraments, Martin Luther explained his attitude toward religious imagery:

> I approached the task of destroying images by first tearing them out of the heart through God's Word and making them worthless and despised. . . . For when they are no longer in the heart, they can do no harm when seen with the eyes. . . . I have allowed and not forbidden the outward removal of images. . . . And I say at the outset that according to the law of Moses no other images are forbidden than an image of God which one worships. A crucifix, on the other hand, or any other holy image is not forbidden.[2]

Two influential Protestant theologians based in Switzerland—Ulrich Zwingli (1484–1531) and French-born John Calvin (Jean

Cauvin, 1509–1564)—were more vociferous in cautioning their followers about the potentially dangerous nature of religious imagery. Zwingli and Calvin's condemnation of religious imagery often led to eruptions of iconoclasm. Particularly violent waves of iconoclastic fervor swept Basel, Zurich, Strasbourg, and Wittenberg in the 1520s. In an episode known as the Great Iconoclasm, bands of Calvinists visited Catholic churches in the Netherlands in 1566, shattering stained-glass windows, smashing statues, and destroying paintings and other artworks they perceived as idolatrous. These strong reactions to art not only reflect the religious fervor of the time but also serve as dramatic demonstrations of the power of art—and of how much art mattered.

LUCAS CRANACH THE ELDER The artist most closely associated with the Protestant Reformation and with Martin Luther in particular was Lucas Cranach the Elder (1472–1553). Cranach and Luther were godfathers to each other's children, and many scholars have dubbed Cranach "the painter of the Reformation." Cranach was also an accomplished graphic artist who used the new, inexpensive medium of prints on paper to promote Lutheran ideology (FIG. 18-8). Cranach's work encompasses a wide range of themes, however. For example, for aristocratic Saxon patrons he produced a large number of paintings of classical myths featuring female nudes in suggestive poses. One classical theme he depicted several times was *Judgment of Paris,* of which the small panel (FIG. **18-9**) now in Karlsruhe is the best example. Homer records the story, but Cranach's source was probably the second-century CE Roman author Lucian's elaboration of the tale. Mercury chose a handsome young shepherd named Paris to be the judge of a beauty contest among three goddesses—Juno, wife of Jupiter; Minerva, Jupiter's virgin daughter and goddess of wisdom and war; and Venus, the goddess of love (see "The Gods and Goddesses of Mount Olympus," Chapter 5, page 107, or on page xxxiii in Volume II). According to Lucian, each goddess attempted to bribe Paris with rich rewards if he chose her. Venus won by offering Paris the most beautiful woman in the world, Helen of Troy, and thus set in motion the epic war between the Greeks and Trojans recounted in Homer's *Iliad.*

Cranach's painting could never be confused with an ancient depiction of the myth. The setting is a German landscape with a Saxon castle in the background, and the seated shepherd is a knight in full armor wearing a fashionable hat. Mercury, an aged man (as he never is in ancient art), also wearing armor, bends over to draw Paris's attention to the three goddesses. They are nude save for their transparent veils, their fine jewelry, and, in the case of Juno, an elegant hat. Loosely based on classical representations of the Three Graces (compare FIG. 16-1)—ancient artists did not depict Juno or Minerva undressed—Cranach's goddesses do not have the proportions (or modesty) of Praxiteles' *Aphro-*

dite of Knidos (FIG. 5-62). Slender, with small heads and breasts and long legs, they pose seductively before the judge. Venus performs a dance for Paris, but he seems indifferent to all three goddesses. Only the rearing horse appears to be excited by the spectacle—a touch of humor characteristic of Cranach.

ALBRECHT ALTDORFER As elsewhere in 16th-century Europe, some artists in the Holy Roman Empire worked in the employ of rulers, and their work promoted the political agendas of their patrons. In 1529, for example, the duke of Bavaria, Wilhelm IV (r. 1508–1550), commissioned Albrecht Altdorfer (ca. 1480–1538) to paint *Battle of Issus* (FIG. **18-10**) at the commencement of his military campaign against the invading Turks. The panel depicts Alexander the Great's defeat of King Darius III of Persia in 333 BCE at a town called Issus on the Pinarus River. Altdorfer announced the subject—which the Greek painter Philoxenos of Eretria (FIG. 5-70) had represented two millennia before—in the Latin inscription suspended in the sky. The parallels between the historical and contemporary conflicts were no doubt significant

18-9 Lucas Cranach the Elder, *Judgment of Paris,* 1530. Oil on wood, 1′ 1½″ × 9½″. Staatliche Kunsthalle, Karlsruhe.

For aristocratic German patrons, Cranach painted many classical myths featuring seductive female nudes. In his *Judgment of Paris,* the Greek shepherd is a knight in armor in a Saxon landscape.

Interweaving history and 16th-century politics, Albrecht Altdorfer painted Alexander the Great's defeat of the Persians for a patron who had just embarked on a military campaign against the Turks.

ALEXANDER·M·DARIVM·VLTIMO·SVPERAT
CÆSISIN·ACIE·PERSARVM·PEDIT·X·M·EQVIT
VERO·AM·INTERFECTIS·MATRE·QVOQVE
CONIVGE·LIBERIS·DARII·REGIS·CVM·M·LXXD
AMPLIVS·EQVITIB·FVGA·DILAPSI·CAPTIS·

1 ft.

to the duke. Both involved Western societies engaged in battles against Eastern foes with different values—the Persians in antiquity and the Turks in 1528. Altdorfer reinforced this connection by attiring the figures in 16th-century armor and depicting them engaged in contemporary military alignments.

Battle of Issus also reveals Altdorfer's love of landscape. The battle takes place in an almost cosmological setting. From a bird's-eye view, the clashing armies swarm in the foreground. In the distance, craggy mountain peaks rise next to still bodies of water. Amid swirling clouds, a blazing sun descends. Although the spectacular

topography may appear invented, Altdorfer derived his depiction of the landscape from maps. Specifically, he set the scene in the eastern Mediterranean with a view from Greece to the Nile in Egypt. In addition, Altdorfer may have acquired his information about this battle from the German scholar Johannes Aventinus (1477–1534), whose account of Alexander's victory describes the bloody daylong battle. Appropriately, given Alexander's designation as the "sun god," the sun sets over the victorious Greeks on the right, while a small crescent moon (a symbol of ancient Persia) hovers in the upper left corner over the retreating enemy forces.

18-11 HANS HOLBEIN THE YOUNGER, *The French Ambassadors*, 1533. Oil and tempera on wood, 6′ 8″ × 6′ 9½″. National Gallery, London. ◼

In this double portrait, Holbein depicted two humanists with a collection of objects reflective of their worldliness and learning, but he also included an anamorphic skull, a reminder of death.

HANS HOLBEIN Also in the employ of the rich and powerful for much of his career was HANS HOLBEIN THE YOUNGER (ca. 1497–1543), who excelled as a portraitist. Trained by his father, Holbein produced portraits consistent with the northern European tradition of close realism that had emerged in 15th-century Flemish art (see Chapter 15). The surfaces of Holbein's paintings are as lustrous as enamel, and the details are exact and exquisitely drawn. Yet he also incorporated Italian ideas about monumental composition and sculpturesque form.

Holbein began his artistic career in Basel, where he knew Erasmus of Rotterdam. Because of the immediate threat of a religious civil war in Basel, Erasmus suggested Holbein leave for England and gave him a recommendation to Thomas More, chancellor of England under Henry VIII. Holbein quickly obtained important commissions, for example, to paint a double portrait of the French ambassadors to England, Jean de

18-11A HOLBEIN THE YOUNGER, *Henry VIII*, 1540.

Dinteville and Georges de Selve (FIG. **18-11**), and within a few years of his arrival, he became the official painter to the English court, producing numerous portraits of Henry VIII (FIG. **18-11A**).

The French Ambassadors (FIG. **18-11**) exhibits Holbein's considerable talents—his strong sense of composition, his subtle linear patterning, his gift for portraiture, his marvelous sensitivity to color, and his faultless technique. The two men, both ardent humanists, stand at opposite ends of a side table covered with an oriental rug and a collection of objects reflective of their worldliness and their interest in learning and the arts. These include mathematical and astronomical models and implements, a lute with a broken string, compasses, a sundial, flutes, globes, and an open hymnbook with Luther's translation of *Veni, Creator Spiritus* and of the Ten Commandments.

Of particular interest is the long gray shape that slashes diagonally across the picture plane and interrupts the stable, balanced, and serene composition. This form is an *anamorphic image,* a distorted image recognizable only when viewed with a special device, such as a cylindrical mirror, or by looking at the painting at an acute angle. In this case, if the viewer stands off to the right, the gray slash becomes a skull. Although scholars disagree on the skull's precise meaning, it certainly refers to death. Artists commonly incorporated skulls into paintings as reminders of mortality. Indeed, Holbein depicted a skull on the metal medallion on Jean de Dinteville's hat. Holbein may have intended the skulls, in conjunction with the crucifix that appears half hidden behind the curtain in the upper left corner, to encourage viewers to ponder death and resurrection.

This painting may also allude to the growing tension between secular and religious authorities. Jean de Dinteville was a titled

landowner, Georges de Selve a bishop. The inclusion of Luther's translations next to the lute with the broken string (a symbol of discord) may subtly refer to this religious strife. In any case, *The French Ambassadors* is a painting of supreme artistic achievement. Holbein rendered the still-life objects with the same meticulous care as he did the men themselves, the woven design of the deep emerald curtain behind them, and the floor tiles, drawn in perfect perspective.

FRANCE

As *The French Ambassadors* illustrates, France in the early 16th century continued its efforts to secure widespread recognition as a political power and cultural force. The French kings were major patrons of art and architecture.

FRANCIS I Under the rule of Francis I (r. 1515–1547), the French established a firm foothold in Milan and its environs. Francis waged a campaign (known as the Habsburg-Valois Wars) against Charles V (the Spanish king and Holy Roman emperor; r. 1516–1558), which occupied him from 1521 to 1544. These wars involved disputed territories—southern France, the Netherlands, the Rhineland, northern Spain, and Italy—and reflect France's central role in the shifting geopolitical landscape.

The French king also took a strong position in the religious controversies of his day. By the mid-16th century, the split between Catholics and Protestants had become so pronounced that subjects often felt compelled either to accept the religion of their sovereign or emigrate to a territory where the sovereign's religion corresponded with their own. France was predominantly Catholic, and in 1534, Francis declared Protestantism illegal. The state persecuted its Protestants, the Huguenots, a Calvinist sect, and drove them underground. (Calvin fled from France to Switzerland two years later.) The Huguenots' commitment to Protestant Calvinism eventually led to one of the bloodiest religious massacres in European history when the Huguenots and Catholics clashed in Paris in August 1572. The violence quickly spread throughout France with the support of many nobles, which presented a serious threat to the king's authority.

In art as well as politics and religion, Francis I was a dominant figure. To elevate his country's cultural profile, he invited several esteemed Italian artists to his court, Leonardo da Vinci among them (see Chapter 17). Under Francis, the Church, the primary patron of art and architecture in medieval France, yielded that position to the French monarchy.

JEAN CLOUET As the rulers of antiquity had done, Francis commissioned portraits of himself to assert his authority. The finest is the portrait (FIG. **18-12**) JEAN CLOUET (ca. 1485–1541) painted about a decade after Francis became king. It portrays the French monarch as a worldly ruler magnificently bedecked in silks and brocades, wearing a gold chain with a medallion of the Order of Saint Michael, a French order Louis XI founded in 1469. Legend has it that Francis (known as the "merry monarch") was a great lover and the hero of hundreds of "gallant" deeds. Appropriately, he appears suave and confident, with his hand resting on the pommel of a dagger. Despite the careful detail, the portrait also exhibits an elegantly formalized quality, the result of Clouet's suppression of modeling, which flattens features, seen particularly in Francis's neck. The disproportion between the king's small head and his broad body, swathed in heavy layers of fabric, adds to the formalized nature.

Francis and his court favored art that was at once elegant, erotic, and unorthodox. Appropriately, Mannerism appealed to them most, and Francis thus brought Benvenuto Cellini (FIGS. 17-52 and 17-52A) to France with the promise of a lucrative retainer. He put two prominent Florentine Mannerists—Rosso Fiorentino and Francesco Primaticcio—in charge of decorating the new royal palace at Fontainebleau.

CHÂTEAU DE CHAMBORD Francis I also indulged his passion for building by commissioning several large *châteaux,* among them the Château de Chambord (FIG. **18-13**). Reflecting more peaceful times, these châteaux, developed from medieval castles, served as country houses for royalty, who usually built them near forests for use as hunting lodges. Many, including Chambord, still featured protective surrounding moats, however. Construction of the Château de Chambord began in 1519, but Francis I never saw its

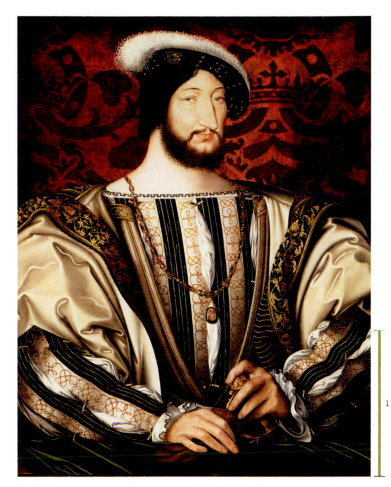

18-12 JEAN CLOUET, *Francis I,* ca. 1525–1530. Tempera and oil on wood, 3′ 2″ × 2′ 5″. Musée du Louvre, Paris.

Clouet's portrait of Francis I in elegant garb reveals the artist's attention to detail but also the flattening of features and disproportion between head and body, giving the painting a formalized quality.

completion. Chambord's plan, originally drawn by a pupil of Giuliano da Sangallo (FIGS. 17-26 and 17-27), includes a central square block with four corridors, in the shape of a cross, and a broad central staircase that gives access to groups of rooms—ancestors of the modern suite of rooms or apartments. At each of the four corners, a

18-13 Château de Chambord (looking northwest), Chambord, France, begun 1519. ◼◀

French Renaissance châteaux, which developed from medieval castles, served as country houses for royalty. King Francis I's Château de Chambord reflects Italian palazzo design, but it has a Gothic roof.

18-14 PIERRE LESCOT, west wing of the Cour Carré (Square Court, looking west) of the Louvre, Paris, France, begun 1546. ◼️◀

Lescot's design for the Louvre palace reflects the Italian Renaissance classicism of Bramante, but the decreasing height of the stories, large windows, and steep roof are northern European features.

round tower punctuates the square plan. From the exterior, Chambord presents a carefully contrived horizontal accent on three levels, with continuous moldings separating its floors. Windows align precisely, one exactly over another. The Italian Renaissance palazzo served as the model for this matching of horizontal and vertical features, but above the third level the structure's lines break chaotically into a jumble of high dormers, chimneys, and lanterns that recall soaring, ragged Gothic silhouettes on the skyline.

LOUVRE, PARIS Chambord, despite its Italian elements, is essentially a French building. During the reign of Francis's successor, Henry II (r. 1547–1559), however, translations of Italian architectural treatises appeared, and Italian architects themselves came to work in France. Moreover, the French turned to Italy for study and travel. These exchanges caused a more extensive revolution in style than had transpired earlier, although certain French elements derived from the Gothic tradition persisted. This incorporation of Italian architectural ideas characterizes the redesigned Louvre in Paris, originally a medieval palace and fortress (FIG. 15-16). Since Charles V's renovation of the Louvre in the mid-14th century, the castle had fallen into a state of disrepair. Francis I initiated the project to update and expand the royal palace, but died before the work was well under way. His architect, PIERRE LESCOT (1510–1578), continued under Henry II and produced the classical style most closely associated with 16th-century French architecture.

Lescot and his associates were familiar with the architectural style of Bramante and his school. In the west wing of the Cour Carré (Square Court; FIG. 18-14) of the Louvre, each of the stories forms a complete order, and the cornices project enough to furnish a strong horizontal accent. The arcading on the ground story reflects the ancient Roman use of arches and produces more shadow than in the upper stories due to its recessed placement, thereby strengthening the design's visual base. On the second story, the pilasters rising from bases and the alternating curved and angular pediments supported by consoles have direct antecedents in several High Renaissance palaces (for example, FIG. 17-26). Yet the decreasing height of the stories, the scale of the windows (proportionally much larger

than in Italian Renaissance buildings), and the steep roof are northern European elements. Especially French are the pavilions jutting from the wall. A motif the French long favored—double columns framing a niche—punctuates the pavilions. The richly ar-

18-14A GOUJON, Fountain of the Innocents, 1547–1549.

ticulated wall surfaces feature relief sculptures by JEAN GOUJON (ca. 1510–1565), who had previously collaborated with Lescot on the Fountain of the Innocents (FIG. 18-14A) in Paris. Other northern European countries imitated this French classical manner—its double-columned pavilions, tall and wide windows, profuse statuary, and steep roofs—although with local variations. The modified classicism the French produced became the model for building projects north of the Alps through most of the 16th century.

THE NETHERLANDS

With the demise of the duchy of Burgundy in 1477 and the division of that territory between France and the Holy Roman Empire, the Netherlands at the beginning of the 16th century consisted of 17 provinces (corresponding to modern Holland, Belgium, and Luxembourg). The Netherlands was among the most commercially advanced and prosperous European countries. Its extensive network of rivers and easy access to the Atlantic Ocean provided a setting conducive to overseas trade, and shipbuilding was one of the most profitable enterprises. The region's commercial center shifted toward the end of the 15th century, partly because of the buildup of silt in the Bruges estuary. Traffic relocated to Antwerp, which became the hub of economic activity in the Netherlands after 1510. As many as 500 ships a day passed through Antwerp's harbor, and large trading companies from England, the Holy Roman Empire, Italy, Portugal, and Spain established themselves in the city.

During the second half of the 16th century, Philip II of Spain (r. 1556–1598) controlled the Netherlands. Philip had inherited the region from his father Charles V, and he sought to force the who traveled to Italy and became fascinated with classical antiquity and mythology (FIG. **18-15**), although he also painted traditional Christian themes (FIG. **18-15A**). Giorgio Vasari, the Italian artist and biographer and Gossaert's contemporary, wrote that "Jean Gossart [sic] of Mabuse

18-15A GOSSAERT, *Saint Luke Drawing the Virgin*, ca. 1520–1525.

was almost the first who took from Italy into Flanders the true method of making scenes full of nude figures and poetical inventions,"[3] although Gossaert derived much of his classicism from Albrecht Dürer.

Indeed, Dürer's *Fall of Man* (FIG. 18-5) inspired the composition and poses in Gossaert's *Neptune and Amphitrite* (FIG. 18-15). However, in contrast to Dürer's exquisitely small engraving, Gossaert's painting is more than six feet tall and four feet wide. The artist executed the painting with characteristic Netherlandish polish, skillfully drawing and carefully modeling the figures. Gossaert depicted the sea god with his traditional attribute, the trident, and wearing a laurel wreath and an ornate conch shell in place of Dürer's fig leaf. Amphitrite is fleshy and, like Neptune, stands in a contrapposto stance. The architectural frame, which resembles the cella of a classical temple (FIG. 5-46), is an unusual mix of Doric and Ionic elements and *bucrania* (ox skull decorations), a common motif in ancient architectural ornamentation.

entire population to become Catholic. His heavy-handed tactics and repressive measures led in 1579 to revolt and the formation of two federations: the Union of Arras, a Catholic union of southern Netherlandish provinces, which remained under Spanish dominion, and the Union of Utrecht, a Protestant union of northern provinces, which became the Dutch Republic (MAP 20-1).

Large-scale altarpieces and other religious works continued to be commissioned for Catholic churches, but with the rise of Protestantism in the Netherlands, artists increasingly favored secular subjects. Netherlandish art of this period provides a wonderful glimpse into the lives of various strata of society, from nobility to peasantry, capturing their activities, environment, and values.

JAN GOSSAERT As in the Holy Roman Empire and France, developments in Italian Renaissance art interested many Netherlandish artists. JAN GOSSAERT (ca. 1478–1535) was one of those

Gossaert likely based the classical setting on sketches he had made of ancient buildings while in Rome. He had traveled to Italy with Philip, bastard of Burgundy, this painting's patron. A Burgundian admiral (hence the Neptune reference), Philip became a bishop and kept this work in the innermost room of his castle.

QUINTEN MASSYS Antwerp's growth and prosperity, along with its wealthy merchants' propensity for collecting and purchasing art, attracted artists to the city. Among them was QUINTEN MASSYS (ca. 1466–1530), who became Antwerp's leading master after 1510. The son of a Louvain blacksmith, Massys demonstrated a willingness to explore the styles and modes of a variety of models, from Jan van Eyck and Rogier van der Weyden to Albrecht Dürer, Hieronymus Bosch, and Leonardo da Vinci. Yet his eclecticism was subtle and discriminating, enriched by an inventiveness that gave a personal stamp to his paintings.

1 ft.

18-16 QUINTEN MASSYS, *Money-Changer and His Wife*, 1514. Oil on wood, 2′ 3¾″ × 2′ 2⅜″. Musée du Louvre, Paris.

Massys's depiction of a secular financial transaction is also a commentary on Netherlandish values. The banker's wife shows more interest in the money-weighing than in her prayer book.

In *Money-Changer and His Wife* (FIG. **18-16**), Massys presented a professional man transacting business. He holds scales, checking the weight of coins on the table. The artist's detailed rendering of the figures, setting, and objects suggests a fidelity to observable fact, and provides insight into developing commercial practices. But *Money-Changer and His Wife* is also a commentary on Netherlandish values and mores. The painting highlights the financial transactions that were an increasingly prominent part of 16th-century secular life in the Netherlands and that distracted Christians from their religious duties. The banker's wife, for example, shows more interest in watching her husband weigh money than in reading her prayer book. Massys incorporated into his painting numerous references to the importance of a moral, righteous, and spiritual life, including a carafe with water and a candlestick, traditional religious symbols. The couple ignores them, focusing solely on money. On the right, through a window, an old man talks with another man, a reference to idleness and gossip. The reflected image in the convex mirror on the counter offsets this image of sloth and foolish chatter. There, a man reads what is most likely a Bible or prayer book. Behind him is a church steeple. An inscription on the original frame (now lost) read, "Let the balance be just and the weights equal" (Lev. 19:36), an admonition that applies both to the money-changer's professional conduct and the eventual last judgment. Nonetheless, the couple in this painting has tipped the balance in favor of the pursuit of wealth.

PIETER AERTSEN This tendency to inject reminders about spiritual well-being into paintings of everyday life emerges again in *Butcher's Stall* (FIG. **18-17**) by PIETER AERTSEN (ca. 1507–1575), who worked in Antwerp for more than three decades. At first glance, this painting appears to be a descriptive *genre* scene (one from daily

18-17 PIETER AERTSEN, *Butcher's Stall*, 1551. Oil on wood, 4′ ⅜″ × 6′ 5¾″. Uppsala University Art Collection, Uppsala.

Butcher's Stall appears to be a genre painting, but in the background, Joseph leads a donkey carrying Mary and the Christ Child. Aertsen balanced images of gluttony with allusions to salvation.

life). On display is an array of meat products—a side of a hog, chickens, sausages, a stuffed intestine, pig's feet, meat pies, a cow's head, a hog's head, and hanging entrails. Also visible are fish, pretzels, cheese, and butter. As did Massys, Aertsen embedded strategically placed religious images in his painting. In the background, Joseph leads a donkey carrying Mary and the Christ Child. The holy family stops to offer alms to a beggar and his son, while the people behind the holy family wend their way toward a church. Furthermore, the crossed fishes on the platter and the pretzels and wine in the rafters on the upper left all refer to "spiritual food" (pretzels were often served as bread during Lent). Aertsen accentuated these allusions to salvation through Christ by contrasting them to their opposite—a life of gluttony, lust, and sloth. He represented this degeneracy with the oyster and mussel shells (which Netherlanders believed possessed aphrodisiacal properties) scattered on the ground on the painting's right side, along with the people seen eating and carousing nearby under the roof. Underscoring the general theme is the placard at the right advertising land for sale—Aertsen's moralistic reference to a recent scandal involving the transfer of land from an Antwerp charitable institution to a land speculator. The sign appears directly above the vignette of the Virgin giving alms to the beggar.

CATERINA VAN HEMESSEN With the accumulation of wealth in the Netherlands, portraits increased in popularity. The self-portrait (FIG. 18-18) by CATERINA VAN HEMESSEN (1528–1587) is the first known northern European self-portrait by a woman. Here, she confidently presented herself as an artist who interrupts her work to gaze at the viewer. She holds brushes, a palette, and a *maulstick* (a stick used to steady the hand while painting) in her left hand, and delicately applies pigment to the canvas with her right hand. The artist ensured proper identification (and credit) through the inscription in the painting: "Caterina van Hemessen painted me / 1548 / her age 20." Professional women artists remained unusual in the 16th century in large part because of the difficulty in obtaining formal training (see "The Artist's Profession in Flanders," Chapter 15, page 433). Caterina was typical in having been trained by her father, Jan Sanders van Hemessen (ca. 1500–1556), a well-known painter.

LEVINA TEERLINC Another Netherlandish woman who achieved a successful career as an artist was LEVINA TEERLINC (1515–1576) of Bruges. She established such a high reputation that Henry VIII and his successors invited her to England to paint miniatures for them. There, she was a formidable rival of some of her male contemporaries at the court, such as Holbein (FIG. 18-11A), and received greater compensation for her work than they did for theirs. Teerlinc's considerable skill is evident in a life-size portrait (FIG. 18-19) attributed to her, which depicts Elizabeth I as a composed, youthful princess. Daughter of Henry VIII and Anne

18-19 Attributed to LEVINA TEERLINC, *Elizabeth I as a Princess,* ca. 1559. Oil on wood, 3' 6¾" × 2' 8¼". Royal Collection, Windsor Castle, Windsor. ◼◄

Teerlinc received greater compensation for her work for the British court than did her male contemporaries. Her considerable skill is evident in this life-size portrait of Elizabeth I as a young princess.

18-18 CATERINA VAN HEMESSEN, *Self-Portrait,* 1548. Oil on wood, 1' ¾" × 9⅞". Kunstmuseum Basel, Basel. ◼◄

In this first known northern European self-portrait by a woman, Caterina van Hemessen represented herself as a confident artist momentarily interrupting her work to look out at the viewer.

18-20 JOACHIM PATINIR, *Landscape with Saint Jerome,* ca. 1520–1524. Oil on wood, 2′ 5⅛″ × 2′ 11⅞″. Museo del Prado, Madrid. ◼▶

Joachim Patinir, a renowned Netherlandish landscape painter, subordinated the story of Saint Jerome to the depiction of craggy rock formations, verdant rolling fields, and expansive bodies of water.

1 ft.

Boleyn, Elizabeth was probably in her late 20s when she posed for this portrait. Appropriate to her station in life, Elizabeth wears an elegant brocaded gown, extravagant jewelry, and a headdress based on a style her mother popularized.

That van Hemessen and Teerlinc enjoyed such success is a testament to their determination and skill, given the difficulties women faced in a profession dominated by men. Women also played an important role as patrons in 16th-century northern Europe. Politically powerful women such as Margaret of Austria (regent of the Netherlands during the early 16th century; 1480–1530) and Mary of Hungary (queen consort of Hungary; 1505–1558) were avid collectors and patrons, and contributed significantly to the thriving state of the arts. As did other art patrons, these women collected and commissioned art not only for the aesthetic pleasure it provided but also for the status it bestowed on them and the cultural sophistication it represented.

JOACHIM PATINIR In addition to portrait and genre painting, landscape painting flourished in the Netherlands. Particularly well known for his landscapes was JOACHIM PATINIR (d. 1524). In fact, the word *Landschaft* (landscape) first emerged in German literature as a characterization of an artistic category when Dürer described Patinir as a "good landscape painter." In *Landscape with Saint Jerome* (FIG. **18-20**), Patinir subordinated the saint, who removes a thorn from a lion's paw in the foreground, to the exotic and detailed landscape. Craggy rock formations, verdant rolling fields, villages with church steeples, expansive bodies of water, and a dramatic sky fill most of the panel. Patinir amplified the sense of distance by masterfully using color to enhance the visual effect of recession and advance.

PIETER BRUEGEL THE ELDER The greatest Netherlandish painter of the mid-16th century was PIETER BRUEGEL THE ELDER (ca. 1528–1569). Influenced by Patinir, Bruegel was also a landscape painter, but in his paintings, no matter how huge a slice of the world he depicted, human activities remain the dominant theme. As did many of his contemporaries, Bruegel traveled to Italy, where he probably spent almost two years, going as far south as Sicily. Unlike other artists, however, Bruegel chose not to incorporate classical elements into his paintings.

Bruegel's *Netherlandish Proverbs* (FIG. **18-21**) depicts a Netherlandish village populated by a wide range of people (nobility, peasants, and clerics). From a bird's-eye view, the spectator encounters a mesmerizing array of activities reminiscent of the topsy-turvy scenes of Bosch (FIG. 18-1), but the purpose and meaning of Bruegel's anecdotal details are clear. By illustrating more than a hundred proverbs in this one painting, the artist indulged his Netherlandish audience's obsession with proverbs and passion for detailed and clever imagery. As the viewer scrutinizes the myriad vignettes within the painting, Bruegel's close observation and deep understanding of human nature become apparent. The proverbs depicted include, on the far left, a man in blue gnawing on a pillar ("He bites the column"—an image of hypocrisy). To his right, a man "beats his head against a wall" (an ambitious idiot). On the roof a man "shoots one arrow after the other, but hits nothing" (a shortsighted fool). In the far distance, the "blind lead the blind"—a subject to which Bruegel returned several years later in one of his most famous paintings (not illustrated).

In contrast to Patinir's Saint Jerome, lost in the landscape, the myriad, raucous cast of characters of Bruegel's *Netherlandish Proverbs* fills the panel, so much so the artist almost shut out the sky. *Hunters in the Snow* (FIG. **18-22**) and *Fall of Icarus*

18-21 PIETER BRUEGEL THE ELDER, *Netherlandish Proverbs*, 1559. Oil on wood, 3′ 10″ × 5′ 4⅛″. Gemäldegalerie, Staatliche Museen zu Berlin, Berlin. ◼️

In this painting of a Netherlandish village, Bruegel indulged his audience's obsession with proverbs and passion for clever imagery, and demonstrated his deep understanding of human nature.

1 ft.

18-22 PIETER BRUEGEL THE ELDER, *Hunters in the Snow*, 1565. Oil on wood, 3′ 10⅛″ × 5′ 3¾″. Kunsthistorisches Museum, Vienna.

In *Hunters in the Snow*, one of a series of paintings illustrating different seasons, Bruegel draws the viewer diagonally deep into the landscape by his mastery of line, shape, and composition.

1 ft.

18-22A BRUEGEL THE ELDER, *Fall of Icarus*, ca. 1555–1556.

(FIG. **18-22A**) are very different in character and illustrate the dynamic variety of Bruegel's work. *Hunters* is one of a series of six paintings (some scholars think there were originally twelve) illustrating seasonal changes. The series grew out of the tradition of depicting seasons and peasants in Books of Hours (FIGS. 15-15 and 15-16). The painting shows human figures and landscape locked in winter cold, reflect-ing the particularly severe winter of 1565, when Bruegel produced the work. The weary hunters return with their hounds, women build fires, skaters skim the frozen pond, and the town and its church huddle in their mantle of snow. Bruegel rendered the landscape in an optically accurate manner. It develops smoothly from foreground to background and draws the viewer diagonally into its depths. The painter's consummate skill in using line and shape and his subtlety in tonal harmony make this one of the great landscape paintings in Western art.

SPAIN

Spain's ascent to power in Europe began in the mid-15th century with the marriage of Isabella of Castile (1451–1504) and Ferdinand of Aragon (1452–1516) in 1469. By the end of the 16th century, Spain had emerged as the dominant European power. Under the Habsburg rulers Charles V and Philip II, the Spanish Empire controlled a territory greater in extent than any ever known—a large part of Europe, the western Mediterranean, a strip of North Africa, and vast expanses in the New World. Spain acquired many of its New World colonies through aggressive overseas exploration. Among the most notable conquistadors sailing under the Spanish flag were Christopher Columbus (1451–1506), Vasco Nuñez de Balboa (ca. 1475–1517), Ferdinand Magellan (1480–1521), Hernán Cortés (1485–1547), and Francisco Pizarro (ca. 1470–1541). The Habsburg Empire, enriched by New World plunder, supported the most powerful military force in Europe. Spain defended and then promoted the interests of the Catholic Church in its battle against the inroads of the Protestant Reformation. Indeed, Philip II earned the title "Most Catholic King." Spain's crusading spirit, nourished by centuries of war with Islam, engaged body and soul in forming the most Catholic civilization of Europe and the Americas. In the 16th century, for good or for ill, Spain left the mark of its power, religion, language, and culture on two hemispheres.

COLEGIO DE SAN GREGORIO During the 15th century and well into the 16th, a Late Gothic style of architecture, the Plateresque, prevailed in Spain. *Plateresque* derives from the Spanish word *platero* (silversmith), and delicately executed ornamentation resembling metalwork is the defining characteristic of the Plateresque style. The Colegio de San Gregorio (Seminary of Saint Gregory; FIG. **18-23**) in the Castilian city of Valladolid handsomely exemplifies the Plateresque manner, which Spanish expansion into the Western Hemisphere also brought to "New Spain" (FIG. **18-23A**). Great carved retables, like the German altarpieces that influenced them (FIGS. 15-19, 15-20, and 18-2, *bottom*), appealed to church patrons and architects in Spain, and the portals of Plateresque facades often resemble elegantly carved retables set into an otherwise blank wall. The Plateresque entrance of San Gregorio is a lofty sculptured stone screen bearing no functional relation to the architecture behind it. On the entrance level, lacelike tracery reminiscent of Moorish design hems the flamboyant ogival arches. (Spanish hatred of the Moors did not prevent Spanish architects from adapting Moorish motifs.) A great screen, paneled into sculptured compartments, rises above the tracery. In the center, the branches of a huge pomegranate tree (symbolizing Granada, the Moorish capital of Spain the Habsburgs captured in 1492; see Chapter 10) wreathe the coat of arms of King Ferdinand and Queen Isabella. Cupids play among the tree branches, and, flanking the central panel, niches frame armed pages of the court, heraldic wild men symbolizing aggression, and armored soldiers, attesting to Spain's proud new militancy. In typical Plateresque and Late Gothic fashion, the activity of a thousand intertwined motifs unifies the whole design, which, in sum, creates an exquisitely carved panel greatly expanded in scale from the retables that inspired it.

18-23A Casa de Montejo, Mérida, 1549.

EL ESCORIAL Under Philip II, the Plateresque style gave way to an Italian-derived classicism that also characterized

18-23 Portal, Colegio de San Gregorio, Valladolid, Spain, ca. 1498.

The Plateresque architectural style takes its name from *platero* (Spanish, "silversmith"). At the center of this portal's Late Gothic tracery is the coat of arms of King Ferdinand and Queen Isabella.

16th-century French architecture (FIG. 18-13). The Italian style is on display in the expansive complex called El Escorial (FIG. **18-24**), which JUAN BAUTISTA DE TOLEDO (d. 1567) and JUAN DE HERRERA (ca. 1530–1597), principally the latter, constructed for Philip II. In his will, Charles V stipulated that a "dynastic pantheon" be built to house the remains of past and future monarchs of Spain. Philip II, obedient to his father's wishes, chose a site some 30 miles northwest of Madrid in rugged terrain with barren mountains. Here, he built El Escorial, not only a royal mausoleum but also a church, a monastery, and a palace. Legend has it that the gridlike plan for the enormous complex, 625 feet wide and 520 feet deep, symbolized the gridiron on which Saint Lawrence, El Escorial's patron saint, suffered his martyrdom.

The vast structure is in keeping with Philip's austere character, his passionate Catholic religiosity, his proud reverence for his dynasty, and his stern determination to impose his will worldwide. He insisted that in designing El Escorial, the architects focus on simplicity of form, severity in the whole, nobility without arrogance, and majesty without ostentation. The result is a classicism of Doric severity, ultimately derived from Italian architecture and with the grandeur of Saint Peter's (FIGS. 19-3 and 19-4) implicit in the scheme, but unique in European architecture.

18-24 JUAN DE HERRERA and JUAN BAUTISTA DE TOLEDO, aerial view (looking southeast) of El Escorial, near Madrid, Spain, 1563–1584.

Conceived by Charles V and built by Philip II, El Escorial is a royal mausoleum, church, monastery, and palace in one. The complex is classical in style with severely plain walls and massive towers.

Only the three entrances, with the dominant central portal framed by superimposed orders and topped by a pediment in the Italian fashion, break the long sweep of the structure's severely plain walls. Massive square towers punctuate the four corners. The stress on the central axis, with its subdued echoes in the two flanking portals, anticipates the three-part organization of later Baroque facades (see Chapter 19). The construction material for the entire complex (including the church)—granite, a difficult stone to work—conveys a feeling of starkness and gravity. The church's massive facade and the austere geometry of the interior complex, with its blocky walls and ponderous arches, produce an effect of overwhelming strength and weight. The entire complex is a monument to the collaboration of a great king and remarkably understanding architects. El Escorial stands as the overpowering architectural expression of Spain's spirit in its heroic epoch and of the character of Philip II, the extraordinary ruler who directed it.

EL GRECO Reflecting the increasingly international character of European art as well as the mobility of artists, the greatest Spanish painter of the era was not a Spaniard. Born on Crete, Domenikos Theotokopoulos, called EL GRECO (ca. 1547–1614), emigrated to Italy as a young man. In his youth, he absorbed the traditions of Late Byzantine frescoes and mosaics. While still young, El Greco went to Venice, where he worked in Titian's studio, although Tintoretto's paintings seem to have made a stronger impression on him (see Chapter 17). A brief trip to Rome explains the influences of Roman and Florentine Mannerism on his work. By 1577, he had left for Spain to spend the rest of his life in Toledo.

El Greco's art is a strong personal blending of Byzantine and Mannerist elements. The intense emotionalism of his paintings, which naturally appealed to Spanish piety, and a great reliance on and mastery of color bound him to 16th-century Venetian art and to Mannerism. El Greco's art was not strictly Spanish (although it appealed to certain sectors of that society), for it had no Spanish antecedents and little effect on later Spanish painters. Nevertheless, El Greco's hybrid style captured the fervor of Spanish Catholicism.

Burial of Count Orgaz (FIG. **18-25**), painted in 1586 for the church of Santo Tomé in El Greco's adoptive home, Toledo, vividly expressed that fervor. El Greco based the painting on the legend that the count of Orgaz, who had died some three centuries before and who had been a great benefactor of Santo Tomé, was buried in the church by Saints Stephen and Augustine, who miraculously descended from Heaven to lower the count's body into its sepulcher. In the painting, El Greco carefully distinguished the terrestrial and celestial spheres. The brilliant Heaven that opens above irradiates the earthly scene. The painter represented the terrestrial realm with a firm realism, whereas he depicted the celestial, in his quite personal manner, with elongated undulating figures, fluttering draperies, and a visionary swirling cloud. Below, the two saints lovingly lower the count's armor-clad body, the armor and heavy draperies painted with all the rich sensuousness of the Venetian school. A solemn chorus of personages dressed in black fills the background. In the carefully individualized features of these figures (who include El Greco himself in a self-portrait, and his young son, Jorge Manuel, as well as the priest who commissioned the painting and the Spanish king Philip II), El Greco demonstrated he was also a great portraitist.

The upward glances of some of the figures below and the flight of an angel above link the painting's lower and upper spheres. The action of the angel, who carries the count's soul in his arms as Saint John and the Virgin intercede for it before the throne of Christ, reinforces this connection. El Greco's deliberate change in style to distinguish between the two levels of reality gives the viewer an opportunity to see the artist's early and late manners in the same work, one below the other. His relatively sumptuous and realistic presentation of the earthly sphere is still strongly rooted in Venetian art,

18-25 El Greco, *Burial of Count Orgaz*, 1586. Oil on canvas, 16′ × 12′. Santo Tomé, Toledo.

El Greco's art is a blend of Byzantine and Italian Mannerist elements. His intense emotional content captured the fervor of Spanish Catholicism, and his dramatic use of light foreshadowed the Baroque style.

but the abstractions and distortions El Greco used to show the immaterial nature of the heavenly realm characterize his later style. His elongated figures existing in undefined spaces, bathed in a cool light of uncertain origin, explain El Greco's usual classification as a Mannerist, but it is difficult to apply that label to him without reservation. Although he used Mannerist formal devices, El Greco's primary concerns were emotion and conveying his religious fervor or arousing that of others. The forcefulness of his paintings is the result of his unique, highly developed expressive style.

VIEW OF TOLEDO El Greco's singular vision is equally evident in one of his latest works, *View of Toledo* (FIG. **18-26**), the only pure landscape he ever painted. As does so much of El Greco's work, this painting breaks sharply with tradition. The Greek-born artist depicted the Spanish city from a nearby hilltop and drew attention to the great spire of Toledo's cathedral by leading the viewer's eye along the diagonal line of the bridge crossing the Tajo and continuing with the city's walls. El Greco knew Toledo intimately, and every building is recognizable, although he rearranged some of their positions, moving, for example, the Alcazar palace to the right of the cathedral. Yet he rendered no structure in meticulous detail, as most Renaissance painters would have done, and the color palette is not true to nature but limited to greens and grays. The atmosphere is eerie. Dramatic bursts of light in the stormy sky cast a ghostly pall over the city. The artist applied oil pigment to canvas in broad brushstrokes typical of his late, increasingly abstract painting style, with the result that the buildings and trees do not have sharp contours and almost seem to shake.

Art historians have compared *View of Toledo* to Giorgione da Castelfranco's *Tempest* (FIG. 17-34) and the dramatic lighting to works by Tintoretto (FIG. 17-48), and indeed, El Greco's Venetian training is evident. Still, the closest parallels lie not in the past but in the future—in paintings such as Vincent van Gogh's *Starry Night* (FIG. 23-18) and in 20th-century Expressionism and Surrealism (see Chapter 24). El Greco's art is impossible to classify using conventional labels. Although he had ties to Mannerism and foreshadowed developments of the Baroque era in Spain and Italy—examined in the next chapter—he was a singular artist with a unique vision.

1 ft.

18-26 El Greco, *View of Toledo,* ca. 1610. Oil on canvas, 3′ 11¾″ × 3′ 6¾″. Metropolitan Museum of Art, New York (H. O. Havemeyer Collection. Bequest of Mrs. H. O. Havemeyer, 1929).

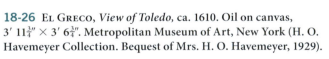

View of Toledo is the only pure landscape El Greco ever produced. The dark, stormy sky casts a ghostly pall over the city. The painting exemplifies the artist's late, increasingly abstract style.

1 ft.

HIGH RENAISSANCE AND MANNERISM IN NORTHERN EUROPE AND SPAIN

HOLY ROMAN EMPIRE

Dürer, *Fall of Man*, 1504

▌ Widespread dissatisfaction with the Church in Rome led to the Protestant Reformation, splitting Christendom in half. Protestants objected to the sale of indulgences and rejected most of the sacraments of the Catholic Church. They also condemned ostentatious church decoration as a form of idolatry that distracted the faithful from communication with God.

▌ As a result, Protestant churches were relatively bare, but art, especially prints, still played a role in Protestantism. Lucas Cranach the Elder, for example, effectively used visual imagery to contrast Catholic and Protestant views of salvation in his woodcut *Law and Gospel*.

▌ The greatest printmaker of the Holy Roman Empire was Albrecht Dürer, who was also a painter. Dürer was the first artist outside Italy to become an international celebrity. His work ranged from biblical subjects to botanical studies. *Fall of Man* reflects Dürer's studies of the Vitruvian theory of human proportions and of classical statuary. Dürer's engravings rival painting in tonal quality.

Holbein, *The French Ambassadors*, 1533

▌ Other German artists, such as Albrecht Altdorfer, achieved fame as landscape painters. Hans Holbein was a renowned portraitist who became court painter in England. His *French Ambassadors* portrays two worldly humanists and includes a masterfully rendered anamorphic skull.

FRANCE

▌ King Francis I fought against Holy Roman Emperor Charles V and declared Protestantism illegal in France. An admirer of Italian art, he invited several prominent Italian painters and sculptors to work at his court and decorate his palace at Fontainebleau.

▌ French architecture of the 16th century mixes Italian and Northern Renaissance elements, as in Pierre Lescot's design of the renovated Louvre palace and Francis's château at Chambord, which combines classical motifs derived from Italian palazzi with a Gothic roof silhouette.

Clouet, *Francis I*, ca. 1525–1530

THE NETHERLANDS

▌ The Netherlands was one of the most commercially advanced and prosperous countries in 16th-century Europe. Much of Netherlandish art of this period provides a picture of contemporary life and values.

▌ Pieter Aertsen of Antwerp, for example, painted *Butcher's Stall,* which seems to be a straightforward genre scene but includes the holy family offering alms to a beggar in the background, providing a stark contrast between gluttony and religious piety.

Bruegel, *Hunters in the Snow*, 1565

▌ Landscapes were the specialty of Joachim Patinir. Pieter Bruegel's repertory also included landscape painting. His *Hunters in the Snow* is one of a series of paintings depicting seasonal changes and the activities associated with them, as in traditional Books of Hours.

▌ Women artists of the period include Caterina van Hemessen, who painted the earliest northern European self-portrait of a woman, and Levina Teerlinc, who produced portraits for the English court.

SPAIN

Colegio de San Gregorio, Valladolid, ca. 1498

▌ At the end of the 16th century, Spain was the dominant power in Europe with an empire greater in extent than any ever known, including vast territories in the New World.

▌ The Spanish Plateresque style of architecture takes its name from *platero* (silversmith) and features delicate ornamentation resembling metalwork.

▌ Under Philip II the Plateresque style gave way to an Italian-derived classicism, seen at its best in El Escorial, a royal mausoleum, monastery, and palace complex near Madrid.

▌ The leading painter of 16th-century Spain was the Greek-born El Greco, who combined Byzantine style, Italian Mannerism, and the religious fervor of Catholic Spain in works such as *Burial of Count Orgaz*.

As water flows from a travertine grotto supporting an ancient Egyptian obelisk, Bernini's marble personifications of major rivers of four continents twist and gesticulate emphatically.

Crowning the grotto is Pope Innocent X's coat of arms and atop the obelisk is the Pamphili family's dove symbolizing the Holy Spirit and Christianity's triumph in all parts of the then-known world.

Each of the four rivers has an identifying attribute. The Ganges (Asia), easily navigable, holds an oar. The Plata (Americas) has a hoard of coins, signifying the wealth of the New World.

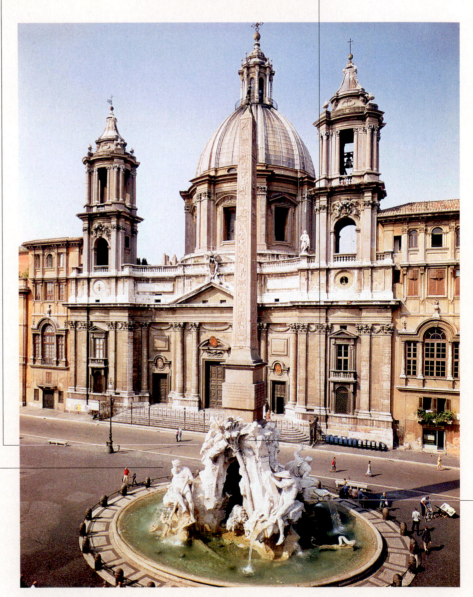

19-1 GIANLORENZO BERNINI, *Fountain of the Four Rivers* (looking southwest with Sant'Agnese in Agone in the background), Piazza Navona, Rome, Italy, 1648–1651. ◼◤

The Danube (Europe) gazes awestruck at the papal arms, and the Nile (Africa) covers his face—Bernini's acknowledgment that the Nile's source was unknown to Europeans at the time.

THE BAROQUE IN ITALY AND SPAIN

BAROQUE ART AND SPECTACLE

One of the most popular tourist attractions in Rome is the Fountain of the Four Rivers (FIG. 19-1) in Piazza Navona by GIANLORENZO BERNINI (1598–1680). Architect, painter, sculptor, playwright, and stage designer, Bernini was one of the most important and imaginative artists of the Baroque era in Italy and its most characteristic and sustaining spirit. Nonetheless, the fountain's patron, Pope Innocent X (r. 1644–1655), did not want Bernini to win this commission. Bernini had been the favorite sculptor of the Pamphili pope's predecessor, Urban VIII (r. 1623–1644), who spent so extravagantly on art and himself and his family that he nearly bankrupted the Vatican treasury. Innocent emphatically opposed the excesses of the Barberini pope and shunned Bernini, awarding new papal commissions to other sculptors and architects. Bernini was also in disgrace at the time because of his failed attempt to erect bell towers for the new facade (FIG. 19-3) of Saint Peter's. When Innocent announced a competition for a fountain in Piazza Navona (MAP 17-1), site of the Pamphili family's palace and parish church, Sant'Agnese in Agone (FIG. 19-1, *rear*), he pointedly did not invite Bernini to submit a design. However, the renowned sculptor succeeded in having a model of his proposed fountain placed where the pope would see it. When Innocent examined it, he was so captivated he declared the only way anyone could avoid employing Bernini was not to look at his work.

Bernini's bold design, executed in large part by his assistants, called for a sculptured travertine grotto supporting an ancient obelisk Innocent had transferred to Piazza Navona from the circus of the Roman emperor Maxentius (r. 305–312) on the Via Appia. The piazza was once the site of the stadium of Domitian (r. 81–96), a long and narrow arena for athletic contests, which explains the piazza's unusual shape and the church's name (*agone* means "foot race" in Italian). Water rushes from the artificial grotto into a basin filled with marble statues personifying major rivers of four continents—the Danube (Europe), Nile (Africa), Ganges (Asia), and Plata (Americas). The reclining figures twist and gesticulate, consistent with Baroque taste for movement and drama. The Nile covers his face—Bernini's way of acknowledging the Nile's source was unknown at the time. The Rio de la Plata has a hoard of coins, signifying the wealth of the New World. The Ganges, easily navigable, holds an oar. The Danube, awestruck, reaches up to the papal coat of arms. A second reference to Innocent X is the Pamphili dove at the apex of the obelisk, which also symbolizes the Holy Spirit and the triumph of Christianity in all parts of the then-known world. The scenic effect of the cascading water would have been heightened whenever Piazza Navona was flooded for festival pageants. Bernini's fountain epitomizes the Baroque era's love for uniting art and spectacle.

"BAROQUE" ART AND ARCHITECTURE

Art historians traditionally describe 17th-century European art as *Baroque*, but the term is problematic because the period encompasses a broad range of styles and genres. Although its origin is unclear, "Baroque" may have come from the Portuguese word *barroco*, meaning an irregularly shaped pearl. Use of the term can be traced to the late 18th century, when critics disparaged the Baroque period's artistic production, in large part because of perceived deficiencies in comparison with the art of the Italian Renaissance. Over time, this negative connotation faded, but the term stuck. "Baroque" remains useful to describe the distinctive new style that emerged during the early 1600s—a style of complexity and drama seen especially in Italian art of this period. Whereas Renaissance artists reveled in the precise, orderly rationality of classical models, Baroque artists embraced dynamism, theatricality, and elaborate ornamentation, all used to spectacular effect, often on a grandiose scale, as in Bernini's Four Rivers Fountain (FIG. 19-1).

ITALY

Although in the 16th century the Roman Catholic Church launched the Counter-Reformation in response to—and as a challenge to—the Protestant Reformation, the considerable appeal of Protestantism continued to preoccupy the popes throughout the 17th century. The Treaty of Westphalia (see Chapter 20) in 1648 had formally recognized the principle of religious freedom, serving to validate Protestantism (predominantly in the German states). With the Catholic Church as the leading art patron in 17th-century Italy, the aim of much of Italian Baroque art was to restore Roman Catholicism's predominance and centrality. The Council of Trent, one 16th-century Counter-Reformation initiative, firmly resisted Protestant objections to using images in religious worship, insisting on their necessity for teaching the laity (see "Religious Art in Counter-Reformation Italy," Chapter 17, page 505). Baroque art in Italy was therefore often overtly didactic.

Architecture and Sculpture

Italian 17th-century art and architecture, especially in Rome, embodied the renewed energy of the Counter-Reformation and communicated it to the populace. At the end of the 16th century, Pope Sixtus V (r. 1585–1590) had played a key role in the Catholic Church's lengthy campaign to reestablish its preeminence. He

19-2 CARLO MADERNO, **facade of Santa Susanna (looking north), Rome, Italy, 1597–1603.**

Santa Susanna's facade is one of the earliest manifestations of the Baroque spirit. The rhythm of the columns and pilasters mounts dramatically toward the emphatically stressed vertical axis.

augmented the papal treasury and intended to rebuild Rome as an even more magnificent showcase of Church power. Between 1606 and 1667, several strong and ambitious popes—Paul V, Urban VIII, Innocent X, and Alexander VII—made many of Sixtus V's dreams a reality. Rome still bears the marks of their patronage everywhere.

SANTA SUSANNA The facade (FIG. **19-2**) CARLO MADERNO (1556–1629) designed at the turn of the century for the Roman church of Santa Susanna stands as one of the earliest manifestations of the

THE BAROQUE IN ITALY AND SPAIN

1600	1625	1650	1675	1700
▍ Paul V commissions Maderno to complete Saint Peter's	▍ Borromini designs San Carlo alle Quattro Fontane and the Chapel of Saint Ivo in Rome	▍ Bernini designs the colonnaded oval piazza in front of Saint Peter's	▍ Gaulli and Pozzo paint illusionistic ceiling frescoes in Il Gesù and Sant'Ignazio	
▍ Carracci introduces quadro riportato fresco painting in the Palazzo Farnese	▍ Gentileschi, the leading woman artist of the 17th century, achieves international renown	▍ Murillo creates the canonical image of the *Virgin of the Immaculate Conception*	▍ Guarini brings the Baroque architectural style of Rome to Turin	
▍ Caravaggio pioneers tenebrism in Baroque painting	▍ Ribera and Zurbarán paint scenes of martyrdom in Catholic Spain	▍ Velázquez paints *Las Meninas*		
▍ Bernini creates *David* and *Apollo and Daphne* for Cardinal Scipione Borghese	▍ Philip IV of Spain appoints Velázquez court painter			

19-3 CARLO MADERNO, east facade of Saint Peter's, Vatican City, Rome, Italy, 1606–1612.

For the facade of Saint Peter's, Maderno elaborated on his design for Santa Susanna (FIG. 19-2), but the two outer bays with bell towers were not part of his plan and detract from the verticality he sought.

Baroque artistic spirit. In its general appearance, Maderno's facade resembles Giacomo della Porta's immensely influential design for Il Gesù (FIG. 17-56), the church of the Jesuits in Rome. But the later facade has a greater verticality that concentrates and dramatizes the major features of its model. The tall central section projects forward from the horizontal lower story, and the scroll buttresses connecting the two levels are narrower and set at a sharper angle. The elimination of an arch framing the pediment over the doorway further enhances the design's vertical thrust. The rhythm of Santa Susanna's vigorously projecting columns and pilasters mounts dramatically toward the emphatically stressed central axis. The recessed niches, which contain statues and create pockets of shadow, heighten the sculptural effect.

MADERNO AND SAINT PETER'S The drama inherent in Santa Susanna's facade appealed to Pope Paul V (r. 1605–1621), who commissioned Maderno in 1606 to complete Saint Peter's in Rome. As the symbolic seat of the papacy, the church Constantine originally built over the first pope's tomb (see Chapter 8) was the very emblem of Western Christendom. In light of Counter-Reformation concerns, the Baroque popes wanted to conclude the already century-long rebuilding project and reap the prestige embodied in the mammoth new church. In many ways Maderno's facade (FIG. 19-3) is a gigantic expansion of the elements of Santa Susanna's first level. But the compactness and verticality of the smaller church's facade are not as prominent because Saint Peter's enormous breadth counterbalances them. Mitigating circumstances must be taken into consideration when assessing this design, however. Because Maderno had to match the preexisting core of an incomplete building, he did not have the luxury of formulating a totally new concept for Saint Peter's. Moreover, the facade's two outer bays with bell towers were not part of Maderno's original design. Hence, had the facade been constructed according to the architect's initial concept, it would have exhibited greater verticality and visual coherence.

Maderno's plan (MAP 19-1) also departed from the Renaissance central plans for Saint Peter's designed by Bramante (FIG. 17-22) and, later, by Michelangelo (FIG. 17-24). Paul V asked Maderno to add three nave bays to the earlier nucleus because Church officials had decided the central plan was too closely associated with ancient temples, such as the Pantheon (FIG. 7-49). Further, the spatial organization of the longitudinal basilican plan of the original

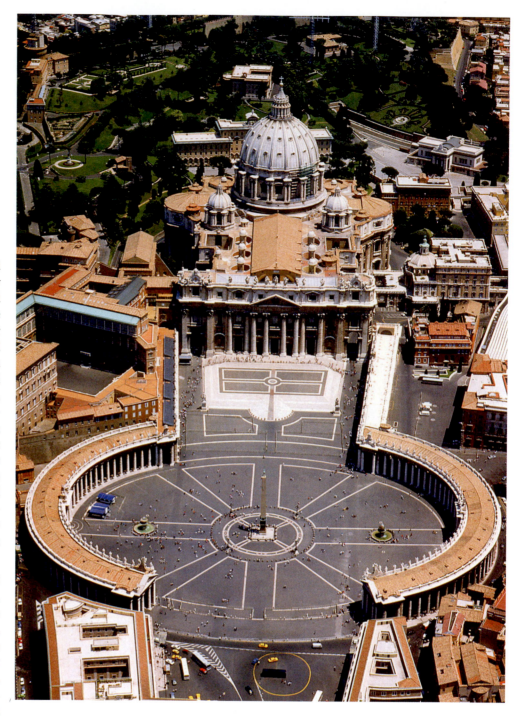

19-4 Aerial view of Saint Peter's (looking west), Vatican City, Rome, Italy. Piazza designed by GIANLORENZO BERNINI, 1656–1667.

The dramatic gesture of embrace Bernini's colonnade makes as worshipers enter Saint Peter's piazza symbolizes the welcome the Catholic Church wished to extend during the Counter-Reformation.

fourth-century church (FIG. 8-9) reinforced the symbolic distinction between clergy and laity and also was much better suited for religious processions. Lengthening the nave, however, pushed the dome farther back from the facade, and all but destroyed the effect Michelangelo had planned—a structure pulled together and dominated by its dome. When viewed at close range, the dome barely emerges above the facade's soaring frontal plane. Seen from farther back (FIG. 19-3), it appears to have no drum. Visitors must move back quite a distance from the front (or fly over the church, FIG. 19-4) to see the dome and drum together. Today, visitors to the Vatican can appreciate the effect Michelangelo intended only by viewing Saint Peter's from the back (FIG. 17-25).

BERNINI AND SAINT PETER'S

Old Saint Peter's had a large forecourt, or *atrium* (FIG. 8-9, *right*), in front of the church proper, and in the mid-17th century, Gianlorenzo Bernini, who had long before established his reputation as a supremely gifted architect and sculptor (see page 557), received the prestigious commission to construct a monumental colonnade-framed *piazza* (plaza; FIG. **19-4**) in front of Maderno's facade. Bernini's design had to incorporate two preexisting structures on the site—an obelisk the ancient Romans had brought from Egypt (which Pope Sixtus V had moved to its present location in 1585 as part of his vision of Christian triumph in Rome) and a fountain Maderno constructed in front of the church. Bernini co-opted these features to define the long axis of a vast oval embraced by two colonnades joined to Maderno's facade. Four rows of huge Tuscan columns make up the two colonnades, which terminate in classical temple fronts. The colonnades extend a dramatic gesture of embrace to all who enter the piazza, symbolizing the welcome the Roman Catholic Church gave its members during the Counter-Reformation. Bernini himself referred to his colonnades as the welcoming arms of Saint Peter's.

Beyond their symbolic resonance, the colonnades served visually to counteract the natural perspective and bring the facade closer to the viewer. (Bernini's mastery of perspective in architecture is even more evident in his contemporaneous design for the Scala Regia [FIG. **19-4A**] of the Vatican palace, a project he undertook at the request of Pope Alexander VII [r. 1655–1667].) Emphasizing the facade's height in this manner, Bernini subtly and effectively compensated for its extensive width. Thus, a Baroque transformation expanded the compact central designs of Bramante and Michelangelo into a dynamic complex of axially ordered elements that reach out and enclose spaces of vast dimension. By its sheer scale and theatricality, the completed Saint Peter's fulfilled the desire of the Counter–Reformation Church to present an awe-inspiring and authoritative vision of itself.

19-4A BERNINI, Scala Regia, Vatican, 1663–1666.

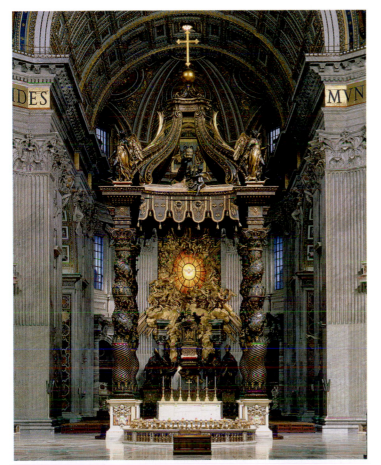

19-5 GIANLORENZO BERNINI, baldacchino (looking west), Saint Peter's, Vatican City, Rome, Italy, 1624–1633.

Bernini's baldacchino serves both functional and symbolic purposes. It marks Saint Peter's tomb and the high altar, and it visually bridges human scale to the lofty vaults and dome above.

BALDACCHINO Prior to being invited to design the piazza in front of Saint Peter's, Bernini had won the commission to erect a gigantic bronze *baldacchino* (FIG. **19-5**) under Giacomo della Porta's dome (FIG. 17-25). Completed between 1624 and 1633, the canopylike structure (*baldacco* is Italian for "silk from Baghdad," such as for a cloth canopy) stands almost 100 feet high (the height of an average eight-story building) and serves both functional and symbolic purposes. It marks the high altar and the tomb of Saint Peter, and it visually bridges human scale to the lofty vaults and dome above. Further, for worshipers entering the nave of the huge church, it provides a dramatic, compelling presence at the crossing. Its columns also create a visual frame for the elaborate sculpture representing the throne of Saint Peter (the Cathedra Petri) at the far end of Saint Peter's (FIG. 19-5, *rear*). On a symbolic level, the structure's decorative elements speak to the power of the Catholic Church and of Pope Urban VIII. Partially fluted and wreathed with vines, the baldacchino's four spiral columns are Baroque versions of the comparable columns of the ancient baldacchino over the same spot in Old Saint Peter's, thereby invoking the past to reinforce the primacy of the Roman Catholic Church in the 17th century. At the top of the vine-entwined columns, four colossal angels stand guard at the upper corners of the canopy. Forming the canopy's apex are four serpentine brackets that elevate the orb and the cross. Since the time of Constantine (FIG. 7-81, *right;* compare FIG. 9-2), the orb and the cross had served as symbols of the Church's triumph. The baldacchino also features numerous bees, symbols of Urban VIII's family, the Barberini. The structure effectively gives visual form to the triumph of Christianity and the papal claim to doctrinal supremacy.

The construction of the baldacchino was itself a remarkable feat. Each of the bronze columns consists of five sections cast from wood models using the *lost-wax process* (see "Hollow-Casting Life-Size Bronze Statues," Chapter 5, page 130). Although Bernini did some of the work himself, including cleaning and repairing the wax molds and doing the final cleaning and *chasing* (engraving and embossing) of the bronze casts, he contracted out much of the project to experienced bronze-casters and sculptors. The superstructure is predominantly cast bronze, although some of the sculptural elements are brass or wood. The enormous scale of the baldacchino required a considerable amount of bronze. On Urban VIII's orders, workmen dismantled the portico of the Pantheon (FIG. 7-49) to acquire the bronze for the baldacchino—ideologically appropriate, given the Church's rejection of polytheism.

The concepts of triumph and grandeur permeate every aspect of the 17th-century design of Saint Peter's. Suggesting a great and solemn procession, the main axis of the complex traverses the piazza (marked by the central obelisk) and enters Maderno's nave. It comes to a temporary halt at the altar beneath Bernini's baldacchino, but it continues on toward its climactic destination at another great altar in the apse.

from those earlier masterpieces, however. Michelangelo portrayed David before his encounter with his gigantic adversary, and Donatello and Verrocchio depicted David after his triumph over Goliath. Bernini chose to represent the combat itself and aimed to catch the split-second of maximum action. Bernini's *David*, his muscular legs widely and firmly planted, begins the violent, pivoting motion that will launch the stone from his sling. (A bag full of stones is at David's left hip, suggesting he thought the fight would be tough and long.) Unlike Myron, the fifth-century BCE Greek sculptor who froze his *Discus Thrower* (FIG. 5-39) at a fleeting moment of inaction, Bernini selected the most dramatic of an implied sequence of poses, requiring the viewer to think simultaneously of the continuum and of this tiny fraction of it. The suggested continuum imparts a dynamic quality to the statue. In Bernini's *David,* the energy confined in Michelangelo's figures (FIGS. 17-14 and 17-15) bursts forth. The Baroque statue seems to be moving through time and through space. This kind of sculpture cannot be inscribed in a cylinder or confined in a niche. Its unrestrained action demands space around it. Nor is it selfsufficient in the Renaissance sense, as its pose and attitude direct attention beyond it to the unseen Goliath. Bernini's *David* moves out into the space surrounding it, as do Apollo and Daphne in the marble group (FIG. **19-6A**) he carved for the same patron, Cardinal Scipione Borghese (1576–1633). Further, the expression

19-6A BERNINI, *Apollo and Daphne,* 1623–1624.

19-6 GIANLORENZO BERNINI, *David,* 1623. Marble, 5′ 7″ high. Galleria Borghese, Rome. ◼◀

Bernini's sculptures are expansive and theatrical, and the element of time plays an important role in them. His emotion-packed *David* seems to be moving through both time and space.

DAVID Bernini's baldacchino is, like his Four Rivers Fountain (FIG. 19-1), a masterpiece of the sculptor's craft even more than the architect's. In fact, although Bernini achieved an international reputation as an architect, his fame rests primarily on his sculpture. The biographer Filippo Baldinucci (1625–1696) observed: "[T]here was perhaps never anyone who manipulated marble with more facility and boldness. He gave his works a marvelous softness . . . making the marble, so to say, flexible."[1] Bernini's sculpture is expansive and theatrical, and the element of time usually plays an important role in it, as in the pronounced movement of the personified rivers—and the cascading water—in his Piazza Navona fountain.

A sculpture that predates both the Four Rivers Fountain and Saint Peter's baldacchino is Bernini's *David* (FIG. **19-6**). The Baroque master surely knew the Renaissance statues of the biblical hero fashioned by Donatello (FIG. 16-12), Verrocchio (FIG. 16-13), and Michelangelo (FIG. 17-13). Bernini's *David* differs fundamentally

19-7 GIANLORENZO BERNINI, *Ecstasy of Saint Teresa,* Cornaro chapel, Santa Maria della Vittoria, Rome, Italy, 1645–1652. Marble, height of group 11′ 6″. ◼◀

The passionate drama of Bernini's depiction of Saint Teresa correlated with the ideas of Ignatius Loyola, who argued that the re-creation of spiritual experience would encourage devotion and piety.

19-8 GIANLORENZO BERNINI, Cornaro chapel, Santa Maria della Vittoria, Rome, Italy, 1645–1652.

In the Cornaro chapel, Bernini, the quintessential Baroque artist, marshaled the full capabilities of architecture, sculpture, and painting to create an intensely emotional experience for worshipers.

conversion occurred after the death of her father, when she fell into a series of trances, saw visions, and heard voices. Feeling a persistent pain, she attributed it to the fire-tipped arrow of divine love an angel had thrust repeatedly into her heart. In her writings, Saint Teresa described this experience as making her swoon in delightful anguish.

In Bernini's hands, the entire Cornaro chapel became a theater for the production of this mystical drama. The niche in which it takes place appears as a shallow *proscenium* (the part of the stage in front of the curtain) crowned with a broken Baroque pediment and ornamented with polychrome marble. On either side of the chapel, sculpted portraits of members of the family of Cardinal Federico Cornaro (1579–1673) watch the heavenly drama unfold from choice balcony seats. Bernini depicted the saint in ecstasy, unmistakably a mingling of spiritual and physical passion, swooning back on a cloud, while the smiling angel aims his arrow. The sculptor's supreme technical virtuosity is evident in the visual differentiation in texture among the clouds, rough nun's cloth, gauzy material, smooth flesh, and feathery wings—all carved from the same white marble. Light from a hidden window of yellow glass pours down on golden rays suggesting the radiance of Heaven, whose painted representation covers the vault.

The passionate drama of Bernini's *Ecstasy of Saint Teresa* correlated with the ideas disseminated earlier by Ignatius Loyola (1491–1556), who founded the Jesuit order in 1534 and whom the Catholic Church canonized as Saint Ignatius in 1622. In his book *Spiritual Exercises*, Ignatius argued that the re-creation of spiritual experiences in artworks would do much to increase devotion and piety. Thus, theatricality and sensory impact were useful vehicles for achieving Counter-Reformation goals (see "Religious Art in Counter-Reformation Italy," Chapter 17, page 505). Bernini was a devout Catholic, which undoubtedly contributed to his understanding of those goals. His inventiveness, technical skill, sensitivity to his patrons' needs, and energy made him the quintessential Italian Baroque artist.

of intense concentration on David's face contrasts vividly with the classically placid visages of Donatello's and Verrocchio's versions and is more emotionally charged even than Michelangelo's. The tension in David's face augments the dramatic impact of Bernini's sculpture.

ECSTASY OF SAINT TERESA Another work displaying the motion and emotion that are hallmarks of Italian Baroque art is Bernini's *Ecstasy of Saint Teresa* (FIG. **19-7**) in the Cornaro chapel (FIG. **19-8**) of the Roman church of Santa Maria della Vittoria. The work exemplifies the Baroque master's refusal to limit his statues to firmly defined spatial settings. For this commission, Bernini marshaled the full capabilities of architecture, sculpture, and painting to charge the entire chapel with palpable tension. In the Cornaro chapel, Bernini drew on the considerable knowledge of the theater he derived from writing plays and producing stage designs. The marble sculpture that serves as the chapel's focus depicts Saint Teresa of Avila (1515–1582), a nun of the Carmelite order and one of the great mystical saints of the Spanish Counter-Reformation. Her

19-9 FRANCESCO BORROMINI, facade of San Carlo alle Quattro Fontane (looking south), Rome, Italy, 1638–1641.

Borromini rejected the notion that a church should have a flat frontispiece. He set San Carlo's facade in undulating motion, creating a dynamic counterpoint of concave and convex elements.

SAN CARLO ALLE QUATTRO FONTANE

As gifted as Bernini was as an architect, FRANCESCO BORROMINI (1599–1667) took Italian Baroque architecture to even greater dramatic heights. In the little church of San Carlo alle Quattro Fontane (Saint Charles at the Four Fountains; FIG. 19-9), Borromini went much further than any of his predecessors or contemporaries in emphasizing a building's sculptural qualities. Although Maderno incorporated sculptural elements in his designs for the facades of Santa Susanna (FIG. 19-2) and Saint Peter's (FIG. 19-3), those church fronts still develop along relatively lateral planes. Borromini set his facade in undulating motion, creating a dynamic counterpoint of concave and convex elements on two levels (for example, the sway of the cornices). He enhanced the three-dimensional effect with deeply recessed niches. This facade is not the traditional flat frontispiece that defines a building's outer limits. It is a pulsating, engaging screen inserted between interior and exterior space, designed not to separate but to provide a fluid transition between the two. In fact, San Carlo has not one but two facades, underscoring the functional interrelation of the building and its environment. The second facade, a narrow bay crowned with its own small tower, turns away from the main facade and, following the curve of the street, faces an intersection. Borromini's innovative style had an enormous influence on later Baroque architects throughout Italy. The Palazzo Carignano (FIG. 19-9A) in Turin, for example, designed by GUARINO GUARINI (1624–1683), depends heavily on Borromini's work in Rome.

19-9A GUARINI, Palazzo Carignano, Turin, 1679–1692.

The interior of San Carlo alle Quattro Fontane is not only Borromini's ingenious response to an awkward site but also a provocative variation on the theme of the centrally planned church. In plan (FIG. 19-10), San Carlo is a hybrid of a *Greek cross* (a cross with four arms of equal length) and an oval, with a long axis between entrance and apse. The side walls move in an undulating flow that reverses the facade's motion. Vigorously projecting columns define the space into which they protrude just as much as they accent the walls to which they are attached. Capping this molded interior space is a deeply coffered oval dome (FIG. 19-11) that seems to float on the light entering through windows hidden in its base. Rich variations on the basic theme of the oval—dynamic curves relative to the static circle—create an interior that flows from entrance to altar, unimpeded by the segmentation so characteristic of Renaissance buildings.

The plan of San Carlo is a hybrid of a Greek cross and an oval. The walls pulsate in a way that reverses the facade's movement. The molded, dramatically lit space flows from entrance to altar.

Dome

Dome

0   10   20   30 feet

0   5   10 meters

N

19-11 FRANCESCO BORROMINI, San Carlo alle Quattro Fontane (view into dome), Rome, Italy, 1638–1641.

In place of a traditional round dome, Borromini capped the interior of San Carlo with a deeply coffered oval dome that seems to float on the light entering through windows hidden in its base.

19-12 FRANCESCO BORROMINI, *Chapel of Saint Ivo (looking east), College of the Sapienza, Rome, Italy, begun 1642.*

In characteristic fashion, Borromini played concave against convex forms on the upper level of the Chapel of Saint Ivo. Pilasters restrain the forces that seem to push the bulging forms outward.

19-13 FRANCESCO BORROMINI, *plan of the Chapel of Saint Ivo, College of the Sapienza, Rome, Italy, begun 1642.*

The interior elevation of Borromini's Saint Ivo chapel fully reflects all the elements of its highly complex plan, which is star-shaped with rounded points and apses on all sides.

CHAPEL OF SAINT IVO Borromini carried the unification of interior space even further in the Chapel of Saint Ivo (FIG. **19-12**) at the east end of the courtyard of the College of the Sapienza (Wisdom) in Rome. In his characteristic manner, Borromini played concave against convex forms on the upper level of the chapel's exterior. The arcaded courtyard, which frames the lower levels of the chapel's facade, had already been constructed when Borromini began work, and he adjusted his design to achieve a harmonious merging of the new and older parts of the college. Above the inward-curving lower two stories of the Saint Ivo chapel rises a convex drumlike structure that supports the dome's lower parts. Clusters of pilasters restrain the forces that seem to push the bulging forms outward. Buttresses above the pilasters curve upward to brace a tall, ornate lantern topped by a spiral that, screwlike, seems to fasten the structure to the sky.

The centralized plan (FIG. **19-13**) of the interior of the Saint Ivo chapel is that of a star with rounded points and apses on all sides. Indentations and projections along the angled curving walls create a highly complex plan, with all the elements fully reflected in the interior elevation. From floor to lantern, the wall panels rise in a continuously tapering sweep halted only momentarily by a single horizontal cornice (FIG. **19-14**). Thus, the dome is not a separate unit placed on a supporting block, as in Renaissance buildings. It is an organic part that evolves out of and shares the qualities of the supporting walls, and it cannot be separated from them. This carefully designed progression up through the lantern creates a dynamic and cohesive shell that encloses and energetically molds a scalloped fragment of space. Few architects have matched Borromini's ability to translate extremely complicated designs into masterfully unified structures, but some later architects, including Guarini, an accomplished mathematician as well as architect, designed even more complex domes (FIG. **19-14A**).

19-14A GUARINI, *Chapel of the Holy Shroud, Turin, 1667–1694.*

Painting

Although architecture and sculpture provided the most obvious vehicles for manipulating space and creating theatrical effects, painting continued to be an important art form in 17th-century Italy. Among the most noted Italian Baroque painters were Annibale Carracci and Caravaggio, whose styles, although different, were both thoroughly in accord with the period.

19-14 FRANCESCO BORROMINI, Chapel of Saint Ivo (view into dome), College of the Sapienza, Rome, Italy, begun 1642.

Unlike Renaissance domes, Borromini's Baroque dome is an organic part that evolves out of and shares the qualities of the supporting walls, and it cannot be separated from them.

cant institution of its kind in the history of Western art. The Carracci established it on the premises that art can be taught—the basis of any academic philosophy of art—and that art instruction must include the classical and Renaissance traditions in addition to the study of anatomy and life drawing.

In *Flight into Egypt* (FIG. **19-15**), based on the biblical narrative from Matthew 2:13–14, Annibale Carracci created the "ideal" or "classical" landscape, in which nature appears ordered by divine law and human reason. Tranquil hills and fields, quietly gliding streams, serene skies, unruffled foliage, shepherds with their flocks—all the props of the pastoral scene and mood familiar in Venetian Renaissance paintings (FIG. 17-35)—expand to fill the picture space in *Flight into Egypt* and similar paintings. Carracci regularly included screens of trees in the foreground, dark against the sky's even light. In contrast to many Renaissance artists, he did not create the sense of deep space through linear perspective but rather by varying light and shadow

ANNIBALE CARRACCI A native of Bologna, ANNIBALE CARRACCI (1560–1609) received much of his training at an art academy founded there by several members of his family, among them his cousin Ludovico Carracci (1555–1619) and brother Agostino Carracci (1557–1602). The Bolognese academy was the first signifi-

19-15 ANNIBALE CARRACCI, *Flight into Egypt*, 1603–1604. Oil on canvas, 4′ × 7′ 6″. Galleria Doria Pamphili, Rome.

Carracci's landscapes idealize antiquity and the idyllic life. Here, the pastoral setting takes precedence over the narrative of Mary, the Christ Child, and Saint Joseph wending their way slowly to Egypt.

19-16 ANNIBALE CARRACCI, *Loves of the Gods,* ceiling frescoes in the gallery, Palazzo Farnese (FIG. 17-26), Rome, Italy, 1597–1601. ◼◀

On the shallow curved vault of this gallery in the Palazzo Farnese, Carracci arranged the mythological scenes in a quadro riportato format resembling easel paintings on a wall.

to suggest expansive atmosphere. In *Flight into Egypt,* streams or terraces, carefully placed one above the other and narrowed, zigzag through the terrain, leading the viewer's eyes back to the middle ground. There, many Venetian Renaissance landscape artists depicted walled towns or citadels, towers, temples, monumental tombs, and villas (as Carracci did in *Flight into Egypt*). These constructed environments captured idealized antiquity and the idyllic life. Although the artists often took the subjects for these classically rendered scenes from religious or heroic stories, they favored pastoral landscapes over narratives. Here, Annibale greatly diminished the size of Mary, the Christ Child, and Saint Joseph, who simply become part of the landscape as they wend their way slowly to Egypt after having been ferried across a stream.

LOVES OF THE GODS Carracci's most notable works are his frescoes (FIG. **19-16**) in the Palazzo Farnese in Rome. Cardinal Odoardo Farnese (1573–1626), a wealthy descendant of Pope Paul III,

who built the palace (FIG. 17-26) in the 16th century, commissioned Annibale to decorate the ceiling of the palace's gallery to celebrate the wedding of the cardinal's brother. Appropriately, the title of the fresco's iconographic program is *Loves of the Gods*—interpretations of the varieties of earthly and divine love in classical mythology.

Carracci arranged the scenes in a format resembling framed easel paintings on a wall, but in the Farnese gallery the paintings cover a shallow curved vault. The term for this type of simulation of easel painting for ceiling design is *quadro riportato* (transferred framed painting). By adapting the northern European and Venetian tradition of easel painting to the Florentine and Roman fresco tradition, Carracci reoriented the direction of painting in central Italy. He made quadro riportato fashionable for more than a century.

Flanking the framed pictures are polychrome seated nude youths, who turn their heads to gaze at the scenes around them, and

The stark contrast of light and dark was a key feature of Caravaggio's style. Here, Christ, cloaked in mysterious shadow, summons Levi the tax collector (Saint Matthew) to a higher calling.

1 ft.

are an important source of information about the artist), Caravaggio received many commissions, both public and private, and numerous painters paid him the supreme compliment of borrowing from his innovations. His influence on later artists, as much outside Italy as within, was immense. In his art, Caravaggio injected naturalism into both religion and the classics, reducing them to human dramas played out in the harsh and dingy settings of his time and place. The unidealized figures he selected from

standing Atlas figures painted to resemble marble statues. Carracci derived these motifs from the Sistine Chapel ceiling (FIG. 17-17), but he did not copy Michelangelo's figures. Notably, the chiaroscuro of the Farnese gallery frescoes differs for the pictures and the figures surrounding them. Carracci modeled the figures inside the panels in an even light. In contrast, light from beneath illuminates the outside figures, as if they were tangible three-dimensional beings or statues lit by torches in the gallery below. This interest in illusion, already manifest in the Renaissance, continued in the grand ceiling compositions (FIGS. 19-21 to 19-24) of the mature Baroque. In the crown of the vault, the long panel, *Triumph of Bacchus,* is an ingenious mixture of Raphael's drawing style and lighting and Titian's more sensuous and animated figures. Carracci succeeded in adjusting their authoritative styles to create something of his own—no easy achievement.

CARAVAGGIO Michelangelo Merisi, known as CARAVAGGIO (1573–1610) after his northern Italian birthplace, developed a unique style that had tremendous influence throughout Europe. His outspoken disdain for the classical masters (probably more rhetorical than real) drew bitter criticism from many painters, one of whom denounced him as the "anti-Christ of painting." Giovanni Pietro Bellori (1613–1696), the most influential critic of the age and an admirer of Annibale Carracci, believed Caravaggio's refusal to emulate the models of his distinguished predecessors threatened the whole classical tradition of Italian painting that had reached its zenith in Raphael's work (see "Giovanni Pietro Bellori on Annibale Carracci and Caravaggio," page 570). Yet despite this criticism and the problems in Caravaggio's troubled life (police records

the fields and the streets of Italy, however, were effective precisely because of their familiarity.

CALLING OF SAINT MATTHEW An early Caravaggio masterpiece, *Calling of Saint Matthew* (FIG. **19-17**), is one of two large canvases honoring Saint Matthew the artist created for the Contarelli chapel in San Luigi dei Francesi (Saint Louis of the French) in Rome. Caravaggio received the commission for the San Luigi paintings upon the recommendation of Cardinal Del Monte, for whom the artist had recently painted *Musicians* (FIG. **19-17A**). The commonplace setting of the painting—a tavern with unadorned walls—is typical of Caravaggio. Into this mundane environment, cloaked in mysterious shadow and almost unseen, Christ, identifiable

19-17A CARAVAGGIO, *Musicians,* ca. 1595.

initially only by his indistinct halo, enters from the right. With a commanding gesture, he summons Levi, the Roman tax collector, to a higher calling. The astonished Levi—his face highlighted for the viewer by the beam of light emanating from an unspecified source above Christ's head and outside the picture—points to himself in disbelief. Although Christ's extended arm is reminiscent of the Lord's in Michelangelo's *Creation of Adam* (FIG. 17-18), the position of his hand and wrist is similar to Adam's. This reference was highly appropriate, because the Church considered Christ to be the second Adam. Whereas Adam was responsible for the fall of humankind, Christ is the vehicle of its redemption. The conversion of Levi (who became Matthew) brought his salvation.

Giovanni Pietro Bellori on Annibale Carracci and Caravaggio

The written sources to which art historians turn as aids in understanding the art of the past are invaluable, but they reflect the personal preferences and prejudices of the writers. Pliny the Elder, for example, claimed in the first century CE that "art ceased" after the death of Alexander the Great—a remark usually interpreted as expressing his disapproval of Hellenistic art in contrast to Classical art (see Chapter 5).* Giorgio Vasari, the biographer and champion of Italian Renaissance artists, condemned Gothic art as "monstrous and barbarous," and considered medieval art in general a distortion of the noble art of the Greeks and Romans (see Chapter 13).† Giovanni Pietro Bellori, the leading biographer of Baroque artists, similarly recorded his admiration for Renaissance classicism as well as his distaste for Mannerism and realism in his opposing evaluations of Annibale Carracci and Caravaggio.

In the opening lines of his *Vita* (Life) of Carracci, Bellori praised "the divine Raphael . . . [whose art] raised its beauty to the summit, restoring it to the ancient majesty of . . . the Greeks and the Romans" and lamented that soon after, "artists, abandoning the study of nature, corrupted art with the *maniera*, that is to say, with the fantastic idea based on practice and not on imitation." But fortunately, Bellori observed, just "when painting was drawing to its end," Annibale Carracci rescued "the declining and extinguished art."‡

Bellori especially lauded Carracci's Palazzo Farnese frescoes (FIG. 19-16):

No one could imagine seeing anywhere else a more noble and magnificent style of ornamentation, obtaining supreme excellence in the compartmentalization and in the figures and executed with the grandest manner in the design with the just proportion and the great strength of chiaroscuro. . . . Among modern works they have no comparison.§

In contrast, Bellori characterized Caravaggio as talented and widely imitated but misguided in his rejection of classicism in favor of realism.

[Caravaggio] began to paint according to his own inclinations; not only ignoring but even despising the superb statuary of antiquity and the famous paintings of Raphael, he considered nature to be the only subject fit for his brush. As a result, when he was shown the most famous statues of [the ancient sculptors] Phidias [FIG. 5-46] and Glykon [FIG. 5-66] in order that he might use them as models, his only answer was to point toward a crowd of people, saying that nature had given him an abundance of masters. . . . [W]hen he came upon someone in town who pleased him he made no attempt to improve on the creations of nature.¨

[Caravaggio] claimed that he imitated his models so closely that he never made a single brushstroke that he called his own, but said rather that it was nature's. Repudiating all other rules, he considered the highest achievement not to be bound to art. For this innovation he was greatly acclaimed, and many talented and educated artists seemed compelled to follow him . . . Nevertheless he lacked *invenzione*, decorum, *disegno*, or any knowledge of the science of painting. The moment the model was taken from him, his hand and his mind became empty. . . . Thus, as Caravaggio suppressed the dignity of art, everybody did as he pleased, and what followed was contempt for beautiful things, the authority of antiquity and Raphael destroyed. . . . Now began the imitation of common and vulgar things, seeking out filth and deformity.††

*Pliny, *Natural History*, 25.52.
†Giorgio Vasari, *Introduzione alle tre arti del disegno* (1550), ch. 3.
‡Giovanni Pietro Bellori, *Le vite de' pittori, scultori e architetti moderni* (Rome, 1672). Translated by Catherine Enggass, *The Lives of Annibale and Agostino Carracci by Giovanni Pietro Bellori* (University Park: Pennsylvania University Press, 1968), 5–6.
§Ibid., 33.
¨Translated by Howard Hibbard, *Caravaggio* (New York: Harper & Row, 1983), 362.
††Ibid., 371–372.

CONVERSION OF SAINT PAUL A piercing ray of light illuminating a world of darkness and bearing a spiritual message is also a central feature of *Conversion of Saint Paul* (FIG. **19-18**), which Caravaggio painted for the Cerasi chapel in Santa Maria del Popolo. He depicted the saint-to-be at the moment of his conversion, flat on his back with his arms thrown up. In the background, an old groom seems preoccupied with caring for the horse. At first inspection, little here suggests the momentous significance of the unfolding spiritual event. The viewer could be witnessing a mere stable accident, not a man overcome by a great miracle. Although many of his contemporaries criticized Caravaggio for departing from traditional depictions of religious scenes, the eloquence and humanity with which he imbued his paintings impressed many others.

To compel worshipers' interest and involvement in Paul's conversion, Caravaggio employed a variety of ingenious formal devices. Here, as in the slightly later *Entombment* (FIG. **19-18A**), he used a perspective and a chiaroscuro intended to bring viewers as close as possible to the scene's space and action, almost as if they

were participants. The low horizon line augments the sense of inclusion. Further, Caravaggio designed *Conversion of Saint Paul* for its specific location on the chapel wall, positioned at the line of sight of an average-height person standing at the chapel entrance. The sharply lit figures emerge from the dark background as if illuminated by the light from the chapel's windows. The lighting resembles that of a stage production and is analogous to the rays in Bernini's *Ecstasy of Saint Teresa* (FIGS. 19-7 and 19-8).

19-18A CARAVAGGIO, *Entombment*, ca. 1603.

Caravaggio's figures are still heroic with powerful bodies and clearly delineated contours in the Renaissance tradition, but the stark and dramatic contrast of light and dark, which at first shocked and then fascinated his contemporaries, obscures the more traditional aspects of his style. Art historians call Caravaggio's use of dark settings enveloping their occupants—which profoundly

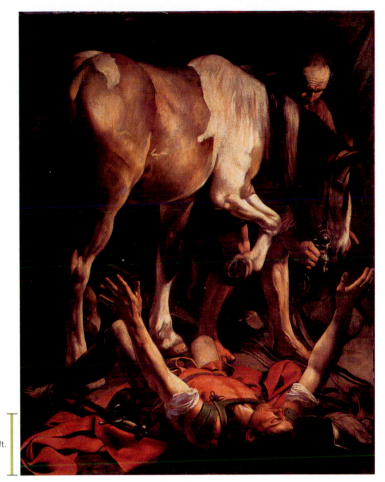

19-18 CARAVAGGIO, *Conversion of Saint Paul*, ca. 1601. Oil on canvas, 7′ 6″ × 5′ 9″. Cerasi chapel, Santa Maria del Popolo, Rome.

Caravaggio used perspective, chiaroscuro, and dramatic lighting to bring viewers into this painting's space and action, almost as if they were participants in Saint Paul's conversion to Christianity.

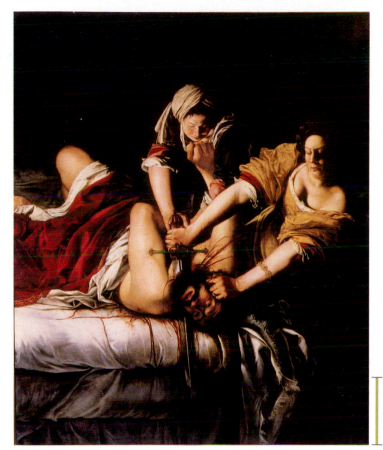

19-19 ARTEMISIA GENTILESCHI, *Judith Slaying Holofernes*, ca. 1614–1620. Oil on canvas, 6′ 6⅓″ × 5′ 4″. Galleria degli Uffizi, Florence. ▪◄

Narratives involving heroic women were a favorite theme of Gentileschi. In *Judith Slaying Holofernes*, the dramatic lighting of the action in the foreground emulates Caravaggio's tenebrism.

influenced European art, especially in Spain and the Netherlands—*tenebrism*, from the Italian word *tenebroso*, or "shadowy" manner. In Caravaggio's work, tenebrism also contributed greatly to the essential meaning of his pictures. In *Conversion of Saint Paul*, the dramatic spotlight shining down upon the fallen Paul is the light of divine revelation converting him to Christianity.

ARTEMISIA GENTILESCHI Caravaggio's combination of naturalism and drama appealed both to patrons and artists, and he had many followers. Among them was the most celebrated woman artist of the era, ARTEMISIA GENTILESCHI (ca. 1593–1653), whose father Orazio (1563–1639), her teacher, was himself strongly influenced by Caravaggio. The daughter's successful career, pursued in Florence, Venice, Naples, and Rome, helped disseminate Caravaggio's style throughout the peninsula.

In *Judith Slaying Holofernes* (FIG. 19-19), Gentileschi adopted the tenebrism and what might be called the "dark" subject matter Caravaggio favored. Significantly, she chose a narrative involving a heroic woman, a favorite theme of hers. The story, from the book of Judith, relates the delivery of Israel from the Assyrians. Having succumbed to Judith's charms, the Assyrian general Holofernes invited her to his tent for the night. When he fell asleep, Judith cut off his head. In this version of the scene (Gentileschi produced more than one painting of the subject), Judith and her maidservant behead Holofernes. Blood spurts everywhere as the two women

summon all their strength to wield the heavy sword. The tension and strain are palpable. The controlled highlights on the action in the foreground recall Caravaggio's work and heighten the drama here as well.

LA PITTURA During the brief period Orazio Gentileschi was the official painter of the English king Charles I (r. 1625–1649), Artemisia painted perhaps her most unusual work, an allegory of Painting (*La Pittura*; FIG. **19-20**). Most art historians believe the painting, which was in the collection of the king at the time of his execution in 1649, is a self-portrait.

Gentileschi's personified image of Painting as a woman closely follows the prescription for representing *La Pittura* in a widely circulated handbook by Cesare Ripa (d. 1622) called *Iconologia*, published in 1593. Until the 16th century, only Poetry and Music had a fixed iconography. The inclusion of Painting in Ripa's handbook reflects the newly elevated status painters held during the Renaissance. He describes *La Pittura* as a beautiful woman with disheveled hair painting with her brush in one hand and holding her palette in the other. She wears a gold chain with a pendant in the form of a mask, because masks imitate faces and painting is the art of imitation. The chain symbolizes the continuous linkage of master to pupil from generation to generation. Gentileschi incorporated all of these traits into her painting, but instead of representing *La Pittura* as a frontal, emblematic figure, she portrayed her as actively

The Letters of Artemisia Gentileschi

Artemisia Gentileschi (FIG. 19-20) was the most renowned woman painter in Europe during the first half of the 17th century and the first woman ever admitted to membership in Florence's Accademia del Disegno (Academy of Design). As did other women who could not become apprentices in all-male studios (see "The Artist's Profession," Chapter 15, page 433), she learned her craft from her father. Never forgotten in subsequent centuries, Artemisia's modern fame stems from the seminal 1976 exhibition *Women Artists: 1550–1950,*[*] which opened a new chapter in feminist art history.

In addition to scores of paintings created for wealthy patrons, among them the king of England and the grand duke of Tuscany, Gentileschi left behind 28 letters, some of which reveal she believed patrons treated her differently because of her gender. Three 1649 letters written in Naples to Don Antonio Ruffo (1610–1678) in Messina make her feelings explicit.

I fear that before you saw the painting you must have thought me arrogant and presumptuous. . . . [I]f it were not for Your Most Illustrious Lordship . . . I would not have been induced to give it for one hundred and sixty, because everywhere else I have been I was paid one hundred *scudi* per figure. . . . You think me pitiful, because a woman's name raises doubts until her work is seen.[†]

I was mortified to hear that you want to deduct one third from the already very low price that I had asked. . . . It must be that in your heart Your Most Illustrious Lordship finds little merit in me.[‡]

As for my doing a drawing and sending it, [tell the gentleman who wishes to know the price for a painting that] I have made a solemn vow never to send my drawings because people have cheated me. In particular, just today I found myself [in the situation] that, having done a drawing of souls in Purgatory for the Bishop of St. Gata, he, in order to spend less, commissioned another painter to do the painting using my work. If I were a man, I can't imagine it would have turned out this way, because when the concept has been real-

19-20 ARTEMISIA GENTILESCHI, *Self-Portrait as the Allegory of Painting,* ca. 1638–1639. Oil on canvas, 3' 2$\frac{7}{8}$" × 2' 5$\frac{5}{8}$". Royal Collection, Kensington Palace, London. ◀

Gentileschi here portrayed herself in the guise of *La Pittura* (Painting) with brush and palette. To paint a self-portrait from the side, Gentileschi had to set up a pair of mirrors to record her features.

ized and defined with lights and darks, and established by means of planes, the rest is a trifle.[§]

[*]Ann Sutherland Harris and Linda Nochlin, *Women Artists: 1550–1950* (Los Angeles: Los Angeles County Museum of Art, 1976), 118–124.
[†]Letter dated Janary 30, 1649. Translated by Mary D. Garrard, *Artemisia Gentileschi: The Image of the Female Hero in Italian Baroque Art* (Princeton, N.J.: Princeton University Press, 1989), 390.
[‡]Letter dated October 23, 1649. Ibid., 395–396.
[§]Letter dated November 13, 1649. Ibid., 397–398.

engaged in her craft, seen from her left side. The viewer's eye follows the line of her left arm through the curve of her shoulders and right arm to her right hand, the instrument of artistic genius. It is noteworthy that the canvas in this painting is blank. This is not a self-portrait of the artist at work on a specific painting (compare FIGS. 18-18, 20-11, 21-15, and 21-16) but a portrait of Gentileschi as Painting herself.

In almost all Renaissance and Baroque self-portraits, the artist gazes at the viewer. The frontal view not only provides the fullest view of the artist's features, but it is also the easiest to paint because the artist needs only to look in a mirror in order to record his or her features (FIG. 17-43). To create this self-portrait, however, Gentileschi had to set up two mirrors in order to paint her likeness from

an angle, a highly original break from tradition and an assertion of her supreme skill in a field dominated by men (see "The Letters of Artemisia Gentileschi," above).

GUIDO RENI Caravaggio was not the only early-17th-century painter to win a devoted following. GUIDO RENI (1575–1642), known to his many admirers as "the divine Guido," trained in the Bolognese art academy founded by the Carracci family. The influence of Annibale Carracci and Raphael is evident in *Aurora* (FIG. 19-21), a ceiling fresco in the Casino Rospigliosi in Rome. Aurora (Dawn) leads Apollo's chariot, while the Hours dance about it. Guido conceived *Aurora* as a quadro riportato, following the format of the paintings in Annibale's *Loves of the Gods* (FIG. 19-16), and

19-21 GUIDO RENI, *Aurora,* ceiling fresco in the Casino Rospigliosi, Rome, Italy, 1613–1614.

The "divine Guido" conceived *Aurora* as a quadro riportato, reflecting his training in the Bolognese art academy. The scene of Dawn leading Apollo's chariot derives from ancient Roman reliefs.

provided the quadro with a complex and convincing illusionistic frame. The fresco exhibits a fluid motion, soft modeling, and sure composition, although without Raphael's sculpturesque strength. It is an intelligent interpretation of the Renaissance master's style. Consistent with the precepts of the Bolognese academy, the painter also looked to antiquity for models. The ultimate sources for the *Aurora* composition were Roman reliefs (FIG. 7-42) and coins depicting emperors in triumphal chariots accompanied by flying Victories and other personifications.

PIETRO DA CORTONA The experience of looking up at a painting is different from viewing a painting hanging on a wall. The considerable height and the expansive scale of most ceiling frescoes induce a feeling of awe. Patrons who wanted to burnish their public image or control their legacy found monumental ceiling frescoes to be perfect vehicles. In 1633, Pope Urban VIII commissioned a ceiling fresco for the Gran Salone (the main reception hall) of the Palazzo Barberini in Rome. The most important decorative commission of the 1630s, the lucrative assignment went to PIETRO DA CORTONA (1596–1669), a Tuscan architect and painter who had moved to Rome two decades before. The grandiose and spectacular *Triumph of the Barberini* (FIG. **19-22**) overwhelms spectators with

19-22 PIETRO DA CORTONA, *Triumph of the Barberini,* ceiling fresco in the Gran Salone, Palazzo Barberini, Rome, Italy, 1633–1639.

In this dramatic ceiling fresco, Divine Providence appears in a halo of radiant light directing Immortality, holding a crown of stars, to bestow eternal life on the family of Pope Urban VIII.

In the nave of Il Gesù, gilded architecture opens up to offer the faithful a glimpse of Heaven. To heighten the illusion, Gaulli painted figures on stucco extensions that project outside the painting's frame.

the glory of the Barberini family (and Urban VIII in particular). The iconographic program for this fresco, designed by the poet Francesco Bracciolini (1566–1645), centered on the accomplishments of the Barberini. Divine Providence appears in a halo of radiant light directing Immortality, holding a crown of stars, to bestow eternal life on the family. The virtues Faith, Hope, and Charity hold aloft a gigantic laurel wreath (also a symbol of immortality), which frames three bees (the Barberini family's symbols, which also appeared in Bernini's baldacchino, FIG. 19-5). Also present are the papal tiara and keys announcing the personal triumphs of Urban VIII.

GIOVANNI BATTISTA GAULLI The dazzling spectacle of ceiling frescoes also proved very effective for commissions illustrating religious themes. Church authorities realized paintings high above the ground offered perfect opportunities to impress on worshipers the glory and power of the Catholic Church. In conjunction with the theatricality of Italian Baroque architecture and sculpture, monumental frescoes on church ceilings contributed to creating transcendent spiritual environments well suited to the needs of the Catholic Church in Counter-Reformation Rome.

Triumph of the Name of Jesus (FIG. **19-23**) in the nave of Il Gesù (FIGS. 17-56 and 17-57) vividly demonstrates the dramatic impact Baroque ceiling frescoes could have. As the mother church of the Jesuit order, Il Gesù played a prominent role in Counter-Reformation efforts. In this immense fresco by GIOVANNI BATTISTA GAULLI (1639–1709), gilded architecture opens up in the center of the ceiling to offer the faithful a stunning glimpse of Heaven. Gaulli represented Jesus as a barely visible monogram (IHS) in a blinding radiant light floating heavenward. In contrast, sinners experience a violent descent back to Earth. The painter glazed the gilded architecture to suggest shadows, thereby enhancing the scene's illusionistic quality. To further heighten the illusion, Gaulli painted many of the sinners on three-dimensional stucco extensions projecting outside the painting's frame.

FRA ANDREA POZZO Another master of ceiling decoration was FRA ANDREA POZZO (1642–1709), a lay brother of the Jesuit order and a master of perspective, on which he wrote an influential treatise. Pozzo designed and executed the vast ceiling fresco *Glorification of Saint Ignatius* (FIG. **19-24**) for the church of Sant'Ignazio in Rome. Like Il Gesù, Sant'Ignazio was a prominent Counter-Reformation church because of its dedication to the founder of the Jesuit order. The Jesuits played a major role in Catholic education and sent legions of missionaries to the New World and Asia. As

Gaulli did in Il Gesù, Pozzo created the illusion of Heaven opening up above the congregation. To accomplish this, the artist painted an extension of the church's architecture into the vault so the roof seems to be lifted off. As Heaven and Earth commingle, Christ receives Saint Ignatius in the presence of figures personifying the four corners of the world. A disk in the nave floor marks the spot where the viewer should stand to gain the whole perspective illusion. For worshipers looking up from this point, the vision is complete. They find themselves in the presence of the heavenly and spiritual.

The effectiveness of Italian Baroque religious art depended on the drama and theatricality of individual images, as well as on the interaction and fusion of architecture, sculpture, and painting. Sound enhanced this experience. Architects designed churches with acoustical effects in mind, and in an Italian Baroque church filled with music, the power of both image and sound must have been immensely moving. Through simultaneous stimulation of both the senses of sight and hearing, the faithful might well have been transported into a trancelike state that would, indeed, as the great English poet John Milton (1608–1674) eloquently stated in *Il Penseroso* (1631), "bring all Heaven before [their] eyes."[2]

19-24 Fra Andrea Pozzo, *Glorification of Saint Ignatius*, ceiling fresco in the nave of Sant'Ignazio, Rome, Italy, 1691–1694.

By merging real and painted architecture, Pozzo created the illusion the vaulted ceiling of Sant'Ignazio has been lifted off and the nave opens to Heaven above the worshipers' heads.

SPAIN

During the 16th century, Spain had established itself as an international power. The Habsburg kings had built a dynastic state encompassing Portugal, part of Italy, the Netherlands, and extensive areas of the New World. By the beginning of the 17th century, however, the Habsburg Empire was struggling, and although Spain mounted an aggressive effort during the Thirty Years' War (see Chapter 20), by 1660 the imperial age of the Spanish Habsburgs was over. In part, the demise of the Habsburg Empire was due to economic woes. The military campaigns Philip III (r. 1598–1621) and his son Philip IV (r. 1621–1665) waged during the Thirty Years' War were costly and led to higher taxes. The increasing tax burden placed on Spanish subjects in turn incited revolts and civil war in Catalonia and Portugal in the 1640s, further straining an already fragile economy.

Painting

Although the dawn of the Baroque period found the Spanish kings struggling to maintain control of their dwindling empire, both Philip III and Philip IV realized the prestige great artworks brought and the value of visual imagery in communicating to a wide audience. Thus, both of them continued to spend lavishly on art.

JUAN SÁNCHEZ COTÁN One painter who made a major contribution to the development of Spanish art, although he did not receive any royal commissions, was JUAN SÁNCHEZ COTÁN (1560–1627). Born in Orgaz, outside Toledo, Sánchez Cotán moved to Granada and became a Carthusian monk in 1603. Although he painted religious subjects, his greatest works are the *still lifes* (paintings of artfully arranged inanimate objects) he produced before entering monastic life (and never thereafter). Few in number, they nonetheless established still-life painting as an important genre in 17th-century Spain.

Still Life with Game Fowl (FIG. **19-25**) is one of Sánchez Cotán's most ambitious compositions, but it conforms to the pattern he adopted for all of his still lifes. A niche or a window—the artist clearly wished the setting to be indeterminate—fills the entire surface of the canvas. At the bottom, fruits and vegetables, including a melon—cut open with a slice removed—rest on a ledge. Above, suspended on strings from a nail or hook outside the frame, are a quince and four game fowl. All are meticulously rendered and

1 ft.

19-25 JUAN SÁNCHEZ COTÁN, *Still Life with Game Fowl*, ca. 1600–1603. Oil on canvas, 2′ 2¾″ × 2′ 10⅞″. Art Institute of Chicago, Chicago (gift of Mr. and Mrs. Leigh B. Block).

Sánchez Cotán established still life as an important genre in Spain. His compositions feature brightly illuminated fruits, vegetables, and birds, hanging or on a ledge, against a dark background.

brightly illuminated, enhancing the viewer's sense of each texture, color, and shape, yet the background is impenetrable shadow. The sharp and unnatural contrast between light and dark imbues the still life with a sense of mystery absent, for example, in Dutch still-life paintings (FIGS. 18-17, 20-1, 20-22, and 20-23). There may, in fact, be a spiritual reference. Sánchez Cotán once described his 11 paintings of fruits, vegetables, and birds as "offerings to the Virgin"—probably a reference to the Virgin as the *fenestra coeli* ("window to Heaven") and the source of spiritual food for the faithful.

BARTOLOMÉ ESTEBAN MURILLO In the 17th century, Spain maintained its passionate commitment to Catholic orthodoxy, and as in Counter-Reformation Italy, Spanish Baroque artists sought ways to move viewers and to encourage greater devotion and piety. BARTOLOMÉ ESTEBAN MURILLO (1617–1682), for example, formulated the canonical image of the *Virgin of the Immaculate Conception* (FIG. 19-25A), in which Mary is a beautiful young woman ascending to Heaven. But scenes of death and martyrdom also had great appeal in Spain. They provided artists with opportunities both to depict extreme emotion and to elicit passionate feelings in viewers. Spain prided itself on its saints—Saint Teresa of Avila (FIG. 19-8) and Saint Ignatius Loyola (FIG. 19-24) were both Spanish-born—and martyrdom scenes surfaced frequently in Spanish Baroque art.

19-25A MURILLO, *Immaculate Conception,* ca. 1661–1670.

JOSÉ DE RIBERA As a young man, JOSÉ (JUSEPE) DE RIBERA (ca. 1588–1652) emigrated to Naples and fell under the spell of Caravaggio, whose innovative style he introduced to Spain. Emulating Caravaggio, Ribera made naturalism and compelling drama primary ingredients of his paintings, which often embraced brutal themes, reflecting the harsh times of the Counter-Reformation and the Spanish taste for stories showcasing courage and devotion. Ribera's *Martyrdom of Saint Philip* (FIG. 19-26) is grim and dark in subject and form. Scorning idealization of any kind, Ribera represented Philip's executioners hoisting him into position after tying him to a cross, the instrument of Christ's own martyrdom. The saint's rough, heavy body and swarthy, plebeian features express a kinship between him and his tormentors, who are similar to the types of figures found in Caravaggio's paintings. The patron of this painting is unknown, but it is possible Philip IV commissioned the work, because Saint Philip was the king's patron saint.

FRANCISCO DE ZURBARÁN Another prominent Spanish painter of dramatic works was FRANCISCO DE ZURBARÁN (1598–1664), whose primary patrons throughout his career were rich Spanish monastic orders. Many of his paintings are quiet and contemplative, appropriate for prayer and devotional purposes. Zurbarán painted *Saint Serapion* (FIG. 19-27) as a devotional image for the funerary chapel of the monastic Order of Mercy in Seville. The saint, who participated in the Third Crusade of 1196, suffered martyrdom while preaching the Gospel to Muslims. According to one account, the monk's captors tied him to a tree and then tortured and decapitated him. The Order of Mercy dedicated itself

19-26 JOSÉ DE RIBERA, *Martyrdom of Saint Philip,* ca. 1639. Oil on canvas, 7′ 8″ × 7′ 8″. Museo del Prado, Madrid.

Martyrdom scenes were popular in Counter-Reformation Spain. Scorning idealization of any kind, Ribera represented Philip's executioners hoisting him into position to die on a cross.

1 ft.

19-27 Francisco de Zurbarán, *Saint Serapion*, 1628. Oil on canvas, 3′ 11½″ × 3′ 4¾″. Wadsworth Atheneum Museum of Art, Hartford (The Ella Gallup Sumner and Mary Catlin Sumner Collection Fund).

The light shining on Serapion calls attention to his tragic death and increases the painting's dramatic impact. The monk's coarse features label him as common, evoking empathy from a wide audience.

to self-sacrifice, and Serapion's membership in this order amplified the resonance of Zurbarán's painting. In *Saint Serapion*, the monk emerges from a dark background and fills the foreground. The bright light shining on him calls attention to the saint's tragic death and increases the dramatic impact of the image. In the background are two barely visible tree branches. A small note next to the saint identifies him for viewers. The coarse features of the Spanish monk label him as common, no doubt evoking empathy from a wide audience.

DIEGO VELÁZQUEZ

The foremost Spanish painter of the Baroque age—and the greatest beneficiary of royal patronage—was Diego Velázquez (1599–1660). An early work, *Water Carrier of Seville* (FIG. **19-28**), painted when Velázquez was only about 20 years old, already reveals his impressive command of the painter's craft. In this genre scene that seems to convey a deeper significance, Velázquez rendered the figures with clarity and dignity, and his careful and convincing depiction of the water jugs in the foreground, complete with droplets of water, adds to the scene's credibility. The plebeian nature of the figures and the contrast of darks and lights again reveal the influence of Caravaggio, whose work Velázquez had studied.

19-28A Velázquez, *Christ on the Cross*, ca. 1631–1632.

As did many other Spanish artists, Velázquez produced religious pictures, for example, *Christ on the Cross* (FIG. **19-28A**), as well as genre scenes, but his renown in his day rested primarily on the works he painted for King Philip IV (see "Velázquez and Philip IV," page 578). After the king appointed Velázquez court painter, the artist largely abandoned both religious and genre subjects in favor of royal portraits (FIG. **19-28B**) and canvases recording historical events.

19-28B Velázquez, *Philip IV*, 1644.

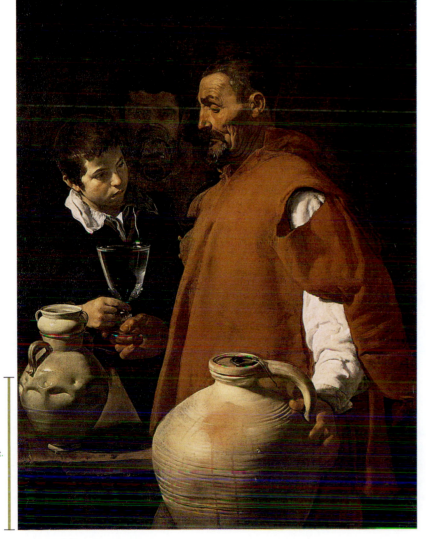

19-28 Diego Velázquez, *Water Carrier of Seville*, ca. 1619. Oil on canvas, 3′ 5½″ × 2′ 7½″. Victoria & Albert Museum, London.

In this early work—a genre scene that seems to convey a deeper significance—the contrast of darks and lights, and the plebeian nature of the figures, reveal Velázquez's debt to Caravaggio.

Velázquez and Philip IV

Trained in Seville, Diego Velázquez was quite young when he came to the attention of Philip IV. The painter's immense talent impressed the king, and Philip named him chief court artist and palace chamberlain, a position that also involved overseeing the rapidly growing royal art collection and advising the king on acquisitions and display. Among the works in Philip IV's possession were paintings by Titian, Annibale Carracci, Guido Reni, Albrecht Dürer, and Velázquez's famous Flemish contemporary, Peter Paul Rubens (see Chapter 20).

With the exception of two extended trips to Italy and a few excursions, Velázquez remained in Madrid for the rest of his life. His close relationship with Philip IV and his high office as chamberlain gave him prestige and a rare opportunity to fulfill the promise of his genius. One sign of Velázquez's fertile imagination as well as mastery of the brush is that he was able to create timeless artworks out of routine assignments to commemorate the achievements of his patron, as he did in his record of the Spanish victory over the Dutch in 1625 (*Surrender of Breda*, FIG. 19-29). Velázquez also painted dozens of portraits of Philip IV (FIG. 19-28B) and his family and retinue, including *Las Meninas* (FIG. 19-30), one of the greatest paintings in the history of Western art, a work Philip admired so much he displayed it in his personal office.

19-29 DIEGO VELÁZQUEZ, *Surrender of Breda,* 1634–1635. Oil on canvas, 10′ 1″ × 12′ ½″. Museo del Prado, Madrid.

As Philip IV's court artist, Velázquez produced many history paintings, including fictional representations such as this one depicting the Dutch mayor of Breda surrendering to the Spanish general.

1 ft.

SURRENDER OF BREDA In 1635, Velázquez painted *Surrender of Breda* (FIG. **19-29**) as part of an extensive program of decoration for the Hall of Realms in Philip IV's new secondary pleasure palace in Madrid, the Palacio del Buen Retiro. The huge canvas (more than 12 feet long and almost as tall) was one of 10 paintings celebrating recent Spanish military successes around the globe. It commemorates the Spanish victory over the Dutch at Breda in 1625. Among the most troublesome situations for Spain was the conflict in the Netherlands. Determined to escape Spanish control, the northern Netherlands broke from the Habsburg Empire in the late 16th century. Skirmishes continued to flare up along the border between the northern (Dutch) and southern (Spanish) Netherlands, and in 1625 Philip IV sent General Ambrogio di Spínola to Breda to reclaim the town for Spain.

Velázquez depicted the victorious Spanish troops, organized and well armed, on the right side of the painting. In sharp contrast, the defeated Dutch on the left appear bedraggled and disorganized. In the center foreground, the mayor of Breda, Justinus of Nassau, hands the city's keys to the Spanish general—although no encounter of this kind ever occurred. Velázquez's fictional record of the event glorifies not only the strength of the Spanish military but the benevolence of Spínola as well. Velázquez did not portray the Spanish general astride his horse, lording over the vanquished Dutch mayor, but rather painted him standing and magnanimously stopping Justinus from kneeling. Indeed, the terms of surrender were notably lenient, and Spínola allowed the Dutch to retain their arms—which they used to recapture the city in 1637.

LAS MENINAS After an extended visit to Rome from 1648 to 1651, Velázquez returned to Spain. In 1656, he painted his greatest work, *Las Meninas* (*The Maids of Honor;* FIG. **19-30**). The setting is the artist's studio in the palace of the Alcázar, the official royal residence in Madrid. After the death of Prince Baltasar Carlos in 1646, Philip IV ordered part of the prince's chambers converted into a studio for Velázquez. The painter represented himself stand-

19-30 DIEGO VELÁZQUEZ, *Las Meninas* (*The Maids of Honor*), 1656. Oil on canvas, 10′ 5″ × 9′. Museo del Prado, Madrid. 📹

Velázquez intended this huge and complex work, with its cunning contrasts of real, mirrored, and picture spaces, to elevate both himself and the profession of painting in the eyes of Philip IV.

ing before a large canvas. The young Infanta (Princess) Margarita appears in the foreground with her two maids-in-waiting, her favorite dwarfs, and a large dog. In the middle ground are a woman in widow's attire and a male escort. In the background, a chamberlain stands in a brightly lit open doorway. Scholars have been able to identify everyone in the room, including the two meninas and the dwarfs.

Las Meninas is noteworthy for its visual and narrative complexity. Indeed, art historians have yet to agree on any particular reading or interpretation. A central issue preoccupying scholars has been what, exactly, is taking place in *Las Meninas*. What is Velázquez depicting on the huge canvas in front of him? He may be painting this very picture—an informal image of the infanta and her entourage. Alternately, Velázquez may be painting a portrait of King Philip IV and Queen Mariana, whose reflections appear in the mirror on the far wall. If so, that would suggest the presence of the king and queen in the viewer's space, outside the confines of the picture. Other scholars have proposed that the mirror image is not a reflection of the royal couple standing in Velázquez's studio but a reflection of the portrait the artist is in the process of painting on the canvas before him. This question will probably never be definitively resolved.

More generally, *Las Meninas* is Velázquez's attempt to elevate both himself and his profession. As first painter to the king and as chamberlain of the palace, Velázquez was conscious not only of the importance of his court office but also of the honor and dignity belonging to his profession as a painter. Throughout his career, Velázquez hoped to be ennobled by royal appointment to membership in the ancient and illustrious Order of Santiago (Saint James). Because he lacked a sufficiently noble lineage, he gained entrance only with difficulty at the very end of his life, and then only through the pope's dispensation. In the painting, Velázquez wears the order's red cross on his doublet, painted there, legend says, by Philip IV. In all likelihood, Velázquez painted it. In the artist's mind, *Las Meninas* might have embodied the idea of the great king visiting his studio, as Alexander the Great visited the studio of the painter Apelles in ancient times. The figures in the painting all appear to acknowledge the royal presence. Placed among them in equal dignity is Velázquez, face-to-face with his sovereign.

The location of the completed painting reinforced this act of looking—of seeing and being seen. *Las Meninas* hung in Philip IV's personal office in another part of the palace. Thus, although occasional visitors admitted to the king's private quarters may have seen this painting, Philip was the primary audience. Each time he stood before the canvas, he again participated in the work as the probable subject of Velázquez's painting within the painting and as the object of the figures' gazes. In *Las Meninas,* Velázquez elevated the art of painting, in the person of the painter, to the highest status. The king's presence enhanced this status—either in person as the viewer of *Las Meninas* or as a reflected image in the painting itself. The paintings that appear in *Las Meninas* further reinforced this celebration of the painter's craft. On the wall above the doorway and the mirror, two faintly recognizable pictures are copies made by Velázquez's son-in-law, Juan del Mazo (ca. 1612–1667), of paintings by Peter Paul Rubens. The paintings depict the immortal gods as the source of art. Ultimately, Velázquez sought ennoblement not for himself alone but for his art as well.

Las Meninas is extraordinarily complex visually. Velázquez's optical report of the event, authentic in every detail, pictorially summarizes the various kinds of images in their different levels and degrees of reality. He portrayed the realities of image on canvas, of mirror image, of optical image, and of the two painted images. This work—with its cunning contrasts of real spaces, mirrored spaces, picture spaces, and pictures within pictures—itself appears to have been taken from a large mirror reflecting the entire scene. This would mean the artist did not paint the princess and her suite as the main subjects of *Las Meninas* but himself in the process of painting them. *Las Meninas* is a pictorial summary and a commentary on the essential mystery of the visual world, as well as on the ambiguity that results when different states or levels interact or are juxtaposed.

Velázquez employed several devices in order to achieve this visual complexity. For example, the extension of the composition's pictorial depth in both directions is noteworthy. The open doorway and its ascending staircase lead the eye beyond the artist's studio, and the mirror and the outward glances of several of the figures incorporate the viewer's space into the picture as well. (Compare how the mirror in Jan van Eyck's *Giovanni Arnolfini and His Wife* [FIG. 15-6] similarly incorporates the area in front of the canvas into the picture, although less obviously and without a comparable extension of space beyond the rear wall of the room.) Velázquez also masterfully observed and represented form and shadow. Instead of putting lights abruptly beside darks, following Caravaggio, Velázquez allowed a great number of intermediate values of gray to come between the two extremes. His matching of tonal gradations approached effects later discovered in the age of photography.

The inclusion of the copies of two Rubens paintings hanging on the wall in Velázquez's studio is the Spanish master's tribute to the great Flemish painter, one of the towering figures who made the 17th century one of the most important in the history of art in northern Europe. The works of Rubens, Rembrandt, and the other leading Baroque painters, sculptors, and architects of Flanders, the Dutch Republic, France, and England are the subject of Chapter 20.

THE BAROQUE IN ITALY AND SPAIN

ITALY

Borromini, San Carlo alle
Quattro Fontane, Rome,
1638–1641

▌ Art historians call the art of 17th-century Italy and Spain *Baroque,* a term that probably derives from the Portuguese word for an irregularly shaped pearl. Baroque art is dynamic and theatrical in vivid contrast to the precision and orderly rationality of Renaissance classicism.

▌ Baroque architects emphatically rejected the classical style. Gianlorenzo Bernini's colonnade framing the piazza in front of Saint Peter's is not a traditional rectangular atrium but two curving arms welcoming worshipers.

▌ Francesco Borromini emphasized the sculptural qualities of buildings. The facades of his churches—for example, San Carlo alle Quattro Fontane—are not flat frontispieces but undulating surfaces that provide a fluid transition from exterior to interior space. The interiors of his buildings pulsate with energy and feature complex domes that grow organically from curving walls.

Bernini, *Ecstasy of
Saint Teresa,* 1645–1652

▌ Guarino Guarini brought Borromini's innovative Baroque architectural style to Turin and designed even more complex domes than those the Roman master created.

▌ Bernini achieved even greater renown as a sculptor. His *David* represents the biblical hero in action, hurling stones at Goliath. In *Ecstasy of Saint Teresa,* Bernini marshaled the full capabilities of architecture, sculpture, and painting to create an intensely emotional experience for worshipers, consistent with the Counter-Reformation principle of using artworks to inspire devotion and piety.

▌ In painting, Caravaggio broke new ground by employing stark and dramatic contrasts of light and dark (tenebrism) and by setting religious scenes in everyday locales filled with rough-looking common people. An early masterpiece, *Calling of Saint Matthew,* for example, takes place in an ordinary tavern.

Caravaggio, *Calling of
Saint Matthew,* ca. 1597–1601

▌ Caravaggio's combination of drama and realism attracted both admiring followers, including Artemisia Gentileschi, the leading woman painter of the 17th century, and harsh critics. The biographer Giovanni Pietro Bellori, for example, deplored Caravaggio's abandonment of the noble style of Raphael and the ancients and his "suppression of the dignity of art." He preferred the more classical style of Annibale Carracci and the Bolognese art academy.

▌ Illusionistic ceiling paintings were very popular in Baroque Italy. The major ceiling painters were Pietro da Cortona, Giovanni Battista Gaulli, and Fra Andrea Pozzo. In Sant'Ignazio in Rome, Pozzo created the illusion that Heaven is opening up above worshipers' heads by merging the church's architecture with the painted nave vault.

Pozzo, *Glorification of Saint Ignatius,*
1691–1694

SPAIN

Velázquez, *Las Meninas,* 1656

▌ Although the power of the Habsburg kings declined during the 17th century, the royal family, which was devoutly Catholic, continued to spend lavishly on art. Spanish artists eagerly embraced the drama and emotionalism of Italian Baroque art. Scenes of death and martyrdom were popular in Counter-Reformation Spain. Painters such as José de Ribera and Francisco de Zurbarán adopted Caravaggio's lighting and realism to produce moving images of martyred saints.

▌ The greatest Spanish Baroque painter was Diego Velázquez, court painter to Philip IV. Velázquez painted themes ranging from genre and religious subjects to royal portraits and historical events. His masterwork, *Las Meninas,* is extraordinarily complex and mixes real spaces, mirrored spaces, picture spaces, and pictures within pictures. It is a celebration of the art of painting itself.

In the 17th century, an important new class of patrons emerged in the Dutch Republic—successful merchants who took pride in their material possessions, the fruit of worldwide trade.

Claesz's mastery of the oil medium is evident in details such as the glass ball on the left side of the table, in which the viewer sees the reflected image of the artist painting this still life.

Dutch Baroque still-life paintings are meticulously crafted images that are both scientific in their accurate portrayal of devices such as this timepiece and poetic in their beauty and lyricism.

1 in.

20-1 PIETER CLAESZ, *Vanitas Still Life,* 1630s. Oil on panel, 1′ 2″ × 1′ 11½″. Germanisches Nationalmuseum, Nuremberg.

Calvinist morality tempered Dutch citizens' delight in accumulated wealth. In this vanitas still life, the skull and timepiece are *mementi mori,* reminders of life's transience.

20

THE BAROQUE IN NORTHERN EUROPE

FRAMING THE ERA

STILL-LIFE PAINTING IN THE DUTCH REPUBLIC

In 1648, after decades of continuous border skirmishes with the Spaniards, the northern Netherlands achieved official recognition as the United Provinces of the Netherlands (the Dutch Republic; MAP **20-1**). The new independent republic owed its ascendance largely to its success in international trade. Dutch ships laden with goods roamed the world, sailing as far as North and South America, western Africa, China, Japan, and the Pacific islands.

Peter Mundy, a widely traveled Englishman, commented in 1640 on the irony that the Dutch Republic produced almost nothing on its own land yet enjoyed great wealth and could afford rare commodities from around the world:

> For although the land (and that with much labour) is brought only to pasture . . . yet by means of their shipping they are plentifully supplied with what the earth affords for the use of man . . . from any part of the world . . . Europe, Asia, Africa or America . . . with the most precious and rich commodities of those parts.[1]

The prosperous Dutch were justifiably proud of their accomplishments, and the popularity of still-life paintings—particularly images of accumulated goods—reflected this pride. These paintings of worldly possessions marked the emergence of an important new class of art patrons—wealthy merchants—who had tastes distinctly different from those of the leading patrons elsewhere in Baroque Europe, namely royalty and the Catholic Church. Dutch still lifes, which were well suited to the Protestant ethic rejecting most religious art, are among the finest ever painted. They are meticulously crafted images both scientific in their optical accuracy and poetic in their beauty and lyricism.

One of the best Dutch paintings of this genre is *Vanitas Still Life* (FIG. **20-1**) by PIETER CLAESZ (1597–1660), in which the painter presented the material possessions of a prosperous household strewn across a tabletop or dresser. The ever-present morality and humility central to the Calvinist faith tempered Dutch pride in worldly goods, however. Thus, although Claesz fostered the appreciation and enjoyment of the beauty and value of the objects he depicted, he also reminded the viewer of life's transience by incorporating references to death. Art historians call works of this type *vanitas* (vanity) paintings, and each feature a *memento mori* (reminder of death). In *Vanitas Still Life*, references to mortality include the skull, timepiece, tipped glass, and cracked walnut. All suggest the passage of time or something or someone that was here but now is gone. Claesz emphasized this element of time (and demonstrated his technical virtuosity) by including a self-portrait reflected in the glass ball on the left side of the table. He appears to be painting this still life. But in an apparent challenge to the message of inevitable mortality that vanitas paintings convey, the portrait serves to immortalize the artist.

WAR AND TRADE IN NORTHERN EUROPE

During the 17th and early 18th centuries, numerous geopolitical shifts occurred in Europe as the fortunes of individual countries waxed and waned. Pronounced political and religious friction resulted in widespread unrest and warfare. Indeed, between 1562 and 1721, all of Europe was at peace for a mere four years. The major conflict of this period was the Thirty Years' War (1618–1648), which ensnared Spain, France, Sweden, Denmark, the Netherlands, Germany, Austria, Poland, the Ottoman Empire, and the Holy Roman Empire. Although the outbreak of the war had its roots in the conflict between militant Catholics and militant Protestants, the driving force quickly shifted to secular, dynastic, and nationalistic concerns. Among the major political entities vying for expanded power and authority in Europe were the Bourbon dynasty of France and the Habsburg dynasties of Spain and the Holy Roman Empire. The war, which concluded with the Treaty of Westphalia in 1648, was largely responsible for the political restructuring of Europe (MAP 20-1). As a result, the United Provinces of the Netherlands (the Dutch Republic), Sweden, and France expanded their authority. Spanish and Danish power diminished. In addition

MAP 20-1 Europe in 1648 after the Treaty of Westphalia.

THE BAROQUE IN NORTHERN EUROPE

1600	1625	1650	1675	1700
▮ Peter Paul Rubens is the leading painter in Catholic Flanders ▮ The founding of the Bank of Amsterdam in 1609 initiates an era of Dutch preeminence in international trade ▮ In the northern Netherlands, Calvinist patrons favor genre scenes, portraits, and still lifes	▮ Frans Hals achieves renown for his group portraits of Dutch burghers ▮ Rembrandt, the foremost Dutch Baroque painter, is also a master of etching ▮ The Treaty of Westphalia concludes the Thirty Years' War in 1648	▮ Jacob van Ruisdael and other Dutch artists specialize in landscape painting ▮ Jan Vermeer uses a camera obscura as an aid in painting domestic interiors ▮ Nicholas Poussin champions classical "grand manner" painting in Rome	▮ Louis XIV, the Sun King, builds the palace at Versailles ▮ Sir Christopher Wren designs Saint Paul's Cathedral in London	

to reconfiguring territorial boundaries, the Treaty of Westphalia in essence granted freedom of religious choice throughout Europe. This treaty thus marked the abandonment of the idea of a united Christian Europe, and accepted the practical realities of secular political systems. The building of today's nation-states was emphatically under way.

The 17th century also brought heightened economic competition to Europe. Much of the foundation for worldwide mercantilism—extensive voyaging and geographic exploration, improved cartography, and advances in shipbuilding—had been laid in the previous century. In the 17th century, however, changes in financial systems, lifestyles, and trading patterns, along with expanding colonialism, fueled the creation of a worldwide marketplace. The Dutch founded the Bank of Amsterdam in 1609, which eventually became the center of European transfer banking. By establishing a system in which merchant firms held money on account, the bank relieved traders of having to transport precious metals as payment. Trading practices became more complex. Rather than simple reciprocal trading, triangular trade (trade among three parties) allowed for a larger pool of desirable goods. Exposure to an ever-growing array of goods affected European diets and lifestyles. Coffee (from island colonies) and tea (from China) became popular beverages during the early 17th century. Equally explosive was the growth of sugar use. Sugar, tobacco, and rice were slave crops, and the slave trade expanded to meet the demand for these goods. Traders captured and enslaved Africans and shipped them to European colonies and the Americas to provide the requisite labor force for producing these commodities.

The resulting worldwide mercantile system permanently changed the face of Europe. The prosperity international trade generated affected social and political relationships, necessitating new rules of etiquette and careful diplomacy. With increased disposable income, more of the newly wealthy spent money on art, significantly expanding the market for artworks, especially small-scale paintings for private homes.

FLANDERS

In the 16th century, the Netherlands had come under the crown of Habsburg Spain when Emperor Charles V retired, leaving the Spanish kingdoms, their Italian and American possessions, and the Netherlandish provinces to his only legitimate son, Philip II (r. 1556–1598). (Charles bestowed his imperial title and German lands on his brother.) Philip's repressive measures against the Protestants led the northern provinces to break from Spain and set up the Dutch Republic. The southern provinces remained under Spanish control and retained Catholicism as their official religion. The political distinction between modern Holland and Belgium more or less reflects this original separation, which in the 17th century signaled not only religious but also artistic differences.

Painting

The leading art of 17th-century Flanders (the Spanish Netherlands) was painting. Flemish Baroque painters retained close connections to the Baroque art of Catholic Europe. The Dutch schools of painting developed their own subjects and styles, consistent with their reformed religion and the new political, social, and economic structure of the Dutch Republic.

PETER PAUL RUBENS The greatest 17th-century Flemish painter was PETER PAUL RUBENS (1577–1640), a towering figure in the history of Western art. Rubens built on the innovations of the Italian Renaissance and Baroque masters to formulate the first truly pan-European painting style. Rubens's art is an original and powerful synthesis of the manners of many masters, especially Michelangelo, Titian, Carracci, and Caravaggio. His style had wide appeal, and his influence was international. Among the most learned individuals of his time, Rubens possessed an aristocratic education and a courtier's manner, diplomacy, and tact, which, with his facility for language, made him the associate of princes and scholars. He became court painter to the dukes of Mantua (descended from Mantegna's patrons), friend of King Philip IV (r. 1621–1665) of Spain and his adviser on collecting art, painter to Charles I (r. 1625–1649) of England and Marie de' Medici (1573–1642) of France, and permanent court painter to the Spanish governors of Flanders. Rubens also won the confidence of his royal patrons in matters of state, and they often entrusted him with diplomatic missions of the highest importance. Rubens employed scores of associates and apprentices to produce a steady stream of paintings for an international clientele. In addition, he functioned as an art dealer, buying and selling contemporary artworks and classical antiquities for royal and aristocratic clients throughout Europe, who competed with one another in amassing vast collections of paintings and sculptures, one of which

20-1A BRUEGHEL and RUBENS, *Allegory of Sight,* ca. 1617–1618.

became the subject of a painting (FIG. **20-1A**) by Rubens and JAN BRUEGEL THE ELDER (1568–1625). Rubens's many enterprises made him a rich man, able to afford a magnificent townhouse in Antwerp and a castle in the countryside. Rubens, like Raphael, was a successful and renowned artist, a consort of kings, a shrewd man of the world, and a learned philosopher.

ELEVATION OF THE CROSS Rubens departed Flanders for Italy in 1600 and remained there until 1608. During these years, he studied the works of Italian Renaissance and Baroque masters and laid the foundations of his mature style. Shortly after returning home, he painted *Elevation of the Cross* (FIG. **20-2**) for the church of Saint Walburga in Antwerp. Later moved to the city's cathedral, the altarpiece is one of numerous commissions for religious works Rubens received at this time. By investing in sacred art, Flemish churches sought to affirm their allegiance to Catholicism and Spanish Habsburg rule after a period of Protestant iconoclastic fervor in the region.

Rubens's interest in Italian art, especially the works of Michelangelo and Caravaggio, is evident in the Saint Walburga triptych. The choice of this episode from the passion cycle provided Rubens with the opportunity to depict heavily muscled men in unusual poses straining to lift the heavy cross with Christ's body nailed to it. Here, as in his *Lion Hunt* (FIG. I-14), Rubens, deeply impressed by Michelangelo's twisting sculpted and painted figures, showed his prowess in representing foreshortened anatomy and the contortions of violent action. Rubens placed the body of Christ on the cross as a diagonal that cuts dynamically across the picture while inclining back into it. The whole composition seethes with a power that comes from strenuous exertion, from elastic human sinew taut with effort. The tension is emotional as well as physical, as reflected

20-2 PETER PAUL RUBENS, *Elevation of the Cross,* from Saint Walburga, Antwerp, 1610. Oil on wood, center panel 15′ 1⅞″ × 11′ 1½″, each wing 15′ 1⅞″ × 4′ 11″. Antwerp Cathedral, Antwerp.

In this triptych, Rubens explored foreshortened anatomy and violent action. The whole composition seethes with a power that comes from heroic exertion. The tension is emotional as well as physical.

not only in Christ's face but also in the features of his followers. Bright highlights and areas of deep shadow inspired by Caravaggio's tenebrism, hallmarks of Rubens's work at this stage of his career, enhance the drama.

20-2A RUBENS, *Garden of Love,* 1630–1632.

Although Rubens later developed a much subtler coloristic style in paintings such as *Garden of Love* (FIG. **20-2A**), the human body in action, draped or undraped, male or female, remained the focus of his art. This interest, combined with his voracious intellect, led Rubens to copy the works of classical antiquity and of the Italian masters. During his last two years in Rome (1606 to 1608), Rubens made many black-chalk drawings of great artworks, including figures in Michelangelo's Sistine Chapel frescoes (FIG. 17-17) and the ancient marble group (FIG. 5-89) of Laocoön and his two sons. In a Latin treatise he wrote titled *De imitatione statuarum* (*On the Imitation of Statues*), Rubens stated: "I am convinced that in order to achieve the highest perfection one needs a full understanding of the [ancient] statues, indeed a complete absorption in them; but one must make judicious use of them and before all avoid the effect of stone."[2]

MARIE DE' MEDICI Rubens's interaction with royalty and aristocracy provided him with an understanding of the ostentation and spectacle of Baroque (particularly Italian) art that appealed to the wealthy and privileged. Rubens, the born courtier, reveled in the pomp and majesty of royalty. Likewise, those in power embraced the lavish spectacle that served the Catholic Church so well in Italy. The magnificence and splendor of Baroque imagery reinforced the authority and right to rule of the highborn. Among Rubens's royal patrons was Marie de' Medici, a member of the famous Florentine house and widow of Henry IV (r. 1589–1610), the first Bourbon king of France. She commissioned Rubens to paint a series of huge canvases memorializing and glorifying her career. Between 1622 and 1626, Rubens, working with amazing creative energy, produced with the aid of his many assistants 21 historical-allegorical pictures designed to hang in the queen's new palace, the Luxembourg, in Paris.

In *Arrival of Marie de' Medici at Marseilles* (FIG. **20-3**), a 13-foot-tall tableau, Marie disembarks at that southern French port after her sea voyage from Italy. An allegorical personification of France, draped in a cloak decorated with the *fleur-de-lis* (the floral symbol of French royalty; compare FIG. 20-24), welcomes her. The sea and sky rejoice at the queen's safe arrival. Neptune

20-3 PETER PAUL RUBENS, *Arrival of Marie de' Medici at Marseilles,* 1622–1625. Oil on canvas, 12′ 11½″ × 9′ 7″. Musée du Louvre, Paris.

Rubens painted 21 large canvases glorifying Marie de' Medici's career. In this historical-allegorical picture of robust figures in an opulent setting, the sea and sky rejoice at the queen's arrival in France.

1 ft.

and the Nereids (daughters of the sea god Nereus) salute her, and the winged and trumpeting personified Fame swoops overhead. Conspicuous in the galley's opulently carved stern-castle, under the Medici coat of arms, stands the imperious commander of the vessel, the only immobile figure in the composition. In black and silver, this figure makes a sharp accent amid the swirling tonality of ivory, gold, and red. Rubens enriched the surfaces with a decorative splendor that pulls the whole composition together. The audacious vigor that customarily enlivens the painter's figures, beginning with the monumental, twisting sea creatures, vibrates through the entire design.

CONSEQUENCES OF WAR Rubens's diplomatic missions gave him great insight into European politics, and he never ceased

Rubens on *Consequences of War*

In the ancient and medieval worlds, artists rarely wrote commentaries on the works they produced. (The Greek sculptor Polykleitos is a notable exception; see "Polykleitos's Prescription for the Perfect Statue," Chapter 5, page 132.) Beginning with the Renaissance, however, the increased celebrity artists enjoyed and the ready availability of paper encouraged artists to record their intentions in letters to friends and patrons.

In March 1638, Peter Paul Rubens wrote a letter to Justus Sustermans (1597–1681), court painter of Grand Duke Ferdinando II de' Medici of Tuscany, explaining his *Consequences of War* (FIG. 20-4) and his attitude toward the European military conflicts of his day.

The principal figure is Mars, who has left the open temple of Janus (which in time of peace, according to Roman custom, remained closed) and rushes forth with shield and blood-stained sword, threatening the people with great disaster. He pays little heed to Venus, his mistress, who, accompanied by Amors and Cupids, strives with caresses and embraces to hold him. From the other side, Mars is dragged forward by the Fury Alekto, with a torch in her hand. Near by are monsters personifying Pestilence and Famine, those inseparable partners of War. On the ground, turning her back, lies a woman with a broken lute, representing Harmony, which is

incompatible with the discord of War. There is also a mother with her child in her arms, indicating that fecundity, procreation and charity are thwarted by War, which corrupts and destroys everything. In addition, one sees an architect thrown on his back, with his instruments in his hand, to show that which in time of peace is constructed for the use and ornamentation of the City, is hurled to the ground by the force of arms and falls to ruin. I believe, if I remember rightly, that you will find on the ground, under the feet of Mars a book and a drawing on paper, to imply that he treads underfoot all the arts and letters. There ought also to be a bundle of darts or arrows, with the band which held them together undone; these when bound form the symbol of Concord. Beside them is the caduceus and an olive branch, attribute of Peace; these are also cast aside. That grief-stricken woman clothed in black, with torn veil, robbed of all her jewels and other ornaments, is the unfortunate Europe who, for so many years now, has suffered plunder, outrage, and misery, which are so injurious to everyone that it is unnecessary to go into detail. Europe's attribute is the globe, borne by a small angel or genius, and surmounted by the cross, to symbolize the Christian world.*

*Translated by Kristin Lohse Belkin, *Rubens* (London: Phaidon, 1998), 288–289.

1 ft.

20-4 PETER PAUL RUBENS, *Consequences of War*, 1638–1639. Oil on canvas, 6′ 9″ × 11′ 3⅞″. Palazzo Pitti, Florence.

Since the Renaissance, artists have left behind many letters shedding light on their lives and work. In a 1638 letter, Rubens explained the meaning of each figure in this allegorical painting.

to promote peace. Throughout most of his career, however, war was constant. When commissioned in 1638 to produce a painting (FIG. 20-4) for Ferdinando II de' Medici, the grand duke of Tuscany (r. 1621–1670), Rubens took the opportunity to express his at-

titude toward the Thirty Years' War (see "Rubens on *Consequences of War*," above). The fluid articulation of human forms in this work and the energy emanating from the chaotic scene are hallmarks of Rubens's mature style.

ANTHONY VAN DYCK Most of the leading painters of the next generation in Flanders were at one time Rubens's assistants. The master's most famous pupil was ANTHONY VAN DYCK (1599–1641). Early on, the younger man, unwilling to be overshadowed by Rubens's undisputed stature, left his native Antwerp for Genoa and then London, where he became court portraitist to Charles I. Although Van Dyck created dramatic compositions of high quality, his specialty became the portrait. He developed a courtly manner of great elegance that influenced many artists throughout Europe and resounded in English portrait painting well into the 19th century.

In one of his finest works, *Charles I Dismounted* (FIG. **20-5**), the ill-fated English king stands in a landscape with the Thames River in the background. An equerry and a page attend him. The portrait is a stylish image of relaxed authority, as if the king is out for a casual ride in his park, but no one can mistake the regal poise and the air of absolute authority that Charles's Parliament resented and was soon to rise against. Here, the king turns his back on his attendants as he surveys his domain. Van Dyck's placement of the monarch is exceedingly artful. He stands off center but balances the composition with a single keen glance at the viewer. Van Dyck even managed to portray Charles I, who was of short stature, in a position to look down on the observer.

CLARA PEETERS Some Flemish 17th-century artists specialized in still-life painting, as did Sánchez Cotán (FIG. 19-25) in Spain. A pioneer of this genre was CLARA PEETERS (1594–ca. 1657), a native of Antwerp who spent time in Holland and laid the groundwork for Pieter Claesz (FIG. 20-1) and other Dutch masters of still-life painting, including Willem Kalf (FIG. 20-22) and Rachel Ruysch (FIG. 20-23). Peeters won renown for her depictions

20-5 ANTHONY VAN DYCK, *Charles I Dismounted*, ca. 1635. Oil on canvas, 8′ 11″ × 6′ 11½″. Musée du Louvre, Paris.

Van Dyck specialized in court portraiture. In this painting, he depicted the absolutist monarch Charles I at a sharp angle so the king, a short man, appears to be looking down at the viewer.

1 ft.

of food and flowers together, and for still lifes featuring bread and fruit, known as *breakfast pieces*. In *Still Life with Flowers, Goblet, Dried Fruit, and Pretzels* (FIG. **20-6**), Peeters's considerable skills are on full display. One of a series of four paintings, each of which depicts a typical early-17th-century meal, this breakfast piece reveals Peeters's virtuosity in depicting a wide variety of objects convincingly, from the smooth, reflective surfaces of the glass and silver goblets to the soft petals of the blooms in the vase. Peeters often painted the objects in her still lifes against a dark background, thereby negating any sense of deep space (compare FIG. 19-25). In this breakfast piece, she enhanced the sense of depth in the foreground by placing the leaves of the flower on the stone ledge as though they were encroaching into the viewer's space.

20-6 CLARA PEETERS, *Still Life with Flowers, Goblet, Dried Fruit, and Pretzels*, 1611. Oil on panel, 1′ 7¾″ × 2′ 1¼″. Museo del Prado, Madrid. ◼◀

Clara Peeters was a pioneer of still-life painting. Although a Flemish artist, she spent time in Holland and laid the groundwork for many Dutch artists (FIGS. 20-1, 20-22, and 20-23).

1 in.

DUTCH REPUBLIC

With the founding of the Bank of Amsterdam in 1609, Amsterdam emerged as the financial center of the Continent. In the 17th century, the city had the highest per capita income in Europe. The Dutch economy also benefited enormously from the country's expertise on the open seas, which facilitated establishing far-flung colonies. By 1650, Dutch trade routes extended to North America, South America, the west coast of Africa, China, Japan, Southeast Asia, and much of the Pacific. Due to this prosperity and in the absence of an absolute ruler, political power increasingly passed into the hands of an urban patrician class of merchants and manufacturers, especially in cities such as Amsterdam, Haarlem, and Delft. All of these bustling cities were located in Holland (the largest of the seven United Provinces), which explains why historians informally use the name "Holland" to refer to the entire country.

Ter Brugghen, van Honthorst, Hals, Leyster

Religious differences were a major consideration during the northern Netherlands' insistent quest for independence during the 16th and early 17th centuries. Whereas Spain and the southern Netherlands were Catholic, the people of the northern Netherlands were predominantly Protestant. The prevailing Calvinism demanded a puritanical rejection of art in churches, and thus artists produced relatively little religious art in the Dutch Republic at this time (especially compared with the volume of commissions created in the wake of the Counter-Reformation in areas dominated by Catholicism; see Chapter 19).

HENDRICK TER BRUGGHEN Some artists in the Dutch Republic did produce religious art, however. HENDRICK TER BRUGGHEN (1588–1629) of Utrecht, for example, painted *Calling of Saint Matthew* (FIG. **20-7**) in 1621 after returning from a trip to Italy, selecting as his subject a theme Caravaggio had painted (FIG. 19-17) for the church of San Luigi dei Francesi in Rome. The moment of the narrative chosen and the naturalistic depiction of the figures echo Caravaggio's work. But although ter Brugghen was an admirer of the Italian master, he dispensed with Caravaggio's stark contrasts of dark and light and instead presented the viewer with a more colorful palette of soft tints. Further, the Dutch painter compressed the figures into a small but well-lit space, creating an intimate effect compared with Caravaggio's more spacious setting.

MERCANTILIST PATRONAGE Given the absence of an authoritative ruler and the Calvinist concern for the potential misuse of religious art, commissions from royalty or the Catholic Church, prominent in the art of other countries, were uncommon in the United Provinces. With the new prosperity, however, an expanding class of merchants with different tastes emerged as art patrons. In contrast to Italian, Spanish, and Flemish Baroque art, 17th-century Dutch art centered on genre scenes, landscapes, portraits of middle-class men and women, and still lifes, all of which appealed to the newly prosperous Dutch merchants (see "Still-Life Painting in the Dutch Republic," page 583, and "Middle-Class Patronage and the Art Market in the Dutch Republic," page 591).

GERRIT VAN HONTHORST Typical of 17th-century Dutch genre scenes is *Supper Party* (FIG. **20-8**) by GERRIT VAN HONTHORST (1590–1656). In this painting, van Honthorst presented an informal gathering of unidealized figures. While a musician serenades the group, his companions delight in watching a young woman feeding a piece of chicken to a man whose hands are both occupied—one holds a jug and the other a glass. Van Honthorst spent several years in Italy, and while there he carefully studied Caravaggio's work, as did fellow Utrecht painter Hendrick ter Brugghen. The Italian artist's influence surfaces in the mundane tavern setting and the nocturnal lighting of *Supper Party*. Fascinated by nighttime effects, van Honthorst frequently placed a hidden light source in his pictures and used it as a pretext to work with dramatic and starkly contrasting dark and light effects. Seemingly lighthearted genre scenes were popular in Baroque Holland, but Dutch viewers could also interpret them moralistically. For example, *Supper Party* can be read as a warning against the sins of gluttony (represented by the man on the right) and lust (the woman feeding the glutton is, in all likelihood, a prostitute with her aged procuress at her side). Or perhaps the painting represents the loose companions of the Prodigal Son (Luke 15:13)—panderers and prostitutes drinking, singing, strumming, and laughing. Strict Dutch Calvinists no doubt approved of such interpretations. Others simply took delight in the immediacy of the scenes and skill of artists such as van Honthorst.

20-7 HENDRICK TER BRUGGHEN, *Calling of Saint Matthew*, 1621. Oil on canvas, 3′ 4″ × 4′ 6″. Centraal Museum, Utrecht.

Although middle-class patrons in the Protestant Dutch Republic preferred genre scenes, still lifes, and portraits, some artists, including Hendrick ter Brugghen, also painted religious scenes.

1 ft.

Middle-Class Patronage and the Art Market in the Dutch Republic

Throughout history, the wealthy have been the most avid art collectors. Indeed, the money necessary to commission major artworks from leading artists can be considerable. During the 17th century in the Dutch Republic, however, the prosperity a large proportion of the population enjoyed significantly expanded the range of art patrons. As a result, one distinguishing hallmark of Dutch art production during the Baroque period was how it catered to the tastes of a middle-class audience, broadly defined. An aristocracy and an upper class of ship owners, rich businesspeople, high-ranking officers, and directors of large companies still existed, and these groups continued to be major patrons of the arts. But with the expansion of the Dutch economy, traders, craftspeople, bureaucrats, and soldiers also commissioned and collected art.

Although steeped in the morality and propriety central to the Calvinist ethic, members of the Dutch middle class sought ways to announce their success and newly acquired status. House furnishings, paintings, tapestries, and porcelain were among the items they collected and displayed in their homes. The Calvinist disdain for excessive ostentation, however, led Dutch collectors to favor small, low-key works—portraits of bourgeois men and women (FIGS. 20-9, 20-10, 20-12, and 20-13), still lifes (FIGS. 20-1, 20-22, and 20-23), genre scenes (FIGS. 20-8, 20-19, and 20-21), and landscapes (FIGS. 20-17, 20-18, 20-18A, and 20-18B). This focus contrasted with the Italian Baroque penchant for large-scale, dazzling ceiling frescoes and opulent room decoration (see Chapter 19). Indeed, the stylistic, as opposed to the chronological, designation "Baroque" is ill suited to these 17th-century northern European artworks.

It is risky to generalize about the spending and collecting habits of the Dutch middle class, but probate records, contracts, and archived inventories reveal some interesting facts. These records suggest an individual earning between 1,500 and 3,000 guilders a year could live quite comfortably. A house could be purchased for 1,000 guilders. Another 1,000 guilders could buy all the necessary furnishings for a middle-class home, including a significant amount of art, particularly paintings. Although there was, of course, considerable variation in prices, many artworks were very affordable. Prints, for example, were extremely cheap because of the high number of copies artists produced of each picture. Paintings of interior and genre scenes were relatively inexpensive in 17th-century Holland, perhaps costing one or two guilders each. Small landscapes fetched between three and four guilders. Commissioned portraits were the most costly. The size of the work and quality of the frame, as well as the reputation of the artist, were other factors in determining the price of a painting, regardless of the subject.

With the exception of portraits, Dutch artists produced most of their paintings for an anonymous market, hoping to appeal to a wide audience. To ensure success, artists in the United Provinces adapted to the changed conditions of art production and sales. They marketed their paintings in many ways, selling their works directly to buyers who visited their studios and through art dealers, exhibitions, fairs, auctions, and even lotteries. Because of the uncertainty of these sales mechanisms (as opposed to the certainty of an ironclad contract for a commission from a church or king), artists became more responsive to market demands. Specialization became common among Dutch artists. For example, painters might limit their practice to portraits, still lifes, or landscapes—the most popular genres among middle-class patrons.

Artists did not always sell their paintings. Frequently they used their work to pay off loans or debts. Tavern debts, in particular, could be settled with paintings, which may explain why many art dealers (such as Jan Vermeer and his father before him) were also innkeepers. This connection between art dealing and other businesses eventually solidified, and innkeepers, for example, often would have art exhibitions in their taverns hoping to make a sale. The institutions of today's open art market—dealers, galleries, auctions, and estate sales—owe their establishment to the emergence in the 17th century of a prosperous middle class in the Dutch Republic.

1 ft.

20-8 GERRIT VAN HONTHORST, *Supper Party,* 1620. Oil on canvas, 4′ 8″ × 7′. Galleria degli Uffizi, Florence.

Genre scenes were popular subjects among middle-class Dutch patrons. Gerrit van Honthorst's *Supper Party* may also have served as a Calvinist warning against the sins of gluttony and lust.

FRANS HALS Many Dutch artists excelled in portraiture in response to popular demand. FRANS HALS (ca. 1581–1666), the leading painter in Haarlem, was one of those who made portraits his specialty. Portrait artists traditionally relied heavily on convention—for example, specific poses, settings, attire, and furnishings—to convey a sense of the sitter. Because the subject was usually someone of status or note, such as a pope, king, duchess, or wealthy banker, the artist's goal was to produce an image appropriate to the subject's station in life. With the increasing number of Dutch middle-class patrons, portrait painting became more challenging. The Calvinists shunned ostentation, instead wearing subdued and dark clothing with little variation or decoration, and the traditional conventions became inappropriate and thus unusable. Despite these difficulties, or perhaps because of them, Hals produced lively portraits that seem far more relaxed than traditional formulaic portraiture. He injected an engaging spontaneity into his images and conveyed the individuality of his sitters as well. His manner of execution intensified the casualness, immediacy, and intimacy in his paintings. Because the touch of Hals's brush was as light and fleeting as the moment he captured the pose, the figure, the highlights on clothing, and the facial expression all seem instantaneously created.

ARCHERS OF SAINT HADRIAN Hals's most ambitious portraits reflect the widespread popularity in the Dutch Republic of vast canvases commemorating the participation of Dutch burghers in civic organizations. These commissions presented greater difficul-

ties to the painter than requests to depict a single sitter. Hals rose to the challenge and achieved great success with this new portrait genre. His *Archers of Saint Hadrian* (FIG. 20-9) is typical in that the subject is one of the many Dutch civic militia groups that claimed credit for liberating the Dutch Republic from Spain. As other companies did, the Archers met on their saint's feast day in dress uniform for a grand banquet. The celebrations sometimes lasted an entire week, prompting an ordinance limiting them to three or four days. These events often included sitting for a group portrait.

In *Archers of Saint Hadrian,* Hals attacked the problem of how to represent each militia member satisfactorily yet retain action and variety in the composition. Whereas earlier group portraits in the Netherlands were rather ordered and regimented images, Hals sought to enliven the depictions. In his portrait of the Saint Hadrian militiamen, each member is both part of the troop and an individual with a distinct physiognomy. The sitters' movements and moods vary markedly. Some engage the viewer directly. Others look away or at a companion. Some are stern, others animated. Each archer is equally visible and clearly recognizable. The uniformity of attire—black military dress, white ruffs, and sashes—did not deter Hals from injecting spontaneity into the work. Indeed, he used those elements to create a lively rhythm extending throughout the composition and energizing the portrait. The impromptu effect—the preservation of every detail and fleeting facial expression—is, of course, the result of careful planning. Yet Hals's vivacious brush appears to have moved instinctively, directed by a plan in his mind but not traceable in any preparatory scheme on the canvas.

1 ft.

20-9 FRANS HALS, *Archers of Saint Hadrian,* ca. 1633. Oil on canvas, 6′ 9″ × 11′. Frans Halsmuseum, Haarlem. ◼◀

In this brilliant composition, Hals succeeded in solving the problem of portraying each individual in a group portrait while retaining action and variety in the painting as a whole.

20-10 FRANS HALS, *The Women Regents of the Old Men's Home at Haarlem*, 1664. Oil on canvas, 5′ 7″ × 8′ 2″. Frans Halsmuseum, Haarlem. ◼◀

Dutch women played a major role in public life as regents of charitable institutions. A stern puritanical sensibility suffuses Hals's group portrait of the regents of Haarlem's old men's home.

1 ft.

WOMEN REGENTS OF HAARLEM Hals also produced group portraits of Calvinist women engaged in charitable work. The finest is *The Women Regents of the Old Men's Home at Haarlem* (FIG. 20-10). Although Dutch women had primary responsibility for the welfare of the family and the orderly operation of the home, they also populated the labor force in the cities. Among the more prominent roles educated Dutch women played in public life were as regents of orphanages, hospitals, old age homes, and prisons. In Hals's portrait, the Haarlem regents sit quietly in a manner becoming of devout Calvinists. Unlike the more relaxed, seemingly informal character of his other group portraits, a stern, puritanical, and composed sensibility suffuses Hals's portrayal of these regents. The women—all carefully distinguished as individuals—gaze out from the painting with expressions ranging from dour disinterest to kindly concern. The somber and virtually *monochromatic* (one-color) palette, punctuated only by the white accents of the clothing, contributes to the painting's restraint. Both the coloration and the mood of Hals's portrait are appropriate for this commission. Portraying the Haarlem regents called for a very different kind of portrait from those Hals made of men at festive militia banquets.

JUDITH LEYSTER Some of Hals's students developed thriving careers of their own as portraitists. One was JUDITH LEYSTER (1609–1660), whose *Self-Portrait* (FIG. 20-11) reveals the strong training she received. It is detailed, precise, and accurate but also imbued with the spontaneity found in her master's works. In her portrait, Leyster succeeded at communicating a great deal about herself. She depicted herself as an artist, seated in front of a painting on an easel. The palette in her left hand and brush in her right announce the painting as her creation. She thus invites the viewer to evaluate her skill, which both the fiddler on the canvas and the image of herself demonstrate as considerable. Although she produced a wide range of paintings, including still lifes and floral pieces, her specialty was genre scenes such as the comic image seen on the easel. Leyster's quick smile and relaxed pose as she stops her work to meet the viewer's gaze reveal her self-assurance. Although presenting herself as an artist, Leyster did not paint herself wearing the traditional artist's smock, as her more famous contemporary Rembrandt did in his 1659–1660 self-portrait (FIG. 20-15). Her elegant attire distinguishes her socially as a member of a well-to-do family, another important aspect of Leyster's identity.

20-11 JUDITH LEYSTER, *Self-Portrait*, ca. 1630. Oil on canvas, 2′ 5 3/8″ × 2′ 1 5/8″. National Gallery of Art, Washington, D.C. (gift of Mr. and Mrs. Robert Woods Bliss). ◼◀

Although presenting herself as an artist specializing in genre scenes, Leyster wears elegant attire instead of a painter's smock, placing her socially as a member of a well-to-do family.

1 ft.

Rembrandt

REMBRANDT VAN RIJN (1606–1669), Hals's younger contemporary and the leading Dutch painter of his time, was an undisputed genius—an artist of great versatility, a master of light and shadow, and a unique interpreter of the Protestant conception of scripture. Born in Leiden, he moved to Amsterdam around 1631, where he could attract a more extensive clientele than possible in his native city. Rembrandt had trained as a history painter in Leiden, but in Amsterdam he immediately entered the lucrative market for portraiture and soon became renowned for that genre.

ANATOMY LESSON OF DR. TULP In a painting he completed shortly after he arrived in Amsterdam, *Anatomy Lesson of Dr. Tulp* (FIG. **20-12**), Rembrandt deviated even further from the traditional staid group portrait than had Hals. Despite Hals's determination to enliven his portraits, he still evenly spread his subjects across the canvas. In contrast, Rembrandt chose to portray the members of the surgeons' guild (who commissioned this group portrait) clustered on the painting's left side. In the foreground appears the corpse Dr. Tulp, a noted physician, is in the act of dissecting. Rembrandt diagonally placed and foreshortened the corpse, activating the space by disrupting the strict horizontal, planar orientation typical of traditional portraiture. He depicted each of the "students" specifically, and although they wear virtually identical attire, their poses and facial expressions suggest the varying degrees of intensity with which they watch Dr. Tulp's demonstration—or ignore it. One, at the apex of Rembrandt's triangular composition of bodies, gazes at the viewer instead of at the operating table. Another directs his attention to the open book (an anatomy manual) at the cadaver's feet. Rembrandt produced this painting when he was 26 and just beginning his career. His innovative approach to group portraiture is therefore all the more remarkable.

NIGHT WATCH Rembrandt amplified the complexity and energy of the group portrait in *The Company of Captain Frans Banning Cocq* (FIG. **20-13**), better known as *Night Watch*. This more commonly used title is a misnomer, however. The painting is not of a nocturnal scene. Rembrandt used light in a masterful way, and dramatic lighting certainly enhances the image. Still, the painting's darkness (which explains the commonly used title) is the result of the varnish the artist used, which darkened considerably over time. It was not the painter's intention to portray his subjects moving about at night.

This painting was one of many civic-guard group portraits Dutch artists produced during this period.

From the limited information available about the commission, it appears the two officers, Captain Frans Banning Cocq and Lieutenant Willem van Ruytenburch, along with 16 members of their militia, contributed to Rembrandt's fee. (Despite the prominence of the girl just to the left of center, scholars have yet to ascertain her identity.) *Night Watch* was one of six paintings by different artists commissioned by various groups around 1640 for the assembly and banquet hall of Amsterdam's new Musketeers Hall, the largest and most prestigious interior space in the city. Unfortunately, in 1715, when city officials moved Rembrandt's painting to Amsterdam's town hall, they trimmed it on all sides, leaving an incomplete record of the artist's resolution of the challenge of portraying this group.

Even in its truncated form, *The Company of Captain Frans Banning Cocq* succeeds in capturing the excitement and frenetic activity of men preparing for a parade. Comparing this militia group portrait with Hals's *Archers of Saint Hadrian* (FIG. 20-9) reveals Rembrandt's inventiveness in enlivening what was, by then, becoming a conventional format for Dutch group portraits. Rather than present assembled men posed in orderly fashion, the younger artist chose to portray the company members rushing about in the act of organizing themselves, thereby animating the image considerably. At the same time, he managed to record the three most important stages of using a musket—loading, firing, and readying the weapon for reloading—details that must have pleased his patrons.

RETURN OF THE PRODIGAL SON The Calvinist injunction against religious art did not prevent Rembrandt from making a series of religious paintings and prints. In the Dutch Republic, paintings depicting biblical themes were not objects of devotion, but they still brought great prestige, and Rembrandt and other artists vied to demonstrate their ability to narrate holy scripture in dramatic new ways. One of Rembrandt's earliest biblical paintings, *Blinding of Samson* (FIG. **20-13A**), reveals the young artist's debt to Rubens and Caravaggio. His mature works, however, differ markedly from the

20-12 REMBRANDT VAN RIJN, *Anatomy Lesson of Dr. Tulp*, 1632. Oil on canvas, 5′ 3¾″ × 7′ 1¼″. Mauritshuis, The Hague. ◼◀

In this early work, Rembrandt used an unusual composition, arranging members of Amsterdam's surgeons' guild clustered on one side of the painting as they watch Dr. Tulp dissect a corpse.

1 ft.

20-13 Rembrandt van Rijn, *The Company of Captain Frans Banning Cocq* (*Night Watch*), 1642. Oil on canvas, 11′ 11″ × 14′ 4″ (trimmed from original size). Rijksmuseum, Amsterdam.

Rembrandt's dramatic use of light contributes to the animation of this militia group portrait in which the artist showed the company members rushing to organize themselves for a parade.

1 ft.

20-13A Rembrandt, *Blinding of Samson,* 1636.

religious art of Baroque Italy and Flanders. Rembrandt had a special interest in probing the states of the human soul. The spiritual stillness of his later religious paintings is that of inward-turning contemplation, far from the choirs and trumpets and the heavenly tumult of Bernini (FIG. 19-7) or Pozzo (FIG. 19-24).

The Dutch artist's psychological insight and his profound sympathy for human affliction produced, at the end of his life, one of the most moving pictures in all religious art, *Return of the Prodigal Son* (FIG. **20-14**). In this biblical parable, the younger of two sons leaves his home and squanders his wealth on a life of sin. When he becomes poor and hungry and sees the error of his ways, he returns home. In Rembrandt's painting, the forgiving father tenderly embraces his lost son, who crouches before him in weeping contrition, while three figures, immersed to varying degrees in the soft shadows, note the lesson of mercy. The light, everywhere mingled with shadow, directs the viewer's attention by illuminating the father and son and largely veiling the witnesses. Its focus is the beautiful, spiritual face of the old man. Secondarily, the light touches the contrasting stern face of the foremost witness. The painting demonstrates the degree to which Rembrandt developed a personal style completely in tune with the simple eloquence of the biblical passage.

20-14 Rembrandt van Rijn, *Return of the Prodigal Son,* ca. 1665. Oil on canvas, 8′ 8″ × 6′ 9″. Hermitage Museum, Saint Petersburg.

The spiritual stillness of Rembrandt's religious paintings is that of inward-turning contemplation, in vivid contrast to the heavenly tumult of Italian Baroque Counter-Reformation works.

1 ft.

20-15 Rembrandt van Rijn, *Self-Portrait,* ca. 1659–1660. Oil on canvas, 3′ 8¾″ × 3′ 1″. Kenwood House, London (Iveagh Bequest). ◼◀

In this late self-portrait, Rembrandt's interest in revealing the soul is evident in the attention given to his expressive face. The controlled use of light and the nonspecific setting contribute to this focus.

GRADATIONS OF LIGHT From the few paintings by Rembrandt discussed thus far, it should be clear the artist's use of light is among the hallmarks of his style. Rembrandt's pictorial method involved refining light and shade into finer and finer nuances until they blended with one another. Earlier painters' use of abrupt lights and darks gave way, in the work of artists such as Rembrandt and Velázquez (FIGS. 19-28 to 19-30), to gradation. Although these later artists sacrificed some of the dramatic effects of sharp chiaroscuro, a greater fidelity to appearances more than offsets those sacrifices. In fact, the recording of light in small gradations is closer to reality because the eye perceives light and dark not as static but as always subtly changing.

In general, Renaissance artists represented forms and faces in a flat, neutral modeling light (even Leonardo's shading is of a standard kind). They represented the *idea* of light, rather than showed how humans perceive light. Artists such as Rembrandt discovered gradations of light and dark as well as degrees of differences in pose, in the movements of facial features, and in psychic states. They arrived at these differences optically, not conceptually or in terms of some ideal. Rembrandt found that by manipulating the direction, intensity, and distance of light and shadow, and by varying the surface texture with tactile brushstrokes, he could render subtle nuances of character and mood, both in individuals and whole scenes. He discovered for the modern world that variation of light and shade, subtly modulated, can be read as emotional differences. In the visible world, light, dark, and the wide spectrum of values

between the two are charged with meanings and feelings that sometimes are independent of the shapes and figures they modify. The theater and the photographic arts have used these discoveries to great dramatic effect.

SELF-PORTRAITS Rembrandt carried over the spiritual quality of his religious works into his later portraits (FIGS. **20-15** and **20-15A**) by the same means—what could be called the "psychology of light." Light and dark are not in conflict in his portraits. They are reconciled, merging softly and subtly to produce the visual equivalent of quietness. Their prevailing mood is one of tranquil meditation, of philosophical resignation, of musing recollection—indeed, a whole cluster of emotional tones heard only in silence.

20-15A Rembrandt, *Self-Portrait,* 1658.

In his self-portrait now in Kenwood House (FIG. 20-15), the light source outside the upper left of the painting bathes the painter's face in soft highlights, leaving the lower part of his body in shadow. The artist depicted himself as possessing dignity and strength, and the portrait serves as a summary of the many stylistic and professional concerns that occupied him throughout his career. Rembrandt's distinctive use of light is evident, as is the assertive brushwork suggesting his confidence and self-assurance. He presented himself as a working artist holding his brushes, palette, and maulstick (compare FIG. 18-18) and wearing his studio garb—a smock and painter's turban. The circles on the wall behind him (the subject of much scholarly debate) may allude to a legendary sign of artistic virtuosity—the ability to draw a perfect circle freehand. Rembrandt's abiding interest in revealing the human soul emerges here in his careful focus on his expressive visage. His controlled use of light and the nonspecific setting contribute to this focus. Further, X-rays of the painting have revealed that Rembrandt originally depicted himself in the act of painting. His final resolution, with the viewer's attention drawn to his face, produced a portrait not just of the artist but of the man as well. Indeed, Rembrandt's nearly 70 self-portraits in various media have no parallel in sheer quantity. They reflect the artist's deeply personal connection to his craft.

ETCHINGS Rembrandt's virtuosity also extended to the graphic media, especially etching (see "Woodcuts, Engravings, and Etchings," Chapter 15, page 444). Many printmakers adopted etching after its perfection early in the 17th century, because the technique afforded greater freedom than engraving in drawing the design. The etcher covers a copper plate with a layer of wax or varnish, and then incises the design into this surface with a pointed tool, exposing the metal below but not cutting into its surface. Next, the artist immerses the plate in acid, which etches, or eats away, the exposed parts of the metal, acting in the same way the burin does in engraving. The medium's softness gives etchers greater carving freedom than woodcutters and engravers have working directly in more resistant wood and metal. If Rembrandt had never painted, he still would be renowned, as he principally was in his lifetime, for his prints. Prints were a major source of income for Rembrandt, as they were for Albrecht Dürer (see Chapter 18), and he often reworked the plates so they could be used to produce a new issue or edition. This constant reworking was unusual within the context of 17th-century printmaking practices.

20-16 REMBRANDT VAN RIJN, *Christ with the Sick around Him, Receiving the Children* (*Hundred-Guilder Print*), ca. 1649. Etching, 11″ × 1′ 3¼″. Pierpont Morgan Library, New York.

Rembrandt's mastery of the newly perfected medium of etching is evident in his expert use of light and dark to draw attention to Christ as he preaches compassionately to the blind and lame.

HUNDRED-GUILDER PRINT One of Rembrandt's most celebrated etchings is *Christ with the Sick around Him, Receiving the Children* (FIG. **20-16**). Indeed, the title by which this work has been known since the early 18th century, *Hundred-Guilder Print*, refers to the high sale price it brought during Rembrandt's lifetime. (As noted, a comfortable house could be purchased for 1,000 guilders.) *Christ with the Sick* demonstrates the artist's mastery of all aspects of the printmaker's craft, for Rembrandt used both engraving and etching to depict the figures and the setting. As in his other religious works, Rembrandt suffused this print with a deep and abiding piety, presenting the viewer not the celestial triumph of the Catholic Church but the humanity and humility of Jesus. Christ appears in the center preaching compassionately to, and simultaneously blessing, the blind, the lame, and the young, who are spread throughout the composition in a dazzling array of standing, kneeling, and lying positions. Also present is a young man in elegant garments with his head in his hand, lamenting Christ's insistence that the wealthy need to give their possessions to the poor in order to gain entrance to Heaven. The tonal range of the print is remarkable. At the right, the figures near the city gate are in deep shadow. At the left, the figures, some rendered almost exclusively in outline, are in bright light—not the light of day but the illumination radiating from Christ himself. A second, unseen source of light comes from the right and casts the shadow of the praying man's arms and head onto Christ's tunic. Technically and in terms of its humanity, *Hundred-Guilder Print* is Rembrandt's supreme achievement as a printmaker.

Cuyp and Ruisdael

Due to topography and politics, the Dutch had a unique relationship to the land, one that differed from attitudes of people living in other European countries. After gaining independence from Spain, the Dutch undertook an extensive reclamation project lasting almost a century. Dikes and drainage systems cropped up across the countryside. Because of the effort expended on these endeavors, the Dutch developed a distinctly direct relationship to the land. The reclamation also affected Dutch social and economic life. The marshy and swampy nature of much of the terrain made it less desirable for large-scale exploitation, so the extensive feudal landowning system elsewhere in Europe never developed in the United Provinces. Most Dutch families owned and worked their own farms, cultivating a feeling of closeness to the land. Consequently, landscape scenes abound in 17th-century Dutch art.

AELBERT CUYP One Dutch artist who established his reputation as a specialist in landscape painting was AELBERT CUYP (ca. 1620–1691). His works were the products of careful observation and a deep respect for and understanding of Dutch topography. *Distant View of Dordrecht, with a Milkmaid and Four Cows, and Other Figures* (FIG. **20-17**) reveals Cuyp's substantial skills. Unlike the idealized classical landscapes in many Italian Renaissance paintings, this landscape is particularized. The church in the background, for example, is a faithful representation of the Grote Kerk in Dordrecht. The dairy cows, shepherds, and milkmaid in the foreground refer to a cornerstone of Dutch agriculture—the demand for dairy products such as butter and cheese, which increased with the development of urban centers. The credibility of this and similar paintings rests on Cuyp's pristine rendering of each detail.

JACOB VAN RUISDAEL Depicting the Dutch landscape with precision and sensitivity was also a specialty of JACOB VAN RUISDAEL (ca. 1628–1682). In *View of Haarlem from the Dunes at Overveen* (FIG. **20-18**), Ruisdael provided an overarching view of this major Dutch city. The specificity of the artist's image—the Saint Bavo church in the background, the numerous windmills that refer to the land reclamation efforts, and the figures in the foreground stretching linen to be bleached (a major industry in Haarlem)—reflects the pride Dutch painters took in recording their homeland and the activities of their fellow citizens. Nonetheless, in this painting the inhabitants and dwellings are so minuscule they blend into the land itself, unlike the figures in Cuyp's view of Dordrecht. Moreover, the horizon line is low, so the sky fills almost three-quarters of the picture space, and the sun illuminates the landscape only in patches, where

it has broken through the clouds above. In *View of Haarlem*, Ruisdael not only captured the appearance of a specific locale but also succeeded in imbuing the work with a quiet serenity that is almost spiritual. Less typical of his work, but also one of the great landscape paintings of the 17th century, is Ruisdael's allegorical *Jewish Cemetery* (FIG. **20-18A**).

20-18A RUISDAEL, *Jewish Cemetery*, ca. 1655–1660.

Vermeer

20-18B VERMEER, *View of Delft*, ca. 1661.

Although he also painted landscapes, such as *View of Delft* (FIG. **20-18B**), JAN VERMEER (1632–1675) made his reputation as a painter of interior scenes, another popular subject among middle-class patrons. These paintings offer the viewer glimpses into the private lives of prosperous, responsible, and cultured citizens of the United Provinces. Despite his fame as a painter today, Vermeer derived much of his income from his work as an innkeeper and art dealer in Delft (see "Middle-Class Patronage and the Art Market," page 591), and he completed no more than 35 paintings that can be definitively attributed to him. He began his career as a painter of biblical and historical themes but soon abandoned those traditional subjects in favor of domestic scenes. Flemish artists of the 15th century also had painted domestic interiors, but sacred personages often occupied those scenes (for example, FIG. **15-1**). In contrast, Vermeer and his contemporaries composed neat, quietly opulent interiors of Dutch middle-class dwellings with men, women, and children engaging in household tasks or at leisure. Women are the primary occupants of Vermeer's homes, and his paintings are highly idealized depictions of the social values of Dutch burghers.

WOMAN HOLDING A BALANCE In one of Vermeer's finest canvases, *Woman Holding a Balance* (FIG. **20-19**), a beautiful young woman wearing a veil and a fur-trimmed jacket stands in a room in her home. Light coming from a window illuminates the scene, as in many of the artist's paintings. The woman stands before a table on which are spread her most precious possessions—pearl necklaces, gold chains, and gold coins, which reflect the sunlight that also shines on the woman's face and the fingers of her right hand. In fact, the perspective orthogonals direct the viewer's attention neither to the woman's head nor to her treasures but to the hand in which she holds a balance for weighing gold. The scales, however, are empty—in perfect balance, the way Ignatius of Loyola advised Catholics (Vermeer was a Catholic convert in the Protestant Dutch Republic) to lead a temperate, self-aware life and to balance one's sins with virtuous behavior. The mirror on the wall may refer to self-knowledge, but it may also symbolize, as do the pearls and gold, the sin of vanity. Bolstering that interpretation is the large framed *Last Judgment* painting on the back wall in which Christ, weigher of souls, appears in a golden aureole directly above the young woman's head. Therefore, this serene domestic scene is pregnant with hidden meaning. The woman holds the scales in balance and contemplates the kind of life (one free from the temptations of worldly riches) she must lead in order to be judged favorably on judgment day.

Vermeer, like Rembrandt, was a master of pictorial light and used it with immense virtuosity. He could render space so convincingly through his depiction of light that in his works the picture surface functions as an invisible glass pane through which the viewer looks into the constructed illusion. Art historians believe Vermeer used as tools both mirrors and the *camera obscura*, an ancestor of the modern camera based on passing light through a tiny pinhole or lens to project an image on a screen or the wall of a room. (In later versions, artists projected the image on a ground-glass wall of a box whose opposite wall contained the pinhole or lens.) Vermeer did not simply copy the camera's image, however. Instead, the camera obscura and the mirrors helped him obtain results he reworked compositionally, placing his figures and the furniture of a room in a beautiful stability of quadrilateral shapes. Vermeer's compositions evoke a matchless classical serenity. Enhancing this quality are colors so true to the optical facts and so subtly modulated they suggest Vermeer was far ahead of his time in color science. For example, Vermeer realized shadows are not colorless and dark, adjoining colors affect each other, and light is composed of colors. Thus, he painted reflections off of surfaces in colors modified by others nearby. Some scholars have suggested Vermeer also perceived the phenomenon modern photographers call "circles of confusion," which appear on out-of-focus negatives. Vermeer could have seen them in images projected by the camera obscura's primitive lenses. He approximated these effects with light dabs that, in close view, give the impression of an image slightly "out of focus." When the observer draws back a step, however, as if adjusting the lens, the color spots cohere, giving an astonishingly accurate illusion of the third dimension.

1 in.

20-19 JAN VERMEER, *Woman Holding a Balance*, ca. 1664. Oil on canvas, 1' 3⅝" × 1' 2". National Gallery of Art, Washington, D.C. (Widener Collection).

Vermeer's woman holding empty scales in perfect balance, ignoring pearls and gold on the table, is probably an allegory of the temperate life. On the wall behind her is a *Last Judgment* painting.

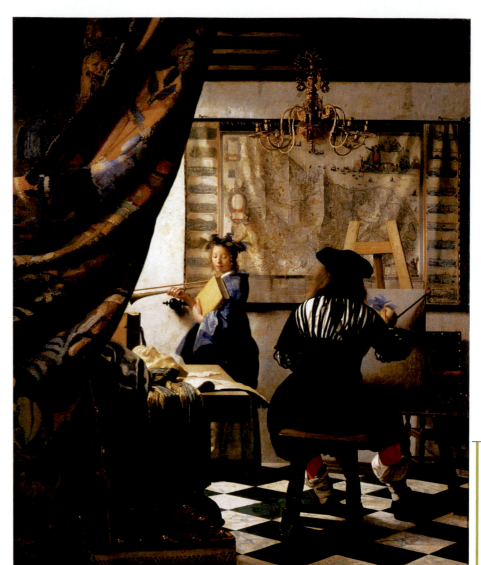

20-20 JAN VERMEER, *Allegory of the Art of Painting*, 1670–1675. Oil on canvas, 4′ 4″ × 3′ 8″. Kunsthistorisches Museum, Vienna.

Dutch painters often specialized in domestic scenes, but Vermeer's mother-in-law described this work as the "Art of Painting." Vermeer's tribute to his craft includes a model holding Clio's attributes.

THE ART OF PAINTING Vermeer's stylistic precision and commitment to his profession are evident in *Allegory of the Art of Painting* (FIG. **20-20**). The artist himself appears in the painting, with his back to the viewer and dressed in "historical" clothing (reminiscent of Burgundian attire). He is hard at work on a painting of the model standing before him wearing a laurel wreath and holding a trumpet and book, traditional attributes of Clio, the muse of history. The map of the provinces (an increasingly common wall adornment in Dutch homes) on the back wall serves as yet another reference to history. As

20-20A VERMEER, *The Letter*, 1666.

in *Woman Holding a Balance* and *The Letter* (FIG. **20-20A**), another of Vermeer's domestic scenes, the viewer is outside the space of the action, looking in through the drawn curtain, which also separates the artist in his studio from the rest of the house. Some art historians have suggested the light radiating from an unseen window on the left, illuminating both the model and the canvas being painted, alludes to the light of artistic inspiration. Accordingly, many scholars have interpreted this painting as an allegory—a reference to painting inspired by history. Vermeer's mother-in-law confirmed this allegorical reading in 1677 while seeking to retain the painting after the artist's death, when 26 of his works were scheduled to be sold to pay his widow's debts. She listed the painting in her written claim as "the piece . . . wherein the Art of Painting is portrayed."[3]

Steen

Whereas Vermeer's paintings reveal the charm and beauty of Dutch domesticity, the works of JAN STEEN (ca. 1625–1679) provide a counterpoint. In *Feast of Saint Nicholas* (FIG. **20-21**), instead of depicting a tidy, calm Dutch household, Steen opted for a scene of chaos and disruption. Saint Nicholas has just visited this residence, and the children are in an uproar as they search their shoes for the

20-21 JAN STEEN, *Feast of Saint Nicholas,* ca. 1660–1665. Oil on canvas, 2′ 8¼″ × 2′ 3¾″. Rijksmuseum, Amsterdam.

Steen's lively scene of Dutch children discovering their Christmas gifts may also have an allegorical dimension. *Feast of Saint Nicholas* probably alludes to selfishness, pettiness, and jealousy.

Christmas gifts he has left. Some children are delighted. The little girl in the center clutches her gifts, clearly unwilling to share with the other children despite her mother's pleas. Others are disappointed. The boy on the left is in tears because he received only a birch rod. An appropriately festive atmosphere reigns, which contrasts sharply with the decorum prevailing in Vermeer's works. As do the paintings of other Dutch artists, Steen's lively scenes often take on an allegorical dimension and moralistic tone. Steen frequently used children's activities as satirical comments on foolish adult behavior. *Feast of Saint Nicholas* is not his only allusion to selfishness, pettiness, and jealousy.

Kalf and Ruysch

As already discussed (see "Still-Life Painting in the Dutch Republic," page 583), Dutch patrons had a keen interest in still lifes. In addition to Peter Claesz (FIG. 20-1), the leading Dutch still-life painters included Willem Kalf and Rachel Ruysch.

WILLEM KALF As Dutch prosperity increased, precious objects and luxury items made their way into still-life paintings. *Still Life with a Late Ming Ginger Jar* (FIG. **20-22**) by WILLEM KALF (1619–1693) reflects the wealth Dutch citizens had accrued and the painter's exquisite skills, both technical and aesthetic. Kalf highlighted the breadth of Dutch maritime trade through his depiction of the Indian floral carpet and the Chinese jar used to store ginger (a luxury item). He delighted in recording the lustrous sheen of fabric and the light glinting off reflective surfaces. As is evident in this image, Kalf's works present an array of ornamental objects, such as the Venetian and Dutch glassware and the silver dish. The inclusion of the watch, Mediterranean peach, and peeled lemon suggests this work, like Claesz's *Vanitas Still Life* (FIG. 20-1), is also a vanitas painting, consistent with Calvinist values.

RACHEL RUYSCH As living objects that soon die, flowers, particularly cut blossoms, appeared frequently in vanitas paintings. However, floral painting as a distinct genre also flourished in the Dutch Republic. One of the leading practitioners of this art was RACHEL RUYSCH (1663–1750), who from 1708 to 1716 served as court painter to the elector Palatine (the ruler of the Palatinate, a former division of Bavaria) in Düsseldorf, Germany. Ruysch's father was a professor of botany and anatomy, which may account for her interest in and knowledge of plants and insects. She acquired an international reputation for her lush paintings, such as *Flower Still Life* (FIG. **20-23**). In this canvas, the lavish floral arrangement is so full, many of the blossoms seem to be spilling out of the vase. Ruysch's careful arrangement of the painting's elements is evident in her composing the flowers to create a diagonal running from the lower left to the upper right corner of the canvas, offsetting the opposing diagonal of the table edge.

1 ft.

20-22 WILLEM KALF, *Still Life with a Late Ming Ginger Jar*, 1669. Oil on canvas, 2′ 6″ × 2′ 1¾″. Indianapolis Museum of Art, Indianapolis (gift in commemoration of the 60th anniversary of the Art Association of Indianapolis, in memory of Daniel W. and Elizabeth C. Marmon).

The opulent objects, especially the Indian carpet and Chinese jar, attest to the prosperous Dutch maritime trade. Kalf's inclusion of a watch suggests this painting may be a vanitas still life.

1 ft.

20-23 RACHEL RUYSCH, *Flower Still Life*, after 1700. Oil on canvas, 2′ 5¾″ × 1′ 11⅞″. Toledo Museum of Art, Toledo (purchased with funds from the Libbey Endowment, gift of Edward Drummond Libbey). ◼◀

Flower paintings were very popular in the Dutch Republic. Ruysch achieved international renown for her lush paintings of floral arrangements, noted also for their careful compositions.

FRANCE

In France, monarchical authority had been increasing for centuries, culminating in the reign of Louis XIV (r. 1661–1715), who sought to determine the direction of French society and culture. Although its economy was not as expansive as the Dutch Republic's, France became Europe's largest and most powerful nation in the 17th century. Against this backdrop, the arts flourished.

Louis XIV

The preeminent French art patron of the 17th century was King Louis XIV himself. Determined to consolidate and expand his power, Louis was a master of political strategy and propaganda. He established a carefully crafted and nuanced relationship with the nobility, granting them sufficient benefits to keep them pacified but simultaneously maintaining rigorous control to avoid insurrection or rebellion. He also ensured subservience by anchoring his rule in *divine right* (belief in a king's absolute power as God's will), rendering Louis's authority incontestable. So convinced was Louis of his importance and centrality to the French kingdom that he eagerly adopted the title "le Roi Soleil" ("the Sun King"). Like the sun, Louis XIV was the center of the universe.

The Sun King's desire for control extended to all realms of French life, including art. Louis and his principal adviser, Jean-Baptiste Colbert (1619–1683), strove to organize art and architecture in the service of the state. They understood well the power of art as propaganda and the value of visual imagery for cultivating a public persona, and they spared no pains to raise great symbols and monuments to the king's absolute power. Louis and Colbert sought to regularize taste and establish the classical style as the preferred French manner. The founding of the Royal Academy of Painting and Sculpture in 1648 served to advance this goal.

PORTRAITURE Louis XIV maintained a workshop of artists, each with a specialization—for example, faces, fabric, architecture, landscapes, armor, or fur. Thus, many of the king's portraits were a group effort, but the finest is the work of one artist. *Louis XIV*

1 ft.

20-24 HYACINTHE RIGAUD, *Louis XIV,* 1701. Oil on canvas, 9′ 2″ × 6′ 3″. Musée du Louvre, Paris. ◼◀

In this portrait set against a stately backdrop, Rigaud portrayed the 5′ 4″ Sun King wearing red high-heeled shoes and with his ermine-lined coronation robes thrown over his left shoulder.

20-25 CLAUDE PERRAULT, LOUIS LE VAU, and CHARLES LE BRUN, east facade of the Louvre (looking southwest), Paris, France, 1667–1670. ◼◀

The design of the Louvre's east facade is a brilliant synthesis of French and Italian classical elements, including a central pavilion resembling an ancient temple front with a pediment.

(FIG. **20-24**) by HYACINTHE RIGAUD (1659–1743) successfully conveys the image of an absolute monarch. The king, age 63 when Rigaud painted this work, stands with his left hand on his hip and gazes directly at the viewer. His elegant ermine-lined fleur-de-lis coronation robes (compare FIG. **20-3**) hang loosely from his left shoulder, suggesting an air of haughtiness. Louis also draws his garment back to expose his legs. (The king was a ballet dancer in his youth and was proud of his well-toned legs.) The portrait's majesty derives in large part from the composition. The Sun King is the unmistakable focal point of the image, and Rigaud placed him so he seems to look down on the viewer. (Louis XIV was only five feet four inches tall—a fact that drove him to invent the red-heeled shoes he wears in the portrait.) The carefully detailed environment in which the king stands also contributes to the painting's stateliness and grandiosity. Indeed, when the king was not present, Rigaud's portrait, which hung over the throne, served in his place, and courtiers knew never to turn their backs on the painting.

THE LOUVRE The first great architectural project Louis XIV and his adviser Colbert undertook was the closing of the east side of the Louvre's Cour Carré (FIG. **18-14**), left incomplete by Pierre Lescot in the 16th century. The king summoned Gianlorenzo Bernini (see Chapter 19) from Rome to submit plans, but Bernini envisioned an Italian palace on a monumental scale, which would have involved the demolition of all previous work. His plan rejected, Bernini indignantly returned to Rome. Louis then turned to three

French architects—CLAUDE PERRAULT (1613–1688), LOUIS LE VAU (1612–1670), and CHARLES LE BRUN (1619–1690)—for the Louvre's east facade (FIG. **20-25**). The design is a brilliant synthesis of French and Italian classical elements, culminating in a new and definitive formula. The facade has a central and two corner projecting columnar pavilions resting on a stately podium. The central pavilion is in the form of a classical temple front. To either side is a giant colonnade of paired columns, resembling the columned flanks of a temple folded out like wings. The designers favored an even roofline, balustraded and broken only by the central pediment, over the traditional French pyramidal roof of the Louvre's west wing (FIG. **18-14**). The emphatically horizontal sweep of the 17th-century facade brushed aside all memory of Gothic verticality. The stately proportions and monumentality of the Baroque design were both an expression of the new official French taste and a symbol of centrally organized authority.

VERSAILLES PALACE Work on the Louvre barely had begun when Louis XIV decided to convert a royal hunting lodge at Versailles, south of Paris, into a great palace. He assembled a veritable army of architects, decorators, sculptors, painters, and landscape designers under the general management of Charles Le Brun. In their hands, the conversion of a simple lodge into the palace of Versailles (FIG. **20-26**) became the greatest architectural project of the age—a defining statement of French Baroque style and an undeniable symbol of Louis XIV's power and ambition.

20-26 JULES HARDOUIN-MANSART, CHARLES LE BRUN, and ANDRÉ LE NÔTRE, aerial view of the palace and gardens (looking northwest), Versailles, France, begun 1669.

Louis XIV ordered his architects to convert a royal hunting lodge at Versailles into a gigantic palace and park with a satellite city whose three radial avenues intersect in the king's bedroom.

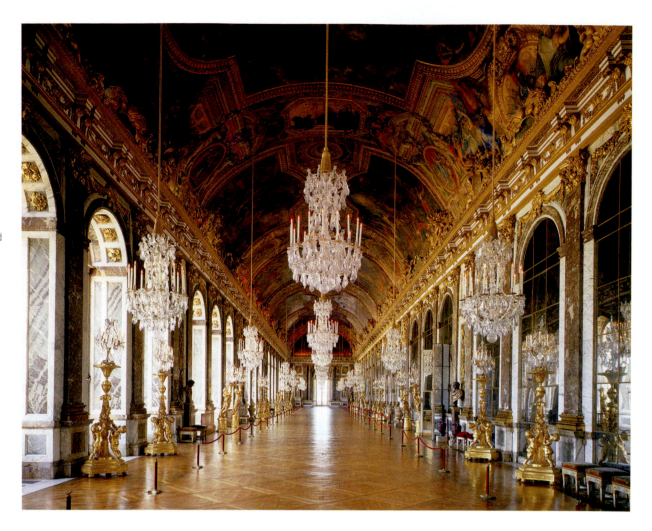

20-27 JULES HARDOUIN-MANSART and CHARLES LE BRUN, Galerie des Glaces (Hall of Mirrors), palace of Versailles, Versailles, France, ca. 1680.

This hall overlooks the Versailles park from the second floor of Louis XIV's palace. Hundreds of mirrors illusionistically extend the room's width and once reflected gilded and jeweled furnishings.

Planned on a gigantic scale, the project called not only for a large palace flanking a vast park but also for the construction of a satellite city to house court and government officials, military and guard detachments, courtiers, and servants (undoubtedly to keep them all under the king's close supervision). Le Brun laid out this town to the east of the palace along three radial avenues that converge on the palace. Their axes, in a symbolic assertion of the ruler's absolute power over his domains, intersected in the king's spacious bedroom, which served as an official audience chamber. The palace itself, more than a quarter mile long, is perpendicular to the dominant east-west axis running through the associated city and park.

Every detail of the extremely rich decoration of the palace's interior received careful attention. The architects and decorators designed everything from wall paintings to doorknobs in order to reinforce the splendor of Versailles and to exhibit the very finest sense of artisanship. Of the literally hundreds of rooms within the palace, the most famous is the Galerie des Glaces, or Hall of Mirrors (FIG. 20-27), designed by JULES HARDOUIN-MANSART (1646–1708) and Le Brun. This hall overlooks the park from the second floor and extends along most of the width of the central block. Although deprived of its original sumptuous furniture, which included gold and silver chairs and bejeweled trees, the Galerie des Glaces retains much of its splendor today. Hundreds of mirrors, set into the wall opposite the windows, alleviate the hall's tunnel-like quality and illusionistically extend the width of the room. The mirror, that ultimate source of illusion, was a favorite element of Baroque interior design. Here, it also enhanced the dazzling extravagance of the great festivals Louis XIV was so fond of hosting.

VERSAILLES PARK The enormous palace might appear unbearably ostentatious were it not for its extraordinary setting in a vast park, which makes the palace seem almost an adjunct. From the Galerie des Glaces, the king and his guests could enjoy a sweeping vista down the park's tree-lined central axis and across terraces, lawns, pools, and lakes toward the horizon. The park of Versailles, designed by ANDRÉ LE NÔTRE (1613–1700), must rank among the world's greatest artworks in both size and concept. Here, the French architect transformed an entire forest into a park. Although its geometric plan may appear stiff and formal, the park in fact offers an almost unlimited assortment of vistas, as Le Nôtre used not only the multiplicity of natural forms but also the terrain's slightly rolling contours with stunning effectiveness.

The formal gardens near the palace provide a rational transition from the frozen architectural forms to the natural living ones. Here, the elegant shapes of trimmed shrubs and hedges define the tightly designed geometric units. Each unit is different from its neighbor and has a focal point in the form of a sculptured group, a pavilion, a reflecting pool, or perhaps a fountain. Farther away from the palace, the design loosens as trees, in shadowy masses, screen or frame views of open countryside. Le Nôtre carefully composed all vistas for maximum effect. Light and shadow, formal and informal, dense growth and open meadows—all play against one another in unending combinations and variations. No photograph or series of photographs can reveal the design's full richness. The park unfolds itself only to those walking through it. In this respect, it is a temporal artwork. Its aspects change with the time of day, the seasons, and the relative position of the observer.

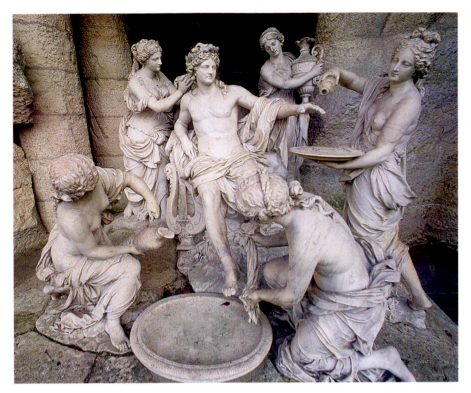

20-28 FRANÇOIS GIRARDON and THOMAS REGNAUDIN, *Apollo Attended by the Nymphs,* Grotto of Thetis, Park of Versailles, Versailles, France, ca. 1666–1672. Marble, life-size.

Girardon's study of ancient sculpture and Poussin's figure compositions influenced the design of this mythological group in a grotto above a dramatic waterfall in the gardens of Versailles.

GROTTO OF THETIS For the Grotto of Thetis above a dramatic waterfall in the gardens of Versailles, FRANÇOIS GIRARDON (1628–1715) designed *Apollo Attended by the Nymphs* (FIG. **20-28**). Both stately and graceful, the nymphs have a compelling charm as they minister to the god Apollo at the end of the day. (The three nymphs in the background are the work of THOMAS REGNAUDIN [1622–1706].) Girardon's close study of Greco-Roman sculpture heavily influenced his design of the figures, and the figure compositions of the most renowned French painter of the era, Nicholas Poussin (FIG. 20-31), inspired their arrangement. Since Apollo was often equated with the sun god (see "The Gods and Goddesses of Mount Olympus," Chapter 5, page 107, or page xxxiii in Volume II), the group refers obliquely to Louis XIV as the Roi Soleil. This doubtless helped to assure the work's success at court. Girardon's classical style and mythological symbolism well suited France's glorification of royal majesty.

ROYAL CHAPEL In 1698, Hardouin-Mansart received the commission to add a Royal Chapel to the Versailles palace complex. The chapel's interior (FIG. **20-29**) is essentially rectangular, but because its apse is as high as the nave, the fluid central space takes on a curved Baroque quality. However, the light entering through the large clerestory windows lacks the directed dramatic effect of the Italian Baroque, instead illuminating the interior's precisely chiseled details brightly and evenly. Pier-supported arcades carry a majestic row of Corinthian columns defining the royal gallery. The royal pew is at the rear, accessible directly from the king's apartments. Amid the restrained decoration, only the illusionistic ceiling paintings, added in 1708 and 1709 by ANTOINE COYPEL (1661–1722), suggest the drama and complexity of Italian Baroque art.

As a symbol of absolute power, Versailles has no equal. It also expresses, in the most monumental terms of its age, the rationalistic creed—based on scientific advances, such as the physics of Sir Isaac

20-29 JULES HARDOUIN-MANSART, interior of the Royal Chapel, with ceiling decorations by ANTOINE COYPEL, palace of Versailles, Versailles, France, 1698–1710.

Because the apse is as high as the nave, the central space of the Royal Chapel at Versailles has a curved Baroque quality. Louis XIV could reach the royal pew directly from his apartments.

20-30 JULES HARDOUIN-MANSART, Église du Dôme (looking north), Church of the Invalides, Paris, France, 1676–1706. ◼◀

Hardouin-Mansart's church marries the Italian and French architectural styles. The grouping of the orders is similar to the Italian Baroque manner but without the dramatic play of curved surfaces.

established for the disabled soldiers of his many wars. Two firmly separated levels, the upper one capped by a pediment, compose the frontispiece. The grouping of the orders and of the bays they frame is not unlike that in Italian Baroque architecture but without the dramatic play of curved surfaces characteristic of many 17th-century Italian churches, for example, Borromini's San Carlo (FIG. 19-9) in Rome. The compact facade is low and narrow in relation to the vast drum and dome, seeming to serve simply as a base for them. The overpowering dome, conspicuous on the Parisian skyline, is itself expressive of the Baroque love for dramatic magnitude, as is the way its designer aimed for theatrical effects of light and space. The dome consists of three shells, the lowest cut off so a visitor to the interior looks up through it to the one above, which is filled with light from hidden windows in the third, outermost dome. CHARLES DE LA FOSSE (1636–1716) painted the second dome in 1705 with an Italian-inspired representation of the heavens opening up to receive Saint Louis, patron of France (see "Louis IX, the Saintly King," Chapter 13, page 385).

Poussin

Louis XIV's embrace of classicism enticed many French artists to study Rome's ancient and Renaissance monuments. But even before the Sun King ascended to the throne in 1661, NICOLAS POUSSIN (1594–1665) of Normandy had spent most of his life in Rome, where he produced grandly severe paintings modeled on those of Titian and Raphael. He also carefully formulated a theoretical explanation of his method and was ultimately responsible for establishing classical painting as an important ingredient of 17th-century French art (see "Poussin's Notes for a Treatise on Painting," page 607). His classical style presents a striking contrast to the contemporaneous Baroque style of his Italian counterparts in Rome (see Chapter 19), underscoring the multifaceted character of the art of 17th-century Europe.

ET IN ARCADIA EGO Poussin's *Et in Arcadia Ego* (*Even in Arcadia, I* [am present]; FIG. 20-31) exemplifies the "grand manner" of painting the artist advocated. It features a lofty subject rooted in the classical world and figures based on antique statuary. Rather than depicting dynamic movement and intense emotions, as his Italian contemporaries in Rome did, Poussin emulated the rational order and stability of Raphael's paintings. Dominating the foreground are three shepherds living in the idyllic land of Arcadia. They study an inscription on a tomb as a statuesque female figure quietly places her hand on the shoulder of one of them. She may be the spirit of death, reminding these mortals, as does the inscription, that death is found even in Arcadia, supposedly a spot of paradisiacal bliss. The countless draped female statues surviving in Italy from Roman times supplied the models for this figure, and the posture of the youth with one foot resting on a boulder derives from Greco-Roman statues of Neptune, the sea god, leaning on his trident. The classically compact and balanced grouping of the figures, the even light, and the thoughtful and reserved mood complement Poussin's classical figure types.

Newton (1642–1727) and the mathematical philosophy of René Descartes (1596–1650)—that all knowledge must be systematic and all science must be the consequence of the intellect imposed on matter. The majestic and rational design of Versailles proudly proclaims the mastery of human intelligence (and the mastery of Louis XIV) over the disorderliness of nature.

ÉGLISE DU DÔME, PARIS Another of Hardouin-Mansart's masterworks, the Église du Dôme (FIG. 20-30), or Church of the Invalides, in Paris, also marries the Italian Baroque and French classical architectural styles. An intricately composed domed square of great scale, the church adjoins the veterans hospital Louis XIV

Poussin's Notes for a Treatise on Painting

As the leading proponent of classical painting in 17th-century Rome, Nicolas Poussin outlined the principles of classicism in notes for an intended treatise on painting, left incomplete at his death. In those notes, Poussin described the essential ingredients necessary to produce a beautiful painting in "the grand manner":

> The grand manner consists of four things: subject-matter or theme, thought, structure, and style. The first thing that, as the foundation of all others, is required, is that the subject-matter shall be grand, as are battles, heroic actions, and divine things. But assuming that the subject on which the painter is laboring is grand, his next consideration is to keep away from minutiae . . . [and paint only] things magnificent and grand . . . Those who elect mean subjects take refuge in them because of the weakness of their talents.*

> The idea of beauty does not descend into matter unless this is prepared as carefully as possible. This preparation consists of three things: arrangement, measure, and aspect or form. Arrangement means the relative position of the parts; measure refers to their size; and form consists of lines and colors. Arrangement and relative position of the parts and making every limb of the body hold its natural place are not sufficient unless measure is added, which gives to each limb its correct size, proportionate to that of the whole body [compare "Polykleitos's Prescription for the Perfect Statue," Chapter 5, page 132], and unless form joins in, so that the lines will be drawn with grace and with a harmonious juxtaposition of light and shadow.†

Poussin applied these principles in paintings such as *Et in Arcadia Ego* (FIG. 20-31), a work peopled with perfectly proportioned statuesque figures attired in antique garb.

*Translated by Robert Goldwater and Marco Treves, eds., *Artists on Art,* 3d ed. (New York: Pantheon Books, 1958), 155.
†Ibid., 156.

1 ft.

20-31 NICOLAS POUSSIN, *Et in Arcadia Ego*, ca. 1655. Oil on canvas, 2′ 10″ × 4′. Musée du Louvre, Paris.

Poussin was the leading proponent of classicism in 17th-century Rome. His "grand manner" paintings are models of "arrangement and measure" and incorporate figures inspired by ancient statuary.

20-32 NICOLAS POUSSIN, *Landscape with Saint John on Patmos,* 1640. Oil on canvas, 3′ 3½″ × 4′ 5⅝″. Art Institute of Chicago, Chicago (A. A. Munger Collection). ◼◀

Poussin placed Saint John in a classical landscape amid broken columns, an obelisk, and a ruined temple, suggesting the decay of great civilizations and the coming of the new Christian era.

1 ft.

SAINT JOHN ON PATMOS In *Et in Arcadia Ego,* monumental figures dominate the landscape setting, but the natural world looms large in many of Poussin's paintings. *Landscape with Saint John on Patmos* (FIG. **20-32**) is one of a pair of canvases Poussin painted for Gian Maria Roscioli (d. 1644), secretary to Pope Urban VIII. The second landscape represents Saint Matthew, reclining in right profile, who faced Saint John when the two canvases, now in different museums on different continents, hung side by side in Rome. An eagle stands behind John, just as an angel, Matthew's attribute, stands beside him. John, near the end of his life on the Greek island of Patmos, composed the book of Revelation, his account of the end of the world and the second coming of Christ, a prophetic vision of violent destruction and the last judgment. Poussin's setting, however, is a serene classical landscape beneath a sunny sky. (He created a similar setting in *Burial of Phocion* [FIG. **20-32A**], which he painted later in the decade.) Saint John reclines in the foreground, posed like a Greco-Roman river god, amid shattered columns and a pedestal for a statue that disappeared long ago. In the middle ground, two oak trees frame the ruins of a classical temple and an Egyptian obelisk, many of which the Romans brought to their capital from the Nile and the popes reused in their building projects, for example, in the piazza in front of Saint Peter's (FIG. 19-4) and in Bernini's Fountain of the Four Rivers (FIG. 19-1). The decaying buildings suggest the decline of great empires—to be replaced by Christianity in a new era. In the distance are hills, sky, and clouds, all of which Poussin represented with pristine clarity, ignoring the rules of atmospheric perspective. His landscapes are not portraits of specific places, as are the Dutch landscapes of Ruisdael (FIG. 20-18) and Vermeer (FIG. 20-18B). Rather, they are imaginary settings constructed according to classical rules of design. Poussin's clouds, for example, echo the contours of his hills.

20-32A POUSSIN, *Burial of Phocion,* 1648.

Claude Lorrain

Claude Gellée, called CLAUDE LORRAIN (1600–1682) after his birthplace in the duchy of Lorraine, rivaled Poussin in fame. Claude modulated in a softer style Poussin's disciplined rational art, with its sophisticated revelation of the geometry of landscape. Unlike the figures in Poussin's pictures, those in Claude's landscapes tell no dramatic story, point out no moral, praise no hero, and celebrate no saint. Indeed, the figures in Claude's paintings often appear to be added as mere excuses for the radiant landscape itself. For the French artist, painting involved essentially one theme—the beauty of a broad sky suffused with the golden light of dawn or sunset glowing through a hazy atmosphere and reflecting brilliantly off rippling water.

In *Landscape with Cattle and Peasants* (FIG. **20-33**), the figures in the right foreground chat in animated fashion. In the left foreground, cattle relax contentedly. In the middle ground, cattle amble slowly away. The well-defined foreground, distinct middle ground, and dim background recede in serene orderliness, until all form dissolves in a luminous mist. Atmospheric and linear perspective reinforce each other to turn a vista into a typical Claudian vision, an ideal classical world bathed in sunlight in infinite space (compare FIG. I-12).

Claude's formalizing of nature with balanced groups of architectural masses, screens of trees, and sheets of water followed the great tradition of classical landscape. It began with the backgrounds of Venetian paintings (FIGS. 17-33 to 17-35) and continued in the art of Annibale Carracci (FIG. 19-15) and Poussin (FIGS. 20-32 and 20-32A). Yet Claude, like the Dutch painters, studied the light and the atmospheric nuances of nature, making a unique contribution. He recorded carefully in hundreds of sketches the look of the Roman countryside, its gentle terrain accented by stone-pines, cypresses, and poplars and by the ever-present ruins of ancient aqueducts, tombs, and towers. He made these the fundamental elements of his compositions. Travelers could understand the picturesque beauties of the outskirts of Rome in Claude's landscapes.

1 ft.

Claude achieved his marvelous effects of light by painstakingly placing tiny value gradations, which imitated, though on a very small scale, the range of values of outdoor light and shade. Avoiding the problem of high-noon sunlight overhead, Claude preferred, and convincingly represented, the sun's rays as they gradually illuminated the morning sky or, with their dying glow, set the pensive mood of evening. Thus, he matched the moods of nature with those of human subjects. Claude's infusion of nature with human feeling and his recomposition of nature in a calm equilibrium greatly appealed to many landscape painters of the 18th and early 19th centuries.

Le Nain, Callot, La Tour

Although classicism was an important element of French art during the 17th and early 18th centuries, not all artists embraced the "grand manner."

LOUIS LE NAIN The works of LOUIS LE NAIN (ca. 1593–1648) have more in common with contemporaneous Dutch art than Renaissance or ancient art. Nevertheless, subjects that in Dutch painting were opportunities for boisterous good humor (FIG. 20-21), Le Nain treated with somber stillness. *Family of Country People* (FIG. **20-34**) reflects the thinking of 17th-century French social theorists who celebrated the natural virtue of peasants who worked the soil. Le Nain's painting expresses the grave dignity of one peasant family made stoic and resigned by hardship. These drab country folk surely had little reason for merriment. The peasant's lot, never easy, was miserable during the Thirty Years' War.

1 ft.

1 in.

20-35 JACQUES CALLOT, *Hanging Tree,* from the *Miseries of War* series, 1629–1633. Etching, $3\frac{3}{4}'' \times 7\frac{1}{4}''$. Biliothèque Nationale, Paris.

Callot's *Miseries of War* etchings were among the first realistic pictorial records of the human disaster of military conflict. *Hanging Tree* depicts a mass execution of thieves in the presence of an army.

The anguish and frustration of the peasantry, suffering from the cruel depredations of unruly armies living off the countryside, often erupted in violent revolts that the same armies savagely suppressed. This family, however, is pious, docile, and calm. Because Le Nain depicted peasants with dignity and quiet resignation, despite their harsh living conditions, some scholars have suggested he intended his paintings to please wealthy urban patrons.

JACQUES CALLOT Two other prominent artists from Lorraine were Jacques Callot and Georges de La Tour. JACQUES CALLOT (ca. 1592–1635) conveyed a sense of military life during these troubled times in a series of prints called *Miseries of War.* Callot confined himself almost exclusively to the art of etching and was widely influential—Rembrandt was among those who knew and learned from his work. Callot perfected the medium of etching, developing a very hard surface for the copper plate to enable fine and precise delineation with the needle. His quick, vivid touch and faultless drawing produced panoramas sparkling with sharp details of life—and death—despite their small size (roughly 4 by 7 inches). In the *Miseries of War* series, he observed these details coolly, presenting without comment images based on events he must have witnessed in the wars in Lorraine.

In *Hanging Tree* (FIG. **20-35**), Callot depicted a mass execution of thieves (identified in the text at the bottom of the etching). The event takes place in the presence of a disciplined army, drawn up on parade with banners, muskets, and lances, their tents in the background. Hanged men sway in clusters from the branches of a huge cross-shaped tree. A monk climbs a ladder, holding up a crucifix to a man while the executioner adjusts the noose around the man's neck. At the foot of the ladder, another victim kneels to receive absolution. Under the crucifix tree, men roll dice on a drumhead, hoping to win the belongings of the executed. (This is probably an allusion to the soldiers who cast lots for the gar-

ments of the crucified Christ.) In the right foreground, a hooded priest consoles a bound man. Callot's *Miseries of War* etchings are among the first realistic pictorial records of the human disaster of armed conflict.

GEORGES DE LA TOUR France, unlike the Dutch Republic, was a Catholic country, and religious themes, although not as common as in Italian and Spanish Baroque art (see Chapter 19), occupied some 17th-century French painters. Among the French artists who painted biblical subjects was GEORGES DE LA TOUR (1593–1652). His work, particularly his use of light, suggests a familiarity with Caravaggio's art, which he may have learned about from painters in Utrecht, such as ter Brugghen and van Honthorst (FIGS. 20-7 and 20-8). Although La Tour used the devices of Caravaggio's Dutch followers, his effects are strikingly different from theirs. His *Adoration of the Shepherds* (FIG. **20-36**) makes use of the night setting favored by the Utrecht school, much as van Honthorst portrayed it. But here, the light, its source shaded by an old man's hand, falls upon a very different company in a very different mood. A group of humble men and women, coarsely clad, gather in prayerful vigil around a luminous baby Jesus. Without the aid of the title, this work might be construed as a genre piece, a narrative of some event from peasant life. Nothing in the environment, placement, poses, dress, or attributes of the figures distinguishes them as the Virgin Mary, Joseph, Christ Child, or shepherds. The artist did not even paint halos. The light is not spiritual but material: it comes from a candle. La Tour's scientific scrutiny of the effects of light, as it throws precise shadows on surfaces intercepting it, nevertheless had religious intention and consequence. The light illuminates a group of ordinary people held in a mystic trance induced by their witnessing the miracle of the incarnation. In this timeless tableau of simple people, La Tour eliminated the dogmatic significance and traditional iconography of the incarnation. Still, these people

20-36 GEORGES DE LA TOUR, *Adoration of the Shepherds*, 1645–1650. Oil on canvas, 3′ 6″ × 4′ 6″. Musée du Louvre, Paris.

Without the aid of the title, this candlelit nighttime scene could be a genre piece instead of a biblical narrative. La Tour did not even paint halos around the heads of the holy figures.

ENGLAND

In England, in sharp distinction to France, the common law and the Parliament kept royal power in check. England also differed from France (and Europe in general) in other significant ways. Although an important part of English life, religion was not the contentious issue it was on the Continent. The religious affiliations of the English included Catholicism, Anglicanism, Protestantism, and Puritanism (the English version of Calvinism). In the economic realm, England was the one country (other than the Dutch Republic) to take advantage of the opportunities overseas trade offered. As an island, Britain (which after 1603 consisted of England, Wales, and Scotland), like the Dutch Republic, possessed a large and powerful navy, as well as excellent maritime capabilities.

reverently contemplate something they regard as holy. The devout of any religious persuasion can read this painting, regardless of their familiarity with the biblical account.

The supernatural calm pervading *Adoration of the Shepherds* is characteristic of the mood of Georges de La Tour's art. He achieved this by eliminating motion and emotive gesture (only the light is dramatic), by suppressing surface detail, and by simplifying body volumes. These stylistic traits are among those associated with classical and Renaissance art. Thus, several apparently contradictory elements meet in the work of La Tour: classical composure, fervent spirituality, and genre realism.

Jones and Wren

In the realm of art, the most significant English achievements were in the field of architecture, much of it, as in France, incorporating classical elements.

INIGO JONES The most important English architect of the first half of the 17th century was INIGO JONES (1573–1652), architect to Kings James I (r. 1603–1625) and Charles I (FIG. 20-5). Jones spent considerable time in Italy. He greatly admired the classical authority and restraint of Andrea Palladio's structures and studied with great care his treatise on architecture (see Chapter 17). Jones took many motifs from Palladio's villas and palaces, and he adopted Palladio's basic design principles for his own architecture. The nature of his achievement is evident in the buildings he designed for his royal patrons, among them the Banqueting House (FIG. 20-37) at Whitehall in London. For this structure, a symmetrical block of great clarity and dignity,

20-37 INIGO JONES, Banqueting House (looking northeast), Whitehall, London, England, 1619–1622.

Jones was a great admirer of the classical architecture of Palladio, and he adopted motifs from the Italian architect's villas and palaces for the buildings he designed for his royal patrons.

20-38 Sir Christopher Wren, west facade of Saint Paul's Cathedral, London, England, 1675–1710.

Wren's cathedral replaced an old Gothic church. The facade design owes much to Palladio (FIG. 17-30) and Borromini (FIG. 19-12). The great dome recalls Saint Peter's in Rome (FIGS. 17-25 and 19-4).

Jones superimposed two orders, using columns in the center and pilasters near the ends. The balustraded roofline, uninterrupted in its horizontal sweep, antedates the Louvre's east facade (FIG. 20-25) by more than 40 years. Palladio would have recognized and approved all of the design elements, but the building as a whole is not a copy of his work. Although relying on the revered Italian's architectural vocabulary and syntax, Jones retained his independence as a designer. For two centuries his influence in English architecture was almost as authoritative as Palladio's.

CHRISTOPHER WREN London's majestic Saint Paul's Cathedral (FIG. **20-38**) is the work of England's most renowned architect, Christopher Wren (1632–1723). A mathematical genius and skilled engineer whose work won Isaac Newton's praise, Wren became professor of astronomy in London at age 25. Mathematics led to architecture, and Charles II (r. 1649–1685) asked Wren to prepare a plan for restoring the old Gothic church of Saint Paul. Wren proposed to remodel the building based on Roman structures. Within a few months, the Great Fire of London, which destroyed the old structure and many churches in the city in 1666, gave Wren his opportunity. Although Jones's work strongly influenced him, Wren also traveled in France, where the splendid palaces and state buildings being created in and around Paris at the time of the com-

petition for the Louvre design must have impressed him. Wren also closely studied prints illustrating Baroque architecture in Italy. In Saint Paul's, he harmonized Palladian, French, and Italian Baroque features.

In view of its size, the cathedral was built with remarkable speed—in little more than 30 years—and Wren lived to see it completed. The building's form underwent constant refinement during construction, and Wren did not determine the final appearance of the towers until after 1700. In the splendid skyline composition, two foreground towers act effectively as foils to the great dome. Wren must have known similar schemes Italian architects had devised for Saint Peter's (FIG. 19-4) in Rome to solve the problem of the relationship between the facade and dome. Certainly, the influence of Borromini (FIG. 19-12) is evident in the upper levels and lanterns of the towers. The lower levels owe a debt to Palladio (FIG. 17-30), and the superposed paired columnar porticos recall the Louvre's east facade (FIG. 20-25). Wren's skillful eclecticism brought all these foreign features into a monumental unity.

Wren designed many other London churches after the Great Fire. Even today, Wren's towers and domes punctuate the skyline of London. Saint Paul's dome is the tallest of all. Wren's legacy was significant and long-lasting, both in England and in colonial America (see Chapter 21).

THE BAROQUE IN NORTHERN EUROPE

FLANDERS

▌ In the 17th century, Flanders remained Catholic and under Spanish control. Flemish Baroque art is more closely tied to the Baroque art of Italy than is the art of much of the rest of northern Europe.

▌ The leading Flemish painter of this era was Peter Paul Rubens, whose work and influence were international in scope. A diplomat as well as an artist, he counted kings and queens among his patrons and friends. His paintings exhibit Baroque splendor in color and ornament, and feature robust and foreshortened figures in swirling motion.

Rubens, *Consequences of War*, 1638–1639

DUTCH REPUBLIC

▌ The Dutch Republic received official recognition of its independence from Spain in the Treaty of Westphalia of 1648. Worldwide trade and banking brought prosperity to its predominantly Protestant citizenry, which largely rejected church art in favor of private commissions of portraits, genre scenes, landscapes, and still lifes.

▌ Frans Hals produced innovative portraits of middle-class patrons in which a lively informality replaced the formulaic patterns of traditional portraiture. Aelbert Cuyp and Jacob van Ruisdael specialized in landscapes depicting specific places, not idealized Renaissance settings. Peter Claesz, Willem Kalf, and others painted vanitas still lifes featuring meticulous depictions of worldly goods amid reminders of death.

▌ Rembrandt van Rijn, the greatest Dutch artist of the age, treated a broad range of subjects, including religious themes and portraits. His oil paintings are notable for their dramatic impact and subtle gradations of light and shade as well as the artist's ability to convey human emotions. Rembrandt was also a master printmaker renowned for his etchings.

▌ Jan Vermeer specialized in painting the occupants of serene, comfortable Dutch homes. His convincing representation of interior spaces depended in part on his employment of the camera obscura. Vermeer was also a master of light and color and understood shadows are not colorless.

Rembrandt, *Hundred-Guilder Print*, ca. 1649

Vermeer, *Woman Holding a Balance*, ca. 1664

FRANCE AND ENGLAND

▌ The major art patron in 17th-century France was the Sun King, the absolutist monarch Louis XIV, who expanded the Louvre and built a gigantic palace-and-garden complex at Versailles featuring sumptuous furnishings and sweeping vistas. Among the architects Louis employed were Charles Le Brun and Jules Hardouin-Mansart, who succeeded in marrying Italian Baroque and French classical styles.

▌ The leading French proponent of classical painting was Nicolas Poussin, who spent most of his life in Rome and championed the "grand manner" of painting. This style called for heroic or divine subjects and classical compositions with figures often modeled on ancient statues.

▌ Claude Lorraine, whose fame rivaled Poussin's, specialized in classical landscapes rendered in linear and atmospheric perspective. His compositions often incorporated ancient ruins.

▌ In 17th-century England, architecture was the most important art form. Two architects who achieved international fame were Inigo Jones and Christopher Wren, who harmonized the architectural principles of Andrea Palladio with the Italian Baroque and French classical styles.

Poussin, *Et in Arcadia Ego*, ca. 1655

Wren, Saint Paul's, London, 1675–1710

Joseph Wright of Derby specialized in dramatically lit paintings celebrating the scientific advances of the Enlightenment era. Here, a man listening to a learned lecture takes careful notes.

At the center of Wright's canvas, a scholar demonstrates an orrery, a mechanical model of the solar system in which each planet revolves around the sun at the correct relative velocity.

Awestruck children crowd close to the orbs representing the planets within the arcing bands symbolizing their orbits. Light from a lamp creates shadows, heightening the drama of the scene.

1 ft.

21-1 JOSEPH WRIGHT OF DERBY, *A Philosopher Giving a Lecture at the Orrery*, ca. 1763–1765. Oil on canvas, 4′ 10″ × 6′ 8″. Derby Museums and Art Gallery, Derby.

The wonders of scientific knowledge mesmerize everyone in Wright's painting, adults as well as children. At the right, two gentlemen pay rapt attention to the demonstration.

ROCOCO TO NEOCLASSICISM: THE 18TH CENTURY IN EUROPE AND AMERICA

FRAMING THE ERA

ART AND SCIENCE IN THE ERA OF ENLIGHTENMENT

The dawn of the *Enlightenment* in the 18th century brought a new way of thinking critically about the world and about humankind, independently of religion, myth, or tradition. Enlightenment thinkers rejected unfounded beliefs in favor of empirical evidence and promoted the questioning of all assertions. Thus, the Enlightenment encouraged and stimulated the habit and application of mind known as the "scientific method" and fostered technological invention. The scientific advances of the Enlightenment era affected the lives of everyone, and most people enthusiastically responded to wonders of the Industrial Revolution such as the steam engine, which gave birth to the modern manufacturing economy and the prospect of a seemingly limitless supply of goods and services.

The fascination science had for ordinary people as well as for the learned is the subject of *A Philosopher Giving a Lecture at the Orrery* (FIG. 21-1) by the English painter JOSEPH WRIGHT OF DERBY (1734–1797). Wright studied painting near Birmingham (MAP 22-2), the center of the Industrial Revolution, and specialized in dramatically lit scenes showcasing modern scientific instruments and experiments. In this painting, a scholar demonstrates a mechanical model of the solar system called an *orrery*, in which each planet (represented by a metal orb) revolves around the sun (a lamp) at the correct relative velocity. Light from the lamp pours forth from in front of the boy silhouetted in the foreground to create shadows that heighten the drama of the scene. Awestruck children crowd close to the tiny orbs representing the planets within the arcing bands symbolizing their orbits. An earnest listener makes notes, while the lone woman seated at the left and the two gentlemen at the right pay rapt attention. Scientific knowledge mesmerizes everyone in Wright's painting. The artist visually reinforced the fascination with the orrery by composing his image in a circular fashion, echoing the device's orbital design. The postures and gazes of all the participants and observers focus attention on the cosmic model. Wright scrupulously and accurately rendered every detail of the figures, the mechanisms of the orrery, and even the books and curtain in the shadowy background.

Wright's choice of subjects and realism in depicting them appealed to the great industrialists of his day, including Josiah Wedgwood (1730–1795), who pioneered many techniques of mass-produced pottery, and Sir Richard Arkwright (1732–1792), whose spinning frame revolutionized the textile industry. Both men often purchased paintings by Wright featuring scientific advances. To them, the Derby artist's elevation of the theories and inventions of the Industrial Revolution to the plane of history painting was exciting and appropriately in tune with the new era of Enlightenment.

A CENTURY OF REVOLUTIONS

In 1700, Louis XIV still ruled France as the Sun King (see Chapter 20), presiding over his realm and French culture from his palatial residence at Versailles (FIG. 20-26). The French king's palace inspired the construction of many other

21-1A VANBRUGH and HAWKSMOOR, Blenheim Palace, 1705–1725.

grandiose homes on the Continent and across the English Channel during the early 18th century, including Blenheim Palace (FIG. 21-1A), which SIR JOHN VANBRUGH (1664–1726) and NICHOLAS HAWKSMOOR (1661–1736) designed for the duke of Marlborough. By 1800, however, revolutions had overthrown the monarchy in France and achieved independence for the British colonies in America (MAP 21-1). The 18th century also gave birth to a revolution of a different kind—the Industrial Revolution, which began in England and soon transformed the economies of continental Europe and North America and eventually the world.

Against this backdrop of revolutionary change, social as well as political, economic, and technological, came major transformations in the arts. Compare, for example, Antoine Watteau's *Pilgrimage to Cythera* (FIG. 21-7), painted 1717–1719, which unfolds in a lush landscape and celebrates the romantic dalliances of the moneyed elite, with Jacques-Louis David's 1784 *Oath of the Horatii* (FIG. 21-25), set in an austere Doric hall and glorifying the civic virtue and heroism of an ancient Roman family. The two works have little in common other than both are French oil paintings. In the 18th century, shifts in style and subject matter were both rapid and significant.

ROCOCO

The death of Louis XIV in 1715 brought many changes in French high society. The elite quickly abandoned the court of Versailles for the pleasures of town life. Although French citizens still owed allegiance to a monarch, the early 18th century brought a resurgence of aristocratic social, political, and economic power. Members of the nobility not only exercised their traditional privileges (for example, exemption from certain taxes and from forced labor on public works) but also sought to expand their power. In the cultural realm, aristocrats reestablished their predominance as art patrons.

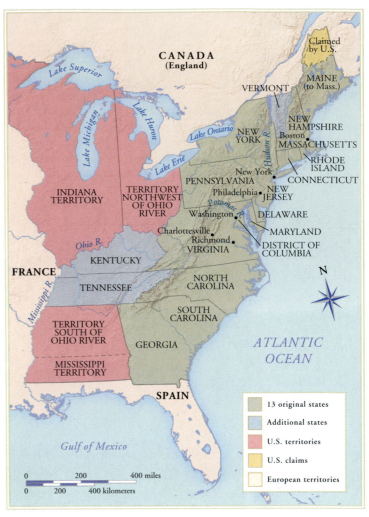

MAP 21-1 The United States in 1800.

The *hôtels* (townhouses) of Paris soon became the centers of a new, softer style called *Rococo*. Associated with the regency (1715–1723) following the death of Louis XIV and with the reign of Louis XV (r. 1723–1774), the Rococo style in art and architecture was the perfect expression of the lighthearted elegance the wealthy cultivated in their opulent homes (see "Femmes Savants and Salon Culture," page 617).

ROCOCO TO NEOCLASSICISM:
THE 18TH CENTURY IN EUROPE AND AMERICA

1700	1725	1750	1775	1800

- The Rococo style becomes the rage in the opulent townhouses of Paris
- Watteau creates a new painting genre—the *fête galante*

- Neumann adapts the intimate Rococo domestic style to ecclesiastical architecture
- Chardin rejects the frivolity of Rococo painting in favor of "natural" art
- Canaletto paints views of Venice as souvenirs of the Grand Tour of Italy

- The Enlightenment admiration for Greece and Rome prompts a Neoclassical revival in architecture
- During the Industrial Revolution, Wright celebrates scientific advances in dramatically lit paintings
- First use of iron in bridge construction at Coalbrookdale, England

- Reynolds achieves renown for Grand Manner portraits
- Vigée-Lebrun and Labille-Guiard gain admission to the French Royal Academy of Painting and Sculpture
- David becomes the painter-ideologist of the French Revolution
- Jefferson promotes Neoclassicism as the official architectural style of the new American republic

Femmes Savants and Salon Culture

The feminine look of the Rococo style suggests the taste and social initiative of women, and to a large extent, women dominated the cultural sphere during the Rococo age. In the 18th century, aristocratic women—including Madame de Pompadour (1721–1764), mistress of Louis XV of France; Maria Theresa (1717–1780), archduchess of Austria and queen of Hungary and Bohemia; and Empresses Elizabeth (r. 1741–1762) and Catherine the Great (r. 1762–1796) of Russia—held some of the most influential positions in Europe. Female taste also was a defining factor in numerous smaller courts as well as in the private sphere.

In the early 1700s, Paris was the social capital of Europe, and the Rococo salon (FIG. 21-2) was the center of Parisian society. Wealthy, ambitious, and clever society hostesses competed to attract the most famous and accomplished people to their salons. The medium of social intercourse was conversation spiced with wit, repartee as quick and deft as a fencing match. Artifice reigned supreme, and participants considered enthusiasm or sincerity in bad taste.

The women who hosted these salons, whether in Paris or elsewhere in Europe (FIG. 21-3), referred to themselves as *femmes savants*—learned women. Chief among them was Julie de Lespinasse (1732–1776), one of the most articulate, urbane, and intelligent French women of the time. She held daily salons from five o'clock until nine in the evening. The memoirs of Jean François Marmontel (1723–1799), published in 1827, documented the liveliness of these gatherings and the remarkable nature of this hostess.

21-2 GERMAIN BOFFRAND, Salon de la Princesse, with paintings by CHARLES-JOSEPH NATOIRE and sculptures by JEAN-BAPTISTE LEMOYNE, Hôtel de Soubise, Paris, France, 1737–1740.

Rococo rooms such as this one, featuring sinuous curves, gilded moldings and mirrors, small sculptures and paintings, and floral ornamentation, were the center of Parisian social and intellectual life.

The circle was formed of persons who were not bound together. She [Julie de Lespinasse] had taken them here and there in society, but so well assorted were they that once [in her salon] they fell into harmony like the strings of an instrument touched by an able hand. Following out that comparison, I may say that she played the instrument with an art that came of genius; she seemed to know what tone each string would yield before she touched it; I mean to say that our minds and our natures were so well known to her that in order to bring them into play she had but to say a word. Nowhere was conversation more lively, more brilliant, or better regulated than at her house. It was a rare phenomenon indeed, the degree of tempered, equable heat which she knew so well how to maintain, sometimes by moderating it, sometimes by quickening it. The continual activity of her soul was communicated to our souls, but measurably; her imagination was the mainspring, her reason the regulator. Remark that the brains she stirred at will were neither feeble nor frivolous. . . . Her talent for casting out a thought and giving it for discussion to men of that class, her own talent in discussing it with precision, sometimes with eloquence, her talent for bringing forward new ideas and varying the topic— always with the facility and ease of a fairy . . . these talents, I say, were not those of an ordinary woman. It was not with the follies of fashion and vanity that daily, during four hours of conversation, without languor and without vacuum, she knew how to make herself interesting to a wide circle of strong minds.*

*Jean François Marmontel, *Memoirs of Marmontel* (1827), translated by Brigit Patmore (London: Routledge, 1930), 270.

Architecture

Rococo appeared in France in about 1700, primarily as a style of interior design. The French Rococo exterior was most often simple, or even plain, but Rococo exuberance took over the interior. The term derived from the French word *rocaille* (pebble), but it referred especially to the small stones and shells used to decorate grotto interiors. Shells or forms resembling shells were the principal motifs in Rococo ornamentation.

SALON DE LA PRINCESSE A typical French Rococo room is the Salon de la Princesse (FIG. **21-2**) in the Hôtel de Soubise in Paris, designed by GERMAIN BOFFRAND (1667–1754) in collaboration with the painter JOSEPH NATOIRE (1700–1777) and the sculptor JEAN-BAPTISTE LEMOYNE (1704–1778). Parisian salons such as this one were the center of Rococo social life. They usurped the role Louis XIV's Versailles palace (FIG. 20-26) played in the 17th century, when the Sun King set the tone for French culture. In the

21-3 François de Cuvilliés, Hall of Mirrors, the Amalienburg, Nymphenburg Palace park, Munich, Germany, early 18th century.

Designed by a French architect, this circular hall in a German lodge displays the Rococo architectural style at its zenith, dazzling the eye with the organic interplay of mirrors, crystal, and stucco relief.

early 18th century, the centralized and grandiose palace-based culture of Baroque France gave way to a much more intimate and decentralized culture based in private homes. The new architectural style mirrored this social and cultural shift. A comparison between the Salon de la Princesse and the Galerie des Glaces (FIG. 20-27) at Versailles reveals how Boffrand softened the strong architectural lines and panels of the earlier style into flexible, sinuous curves luxuriantly multiplied in mirror reflections. The walls melt into the vault. Irregular painted shapes, surmounted by sculpture and separated by the ubiquitous rocaille shells, replace the hall's cornices. Painting, architecture, and sculpture combine to form a single ensemble. The profusion of curving tendrils and sprays of foliage blend with the shell forms to give an effect of freely growing nature, suggesting the designer permanently bedecked the Rococo room for a festival.

French Rococo interiors were lively total works of art. Exquisitely wrought furniture, enchanting small sculptures, ornamented mirror frames, delightful ceramics and silver, small paintings, and decorative *tapestries* complemented the architecture, relief sculptures, and mural paintings. Unfortunately, the Salon de la Princesse has lost most of the moveable furnishings that once contributed so much to its total ambience. Visitors can imagine, however,

how this and similar Rococo rooms—with their alternating gilded moldings, vivacious relief sculptures, and daintily colored ornamentation of flowers and garlands—must have harmonized with the chamber music played in them, with the elaborate costumes of satin and brocade, and with the equally elegant etiquette and sparkling wit of the people who graced them.

AMALIENBURG The French Rococo style quickly spread beyond Paris. The Amalienburg, a small lodge the French architect François de Cuvilliés (1695–1768) built in the park of the Nymphenburg Palace in Munich, is a prime example of Germany's adoption of the Parisian style. The most spectacular room in the lodge is the circular Hall of Mirrors (FIG. **21-3**), a silver-and-blue ensemble of architecture, stucco relief, silvered bronze mirrors, and crystal. The hall dazzles the eye with myriad scintillating motifs, forms, and figurations and showcases the full ornamental repertoire of the Rococo style at its zenith. Silvery light, reflected and amplified by windows and mirrors, bathes the room and creates shapes and contours that weave rhythmically around the upper walls and the ceiling coves. Everything seems organic, growing, and in motion, an ultimate refinement of illusion the architect, artists, and artisans created with virtuoso flourishes.

21-4 BALTHASAR NEUMANN, interior of the pilgrimage church of Vierzehnheiligen (looking east), near Staffelstein, Germany, 1743–1772.

Neumann adapted the intimate Rococo style to ecclesiastical architecture. Vierzehnheiligen's interior is light and delicate in contrast to the dynamic energy of Italian Baroque church designs.

21-5 BALTHASAR NEUMANN, plan of the pilgrimage church of Vierzehnheiligen, near Staffelstein, Germany, 1743–1772.

Vierzehnheiligen's plan features undulating lines and a dynamic composition of tangent ovals and circles. It is even more complex than Borromini's influential church plans (FIGS. 19-10 and 19-13).

21-3A FISCHER VON ERLACH, Karlskirche, Vienna, 1716–1737.

21-5A NEUMANN, Kaisersaal, Würzburg, 1719–1744.

21-5B ZIMMERMANN, Wieskirche, Füssen, 1745–1754.

VIERZEHNHEILIGEN Rococo style was not exclusively a domestic phenomenon, however. Although in the early 18th century, some architects, such as JOHANN BERNHARD FISCHER VON ERLACH (1656–1723), continued to design churches incorporating Baroque and classical elements—for example, Karlskirche (FIG. **21-3A**) in Vienna—others eagerly adopted the Rococo style for ecclesiastical architecture. One of the most splendid examples is the pilgrimage church of Vierzehnheiligen (Fourteen Saints; FIGS. **21-4** and **21-5**) near Staffelstein (MAP 20-1), which the German architect BALTHASAR NEUMANN (1687–1753) began as construction was about to be concluded on the grandiose palace (FIG. **21-5A**) he had designed in 1719 for the prince-bishops of Würzburg. The interior (FIG. 21-4) of Neumann's church exhibits a vivacious play of architectural fantasy that retains the dynamic energy of Italian Baroque architecture (see Chapter 19) but not its drama. Numerous large windows in the richly decorated walls of Vierzehnheiligen flood the interior with an even, bright, and cheerful light. The feeling is one of lightness and delicacy.

Vierzehnheiligen's plan (FIG. 21-5) reveals the influence of Francesco Borromini (FIGS. 19-10 and 19-13), as does the contemporaneous Wieskirche (Church of the Meadow; FIG. **21-5B**) by DOMINIKUS ZIMMERMANN (1685–1766). The Staffelstein plan, however, is even more complex than the plans for Borromini's churches in Rome. Neumann, perhaps deliberately, banished all straight lines. The composition, made up of tangent ovals and circles, achieves a quite different interior effect within the essential outlines of a traditional rectilinear basilican church with a nave, transept, and apse. Undulating space is in continuous motion, creating unlimited vistas bewildering in their variety and surprise effects. The structure's features pulse, flow, and commingle as if they were ceaselessly in the process of being molded. The design's fluidity of line, the floating and hovering surfaces, the interwoven spaces, and the dematerialized masses combine to suggest a "frozen" counterpart to the intricacy of voices in a Baroque fugue by Johann Sebastian Bach (1685–1750). The church is a brilliant ensemble of architecture, painting, sculpture, and music that dissolves the boundaries among the arts.

Painting and Sculpture

The unification of diverse artistic media that characterizes the Rococo style did not preclude the rise to prominence of painters of independent works. Chief among them were Antoine Watteau, François Boucher, and Jean-Honoré Fragonard in France.

ANTOINE WATTEAU The painter whom scholars most closely associate with French Rococo is ANTOINE WATTEAU (1684–1721). The sharp differences between the Rococo and Baroque ages in France quickly become evident by contrasting Watteau's *L'Indifférent* (*The Indifferent One;* FIG. 21-6) with Rigaud's portrait of Louis XIV (FIG. 20-24). Rigaud portrayed pompous majesty in supreme glory, as if the French monarch were reviewing throngs of bowing courtiers at Versailles. Watteau's painting is more delicate and lighter in both color and tone. The artist presented a languid, gliding dancer whose stilted minuet might constitute a parody of the monarch's solemnity if the paintings were hung together. (The contrast in scale would be equally stark: The portrait of Louis XIV is almost 10 feet tall. Watteau's dancer is 10 inches tall.) In Rigaud's portrait, stout architecture, bannerlike curtains, flowing ermine, and fleur-de-lis exalt the king. In Watteau's painting, the dancer moves in a rainbow shimmer of color, emerging onto the stage of the intimate comic opera to the silken sounds of strings. As in architecture, this contrast of paintings also highlights the shift in artistic patronage from one era to the next.

21-6 ANTOINE WATTEAU, *L'Indifférent,* ca. 1716. Oil on canvas, 10″ × 7″. Musée du Louvre, Paris. ◼◀

This small Rococo painting of a dancer exhibits lightness and delicacy in both color and tone. It differs significantly from Rigaud's majestic portrait (FIG. 20-24) of the pompous Louis XIV.

1 in.

21-7 ANTOINE WATTEAU, *Pilgrimage to Cythera,* 1717. Oil on canvas, 4′ 3″ × 6′ 4½″. Musée du Louvre, Paris. ◼◀

Watteau's *fête galante* paintings depict the outdoor amusements of French upper-class society. The haze of color, subtly modeled shapes, gliding motion, and air of suave gentility match Rococo taste.

1 ft.

Whereas royal patronage, particularly on the part of Louis XIV, dominated the French Baroque period, Rococo was the culture of a wider aristocracy in which private patrons dictated taste.

PILGRIMAGE TO CYTHERA Watteau was largely responsible for creating a specific type of Rococo painting, called a *fête galante* (amorous festival) painting. These paintings depicted the outdoor entertainment or amusements of French high society. The premier example of a fête galante painting is Watteau's masterpiece (painted in two versions), *Pilgrimage to Cythera* (FIG. **21-7**). The painting was the artist's entry for admission to the French Royal Academy of Painting and Sculpture (see "Academic Salons," Chapter 23, page 690). In 1717 the fête galante was not an acceptable category for submission, but rather than reject Watteau's candidacy, the academy created a new category to accommodate his entry. At the turn of the 18th century, two competing doctrines sharply divided the membership of the French academy. Many members followed Nicolas Poussin in teaching that form was the most important element in painting, whereas "colors in painting are as allurements for persuading the eyes."[1] Colors were additions for effect and not really essential. The other group took Rubens as its model and proclaimed the natural supremacy of color and the coloristic style as the artist's proper guide. Depending on which doctrine they supported, academy members were either *Poussinistes* or *Rubénistes*. Watteau was Flemish and Rubens's coloristic style heavily influenced his work. With Watteau in their ranks, the Rubénistes carried the day, establishing Rococo painting as the preferred style of the early 18th century.

Watteau's *Pilgrimage to Cythera* (FIG. 21-7) presents luxuriously costumed lovers who have made a "pilgrimage" to Cythera, the island of eternal youth and love, sacred to Aphrodite. (Some art historians think the lovers are returning from Cythera rather than having just arrived. Watteau provided few clues to settle the question definitively.) The elegant figures move gracefully from the protective shade of a woodland park, filled with amorous cupids and voluptuous statuary. Watteau's figural poses blend elegance and sweetness. He composed his generally quite small paintings from albums of drawings in which he sought to capture slow movement from difficult and unusual angles, searching for the smoothest, most poised, and most refined attitudes. As he experimented with nuances of posture and movement, Watteau also strove for the most exquisite shades of color difference, defining in a single stroke the shimmer of silk at a bent knee or the iridescence that touches a glossy surface as it emerges from shadow. The haze of color, the subtly modeled shapes, the gliding motion, and the air of suave gentility appealed greatly to Watteau's wealthy patrons, whom, as he was dying from tuberculosis, he still depicted as carefree and at leisure in his most unusual painting, *Signboard of Gersaint* (FIG. **21-7A**).

21-7A WATTEAU, *Signboard of Gersaint*, 1721.

FRANÇOIS BOUCHER After Watteau's death at age 36 brought his brilliant career to a premature end, FRANÇOIS BOUCHER (1703–1770) rose to the dominant position in French painting, in large part because he was Madame de Pompadour's favorite artist. Although Boucher was an excellent portraitist,

his success rested primarily on his graceful canvases depicting Arcadian shepherds, nymphs, and goddesses cavorting in shady glens engulfed in pink and sky-blue light. *Cupid a Captive* (FIG. **21-8**) presents a rosy pyramid of infant and female flesh set off against a cool, leafy background, with fluttering draperies both hiding and revealing the nudity of the figures. Boucher used the full range of Italian

21-8 FRANÇOIS BOUCHER, *Cupid a Captive*, 1754. Oil on canvas, 5′ 6″ × 2′ 10″. Wallace Collection, London. ◼◄

Boucher was Madame de Pompadour's favorite artist. In this Rococo tableau, he painted a pyramid of rosy infant and female flesh and fluttering draperies set off against a cool, leafy background.

1 ft.

Rococo   **621**

and French Baroque devices—the dynamic play of crisscrossing diagonals, curvilinear forms, and slanting recessions—to create his masterly composition. But he dissected powerful Baroque curves into a multiplicity of decorative flourishes, dissipating Baroque drama into sensual playfulness. Lively and lighthearted, Boucher's artful Rococo fantasies became mirrors for his affluent French patrons to behold the ornamental reflections of their cherished pastimes.

JEAN-HONORÉ FRAGONARD Boucher's greatest student, JEAN-HONORÉ FRAGONARD (1732–1806), was a first-rate colorist whose decorative skill almost surpassed his master's. An example of his manner can stand as characteristic not only of his work but also of the later Rococo in general. In *The Swing* (FIG. **21-9**), a young gentleman has convinced an unsuspecting old bishop to swing the young man's pretty sweetheart higher and higher, while her lover (and the work's patron), in the lower left corner, stretches out to admire her ardently from a strategic position on the ground. The young lady flirtatiously and boldly kicks off her shoe toward the little statue of Cupid. The infant love god holds his finger to his lips. The landscape emulates Watteau's—a luxuriant perfumed bower in

21-9 JEAN-HONORÉ FRAGONARD, *The Swing*, 1766. Oil on canvas, 2′ 8⅝″ × 2′ 2″. Wallace Collection, London. ◼◖

Fragonard's *Swing* epitomizes Rococo style. Pastel colors and soft light complement a scene in which a young lady flirtatiously kicks off her shoe at a statue of Cupid while her lover watches.

1 ft.

10 ft.

21-10 GIAMBATTISTA TIEPOLO, *Apotheosis of the Pisani Family,* ceiling painting in the Villa Pisani, Stra, Italy, 1761–1762. Fresco, 77′ 1″ × 44′ 3″.

A master of illusionistic ceiling painting in the Baroque tradition, Tiepolo adopted the bright and cheerful colors and weightless figures of Rococo easel paintings for huge frescoes.

1 in.

21-11 CLODION, *Nymph and Satyr Carousing,* ca. 1780–1790. Terracotta, 1′ 11¼″ high. Metropolitan Museum of Art, New York (bequest of Benjamin Altman, 1913).

The erotic playfulness of Boucher and Fragonard is evident in Clodion's tabletop terracotta sculptures representing sensuous fantasies often involving satyrs and nymphs, the followers of Bacchus.

a park that very much resembles a stage scene for comic opera. The glowing pastel colors and soft light convey, almost by themselves, the theme's sensuality.

GIAMBATTISTA TIEPOLO *The Swing* is less than 3 feet in height and Watteau's *L'Indifférent* (FIG. 21-6), as already noted, barely 10 inches tall. But the intimate Rococo style could also be adapted for paintings of huge size, as the work of GIAMBATTISTA TIEPOLO (1696–1770) demonstrates. A Venetian, Tiepolo worked for patrons in Austria, Germany, and Spain, as well as in Italy. He was a master of illusionistic ceiling decoration in the Baroque tradition, but favored the bright, cheerful colors and relaxed compositions of Rococo easel paintings. In *Apotheosis of the Pisani Family* (FIG. 21-10), a ceiling fresco in the Villa Pisani at Stra in northern Italy (MAP 20-1), Tiepolo depicted seemingly weightless figures fluttering through vast sunlit skies and fleecy clouds, their forms casting dark accents

against the brilliant light of high noon. The painter elevated Pisani family members to the rank of gods in a heavenly scene recalling the ceiling paintings of Pozzo (FIG. 19-24). But while retaining 17th-century illusionism in his works, Tiepolo softened the rhetoric and created pictorial schemes of great elegance and grace, unsurpassed for their sheer effectiveness as decor.

CLODION Rococo was nonetheless a style best suited for small-scale works projecting a mood of sensual intimacy. Claude Michel, called CLODION (1738–1814), specialized in small, lively sculptures representing sensuous Rococo fantasies. Clodion lived and worked in Rome for several years after winning a cherished Prix de Rome (Rome Prize) from the French royal academy to study art and paint or sculpt in the eternal city. Clodion's work incorporates echoes of Italian Mannerist sculpture. His small group, *Nymph and Satyr Carousing* (FIG. 21-11), depicts two followers of Bacchus, the Roman god of wine. The sensuous nymph who rushes to pour wine from a cup into the open mouth of a semihuman goat-legged satyr is reminiscent of the nude female figures of Benvenuto Cellini (FIGS. 17-52 and 17-52A), who worked at Fontainebleau for Francis I, and of Giovanni da Bologna (FIG. 17-53), a French Mannerist sculptor who moved to Italy. The erotic playfulness of Boucher and Fragonard is also evident in Clodion's 2-foot-tall terracotta group destined for display on a marble tabletop in an elegant Rococo salon.

THE ENLIGHTENMENT

The aristocratic culture celebrated in Rococo art did not go unchallenged during the 18th century. Indeed, the feudal system that served as the foundation of social and economic life in Europe dissolved, and the rigid social hierarchies that provided the basis for Rococo art and patronage relaxed. By the end of the 18th century, revolutions had erupted in France and America. A major factor in these political, social, and economic changes was the Enlightenment.

Philosophy and Science

Enlightenment thinkers championed an approach to the acquisition of knowledge based on empirical observation and scientific experimentation (see "Art and Science in the Era of Enlightenment," page 615). Enlightenment-era science had roots in the work of René Descartes (1596–1650), Blaise Pascal (1623–1662), Isaac Newton (1642–1727), and Gottfried Wilhelm von Leibnitz (1646–1716) in the 17th century. England and France were the principal centers of the Enlightenment, though its dictums influenced the thinking of intellectuals throughout Europe and in the American colonies. Benjamin Franklin (1706–1790), Thomas Jefferson (1743–1826), and other American notables embraced its principles.

NEWTON AND LOCKE Of particular importance for Enlightenment thought was the work of Isaac Newton and John Locke (1632–1704) in England. In his scientific studies, Newton insisted on empirical proof of his theories and encouraged others to avoid metaphysics and the supernatural—realms that extended beyond the natural physical world. This emphasis on both tangible data and concrete experience became a cornerstone of Enlightenment thought. In addition, Newton's experiments revealed rationality in the physical world, and Enlightenment thinkers transferred that concept to the sociopolitical world by promoting a rationally organized society. Locke, whose works acquired the status of Enlightenment gospel, developed these ideas further. According to Locke's "doctrine of empiricism," knowledge comes through sensory perception of the material world. From these perceptions alone people form ideas. Locke asserted human beings are born good, not cursed by original sin. The laws of nature grant them the natural rights of life, liberty, and property as well as the right to freedom of conscience. Government is by contract, and its purpose is to protect these rights. If and when government abuses these rights, the citizenry has the further natural right of revolution. Locke's ideas empowered people to take control of their own destinies.

PHILOSOPHES The work of Newton and Locke also inspired many French intellectuals, or *philosophes*. These thinkers conceived of individuals and societies at large as parts of physical nature. They shared the conviction the ills of humanity could be remedied by applying reason and common sense to human problems. They criticized the powers of church and state as irrational limits placed on political and intellectual freedom. They believed by accumulating and propagating knowledge, humanity could advance by degrees to a happier state than it had ever known. This conviction matured into the "doctrine of progress" and its corollary doctrine, the "perfectibility of humankind." Previous societies, for the most part, perceived the future as inevitable—the cycle of life and death. They believed religious beliefs determined fate. The notion of progress—the systematic and planned improvement of society—first developed during the 18th century and continues to influence 21st-century thought.

DIDEROT Animated by their belief in human progress and perfectibility, the philosophes took on the task of gathering knowledge and making it accessible to all who could read. Their program was, in effect, the democratization of knowledge. Denis Diderot (1713–1784) greatly influenced the Enlightenment's rationalistic and materialistic thinking. He became editor of the pioneering *Encyclopédie*, a compilation of articles written by more than a hundred contributors, including all the leading philosophes. The *Encyclopédie* was truly comprehensive (its formal title was *Systematic Dictionary of the Sciences, Arts, and Crafts*) and included all available knowledge—historical, scientific, and technical as well as religious and moral—and political theory. The first volume appeared in 1751 and the last of the 35 volumes of text and illustrations in 1780. Other Enlightenment authors produced different compilations of knowledge. Diderot's contemporary, Georges-Louis Leclerc (1707–1788), Comte de Buffon, undertook a kind of encyclopedia of the natural sciences. His *Natural History*, a monumental work of 44 volumes, was especially valuable for its zoological study. Buffon's contemporary, the Swedish botanist Carolus Linnaeus (1707–1778), established a system of plant classification.

The political, economic, and social consequences of this increase in knowledge and the doctrine of progress were explosive. It is no coincidence the French Revolution, the American Revolution, and the Industrial Revolution in England all occurred during this period. These upheavals precipitated yet other major changes, including the growth of cities and of an urban working class, and the expansion of colonialism as the demand for cheap labor and raw materials increased. This enthusiasm for growth gave birth to the doctrine of Manifest Destiny—the ideological justification for continued territorial expansion. Thus, the Age of Enlightenment ushered in a new way of thinking and affected historical developments worldwide.

VOLTAIRE François Marie Arouet, better known as Voltaire (1694–1778), was the most representative figure—almost the personification—of the Enlightenment spirit. Voltaire was instrumental in introducing Newton and Locke to the French intelligentsia. He hated, and attacked through his writings, the arbitrary despotic rule of kings, the selfish privileges of the nobility and the church, religious intolerance, and, above all, the injustice of the French *ancien regime* (the "old order"). In his numerous books and pamphlets, which the authorities regularly condemned and burned, he protested against government persecution of the freedoms of thought and religion. Voltaire believed humankind could never be happy until an enlightened society removed the traditional obstructions to the progress of the human mind. His personal and public involvement in the struggle against established political and religious authority gave authenticity to his ideas. Voltaire persuaded a whole generation that fundamental changes were necessary, paving the way for a revolution in France he never intended and probably would never have approved. Voltaire did not believe "all men are created equal," the credo of Jean-Jacques Rousseau, Thomas Jefferson, and the American Declaration of Independence.

INDUSTRIAL REVOLUTION The Enlightenment emphasis on scientific investigation and technological invention opened up new possibilities for human understanding of the world and for control of its material forces. Research into the phenomena of electricity and combustion, along with the discovery of oxygen and the power of steam, had enormous consequences. Steam power as an adjunct to, or replacement for, human labor initiated a new era in world history, beginning with the Industrial Revolution in England. These and other technological advances—admiringly recorded in the paintings of Joseph Wright of Derby (FIGS. 21-1 and **21-11A**)—epitomized the Enlightenment notion of progress and gave birth to the Industrial Revolution. Most scholars mark the dawn of that technological revolution in the 1740s with the invention of steam engines in England for industrial production. By 1850, England could boast the world's first manufacturing economy. Within a century, the harnessed power of steam, coal, oil, iron, steel, and electricity working in concert transformed Europe. These scientific and technological advances also affected the arts, particularly through the invention of photography (see Chapter 22) and the use of new materials for constructing buildings.

COALBROOKDALE BRIDGE The first use of iron in bridge design was in the cast-iron bridge (FIG. 21-12) built over the Severn River, near Coalbrookdale in England (MAP 25-1), where ABRAHAM DARBY III (1750–1789), one of the bridge's two designers, ran his family's cast-iron business. The Darby family had spearheaded the evolution of the iron industry in England, and they vigorously supported the investigation of new uses for the material. The fabrication of cast-iron rails and bridge elements inspired Darby to work with architect THOMAS F. PRITCHARD (1723–1777) in designing the Coalbrookdale Bridge. The cast-iron armature supporting the roadbed springs from stone pier to stone pier until it leaps the final 100 feet across the Severn River gorge. The style of

the graceful center arc echoes the grand arches of Roman aqueducts (FIG. 7-33). At the same time, the exposed structure of the bridge's cast-iron parts prefigured the skeletal use of iron and steel in the 19th century, when exposed structural armatures became expressive factors in the design of buildings such as the Crystal Palace (FIG. 22-47) in England and the Eiffel Tower (FIG. 23-38) in France.

ROUSSEAU The second key figure of the French Enlightenment, who was also instrumental in preparing the way ideologically for the French Revolution, was Jean-Jacques Rousseau (1712–1778). Voltaire believed the salvation of humanity lay in the advancement of science and the rational improvement of society. In contrast, Rousseau argued the arts, sciences, society, and civilization in general had corrupted "natural man"—people in their primitive state. He was convinced humanity's only salvation lay in a return to something like "the ignorance, innocence and happiness" of its original condition. According to Rousseau, human capacity for feeling, sensibility, and emotions came before reason: "To exist is to feel; our feeling is undoubtedly earlier than our intelligence, and we had feelings before we had ideas." Nature alone must be the guide: "All our natural inclinations are right." Fundamental to Rousseau's thinking was the notion "Man by nature is good . . . he is depraved and perverted by society." He rejected the idea of progress, insisting "Our minds have been corrupted in proportion as the arts and sciences have improved."[2] Rousseau's elevation of feelings above reason as the most primitive—and hence the most "natural"—of human expressions led him to exalt as the ideal the peasant's simple life, with its honest and unsullied emotions.

21-12 ABRAHAM DARBY III and THOMAS F. PRITCHARD, iron bridge (looking northwest), Coalbrookdale, England, 1776–1779.

The first use of iron in bridge design was in this bridge over the Severn River. The Industrial Revolution brought engineering advances and new materials that revolutionized architectural construction.

Diderot on Chardin and Boucher

Denis Diderot was a pioneer in the field of art criticism as well as in the encyclopedic compilation of human knowledge. Between 1759 and 1781, he contributed reviews of the biennial Salon of the French Royal Academy of Painting and Sculpture (see "Academic Salons," Chapter 23, page 690) to the Parisian journal *Correspondence littéraire*. In his review of the 1763 Salon, Diderot had the following praise for Chardin's still lifes and for naturalism in painting.

There are many small pictures by Chardin at the Salon, almost all of them depicting fruit with the accoutrements for a meal. This is nature itself. The objects stand out from the canvas and they are so real that my eyes are fooled by them. . . . In order to look at other people's paintings, I feel as though I need different eyes; but to look at Chardin's, I need only keep the ones nature gave me and use them properly. If I had painting in mind as a career for my child, I'd buy this one [and have him copy it]. . . . Yet nature itself may be no more difficult to copy. . . . O Chardin, it's not white, red or black pigment that you grind on your palette but rather the very substance of objects; it's real air and light that you take onto the tip of your brush and transfer onto the canvas. . . . It's magic, one can't understand how it's done: thick layers of colour, applied one on top of the other, each one filtering through from underneath to create the effect. . . . Close up, everything blurs, goes flat and disappears. From a distance, everything comes back to life and reappears.*

Diderot could write scathing reviews as well as lavish praise on the leading artists of his day. He admired Chardin (FIG. 21-13) because his work was the antithesis of the Rococo manner in painting, which Diderot deplored. Here, for example, is what Diderot had to say about François Boucher (FIG. 21-8), who also exhibited in the Salon of 1763, and his younger protégés emulating his Rococo style:

What a misuse of talent! How much time gone to waste! You could have had twice the effect for half the effort. . . . When one writes, does one have to write everything? And when one paints, does one have to paint everything? . . . This man is the ruination of all young

21-13 JEAN-BAPTISTE-SIMÉON CHARDIN, *Saying Grace*, 1740. Oil on canvas, 1' 7" × 1' 3". Musée du Louvre, Paris.

Chardin embraced naturalism and celebrated the simple goodness of ordinary people, especially mothers and children, who lived in a world far from the frivolous Rococo salons of Paris.

1 in.

apprentice painters. Barely able to handle a brush and hold a palette, they torture themselves stringing together infantile garlands, painting chubby crimson bottoms, and hurl themselves headlong into all kinds of follies which cannot be redeemed by originality, fire, tenderness nor by any magic in their models. For they lack all of these.†

*Translated by Kate Tunstall, in Charles Harrison, Paul Wood, and Jason Gaiger, eds., *Art in Theory 1648–1815: An Anthology of Changing Ideas* (Oxford: Blackwell, 2000), 604.
†Ibid., 603–604.

"NATURAL" ART

Rousseau's views, popular and widely read, were largely responsible for the turning away from the Rococo sensibility in the arts and the formation of a taste for the "natural," as opposed to the artificial and frivolous.

CHARDIN Reflecting Rousseau's values, JEAN-BAPTISTE-SIMÉON CHARDIN (1699–1779) painted quiet scenes of domestic life, which offered the opportunity to praise the simple goodness of ordinary people, especially mothers and young children, who in spirit, occupation, and environment lived far from corrupt society. In

Saying Grace (FIG. **21-13**), Chardin ushers the viewer into a modest room where a mother and her two daughters are about to dine. The mood of quiet attention is at one with the hushed lighting and mellow color and with the closely studied still-life accessories whose worn surfaces tell their own humble domestic history. The viewer witnesses a moment of social instruction, when mother and older sister supervise the younger sister in the simple, pious ritual of giving thanks to God before a meal. The simplicity of the composition reinforces the subdued charm of this scene, with the three figures highlighted against the dark background. Chardin was the poet of the commonplace and the master of its nuances. A gentle sentiment

21-14 Jean-Baptiste Greuze, *Village Bride*, 1761. Oil on canvas, 3′ × 3′ 10½″. Musée du Louvre, Paris.

Greuze was a master of sentimental narrative, which appealed to a new audience that admired "natural" virtue. Here, in an unadorned room, a father blesses his daughter and her husband-to-be.

prevails in all his pictures, an emotion not contrived and artificial but born of the painter's honesty, insight, and sympathy. Chardin's paintings had wide appeal, even in unexpected places. Louis XV, the royal personification of the Rococo in his life and tastes, once owned *Saying Grace*. The painter was also a favorite of Diderot, the leading art critic of the day as well as the editor of the *Encyclopédie* (see "Diderot on Chardin and Boucher," page 626).

JEAN-BAPTISTE GREUZE The sentimental narrative in art became the specialty of French artist JEAN-BAPTISTE GREUZE (1725–1805), whose most popular work, *Village Bride* (FIG. **21-14**), sums up the characteristics of the genre. The setting is an unadorned room in a rustic dwelling. In a notary's presence, the elderly father has passed his daughter's dowry to her youthful husband-to-be and blesses the pair, who gently take each other's arms. The old mother tearfully gives her daughter's arm a farewell caress, while the youngest sister melts in tears on the shoulder of the demure bride. An envious older sister broods behind her father's chair. Rosy-faced, healthy children play around the scene. The picture's story is simple—the happy climax of a rural romance. The picture's moral is just as clear—happiness is the reward of "natural" virtue.

Greuze produced this work at a time when the audience for art was expanding. The strict social hierarchy that provided the foundation for Rococo art and patronage gave way to a bourgeois economic and social system. The newly important bourgeois class embraced art, and paintings such as *Village Bride* particularly appealed to ordinary hard-working people. They carefully analyzed each gesture and each nuance of sentiment and reacted with tumultuous enthusiasm. At the 1761 Salon of the Royal Academy, Greuze's picture received enormous attention. Diderot, who reviewed the exhibition for *Correspondence littéraire,* reported it was difficult to get near the canvas because of the throngs of admirers.

ÉLISABETH-LOUISE VIGÉE-LEBRUN Another manifestation of the "naturalistic" impulse in 18th-century French art was the emergence of a new mode of portraiture exemplified by *Self-Portrait* (FIG. **21-15**) by ÉLISABETH-LOUISE VIGÉE-LEBRUN (1755–1842). The painter looks directly at viewers and pauses in her work to return their gaze. Although her mood is lighthearted and her costume's details echo the serpentine curve Rococo artists and wealthy patrons loved, nothing about Vigée-Lebrun's pose or her mood speaks of Rococo frivolity. Hers is the self-confident stance of a woman whose art has won her an independent role in society. She

21-15 Élisabeth-Louise Vigée-Lebrun, *Self-Portrait*, 1790. Oil on canvas, 8′ 4″ × 6′ 9″. Galleria degli Uffizi, Florence.

Vigée-Lebrun was one of the few women admitted to the Royal Academy of Painting and Sculpture. In this self-portrait, she depicted herself confidently painting the likeness of Queen Marie Antoinette.

21-15A VIGÉE-LEBRUN, *Marie Antoinette,* 1787.

portrayed herself in a close-up, intimate view at work on one of the many portraits (for example, FIG. **21-15A**) she painted of her most important patron, Queen Marie Antoinette (1755–1793). Like many of her contemporaries, Vigée-Lebrun lived a life of extraordinary personal and economic independence, working for the nobility throughout Europe. She was famous for the force and grace of her portraits, especially those of highborn ladies and royalty. She was successful during the age of the late monarchy in France and was one of the few women admitted to the Royal Academy of Painting and Sculpture. After the French Revolution, however, the academy rescinded her membership, because women were no longer welcome, but she enjoyed continued success owing to her talent, wit, and ability to forge connections with those in power in the postrevolutionary period.

ADÉLAÏDE LABILLE-GUIARD Six years older than Vigée-Lebrun, ADÉLAÏDE LABILLE-GUIARD (1749–1803) was the second-most important woman painter in Paris at the end of the 18th century, but she never achieved the renown enjoyed by her younger rival. She trained with François-Élie Vincent (1708–1790) and later with his son François-André Vincent (1746–1816), whom she married after her divorce from her first husband, Louis-Nicolas Guiard, a clerk. Like Vigée-Lebrun, Labille-Guiard boasted royal patronage but not of the same order. She became the official painter of the "mesdames"—the aunts of King Louis XVI—in 1787, four years after she was admitted to the royal painting academy on the same day as Vigée-Lebrun. The two painters captured the remaining two of four memberships reserved for women, a quota Labille-Guiard worked hard to lift after gaining admission. The two artists took opposite sides during the French Revolution, and Labille-Guiard painted portraits of some of the uprising's leaders, including one of the few known portraits of Maximilien Robespierre (1758–1794), the most prominent figure calling for the death of King Louis XVI.

A comparison between Labille-Guiard's *Self-Portrait with Two Pupils* (FIG. **21-16**) and Vigée-Lebrun's *Self-Portrait* (FIG. 21-15) underscores the two women's different self-images. The younger painter presented herself at work on a portrait of her most important patron, Marie Antoinette. The subject of the canvas Labille-Guiard is painting is unknown. Her self-portrait focuses instead on her role as a teacher. She had as many as nine women in her studio at one time. Here, two apprentices—dressed more simply than their elegantly clad instructor—cluster behind her, one intently studying the painting in progress, the other, as Labille-Guiard, gazing at the viewer. The three figures form a classical pyramidal composition, echoed by the easel. In the V formed by the two triangles is a portrait bust of the artist's father. Appropriately for this early feminist, her muse is a man, a reversal of the traditional gender roles.

WILLIAM HOGARTH Across the Channel, a truly English style of painting emerged with WILLIAM HOGARTH (1697–1764), who satirized the lifestyle of the newly prosperous middle class with comic zest. Traditionally, the British imported painters from the Continent—Holbein, Rubens, and Van Dyck among them. Hogarth waged a lively campaign throughout his career against the English feeling of dependence on, and inferiority to, these artists. Although Hogarth would have been the last to admit it, his own painting owed much to the work of his contemporaries in France, the Rococo

21-16 ADÉLAÏDE LABILLE-GUIARD, *Self-Portrait with Two Pupils,* 1785. Oil on canvas, 6′ 11″ × 4′ 11½″. Metropolitan Museum of Art, New York (gift of Julia A. Berwind, 1953).

In contrast to Vigée-Lebrun (FIG. 21-15), Labille-Guiard, her older contemporary, depicted herself as a teacher. Her father's bust portrait serves as her muse in a reversal of traditional gender roles.

artists. Yet his subject matter, frequently moral in tone, was distinctively English. This was the great age of English satirical writing, and Hogarth—who admired that literary genre and included Henry Fielding (1701–1754), the author of *Tom Jones,* among his closest friends—clearly saw himself as translating satire into the visual arts.

Hogarth's favorite device was to make a series of narrative paintings and prints, in a sequence similar to chapters in a book or scenes in a play, following a character or group of characters in their encounters with some social evil. *Breakfast Scene* (FIG. **21-17**), from *Marriage à la Mode,* is one in a sequence of six paintings satirizing the marital immoralities of the moneyed classes in England. In it, the marriage of a young viscount is just beginning to founder. The husband and wife are tired after a long night spent in separate pursuits. While the wife stayed at home for an evening of cards and music-making, her young husband had been away from the house for a night of suspicious business. He thrusts his hands deep into the empty money-pockets of his breeches, while his wife's small dog sniffs inquiringly at a woman's lacy cap protruding from his coat pocket. A steward, his hands full of unpaid bills, raises his eyes in despair at the actions of his noble master and mistress. The house is palatial, but Hogarth filled it with witty clues to the dubious taste of

21-17 William Hogarth, *Breakfast Scene,* from *Marriage à la Mode,* ca. 1745. Oil on canvas, 2′ 4″ × 3′. National Gallery, London.

Hogarth won fame for his paintings and prints satirizing English life with comic zest. This is one of a series of six paintings in which he chronicled the marital immoralities of the moneyed class.

its occupants. For example, the row of pious religious paintings on the upper wall of the distant room concludes with a curtained canvas undoubtedly depicting an erotic subject. According to the custom of the day, ladies could not view this discretely hidden painting, but at the pull of a cord, the master and his male guests could enjoy a tableau of cavorting figures. In *Breakfast Scene,* as in all his work, Hogarth proceeded as a novelist might, elaborating on his subject with carefully chosen detail, the discovery of which heightens the comedy.

Hogarth designed the marriage series to be published as a set of engravings. The prints of this and his other moral narratives were so popular that unscrupulous entrepreneurs produced unauthorized versions almost as fast as the artist created his originals. The popularity of these prints speaks not only to the appeal of their subjects but also to the democratization of knowledge and culture the Enlightenment fostered and to the exploitation of new printing technologies that opened the way for a more affordable and widely disseminated visual culture.

THOMAS GAINSBOROUGH

A contrasting blend of "naturalistic" representation and Rococo setting is found in *Mrs. Richard Brinsley Sheridan* (FIG. **21-18**), a characteristic portrait by British painter THOMAS GAINSBOROUGH (1727–1788). Gainsborough presented Mrs. Sheridan as a lovely, informally dressed woman seated in a rustic landscape faintly reminiscent of Watteau (FIG. **21-7**) in its soft-hued light and feathery brushwork. Gainsborough's goal was to match the natural, unspoiled

21-18 Thomas Gainsborough, *Mrs. Richard Brinsley Sheridan,* 1787. Oil on canvas, 7′ 2⅝″ × 5′ 5⅝″. National Gallery of Art, Washington, D.C. (Andrew W. Mellon Collection).

In this life-size portrait, Gainsborough sought to match Mrs. Sheridan's natural beauty with that of the landscape. The rustic setting, soft-hued light, and feathery brushwork recall Rococo painting.

beauty of the landscape with that of his sitter. Mrs. Sheridan's dark brown hair blows freely in the slight wind, and her clear "English complexion" and air of ingenuous sweetness contrast sharply with the pert sophistication of the subjects of Continental Rococo portraits. Gainsborough planned to give the picture a more pastoral air by adding several sheep, but he did not live long enough to complete the canvas. Even without the sheep, the painting clearly expresses Gainsborough's deep interest in the landscape setting. Although he won greater fame in his time for his portraits, he had begun as a landscape painter and always preferred painting scenes of nature to depicting individual likenesses.

JOSHUA REYNOLDS Morality of a more heroic tone than found in the work of Greuze, yet in harmony with "naturalness," included the virtues of honor, valor, and love of country. The Enlightenment concept of "nobility," especially in the view of Rousseau, referred to character, not to aristocratic birth. As the century progressed and people felt the tremors of coming revolutions, the virtues of courage and resolution, patriotism, and self-sacrifice assumed greater importance. Having risen from humble origins, the modern military hero, not the decadent aristocrat, brought the excitement of war into the company of the "natural" emotions.

Sir Joshua Reynolds (1723–1792) specialized in what became known as *Grand Manner portraiture* and often painted likenesses of key participants in the great events of the latter part of the 18th century. Although clearly depicting specific individuals, Grand Manner portraits elevated the sitters by conveying refinement and elegance. Painters communicated a person's grace and class through certain standardized conventions, such as the large scale of the figure relative to the canvas, the controlled pose, the landscape setting, and the low horizon line.

Reynolds painted *Lord Heathfield* (FIG. **21-19**) in 1787. The sitter was a perfect subject for a Grand Manner portrait—a burly, ruddy English officer, the commandant of the fortress at Gibraltar. Heathfield had doggedly defended the British stronghold against the Spanish and French, and later received the honorary title Baron Heathfield of Gibraltar. Here, he holds the huge key to the fortress, the symbol of his victory. He stands in front of a curtain of dark smoke rising from the battleground, flanked by one cannon pointing ineffectively downward and another whose tilted barrel indicates it lies uselessly on its back. Reynolds portrayed the features of the general's heavy, honest face and his uniform with unidealized realism. But Lord Heathfield's posture and the setting dramatically suggest the heroic themes of battle, courage, and patriotism.

BENJAMIN WEST Some American artists also became well known in England. Benjamin West (1738–1820), born in Pennsylvania on what was then the colonial frontier (MAP 21-1), traveled to Europe early in life to study art and then went to England, where he met with almost immediate success. A cofounder of the Royal Academy of Arts, West succeeded Reynolds as its president. He became official painter to George III (r. 1760–1801) and retained that position even during the strained period of the American Revolution.

In *Death of General Wolfe* (FIG. **21-20**), West depicted the mortally wounded young English commander just after his defeat of the French in the decisive battle of Quebec in 1759, which gave Canada to Great Britain. Because his subject was a recent event, West clothed his characters in contemporary costumes (although the military uniforms are not completely accurate in all details). However, West blended this realism of detail with the grand tradition of history painting by arranging his figures in a complex and

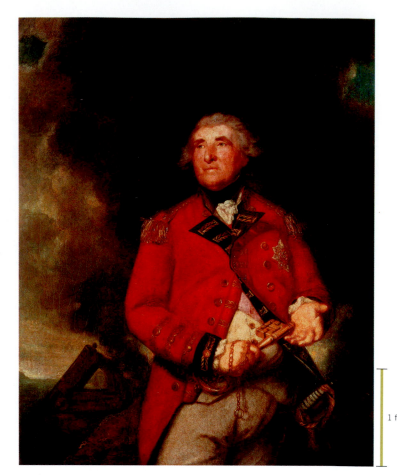

21-19 Sir Joshua Reynolds, *Lord Heathfield*, 1787. Oil on canvas, 4′ 8″ × 3′ 9″. National Gallery, London.

In this Grand Manner portrait, Reynolds depicted the English commander who defended Gibraltar. As is typical for this genre, Heathfield stands in a dramatic pose and his figure takes up most of the canvas.

1 ft.

theatrically ordered composition. His modern hero dies among grieving officers on the field of victorious battle in a way that suggests the death of a saint. (The composition, in fact, derives from paintings of the lamentation over the dead Christ.) West wanted to present this hero's death in the service of the state as a martyrdom charged with religious emotions. His innovative and highly effective combination of the conventions of traditional heroic painting with a look of modern realism influenced history painting well into the 19th century.

JOHN SINGLETON COPLEY American artist John Singleton Copley (1738–1815) matured as a painter in the Massachusetts Bay Colony. Like West, Copley later emigrated to England, where he absorbed the fashionable English portrait style. But unlike Grand Manner portraiture, Copley's *Paul Revere* (FIG. **21-21**), painted before the artist left Boston, conveys a sense of directness and faithfulness to visual fact that marked the taste for honesty and plainness noted by many late-18th- and 19th-century visitors to America. When Copley painted his portrait, Revere was not yet the familiar hero of the American Revolution. In the picture, he is working at his profession of silversmithing. The setting is plain, the lighting clear and revealing. Revere sits in his shirtsleeves, bent over a teapot in progress. He pauses and turns his head to look the observer straight in the eyes. The painter treated the reflections in the polished wood of the tabletop with as much care as he did Revere's

21-20 BENJAMIN WEST, *Death of General Wolfe,* 1771. Oil on canvas, 4′ 11½″ × 7′. National Gallery of Canada, Ottawa (gift of the Duke of Westminster, 1918).

West's great innovation was to blend contemporary subject matter and costumes with the grand tradition of history painting. Here, the painter likened General Wolfe's death to that of a martyred saint.

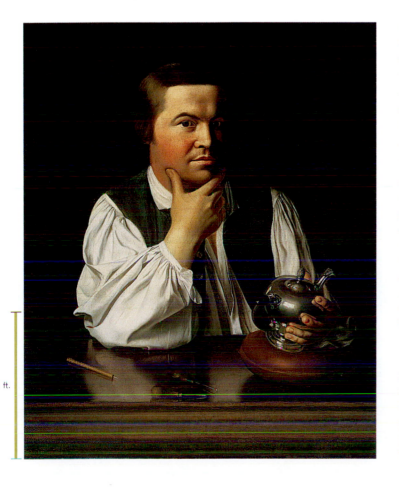

figure, his tools, and the teapot resting on its leather graver's pillow. Copley gave special prominence to Revere's eyes by reflecting intense reddish light onto the darkened side of his face and hands. The informality and the sense of the moment link this painting to contemporaneous English and Continental portraits. But the spare style and the emphasis on the sitter's down-to-earth character differentiate this American work from its European counterparts.

THE GRAND TOUR The 18th-century public also sought "naturalness" in artists' depictions of landscapes. Documentation of specific places became popular, in part due to growing travel opportunities and expanding colonialism. These depictions of geographic settings also served the needs of the many scientific expeditions mounted during the century and satisfied the desires of genteel tourists for mementos of their journeys. By this time, a Grand Tour of the major sites of Europe was an essential part of every well-bred person's education (see "The Grand Tour and Veduta Painting," page 632). Those who embarked on a tour of the Continent wished to return with souvenirs to help them remember their experiences and impress those at home with the wonders

21-21 JOHN SINGLETON COPLEY, *Paul Revere,* ca. 1768–1770. Oil on canvas, 2′ 11⅛″ × 2′ 4″. Museum of Fine Arts, Boston (gift of Joseph W., William B., and Edward H. R. Revere).

In contrast to Grand Manner portraiture, Copley's *Paul Revere* emphasizes his subject's down-to-earth character, differentiating this American work from its European counterparts.

The Grand Tour and Veduta Painting

Although travel throughout Europe was commonplace in the 18th century, Italy became an especially popular destination. This "pilgrimage" of aristocrats, the wealthy, politicians, and diplomats from France, England, Germany, Flanders, Sweden, the United States, Russia, Poland, and Hungary came to be known as the Grand Tour. Italy's allure fueled the revival of classicism, and the popularity of Neoclassical art drove the fascination with Italy. One British observer noted: "All our religion, all our arts, almost all that sets us above savages, has come from the shores of the Mediterranean."*

The Grand Tour was not simply leisure travel. The education available in Italy to the inquisitive mind made such a tour an indispensable experience for anyone who wished to make a mark in society. The Enlightenment had made knowledge of ancient Rome and Greece imperative, and a steady stream of Europeans and Americans traveled to Italy in the late 18th and early 19th centuries. These tourists aimed to increase their knowledge of literature, the visual arts, architecture, theater, music, history, customs, and folklore. Given this extensive agenda, it is not surprising a Grand Tour could take a number of years to complete. Most travelers moved from location to location, following an established itinerary.

The British were the most avid travelers, and they conceived the initial "tour code," including required itineraries to important destinations. Although they designated Rome early on as the primary destination in Italy, visitors traveled as far north as Venice and as far south as Naples. Eventually, Paestum, Sicily, Florence, Siena, Pisa, Genoa, Milan, Bologna, and Parma (MAP 20-1) all appeared in guidebooks and in paintings. Joseph Wright of Derby (FIGS. 21-1 and 21-11A) and Joseph Mallord William Turner (FIG. 22-22) were among the many British artists to undertake a Grand Tour.

Many visitors to Italy returned home from their Grand Tour with a painting by Antonio Canaletto, the leading painter of scenic views (*vedute*) of Venice. It must have been very cheering on a gray winter afternoon in England to look up and see a sunny, panoramic view such as that in Canaletto's *Riva degli Schiavoni, Venice* (FIG. 21-22), with its cloud-studded sky, picturesque water traffic, and well-known Venetian landmarks painted in scrupulous perspective and minute detail. (The Doge's Palace [FIG. 14-21] is at the left in *Riva degli Schiavoni*.) Canaletto usually made drawings "on

21-22 ANTONIO CANALETTO, *Riva degli Schiavoni, Venice*, ca. 1735–1740. Oil on canvas, $1' 6\frac{1}{2}'' \times 2' \frac{7}{8}''$. Toledo Museum of Art, Toledo.

Canaletto was the leading painter of Venetian *vedute*, which were treasured souvenirs for 18th-century travelers visiting Italy on a Grand Tour. He used a camera obscura for his on-site drawings.

location" to take back to his studio and use as sources for paintings. To help make the on-site drawings true to life, he often used a camera obscura, as Vermeer (FIGS. 20-19 to 20-20A) did before him. These instruments were darkened chambers (some of them virtually portable closets) with optical lenses fitted into a hole in one wall through which light entered to project an inverted image of the subject onto the chamber's opposite wall. The artist could trace the main details from this image for later reworking and refinement. The camera obscura enabled artists to create convincing representations incorporating the variable focus of objects at different distances. Canaletto's paintings give the impression of capturing every detail, with no "editing." In fact, he presented each site according to Renaissance perspective conventions and exercised great selectivity about which details to include and which to omit to make a coherent and engagingly attractive veduta.

*Cesare de Seta, "Grand Tour: The Lure of Italy in the Eighteenth Century," in Andrew Wilton and Ilaria Bignamini, eds., *Grand Tour: The Lure of Italy in the Eighteenth Century* (London: Tate Gallery, 1996), 13.

they had seen. The English were especially eager collectors of travel pictures. Venetian artists in particular found it profitable to produce paintings of the most characteristic *vedute* (scenic views) of their city to sell to British visitors. Chief among those artists was

ANTONIO CANALETTO (1697–1768), whose works, for example *Riva degli Schiavoni, Venice* (*Bank of the Slaves, Venice*; FIG. **21-22**), English tourists avidly acquired as evidence of their visit to Italy's magical city of water.

The Excavations of Herculaneum and Pompeii

Among the developments stimulating the European fascination with classical antiquity was the initiation of systematic excavations at two ancient Roman cities on the Bay of Naples—Herculaneum and Pompeii—in 1738 and 1748, respectively. The violent eruption of Mount Vesuvius in August 79 CE had buried both cities under volcanic ash and lava (see "An Eyewitness Account of the Eruption of Mount Vesuvius," Chapter 7, page 188), protecting the sites for hundreds of years from looters and the ravages of nature. Consequently, the 18th-century excavations yielded an unprecedented number of well-preserved paintings, sculptures, vases, and other household objects, and provided rich evidence for reconstructing Roman art and life. As a result, European ideas about and interest in ancient Rome expanded tremendously, and collectors eagerly acquired as many of the newly discovered antiquities as they could. One of the most avid collectors was Sir William Hamilton (1731–1803), British consul in Naples from 1764 to 1800, who purchased numerous painted vases and other ancient objects and then sold them to the British Museum in 1772. The finds at Pompeii and Herculaneum, therefore, quickly became available to a wide public.

"Pompeian" style soon became all the rage in England, as is evident, for example, in Robert Adam's Etruscan Room (FIG. 21-23) at Osterley Park House, which was inspired by the frescoes of the Third and early Fourth Styles of Roman mural painting (FIGS. 7-21 and 7-22). Adam took decorative motifs (medallions, urns, vine scrolls, sphinxes, and tripods) from Roman art and arranged them sparsely within broad, neutral spaces and slender margins, as in his elegant, linear ancient models. This new Neoclassical style almost entirely displaced the curvilinear Rococo (FIGS. 21-2 and 21-3) in the homes of the wealthy after midcentury. Adam was also an archaeologist, and he had explored and written accounts of the ruins of Diocletian's palace (FIG. 7-74) at Split. Kedleston House in Derbyshire, Adelphi Terrace in London, and a great many other structures he designed show how the Split palace influenced his work.

The archaeological finds from Herculaneum and Pompeii also affected garden and landscape design, fashion, and tableware.

21-23 ROBERT ADAM, Etruscan Room, Osterley Park House, Middlesex, England, begun 1761. Reconstructed in the Victoria & Albert Museum, London.

Inspired by archaeological discoveries at Herculaneum and Pompeii in the mid-18th century, Adam incorporated decorative motifs from Roman mural painting into his Etruscan Room at Osterley Park.

Clothing based on classical garb became popular, and Emma, Lady Hamilton (1761–1815), Sir William's wife, often gave lavish parties dressed in delicate Greek-style drapery. Neoclassical taste also determined the pottery designs of John Flaxman (1755–1826) and Josiah Wedgwood. Wedgwood established his reputation in the 1760s with his creamware inspired by ancient art. He eventually produced vases based on what were then thought to be Etruscan designs (they were, in fact, imported Greek vases deposited in Etruscan tombs) and expanded his business by producing small busts of classical figures as well as cameos and medallions adorned with copies of antique reliefs and statues.

NEOCLASSICISM

One of the defining characteristics of the late 18th century was a renewed admiration for classical antiquity, which the Grand Tour was instrumental in fueling. This interest gave rise to the artistic movement known as *Neoclassicism*, which incorporated the subjects and styles of ancient art. Painting, sculpture, and architecture, however, were only the most prominent manifestations of Neoclassicism. Fascination with Greek and Roman culture was widespread and extended to the public culture of fashion and home decor. The Enlightenment's emphasis on rationality in part explains this classical focus, because the geometric harmony of classical art and architecture embodied Enlightenment ideals. In addition, classical cultures represented the pinnacle of civilized society. Greece and Rome served as models of enlightened political organization. With their traditions of liberty, civic virtue, morality, and sacrifice, these cultures were ideal models during a period of great political upheaval. Given these traditional associations, it is not coincidental that Neoclassicism was particularly appealing during the French and American revolutions.

Further whetting the public appetite for classicism were the excavations near Naples of Herculaneum and Pompeii, which the volcanic eruption of Mount Vesuvius had buried (see "The Excavations of Herculaneum and Pompeii," above). Soon, murals based on the paintings unearthed in the excavations began to appear in European townhouses, such as the Etruscan Room (FIG. **21-23**) by ROBERT ADAM (1728–1792) in Osterley Park House in Middlesex, begun in 1761.

21-24 ANGELICA KAUFFMANN, *Cornelia Presenting Her Children as Her Treasures,* or *Mother of the Gracchi,* ca. 1785. Oil on canvas, 3′ 4″ × 4′ 2″. Virginia Museum of Fine Arts, Richmond (Adolph D. and Wilkins C. Williams Fund).

Kauffmann's painting of a virtuous Roman mother who presented her children to a visitor as her jewels exemplifies the Enlightenment fascination with classical antiquity and with classical art.

1 ft.

WINCKELMANN The enthusiasm for classical antiquity also permeated much of the scholarship of the time. In the late 18th century, the ancient world increasingly became the focus of academic research. A visit to Rome inspired Edward Gibbon (1737–1794) to begin his monumental *Decline and Fall of the Roman Empire,* which appeared between 1776 and 1788. Earlier, in 1755, Johann Joachim Winckelmann (1717–1768), widely recognized as the first modern art historian, published *Reflections on the Imitation of Greek Works in Painting and Sculpture,* in which the German scholar unequivocally designated Greek art as the most perfect to come from human hands. For Winckelmann, classical art was far superior to the "natural" art of his day.

> Good taste, which is becoming more prevalent throughout the world, had its origins under the skies of Greece. . . . The only way for us to become great . . . is to imitate the ancients. . . . In the masterpieces of Greek art, connoisseurs and imitators find not only nature at its most beautiful but also something beyond nature, namely certain ideal forms of its beauty. . . . A person enlightened enough to penetrate the innermost secrets of art will find beauties hitherto seldom revealed when he compares the total structure of Greek figures with most modern ones, especially those modelled more on nature than on Greek taste.[3]

In his later *History of Ancient Art* (1764), Winckelmann carefully described major works of classical art and positioned each one within a huge inventory organized by subject matter, style, and period. Before Winckelmann, art historians had focused on biography, as did Giorgio Vasari and Giovanni Pietro Bellori in the 16th and 17th centuries (see "Giovanni Pietro Bellori on Annibale Carracci and Caravaggio," Chapter 19, page 570). Winckelmann thus initiated one modern art historical method thoroughly in accord with Enlightenment ideas of ordering knowledge—a system of description and classification that provided a pioneering model for the understanding of stylistic evolution. Winckelmann's familiarity with classical art derived predominantly (as was the norm) from Roman works and Roman copies of Greek art in Italy. Yet Winckelmann was instrumental in bringing to scholarly attention the differences between Greek and Roman art. Thus, he paved the way for more thorough study of the distinct characteristics of the art and architecture of these two cultures.

Painting

Winckelmann's influence extended beyond the world of scholarship. He also was instrumental in promoting Neoclassicism as a major stylistic movement in late-18th-century painting. He was, for example, the scholar who advised his countryman ANTON RAPHAEL MENGS (1728–1779) on classical iconography when Mengs painted *Parnassus* (FIG. **21-23A**), the fresco many art historians regard as the first Neoclassical painting.

21-23A MENGS, *Parnassus,* 1761.

ANGELICA KAUFFMANN Another pioneer of Neoclassical painting was ANGELICA KAUFFMANN (1741–1807). Born in Switzerland and trained in Italy, Kauffmann spent many of her productive years in England. A student of Reynolds (FIG. 21-19), she was a founding member of the British Royal Academy of Arts and enjoyed an enviable reputation. Her *Cornelia Presenting Her Children as Her Treasures,* or *Mother of the Gracchi* (FIG. **21-24**), is an *exemplum virtutis* (example or model of virtue) drawn from Greek and Roman history and literature. The moralizing pictures of Greuze (FIG. 21-14) and Hogarth (FIG. 21-17) already had marked a change in taste, but Kauffmann replaced the modern setting and character of their works. She clothed her actors in ancient Roman garb and posed them in statuesque attitudes within Roman interiors. The theme of *Mother of the Gracchi* is the virtue of Cornelia, mother of the future political leaders Tiberius and Gaius Gracchus, who, in the second century BCE, attempted to reform the Roman Republic. Cornelia reveals her character in this scene, which takes place after a visitor had shown off her fine jewelry and then haughtily insisted Cornelia show hers. Instead of taking out her own precious adornments, Cornelia brought her sons forward, presenting them as her jewels. The architectural setting is severely Roman, with no

David on Greek Style and Public Art

Jacques-Louis David was the leading Neoclassical painter in France at the end of the 18th century. He championed a return to Greek style and the painting of inspiring heroic and patriotic subjects. In 1796 he made the following statement to his pupils:

> I want to work in a pure Greek style. I feed my eyes on antique statues, I even have the intention of imitating some of them. The Greeks had no scruples about copying a composition, a gesture, a type that had already been accepted and used. They put all their attention and all their art on perfecting an idea that had been already conceived. They thought, and they were right, that in the arts the way in which an idea is rendered, and the manner in which it is expressed, is much more important than the idea itself. To give a body and a perfect form to one's thought, this—and only this—is to be an artist.*

David also strongly believed paintings depicting noble events in ancient history, such as his *Oath of the Horatii* (FIG. 21-25), would serve to instill patriotism and civic virtue in the public at large in postrevolutionary France. In November 1793 he wrote:

> [The arts] should help to spread the progress of the human spirit, and to propagate and transmit to posterity the striking examples of the efforts of a tremendous people who, guided by reason and philosophy, are bringing back to earth the reign of liberty, equality, and law. The arts must therefore contribute forcefully to the education of the public. . . . The arts are the imitation of nature in her most beautiful and perfect form. . . .

> [T]hose marks of heroism and civic virtue offered the eyes of the people [will] electrify the soul, and plant the seeds of glory and devotion to the fatherland.†

*Translated by Robert Goldwater and Marco Treves, eds., *Artists on Art,* 3d ed. (New York: Pantheon Books, 1958), 206.
†Ibid., 205.

21-25 JACQUES-LOUIS DAVID, *Oath of the Horatii*, 1784. Oil on canvas, 10′ 10″ × 13′ 11″. Musée du Louvre, Paris. ◼◀

David was the Neoclassical painter-ideologist of the French Revolution. This huge canvas celebrating ancient Roman patriotism and sacrifice features statuesque figures and classical architecture.

1 ft.

Rococo motif in evidence, and the composition and drawing have the simplicity and firmness of low-relief carving, qualities shared with Mengs's *Parnassus* (FIG. 21-23A).

JACQUES-LOUIS DAVID The Enlightenment idea of a participatory and knowledgeable citizenry lay behind the revolt against the French monarchy in 1789, but the immediate causes of the French Revolution were France's economic crisis and the clash between the Third Estate (bourgeoisie, peasantry, and urban and rural workers) and the First and Second Estates (the clergy and nobility, respectively). They fought over the issue of representation in the legislative body, the Estates-General, which had been convened to discuss taxation as a possible solution to the economic problem. However, the ensuing revolution revealed the instability of the monarchy and of French society's traditional structure and resulted in a succession of republics and empires as France struggled to find a way to adjust to these fundamental changes.

JACQUES-LOUIS DAVID (1748–1825) became the Neoclassical painter-ideologist of the French Revolution. A distant relative of François Boucher (FIG. 21-8), he followed the Rococo painter's style until a period of study in Rome won the younger man over to the classical art tradition. David favored academic teachings about using the art of the ancients and of the great Renaissance masters as models. He, as Winckelmann, rebelled against Rococo style as an "artificial taste" and exalted the "perfect form" of Greek art (see "David on Greek Style and Public Art," above).

OATH OF THE HORATII David concurred with the Enlightenment belief that the subject of an artwork should have a moral. Paintings representing noble deeds in the past could inspire virtue in the present. A milestone painting in the Neoclassical master's career, *Oath of the Horatii* (FIG. 21-25), depicts a story from pre-Republican Rome, the heroic phase of Roman history. The topic was not too obscure for David's audience. Pierre Corneille (1606–1684) had retold this story of conflict between love and patriotism, first recounted by the ancient Roman historian Livy, in a play performed in Paris several years earlier. According to the story, the leaders of the warring cities of Rome and Alba decided to resolve their conflicts in a series of encounters waged by three representatives from each side. The Romans chose as their champions the three Horatius brothers, who had to face the three sons of the Curatius family from Alba. A sister of the Horatii, Camilla, was the bride-to-be of one of the Curatius sons, and the wife of the youngest Horatius was the sister of the Curatii. David's painting shows the Horatii as they swear on their swords, held high by their father, to win or die for Rome, oblivious to the anguish and sorrow of the Horatii women.

Oath of the Horatii is a paragon of the Neoclassical style. Not only does the subject matter deal with a narrative of patriotism and sacrifice excerpted from Roman history, but the painter also employed formal devices to present the image with force and clarity. The action unfolds in a shallow space much like a stage setting, defined by a severely simple architectural framework. David deployed his statuesque and carefully modeled figures across the space, close to the foreground, in a manner reminiscent of ancient relief sculpture. The rigid, angular, and virile forms of the men on the left effectively contrast with the soft curvilinear shapes of the distraught women on the right. This juxtaposition visually pits virtues the Enlightenment leaders ascribed to men (such as courage, patriotism, and unwavering loyalty to a cause) against the emotions of love, sorrow, and despair the women in the painting express. The French viewing audience perceived such emotionalism as characteristic of the female nature. The message was clear and of a type readily identifiable to the prerevolutionary French public. The picture created a sensation at its first exhibition in Paris in 1785. Although David had painted it under royal patronage and did not intend the painting as a revolutionary statement, *Oath of the Horatii* aroused his audience to patriotic zeal. The Neoclassical style soon became the semiofficial voice of the French Revolution.

DEATH OF MARAT When the revolution broke out in 1789, David threw in his lot with the Jacobins, the radical and militant revolutionary faction. He accepted the role of de facto minister of propaganda, organizing political pageants and ceremonies requiring floats, costumes, and sculptural props. David believed art could play an important role in educating the public and that dramatic paintings emphasizing patriotism and civic virtue would prove effective as rallying calls. However, rather than continuing to create artworks focused on scenes from antiquity, David began to portray scenes from the French Revolution itself.

In 1793, David painted *Death of Marat* (FIG. **21-26**), which he wanted not only to serve as a record of an important event in the struggle to overthrow the monarchy but also to provide inspiration and encouragement to the revolutionary forces. The painting commemorates the assassination that year of Jean-Paul Marat (1743–1793), an influential writer who was David's friend. The artist depicted the martyred revolutionary in his bathtub after Charlotte Corday (1768–1793), a member of a rival political faction, stabbed him to death. (Marat suffered from a painful skin disease and required frequent medicinal baths.) David presented the scene with directness and clarity. The cold neutral space above Marat's figure slumped in the tub produces a chilling oppressiveness. The painter vividly placed all narrative details in the foreground—the knife, the wound, the blood, the letter with which Corday gained entrance—to sharpen the sense of pain and outrage. David masterfully composed the painting to present Marat as a tragic martyr who died

21-26 JACQUES-LOUIS DAVID, *Death of Marat*, 1793. Oil on canvas, 5′ 5″ × 4′ 2½″. Musées Royaux des Beaux-Arts de Belgique, Brussels. ◼◀

David depicted the revolutionary Marat as a tragic martyr, stabbed to death in his bath. Although the painting displays severe Neoclassical spareness, its convincing realism conveys pain and outrage.

in the service of the revolution. He based Marat's figure on Christ in Michelangelo's *Pietà* (FIG. 17-12) in Saint Peter's in Rome. The reference to Christ's martyrdom made the painting a kind of "altarpiece" for the new civic "religion," inspiring the French people with the saintly dedication of their slain leader.

Architecture and Sculpture

Architects in the Enlightenment era also formed a deep admiration for the Greco-Roman past. Fairly early in the 18th century, they began to turn away from the theatricality and ostentation of Baroque design, still evident in grandiose structures such as Blenheim Palace (FIG. 21-1A) in England and Karlskirche (FIG. 21-3A) in Austria, as well as from the delicate flourishes of Rococo salons (FIGS. 21-2 and 21-3), palaces (FIG. 21-5A), and churches (FIGS. 21-4 and 21-5B). The style they instead embraced offered a more streamlined antique look.

PANTHÉON The Parisian church of Sainte-Geneviève, now the Panthéon (FIG. **21-27**), by JACQUES-GERMAIN SOUFFLOT (1713–1780) stands as testament to the revived interest in classical architecture. The Roman ruins at Baalbek in Lebanon, especially the titanic colonnade of the temple of Jupiter, provided much of the inspiration for Soufflot's design. The columns, reproduced with studied archaeological precision, stand out from walls that are severely blank, except for a repeated garland motif near the top. The colonnaded dome, a Neoclassical version of the domes of Saint

21-27 JACQUES-GERMAIN SOUFFLOT, Panthéon (Sainte-Geneviève; looking northeast), Paris, France, 1755–1792.

Soufflot's Panthéon is a testament to the Enlightenment admiration for Greece and Rome. It combines a portico based on an ancient Roman temple with a colonnaded dome and a Greek-cross plan.

cal systems ranging from Athenian democracy to Roman imperial rule. Thus, parliamentary England joined revolutionary France in embracing Neoclassicism. In England, Neoclassicism's appeal also was due to its clarity and simplicity. These characteristics provided a stark contrast to the complexity and opulence of Baroque art, then associated with the flamboyant rule of absolute monarchy. In English architecture, the preference for a simple and rational style derived indirectly from the authority of the ancient Roman architect Vitruvius through Andrea Palladio (FIGS. 17-28 to 17-31) in the 16th century and Inigo Jones (FIG. 20-37) in the 17th.

RICHARD BOYLE (1695–1753), earl of Burlington, strongly restated Jones's Palladian doctrine in the new Neoclassical idiom in Chiswick House (FIG. 21-28), which he built on London's outskirts with the help of WILLIAM KENT (ca. 1686–1748). Paving the way for this shift in style was, among other things, the publication of Colin Campbell's *Vitruvius Britannicus* (1715), three volumes of engravings of ancient buildings, prefaced by a denunciation of Italian Baroque and high praise for Palladio and Jones. Chiswick House is a free variation on the theme of Palladio's Villa Rotonda (FIG. 17-28). The exterior design provided a clear alternative to the colorful splendor of Versailles (FIG. 20-26). In its simple symmetry, unadorned planes, right angles, and precise proportions, Chiswick looks very classical and rational. But the Palladian-style villa's setting within informal gardens, where a charming irregularity of layout and freely growing uncropped foliage dominate the scene, mitigates the classical severity and rationality. Just as the owners of English villas cultivated irregularity in the landscaping surrounding their homes, they sometimes preferred interiors ornamented in a style more closely related to Rococo decoration. At Chiswick, the interior design creates a luxurious Baroque foil to the stern symmetry of the exterior and the plan.

Palladian classicism prevailed in English architecture until about 1760, when it began to evolve into Neoclassicism. Playing a pivotal role in the shift from a dependence on Renaissance examples to ancient models was the publication in 1762 of the first volume of *Antiquities of Athens*

21-28 RICHARD BOYLE and WILLIAM KENT, Chiswick House (looking northwest), near London, England, begun 1725.

For this English villa, Boyle and Kent emulated the simple symmetry and unadorned planes of the Palladian architectural style. Chiswick House is a free variation on the Villa Rotonda (FIG. 17-28).

21-27A WALPOLE, Strawberry Hill, Twickenham, 1749–1777.

Peter's (FIG. 17-25) in Rome, the Église du Dôme (FIG. 20-30) in Paris, and Saint Paul's (FIG. 20-38) in London, rises above a Greek-cross plan. Both the dome and the vaults rest on an interior grid of splendid freestanding Corinthian columns, as if the portico's colonnade continued within. Although the whole effect, inside and out, is Roman, the structural principles employed were essentially Gothic. Soufflot was one of the first 18th-century builders to apply the logical engineering of Gothic cathedrals (see "The Gothic Cathedral," Chapter 13, page 373) to modern buildings. With few exceptions, however, such as Strawberry Hill (FIG. 21-27A), owned and largely designed by HORACE WALPOLE (1717–1797), the revival of interest in the Gothic architectural style did not take hold until the following century (see Chapter 22 and FIGS. 22-43 and 22-43A).

CHISWICK HOUSE The appeal of classical architecture extended well beyond French borders. The popularity of Greek and Roman cultures was due not only to their association with morality, rationality, and integrity but also to their connection to politiby two British painters and architects, JAMES STUART (1713–1788) and Nicholas Revett (1720–1804). Indeed, the purest expression of Greek-inspired architecture in 18th-century England was Stuart's design for the Doric portico (FIG. 21-28A) at Hagley Park.

STOURHEAD PARK English architects also made a significant contribution to the history of architecture by developing the *picturesque garden* in the 18th century, a garden designed in accord with the Enlightenment taste for the "natural." This approach to landscape architecture was in strong opposition to the formality and symmetry of Continental gardens such as those of the palace at Versailles (FIG. 20-26), which epitomized the imposition of rational order on untamed nature. Despite their "unordered" appearance, English gardens were carefully planned and often made allusions to classical antiquity, satisfying the demands of their patrons to surround themselves with mementos of the Grand Tour (see "The Grand Tour," page 632) they undertook in their youth.

An early masterpiece of this genre is the park at Stourhead (FIG. 21-29), designed by HENRY FLITCROFT (1697–1769) in collaboration with the property's owner, HENRY HOARE (1705–1785), the son of a wealthy banker. Hoare's country estate in Wiltshire overlooked a lush valley in which Flitcroft created an irregularly shaped artificial lake by damming up the Stour River. Around it, he placed a winding path leading to and from a grotto adorned with statues of a river god and a nymph. The twisting road and the grotto conjured for Hoare the voyage of Aeneas and the entrance to the Underworld in Virgil's *Aeneid,* required reading (in the original Latin) for any properly educated British gentleman. Flitcroft also placed around Hoare's version of Lake Avernus a bridge with five arches modeled on Andrea Palladio's bridge at Vicenza and pavilions that are free variations on famous classical buildings, including the Temple of Venus (FIG. 7-72) at Baalbek and the Pantheon (FIG. 7-49) in Rome.

Flitcroft sited all the structures strategically to create vistas resembling those in the paintings of Claude Lorrain (FIG. 20-33), beloved by those who had completed a Grand Tour. In fact, the view reproduced here of Flitcroft's Pantheon beyond the Palladian bridge on the far side of the lake at Stourhead specifically emulates Claude's 1672 *Landscape with Aeneas at Delos* in the National Gallery in London, in turn inspired by the *Aeneid.* Still, consistent with the eclectic tastes of 18th-century patrons, Hoare's park also contains Chinese bridges, a Turkish tent, and a Gothic tower.

THOMAS JEFFERSON Because the appeal of Neoclassicism was due in part to the values with which it was associated—morality, idealism, patriotism, and civic virtue—it is not surprising that in the new American republic (MAP 21-1), THOMAS JEFFERSON (1743–1826) spearheaded a movement to adopt Neoclassicism as the national architectural style. Jefferson—economist, educational theorist, gifted amateur architect, as well as stateman—admired Palladio immensely and read carefully the Italian architect's *Four Books of Architecture.* Later, while minister to France, he studied 18th-century French classical architecture and city planning and visited the Maison Carrée (FIG. 7-32), an ancient Roman temple at Nîmes. After his European sojourn, Jefferson completely remodeled Monticello (FIG. 21-30), his home near Charlottesville, Virginia, which he originally had designed in a different style. The final version of Monticello is somewhat reminiscent of Palladio's Villa Rotonda (FIG. 17-28) and of Chiswick House (FIG. 21-28), but its materials are the local wood and brick used in Virginia.

UNIVERSITY OF VIRGINIA Jefferson's Neoclassicism was an extension of the Enlightenment belief in the perfectibility of human beings and in the power of art to help achieve that perfection. When he became president, he selected Benjamin Latrobe (1764–1820) to build the U.S. Capitol in Washington, D.C., specifying that Latrobe use a Roman style. Jefferson's choice in part reflected his admiration for the beauty of the Roman buildings he had seen in Europe and in part his association of those buildings

21-29 HENRY FLITCROFT and HENRY HOARE, the park at Stourhead, England, 1743–1765.

Flitcroft's design for Hoare's Wiltshire estate included a replica of the Pantheon overlooking an artificial lake and a grotto alluding to Aeneas's journey to the Underworld from Lake Avernus.

21-30 THOMAS JEFFERSON, Monticello, Charlottesville, Virginia, 1770–1806. ◀◼

Jefferson led the movement to adopt Neoclassicism as the architectural style of the United States. Although built of local materials, his Palladian Virginia home recalls Chiswick House (FIG. 21-28).

with an idealized Roman republican government and, through that, with the democracy of ancient Greece.

In his own designs for public buildings, Jefferson also looked to Rome for models. He modeled the State Capitol in Richmond, Virginia, on the Maison Carrée (FIG. 7-32). For the University of Virginia, which he founded, Jefferson turned to the Pantheon (FIG. 7-49). The Rotunda (FIG. 21-31) is the centerpiece of Jefferson's "academical village" in Charlottesville. It sits on an elevated platform at one end of a grassy quadrangle ("the Lawn"), framed by Neoclassical pavilions and colonnades—just as temples in Roman forums (FIGS. 7-12 and 7-44) stood at one short end of a colonnaded square. Each of the ten pavilions (five on each side) resembles a small classical temple. No two are exactly alike. Jefferson ex-

perimented with variations of all the different classical orders in his pavilions. He had thoroughly absorbed the principles of classical architecture and clearly delighted in borrowing motifs from major buildings. Jefferson was no mere copyist, however. His designs were highly original—and, in turn, frequently emulated.

JEAN-ANTOINE HOUDON Neoclassicism also became the preferred style for public sculpture in the new American republic. When members of the Virginia legislature wanted to erect a life-size marble statue of Virginia-born George Washington (1732–1799), they awarded the commission to the leading French Neoclassical sculptor of the late 18th century, JEAN-ANTOINE HOUDON (1741–1828). Houdon had already carved a bust portrait of Benjamin Franklin

21-31 THOMAS JEFFERSON, Rotunda and Lawn (looking north), University of Virginia, Charlottesville, Virginia, 1819–1826.

Modeled on the Pantheon (FIG. 7-49), Jefferson's Rotunda sits like a temple in a Roman forum on an elevated platform overlooking the colonnaded Lawn of the University of Virginia.

1 ft.

21-32 JEAN-ANTOINE HOUDON, *George Washington*, 1788–1792. Marble, 6′ 2″ high. State Capitol, Richmond.

Houdon portrayed Washington in contemporary garb, but he incorporated the Roman *fasces* and Cincinnatus's plow in the statue, because Washington similarly had returned to his farm after his war service.

1 ft.

21-33 HORATIO GREENOUGH, *George Washington*, 1840. Marble, 11′ 4″ high. Smithsonian American Art Museum, Washington, D.C.

In this posthumous portrait, Greenough likened Washington to a god by depicting him seminude and enthroned in the manner of Phidias's Olympian statue of Zeus, king of the Greek gods.

(1706–1790) when he was America's ambassador to France. His portrait of Washington (FIG. **21-32**) is the sculptural equivalent of a painted Grand Manner portrait (FIG. 21-19). But although Washington wears 18th-century garb, the statue makes overt reference to the Roman Republic. The "column" on which Washington leans is a bundle of rods with an ax attached—the ancient Roman *fasces*, an emblem of authority (used much later as the emblem of Mussolini's Fascist—the term derives from "fasces"—government in 20th-century Italy). The 13 rods symbolize the 13 original states. The plow behind Washington alludes to Cincinnatus, a patrician of the early Roman Republic who was elected dictator during a time of war and resigned his position as soon as victory had been achieved in order to return to his farm. Washington wears the badge of the Society of the Cincinnati (visible beneath the bottom of his waistcoat), an association founded in 1783 for officers in the revolutionary army who had resumed their peacetime roles. Tellingly, Washington no longer holds his sword in Houdon's statue.

HORATIO GREENOUGH After his death, Washington gradually took on almost godlike stature as the "father of his country." In 1840 the U.S. Congress commissioned American sculptor HORATIO GREENOUGH (1805–1852) to create a statue (FIG. **21-33**) of the country's first president for the Capitol. Greenough used Houdon's portrait as his model for the head, but he portrayed Washington as seminude and enthroned, as Phidias depicted Zeus in the famous lost statue he made for the god's temple at Olympia in ancient Greece. The colossal statue—Washington is more than 11 feet tall, seated—epitomizes the Neoclassical style, but it did not win favor with either the Congress that commissioned it or the public. Although no one ever threw Greenough's statue into the Potomac River, as one congressman suggested, the legislators never placed it in its intended site beneath the Capitol dome. In fact, by 1840 the Neoclassical style itself was no longer in vogue. The leading artists of Europe and America had embraced a new style, Romanticism, examined in the next chapter.

ROCOCO TO NEOCLASSICISM: THE 18TH CENTURY IN EUROPE AND AMERICA

ROCOCO

▌ In the early 18th century, the centralized and grandiose palace-based culture of Baroque France gave way to the much more intimate Rococo culture based in the townhouses of Paris. There, aristocrats and intellectuals gathered for witty conversation in salons featuring delicate colors, sinuous lines, gilded mirrors, elegant furniture, and small paintings and sculptures.

▌ The leading Rococo painter was Antoine Watteau, whose usually small canvases feature light colors and elegant figures in ornate costumes moving gracefully through lush landscapes. His *fête galante* paintings depict the outdoor amusements of French high society.

▌ Watteau's successors included François Boucher and Jean-Honoré Fragonard, who carried on the Rococo style late into the 18th century. In Italy, Giambattista Tiepolo adapted the Rococo manner to huge ceiling frescoes in the Baroque tradition.

Boffrand, Salon de la Princesse, Paris 1737–1740

THE ENLIGHTENMENT

▌ By the end of the 18th century, revolutions had overthrown the monarchy in France and achieved independence for the British colonies in America. A major factor was the Enlightenment, a new way of thinking critically about the world independently of religion and tradition.

▌ The Enlightenment promoted scientific questioning of all assertions and embraced the doctrine of progress, epitomized by the Industrial Revolution, which began in England in the 1740s. The paintings of Joseph Wright of Derby celebrated the scientific inventions of the Enlightenment era.

▌ The Enlightenment also made knowledge of ancient Rome imperative for the cultured elite, and Europeans and Americans in large numbers undertook a Grand Tour of Italy. Among the most popular souvenirs of the Grand Tour were Antonio Canaletto's *vedute* of Venice rendered in precise Renaissance perspective with the aid of a camera obscura.

▌ Rejecting the idea of progress, Rousseau, one of the leading French *philosophes,* argued for a return to natural values and exalted the simple, honest life of peasants. His ideas had a profound impact on artists such as Jean-Baptiste-Siméon Chardin and Jean-Baptiste Greuze, who painted sentimental narratives about rural families.

▌ The taste for naturalism also led to the popularity of portrait paintings with landscape backgrounds, a specialty of Thomas Gainsborough, and to a reawakening of interest in realism. Benjamin West represented the protagonists in his history paintings wearing contemporary costumes.

Wright, *A Lecture at the Orrery,* ca. 1763–1765

Canaletto, *Riva degli Schiavoni, Venice,* ca. 1735–1740

NEOCLASSICISM

▌ The Enlightenment revival of interest in Greece and Rome, which spurred systematic excavations at Herculaneum and Pompeii, also gave rise in the late 18th century to the artistic movement known as Neoclassicism, which incorporated the subjects and styles of ancient art.

▌ One pioneer of the new style was Angelica Kauffmann, who often chose subjects drawn from Roman history for her paintings. Jacques-Louis David, who exalted classical art as "the imitation of nature in her most beautiful and perfect form," also favored ancient Roman themes. Painted on the eve of the French Revolution, *Oath of the Horatii,* set in a severe classical hall, served as an example of patriotism and sacrifice.

▌ Architects also eagerly embraced the Neoclassical style. Ancient Roman and Italian Renaissance structures inspired Jacques-Germain Soufflot's Panthéon in Paris and Richard Boyle's Chiswick House near London. A Greek temple in Athens was the model for James Stuart's Doric portico in Worcestershire.

▌ In the United States, Thomas Jefferson adopted the Neoclassical style in his designs for Monticello and the University of Virginia. He championed Neoclassicism as the official architectural style of the new American republic because it represented for him idealism, patriotism, and civic virtue.

Kauffmann, *Mother of the Gracchi,* ca. 1785

Soufflot, Panthéon, Paris, 1755–1792

In the shadows of the left side of the huge canvas are dying and dead Arabs, including a seated man in despair. Gros based the figure on one of the damned in Michelangelo's *Last Judgment* (FIG. 17-19).

Napoleon, fearless among the plague-stricken, reaches out to touch one man's sores. Gros portrayed the French general as Christlike, implying he possessed miraculous power to heal the sick.

Foreshadowing Romanticism, Gros carefully recorded the exotic people, costumes, and architecture of Jaffa, including the distinctive Islamic striped horseshoe arches of the mosque-hospital.

1 ft.

22-1 ANTOINE-JEAN GROS, *Napoleon at the Plague House at Jaffa,* 1804. Oil on canvas, 17′ 5″ × 23′ 7″. Musée du Louvre, Paris.

Among the dying whom Napoleon has come to comfort is a kneeling nude man with left arm extended. His posture recalls that of the dead Christ in Michelangelo's emotional *Pietà* (FIG. 17-20).

ROMANTICISM, REALISM, PHOTOGRAPHY: EUROPE AND AMERICA, 1800 TO 1870

FRAMING THE ERA

NAPOLEON AT JAFFA

In the opening decade of the 19th century, many of the leading French artists produced major artworks glorifying the most powerful man in Europe at the time—Napoleon Bonaparte (1769–1821), since 1799 First Consul of the French Republic and from 1804 to 1815, Emperor of the French. One of those artists was ANTOINE-JEAN GROS (1771–1835), a pupil of Jacques-Louis David (FIGS. 21-25 and 21-26), Napoleon's favorite painter. Gros, like David, produced several paintings that contributed to Napoleon's growing mythic status. In *Napoleon at the Plague House at Jaffa* (FIG. **22-1**), the artist, at Napoleon's request, recorded an incident during an outbreak of the bubonic plague in the course of the general's Syrian campaign of 1799. This fearsome disease struck Muslim and French forces alike, and to quell the growing panic and hysteria, on March 11, 1799, Napoleon himself visited the mosque at Jaffa that had been converted into a hospital for those who had contracted the dreaded disease. Gros depicted Napoleon's staff officers covering their noses against the stench of the place, whereas Napoleon, amid the dead and dying, is fearless and in control. He comforts those still alive, who are clearly awed by his presence and authority. Indeed, by depicting the French leader having removed his glove to touch the sores of a plague victim, Gros implied Napoleon possessed the miraculous power to heal. The composition recalls scenes of the doubting Thomas touching Christ's wound. Here, however, Napoleon is not Saint Thomas but a Christlike figure tending to the sick, as in Rembrandt's *Hundred-Guilder Print* (FIG. 20-16), which Gros certainly knew. The French painter also based the despairing seated figure at the lower left on the comparable figure (one of the damned) in Michelangelo's *Last Judgment* (FIG. 17-19). The kneeling nude man with extended arm at the right recalls the dead Christ in Michelangelo's late *Pietà* (FIG. 17-20).

The action in *Napoleon at the Plague House in Jaffa* unfolds against the exotic backdrop of the horseshoe arches and Moorish arcades of the mosque-hospital's courtyard (compare FIG. 10-9). On the left are Muslim doctors distributing bread and ministering to plague-stricken Arabs in the shadows. On the right, in radiant light, are Napoleon and his soldiers in their splendid tailored uniforms. David had used this polarized compositional scheme and an arcaded backdrop to great effect in his *Oath of the Horatii* (FIG. 21-25), and Gros emulated these features in this painting. However, the younger artist's fascination with the exoticism of the Muslim world, as is evident in his attention to the details of architecture and costume, represented a departure from Neoclassicism. This, along with Gros's emphasis on death, suffering, and an emotional rendering of the scene, presaged core elements of the artistic movement that would soon displace Neoclassicism—Romanticism.

ART UNDER NAPOLEON

The revolution of 1789 initiated a new era in France, but the overthrow of the monarchy also opened the door for Napoleon Bonaparte to exploit the resulting disarray and establish a different kind of monarchy with himself at its head. In 1799, after serving in various French army commands and leading major campaigns in Italy and Egypt, Napoleon became First Consul of the French Republic, a title with clear and intentional links to the ancient Roman Republic (see Chapter 7). During the next 15 years, the ambitious general gained control of almost all of continental Europe in name or through alliances

(MAP 22-1). In May 1804, for example, he became king of Italy. Later that year, the pope journeyed to Paris for Napoleon's coronation as Emperor of the French (FIG. 22-2). In 1812, however, Napoleon launched a disastrous invasion of Russia that ended in retreat, and in 1815 he suffered a devastating defeat at the hands of the British at Waterloo in present-day Belgium. Forced to abdicate the imperial throne, Napoleon went into exile on the island of Saint Helena in the South Atlantic, where he died six years later.

After Napoleon's death, the political geography of Europe changed dramatically (MAP 22-2, page 646), but in many ways the more significant changes during the first half of the 19th century

MAP 22-1 The Napoleonic Empire in 1815.

ROMANTICISM, REALISM, PHOTOGRAPHY: EUROPE AND AMERICA, 1800 TO 1870

1800	1815	1840	1870
▌ Napoleon appoints David as First Painter of the Empire and brings Canova from Rome to Paris ▌ Vignon designs La Madeleine, Napoleon's Neoclassical "temple of glory" ▌ Gros, Girodet, and Ingres form a bridge between Neoclassicism and Romanticism	▌ Romanticism is the leading art movement in Europe. Delacroix and other painters favor exotic and fantastic subjects featuring unleashed emotion, vibrant color, and bold brushstrokes ▌ Friedrich, Turner, Cole, and other Romantic artists specialize in painting transcendental landscapes ▌ Gothic style enjoys a revival in architecture ▌ Daguerre and Talbot invent photography	▌ Courbet exhibits his work in the Pavilion of Realism. He and other Realist painters in Europe and America insist people and events of their own time are the only valid subjects for art ▌ Manet's paintings get a hostile reception because of their shocking subject matter and nonillusionistic style ▌ Paxton pioneers prefabricated glass-and-iron construction in the Crystal Palace ▌ Technological advances enable artists to make on-the-spot photographs of the Civil War	

were technological and economic. The Industrial Revolution caused a population boom in European cities, and railroads spread to many parts of the Continent, facilitating the transportation of both goods and people. Transformation also occurred in the art world. The century opened with Neoclassicism still supreme, but by 1870 Romanticism and Realism in turn had captured the imagination of artists and public alike. New construction techniques had a major impact on architectural design, and the invention of photography revolutionized picturemaking of all kinds.

22-1A DAVID, *Napoleon Crossing Saint-Bernard,* 1800–1801.

DAVID AND NAPOLEON At the fall of the French revolutionary Maximilien Robespierre and his party in 1794, Jacques-Louis David, who had aligned himself personally and through his work with the revolutionary forces, barely escaped with his life. He stood trial and went to prison. After his release in 1795, he worked hard to resurrect his career. When Napoleon approached David in 1804 and offered him the position of First Painter of the Empire, David seized the opportunity. The artist, who had earlier painted a series of portraits of the emperor on horseback crossing the Alps (FIG. 22-1A), exemplified Neoclassicism, the artistic style Napoleon favored because he aspired to rule an empire that might one day rival ancient Rome's. The French emperor consequently embraced all links with the classical past as symbolic sources of authority.

CORONATION OF NAPOLEON The new emperor was well aware of the power of art for constructing a public image and of David's ability to produce inspiring patriotic images. The most grandiose work First Painter David produced for his new imperial patron was *Coronation of Napoleon* (FIG. 22-2), an immense (20 by 32 feet) canvas documenting the pomp and pageantry of the crowning ceremony of December 1804. To a large extent, David adhered to historical fact in depicting Napoleon's coronation, duly recording, for example, the appearance of the interior of Paris's Notre Dame Cathedral as the emperor's architects Charles Percier (1764–1838) and Pierre-François-Léonard Fontaine (1762–1853) had decorated it for the occasion. David also faithfully portrayed those in attendance: Napoleon; his wife Josephine (1763–1814), who kneels to receive her crown; Pope Pius VII (r. 1800–1823), seated behind Napoleon; Joseph (1768–1814) and Louis (1778–1846) Bonaparte; Napoleon's ministers; the retinues of the emperor and empress; a representative group of the clergy; and David himself, seated among the rows of spectators in the balconies. Preliminary studies and drawings reveal, however, that, at Napoleon's request, David made changes to his initially accurate record of the event. For example, the emperor insisted the painter depict the pope with his hand raised in blessing. Further, Napoleon's mother, who had refused to attend the coronation, appears prominently in the center background.

Given the number of figures and details David had to incorporate in his painting, it is remarkable he was able to impose upon the lavish pageant the structured composition central to the Neoclassical style. As in his *Oath of the Horatii* (FIG. 21-25), David presented

22-2 JACQUES-LOUIS DAVID, *Coronation of Napoleon,* 1805–1808. Oil on canvas, 20' $4\frac{1}{2}$" × 32' $1\frac{3}{4}$". Musée du Louvre, Paris.

As First Painter of the Empire, David recorded Napoleon at his December 1804 coronation crowning his wife with the pope as witness, thus underscoring the authority of the state over the church.

1 ft.

Art under Napoleon **645**

MAP 22-2 Europe around 1850.

the action as if on a theater stage—which in this instance was literally the case, even if the stage Percier and Fontaine constructed was inside a church. In addition, as he did in his arrangement of the men and women in *Oath of the Horatii,* David conceptually divided the painting to highlight polarities. The pope, prelates, and priests representing the Catholic Church appear on the right. The members of Napoleon's imperial court are on the left. The relationship between church and state was one of this period's most contentious issues. Napoleon's decision to crown himself, rather than to allow the pope to perform the coronation, as was traditional, reflected Napoleon's concern about the church-state power relationship. For the painting commemorating the occasion, the emperor insisted David depict the moment when, having already crowned himself, Napoleon placed a crown on his wife's head, further underscoring his authority. Thus, although this painting appears at first to be a detailed, objective record of a historical event, it is, in fact, a carefully crafted tableau designed to present Napoleon in the way he wished to be seen. In that respect, as well as stylistically, David was emulating the artists in the employ of the ancient Roman emperors (see Chapter 7), as did his pupil, JEAN-AUGUSTE-DOMINIQUE INGRES (1780–1867) in a contemporaneous portrait (FIG. **22-2A**) of Napoleon enthroned.

22-2A INGRES, *Napoleon on His Imperial Throne,* 1806.

LA MADELEINE Napoleon also embraced Neoclassical architecture as an ideal vehicle for expressing his imperial authority. For example, the emperor resumed construction of the church of La Madeleine (FIG. **22-3**) in Paris, which had been interrupted in 1790. However, he converted the building into a "temple of glory" for France's imperial armies. (The structure reverted again to a church after Napoleon's defeat and long before its completion in 1842.) Designed by PIERRE VIGNON (1763–1828), the grandiose Napoleonic temple includes a high podium and broad flight of stairs leading to a deep porch in the front. These architectural features, coupled with the Corinthian columns, recall Roman temples in France, such as the Maison Carrée (FIG. 7-32) at Nîmes, making La Madeleine a symbolic link between the Napoleonic and Roman empires. Curiously, the building's classical shell surrounds an interior covered by a sequence of three domes, a feature found in Byzantine and Romanesque churches. Vignon in essence clothed a traditional church in the costume of imperial Rome.

ANTONIO CANOVA Neoclassical sculpture also was in vogue under Napoleon. His favorite sculptor was ANTONIO CANOVA (1757–1822), who somewhat reluctantly left a successful career in Italy to settle in Paris and serve the emperor. Once in France, Canova became Napoleon's admirer and made numerous portraits, all in the Neoclassical style, of the emperor and his family. The most remarkable is the marble portrait (FIG. **22-4**) of Napoleon's sister, Pauline Borghese (1780–1825), as Venus. Initially, Canova, who had gained renown for his sculptures of classical gods and heroes—for

Napoleon constructed La Madeleine as a "temple of glory" for his armies. Based on ancient temples (FIG. 7-32) in France, Vignon's Neoclassical design linked the Napoleonic and Roman empires.

The French public never got to admire Canova's portrait, however. Napoleon had arranged the marriage of his sister to an heir of the noble Roman Borghese family. Once Pauline was in Rome, her behavior was less than dignified, and the public gossiped extensively about her affairs. Pauline's insistence on being represented as the goddess of love reflected her self-perception. Because of his wife's questionable reputation, Prince Camillo Borghese (1775–1832), the work's official patron, kept the sculpture sequestered in the Villa Borghese in Rome (where it still is). Borghese allowed relatively few people to see the portrait. Still, knowledge of the existence of the sculpture was widespread and increased the notoriety of both artist and subject.

22-4A CANOVA, *Cupid and Psyche*, 1787–1793.

example, *Cupid and Psyche* (FIG. **22-4A**)—had suggested depicting Borghese as Diana, goddess of the hunt. Pauline, however, demanded she be portrayed as Venus, the goddess of love. Thus she appears, reclining on a divan and gracefully holding the golden apple, the symbol of the goddess's triumph in the judgment of Paris. Canova clearly based his work on Greek statuary—the sensuous pose and seminude body recall Hellenistic works such as *Venus de Milo* (FIG. 5-83)—and the reclining figure has parallels on Roman sarcophagus lids (FIG. 7-61; compare FIG. 6-5).

DAVID'S STUDENTS Given David's stature as an artist in Napoleonic France, along with the popularity of Neoclassicism, it is not surprising the First Painter attracted numerous students and developed an active and flourishing teaching studio (see "David on Greek Style," Chapter 21, page 635). He gave practical instruction to and deeply influenced many important artists of the period. So strong was David's commitment to classicism that he encouraged all his students to learn Latin, the better to immerse themselves in and understand classical culture. David even initially demanded his pupils select their subjects from Plutarch, the ancient author of *Lives of the Noble Greeks and Romans* and a principal source of Neoclassical subject matter. Due to this thorough classical foundation, David's students all produced work that at its core retains Neoclassical elements. Yet David was far from authoritarian in his teaching, and he encouraged his students to find their own artistic identities. The work of his three most famous students—Gros (FIG. 22-1), Ingres (FIGS. 22-2A, 22-6, and 22-7), and Girodet-Trioson (FIGS. 22-5 and 22-5A)—represents a departure from the structured confines of Neoclassicism. David's pupils laid the foundation for the Romantic movement (see page 650) by exploring the realm of the exotic and the erotic, and often by turning to fictional narratives for the subjects of their paintings, as the Romantic artists would also do.

1 ft.

22-4 ANTONIO CANOVA, *Pauline Borghese as Venus*, 1808. Marble, 6′ 7″ long. Galleria Borghese, Rome.

Canova was Napoleon's favorite sculptor. Here, the artist depicted the emperor's sister—at her request—as the nude Roman goddess of love in a marble statue inspired by classical models.

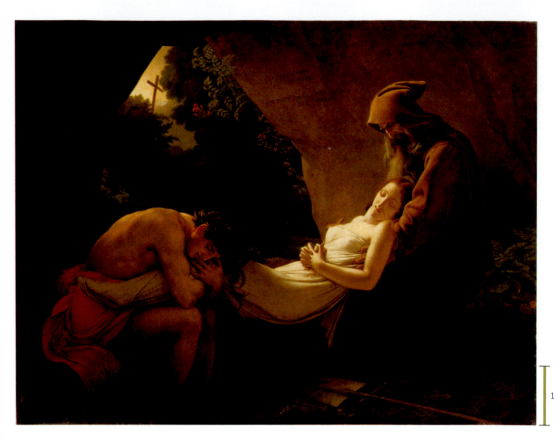

22-5 Anne-Louis Girodet-Trioson, *Burial of Atala*, 1808. Oil on canvas, 6′ 11″ × 8′ 9″. Musée du Louvre, Paris.

Girodet's depiction of Native American lovers in the Louisiana wilderness appealed to the French public's fascination with what it perceived as the passion and primitivism of the New World.

1 ft.

GIRODET-TRIOSON *Burial of Atala* (FIG. **22-5**) by ANNE-LOUIS GIRODET-TRIOSON (1767–1824) is an important bridge between Neoclassicism and Romanticism. Girodet based the painting on *The Genius of Christianity,* a novel by François René de Chateaubriand (1768–1848). The section of the novel dealing with Atala appeared as an excerpt a year before the publication of the entire book in 1802. Both the excerpt and the novel were enormously successful, and as a result, Atala became almost a cult figure. The exoticism and eroticism integral to the narrative accounted in large part for the public's interest in *The Genius of Christianity*. Set in Louisiana, Chateaubriand's work focuses on two young Native Americans, Atala and Chactas. The two, from different tribes, fall in love and run away together through the wilderness. Erotic passion permeates the story, and Atala, sworn to lifelong virginity, finally commits suicide rather than break her oath. Girodet's painting depicts this tragedy. Atala's grief-stricken lover, Chactas, buries the heroine in the shadow of a cross. Assisting in the burial is a cloaked priest, whose presence is appropriate given Chateaubriand's emphasis on the revival of Christianity (and the Christianization of the New World) in his novel. Like Gros's depiction of the exotic Muslim world of Jaffa (FIG. 22-1), Girodet's representation of American Indian lovers in the Louisiana wilderness appealed to the public's fascination (whetted by the Louisiana Purchase in 1803) with what it perceived as the passion and primitivism of Native American life in the New World. *Burial of*

22-5A Girodet-Trioson, *Jean-Baptiste Belley,* 1797.

Atala speaks here to emotions, rather than inviting philosophical meditation or revealing some grand order of nature and form. Unlike David's appeal in *Oath of the Horatii* (FIG. 21-25) to feelings that inspire public action, the appeal here is to the viewer's private world of fantasy and emotion. But Girodet-Trioson also occasionally addressed contemporary themes in his work, as he did in his portrait (FIG. **22-5A**) of Jean-Baptiste Belley, a French legislator and former slave.

INGRES David's greatest pupil, J.-A.-D. Ingres (FIG. 22-2A), arrived at David's studio in the late 1790s after Girodet-Trioson had left to

establish an independent career. Ingres's study there was to be short-lived, however, as he soon broke with David on matters of style. Ingres adopted what he believed to be a truer and purer Greek style than David's Neoclassical manner. The younger artist employed flat, linear forms approximating those found in Greek vase painting (see Chapter 5), and often placed the main figures in the foreground of his composition, emulating classical low-relief sculpture.

APOTHEOSIS OF HOMER Ingres exhibited his huge composition *Apotheosis of Homer* (FIG. **22-6**) at the Salon of 1827 (see "Academic Salons," Chapter 23, page 690). The painting presented in a single statement the doctrines of ideal form and of Neoclassical taste, and generations of academic painters remained loyal to that style. Winged Victory (or Fame) crowns the epic poet Homer, who sits like a god on a throne before an Ionic temple. At Homer's feet are two statuesque women, personifications of the *Iliad* and the *Odyssey,* the offspring of his imagination. Symmetrically grouped about him is a company of the "sovereign geniuses"—as Ingres called them—who expressed humanity's highest ideals in philosophy, poetry, music, and art. To Homer's left are the Greek poet Anacreon with his lyre, Phidias with his sculptor's hammer, the philosophers Plato and Socrates, and other ancient worthies of different eras. They gather together in the painter's world of suspended time as Raphael united them in *School of Athens* (FIG. 17-9), which was the inspiration for *Apotheosis of Homer*. To the far right in Ingres's assembly of literary and artistic giants are the Roman poets Horace and Vergil, and two Italians: Dante, and, conspicuously, Raphael. Among the forward group on the painting's left side are Poussin (pointing) and Shakespeare (half concealed). At the right are French writers Jean Baptiste Racine, Molière, Voltaire, and François de Salignac de la Mothe Fénelon. Ingres had planned a much larger and more inclusive group, but he never completed the project.

22-6 JEAN-AUGUSTE-DOMINIQUE INGRES, *Apotheosis of Homer*, 1827. Oil on canvas, 12′ 8″ × 16′ 10¾″. Musée du Louvre, Paris. ◼◀

Inspired by *School of Athens* (FIG. 17-9) by Raphael, Ingres's favorite painter, this monumental canvas is a Neoclassical celebration of Homer and other ancient worthies, Dante, and select French authors.

1 ft.

languid pose, small head and elongated limbs, and the generally cool color scheme reveal the painter's debt to Parmigianino (FIG. 17-44) and the Italian Mannerists. However, by converting the figure to an *odalisque* (woman in a Turkish harem), Ingres, unlike Canova, made a strong concession to the burgeoning Romantic taste for the exotic.

This rather strange mixture of artistic allegiances—the combination of precise classical form and Romantic themes—prompted

GRANDE ODALISQUE Despite his commitment to ideal form and careful compositional structure, Ingres also produced works that, like those of Gros and Girodet, his contemporaries saw as departures from Neoclassicism. The most famous is *Grande Odalisque* (FIG. 22-7). The subject—the reclining nude female figure—followed the grand tradition of antiquity and the Renaissance (FIGS. 17-16 and 17-39) in sculpture as well as painting, as did Canova's *Pauline Borghese as Venus* (FIG. 22-4). *Grande Odalisque* again shows Ingres's admiration for Raphael in his borrowing of that master's type of female head (FIGS. 17-7 and 17-8). The figure's

confusion, and when Ingres first exhibited *Grande Odalisque* in 1814, the painting drew acid criticism. Critics initially saw Ingres as a rebel in terms of both the form and content of his works. They did not cease their attacks until the mid-1820s, when a greater enemy of David's Neoclassical style, Eugène Delacroix, appeared on the scene. Then critics suddenly perceived that Ingres's art, despite its innovations and deviations, still contained crucial elements adhering to the Neoclassical taste for the ideal. In fact, Ingres soon became the leader of the academic forces in their battle against the "barbarism" of Delacroix, Théodore Géricault, and the Romantic movement.

22-7 JEAN-AUGUSTE-DOMINIQUE INGRES, *Grande Odalisque*, 1814. Oil on canvas, 2′ 11⅞″ × 5′ 4″. Musée du Louvre, Paris. ◼◀

The reclining female nude was a Greco-Roman subject, but Ingres converted his Neoclassical figure into an odalisque in a Turkish harem, consistent with the new Romantic taste for the exotic.

1 ft.

ROMANTICISM

Whereas Neoclassicism's rationality reinforced Enlightenment thought (see Chapter 21), particularly Voltaire's views, Rousseau's ideas contributed to the rise of *Romanticism*. Rousseau's exclamation "Man is born free, but is everywhere in chains!"—the opening line of his *Social Contract* (1762)—summarizes a fundamental Romantic premise. Romanticism emerged from a desire for freedom—not only political freedom but also freedom of thought, of feeling, of action, of worship, of speech, and of taste. Romantics asserted freedom was the right and property of all. They believed the path to freedom was through imagination rather than reason and functioned through feeling rather than through thinking.

The allure of the Romantic spirit grew dramatically during the late 18th century, when the term originated among German literary critics. Their aim was to distinguish peculiarly "modern" traits from the Neoclassical traits that already had displaced Baroque and Rococo design elements. Consequently, some scholars refer to Romanticism as a phenomenon that began around 1750 and ended about 1850, but most use the term more narrowly to denote a movement that flourished from about 1800 to 1840, between Neoclassicism and Realism.

Roots of Romanticism

The transition from Neoclassicism to Romanticism represented a shift in emphasis from reason to feeling, from calculation to intuition, and from objective nature to subjective emotion. Among Romanticism's manifestations were the interests in the medieval period and in the sublime. For people living in the 18th century, the Middle Ages were the "dark ages," a time of barbarism, superstition, dark mystery, and miracle. The Romantic imagination stretched its perception of the Middle Ages into all the worlds of fantasy open to it, including the ghoulish, the infernal, the terrible, the nightmarish, the grotesque, the sadistic, and all the imagery that comes from the chamber of horrors when reason sleeps. Related to the imaginative sensibility was the period's notion of the sublime. Among the individuals most involved in studying the sublime was the British politician and philosopher Edmund Burke (1729–1797). In *A Philosophical Enquiry into the Origins of Our Ideas of the Sublime and Beautiful* (1757), Burke articulated his definition of the sublime—feelings of awe mixed with terror. Burke observed that pain or fear evoked the most intense human emotions and that these emotions could also be thrilling. Thus, raging rivers and great storms at sea could be sublime to their viewers.

Accompanying this taste for the sublime was the taste for the fantastic, the occult, and the macabre—for the adventures of the soul voyaging into the dangerous reaches of the imagination.

HENRY FUSELI The concept of the nightmare is the subject of a 1781 painting (FIG. **22-8**) by HENRY FUSELI (1741–1825). Swiss by birth, Fuseli settled in England and eventually became a member of the Royal Academy and an instructor there. Largely self-taught, he contrived a distinctive manner to express the fantasies of his vivid imagination. Fuseli specialized in night moods of horror and in dark fantasies—in the demonic, in the macabre, and often in the sadistic. In *The Nightmare,* a beautiful young woman lies asleep, draped across the bed with her limp arm dangling over the side. An *incubus,* a demon believed in medieval times to prey, often sexually, on sleeping women, squats ominously on her body. In the background, a ghostly horse with flaming eyes bursts into the scene from beyond the curtain. Despite the temptation to see the painting's title as a pun because of this horse, the word *nightmare* in fact derives from "night" and "Mara." Mara was a spirit in Scandinavian mythology who tormented and suffocated sleepers. Fuseli was among the first to attempt to depict the dark terrain of the human subconscious that became fertile ground for later artists to harvest.

WILLIAM BLAKE In their images of the sublime and the terrible, Romantic artists often combined something of Baroque dynamism with naturalistic details in their quest for grippingly moving visions. These elements became the mainstay of Romantic art and contrasted with the more intellectual, rational Neoclassical themes and compositions. The two were not mutually exclusive, however. Gros, Girodet-Trioson, and Ingres effectively integrated elements of Neoclassicism with Romanticism. So, too, did the visionary English poet, painter, and engraver WILLIAM BLAKE (1757–1827). Blake greatly admired ancient Greek art because it exemplified for him the mathematical and thus the eternal, and his work often incorporated classical references. Yet Blake did not align himself with prominent Enlightenment figures. Like many other Romantic

22-8 HENRY FUSELI, *The Nightmare,* 1781. Oil on canvas, 3′ 3¾″ × 4′ 1½″. Detroit Institute of the Arts (Founders Society purchase with funds from Mr. and Mrs. Bert L. Smokler and Mr. and Mrs. Lawrence A. Fleishman).

The transition from Neoclassicism to Romanticism marked a shift in emphasis from reason to feeling. Fuseli was among the first painters to depict the dark terrain of the human subconscious.

1 ft.

of his Michelangelesque physique keeps him firmly planted on his heavenly perch. In this image Blake merged ideal classical anatomy with the inner dark dreams of Romanticism.

Spain and France

From its roots in the work of Fuseli, Blake, and other late-18th-century artists, Romanticism gradually displaced Neoclassicism as the dominant painting style of the first half of the 19th century. Romantic artists, including Francisco Goya in Spain and Théodore Géricault and Eugène Delacroix in France, reveled in exploring the exotic, erotic, and fantastic.

FRANCISCO GOYA Although FRANCISCO JOSÉ DE GOYA Y LUCIENTES (1746–1828) was David's contemporary, their work has little in common. Goya, however, did not arrive at his general dismissal of Neoclassicism without considerable thought about the Enlightenment and the Neoclassical penchant for rationality and order. In *The Sleep of Reason Produces Monsters* (FIG. **22-10**), an

1 in.

22-9 WILLIAM BLAKE, *Ancient of Days,* frontispiece of *Europe: A Prophecy,* 1794. Metal relief etching, hand colored, $9\frac{1}{2}'' \times 6\frac{3}{4}''$. Pierpont Morgan Library, New York.

Although art historians classify Blake as a Romantic artist, he incorporated classical references in his works. Here, ideal classical anatomy merges with the inner dark dreams of Romanticism.

artists, he also found the art of the Middle Ages appealing. Blake derived the inspiration for many of his paintings and poems from his dreams. The importance he attached to these nocturnal experiences led him to believe the rationalist search for material explanations of the world stifled the spiritual side of human nature. He also believed the stringent rules of behavior that orthodox religions imposed killed the individual creative impulse.

Blake's vision of the Almighty in *Ancient of Days* (FIG. **22-9**) combines his ideas and interests in a highly individual way. For Blake, this figure united the concept of the Creator with that of wisdom as a part of God. He chose *Ancient of Days* as the frontispiece for his book *Europe: A Prophecy,* and juxtaposed it with a quotation ("When he set a compass upon the face of the deep") from Proverbs 8:27. The speaker is Wisdom, who tells the reader how she was with the Lord through all the time of the creation (Prov. 8:22–23, 27–30). Energy fills Blake's composition. The Almighty leans forward from a fiery orb, peering toward earth and unleashing power through his outstretched left arm into twin rays of light. These emerge between his spread fingers like an architect's measuring instrument—a conception of creation with precedents in Gothic manuscript painting (FIG. 13-32). Here, however, a mighty wind surges through the Creator's thick hair and beard. Only the strength

1 in.

22-10 FRANCISCO GOYA, *The Sleep of Reason Produces Monsters,* from *Los Caprichos,* ca. 1798. Etching and aquatint, $8\frac{1}{2}'' \times 5\frac{7}{8}''$. Metropolitan Museum of Art, New York (gift of M. Knoedler & Co., 1918).

In this print, Goya depicted himself asleep while threatening creatures converge on him, revealing his commitment to the Romantic spirit—the unleashing of imagination, emotions, and nightmares.

etching from a series titled *Los Caprichos* (*The Caprices*), Goya depicted himself asleep, slumped onto a desk, while threatening creatures converge on him. Seemingly poised to attack the artist are owls (symbols of folly) and bats (symbols of ignorance). The viewer might read this as a portrayal of what emerges when reason is suppressed and, therefore, as advocating Enlightenment ideals. However, the print also can be interpreted as Goya's commitment to the creative process and the Romantic spirit—the unleashing of imagination, emotions, and even nightmares.

22-10A GOYA, *Family of Charles IV*, 1800.

THIRD OF MAY, 1808 Much of Goya's multifaceted work deals not with Romantic fantasies but with contemporary events. In 1786, he became an official artist in the court of Charles IV (r. 1788–1808) and produced portraits of the king and his family (FIG. **22-10A**). Dissatisfaction with the king's rule increased dramatically during Goya's tenure at the court, and the Spanish people eventually threw their support behind the king's son, Ferdinand VII, in the hope he would initiate reform. To overthrow his father and mother, Queen Maria Luisa (1751–1819), Ferdinand enlisted the aid of Napoleon Bonaparte, who possessed uncontested authority and military expertise at that time. Napoleon had designs on the Spanish throne and thus readily agreed to send French troops to Spain. Not surprisingly, as soon as he ousted Charles IV, Napoleon revealed his plan to rule Spain himself by installing his brother Joseph Bonaparte (r. 1808–1813) on the Spanish throne.

The Spanish people, finally recognizing the French as invaders, sought a way to expel the foreign troops. On May 2, 1808, Spaniards attacked Napoleon's soldiers in a chaotic and violent clash. In retaliation and as a show of force, the French responded the next day by rounding up and executing Spanish citizens. This tragic event is the subject of Goya's most famous painting, *Third of*

May, 1808 (FIG. **22-11**), commissioned in 1814 by Ferdinand VII (r. 1813–1833), who had reclaimed the throne after the ouster of the French. In emotional fashion, Goya depicted the anonymous murderous wall of Napoleonic soldiers ruthlessly executing the unarmed and terrified Spanish peasants. The artist encouraged empathy for the Spaniards by portraying horrified expressions and anguish on their faces, endowing them with a humanity lacking in the French firing squad. Moreover, the peasant about to be shot throws his arms out in a cruciform gesture reminiscent of Christ's position on the cross. Goya enhanced the emotional drama of the massacre by using stark darks and lights and by extending the time frame depicted. Although Goya captured the specific moment when one man is about to be executed, he also recorded the bloody bodies of others lying dead on the ground. Still others have been herded together to be shot in a few moments.

SATURN Over time, Goya became increasingly disillusioned and pessimistic, and his declining health further contributed to this state of mind. Among Goya's later works are the "Black Paintings," frescoes he painted on the walls of his farmhouse in Quinta del Sordo, outside Madrid. Because Goya created these works solely on his terms and for his private viewing, they provide great insight into the artist's outlook, which is terrifying and disturbing. *Saturn Devouring One of His Children* (FIG. **22-12**) depicts the raw carnage and violence of Saturn (the Greek god Kronos; see "The Gods and Goddesses of Mount Olympus," Chapter 5, page 107, or page xxxiii in Volume II), wild-eyed and monstrous, as he consumes one of his offspring. Because of the similarity of Kronos and *khronos* (the Greek word for "time"), Saturn has come to be associated with time. This has led some to interpret Goya's painting as an expression of the artist's despair over the passage of time. Despite the simplicity of the image, it conveys a wildness, boldness, and brutality that evokes an elemental response from all viewers. Goya's work, rooted both in personal and national history, presents darkly emotional images well in keeping with Romanticism.

22-11 FRANCISCO GOYA, *Third of May, 1808*, 1814–1815. Oil on canvas, 8′ 9″ × 13′ 4″. Museo del Prado, Madrid. ◼◀

Goya encouraged empathy for the massacred Spanish peasants by portraying horrified expressions on their faces, endowing them with a humanity lacking in the French firing squad.

1 ft.

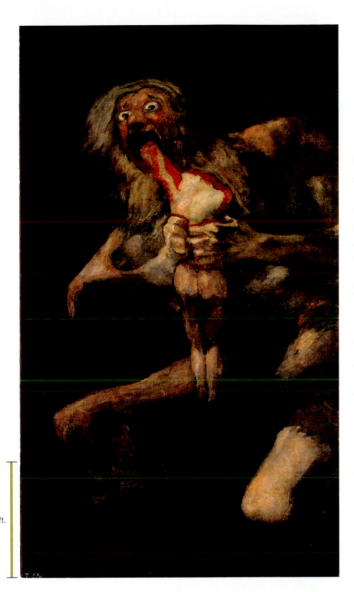

22-12 Francisco Goya, *Saturn Devouring One of His Children*, 1819–1823. Fresco, later detached and mounted on canvas, 4′ 9⅛″ × 2′ 8⅝″. Museo del Prado, Madrid.

This disturbing fresco in Goya's farmhouse uses a mythological tale to express the aging artist's despair over the passage of time. Saturn's Greek name *Kronos* is similar to the Greek word for "time."

THÉODORE GÉRICAULT In France, one of the artists most closely associated with the Romantic movement was THÉODORE GÉRICAULT (1791–1824), who studied with an admirer of David, PIERRE-NARCISSE GUÉRIN (1774–1833). Although Géricault retained an interest in the heroic and the epic and completed rigorous training in classical drawing, he chafed at the rigidity of the Neoclassical style, instead producing works that captivate viewers with their drama, visual complexity, and emotional force.

RAFT OF THE MEDUSA Géricault's most ambitious project was a gigantic canvas (approximately 16 by 23 feet) titled *Raft of the Medusa* (FIG. **22-13**), exhibited in the Salon of 1819, seven years after he burst onto the Parisian art scene with *Charging Chasseur* (FIG. **22-13A**). In both works, Géricault abandoned the idealism of Neoclassicism and embraced the theatricality of Romanticism. The subject of *Raft of the Medusa* is the 1816 shipwreck off the African coast of the French frigate *Medusa,* which ran aground on a reef due to the incompetence of the captain, a political appointee. In an attempt to sur-

22-13A GÉRICAULT, *Charging Chasseur,* 1812.

vive, 150 passengers built a makeshift raft from pieces of the disintegrating ship. The raft drifted for 12 days, and the number still alive dwindled to 15. Finally, a ship spotted the raft and rescued the emaciated survivors. This horrendous event was political dynamite once it became public knowledge.

In *Raft of the Medusa*, which took Géricault eight months to complete, the artist sought to capture the horror, chaos, and emotion of the tragedy yet invoke the grandeur and impact of Neoclassical history painting.

22-13 THÉODORE GÉRICAULT, *Raft of the Medusa*, 1818–1819. Oil on canvas, 16′ 1″ × 23′ 6″. Musée du Louvre, Paris. ◼◂

In this gigantic history painting, Géricault rejected Neoclassical compositional principles and, in the Romantic spirit, presented a jumble of writhing bodies in every attitude of suffering, despair, and death.

1 ft.

Romanticism **653**

Géricault went to great lengths to ensure the accuracy of his representation. He visited hospitals and morgues to examine corpses, interviewed the survivors, and had a model of the raft constructed in his studio. In the painting, the few despairing survivors summon what little strength they have left to flag down the passing ship far on the horizon. The subdued palette and prominent shadows lend an ominous pall to the scene. Géricault departed from the straightforward organization of Neoclassical compositions and instead presented a jumble of writhing bodies. He arranged the survivors and several corpses in a powerful X-shaped composition, and piled one body on another in every attitude of suffering, despair, and death (recalling the plague-stricken figures in Gros's *Napoleon at the Plague House at Jaffa*, FIG. 22-1). One light-filled diagonal axis stretches from bodies at the lower left up to the black man raised on his comrades' shoulders and waving a piece of cloth toward the horizon. The cross axis descends from the dark, billowing sail at the upper left to the shadowed upper torso of the body trailing in the open sea. Géricault's decision to place the raft at a diagonal so that a corner juts outward further draws viewers into the tragic scene. Indeed, it seems as though some of the corpses are sliding off the raft into the viewing space.

Raft of the Medusa is also the artist's commentary on the practice of slavery. Géricault was a member of an abolitionist group that sought ways to end the slave trade in the colonies, the cause promoted in the French legislature by Jean-Baptiste Belley (FIG. 22-5A). Given Géricault's antipathy to slavery, it is appropriate he placed Jean Charles, a black soldier who was one of the few survivors, at the top of the pyramidal heap of bodies.

22-14 THÉODORE GÉRICAULT, *Insane Woman*, 1822–1823. Oil on canvas, 2′ 4″ × 1′ 9″. Musée des Beaux-Arts, Lyons.

The insane and the influence of aberrant states of mind on the appearance of the human face fascinated Géricault and other Romantic artists, who rebelled against Enlightenment rationality.

INSANE WOMAN Mental aberration and irrational states of mind could not fail to interest the rebels against Enlightenment rationality. Géricault, like Goya, examined the influence of mental states on the human face and believed, as many of his contemporaries did, that a face accurately revealed character, especially at the moment of death (FIG. 22-11) and in madness (FIG. 22-12). Géricault made many studies of the inmates of hospitals and institutions for the criminally insane, and he studied the severed heads of guillotine victims. Scientific and artistic curiosity often accompanied the morbidity of the Romantic interest in derangement and death.

Insane Woman (FIG. **22-14**) is one of several of Géricault's portraits of the insane possessing a peculiar hypnotic power. The woman looks away from the viewer, her mouth tense and her eyes red-rimmed with suffering. The portrait presents the psychic facts with astonishing authenticity and breaks sharply with traditional portraiture in which the sitter's visage is idealized, the expression placid, and the setting designed to communicate the elevated stature of the person portrayed.

EUGÈNE DELACROIX Art historians often present the history of painting during the first half of the 19th century as a contest between two major artists—Ingres, the Neoclassical draftsman, and EUGÈNE DELACROIX (1798–1863; FIG. 22-50), the Romantic colorist. Their dialogue recalls the quarrel between the Poussinistes and the Rubénistes at the end of the 17th century and the beginning of the 18th (see Chapter 21). The Poussinistes were conservative defenders of academism who insisted that drawing was superior to color, whereas the Rubénistes proclaimed the importance of color over line (line quality being more intellectual and thus more restrictive than color). Delacroix's works were products of his view that the artist's powers of imagination would in turn capture and inflame the viewer's imagination. Literature of imaginative power served Delacroix (and many of his contemporaries) as a useful source of subject matter (see "The Romantic Spirit in Art, Music, and Literature," page 655). Théophile Gautier (1811–1872), the prominent Romantic critic and novelist, recalled:

> In those days painting and poetry fraternized. The artists read the poets, and the poets visited the artists. We found Shakespeare, Dante, Goethe, Lord Byron and Walter Scott in the studio as well as in the study. There were as many splashes of color as there were blots of ink in the margins of those beautiful books which we endlessly perused. Imagination, already excited, was further fired by reading those foreign works, so rich in color, so free and powerful in fantasy.[1]

DEATH OF SARDANAPALUS Delacroix's 1827 *Death of Sardanapalus* (FIG. **22-15**) is perhaps the grandest Romantic pictorial drama ever painted. Although inspired by the 1821 narrative poem *Sardanapalus* by Lord Byron (1788–1824), the painting does not illustrate that text faithfully. Delacroix depicted the last hour of the Assyrian king Ashurbanipal (r. 668–627 BCE; FIG. 2-23), whom the Greeks called Sardanapalus. The king has just received news of his armies' defeat and the enemies' entry into his city. The setting Delacroix painted is much more tempestuous and crowded than Byron described, and orgiastic destruction has replaced the sacrificial suicide of the poem. Sardanapalus reclines on his funeral pyre, soon to be set alight, and gloomily watches the destruction of all of his most precious possessions—his women, slaves, horses, and treasure. The king's favorite concubine throws herself on the bed, determined to go up in flames with her master. The Assyrian ruler presides like a genius of evil over the tragic scene. Most conspicuous

The Romantic Spirit in Art, Music, and Literature

The appeal of Romanticism, with its emphasis on freedom and feeling, extended well beyond the realm of the visual arts. The imagination and vision that characterized Romantic paintings and sculptures were equally moving and riveting in musical or written form. In European music, literature, and poetry, the Romantic spirit was a dominant presence during the late 18th and early 19th centuries. Composers and authors alike rejected classicism's structured order in favor of the emotive and expressive. In music, the compositions of Franz Schubert (1797–1828), Franz Liszt (1811–1886), Frédéric Chopin (1810–1849), and Johannes Brahms (1833–1897) emphasized the melodic or lyrical. For these composers, music had the power to express the unspeakable and to communicate the subtlest and most powerful human emotions.

In literature, Romantic poets such as John Keats (1795–1821), William Wordsworth (1770–1850), and Samuel Taylor Coleridge (1772–1834) published volumes of poetry manifesting the Romantic interest in lyrical drama. *Ozymandias,* by Percy Bysshe Shelley (1792–1822), transported readers to faraway, exotic locales. The setting of Lord Byron's *Sardanapalus* is the ancient Assyrian Empire (see Chapter 2). Byron's poem conjures images of eroticism and fury unleashed—images Eugène Delacroix made concrete in his painting *Death of Sardanapalus* (FIG. 22-15). One of the best examples of the Romantic spirit is the engrossing novel *Frankenstein,* written in 1818 by Shelley's wife, Mary Wollstonecraft Shelley (1797–1851). This fantastic tale of a monstrous creature run amok remains popular to the present day. As was true of many Romantic artworks, the novel not only embraced emotionalism but also rejected the rationalism underlying Enlightenment thought. Dr. Frankenstein's monster was a product of science, and the novel is an indictment of the tenacious belief in science that Voltaire and other Enlightenment thinkers promoted. *Frankenstein* served as a cautionary tale of the havoc that could result from unrestrained scientific experimentation and from the arrogance of scientists.

1 ft.

22-15 Eugène Delacroix, *Death of Sardanapalus,* 1827. Oil on canvas, 12′ 1½″ × 16′ 2⅞″. Musée du Louvre, Paris. ◼◀

Inspired by Byron's 1821 poem, Delacroix painted the Romantic spectacle of an Assyrian king on his funeral pyre. The richly colored and emotionally charged canvas is filled with exotic figures.

are the tortured and dying bodies of the harem women. In the foreground, a muscular slave plunges his knife into the neck of one woman. Delacroix filled this awful spectacle of suffering and death with the most daringly difficult and tortuous poses, and chose the richest intensities of hue. With its exotic and erotic overtones, *Death of Sardanapalus* tapped into the Romantic fantasies of 19th-century viewers.

Although *Death of Sardanapalus* is a seventh-century BCE drama, Delacroix, as Géricault, also turned to current events, particularly tragic or sensational ones, for his subject matter. For example, he produced several images based on the Greek War for Independence (1821–1829), including a huge canvas painted while the war was in progress recording the Turkish massacre of the Greeks of Chios (FIG. **22-15A**). The French perception of the Greeks locked in a brutal struggle for freedom from the cruel and exotic Ottoman Turks generated great interest in Romantic circles.

22-15A Delacroix, *Massacre at Chios,* 1822–1824.

22-16 EUGÈNE DELACROIX, *Liberty Leading the People,* 1830. Oil on canvas, 8′ 6″ × 10′ 8″. Musée du Louvre, Paris. ◼◀

In a balanced mix of history and poetic allegory, Delacroix captured the passion and energy of the 1830 revolution in this painting of Liberty leading the Parisian uprising against Charles X.

1 ft.

LIBERTY LEADING THE PEOPLE Closer to home, Delacroix captured the passion and energy of the 1830 revolution in *Liberty Leading the People* (FIG. **22-16**). Based on the Parisian uprising against Charles X (r. 1824–1830) at the end of July 1830, it depicts the allegorical personification of Liberty defiantly thrusting forth the republic's tricolor banner as she urges the masses to fight on. The scarlet Phrygian cap (the symbol of a freed slave in antiquity) she wears reinforces the urgency of this struggle. Arrayed around Liberty are bold Parisian types—the street boy brandishing his pistols, the menacing worker with a cutlass, and the intellectual dandy in a top hat brandishing a musket. As in Géricault's *Raft of the Medusa* (FIG. 22-13), dead bodies are all around. In the background, the towers of Notre-Dame (FIG. 13-11) rise through the smoke and haze. The painter's inclusion of this recognizable Parisian landmark announces the specificity of locale and event, balancing contemporary historical fact with poetic allegory.

22-17A DELACROIX, *Women of Algiers,* 1834.

TIGER HUNT An enormously influential event in Delacroix's life that affected his art in both subject and form was his visit to North Africa in 1832 (see "Delacroix in Morocco," page 657). Things he saw there shocked his imagination with fresh impressions that lasted throughout his life and resulted in paintings such as *Tiger Hunt* (FIG. **22-17**), which he completed more than two decades after his trip. Among the canvases he painted immediately upon his return is *Women of Algiers* (FIG. **22-17A**), which captivated the public

when exhibited in the 1834 Salon. Delacroix's African experience further heightened his already considerable awareness of the expressive power of color and light. What Delacroix knew about color he passed on to later painters of the 19th century, particularly the Impressionists (see Chapter 23). He observed that pure colors are as rare in nature as lines and that color appears only in an infinitely varied scale of different tones, shadings, and reflections, which he tried to re-create in his paintings. He recorded his observations in his journal, which became for later painters and scholars a veritable handbook of pre-Impressionist color theory. Although Delacroix anticipated the later development of Impressionist color science, that art-science had to await the discoveries by Michel Eugène Chevreul (1786–1889) and Hermann von Helmholtz (1821–1894) of the laws of light decomposition and the properties of complementary colors. Only then could the problems of color perception and juxtaposition in painting be properly formulated (see "19th-Century Color Theory," Chapter 23, page 701). Nevertheless, Delacroix's observations were significant, and he advised other artists not to fuse their brushstrokes, as those strokes would appear to fuse naturally from a distance.

No other painter of the time explored the domain of Romantic subject and mood as thoroughly and definitively as Delacroix. His technique was impetuous, improvisational, and instinctive, rather than deliberate, studious, and cold. It epitomized Romantic colorist painting, catching the impression quickly and developing it in the execution process. His contemporaries commented on how furiously Delacroix worked once he had an idea, keeping the whole painting progressing at once. The fury of his attack matched the fury of his imagination and his subjects.

Delacroix in Morocco

Romantic painters often depicted exotic faraway places they had never seen, but Eugène Delacroix journeyed to Morocco in 1832 and discovered in the sun-drenched landscape—and in the hardy and colorful Moroccans dressed in robes reminiscent of the Roman toga—new insights into a culture built on proud virtues. He found in North Africa a culture more classical than anything European Neoclassicism could conceive. In a letter to his friend Fréderic Villot dated February 29, 1832, he wrote:

> This place is made for painters. . . . [B]eauty abounds here; not the over-praised beauty of fashionable paintings. The heroes of David and Co. with their rose-pink limbs would cut a sorry figure beside these children of the sun, who moreover wear the dress of classical antiquity with a nobler air, I dare assert.*

In a second letter, written June 4, 1832, he reported to Auguste Jal:

> You have seen Algiers and you can imagine what the natives of these regions are like. Here there is something even simpler and more primitive; there is less of the Turkish alloy; I have Romans and Greeks on my doorstep: it makes me laugh heartily at David's Greeks, apart, of course, from his sublime skill as a painter. I know now what they were really like; . . . If painting schools persist in [depicting classical subjects], I am convinced, and you will agree

with me, that they would gain far more from being shipped off as cabin boys on the first boat bound for the Barbary coast than from spending any more time wearing out the classical soil of Rome. Rome is no longer to be found in Rome.†

The gallantry, valor, and fierce love of liberty of the Moroccans made them, in Delacroix's eyes, unspoiled heroes uncontaminated by European decadence. The Moroccan voyage reinforced Delacroix's Romantic conviction that beauty exists in the fierceness of nature, natural processes, and natural beings, especially animals. After he experienced Morocco, more and more of Delacroix's subjects involved combats between beasts or between beasts and men. He painted snarling tangles of lions and tigers, battles between horses, and clashes of Muslims with great cats in swirling hunting scenes using compositions reminiscent of those of Rubens (FIG. I-14), as in his 1854 painting *Tiger Hunt* (FIG. 22-17), which clearly speaks to the Romantic interest in faraway lands and exotic cultures.

---

*Translated by Jean Stewart, in Charles Harrison, Paul Wood, and Jason Gaiger, eds., *Art in Theory 1815–1900: An Anthology of Changing Ideas* (Oxford: Blackwell, 1998), 87.
†Ibid., 88.

1 ft.

22-17 EUGÈNE DELACROIX, *Tiger Hunt*, 1854. Oil on canvas, 2′ 5″ × 3′. Musée d'Orsay, Paris.

Delacroix's 1832 trip to Morocco inspired *Tiger Hunt* and had a lasting impact on his art. His paintings of men battling ferocious beasts are consistent with the Romantic interest in exotic places.

FRANÇOIS RUDE The Romantic spirit pervaded all media during the early 19th century. As did the painters of the period, many sculptors produced work incorporating both Neoclassical and Romantic elements. The colossal limestone group *Departure of the Volunteers of 1792* (FIG. **22-18**), also called *La Marseillaise*, is one example. The relief, the work of FRANÇOIS RUDE (1784–1855), decorates one of the gigantic piers of the Arc de Triomphe in Paris. This French landmark was an 1806 Napoleonic commission designed by Jean François Thérèse Chalgrin (1739–1811) on the model of the triumphal arches of ancient Rome (FIGS. 7-40, 7-44B, and 7-75). Work on the arch stopped after Napoleon's defeat but resumed in 1833. Three years later, workmen inserted Rude's group (and three similar ones by other sculptors) into the completed arch. The sculpture depicts the volunteers of 1792 departing to defend France's borders against the foreign enemies of the revolution. The Roman goddess of war, Bellona (who here personifies liberty as well as the "Marseillaise," the revolutionary hymn that is now France's national anthem), soars above patriots of all ages, exhorting them forward with her thundering battle cry. The figures recall David's classically armored (FIG. 21-25) or nude heroes, as do the rhetorical gestures of the wide-flung arms and the striding poses. Yet the violence of motion, the jagged contours, and the densely packed, overlapping

masses relate more closely to the compositional method of dramatic Romanticism, as found in the canvases of Géricault (FIG. 22-13) and Delacroix (FIG. 22-16). Indeed, the allegorical figure in *La Marseillaise* is the spiritual sister of Delacroix's Liberty. Rude's stone figure shares the same Phrygian cap, the badge of liberty, with Delacroix's earlier painted figure, but Rude's soldiers wear classical costumes or are heroically nude, whereas those in Delacroix's painting appear in modern Parisian dress. Both works are allegorical, but one looks to the past and the other to the present.

Landscape Painting

Landscape painting came into its own in the 19th century as a fully independent and respected genre. Briefly eclipsed at the century's beginning by the taste for ideal form, which favored figural composition and history, landscape painting flourished as leading painters adopted the genre as their specialty. Increasing tourism, which came courtesy of improved and expanded railway systems both in Europe (MAP 22-2) and America, contributed to the popularity of landscape painting.

The notion of the picturesque became particularly resonant in the Romantic era. Already in the 18th century, artists had regarded the pleasurable, aesthetic mood that natural landscape inspired as making the landscape itself "picturesque"—that is, worthy of being painted. Rather than simply describe nature, Romantic poets and artists often used nature as allegory. In this manner, artists commented on spiritual, moral, historical, or philosophical issues. Landscape painting was a particularly effective vehicle for such commentary.

In the early 19th century, most northern European (especially German) landscape painting to some degree expressed the Romantic view (first extolled by Rousseau) of nature as a "being" that included the totality of existence in organic unity and harmony. In nature—"the living garment of God," as German poet and dramatist Johann Wolfgang von Goethe (1749–1832) called it—artists found an ideal subject to express the Romantic theme of the soul unified with the natural world. As all nature was mysteriously permeated by "being," landscape artists had the task of interpreting the signs, symbols, and emblems of universal spirit disguised within visible material things. Artists no longer merely beheld a landscape but participated in its spirit, becoming translators of nature's transcendent meanings.

CASPAR DAVID FRIEDRICH Among the first northern European artists to depict the Romantic transcendental landscape was CASPAR DAVID FRIEDRICH (1774–1840). For Friedrich, landscapes were temples, and his paintings were altarpieces. The reverential mood of his works demands from the viewer the silence appropriate to sacred places filled with a divine presence. *Abbey in the Oak Forest* (FIG. **22-19**) serves as a solemn requiem. Under a winter sky, through the leafless oaks of a snow-covered cemetery, a funeral procession bears a coffin into the ruins of a Gothic church Friedrich based on the remains of Eldana Abbey in Greifswald. The emblems of death are everywhere—the season's desolation, the leaning crosses and tombstones, the black of mourning the grieving wear, the skeletal trees, and the destruction time has wrought on the church. The painting is a kind of meditation on human mortality. As Friedrich himself remarked: "Why, it has often occurred to me to ask myself, do I so frequently choose death, transience, and the grave as subjects for my paintings? One must submit oneself many times to death in order some day to attain life everlasting."[2] The artist's sharp-focused rendering of details demonstrates his keen perception of everything in the physical environment relevant to his message. Friedrich's work

10 ft.

22-18 FRANÇOIS RUDE, *Departure of the Volunteers of 1792* (*La Marseillaise*), Arc de Triomphe, Paris, France, 1833–1836. Limestone, 41′ 8″ high. ◼◀

This historical-allegorical sculpture features the Roman war goddess Bellona, but the violent motion, jagged contours, and densely packed masses typify Romantic painting compositions.

22-19 CASPAR DAVID FRIEDRICH, *Abbey in the Oak Forest,* 1810. Oil on canvas, 4′ × 5′ 8½″. Nationalgalerie, Staatliche Museen zu Berlin, Berlin. ◼️▶️

Friedrich was a master of the Romantic transcendental landscape. The reverential mood of this winter scene with a ruined Gothic church and cemetery demands the silence appropriate to sacred places.

balances inner and outer experience. "The artist," he wrote, "should not only paint what he sees before him, but also what he sees within him. If he does not see anything within him, he should give up painting what he sees before him."[3] Although Friedrich's works may not have the theatrical energy of the paintings of Géricault or Delacroix, a resonant and deep emotion pervades them.

WANDERER ABOVE A SEA OF MIST In *Abbey in the Oak Forest* and many of Friedrich's landscapes, the human figure plays an insignificant role. Indeed, in many instances the human actors are difficult even to discern. But in other paintings, one or more figures seen from behind gazing at the natural vista dominate the canvas. In *Wanderer above a Sea of Mist* (FIG. **22-20**), probably Friedrich's most famous painting, a solitary man dressed in German attire suggestive of a bygone era stands on a rocky promontory and leans on his cane. He surveys a vast panorama of clouds, mountains, and thick mist. Because Friedrich chose a point of view on the level of the man's head, the viewer has the sensation of hovering in space behind him—an impossible position that enhances the aura of mystery the scene conveys. Scholars dispute whether Friedrich intended the viewer to identify with the man seen from behind or if he wanted the viewer to contemplate the man gazing at the misty landscape. In either case, the painter communicated an almost religious awe at the beauty and vastness of the natural world. *Wanderer above a Sea of Mist* perfectly expresses the Romantic notion of the sublime in nature.

JOHN CONSTABLE In England, one of the most momentous developments in Western history—the Industrial Revolution—had a profound impact on the evolution of Romantic landscape painting. Although discussion of the Industrial Revolution invariably focuses on technological advances, factory development, and growth of urban centers (see Chapter 21), industrialization had no less pronounced an effect on the countryside and the land itself. The detrimental economic effect the Industrial Revolution had

22-20 CASPAR DAVID FRIEDRICH, *Wanderer above a Sea of Mist,* 1817–1818. Oil on canvas, 3′ 1¾″ × 2′ 5⅜″. Hamburger Kunsthalle, Hamburg.

Friedrich's painting of a solitary man on a rocky promontory gazing at a vast panorama of clouds, mountains, and thick mist perfectly expresses the Romantic notion of the sublime in nature.

22-21 John Constable, *The Haywain,* 1821. Oil on canvas, 4′ 3¼″ × 6′ 1″. National Gallery, London.

The Haywain is a nostalgic view of the disappearing English countryside during the Industrial Revolution. Constable had a special gift for capturing the texture that climate and weather give to landscape.

1 ft.

on prices for agrarian products produced significant unrest in the English countryside. In particular, increasing numbers of displaced farmers could no longer afford to farm their small land plots.

John Constable (1776–1837) addressed this agrarian crisis in his landscape paintings. He made countless studies from nature for each of his canvases, which helped him produce in his paintings the convincing sense of reality that won so much praise from his contemporaries. In his quest for the authentic landscape, Constable studied it as a meteorologist (which he was by avocation). His special gift was for capturing the texture that climate and weather, which delicately veil what is seen, give to landscape. Constable's use of tiny dabs of local color, stippled with white, created a sparkling shimmer of light and hue across the canvas surface—the vibration itself suggestive of movement and process.

The Haywain (FIG. **22-21**) is representative of Constable's art and reveals much about his outlook. A small cottage sits on the left of this placid, picturesque scene of the countryside, and in the center foreground, a man leads a horse and wagon across the stream. Billowy clouds float lazily across the sky. The muted greens and golds and the delicacy of Constable's brushstrokes complement the scene's tranquility. The artist portrayed the oneness with nature the Romantic poets sought. The relaxed figures are not observers but participants in the landscape's "being."

In terms of content, *The Haywain* is significant for precisely what it does not show—the civil unrest of the agrarian working class and the resulting outbreaks of violence and arson. The people populating Constable's landscapes blend into the scenes and are at one with nature. Rarely does the viewer see workers engaged in tedious labor. Indeed, this painting has a nostalgic, wistful air to it, and reflects Constable's memories of a disappearing rural pastoralism. The artist's father was a rural landowner of considerable wealth, and many of the scenes Constable painted (*The Haywain* included) depict his family's property near East Bergholt in Suffolk, East Anglia. This nostalgia, presented in such naturalistic terms, renders Constable's works Romantic in tone. That the painter felt a kindred spirit with the Romantic artists is revealed by his comment, "Painting is but another word for feeling."[4]

J.M.W. TURNER Constable's contemporary in the English school of landscape painting, Joseph Mallord William Turner (1775–1851), produced work that also responded to encroaching industrialization. However, whereas Constable's paintings are serene and precisely painted, Turner's feature turbulent swirls of frothy pigment. The passion and energy of Turner's works reveal the Romantic sensibility that was the foundation for his art and also clearly illustrate Edmund Burke's concept of the sublime—awe mixed with terror.

Among Turner's most notable works is *The Slave Ship* (FIG. **22-22**). Its subject is a 1783 incident reported in a widely read book titled *The History of the Abolition of the Slave Trade,* by Thomas Clarkson. Because the book had just been reprinted in 1839, Clarkson's account probably prompted Turner's choice of subject for this 1840 painting. The incident involved the captain of a slave ship who, on realizing his insurance company would reimburse him only for slaves lost at sea but not for those who died en route, ordered the sick and dying slaves thrown overboard. Appropriately, the painting's full title is *The Slave Ship* (*Slavers Throwing Overboard the Dead and Dying, Typhoon Coming On*). Turner's frenzied emotional depiction of this act matches its barbaric nature. The artist transformed the sun into an incandescent comet amid flying scarlet clouds. The slave ship moves into the distance, leaving in its wake a turbulent sea choked with the bodies of slaves sinking to their deaths. The relative scale of the minuscule human forms compared with the vast sea and overarching sky reinforces the sense of the sublime, especially the immense power of nature over humans. Almost lost in the boiling colors are the event's particulars, but on close inspection, the viewer can discern the iron shackles and manacles around the wrists and ankles of the drowning slaves, cruelly denying them any chance of saving themselves.

A key ingredient of Turner's highly personal style is the emotive power of pure color. The haziness of the painter's forms and the indistinctness of his compositions intensify the colors and energetic brushstrokes. Turner's innovation in works such as *The Slave Ship* was to release color from any defining outlines so as to express both the forces of nature and the painter's emotional response to them. In his paintings, the reality of color is at one with the reality of feeling. Turner's methods had an incalculable effect on the later

1 ft.

22-22 JOSEPH MALLORD WILLIAM TURNER, *The Slave Ship* (*Slavers Throwing Overboard the Dead and Dying, Typhoon Coming On*), 1840. Oil on canvas, 2′ 11¼″ × 4′. Museum of Fine Arts, Boston (Henry Lillie Pierce Fund).

The essence of Turner's innovative style is the emotive power of color. He released color from any defining outlines to express both the forces of nature and the painter's emotional response to them.

ongoing exploration of the individual's and the country's relationship to the land. American landscape painters frequently focused on identifying qualities that made America unique. One American painter of English birth, THOMAS COLE (1801–1848), often referred to as the leader of the Hudson River School, articulated this idea:

development of painting. His discovery of the aesthetic and emotive power of pure color and his pushing of the medium's fluidity to a point where the paint itself is almost the subject were important steps toward 20th-century abstract art, which dispensed with shape and form altogether (see Chapter 25).

THOMAS COLE In America, landscape painting was the specialty of a group of artists known as the Hudson River School, so named because its members drew their subjects primarily from the uncultivated regions of New York's Hudson River Valley, although many of these painters depicted scenes from across the country. As did the early-19th-century landscape painters in Germany and England, the artists of the Hudson River School not only presented Romantic panoramic landscape views but also participated in the

Whether he [an American] beholds the Hudson mingling waters with the Atlantic—explores the central wilds of this vast continent, or stands on the margin of the distant Oregon, he is still in the midst of American scenery—it is his own land; its beauty, its magnificence, its sublimity—all are his; and how undeserving of such a birthright, if he can turn towards it an unobserving eye, an unaffected heart![5]

Another issue that surfaced frequently in Hudson River School paintings was the moral question of America's direction as a civilization. Cole addressed this question in *The Oxbow* (*View from Mount Holyoke, Northampton, Massachusetts, after a Thunderstorm*; FIG. 22-23). A splendid scene opens before the viewer, dominated by the lazy oxbow-shaped turning of the Connecticut River. Cole divided the composition in two, with the dark, stormy wilderness on the left and the more developed civilization on the right. The minuscule artist in the bottom center of the painting (wearing a top hat), dwarfed by the landscape's scale, turns to the viewer as if to ask for input in deciding the country's future course. Cole's depictions of expansive wilderness incorporated reflections and moods romantically appealing to the public.

1 ft.

22-23 THOMAS COLE, *The Oxbow* (*View from Mount Holyoke, Northampton, Massachusetts, after a Thunderstorm*), 1836. Oil on canvas, 4′ 3½″ × 6′ 4″. Metropolitan Museum of Art, New York (gift of Mrs. Russell Sage, 1908). ◼▶

Cole divided his canvas into dark wilderness on the left and sunlit civilization on the right. The minuscule painter at the bottom center seems to be asking for advice about America's future course.

22-24 ALBERT BIERSTADT, *Among the Sierra Nevada Mountains, California*, 1868. Oil on canvas, 6′ × 10′. National Museum of American Art, Smithsonian Institution, Washington, D.C.

Bierstadt's panoramic landscape presents the breathtaking natural beauty of the American West, reinforcing the 19th-century doctrine of Manifest Destiny, which justified America's western expansion.

1 ft.

ALBERT BIERSTADT Other Hudson River artists used the landscape genre as an allegorical vehicle to address moral and spiritual concerns. ALBERT BIERSTADT (1830–1902) traveled west in 1858 and produced many paintings depicting the Rocky Mountains, Yosemite Valley, and other dramatic locales. These works, such as *Among the Sierra Nevada Mountains, California* (FIG. **22-24**), present breathtaking scenery and natural beauty. This panoramic view (the painting is 10 feet wide) is awe-inspiring. Deer and waterfowl appear at the edge of a placid lake, and steep and rugged mountains soar skyward on the left and in the distance. A stand of trees, uncultivated and wild, frames the lake on the right. To underscore the almost transcendental nature of this scene, Bierstadt depicted the sun's rays breaking through the clouds overhead, which suggests a heavenly consecration of the land. That Bierstadt's focus was the American West is not insignificant. By

calling national attention to the splendor and uniqueness of the regions beyond the Rocky Mountains, Bierstadt's paintings reinforced the idea of Manifest Destiny. This popular 19th-century doctrine held that westward expansion across the continent was the logical destiny of the United States. As John L. O'Sullivan (1813–1895) expounded in the earliest known use of the term in 1845, "Our manifest destiny [is] to overspread the continent allotted by Providence for the free development of our yearly multiplying millions."[6] Paintings of the scenic splendor of the West helped to mute growing concerns over the realities of conquest, the displacement of Native Americans, and the exploitation of the environment. It should come as no surprise that among those most eager to purchase Bierstadt's work were mail-service magnates and railroad builders—entrepreneurs and financiers involved in westward expansion.

22-25 FREDERIC EDWIN CHURCH, *Twilight in the Wilderness*, 1860s. Oil on canvas, 3′ 4″ × 5′ 4″. Cleveland Museum of Art, Cleveland (Mr. and Mrs. William H. Marlatt Fund).

Church's paintings eloquently express the Romantic notion of the sublime. Painted during the Civil War, this wilderness landscape presents an idealistic view of America free of conflict.

1 ft.

FREDERIC CHURCH Another painter usually associated with the Hudson River School was FREDERIC EDWIN CHURCH (1826–1900), but his interest in landscape scenes extended beyond America. He traveled widely—to South America, Mexico, Europe, the Middle East, Newfoundland, and Labrador. Church's paintings are firmly in the idiom of the Romantic sublime, yet they also reveal contradictions and conflicts in the constructed mythology of American providence and character. *Twilight in the Wilderness* (FIG. **22-25**) presents a panoramic view of the sun setting over the majestic landscape. Beyond Church's precise depiction of the magnificent spectacle of nature, the painting, like Constable's *Haywain* (FIG. **22-21**), is remarkable for what it does not depict. As did Constable, Church and the other Hudson River School painters worked in a time of great upheaval. *Twilight in the Wilderness* dates to the 1860s, when the Civil War was tearing apart the no-longer-united states. Yet this painting does not display evidence of turbulence or discord. Indeed, it does not include even a single figure. By constructing such an idealistic and comforting view, Church contributed to the national mythology of righteousness and divine providence—a mythology that had become increasingly difficult to maintain in the face of conflict.

Landscape painting was immensely popular in the late 18th and early 19th centuries, in large part because it provided viewers with breathtaking and sublime spectacles of nature. Artists also could allegorize nature, and it was rare for a landscape painting not to touch on spiritual, moral, historical, or philosophical issues. Landscape painting became the perfect vehicle for artists (and the viewing public) to "naturalize" conditions, rendering debate about contentious issues moot and eliminating any hint of conflict.

REALISM

Advances in industrial technology during the early 19th century reinforced Enlightenment faith in the connection between science and progress. Both intellectuals and the general public increasingly embraced *empiricism* and *positivism*. To empiricists, the basis of knowledge is observation and direct experience. Positivists

ascribed to the philosophical model developed by Auguste Comte (1798–1857), who believed scientific laws governed the environment and human activity and could be revealed through careful recording and analysis of observable data. Comte's followers promoted science as the mind's highest achievement and advocated a purely empirical approach to nature and society.

France

Realism was a movement that developed in France around mid-century against this backdrop of an increasing emphasis on science. Consistent with the philosophical tenets of the empiricists and positivists, Realist artists argued that only the contemporary world—what people can see—was "real." Accordingly, Realists focused their attention on the people and events of their own time and disapproved of historical and fictional subjects on the grounds they were neither visible nor present and therefore were not real.

GUSTAVE COURBET The leading figure of the Realist movement in 19th-century art was GUSTAVE COURBET (1819–1877). In fact, even though he shunned labels, Courbet used the term *Realism* when exhibiting his own works (see "Courbet on Realism," page 664). The Realists' sincerity about scrutinizing their environment led them to paint subjects artists had traditionally deemed unworthy of depiction—the mundane and trivial, working-class laborers and peasants, and so forth. Moreover, by depicting these subjects on a scale and with an earnestness and seriousness previously reserved for historical, mythological, and religious painting, Realist artists sought to establish parity between contemporary subject matter and the traditional themes of "high art."

THE STONE BREAKERS An early work that exemplifies Courbet's championing of everyday life as the only valid subject for the modern artist is *The Stone Breakers* (FIG. **22-26**), in which the Realist painter presented a glimpse into the life of rural menial laborers. Courbet represented in a straightforward manner two men—one about 70, the other quite young—in the act of breaking stones, traditionally the lot of the lowest members of French society. By juxtaposing youth and age, Courbet suggested those born

22-26 GUSTAVE COURBET, *The Stone Breakers*, 1849. Oil on canvas, 5′ 3″ × 8′ 6″. Formerly Gemäldegalerie, Dresden (destroyed in 1945).

Courbet was the leading figure in the Realist movement. Using a palette of dirty browns and grays, he conveyed the dreary and dismal nature of menial labor in mid-19th-century France.

1 ft.

Courbet on Realism

The academic jury selecting work for the 1855 Salon (part of the Exposition Universelle in Paris that year) rejected two of Courbet's paintings, declaring his subjects and figures were too coarse (so much so as to be plainly "socialistic") and too large. Typical of Courbet's work are *The Stone Breakers* (FIG. 22-26), which depicts menial laborers, and *Burial at Ornans* (FIG. 22-27), which represents the funeral of an ordinary man and is nearly 22 feet long. In response to the jury's decision, Courbet withdrew all of his works, including those that had been accepted, and set up his own exhibition outside the grounds, calling it the Pavilion of Realism. This was in itself a bold action. Courbet was the first artist ever known to have staged a private exhibition of his own work. His pavilion and the statement he issued to explain the paintings shown there amounted to the Realist movement's manifesto. Although Courbet maintained he founded no school and was of no school, he did, as the name of his pavilion suggests, accept the term *Realism* as descriptive of his art.

The statement Courbet distributed at his pavilion reads in part:

The title of "realist" has been imposed upon me . . . Titles have never given a just idea of things; were it otherwise, the work would be superfluous. . . . I have studied the art of the moderns, avoiding any preconceived system and without prejudice. I have no more wanted to imitate the former than to copy the latter; nor have I thought of achieving the idle aim of "art for art's sake." No! I have simply wanted to draw from a thorough knowledge of tradition the reasoned and free sense of my own individuality. . . . To be able to translate the customs, ideas, and appearances of my time as I see them—in a word, to create a living art—this has been my aim.*

Six years later, on Christmas Day, 1861, Courbet wrote an open letter, published a few days later in the *Courier du dimanche,* addressed to prospective students. In the letter, the painter reflected on the nature of his art.

[An artist must apply] his personal faculties to the ideas and the events of the times in which he lives. . . . [A]rt in painting should consist only of the representation of things that are visible and tangible to the artist. Every age should be represented only by its own artists, that is to say, by the artists who have lived in it. I also maintain that painting is an essentially concrete art form and can consist only of the representation of both real and existing things. . . . An abstract object, not visible, nonexistent, is not within the domain of painting.†

Courbet's most famous statement, however, is his blunt dismissal of academic painting, in which he concisely summed up the core principle of Realist painting:

I have never seen an angel. Show me an angel, and I'll paint one.‡

*Translated by Robert Goldwater and Marco Treves, eds., *Artists on Art from the XIV to the XX Century* (New York: Pantheon, 1958), 295.
†Translated by Petra ten-Doesschate Chu, *Letters of Gustave Courbet* (Chicago: University of Chicago Press, 1992), 203–204.
‡Quoted by Vincent van Gogh in a July 1885 letter to his brother Theo, in Ronald de Leeuw, *The Letters of Vincent van Gogh* (New York: Penguin, 1996), 302.

1 ft.

22-27 GUSTAVE COURBET, *Burial at Ornans*, 1849. Oil on canvas, 10′ 3½″ × 21′ 9½″. Musée d'Orsay, Paris.

Although as monumental in scale as a traditional history painting, *Burial at Ornans* horrified critics because of the ordinary nature of the subject and Courbet's starkly antiheroic composition.

to poverty remain poor their entire lives. The artist neither romanticized nor idealized the men's work but depicted their thankless toil with directness and accuracy. Courbet's palette of dirty browns and grays further conveys the dreary and dismal nature of the task, and the angular positioning of the older stone breaker's limbs suggests a mechanical monotony.

Courbet's interest in the working poor as subject matter had a special resonance for his mid-19th-century French audience. In 1848, laborers rebelled against the bourgeois leaders of the newly formed Second Republic and against the rest of the nation, demanding better working conditions and a redistribution of property. The army quelled the uprising in three days, but not without long-lasting trauma and significant loss of life. The 1848 revolution raised the issue of labor as a national concern. Courbet's depiction of stone breakers in 1849 was thus timely and populist.

BURIAL AT ORNANS Many art historians regard Courbet's *Burial at Ornans* (FIG. **22-27**) as his masterpiece. The huge (10 by 22 feet) canvas depicts a funeral set in a bleak provincial landscape outside the artist's home town. Attending the funeral are the types of ordinary people Honoré de Balzac (1799–1850) and Gustave Flaubert (1821–1880) presented in their novels. While an officious clergyman reads the Office of the Dead, those attending cluster around the excavated gravesite, their faces registering all degrees of response to the ceremony. Although the painting has the monumental scale of a traditional history painting, the subject's ordinariness and the starkly antiheroic composition horrified critics. Arranged in a wavering line extending across the enormous breadth of the canvas are three groups—the somberly clad women at the back right, a semicircle of similarly clad men by the open grave, and assorted churchmen at the left. This wall of figures blocks any view into deep space. The faces are portraits. Some of the models were Courbet's sisters (three of the women in the front row, toward the right) and friends. Behind and above the figures are bands of overcast sky and barren cliffs. The dark pit of the grave opens into the viewer's space in the center foreground. Despite the unposed look of the figures, Courbet controlled the composition in a masterful way by his sparing use of bright color. In place of the heroic, the sublime, and the dramatic, Courbet aggressively presented the viewer with the mundane realities of daily life and death. In 1857, Jules-François-Félix Husson Champfleury (1821–1889), one of the first critics to recognize and appreciate Courbet's work, wrote of *Burial at Ornans*, "[I]t represents a small-town funeral and yet reproduces the funerals of *all* small towns."[7] Unlike the theatricality of Romanticism, Realism captured the ordinary rhythms of daily life.

Of great importance for the later history of art, Realism also involved a reconsideration of the painter's primary goals and departed from the established emphasis on illusionism. Accordingly, Realists called attention to painting as a pictorial construction by the ways they applied pigment or manipulated composition. Courbet's intentionally simple and direct methods of expression in composition and technique seemed unbearably crude to many of his more traditional contemporaries, who called him a primitive. Although his bold, somber palette was essentially traditional, Courbet often used the *palette knife* for quickly placing and unifying large daubs of paint, producing a roughly wrought surface. His example inspired the young artists who worked for him (and later Impressionists such as Claude Monet and Auguste Renoir; see Chapter 28), but the public accused him of carelessness and critics wrote of his "brutalities."

JEAN-FRANÇOIS MILLET As did Courbet, JEAN-FRANÇOIS MILLET (1814–1878) found his subjects in the people and occupations of the everyday world. Millet was one of a group of French painters of country life who, to be close to their rural subjects, settled near the village of Barbizon in the forest of Fontainebleau. This Barbizon School specialized in detailed pictures of forest and countryside. Millet, their most prominent member, was of peasant stock and identified with the hard lot of the country poor. In *The Gleaners* (FIG. **22-28**), he depicted three impoverished women—members of the lowest level of peasant society—performing the backbreaking task of gleaning. Landowning nobles traditionally permitted peasants to glean, or collect, the wheat scraps left in the field after the harvest. Millet characteristically placed his monumental figures in the foreground, against a broad sky. Although the field stretches back to a rim of haystacks, cottages, trees, distant workers, and a flat horizon, the gleaners quietly doing their tedious and time-consuming work dominate the canvas.

1 ft.

22-28 JEAN-FRANÇOIS MILLET, *The Gleaners,* 1857. Oil on canvas, 2′ 9″ × 3′ 8″. Musée d'Orsay, Paris.

Millet and the Barbizon School painters specialized in depictions of French country life. Here, Millet portrayed three impoverished women gathering the scraps left in the field after a harvest.

Lithography

In 1798, the German printmaker Alois Senefelder (1771–1834) created the first prints using stone instead of metal plates or wooden blocks. In contrast to earlier printing techniques (see "Woodcuts, Engravings, and Etchings," Chapter 15, page 444), in which the artist applied ink either to a raised or incised surface, in *lithography* (Greek, "stone writing") the printing and nonprinting areas of the plate are on the same plane.

The chemical phenomenon fundamental to lithography is the repellence of oil and water. The lithographer uses a greasy, oil-based crayon to draw directly on a stone plate and then wipes water onto the stone, which clings only to the areas the drawing does not cover.

Next, the artist rolls oil-based ink onto the stone, which adheres to the drawing but is repelled by the water. When the artist presses the stone against paper, only the inked areas—the drawing—transfer to the paper. Color lithography requires multiple plates, one for each color, and the printmaker must take special care to make sure each impression lines up perfectly with the previous one so that each color prints in its proper place.

One of the earliest masters of this new printmaking process was Honoré Daumier, whose politically biting lithographs (FIG. 22-29) published in a widely read French journal reached an audience of unprecedented size.

22-29 HONORÉ DAUMIER, *Rue Transnonain*, 1834. Lithograph, 1′ × 1′ 5½″. Philadelphia Museum of Art, Philadelphia (bequest of Fiske and Marie Kimball).

RUE TRANSNONAIN, LE 15 AVRIL, 1834

1 in.

Daumier used the recent invention of lithography to reach a wide audience for his social criticism and political protest. This print records the horrific 1834 massacre in a workers' housing block.

Although Millet's paintings evoke a sentimentality absent from Courbet's, the French public still reacted to his work with disdain and suspicion. In the aftermath of the 1848 revolution, Millet's investiture of the poor with solemn grandeur did not meet with approval from the prosperous classes. In particular, middle-class landowners resisted granting gleaning rights, and thus Millet's relatively dignified depiction of gleaning antagonized them. The middle class also linked the poor with the dangerous, newly defined working class, which was finding outspoken champions in men such as Karl Marx (1818–1883), Friedrich Engels (1820–1895), and the novelists Émile Zola (1840–1902) and Charles Dickens (1812–1870). Socialism was a growing movement, and both its views on property and its call for social justice, even economic equality, threatened and frightened the bourgeoisie. Millet's sympathetic portrayal of the poor seemed to much of the public to be a political manifesto.

HONORÉ DAUMIER Because people widely recognized the power of art to serve political ends, the political and social agitation accompanying the violent revolutions in France and the rest of Europe in the later 18th and early 19th centuries prompted the French people to suspect artists of subversive intention. A person could be jailed for too bold a statement in the press, in literature, in art—even in music and drama. Realist artist HONORÉ DAUMIER (1808–1879) was a defender of the urban working classes, and in his art he boldly confronted authority with social criticism and political protest. In response, the authorities imprisoned the artist. A painter, sculptor, and, like Dürer, Rembrandt, and Goya, one of history's great printmakers, Daumier produced *lithographs* (see "Lithography," above) that enabled him to create an unprecedented number of prints, thereby reaching an exceptionally large and broad audience. In addition to producing individual prints for sale,

1 ft.

22-30 Honoré Daumier, *Third-Class Carriage,* ca. 1862. Oil on canvas, 2′ 1¾″ × 2′ 11½″. Metropolitan Museum of Art, New York (H. O. Havemeyer Collection, bequest of Mrs. H. O. Havemeyer, 1929).

Daumier frequently depicted the plight of the disinherited masses of 19th-century industrialization. Here, he portrayed the anonymous poor cramped together in a grimy third-class railway carriage.

Daumier also contributed satirical lithographs to the widely read, liberal French Republican journal *Caricature,* further increasing the number of people exposed to his work. In *Caricature,* Daumier mercilessly lampooned the foibles and misbehavior of politicians, lawyers, doctors, and the rich bourgeoisie in general.

RUE TRANSNONAIN Daumier's lithograph *Rue Transnonain* (FIG. **22-29**) depicts an atrocity having the same shocking impact as Goya's *Third of May, 1808* (FIG. 22-11). The title refers to a street in Paris where an unknown sniper killed a civil guard, part of a government force trying to repress a worker demonstration. Because the fatal shot had come from a workers' housing block, the remaining guards immediately stormed the building and massacred all of its inhabitants. With Goya's power, Daumier created a view of the slaughter from a sharp angle of vision. But unlike Goya, he depicted not the dramatic moment of execution but the terrible, quiet aftermath. The limp bodies of the workers—and of a child crushed beneath his father's corpse—lie amid violent disorder. The print's power lies in its factualness. Daumier's pictorial manner is rough and spontaneous, and that approach to representation, which is a central characteristic of Realist art, accounts in large measure for its remarkable force.

THIRD-CLASS CARRIAGE For his paintings, Daumier chose the same kind of subjects and representational manner as in his graphic work, especially after the 1848 revolution. His unfinished *Third-Class Carriage* (FIG. **22-30**) provides a glimpse into the cramped and grimy railway cars of the 1860s. The riders are poor and can afford only third-class tickets. First- and second-class carriages had closed compartments, but third-class passengers had to cram together on hard benches stretching from one end of their carriage to the other. The disinherited masses of 19th-century industrialization were Daumier's indignant concern. He depicted them in the unposed attitudes and unplanned arrangements of the millions thronging the modern cities—anonymous, insignificant, dumbly patient with a lot they could not change. Daumier saw people as they ordinarily appeared, their faces vague, impersonal, and blank—unprepared for any observers. He tried to achieve the real by isolating a random collection of the unrehearsed details of human existence from the continuum of ordinary life. Daumier's vision anticipated the spontaneity and candor of scenes captured with the camera by the end of the century.

ROSA BONHEUR The most celebrated woman artist of the 19th century was MARIE-ROSALIE (ROSA) BONHEUR (1822–1899). The winner of the gold medal at the Salon of 1848, Bonheur became in 1894 the first woman officer in the French Legion of Honor. As was typical for women since the Renaissance (see "The Artist's Profession," Chapter 15, page 433), Bonheur received her artistic training from her father, Oscar-Raymond Bonheur (1796–1849), who was a proponent of *Saint-Simonianism,* an early-19th-century utopian socialist movement that championed the education and enfranchisement of women. As a result of her father's influence, Bonheur launched her career believing that as a woman and an artist, she had a special role to play in creating a new and perfect society. A Realist passion for accuracy in painting drove Bonheur, but she resisted depicting the problematic social and political themes seen in the work of Courbet, Millet, Daumier, and other Realists. Rather, she turned to the animal world—not, however, to the exotic wild animals that so fascinated Delacroix (FIG. 22-17), but to animals common in the French countryside, especially horses, but also rabbits, cows, and sheep. She went to great lengths to observe the anatomy of living horses at the great Parisian horse fair and spent long hours studying the anatomy of carcasses in the Paris slaughterhouses.

22-31 ROSA BONHEUR, *The Horse Fair,* 1853–1855. Oil on canvas, 8' ¼" × 16' 7½". Metropolitan Museum of Art, New York (gift of Cornelius Vanderbilt, 1887).

Bonheur was the most celebrated woman artist of the 19th century. A Realist, she went to great lengths to record accurately the anatomy of living horses, even studying carcasses in slaughterhouses.

1 ft.

For *The Horse Fair* (FIG. 22-31), Bonheur's best-known work, the artist chose a panoramic composition similar to that in Courbet's *Burial at Ornans* (FIG. 22-27). She filled her broad canvas with the sturdy farm Percherons and their grooms seen on parade at the annual Parisian horse sale. Some horses, not quite broken, rear up. Others plod or trot, guided on foot or ridden by their keepers. Bonheur recorded the Percherons' uneven line of march, their thunderous pounding, and their seemingly overwhelming power based on her close observation of living animals, even though she acknowledged some inspiration from the Parthenon frieze (FIG. 5-50, *top*). The dramatic lighting, loose brushwork, and rolling sky also reveal her admiration of Géricault's style (FIGS. 22-13 and 22-13A). The equine drama in *The Horse Fair* captivated viewers, who eagerly bought engraved reproductions of Bonheur's painting, making it one of the most popular artworks of the century.

ÉDOUARD MANET As pivotal a figure in 19th-century European art as Gustave Courbet was the painter ÉDOUARD MANET (1832–1883). Like Courbet, Manet was influential in articulating Realist principles, but the younger artist also played an important role in the development of Impressionism in the 1870s (see Chapter 23). Manet's *Le Déjeuner sur l'Herbe* (*Luncheon on the Grass;* FIG. 22-32), widely recognized only later as a seminal work in the history of art, depicts two clothed men and one nude and one clothed woman at a picnic. Consistent with Realist principles, Manet based all four figures on real people. The seated nude is Victorine Meurend (Manet's favorite model at the time), and the gentlemen are his brother Eugène (with cane) and probably the sculptor Ferdinand Leenhof, although scholars have suggested other identifications. The two men wear fashionable Parisian attire of the 1860s. The nude woman is a distressingly unidealized figure who also seems disturbingly unabashed and at ease, gazing directly at the viewer without shame or flirtatiousness.

This audacious painting outraged the French public. Rather than a traditional pastoral scene, for example, Titian's *Pastoral Symphony* (FIG. 17-35), populated by anonymous idealized figures in an idyllic setting, *Le Déjeuner* featured ordinary men and promiscuous women in a Parisian park. One hostile critic, no doubt voicing public opinion, said: "A commonplace woman of the demimonde, as naked as can be, shamelessly lolls between two dandies dressed to the teeth. These latter look like schoolboys on a holiday, perpetrating an outrage to play the man. . . . This is a young man's practical joke—a shameful, open sore."[8] Manet surely anticipated criticism of his painting, but shocking the public was not his primary aim. His goal was more complex and far more ambitious. With *Le Déjeuner,* he sought to reassess the nature of painting. The work contains sophisticated references and allusions to many artistic genres—history painting, portraiture, pastoral scenes, nudes, and even religious scenes. *Le Déjeuner* is Manet's impressive synthesis and critique of the entire history of painting.

The negative response to Manet's painting on the part of public and critics alike extended beyond subject matter. The painter's manner of presenting his figures also elicited severe criticism. He rendered the men and women in soft focus and broadly painted the landscape, including the pool in which the second woman bathes. The loose manner of painting contrasts with the clear forms of the harshly lit foreground trio and of the pile of discarded female clothes and picnic foods at the lower left. The lighting creates strong contrasts between dark and highlighted areas. In the main figures, many values are summed up in one or two lights or darks. The effect is both to flatten the forms and set them off sharply from the setting. Form, rather than a matter of line, is only a function of paint and light. Manet aimed to move away from illusionism toward an open acknowledgment of painting's properties, such as the flatness of the painting surface, which would become a core principle of many later 19th-century painters as well as their successors

22-32 ÉDOUARD MANET, *Le Déjeuner sur l'Herbe* (*Luncheon on the Grass*), 1863. Oil on canvas, 7′ × 8′ 8″. Musée d'Orsay, Paris.

Manet shocked his contemporaries with both his subject matter and manner of painting. Moving away from illusionism, he used colors to flatten form and to draw attention to the painting surface.

1 ft.

to the present day. The mid-19th-century French public, however, saw only a crude sketch lacking the customary finish of paintings exhibited in the Paris Salon. The style of the painting, coupled with the unorthodox subject matter, made *Le Déjeuner sur l'Herbe* one of the most controversial artworks ever created.

OLYMPIA Even more scandalous to the French viewing public, however, was Manet's *Olympia* (FIG. **22-33**), painted the same year. Manet's subject was a young white prostitute (Olympia was a common "professional" name for prostitutes in 19th-century France). She reclines on a bed that extends across the full width of

22-33 ÉDOUARD MANET, *Olympia*, 1863. Oil on canvas, 4′ 3″ × 6′ 2¼″. Musée d'Orsay, Paris. ◄

Manet's painting of a nude prostitute and her black maid carrying a bouquet from a client scandalized the public. Critics also faulted his rough brushstrokes and abruptly shifting tonalities.

1 ft.

the painting (and beyond) and is nude except for a thin black ribbon tied around her neck, a bracelet on her arm, an orchid in her hair, and fashionable slippers on her feet. Like the seated nude in *Le Déjeuner*, Olympia meets the viewer's eye with a look of cool indifference. The only other figure in the painting is a black maid, who presents Olympia a bouquet of flowers from a client.

Olympia horrified public and critics alike. Although images of prostitutes were not unheard of during this period, the shamelessness of Olympia and her look verging on defiance shocked viewers. The depiction of a black woman was also not new to painting, but the French public perceived Manet's inclusion of both a black maid and a nude prostitute as evoking moral depravity, inferiority, and animalistic sexuality. The contrast of the black servant with the fair-skinned courtesan also conjured racial divisions. One critic described Olympia as "a courtesan with dirty hands and wrinkled feet . . . her body has the livid tint of a cadaver displayed in the morgue; her outlines are drawn in charcoal and her greenish, bloodshot eyes appear to be provoking the public, protected all the while by a hideous Negress."[9] From this statement, it is clear viewers were responding not solely to the subject matter but to Manet's artistic style as well. The painter's brushstrokes are much rougher and the shifts in tonality are far more abrupt than those found in traditional academic painting. This departure from accepted practice exacerbated the audacity of the subject matter. *Olympia*—indeed, all of Manet's work—represented a radical departure from the academic style then in favor, as exemplified by the work of ADOLPHE-WILLIAM BOUGUEREAU (1825–1905; FIG. **22-33A**), an artist largely forgotten today, although he was a towering figure in the French art world during the second half of the 19th century.

22-33A BOUGUEREAU, *Nymphs and a Satyr*, 1873.

Germany and the United States

Although French artists took the lead in promoting the depiction of the realities of modern life as the only valid goal for artists, the Realist movement was neither exclusively French nor confined to Europe.

WILHELM LEIBL In Germany, WILHELM LEIBL (1844–1900) shared French Realists' commitment to representing the contemporary world and real people in his paintings. *Three Women in a Village Church* (FIG. **22-34**) is typical of Leibl's work, which focused on country life. The painting records a sacred moment—the moment of prayer—in the life of three women of different generations. Dressed in rustic costume, their Sunday-church best, they quietly pursue their devotions, their prayer books held in large hands roughened by work. Their manners and their dress reflect their unaffected nature, untouched by the refinements of urban life. Leibl highlighted their natural virtues: simplicity, honesty, steadfastness, patience. He spent three years working on this image of peasants in their village church, often under impossible conditions of lighting and temperature. Despite the meticulous application of paint and sharpness of focus, the picture is a moving expression of the artist's compassionate view of his subjects, a reading of character without sentimentality.

WINSLOW HOMER Realism received an especially warm welcome in the United States. One of the leading American Realist painters was WINSLOW HOMER (1836–1910) of Boston. Homer

22-34 WILHELM LEIBL, *Three Women in a Village Church*, 1878–1882. Oil on canvas, 2′ 5″ × 2′ 1″. Hamburger, Kunsthalle, Hamburg.

French Realism spread quickly to Germany, where Leibl painted this moving depiction of simple peasant women of different generations holding their prayer books in hands roughened by work.

1 ft.

experienced at first hand the most momentous event of his era— the Civil War. In 1860, he joined the Union campaign as an artist-reporter for *Harper's Weekly*. At the end of the war, he painted *Veteran in a New Field* (FIG. **22-35**). Although it is relatively simple and direct, Homer's painting is a significant commentary on the effects and aftermath of America's catastrophic national conflict. At the center of the canvas is a man with his back to the viewer, harvesting wheat. Homer identified him as a veteran by including his uniform and canteen carelessly thrown on the ground in the lower right corner. The man's current occupation, however, is as a farmer, and he has cast aside his former role as a soldier. The veteran's involvement in meaningful and productive work implies a smooth transition from war to peace. This postwar transition to work and the fate of disbanded soldiers were national concerns. Echoing the sentiments behind Houdon's portrayal of George Washington as the new Cincinnatus (FIG. 21-32), the *New York Weekly Tribune* commented: "Rome took her great man from the plow, and made him a dictator—we must now take our soldiers from the camp and make them farmers."[10] America's ability to effect a smooth transition was seen as evidence of its national strength. "The peaceful and harmonious

1 ft.

22-35 WINSLOW HOMER, *Veteran in a New Field*, 1865. Oil on canvas, 2′ $\frac{1}{8}$″ × 3′ 2$\frac{1}{8}$″. Metropolitan Museum of Art, New York (bequest of Miss Adelaide Milton de Groot, 1967).

This veteran's productive work implies a smooth transition to peace after the Civil War, but Homer placed a single-bladed scythe—the Grim Reaper's tool— in his hands, symbolizing the deaths of soldiers.

Veteran in a New Field also comments symbolically about death. By the 1860s, farmers used cradled scythes to harvest wheat. For this detail, however, Homer rejected realism in favor of symbolism. The former soldier's tool

disbanding of the armies in the summer of 1865," poet Walt Whitman (1819–1892) wrote, was one of the "immortal proofs of democracy, unequall'd in all the history of the past."[11] Homer's painting thus reinforced the perception of the country's greatness.

is a single-bladed scythe. The artist thus transformed the man who lived through the Civil War into a symbol of Death—the Grim Reaper himself. In addition to being a tribute to the successful transition to peace, *Veteran in a New Field* is an elegy to the thousands of soldiers who did not return from the war. It may also be a lamentation on the recent assassination of President Abraham Lincoln.

THOMAS EAKINS Even more resolutely a Realist than Homer was Philadelphia-born THOMAS EAKINS (1844–1916), whose work reflects his keen appetite for recording the realities of the human experience. Eakins studied both painting and medical anatomy in Philadelphia before undertaking further study under French artist Jean-Léon Gérôme (1824–1904). Eakins aimed to paint things as he saw them rather than as the public might wish them portrayed. This attitude was very much in tune with 19th-century American taste, combining an admiration for accurate depiction with a hunger for truth.

The too-brutal Realism of Eakins's early masterpiece, *The Gross Clinic* (FIG. **22-36**), prompted the art jury to reject it for the Philadelphia exhibition celebrating the American independence centennial in 1876. The painting portrays the renowned surgeon Dr. Samuel Gross in the operating amphitheater of the Jefferson Medical College in Philadelphia, where the painting hung for 130 years until its sale in 2006 to raise funds for the college. Eakins's decision to depict

1 ft.

22-36 THOMAS EAKINS, *The Gross Clinic*, 1875. Oil on canvas, 8′ × 6′ 6″. Philadelphia Museum of Art, Philadelphia. ◼◂

The too-brutal realism of Eakins's depiction of a medical college operating amphitheater caused this painting's rejection from the Philadelphia exhibition celebrating America's centennial.

an operation in progress reflects the public's increasing faith that scientific and medical advances could enhance—and preserve—lives. Dr. Gross, with bloody fingers and scalpel, lectures about his surgery on a young man's leg. The patient suffered from osteomyelitis, a bone infection. Watching the surgeon, acclaimed for his skill in this particular operation, are several colleagues—all of whom historians have identified—and the patient's mother, who covers her face. Also present is an anesthetist, who holds a cloth over the patient's face. Anesthetics had been introduced in 1846, and their development eliminated a major obstacle to extensive surgery. The painting is an unsparing description of an unfolding event, with a good deal more reality than many viewers could endure. "It is a picture," one critic said, "that even strong men find difficult to look at long, if they can look at it at all."[12]

Consistent with the dominance of empiricism in the latter half of the 19th century, Eakins believed careful observation—and, where relevant, scientific knowledge—were prerequisites for his art, and he created his paintings in a deliberate, methodical way based on firsthand study of his subject. For example, Eakins's focus on anatomical correctness led him to investigate the human form and humans in motion, both with regular photographic apparatuses and with a special camera devised by the French kinesiologist (a person who studies the physiology of body movement) Étienne-Jules Marey (1830–1904). Eakins later collaborated with Eadweard Muybridge (FIG. 22-54) in the photographic study of animal and human action of all types, anticipating the 20th-century invention of the motion picture.

JOHN SINGER SARGENT The expatriate American artist JOHN SINGER SARGENT (1856–1925), born in Florence, Italy, was a younger contemporary of Eakins. Sargent developed a looser, more dashing Realist portrait style, in contrast to Eakins's carefully rendered details. Sargent studied art in Paris before settling in London, where he won renown both as a cultivated and cosmopolitan gentleman and as an accomplished portrait painter. He learned his adept application of paint in thin layers and his effortless achievement of quick and lively illusion from his study of Velázquez, whose masterpiece, *Las Meninas* (FIG. 19-30), may have influenced Sargent's family portrait *The Daughters of Edward Darley Boit* (FIG. **22-37**). The four girls (the children of one of Sargent's close friends) appear in a hall and small drawing room in their Paris home. The informal, eccentric arrangement of their slight figures suggests how much at ease they are within this familiar space and with objects such as the monumental Japanese vases, the red screen, and the fringed rug, whose scale subtly emphasizes the children's diminutive stature. Sargent must have known the Boit daughters well. Relaxed and trustful, they gave the artist an opportunity to record a gradation of young innocence. He sensitively captured the naive, wondering openness of the little girl in the foreground, the grave artlessness of the 10-year-old child, and the slightly self-conscious poise of the adolescents. Sargent's casual positioning of the figures and seemingly random choice of the setting communicate a sense of spontaneity. The children seem to be attending momentarily to an adult who has asked them to interrupt their activity. The painting embodies the Realist belief that the artist's business is to record modern people in modern contexts.

HENRY OSSAWA TANNER Typical of the Realist painter's desire to depict the lives of ordinary people engaged in everyday activities is the early work of African American artist HENRY OSSAWA TANNER (1859–1937). Tanner studied art with Eakins before moving to Paris. There he combined Eakins's belief in careful study from nature with a desire to portray with dignity the life of the working people he had been raised among as a minister's son in Pennsylvania. The mood in *The Thankful Poor* (FIG. **22-38**) is one of quiet devotion not far removed from the Realism of Millet (FIG. 22-28) and

1 ft.

22-37 JOHN SINGER SARGENT, *The Daughters of Edward Darley Boit,* 1882. Oil on canvas, 7′ 3⅜″ × 7′ 3⅝″. Museum of Fine Arts, Boston (gift of Mary Louisa Boit, Florence D. Boit, Jane Hubbard Boit, and Julia Overing Boit, in memory of their father, Edward Darley Boit).

Sargent's casual positioning of the Boit sisters creates a sense of the momentary and spontaneous, consistent with Realist painters' interest in recording modern people in modern contexts.

22-38 Henry Ossawa Tanner, *The Thankful Poor*, 1894. Oil on canvas, 2′ 11½″ × 3′ 8¼″. Collection of William H. and Camille Cosby.

Tanner combined the Realists' belief in careful study from nature with a desire to portray with dignity the life of African American families. Expressive lighting reinforces the painting's reverent spirit.

1 ft.

Leibl (FIG. 22-34). Tanner painted the grandfather, grandchild, and main objects in the room in great detail, whereas everything else dissolves into loose strokes of color and light. Expressive lighting reinforces the painting's reverent spirit, with deep shadows intensifying the man's devout concentration and golden light pouring in the window to illuminate the quiet expression of thanksgiving on the younger face. The deep sense of sanctity expressed here in terms of everyday experience became increasingly important for Tanner. Within a few years of completing *The Thankful Poor,* he began painting biblical subjects grounded in direct study from nature and in the love of Rembrandt that had inspired him from his days as a Philadelphia art student.

EDMONIA LEWIS About 15 years older than Tanner, the sculptor EDMONIA LEWIS (ca. 1845–after 1909), the daughter of a Chippewa mother and African American father, produced work stylistically indebted to Neoclassicism but depicting contemporary Realist themes. *Forever Free* (FIG. **22-39**) is a marble sculpture Lewis carved while living in Rome, surrounded by examples of both classical and Renaissance art. It represents two freed African American slaves. The man stands heroically in a contrapposto stance reminiscent of classical statues. His right hand rests on the shoulder of the kneeling woman, and his left hand holds aloft a broken manacle and chain as literal and symbolic references to his former servitude. Produced four years after President Lincoln's issuance of the Emancipation Proclamation, *Forever Free* (originally titled *The Morning*

22-39 EDMONIA LEWIS, *Forever Free*, 1867. Marble, 3′ 5¼″ high. James A. Porter Gallery of Afro-American Art, Howard University, Washington, D.C.

Lewis was a sculptor whose work owes a stylistic debt to Neoclassicism but depicts contemporary Realist themes. She carved *Forever Free* four years after Lincoln's Emancipation Proclamation.

1 ft.

22-40 JOHN EVERETT MILLAIS, *Ophelia*, 1852. Oil on canvas, 2′ 6″ × 3′ 8″. Tate Gallery, London. ◼◣

Millet was a founder of the Pre-Raphaelite Brotherhood, whose members refused to be limited to the contemporary scenes that strict Realists portrayed. The drowning of Ophelia is a Shakespearean subject.

1 ft.

of Liberty) was widely perceived as an abolitionist statement. However, other factors caution against an overly simplistic reading. For example, scholars have debated the degree to which the sculptor attempted to inject a statement about gender relationships into this statue and whether the kneeling position of the woman is a reference to female subordination in the African American community.

Lewis's accomplishments as a sculptor speak to the increasing access to training available to women in the 19th century. Educated at Oberlin College (the first American college to grant degrees to women), Lewis financed her trip to Rome with the sale of medallions and marble busts. Her success in a field dominated by white male artists is a testament to both her skill and her determination.

Pre-Raphaelite Brotherhood

Realism did not appeal to all artists, of course. In England, a group of painters who called themselves the *Pre-Raphaelite Brotherhood* refused to be limited to the contemporary scenes strict Realists portrayed. These artists chose instead to represent fictional, historical, and fanciful subjects, albeit with a significant degree of convincing illusion.

JOHN EVERETT MILLAIS One of the founders of the Pre-Raphaelite Brotherhood was JOHN EVERETT MILLAIS (1829–1896). So painstakingly careful was Millais in his study of visual facts closely observed from nature that Charles Baudelaire (1821–1867) called him "the poet of meticulous detail." The Pre-Raphaelite Brotherhood, organized in 1848, wished to create fresh and sincere art, free from what its members considered the tired and artificial manner propagated in the academies by the successors of Raphael. Influenced by the critic, artist, and writer John Ruskin (1819–1900), the Pre-Raphaelites shared his distaste for the materialism and ugliness of the contemporary industrializing world. They also expressed appreciation for the spirituality and idealism (as well as the art and artisanship) of past times, especially the Middle Ages and the Early Renaissance.

Millais's *Ophelia* (FIG. **22-40**) garnered enthusiastic praise when the painter exhibited it in the Exposition Universelle in Paris in 1855—the exhibition at which Courbet set up his Pavilion of Realism. The subject, from Shakespeare's *Hamlet* (4.7.176–179), is the drowning of Ophelia, who, in her madness, is unaware of her plight:

> *Her clothes spread wide,*
> *And mermaidlike awhile they bore her up—*
> *Which time she chanted snatches of old tunes,*
> *As one incapable of her own distress.*

To make the pathos of the scene visible, Millais became a faithful and feeling witness of its every detail, reconstructing it with a lyricism worthy of the original poetry. Although the scene is fictitious and therefore one Realist painters would have rejected, Millais worked diligently to present it with unswerving fidelity to visual fact. He painted the background on site at a spot along the Hogsmill River in Surrey. For the figure of Ophelia, Millais had a friend lie in a heated bathtub full of water for hours at a time.

DANTE GABRIEL ROSSETTI Another founder of the Pre-Raphaelite Brotherhood was DANTE GABRIEL ROSSETTI (1828–1882), who established an enviable reputation as both a painter and poet. Like other members of the group, Rossetti focused on literary and biblical themes in his art. He also produced numerous portraits of women that projected an image of ethereal beauty and melded apparent opposites—for example, a Victorian prettiness with sensual allure. His *Beata Beatrix* (FIG. **22-41**) is ostensibly a portrait of a literary figure—Beatrice, from Dante's *Vita Nuova*—as she overlooks Florence in a trance after being mystically transported to Heaven. Yet the portrait also had personal resonance for Rossetti. It served as a memorial to his wife, Elizabeth Siddal (the model for Millais's *Ophelia*). Siddal had died shortly before Rossetti began this painting in 1862. In the image, the woman (Siddal-Beatrice) sits in a trancelike state, while a red dove (a messenger of both love

1 ft.

22-41 DANTE GABRIEL ROSSETTI, *Beata Beatrix*, ca. 1863. Oil on canvas, 2′ 10″ × 2′ 2″. Tate Gallery, London.

This painting of a beautiful and sensuous woman is ostensibly a literary portrait of Dante's Beatrice, but the work also served as a memorial to Rossetti's wife, who died of an opium overdose.

and death) deposits a poppy (symbolic of sleep and death) in her hands. Because Siddal died of an opium overdose, the presence of the poppy assumes greater significance.

ARCHITECTURE

At the opening of the 19th century, Napoleon had co-opted the classical style as the official architectural expression of his empire. Neoclassicism was in vogue elsewhere in Europe and in the new American republic too, but other historical styles also enjoyed revivals at the same time architects were exploring the expressive possibilities that new construction technologies had fostered. The buildings constructed during the 19th century are consequently among the most stylistically diverse in history.

ALTES MUSEUM, BERLIN After the fall of Napoleon, who had occupied the Prussian capital of Berlin from 1806 to 1808, a fervent nationalistic spirit emerged in Germany. One manifestation of Prussian nationalism was the decision to build Europe's first public art museum to house the extensive and growing royal collection. The commission went to KARL FRIEDRICH SCHINKEL (1781–1841), who worked in many revival styles during his career, including Romanesque, Gothic, and Italian Renaissance, but who chose the Neoclassical style for what he and Crown Prince Friedrich Wilhelm III (1755–1861) conceived as a "temple of culture."

The Altes (Old) Museum (FIG. **22-42**), constructed on an island in the Spree River across from the royal palace in Berlin, is not truly templelike, however. Rather, with its broad facade of 18 Ionic columns on a high podium, it more closely resembles a Greek stoa (FIG. 5-77) than a pediment-capped classical temple. Noteworthy for its perfect proportions, Schinkel's austere design expresses nobility, tradition, and elite culture, now made accessible to the public in a building whose style Europeans associated with the democratic values of ancient Greece and Rome.

22-42 KARL FRIEDRICH SCHINKEL, Altes Museum, Berlin, Germany, 1822–1830.

Schinkel conceived the first public art museum in Europe as a Neoclassical "temple of culture." The Altes Museum's facade of 18 Ionic columns resembles an ancient Greek stoa (FIG. 5-77).

22-43 CHARLES BARRY and AUGUSTUS WELBY NORTHMORE PUGIN, Houses of Parliament, London, England, designed 1835. ◼◀

During the 19th century, architects revived many historical styles, often reflecting nationalistic pride. The Houses of Parliament have an exterior veneer and towers that recall English Late Gothic style.

The Neoclassical facade masks a very practical plan that has no model in classical temples or stoas. A broad central staircase leads into a foyer and then a cubical central block, which projects above the facade's colonnade. The central block houses a sculpture-filled domed rotunda loosely based on the Pantheon (FIGS. 7-50 and 7-51) in Rome. To either side is a courtyard whose windows provide light to the painting galleries all around. Large windows on the side and rear walls of the Altes Museum also illuminate the galleries. The museum was revolutionary in organizing the artworks it contained in chronological order, emphasizing the history of art, as opposed to simply displaying aesthetic treasures (compare FIG. 20-1A).

GOTHIC REVIVAL As 19th-century scholars gathered the documentary materials of European history in encyclopedic enterprises, each nation came to value its past as evidence of the validity of its ambitions and claims to greatness. Intellectuals appreciated the art of the remote past as a product of cultural and national genius. Italy, of course, had its Roman ruins, which had long inspired later architects. A reawakening of interest in Gothic architecture also surfaced at this time, even in France under Napoleon. In 1802, Chateaubriand published his influential *Genius of Christianity*—the source for Girodet-Trioson's *Burial of Atala* (FIG. 22-5)—which defended religion on the grounds of its beauty and mystery rather than on the grounds of truth. Gothic cathedrals, according to Chateaubriand, were translations of the sacred groves of the ancient Gauls into stone and should be cherished as manifestations of France's holy history. One result of this new nationalistic respect for the Gothic style was that Eugène Emmanuel Viollet-le-Duc (1814–1879) received a commission in 1845 to restore the interior of Paris's Notre Dame to its Gothic splendor after removing the Baroque and Napoleonic (FIG. 22-2) alterations.

HOUSES OF PARLIAMENT England also celebrated its medieval heritage with *Neo-Gothic* buildings. In London, when the old Houses of Parliament burned in 1834, the Parliamentary Commission decreed that designs for the new building be either Gothic or Elizabethan. CHARLES BARRY (1795–1860), with the assistance of AUGUSTUS WELBY NORTHMORE PUGIN (1812–1852), submitted

the winning design (FIG. **22-43**) in 1835. By this time, architectural style had become a matter of selection from the historical past. Barry had traveled widely in Europe, Greece, Turkey, Egypt, and Palestine, studying the architecture of each place. He preferred the classical Renaissance styles, but he had designed some earlier Neo-Gothic buildings, and Pugin successfully influenced him in the direction of English Late Gothic. Pugin was one of a group of English artists and critics who saw moral purity and spiritual authenticity in the religious architecture of the Middle Ages and revered the careful medieval artisans who built the great cathedrals. The Industrial Revolution was flooding the market with cheaply made and ill-designed commodities. Machine work was replacing handicraft. Many, Pugin included, believed in the necessity of restoring the old artisanship, which they felt embodied honesty as well as quality. Pugin was also the author of the influential *True Principles of Pointed or Christian Architecture* (1841), which RICHARD UPJOHN (1802–1878) consulted for his Neo-Gothic Trinity Church (FIG. **22-43A**) in New York City. The design of the Houses of Parliament, however, is not genuinely Gothic, despite its picturesque tower groupings (the Clock Tower, housing Big Ben, at one end, and the Victoria Tower at the other). The building has a formal axial plan and a kind of Palladian regularity beneath its Neo-Gothic detail. Pugin himself said of it, "All Grecian, Sir. Tudor [English Late Gothic] details on a classical body."[13]

22-43A UPJOHN, Trinity Church, New York, 1841–1852.

ROYAL PAVILION Although the Neoclassical and Neo-Gothic styles dominated early-19th-century architecture, exotic new approaches of all manner soon began to appear, due in part to European imperialism and in part to the Romantic spirit permeating all the arts. Great Britain's forays throughout the world, particularly India, had exposed English culture to a broad range of non-Western artistic styles. The Royal Pavilion (FIG. **22-44**), designed

22-44 JOHN NASH, Royal Pavilion, Brighton, England, 1815–1818.

British territorial expansion brought a familiarity with many exotic styles. This palatial "Indian Gothic" seaside pavilion is a conglomeration of Islamic domes, minarets, and screens.

by JOHN NASH (1752–1835), exhibits a wide variety of these styles. Nash was an established architect, known for Neoclassical buildings in London, when the prince regent (later King George IV) asked him to design a royal pleasure palace in the seaside resort of Brighton. The architecture of Greece, Egypt, and China influenced the interior décor of the Royal Pavilion, but the fantastic exterior is a conglomeration of Islamic domes, minarets, and screens architectural historians describe as "Indian Gothic." Underlying the exotic facade is a cast-iron skeleton, an early (if hidden) use of this material in noncommercial construction. Nash also put this metal to fanciful use, creating life-size palm-tree columns in cast iron to support the Royal Pavilion's kitchen ceiling. The building, an appropriate enough backdrop for gala throngs pursuing pleasure by the seaside, has served as a prototype for countless playful architectural exaggerations still found in European and American resorts.

PARIS OPÉRA Another style that found favor in 19th-century architecture was the Baroque, because it was well suited to convey-ing a grandeur worthy of the riches the European elite acquired during this age of expansion. The Paris Opéra (FIG. **22-45**), designed by CHARLES GARNIER (1825–1898), mirrored the opulent lives of these privileged few. The opera house has a festive and spectacularly theatrical Neo-Baroque front and two wings resembling Baroque domed central-plan churches. Inside, intricate arrangements of corridors, vestibules, stairways, balconies, alcoves, entrances, and exits facilitate easy passage throughout the building and provide space for entertainment and socializing at intermissions.

The Baroque grandeur of the layout and of the building's ornamental appointments are characteristic of an architectural style called *Beaux-Arts,* which flourished in the late 19th and early 20th centuries in France. Based on ideas taught at the dominant École des Beaux-Arts (School of Fine Arts) in Paris, the Beaux-Arts style incorporated classical principles (such as symmetry in design, including interior spaces extending radially from a central core or axis) and featured extensive exterior ornamentation. As an example of a Beaux-Arts building, Garnier's Opéra proclaims, through its majesty and lavishness, its function as a gathering place for fashionable audiences in an era of conspicuous wealth. The style was so attractive to the moneyed classes who supported the arts that theaters and opera houses continued to reflect the Paris Opéra's design until World War I transformed society (see Chapter 24).

22-45 CHARLES GARNIER, Opéra (looking north), Paris, France, 1861–1874. ◼◀

For Paris's opera house, Garnier chose a festive and spectacularly theatrical Neo-Baroque facade well suited to a gathering place for fashionable audiences in an age of conspicuous wealth.

The exterior of this Parisian library looks like a Renaissance palazzo, but the interior has an exposed cast-iron skeleton, which still incorporates classical Corinthian capitals and Renaissance scrolls.

SAINTE-GENEVIÈVE LIBRARY

Work on Garnier's opera house began in 1861, but by the middle of the 19th century, many architects had already abandoned sentimental and Romantic designs from the past. Since the 18th century, bridges had been constructed of cast iron (FIG. 21-12) because of its tensile strength and resistance to fire, and steel became available after 1860 as a building material that enabled architects to create new designs involving vast enclosed spaces, as in the great train sheds of railroad stations (FIG. 23-4) and in exposition halls. Most other utilitarian architecture—factories, warehouses, dockyard structures, mills, and the like—long had been built simply and without historical ornamentation.

The Bibliothèque Sainte-Geneviève, built by HENRI LABROUSTE (1801–1875), is an interesting mix of Renaissance revival style and modern cast-iron construction. The library's two-story facade with arched windows recalls Renaissance palazzo designs, but Labrouste exposed the structure's metal skeleton on the interior. The lower story of the building housed the book stacks. The upper floor featured a spacious reading room (FIG. **22-46**) consisting essentially of two barrel-vaulted halls, roofed in terracotta and separated by a row of slender cast-iron columns on concrete pedestals. The columns, recognizably Corinthian, support the iron roof arches pierced with intricate vine-scroll ornamentation derived from the Renaissance

22-47 JOSEPH PAXTON, Crystal Palace, London, England, 1850–1851; enlarged and relocated at Sydenham, England, 1852–1854. Detail of a color lithograph by ACHILLE-LOUIS MARTINET, ca. 1862. Private collection.

The tensile strength of iron enabled Paxton to experiment with a new system of glass-and-metal roof construction. Constructed of prefabricated parts, the vast Crystal Palace required only six months to build.

22-46A ROEBLING, Brooklyn Bridge, 1867–1883.

architectural repertoire. Labrouste's design highlights how the peculiar properties of the new structural material aesthetically transformed the shapes of traditional masonry architecture. But it is also clear how reluctant some 19th-century architects were to surrender traditional forms, even when fully aware of new possibilities for design and construction. Architects scoffed at "engineers' architecture" for many years and continued to clothe their steel-and-concrete structures in the Romantic "drapery" of a historical style. For example, the designer of the Brooklyn Bridge (FIG. **22-46A**), JOHN AUGUSTUS ROEBLING (1806–1869), combined the latest steel technology with motifs from Gothic and Egyptian architecture.

CRYSTAL PALACE Completely "undraped" construction first became popular in the conservatories (greenhouses) of English country estates. JOSEPH PAXTON (1801–1865) built several of these structures for his patron, the duke of Devonshire. In the largest—300 feet long—he used an experimental system of glass-and-metal roof construction. Encouraged by the success of this system, Paxton submitted a winning glass-and-iron building design in the competition for the hall to house the Great Exhibition of 1851 in London, organized to present "works of industry of all nations." Paxton constructed the exhibition building, the Crystal Palace (FIG. **22-47**), with prefabricated parts. This enabled workers to build the vast structure in the then-unheard-of time of six months and to dismantle it quickly at the exhibition's closing to avoid permanent obstruction of the park. The plan borrowed much from Roman and Christian basilicas, with a central flat-roofed "nave" and a barrel-vaulted crossing "transept." The design provided ample interior space to contain displays of huge machines as well as to accommodate decorative touches in the form of large working fountains and giant trees. The public admired the Crystal Palace so much that the workers who dismantled it put up an enlarged version of the glass-and-steel exhibition hall at a new location on the outskirts of London at Sydenham, where it remained until fire destroyed it in 1936. Fortunately, a few old black-and-white photographs and several color lithographs (FIG. 22-47) preserve a record of the Crystal Palace's appearance.

PHOTOGRAPHY

A technological device of immense consequence for the modern experience was invented shortly before the mid-19th century: the camera, with its attendant art of photography. From the time Frenchman LOUIS-JACQUES-MANDÉ DAGUERRE (1789–1851) and Briton WILLIAM HENRY FOX TALBOT (1800–1877) announced the first practical photographic processes in 1839, people have celebrated photography's ability to make convincing pictures of people, places, and things. The relative ease of the process, even in its earliest and most primitive form, seemed a dream come true for scientists and artists, who for centuries had grappled with less satisfying methods of capturing accurate images of their subjects. Photography also perfectly suited an age that saw the emergence of Realism as an art movement and a pronounced shift of artistic patronage away from the elite few toward a broader base of support. The growing and increasingly powerful middle class

embraced both the comprehensible images of the new artistic medium and their lower cost.

For the traditional artist, photography suggested new answers to the great debate about what is real and how to represent the real in art. Because photography easily and accurately enabled the reproduction of three-dimensional objects on a two-dimensional surface, the new medium also challenged the place of traditional modes of pictorial representation originating in the Renaissance. Artists as diverse as Delacroix, Ingres, Courbet, and the Impressionist Edgar Degas (see Chapter 23) welcomed photography as a helpful auxiliary to painting. Other artists, however, feared the camera was a mechanism that would displace the painstaking work of skilled painters. From the moment of its invention, photography threatened to expropriate the realistic image, until then the exclusive property of painting. But just as some painters looked to the new medium of photography for answers on how best to render an image in paint, so some photographers looked to painting for suggestions about ways to imbue the photographic image with qualities beyond simple reproduction. Indeed, the first subjects photographers chose to record were traditional painting themes, for example, still lifes and portraits—in part to establish photography as a legitimate artistic medium on a par with painting. A debate immediately began over whether the photograph was an art form or if the camera was merely a scientific instrument. An 1862 court case provided the answer: Photography was an art, and photographs were entitled to copyright protection.

Artists themselves were instrumental in the development of the new photographic technology. The camera obscura was familiar to 18th-century artists. In 1807, the invention of the *camera lucida* (lighted room) replaced the enclosed chamber of the camera obscura. Now the photographer aimed a small prism lens, hung on a stand, downward at an object. The lens projected the image of the object onto a sheet of paper. Artists using either of these devices found the process long and arduous, no matter how accurate the resulting work. All yearned for a more direct way to capture a subject's image. Two very different scientific inventions that accomplished this—the *daguerreotype* and the *calotype* (see "Daguerreotypes, Calotypes, and Wet-Plate Photography," page 680)—appeared almost simultaneously in France and England in 1839.

DAGUERREOTYPES The French government presented the new daguerreotype process at the Academy of Science in Paris on January 7, 1839, with the understanding that its details would be made available to all interested parties without charge (although the inventor received a large annuity in appreciation). Soon, people worldwide began making pictures with the daguerreotype "camera" (a name shortened from camera obscura) in a process almost immediately christened "photography," from the Greek *photos* (light) and *graphos* (writing). From the start, the possibilities of the process as a new art medium intrigued painters. Paul Delaroche (1797–1856), a leading academic painter of the day, wrote in an official report to the French government that anticipated the 1862 legal ruling:

> Daguerre's process completely satisfies all the demands of art, carrying certain essential principles of art to such perfection that it must become a subject of observation and study even to the most accomplished painters. The pictures obtained by this method are as remarkable for the perfection of the details as for the richness and harmony of the general effect. Nature is reproduced in them not only with truth, but also with art.[14]

Daguerreotypes, Calotypes, and Wet-Plate Photography

The earliest photographic processes were the *daguerreotype* (FIGS. 22-48 and 22-49), named after L.J.M. Daguerre, and the *calotype* (FIG. 22-54). Daguerre was an architect and theatrical set painter and designer. This background led Daguerre and a partner to open a popular entertainment called the Diorama. Audiences witnessed performances of "living paintings" created by changing the lighting effects on a "sandwich" composed of a painted backdrop and several layers of painted translucent front curtains. Daguerre used a camera obscura for the Diorama, but he wanted to find a more efficient and effective procedure. Through a mutual acquaintance, he met Joseph Nicéphore Niépce (1765–1833), who in 1826 had successfully made a permanent picture of the cityscape outside his upper-story window by exposing, in a camera obscura, a metal plate covered with a light-sensitive coating. Niépce's process, however, had the significant drawback that it required an eight-hour exposure time. After Niépce died in 1833, Daguerre continued his work, making two important discoveries. Latent development—that is, bringing out the image through treatment in chemical solutions—considerably shortened the length of time needed for exposure. Daguerre also discovered a better way to "fix" the image by chemically stopping the action of light on the photographic plate, which otherwise would continue to darken until the image turned solid black.

The daguerreotype reigned supreme in photography until the 1850s, but the second major photographic invention, the ancestor of the modern negative-print system, eventually replaced it. On January 31, 1839, less than three weeks after Daguerre unveiled his method in Paris, William Henry Fox Talbot presented a paper on his "photogenic drawings" to the Royal Institution in London. As early as 1835, Talbot made "negative" images by placing objects on sensitized paper and exposing the arrangement to light. This created a design of light-colored silhouettes recording the places where opaque or translucent objects had blocked light from darkening the paper's emulsion. In his experiments, Talbot next exposed sensitized papers inside simple cameras and, with a second sheet, created "positive" images. He further improved the process with more light-sensitive chemicals and a chemical development of the negative image. This technique enabled multiple prints. However, in Talbot's process, which he named the calotype (from the Greek word *kalos,* "beautiful"), the photographic images incorporated the texture of the paper. This produced a slightly blurred, grainy effect very different from the crisp detail and wide tonal range available with the daguerreotype. Also discouraging widespread adoption of the calotype were the stiff licensing and equipment fees charged for many years after Talbot patented his new process in 1841.

One of the earliest masters of an improved kind of calotype photography was the multitalented Frenchman known as Nadar (FIGS. 22-50 and 22-51). He used glass negatives and albumen (prepared with egg white) printing paper (FIGS. 22-52 and 22-53), which could record finer detail and a wider range of light and shadow than Talbot's calotype process. The new *wet-plate* technology (so named because the photographic plate was exposed, developed, and fixed while wet) almost at once became the universal way of making negatives until 1880. However, wet-plate photography had drawbacks. The plates had to be prepared and processed on the spot. Working outdoors meant taking along a portable darkroom—a wagon, tent, or box with light-tight sleeves for the photographer's arms.

Refinements of these early processes served photographers well for a century and a half but have been largely supplanted today by digital photography (see Chapter 26).

22-48 LOUIS-JACQUES-MANDÉ DAGUERRE, *Still Life in Studio,* 1837. Daguerreotype, $6\frac{1}{4}'' \times 8\frac{1}{4}''$. Société Française de Photographie, Paris. ◼◀

One of the first plates Daguerre produced after perfecting his new photographic process was this still life, in which he was able to capture amazing detail and finely graduated tones of light and shadow.

1 in.

22-49 Josiah Johnson Hawes and Albert Sands Southworth, *Early Operation under Ether, Massachusetts General Hospital*, ca. 1847. Daguerreotype, $6\frac{1}{2}'' \times 8\frac{1}{2}''$. Massachusetts General Hospital Archives and Special Collections, Boston.
▪️📹

In this early daguerreotype, which predates Eakins's *The Gross Clinic* (FIG. 22-36) by almost 30 years, Hawes and Southworth demonstrated the documentary power of the new medium of photography.

1 in.

Unlike photographs people make today, whether printed from traditional film negatives or from computerized digital images, each daguerreotype is a unique work. *Still Life in Studio* (FIG. **22-48**) is one of the first successful plates Daguerre produced after perfecting his method. The process captured every detail—the subtle forms, the varied textures, the finely graduated tones of light and shadow—in Daguerre's carefully constructed tableau. The three-dimensional forms of the sculptures, the basket, and the bits of cloth spring into high relief. The inspiration for the composition came from 17th-century Dutch vanitas still lifes, such as those of Pieter Claesz (FIG. 20-1). As did Claesz, Daguerre arranged his objects to reveal their textures and shapes clearly. Unlike a painter, Daguerre could not alter anything within his arrangement to create a stronger image. However, he could suggest a symbolic meaning through his choice of objects. Like the skull and timepiece in Claesz's painting, Daguerre's sculptural and architectural fragments and the framed print of an embrace suggest even art is vanitas and will not endure forever.

HAWES AND SOUTHWORTH In the United States, photographers began to make daguerreotypes within two months of Daguerre's presentation in Paris. Two particularly avid and resourceful advocates of the new medium were JOSIAH JOHNSON HAWES (1808–1901), a painter, and ALBERT SANDS SOUTHWORTH (1811–1894), a pharmacist and teacher. Together, they ran a daguerreotype studio in Boston specializing in portraiture, then popular due to the shortened exposure time required for the process (although it was still long enough to require head braces to help subjects remain motionless while photographers recorded their images).

The partners also took their equipment outside the studio to record places and events of particular interest to them. One resultant image is *Early Operation under Ether, Massachusetts General Hospital* (FIG. **22-49**). This daguerreotype, taken from the vantage point of the gallery of a hospital operating room, put the viewer in the position of medical students looking down on a lecture-demonstration typical throughout the 19th century. An image of historical record, this early daguerreotype predates Eakins's *Gross Clinic* (FIG. 22-36) by almost three decades. The focus of attention in *Early Operation* is the white-draped patient surrounded by a circle of darkly clad doctors. The details of the figures and the room's furnishings are in sharp focus, but the slight blurring of several of the figures betrays motion during the exposure. The elevated viewpoint flattens the spatial perspective and emphasizes the relationships of the figures in ways the Impressionists, especially Degas, found intriguing.

NADAR Portraiture was one of the first photography genres to use a technology that improved the calotype. Making portraits was an important economic opportunity for most photographers, as Southworth and Hawes proved, but the greatest of the early portrait photographers was undoubtedly Gaspar-Félix Tournachon. Known simply as NADAR (1820–1910), Tournachon was a French novelist, journalist, enthusiastic balloonist, and caricaturist, who became an early champion of photography. Photographic studies for his caricatures led Nadar to open a portrait studio. So talented was he at capturing the essence of his subjects that the most important people in France, including Delacroix, Daumier, Courbet, and Manet, flocked to his studio to have their portraits made. Nadar said he sought in his work "that instant of understanding that puts you in touch with the model—helps you sum him up,

1 in.

22-50 NADAR, *Eugène Delacroix*, ca. 1855. Modern print, $8\frac{1}{2}'' \times 6\frac{2}{3}''$, from the original negative. Bibliothèque Nationale, Paris.

Nadar was one of the earliest portrait photographers. His prints of the leading artists of the day, such as this one of Delacroix, reveal the sitters' personalities as well as record their features.

NADAR. élevant la Photographie à la hauteur de l'Art

1 in.

22-51 HONORÉ DAUMIER, *Nadar Raising Photography to the Height of Art*, 1862. Lithograph, $10\frac{3}{4}'' \times 8\frac{3}{4}''$. Museum of Fine Arts, Boston.

Daumier's lithograph of Nadar (FIG. 22-50) in a balloon "elevating the art of photography" commemorates a court decision acknowledging photographs as artworks protected by copyright.

guides you to his habits, his ideas, and character and enables you to produce . . . a really convincing and sympathetic likeness, an intimate portrait."[15]

Nadar's *Eugène Delacroix* (FIG. 22-50) shows the painter at the height of his career. In this photograph, the artist appears with remarkable presence. Even in half-length, his gesture and expression create a mood that seems to reveal much about him. Perhaps Delacroix responded to Nadar's famous gift for putting his clients at ease by assuming the pose that best expressed his personality. The new photographic materials made possible the rich range of tones in Nadar's images.

Nadar achieved so much fame for his wet-plate photographic portraits (see "Daguerreotypes, Calotypes, and Wet-Plate Photography," page 680) that he became the subject of a Daumier lithograph (FIG. 22-51) that provides incisive and amusing commentary about the struggle of photography to be recognized as a fine art. Daumier made his print in response to the 1862 court decision acknowledging photographs were indeed artworks. In the lithograph, Nadar energetically takes pictures with his camera as his balloon rises over Parisian rooftops—Daumier's literal representation of the elevation of photography's status the French judge reaffirmed. The image also refers to the fact that Nadar was a staunch advocate of balloon transportation and aerial reconnaissance. He produced the first aerial photographs of Paris in 1858 from his balloon *Le Géant* (The Giant).

JULIA MARGARET CAMERON Among the most famous portrait photographers in 19th-century England was JULIA MARGARET CAMERON (1815–1879), who did not take up photography seriously until the age of 48. Although she produced images of many well-known men of the period, including Charles Darwin, Alfred Tennyson, and Thomas Carlyle, she photographed more women than men, as was true of many women photographers. *Ophelia, Study No. 2* (FIG. 22-52) typifies her portrait style. Cameron often depicted her female subjects as characters in literary or biblical narratives. The slightly blurred focus also became a distinctive feature of her work—the byproduct of photographing with a lens with a short focal length, which allowed only a small area of sharp focus. The blurriness adds an ethereal, dreamlike tone to the photographs, appropriate for Cameron's fictional "characters." Her photograph of Ophelia has a mysterious, fragile quality reminiscent of Pre-Raphaelite paintings (FIG. 22-41) of literary heroines.

TIMOTHY O'SULLIVAN Photographers were quick to realize the documentary power of their new medium. Thus began the story of photography's influence on modern life and of the immense changes it brought to communication and information management. Historical events could be recorded in permanent form on the spot for the first time. The photographs taken of the Crimean War (1856) by Roger Fenton (1819–1869) and of the American Civil War by Mathew B. Brady (1823–1896), ALEXANDER GARDNER (1821–1882),

22-52 Julia Margaret Cameron, *Ophelia, Study No. 2*, 1867. Albumen print, 1′ 1″ × 10⅔″. George Eastman House, Rochester (gift of Eastman Kodak Company; formerly Gabriel Cromer Collection).

Cameron was a prominent 19th-century photographer who often depicted her female subjects as characters in literary or biblical narratives. The slightly blurred focus is a distinctive feature of her work.

and Timothy O'Sullivan (1840–1882) remain unsurpassed as incisive accounts of military life, unsparing in their truth to detail and poignant as expressions of human experience.

Of the Civil War photographs, the most moving are the inhumanly objective records of combat deaths. Perhaps the most reproduced of these Civil War photographs is Gardner's print of O'Sullivan's *A Harvest of Death, Gettysburg, Pennsylvania* (FIG. 22-53). Although viewers could regard this image as simple reportage, it also functions to impress on people the high price of war. Corpses litter the battlefield as far as the eye can see. O'Sullivan presented a scene stretching far to the horizon. As the photograph modulates from the precise clarity of the bodies of Union soldiers in the foreground, boots stolen and pockets picked, to the indistinct corpses in the distance, the suggestion of innumerable other dead soldiers is unavoidable. This "harvest" is far more sobering and depressing than that in Winslow Homer's Civil War painting, *Veteran in a New Field* (FIG. 22-35). Though it was years before photolithography could reproduce photographs such as this in newspapers, photographers exhibited them publicly. They made an impression newsprint engravings never could.

22-53 Timothy O'Sullivan, *A Harvest of Death, Gettysburg, Pennsylvania*, 1863. Negative by Timothy O'Sullivan. Albumen print by Alexander Gardner, 6¾″ × 8¾″. New York Public Library (Astor, Lenox and Tilden Foundations, Rare Books and Manuscript Division), New York. ◼◀

Wet-plate technology enabled photographers to record historical events on the spot— and to comment on the high price of war, as in this photograph of dead Union soldiers at Gettysburg in 1863.

Negative by T. H. O'Sullivan. Entered according to act of Congress, in the year 1865, by A. Gardner, in the Clerk's Office of the District Court of the District of Columbia. Positive by A. Gardner, 511 7th st., Washington.

A HARVEST OF DEATH, GETTYSBURG, PENNSYLVANIA.

22-54 EADWEARD MUYBRIDGE, *Horse Galloping*, 1878. Calotype print, 9″ × 12″. George Eastman House, Rochester. ◼◀

Muybridge specialized in photographic studies of the successive stages in human and animal motion—details too quick for the human eye to capture. Modern cinema owes a great deal to his work.

EADWEARD MUYBRIDGE The Realist photographer and scientist EADWEARD MUYBRIDGE (1830–1904) came to the United States from England in the 1850s and settled in San Francisco, where he established a prominent international reputation for his photographs of the western United States. In 1872, the governor of California, Leland Stanford (1824–1893), sought Muybridge's assistance in settling a bet about whether, at any point in a stride, all four feet of a horse galloping at top speed are off the ground. Through his sequential photography, as seen in *Horse Galloping* (FIG. 22-54), Muybridge proved they were. This experience was the beginning of Muybridge's photographic studies of the successive stages in human and animal motion—details too quick for the human eye to capture. These investigations culminated in 1885 at the University of Pennsylvania with a series of multiple-camera motion studies that recorded separate photographs of progressive moments in a single action. Muybridge's discoveries received extensive publicity through the book *Animal Locomotion* (1887), and his motion photographs earned him a place in the history of science, as well

as art. These sequential motion studies, along with those of Eakins and Marey, influenced many other artists, including their contemporary, the painter and sculptor Edgar Degas (FIG. 23-10), and 20th-century artists such as Marcel Duchamp (FIG. 24-35).

Muybridge presented his work to scientists and general audiences with a device called the *zoopraxiscope,* which he invented to project his sequences of images (mounted on special glass plates) onto a screen. The result was so lifelike one viewer said it "threw upon the screen apparently the living, moving animals. Nothing was wanting but the clatter of hoofs upon the turf."[16] The illusion of motion in Muybridge's photographic exhibits was the result of a physical fact of human eyesight called "persistence of vision." Stated simply, it means the brain retains whatever the eye sees for a fraction of a second after the eye stops seeing it. Thus, viewers saw a rapid succession of different images merging one into the next, producing the illusion of continuous change. This illusion lies at the heart of the motion-picture industry that debuted in the 20th century. Thus, with Muybridge's innovations in photography, yet another new art form was born—the cinema.

ROMANTICISM, REALISM, PHOTOGRAPHY: EUROPE AND AMERICA, 1800 TO 1870

ART UNDER NAPOLEON

▌ As Emperor of the French from 1804 to 1815, Napoleon embraced the Neoclassical style in order to associate his regime with the empire of ancient Rome. Roman temples were the models for La Madeleine in Paris, which Pierre Vignon built as a temple of glory for France's imperial armies.

▌ Napoleon chose Jacques-Louis David as First Painter of the Empire. His favorite sculptor was Antonio Canova, who carved marble Neoclassical portraits of the imperial family, including a reclining image of Napoleon's sister, Pauline Borghese, in the guise of Venus.

▌ The beginning of a break from Neoclassicism can already be seen in the work of some of David's students, including Gros, Girodet-Trioson, and Ingres, all of whom painted some exotic subjects reflecting Romantic taste.

Vignon, La Madeleine, Paris, 1807–1842

ROMANTICISM

▌ The roots of Romanticism are in the 18th century, but usually the term more narrowly denotes the artistic movement that flourished from 1800 to 1840, between Neoclassicism and Realism. Romantic artists gave precedence to feeling and imagination over Enlightenment reason. Romantic painters explored the exotic, erotic, and fantastic in their art.

▌ In Spain, Francisco Goya's *Los Caprichos* series celebrated the unleashing of imagination, emotions, and even nightmares. In France, Eugène Delacroix led the way in depicting Romantic narratives set in faraway places and distant times. Ancient Assyria, for example, is the subject of his colorful *Death of Sardanapalus*.

▌ Romantic painters often chose landscapes as an ideal subject to express the theme of the soul unified with the natural world. Masters of the transcendental landscape include Friedrich in Germany, Constable and Turner in England, and Cole, Bierstadt, and Church in the United States.

Delacroix, *Death of Sardanapalus*, 1827

REALISM

▌ Realism developed as an artistic movement in mid-19th-century France. Its leading proponent was Gustave Courbet, whose paintings of menial laborers and ordinary people exemplify his belief that painters should depict only their own time and place. Honoré Daumier boldly confronted authority with his satirical lithographs commenting on the plight of the urban working classes. Édouard Manet shocked the public with his paintings featuring promiscuous women, and his rough brushstrokes, which emphasized the flatness of the painting surface, paved the way for modern abstract art.

▌ Among the leading American Realists were Winslow Homer, Thomas Eakins, and John Singer Sargent. Eakins's painting of surgery in progress was too brutally realistic for the Philadelphia art jury that rejected it.

Courbet, *The Stone Breakers,* 1849

ARCHITECTURE

▌ Territorial expansion, the Romantic interest in exotic locales and earlier eras, and nationalistic pride led to the revival in the 19th century of older architectural styles, especially the Gothic, exemplified by London's Houses of Parliament.

▌ By the middle of the century, many architects had already abandoned sentimental and Romantic designs from the past in favor of exploring the possibilities of cast-iron construction, as in Henri Labrouste's Saint-Geneviève Library in Paris and Joseph Paxton's Crystal Palace in London.

Barry and Pugin, Houses of Parliament, London, 1835

PHOTOGRAPHY

▌ In 1839, Daguerre in Paris and Talbot in London invented the first practical photographic processes. In 1862, a French court formally recognized photography as an art form subject to copyright protection. Many of the earliest photographers, including Nadar and Cameron, specialized in portrait photography, but others, including Hawes, Southworth, and O'Sullivan in the United States quickly realized the documentary power of the new medium. Muybridge's sequential photos of human and animal motion were the forerunners of the modern cinema.

Daguerre, *Still Life in Studio,* 1837

In summer 1874, Manet recorded Monet painting—*en plein air* directly on canvas without any preliminary sketchpreliminar—in his floating studio on the Seine at Argenteuil, 22 minutes from Paris by train.

With Monet is his wife, Camille Doncieux. Monet, underappreciated as an artist, had recently sold some paintings, enabling the couple to purchase the small boat he equipped with a cabin and easel.

In this painting, Manet adopted not only Monet's Impressionist subject matter but also the younger artist's short brushstrokes and fascination with the reflection of sunlight on water.

1 ft.

23-1 ÉDOUARD MANET, *Claude Monet in His Studio Boat,* 1874. Oil on canvas, 2′ 8″ × 3′ 3¼″. Neue Pinakothek, Munich. ◼◀

IMPRESSIONISM, POST-IMPRESSIONISM, SYMBOLISM: EUROPE AND AMERICA, 1870 TO 1900

In the distance are the factories and smokestacks of Argenteuil. Manet thus recorded the two poles of modern life— the leisure activities of the bourgeosie and the industrialization along the Seine.

IMPRESSIONS OF MODERN LIFE

Impressionism was an art movement born in late-19th-century industrialized, urbanized Paris as a reaction to the sometimes brutal and chaotic transformation of French life, which made the world seem unstable and insubstantial. As the poet and critic Charles Baudelaire (1821–1867) observed in his 1860 essay *The Painter of Modern Life:* "[M]odernity is the transitory, the fugitive, the contingent."[1] Accordingly, Impressionist painters built upon the innovations of the Realists in turning away from traditional mythological and religious themes in favor of daily life, but they sought to convey the elusiveness and impermanence of the subjects they portrayed.

In 1872, the painter CLAUDE MONET (1840–1926), a leading Impressionist, moved to Argenteuil, a prosperous industrial town on the Seine (MAP **23-1**) that was also a favorite leisure destination of the city dwellers of Paris—only 22 minutes by train from the Saint-Lazare train station (FIG. 23-4). Situated at a point where the river widened into a deep basin, Argenteuil was an ideal spot for boating of all kinds, from casual rowing to formal regattas. In 1873, after accumulating enough money from recent sales of his paintings, the underappreciated and financially strapped Monet was able to purchase a small boat, which he equipped with a tiny wooden cabin and a striped awning and used as his floating studio.

During the summer of 1874, Édouard Manet (FIGS. 22-32 and 22-33) joined Monet at Argenteuil and painted side-by-side with the younger artist. One day, Manet recorded Monet in his studio boat (FIG. **23-1**) at work on *Sailboats on the Seine, Argenteuil*, a painting now in the Fine Arts Museum of San Francisco. Monet, wearing a straw hat, sits at the front of the boat with his easel before him. Camille Doncieux, Monet's wife (compare FIG. 23-2A), is at once the painter's admirer and his muse. In the distance are the factories and smokestacks that represent the opposite pole of life at Argenteuil. In capturing both the leisure activities of the bourgeoisie and the industrialization along the Seine in the 1870s on the same canvas, Manet, like Monet, was fulfilling Baudelaire's definition of "the painter of modern life."

Claude Monet in His Studio Boat is noteworthy as a document of Monet's preference for painting outdoors (*en plein air*)—a radical practice at the time—in order to record his "impression" of the Seine by placing colors directly on a white canvas without any preliminary sketch—also a sharp break from traditional studio techniques. The painting further attests to Monet's influence on his older friend Manet, who here adopted the younger painter's subject matter, short brushstrokes, and fascination with the reflection of light on water.

MARXISM, DARWINISM, MODERNISM

The momentous developments of the early 19th century in Europe—industrialization, urbanization, and increased economic and political interaction worldwide—matured during the latter half of the century. The Industrial Revolution born in England spread so rapidly to the Continent and the United States that historians often refer to the third quarter of the 19th century as the second Industrial Revolution. Whereas the first Industrial Revolution centered on textiles, steam, and iron, the second focused on steel, electricity, chemicals, and oil. The discoveries in these fields provided the foundation for developments in plastics, machinery, building construction, and automobile manufacturing and paved the way for the invention of the radio, electric light, telephone, and electric streetcar.

A significant consequence of industrialization was urbanization. The number and size of Western cities grew dramatically during the latter part of the 19th century, largely due to migration from the countryside. Farmers in large numbers relocated to urban centers because expanded agricultural enterprises squeezed smaller property owners from their land. The widely available work opportunities in the cities, especially in the factories, were also a major factor in this population shift. Improving health and living conditions in the cities further contributed to their explosive growth.

MAP 23-1 France around 1870.

MARXISM AND DARWINISM The rise of the urban working class was fundamental to the ideas of Karl Marx (1818–1883), one of the era's dominant figures. Born in Trier, Germany, Marx received a doctorate in philosophy from the University of Berlin. After moving to Paris, he met fellow German Friedrich Engels (1820–1895), who became his lifelong collaborator. Together they wrote *The Communist Manifesto* (1848), which called for the working class to overthrow the capitalist system. As did other 19th-century empiricists, Marx believed scientific, rational law governed nature and, indeed, all human history. For Marx, economic forces based on class struggle induced historical change. Throughout history, insisted Marx, those who controlled the means of production conflicted with those whose labor they exploited for their own enrichment—a dynamic he called "dialectical materialism." Marx advocated the creation of a socialist state in which the working class seized power and destroyed capitalism. This new political, social, and economic system—Marxism—held great appeal for the oppressed as well as for many intellectuals.

Equally influential was the English naturalist Charles Darwin (1809–1882), whose theory of natural selection did much to increase interest in science. Darwin and his compatriot Alfred Russel Wallace (1823–1913), working independently, proposed a model for the process of evolution based on mechanistic laws, rather than attributing evolution to random chance or God's plan. They postulated a competitive system in which only the fittest survived. Darwin's controversial ideas, as presented in *On the Origin of Species by Means of Natural Selection* (1859), contradicted the biblical narrative of creation. By challenging traditional religious beliefs, Darwinism contributed to growing secularism.

IMPRESSIONISM, POST-IMPRESSIONISM, SYMBOLISM: EUROPE AND AMERICA, 1870 TO 1900

1870	1880	1890	1900

- Claude Monet and the Impressionists mount their first independent exhibition in Paris
- Monet, Pierre-Auguste Renoir, Berthe Morisot, and other Impressionists paint landscapes and bourgeois life outdoors
- European artists begin to collect Japanese prints
- Gustave Moreau explores eroticism and fantasy in Symbolist paintings

- Georges Seurat develops pointillism
- Vincent van Gogh moves to France and explores the expressive power of color
- Auguste Rodin receives the commission for *Gates of Hell*
- Alexandre-Gustave Eiffel builds the Eiffel Tower in Paris

- Paul Cézanne seeks "to do Poussin over entirely from nature"
- The Art Nouveau movement emerges in architecture and the decorative arts
- Gustav Klimt's paintings epitomize fin-de-siècle culture in Austria
- Louis Sullivan builds steel, glass, and stone skyscrapers in America

Other theorists and social thinkers, most notably British philosopher Herbert Spencer (1820–1903), applied Darwin's principles to the rapidly changing socioeconomic realm. As in the biological world, they asserted, industrialization's intense competition led to the survival of the most economically fit companies, enterprises, and countries. The social Darwinists provided Western nations with justification for the colonization of peoples and cultures they deemed less advanced. By 1900, the major economic and political powers had divided up much of the world. The French had colonized most of North Africa and Indochina, while the British occupied India, Australia, and large areas of Africa, including Nigeria, Egypt, Sudan, Rhodesia, and the Union of South Africa. The Dutch were a major presence in the Pacific, and the Germans, Portuguese, Spanish, and Italians all established themselves in various areas of Africa.

MODERNISM The combination of extensive technological changes and increased exposure to other cultures, coupled with the rapidity of these changes, led to an acute sense in Western cultures of the world's impermanence. Darwin's ideas of evolution and Marx's emphasis on a continuing sequence of conflicts reinforced this awareness of a constantly shifting reality. These societal changes in turn fostered a new and multifaceted artistic approach that art historians call *modernism*. Modernist artists seek to capture the images and sensibilities of their age, but modernism transcends the simple depiction of the contemporary world—the goal of Realism (see Chapter 22). Modernist artists also critically examine the premises of art itself, as Manet did in his seminal 1863 painting *Le Déjeuner sur l'Herbe* (FIG. 22-32). Modernism thus implies certain concerns about art and aesthetics internal to art production, regardless of whether the artist is portraying modern life. Clement Greenberg (1909–1994), an influential American art critic who wrote about the revolutionary art movements of the decades following World War II (see Chapter 25), explained:

> The essence of Modernism lies . . . in the use of the characteristic methods of a discipline to criticize the discipline itself—not in order to subvert it, but to entrench it more firmly in its area of competence. . . . Realistic, illusionist art had dissembled the medium, using art to conceal art. Modernism used art to call attention to art. The limitations that constitute the medium of painting—the flat surface, the shape of the support, the properties of pigment—were treated by the Old Masters as negative factors that could be acknowledged only implicitly or indirectly. Modernist painting has come to regard these same limitations as positive factors that are to be acknowledged openly.[2]

Although the work of Gustave Courbet and the Realists already expressed this modernist viewpoint, modernism emerged even more forcefully in the late-19th-century movements that art historians call Impressionism, Post-Impressionism, and Symbolism.

IMPRESSIONISM

A hostile critic applied the term *Impressionism* in response to Claude Monet's *Impression: Sunrise* (FIG. 23-2), exhibited in the first Impressionist show in 1874 (see "Academic Salons and Independent Art Exhibitions," page 690). Although the critic intended the label to be derogatory, by the third Impressionist show in 1878, the artists had embraced it and were calling themselves Impressionists.

CLAUDE MONET Artists and critics had used the term *Impressionism* before, but only in relation to sketches. Impressionist paintings do incorporate the qualities of sketches—abbreviation, speed, and spontaneity. This is apparent in *Impression: Sunrise* (FIG. 23-2), in which Monet made no attempt to disguise the brushstrokes or blend the pigment to create smooth tonal gradations and an optically accurate scene. This concern with acknowledging the paint and the canvas surface continued the modernist exploration the Realists began. Beyond this connection to the sketch, Impressionism operated at the intersection of what the artists saw and what they felt. In other words, the "impressions" these artists recorded in their paintings were neither purely objective descriptions of the exterior world nor solely subjective responses, but the interaction between the two. They were sensations—the Impressionists' subjective and personal responses to nature.

23-2A MONET, *Bank of the Seine, Bennecourt*, 1868.

In sharp contrast to traditional studio artists, Monet painted outdoors, often on the banks of the Seine (FIG. **23-2A**) northwest of Paris or in a boat on the river (FIG. 23-1). Painting *en plein air* sharpened Monet's focus on the roles light and color play in capturing an instantaneous representation of atmosphere and climate. Monet carried the systematic investigation of light and color further than any other Impressionist, but all of them recognized the importance of carefully observing and understanding how light and color operate. Such thorough study enabled the Impressionists to present images that truly conveyed a sense of the momentary and transitory. Lila Cabot Perry (1848–1933), a student of Monet's late in his career, gave this description of Monet's approach:

> I remember his once saying to me: "When you go out to paint, try to forget what objects you have before you—a tree, a house, a field, or whatever. Merely think, here is a little square of blue, here an oblong of pink, here a streak of yellow, and paint it just as it looks to you, the exact color and shape, until it gives your own naïve impression of the scene before you."[3]

Scientific studies of light and the invention of chemically synthesized pigments increased artists' sensitivity to the multiplicity of colors in nature and gave them new colors for their work. After scrutinizing the effects of light and color on forms, the Impressionists concluded that *local color*—an object's color in white light—becomes modified by the quality of the light shining on it, by reflections from other objects, and by the effects juxtaposed colors produce. Shadows do not appear gray or black, as many earlier painters thought, but seem to be composed of colors modified by reflections or other conditions. If artists use complementary colors (see "19th-Century Color Theory," page 701) side by side over large enough areas, the colors intensify each other, unlike the effect of small quantities of adjoining mixed pigments, which blend into neutral tones. Furthermore, the "mixing" of colors by juxtaposing them on a canvas produces a more intense hue than the same colors mixed on the palette. It is not strictly true the Impressionists used only primary hues, placing them side by side to create secondary colors (blue and yellow, for example, to create green). But they did achieve remarkably brilliant effects with their characteristically short, choppy brushstrokes, which so accurately caught the vibrating quality of light. The fact their canvas surfaces look unintelligible at close range and their forms and objects appear only when the eye fuses the strokes at a certain distance accounts for much of the early adverse criticism leveled at their work. Some critics even accused the Impressionists of firing their paint at the canvas with pistols.

Academic Salons and Independent Art Exhibitions

For both artists and art historians, modernist art stands in marked contrast—indeed in forceful opposition—to academic art, that is, to the art promoted by the established art schools such as the Royal Academy of Painting and Sculpture in France (founded in 1648) and the Royal Academy of Arts in Britain (founded in 1768). These academies provided instruction for art students and sponsored exhibitions, exerting tight control over the art scene. The annual exhibitions, called "Salons" in France, were highly competitive, as was membership in these academies. Subsidized by the government, the French Royal Academy supported a limited range of artistic expression, focusing on traditional subjects and highly polished technique. Because of the challenges modernist art presented to established artistic conventions, the juries for the Salons and other exhibitions often rejected the works more adventurous artists wished to display, thereby preventing the public from viewing any art other than the officially sanctioned forms of expression. When, however, the 1855 jury rejected some of Gustave Courbet's paintings, the artist reacted by setting up his own Pavilion of Realism (see "Courbet on Realism," Chapter 22, page 664). Years later, he wrote:

> [I]t is high time that someone have the courage to be an honest man and that he say that the Academy is a harmful, all-consuming institution, incapable of fulfilling the goal of its so-called mission.*

Growing dissatisfaction with the decisions of the French Academy's jurors prompted Napoleon III (r. 1852–1870) in 1863 to establish the Salon des Refusés (Salon of the Rejected) to show all of the works not accepted for exhibition in the regular Salon. Édouard Manet's *Le Déjeuner sur l'Herbe* (FIG. 22-32) was among them. The public greeted it and the entire exhibition with derision. One reviewer of the rejected works summed up the prevailing attitude:

> This exhibition, at once sad and grotesque, . . . offers abundant proof . . . that the jury always displays an unbelievable leniency. Save for one or two questionable exceptions there is not a painting which deserves the honor of the official galleries . . . There is even something cruel about this exhibition; people laugh as they do at a farce.†

In 1867, after further rejections, Manet, following Courbet, mounted a private exhibition of 50 of his paintings outside the Paris World's Fair. Six years later, Claude Monet (FIG. 23-2) and the other Impressionists formed their own society and began mounting shows of their works in Paris. This action provided the Impressionists much freedom, for they did not have to contend with the Royal Academy's authoritative and confining viewpoint. The Impressionist exhibitions took place at one- or two-year intervals from 1874 until 1886.

Another group of artists unhappy with the official Salon's conservative nature adopted the same renegade idea. In 1884, these artists formed the Société des Artistes Indépendants (Society of Independent Artists) and held annual Salons des Indépendants. Georges Seurat's *A Sunday on La Grande Jatte* (FIG. 23-16) was one of the paintings in the Independents' 1886 salon.

As the art market expanded, venues for the exhibition of art increased. Art circles and societies sponsored private shows in which both amateurs and professionals participated. Dealers became more aggressive in promoting the artists they represented by mounting exhibitions in a variety of spaces, some fairly intimate and small, others large and grandiose. All of these proliferating opportunities for exhibition gave French artists alternatives to the traditional constraints of the Salon and provided fertile breeding ground for the development of radically new art forms and styles.

*Letter to Jules-Antoine Castagnary, October 17, 1868. Translated by Petra ten-Doesschate Chu, *Letters of Gustave Courbet* (Chicago: University of Chicago Press, 1992), 346.
†Maxime du Camp, in *Revue des deux mondes,* 1863, quoted in George Heard Hamilton, *Manet and His Critics* (New Haven: Yale University Press, New Haven, Conn., 1986), 42–43.

23-2 CLAUDE MONET, *Impression: Sunrise,* 1872. Oil on canvas, 1′ 7½″ × 2′ 1½″. Musée Marmottan, Paris.

A hostile critic applied the derogatory term *Impressionism* to this painting because of its sketchy quality and undisguised brushstrokes. Monet and his circle embraced the label for their movement.

1 in.

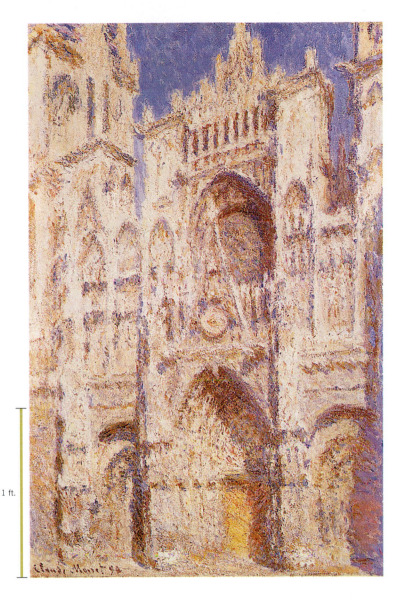

1 ft.

23-3 CLAUDE MONET, *Rouen Cathedral: The Portal (in Sun)*, 1894. Oil on canvas, 3′ 3¼″ × 2′ 1⅞″. Metropolitan Museum of Art, New York (Theodore M. Davis Collection, bequest of Theodore M. Davis, 1915).

Monet painted a series of views of Rouen Cathedral at different times of day and under various climatic conditions. The real subject of this painting is not the building but the sunlight shining on it.

ROUEN CATHEDRAL Monet's intensive study of the phenomena of light and color is especially evident in several series of paintings he made of the same subject. In one series, he painted more than three dozen views of Rouen Cathedral, northwest of Paris. For each canvas in the series, Monet observed the cathedral from nearly the same viewpoint but at different times of the day or under various climatic conditions. In the painting illustrated here (FIG. 23-3), Monet depicted the church bathed in bright light. With scientific precision, he carefully recorded the passing of time as seen in the movement of light over identical forms. In fact, the real subject of Monet's painting—as the title *Rouen Cathedral: The Portal (in Sun)* implies—is not the cathedral, which he showed only in part, but the sunlight on the building's main portal. Later critics accused Monet and his companions of destroying form and order for fleeting atmospheric effects, but Monet focused on light and color precisely to reach a greater understanding of the appearance of form.

SAINT-LAZARE Most of the Impressionists painted scenes in and around Paris, the heart of modern life in France. Monet's *Saint-Lazare Train Station* (FIG. 23-4) depicts a dominant aspect of the contemporary urban scene. The expanding railway network had made travel more convenient, bringing throngs of people into Paris and enabling city dwellers to reach rural areas quickly. In this painting, Monet captured the energy and vitality of Paris's modern transportation hub. The train, emerging from the steam and smoke it emits, rumbles into the station. In the background haze are the tall buildings that were becoming a major component of the Parisian landscape. Monet's agitated paint application contributes to the sense of energy and conveys the atmosphere of urban life.

1 ft.

23-4 CLAUDE MONET, *Saint-Lazare Train Station*, 1877. Oil on canvas, 2′ 5¾″ × 3′ 5″. Musée d'Orsay, Paris. ◼

Impressionist paintings are unintelligible at close range, but the eye fuses the brushstrokes at a distance. The agitated application of paint contributes to the sense of energy in this urban scene.

Georges Rivière (1855–1943), a critic and friend of some of the Impressionists, saw this painting in the third Impressionist exhibition and recorded the essence of what Monet had tried to achieve:

> Like a fiery steed, stimulated rather than exhausted by the long trek that it has only just finished, [the locomotive] tosses its mane of smoke, which lashes the glass roof of the main hall. . . . We see the vast and manic movements at the station where the ground shakes with every turn of the wheel. The platforms are sticky with soot, and the air is full of that bitter scent exuded by burning coal. As we look at this magnificent picture, we are overcome by the same feelings as if we were really there, and these feelings are perhaps even more powerful, because in the picture the artist has conveyed his own feelings as well.[4]

GUSTAVE CAILLEBOTTE Other Impressionists also represented facets of city life, although not always using Monet's impressionistic brushstrokes. The setting of *Paris: A Rainy Day* (FIG. **23-5**) by GUSTAVE CAILLEBOTTE (1849–1893) is a junction of spacious boulevards resulting from the redesigning of Paris begun in 1852. The city's population had reached close to 1.5 million by midcentury. To accommodate this congregation of humanity—and to facilitate the movement of troops in the event of another revolution—Napoleon III ordered Paris rebuilt. The emperor named Baron Georges Haussmann (1809–1891), a city superintendent, to oversee the entire project. In addition to new water and sewer systems, street lighting, and new residential and commercial buildings, a major component of the new Paris was the creation of the wide, open boulevards seen in Caillebotte's painting. These great avenues, whose construction caused the demolition of thousands of old buildings and streets, transformed medieval Paris into the present-day city, with its superb vistas and wide uninterrupted arteries for the flow of vehicular and pedestrian traffic. Caillebotte chose to focus on these markers of the city's rapid urbanization.

Although Caillebotte did not dissolve his image into the broken color and brushwork characteristic of Impressionism, he did use an informal and asymmetrical composition. The figures seem randomly placed, with the frame cropping them arbitrarily, suggesting the transitory nature of the street scene. Well-dressed Parisians of the leisure class share the viewer's space. Despite the sharp focus of *Paris: A Rainy Day*, the picture captures the artist's "impression" of urban life.

CAMILLE PISSARRO Other Impressionists also found Paris's spacious boulevards and avenues—the product of "Haussmannization"—attractive subjects for paintings. *La Place du Théâtre Français* (FIG. **23-6**) is one of many panoramic scenes of the city CAMILLE PISSARRO (1830–1903) painted. The artist recorded the blurred dark accents against a light ground that constituted his visual sensations of a crowded Parisian square viewed from several stories above street level. The moment Pissarro captured on his canvas is not so much of fugitive light effects as it is of the street life, achieved through a deliberate casualness in the arrangement of figures. To accomplish this sense of spontaneity, Pissarro sometimes used photography to record the places he wished to paint, as did many of his fellow Impressionists. Indeed, the visual parallels between Impressionist paintings and photographs are striking. In *La Place du Théâtre Français*, these parallels include the arbitrary cutting off of figures at the edges of the painting and the curious flattening spatial effect produced by the high viewpoint.

BERTHE MORISOT Many Impressionist paintings depict scenes from resort areas on the seashore or along the Seine River, such as Argenteuil (FIG. 23-1), Bennencourt (FIG. 23-2A), Bougival, and Chatou (MAP 23-1). The railway line running to and from Saint-Lazare station connected Argenteuil to Paris, so transportation was not an obstacle. Parisians often would take the train out to these resort areas for a day of sailing, picnicking, and strolling

23-5 GUSTAVE CAILLEBOTTE, *Paris: A Rainy Day,* 1877. Oil on canvas, 6′ 9″ × 9′ 9″. Art Institute of Chicago, Chicago (Worcester Fund).

Although Caillebotte did not use Impressionistic broken brushstrokes, the seemingly randomly placed figures and the arbitrary cropping of the vista suggest the transitory nature of modern life.

1 ft.

along the Seine. BERTHE MORISOT (1841–1895), Édouard Manet's sister-in-law, regularly exhibited with the Impressionists. Most of her paintings focus on domestic subjects, the one realm of Parisian life where society allowed an upper-class woman such as Morisot free access, but she also produced many outdoor scenes, including *Villa at the Seaside* (FIG. 23-7), painted in 1874, and *Summer's Day* (FIG. 23-7A), in 1879. The subject and style of both works correlate well with Impressionist concerns.

The setting of *Villa at the Seaside* is the shaded veranda of a summer hotel at a fashionable seashore resort. A woman elegantly but not ostentatiously dressed sits gazing out across the railing to a sun-lit beach. Her child, its discarded toy boat a splash of red, gazes at the passing sails on the placid sea. The mood is of relaxed leisure. Morisot used the

23-7A MORISOT, *Summer's Day*, 1879. ◼◀

open brushwork and the *plein air* lighting characteristic of Impressionism. Sketchy brushstrokes record her quick perceptions. Nowhere did Morisot linger on contours or enclosed details. She presented the scene in a slightly filmy, soft focus conveying a feeling of airiness. The composition also recalls the work of other Impressionists. The figures fall informally into place, as someone who shared their intimate space would perceive them. Morisot was both immensely ambitious and talented, as her ability to catch the pictorial moment demonstrates. She escaped the hostile criticism directed at most of the other Impressionists. People praised her work for its sensibility, grace, and delicacy.

Renoir on the Art of Painting

Many 19th-century artists were concerned with the theoretical basis of picturemaking. One of the most cogent statements on this subject is Pierre-Auguste Renoir's concise summary of how he, as an Impressionist, painted pictures and what he hoped to achieve as an artist.

I arrange my subject as I want it, then I go ahead and paint it, like a child. I want a red to be sonorous, to sound like a bell; if it doesn't turn out that way, I add more reds and other colors until I get it. I am no cleverer than that. I have no rules and no methods; . . . I have no secrets. I look at a nude; there are myriads of tiny tints. I must find the ones that will make the flesh on my canvas live and quiver. . . . [I]f they could explain a picture, it wouldn't be art. Shall I tell you what I think are the two qualities of art? It must be indescribable and it must be inimitable. . . . The work of art must seize upon you, wrap you up in itself, carry you away. It is the means by which the artist conveys his passions. . . . I want people to feel that neither the setting nor the figures are dull and lifeless.*

There is certainly nothing dull or lifeless about *Le Moulin de la Galette* (FIG. 23-8), in which Renoir depicted throngs of people gathered in a popular Parisian dance hall. Some crowd the tables and chatter, while others dance energetically. So lively is the atmosphere the viewer can virtually hear the sounds of music, laughter, and tinkling glasses. The painter dappled the whole scene with sunlight and shade, artfully blurred into the figures to produce precisely the effect of floating and fleeting light the Impressionists so cultivated. Renoir's casual unposed placement of the figures and the suggested continuity of space, spreading in all directions and only accidentally limited by the frame, position the viewer as a participant rather than as an outsider. Whereas classical art sought to express universal and timeless qualities, Impressionism attempted to depict just the opposite—the incidental, momentary, and passing aspects of reality.

*Quoted in Eric Protter, ed., *Painters on Painting* (New York: Grosset & Dunlap, 1971), 145.

23-8 Pierre-Auguste Renoir, *Le Moulin de la Galette,* 1876. Oil on canvas, 4′ 3″ × 5′ 8″. Musée d'Orsay, Paris. ◼◀

Renoir's painting of this popular Parisian dance hall is dappled by sunlight and shade, artfully blurred into the figures to produce the effect of floating and fleeting light the Impressionists cultivated.

1 ft.

PIERRE-AUGUSTE RENOIR Ample time for leisure activities was another facet of the new, industrialized Paris, and scenes of dining and dancing, café-concerts, opera, ballet, and other forms of urban recreation became mainstays of Impressionism. Although seemingly unrelated, industrialization facilitated these pursuits. With the advent of set working hours, people's schedules became more regimented, enabling them to plan their favorite pastimes. One Impressionist who turned repeatedly to Parisian nightlife for the subjects of his canvases was Pierre-Auguste Renoir (1841–1919), who in 1874 painted *en plein air* alongside Monet and Manet at Argenteuil (FIG. 23-1) and was also one of the most eloquent writers on the aims of Impressionism (see "Renoir on the Art of Painting," above). His *Le Moulin de la Galette* (FIG. **23-8**) of 1876 is a superb example of this Impressionist genre.

23-9 Édouard Manet, *A Bar at the Folies-Bergère,* 1882. Oil on canvas, 3′ 1″ × 4′ 3″. Courtauld Institute of Art Gallery, London. ◼◀

In this painting set in a Parisian café, Manet called attention to the canvas surface by creating spatial inconsistencies, such as the relationship between the barmaid and her apparent reflection in a mirror.

1 ft.

of modeling and perspective are minimal. This painting method further calls attention to the surface by forcing the viewer to scrutinize the work to make sense of the scene. But it is difficult to do so, because visual discrepancies immediately emerge. For example, what initially seems easily recognizable as a mirror behind the barmaid creates confusion throughout the rest of the painting. Is the woman on the right the barmaid's reflection? If both figures are the same person, it is impossible to reconcile the spatial relationship between the barmaid, the mirror, the bar's frontal horizontality, and the barmaid's seemingly displaced reflection. These visual contradictions reveal Manet's insistence on calling attention to the pictorial structure of his painting, in keeping with his modernist interest in examining the basic premises of the medium.

ÉDOUARD MANET The immensely versatile Manet, whose career bridged Realism (FIGS. 22-32 and 22-33) and Impressionism (FIG. 23-1), also depicted Parisian nightlife. One of his later works in the Impressionist mode is *A Bar at the Folies-Bergère* (FIG. 23-9), painted in 1882. The Folies-Bergère was a popular café with music-hall performances, one of the fashionable gathering places for Parisian revelers that many Impressionists frequented. In Manet's painting, a barmaid, centrally placed, looks out from the canvas but seems disinterested or lost in thought, divorced from her patrons as well as from the viewer. Manet blurred and roughly applied the brushstrokes, particularly those in the background, and the effects

EDGAR DEGAS Impressionists also depicted more-formal leisure activities. The fascination EDGAR DEGAS (1834–1917) had with patterns of motion brought him to the Paris Opéra (FIG. 22-45) and its ballet school. There, his keen observational power took in the formalized movements of classical ballet, one of his favorite subjects. In *The Rehearsal* (FIG. 23-10), Degas used several devices to bring the observer into the pictorial space. The frame cuts off the spiral stair, the windows in the background, and the group of figures in the right foreground. The figures are not at the center of a

23-10 EDGAR DEGAS, *The Rehearsal,* 1874. Oil on canvas, 1′ 11″ × 2′ 9″. Glasgow Art Galleries and Museum, Glasgow (Burrell Collection). ◼◀

The arbitrarily cut-off figures of dancers, the patterns of light splotches, and the blurry images reveal Degas's interest in reproducing fleeting moments, as well as his fascination with photography.

1 in.

Japonisme

Despite Europe's and America's extensive colonization during the 19th century, Japan avoided Western intrusion until 1853–1854, when Commodore Matthew Perry (1794–1858) and American naval forces exacted trading and diplomatic privileges from Japan. From the increased contact, Westerners became familiar with Japanese culture. So intrigued were the French with Japanese art and culture that they coined a specific term—*Japonisme*—to describe the Japanese aesthetic, which, because of both its beauty and exoticism, greatly appealed to the fashionable segment of Parisian society. In 1867 at the Exposition Universelle in Paris, the Japanese pavilion garnered more attention than any other. Soon, Japanese kimonos, fans, lacquer cabinets, tea caddies, folding screens, tea services, and jewelry flooded Paris. Japanese-themed novels and travel books were immensely popular as well. As demand for Japanese merchandise grew in the West, the Japanese began to develop import-export businesses, and the foreign currency flowing into Japan helped to finance much of its industrialization.

Artists in particular were great admirers of Japanese art. Among those the Japanese aesthetic influenced were the Impressionists and Post-Impressionists, especially Édouard Manet, Edgar Degas, Mary Cassatt, James Abbott McNeill Whistler, Henri de Toulouse-Lautrec, Paul Gauguin, and Vincent van Gogh. Indeed, van Gogh collected and copied Japanese prints (FIG. 23-16B). For the most part, the Japanese presentation of space in woodblock prints, which were more readily available in the West than any other Asian art form, intrigued these artists. Because of the simplicity of the woodblock printing process, the Japanese prints feature broad areas of flat color with a limited amount of modulation or gradation. This flatness interested modernist painters, who sought ways to call attention to the picture surface. The right side of Degas's *The Tub* (FIG. 23-11), for example, has this two-dimensional quality. Degas, in fact, owned a print by Japanese artist Torii Kiyonaga depicting eight women at a bath in various poses and states of undress. That print inspired Degas's painting. A comparison between Degas's bather and a detail (FIG. 23-12) of a bather from another of Kiyonaga's prints is striking, although Degas did not closely copy any of the Japanese artist's figures. Instead, he absorbed the essence of Japanese compositional style and the distinctive angles employed in representing human figures, and he translated them into the Impressionist mode.

The decorative quality of Japanese images also appealed to the artists associated with the Arts and Crafts movement in England. Artists such as William Morris (FIG. 23-34) and Charles Rennie Mackinstosh (FIG. 23-35) found Japanese prints attractive because those artworks intersected nicely with two fundamental Arts and Crafts principles: art should be available to the masses, and functional objects should be artistically designed.

23-11 EDGAR DEGAS, *The Tub*, 1886. Pastel, 1′ 11½″ × 2′ 8⅜″. Musée d'Orsay, Paris. ◼◗

The Tub reveals the influence of Japanese prints, especially the sharp angles that artists such as Kiyonaga used in representing figures. Degas translated his Japanese model into the Impressionist mode.

23-12 TORII KIYONAGA, detail of *Two Women at the Bath*, ca. 1780. Color woodblock, full print 10½″ × 7½″, detail 3¾″ × 3½″. Musée Guimet, Paris.

classically balanced composition. Instead, Degas arranged them in a seemingly random manner. The prominent diagonals of the wall bases and floorboards lead the viewer's eye into and along the directional lines of the dancers. Finally, as is customary in Degas's ballet pictures, a large, off-center, empty space creates the illusion of a continuous floor connecting the observer with the pictured figures.

The often arbitrarily cut-off figures, the patterns of light splotches, and the blurriness of the images in this and other Degas works indicate the artist's interest in reproducing single moments. They also reveal his fascination with photography. Degas not only studied the photographs of others but regularly used a camera to make preliminary studies for his works, particularly photographing figures in interiors. Japanese woodblock prints (see "Japonisme," page 696) were another inspirational source for paintings such as *The Rehearsal.* The cunning spatial projections in Degas's paintings probably derived in part from Japanese prints, such as those by Suzuki Harunobu. Japanese artists used diverging lines not only to organize the flat shapes of figures but also to direct the viewer's attention into the picture space. The Impressionists, acquainted with these woodblocks as early as the 1860s, greatly admired the spatial organization, familiar and intimate themes, and flat unmodeled color areas of the Japanese prints, and avidly incorporated these features into their own paintings.

THE TUB Although color and light were major components of the Impressionists' quest to capture fleeting sensations, these artists considered other formal elements as well. Degas, for example, became a master of line, so much so his works often differ significantly from those of Monet and Renoir. Degas specialized in studies of figures in rapid and informal action, recording the quick impression of arrested motion, as is evident in *The Rehearsal* (FIG. 23-10). He often employed lines to convey this sense of movement. In *The Tub* (FIG. **23-11**), inspired by a Japanese print similar to the one illustrated here (FIG. **23-12**) by TORII KIYONAGA (1752–1815), a young woman crouches in a washing tub. Degas outlined the major objects in the painting—the woman, tub, and pitchers—and covered all surfaces with linear hatch marks. He was able to achieve this leaner quality by using *pastels,* his favorite medium. With these dry sticks of powdered pigment, Degas drew directly on the paper, as one would with a piece of chalk, thus accounting for the linear basis of his work. Although the applied pastel is subject to smudging, the colors tend to retain their autonomy, so they appear fresh and bright.

The Tub also reveals how Degas's work, like that of the other Impressionists, continued the modernist exploration of the premises of painting by acknowledging the artwork's surface. Although the viewer clearly perceives the woman as a depiction of a three-dimensional form in space, the tabletop or shelf on the right of the image appears severely tilted, so much so it seems to parallel the picture plane. The two pitchers on the table complicate this visual conflict between the table's flatness and the illusion of the bathing woman's three-dimensional volume. The limited foreshortening of the pitchers and their shared edge, in conjunction with the rest of the image, create a visual perplexity for the viewer.

MARY CASSATT In the Salon of 1874, Degas admired a painting by a young American artist, MARY CASSATT (1844–1926), the daughter of a Philadelphia banker. Degas befriended and influ-

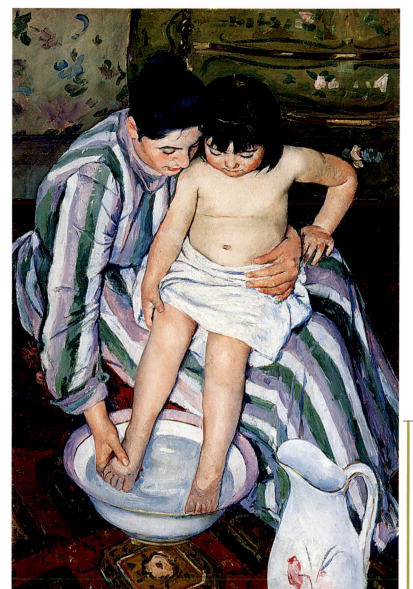

23-13 MARY CASSATT, *The Bath,* ca. 1892. Oil on canvas, 3′ 3″ × 2′ 2″. Art Institute of Chicago, Chicago (Robert A. Walker Fund). ◼◀

Cassatt's compositions owe much to Degas and Japanese prints, but her subjects differ from those of most Impressionist painters, in part because, as a woman, she could not frequent cafés.

1 ft.

enced Cassatt, who exhibited regularly with the Impressionists. She had trained as a painter before moving to Europe to study masterworks in France and Italy. As a woman, she could not easily frequent the cafés with her male artist friends, and she had the responsibility of caring for her aging parents, who had moved to Paris to join her. Because of these restrictions, Cassatt's subjects, like Morisot's (FIG. 23-7), were principally women and children, whom she presented with a combination of objectivity and genuine sentiment. Works such as *The Bath* (FIG. **23-13**) show the tender relationship between a mother and child. As in Degas's *The Tub,* the visual solidity of the mother and child contrasts with the flattened patterning of the wallpaper and rug. Cassatt's style in this work owed much to the compositional devices of Degas and of Japanese prints, but the painting's design has an originality and strength all its own.

Whistler on "Artistic Arrangements"

Underscoring the insistence by late-19th-century artists, both in Europe and America, that paintings are independent two-dimensional artworks and not windows opening onto the three-dimensional world, American-born James Abbott McNeill Whistler, who produced his most famous works in London, called his paintings "arrangements" or "nocturnes." *Nocturne in Black and Gold* (FIG. 23-14) is a daring painting with gold flecks and splatters representing an exploded firework punctuating the darkness of the night sky. More interested in conveying the atmospheric effects than in providing details of the scene, Whistler emphasized creating a harmonious arrangement of shapes and colors on the rectangle of his canvas, an approach many 20th-century artists adopted. Whistler's works angered many 19th-century viewers, however. The British critic John Ruskin (1819–1900) responded to this painting by writing a scathing review accusing Whistler of "flinging a pot of paint in the public's face" with his style. In reply, Whistler sued Ruskin for libel. During the trial, Ruskin's attorney asked Whistler about the subject of *Nocturne*:

"What is your definition of a Nocturne?"

"It is an arrangement of line, form, and colour first; . . . Among my works are some night pieces; and I have chosen the word Nocturne because it generalizes and amplifies the whole set of them. . . . The nocturne in black and gold is a night piece and represents the fireworks at Cremorne [Gardens in London]."

"Not a view of Cremorne?"

"If it were a view of Cremorne, it would certainly bring about nothing but disappointment on the part of the beholders. It is an artistic arrangement."*

The court transcript notes the spectators in the courtroom laughed at that response, but Whistler won the case. However, his victory

23-14 JAMES ABBOTT MCNEILL WHISTLER, *Nocturne in Black and Gold (The Falling Rocket)*, ca. 1875. Oil on panel, 1′ 11⅝″ × 1′ 6½″. Detroit Institute of Arts, Detroit (gift of Dexter M. Ferry Jr.).

In this painting, Whistler displayed an Impressionist's interest in conveying the atmospheric effects of fireworks at night, but he also emphasized the abstract arrangement of shapes and colors.

had sadly ironic consequences for him. The judge in the case, showing where his—and the public's—sympathies lay, awarded the artist only one farthing (less than a penny) in damages and required him to pay all of the court costs, which ruined him financially.

*Quoted in Charles Harrison, Paul Wood, and Jason Gaiger, *Art in Theory, 1815–1900* (Oxford: Blackwell, 1998), 835–836.

JAMES WHISTLER Another American expatriate artist in Europe was JAMES ABBOTT MCNEILL WHISTLER (1834–1903), who spent time in Paris before settling finally in London. He met many of the French Impressionists, and his art, for example, *Nocturne in Black and Gold,* or *The Falling Rocket* (FIG. 23-14), is a unique combination of some of their concerns and his own (see "Whistler on 'Artistic Arrangements,'" above). Whistler shared the Impressionists' interests in the subject of contemporary life and the sensations color produces on the eye. To these influences he added his own desire to create harmonies paralleling those achieved in music.

Nature contains the elements, in color and form, of all pictures, as the keyboard contains the notes of all music. But the artist is born to pick, and choose, and group with science, these elements, that the result may be beautiful—as the musician gathers his notes, and forms his chords, until he brings forth from chaos glorious harmony.[5]

23-15 HENRI DE TOULOUSE-LAUTREC, *At the Moulin Rouge*, 1892–1895. Oil on canvas, 4′ × 4′ 7″. Art Institute of Chicago, Chicago (Helen Birch Bartlett Memorial Collection).

Degas, Japanese prints, and photography influenced this painting's oblique composition, but the glaring lighting, masklike faces, and dissonant colors are distinctly Toulouse-Lautrec's.

1 ft.

POST-IMPRESSIONISM

By 1886 most critics and a large segment of the public accepted the Impressionists as serious artists. Just when their images of contemporary life no longer seemed crude and unfinished, however, some of these painters and a group of younger followers came to feel the Impressionists were neglecting too many of the traditional elements of picturemaking in their attempts to capture momentary sensations of light and color on canvas. In a conversation with the influential art dealer Ambroise Vollard (1866–1939) in about 1883, Renoir commented: "I had wrung impressionism dry, and I finally came to the conclusion that I knew neither how to paint nor how to draw. In a word, impressionism was a blind alley, as far as I was concerned."[6] By the 1880s, some artists were more systematically examining the properties and the expressive qualities of line, pattern, form, and color. Among them were Dutch-born Vincent van Gogh and the French painter Paul Gauguin, who focused their artistic efforts on exploring the expressive capabilities of formal elements, and Georges Seurat and Paul Cézanne, also from France, who were more analytical in orientation. Because their art had its roots in Impressionist precepts and methods, but was not stylistically homogeneous, these artists and others, including Henri de Toulouse-Lautrec, became known as the *Post-Impressionists*.

HENRI DE TOULOUSE-LAUTREC Closest to the Impressionists in many ways was the French artist HENRI DE TOULOUSE-LAUTREC (1864–1901), who deeply admired Degas and shared the Impressionists' interest in capturing the sensibility of modern life. His work, however, has an added satirical edge to it and often borders on caricature. Genetic defects stunted his growth and partially crippled him, leading to his self-exile from the high society his ancient aristocratic name entitled him to enter. He became a denizen of the night world of Paris, consorting with a tawdry population of entertainers, prostitutes, and other social outcasts. He reveled in the energy of the city's music halls, such as the Moulin Rouge (FIG. **23-15**) and the Jardin de Paris (FIG. **23-15A**), cafés, and bordellos. *At the Moulin Rouge* reveals the influ-

23-15A TOULOUSE-LAUTREC, *Jane Avril*, 1893.

ences of Degas, of Japanese prints, and of photography in the oblique and asymmetrical composition, the spatial diagonals, and the strong line patterns with added dissonant colors. But although Toulouse-Lautrec based everything he painted on firsthand observation and the scenes he captured were already familiar to viewers in the work of the Impressionists, he so emphasized or exaggerated each element that the tone is new. Compare, for instance, the mood of *At the Moulin Rouge* with the relaxed and casual atmosphere of Renoir's *Le Moulin de la Galette* (FIG. 23-8). Toulouse-Lautrec's scene is nightlife, with its glaring artificial light, brassy music, and assortment of corrupt, cruel, and masklike faces. (He included himself in the background—the diminutive man wearing a derby hat accompanying the very tall man, his cousin.) Such distortions by simplification of the figures and faces anticipated Expressionism (see Chapter 24), when artists' use of formal elements—for example, brighter colors and bolder lines than ever before—increased the effect of the images on observers.

1 ft.

23-16 GEORGES SEURAT, *A Sunday on La Grande Jatte*, 1884–1886. Oil on canvas, 6′ 9″ × 10′. Art Institute of Chicago, Chicago (Helen Birch Bartlett Memorial Collection, 1926).

Seurat's color system—pointillism—involved dividing colors into their component parts and applying those colors to the canvas in tiny dots. The forms become comprehensible only from a distance.

GEORGES SEURAT The themes GEORGES SEURAT (1859–1891) addressed in his paintings were also Impressionist subjects, but he depicted them in a resolutely intellectual way. He devised a disciplined and painstaking system of painting focused on color analysis. Seurat was less concerned with the recording of immediate color sensations than he was with their careful and systematic organization into a new kind of pictorial order. He disciplined the free and fluent play of color characterizing Impressionism into a calculated arrangement based on scientific color theory. Seurat's system, known as *pointillism* or *divisionism,* involved carefully observing color and separating it into its component parts (see "Pointillism and 19th-Century Color Theory," page 701). The artist then applies these pure component colors to the canvas in tiny dots (points) or daubs. Thus, the shapes, figures, and spaces in the image become comprehensible only from a distance, when the viewer's eyes blend the many pigment dots.

Seurat introduced pointillism to the French public at the eighth and last Impressionist exhibition in 1886, where he displayed *A Sunday on La Grande Jatte* (FIG. **23-16**). The subject of the painting is consistent with Impressionist recreational themes, and Seurat also shared the Impressionists' interest in analyzing light and color. But Seurat's rendition of Parisians at leisure is rigid and remote, unlike the spontaneous representations of Impressionism. Seurat's pointillism instead produced a carefully composed and painted image. By using meticulously calculated values, the painter carved out a deep rectangular space. He played on repeated motifs both to create flat patterns and to suggest spatial depth. Reiterating the profile of the female form, the parasol, and the cylindrical forms of the figures, Seurat placed each in space to set up a rhythmic movement in depth as well as from side to side. Sunshine fills the picture, but the painter did not break the light into transient patches of color. Light, air, people, and landscape are formal elements in an abstract design in which line, color, value, and shape cohere in a precise and tightly controlled organization. Seurat's orchestration of the many forms across the monumental (almost 7 by 10 feet) canvas created a rhythmic cadence harmonizing the entire composition.

Seurat once stated: "They see poetry in what I have done. No, I apply my method, and that is all there is to it."[7] Despite this claim, Seurat's art is much more than a scientifically based system. *La Grande Jatte* reveals the painter's recognition of the tenuous and shifting social and class relationships at the time. La Grande Jatte (The Big Bowl) is an island in the Seine River near Asnières, one of late-19th-century Paris's rapidly growing industrial suburbs. Seurat's painting captures public life on a Sunday—a congregation of people from various classes, from the sleeveless worker lounging in the left foreground, to the middle-class man and woman seated next to him. Most of the people wear their Sunday best, making class distinctions less obvious.

VINCENT VAN GOGH In marked contrast to Seurat, VINCENT VAN GOGH (1853–1890) explored the capabilities of colors

Pointillism and 19th-Century Color Theory

In the 19th century, advances in the sciences contributed to changing theories about color and how people perceive it. Many physicists and chemists immersed themselves in studying optical reception and the behavior of the human eye in response to light of differing wavelengths. They also investigated the psychological dimension of color. These new ideas about color and its perception provided a framework within which artists such as Georges Seurat (FIG. 23-16) worked. Although historians do not know which publications on color Seurat himself read, he no doubt relied on aspects of these evolving theories to develop pointillism.

Discussions of color often focus on *hue* (for example, red, yellow, and blue), but it is important to consider the other facets of color—*saturation* (the hue's brightness or dullness) and *value* (the hue's lightness or darkness). Most artists during the 19th century understood the concepts of *primary colors* (red, yellow, and blue), *secondary colors* (orange, purple, and green), and *complementary colors* (red and green, yellow and purple, blue and orange; see Introduction, page 7).

Chemist Michel-Eugène Chevreul (1786–1889) extended artists' understanding of color dynamics by formulating the law of *simultaneous contrasts* of colors. Chevreul asserted juxtaposed colors affect the eye's reception of each, making the two colors as dissimilar as possible, both in hue and value. For example, placing light green next to dark green has the effect of making the light green look even lighter and the dark green darker. Chevreul further provided an explanation of *successive contrasts*—the phenomenon of colored afterimages. When a person looks intently at a color (green, for example) and then shifts to a white area, the fatigued eye momentarily perceives the complementary color (red).

Charles Blanc (1813–1882), who coined the term *optical mixture* to describe the visual effect of juxtaposed complementary colors, asserted the smaller the areas of adjoining complementary colors, the greater the tendency for the eye to "mix" the colors, so that the viewer perceives a grayish or neutral tint. Seurat used this principle frequently in his paintings.

Also influential for Seurat was the work of physicist Ogden Rood (1831–1902), who published his ideas in *Modern Chromatics, with Applications to Art and Industry* in 1879. Expanding on the ideas of Chevreul and Blanc, Rood constructed an accurate and understandable diagram of contrasting colors. Further (and particularly significant to Seurat), Rood explored representing color gradation. He suggested artists could achieve gradation by placing small

Detail of *A Sunday on La Grande Jatte* (FIG. 23-16).

1 ft.

dots or lines of color side by side, which he observed blended in the eye of the beholder when viewed from a distance.

The color experiments of Seurat and other late-19th-century artists were also part of a larger discourse about human vision and how people see and understand the world. The theories of physicist Ernst Mach (1838–1916) focused on the psychological experience of sensation. He believed humans perceive their environments in isolated units of sensation the brain then recomposes into a comprehensible world. Another scientist, Charles Henry (1859–1926), also pursued research into the psychological dimension of color—how colors affect people, and under what conditions. He went even further to explore the physiological effects of perception. Seurat's work, though characterized by a systematic and scientifically minded approach, also incorporated his concerns about the emotional tone of the images.

and distorted forms to express his emotions as he confronted nature. The son of a Dutch Protestant pastor, van Gogh believed he had a religious calling and did missionary work in the coal-mining area of Belgium. Repeated professional and personal failures brought him close to despair. Only after he turned to painting did he find a way to communicate his experiences. He completed his first major work, *The Potato Eaters* (FIG. 23-16A), when he was 32 years old. Five years later, considering himself a failure as an artist and an outcast not only from artistic circles but also from society at large, van Gogh fatally shot himself. He sold only one painting during his lifetime. Since his death, however, van Gogh's reputation and the

appreciation of his art have grown dramatically. Subsequent painters, especially the Fauves and German Expressionists (see Chapter 24), built on van Gogh's use of color and the expressiveness of his art. This kind of influence is an important factor in determining artistic significance, and it is no exaggeration to state that today van Gogh is one of the most revered artists in history.

23-16A VAN GOGH, *The Potato Eaters*, 1885.

The Letters of Vincent van Gogh

Throughout his life, Vincent van Gogh wrote letters to his brother Theo van Gogh (1857–1891), a Parisian art dealer, on matters both mundane and philosophical. The letters are precious documents of the vicissitudes of the painter's life and reveal his emotional anguish. In many of the letters, van Gogh also forcefully stated his views about art, including his admiration for Japanese prints (FIG. 23-16B). In one letter, he told Theo: "In both my life and in my painting, I can very well do without God but I cannot, ill as I am, do without something which is greater than I, . . . the power to create."[*] For van Gogh, the power to create involved the expressive use of color. "Instead of trying to reproduce exactly what I have before my eyes, I use color more arbitrarily so as to express myself forcibly."[†] Color in painting, he argued, is "not locally true from the point of view of the delusive realist, but color suggesting some emotion of an ardent temperament."[‡]

Some of van Gogh's letters contain vivid descriptions of his paintings, which are invaluable to art historians in gauging his intentions and judging his success. For example, about *Night Café* (FIG. 23-17), he wrote:

I have tried to express the terrible passions of humanity by means of red and green. The room is blood red and dark yellow with a green billiard table in the middle; there are four citron-yellow lamps with a glow of orange and green. Everywhere there is a clash and contrast of the most disparate reds and greens in the figures

23-17 VINCENT VAN GOGH, *Night Café*, 1888. Oil on canvas, 2′ 4½″ × 3′. Yale University Art Gallery, New Haven (bequest of Stephen Carlton Clark).

In *Night Café*, van Gogh explored ways colors and distorted forms can express emotions. The thickness, shape, and direction of the brushstrokes create a tactile counterpart to the intense colors.

1 ft.

of little sleeping hooligans, in the empty, dreary room, in violet and blue. The blood-red and the yellow-green of the billiard table, for instance, contrast with the soft, tender Louis XV green of the counter, on which there is a pink nosegay. The white coat of the landlord, awake in a corner of that furnace, turns citron-yellow, or pale luminous green.[§]

[*]Vincent van Gogh to Theo van Gogh, September 3, 1888, in W. H. Auden, ed., *Van Gogh: A Self-Portrait. Letters Revealing His Life as a Painter* (New York: Dutton, 1963), 319.
[†]August 11, 1888. Ibid., 313.
[‡]September 8, 1888. Ibid., 321.
[§]September 8, 1888. Ibid., 320.

23-16B VAN GOGH, *Flowering Plum Tree*, 1887.

NIGHT CAFÉ Van Gogh moved to Paris in 1886, where he began to collect—and copy (FIG. 23-16B)—Japanese prints. In 1888, he relocated to Arles in southern France, where he painted *Night Café* (FIG. 23-17), one of his most important and innovative canvases. Although the subject is apparently benign, van Gogh invested it with a charged energy. As he stated in a letter to his brother Theo (see "The Letters of Vincent van Gogh," above), he wanted the painting to convey an oppressive atmosphere—" a place where one can ruin oneself, go mad, or commit a crime."[8] The proprietor rises like a specter from the edge of the billiard table, which the painter depicted in such a steeply tilted perspective that it threatens to slide out of the painting into the viewer's space. Van Gogh communicated the "madness" of the place by selecting vivid hues whose juxtaposition augmented their intensity. His insistence

on the expressive values of color led him to develop a corresponding expressiveness in his paint application. The thickness, shape, and direction of his brushstrokes created a tactile counterpart to his intense color schemes. He moved the brush vehemently back and forth or at right angles, giving a textilelike effect, or squeezed dots or streaks onto his canvas from his paint tube. This bold, almost slapdash attack enhanced the intensity of his colors.

STARRY NIGHT Similarly illustrative of van Gogh's "expressionist" method is *Starry Night* (FIG. 23-18), which the artist painted in 1889, the year before his death. At this time, van Gogh was living at the asylum of Saint-Paul-de-Mausole in Saint-Rémy, near Arles, where he had committed himself. In *Starry Night,* the artist did not represent the sky's appearance. Rather, he communicated his feelings about the electrifying vastness of the universe, filled with whirling and exploding stars, with the earth and humanity huddling beneath it. The church nestled in the center of the village is, perhaps, van

23-18 Vincent van Gogh, *Starry Night*, 1889. Oil on canvas, 2′ 5″ × 3′ ¼″. Museum of Modern Art, New York (acquired through the Lillie P. Bliss Bequest). ◼◀

In this late work, van Gogh painted the vast night sky filled with whirling and exploding stars, the earth huddled beneath it. The painting is an almost abstract pattern of expressive line, shape, and color.

Gogh's attempt to express or reconcile his conflicted views about religion. Although the style of *Starry Night* suggests a very personal vision, this work does correspond in many ways to the view available to the painter from the window of his room in Saint-Paul-de-Mausole. The existence of cypress trees and the placement of the constellations have been confirmed as matching the view visible to van Gogh during his stay in the asylum. Still, the artist translated everything he saw into his unique vision. Given van Gogh's determination to "use color . . . to express [him]self forcibly," the dark, deep blue suffusing the entire painting cannot be overlooked. Together with the turbu-

lent brushstrokes, the color suggests a quiet but pervasive depression. A letter van Gogh wrote to his brother on July 16, 1888, reveals his contemplative state of mind:

Perhaps death is not the hardest thing in a painter's life. . . . [L]ooking at the stars always makes me dream, as simply as I dream over the black dots representing towns and villages on a map. Why, I ask myself, shouldn't the shining dots of the sky be as accessible as the black dots on the map of France? Just as we take the train to get to Tarascon or Rouen, we take death to reach a star.[9]

PAUL GAUGUIN After painting as an amateur, Paul Gauguin (1848–1903) took lessons with Camille Pissarro and then resigned from his prosperous brokerage business in 1883 to devote his time entirely to painting. As van Gogh did, Gauguin rejected objective representation in favor of subjective expression. He also broke with the Impressionists' studies of minutely contrasted hues because he believed color above all must be expressive. For Gauguin, the artist's power to determine the colors in a painting was a central element of creativity. However, whereas van Gogh's heavy, thick brushstrokes were an important component of his expressive style, Gauguin's color areas appear flatter, often visually dissolving into abstract patches or patterns.

In 1886, attracted by Brittany's unspoiled culture, its ancient Celtic folkways, and the still-medieval Catholic piety of its people, Gauguin moved to Pont-Aven. Although in the 1870s and 1880s, Brittany had been transformed into a profitable market economy, Gauguin still viewed the Bretons as "natural" men and women, perfectly at ease in their unspoiled peasant environment. At Pont-Aven, he painted *Vision after the Sermon* (FIG. **23-19**), also known as *Jacob Wrestling with the Angel,* a work in which he decisively rejected both Realism and Impressionism. The painting shows Breton women, wearing their starched white Sunday caps and black dresses, visualizing the

23-19 Paul Gauguin, *Vision after the Sermon* (*Jacob Wrestling with the Angel*), 1888. Oil on canvas, 2′ 4¾″ × 3′ ½″. National Gallery of Scotland, Edinburgh. ◼◀

Gauguin admired Japanese prints, stained glass, and cloisonné enamels. Their influences are evident in this painting of Breton women, in which firm outlines enclose large areas of unmodulated color.

Gauguin on *Where Do We Come From?*

Paul Gauguin's *Where Do We Come From? What Are We? Where Are We Going?* (FIG. 23-20), painted in Tahiti in 1897, was, in the artist's judgment, his most important work. It can be read as a summary of his artistic methods and of his views on life. The scene is a tropical landscape, populated with native women and children. Despite the setting, most of the canvas surface, other than the figures, consists of broad areas of flat color, which convey a lushness and intensity.

Two of Gauguin's letters to friends contain lengthy discussions of this work and shed important light on the artist's intentions and on the painting's meaning.

> Where are we going? Near to death an old woman. . . . What are we? Day to day existence. . . . Where do we come from? Source. Child. Life begins. . . . Behind a tree two sinister figures, cloaked in garments of sombre colour, introduce, near the tree of knowledge, their note of anguish caused by that very knowledge in contrast to some simple beings in a virgin nature, which might be paradise as conceived by humanity, who give themselves up to the happiness of living.*

> I wanted to kill myself. I went to hide in the mountains, where my corpse would have been eaten up by ants. I didn't have a revolver but I did have arsenic . . . Was the dose too large, or was it the fact of vomiting, which overcame the effects of the poison by getting rid of it? I know not. . . . . Before I died I wanted to paint a large canvas that I had worked out in my head, and all month long I worked day and night at fever pitch. I can assure you it's nothing like a canvas by Puvis de Chavannes [FIG. 23-23], with studies from nature, then a preparatory cartoon, etc. No, it's all done without a model, feeling my way with the tip of the brush on a piece of sackcloth that is full of knots and rough patches; so it looks terribly unpolished. [Contrary to this assertion, Gauguin did make a detailed preliminary drawing, now in the Louvre, for *Where Do We Come From?* He is here altering the facts in order to establish a persona for himself as an inspired genius who created great works without recourse to traditional studio methods.] People will say it is slipshod, unfinished . . . [but] I do believe that not only is this painting worth more than all the previous ones but also that I will never do a better one or another like it. I put all my energy into it before dying, such painful passion amid terrible circumstances . . . and life burst from it.†

Where Do We Come From? is, therefore, a sobering, pessimistic image of the life cycle's inevitability.

*Letter to Charles Morice, March 1898. Translated by Belinda Thompson, *Gauguin by Himself* (Boston: Little, Brown, 1993), 270–271.
†Letter to Daniel de Monfreid, February 1898. Translated by Thompson, ibid., 257–258.

23-20 PAUL GAUGUIN, *Where Do We Come From? What Are We? Where Are We Going?* 1897. Oil on canvas, 4′ 6¾″ × 12′ 3″. Museum of Fine Arts, Boston (Tompkins Collection).

In search of a place far removed from European materialism, Gauguin moved to Tahiti, where he used native women and tropical colors to present a pessimistic view of the inevitability of the life cycle.

sermon they have just heard in church on Jacob's encounter with the Holy Spirit (Gen. 32:24–30). The women pray devoutly before the apparition, as they would have before the roadside crucifix shrines that were characteristic features of the Breton countryside. Gauguin departed from optical realism and composed the picture elements to focus the viewer's attention on the idea and intensify its message.

The images are not what the Impressionist eye would have seen and replicated but what memory would have recalled and imagination would have modified. Thus the artist twisted the perspective and allotted the space to emphasize the innocent faith of the unquestioning women, and he shrank Jacob and the angel, wrestling in a ring enclosed by a Breton stone fence, to the size of fighting cocks.

Wrestling matches were regular features at the entertainment held after high mass, so Gauguin's women are spectators at a contest that was, for them, a familiar part of their culture.

Gauguin did not unify the picture with a horizon perspective, light and shade, or naturalistic use of color. Instead, he abstracted the scene into a pattern. Pure unmodulated color fills flat planes and shapes bounded by firm line: white caps, black dresses, and the red field of combat. The shapes are angular, even harsh. The caps, the sharp fingers and profiles, and the hard contours suggest the austerity of peasant life and ritual. Gauguin admired Japanese prints, stained glass, and *cloisonné* metalwork (FIGS. 11-2 and 11-3). These art forms contributed to his daring experiment to transform traditional painting and Impressionism into abstract, expressive patterns of line, shape, and pure color. His revolutionary method found its first authoritative expression in *Vision after the Sermon*.

WHERE DO WE COME FROM?

After a brief period of association with van Gogh in Arles in 1888, Gauguin, in his restless search for provocative subjects and for an economical place to live, settled in Tahiti. The South Pacific island attracted Gauguin because he believed it offered him a life far removed from materialistic Europe and an opportunity to reconnect with nature. Upon his arrival, he discovered that Tahiti, under French control since 1842, had been extensively colonized. Disappointed, Gauguin tried to maintain his vision of an untamed paradise by moving to the Tahitian countryside, where he expressed his fascination with primitive life in a series of canvases in which he often based the design, although indirectly, on native motifs. The tropical flora of the island inspired the colors he chose for these paintings—unusual harmonies of lilac, pink, and lemon.

Despite the allure of the South Pacific, Gauguin continued to struggle with life. His health suffered, and his art had a hostile reception. In 1897, worn down by these obstacles, Gauguin decided to take his own life, but not before painting a large canvas titled *Where Do We Come From? What Are We? Where Are We Going?* (FIG. 23-20), which he wrote about in letters to his friends (see "Gauguin on *Where Do We Come From?*" page 704). His attempt to commit suicide in Tahiti was unsuccessful, but Gauguin died a few years later, in 1903, in the Marquesas Islands, his artistic genius still unrecognized.

PAUL CÉZANNE Although a lifelong admirer of Delacroix, PAUL CÉZANNE (1839–1906) allied himself early in his career with the Impressionists, especially Pissarro (FIG. 23-6). He at first accepted their color theories and their faith in subjects chosen from everyday life, but his own studies of the Old Masters in the Louvre persuaded him Impressionism lacked form and structure. Cézanne declared he wanted to "make of Impressionism something solid and durable like the art of the museums."[10]

The basis of Cézanne's art was his unique way of studying nature in works such as *Mont Sainte-Victoire* (FIG. 23-21), one of many views he painted of this mountain near his home in Aix-en-Provence. His aim was not truth in appearance, especially not photographic truth, nor was it the "truth" of Impressionism. Rather, he sought a lasting structure behind the formless and fleeting visual information the eyes absorb. Instead of employing the Impressionists' random approach when he was face-to-face with nature, Cézanne developed a more analytical style. His goal was to order the lines, planes, and colors comprising nature. He constantly and painstakingly checked his painting against the part of the scene—he called it the "motif"—he was studying at the moment. In a March 1904 letter, Cézanne stated his goal as a painter: "[to do] Poussin over entirely from nature . . . in the open air, with color and light, instead of one of those works imagined in a studio, where

23-21 PAUL CÉZANNE, *Mont Sainte-Victoire*, 1902–1904. Oil on canvas, 2′ 3½″ × 2′ 11¼″. Philadelphia Museum of Art, Philadelphia (George W. Elkins Collection). ◼◀

In his landscapes, Cézanne replaced the transitory visual effects of changing atmospheric conditions—the Impressionists' focus—with careful analysis of the lines, planes, and colors of nature.

1 ft.

everything has the brown coloring of feeble daylight without reflections from the sky and sun."[11] He sought to achieve Poussin's effects of distance, depth, structure, and solidity not by using traditional perspective and chiaroscuro but by recording the color patterns he deduced from an optical analysis of nature.

With special care, Cézanne explored the properties of line, plane, and color and their interrelationships. He studied the effect of every kind of linear direction, the capacity of planes to create the sensation of depth, the intrinsic qualities of color, and the power of colors to modify the direction and depth of lines and planes. To create the illusion of three-dimensional form and space, Cézanne focused on carefully selecting colors. He understood the visual properties—hue, saturation, and value—of different colors vary (see "Color Theory," page 701). Cool colors tend to recede, whereas warm ones advance. By applying to the canvas small patches of juxtaposed colors, some advancing and some receding, Cézanne created volume and depth in his works. On occasion, the artist depicted objects chiefly in one hue and achieved convincing solidity by modulating the intensity (or saturation). At other times, he juxtaposed contrasting colors—for example, green, yellow, and red—of similar saturation (usually in the middle range rather than the highest intensity) to compose specific objects, such as fruit or bowls.

In *Mont Sainte-Victoire,* Cézanne replaced the transitory visual effects of changing atmospheric conditions, effects that preoccupied Monet, with a more concentrated, lengthier analysis of the colors in large lighted spaces. The main space stretches out behind and beyond the canvas plane and includes numerous small elements, such as roads, fields, houses, and the viaduct at the far right, each seen from a slightly different viewpoint. Above this shifting, receding perspective rises the largest mass of all, the mountain, with an effect—achieved by equally stressing background and foreground contours—of being simultaneously near and far away. This portrayal approximates the experience a person has when viewing the landscape forms piecemeal. The relative proportions of objects vary rather than being fixed by strict perspective, such as that normally found in a photograph. Cézanne immobilized the shifting colors of Impressionism into an array of clearly defined planes composing the objects and spaces in his scene. Describing his method in a letter to a fellow painter, he wrote:

> [T]reat nature by the cylinder, the sphere, the cone, everything in proper perspective so that each side of an object or a plane is directed towards a central point. Lines parallel to the horizon give breadth . . . Lines perpendicular to this horizon give depth. But nature for us men is more depth than surface, whence the need of introducing into our light vibrations, represented by reds and yellows, a sufficient amount of blue to give the impression of air.[12]

BASKET OF APPLES Still life was another good vehicle for Cézanne's experiments, as he could arrange a limited number of selected objects to provide a well-ordered point of departure. So analytical was Cézanne in preparing, observing, and painting still lifes (in contrast to the Impressionist emphasis on spontaneity) that he had to abandon using real fruit and flowers because they tended to rot. In *Basket of Apples* (FIG. **23-22**), the objects have lost something of their individual character as bottles and fruit and have almost become cylinders and spheres. Cézanne captured the solidity of each object by juxtaposing color patches. His interest in the study of volume and solidity is evident from the disjunctures in the painting—the table edges are discontinuous, and various objects seem to be depicted from different vantage points. In his zeal to understand three-dimensionality and to convey the placement of forms relative to the space around them, Cézanne explored his still-life arrangements from different viewpoints. This resulted in paintings that, though conceptually coherent, do not appear optically realistic. Cézanne created what might be called, paradoxically, an architecture of color.

In keeping with the modernist concern with the integrity of the painting surface, Cézanne's methods never allow the viewer to disregard the actual two-dimensionality of the picture plane.

23-22 PAUL CÉZANNE, *Basket of Apples,* ca. 1895. Oil on canvas, 2′ ⅜″ × 2′ 7″. Art Institute of Chicago, Chicago (Helen Birch Bartlett Memorial Collection, 1926). ◼◄

Cézanne's still lifes reveal his analytical approach to painting. He captured the solidity of bottles and fruit by juxtaposing color patches, but the resulting abstract shapes are not optically realistic.

1 ft.

23-22A CÉZANNE, *Large Bathers*, 1906.

In this manner, Cézanne achieved a remarkable feat—presenting the viewer with two-dimensional and three-dimensional images simultaneously. His late works, such as his unfinished *The Large Bathers* (FIG. **23-22A**), profoundly influenced the development of Cubism in the early 20th century (see Chapter 24).

SYMBOLISM

The Impressionists and Post-Impressionists believed their emotions and sensations were important elements for interpreting nature, but the depiction of nature remained a primary focus of their efforts. By the end of the 19th century, the representation of nature became completely subjective. Artists no longer sought to imitate nature but created free interpretations of it, concerned solely with expressing their individual spirit. They rejected the optical world as observed in favor of a fantasy world, of forms they conjured in their free imagination, with or without reference to things conventionally seen. Color, line, and shape, divorced from conformity to the optical image, became symbols of personal emotions in response to the world. Deliberately choosing to stand outside of convention and tradition, artists spoke in signs and symbols, as if they were prophets.

Many of the artists following this path adopted an approach to subject and form that associated them with a general European movement called *Symbolism*. Symbolists, whether painters or writers, disdained Realism as trivial. The task of Symbolist artists, both visual and verbal, was not to see things but to see through them to a significance and reality far deeper than what superficial appearance revealed. In this function, as the poet Arthur Rimbaud (1854–1891) insisted, artists became beings of extraordinary insight. (One group of Symbolist painters called itself the *Nabis*, the Hebrew word for

"prophet.") Rimbaud, whose poems had great influence on the artistic community, went so far as to say, in his *Letter from a Seer* (1871), that to achieve the seer's insight, artists must become deranged. In effect, they must systematically unhinge and confuse the everyday faculties of sense and reason, which served only to blur artistic vision. The artists' mystical vision must convert the objects of the commonsense world into symbols of a reality beyond that world and, ultimately, a reality from within the individual. Elements of Symbolism appeared in the works of van Gogh and Gauguin, but their art differed from mainstream Symbolism in their insistence on showing unseen powers as linked to a physical reality, instead of attempting to depict an alternate, wholly interior life.

The extreme subjectivism of the Symbolists led them to cultivate all the resources of fantasy and imagination, no matter how deeply buried or obscure. Moreover, they urged artists to stand against the vulgar materialism and conventional mores of industrial and middle-class society. Above all, the Symbolists wished to purge literature and art of anything utilitarian, to cultivate an exquisite aesthetic sensitivity. The subjects of the Symbolists, conditioned by this reverent attitude toward art and exaggerated aesthetic sensation, became increasingly esoteric and exotic, mysterious, visionary, dreamlike, and fantastic. Perhaps not coincidentally, contemporary with the Symbolists, Sigmund Freud (1856–1939), the founder of psychoanalysis, began the age of psychiatry with his *Interpretation of Dreams* (1900), an introduction to the concept and the world of unconscious experience.

PIERRE PUVIS DE CHAVANNES Although he never formally identified himself with the Symbolists, the French painter PIERRE PUVIS DE CHAVANNES (1824–1898) became the "prophet" of those artists. Puvis rejected Realism and Impressionism and went his own way in the 19th century, serenely unaffected by these movements. He produced an ornamental and reflective art—a dramatic rejection of Realism's noisy everyday world. In *Sacred Grove* (FIG. **23-23**), which may have influenced Seurat's *Grande Jatte*

1 ft.

23-23 PIERRE PUVIS DE CHAVANNES, *Sacred Grove,* 1884. Oil on canvas, 2′ 11½″ × 6′ 10″. Art Institute of Chicago, Chicago (Potter Palmer Collection).

The Symbolists revered Puvis de Chavannes for his rejection of Realism. His statuesque figures in timeless poses inhabit a tranquil landscape, their gestures suggesting a symbolic ritual significance.

(FIG. 23-16), he deployed statuesque figures in a tranquil landscape with a classical shrine. Suspended in timeless poses, the figures' contours are simple and sharp, and their modeling is as shallow as *bas-relief*. The calm and still atmosphere suggests some consecrated place where all movements and gestures have a permanent ritual significance. The stillness and simplicity of the forms, the linear patterns their rhythmic contours create, and the suggestion of their symbolic weight constitute a type of anti-Realism. Puvis garnered support from a wide range of artists. The conservative French Academy and the government applauded his classicism. The Symbolists revered Puvis for his vindication of imagination and his independence from the capitalist world of materialism and the machine.

GUSTAVE MOREAU In keeping with Symbolist tenets, GUSTAVE MOREAU (1826–1898) gravitated toward subjects inspired by dreaming, which was as remote as possible from the everyday world. Moreau presented these subjects sumptuously, and his natural love of sensuous design led him to incorporate gorgeous color, intricate line, and richly detailed shape in all his paintings.

The Apparition (FIG. **23-24**), one of two versions of the same subject Moreau submitted to the Salon of 1876, treats a theme that fascinated him and many of his contemporaries—the *femme fatale* (fatal woman), the destructive temptress of men. The seductive heroine here is the biblical Salome (Mark 6:211–28), who danced enticingly before her stepfather, King Herod, and demanded in return the head of Saint John the Baptist (compare FIG. 16-8). In Moreau's representation of the story, Herod sits in the background, enthroned not in a Middle Eastern palace but in a classical columnar hall resembling a Roman triumphal arch. Salome is in the foreground, scantily clad in a gold- and gemencrusted costume. She points to an apparition hovering in the air at the level of Herod's head. In a radiant circle of light is the halo-framed head of John the Baptist that Salome desired, dripping with blood but with eyes wide open. The combination of hallucinatory imagery, eroticism, precise drawing, rich color, and opulent setting is the hallmark of Moreau's highly original style (compare FIG. **23-24A**). His paintings foreshadow the work of the Surrealists in the next century (see Chapter 24).

23-24A MOREAU, *Jupiter and Semele*, ca. 1875.

ODILON REDON Like Moreau, fellow French Symbolist ODILON REDON (1840–1916) was a visionary. He had been aware of an intense inner world since childhood and later wrote of "imaginary things" haunting him. Redon adapted the Impressionist palette and stippling brushstroke for a very different purpose. In *The Cyclops* (FIG. **23-25**), Redon projected a figment of the imagination as if it were visible, coloring it whimsically with a rich profusion of fresh saturated hues that harmonized with the mood he felt fit the subject. The fetal head of the shy, simpering Polyphemus, with its single huge loving eye, rises balloonlike above the sleeping Galatea. The image born of the dreaming world and the color

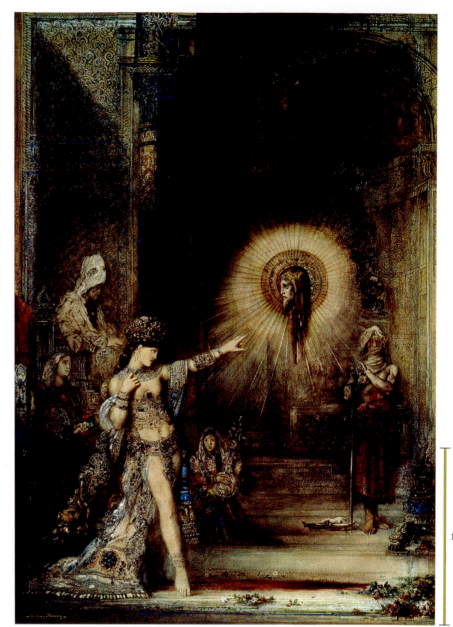

1 ft.

23-24 GUSTAVE MOREAU, *The Apparition*, 1874–1876. Watercolor on paper, 3′ 5¾″ × 2′ 4⅜″. Musée du Louvre, Paris.

Moreau's painting of Salome, a biblical femme fatale, combines hallucinatory imagery, eroticism, precise drawing, rich color, and an opulent setting—hallmarks of Moreau's Symbolist style.

analyzed and disassociated from the waking world come together here at the artist's will. The contrast with Raphael's representation of the same subject (FIG. 17-11) could hardly be more striking. As Redon himself observed: "All my originality consists . . . in making unreal creatures live humanly by putting, as much as possible, the logic of the visible at the service of the invisible."[13]

HENRI ROUSSEAU The imagination of HENRI ROUSSEAU (1844–1910) engaged a different but equally powerful world of personal fantasy. Gauguin had journeyed to the South Seas in search of primitive innocence. Rousseau was a "primitive" without leaving Paris—a self-taught amateur who turned to painting full-time only after his retirement from service in the French government. Nicknamed "Le Douanier" (The Customs Inspector), he first exhibited in the Salon of 1885 when he was 41. Derided by the critics, Rousseau turned to the Salon des Indépendants in 1886 and thereafter

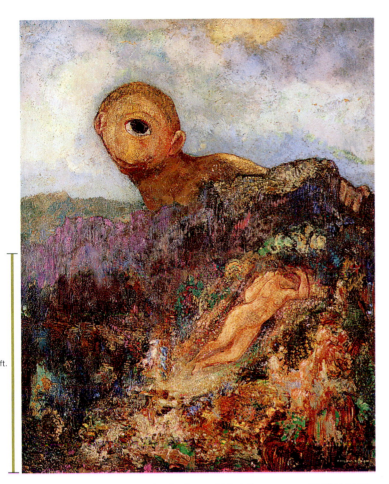

23-25 ODILON REDON, *The Cyclops,* 1898. Oil on canvas, 2′ 1″ × 1′ 8″. Kröller-Müller Foundation, Otterlo.

In *The Cyclops,* the Symbolist painter Odilon Redon projected a figment of the imagination as if it were visible, coloring it whimsically with a rich profusion of hues adapted from the Impressionist palette.

exhibited his works there almost every year until his death. Even in that more liberal venue, Rousseau still received almost universally unfavorable reviews because of his lack of formal training, imperfect perspective, doll-like figures, and settings resembling constructed theater sets more than natural landscapes. Rousseau compensated for his apparent visual, conceptual, and technical naïveté with a natural talent for design and an imagination teeming with exotic images of mysterious tropical landscapes, which are the setting for two of his most famous works, *Sleeping Gypsy* (FIG. **23-26**) of 1897 and *The Dream* (FIG. **23-26A**), painted 13 years later. In the earlier painting, the recumbent figure occupies a desert

23-26A ROUSSEAU, *The Dream,* 1910.

world, silent and secret, and dreams beneath a pale, perfectly round moon. In the foreground, a lion resembling a stuffed, but somehow menacing, animal doll sniffs at the gypsy. A critical encounter impends—an encounter of the type that recalls the uneasiness of a person's vulnerable subconscious self during sleep—a subject of central importance to Rousseau's contemporary, Sigmund Freud. Rousseau's art of drama and fantasy has its own sophistication and, after the artist's death, influenced the development of Surrealism (see Chapter 24).

JAMES ENSOR Not all Symbolist artists were French. The leading Belgian painter of the late 19th century was JAMES ENSOR (1860–1949), the son of an expatriate Englishman and a Flemish mother, who spent most of his life in the seaside resort village of Ostend, far from the artistic centers of Europe. In 1883 he cofounded Les Vingts (The Twenty), a group of Belgian artists who staged unjuried exhibitions in Brussels modeled on the independent salons of Paris. A fervent nationalist, he left the group when it began to exhibit the work of foreign artists. In fact, Ensor's most monumental

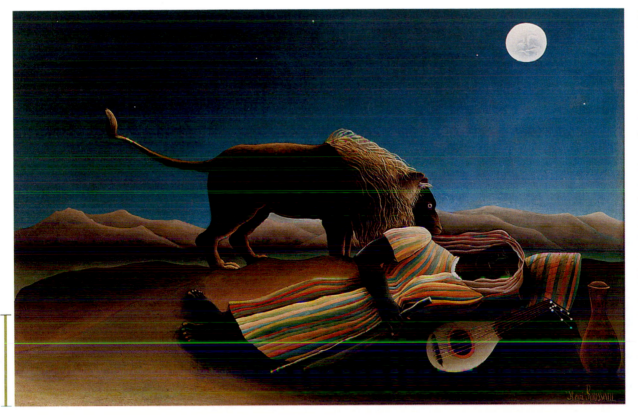

23-26 HENRI ROUSSEAU, *Sleeping Gypsy,* 1897. Oil on canvas, 4′ 3″ × 6′ 7″. Museum of Modern Art, New York (gift of Mrs. Simon Guggenheim).

In *Sleeping Gypsy,* Rousseau depicted a doll-like but menacing lion sniffing at a recumbent dreaming figure in a mysterious landscape. The painting suggests the vulnerable subconscious during sleep.

23-27 James Ensor, *Christ's Entry into Brussels in 1889,* 1888. Oil on canvas, 8' 3½" × 14' 1½". J. Paul Getty Museum, Los Angeles.

Ensor's gigantic canvas is an indictment of corrupt modern values. Christ enters Brussels on a donkey in 1889, ignored by the dense crowd of soldiers and citizens wearing grotesque, grimacing masks.

work, *Christ's Entry into Brussels in 1889* (FIG. **23-27**), is very likely a critical response to Georges Seurat's *La Grande Jatte* (FIG. 23-16), exhibited by Les Vingt in 1887.

Whereas Seurat's canvas celebrates the leisure activities of contented bourgeois Parisians, Ensor's even larger (14 feet long) painting is a socialist commentary on the decadence and alienation of urban life at the end of the 19th century. The giant canvas is the artist's pessimistic vision of how Christ would be greeted if he entered the Belgian capital in 1889. Christ is a small and insignificant figure on a donkey in the background of the painting, ignored by the dense crowd of soldiers and citizens wearing grotesque masks inspired by the papier-mâché carnival masks Ensor's family sold in their curio shop in Ostend. Some of the people carry banners and signs. One reads "Long Live Jesus, King of Brussels," another "Long Live Socialism." Complementing the ugly, grimacing masked faces of the anonymous crowd, which eloquently express Ensor's condemnation of the corrupt values of modern society, are the discordant combination of reds, blues, and greens and the coarse texture of the thickly applied oil pigment. As an indictment of the immorality of modern life, Ensor's canvas has few equals.

EDVARD MUNCH Also linked in spirit to the Symbolists were the English artist AUBREY BEARDSLEY (1872–1898; FIG. **23-27A**) and the Norwegian EDVARD MUNCH (1863–1944). Munch felt deeply the pain of human life. He believed humans were powerless before the great natural forces of death and love. The emotions associated with them—jealousy, loneliness, fear, desire, despair— became the theme of most of his art. Because Munch's goal was

to describe the conditions of "modern psychic life," as he put it, Realist and Impressionist techniques were inappropriate, focusing as they did on the tangible world. In the spirit of Symbolism, Munch used color, line, and figural distortion for expressive ends. Influenced by Gauguin, Munch produced both paintings and prints whose high emotional charge was a major source of inspiration for the German Expressionists in the early 20th century (see Chapter 24).

23-27A BEARDSLEY, *The Peacock Skirt,* 1894.

Munch's *The Scream* (FIG. **23-28**) exemplifies his style. The image—a man standing on a bridge or jetty in a landscape—comes from the real world, but Munch's treatment of the image departs significantly from visual reality. *The Scream* evokes a visceral, emotional response from the viewer because of the painter's dramatic presentation. The man in the foreground, simplified to almost skeletal form, emits a primal scream. The landscape's sweeping curvilinear lines reiterate the shapes of the man's mouth and head, almost like an echo, as the cry seems to reverberate through the setting. The fiery red and yellow stripes that give the sky an eerie glow also contribute to this work's resonance. Munch wrote a revealing epigraph to accompany the painting: "I stopped and leaned against the balustrade, almost dead with fatigue. Above the blue-black fjord hung the clouds, red as blood and tongues of fire. My friends had left me, and alone, trembling with anguish, I became aware of the vast, infinite cry of nature."[14] Appropriately, the original title of this work was *Despair.*

23-28 EDVARD MUNCH, *The Scream*, 1893. Tempera and pastels on cardboard, 2′ 11¾″ × 2′ 5″. National Gallery, Oslo.

Although grounded in the real world, *The Scream* departs significantly from visual reality. Munch used color, line, and figural distortion to evoke a strong emotional response from the viewer.

FIN-DE-SIÈCLE Historians have adopted the term *fin-de-siècle,* which literally means "end of the century," to describe the spirit of dissolution and anxiety that characterized European, and especially Austrian, culture of the late 1800s. This designation is not merely chronological but also refers to a certain sensibility. The increasingly large and prosperous middle classes aspired to the advantages the aristocracy traditionally enjoyed. They too strove to live "the good life," which evolved into a culture of decadence and indulgence. Characteristic of the fin-de-siècle period was an intense preoccupation with sexual drives, powers, and perversions. People at the end of the century also immersed themselves in an exploration of the unconscious. This culture was unrestrained and freewheeling, but the determination to enjoy life masked an anxiety prompted by significant political upheaval and an uncertain future. The country most closely associated with fin-de-siècle culture was Austria.

GUSTAV KLIMT The Viennese artist GUSTAV KLIMT (1863–1918) captured this period's flamboyance in his work but tempered it with unsettling undertones. In *The Kiss* (FIG. **23-29**), his best-known work, Klimt depicted a couple locked in an embrace. The setting is ambiguous, an indeterminate place apart from time and space. Moreover, all the viewer sees of the embracing couple is a small segment of each body—and virtually nothing of the man's face. The rest of the canvas dissolves into shimmering, extravagant flat patterning. This patterning has clear ties to Art Nouveau and to the Arts and Crafts movement (discussed later) and also evokes the conflict between two- and three-dimensionality intrinsic to the work of Degas and other modernists. In *The Kiss,* however, those patterns also signify gender contrasts—rectangles for the man's garment, circles for the woman's. Yet the patterning also unites the two lovers into a single formal entity, underscoring their erotic union.

GERTRUDE KÄSEBIER Photography, which during the 19th century most people regarded as the ultimate form of Realism, could also be manipulated by artists to produce effects more akin to painting than to factual records of contemporary life. After the first great breakthroughs (see Chapter 22), which bluntly showed what was before the eye, some photographers began to pursue

23-29 GUSTAV KLIMT, *The Kiss*, 1907–1908. Oil on canvas, 5′ 10¾″ × 5′ 10¾″. Österreichische Galerie Belvedere, Vienna. ◼◂

In this opulent Viennese painting, Klimt revealed only a small segment of each lover's body. The rest of his painting dissolves into shimmering, extravagant flat patterning.

entire image slightly. In *Blessed Art Thou among Women*, the soft focus invests the whole scene with an aura of otherworldly peace. The photograph showcases Käsebier's ability to inject a sense of the spiritual and the divine into scenes from everyday life.

SCULPTURE

The three-dimensional art of sculpture could not capture the optical sensations many painters favored in the later 19th century. Its very nature—its tangibility and solidity—suggests permanence. Consequently, the sculptors of this period pursued artistic goals markedly different from those of contemporaneous painters and photographers.

JEAN-BAPTISTE CARPEAUX In France, JEAN-BAPTISTE CARPEAUX (1827–1875) combined an interest in Realism with a love of ancient, Renaissance, and Baroque sculpture. He based his group *Ugolino and His Children* (FIG. 23-31) on a passage in Dante's *Inferno* (33.58–75) in which Count Ugolino and his four sons starve to death while shut up in a tower. In Hell, Ugolino relates to Dante how, in a moment of extreme despair, he bit both his hands in grief. His children, thinking he did it because of his hunger, offered him

23-30 GERTRUDE KÄSEBIER, *Blessed Art Thou among Women*, 1899. Platinum print on Japanese tissue, $9\frac{3}{8}'' \times 5\frac{1}{2}''$. Museum of Modern Art, New York (gift of Mrs. Hermine M. Turner).

Symbolist Käsebier injected a sense of the spiritual and the divine into scenes from everyday life. The deliberately soft focus of this photograph invests the scene with an aura of otherworldly peace.

new ways of using the medium as a vehicle of artistic expression. A leading practitioner of what might be called the pictorial style in photography was the American GERTRUDE KÄSEBIER (1852–1934), who took up the camera in 1897 after raising a family and working as a portrait painter. She soon became famous for photographs with Symbolist themes, such as *Blessed Art Thou among Women* (FIG. 23-30). The title repeats the phrase the angel Gabriel used to announce to the Virgin Mary that she will be the mother of Jesus. In the context of Käsebier's photography, the words suggest a parallel between the biblical Mother of God and the modern mother in the image, who both protects and sends forth her daughter. The white setting and the mother's pale gown shimmer in soft focus behind the serious girl, who wears darker tones and whom the photographer captured with sharper focus. Käsebier deliberately combined an out-of-focus background with a sharp or almost-sharp foreground in order to achieve an expressive effect by blurring the

23-31 JEAN-BAPTISTE CARPEAUX, *Ugolino and His Children*, 1865–1867. Marble, 6′ 5″ high. Metropolitan Museum of Art, New York (Josephine Bay Paul and C. Michael Paul Foundation, Inc., and the Charles Ulrich and Josephine Bay Foundation, Inc., gifts, 1967).

As in Dante's *Inferno*, Carpeaux represented Ugolino biting his hands in despair as he and his sons await death by starvation. The twisted forms suggest the self-devouring torment of frustration.

Rodin on Movement in Art and Photography

Photography had a profound effect on 19th-century art, and many artists used photographs as an aid in capturing "reality" on canvas or in stone. Eadweard Muybridge's photographs of a galloping horse (FIG. 22-54), for example, definitively established that at certain times all four hooves of the animal are in the air. But not all artists believed photography was "true to life." The sculptor Auguste Rodin (FIGS. 23-32, 23-32A, and 23-33) was one of the doubters.

> I have always sought to give some indication of movement [in my statues]. I have very rarely represented complete repose. I have always endeavoured to express the inner feelings by the mobility of the muscles. . . . The illusion of life is obtained in our art by good modelling and by movement. . . . [M]ovement is the transition from one attitude to another. . . . Have you ever attentively examined instantaneous photographs of walking figures? . . . [Photographs] present the odd appearance of a man suddenly stricken with paralysis and petrified in his pose. . . . If, in fact, in instantaneous photographs, the figures, though taken while moving, seem suddenly fixed in mid-air, it is because, all parts of the body being reproduced exactly at the same twentieth or fortieth of a second, there is no progressive development of movement as there is in art. . . . [I]t is the artist who is truthful and it is photography which lies, for in reality time does not stop.*

* Translated by Robin Fedden, in Elizabeth Gilmore Holt, ed., *From the Classicists to the Impressionists: Art and Architecture in the 19th Century* (New Haven, Conn.: Yale University Press, 1966; reprint 1986), 406–409.

23-32 Auguste Rodin, *Walking Man,* 1905. Bronze, 6′ 11¾″ high. Musée d'Orsay, Paris.

In this study for a statue of Saint John the Baptist, Rodin depicted a headless and armless figure in midstride. *Walking Man* demonstrates Rodin's mastery of anatomy and ability to capture transitory motion.

1 ft.

---

their own flesh as food. In Carpeaux's statuary group, the powerful forms—twisted, intertwined, and densely concentrated—suggest the self-devouring torment of frustration and despair wracking the unfortunate Ugolino. A careful student of Michelangelo's male figures, Carpeaux also said he had the Laocoön group (FIG. 5-89) in mind. Certainly, the storm and stress of *Ugolino and His Children* recall similar characteristics of that ancient work. Regardless of these influences, the sense of vivid reality in the anatomy of Carpeaux's figures shows the artist's interest in study from life. The French public did not share that interest, however, and preferred the idealized bodies of classical sculptures—one of the reasons Carpeaux was forced to remove *The Dance* (FIG. 23-31A) from the facade of the Paris opera house (FIG. 22-45).

AUGUSTE RODIN The leading French sculptor of the later 19th century was Auguste Rodin (1840–1917), who conceived and executed his sculptures with a Realist sensibility. The human body in

23-31A Carpeaux, *The Dance,* 1867–1869.

motion (see "Rodin on Movement in Art and Photography," above) fascinated Rodin, as it did Eakins and Muybridge (FIG. 22-54) before him. Rodin was also well aware of the Impressionists' innovations. Although color was not a significant factor in Rodin's work, the influence of Impressionism is evident in the artist's abiding concern for the effect of light on sculpted surfaces. When focusing on the human form, he joined his profound knowledge of anatomy and movement with special attention to the body's exterior, saying, "The sculptor must learn to reproduce the surface, which means all that vibrates on the surface, soul, love, passion, life. . . . Sculpture is thus the art of hollows and mounds, not of smoothness, or even polished planes."[15] Primarily a modeler of pliable material rather than a carver of hard wood or stone, Rodin worked his surfaces with fingers sensitive to the subtlest variations of surface, catching the fugitive play of constantly shifting light on the body. In his studio, he often would have a model move around in front of him while he created preliminary versions of his sculptures with coils of clay.

In *Walking Man* (FIG. 23-32), a preliminary study for the sculptor's *Saint John the Baptist Preaching,* Rodin succeeded in representing a fleeting moment in cast bronze. He portrayed a headless and armless figure in midstride at the moment when weight is transferred across the pelvis from the back leg to the front. In addition to capturing the sense of the transitory, Rodin demonstrated his mastery of realistic detail in his meticulous rendition of muscle, bone, and tendon.

GATES OF HELL Rodin also made many nude and draped studies for each of the figures in two of his most ambitious works—the life-size group *Burghers of Calais* (FIG. 23-32A) and the *Gates of Hell* (FIG. 23-33), which occupied the sculptor for two decades. After he failed to gain admission to the École des Beaux-Arts, Rodin enrolled in the École Impériale Spéciale de Dessin et Mathématiques, the French school of decorative arts, known as the "Petit École" (Little School) because it was a lesser version of the more prestigious Beaux-Arts academy. Nonetheless, Rodin gained attention for the outstanding realism of some of his early sculptures, and on August 16, 1880, he received a major governmental commission to design a pair of doors for a planned Museum of Decorative Arts in Paris. Rodin worked on the project for 20 years, but the museum was never built (the Musée d'Orsay now occupies the intended site). It was not until after the sculptor's death that others cast his still-unfinished doors in bronze.

23-32A Rodin, *Burghers of Calais*, 1884–1889.

The commission permitted Rodin to choose his own subject. He selected *The Gates of Hell*, based on Dante's *Inferno* and Baudelaire's *Flowers of Evil*. Originally inspired by Lorenzo Ghiberti's *Gates of Paradise* (FIG. 16-9), which he had seen in Florence, Rodin quickly abandoned the idea of a series of framed narrative panels and decided instead to cover each of the doors with a continuous writhing mass of tormented men and women, sinners condemned to Dante's second circle of Hell for their lust. Because of the varying height of the relief and the variegated surfaces, the figures seem to be in flux, moving in and out of an undefined space in a reflection of their psychic turmoil. The dreamlike (or rather, the nightmarish) vision connects Rodin with the Symbolists, and the pessimistic mood exemplifies the fin-de-siècle spirit. The swirling composition and emotionalism recall Eugène Delacroix's *Death of Sardanapalus* (FIG. 22-15) and Michelangelo's *Last Judgment* (FIG. 17-19). But Rodin's work defies easy stylistic classification.

The nearly 200 figures of *The Gates of Hell* spill over onto the jambs and the lintel. Rodin also included freestanding figures, which, cast separately in multiple versions, are among his most famous works. Above the doors, *The Three Shades* is a trio of twisted nude male figures, essentially the same figure with elongated arms in three different positions. The group evokes Jean Baptiste Carpeaux's *Ugolino and His Children* (FIG. 23-31). *The Thinker,* Rodin's famous seated nude man with a powerful body who rests his chin

1 ft.

23-33 AUGUSTE RODIN, *The Gates of Hell,* 1880–1900 (cast in 1917). Bronze, 20′ 10″ × 13′ 1″. Musée Rodin, Paris.

Rodin's most ambitious work, inspired by Dante's *Inferno* and Ghiberti's *Gates of Paradise* (FIG. 16-9), presents nearly 200 tormented sinners in relief below *The Three Shades* and *The Thinker.*

on his clenched right hand, ponders the fate of the tormented souls on the doors below. *The Gates of Hell,* more than 20 feet tall, was Rodin's most ambitious project. It greatly influenced the painters and sculptors of the Expressionist movements of the early 20th century (see Chapter 24).

Rodin's ability to capture the quality of the transitory through his highly textured surfaces while revealing larger themes and deeper, lasting sensibilities is one of the reasons he had a strong influence on 20th-century artists. Because many of his works, such as

23-33A SAINT-GAUDENS, *Adams Memorial*, 1886–1891.

Walking Man, were deliberate fragments, he was also instrumental in creating a taste for the incomplete, an aesthetic many later sculptors embraced enthusiastically.

AUGUSTUS SAINT-GAUDENS

Other leading sculptors of the late 19th century pursued more traditional goals, however. In America, for example, AUGUSTUS SAINT-GAUDENS (1848–1907) produced monumental statues expressing the majestic calm of ancient Greek and Roman sculpture, as in his *Adams Memorial* (FIG. 23-33A) in Washington, D.C.

ARCHITECTURE AND DECORATIVE ARTS

The decisive effects of industrialization were impossible to ignore, and although many artists embraced this manifestation of "modern life" or at least explored its effects, other artists, especially those associated with the Arts and Crafts movement in England, decried the impact of rampant industrialism. This movement, which developed during the last decades of the 19th century, was shaped by the ideas of John Ruskin, the critic who skewered Whistler's "arrangements" (see "Whistler," page 698), and the artist William Morris. Both men shared a distrust of machines and industrial capitalism, which they believed alienated workers from their own nature. Accordingly, they advocated an art "made by the people for the people

as a joy for the maker and the user."[16] This condemnation of capitalism and support for manual laborers were consistent with the tenets of socialism, and many artists in the Arts and Crafts movement, especially in England, considered themselves socialists and participated in the labor movement.

This democratic, or at least populist, attitude carried over to the art they produced as well. Members of the Arts and Crafts movement dedicated themselves to making functional objects with high aesthetic value for a wide public. They advocated a style based on natural, rather than artificial, forms, which often consisted of repeated designs of floral or geometric patterns. For Ruskin, Morris, and others in the Arts and Crafts movement, high-quality artisanship and honest labor were crucial ingredients of superior works of decorative art.

WILLIAM MORRIS To promote these ideals, WILLIAM MORRIS (1834–1896) formed a decorating firm dedicated to Arts and Crafts principles: Morris, Marshall, Faulkner, and Company, Fine Arts Workmen in Painting, Carving, Furniture, and Metals. His company did a flourishing business producing wallpaper, textiles, furniture, books, rugs, stained glass, tiles, and pottery. In 1867, Morris received the commission to decorate the Green Dining Room (FIG. 23-34) at London's South Kensington Museum (now the Victoria & Albert Museum), the center of public art education and home of decorative art collections. The range of room features—windows, lights, and *wainscoting* (paneling on the lower part of interior walls)—Morris created for this unified, beautiful, and functional environment was all-encompassing. Nothing escaped his eye. Morris's design for this room also reveals the penchant of Arts and Crafts designers for intricate patterning.

23-34 WILLIAM MORRIS, Green Dining Room, South Kensington Museum (now Victoria & Albert Museum), London, England, 1867.

William Morris was a founder of the Arts and Crafts movement. His Green Dining Room exemplifies the group's dedication to creating intricately patterned yet unified and functional environments.

23-35 Charles Rennie Mackintosh and Margaret Macdonald Mackintosh, Ladies' Luncheon Room, Ingram Street Tea Room, Glasgow, Scotland, 1900–1912. Reconstructed (1992–1995) in the Glasgow Art Galleries and Museum, Glasgow.

The Mackintoshes' Ladies' Luncheon Room in Glasgow features functional and exquisitely designed Arts and Crafts decor, including stained-glass windows and pristinely geometric furnishings.

CHARLES RENNIE MACKINTOSH Numerous Arts and Crafts societies in America, England, and Germany carried on this ideal of artisanship. In Scotland, CHARLES RENNIE MACKINTOSH (1868–1929) designed a number of tea rooms, including the Ladies' Luncheon Room (FIG. **23-35**) located in the Ingram Street Tea Room in Glasgow. The room decor is consistent with Morris's vision of a functional, exquisitely designed art. The chairs, stained-glass windows, and large panels of colored gesso with twine, glass beads, thread, mother-of-pearl, and tin leaf—made by MARGARET MACDONALD MACKINTOSH (1864–1933), an artist-designer and Mackintosh's wife, who collaborated with him on many projects—are all pristinely geometric and rhythmical in design.

ART NOUVEAU An important international architectural and design movement that developed out of the ideas the Arts and Crafts movement promoted was *Art Nouveau* (New Art), which took its name from a shop in Paris called L'Art Nouveau. Known by that name in France, Belgium, Holland, England, and the United States, the style had other names in other places: *Jugendstil* in Austria and Germany (after the magazine *Jugend,* "youth"), *Modernismo* in Spain, and *Floreale* in Italy. Proponents of this movement tried to synthesize all the arts in a determined attempt to create art based on natural forms that could be mass-produced for a large audience. The Art Nouveau style adapted the twining plant form to the needs of architecture, painting, sculpture, and all of the decorative arts.

23-36 VICTOR HORTA, staircase in the Van Eetvelde House, Brussels, 1895.

The Art Nouveau movement was an attempt to create art and architecture based on natural forms. Here, every detail conforms to the theme of the twining plant and functions as part of a living whole.

23-36A HORTA, Tassel House, Brussels, 1892–1893.

23-36B TIFFANY, water lily lamp, 1904–1915.

VICTOR HORTA The mature Art Nouveau style of the 1890s is on display in the houses the Belgian architect VICTOR HORTA (1861–1947) designed. A characteristic example is the staircase (FIG. **23-36**) in the Van Eetvelde House, which Horta built in Brussels in 1895, three years after designing the Tassel House (FIG. **23-36A**), his first major commission. Every detail of the Van Eetvelde interior functions as part of a living whole. Furniture, drapery folds, veining in the lavish stone paneling, and the patterning of the door moldings join with real plants to provide graceful counterpoints for the twining-plant theme. Metallic tendrils curl around the railings and posts, delicate metal tracery fills the glass dome, and floral and leaf motifs spread across the fabric panels of the screen. Flower and plant motifs also figure prominently in the immensely popular stained-glass lamps (FIG. **23-36B**) of LOUIS COMFORT TIFFANY (1848–1933).

The Art Nouveau style reflects several influences. In addition to the rich, foliated two-dimensional ornamentation of Arts and Crafts design and that movement's respect for materials, the sinuous whiplash curve of Japanese print designs inspired Art Nouveau artists. Art Nouveau also borrowed from the expressively patterned styles of van Gogh (FIGS. 23-17 and 23-18), Gauguin (FIGS. 23-19 and 23-20), and their Post-Impressionist and Symbolist contemporaries.

ANTONIO GAUDI Art Nouveau achieved its most personal expression in the work of the Spanish architect ANTONIO GAUDI (1852–1926). Before becoming an architect, Gaudi had trained as an ironworker. As many young artists of his time, he longed to create a style both modern and appropriate to his country. Taking inspiration from Moorish architecture and from the simple architecture of his native Catalonia, Gaudi developed a personal aesthetic. He conceived a building as a whole and molded it almost as a sculptor might shape a figure from clay. Although work on his designs proceeded slowly under the guidance of his intuition and imagination, Gaudi was a master who invented many new structural techniques that facilitated construction of his visions. His Barcelona apartment house, Casa Milá (FIG. **23-37**), is a wondrously free-form mass wrapped around a street corner. Lacy iron railings enliven the swelling curves of the cut-stone facade. Dormer windows peep from the undulating tiled roof, from which fantastically writhing chimneys poke energetically into the air above. The rough surfaces of the stone walls suggest naturally worn rock. The entrance portals look like eroded sea caves, but their design also may reflect the excitement that swept Spain following the 1879 discovery of Paleolithic cave paintings at Altamira (FIG. 1-9). Gaudi felt each of his buildings was symbolically a living thing, and the passionate naturalism of his Casa Milá is the spiritual kin of early-20th-century Expressionist painting and sculpture (see Chapter 24).

23-37 ANTONIO GAUDI, Casa Milá (looking north), Barcelona, Spain, 1907.

Spanish Art Nouveau architect Gaudi conceived this apartment house as if it were a gigantic sculpture to be molded from clay. Twisting chimneys cap the undulating roof and walls.

23-38 ALEXANDRE-GUSTAVE EIFFEL, Eiffel Tower (looking southeast), Paris, France, 1889. ◼◀

New materials and technologies and the modernist aesthetic fueled radically new architectural designs in the late 19th century. Eiffel jolted the world with the exposed iron skeleton of his tower.

ALEXANDRE-GUSTAVE EIFFEL In the later 19th century, new technologies and the changing needs of urbanized, industrialized society affected architecture throughout the Western world. Since the 18th century, bridges had been built of cast iron (FIG. 21-12), which enabled engineering advancements in the construction of larger, stronger, and more fire-resistant structures. Steel, available after 1860, made it possible for architects to enclose ever larger spaces, such as those found in railroad stations (FIG. 23-4) and exposition halls. The Realist impulse also encouraged architectural designs that honestly expressed a building's purpose, rather than elaborately disguising its function. The elegant metal-skeleton structures of the French engineer-architect ALEXANDRE-GUSTAVE EIFFEL (1832–1923) were responses to this idea, and they constituted an important contribution to the development of the 20th-century skyscraper. A native of Burgundy, Eiffel trained in Paris before beginning a distinguished career designing exhibition halls, bridges, and the interior armature for France's anniversary gift to the United States—the *Statue of Liberty* by Frédéric Auguste Bartholdi (1834–1904).

Eiffel designed his best-known work, the Eiffel Tower (FIG. **23-38**), for an exhibition in Paris in 1889. Originally seen as a symbol of modern Paris and still considered a symbol of 19th-century civilization, the elegant iron tower thrusts its needle shaft 984 feet above the city, making it at the time of its construction (and for some time thereafter) the world's tallest structure. The tower rests on four giant supports connected by gracefully arching open-frame skirts that provide a pleasing mask for the heavy horizontal girders needed to strengthen the legs. Visitors can take two successive elevators to the top, or they can use the internal staircase. Either way, the view of Paris and the Seine from the tower is incomparable, as is the design of the tower itself. The transparency of Eiffel's structure blurs the distinction between interior and exterior to an extent never before achieved or even attempted. This interpenetration of inner and outer space became a hallmark of 20th-century art and architecture. Eiffel's tower and the earlier iron skeletal frames designed by Labrouste (FIG. 22-46) and Paxton (FIG. 22-47) jolted the architectural profession into a realization that modern materials and processes could germinate a completely new style and a radically innovative approach to architectural design.

AMERICAN SKYSCRAPERS The desire for greater speed and economy in building, as well as for a reduction in fire hazards, prompted the use of cast and wrought iron for many building programs, especially commercial ones. Designers in both England and the United States enthusiastically developed cast-iron architecture until a series of disastrous fires in the early 1870s in New York, Boston, and Chicago demonstrated that cast iron by itself was far from impervious to fire. This discovery led to encasing the metal in masonry, combining the first material's strength with the second's fire resistance.

In cities, convenience required closely grouped buildings, and increased property values forced architects literally to raise the roof. Even an attic could command high rentals if the builders installed one of the new elevators, used for the first time in the Equitable Building in New York (1868–1871). Metal, which could support these towering structures, gave birth to the American skyscraper.

23-39 **Henry Hobson Richardson, Marshall Field wholesale store, Chicago, 1885–1887 (demolished 1930).**

Richardson was a pioneer in designing commercial structures using a cast-iron skeleton encased in fire-resistant masonry. This construction technique enabled the insertion of large windows in the walls.

HENRY HOBSON RICHARDSON One of the pioneers in designing these modern commercial structures was Henry Hobson Richardson (1838–1886), but he also had a profound respect for earlier architectural styles. Because Richardson had a special fondness for the Romanesque architecture of the Auvergne area in France, he frequently used heavy round arches and massive masonry walls. Architectural historians sometimes consider his work to constitute a Romanesque revival related to the Neo-Gothic style (FIGS. 22-43 and 22-43A). This designation does not do credit to the originality and quality of most of the buildings Richardson designed during his brief 18-year practice. Trinity Church in Boston and his smaller public libraries, residences, railroad stations, and courthouses in New England and elsewhere best demonstrate his vivid imagination and the solidity (the sense of enclosure and permanence) so characteristic of his style. However, his most important and influential building was the Marshall Field wholesale store (FIG. **23-39**) in Chicago, begun in 1885 and demolished in 1930. This vast building occupied an entire city block. Designed for the most practical of purposes, it nonetheless recalled historical styles without imitating them. The tripartite elevation of a Renaissance palace (FIG. 16-37) or of the Roman aqueduct (FIG. 7-33) near Nîmes, France, may have been close to Richardson's mind. But he used no classical ornamentation, made much of the massive courses of masonry, and, in the strong horizontality of the window-sills and the interrupted courses defining the levels, stressed the long sweep of the building's lines, as well as the edifice's ponderous weight. Although the structural frame still lay behind and in conjunction with the masonry screen, the great glazed arcades opened up the walls of the monumental store. They pointed the way to the modern total penetration of walls and the transformation of them into mere screens or curtains that serve both to echo the underlying structural grid and to protect it from the weather.

LOUIS HENRY SULLIVAN As skyscrapers proliferated, architects refined the visual vocabulary of these buildings. Louis Henry Sullivan (1856–1924), whom many architectural historians call the first truly modern architect, arrived at a synthesis of industrial structure and ornamentation that perfectly expressed the spirit of late-19th-century commerce. To achieve this, he used the latest technological developments to create light-filled, well-ventilated office buildings and adorned both exteriors and interiors with ornate embellishments. Such decoration served to connect commerce and culture, and imbued these white-collar workspaces with a sense of refinement and taste. These characteristics are evident in the Guaranty (Prudential) Building (FIG. **23-40**) in Buffalo, built

23-40 **Louis Henry Sullivan, Guaranty (Prudential) Building (looking southwest), Buffalo, New York, 1894–1896.**

Sullivan drew on the latest technologies to create this light-filled, well-ventilated Buffalo office building. He added ornate surface embellishments to impart a sense of refinement and taste.

23-41 LOUIS HENRY SULLIVAN, Carson, Pirie, Scott Building (looking southeast), Chicago, 1899–1904.

Sullivan's slogan was "form follows function." He tailored the design of this steel, glass, and stone Chicago department store to meet the needs of its employees and customers.

23-40A SULLIVAN, Wainwright Building, St. Louis, 1890–1891.

between 1894 and 1896, and in his earlier Wainwright Building (FIG. **23-40A**) in St. Louis. The Buffalo skyscraper is steel, sheathed with terracotta. The imposing scale of the building and the regularity of the window placements served as an expression of the large-scale, refined, and orderly office work taking place within. Sullivan tempered the severity of the structure with lively ornamentation, both on the piers and cornice on the exterior of the building and on the stairway balustrades, elevator cages, and ceiling in the interior. The Guaranty Building illustrates Sullivan's famous dictum "form follows function," which became the slogan of many early-20th-century architects. Still, Sullivan did not advocate a rigid and doctrinaire correspondence between exterior and interior design. Rather, he espoused a free and flexible relationship—one his pupil

Frank Lloyd Wright (see Chapter 24) later described as similar to that between the hand's bones and tissue.

Sullivan also designed the Carson, Pirie, Scott Building (FIG. **23-41**) in Chicago. Built between 1899 and 1904, this department store required broad, open, well-illuminated display spaces. Sullivan again used a minimal structural steel skeleton to achieve this goal. The architect gave over the lowest two levels of the building to an ornament in cast iron (of his invention) made of wildly fantastic motifs. He regarded the display windows as pictures, which merited elaborate frames. As in the Guaranty Building, Sullivan revealed his profound understanding of the maturing consumer economy and tailored the Carson, Pirie, Scott Building to meet the functional and symbolic needs of its users.

Thus, in architecture as well as in the pictorial arts, the late 19th century was a period during which artists challenged traditional modes of expression, often emphatically rejecting the past. Architects and painters as different as Sullivan, Monet, van Gogh, and Cézanne, each in his own way, contributed significantly to the entrenchment of modernism as the new cultural orthodoxy of the early 20th century (see Chapter 24).

IMPRESSIONISM, POST-IMPRESSIONISM, SYMBOLISM: EUROPE AND AMERICA, 1870 TO 1900

IMPRESSIONISM

▌ A hostile critic applied the term *Impressionism* to the paintings of Claude Monet because of their sketchy quality. The Impressionists—Monet, Pierre-Auguste Renoir, Edgar Degas, and others—strove to capture fleeting moments and transient effects of light and climate on canvas. They also focused on recording the contemporary urban scene in Paris, frequently painting bars, dance halls, the ballet, wide boulevards, and railroad stations.

▌ Complementing the Impressionists' sketchy, seemingly spontaneous brushstrokes are the compositions of their paintings. Reflecting the influence of Japanese prints and photography, Impressionist works often have arbitrarily cut-off figures and settings seen at sharply oblique angles.

Renoir, *Le Moulin de la Galette,* 1876

POST-IMPRESSIONISM AND SYMBOLISM

▌ Post-Impressionism is not a unified style. The term refers to the group of late-19th-century artists, including Georges Seurat, Vincent van Gogh, Paul Gauguin, and Paul Cézanne, who followed the Impressionists and took painting in new directions. Seurat refined the Impressionist approach to color and light into pointillism—the disciplined application of pure color in tiny daubs. Van Gogh explored the capabilities of colors and distorted forms to express emotions. Gauguin, an admirer of Japanese prints, moved away from Impressionism in favor of large areas of flat color bounded by firm lines. Cézanne replaced the transitory visual effects of the Impressionists with a rigorous analysis of the lines, planes, and colors that make up landscapes and still lifes.

▌ Gustave Moreau, Odilon Redon, and Henri Rousseau were the leading French Symbolists. They disdained Realism as trivial and sought to depict a reality beyond that of the everyday world, rejecting materialism and celebrating fantasy and imagination. Their subjects were often mysterious, exotic, and sensuous.

van Gogh, *Starry Night,* 1889

Rousseau, *Sleeping Gypsy,* 1897

SCULPTURE

▌ Sculpture cannot capture transitory optical effects or explore the properties of color and line, and late-19th-century sculptors pursued goals different from those of contemporaneous painters.

▌ The leading figure of the era was Auguste Rodin, who explored Realist themes and the representation of movement. His vision of tormented, writhing figures in Hell connects his work with the Symbolists. Rodin also made statues that were deliberate fragments, creating a taste for the incomplete that appealed to many later sculptors.

Rodin, *Gates of Hell,* 1880–1900

ARCHITECTURE AND DECORATIVE ARTS

▌ Not all artists embraced the industrialization transforming daily life during the 19th century. The Arts and Crafts movement in England and the international Art Nouveau style formed in opposition to modern mass production. Both schools advocated natural forms and high-quality craftsmanship.

▌ New technologies and the changing needs of urbanized, industrialized society transformed architecture in the late 19th century. The exposed iron skeleton of the Eiffel Tower jolted architects into realizing how modern materials and processes could revolutionize architectural design. Henry Hobson Richardson and Louis Sullivan were pioneers in designing the first metal, stone, and glass skyscrapers.

Eiffel, Eiffel Tower, Paris, 1889

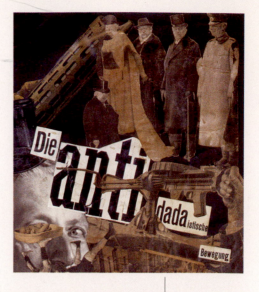

The cut-out photos in Höch's photomontage appear to be randomly selected, but they are carefully arranged. The leading figures of the Weimar Republic (the "anti-Dadaists") are at the top right.

The many photos pasted together in *Cut with a Kitchen Knife* include mass-produced machine parts. In the lower left of this detail, the artist Käthe Kollwitz's head floats above a dancer's body.

The letters cut from various publications are of different typefaces and font sizes, contributing to the sense of dislocation throughout. Near the center are the words "The great Dada world."

24-1 Hannah Höch, *Cut with the Kitchen Knife Dada through the Last Weimar Beer Belly Cultural Epoch of Germany*, 1919–1920. Photomontage, 3′ 9″ × 2′ 11½″. Neue Nationalgalerie, Staatliche Museen zu Berlin, Berlin. ◼◀

1 ft.

At the lower right, in the section labeled "Dadaists," Höch juxtaposed a photo of her own face with a map of Europe showing those countries that had granted women the right to vote.

MODERNISM IN EUROPE AND AMERICA, 1900 TO 1945

GLOBAL WAR, ANARCHY, AND DADA

World War I—the "Great War"—broke out in 1914, unleashing slaughter and devastation on a scale unprecedented in history. More than nine million soldiers died in four years. Britain alone lost 60,000 men on the opening day of the battle of the Somme. The negotiated formal end of hostilities in 1919 redrew the political map of Europe (MAP 24-1). Peace, however, could not erase the scars of a global conflict that had altered the worldview of millions. One major consequence of the Great War was the emergence of an artistic movement known as *Dada*. The Dadaists believed reason and logic had been responsible for the insane spectacle of collective homicide that was World War I, and they concluded the only route to salvation was through political anarchy, the irrational, and the intuitive.

In Berlin, Dada took on an activist political edge. The Berlin Dadaists pioneered a variation of the technique called *collage* in French (FIG. 24-17)—creating artistic compositions from cut pieces of paper. The Berliners christened their version *photomontage*, because their assemblages consisted almost entirely of pieces of magazine photographs, usually combined into deliberately antilogical compositions. Collage lent itself well to the Dada desire to exploit chance in the creation of art—and anti-art.

One of the Berlin Dadaists who perfected the photomontage technique was HANNAH HÖCH (1889–1978). Höch's photomontages advanced the absurd illogic of Dada by presenting viewers with chaotic, contradictory, and satiric compositions. They also provided scathing and insightful commentary on two of the most dramatic developments during the Weimar Republic (1918–1933) in Germany—the redefinition of women's social roles and the explosive growth of mass print media. Höch incorporated both themes in *Cut with the Kitchen Knife Dada through the Last Weimar Beer Belly Cultural Epoch of Germany* (FIG. 24-1), in which she arranged in seemingly haphazard fashion—often with a touch of typically wicked Dada humor—an eclectic mixture of cutout photos. Closer inspection, however, reveals the artist's careful selection and placement of the photographs. For example, the key figures in the Weimar Republic are together at the upper right (identified as the "anti-Dada movement"). Some of Höch's fellow Dadaists appear among images of Karl Marx and Vladimir Lenin, aligning Dada with other revolutionary forces in what she prominently labeled with cutout lettering "Die grosse Welt dada" (the great Dada world). Höch also positioned herself in the topsy-turvy Dada world she created. A photograph of her head appears in the lower right corner, juxtaposed with a map of Europe showing which countries had granted women the right to vote—a commentary on the power both women and Dada had to destabilize society.

GLOBAL UPHEAVAL
AND ARTISTIC REVOLUTION

The first half of the 20th century was a period of significant upheaval worldwide. Between 1900 and 1945, the major industrial powers fought two global wars, witnessed the rise of Communism, Fascism, and Nazism, and suffered the Great Depression. These decades were also a time of radical change in the arts when painters and sculptors challenged some of the most basic assumptions about the purpose of art and what form an artwork should take. Throughout history, artistic revolution has often accompanied political, social, and economic upheaval, but never before had the new directions artists explored been as pronounced or as long-lasting as those born during the first half of the last century.

AVANT-GARDE As did other members of society, artists felt deeply the effects of the political and economic disruptions of the early 20th century. As the old social orders collapsed and new ones, from communism to corporate capitalism, took their places, artists searched for new definitions of and uses for art in a changed world. Already in the 19th century, each successive modernist movement had challenged artistic conventions with ever-greater intensity. This relentless questioning of the status quo gave rise to the notion of an artistic *avant-garde*. The term, which means "front guard," derives from 19th-century French military usage. The avant-garde were the troops sent ahead of the army's main body to reconnoiter and make occasional raids on the enemy. Politicians who deemed themselves visionary and forward-thinking subsequently adopted the term. It then migrated to the art world in the 1880s, when artists and critics used it to refer to the Realists, Impressionists, and Post-Impressionists—artists who were ahead of their time and who transgressed the limits of established art forms.

These trailblazing rebels rejected the classical, academic, and traditional, and zealously explored the premises and formal qualities of painting, sculpture, and other media. Although the general public found avant-garde art incomprehensible, the principles underlying 19th-century modernism appealed to increasing numbers of artists as the 20th century dawned.

EUROPE, 1900 TO 1920

Avant-garde artists in all their diversity became a major force during the opening decades of the 20th century, beginning with the artistic movement known as *Fauvism*.

Fauvism

In 1905, at the third Salon d'Automne (Autumn Salon) in Paris, a group of young painters exhibited canvases so simplified in design and so shockingly bright in color that a startled critic, Louis Vauxcelles (1870–1943), described the artists as *fauves* (wild beasts). The Fauves were totally independent of the French Academy and the "official" Salon (see "Academic Salons and Independent Art Exhibitions," Chapter 23, page 690). Driving the Fauve movement was a desire to develop an art having the directness of Impressionism but employing intense color juxtapositions for expressive ends.

Building on the legacy of artists such as Vincent van Gogh and Paul Gauguin (see Chapter 23), the Fauves went even further in liberating color from its descriptive function and exploring the effects different colors have on emotions. The Fauves produced portraits, landscapes, still lifes, and nudes of spontaneity and verve, with rich surface textures, lively linear patterns, and, above all, bold colors. They employed startling contrasts of vermilion and emerald green and of cerulean blue and vivid orange held together by sweeping brushstrokes and bold patterns in an effort to release internal feelings.

The Fauve painters never officially organized, and the looseness of both personal connections and stylistic affinities caused the Fauve movement to begin to disintegrate almost as soon as it emerged. Within five years, most of the artists had departed from a strict adherence to Fauve principles and developed their own more

MODERNISM IN EUROPE AND AMERICA, 1900 TO 1945

1900	1910	1920	1930	1945
▪ European artists build on the innovations of the Impressionists and Post-Impressionists and explore new avenues of artistic expression ▪ Henri Matisse and the Fauves free color from its descriptive function ▪ German Expressionist groups—Die Brücke and Der Blaue Reiter—produce paintings featuring bold colors and distorted forms ▪ In America, Frank Lloyd Wright promotes "natural architecture" in his expansive "prairie houses"	▪ Pablo Picasso and Georges Braque radically challenge the traditional Western way of making pictures with their Cubist dissection of forms ▪ The Italian Futurists celebrate dynamic motion and modern technology in paintings and statues ▪ Vassily Kandinsky pursues complete abstraction in painting ▪ The Dadaists explore the role of chance in often irreverent artworks ▪ The Armory Show introduces American artists and the public to avant-garde developments in Europe	▪ In the wake of World War I, German Neue Sachlichkeit painters depict the horrors of global conflict ▪ The Surrealists seek ways to visualize the world of the unconscious and investigate automatism as a means of creating art ▪ De Stijl artists create "pure plastic art" using geometric forms and primary colors ▪ Constantine Brancusi and Barbara Hepworth promote abstraction in sculpture ▪ The Bauhaus advocates the integration of all the arts in its vision of "total architecture" ▪ Photography emerges as an important art form in the work of Alfred Stieglitz and Edward Weston	▪ Aaron Douglas and Jacob Lawrence explore African American history in the Harlem Renaissance ▪ Alexander Calder creates abstract sculptures with moving parts ▪ Grant Wood and the Regionalists celebrate life in rural America in paintings rejecting European abstraction ▪ José Orozco and Diego Rivera paint vast mural cycles recording Mexican history ▪ Dorothea Lange and Margaret Bourke-White achieve renown for their documentary photography	

MAP 24-1 Europe at the end of World War I

Lost immediately after World War I

By Russia
By Germany
By Bulgaria
By Austria-Hungary

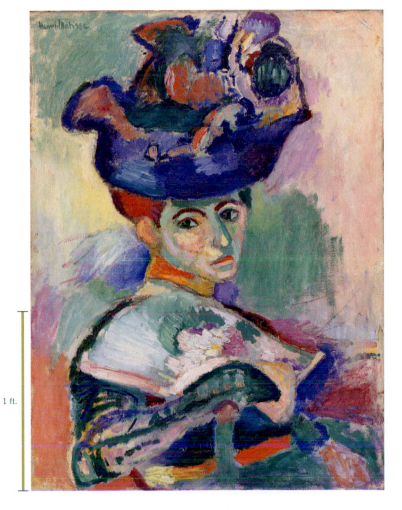

1 ft.

personal styles. During its brief existence, however, Fauvism made a remarkable contribution to the direction of art by demonstrating color's structural, expressive, and aesthetic capabilities.

HENRI MATISSE The dominant figure of the Fauve group was HENRI MATISSE (1869–1954), who believed color could play a primary role in conveying meaning and focused his efforts on developing this notion. In an early painting, *Woman with the Hat* (FIG. **24-2**), Matisse depicted his wife, Amélie, in a rather

24-2A MATISSE, *Le Bonheur de Vivre,* 1905–1906.

conventional manner compositionally, but the seemingly arbitrary colors immediately startle the viewer, as does the sketchiness of the forms. The entire image—the woman's face, clothes, hat, and background—consists of patches and splotches of color juxtaposed in ways that sometimes produce jarring contrasts. Matisse explained his approach: "What characterized fauvism was that we rejected imitative colors, and that with pure colors we obtained stronger reactions."[1] For Matisse and the Fauves, therefore, color became the formal element most responsible for pictorial coherence and the primary conveyor of meaning (see "Matisse on Color," page 726, and FIG. **24-2A**).

24-2 HENRI MATISSE, *Woman with the Hat,* 1905. Oil on canvas, 2′ 7¾″ × 1′ 11½″. San Francisco Museum of Modern Art, San Francisco (bequest of Elise S. Haas).

Matisse's portrayal of his wife, Amélie, features patches and splotches of seemingly arbitrary colors. He and the other Fauve painters used color not to imitate nature but to produce a reaction in the viewer.

Matisse on Color

In an essay entitled "Notes of a Painter," published in the Parisian journal *La Grande Revue* on Christmas Day, 1908, Henri Matisse responded to his critics and set forth his principles and goals as a painter. The following excerpts help explain what Matisse was trying to achieve in paintings such as *Harmony in Red* (FIG. 24-3).

What I am after, above all, is expression. . . . Expression, for me, does not reside in passions glowing in a human face or manifested by violent movement. The entire arrangement of my picture is expressive: the place occupied by the figures, the empty spaces around them, the proportions, everything has its share. Composition is the art of arranging in a decorative manner the diverse elements at the painter's command to express his feelings. . . .

Both harmonies and dissonances of colour can produce agreeable effects. . . . Suppose I have to paint an interior: I have before me a cupboard; it gives me a sensation of vivid red, and I put down a red which satisfies me. A relation is established between this red and the white of the canvas. Let me put a green near the red, and make the floor yellow; and again there will be relationships between the green or yellow and the white of the canvas which will satisfy me. . . . A new combination of colours will succeed the first and render the totality of my representation. I am forced to transpose until finally my picture may seem completely changed when, after successive modifications, the red has succeeded the green as the dominant colour. I cannot copy nature in a servile way; I am forced to interpret nature and submit it to the spirit of the picture. From the relationship I have found in all the tones there must result a living harmony of colours, a harmony analogous to that of a musical composition. . . .

The chief function of colour should be to serve expression as well as possible. . . . My choice of colours does not rest on any scientific theory; it is based on observation, on sensitivity, on felt experiences. . . . I simply try to put down colours which render my sensation. There is an impelling proportion of tones that may lead me to change the shape of a figure or to transform my composition. Until I have achieved this proportion in all parts of the composition I strive towards it and keep on working. Then a moment comes when all the parts have found their definite relationships, and from then on it would be impossible for me to add a stroke to my picture without having to repaint it entirely.*

*Translated by Jack D. Flam, *Matisse on Art* (London: Phaidon, 1973), 32–40.

24-3 Henri Matisse, *Red Room* (*Harmony in Red*), 1908–1909. Oil on canvas, 5′ 11″ × 8′ 1″. State Hermitage Museum, Saint Petersburg. ◼◀

Matisse believed painters should choose compositions and colors that express their feelings. Here, the table and wall seem to merge because they are the same color and have identical patterning.

1 ft.

Derain worked closely with Matisse, but the tropical setting and the bold colors of *The Dance* also reflect Derain's study of Gauguin's paintings (FIGS. 23-19 and 23-20), as does the flattened perspective.

1 ft.

HARMONY IN RED These color discoveries reached maturity in Matisse's *Red Room* (*Harmony in Red;* FIG. **24-3**). The subject is the interior of a comfortable, prosperous household with a maid placing fruit and wine on the table, but Matisse's canvas is radically different from traditional paintings of domestic interiors (for example, FIGS. 25-19 and 25-20A). The Fauve painter depicted objects in simplified and schematized fashion and flattened out the forms. For example, Matisse eliminated the front edge of the table, rendering the table, with its identical patterning, as flat as the wall behind it. The window at the upper left could also be a painting on the wall, further flattening the space. Everywhere, the colors contrast richly and intensely. Matisse's process of overpainting reveals the importance of color for striking the right chord in the viewer. Initially, this work was predominantly green. Then Matisse repainted it blue, but blue also did not seem appropriate. Not until he repainted the canvas red did Matisse feel he had found the right color for the "harmony" he wished to compose.

ANDRÉ DERAIN Another leading Fauve painter was ANDRÉ DERAIN (1880–1954). As did Matisse, with whom he worked closely, Derain sought to employ color for aesthetic and compositional coherence and to elicit emotional responses. *The Dance* (FIG. **24-4**), in which several figures, some nude, others clothed, frolic in a lush

24-4A DERAIN, *Mountains at Collioure*, 1905.

landscape (compare FIG. **24-4A**), is one of Derain's best paintings. The tropical setting and the bold colors reflect in part Derain's study of Gauguin's canvases (FIGS. 23-19 and 23-20), as does the flattened perspective. Derain used color to delineate space, and he indicated light and shadow not by differences in value but by contrasts of hue. For the Fauves, as for Gauguin and van Gogh, color does not describe the local tones of objects but expresses the picture's content.

German Expressionism

The immediacy and boldness of the Fauve images appealed to many artists, including the German *Expressionists*. However, although color plays a prominent role in German painting of the early 20th century, the "expressiveness" of the German images is due as much to the Expressionists' wrenching distortions of form, ragged outlines, and agitated brushstrokes.

ERNST LUDWIG KIRCHNER The first group of German Expressionists—*Die Brücke* (The Bridge)—gathered in Dresden in 1905 under the leadership of ERNST LUDWIG KIRCHNER (1880–1938). The group members thought of themselves as paving the way for a more perfect age by bridging the old age and the new, hence their name. Kirchner's early studies in architecture, painting, and the graphic arts had instilled in him a deep admiration for German medieval art. As did the British artists associated with the Arts and Crafts movement, such as William Morris (FIG. 23-34), Die Brücke artists modeled themselves on medieval craft guilds whose members lived together and practiced all the arts equally. Kirchner described their lofty goals in a ringing 1913 statement published in the form of a woodcut titled *Chronik der Brücke:*

> With faith in progress and in a new generation of creators and spectators we call together all youth. As youth, we carry the future and want to create for ourselves freedom of life and of movement against the long-established older forces. Everyone who reproduces that which drives him to creation with directness and authenticity belongs to us.[2]

Die Brücke artists protested the hypocrisy and materialistic decadence of those in power. Kirchner, in particular, focused much of his attention on the detrimental effects of industrialization, such as the alienation of individuals in cities, which he felt fostered a mechanized and impersonal society. The tensions leading to World War I further exacerbated the discomfort and anxiety of the German Expressionists.

24-5 ERNST LUDWIG KIRCHNER, *Street, Dresden*, 1908 (dated 1907). Oil on canvas, 4′ 11¼″ × 6′ 6⅞″. Museum of Modern Art, New York. ◼◀

Kirchner's perspective distortions, disquieting figures, and color choices reflect the influence of the Fauves and of Edvard Munch (FIG. 23-28), who made similar expressive use of formal elements.

Kirchner's *Street, Dresden* (FIG. **24-5**) provides a glimpse into the frenzied urban activity of a bustling German city before World War I. Rather than offering the distant, panoramic urban view of the Impressionists (FIG. 23-5), Kirchner's street scene is jarring and dissonant in both composition and color. The women in the foreground loom large, approaching somewhat menacingly. The steep perspective of the street, which threatens to push the women directly into the viewer's space, increases their confrontational nature. Harshly rendered, the women's features make them appear ghoulish, and the garish, clashing colors—juxtapositions of bright orange, emerald green, chartreuse, and pink—add to the expressive impact of the image. Kirchner's perspective distortions, disquieting figures, and color choices reflect the influence of the work of Edvard Munch, who made similar expressive use of formal elements in *The Scream* (FIG. 23-28).

EMIL NOLDE Much older than most Die Brücke artists was Emil Hansen, who changed his name in 1902 to EMIL NOLDE (1867–1956) after his birthplace in northern Germany. The younger artists invited him to join their group in 1906, but Nolde, an introvert who preferred to work alone, left Die Brücke the next year. By 1913, the group had dissolved, but a commonality of interests and painterly style continued to link Nolde and the other Die Brücke artists throughout their careers. The content of Nolde's work centered, for the most part, on religious imagery. In contrast to the quiet spirituality and restraint of traditional religious images, however, Nolde's paintings, for example, *Saint Mary of Egypt among Sinners* (FIG. **24-6**), are visceral and forceful. Mary, before her conversion, entertains lechers whose lust magnifies their brutal ugliness. The distortions of form and color (especially the jarring juxtaposition of blue and orange) and the rawness of the brushstrokes amplify the harshness of the leering faces.

Borrowing ideas from van Gogh, Munch, the Fauves, and African and Oceanic art (see "Primi-

tivism and Colonialism," page 734, and FIG. **24-6A**), Nolde and the other Die Brücke artists created images that derive much of their power from a dissonance and seeming lack of finesse. The harsh colors, aggressively brushed paint, and distorted forms expressed the painters' feelings about the injustices of society and their belief in a healthful union of human beings and nature.

24-6A NOLDE, *Masks*, 1911.

24-6 EMIL NOLDE, *Saint Mary of Egypt among Sinners*, 1912. Left panel of a triptych, oil on canvas, 2′ 10″ × 3′ 3″. Hamburger Kunsthalle, Hamburg.

In contrast to the quiet spirituality of traditional religious images, Nolde's paintings produce visceral emotions and feature distorted forms, jarring color juxtapositions, and raw brushstrokes.

Science and Art in the Early 20th Century

In the early 20th century, radical new ways of thinking emerged in both science and art, forcing people to revise how they understood the world. In particular, the values and ideals that were the legacy of the Enlightenment (see Chapter 21) began to yield to new perspectives. Intellectuals countered 18th- and 19th-century assumptions about progress and reason with ideas challenging traditional notions about the physical universe, the structure of society, and human nature. Modernist artists fully participated in this reassessment and formulated innovative theoretical bases for their work. Accordingly, much early-20th-century Western art is a rejection of traditional limitations and definitions both of art and of the universe.

Fundamental to the Enlightenment was faith in science. Because of its basis in empirical, or observable, fact, science provided a mechanistic conception of the universe, which reassured a populace that was finding traditional religions less certain. As promoted in the classic physics of Isaac Newton (1642–1727), the universe was a huge machine consisting of time, space, and matter. In the early 20th century, many scientists challenged this model of the universe in what amounted to a second scientific and technological revolution. Particularly noteworthy was the work of physicists Max Planck (1858–1947), Albert Einstein (1879–1955), Ernest Rutherford (1871–1937), and Niels Bohr (1885–1962). With their discoveries, each of these scientists shattered the existing faith in the objective reality of matter and, in so doing, paved the way for a new model of the universe. Planck's quantum theory (1900) raised questions about the emission of atomic energy. In his 1905 paper "The Electrodynamics of Moving Bodies," Einstein carried Planck's work further by introducing his theory of relativity. He argued that space and time are not absolute, as postulated in Newtonian physics. Rather, Einstein explained, time and space are relative to the observer and linked in

24-7 Vassily Kandinsky, *Improvisation 28* (second version), 1912. Oil on canvas, 3′ 7⅞″ × 5′ 3⅞″. Solomon R. Guggenheim Museum, New York (gift of Solomon R. Guggenheim, 1937).

The theories of Einstein and Rutherford convinced Kandinsky that material objects had no real substance. He was one of the first painters to explore complete abstraction in his canvases.

what he called a four-dimensional space-time continuum. He also concluded that matter, rather than a solid, tangible reality, was another form of energy. Einstein's famous equation, $E = mc^2$, where E stands for energy, m for mass, and c for the speed of light, provided a formula for understanding atomic energy. Rutherford's and Bohr's exploration of atomic structure between 1906 and 1913 contributed to this new perception of matter and energy. Together, all these scientific discoveries constituted a changed view of physical nature and contributed to the growing interest in abstraction, as opposed to the mimetic representation of the world, among early-20th-century artists such as Vassily Kandinsky (FIG. 24-7).

VASSILY KANDINSKY A second major German Expressionist group, *Der Blaue Reiter* (The Blue Rider), formed in Munich in 1911. The two founding members, Vassily Kandinsky and Franz Marc, whimsically selected this name because of their mutual interest in the color blue and horses. As did Die Brücke, this group produced paintings that captured their feelings in visual form while also eliciting intense visceral responses from viewers.

Born in Russia, VASSILY KANDINSKY (1866–1944) moved to Munich in 1896 and soon developed a spontaneous and aggressively avant-garde expressive style. Indeed, Kandinsky was one of the first artists to explore complete abstraction, as in *Improvisation 28* (FIG. 24-7), painted in 1912. Kandinsky fueled his elimination of representational elements with his interest in theosophy (a religious and philosophical belief system incorporating a wide

range of tenets from, among other sources, Buddhism and mysticism) and the occult, as well as with advances in the sciences. A true intellectual, widely read in philosophy, religion, history, and the other arts, especially music, Kandinsky was also one of the few early modernists to read with some comprehension the new scientific theories of the era (see "Science and Art in the Early 20th Century," above). Scientists' exploration of atomic structure, for example, convinced Kandinsky that material objects had no real substance, thereby shattering his faith in a world of tangible things. He articulated his ideas in an influential treatise, *Concerning the Spiritual in Art*, published in 1912. Artists, Kandinsky believed, must express their innermost feelings by orchestrating color, form, line, and space. *Improvisation 28* is one of numerous works Kandinsky produced that convey feelings with color juxtapositions, intersecting

24-8 Franz Marc, *Fate of the Animals,* 1913. Oil on canvas, 6′ 4¾″ × 8′ 9½″. Kunstmuseum Basel, Basel.

Marc developed a system of correspondences between specific colors and feelings or ideas. In this apocalyptic scene of animals trapped in a forest, the colors of severity and brutality dominate.

1 ft.

linear elements, and implied spatial relationships. Ultimately, Kandinsky saw these abstractions as evolving blueprints for a more enlightened and liberated society emphasizing spirituality.

FRANZ MARC As did many of the other German Expressionists, Franz Marc (1880–1916), the cofounder of Der Blaue Reiter, grew increasingly pessimistic about the state of humanity, especially as World War I loomed on the horizon. His perception of human beings as deeply flawed led him to turn to the animal world for his subjects. Animals, he believed, were more pure than humanity and thus more appropriate vehicles to express an inner truth. In his quest to imbue his paintings with greater emotional intensity, Marc focused on color and developed a system of correspondences between specific colors and feelings or ideas. In a letter to a fellow Blaue Reiter, Marc explained: "Blue is the *male* principle, severe and spiritual. Yellow is the *female* principle, gentle, happy and sensual. Red is *matter,* brutal and heavy."[3]

Fate of the Animals (FIG. **24-8**) represents the culmination of Marc's efforts to create, in a sense, an iconography of color. Painted in 1913, when the tension of impending cataclysm had pervaded society, the animals appear trapped in a forest amid falling trees, some apocalyptic event destroying both the forest and the animals inhabiting it. The painter distorted the entire scene and shattered it into fragments. Significantly, the lighter and brighter colors—the passive, gentle, and cheerful ones—are absent, and the colors of severity and brutality dominate the work. On the back of the canvas Marc wrote: "All being is flaming suffering." The artist discovered just how well his painting portended war's anguish and tragedy when he ended up at the front the following year. His experiences in battle prompted him to tell his wife in a letter: "[*Fate of the Animals*] is like a premonition of this war—horrible and shattering. I can hardly conceive that I painted it."[4] Marc's contempt for people's inhumanity and his attempt to express that through his art ended, with tragic irony, in his death in action in 1916.

KÄTHE KOLLWITZ The emotional range of German Expressionism extends from passionate protest and satirical bitterness to the poignantly expressed pity for the poor in the prints of Käthe Kollwitz (1867–1945), for example, *Woman with Dead Child* (FIG. **24-9**). Kollwitz and her younger contemporary Paula Modersohn-Becker (1876–1907; FIG. **24-9A**) studied at the Union of Berlin Women Artists and had no formal association with any Expressionist group. Working in a variety of printmaking techniques, including woodcut, lithography, and etching, Kollwitz explored a range of issues from the overtly political to the deeply personal.

24-9A Modersohn-Becker, *Self-Portrait,* 1906.

One image Kollwitz explored in depth, producing a number of print variations, was a mother with her dead child. Although she initially derived the theme from the Christian *Pietà,* Kollwitz transformed it into a universal statement of maternal loss and grief. In the etching and lithograph illustrated here (FIG. 24-9), she replaced the reverence and grace pervading most depictions of Mary holding the dead Christ (FIG. 17-12) with an animalistic passion. The grieving mother ferociously grips the body of her dead child. The primal nature of the undeniably powerful image is in keeping with the aims of the Expressionists. Not since the Gothic age in Germany (FIG. 13-50) had any artist produced a mother-and-son group with a comparable emotional impact. Because Kollwitz used her son Peter as the model for the dead child, the image was no doubt all the more personal to her. The print stands as a poignant premonition. Peter died fighting in World War I at age 21.

EGON SCHIELE Also related in spirit to but not associated with any German Expressionist group was the Austrian artist Egon Schiele (1890–1918), who during his tragically brief but

24-9 KÄTHE KOLLWITZ, *Woman with Dead Child,* 1903. Etching and soft-ground etching, overprinted lithographically with a gold tone plate, 1′ 4⅝″ × 1′ 7⅛″. British Museum, London.

The theme of a mother mourning over her dead child comes from images of the *Pietà* in Christian art, but Kollwitz transformed it into a powerful universal statement of maternal loss and grief.

prolific career produced more than 3,000 paintings and drawings. The bulk of them are nude figure studies of men and women in *gouache* and watercolor on paper, including approximately a hundred self-portraits (FIG. **24-10**) exemplifying early-20th-century Expressionist painters' intense interest in emotional states. As a teenager, Schiele watched the slow, painful deterioration of his father, who contracted syphilis and died when Egon was 15. The experience had a profound impact on the artist, who ever after associated sex with physical and emotional pain and death.

Schiele began formal art training the year after his father died. He enrolled in Vienna's Academy of Fine Art in 1906, where he became a protégé of Gustav Klimt (FIG. 23-29), who invited Schiele to exhibit some of his works with his own and those of, among others, Vincent van Gogh and Edvard Munch. The emotional content of their work made a deep impression upon Schiele, who nonetheless far surpassed van Gogh, Munch, and all of his contemporaries, including the sculptor WILHELM LEHMBRUCK (1881–1919; FIG. **24-10A**), in the portrayal of emaciated bodies and tormented psyches. Indeed, Schiele once spent 24 days in prison for producing what a judge ruled was pornographic art.

24-10A LEHMBRUCK, *Seated Youth,* 1917.

Schiele's 1910 nude portrait of himself grimacing (FIG. 24-10) is a characteristic example of his mature work. He stands frontally, staring at himself in the large mirror he kept in his studio. There is no background. The edges of the paper sever his lower legs and right elbow. In some portraits Schiele portrayed himself with amputated limbs, and his body is always that of a malnourished man whose muscles show through transparent flesh. The pose is awkward, twisted, and pained. The elongated fingers of the hands seem useless, incapable of holding anything. It is hard to imagine a nude body breaking more sharply with the classical tradition of heroic male nudity. Schiele's self-portrait is that of a martyr who has suffered both physically and psychologically. (He portrayed himself in several paintings as Saint Sebastian pierced by arrows.) Schiele's unhappy life ended when he contracted the Spanish flu in 1918. He was only 28 years old.

24-10 EGON SCHIELE, *Nude Self-Portrait, Grimacing,* 1910. Gouache, watercolor, and pencil on paper, 1′ 10″ × 1′ 2¾″. Albertina, Vienna.

Breaking sharply with the academic tradition of heroic male nudity, Schiele, a Viennese Expressionist, often portrayed himself with an emaciated body, twisted limbs, and a grimacing expression.

Europe, 1900 to 1920   **731**

Gertrude and Leo Stein and the Avant-Garde

One of the many unexpected developments in the history of art is that two Americans—Gertrude (1874–1946) and Leo (1872–1947) Stein—played pivotal roles in the history of the European avant-garde. The Steins provided a hospitable environment in their Paris home for artists, writers, musicians, collectors, and critics to socialize and discuss progressive art and ideas. Born in Pennsylvania, the Stein siblings moved to 27 rue de Fleurus in Paris in 1903. Gertrude's experimental writing stimulated her interest in the latest developments in the arts. Conversely, the avant-garde ideas discussed in her home influenced Gertrude's unique poetry, plays, and other works. She is perhaps best known for *The Autobiography of Alice B. Toklas* (1933), a unique memoir written in the persona of her longtime lesbian companion.

The Steins' interest in the exciting and invigorating debates taking place in avant-garde circles led them to welcome visitors to their Saturday salons, which included lectures, thoughtful discussions, and spirited arguments. Often, these gatherings lasted until dawn and included not only their French friends but also visiting Americans, Britons, Swedes, Germans, Hungarians, Spaniards, Poles, and Russians. Among the hundreds who visited the Steins were artists Henri Matisse, Pablo Picasso, Georges Braque, Mary Cassatt, Marcel Duchamp, Alfred Stieglitz, and Arthur B. Davies; writers Ernest Hemingway, F. Scott Fitzgerald, John dos Passos, Jean Cocteau, and Guillaume Apollinaire; art dealers Daniel Kahnweiler and Ambroise Vollard; critics Roger Fry and Clive Bell; and collectors Sergei Shchukin and Ivan Morozov.

The Steins were avid art collectors, and the works they hung in their home attracted many visitors. One of the first paintings Leo purchased was Matisse's notorious *Woman with the Hat* (FIG. 24-2), and he subsequently bought many more by Matisse—including *Le Bonheur de Vivre* (FIG. 24-2A)—along with works by Gauguin, Cézanne, Renoir, Picasso, and Braque. Picasso, who developed a close friendship with Gertrude, painted her portrait (FIG. 24-11) in 1907. Gertrude loved the painting so much she kept it by her all her life and bequeathed it to the Metropolitan Museum of Art only upon her death in 1946.

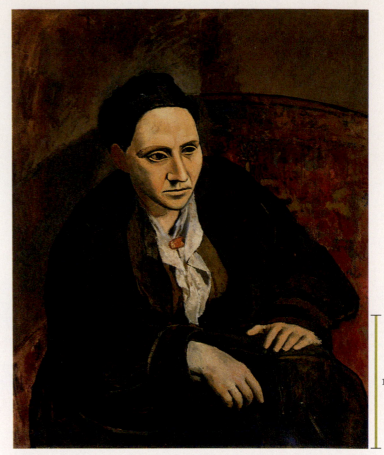

1 ft.

24-11 PABLO PICASSO, *Gertrude Stein,* 1906–1907. Oil on canvas, 3′ 3⅜″ × 2′ 8″. Metropolitan Museum of Art, New York (bequest of Gertrude Stein, 1947). ■◀

Picasso had left this portrait of his friend and patron unfinished until he decided to incorporate the planar simplicity of ancient Iberian stone sculptures into his depiction of her face.

Primitivism and Cubism

The Expressionist departure from any strict adherence to illusionism in art was a path other artists followed. Among those who most radically challenged prevailing artistic conventions and moved most aggressively into the realm of abstraction was Pablo Picasso.

PABLO PICASSO Born in Spain four years after Gustave Courbet's death, PABLO PICASSO (1881–1973) mastered all aspects of late-19th-century Realist technique by the time he entered the Barcelona Academy of Fine Art in the late 1890s. His prodigious talent led him to experiment with a wide range of visual expression, first in Spain and then in Paris, where he settled in 1904. An artist whose importance to the history of art is uncontested, Picasso made staggering contributions to new ways of representing the surrounding world. Perhaps the most prolific artist in history, he explored virtually every artistic medium during his lengthy career, but remained a traditional artist in making careful preparatory studies for each major work. Nonetheless, Picasso epitomized

modernism in his enduring quest for innovation, which resulted in sudden shifts from one style to another. By the time he settled permanently in Paris, Picasso's work had evolved from Spanish painting's sober Realism through an Impressionistic phase to the so-called Blue Period (1901–1904), when, in a melancholy state of mind, he used primarily blue colors to depict worn, pathetic, and alienated figures. In 1904, Picasso's palette changed to lighter and brighter colors during his Rose (or Pink) Period (1904–1906), but some of the canvases he painted during those years, such as *Family of Saltimbanques* (FIG. 24-11A), retain the pessimistic overtones of the Blue Period.

24-11A PICASSO, *Family of Saltimbanques,* 1905.

GERTRUDE STEIN By 1906, Picasso was searching restlessly for new ways to depict form. He found clues in the ancient Iberian sculpture of his homeland and other "primitive" cultures.

1 ft.

Inspired by these sources, Picasso returned to a portrait of *Gertrude Stein* (FIG. **24-11**), his friend and patron (see "Gertrude and Leo Stein and the Avant-Garde," page 732). Picasso had left the portrait unfinished after Stein posed for more than 80 sittings earlier in the year. On resuming work, Picasso painted Stein's head as a simplified planar form, incorporating aspects derived from Iberian stone heads. Although the disparity between the style of the face and the rest of the figure is striking, together they provide an insightful portrait of a forceful, vivacious woman. More important, Picasso had discovered a new approach to the representation of the human form.

DEMOISELLES D'AVIGNON The influence of "primitive" art also surfaces in *Les Demoiselles d'Avignon (The Young Ladies of Avignon;* FIG. **24-12**), which opened the door to a radically new method of representing form in space. Picasso began the work as a symbolic picture to be titled *Philosophical Bordello,* portraying two male clients (who, based on surviving drawings, had features resembling Picasso's) intermingling with women in the reception room of a brothel on Avignon Street in Barcelona. One was a sailor. The other carried a skull, an obvious reference to death. By the time the artist finished, he had eliminated the male figures and simpli-

fied the room's details to a suggestion of drapery and a schematic foreground still life. Picasso had become wholly absorbed in the problem of finding a new way to represent the five female figures in their interior space. Instead of depicting the figures as continuous volumes, he fractured their shapes and interwove them with the equally jagged planes representing drapery and empty space. Indeed, the space, so entwined with the bodies, is virtually illegible. Here Picasso pushed Cézanne's treatment of form and space (FIGS. 23-21 to 23-22A) to a new level. The tension between Picasso's representation of three-dimensional space and his conviction a painting is a two-dimensional design on the surface of a stretched canvas is a tension between representation and abstraction.

The artist extended the radical nature of *Les Demoiselles d'Avignon* even further by depicting the figures inconsistently. Ancient Iberian sculptures inspired the calm, ideal features of the three young women at the left, as they had the head of Gertrude Stein (FIG. 24-11). The energetic, violently striated features of the two heads to the right emerged late in Picasso's production of the work and grew directly from his increasing fascination with the power of African sculpture (see "'Primitivism' and Colonialism," page 734), which the artist studied in Paris's Trocadéro ethnography museum

Primitivism and Colonialism

The art of Africa, Oceania, and the native peoples of the Americas was a major source of inspiration for many early-20th-century modernist artists. Art historians refer to the incorporation of stylistic elements from these "non-Western" cultures as *primitivism*. Both terms imply the superiority of Western civilization and Western art, but many modernist artists admired these artworks precisely because they embodied different stylistic preferences and standards. Some artists, for example Henri Matisse and Pablo Picasso (FIG. 24-13), became enthusiastic collectors of "primitive art," but all of them could view non-Western objects in the many European and American anthropological and ethnographic museums that had begun to proliferate during the second half of the 19th century.

In 1882, the Musée d'Ethnographie du Trocadéro (now the Musée du quai Branly) in Paris opened its doors to the public. The Musée Permanent des Colonies (now the Musée National des Arts d'Afrique et d'Océanie) in Paris also provided the public with a wide array of objects—weapons, tools, basketwork, headdresses—from colonial territories, as did the Musée Africain in Marseilles. In Berlin, the Museum für Völkerkunde housed almost 10,000 African objects by 1886, when it opened for public viewing. Even the Expositions Universelles—regularly scheduled exhibitions in France designed to celebrate industrial progress—included products from Oceania and Africa after 1851. By the beginning of the 20th century, significant non-Western collections were on view in museums in Liverpool, Glasgow, Edinburgh, London, Hamburg, Stuttgart, Vienna, Berlin, Munich, Leiden, Copenhagen, and Chicago.

The formation of these collections was a by-product of the frenzied imperialist expansion central to the geopolitical dynamics of the 19th century and much of the 20th century. Most of the Western powers maintained colonies as raw-material sources, as manufacturing markets, and as territorial acquisitions. For example, the United States, France, and Holland all kept a colonial presence in the Pacific. Britain, France, Germany, Belgium, Holland, Spain, and Portugal divided up the African continent. People often perceived these colonial cultures as "primitive" and referred to many of the non-Western artifacts displayed in museums as "artificial curiosities" or "fetish objects." Indeed, the exhibition of these objects collected during expeditions to the colonies served to reinforce the "need" for a colonial presence in these countries. Colonialism often had a missionary dimension. These objects, which often depicted strange gods or creatures, reinforced the perception these peoples were "barbarians" who needed to be "civilized" or "saved," and this perception justified colonialism and its missionary aspects worldwide.

Whether avant-garde artists were aware of the imperialistic implications of their appropriation of non-Western culture is unclear. Certainly, however, many artists reveled in the energy and freshness of non-Western images and forms. These different cultural products provided Western artists with new ways of looking at their own art. Matisse always maintained he saw African sculptures as simply "good sculptures . . . like any other."* Picasso, in contrast, believed "the masks weren't just like any other pieces of

24-13 FRANK GELETT BURGESS, photograph of Pablo Picasso in his studio in the rue Ravignan, Paris, France, 1908. Musée Picasso, Paris. ◼◂

Picasso was familiar with ancient Iberian art from his homeland and studied African and other "primitive" art in Paris's Trocadéro museum. He kept his own collection of primitive art in his studio.

sculpture. Not at all. They were magic things. . . . mediators" between humans and the forces of evil, and he sought to capture their power as well as their forms in his paintings. "[In the Trocadéro] I understood why I was a painter. . . . All alone in that awful museum, with masks, dolls . . . *Les Demoiselles d'Avignon* [FIG. 24-12] must have come to me that day."† "Primitive art" seemed to embody a directness, closeness to nature, and honesty that appealed to modernist artists determined to reject conventional models. Non-Western art served as an important revitalizing and energizing force in Western art.

*Jean-Louis Paudrat, "From Africa," in William Rubin, ed., *"Primitivism" in 20th Century Art: Affinity of the Tribal and the Modern* (New York: Museum of Modern Art, 1984), 1:141.
†Ibid.

and collected and kept in his Paris studio (FIG. **24-13**). Perhaps responding to the energy of these two new heads, Picasso also revised their bodies. He broke them into more ambiguous planes suggesting a combination of views, as if the observer sees the figures from more than one place in space at once. The woman seated at the lower right shows these multiple angles most clearly, seeming to present the viewer simultaneously with a three-quarter back view from the left, another from the right, and a front view of the head that suggests seeing the figure frontally as well. Gone is the traditional concept of an orderly, constructed, and unified pictorial space mirroring the world. In its place are the rudimentary beginnings of a new representation of the world as a dynamic interplay of time and space. Clearly, *Les Demoiselles d'Avignon* represents a dramatic departure from the careful presentation of a visual reality. Explained Picasso: "I paint forms as I think them, not as I see them."[5]

GEORGES BRAQUE AND CUBISM

For many years, Picasso showed *Les Demoiselles* only to other painters. One of the first to see it was GEORGES BRAQUE (1882–1963), a Fauve painter who found it so challenging he began to rethink his own painting style. Using the painting's revolutionary elements as a point of departure, together Braque and Picasso formulated *Cubism* around 1908 in the belief the art of painting had to move far beyond the description of visual reality. Cubism represented a radical turning point in the history of art, nothing less than a dismissal of the pictorial illusionism that had dominated Western art since the Renaissance. The Cubists rejected naturalistic depictions, preferring compositions of shapes and forms abstracted from the conventionally perceived world. They pursued the analysis of form central to Cézanne's artistic explorations by dissecting everything around them into their many constituent features, which they then recomposed, by a new logic of design, into a coherent, independent aesthetic picture. The Cubists' rejection of accepted artistic practice illustrates both the period's aggressive avant-garde critique of pictorial convention and the public's dwindling faith in a safe, concrete Newtonian world in the face of the physics of Einstein and others (see "Science and Art," page 729).

The new style received its name after Matisse described some of Braque's work to the critic Louis Vauxcelles as having been painted "with little cubes." In his review, Vauxcelles described the new paintings as "cubic oddities."[6] The French writer and theorist Guillaume Apollinaire (1880–1918) summarized well the central concepts of Cubism in 1913:

> Authentic cubism [is] the art of depicting new wholes with formal elements borrowed not from the reality of vision, but from that of conception. This tendency leads to a poetic kind of painting which stands outside the world of observation; for, even in a simple cubism, the geometrical surfaces of an object must be opened out in order to give a complete representation of it. . . . Everyone must agree that a chair, from whichever side it is viewed, never ceases to have four legs, a seat and a back, and that, if it is robbed of one of these elements, it is robbed of an important part.[7]

Most art historians refer to the first phase of Cubism, developed jointly by Picasso and Braque, as *Analytic Cubism*, because in essence it is a painterly analysis of the structure of form. Because Cubists could not achieve the kind of total view Apollinaire described by the traditional method of drawing or painting models from one position, they began to dissect the forms of their subjects and to present their analysis of form across the canvas surface.

THE PORTUGUESE Georges Braque's painting *The Portuguese* (FIG. **24-14**) exemplifies Analytic Cubism. The subject is a Portuguese musician the artist recalled seeing years earlier in a bar in Marseilles. Braque dissected the man and his instrument and placed the resulting forms in dynamic interaction with the space around them. Unlike the Fauves and German Expressionists, who used vibrant colors, the Cubists chose subdued hues—here solely brown tones—in order to focus attention on form. In *The Portuguese*, Braque carried his analysis so far viewers must work diligently to discover clues to the subject. The construction of large intersecting planes suggests the forms of a man and a guitar. Smaller shapes interpenetrate and hover in the large planes. The way Braque treated light and shadow reveals his departure from conventional artistic practice. Light and dark passages suggest both chiaroscuro modeling and transparent planes that enable viewers to see through one level to another. Solid forms emerge only to be canceled almost immediately by a different reading of the subject.

The stenciled letters and numbers Braque included add to the painting's complexity. Letters and numbers are flat shapes, but as elements of a Cubist painting such as *The Portuguese*, they enable the

24-14 GEORGES BRAQUE, *The Portuguese*, 1911. Oil on canvas, 3' 10⅛" × 2' 8". Kunstmuseum Basel, Basel (gift of Raoul La Roche, 1952). ◼◀

The Cubists rejected the pictorial illusionism that had dominated Western art for centuries. Here, Braque concentrated on dissecting form and placing it in dynamic interaction with space.

painter to play with viewers' perception of two- and three-dimensional space. The letters and numbers lie flat on the painted canvas surface, yet the shading and shapes of other forms seem to flow behind and underneath them, pushing the letters and numbers forward into the viewing space. Occasionally, they seem attached to the surface of some object within the painting. Ultimately, the constantly shifting imagery makes it impossible to arrive at any definitive or final reading of the image. Examining this kind of painting is a disconcerting excursion into ambiguity and doubt, especially since the letters and numbers seem to anchor the painting in the world of representation, thereby exacerbating the tension between representation and abstraction. Analytical Cubist paintings radically disrupt expectations about the representation of space and time.

ROBERT DELAUNAY Art historians generally regard the suppression of color as crucial to Cubism's success, but ROBERT DELAUNAY (1885–1941), Picasso's and Braque's contemporary, worked toward a kind of color Cubism. Apollinaire gave the name *Orphism* to Delaunay's version of Cubism, after Orpheus, the Greek god of music. Apollinaire believed art, like music, was distinct from the representation of the visible world. But Delaunay's own name for his art was *Simultanéisme.* "Simultaneity" for Delaunay meant the application of 19th-century theories about the perception and psychology of color (see "19th-Century Color Theory," Chapter 23, page 701) to create spatial effects and kaleidoscopic movement solely through color contrasts. He insisted color in painting was both form and subject, and as early as 1912 he began to paint purely abstract compositions with titles such as *Simultaneous Disks, Simultaneous Windows,* and *Simultaneous Contrasts.* Delaunay developed his ideas about color use in dialogue with his Russian-born wife, Sonia (1885–1974), also an important modernist artist. She created paintings, quilts, and other textile arts, and book covers that exploited the expressive capabilities of color. As a result of their artistic explorations, both Delaunays became convinced the rhythms of modern life could best be expressed through color harmonies and dissonances.

A salient feature of modern life for Delaunay was technological innovation, and the engineering marvels of the late 19th and early 20th centuries figure prominently in his paintings. In 1914 he immortalized the engineer, inventor, and aviator Louis Blériot (1872–1936) in one of his boldest Orphic canvases. *Homage to Blériot* (FIG. **24-15**) is an almost purely abstract composition that celebrates Blériot's great achievement of being the first person to fly across the English Channel, which he accomplished in a monoplane of his own design. The 22-mile flight from Les Barraques, near Calais, France, to Dover, England, on July 25, 1909, lasted 37 minutes and made Blériot an instant international celebrity. It also brought him a prize of 1,000 British pounds, which a London newspaper had offered as a challenge to all aviators. At the time Delaunay commemorated the event, Blériot was manufacturing warplanes for use by French pilots and their allies during World War I. Blériot's monoplane appears at the upper right of Delaunay's painting, above another triumph of French engineering, the Eiffel

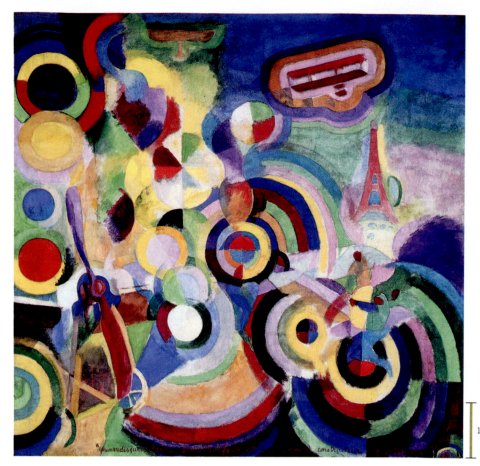

24-15 ROBERT DELAUNAY, *Homage to Blériot,* 1914. Oil on canvas, 8' 2½" × 8' 3". Kunstmuseum Basel, Basel (Emanuel Hoffman Foundation).

In this Orphic Cubist composition, Delaunay paid tribute to Louis Blériot, the first person to fly across the English Channel. Blériot's monoplane is at the upper right, above the Eiffel Tower.

Tower (FIG. 23-38), one of Delaunay's favorite subjects (FIG. **24-15A**). Filling the rest of the canvas are a propeller (at the lower left) and mostly circular abstract shapes suggestive of whirling propellers and blazing suns.

SYNTHETIC CUBISM In 1912, Cubism entered a new phase that art historians have dubbed *Synthetic Cubism.* In this later Cubist style, instead of dissecting forms, artists constructed paintings and

24-15A DELAUNAY, *Champs de Mars,* 1911.

drawings from objects and shapes cut from paper or other materials. The work marking the point of departure for this new style was Picasso's *Still Life with Chair-Caning* (FIG. **24-16**), a mixed-media painting in which Picasso imprinted a photolithographed pattern of a cane chair seat on the canvas and then pasted a piece of oilcloth on it. Framed with rope, this work challenges viewers' understanding of reality. The photographically replicated chair caning seems so "real" one expects the holes to break any brushstrokes laid upon it. But the chair caning, although optically suggestive of the real, is only an illusion or representation of an object. In contrast, the painted abstract areas do not refer to tangible objects in the real world. Yet the fact they do not imitate anything makes them more "real" than the chair caning. No pretense exists. Picasso extended the visual play by making the letter *U* escape from the space of the accompanying *J* and *O*

Picasso on Cubism

In 1923, almost a decade after Picasso and Braque launched an artistic revolution with their Analytic (FIG. 24-14) and Synthetic (FIG. 24-16) Cubist paintings, Picasso granted an interview to the painter and critic Marius de Zayas (1880–1961). Born in Mexico, de Zayas had settled in New York City in 1907, and in 1911 had been instrumental in mounting the first exhibition in the United States of Picasso's works. In their conversation, the approved English translation of which appeared in the journal *The Arts* under the title "Picasso Speaks," the artist set forth his views about Cubism and the nature of art in general.

We all know that Art is not truth. Art is a lie that makes us realize truth, at least the truth that is given us to understand. The artist must know the manner whereby to convince others of the truthfulness of his lies. . . . They speak of naturalism in opposition to modern painting. I would like to know if anyone has ever seen a natural work of art. Nature and art, being two different things, cannot be the same thing. Through art we express our conception of what nature is not. . . .

Cubism is no different from any other school of painting. The same principles and the same elements are common to all. . . . Many think that Cubism is an art of transition, an experiment which is to bring ulterior results. Those who think that way have not understood it. Cubism is not either a seed or a foetus, but an art dealing primarily with forms, and when a form is realized it is there to live its own life. . . . Mathematics, trigonometry, chemistry, psychoanalysis, music, and whatnot, have been related to Cubism to give it an easier interpretation. All this has been pure literature, not to say nonsense, . . . Cubism has kept itself within the limits and limitations of painting, never pretending to go beyond it. Drawing, design, and color are understood and practiced in Cubism in the spirit and manner that they are understood and practiced in all other schools. Our subjects might be different, as we have introduced into painting objects and forms that were formerly ignored. . . . [I]n our subjects, we keep the joy of discovery, the pleasure of the unexpected; our subject itself must be a source of interest.*

*Marius de Zayas, "Picasso Speaks," *The Arts* (May 1923), 315–326. Reprinted in Herschel B. Chipp, *Theories of Modern Art: A Source Book by Artists and Critics* (Berkeley and Los Angeles: University of California Press, 1968), 263–266.

24-16 PABLO PICASSO, *Still Life with Chair-Caning*, 1912. Oil, oilcloth, and rope on canvas, $10\frac{5}{8}'' \times 1' 1\frac{3}{4}''$. Musée Picasso, Paris. ◼◀

This painting includes a piece of oilcloth imprinted with the photolithographed pattern of a cane chair seat. Framed with a piece of rope, the still life challenges the viewer's understanding of reality.

1 in.

and partially covering it with a cylindrical shape that pushes across its left side. The letters *JOU*, which appear in many Cubist paintings, formed part of the masthead of the daily French newspapers (*journaux*) often found among the objects represented. Picasso and Braque especially delighted in the punning references to *jouer* and *jouir*—the French verbs meaning "to play" and "to enjoy."

Although most discussions of Cubism focus on the formal innovations of Picasso, Braque, and Delaunay, it is important to note that the public also viewed the revolutionary nature of Cubism in sociopolitical terms. Many people considered Cubism's challenge to artistic convention and tradition a subversive attack on 20th-century society. In fact, many modernist artists and writers of the period allied themselves with various anarchist groups whose social critiques and utopian visions appealed to progressive thinkers. It was, therefore, not difficult to see radical art, such as Cubism, as having political ramifications. Many critics in the French press consistently equated Cubism's disdain for tradition with anarchism and revolution. Picasso himself, however, never viewed Cubism as a protest movement or even different in kind from traditional painting (see "Picasso on Cubism," above).

24-17 GEORGES BRAQUE, *Bottle, Newspaper, Pipe, and Glass,* 1913. Charcoal and various papers pasted on paper, 1′ 6⅞″ × 2′ 1¼″. Private collection, New York. ∎◀

This Cubist collage of glued paper is a visual game to be deciphered. The pipe in the foreground, for example, seems to lie on the newspaper, but it is a cutout revealing the canvas surface.

1 in.

COLLAGE After *Still Life with Chair-Caning,* both Picasso and Braque continued to explore the medium of *collage* introduced into the realm of "high art" (as opposed to unselfconscious "folk art") in that work. From the French word *coller,* meaning "to stick," a collage is a composition of bits of objects, such as newspaper or cloth, glued to a surface. Braque's *Bottle, Newspaper, Pipe, and Glass* (FIG. **24-17**) is a type of collage called *papier collé* ("stuck paper") in which the artist glues assorted paper shapes to a drawing or painting. In Braque's papier collé, charcoal lines and shadows provide clues to the Cubist multiple views of various surfaces and objects. Roughly rectangular strips of printed and colored paper dominate the composition. The paper imprinted with wood grain and moldings provides an illusion whose concreteness contrasts with the lightly rendered objects on the right. Five pieces of paper overlap one another in the center of the composition to create a layering of flat planes that both echo the space the lines suggest and establish the flatness of the work's surface. All shapes in the image seem to oscillate, pushing forward and dropping back in space. Shading seems to carve space into flat planes in some places and to turn planes into transparent surfaces in others. The pipe in the foreground illustrates this complex visual interplay especially well. Although it appears to lie on the newspaper, it is in fact a form cut through the printed paper to reveal the canvas surface, which Braque lightly modeled with charcoal. The artist thus kept his audience aware that *Bottle, Newspaper, Pipe, and Glass* is an artwork, a visual game to be deciphered, and not an attempt to reproduce nature.

Picasso explained the goals of Cubist collage in this way:

> Not only did we try to displace reality; reality was no longer in the object. . . . [In] the *papier collé* . . . [w]e didn't any longer want to fool the eye; we wanted to fool the mind. . . . If a piece of newspaper can be a bottle, that gives us something to think about in connection with both newspapers and bottles, too.[8]

Like all collage, the papier collé technique was modern in its medium—mass-produced materials never before found in high art—and modern in the way the artist embedded the art's "message" in the imagery and in the nature of these everyday materials.

GUERNICA Picasso continued to experiment with different artistic styles and media right up until his death in 1973. Celebrated primarily for his brilliant formal innovations, he was nonetheless acutely aware of politics throughout his life. As Picasso watched his homeland descend into civil war in the late 1930s, his involvement in political issues grew even stronger. He declared: "[P]ainting is not made to decorate apartments. It is an instrument for offensive and defensive war against the enemy."[9] Picasso got the opportunity to use art as a weapon in January 1937 when the Spanish Republican government-in-exile in Paris asked Picasso to produce a major work for the Spanish Pavilion at the Paris International Exposition that summer. He did not formally accept the invitation, however, until he received word that Guernica, the capital of the Basque region (an area in southern France and northern Spain populated by Basque speakers), had been almost totally destroyed in an air raid on April 26, 1937. Nazi pilots acting on behalf of the rebel general Francisco Franco (1892–1975) bombed the city at the busiest hour of a market day, killing or wounding many of Guernica's 7,000 citizens as well as leveling buildings. The event jolted Picasso into action. By the end of June, he had completed *Guernica* (FIG. **24-18**), a mural-sized canvas of immense power.

Despite the painting's title, Picasso made no specific reference to the event in *Guernica.* The imagery includes no bombs and no German planes. It is a universal visceral outcry of human grief. In the center, along the lower edge of the painting, lies a slain warrior clutching a broken and useless sword. A gored horse tramples him and rears back in fright as it dies. On the left, a shrieking, anguished woman cradles her dead child. On the far right, a woman on fire runs screaming from a burning building, while another woman flees mindlessly. In the upper right corner, a woman, represented by only a head, emerges from the burning building, thrusting forth a light to illuminate the horror. Overlooking the destruction is a bull, which, according to the artist, represents "brutality and darkness."[10]

In *Guernica,* Picasso brilliantly used aspects of his earlier Cubist discoveries to expressive effect, particularly the fragmentation of objects and the dislocation of anatomical features. This Cubist

24-18 PABLO PICASSO, *Guernica*, 1937. Oil on canvas, 11′ 5½″ × 25′ 5¾″. Museo Nacional Centro de Arte Reina Sofía, Madrid. ◼◀

Picasso used Cubist techniques, especially the fragmentation of objects and dislocation of anatomical features, to expressive effect in this condemnation of the Nazi bombing of the Basque capital.

fragmentation gave visual form to the horror of the aerial bombardment of the Basque people. What happened to these figures in the artist's act of painting—the dissections and contortions of the human form—paralleled what happened to them in real life. To emphasize the scene's severity and starkness, Picasso reduced his palette to black, white, and shades of gray, suppressing color once again, as he had in his Analytic Cubist works.

GUITAR Cubism not only opened new avenues for representing form on two-dimensional surfaces. It also inspired new approaches to sculpture. Picasso created *Guitar* (FIG. **24-19**) in 1912. As in his Cubist paintings, this sculpture operates at the intersection of two- and three-dimensionality. Picasso took the form of a guitar—an image that surfaces in many of his paintings as well, including *Three Musicians* (FIG. **24-19A**)—

24-19A PICASSO, *Three Musicians*, 1921.

and explored its volume via flat planar cardboard surfaces. (FIG. 24-19 reproduces the *maquette*, or model. The finished sculpture was to be made of sheet metal.) By presenting what is essentially a cutaway view of a guitar, Picasso allowed viewers to examine both surface and interior space, both mass and void. This, of course, was completely in keeping with the Cubist program. Some scholars have suggested Picasso derived the cylindrical form that serves as the sound hole on the guitar from the eyes on masks from the Ivory Coast of Africa. African masks were a continuing and persistent source of inspiration for the artist (see "Primitivism," page 734). Here, however, Picasso seems to have transformed the anatomical features of African masks into a part of a musical instrument—dramatic evidence of his unique, innovative artistic vision. Ironically—and intentionally—the sound hole, the central void in a real guitar, is, in Picasso's *Guitar*, the only solid form.

24-19 PABLO PICASSO, maquette for *Guitar*, 1912. Cardboard, string, and wire (restored), 2′ 1¼″ × 1′ 1″ × 7½″. Museum of Modern Art, New York.

In this model for a sculpture of sheet metal, Picasso presented what is essentially a cutaway view of a guitar, allowing the viewer to examine both surface and interior space, both mass and void.

24-20 ALEKSANDR ARCHIPENKO, *Woman Combing Her Hair*, 1915. Bronze, 1' 1¾" × 3¼" × 3⅛". Museum of Modern Art, New York (acquired through the Lillie P. Bliss Bequest).

In this statuette, Archipenko introduced, in place of the head, a void with a shape of its own that figures importantly in the whole design. The void is not simply the negative counterpart of the volume.

1 in.

1 ft.

24-21 JULIO GONZÁLEZ, *Woman Combing Her Hair*, 1936. Iron, 4' 4" × 1' 11½" × 2' ⅝". Museum of Modern Art, New York (Mrs. Simon Guggenheim Fund).

Using prefabricated metal pieces, González reduced his figure to an interplay of curves, lines, and planes—virtually a complete abstraction without any vestiges of traditional representational art.

ALEKSANDR ARCHIPENKO The Russian sculptor ALEKSANDR ARCHIPENKO (1887–1964) similarly explored the Cubist notion of spatial ambiguity and the relationship between solid forms and space. In *Woman Combing Her Hair* (FIG. 24-20), Archipenko introduced, in place of the head, a void with a shape of its own that figures importantly in the whole design. Enclosed spaces have always existed in figurative sculpture—for example, the space between the arm and the body when the hand rests on the hip (FIG. 16-13). But in Archipenko's statuette the space penetrates the figure's continuous mass and is a defined form equal in importance to the mass of the bronze. It is not simply the negative counterpart to the volume as it is in traditional statues. Archipenko's *Woman* shows the same fluid intersecting planes seen in Cubist painting, and the relation of the planes to each other is equally complex. Thus, both in painting and sculpture, the Cubists broke through traditional limits and transformed these media.

JULIO GONZÁLEZ Among the other notable sculptors of the early 20th century were JULIO GONZÁLEZ (1876–1942; FIG. 24-21) and JACQUES LIPCHITZ (1891–1973). Lipchitz's works, such as *Bather* (FIG. 24-21A), are three-dimensional equivalents of the Analytical Cubist canvases of Picasso and Braque (FIG. 24-14). González was a friend of Picasso who shared his interest in the artistic possibilities of new materials and new methods borrowed from both industrial technology and

24-21A LIPCHITZ, *Bather*, 1917.

24-22 FERNAND LÉGER, *The City,* 1919. Oil on canvas, 7′ 7″ × 9′ 9½″. Philadelphia Museum of Art, Philadelphia (A. E. Gallatin Collection).

Léger championed the "machine aesthetic." In *The City,* he captured the mechanical commotion of urban life, incorporating the effects of billboard ads, flashing lights, and noisy traffic.

1 ft.

traditional metalworking. Born into a family of metalworkers in Barcelona, González helped Picasso construct a number of welded sculptures. This contact with Picasso in turn enabled González to refine his own sculptural vocabulary. Using prefabricated bars, sheets, or rods of welded or wrought iron and bronze, González created dynamic sculptures with both linear elements and volumetric forms. A comparison between his *Woman Combing Her Hair* (FIG. 24-21) and Archipenko's version of the same subject (FIG. 24-20) is instructive. Archipenko's figure still incorporates the basic shapes of a woman's body. González reduced his figure to an interplay of curves, lines, and planes—virtually a complete abstraction without any vestiges of traditional representational art. Although González's sculpture received only limited exposure during his lifetime, his work greatly influenced later abstract artists working in welded metal (FIG. 25-16).

FERNAND LÉGER AND PURISM Best known today as one of the most important modernist architects, Le Corbusier (FIG. 24-68) was also a painter. In 1918 he founded a movement called *Purism,* which opposed Synthetic Cubism on the grounds it was becoming merely an esoteric, decorative art out of touch with the machine age. Purists maintained machinery's clean functional lines and the pure forms of its parts should direct artists' experiments in design, whether in painting, architecture, or industrially produced objects. This "machine aesthetic" inspired FERNAND LÉGER (1881–1955), a French artist who had painted with the Cubists. He devised an effective compromise of tastes, bringing together meticulous Cubist analysis of form with Purism's broad simplification and machinelike finish of the design components. He retained from his Cubist practice a preference for cylindrical and tube-shaped motifs, suggestive of machined parts such as pistons and cylinders.

Léger's works have the sharp precision of the machine, whose beauty and quality he was one of the first artists to appreciate. For example, in his film *Ballet Mécanique* (1924), Léger contrasted inanimate objects such as functioning machines with humans in dancelike variations. Preeminently the painter of modern urban life, Léger incorporated into works such as *The City* (FIG. **24-22**) the massive effects of modern posters and billboard advertisements, the harsh flashing of electric lights, and the noise of traffic. The monumental scale of *The City,* an early work incorporating the aesthetic of Synthetic Cubism, suggests Léger, had he been given the opportunity, would have been one of the great mural painters of his age. In a definitive way, he depicted the mechanical commotion of urban life, including the robotic movements of mechanized people (FIG. **24-22A**).

24-22A LÉGER, *Three Women*, 1921.

Futurism

Artists associated with another early-20th-century movement, *Futurism,* pursued many of the ideas the Cubists explored. Equally important to the Futurists, however, was their well-defined sociopolitical agenda. Inaugurated and given its name by the charismatic Italian poet and playwright Filippo Tommaso Marinetti (1876–1944) in 1909, Futurism began as a literary movement but soon encompassed the visual arts, cinema, theater, music, and architecture. Indignant over the political and cultural decline of Italy, the Futurists published numerous manifestos in which they aggressively

Futurist Manifestos

On April 11, 1910, a group of young Italian artists published *Futurist Painting: Technical Manifesto* in Milan in an attempt to apply the writer Filippo Tommaso Marinetti's views on literature to the visual arts. Signed jointly by Umberto Boccioni, Carlo Carrà, Luigi Russolo, Giacomo Balla, and Gino Severini, the manifesto also appeared in an English translation supervised by Marinetti himself. It states in part:

On account of the persistency of an image on the retina, moving objects constantly multiply themselves [and] their form changes . . . Thus a running horse has not four legs, but twenty. . . .

What was true for the painters of yesterday is but a falsehood today. . . . To paint a human figure you must not paint it; you must render the whole of its surrounding atmosphere. . . . [T]he vivifying current of science [must] soon deliver painting from academic tradition. . . . The shadows which we shall paint shall be more luminous than the highlights of our predecessors, and our pictures, next to those of the museums, will shine like blinding daylight compared with deepest night. . . .

We declare . . . that all forms of imitation must be despised, all forms of originality glorified . . . that all subjects previously used must be swept aside in order to express our whirling life of steel, of pride, of fever and of speed . . . that movement and light destroy the materiality of bodies.*

Two years later, Boccioni published a *Technical Manifesto of Futurist Sculpture,* in which he argued traditional sculpture was "a monstrous anachronism" and modern sculpture should be

a translation, in plaster, bronze, glass, wood or any other material, of those atmospheric planes which bind and intersect things. . . . Let's . . . proclaim the absolute and complete abolition of finite lines and the contained statue. Let's split open our figures and place the environment inside them. We declare that the environment must form part of the plastic whole.†

24-23 Giacomo Balla, *Dynamism of a Dog on a Leash,* 1912. Oil on canvas, 2′ 11⅜″ × 3′ 7¼″. Albright-Knox Art Gallery, Buffalo (bequest of A. Conger Goodyear, gift of George F. Goodyear, 1964). ◼◣

The Futurists' interest in motion and in the Cubist dissection of form is evident in Balla's painting of a passing dog and its owner. Simultaneity of views was central to the Futurist program.

The sculptures of Boccioni (FIG. 24-24) and the paintings of Balla (FIG. 24-23) and Severini (FIG. 24-25) are the perfect expressions of these Futurist principles and goals.

*Futurist Painting: Technical Manifesto (Poesia, April 11, 1910). Translated by Filippo Tommaso Marinetti, in Umbro Apollonio, ed., *Futurist Manifestos* (Boston: Museum of Fine Arts, 1970), 27–31.
†Translated by Robert Brain, in Apollonio, *Futurist Manifestos,* 51–65.

---

advocated revolution, both in society and in art. As did Die Brücke, the Futurists aimed at ushering in a new, more enlightened era.

In their quest to launch Italian society toward a glorious future, the Futurists championed war as a means of washing away the stagnant past. Indeed, they saw war as a cleansing agent. Marinetti declared: "We will glorify war—the only true hygiene of the world."[11] The Futurists agitated for the destruction of museums, libraries, and similar repositories of accumulated culture, which they described as mausoleums. They also called for radical innovation in the arts. Of particular interest to the Futurists were the speed and dynamism of modern technology, an interest shared by Delaunay (FIGS. 24-15 and 24-15A) and Léger (FIGS. 24-22 and 24-22A). Marinetti insisted a racing "automobile adorned with great pipes like serpents with explosive breath . . . is more beautiful than the *Victory of Samothrace*"[12]—a reference to the Greek statue (FIG. 5-82) in the Musée du Louvre that for early-20th-century artists represented classicism and the glories of past civilizations.

Appropriately, Futurist art often focused on motion in time and space, incorporating the Cubist discoveries derived from the analysis of form.

GIACOMO BALLA The Futurists' interest in motion and in the Cubist dissection of form is evident in *Dynamism of a Dog on a Leash* (FIG. **24-23**), in which GIACOMO BALLA (1871–1958) represented a passing dog and its owner, whose skirts are just within visual range. Balla achieved the effect of motion by repeating shapes, for example, the dog's legs and tail and the swinging line of the leash. Simultaneity of views, as in Cubism, was central to the Futurist program (see "Futurist Manifestos," above).

UMBERTO BOCCIONI One of the cosigners of the Futurist manifesto was UMBERTO BOCCIONI (1882–1916), who produced what is perhaps the definitive work of Futurist sculpture, *Unique Forms of Continuity in Space* (FIG. 24-24). This piece highlights the formal and spatial effects of motion rather than their source,

24-24 UMBERTO BOCCIONI, *Unique Forms of Continuity in Space*, 1913 (cast 1931). Bronze, 3′ 7⅞″ × 2′ 10⅞″ × 1′ 3¾″. Museum of Modern Art, New York (acquired through the Lillie P. Bliss Bequest). ◼◀

Boccioni's Futurist manifesto for sculpture advocated abolishing the enclosed statue. This running figure's body is so expanded it almost disappears behind the blur of its movement.

24-25 GINO SEVERINI, *Armored Train*, 1915. Oil on canvas, 3′ 10″ × 2′ 10⅛″. Collection of Richard S. Zeisler, New York. ◼◀

Severini's glistening armored train with protruding cannon reflects the Futurist faith in the cleansing action of war. The painting captures the dynamism and motion central to the Futurist manifesto.

the striding human figure. The figure is so expanded, interrupted, and broken in plane and contour it almost disappears behind the blur of its movement—just as people, buildings, and stationary objects become blurred when seen from an automobile traveling at great speed on a highway. Boccioni's search for sculptural means for expressing dynamic movement reached a monumental expression in *Unique Forms*. In its power and sense of vital activity, this sculpture surpasses similar efforts in Futurist painting to create images symbolic of the dynamic quality of modern life. Although Boccioni's figure bears a curious resemblance to the *Nike of Samothrace* (FIG. 5-82), the ancient sculptor suggested motion only through posture and agitated drapery, not through distortion and fragmentation of the human body.

This Futurist representation of motion in sculpture has its limitations, however. The eventual development of the motion picture, based on the rapid sequential projection of fixed images, produced more convincing illusions of movement. And several decades later in sculpture, Alexander Calder (FIG. 24-78) pioneered the development of kinetic sculpture—sculptures with parts that really move. But in the early 20th century, Boccioni was unsurpassed for his ability to capture the sensation of motion in statuary.

GINO SEVERINI The painting *Armored Train* (FIG. **24-25**) by GINO SEVERINI (1883–1966) also encapsulates the Futurist program—politically as well as artistically. Severini depicted a high-tech armored train with its rivets glistening and a huge booming cannon protruding from the top. Submerged in the bowels of the train, soldiers in a row point guns at an unseen target. In Cubist fashion, Severini depicted all of the elements of the painting, from the soldiers to the smoke emanating from the cannon, broken into facets and planes, suggesting action and movement. *Armored Train* reflects the Futurists' passion for speed and the "whirling life of steel," and their faith in the cleansing action of war. Not only are the colors predominantly light and bright, but death and destruction—the tragic consequences of war—are absent from Severini's painting. This sanitized depiction of armed conflict contrasts sharply with Francisco Goya's *The Third of May, 1808* (FIG. 22-11), which also depicts a uniform row of anonymous soldiers in the act of shooting. Goya, however, graphically presented the dead and those about to be shot, and the dark tones he used cast a dramatic and sobering pall.

Once World War I broke out, the Futurist group began to disintegrate, largely because so many of them felt compelled (given the Futurist support for the war) to join the Italian Army. Some of them, including Umberto Boccioni, died in the war.

Dada

Although the Futurists celebrated World War I and the changes they hoped it would effect, the mass destruction and chaos that conflict unleashed horrified other artists. Humanity had never before witnessed such wholesale slaughter on so grand a scale over such an extended period. Millions died or sustained grievous wounds in great battles. For example, in 1916, the battle of Verdun (lasting five months) produced a half million casualties. The new technology of armaments, bred from the age of steel, made the Great War a "war of the guns." In the face of massed artillery hurling millions of tons of high explosives and gas shells and in the sheets of fire from thousands of machine guns in armored vehicles of the kind celebrated in Futurist canvases (FIG. 24-25), attack was suicidal. Battle movement congealed into the stalemate of trench warfare, stretching from the English Channel almost to Switzerland. The mud, filth, and blood of the trenches, the pounding and shattering of incessant shell fire, and the terrible deaths and mutilations were a devastating psychological, as well as physical, experience for a generation brought up with the doctrine of progress and a belief in the fundamental values of civilization. The introduction of poison gas in 1915 added to the horror of humankind's inhumanity.

With the war as a backdrop, many artists contributed to the artistic and literary movement that became known as *Dada* (see page 723). This movement emerged, in large part, in reaction to what many of these artists saw as nothing more than an insane spectacle of collective homicide. Although Dada began independently in New York and Zurich, it also emerged in Paris, Berlin, and Cologne, among other cities. Dada was more a mind-set or attitude than a single identifiable style. As André Breton (1896–1966), founder of the slightly later Surrealist movement, explained: "Cubism was a school of painting, futurism a political movement: DADA is a state of mind."[13] The Dadaists believed Enlightenment reasoning had produced global devastation, and consequently they turned away from logic in favor of the irrational. Thus, an element of absurdity is a cornerstone of Dada—reflected in the movement's very name. Many explanations exist for the choice of "Dada," but according to an oft-repeated anecdote, the Dadaists chose the word at random by sticking a knife into a French-German dictionary (hence the title Hannah Höch chose for her Dada photomontage (FIG. 24-1). *Dada* is French for "a child's hobby horse." The word satisfied the Dadaists' desire for something nonsensical.

The Dadaists' pessimism and disgust surfaced in their disdain for convention and tradition. These artists made a concerted and sustained attempt to undermine cherished notions and assumptions about art. Because of this destructive dimension, art historians often describe Dada as a nihilistic enterprise. Dada's nihilism and its derisive iconoclasm can be read at random from the Dadaists' numerous manifestos and declarations of intent:

> Dada knows everything. Dada spits on everything. Dada says "knowthing," Dada has no fixed ideas. Dada does not catch flies. Dada is bitterness laughing at everything that has been accomplished, sanctified. . . . Dada is never right. . . . No more painters, no more writers, no more religions, no more royalists, no more anarchists, no more socialists, no more police, no more airplanes, no more urinary passages. . . . Like everything in life, Dada is useless, everything happens in a completely idiotic way. . . . We are incapable of treating seriously any subject whatsoever, let alone this subject: ourselves.[14]

Although cynicism and pessimism inspired the Dadaists, what they developed was phenomenally influential and powerful. By attacking convention and logic, the Dada artists unlocked new avenues for creative invention, thereby fostering a more serious examination of the basic premises of art than had prior movements. But the Dadaists could also be lighthearted in their subversiveness. Although horror and disgust about the war initially prompted Dada, an undercurrent of humor and whimsy—sometimes sardonic or irreverent—runs through much of the art. For example, Marcel Duchamp painted a moustache and goatee on a reproduction of Leonardo's *Mona Lisa* (FIG. 24-27A). The French painter Francis Picabia (1879–1953), Duchamp's collaborator in setting up Dada in New York, nailed a toy monkey to a board and labeled it *Portrait of Cézanne*.

In its emphasis on the spontaneous and intuitive, Dada paralleled the views of Sigmund Freud (1856–1939) and Carl Jung (1875–1961). Freud was a Viennese doctor who developed the fundamental principles for what became known as psychoanalysis. In his book *The Interpretation of Dreams* (1900), Freud argued unconscious and inner drives (of which people are largely unaware) control human behavior. Jung, a Swiss psychiatrist who developed Freud's theories further, believed the unconscious is composed of two facets, a personal unconscious and a collective unconscious. The collective unconscious comprises memories and associations all humans share, such as archetypes and mental constructions. According to Jung, the collective unconscious accounts for the development of myths, religions, and philosophies.

Particularly interested in the exploration of the unconscious that Freud advocated, the Dada artists believed art was a powerfully practical means of self-revelation and catharsis, and the images arising out of the subconscious mind had a truth of their own, independent of conventional vision. A Dada filmmaker, Hans Richter (1888–1976), summarized the attitude of the Dadaists:

> Possessed, as we were, of the ability to entrust ourselves to "chance," to our conscious as well as our unconscious minds, we became a sort of public secret society. . . . We laughed at everything. . . . But laughter was only the expression of our new discoveries, not their essence and not their purpose. Pandemonium, destruction, anarchy, anti-everything of the World War? How could Dada have been anything but destructive, aggressive, insolent, on principle and with gusto?[15]

JEAN ARP One prominent Dada artist whose works illustrate Richter's element of chance was Zurich-based JEAN (HANS) ARP (1887–1966). Arp pioneered the use of chance in composing his images. Tiring of the look of some Cubist-related collages he was making, he took some sheets of paper, tore them into roughly shaped squares, haphazardly dropped them onto a sheet of paper on the floor, and glued them into the resulting arrangement. The rectilinearity of the shapes guaranteed a somewhat regular design (which Arp no doubt enhanced by adjusting the random arrangement into a quasi-grid), but chance had introduced an imbalance that seemed to Arp to restore to his work a special mysterious vitality he wanted to preserve. *Collage Arranged According to the Laws of Chance* (FIG. **24-26**) is one of the works he created by this method. The operations of chance were for Dadaists a crucial part of this kind of improvisation. As Richter stated: "For us chance was the 'unconscious mind' that Freud had discovered in 1900. . . . Adoption of chance had another purpose, a secret one. This was to restore to the work of art its primeval magic power and to find a way back to the immediacy it had lost through contact with . . . classicism."[16] Arp's

In this collage, Arp dropped torn paper squares onto a sheet of paper and then glued them where they fell. His reliance on chance in composing images reinforced the anarchy inherent in Dada.

renunciation of artistic control and reliance on chance when creating his compositions reinforced the anarchy and subversiveness inherent in Dada.

MARCEL DUCHAMP Perhaps the most influential Dadaist was MARCEL DUCHAMP (1887–1968), a Frenchman who became the central artist of New York Dada but was also active in Paris. In 1913, he exhibited his first "readymade" sculptures, which were mass-produced common objects—"found objects" the artist selected and sometimes "rectified" by modifying their substance or combining them with another object. The creation of readymades, he insisted, was free from any consideration of either good or bad taste, qualities shaped by a society he and other Dada artists found aesthetically bankrupt. Perhaps his most outrageous readymade was *Fountain* (FIG. 24-27), a porcelain urinal presented on its back, signed "R. Mutt," and dated (1917). The "artist's signature" was, in fact, a witty pseudonym derived from the Mott plumbing company's name and that of the shorter man of the then-popular Mutt and Jeff comic-strip duo. As with Duchamp's other readymades and "assisted readymades" such as *L.H.O.O.Q.* (FIG. 24-27A), he did not select the urinal for exhibition because of its aesthetic qualities. The "art" of this "artwork" lay in the artist's choice of object, which had the effect of conferring the status of art on it and forcing viewers to see the object in a new light. As Duchamp wrote in a "defense" published in 1917, after an exhibition committee rejected *Fountain* for display: "Whether Mr. Mutt with his own hands made the fountain or not has no importance. He CHOSE it. He took an ordinary article of life, placed it so that its useful significance disappeared under the new title and point of view—created a new thought for that object."[17] It is hard to imagine a more aggressive challenge to artistic conventions than Dada works such as *Fountain*.

24-27A Duchamp, *L.H.O.O.Q.*, 1919.

24-27 MARCEL DUCHAMP, *Fountain* (second version), 1950 (original version produced 1917). Glazed sanitary china with black paint, 1' high. Philadelphia Museum of Art, Philadelphia.

Duchamp's "readymade" sculptures were mass-produced objects the Dada artist modified. In *Fountain*, he conferred the status of art on a urinal and forced people to see the object in a new light.

1 ft.

24-28 MARCEL DUCHAMP, *The Bride Stripped Bare by Her Bachelors, Even (The Large Glass)*, 1915–1923. Oil, lead, wire, foil, dust, and varnish on glass, 9′ 1½″ × 5′ 9⅛″. Philadelphia Museum of Art, Philadelphia (Katherine S. Dreier Bequest).

The Large Glass is a simultaneously playful and serious examination of humans as machines. The bride is a motor fueled by "love gasoline," and the male figures in the lower half also move mechanically.

THE LARGE GLASS Among the most visually and conceptually challenging of Duchamp's works is *The Bride Stripped Bare by Her Bachelors, Even* (FIG. **24-28**), often called *The Large Glass.* Begun in 1915 and abandoned by Duchamp as unfinished in 1923, *The Large Glass* is a simultaneously playful and serious examination of humans as machines. Consisting of oil paint, wire, and lead foil sandwiched in between two large glass panels, the artwork presents an array of images, some apparently mechanical, others diagrammatic, and yet others seemingly abstract in nature. Duchamp provided some clues to the intriguing imagery in a series of notes accompanying the work. The top half of *The Large Glass* represents "the bride," whom Duchamp has depicted as "basically a motor" fueled by "love gasoline." In contrast, the bachelors appear as uniformed male figures in the lower half of the composition. They too move mechanically. The chocolate grinder in the center of the lower glass pane represents masturbation ("the bachelor grinds his own chocolate"). In *The Large Glass,* Duchamp provided his own whimsical but insightful ruminations into the ever-confounding realm of desire and sexuality. In true

Dadaist fashion, chance completed the work. During the transportation of *The Large Glass* from an exhibition in 1927, the glass panes shattered. Rather than replace the broken glass, Duchamp painstakingly pieced together the glass fragments. After encasing the reconstructed work, broken panes and all, between two heavier panes of glass, Duchamp declared the work completed "by chance."

Duchamp (and the generations of artists after him profoundly influenced by his art and especially his attitude) considered life and art matters of chance and choice freed from the conventions of society and tradition. In Duchamp's approach to art and life, each act was individual and unique. Every person's choice of found objects would be different, for example, and each person's throw of the dice would be at a different instant and probably would yield a different number. This philosophy of utter freedom for artists was fundamental to the history of art in the 20th century—in America as well as Europe. Duchamp spent much of World War I in New York, where he painted *Nude Descending a Staircase* (FIG. 24-35) and inspired a group of American artists and collectors with his radical rethinking of the role of artists and of the nature of art.

KURT SCHWITTERS Early on, Dada spread to Germany. In Berlin, Hannah Höch produced photomontages (FIG. 24-1) featuring sharp political commentary. In Hanover, KURT SCHWITTERS (1887–1948) followed a gentler muse. Inspired by Cubist collage but working nonobjectively, Schwitters found visual poetry in the cast-off junk of modern society and scavenged in trash bins for materials, which he pasted and nailed together into designs such as *Merz 19* (FIG. **24-29**). The term *Merz,* which Schwitters used as a generic title for a whole series of collages, derived nonsensically from the German word *Kommerzbank* (commerce bank) and appeared as a word fragment in one of his compositions. Although nonobjective, his collages still resonate with the meaning of the fragmented found objects they contain. The recycled elements of Schwitters's collages, like Duchamp's readymades, acquire new meanings through their new uses and locations. Elevating objects that are essentially trash to the status of high art certainly fits within the parameters of the Dada program and parallels the absurdist dimension of much of Dada art. Contradiction, paradox, irony, and even blasphemy were Dada's bequest to later artists.

Suprematism and Constructivism

Dada was a movement born of pessimism and cynicism. Not all early-20th-century artists, however, reacted to the profound turmoil of the times by retreating from society. Some artists promoted utopian ideals, believing staunchly in art's ability to contribute to improving society and all humankind. These efforts often surfaced in the face of significant political upheaval, as was the case with Suprematism and Constructivism in Russia.

KAZIMIR MALEVICH Despite Russia's distance from Paris, the center of the international art world in the early 20th century, Russians had a long history of cultural contact and interaction with western Europe. Wealthy Russians, such as Ivan Morozov (1871–1921) and Sergei Shchukin (1854–1936), amassed extensive collections of Impressionist, Post-Impressionist, and avant-garde paintings. Shchukin, who participated in the salons at the Steins' home in Paris (see "Gertrude and Leo Stein," page 732), became particularly enamored with the work of both Picasso and Matisse. By the mid-1910s, he had acquired 37 paintings by Matisse and 51 by Picasso. Because of their access to collections such as these, Russian artists were familiar with the latest artistic developments, especially Fauvism, Cubism, and Futurism.

One Russian artist who pursued the revolutionary direction Cubism introduced was KAZIMIR MALEVICH (1878–1935). Malevich

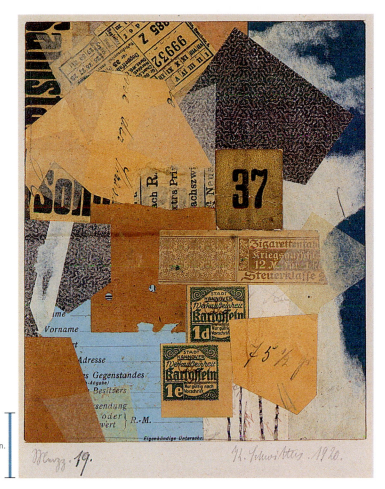

1 in.

24-29 KURT SCHWITTERS, *Merz 19,* 1920. Paper collage, 7¼″ × 5⅞″. Yale University Art Gallery, New Haven (gift of Collection Société Anonyme).

Inspired by Cubist collage but working nonobjectively, Schwitters found visual poetry in the cast-off junk of modern society, which he pasted and nailed together into striking Dada compositions.

1 in.

24-30 KAZIMIR MALEVICH, *Suprematist Composition: Airplane Flying,* 1915 (dated 1914). Oil on canvas, 1′ 10⅞″ × 1′ 7″. Museum of Modern Art, New York. ◼◀

Malevich developed an abstract style he called Suprematism to convey that the supreme reality in the world is pure feeling. Here, the brightly colored rectilinear shapes float against white space.

developed an abstract style to convey his belief that the supreme reality in the world is "pure feeling," which attaches to no object. Thus, this belief called for new, nonobjective forms in art—shapes not related to objects in the visible world. Malevich had studied painting, sculpture, and architecture and had worked his way through most of the avant-garde styles of his youth before deciding none could express pure feeling. He christened his new artistic approach *Suprematism,* explaining: "Under Suprematism I understand the supremacy of pure feeling in creative art. To the Suprematist, the visual phenomena of the objective world are, in themselves, meaningless; the significant thing is feeling, as such, quite apart from the environment in which it is called forth."[18]

The basic form of Malevich's new Suprematist nonobjective art was the square. Combined with its relatives, the straight line and the rectangle, the square soon filled his paintings, such as *Suprematist Composition: Airplane Flying* (FIG. **24-30**). In this work, the brightly colored shapes float against and within a white space, and the artist placed them in dynamic relationship to one another. Malevich believed all peoples would easily understand his new art because of the universality of its symbols. It used the pure language of shape and color, to which everyone could respond intuitively.

Having formulated his artistic approach, Malevich welcomed the Russian Revolution, which broke out in 1917 as a result of

widespread dissatisfaction with the regime of Tsar Nicholas II (r. 1894–1917). Russian workers staged a general strike in protest, and the tsar abdicated in March. In late 1917, the Bolsheviks, a faction of Russian Social Democrats that promoted violent revolution, wrested control of the country from the ruling provisional government. Once in power, their leader, Vladimir Lenin (1870–1924), nationalized the land and turned it over to the local rural soviets (councils of workers' and soldiers' deputies). After extensive civil war, the Communists, as they now called themselves, succeeded in retaining control of Russia and taking over an assortment of satellite countries in eastern Europe. This new state adopted the official name Union of Soviet Socialist Republics (USSR, or Soviet Union) in 1923.

Malevich viewed the revolution as an opportunity to wipe out past traditions and begin a new culture. He believed his art could play a major role in that effort because of its universal accessibility. But, after a short period when the new regime heralded avant-garde art, the political leaders of the Soviet Union decided their new communist society needed a more "practical" art. Soviet authorities promoted a "realistic," illusionistic art that they thought a wide public could understand and that they hoped would teach citizens about their new government. This horrified Malevich. To him, true art could never have a practical connection with life:

Every social idea, however great and important it may be, stems from the sensation of hunger; every art work, regardless of how small and insignificant it may seem, originates in pictorial or plastic feeling. It is high time for us to realize that the problems of art lie far apart from those of the stomach or the intellect.[19]

24-30A POPOVA, *Architectonic Painting*, 1916–1917.

Disappointed and unappreciated by the public, Malevich eventually gravitated toward other disciplines, such as mathematical theory and geometry, logical fields given his interest in pure abstraction, but his work and his theories made a profound impression on other artists, especially in Russia. These included LYUBOV POPOVA (1889–1924), who joined Malevich's Suprematist movement in 1916. Popova's most notable works are the series of canvases she named *Architectonic Paintings* (FIG. **24-30A**).

NAUM GABO The Russian-born sculptor NAUM GABO (1890–1977) also wanted to create an innovative art to express a new reality, and like Malevich, he believed art should spring from sources separate from the everyday world. For Gabo, the new reality was the space-time world described by early-20th-century scientists (see "Science and Art," page 729). As he wrote in *The Realistic Manifesto*, published with his brother Anton Pevsner (1886–1962) in 1920:

> Space and time are the only forms on which life is built and hence art must be constructed.... The realization of our perceptions of the world in the forms of space and time is the only aim of our pictorial and plastic art.... We renounce the thousand-year-old delusion in art that held the static rhythms as the only elements of the plastic and pictorial arts. We affirm in these arts a new element, the kinetic rhythms, as the basic forms of our perception of real time.[20]

Gabo was one of the Russian sculptors known as Constructivists. The name *Constructivism* may have come originally from the title *Construction*, which the Russian artist Vladimir Tatlin (FIG. 24-32) used for some relief sculptures he made in 1913 and 1914. Gabo explained he called himself a Constructivist partly because he built up his sculptures piece by piece in space, instead of carving or modeling them in the traditional way. Although Gabo experimented briefly with real motion in his work, most of his sculptures relied on the relationship of mass and space to suggest the nature of space-time. To indicate the volumes of mass and space more clearly in his sculpture, Gabo used some of the new synthetic plastic materials, including celluloid, nylon, and Lucite, to create constructions whose space seems to flow through as well as around the transparent materials. In works such as *Column* (FIG. **24-31**), Gabo opened up the column's circular mass so viewers could experience the volume of space it occupies. Two transparent planes extend through its diameter, crossing at right angles at the center of the implied cylindrical column shape. The opaque colored planes at the base and the inclined open ring set up counter-rhythms to the crossed upright planes. They establish the sense of dynamic kinetic movement Gabo always sought to express as an essential part of reality.

Architecture

A third art movement that emerged in the Soviet Union in the years immediately following the Russian Revolution was *Productivism*, which was an offshoot of the Constructivist movement. The Productivists sought to design a better environment for human beings.

VLADIMIR TATLIN One of the most gifted leaders of the Productivism movement was VLADIMIR TATLIN (1885–1953). The Russian Revolution was the signal to Tatlin, as it had been to Malevich, that the hated old order was about to end. In utopian fashion, he and the other Productivists aspired to play a significant role in creating

24-31 NAUM GABO, *Column*, ca. 1923 (reconstructed 1937). Perspex, wood, metal, glass, 3′ 5″ × 2′ 5″ × 2′ 5″. Solomon R. Guggenheim Museum, New York.

Gabo's Constructivist sculptures rely on the relationship of mass and space to suggest the nature of space-time. Space seems to flow through as well as around the transparent materials he used.

a new world, one that would fully use the power of industrialization to benefit all people. Initially, like Malevich and Gabo, Tatlin believed nonobjective art was ideal for the new society, free as such art was from any past symbolism. But after the 1917 revolution, Tatlin enthusiastically abandoned abstract art for "functional art" and designed products such as an efficient stove and workers' clothing.

Tatlin's most famous work is *Monument to the Third International* (FIG. **24-32**), which, in its reductive geometry, connects Productivism to the artistic programs of the Suprematists and Constructivists. Tatlin received the commission from the Department of Artistic Work of the People's Commissariat for Enlightenment in early 1919 to honor the Russian Revolution. He envisioned a huge glass-and-iron building that—at 1,300 feet—would have been one-third taller than the Eiffel Tower (FIG. 23-38). Widely influential, "Tatlin's Tower," as it became known, served as a model for those seeking to encourage socially committed and functional art. On its proposed site in the center of Moscow, it would have functioned as a propaganda and news center for the Soviet people. Within a dynamically tilted spiral cage, three geometrically shaped chambers were to rotate around a central axis, each chamber housing

24-32 VLADIMIR TATLIN, *Monument to the Third International*, 1919–1920. Reconstruction of the lost model, 1992-1993. Kunsthalle, Düsseldorf.

"Tatlin's Tower" was an ambitious avant-garde design for a Soviet governmental building with three geometrically shaped chambers rotating at different speeds within a dynamically tilted spiral cage.

ADOLF LOOS In Germany, ADOLF LOOS (1870–1933) was the most influential architectural theorist during the opening decades of the 20th century. Loos trained as an architect at the Dresden College of Technology and then traveled to the United States to attend the 1893 Columbia Exposition in Chicago. Although he apparently found no work as an architect in Chicago, he remained there three years. During that time he became familiar with the buildings (FIGS. 23-40, 23-40A, and 23-41) and theories of Louis Sullivan, whose 1892 essay *Ornament in Architecture* affected Loos profoundly. In that treatise, Sullivan suggested architects consider banishing all ornamentation from their buildings for a period of years "in order that our thought might concentrate acutely upon the production of buildings well formed and comely in the nude."

Loos carried Sullivan's ideas even further in a series of essays in which he railed against the excesses of the Art Nouveau style (FIGS. 23-40 and 23-40A), which was the rage in Europe at the turn of the century. He published his major statement on the subject in 1908 under the title *Ornament and Crime*. Loos equated architectural ornamentation with the "amoral" tattoos of Papua New Guinea (see FIG. I-19) and asserted that modern men who tattooed themselves were either criminals or degenerates. Ornamentation in architecture was also a crime, both on aesthetic grounds and because it wasted labor and materials.

Loos put his ideas to work in his 1910 design for the Viennese home of the painter Lilly Steiner (1884–1962). Cubical in form with a garden facade in the shape of a shallow U, the Steiner House (FIG. **24-33**) has a reinforced-concrete skeleton and a severe white stucco shell devoid of ornamentation of any kind, even moldings separating the floors. The windows are simple unframed sheets of plate glass, symmetrically arranged. Walter Gropius would later build upon Loos's ideas about pure, functional architectural design at the Bauhaus (see "Walter Gropius and the Bauhaus," page 773, and FIG. 24-66), where he promoted "avoiding all romantic embellishment and whimsy."

facilities for a different type of governmental activity and rotating at a different speed. The one at the bottom, a huge cylindrical glass structure for lectures and meetings, was to revolve once a year. Higher up was a cone-shaped chamber that would rotate monthly and serve administrative functions. At the top, a cubic information center would have revolved daily, issuing news bulletins and proclamations via the most modern means of communication. These included an open-air news screen (illuminated at night) and a special instrument designed to project words on the clouds on any overcast day. The proposed decreasing size of the chambers as visitors ascended the monument paralleled the decision-making hierarchy in the political system, with the most authoritative, smallest groups near the building's apex. The design thus served as a visual reinforcement of a social and political reality. Unfortunately, due to Russia's desperate economic situation in the 1920s, Tatlin's Tower was never built. But Tatlin worked out his ambitious design in now-lost metal and wood models exhibited on various official occasions. The only records of these models are a few drawings and photographs, but they have permitted faithful reconstructions of the design, such as the one reproduced in FIG. 24-32.

24-33 ADOLF LOOS, garden facade of the Steiner House (looking northwest), Vienna, Austria, 1910.

For Loos, decoration was a "criminal" waste of labor and materials. His Steiner House is a cubical mass with a white stucco shell devoid of ornamentation and without even moldings separating floors.

UNITED STATES, 1900 TO 1930

Avant-garde experiments in the arts were not limited to Europe. Increasingly common transatlantic travel during the later 19th and early 20th centuries resulted in a lively exchange of artistic ideas among European and American artists. For example, John Singer Sargent (FIG. 22-37), Mary Cassatt (FIG. 23-13), and James Abbott McNeill Whistler (FIG. 23-14) spent much of their productive careers in Europe, whereas many European artists ended their careers in the United States, especially in anticipation of and, later, in the wake of World War I. American artists wishing to pursue modernist ideas at home received encouragement from a number of wealthy and visionary patrons, mostly women (see "Art 'Matronage' in the United States," page 753).

Painting and Sculpture

In the opening decade of the 20th century, when most American artists knew little about the revolutionary work of their European counterparts, the goal of many of the leading painters was to present a realistic, unvarnished look at American life. In this regard, their work paralleled that of the French Realists in the mid-19th century (see Chapter 22).

JOHN SLOAN AND THE EIGHT The most important group of American Realist artists was The Eight—eight painters who gravitated into the circle of the influential and evangelical artist and teacher Robert Henri (1865–1929). Henri urged his followers to make "pictures from life,"[21] and accordingly, these artists pursued with zeal the production of images depicting the rapidly changing urban landscape of New York City. Because these vignettes often captured the bleak and seedy aspects of city life, The Eight eventually became known as the Ash Can School. Some critics referred to them as "the apostles of ugliness."

A prominent member of The Eight was JOHN SLOAN (1871–1951). A self-described "incorrigible window watcher,"[22] Sloan constantly wandered the streets of New York, observing human drama. He focused much of his attention on the working class, which he perceived as embodying the realities of life. So sympathetic was Sloan to the plight of workers that he joined the Socialist Party in 1909 and eventually ran for public office on the Socialist ticket. In paintings such as *Sixth Avenue and 30th Street* (FIG. **24-34**), Sloan revealed his ability to capture both the visual and social realities of American urban life. When he painted this image in 1907, Sloan lived on West 23rd Street, on the outskirts of the Tenderloin District, an area cluttered with brothels, dance halls, saloons, gambling dens, and cheap hotels. *Sixth Avenue* depicts a bustling intersection. Bracketing the throngs of people filling the intersection are elevated train tracks on the left and a row of storefronts and apartment buildings on the right. These two defining elements of city life converge in the far center background of the painting. Sloan's portrayals of New York also feature a cross-section of the population of the city at the opening of the 20th century. In the foreground of *Sixth Avenue,* Sloan prominently placed three women. One, in a shabby white dress, is a drunkard, stumbling along with her pail of beer. Two streetwalkers stare at her. In turn, two well-dressed men gaze at the prostitutes. Sloan's depiction of the women allied him with reformers of the time, who saw streetwalkers not as immoral but as victims of an unfair social and economic system. At a time when traditional art centered on genteel and proper society, Sloan's forthright depiction of prostitutes was categorically "Realist."

24-34 JOHN SLOAN, *Sixth Avenue and Thirtieth Street, New York City,* 1907. Oil on canvas, 2' ¼" × 2' 8". Philadelphia Museum of Art, Philadelphia (gift of Meyer P. Potamkin and Vivian O. Potamkin, 2000).

A prominent member of the American Realist group called The Eight, Sloan captured in his paintings the bleak and seedy aspects of the rapidly changing urban landscape of New York City.

1 ft.

The Armory Show

From February 17 to March 15, 1913, the American public flocked in large numbers to view the International Exhibition of Modern Art at the 69th Regiment Armory in New York City. The "Armory Show," as it came universally to be called, was an ambitious endeavor organized primarily by two artists, Walt Kuhn (1877–1949) and Arthur B. Davies (1862–1928). The show included more than 1,600 artworks by American and European artists. Among the European artists represented were Matisse, Derain, Picasso, Braque, Duchamp (FIG. 24-35), Kandinsky, Kirchner, Lehmbruck, and Brancusi. In addition to exposing Americans to the latest European artistic developments, the Armory Show also provided American artists with a prime showcase for their work. The foreword to the exhibition catalog spelled out the goals of the organizers:

> The American artists exhibiting here consider the exhibition of equal importance for themselves as for the public. The less they find their work showing signs of the developments indicated in the Europeans, the more reason they will have to consider whether or not painters or sculptors here have fallen behind . . . the forces that have manifested themselves on the other side of the Atlantic.*

On its opening, this provocative exhibition served as a lightning rod for commentary, immediately attracting heated controversy. The *New York Times* described the show as "pathological" and called the modernist artists "cousins to the anarchists," while the magazine *Art and Progress* compared them to "bomb throwers, lunatics, depravers."† Other critics demanded the exhibition be closed as a menace to public morality. The *New York Herald,* for example, asserted: "The United States is invaded by aliens, thousands of whom constitute so many perils to the health of the body politic. Modernism is of precisely the same heterogeneous alien origin and is imperiling the republic of art in the same way."‡

Nonetheless, the exhibition was an important milestone in the history of art in the United States. The Armory Show traveled to Chicago and Boston after it closed in New York and was a significant catalyst for the reevaluation of the nature and purpose of American art.

*Quoted in Herschel B. Chipp, *Theories of Modern Art: A Source Book by Artists and Critics* (Berkeley and Los Angeles: University of California Press, 1968), 503.
†Quoted in Sam Hunter, John Jacobus, and Daniel Wheeler, *Modern Art,* rev. 3d. ed. (Upper Saddle River, N.J.: Prentice Hall, 2005), 250.
‡Quoted in Francis K. Pohl, *Framing America: A Social History of American Art,* 2d ed. (New York: Thames & Hudson, 2002), 341.

1 ft.

24-35 MARCEL DUCHAMP, *Nude Descending a Staircase, No. 2,* 1912. Oil on canvas, 4′ 10″ × 2′ 11″. Philadelphia Museum of Art, Philadelphia (Louise and Walter Arensberg Collection).

The Armory Show introduced European modernism to America. Duchamp's figure moving in a time continuum owes a debt to Cubism and Futurism. The press gave it a hostile reception.

ARMORY SHOW The relative isolation of American artists from developments across the Atlantic came to an abrupt end in early 1913 when the Armory Show opened in New York City (see "The Armory Show," above). Although later recognized as the seminal event in the development of American modernist art, the exhibition received a hostile response from the press. The work the journalists and critics most maligned was Marcel Duchamp's *Nude Descending a Staircase, No. 2* (FIG. 24-35). The painting represents a single figure in motion down a staircase in a time continuum and suggests the effect of a sequence of overlaid film stills. Unlike the Dada works by Duchamp (FIGS. 24-27, 24-27A, and 24-28), *Nude Descending a Staircase* shares many characteristics with the work of the Cubists and the Futurists. The monochromatic palette is reminiscent of Analytic Cubism, as is Duchamp's faceted presentation of the human form. The artist's interest in depicting the figure in motion reveals an affinity for the Futurists' ideas. One critic described this work as "an explosion in a shingle factory,"[23] and newspaper cartoonists delighted in lampooning the painting.

24-36 ARTHUR DOVE, *Nature Symbolized No. 2*, ca. 1911. Pastel on paper, 1′ 6″ × 1′ 9⅝″. Art Institute of Chicago, Chicago (Alfred Stieglitz Collection).

Dove was one of the first painters to produce completely nonobjective canvases. Using only abstract shapes and color, he sought to capture the essence of nature and of pulsating organic growth.

ARTHUR DOVE Among the American modernists who exhibited their work in the Armory Show was ARTHUR DOVE (1880–1946). After graduating from Cornell University, Dove worked briefly as a commercial artist in New York and then in 1907 left for Paris, where he encountered the paintings of Henri Matisse (FIGS. 24-2, 24-2A, and 24-3) and André Derain (FIGS. 24-4 and 24-4A). Dove returned to New York in 1910. He occupies a special place in the evolution of modernist art in the United States because he began painting completely nonobjective paintings at about the same time as Vassily Kandinsky but apparently without any knowledge of Kandinsky's *Improvisation* series (FIG. 24-7).

Dove spent most of his life on farms in rural New York and Connecticut and loved the textures and colors of the American landscape. He sought to capture in his paintings the essence of nature, especially its pulsating energy, but without representing nature directly. A characteristic and aptly named example of his abstract renditions of fields, vegetation, and sky is *Nature Symbolized No. 2* (FIG. **24-36**), which he probably painted in 1911. Incorporating some of the principles and forms of Cubism but without representing any identifiable objects or landscape elements, Dove used swirling and jagged lines and a palette of mostly green, black, and sandy yellow to capture the essence of vegetation sprouting gloriously from fertile soil beneath patches of blue sky. He once described his goal as the creation of "rhythmic paintings" expressing nature's "spirit" through shape and color.

MAN RAY Another American artist who incorporated the latest European trends in his work was Emmanuel Radnitzky, who assumed the name MAN RAY (1890–1976). Ray was a close associate of Duchamp's in the 1920s. During that decade, Ray produced art having a decidedly Dada spirit, and he often incorporated found objects in his paintings, sculptures, movies, and photographs.

Trained as an architectural draftsman and engineer, Ray earned his living as a graphic designer and portrait photographer, and developed an innovative photographic technique relying on chance. In contrast to traditional photographs, Ray produced his images without using a camera. He placed objects directly on photographic paper and then exposed the paper to light. Ray dubbed these photographs, which in effect created themselves, *Rayographs.*

As did many other artists of this period, Ray had a keen interest in mass-produced objects and technology, as well as a dedication to exploring the psychological realm of human perception of the exterior world. Like Schwitters, he used the dislocation of ordinary things from their everyday settings to surprise his viewers into new awareness. His displacement of found objects was particularly effective in works such as *Cadeau* (*Gift;* FIG. **24-37**). For this sculpture, with characteristic Dada humor, he equipped a laundry iron with a row of wicked-looking tacks, subverting its proper function. Ray's "gift" would rip to shreds any garment the recipient tried to press with it.

Art "Matronage" in the United States

Until the 20th century, a leading reason for the dearth of women artists was that professional institutions restricted women's access to artistic training. For example, the proscription against women participating in life-drawing classes, a staple of academic artistic training, in effect denied women the opportunity to become professional artists. Another explanation for the absence of women from the traditional art historical canon is that art historians have not considered as "high art" many of the art objects women have traditionally produced (for example, quilts or basketry).

By the early 20th century, however, many of the impediments to a woman's becoming a recognized artist had been removed. Today, women are a major presence in the art world. One of the developments in the early 20th century that laid the groundwork for this change was the prominent role American women played as art patrons. These "art matrons" provided financial, moral, and political support to cultivate the advancement of the arts in America. Chief among them were Gertrude Vanderbilt Whitney, Lillie P. Bliss, Mary Quinn Sullivan, Abby Aldrich Rockefeller, Isabella Stewart Gardner, Peggy Guggenheim, and Jane Stanford.*

Gertrude Vanderbilt Whitney (1875–1942) was a practicing sculptor and enthusiastic collector. To assist young American artists such as Robert Henri and John Sloan (FIG. 24-34) in exhibiting their work, she opened the Whitney Studio in 1914. By 1929, dissatisfied with the recognition accorded young, progressive American artists, she offered her entire collection of 500 works to the Metropolitan Museum of Art in New York City. Her offer rejected, she founded her own museum in New York, the Whitney Museum of American Art. She chose as the first director a visionary and energetic woman, Juliana Force (1876–1948), who inaugurated a pioneering series of monographs on living American artists and organized lecture series by influential art historians and critics. Through the efforts of these two women, the Whitney Museum became a major force in American art.

A trip to Paris in 1920 whetted the interest of Peggy Guggenheim (1898–1979) in avant-garde art. As did Whitney, Guggenheim collected art and eventually opened a gallery in England to exhibit the work of innovative artists. She continued her support for modernist art after her return to the United States. Guggenheim's New York gallery, called Art of This Century, was instrumental in advancing the careers of many artists, including her husband, Max Ernst (FIG. 24-53). She eventually moved her art collection to a lavish Venetian palace, where the public can still view the important artworks she acquired.

Other women who contributed significantly to the arts were Lillie P. Bliss (1864–1931), Mary Quinn Sullivan (1877–1939), and Abby Aldrich Rockefeller (1874–1948). Philanthropists, art collectors, and educators, these influential and far-sighted women saw the need for a museum to collect and exhibit modernist art. Together they established the Museum of Modern Art in New York City in 1929, which became (and continues to be) the most influential museum of modern art in the world (see "The Museum of Modern Art," page 783), and collects American as well as European modernist art, for example, Man Ray's *Cadeau* (FIG. 24-37).

Isabella Stewart Gardner (1840–1924) and Jane Stanford (1828–1905) also undertook the ambitious project of founding museums. The Isabella Stewart Gardner Museum in Boston, established in 1903,

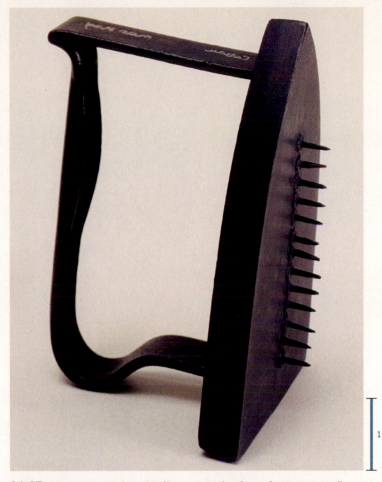

1 in.

24-37 MAN RAY, *Cadeau* (*Gift*), ca. 1958 (replica of 1921 original). Painted flatiron with row of 13 tacks with heads glued to the bottom, $6\frac{1}{8}'' \times 3\frac{5}{8}'' \times 4\frac{1}{2}''$. Museum of Modern Art, New York (James Thrall Soby Fund).

With characteristic Dada humor, the American artist Man Ray equipped a laundry iron with a row of wicked-looking spikes, subverting its proper function of smoothing and pressing.

houses a well-chosen and comprehensive collection of art of many periods. The Stanford Museum, the first American museum west of the Mississippi, got its start in 1905 on the grounds of Stanford University, which Leland Stanford Sr. and Jane Stanford founded after the tragic death of their son. The Stanford Museum houses a wide range of objects, including archaeological and ethnographic artifacts. These two driven women committed much of their time, energy, and financial resources to ensure the success of their museums, and were intimately involved in their institutions' day-to-day operations.

The museums these women established flourish today, attesting to the extraordinary vision of these "art matrons" and the remarkable contributions they made to the advancement of art in the United States.

*Art historian Wanda Corn coined the term *art matronage* in the catalog *Cultural Leadership in America: Art Matronage and Patronage* (Boston: Isabella Stewart Gardner Museum, 1997).

24-38 MARSDEN HARTLEY, *Portrait of a German Officer,* 1914. Oil on canvas, 5' 8¼" × 3' 5⅜". Metropolitan Museum of Art, New York (Alfred Stieglitz Collection).

In this elegy to a lover killed in battle, Hartley arranged military-related images against a somber black background. The flattened, planar presentation reveals the influence of Synthetic Cubism.

24-39 STUART DAVIS, *Lucky Strike,* 1921. Oil on canvas, 2' 9¼" × 1' 6". Museum of Modern Art, New York (gift of the American Tobacco Company, Inc.). © Estate of Stuart Davis/Licensed by VAGA, New York.

Tobacco products fascinated Davis, a heavy smoker. In *Lucky Strike,* he depicted a cigarette package in fragmented form, recalling Cubism, and imbued his painting with an American jazz rhythm.

MARSDEN HARTLEY One American artist who developed a personal style influenced by Cubism and German Expressionism was MARSDEN HARTLEY (1877–1943). In 1912, Hartley traveled to Europe, visiting Paris, where he became acquainted with the work of the Cubists, and Munich, where he gravitated to the Blaue Reiter circle. Kandinsky's work particularly impressed Hartley, and he developed a style he called "Cosmic Cubism." In 1913, he moved to Berlin. With the heightened militarism in Germany and the eventual outbreak of World War I, Hartley immersed himself in military imagery.

Portrait of a German Officer (FIG. 24-38) is one of Hartley's best paintings of this period. It depicts an array of military-related images: German imperial flags, regimental insignia, badges, and emblems such as the Iron Cross. Although this image resonates in the general context of wartime militarism, important elements in the painting had personal significance for Hartley. In particular,

the painting includes references to his lover, Lieutenant Karl von Freyberg, who lost his life in battle a few months before Hartley painted this "portrait." Von Freyberg's initials appear in the lower left corner. His age when he died (24) appears in the lower right corner, and his regiment number (4) appears in the center of the painting. Also incorporated is the letter E for von Freyberg's regiment, the Bavarian Eisenbahn. The influence of Synthetic Cubism is evident in the flattened, planar presentation of the elements, which almost appear as abstract patterns. The somber black background against which the artist placed the colorful stripes, patches, and shapes casts an elegiac pall over the painting.

24-40 Aaron Douglas, *Noah's Ark,* ca. 1927. Oil on Masonite, 4′ × 3′. Fisk University Galleries, University of Tennessee, Nashville.

In *Noah's Ark* and other paintings of the cultural history of African Americans, Douglas incorporated motifs from African sculpture and the transparent angular planes characteristic of Synthetic Cubism.

STUART DAVIS Philadelphia-born Stuart Davis (1894–1964) created what he believed was a modern American art style by combining the flat shapes of Synthetic Cubism with his sense of jazz tempos and his perception of the energy of fast-paced American culture. *Lucky Strike* (FIG. **24-39**) is one of several tobacco still lifes Davis began in 1921. Davis was a heavy smoker, and tobacco products and their packaging fascinated him. He insisted the introduction of packaging in the late 19th century was evidence of high civilization and therefore, he concluded, of the progressiveness of American culture. Davis depicted the Lucky Strike package in fragmented form, reminiscent of Synthetic Cubist collages. However, although the work does incorporate flat printed elements, these are illusionistically painted, rather than glued onto the canvas. The discontinuities and the interlocking planes imbue *Lucky Strike* with a dynamism and rhythm not unlike American jazz or the pace of life in a lively American metropolis. *Lucky Strike* is resolutely both American and modern.

AARON DOUGLAS Also deriving his personal style from Synthetic Cubism was African American artist Aaron Douglas (1898–1979), who used the style to represent symbolically the historical and cultural memories of his people. Born in Kansas,

Douglas studied in Nebraska and Paris before settling in New York City, where he became part of the flowering of art and literature in the 1920s known as the Harlem Renaissance. Spearheaded by writers and editors Alain Locke (1886–1953) and Charles Spurgeon Johnson (1883–1956), the Harlem Renaissance was a manifestation of the desire of African Americans to promote their cultural accomplishments. They also aimed to cultivate pride among fellow African Americans and to foster racial tolerance across the United States. Expansive and diverse, the fruits of the Harlem Renaissance included the writings of authors such as Langston Hughes, Countee Cullen, and Zora Neale Hurston; the jazz and blues of Duke Ellington, Bessie Smith, Eubie Blake, Fats Waller, and Louis Armstrong; the photographs of James Van Der Zee and Prentice H. Polk; and the paintings and sculptures of Meta Warrick Fuller and Augusta Savage.

Douglas arrived in New York City in 1924 and became one of the most sought-after graphic artists in the African American community. Encouraged to create art that would express the cultural history of his race, Douglas incorporated motifs from African sculpture into compositions painted in a version of Synthetic Cubism stressing transparent angular planes. *Noah's Ark* (FIG. **24-40**) was one of seven paintings based on a book of poems by James Weldon Johnson (1871–1938) called *God's Trombones: Seven Negro Sermons in Verse.* Douglas used flat planes to evoke a sense of mystical space and miraculous happenings. In *Noah's Ark,* lightning strikes and rays of light crisscross the pairs of animals entering the ark, while men load supplies in preparation for departure. The artist suggested deep space by differentiating the size of the large human head and shoulders of the worker at the bottom and the small person at work on the far deck of the ship. Yet the composition's unmodulated color shapes create a pattern on the Masonite surface that cancels any illusion of three-dimensional depth. Here, Douglas used Cubism's formal language to express a powerful religious vision. Seven years later, employed by the U.S. government to create murals for the Harlem branch of the New York Public Library, he addressed a contemporary rather than a biblical subject: the history of Africans in America (FIG. **24-40A**).

24-40A Douglas, *Slavery through Reconstruction,* 1934.

PRECISIONISM Another distinctly American art movement in the post–Armory Show period was *Precisionism.* Although not an organized group, the Precisionists shared a fascination with the machine's "precision" and its importance in modern life. Although new technologies captured the imaginations of many European artists, especially the Futurists, Americans generally seemed more enamored by the prospects of a mechanized society than did Europeans. Even the Frenchman Francis Picabia, Duchamp's collaborator, noted: "Since machinery is the soul of the modern world, and since the genius of machinery attains its highest expression in America, why is it not reasonable to believe that in America the art of the future will flower most brilliantly?"[24] Precisionism, however, expanded beyond the exploration of machine imagery. Many artists associated with this group gravitated toward Synthetic Cubism's flat, sharply delineated planes as an appropriate visual idiom for their imagery, adding to the clarity and precision of their work. Eventually, Precisionism came to be characterized by a merging of a familiar native style in American architecture and artifacts with a modernist vocabulary derived largely from Synthetic Cubism.

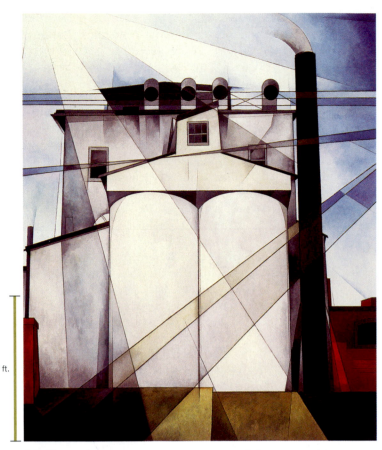

1 ft.

24-41 CHARLES DEMUTH, *My Egypt,* 1927. Oil on composition board, 2′ 11¾″ × 2′ 6″. Whitney Museum of American Art, New York (purchased with funds from Gertrude Vanderbilt Whitney).

Demuth was one of the leading Precisionists—American artists who extolled the machine age. This painting depicts grain elevators reduced to geometric forms amid Cubist transparent diagonal planes.

CHARLES DEMUTH Two of the leading Precisionists hailed from Pennsylvania—Charles Sheeler (1883–1965) and CHARLES DEMUTH (1883–1935). Sheeler traveled to Italy and France in 1909, and Demuth spent the years 1912–1914 in Paris, but both artists rejected pure abstraction and favored American subjects, especially industrial landscapes. Demuth's *My Egypt* (FIG. **24-41**) incorporates the spatial discontinuities characteristic of Cubism into a typically Precisionist depiction of an industrial site near Lancaster, the painter's birthplace. Demuth reduced the John W. Eshelman and Sons grain elevators to simple geometric forms. The grain elevators remain recognizable and solid, but the "beams" of transparent planes and the diagonal force lines threaten to destabilize the image and recall Cubist fragmentation of space. The degree to which Demuth intended to extol the American industrial scene is unclear. The title, *My Egypt,* is sufficiently ambiguous in tone to accommodate differing readings. On the one hand, Demuth could have been suggesting a favorable comparison between the Egyptian pyramids and American grain elevators as cultural icons. On the other hand, the title could be read cynically, as a negative comment on the limitations of American culture.

GEORGIA O'KEEFFE The work of Wisconsin-born GEORGIA O'KEEFFE (1887–1986) changed stylistically throughout her career. During the 1920s, O'Keeffe was a Precisionist. She had moved from the tiny town of Canyon, Texas, to New York City in 1918, and although she had visited the city before, what she found there excited her. "You have to live in today," she told a friend. "Today the

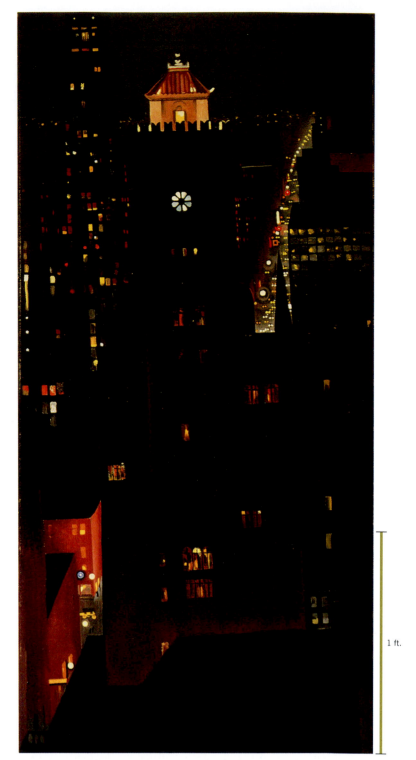

1 ft.

24-42 GEORGIA O'KEEFFE, *New York, Night,* 1929. Oil on canvas, 3′ 4⅛″ × 1′ 7⅞″. Sheldon Memorial Art Gallery, Lincoln (Nebraska Art Association, Thomas C. Woods Memorial Collection).

O'Keeffe's Precisionist representation of New York's soaring skyscrapers reduces the buildings to large, simple, dark planes punctuated by small windows that add rhythm and energy to the image.

city is something bigger, more complex than ever before in history. And nothing can be gained from running away. I couldn't even if I could."[25] While in New York, O'Keeffe met Alfred Stieglitz (FIGS. 24-43 and 24-43A), who played a major role in promoting the avant-garde in the United States. Stieglitz had established an art gallery at 291 Fifth Avenue in New York. In "291," as the gallery came to be called, he exhibited the latest in both European and

American art. Thus, 291, like the Armory Show, played an important role in the history of early-20th-century art in America. Stieglitz had seen and exhibited some of O'Keeffe's earlier work, and he drew her into his avant-garde circle of painters and photographers. He became one of O'Keeffe's staunchest supporters and, eventually, her husband. The interest of Stieglitz and his circle in capturing the sensibility of the machine age intersected with O'Keeffe's fascination with the fast pace of city life, and she produced paintings during this period, such as *New York, Night* (FIG. **24-42**), featuring the soaring skyscrapers dominating the city. As did other Precisionists, O'Keeffe reduced her images to simple planes, here punctuated by small rectangular windows that add rhythm and energy to the image, countering the monolithic darkness of the looming buildings.

Despite O'Keeffe's affiliation with the Precisionist movement and New York, she is best known for her paintings of cow skulls and of flowers. For example, in *Jack in the Pulpit No. 4* (FIG. I-5), she reveals her interest in stripping subjects to their purest forms and colors to heighten their expressive power. In this work, O'Keeffe reduced the incredible details of a flower to a symphony of basic colors, shapes, textures, and vital rhythms. Exhibiting the natural flow of curved planes and contour, O'Keeffe simplified the form almost to the point of complete abstraction. The fluid planes unfold like undulant petals from a subtly placed axis—the white jetlike streak—in a vision of the slow, controlled motion of growing life. O'Keeffe's painting, in its graceful, quiet poetry, reveals the organic reality of the object by strengthening its characteristic features.

Photography

Among the most significant artistic developments during the decades between the two world wars was the emergence of photography as a respected branch of the fine arts. The person most responsible for elevating the stature of photography was Alfred Stieglitz.

ALFRED STIEGLITZ Taking his camera everywhere he went, ALFRED STIEGLITZ (1864–1946) photographed whatever he saw around him, from the bustling streets of New York City to cloudscapes in upstate New York and the faces of friends and relatives. He believed in making only "straight, unmanipulated" photographs. Thus, he exposed and printed them using basic photographic processes, without resorting to techniques such as double-exposure or double-printing that would add information absent in the subject when he released the shutter. Stieglitz said he wanted the photographs he made with this direct technique "to hold a moment, to record something so completely that those who see it would relive an equivalent of what has been expressed."[26]

Stieglitz began a lifelong campaign to win a place for photography among the fine arts while he was a student of photochemistry in Germany. Returning to New York, he founded the Photo-Secession group, which mounted traveling exhibitions in the United States and sent loan collections abroad, and he published an influential journal titled *Camera Work*. In his own works, Stieglitz specialized in photographs of his environment and saw these subjects in terms of arrangements of forms and of the "colors" of his black-and-white materials. His aesthetic approach crystallized during the making of *The Steerage* (FIG. **24-43**), taken during a voyage to Europe with his first wife and daughter in 1907. Traveling first class, Stieglitz rapidly grew bored with the company of the prosperous passengers in his section of the ship. He walked as far forward on the first-class level as he could, when the rail around the opening onto the lower deck brought him up short. This level was for the steerage passengers the U.S. government sent back to Europe after refusing them entrance into the country. Later, Stieglitz described what happened next:

24-43 ALFRED STIEGLITZ, *The Steerage*, 1907 (print 1915). Photogravure (on tissue), 1' $\frac{3}{8}$" × 10$\frac{1}{8}$". Amon Carter Museum, Fort Worth. ◼◀

Stieglitz waged a lifelong campaign to win a place for photography among the fine arts. This 1907 image is a haunting mixture of found patterns of forms and human activity. It stirs deep emotions.

The scene fascinated me: A round hat; the funnel leaning left, the stairway leaning right; the white drawbridge, its railing made of chain; white suspenders crossed on the back of a man below; circular iron machinery; a mast that cut into the sky, completing a triangle. I stood spellbound. I saw shapes related to one another—a picture of shapes, and underlying it, a new vision that held me: simple people; the feeling of ship, ocean, sky; a sense of release that I was away from the mob called rich. Rembrandt came into my mind and I wondered would he have felt as I did. . . . I had only one plate holder with one unexposed plate. Could I catch what I saw and felt? I released the shutter. If I had captured what I wanted, the photograph would go far beyond any of my previous prints. It would be a picture based on related shapes and deepest human feeling—a step in my own evolution, a spontaneous discovery.[27]

This description reveals Stieglitz's abiding interest in the formal elements of the photograph—an insistently modernist focus that emerges in even more extreme form in his *Equivalent* series (FIG. **24-43A**) of the 1920s. The finished print fulfilled Stieglitz's vision so well that it shaped his future photographic work, and its haunting mixture of found patterns and human activity has continued to stir viewers' emotions to this day.

24-43A STIEGLITZ, *Equivalent*, 1923. ◼◀

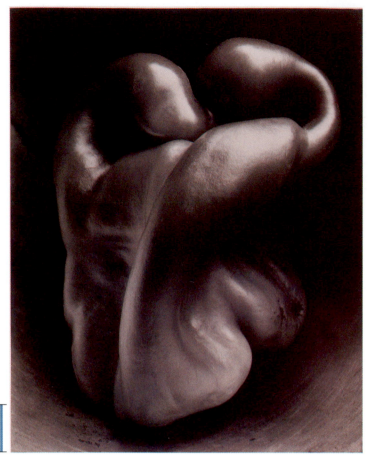

24-44 EDWARD WESTON, *Pepper No. 30,* 1930. Gelatin silver print, 9½″ × 7½″. Center for Creative Photography, University of Arizona, Tucson.

Weston "previsualized" his still lifes, choosing the exact angle, lighting, and framing he desired. His vegetables often resemble human bodies, in this case a seated nude seen from behind.

EDWARD WESTON Like Alfred Stieglitz, in whose 291 Gallery he exhibited his work, EDWARD WESTON (1886–1958) played a major role in establishing photography as an important artistic medium. But unlike Stieglitz, who worked outdoors and sought to capture transitory moments in his photographs, Weston meticulously composed and carefully lit his subjects in a controlled studio setting, whether he was doing still lifes of peppers, shells, and other natural forms of irregular shape, or figure studies. The 1930 photograph of a pepper illustrated here (FIG. 24-44) is the 30th in a large series and an outstanding example of this genre. In contrast to Weston's photographs of sections of nude human bodies (FIG. 24-44A), his still-life photographs show the entire object, albeit tightly framed. (Compare Georgia O'Keeffe's *Jack-in-the-Pulpit No. 4* [FIG. I-5] painted the same year.) The artificial lighting accentuates the undulating surfaces and crevices of the vegetable. Weston left nothing to chance, choosing the exact angle and play of light over the object, "previsualizing" the final photographic print before snapping the camera's shutter.

24-44A WESTON, *Nude,* 1925.

In a kind of reversal of his approach to photographing nudes, which he often transformed into landscapes, Weston frequently chose peppers whose shapes reminded him of human bodies. *Pepper No. 30* looks like a seated nude figure seen from behind with raised arms emerging from broad shoulders. Viewers can read the vertical crease down the center of the vegetable as the spinal column leading to the buttocks. Although highly successful as a purely abstract composition of shapes and of light and dark, Weston's still life also conveys mystery and sensuality through its dramatic lighting and rich texture.

Architecture

As did other artists, many early-20th-century architects in the United States looked to Europe for inspiration, but distinctive American styles also emerged that in turn had a major influence on architectural design worldwide.

FRANK LLOYD WRIGHT One of the most striking personalities in the development of modern architecture on either side of the Atlantic was FRANK LLOYD WRIGHT (1867–1959). Born in Wisconsin, Wright moved to Chicago, where he eventually joined the firm headed by Louis Sullivan (FIGS. 23-40, 23-40A, and 23-41). Wright set out to create an American "architecture of democracy."[28] Always a believer in "natural" and "organic" buildings, Wright saw architecture as serving free individuals who have the right to move within a "free" space, envisioned as a nonsymmetrical design interacting spatially with its natural surroundings. He sought to develop an organic unity of planning, structure, materials, and site. Wright identified the principle of continuity as fundamental to understanding his view of organic unity:

> Classic architecture was all fixation. . . . Now why not let walls, ceilings, floors become seen as component parts of each other? . . . You may see the appearance in the surface of your hand contrasted with the articulation of the bony structure itself. This ideal, profound in its architectural implications . . . I called . . . continuity.[29]

Wright manifested his vigorous originality early, and by 1900 he had arrived at a style entirely his own. In his work during the first decade of the 20th century, his cross-axial plan and his fabric of continuous roof planes and screens defined a new American domestic architecture.

ROBIE HOUSE Wright fully expressed these elements and concepts in the Robie House (FIG. 24-45), built between 1907 and 1909. Like other buildings in the Chicago area Wright designed at about the same time, he called this home a "prairie house." Wright conceived the long, sweeping, ground-hugging lines, unconfined by abrupt wall limits, as reaching out toward and capturing the expansiveness of the Midwest's great flatlands. Abandoning all symmetry, he eliminated a facade, extended the roofs far beyond the walls, and all but concealed the entrance. Wright filled the house's "wandering" plan (FIG. 24-46) with intricately joined spaces (some large and open, others closed), grouped freely around a great central fireplace. (He believed strongly in the hearth's age-old domestic significance.) Wright designed enclosed patios, overhanging roofs, and strip windows to provide unexpected light sources and glimpses of the outdoors as the inhabitants moved through the interior space. These elements, together with the open ground plan, created a sense of space in motion, inside and out. Wright matched his new and fundamental interior spatial arrangement in his exterior treatment. For example, the flow of interior space determined the sharp angular placement of exterior walls.

24-45 FRANK LLOYD WRIGHT, Robie House (looking northeast), Chicago, Illinois, 1907–1909.

The Robie House is an example of Wright's "architecture of democracy," in which free individuals move within a "free" space—a nonsymmetrical design interacting spatially with its natural surroundings.

24-46 FRANK LLOYD WRIGHT, plan of the second (main) level of the Robie House, Chicago, Illinois, 1907–1909.

Typical of Wright's "prairie houses," the Robie House has a bold "wandering" asymmetrical plan with intricately joined open and closed spaces grouped freely around a great central fireplace.

ART DECO Although Adolf Loos (FIG. 24-33) had strongly condemned ornamentation in the design of buildings, popular taste still favored decoration as an important element in architecture. *Art Deco* was a movement in the 1920s and 1930s whose adherents sought to upgrade industrial design in competition with "fine art." Proponents wanted to work new materials into decorative patterns that could be either machined or handcrafted and could, to a degree, reflect the simplifying trend in architecture. A remote descendant of Art Nouveau, Art Deco acquired its name at the Exposition des Arts Décoratifs et Industriels Modernes (Exposition of Modern Decorative and Industrial Arts), held in Paris in 1925. Art Deco had universal application—to buildings, interiors, furniture, utensils, jewelry, fashions, illustration, and commercial products of every sort. Art Deco products have a "streamlined," elongated symmetrical aspect. Simple flat shapes alternate with shallow volumes in hard patterns. Derived from nature, these simple forms are inherently aerodynamic, making them technologically efficient (because of their reduced resistance as they move through air or water) as well as aesthetically pleasing. Designers adopted streamlined designs for trains and cars, and the popular appeal of these designs led to their use in an array of objects, from machines to consumer products.

Art Deco's exemplary masterpiece is the stainless-steel spire of the Chrysler Building (FIG. **24-47**) in New York City, designed by WILLIAM VAN ALEN (1882–1954). The building and spire are

24-47 WILLIAM VAN ALEN, Art Deco spire of the Chrysler Building (looking south), New York, New York, 1928–1930. ▪◀

The Chrysler Building's stainless steel spire epitomizes Art Deco architecture. The skyscraper's glittering crown of diminishing fan shapes has a streamlined form popular during the 1920s.

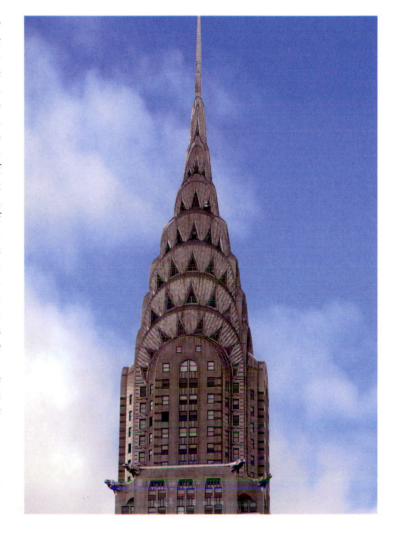

monuments to the fabulous 1920s, when American millionaires and corporations competed with one another to raise the tallest skyscrapers in the biggest cities. Built up of diminishing fan shapes, the spire glitters triumphantly in the sky, a resplendent crown honoring the business achievements of the great auto manufacturer. As a temple of commerce, the Chrysler Building celebrated the principles and success of American business before the onset of the Great Depression.

EUROPE, 1920 TO 1945

Because World War I was fought entirely on European soil, European artists experienced its devastating effects to a much greater degree than did American artists. The war had a profound effect on Europe's geopolitical terrain, on individual and national psyches, and on the art of the 1920s and 1930s.

Neue Sachlichkeit

In Germany, World War I gave rise to an artistic movement called *Neue Sachlichkeit* (New Objectivity). All of the artists associated with Neue Sachlichkeit served, at some point, in the German army. Their military experiences deeply influenced their worldviews and informed their art. "New Objectivity" captures the group's aim—to present a clear-eyed, direct, and honest image of the war and its effects.

GEORGE GROSZ One of the Neue Sachlichkeit artists was GEORGE GROSZ (1893–1958), who was, for a time, associated with the Dada group in Berlin. Grosz observed the onset of World War I with horrified fascination that soon turned to anger and frustration. He reported:

Of course, there was a kind of mass enthusiasm at the start. But this intoxication soon evaporated, leaving a huge vacuum. . . . And then after a few years when everything bogged down, when we were defeated, when everything went to pieces, all that remained, at least for me and most of my friends, were disgust and horror.[30]

The largest canvas Grosz ever painted— *The Eclipse of the Sun* (FIG. **24-48**)—does not depict the Great War itself, but, as are many of his other paintings and drawings (FIG. **24-48A**), it is a stinging indictment of the militarism and capitalism he believed were the root causes of the global conflict. The painting takes its name from the large red German coin at the upper left blocking the sun and signifying capitalism has

24-48A GROSZ, *Fit for Active Service*, 1916–1917.

brought darkness to the world. Also at the top are burning buildings. At the lower right are a skull and bones. Filling the rest of the canvas are the agents of this destruction seated at a table seen at a sharp angle from above. The main figure is the president of Germany, Paul von Hindenburg (r. 1925–1934), who wears his army uniform and war medals. His bloody sword is on the table before him, and on his head is the laurel wreath of victory. He presides over a meeting with four headless ministers—men who act on his orders without question. Grosz, however, also portrayed the president as a puppet leader. A wealthy industrialist wearing a top hat whispers instructions in von Hindenburg's ear. The painting is also a commentary on the gullibility of the public, personified here as a donkey who eats newspapers, that is, as a mindless creature who swallows the propagandistic lies promoted by the government- and business-friendly press.

1 ft.

24-48 **GEORGE GROSZ**, *The Eclipse of the Sun*, 1926. Oil on canvas, 6′ 9⅝″ × 5′ 11⅞″. **Heckscher Museum of Art, Huntington.**

In Grosz's indictment of militarism and capitalism, an industrialist whispers instructions in the ear of the uniformed president of Germany, who meets with four of his headless ministers.

24-49 Max Beckmann, *Night,* 1918–1919. Oil on canvas, 4′ 4⅜″ × 5′ ¼″. Kunstsammlung Nordrhein-Westfalen, Düsseldorf.

Beckmann's treatment of forms and space in *Night* matched his view of the brutality of early-20th-century society. Objects seem dislocated and contorted, and the space appears buckled and illogical.

MAX BECKMANN Another major German artist who enlisted in the German army and initially rationalized the Great War was Max Beckmann (1884–1950). He believed the chaos would lead to a better society, but over time the massive loss of life and widespread destruction increasingly disillusioned him. Soon his work began to emphasize the horrors of war and of a society he saw descending into madness. His disturbing view of society is evident in *Night* (FIG. 24-49), which depicts a cramped room three intruders have forcefully invaded. A bound woman, apparently raped, is splayed across the foreground of the painting. Her husband appears on the left. One of the intruders hangs him, while another one twists his left arm out of its socket. An unidentified woman cowers in the background. On the far right, the third intruder prepares to flee with the child.

Although this image does not depict a war scene, the wrenching brutality and violence pervading the home are searing and horrifying comments on society's condition. Beckmann also injected a personal reference by using himself, his wife, and his son as the models for the three family members. The stilted angularity of the figures and the roughness of the paint surface contribute to the image's savageness. In addition, the artist's treatment of forms and space reflects the world's violence. Objects seem dislocated and contorted, and the

space appears buckled and illogical. For example, the woman's hands are bound to the window opening from the room's back wall, but her body appears to hang vertically, rather than lying across the plane of the intervening table.

OTTO DIX The third artist most closely associated with Neue Sachlichkeit was Otto Dix (1891–1959). Having served as both a machine gunner and an aerial observer, Dix was well acquainted with war's effects. As did Grosz and Beckmann, Dix initially tried to find redeeming value in the apocalyptic event: "The war was a horrible thing, but there was something tremendous about it, too. . . . You have to have seen human beings in this unleashed state to know what human nature is. . . . I need to experience all the depths of life for myself, that's why I go out, and that's why I volunteered."[31] This idea of experiencing the "depths of life" stemmed from Dix's interest in the philosophy of Friedrich Nietzsche (1844–1900). In particular, Dix avidly read Nietzsche's *The Joyous Science,* deriving from it a belief in life's cyclical nature—procreation and death, building up and tearing down, and growth and decay.

As the war progressed, however, Dix's faith in the potential improvement of society dissipated, and he began to produce

24-50 OTTO DIX, *Der Krieg* (*The War*), 1929–1932. Oil and tempera on wood, 6′ 8⅓″ × 13′ 4¾″. Staatliche Kunstsammlungen, Gemäldegalerie Neue Meister, Dresden.

In this triptych recalling earlier altarpieces, Dix captured the panoramic devastation war inflicts on the terrain and on humans. He depicted himself as a soldier dragging a comrade to safety.

unflinchingly direct and provocative artworks. His triptych titled *Der Krieg* (*The War;* FIG. **24-50**) vividly captures the panoramic devastation war inflicts, both on the terrain and on humans. In the left panel, armed and uniformed soldiers march off into the distance. Dix graphically displayed the horrific results in the center and right panels, where mangled bodies, many riddled with bullet holes, are scattered throughout the eerily lit apocalyptic landscape. As if to emphasize the intensely personal nature of this scene, the artist painted himself into the right panel as the ghostly but determined soldier who drags a comrade to safety. In the bottom panel, in a coffinlike bunker, lie soldiers asleep—or perhaps dead. Dix significantly chose to present this sequence of images in the format of an altarpiece, and the work recalls triptychs such as Matthias Grünewald's *Isenheim Altarpiece* (FIG. 18-2). However, Dix's "altarpiece" presents a bleaker outlook than Grünewald's. The hope of salvation extended to viewers of the *Isenheim Altarpiece* through Christ's eventual resurrection is absent from *Der Krieg.* As did his fellow Neue Sachlichkeit artists, Dix felt compelled to lay bare the realities of his time, which the war's violence dominated. Even years later, Dix still maintained:

> You have to see things the way they are. You have to be able to say yes to the human manifestations that exist and will always exist. That doesn't mean saying yes to war, but to a fate that approaches you under certain conditions and in which you have to prove yourself. Abnormal situations bring out all the depravity, the bestiality of human beings. . . . I portrayed states, states that the war brought about, and the results of war, as states.[32]

ERNST BARLACH A work more spiritual in its expression is the *War Monument* (FIG. **24-51**), which the German sculptor ERNST BARLACH (1870–1938) created for the cathedral in his hometown of Güstrow in 1927. Working often in wood, Barlach sculpted single figures usually dressed in flowing robes and portrayed in strong, simple poses embodying deep human emotions and experiences such as grief, vigilance, or self-comfort. Barlach's works combine sharp, smoothly planed forms with intense expression. The cast-bronze hovering figure of his *War Monument* is one of the poignant memorials of World War I. Unlike traditional war memorials depicting heroic military figures, often engaged in battle, the hauntingly symbolic figure Barlach created speaks to the experience of all caught in the conflict of war. The floating human form, suspended above a tomb inscribed with the dates 1914–1918 (and later also 1939–1945), suggests a dying soul at the moment when it is about to awaken to everlasting life—the theme of death and transfiguration. The rigid economy of surfaces concentrates attention on the simple but expressive head. So powerful was this sculpture the Nazis had it removed from the cathedral in 1937 and melted it down for ammunition. Luckily, a friend hid another version Barlach made. A Protestant parish in Cologne purchased it, and bronze workers made a new cast of the figure for the Güstrow cathedral.

Surrealism

The exuberantly aggressive momentum of the Dada movement that emerged during World War I lasted for only a short time. By 1924, with the publication in France of the *First Surrealist Manifesto,*

24-51 ERNST BARLACH, *War Monument,* Güstrow Cathedral, Güstrow, Germany, 1927. Bronze.

In this World War I memorial, which the Nazis melted down for ammunition, a human form floating above a tomb suggests a dying soul at the moment it is about to awaken to everlasting life.

most of the artists associated with Dada joined the *Surrealism* movement and its determined exploration of ways to express in art the world of dreams and the unconscious. Not surprisingly, the Surrealists incorporated many of the Dadaists' improvisational techniques. They believed these methods important for engaging the elements of fantasy and activating the unconscious forces deep within every human being. The Surrealists sought to explore the inner world of the psyche, the realm of fantasy and the unconscious. Inspired in part by the ideas of the psychoanalysts Sigmund Freud and Carl Jung, the Surrealists had a special interest in the nature of dreams. They viewed dreams as occurring at the level connecting all human consciousness and as constituting the arena in which people could move beyond their environment's constricting forces to reengage with the deeper selves society had long suppressed. In the words of André Breton, one of the leading Surrealist thinkers:

> Surrealism is based on the belief in the superior reality of certain forms of association heretofore neglected, in the omnipotence of dreams, in the undirected play of thought. . . . I believe in the future resolution of the states of dream and reality, in appearance so contradictory, in a sort of absolute reality, or surreality.[33]

Thus, the Surrealists' dominant motivation was to bring the aspects of outer and inner "reality" together into a single position, in much the same way life's seemingly unrelated fragments combine in the vivid world of dreams. The projection in visible form of this new conception required new techniques of pictorial construction. The Surrealists adapted some Dada devices and invented new

methods such as automatic writing (spontaneous writing using free association), not so much to reveal a world without meaning as to provoke reactions closely related to subconscious experience.

Surrealism developed along two lines. In *Naturalistic Surrealism,* artists presented recognizable scenes that seem to have metamorphosed into a dream or nightmare image. The artists Salvador Dalí (FIG. 24-55) and René Magritte (FIGS. 24-56 and 24-56A) were the most famous practitioners of this variant of Surrealism. In contrast, some artists gravitated toward an interest in *Biomorphic Surrealism.* In Biomorphic (life forms) Surrealism, *automatism*—the creation of art without conscious control—predominated. Biomorphic Surrealists such as Joan Miró (FIG. 24-58) produced largely abstract compositions, although the imagery sometimes suggests organisms or natural forms.

GIORGIO DE CHIRICO The widely recognized precursor of Surrealism was the Italian painter GIORGIO DE CHIRICO (1888–1978). De Chirico's emphatically ambiguous paintings of cityscapes are the most famous examples of a movement called *Pittura Metafisica,* or Metaphysical Painting. Returning to Italy after studying in Munich, de Chirico found hidden reality revealed through strange juxtapositions, such as those seen on late autumn afternoons, when the long shadows of the setting sun transformed vast open squares and silent public monuments into what the painter called "metaphysical towns." De Chirico translated this vision into paint in works such as *The Song of Love* (FIG. **24-52**), a dreamlike scene set in the deserted piazza of an Italian town. A huge marble head—a fragment of the

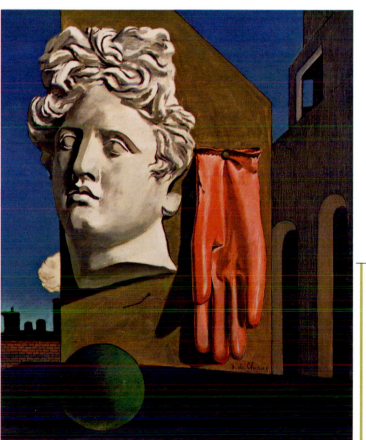

24-52 GIORGIO DE CHIRICO, *The Song of Love,* 1914. Oil on canvas, 2' 4¾" × 1' 11⅜". Museum of Modern Art, New York (Nelson A. Rockefeller bequest).

De Chirico's Metaphysical Painting movement was a precursor of Surrealism. Here, a classical head of Apollo floats mysteriously next to a gigantic red glove in a deserted, shadow-filled Italian city square.

famous *Apollo Belvedere* in the Vatican—is suspended in midair above a large green ball. To the right is a gigantic red glove nailed to a wall. The buildings and the three over-life-size objects cast shadows that direct the viewer's eye to the left and to a locomotive puffing smoke—a favorite Futurist motif, here shown in slow motion and incongruously placed near the central square. The choice of the term *metaphysical* to describe de Chirico's paintings suggests these images transcend their physical appearances. *The Song of Love,* for all of its clarity and simplicity, takes on a rather sinister air. The sense of strangeness de Chirico could conjure with familiar objects and scenes recalls Nietzsche's "foreboding that underneath this reality in which we live and have our being, another and altogether different reality lies concealed."[34]

Reproductions of De Chirico's paintings appeared in periodicals almost as soon as he completed them, and his works quickly influenced artists outside Italy, including both the Dadaists and, later, the Surrealists. The incongruities in his work intrigued the Dadaists, whereas the eerie mood and visionary quality of paintings such as *The Song of Love* excited and inspired Surrealist artists who sought to portray the world of dreams.

MAX ERNST Originally a Dada activist in Germany, Max Ernst (1891–1976) became one of the early adherents of the Surrealist circle André Breton anchored. As a child living in a small community near Cologne, Ernst had found his existence fantastic and filled with marvels. In autobiographical notes, written mostly in the third person, he said of his birth: "Max Ernst had his first

contact with the world of sense on the 2nd April 1891 at 9:45 a.m., when he emerged from the egg which his mother had laid in an eagle's nest and which the bird had incubated for seven years."[35] Ernst's service in the German army during World War I swept away his early success as an Expressionist. In his own words:

> Max Ernst died on 1st August 1914. He returned to life on 11th November 1918, a young man who wanted to become a magician and find the central myth of his age. From time to time he consulted the eagle which had guarded the egg of his prenatal existence. The bird's advice can be detected in his work.[36]

Before joining the Surrealists, Ernst explored every means to achieve the sense of the psychic in his art. As other Dadaists did, Ernst set out to incorporate found objects and chance into his works, often combining fragments of images he had cut from old books, magazines, and prints to form one hallucinatory collage. He also began making paintings that shared the mysterious dreamlike effect of his collages.

In 1920, Ernst met Breton, who instantly recognized the German artist's affinity with the Surrealist group. In 1922, Ernst moved to Paris, where he painted *Two Children Are Threatened by a Nightingale* (FIG. **24-53**). In it, Ernst displayed a private dream challenging the post-Renaissance idea that a painting should resemble a window looking into a "real" scene rendered illusionistically three-dimensional through mathematical perspective. He painted the landscape, the distant city, and the tiny flying bird in conventional fashion, following all the established rules of linear and atmospheric perspective. The three sketchily rendered figures, however, clearly belong to a dream world, and the literally three-dimensional miniature gate, the odd button knob, and the strange closed building "violate" the bulky frame's space. Additional dislocation occurs in the traditional museum identification label, which Ernst displaced into a cutaway part of the frame. Handwritten, it announces the work's title (taken from a poem Ernst wrote before he painted this), adding another note of irrational mystery.

As is true of many Surrealist works, the title, *Two Children Are Threatened by a Nightingale,* is ambiguous and relates uneasily to what the spectator sees. The viewer must struggle to decipher connections between the image and the words. When Surrealists (and Dadaists and Metaphysical artists before them) used puzzling titles, they intended the seeming contradiction between title and picture to knock the audience off balance with all expectations challenged. Much of the impact of Surrealist works begins with the viewer's sudden awareness of the incongruity and absurdity of what the artist pictured. These were precisely the qualities that subjected the Dadaists and

1 ft.

24-53 Max Ernst, *Two Children Are Threatened by a Nightingale,* 1924. Oil on wood with wood construction, 2′ 3½″ × 1′ 10½″ × 4½″. Museum of Modern Art, New York.

In this early Surrealist painting with an intentionally ambiguous title, Ernst used traditional perspective to represent the setting, but the three sketchily rendered figures belong to a dream world.

Degenerate Art

Although avant-garde artists often had to endure public ridicule both in Europe and America (see "The Armory Show," page 751), they suffered outright political persecution in Germany in the 1930s and 1940s. The most dramatic example of this persecution was the infamous "Entartete Kunst" (Degenerate Art) exhibition Adolf Hitler (1889–1945) and the Nazis mounted in 1937.

Hitler aspired to become an artist himself and produced numerous drawings and paintings reflecting his firm belief that 19th-century realistic genre painting represented the zenith of Aryan art development. Accordingly, Hitler denigrated anything that did not conform to that standard—in particular, avant-garde art. Turning his criticism into action, Hitler ordered the confiscation of more than 16,000 artworks he considered "degenerate." To publicize his condemnation of this art, he ordered his minister for public enlightenment and propaganda, Joseph Goebbels (1897–1945), to organize a massive exhibition of this "degenerate art." Hitler designated as degenerate those artworks that "insult German feeling, or destroy or confuse natural form, or simply reveal an absence of adequate manual and artistic skill."* The term *degenerate* also had other specific connotations at the time. The Nazis used it to identify supposedly inferior racial, sexual, and moral types. Hitler's order to Goebbels to target 20th-century avant-garde art for inclusion in the Entartete Kunst exhibition aimed to impress on the public the general inferiority of the artists producing this work. To make that point all the more dramatic, Hitler ordered the organization of another exhibition, the Grosse Deutsche Kunstausstellung (Great German Art Exhibition), which ran concurrently and presented an extensive array of Nazi-approved conservative art.

Entartete Kunst opened in Munich on July 19, 1937, and included more than 650 paintings, sculptures, prints, and books. The exhibition was immensely popular. Roughly 20,000 viewers visited the show daily. By the end of its four-month run, it had attracted more than two million viewers, and nearly a million more viewed it as it traveled through Germany and Austria. Among the 112 artists whose works the Nazis presented for ridicule were Ernst Barlach, Max Beckmann, Otto Dix, Max Ernst, George Grosz, Vassily Kandinsky, Ernst Kirchner, Paul Klee, Wilhelm Lehmbruck, Franz Marc, Emil Nolde, and Kurt Schwitters. In a memorable photograph (FIG. 24-54) taken during Hitler's preview visit to the exhibition on July 16, 1937, the Nazi leader pauses in front of the Dada wall. Behind him are works by Schwitters, Klee, and Kandinsky, which the organizers deliberately hung askew on the wall. (They subsequently straightened them for the duration of the exhibition.)

24-54 Adolf Hitler, accompanied by Nazi commission members, including photographer Heinrich Hoffmann, Wolfgang Willrich, Walter Hansen, and painter Adolf Ziegler, viewing the "Entartete Kunst" show on July 16, 1937.

For Hitler's visit, the curators deliberately hung askew the works of Kandinsky, Klee, and Schwitters. In Nazi Germany, no modernist artist was safe from persecution, and many fled the country.

In Germany in the 1930s and 1940s, in the face of Nazi persecution, artists committed to pursuing avant-garde ideas required courage and a resoluteness that extended beyond issues of aesthetics and beyond the confines of the art world. No modernist artist was safe from Hitler's attack. (Only six of the artists in the exhibition were Jewish.) For example, despite his status as a charter member of the Nazi party, Emil Nolde received particularly harsh treatment. The Nazis confiscated more than 1,000 of Nolde's works from German museums and included 27 of them in the exhibition, more than for almost any other artist. Max Beckmann and his wife fled to Amsterdam on the opening day of the Entartete Kunst exhibit, never to return to their homeland. Ernst Kirchner responded to the stress of Nazi pressure by destroying all his woodblocks and burning many of his works. A year later, in 1938, he committed suicide.

*Stephanie Barron, *"Degenerate Art": The Fate of the Avant-Garde in Nazi Germany* (Los Angeles: Los Angeles County Museum of Art, 1991), 19.

Surrealists to public condemnation and, in Germany under Adolf Hitler (1889–1945), to governmental persecution (see "Degenerate Art," above, and FIG. 24-54).

SALVADOR DALÍ The Surrealists' exploration of the human psyche and dreams reached new heights in the works of Spanish-born SALVADOR DALÍ (1904–1989). In his paintings, sculptures, jewelry, and designs for furniture and movies, Dalí probed a deeply erotic dimension, studying the writings of Richard von Krafft-Ebing (1840–1902) and Sigmund Freud, and inventing what he called the "paranoiac-critical method" to assist his creative process. As he described it, in his painting he aimed "to materialize the images of concrete irrationality with the most imperialistic fury of precision . . . in order that the world of imagination and of concrete irrationality may be as objectively evident . . . as that of the exterior world of phenomenal reality."[37]

In *The Persistence of Memory* (FIG. **24-55**), Dalí created a haunting allegory of empty space where time has ended. An eerie, never-setting sun illuminates the barren landscape. An amorphous creature draped with a limp pocket watch sleeps in the foreground. Another watch hangs from the branch of a dead tree springing unexpectedly from a blocky architectural form. A third watch hangs half over the edge of the rectangular form, beside a small timepiece resting dial-down on the block's surface. Ants swarm mysteriously over the small watch, while a fly walks along the face of its large neighbor, almost as if this assembly of watches were decaying organic life—soft and sticky. Dalí rendered every detail of this dreamscape with precise control, striving to make the world of his paintings convincingly real—in his words, to make the irrational concrete.

RENÉ MAGRITTE The Belgian painter RENÉ MAGRITTE (1898–1967) encountered the work of Giorgio de Chirico (FIG. 24-52) in 1922. The Italian artist's disquieting combinations of motifs rendered in a realistic manner deeply impressed the younger Belgian artist, who produced his first Surrealist painting, *The Lost Jockey*, in 1926. The next year Magritte moved to Paris, where he joined the intellectual circle of André Breton and remained in France until 1930. In 1929, Magritte published an important essay in the Surrealist journal *La revolution surréaliste* in which he discussed the disjunction between objects, pictures of objects, and names of objects and pictures. The essay explains the intellectual basis for *The Treachery* (or *Perfidy*) *of Images* (FIG. 24-56), in which Magritte presented a meticulously rendered *trompe l'oeil* depiction of a briar pipe. The caption beneath the image, however, contradicts what seems obvious: "Ceci n'est pas une pipe" ("This is not a pipe"). The discrepancy between image and caption clearly challenges the assumptions underlying the reading of visual art. As is true of the other Surrealists' work, Magritte's paintings for example, *The False Mirror* (FIG. **24-56A**), wreak havoc on the viewer's reliance on the conscious and the rational.

1 ft.

Ceci n'est pas une pipe.

1 in.

24-57 MERET OPPENHEIM, *Object* (*Le Déjeuner en fourrure*), 1936. Fur-covered cup, $4\frac{3}{8}''$ diameter; saucer, $9\frac{3}{8}''$ diameter; spoon, $8''$ long. Museum of Modern Art, New York.

The Surrealists loved the concrete tangibility of sculpture, which made their art even more disquieting. Oppenheim's functional fur-covered object captures the Surrealist flair for magical transformation.

MERET OPPENHEIM Sculpture especially appealed to the Surrealists because its concrete tangibility made their art all the more disquieting. *Object* (FIG. 24-57), also called *Le Déjeuner en fourrure* (*Luncheon in Fur*), by Swiss artist MERET OPPENHEIM (1913–1985) captures the incongruity, humor, visual appeal, and, often, eroticism characterizing Surrealism. The artist presented a fur-lined teacup inspired by a conversation she had with Picasso.

After admiring a bracelet Oppenheim had made from a piece of brass covered with fur, Picasso noted anything might be covered with fur. When her tea grew cold, Oppenheim responded to Picasso's comment by ordering "un peu plus de fourrure" (a little more fur), and the sculpture had its genesis. *Object* takes on an anthropomorphic quality, animated by the quirky combination of the fur with a functional object. Further, the sculpture captures the Surrealist flair for alchemical, seemingly magical or mystical, transformation. It incorporates a sensuality and eroticism (seen here in the seductively soft, tactile fur lining the concave form) that are also components of much of Surrealist art.

JOAN MIRÓ Like the Dadaists, the Surrealists used many methods to free the creative process from reliance on the kind of conscious control they believed society had shaped too much. Dalí used his paranoiac-critical approach to encourage the free play of association as he worked. Other Surrealists used automatism and various types of planned "accidents" to provoke reactions closely related to subconscious experience. Dalí's older countryman JOAN MIRÓ (1893–1983) was a master of this approach. Although Miró resisted formal association with any movement or group, including the Surrealists, André Breton identified him as "the most Surrealist of us all."[38] From the beginning, Miró's work contained an element of fantasy and hallucination. After Surrealist poets in Paris introduced him to the use of chance in the creation of art, the young Spaniard devised a new painting method that enabled him to create works such as *Painting* (FIG. 24-58). Miró began this painting by making a scattered collage composition with assembled fragments cut from a catalog for machinery. The shapes in the collage became motifs the artist freely reshaped on the canvas to create black silhouettes—solid or in outline, with dramatic accents of white and vermilion. They suggest, in the painting, a host of amoebic organisms or constellations in outer space floating in an immaterial background space filled with soft reds, blues, and greens.

Miró described his creative process as a switching back and forth between unconscious and conscious image-making: "Rather than setting out to paint something, I begin painting and as I paint the picture begins to assert itself, or suggest itself under my brush. The form becomes a sign for a woman or a bird as I work. . . . The first stage is free, unconscious. . . . The second stage is carefully calculated."[39] Even the artist could not always explain the meanings of pictures such as *Painting*. They are, in the truest sense, spontaneous and intuitive expressions of the little-understood, submerged unconscious part of life.

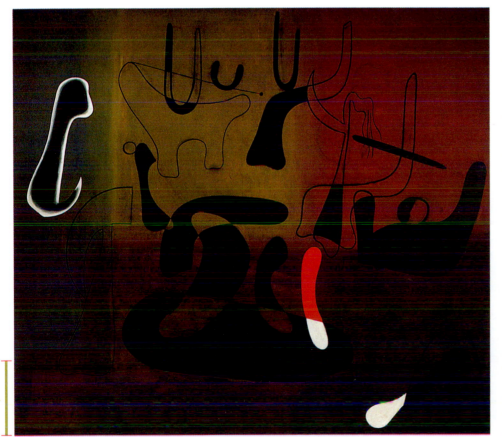

24-58 JOAN MIRÓ, *Painting*, 1933. Oil on canvas, $5'\ 8'' \times 6'\ 5''$. Museum of Modern Art, New York (Loula D. Lasker bequest by exchange). ◼◀

Miró promoted automatism, the creation of art without conscious control. He began this painting with a scattered collage and then added forms suggesting floating amoebic organisms.

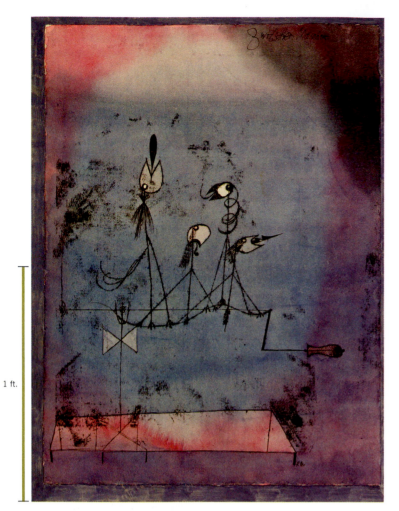

24-59 PAUL KLEE, *Twittering Machine*, 1922. Watercolor and pen and ink, on oil transfer drawing on paper, mounted on cardboard, 2′ 1″ × 1′ 7″. Museum of Modern Art, New York. ◼◣

Although based on forms in the tangible world easily read as birds, Klee's *Twittering Machine* is a fanciful vision of a mysterious world presented in a simplified, almost childlike manner.

PAUL KLEE Perhaps the most inventive artist using fantasy images to represent the nonvisible world was the Swiss-German painter PAUL KLEE (1879–1940). Like Miró, he shunned formal association with groups such as the Dadaists and Surrealists but pursued their interest in the subconscious. Klee sought clues to humanity's deeper nature in primitive shapes and symbols. Like Jung, Klee seems to have accepted the existence of a collective unconscious that reveals itself in archaic signs and patterns and is everywhere evident in the art of "primitive" cultures (see "Primitivism," page 734). The son of a professional musician and himself an accomplished violinist, Klee thought of painting as similar to music in its ability to express feelings through color, form, and line. In 1920, Klee set down his "creative credo," which reads in part:

> Art does not reproduce the visible; rather it makes visible. . . . The formal elements of graphic art are dot, line, plane, and space—the last three charged with energy of various kinds. . . . Formerly we used to represent things visible on earth, things we either liked to look at or would have liked to see. Today we reveal the reality that is behind visible things.[40]

To penetrate the reality behind visible things, Klee studied nature avidly, taking special interest in analyzing processes of growth and change. He coded these studies in diagrammatic form

in notebooks. The root of his work was thus nature, but nature filtered through his mind. Upon starting an image, he would allow the pencil or brush to lead him until an image emerged, to which he would then respond to complete the idea.

Twittering Machine (FIG. 24-59) reveals Klee's fanciful vision. The painting, although based on forms in the tangible world easily read as birds, is far from illusionistic. Klee presented the scene in a simplified, almost childlike manner, imbuing the work with a poetic lyricism. The inclusion of a crank-driven mechanism added a touch of whimsy. The small size of Klee's works enhances their impact. A viewer must draw near to decipher the delicately rendered forms and enter his mysterious dream world. Perhaps no other artist of the 20th century matched Klee's subtlety as he deftly created a world of ambiguity and understatement that draws each viewer into finding a unique interpretation of the work.

Also associated with the Surrealists was WIFREDO LAM (1902–1982), a Cuban painter who studied in Madrid and Paris and whose work (FIG. 24-59A) was greatly influenced by Picasso. It was Picasso who introduced Lam to Braque, Breton, and other avant-garde artists and critics.

24-59A LAM, *The Jungle*, 1943.

De Stijl

The utopian spirit and ideals of the Suprematists and Constructivists (FIGS. 24-30 and 24-31) in Russia were shared in western Europe by a group of young Dutch artists. They formed a new movement in 1917 and began publishing a magazine, calling both movement and magazine *De Stijl* (*The Style*). The group's cofounders were the painters Piet Mondrian (FIG. 24-60) and Theo van Doesburg (1883–1931). In addition to promoting utopian ideals, De Stijl artists believed in the birth of a new age in the wake of World War I. They felt it was a time of balance between individual and universal values, when the machine would assure ease of living. In their first manifesto of De Stijl, the artists declared: "There is an old and a new consciousness of time. The old is connected with the individual. The new is connected with the universal."[41] The goal, according to van Doesburg and architect Cor van Eesteren (1897–1988), was a total integration of art and life:

> We must realize that life and art are no longer separate domains. That is why the "idea" of "art" as an illusion separate from real life must disappear. The word "Art" no longer means anything to us. In its place we demand the construction of our environment in accordance with creative laws based upon a fixed principle. These laws, following those of economics, mathematics, technique, sanitation, etc., are leading to a new, plastic unity.[42]

PIET MONDRIAN Toward this goal of integration, PIET MONDRIAN (1872–1944) created a new style based on a single ideal principle. The choice of the term *De Stijl* reflected Mondrian's confidence that this style—*the* style—revealed the underlying eternal structure of existence. Accordingly, De Stijl artists reduced their artistic vocabulary to simple geometric elements. Time spent in Paris, just before World War I, introduced Mondrian to Cubism and other modes of abstraction. However, as his attraction to theological writings grew, Mondrian sought to purge his art of every overt reference to individual objects in the external world. He initially favored the teachings of theosophy, a tradition basing knowledge of nature and the human condition on knowledge of the divine nature or spiritual powers. (His fellow theosophist Vassily Kandinsky pursued a similar path.) Mondrian, however, quickly abandoned the strictures of

24-60 PIET MONDRIAN, *Composition with Red, Blue, and Yellow*, 1930. Oil on canvas, 1' 6⅛" × 1' 6⅛". Kunsthaus, Zürich. © Mondrian/ Holtzman Trust c/o HCR International, VA, USA. ▪◀

Mondrian's "pure plastic" paintings consist of primary colors locked into a grid of intersecting vertical and horizontal lines. By altering the grid patterns, he created a dynamic tension.

theosophy and turned toward a conception of nonobjective design— "pure plastic art"—that he believed expressed universal reality. He articulated his credo with great eloquence in 1914:

> What first captivated us does not captivate us afterward (like toys). If one has loved the surface of things for a long time, later on one will look for something more. . . . The interior of things shows through the surface; thus as we look at the surface the inner image is formed in our soul. It is this inner image that should be represented. For the natural surface of things is beautiful, but the imitation of it is without life. . . . Art is higher than reality and has no direct relation to reality. . . . To approach the spiritual in art, one will make as little use as possible of reality, because reality is opposed to the spiritual. . . . [W]e find ourselves in the presence of an abstract art. Art should be above reality, otherwise it would have no value for man.[43]

Mondrian soon moved beyond Cubism because he felt "Cubism did not accept the logical consequences of its own discoveries; it was not developing towards its own goal, the expression of pure plastics."[44] Caught by the outbreak of hostilities while on a visit to Holland, Mondrian remained there during World War I, developing his theories for what he called *Neoplasticism*—the new "pure plastic art." He believed all great art had polar but coexistent goals, the attempt to create "universal beauty" and the desire for "aesthetic expression of oneself."[45] The first goal is objective in nature, whereas the second is subjective, existing within the individual's mind and heart. To create a universal expression, an artist must communicate "a real equation of the universal and the individual."[46]

To express this vision, Mondrian eventually limited his formal vocabulary to the three primary colors (red, yellow, and blue), the three primary values (black, white, and gray), and the two primary directions (horizontal and vertical). Basing his ideas on a combination of teachings, he concluded primary colors and values are the

purest colors and therefore are the perfect tools to help an artist construct a harmonious composition. Using this system, he created numerous paintings locking color planes into a grid of intersecting vertical and horizontal lines, as in *Composition with Red, Blue, and Yellow* (FIG. **24-60**). In each of these paintings, Mondrian altered the grid patterns and the size and placement of the color planes to create an internal cohesion and harmony. This did not mean inertia. Rather, Mondrian worked to maintain a dynamic tension in his paintings from the size and position of lines, shapes, and colors.

Sculpture

It was impossible for early-20th-century artists to ignore the increasingly intrusive expansion of mechanization and growth of technology. However, not all artists embraced these developments, as had the Futurists. In contrast, many artists attempted to overcome the predominance of mechanization in society by immersing themselves in a search for the organic and natural.

CONSTANTIN BRANCUSI

One artist who was eager to produce works emphasizing the natural or organic was Romanian sculptor CONSTANTIN BRANCUSI (1876–1957). Brancusi sought to move beyond surface appearances to capture the essence or spirit of the object depicted (see "Brancusi, Hepworth, and Moore on Abstract Sculpture," page 770) in rhythmic, elegant sculptures. The softly curving surfaces and ovoid form of his sculptures refer, directly or indirectly, to the cycle of life. *Bird in Space* (FIG. **24-61**) is not a literal depiction of a bird, nor does his *Newborn* (FIG. **24-61A**) mimic a real baby's head. The abstract form of both works is the final result of a long process. For *Bird in Space*, Brancusi started with the image of a bird at rest with its wings folded at its sides and ended with a gently

24-61A BRANCUSI, *The Newborn*, 1915.

24-61 CONSTANTIN BRANCUSI, *Bird in Space*, 1924. Bronze, 4' 2⁵⁄₁₆" high. Philadelphia Museum of Art, Philadelphia (Louise and Walter Arensberg Collection, 1950). ▪◀

Although not a literal depiction of a bird, Brancusi's softly curving light-reflecting abstract sculpture in polished bronze suggests a bird about to soar in free flight through the heavens.

Brancusi, Hepworth, and Moore on Abstract Sculpture

Many early-20th-century sculptors rejected the notion that reproducing the physical world of nature was the purpose of sculpture. Instead, they championed abstraction as the sculptor's proper goal. Among those who not only produced enduring masterpieces of abstract sculpture but also wrote eloquently about the theoretical basis of their work were Constantin Brancusi (FIG. 24-61), Barbara Hepworth (FIG. 24-62), and Henry Moore (FIG. 24-63). Some excerpts from their writings on sculpture illustrate their commitment to abstraction as their guiding principle.

Constantin Brancusi Simplicity is not an objective in art, but one achieves simplicity despite oneself by entering into the real sense of things.* . . . What is real is not the external form but the essence of things. Starting from this truth it is impossible for anyone to express anything essentially real by imitating its exterior surface.†

Barbara Hepworth The forms which have had special meaning for me since childhood have been the standing form (which is the translation of my feeling towards the human being standing in landscape); the two forms (which is the tender relationship of one living thing beside another); and the closed form, such as the oval, spherical, or pierced form (sometimes incorporating colour) which translates for me the association and meaning of gesture in the landscape. . . . In all these shapes the translation of what one feels about man and nature must be conveyed by the sculptor in terms of mass, inner tension, and rhythm, scale in relation to our human size, and the quality of surface which speaks through our hands and eyes.‡

Henry Moore Since the Gothic, European sculpture had become overgrown with moss, weeds—all sorts of surface excrescences which completely concealed shape. It has been Brancusi's special mission to get rid of this overgrowth, and to make us once more shape-conscious. To do this he has had to concentrate on very simple direct shapes . . . Abstract qualities of design are essential to the value of a work . . . Because a work does not aim at reproducing natural appearances, it is not, therefore, an escape from life—but may be a penetration into reality. . . . My sculpture is becoming less representational, less an outward visual copy . . . but only because I believe that in this way I can present the

24-62 BARBARA HEPWORTH, *Oval Sculpture* (*No. 2*), 1943, cast 1958, plaster, $11\frac{1}{4}" \times 1' \, 4\frac{1}{4}" \times 10"$. Tate.

Hepworth's major contribution to the history of sculpture was the introduction of the hole, or negative space, as an abstract element that is as integral and important to the sculpture as its mass.

human psychological content of my work with greatest directness and intensity.§

*Quoted in Herschel B. Chipp, *Theories of Modern Art: A Source Book by Artists and Critics* (Berkeley and Los Angeles: University of California Press, 1968), 364–365.
†Quoted in George Heard Hamilton, *Painting and Sculpture in Europe, 1880–1940*, 6th ed. (New Haven, Conn.: Yale University Press, 1993), 426.
‡Barbara Hepworth, *A Pictorial Autobiography* (London: Tate Gallery, 1978), 9, 53.
§Quoted in Robert L. Herbert, *Modern Artists on Art*, 2d ed. (Mineola, N.Y.: Dover, 2000), 173–179.

curving columnar form sharply tapered at each end. Despite the abstraction, the sculpture retains the suggestion of a bird about to soar in free flight through the heavens. The highly reflective surface of the polished bronze does not allow the viewer's eye to linger on the sculpture itself (as do, for example, Rodin's agitated and textured surfaces; FIGS. 23-32, 23-32A, and 23-33). Instead, the eye follows the gleaming reflection along the delicate curves right off the tip of the work, thereby inducing a feeling of flight. Brancusi stated, "All my life I have sought the essence of flight. Don't look for mysteries. I give you pure joy. Look at the sculptures until you see them. Those nearest to God have seen them."[47]

BARBARA HEPWORTH In England, BARBARA HEPWORTH (1903–1975) developed her own kind of essential sculptural form,

combining pristine shape with a sense of organic vitality. She sought a sculptural idiom that would express her sense both of nature and the landscape and of the person who is in and observes nature (see "Brancusi, Hepworth, and Moore," above). By 1929, Hepworth arrived at a breakthrough that evolved into an enduring and commanding element in her work from that point on. It represents her major contribution to the history of sculpture: the use of the hole, or void. Earlier sculptors, such as Archipenko (FIG. 24-20) had experimented with sculptural voids, but Hepworth introduced holes in her sculptures as abstract elements. The holes do not represent anything specific. They are simply negative space, but are as integral and important to the sculptures as their mass. *Oval Sculpture* (*No. 2*) is a plaster cast (FIG. **24-62**) of an earlier wood sculpture Hepworth carved in 1943. Pierced in four places, the work is as

The reclining female figure was a major theme in Moore's sculptures. Inspired by a Mexican chacmool, he simplified and abstracted the body form in a way that recalls Biomorphic Surrealism.

much defined by the smooth, curving holes as by the volume of white plaster. Like the forms in all of Hepworth's mature works, those in *Oval Sculpture* are basic and universal, expressing a sense of eternity's timelessness.

HENRY MOORE Fellow Briton HENRY MOORE (1898–1986) shared Hepworth's interest in the hole, or void, as an important element in sculptural design, but his sculptures, such as *Reclining Figure* (FIG. **24-63**), although abstracted, always remain recognizable. This statue is one of a long series of reclining female nudes inspired originally by a photograph Moore acquired of a *chacmool* from pre-Columbian Mexico. Moore believed the simple and massive shapes of his statues expressed a universal truth beyond the physical world (see "Brancusi, Hepworth, and Moore," page 770).

Reclining Figure is also characteristic of Moore's work in exploiting the natural beauty of different materials—here, elm. Moore maintained every "material has its own individual qualities" and these qualities could play a role in the creative process: "It is only when the sculptor works direct, when there is an active relationship with his material, that the material can take its part in the shaping of an idea."[48] Accordingly, the contours of *Reclining Figure* follow the grain of the wood. The abstracted shapes suggest Surrealist biomorphic forms (FIG. 24-58), but Moore's recumbent woman is also a powerful earth mother whose undulant forms and hollows suggest nurturing human energy. Similarly, the body shapes evoke the contours of the Yorkshire hills of Moore's childhood and the wind-polished surfaces of weathered wood and stone. Moore heightened the allusions to landscape and to Surrealist organic forms in his work by interplaying mass and void, based on the intriguing qualities of cavities in nature. For Moore, the hole was not an abstract shape. It represented "the mysterious fascination of caves in hillsides and cliffs."[49] *Reclining Figure* combines the organic vocabulary central to Moore's philosophy—bone shapes, eroded rocks, and geologic formations—to communicate the human form's fluidity, dynamism, and evocative nature.

VERA MUKHINA Not all European sculptors of this period pursued abstraction, however. *The Worker and the Collective Farm Worker* (FIG. **24-64**) by Russian artist VERA MUKHINA (1889–1963) presents a vivid contrast with the work of Brancusi, Hepworth, and Moore. Produced in 1937 for the International Exposition

24-64 VERA MUKHINA, *The Worker and the Collective Farm Worker*, Soviet Pavilion, Paris Exposition, 1937. Stainless steel, 78′ high. © Estate of Vera Mukhina/RAO, Moscow/VAGA, New York.

In contrast to contemporaneous abstract sculpture, Mukhina's realistic representation of a male factory worker and a female farm worker glorified the communal labor of the Soviet people.

in Paris—the same venue in which Picasso displayed *Guernica* (FIG. 24-18)—Mukhina's monumental stainless-steel sculpture glorifies the communal labor of the Soviet people. Whereas Picasso employed Cubist abstraction to convey the horror of wartime bombing, Mukhina relied on realism to represent exemplars of the Soviet citizenry. Her sculpture, which stood on the top of the Soviet Pavilion at the exposition, depicts a male factory worker, holding aloft the tool of his trade, the hammer. Alongside him is a female farm worker, raising her sickle to the sky. The juxtaposed hammer and sickle at the apex of the sculpture replicate their appearance on the Soviet flag. Mukhina augmented the heroic tenor of the work by emphasizing the solidity of the figures, who stride forward with their clothes blowing dramatically behind them. Mukhina had studied in Paris and was familiar with abstraction, especially Cubism, but felt a commitment to realism produced the most powerful sculpture. The Soviet government officially approved this realist style and Mukhina earned high praise for her sculpture. Indeed, Russian citizens celebrated the work as a national symbol for decades.

Architecture

As in the opening decades of the century, developments in European architecture after World War I closely paralleled the stylistic and theoretical concerns of painters and sculptors.

GERRIT THOMAS RIETVELD The ideas Piet Mondrian, Theo van Doesburg, and De Stijl artists advanced found their architectural equivalent in the designs of GERRIT THOMAS RIETVELD (1888–1964). His Schröder House (FIG. **24-65**) in Utrecht, built in 1924, perfectly expresses van Doesburg's definition of De Stijl architecture:

> The new architecture is anti-cubic, i.e., it does not strive to contain the different functional space cells in a single closed cube, but it throws the functional space (as well as canopy planes, balcony volumes, etc.) out from the centre of the cube, so that height, width, and depth plus time become a completely new plastic expression in open spaces. . . . The plastic architect . . . has to construct in the new field, time-space.[50]

The main living rooms of the Schröder House are on the second floor, with more private rooms on the ground floor. However, Rietveld's house has an open plan and a relationship to nature more like the houses of American architect Frank Lloyd Wright (FIGS. 24-45 and 24-46). Rietveld designed the entire second floor with sliding partitions that can be closed to define separate rooms or pushed back to create one open space broken into units only by the furniture arrangement. This shifting quality appears also on the outside, where railings, free-floating walls, and long rectangular windows give the effect of cubic units breaking up before the viewer's eyes. Rectangular planes seem to slide across each other on the Schröder House facade like movable panels, making this structure a kind of three-dimensional projection of

the rigid but carefully proportioned flat color rectangles in Mondrian's paintings (FIG. 24-60).

WALTER GROPIUS De Stijl architects not only developed an appealing simplified geometric style but also promoted the notion art should be thoroughly incorporated into living environments. As Mondrian had insisted, "[A]rt and life are *one*; art and life are both expressions of truth."[51] In Germany, WALTER GROPIUS (1883–1969) developed a particular vision of "total architecture." He made this concept the foundation of not only his own work but also the work of generations of pupils under his influence at a school called the *Bauhaus* (see "Walter Gropius and the Bauhaus," page 773).

The building Gropius designed for the Bauhaus in 1925 after the school relocated to Dessau was the Bauhaus's architectural manifesto. The Dessau Bauhaus consisted of workshop and class areas, a dining room, a theater, a gymnasium, a wing with studio apartments, and an enclosed two-story bridge housing administrative offices. Of the major wings, the most dramatic was the Shop Block (FIG. 24-66). Three stories tall, the Shop Block housed a printing shop and dye works facility, in addition to other work areas. The builders constructed the skeleton of reinforced concrete but set these supports well back, sheathing the entire structure in glass, creating a streamlined and light effect. This design's simplicity followed Gropius's dictum that architecture should avoid "all romantic embellishment and whimsy." Further, he realized the "economy in the use of space" articulated in his list of Bauhaus principles in his interior layout of the Shop Block, which consisted of large areas of free-flowing undivided space. Gropius believed this kind of spatial organization encouraged interaction and the sharing of ideas.

24-65 GERRIT THOMAS RIETVELD, Schröder House (looking northwest), Utrecht, the Netherlands, 1924.

The De Stijl Schröder House has an open plan and an exterior that is a kind of three-dimensional projection of the carefully proportioned flat color rectangles in Mondrian's paintings (FIG. 24-60).

Walter Gropius and the Bauhaus

In 1919, Walter Gropius became the director of the Weimar School of Arts and Crafts in Germany, founded in 1906. Under Gropius, the school assumed a new name—Das Staatliche Bauhaus (State School of Building). Gropius's goal was to train artists, architects, and designers to accept and anticipate 20th-century needs. He developed an extensive curriculum based on certain principles set forth in a formal Bauhaus *Manifesto* published in April 1919.

BAUHAUS MANIFESTO

The first principle Gropius staunchly advocated in the 1919 manifesto was the importance of strong basic design (including principles of composition, two- and three-dimensionality, and color theory) and craftsmanship as fundamental to good art and architecture. He asserted there was no essential difference between the artist and the craftsperson.

> The Bauhaus strives to coordinate all creative effort, to achieve, in a new architecture, the unification of all training in art and design. The ultimate, if distant, goal of the Bauhaus is the collective work of art—the Building—in which no barriers exist between the structural and the decorative arts.*

24-66 WALTER GROPIUS, Shop Block (looking northeast), the Bauhaus, Dessau, Germany, 1925–1926.

Gropius constructed this Bauhaus building by sheathing a reinforced concrete skeleton in glass. The design followed his dictum that architecture should avoid "all romantic embellishment and whimsy."

24-66A BREUER, Wassily chair, 1925.

24-66B STÖLZL, Gobelin tapestry, 1927–1928.

To encourage the elimination of those boundaries that traditionally separated art from architecture and art from craft, the Bauhaus offered courses in a wide range of artistic disciplines. These included carpentry, furniture design (by MARCEL BREUER [1902–1981]; FIG. **24-66A**), weaving (by GUNTA STÖLZL [1897–1983]; FIG. **24-66B**), pottery, bookbinding, metalwork, stained glass, mural painting, stage design, and advertising and typography, in addition to painting, sculpture, and architecture. Both a technical instructor and a "teacher of form"—an artist—taught in each department. Among the teachers Gropius hired were Vassily Kandinsky (FIG. 24-7) and Paul Klee (FIG. 24-59).

In addition, because Gropius wanted the Bauhaus to produce graduates who could design progressive environments that satisfied 20th-century needs, he emphasized thorough knowledge of machine-age technologies and materials. He felt that to produce truly successful designs, the artist-architect-craftsperson had to understand industry and mass production. Ultimately, Gropius hoped for a marriage between art and industry—a synthesis of design and production. As did the De Stijl movement, the Bauhaus philosophy had its roots in utopian principles. Gropius's declaration reveals the idealism of the entire Bauhaus enterprise:

> Let us collectively desire, conceive, and create the new building of the future, which will be everything in one structure: architecture and sculpture and painting, which, from the million hands of craftsmen, will one day rise towards heaven as the crystalline symbol of a new and coming faith.†

In its reference to a unity of workers, this statement also reveals the undercurrent of socialism present in Germany at the time.

BAUHAUS IN DESSAU

After encountering increasing hostility from a new government elected in 1924, the Bauhaus moved north from Weimar to Dessau (FIG. 24-66) in early 1925. By this time, the Bauhaus program had matured. In a new statement, Gropius listed the school's goals more clearly:

- A decidedly positive attitude to the living environment of vehicles and machines
- The organic shaping of things in accordance with their own current laws, avoiding all romantic embellishment and whimsy
- Restriction of basic forms and colors to what is typical and universally intelligible
- Simplicity in complexity, economy in the use of space, materials, time, and money‡

*Quoted in Charles Harrison and Paul Wood, eds., *Art in Theory, 1900–2000: An Anthology of Changing Ideas*, 2d ed. (Oxford: Blackwell, 2003), 311.
†Translated by Charles W. Haxthausen, in Barry Bergdoll, ed., *Bauhaus 1919–1933* (New York: Museum of Modern Art, 2009), 64.
‡Quoted in John Willett, *Art and Politics in the Weimar Period: The New Sobriety, 1917–1933* (New York: Da Capo Press, 1978), 119.

24-67 LUDWIG MIES VAN DER ROHE, **model for a glass skyscraper, Berlin, Germany, 1922 (no longer extant).**

In this technically and aesthetically adventurous design, the architect whose motto was "less is more" proposed a transparent building that revealed its cantilevered floor planes and thin supports.

LUDWIG MIES VAN DER ROHE In 1928, Gropius left the Bauhaus, and LUDWIG MIES VAN DER ROHE (1886–1969) eventually took over the directorship, moving the school to Berlin. Taking as his motto "less is more" and calling his architecture "skin and bones," the new Bauhaus director had already fully formed his aesthetic when he conceived the model (FIG. **24-67**) for a glass skyscraper building in 1921. In the glass model, which was on display at the first Bauhaus exhibition in 1923, three irregularly shaped towers flow outward from a central court designed to hold a lobby, a porter's room, and a community center. Two cylindrical entrance shafts rise at the ends of the court, each containing elevators, stairways, and toilets. Wholly transparent, the perimeter walls reveal the regular horizontal patterning of the cantilevered floor planes and their thin vertical supporting elements. The bold use of glass sheathing and inset supports was, at the time, technically and aesthetically adventurous. The weblike delicacy of the lines of the model, as well as the illusion of movement created by reflection and by light changes seen through the glass, appealed to many other architects. A few years later, Gropius pursued it in his design for the Bauhaus building (FIG. 24-66) in Dessau. The legacy of Mies van der Rohe's design can be seen in the glass-and-steel skyscrapers found in major cities throughout the world today.

END OF THE BAUHAUS One of Hitler's first acts after coming to power was to close the Bauhaus in 1933. During its 14-year existence, the beleaguered school graduated fewer than 500 students, yet it achieved legendary status. Its phenomenal influence extended beyond painting, sculpture, and architecture to interior design, graphic design, and advertising. Moreover, art schools everywhere began to structure their curricula in line with the program the Bauhaus pioneered. The numerous Bauhaus instructors who fled Nazi Germany disseminated the school's philosophy and aesthetic. Many Bauhaus members came to the United States. Gropius and Breuer (FIG. 24-66A) ended up at Harvard University. Mies van der Rohe moved to Chicago and taught there.

LE CORBUSIER The simple geometric aesthetic developed by Gropius and Mies van der Rohe became known as the *International style* because of its widespread popularity. The first and purest exponent of this style was the Swiss architect Charles-Edouard Jeanneret, who adopted his maternal grandfather's name— LE CORBUSIER (1887–1965). Trained in Paris and Berlin, he was also a painter, but Le Corbusier had the greatest influence as an architect and theorist on modern architecture. As such, he applied himself to designing a functional living space, which he described as a "machine for living."[52]

Le Corbusier maintained the basic physical and psychological needs of every human being were sun, space, and vegetation combined with controlled temperature, good ventilation, and insulation against harmful and undesired noise. He also advocated basing dwelling designs on human scale, because the house is humankind's assertion within nature. All these qualities characterize Le Corbusier's Villa Savoye (FIG. **24-68**), located at Poissy-sur-Seine near Paris. The country house sits at the center of a large plot of land cleared of trees and shrubs, but windows on all sides and the villa's roof-terrace provide the residents with broad views of the surrounding landscape. Several colors appear on the exterior—originally, a dark-green base, cream walls, and a rose-and-blue windscreen on top. They were a deliberate analogy for the colors in the machine-inspired Purist style of painting (FIG. 24-22) Le Corbusier practiced.

A cube of lightly enclosed and deeply penetrated space, the Villa Savoye has only a partially confined ground floor (containing, originally, a three-car garage, bedrooms, a bathroom, and utility rooms, and today a ticket counter and small gift shop for visitors). Much of the house's interior is open space, with thin columns supporting the main living floor and the roof garden area. The major living rooms in the Villa Savoye are on the second floor, wrapping around an open central court. Strip windows running along the membranelike exterior walls provide illumination to the rooms as well as views out to nature. From the second floor court, a ramp leads up to the roof-terrace and an interior garden protected by a curving windbreak along the north side.

The Villa Savoye has no traditional facade. The ostensible approach to the house does not define an entrance. Visitors must walk around and through the house to comprehend its layout, which incorporates several changes of direction and spiral staircases. Spaces and masses interpenetrate so fluidly that inside and outside space intermingle. The machine-planed smoothness of the unadorned

24-68 Le Corbusier, Villa Savoye (looking southeast), Poissy-sur-Seine, France, 1929. ◼◀

Steel and ferroconcrete made it possible for Le Corbusier to invert the traditional practice of placing light architectural elements above heavy ones and to eliminate weight-bearing walls on the ground story.

surfaces, the slender ribbons of continuous windows, and the buoyant lightness of the whole fabric—all combine to reverse the effect of traditional country houses (FIG. 17-28). By placing heavy elements above and light ones below, and by refusing to enclose the ground story of the Villa Savoye with masonry walls, Le Corbusier inverted traditional design practice. This openness, made possible by the use of steel and ferroconcrete as construction materials, makes the "load" of the Villa Savoye's upper stories appear to hover lightly on the slender columnar supports.

MARSEILLES AND CHANDIGARH Le Corbusier designed the Villa Savoye as a private home, but as did De Stijl architects, he dreamed of extending his ideas of the house as a "machine for living" to designs for efficient and humane cities. He saw great cities as spiritual workshops and he proposed to correct the deficiencies in existing cities caused by poor traffic circulation, inadequate living units, and the lack of space for recreation and exercise. He proposed replacing traditional cities with three types of new communities. Vertical cities would house workers and the business and service industries. Linear-industrial cities would run as belts along the routes between the vertical cities and would serve as centers for the people and processes involved in manufacturing. Finally, separate centers would be constructed for people involved in intensive agricultural activity. Le Corbusier's cities would provide for human cultural needs in addition to serving every person's physical, mental, and emotional comfort needs.

Later in his career, Le Corbusier designed a few vertical cities, most notably the Unité d'Habitation in Marseilles (1945–1952). He also created the master plan for the entire city of Chandigarh, the capital city of the Punjab, India (1950–1957). He ended his career with a personal expressive style in his design of the Chapel of Notre Dame du Haut (FIG. 25-40) at Ronchamp, France.

UNITED STATES AND MEXICO, 1930 TO 1945

In the 1930s, much of the Western world was plunged into the Great Depression, which had a particularly acute effect in the United States. The decade following the catastrophic stock market crash of October 1929 dramatically changed the nation, and artists were among the millions of economic victims. The limited art market virtually disappeared, and museums curtailed both their purchases and exhibition schedules. Many artists sought financial support from the federal government, which established numerous programs to provide relief, assist recovery, and promote reform. Among the programs supporting artists were the Treasury Relief Art Project, founded in 1934 to commission art for federal buildings, and the Works Progress Administration (WPA), founded in 1935 to relieve widespread unemployment. Under the WPA, varied activities of the Federal Art Project paid artists, writers, and theater people a regular wage in exchange for work in their professions.

Despite the economic hardships facing artists during the Great Depression, the United States became a haven for European painters, sculptors, and architects seeking to escape from Hitler and the Nazis. Among those who abandoned their homelands for America during the years leading up to World War II in search of freedom from political and religious persecution and a more hospitable environment for their art were Léger, Lipchitz, Beckmann, Grosz, Ernst, and Dalí. This influx of European artists was as significant a factor in exposing American artists to modernist European art as was the Armory Show of 1913 (see "The Armory Show," page 751).

A complementary factor was the desire on the part of American museums to demonstrate their familiarity and connection with the most progressive European art by mounting exhibitions centered on the latest European artistic developments. In 1938, for example, the City Art Museum of Saint Louis presented an exhibition of Beckmann's work, and the Art Institute of Chicago organized *George Grosz: A Survey of His Art from 1918–1938*. This interest in exhibiting the work of persecuted artists driven from their homelands also had political overtones. In the highly charged atmosphere of the late 1930s leading to the onset of World War II, Americans often perceived support for these artists and their work as support for freedom and democracy. In 1942, Alfred H. Barr Jr. (1902–1981), the director of the Museum of Modern Art, stated:

> Among the freedoms which the Nazis have destroyed, none has been more cynically perverted, more brutally stamped upon, than the Freedom of Art. For not only must the artist of Nazi Germany bow to political tyranny, he must also conform to the personal taste of that great art connoisseur, Adolf Hitler. . . . But German artists of spirit and integrity have refused to conform. They have gone into exile or slipped into anxious obscurity. . . . Their paintings and sculptures, too, have been hidden or exiled. . . . But in free countries they can still be seen, can still bear witness to the survival of a free German culture.[53]

Despite this moral support for exiled artists, once the United States formally entered the war, Germany officially became the enemy. It became much more difficult for the American art world to promote German artists, however persecuted. Many émigré artists, including Léger, Grosz, Ernst, and Dalí, returned to Europe after the war ended. Their collective presence in the United States until then, however, was critical for the development of American art.

Painting

Although the political, social, and economic developments of the 1930s and 1940s brought many modernist European artists to the United States, the leading American painters of this period were primarily figural artists who had only a limited interest in abstract composition.

BEN SHAHN Born in Lithuania, BEN SHAHN (1898–1969) came to the United States in 1906 and trained as a lithographer before broadening the media in which he worked to include easel painting, photography, and murals. He focused on the lives of ordinary people and the injustices often done to them by the structure of an impersonal, bureaucratic society. In the early 1930s, he completed a cycle of 23 paintings and prints inspired by the trial and execution of the two Italian anarchists Nicola Sacco and Bartolomeo Vanzetti. Accused of killing two men in a holdup in 1920 in South Braintree, Massachusetts, the Italians were convicted in a trial many people thought resulted in a grave miscarriage of justice. Shahn felt he had found in this story a subject the equal of any in Western art history: "Suddenly I realized . . . I was living through another crucifixion."[54] Basing many of the works in this cycle on newspaper photographs of the events, Shahn devised a style that adapted his knowledge of Synthetic Cubism and his training in commercial art to an emotionally expressive use of flat, intense color in figural compositions filled with sharp, dry, angular forms. He called the major work in the series *The Passion of Sacco and Vanzetti* (FIG. I-6), drawing a parallel to Christ's Passion. This tall, narrow painting condenses the narrative in terms of both time and space. The two executed men lie in coffins at the bottom of the composition. Presiding over them are the three members of the commission chaired by Harvard University president A. Laurence Lowell, who declared the original trial fair and cleared the way for the executions to take place. A framed portrait of Judge Webster Thayer, who handed down the initial sentence, hangs on the wall of a simplified government building. The gray pallor of the dead men, the stylized mask-faces of the mock-pious mourning commissioners, and the sanctimonious, distant judge all contribute to the mood of anguished commentary making this image one of Shahn's most powerful works.

EDWARD HOPPER Trained as a commercial artist, EDWARD HOPPER (1882–1967) studied painting and printmaking in New York and then in Paris. When he returned to the United States, he concentrated on scenes of contemporary American city and

24-69 EDWARD HOPPER, *Nighthawks*, 1942. Oil on canvas, 2′ 6″ × 4′ 8 11/16″. Art Institute of Chicago, Chicago (Friends of American Art Collection).

The seeming indifference of Hopper's characters to one another, and the echoing spaces surrounding them, evoke the overwhelming loneliness and isolation of Depression-era life in the United States.

1 ft.

country life. His paintings depict buildings, streets, and landscapes that are curiously muted, still, and filled with empty spaces, evoking the national mind-set during the Depression era. Hopper did not paint historically specific scenes. He took as his subject the more generalized theme of the overwhelming loneliness and echoing isolation of modern life in the United States. In his paintings, motion is stopped and time suspended.

From the darkened streets outside a restaurant in Hopper's *Nighthawks* (FIG. **24-69**), the viewer glimpses the lighted interior through huge plate-glass windows, which lend the inner space the paradoxical sense of being both a safe refuge and a vulnerable place for the three customers and the man behind the counter. The seeming indifference of Hopper's characters to one another as well as the echoing spaces surrounding them evoke the pervasive loneliness of modern humans. In *Nighthawks* and other works, Hopper created a Realist vision recalling that of 19th-century artists such as Thomas Eakins (FIG. 22-36) and Henry Ossawa Tanner (FIG. 22-38), but in keeping with more recent trends in painting, he simplified the shapes, moving toward abstraction.

JACOB LAWRENCE African American artist JACOB LAWRENCE (1917–2000) moved to Harlem, New York, in 1927 while still a boy. There, he came under the spell of the African art and the African American history he found in lectures and exhibitions and in the special programs sponsored by the 135th Street branch of the New York Public Library, which had outstanding collections of African American art and archival data. Inspired by the politically oriented art of Goya (FIG. 22-11), Daumier (FIG. 22-29), and Orozco (FIG. 24-73), and influenced by the many artists and writers of the Harlem Renaissance whom he met, including Aaron Douglas (FIGS. 24-40 and 24-40A), Lawrence found his subjects in the everyday life of Harlem and in African American history.

In 1941, Lawrence began a 60-painting series titled *The Migration of the Negro* in which he defined his vision of the continuing African American struggle against discrimination. Unlike his earlier historical paintings depicting important figures in American history, such as the abolitionists Frederick Douglass and Harriet Tubman, this series called attention to a contemporaneous event— the ongoing exodus of black labor from the southern United States. Disillusioned with their lives in the South, hundreds of thousands of African Americans migrated north in the years following World War I, seeking improved economic opportunities and a more hospitable political and social environment. But the conditions African Americans encountered both during their migration and in the North were often as difficult and discriminatory as those they had left behind in the South, as Lawrence knew from his own experience:

> I was part of the migration, as was my family, my mother, my sister, and my brother. . . . I grew up hearing tales about people "coming up," another family arriving. . . . I didn't realize what was happening until about the middle of the 1930s, and that's when the *Migration* series began to take form in my mind.[55]

Lawrence's *Migration* paintings provide numerous vignettes capturing the experiences of the African Americans who had moved to the North. Often, a sense of the bleakness and degradation of their new life dominates the images. *No. 49* (FIG. **24-70**) of this series bears the caption "They also found discrimination in the North although it was much different from that which they had known in the South." Lawrence depicted a blatantly segregated dining room with a barrier running down the room's center separating

1 in.

24-70 JACOB LAWRENCE, *No. 49* from *The Migration of the Negro*, 1940–1941. Tempera on Masonite, 1′ 6″ × 1′. Phillips Collection, Washington, D.C.

The 49th in a series of 60 paintings documenting African American life in the North, Lawrence's depiction of a segregated dining room underscored that the migrants had not left discrimination behind.

the whites on the left from the African Americans on the right. To ensure a continuity and visual integrity among all 60 paintings, Lawrence interpreted his themes systematically in rhythmic arrangements of bold, flat, and strongly colored shapes. His style drew equally from his interest in the push-pull effects of Cubist space and his memories of the patterns made by the colored scatter rugs brightening the floors of his childhood homes. He unified the narrative with a consistent palette of bluish green, orange, yellow, and grayish brown throughout the entire series.

GRANT WOOD Although many American artists, such as the Precisionists (FIGS. 24-41 and 24-42), preferred to depict the city or rapidly developing technological advances, others avoided subjects tied to modern life. At a 1931 arts conference, GRANT WOOD (1891–1942) announced a new movement developing in the Midwest, known as *Regionalism*, which he described as focused on American subjects and as standing in reaction to the modernist abstraction of Europe and New York. Four years later, Wood published an essay titled "Revolt against the City" that underscored their new focus.

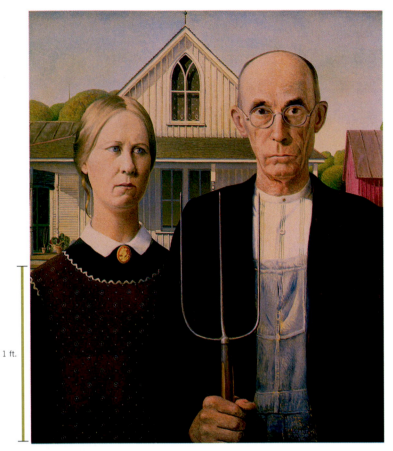

1 ft.

24-71 GRANT WOOD, *American Gothic*, 1930. Oil on beaverboard, 2′ 5⅞″ × 2′ ⅞″. Art Institute of Chicago, Chicago (Friends of American Art Collection). ◼◁

In reaction to modernist abstract painting, the Midwestern Regionalism movement focused on American subjects. Wood's painting of an Iowa farmer and his daughter became an American icon.

Wood and the Regionalists, sometimes referred to as the American Scene Painters, turned their attention instead to rural life as America's cultural backbone. Wood's paintings, for example, portray the people of rural Iowa, where he was born and raised.

The work that catapulted Wood to national prominence was *American Gothic* (FIG. **24-71**), which became an American icon. The artist depicted a farmer and his spinster daughter standing in front of a neat house with a small *lancet* window, a motif originating in Gothic architecture and associated with churches and religious piety. The man and woman wear traditional attire. He appears in worn overalls and she in an apron trimmed with rickrack. The dour expression on both faces gives the painting a severe quality, which Wood enhanced with his meticulous brushwork. The public and professional critics agreed *American Gothic* was "quaint, humorous, and AMERICAN" and embodied "strength, dignity, fortitude, resoluteness, integrity," qualities that represented the true spirit of America.[56]

Wood's Regionalist vision involved more than his subjects. It extended to a rejection of avant-garde styles in favor of a clearly readable, Realist style. Surely this approach appealed to many people alienated by the increasing presence of abstraction in art. However, despite the accolades this painting received, it also attracted criticism. Not everyone saw the painting as a sympathetic portrayal of Midwestern life. Indeed, some Iowans considered the depiction of life in their state insulting. In addition, despite the seemingly reportorial nature of *American Gothic,* some viewed it as a political statement—one of staunch nationalism. In light of the problematic

nationalism in Germany at the time, many observers found Wood's nationalistic attitude disturbing. Nonetheless, during the Great Depression, Regionalist paintings had a popular appeal because they often projected a reassuring image of America's heartland. The public saw Regionalism as a means of coping with the national crisis through a search for cultural roots. Thus, people deemed acceptable any nostalgia implicit in Regionalist paintings or mythologies these works perpetuated because they served a larger purpose.

THOMAS HART BENTON Another major Regionalist artist was THOMAS HART BENTON (1889–1975). Whereas Wood focused his attention on Iowa, Benton turned to scenes from his native Missouri. He produced one of his major works, a series of murals titled *A Social History of the State of Missouri*, in 1936 for the Missouri State Capitol. The murals depict a collection of images from the state's historic and legendary past, such as primitive agriculture, horse trading, a vigilante lynching, and an old-fashioned political meeting. Other scenes portray the mining industry, grain elevators, Native Americans, and family life. One segment, *Pioneer Days and Early Settlers* (FIG. **24-72**), shows a white man using whisky as a bartering tool with a Native American (*left*), along with scenes documenting the building of Missouri (*right*). Part documentary and part invention, Benton's images include both positive and negative aspects of Missouri's history, as these examples illustrate. Although the public perceived the Regionalists as dedicated to glorifying Midwestern life, that was not their aim. Indeed, Grant Wood observed, "Your true regionalist is not a mere eulogist; he may even be a severe critic."[57] Benton, like Wood, championed a visually accessible style, but he developed a highly personal aesthetic that included complex compositions, a fluidity of imagery, and simplified figures depicted with a rubbery distortion.

JOSÉ CLEMENTE OROZCO During the period between the two world wars, several Mexican painters achieved international renown for their work both in Mexico and the United States. The eldest of the three was JOSÉ CLEMENTE OROZCO (1883–1949), one of a group of Mexican artists determined to base their art on the indigenous history and culture existing in Mexico before Europeans arrived. The movement these artists formed was part of the idealistic rethinking of society that occurred in conjunction with the Mexican Revolution (1910–1920) and the lingering political turmoil of the 1920s. Among the projects these politically motivated artists undertook were vast mural cycles placed in public buildings to dramatize and validate the history of Mexico's native peoples. Orozco worked on one of the first major cycles, painted in 1922 on the walls of the National Training School in Mexico City. He carried the ideas of this mural revolution to the United States, completing many commissions for wall paintings between 1927 and 1934. From 1932 to 1934, he painted a major mural cycle in the Baker Library at Dartmouth College in New Hampshire. The college let Orozco choose the subject, and he designed 14 large panels and 10 smaller ones that together formed a panoramic and symbolic history of ancient and modern Mexico. The murals recount Mexican history from the early mythic days of the feathered-serpent god Quetzalcoatl to a contemporary and bitterly satiric vision of modern education.

The imagery in panel 16, *Epic of American Civilization: Hispano-America* (FIG. **24-73**), revolves around the monumental figure of a heroic Mexican peasant armed to participate in the Mexican Revolution. Looming on either side of him are mounds crammed with symbolic figures of his oppressors—bankers, government soldiers, officials, gangsters, and the rich. Money-grubbers empty huge bags of gold coins at the incorruptible peon's feet, cannons threaten him,

24-72 THOMAS HART BENTON, *Pioneer Days and Early Settlers,* fresco in the State Capitol, Jefferson City, Missouri, 1936. © T. H. Benton and R. P. Benton Testamentary Trusts/UMB Bank Trustee/Licensed by VAGA, New York.

Benton's mural for Missouri's State Capitol is one of the major Regionalist artworks. Part documentary and part invention, the images include both positive and negative aspects of state history.

and a general bedecked with medals raises a dagger to stab him in the back. Orozco's training as an architect gave him a sense of the framed wall surface, which he easily commanded, projecting his clearly defined figures onto the solid mural plane in monumental scale. In addition, Orozco's early experience as a maker of politi-cal prints and as a newspaper artist had taught him the rhetorical strength of graphic brevity, which he used here to assure his alle-gory could be read easily. His special merging of the graphic and mural media effects gives his work an originality and force rarely seen in mural painting after the Renaissance and Baroque periods.

24-73 JOSÉ CLEMENTE OROZCO, *Epic of American Civilization: Hispano-America* (panel 16), fresco in Baker Memorial Library, Dartmouth College, Hanover, New Hampshire, ca. 1932–1934.

One of 24 panels depicting the history of Mexico from ancient times, this scene focuses on a heroic peasant soldier of the Mexican Revolution surrounded by symbolic figures of his oppressors.

Rivera on Art for the People

Diego Rivera was an avid proponent of a social and political role for art in the lives of common people and wrote passionately about the proper goals for an artist—goals he fully met in his own murals depicting Mexican history (FIG. 24-74). Rivera's views stand in sharp contrast to the growing interest in abstraction on the part of many early-20th-century painters and sculptors.

Art has always been employed by the different social classes who hold the balance of power as one instrument of domination—hence, as a political instrument. One can analyze epoch after epoch—from the stone age to our own day—and see that there is no form of art which does not also play an essential political role. . . . What is it then that we really need? . . . An art with revolution as its subject:

because the principal interest in the worker's life has to be touched first. It is necessary that he find aesthetic satisfaction and the highest pleasure appareled in the essential interest of his life. . . . The subject is to the painter what the rails are to a locomotive. He cannot do without it. In fact, when he refuses to seek or accept a subject, his own plastic methods and his own aesthetic theories become his subject instead. . . . [H]e himself becomes the subject of his work. He becomes nothing but an illustrator of his own state of mind . . . That is the deception practiced under the name of "Pure Art."*

*Quoted in Robert Goldwater and Marco Treves, eds., *Artists on Art from the XIV to the XX Century* (New York: Pantheon, 1945), 475–477.

24-74 DIEGO RIVERA, *Ancient Mexico,* detail of *History of Mexico,* fresco in the Palacio Nacional, Mexico City, 1929–1935.

A staunch Marxist, Rivera painted vast mural cycles in public buildings to dramatize the history of his native land. This fresco depicts the conflicts between indigenous Mexicans and Spanish colonizers.

DIEGO RIVERA A second Mexican who received great acclaim for his murals, both in Mexico and in the United States was DIEGO RIVERA (1886–1957). A staunch Marxist, Rivera strove to develop an art that served his people's needs (see "Rivera on Art for the People," page 780). Toward that end, he sought to create a national Mexican style focusing on Mexico's history and also incorporating a popular, generally accessible aesthetic in keeping with the socialist spirit of the Mexican Revolution. Rivera produced numerous large murals in public buildings, among them a series lining the staircase of the National Palace in Mexico City. In these images, painted between 1929 and 1935, he depicted scenes from Mexico's history, of which *Ancient Mexico* (FIG. **24-74**) is one. This section of the mural represents the conflicts between the indigenous people and the Spanish colonizers. Rivera included portraits of important figures in Mexican history, especially those involved in the struggle for Mexican independence. Although the composition is complex, the simple monumental shapes and areas of bold color make the story easily legible.

FRIDA KAHLO Born to a Mexican mother and German father, the painter FRIDA KAHLO (1907–1954), who married Diego Rivera, used the details of her life as powerful symbols for the psychological pain of human existence. Art historians often consider Kahlo a Surrealist due to the psychic, autobiographical issues she dealt with in her art. Indeed, André Breton himself deemed her

a Natural Surrealist. (The work of her older contemporary, RUFINO TAMAYO [1899–1991; FIG. **24-74A**] has also been compared to Natural Surrealism.) Kahlo herself, however, rejected any association with the Surrealists. She began painting seriously as a young student, during convalescence from an accident that tragically left her in constant pain. Her life became a heroic and tumultuous battle for survival against illness and stormy personal relationships.

24-74A TAMAYO, *Friend of the Birds*, 1944.

Typical of her long series of unflinching self-portraits is *The Two Fridas* (FIG. **24-75**), one of the few large-scale canvases Kahlo ever produced. The twin figures sit side by side on a low bench in a barren landscape under a stormy sky. The figures suggest different sides of the artist's personality, inextricably linked by the clasped hands and by the thin artery stretching between them, joining their exposed hearts. The artery ends on one side in surgical forceps and on the other in a miniature portrait of her husband as a child. Her deeply personal paintings touch sensual and psychological memories in her audience.

To read Kahlo's paintings solely as autobiographical overlooks the powerful political dimension of her art. Kahlo was deeply nationalistic and committed to her Mexican heritage. Politically active, she joined the Communist Party in 1920 and participated in public political protests. *The Two Fridas* incorporates Kahlo's commentary on the struggle facing Mexicans in the early 20th century in defining their national cultural identity. The Frida on the right (representing indigenous culture) appears in a Tehuana dress, the traditional costume of Zapotec women from the Isthmus of Tehuantepec, whereas the Frida on the left (representing imperialist forces) wears a European-style white lace dress. The heart, depicted here in such dramatic fashion, was an important symbol in the art of the Aztecs, whom Mexican nationalists idealized as the last independent rulers of their land. Thus *The Two Fridas* represents both Kahlo's personal struggles and the struggles of her homeland.

24-75 FRIDA KAHLO, *The Two Fridas,* 1939. Oil on canvas, 5′ 7″ × 5′ 7″. Museo de Arte Moderno, Mexico City.

Kahlo's deeply personal paintings touch sensual and psychological memories in her audience. Here, twin self-portraits linked by clasped hands and a common artery suggest two sides of her personality.

1 ft.

Photography

Frida Kahlo is the most famous female artist of her generation, but other women achieved prominence in the arts, especially the photographers Dorothea Lange and Margaret Bourke-White.

DOROTHEA LANGE One of the most important programs the U.S. government initiated during the 1930s was the Resettlement Administration (RA), better known by its later name, the Farm Security Administration. The RA oversaw emergency aid programs for farm families struggling to survive the Great Depression. The RA hired DOROTHEA LANGE (1895–1965) in 1936, and dispatched her to document the deplorable living conditions of the rural poor. At the end of an assignment photographing migratory pea pickers in California, Lange stopped at a camp in Nipomo and found the migrant workers there starving because the crops had frozen in the fields. Among the pictures Lange made on this occasion was *Migrant Mother, Nipomo Valley* (FIG. **24-76**), in which she captured the mixture of strength and worry in the raised hand and careworn face of a young mother, who holds a baby on her lap. Two older children cling to their mother trustfully while turning their faces away from the camera. Lange described how she got the picture:

> [I] saw and approached the hungry and desperate mother, as if drawn by a magnet. I do not remember how I explained my presence or my camera to her, but I remember she asked me no questions. I made five exposures, working closer and closer from the same direction. . . . There she sat in that lean-to tent with her children huddled around her, and she seemed to know that my pictures might help her, and so she helped me.[58]

Within days after Lange's photograph appeared in a San Francisco newspaper, people rushed food to Nipomo to feed the hungry workers.

MARGARET BOURKE-WHITE Almost 10 years younger than Dorothea Lange, MARGARET BOURKE-WHITE (1904–1971) also made her reputation as a photojournalist in Depression-era America. She was the first staff photographer Henry Luce (1898–1967) hired to furnish illustrations for the magazines in his publishing empire. Beginning in 1929, Bourke-White worked for *Fortune*, then for *Life* when Luce launched the famous newsweekly in 1936. During her long career, she photographed Midwestern farmers in their drought-stricken fields, impoverished Southern sharecroppers, black gold miners in South Africa, the Nazi concentration camp at Buchenwald, and the Korean War.

Bourke-White's most famous photographs, however, were not of people or events but of the triumphs of 20th-century engineering, many of which appeared in Luce's magazines and served to instill pride in an American public severely lacking in confidence during the Depression. She photographed the Chrysler Building (FIG. 24-47) while it was under construction in New York, attracting media attention for her daring balancing act on steel girders high above the pavement. She also achieved renown as the first woman to fly a combat mission when she was an official U.S. Air Force photographer during World War II.

For the first issue of *Life* (November 23, 1936), Bourke-White not only provided the cover photograph (FIG. **24-77**) of *Fort Peck Dam*,

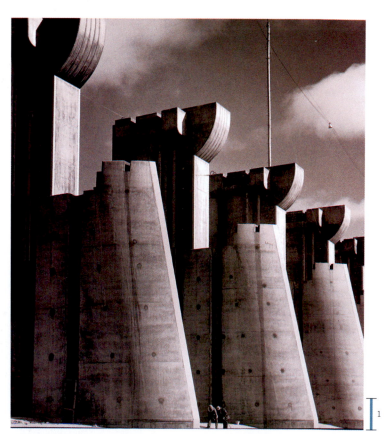

24-76 DOROTHEA LANGE, *Migrant Mother, Nipomo Valley*, 1935. Gelatin silver print, 1′ 1″ × 9″. Oakland Museum of California, Oakland (gift of Paul S. Taylor). ◼◀

While documenting the lives of migratory farm workers during the Depression, Lange made this unforgettable photograph of a mother in which she captured the woman's strength and worry.

24-77 MARGARET BOURKE-WHITE, *Fort Peck Dam, Montana*, 1936. Gelatin silver print, 1′ 1″ × 10½″. Metropolitan Museum of Art, New York (gift of Ford Motor Company and John C. Waddell, 1987).

Bourke-White's dramatic photograph of Fort Peck Dam graced the cover of the first issue of *Life* magazine and celebrated the achievements of modern industry at the height of the Great Depression.

The Museum of Modern Art and the Avant-Garde

Established in 1929, the Museum of Modern Art (MoMA) in New York City owes its existence to a trio of women—Lillie P. Bliss, Mary Quinn Sullivan, and Abby Aldrich Rockefeller (see "Art 'Matronage' in the United States," page 753)—who saw the need for a museum to collect and exhibit modernist art. Together they founded MoMA, which quickly became the most influential museum of modern art in the world. Their success was extraordinary considering the skepticism and hostility greeting modernist art at the time of the museum's inception. Indeed, in the 1920s and 1930s, few American museums exhibited any late-19th- and 20th-century art.

In its quest to expose the public to the energy and challenge of modernist, particularly avant-garde, art, MoMA developed unique and progressive exhibitions. Among those the museum mounted during the early years of its existence were *Cubism and Abstract Art* and *Fantastic Art, Dada, Surrealism* (1936). Two other noteworthy shows were *American Sources of Modern Art* (*Aztec, Maya, Inca*) in 1933 and *African Negro Art* in 1935, both among the first exhibitions to deal with "primitive" artifacts in artistic rather than anthropological terms (see "Primitivism and Colonialism," page 734).

The organization of MoMA's administrative structure and the scope of the museum's early activities were also remarkable. MoMA's first director, Alfred H. Barr Jr., insisted on establishing departments not only for painting and sculpture but also for photography, prints and drawing, architecture, and the decorative arts. He developed a library of books on modern art and a film library, both of which have become world-class collections, as well as an extensive publishing program.

It is the museum's art collection, however, that has drawn the most attention. By cultivating an influential group of patrons, MoMA has developed an extensive and enviable collection of late-19th- and 20th-century art. The museum boasts such important works as van Gogh's *Starry Night* (FIG. 23-18), Picasso's *Les Demoi-*

24-78 ALEXANDER CALDER, *Lobster Trap and Fish Tail*, 1939. Painted sheet aluminum and steel wire, 8′ 6″ × 9′ 6″. Museum of Modern Art, New York.

Using his thorough knowledge of engineering to combine nonobjective organic forms and motion, Calder created a new kind of sculpture—the mobile—that expressed nature's innate dynamism.

selles d'Avignon (FIG. 24-12), and Dalí's *The Persistence of Memory* (FIG. 24-55), as well as many others illustrated in this book, including 22 in this chapter alone. MoMA has also served as an art patron itself. For example, in 1939, just a decade after the institution's founding, it commissioned Alexander Calder to produce the mobile *Lobster Trap and Fish Tail* (FIG. 24-78).

Montana, but also wrote and illustrated with 16 additional photographs the lead story on the town of New Deal, home to the workers who constructed the dam during the depths of the Depression. Fort Peck Dam was at the time the largest earth-filled dam in the world. Bourke-White photographed its towers (designed to conjure a crenellated medieval fortress) at a sharp angle from below to communicate the dam's soaring height, underscoring the immense scale by including two dwarfed figures of men in the foreground. The tight framing, which shuts out all of the landscape and much of the sky, transforms the dam into an almost-abstract composition, a kind of still life, like Edward Weston's peppers (FIG. 24-44). Bourke-White's photographs celebrate modern industry as heir to the architectural achievements of the ancient world's great civilizations, and bear comparison with the paintings of Charles Demuth (FIG. 24-41).

Sculpture

In striking contrast to the leading American painters and photographers of the 1930s, the most renowned sculptor of this period rose to international prominence because of his contributions to the development of abstract art.

ALEXANDER CALDER The son and grandson of sculptors, ALEXANDER CALDER (1898–1976) initially studied mechanical engineering. Fascinated all his life by motion, he explored movement in relationship to three-dimensional form in much of his work. As a young artist in Paris in the late 1920s, Calder invented a circus full of wire-based miniature performers he activated into analogues of the motion of their real-life counterparts. After a visit to Piet Mondrian's studio in the early 1930s, Calder set out to put the Dutch painter's brightly colored rectangular shapes (FIG. 24-60) into motion. (Marcel Duchamp, intrigued by Calder's early motorized and hand-cranked examples of moving abstract pieces, named them *mobiles*.) Calder's engineering skills soon helped him to fashion a series of balanced structures hanging from rods, wires, and colorful, organically shaped plates. This new kind of sculpture, which combined nonobjective organic forms and motion, succeeded in expressing the innate dynamism of the natural world.

An early Calder mobile is *Lobster Trap and Fish Tail* (FIG. 24-78), which the artist created in 1939 under a commission from the Museum of Modern Art in New York City for the stairwell of the museum's new building on West 53rd Street (see "The

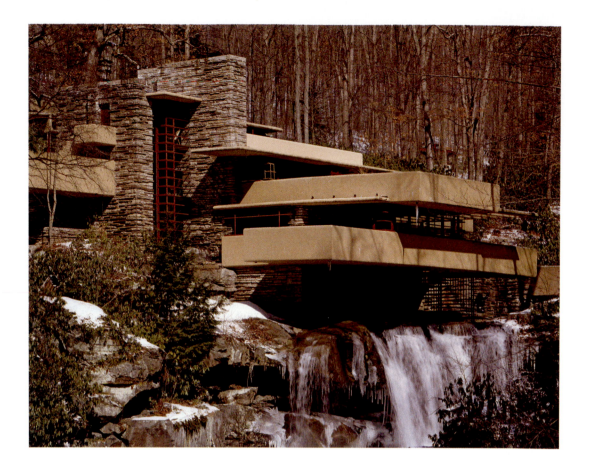

24-79 FRANK LLOYD WRIGHT, Kaufmann House (Fallingwater; looking northeast), Bear Run, Pennsylvania, 1936–1939.

Perched on a rocky hillside over a waterfall, Wright's Fallingwater has long sweeping lines, unconfined by abrupt wall limits, reaching out and capturing the expansiveness of the natural environment.

Museum of Modern Art and the Avant-Garde," page 783). Calder carefully planned each nonmechanized mobile so any air current would set the parts moving to create a constantly shifting dance in space. Mondrian's studio may have provided the initial inspiration for the mobiles, but their organic shapes resemble those in Joan Miró's Surrealist paintings (FIG. 24-58). Indeed, viewers can read Calder's forms as either geometric or organic. Geometrically, the lines suggest circuitry and rigging, and the shapes derive from circles and ovoid forms. Organically, the lines suggest nerve axons, and the shapes resemble cells, leaves, fins, wings, and other bioforms.

Architecture

The most influential American architect of the 1930s, as during the opening decades of the century, was the ever-inventive Frank Lloyd Wright.

FALLINGWATER Wright's universally acclaimed masterpiece of this period is the Kaufmann House (FIG. **24-79**), which he designed as a weekend retreat at Bear Run, Pennsylvania, for Pittsburgh department store magnate Edgar Kaufmann Sr. Perched on a rocky hillside over a small waterfall, the house, nicknamed Fallingwater, has become an icon of modernist architectural design. In keeping with his commitment to an "architecture of democracy," Wright sought to find a way to incorporate the structure fully into its site in order to ensure a fluid, dynamic exchange between the interior of the house and the natural environment outside. Rather than build the house overlooking or next to the waterfall, Wright decided to build it over the waterfall, because he believed the inhabitants would become desensitized to the waterfall's presence and power if they merely overlooked it. In Fallingwater, Wright took the blocky masses characterizing his earlier Robie House (FIGS. 24-45 and 24-46) and extended them in all four directions. To take ad-

vantage of the location, he designed a series of terraces that extend on three levels from a central core structure. The contrast in textures among concrete, painted metal, and natural stones in the house's terraces and walls enlivens its shapes, as does Wright's use of full-length strip windows to create a stunning interweaving of interior and exterior space.

The implied message of Wright's new architecture was space, not mass—a space designed to fit the patron's life and enclosed and divided as required. Wright took special pains to meet his clients' requirements, often designing all the accessories of a house (including, in at least one case, gowns for his client's wife). In the late 1930s, he acted on a cherished dream to provide good architectural design for less prosperous people by adapting the ideas of his prairie houses (see page 758) to plans for smaller, less expensive dwellings with neither attics nor basements. These residences, known as *Usonian* houses (for "United States of North America"), became templates for suburban housing developments in the post–World War II housing boom.

The publication of Wright's plans brought him a measure of fame in Europe, especially in Holland and Germany. The issuance in Berlin in 1910 of a portfolio of his work and an exhibition of his designs the following year stimulated younger architects to adopt some of his ideas about open plans that afforded clients freedom. Some 40 years before his career ended, his work was already of revolutionary significance. Mies van der Rohe wrote in 1940: "[The] dynamic impulse from [Wright's] work invigorated a whole generation. His influence was strongly felt even when it was not actually visible."[59]

Frank Lloyd Wright's influence in Europe was exceptional, however, for any American artist before World War II. But in the decades following that global conflict, American painters, sculptors, and architects often took the lead in establishing new styles artists elsewhere quickly emulated. This new preeminence of the United States in the arts is the subject of Chapter 25.

MODERNISM IN EUROPE AND AMERICA, 1900 TO 1945

EUROPE 1900 to 1920

- In the early 1900s, avant-garde artists searched for new definitions of art in a changed world. Matisse and the Fauves used bold colors as the primary means of conveying feeling. German Expressionist paintings featured clashing colors, disquieting figures, and perspective distortions.

- Pablo Picasso and Georges Braque radically challenged prevailing artistic conventions with Cubism, in which artists dissect forms and place them in interaction with the space around them.

- The Futurists focused on motion in time and space in their effort to create paintings and sculptures that captured the dynamic quality of modern life. The Dadaists celebrated the spontaneous and intuitive, exploring the role of chance in art and often incorporating found objects in their works.

Braque, *The Portuguese*, 1911

UNITED STATES 1900 to 1930

- The Armory Show of 1913 introduced avant-garde European art to American artists. Man Ray, for example, embraced Dada's fondness for chance and the displacement of ordinary items, and Stuart Davis adopted the Cubist interest in fragmented form.

- The Harlem Renaissance brought African American artists to the forefront, including Aaron Douglas, whose paintings drew on Cubist principles. Charles Demuth, Georgia O'Keeffe, and the Precisionists used European modernist techniques to celebrate contemporary American subjects.

- Photography emerged as an important American art form in the work of Alfred Stieglitz and Edward Weston, who emphasized the careful arrangement of forms and patterns of light and dark.

Weston, *Pepper No. 30*, 1930

EUROPE 1920 to 1945

- World War I gave rise to the Neue Sachlichkeit movement in Germany. "New Objectivity" artists depicted the horrors of war and explored the themes of death and transfiguration.

- The Surrealists investigated ways to express in art the world of dreams and the unconscious. Natural Surrealists aimed for "concrete irrationality" in their naturalistic paintings of dreamlike scenes. Biomorphic Surrealists experimented with automatism and employed abstract imagery.

- Many European modernists pursued utopian ideals. The Suprematists developed an abstract style to express pure feeling. The Constructivists used nonobjective forms to suggest the nature of space-time. De Stijl artists reduced their formal vocabulary to simple geometric forms in their search for "pure plastic art."

- Brancusi, Hepworth, Moore, and other sculptors increasingly turned to abstraction, often emphasizing voids as well as masses in their work.

- The Bauhaus in Germany promoted the vision of "total architecture," which called for the integration of all the arts in constructing modern living environments. Bauhaus buildings were simple glass and steel designs devoid of "romantic embellishment and whimsy." In France, Le Corbusier used modern construction materials to build "machines for living"—simple houses with open plans and unadorned surfaces.

Moore, *Reclining Figure*, 1939

Gropius, Bauhaus, Dessau, 1925–1926

UNITED STATES AND MEXICO 1930 to 1945

- Although Alexander Calder created abstract works between the wars, other American artists favored figural art. Lange and Shahn chronicled social injustice. Hopper explored the loneliness of life in the Depression era. Lawrence recorded the struggle of African Americans. Wood depicted life in rural Iowa.

- Mexican artists Orozco and Rivera painted epic mural cycles of the history of Mexico. Kahlo's powerful paintings explored the human psyche and were frequently autobiographical.

- The leading American architect of the first half of the 20th century was Frank Lloyd Wright, who promoted the "architecture of democracy," in which free individuals move in a "free" space.

Kahlo, *The Two Fridas*, 1939

Toying with mass-media imagery typifies British Pop Art. The central motif in Hamilton's modern home is the body builder Charles Atlas, who holds a Tootsie Pop in place of a weightlifter's barbell.

Hanging on the wall like a framed traditional painting is a cutout of a page from a 1950s romance comic book. Modern mass media fascinated Pop artists as an aspect of popular culture.

The fantasy interior in Hamilton's collage reflects the values of modern consumer culture. The figures and objects cut from glossy magazines include an advertisement for Hoover vacuum cleaners.

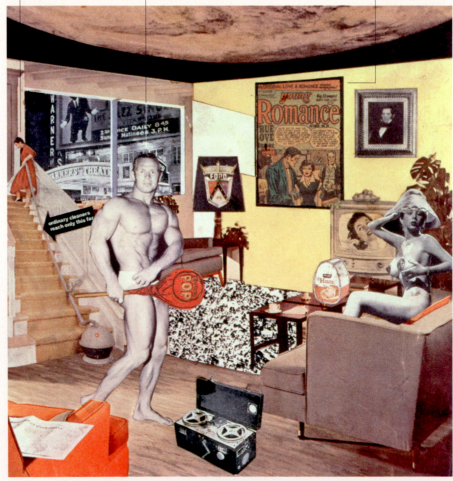

1 in.

25-1 RICHARD HAMILTON, *Just What Is It That Makes Today's Homes So Different, So Appealing?* 1956. Collage, 10¼″ × 9¾″. Kunsthalle Tübingen, Tübingen.

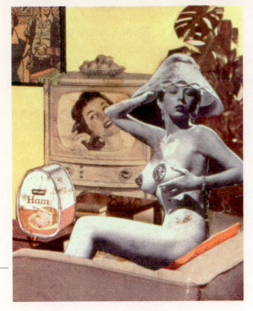

MODERNISM AND POSTMODERNISM IN EUROPE AND AMERICA, 1945 TO 1980

Also included in Hamilton's "appealing" modern home are a television, a can of Armour ham, and a photograph taken from a "girlie magazine" to stimulate speculation about society's values.

ART AND CONSUMER CULTURE

The interest in abstraction that emerged so forcefully in avant-garde artistic circles during the first half of the 20th century gained even greater momentum in the decades after the end of World War II. However, a reaction to pure formalism in painting and sculpture also set in. The artists of the *Pop Art* movement reintroduced all of the devices the postwar abstractionists had purged from their artworks. Pop artists revived the tools traditionally used to convey meaning in art, such as signs, symbols, metaphors, allusions, illusions, and figural imagery. They not only embraced representation but also firmly grounded their art in the consumer culture and mass media of the postwar period, thereby making it much more accessible and understandable to the average person. Indeed, the name "Pop Art"—credited to the British art critic Lawrence Alloway (1926–1990)—is short for "popular art" and referred to the popular mass culture and familiar imagery of the contemporary urban environment.

Art historians trace the roots of Pop Art to the young British artists, architects, and writers who formed the Independent Group at the Institute of Contemporary Art in London in the early 1950s. They sought to initiate fresh thinking in art, in part by sharing their fascination with the aesthetics and content of such facets of popular culture as advertising, comic books, and movies. In 1956, an Independent Group member, RICHARD HAMILTON (b. 1922), made a small collage, *Just What Is It That Makes Today's Homes So Different, So Appealing?* (FIG. **25-1**), which exemplifies British Pop Art. Trained as an engineering draftsman, exhibition designer, and painter, Hamilton studied the way advertising shapes public attitudes. Long intrigued by Marcel Duchamp's ideas (see Chapter 24), Hamilton consistently combined elements of popular art and fine art, seeing both as belonging to the whole world of visual communication. He created *Just What Is It?* for the poster and catalog of one section of an exhibition titled *This Is Tomorrow,* which included images from Hollywood cinema, science fiction, and the mass media.

The fantasy interior in Hamilton's collage reflects the values of mid-20th-century consumer culture through figures and objects cut from glossy magazines. *Just What Is It?* includes references to mass media (the television, the theater marquee outside the window, the newspaper), to advertising (Hoover vacuum cleaners, Ford cars, Armour hams, Tootsie Pops), and to popular culture (the "girlie magazine," the body builder Charles Atlas, romance comic books). Artworks of this sort stimulated viewers' wide-ranging speculation about society's values. This kind of intellectual toying with mass-media meaning and imagery typified Pop Art both in Europe and America.

THE AFTERMATH OF WORLD WAR II

World War II, with the global devastation it unleashed on all dimensions of life—political, economic, and psychological—set the stage for the second half of the 20th century. The dropping of atomic bombs by the United States on the Japanese cities of Hiroshima and Nagasaki in 1945 signaled a turning point not only in the war itself but in the geopolitical balance and the nature of international conflict as well. For the postwar generation, nuclear attack became a very real threat. Indeed, the two nuclear superpowers, the United States and the Soviet Union, divided the world into spheres of influence, and each regularly intervened politically, economically, and militarily wherever and whenever it considered its interests to be at stake.

The cessation of global warfare did not bring global peace. On the contrary, regional conflicts erupted throughout the world during the decades after World War II. In 1947, the British left India, which precipitated a murderous Hindu-Muslim war that divided South Asia into two new hostile nations—India and Pakistan. After a bloody civil war, Communists came to power in China in 1949. North Korea invaded South Korea in 1950 and fought a grim war with the United States and its allies. The Soviets brutally suppressed uprisings in their subject nations—East Germany, Poland, Hungary, and Czechoslovakia. The United States intervened in disputes in Central and South America. Almost as soon as many colonized nations of Africa—Kenya, Uganda, Nigeria, Angola, Mozambique, the Sudan, Rwanda, and the Congo—won their independence, civil wars devastated them. In Indonesia, civil war left more than 100,000 dead. Algeria expelled France in 1962 after the French waged a prolonged war with Algeria's Muslim natives. After 15 years of bitter war in Southeast Asia, the United States suffered defeat in Vietnam.

The period from 1945 to 1980 also brought upheaval in the cultural sphere. In the United States, for example, various groups forcefully questioned the status quo. The struggles for civil rights for African Americans, for free speech on university campuses, and for disengagement from the Vietnam War led to a rebellion of the young, who took to the streets in often raucous demonstrations, some with violent repercussions. The prolonged ferment produced a new system of values, a "youth culture," expressed in the radical rejection not only of national policies but often also of the society generating them. Young Americans derided their elders' lifestyles and adopted unconventional dress, manners, habits, and morals deliberately subversive of mainstream social standards. The youth era witnessed the sexual revolution, the widespread use and abuse of drugs, and the development of rock music, then an exclusively youthful art form. Young people "dropped out" of regulated society, embraced alternative belief systems, and rejected Western university curricula as irrelevant.

This counterculture had considerable societal impact. The civil rights movement of the 1960s and later the women's liberation movement of the 1970s reflected the spirit of rebellion, coupled with the rejection of racism and sexism. In keeping with the growing resistance to established authority, women systematically began to challenge the male-dominated culture, which they perceived as having limited their political power and economic opportunities for centuries. Feminists charged that the institutions of Western society, particularly the traditional family unit headed by a patriarch, perpetuated male power and the subordination of women. They further contended that monuments of Western culture—its arts and sciences, as well as its political, social, and economic institutions—masked the realities of male power.

Increasingly, individuals and groups actively sought to combat the inappropriate exercise of power or to change the balance of power. For example, following patterns developed first in the civil rights movement and later in feminism, various ethnic groups and gays and lesbians mounted challenges to discriminatory policies and attitudes. These groups fought for recognition, respect, and legal protection and battled discrimination with political action. In addition, the growing scrutiny in numerous academic fields—cultural studies, literary theory, and colonial and postcolonial studies—of the dynamics and exercise of power also contributed to the dialogue on these issues. As a result of this concern for the dynamics of power, identity (both individual and group) emerged as a potent arena for discussion and action—and as a persistent and compelling subject for painters, sculptors, and photographers.

PAINTING, SCULPTURE, AND PHOTOGRAPHY

The end of World War II in 1945 left devastated cities, ruptured economies, and governments in chaos throughout Europe. These factors, coupled with the massive loss of life and the indelible horrors of the bombing of Hiroshima and Nagasaki and of the

MODERNISM AND POSTMODERNISM IN EUROPE AND AMERICA, 1945 TO 1980

1945	1960	1970	1980

- European Expressionists capture in their paintings and sculptures the revulsion and cynicism that emerged in the wake of World War II
- New York School painters develop Abstract Expressionism, emphasizing form and raw energy over subject matter
- Sleek, geometrically rigid modernist skyscrapers become familiar sights in cities throughout the world

- Post-Painterly Abstractionists reject the passion and texture of action painting and celebrate the flatness of pigment on canvas
- Op artists produce the illusion of motion and depth using only geometric forms
- Minimalists reduce sculpture to basic shapes and emphasize their works' "objecthood"
- Pop artists find inspiration in popular culture and commonplace commercial products
- Superrealists create paintings and sculptures characterized by scrupulous reproduction of the appearance of people and objects
- Performance artists replace traditional stationary artworks with temporal action-artworks

- Artists play a leading role in the feminist movement by promoting women's themes and employing materials traditionally associated with women, such as china and fabric
- Postmodern architects erect complex and eclectic buildings that often incorporate references to historical styles
- Environmental artists redefine what constitutes "art" by manipulating natural materials in monumental earthworks
- Artists increasingly embrace new media—video recorders, computers—as tools for creating artworks

Holocaust, in which six million Jews died at the hands of the Nazis, resulted in a pervasive sense of despair, disillusionment, and skepticism. Although many people (for example, the Futurists in Italy; see Chapter 24) had tried to find redemptive value in World War I, it was nearly impossible to do the same with World War II, coming as it did so soon after the "war to end all wars." Additionally, World War I was largely a European conflict that left roughly 10 million people dead, whereas World War II was a truly global catastrophe, claiming 35 million lives.

Postwar Expressionism in Europe

The cynicism pervading Europe in the 1940s found voice in existentialism, a philosophy asserting the absurdity of human existence and the impossibility of achieving certitude. Many who embraced existentialism also promoted atheism and questioned the possibility of situating God within a systematic philosophy. Scholars trace the roots of existentialism to the Danish theologian Søren Kierkegaard (1813–1855), but in the postwar period, the writings of French author Jean-Paul Sartre (1905–1980) most clearly captured the existentialist spirit. According to Sartre, if God does not exist, then individuals must constantly struggle in isolation with the anguish of making decisions in a world without absolutes or traditional values. This spirit of pessimism and despair emerged frequently in European art of the immediate postwar period. A brutality or roughness appropriately expressing both the artist's state of mind and the larger cultural sensibility characterized the work of many European sculptors and painters.

ALBERTO GIACOMETTI The sculpture of Swiss artist ALBERTO GIACOMETTI (1901–1966) perhaps best expresses the spirit of existentialism. Although Giacometti never claimed he pursued existentialist ideas in his art, his works capture the spirit of that philosophy. Indeed, Sartre, Giacometti's friend, saw the artist's figurative sculptures as the epitome of existentialist humanity—alienated, solitary, and lost in the world's immensity. Giacometti's sculptures of the 1940s, such as *Man Pointing, No. 5* (FIG. **25-2**), are thin, nearly featureless figures with rough, agitated surfaces. Rather than conveying the solidity and mass of conventional bronze sculpture, these severely attenuated figures seem swallowed up by the space surrounding them, imparting a sense of isolation and fragility. Giacometti's evocative, moving sculptures spoke to the pervasive despair that emerged in the aftermath of world war.

FRANCIS BACON Although born in Dublin, Ireland, FRANCIS BACON (1910–1992) was the son of a well-to-do Englishman. He spent most of his life in London, where he experienced firsthand the destruction of lives and property the Nazi bombing wrought on the city during World War II. *Painting* (FIG. **25-3**) is Bacon's indictment of humanity and a reflection of war's butchery. The artist presented a compelling and revolting image of a powerful, stocky man with a gaping mouth and a vivid red stain on his upper lip, as if he were a carnivore devouring the raw meat sitting on the railing

25-2 ALBERTO GIACOMETTI, *Man Pointing No. 5,* 1947. Bronze, 5′ 10″ high. Des Moines Art Center, Des Moines (Nathan Emory Coffin Collection).

The writer Jean-Paul Sartre saw Giacometti's thin and virtually featureless sculpted figures as the epitome of existentialist humanity—alienated, solitary, and lost in the world's immensity.

1 ft.

25-3 FRANCIS BACON, *Painting,* 1946. Oil and pastel on linen, 6′ 5⅞″ × 4′ 4″. Museum of Modern Art, New York.

Painted in the aftermath of World War II, this intentionally revolting image of a powerful figure presiding over a slaughter is Bacon's indictment of humanity and a reflection of war's butchery.

1 ft.

Painting, Sculpture, and Photography **789**

25-4 Jean Dubuffet, *Vie Inquiète*, 1953. Oil on canvas, 4′ 3″ × 6′ 4″. Tate Modern, London (gift of the artist, 1966).

Dubuffet expressed a tortured vision of the world through thickly encrusted painted surfaces and crude images of the kind children and the insane produce. He called it "art brut"—untaught and coarse art.

25-3A Bacon, *Figure with Meat*, 1954.

surrounding him (compare FIG. **25-3A**). Bacon may have based his depiction of this central figure on news photos of similarly dressed European and American officials. The umbrella in particular recalls images of Neville Chamberlain (1869–1940), the wartime British prime minister who frequently appeared in photographs with an umbrella. Bacon added to the visceral impact of the painting by depicting the flayed carcass hanging behind the central figure like a crucified human form. Although the specific sources for the imagery in *Painting* are uncertain, the work is unmistakably "an attempt to remake the violence of reality itself," as Bacon often described his art, based on what he referred to as "the brutality of fact."[1]

JEAN DUBUFFET Although less specific, the works of French artist JEAN DUBUFFET (1901–1985) also express a tortured vision of the world through manipulated materials. In works such as *Vie Inquiète* (*Uneasy Life*; FIG. **25-4**), Dubuffet first built up an *impasto* (a layer of thickly applied pigment) of plaster, glue, sand, asphalt, and other common materials, over which he painted or incised crude images of the kind produced by children, the insane, and scrawlers of graffiti. Scribblings interspersed with the images heighten the impression of smeared and gashed surfaces of crumbling walls and worn pavements marked by random individuals. Dubuffet believed the art of children, the mentally unbalanced, prisoners, and outcasts was more direct and genuine because those who created it did so unrestrained by conventional standards of art. He promoted "art brut"—untaught and coarse art.

Abstract Expressionism

In the 1960s, the center of the Western art world shifted from Paris to New York because of the devastation World War II had inflicted across Europe and the resulting influx of émigré artists escaping to the United States. It was in New York that the first major American avant-garde art movement—Abstract Expressionism—emerged. The most important forerunner of the Abstract Expressionists, however, was an Armenian immigrant who arrived in New York in 1924.

ARSHILE GORKY Born a Christian in Islamic Turkish Armenia, Vosdanik Manoog Adoian was four years old when his father escaped being drafted into the Turkish army by fleeing the country. His mother died of starvation in her 15-year-old son's arms in a refugee camp for victims of the Turkish campaign of genocide against the Christian minority. The penniless Vosdanik managed in 1920 to make his way to America, where a relative

took him into his home near Boston. Four years later, then a young man, Vosdanik changed his name to ARSHILE GORKY (1904–1948)—"Bitter Achilles" in Russian—and moved to New York City, where he continued the art education he had begun in Boston. In 1948, he hanged himself after an automobile accident robbed him of the use of his right arm. The injury might have been only temporary, but the depressed Gorky thought he would never be able to paint again. In a career lasting only two decades, Gorky contributed significantly to the artistic revolution born in New York. His work is the bridge between the Biomorphic Surrealism of Joan Miró (FIG. 24-58) and the totally abstract canvases of Jackson Pollock (FIG. 25-6).

Garden in Sochi (FIG. **25-5**), painted in 1943, is the third in a series of canvases with identical titles named after a Black Sea resort but inspired by Gorky's childhood memories of the Garden of Wish Fulfillment in his birthplace. The women of the Armenian village of Khorkom believed their wishes would be granted if they rubbed their bare breasts against a rock in that garden beneath a tree to which they tied torn strips of their clothing. The brightly colored and thinly outlined forms in *Garden in Sochi,* which initially appear to be purely abstract biomorphic shapes, are loose sketches representing, at the left, a bare-breasted woman, and, at the center, a tree trunk with fluttering fabric. At the bottom are two oversized shoes—the Armenian slippers Gorky's father gave his son shortly before abandoning the family.

CLEMENT GREENBERG The few traces of representational art in Gorky's work disappeared in *Abstract Expressionism*. As the name suggests, the artists associated with the New York School of Abstract Expressionism produced paintings that are, for the most part, abstract but express the artist's state of mind, with the goal also of striking emotional chords in the viewer. The most important champion of this strict *formalism*—an emphasis on an artwork's visual elements rather than its subject—was the American art critic Clement Greenberg (1909–1994), who wielded considerable influence from the 1940s through the 1970s. Greenberg helped redefine the parameters of modernism by advocating the rejection of illusionism and the exploration of the properties of each artistic medium. So dominant was Greenberg that scholars often refer to the general modernist tenets during this period as Greenbergian formalism.

1 ft.

25-5 ARSHILE GORKY, *Garden in Sochi,* ca. 1943. Oil on canvas, 2′ 7″ × 3′ 3″. Museum of Modern Art, New York (acquired through the Lillie P. Bliss Bequest).

Gorky's paintings of the 1940s, which still incorporate recognizable forms, are the bridge between the Biomorphic Surrealist canvases of Miró and the Abstract Expressionist paintings of Pollock.

Among other things, this means renouncing illusion and explicit subject matter. The arts are to achieve concreteness, "purity," by dealing solely with their respective selves—that is, by becoming "abstract" or nonfigurative.[3]

The Abstract Expressionists turned inward to create, and the resulting works convey a rough spontaneity and palpable energy. The New York School painters wanted the viewer to grasp the content of their art intuitively, in a mental state free from structured thinking. One of the leading painters of this group, Mark Rothko (FIG. 25-10), eloquently wrote:

Although Greenberg modified his complex ideas about art over the years, he consistently expounded certain basic concepts. In particular, Greenberg promoted the idea of artistic purity: "Purity in art consists in the acceptance, willing acceptance, of the limitations of the medium of the specific art."[2] In other words, Greenberg believed artists should strive for a more explicit focus on the properties exclusive to each medium—for example, two-dimensionality or flatness in painting, and three-dimensionality in sculpture.

> It follows that a modernist work of art must try, in principle, to avoid communication with any order of experience not inherent in the most literally and essentially construed nature of its medium.

We assert man's absolute emotions. We don't need props or legends. We create images whose realities are self evident. Free ourselves from memory, association, nostalgia, legend, myth. Instead of making cathedrals out of Christ, man or life, we make it out of ourselves, out of our own feelings. The image we produce is understood by anyone who looks at it without nostalgic glasses of history.[4]

The Abstract Expressionist movement developed along two lines—*gestural abstraction* and *chromatic abstraction.* The gestural abstractionists relied on the expressiveness of energetically applied pigment. In contrast, the chromatic abstractionists focused on color's emotional resonance.

JACKSON POLLOCK The artist whose work best exemplifies gestural abstraction is JACKSON POLLOCK (1912–1956), who developed his signature style in the mid-1940s. By 1950, Pollock had refined his technique and was producing large-scale abstract paintings such as *Number 1, 1950* (*Lavender Mist;* FIG. **25-6**), which consist of rhythmic drips, splatters, and dribbles of paint. The mural-sized fields of energetic skeins of pigment envelop viewers, drawing them into a lacy spider web. Using sticks or brushes, Pollock flung,

25-6 JACKSON POLLOCK, *Number 1, 1950* (*Lavender Mist*), 1950. Oil, enamel, and aluminum paint on canvas, 7′ 3″ × 9′ 10″. National Gallery of Art, Washington, D.C. (Ailsa Mellon Bruce Fund).

Pollock's paintings emphasize the creative process. His mural-size canvases consist of rhythmic drips, splatters, and dribbles of paint that envelop viewers, drawing them into a lacy spider web.

Jackson Pollock on Easel and Mural Painting

Jackson Pollock's canvases (FIG. 25-6) constitute a revolution in the art of painting not only because of their purely abstract form but also in the artist's rejection of the centuries-old tradition of applying pigment to stretched canvases supported vertically before the painter on an easel. In two statements Pollock made in 1947, one as part of his application for a Guggenheim Fellowship and one in a published essay, the artist explained the motivations for his new kind of "action painting" and described the tools he used and the way he produced his monumental canvases (FIG. 25-7).

I intend to paint large movable pictures which will function between the easel and mural.... I believe the easel picture to be a dying form, and the tendency of modern feeling is towards the wall picture or mural.*

My painting does not come from the easel. I hardly ever stretch my canvas before painting. I prefer to tack the unstretched canvas to the hard wall or the floor. I need the resistance of a hard surface. On the floor I am more at ease. I feel nearer, more a part of the painting, since this way I can walk around it, work from the four sides and literally be *in* the painting. This is akin to the method of the Indian sand painters of the West. I continue to get further away from the usual painter's tools such as easel, palette, brushes, etc. I prefer sticks, trowels, knives and dripping fluid paint or a heavy impasto with sand, broken glass and other foreign matter added. When I am *in* my painting, I'm not aware of what I'm doing.... [T]he painting has a life of its own. I try to let it come through.... The source of my painting is the unconscious.†

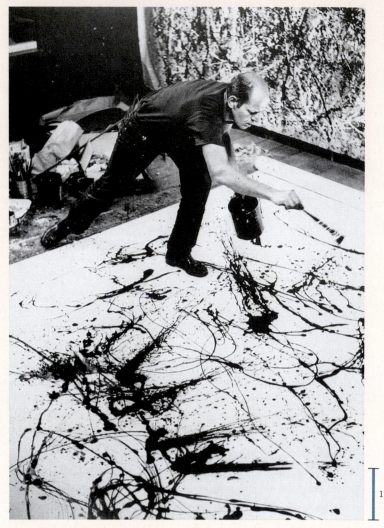

25-7 HANS NAMUTH, Jackson Pollock painting in his studio in Springs, Long Island, New York, 1950. Gelatin silver print, 10″ × 8″. Center for Creative Photography, University of Arizona, Tucson.

"Gestural abstraction" nicely describes Pollock's working technique. Using sticks or brushes, he flung, poured, and dripped paint onto a section of canvas he simply unrolled across his studio floor.

1 in.

*Quoted in Francis V. O'Connor, *Jackson Pollock* (New York: Museum of Modern Art, 1967), 39.
†Ibid., 39-40.

poured, and dripped paint (not only traditional oil paints but aluminum paints and household enamels as well) onto a section of canvas he simply unrolled across his studio floor (FIG. **25-7**). This working method earned Pollock the derisive nickname "Jack the Dripper." Responding to the image as it developed, he created art that was spontaneous yet choreographed. Pollock's painting technique highlights the most significant aspect of gestural abstraction—its emphasis on the creative process. Indeed, Pollock literally immersed himself in the painting during its creation.

Art historians have linked Pollock's ideas about improvisation in the creative process to his interest in what psychiatrist Carl Jung called the collective unconscious. The improvisational nature of Pollock's work and his reliance on the subconscious also have parallels in the "psychic automatism" of Surrealism and the work of Vassily Kandinsky (FIG. 24-7), whom critics described as an Abstract Expressionist as early as 1919. In addition to Pollock's

unique working methods and the expansive scale of his canvases, the lack of a well-defined compositional focus in his paintings significantly departed from conventional easel painting (see "Jackson Pollock on Easel and Mural Painting," above). A towering figure in 20th-century art, Pollock tragically died in a car accident at age 44, cutting short the development of his innovative artistic vision. Surviving him was his wife, LEE KRASNER (1908–1984), whom art historians recognize as a major Abstract Expressionist painter (FIG. **25-7A**), although overshadowed by Pollock during her lifetime.

25-7A KRASNER, *The Seasons*, 1957.

WILLEM DE KOONING Despite the public's skepticism about Pollock's art, other artists enthusiastically pursued similar avenues of expression. Dutch-born WILLEM DE KOONING (1904–1997)

1 ft.

25-8 Willem de Kooning, *Woman I*, 1950–1952. Oil on canvas, 6′ 3 7/8″ × 4′ 10″. Museum of Modern Art, New York. ◼◀

Although rooted in figuration, including pictures of female models on advertising billboards, de Kooning's *Woman I* displays the energetic application of pigment typical of gestural abstraction.

also developed a gestural abstractionist style. Even images such as *Woman I* (FIG. **25-8**), although rooted in figuration, display the sweeping gestural brushstrokes and energetic application of pigment typical of gestural abstraction. Out of the jumbled array of slashing lines and agitated patches of color appears a ferocious-looking woman with staring eyes and ponderous breasts. Her toothy smile, inspired by an ad for Camel cigarettes, seems to devolve into a grimace. Female models on advertising billboards partly inspired *Woman I,* one of a series of images of women, but de Kooning's female forms also suggest fertility figures and a satiric inversion of the traditional image of Venus, goddess of love.

Process was important to de Kooning, as it was to Pollock. Continually working on *Woman I* for almost two years, de Kooning painted an image and then scraped it away the next day and began anew. His wife Elaine, also an accomplished painter, estimated he painted approximately 200 scraped-away images of women on this canvas before settling on the final one.

In addition to this *Woman* series, de Kooning created nonrepresentational works dominated by huge swaths and splashes of pigment. The images suggest rawness and intensity. His dealer, Sidney Janis (1896–1989), confirmed this impression, recalling de Kooning occasionally brought him paintings with ragged holes in them, the result of overly vigorous painting. Like Pollock, de Kooning was very much "in" his paintings. Vigorous physical interaction between the painter and the canvas led the critic Harold Rosenberg (1906–1978) to describe the work of the New York School as *action painting.* In his influential 1952 article "The American Action Painters," Rosenberg described the attempts of Pollock, de Kooning, and others to get "inside the canvas."

At a certain moment the canvas began to appear to one American painter after another as an arena in which to act—rather than as a space in which to reproduce, re-design, analyze or "express" an object, actual or imagined. What was to go on the canvas was not a picture but an event. The painter no longer approached his easel with an image in his mind; he went up to it with material in his hand to do something to that other piece of material in front of him. The image would be the result of this encounter.[5]

Among the other prominent New York School Abstract Expressionists were Pennsylvania-born Franz Kline (1910–1962), whose predominantly black-and-white paintings (FIG. **25-8A**) resemble Chinese and Japanese calligraphy; Robert Motherwell (1915–1991), best known for his series of paintings inspired by the Spanish civil war (FIG. **25-8B**); and Joan Mitchell (1925–1992), the leading woman action painter (FIG. **25-8C**) of the 1950s. In the 1970s and later, a new generation of artists, including Susan Rothenberg (b. 1945; FIG. **25-8D**) reinvigorated Abstract Expressionism in a movement art historians have dubbed *Neo-Expressionism* (see Chapter 26).

25-8A Kline, *Mahoning,* 1956.

25-8B Motherwell, *Elegy to the Spanish Republic,* 1953–1954.

25-8C Mitchell, *Untitled,* ca. 1953–1954.

25-8D Rothenberg, *Tattoo,* 1979. ◼◀

BARNETT NEWMAN In contrast to the aggressively energetic images of the gestural abstractionists, the work of the chromatic abstractionists exudes a quieter aesthetic, exemplified by the work of Barnett Newman and Mark Rothko. The emotional resonance of their works derives from their eloquent use of color. In his early paintings, New York native Barnett Newman (1905–1970) presented organic abstractions inspired by his study of biology and his fascination with Native American art. He soon simplified his

25-9 BARNETT NEWMAN, *Vir Heroicus Sublimis*, 1950–1951. Oil on canvas, 7′ 11$\frac{3}{8}$″ × 17′ 9$\frac{1}{4}$″. Museum of Modern Art, New York (gift of Mr. and Mrs. Ben Heller). ■◀

Newman's canvases consist of a single slightly modulated color field split by "zips" (narrow bands) running from one edge of the painting to the other, energizing the color field and giving it scale.

compositions so that each canvas—for example, the monumental (almost 8 by 18 feet) Latin-titled *Vir Heroicus Sublimis* (*Sublime Heroic Man;* FIG. **25-9**)—consists of a single slightly modulated color field split by narrow bands the artist called "zips," which run from one edge of the painting to the other. As Newman explained it, "The streak was always going through an atmosphere; I kept trying to create a world around it."[6] He did not intend the viewer to perceive the zips as specific entities, separate from the ground, but as accents energizing the field and giving it scale. By simplifying his compositions, Newman increased color's capacity to communicate and to express his feelings about the tragic condition of modern life and the human struggle to survive. He claimed "the artist's problem . . . [is] the idea-complex that makes contact with mystery—of life, of men, of nature, of the hard black chaos that is death, or the grayer, softer chaos that is tragedy."[7] Confronted by one of Newman's grandiose colored canvases, viewers truly feel as if they are in the presence of the epic.

MARK ROTHKO The work of MARK ROTHKO (1903–1970) also deals with universal themes. Born in Russia, Rothko moved with his family to the United States when he was 10. His early paintings were figural, but he soon came to believe that references to anything specific in the physical world conflicted with the sublime idea of the universal, supernatural "spirit of myth," which he saw as the core of meaning in art. In a statement cowritten with Newman and artist Adolph Gottlieb (1903–1974), Rothko expressed his beliefs about art:

> We favor the simple expression of the complex thought. We are for the large shape because it has the impact of the unequivocal. . . . We assert that . . . only that subject matter is valid which is tragic and timeless. That is why we profess spiritual kinship with primitive and archaic art.[8]

Rothko's paintings became compositionally simple, and he increasingly focused on color as the primary conveyor of meaning. In works such as *No. 14* (FIG. **25-10**), Rothko created compelling visual experiences consisting of two or three large rectangles of pure color with hazy edges that seem to float on the canvas surface, hovering in front of a colored background. His compositions present shimmering veils of intensely luminous colors that appear to be suspended in front of the canvases. Although the color juxtapositions are visually captivating, Rothko intended them as more than decorative. He saw

25-10 MARK ROTHKO, *No. 14*, 1960. Oil on canvas, 9′ 6″ × 8′ 9″. San Francisco Museum of Modern Art, San Francisco (Helen Crocker Russell Fund Purchase).

Rothko's chromatic abstractionist paintings—consisting of hazy rectangles of pure color hovering in front of a colored background—are compositionally simple but compelling visual experiences.

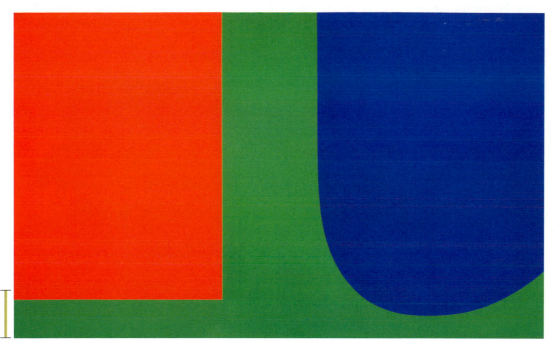

25-11 ELLSWORTH KELLY, *Red Blue Green*, 1963. Oil on canvas, 6′ 11⅝″ × 11′ 3⅞″. Museum of Contemporary Art, San Diego (gift of Dr. and Mrs. Jack M. Farris).

Hard-edge painting is one variant of Post-Painterly Abstraction. Kelly used razor-sharp edges and clearly delineated areas of color to distill painting to its essential two-dimensional elements.

Post-Painterly Abstraction. Greenberg saw this art as contrasting with "painterly" art, characterized by loose, visible pigment application. Evidence of the artist's hand, so prominent in gestural abstraction, is conspicuously absent in Post-Painterly Abstraction. Greenberg championed this art form because it embodied his idea of purity in art.

1 ft.

color as a doorway to another reality, and insisted color could express "basic human emotions—tragedy, ecstasy, doom. . . . The people who weep before my pictures are having the same religious experience I had when I painted them. And if you, as you say, are moved only by their color relationships, then you miss the point."[9] Like the other Abstract Expressionists, Rothko produced highly evocative paintings reliant on formal elements rather than on specific representational content to elicit emotional responses in the viewer.

Post-Painterly Abstraction

Post-Painterly Abstraction, another postwar American art movement, developed out of Abstract Expressionism. Indeed, many of the artists associated with Post-Painterly Abstraction produced Abstract Expressionist work early in their careers. Yet Post-Painterly Abstraction, a term Clement Greenberg coined, manifests a radically different sensibility from Abstract Expressionism. Whereas Abstract Expressionism conveys a feeling of passion and visceral intensity, a cool, detached rationality emphasizing tighter pictorial control characterizes

ELLSWORTH KELLY Attempting to arrive at pure painting, the Post-Painterly Abstractionists distilled painting down to its essential elements, producing spare, elemental images. One of the primary practitioners of one variant of Post-Painterly Abstraction, *hard-edge painting*, was ELLSWORTH KELLY (b. 1923). Born in Newburgh on the Hudson River north of New York City, Kelly studied at the Pratt Institute in Brooklyn and later in Boston and Paris. *Red Blue Green* (FIG. **25-11**) is a characteristic example of his work. With its razor-sharp edges and clearly delineated shapes, the painting is completely abstract and extremely simple in composition. Further, the composition contains no suggestion of the illusion of depth. The color shapes appear resolutely two-dimensional.

FRANK STELLA Another artist associated with the hard-edge painters of the 1960s is Massachusetts-born FRANK STELLA (b. 1936). Stella studied history at Princeton University and moved to New York City in 1958, but did not favor the rough, expressive brushwork of the Abstract Expressionists. In works such as *Mas o Menos* (*More or Less;* FIG. **25-12**), Stella eliminated many of the variables associated with painting. His simplified images of thin, evenly spaced pinstripes on colored grounds have no central focus, no painterly or expressive elements, only limited surface modulation, and no tactile quality. His systematic painting illustrates Greenberg's insistence on purity in art. The artist's own famous comment on his work, "What you see is what you see," reinforces the notions that painters interested in producing advanced art must reduce their work to its essential elements and that the viewer must acknowledge a painting is simply pigment on a flat surface.

25-12 FRANK STELLA, *Mas o Menos*, 1964. Metallic powder in acrylic emulsion on canvas, 9′ 10″ × 13′ 8½″. Musée National d'Art Moderne, Centre Georges Pompidou, Paris (purchase 1983 with participation of Scaler Foundation).

Stella tried to achieve purity in painting using evenly spaced pinstripes on colored grounds. His canvases have no central focus, no painterly or expressive elements, and no tactile quality.

1 ft.

Helen Frankenthaler on Color-Field Painting

Helen Frankenthaler, the daughter of a New York State Supreme Court justice, began her study of art at the Dalton School in New York City under Rufino Tamayo (FIG. 24-74A). She has painted in New York for virtually her entire career. In 1965, the art critic Henry Geldzahler (1935–1994) interviewed Frankenthaler about her work as an abstract painter. In the following excerpt, Frankenthaler described the approach she took to placing color on canvas in *The Bay* (FIG. 25-13) and similar color-field paintings she produced in the early 1960s, and compared her method with the way earlier modernist artists used color in their paintings.

> I will sometimes start a picture feeling "What will happen if I work with three blues and another color, and maybe more or less of the other color than the combined blues?" And very often midway through the picture I have to change the basis of the experience. . . .
>
> When you first saw a Cubist or Impressionist picture there was a whole way of instructing the eye or the subconscious. Dabs of color had to stand for real things; it was an abstraction of a guitar or a hillside. The opposite is going on now. If you have bands of blue, green, and pink, the mind doesn't think sky, grass, and flesh. These are colors and the question is what are they doing with themselves and with each other. Sentiment and nuance are being squeezed out.*

*Henry Geldzahler, "Interview with Helen Frankenthaler," *Artforum* 4, no. 2 (October 1965), 37–38.

1 ft.

25-13 Helen Frankenthaler, *The Bay*, 1963. Acrylic on canvas, 6′ 8⅞″ × 6′ 9⅞″. Detroit Institute of Arts, Detroit.

Frankenthaler and other color-field painters poured paint onto unprimed canvas, allowing the pigments to soak into the fabric. Their works underscore that a painting is simply pigment on a flat surface.

HELEN FRANKENTHALER *Color-field painting,* another variant of Post-Painterly Abstraction, also emphasized painting's basic properties. However, rather than produce sharp, unmodulated shapes as the hard-edge artists had done, the color-field painters poured diluted paint onto unprimed canvas and allowed the pigments to soak in. It is hard to conceive of another painting method resulting in such literal flatness. The images created, such as *The Bay* (FIG. **25-13**) by Helen Frankenthaler (b. 1928), appear spontaneous and almost accidental (see "Helen Frankenthaler on Color-Field Painting," above). These works differ from those by Rothko and Newman in that Frankenthaler subordinated the emotional component, so integral to hard-edge painting, in favor of resolving formal problems.

MORRIS LOUIS Baltimore native Morris Louis (1912–1962), who spent most of his career in Washington, D.C., also became a champion of color-field painting. Clement Greenberg, an admirer of Frankenthaler's paintings, took Louis to her studio, where she introduced him to the possibilities presented by the staining technique. Louis used this method of pouring diluted paint onto the surface of unprimed canvas in several series of paintings. *Saraband* (FIG. **25-14**) is one of the works in Louis's *Veils* series. By holding up the canvas edges and pouring diluted acrylic resin, Louis created billowy, fluid, transparent shapes running down the length of the

canvas. As did Frankenthaler, Louis reduced painting to the concrete fact of the paint-impregnated material.

CLYFFORD STILL Although not a member of the New York School, another American painter whose work art historians usually classify as Post-Painterly Abstraction was Clyfford Still (1904–1980). Born in North Dakota, Still spent most of his career on the West Coast or in Maryland. He is best known for the large series of canvases he titled simply with their dates, underscoring his rejection of the very notion that the purpose of art is to represent places, people, or objects. Nonetheless, Still's paintings remind many viewers of vast landscapes seen from the air. But the artist's canvases make no reference to any forms in nature. His paintings, for example, *1948-C* (FIG. I-2), are pure exercises in the expressive use of color, shape, and texture.

Op Art

A major artistic movement of the 1960s was *Op Art* (short for *Optical Art*), in which painters sought to produce optical illusions of motion and depth using only geometric forms on two-dimensional surfaces. Among the primary sources of the movement was the work of Josef Albers, whose series of paintings called *Homage to the Square* (FIG. I-11) explored the optical effects of placing different

25-14 MORRIS LOUIS, *Saraband*, 1959. Acrylic resin on canvas, 8' 5⅛" × 12' 5". Solomon R. Guggenheim Foundation, New York.

Louis created his color-field paintings by holding up the canvas edges and pouring diluted acrylic resin to produce billowy, fluid, transparent shapes running down the length of the fabric.

colors next to each other. Ultimately, Op Art can be traced to 19th-century theories of color perception and the pointillism of Georges Seurat (see "Pointillism and 19th-Century Color Theory," Chapter 23, page 701, and FIG. 23-16).

25-15 BRIDGET RILEY, *Fission*, 1963. Tempera on composition board, 2' 11" × 2' 10". Museum of Modern Art, New York (gift of Philip Johnson).

Op Art paintings create the illusion of motion and depth using only geometric forms. The effect can be disorienting. The pattern of black dots in Riley's *Fission* appears to cave in at the center.

BRIDGET RILEY The artist whose name is synonymous with Op Art is the British artist BRIDGET RILEY (b. 1931), who painted in a neo-pointillist manner in the 1950s before developing her signature black-and-white Op Art style. Her paintings, for example, *Fission* (FIG. 25-15) of 1963, came to the public's attention after being featured in the December 1964 issue of *Life* magazine. The publicity unleashed a craze for Op Art designs in clothing. In 1965, the exhibition *The Responsive Eye* at the Museum of Modern Art, which also featured paintings by Ellsworth Kelly and Morris Louis, among others, bestowed an official stamp of approval on the movement.

In *Fission*, Riley filled the canvas with black dots of varied sizes and shapes, creating the illusion of a pulsating surface that caves in at the center (hence the painting's title). The effect on the viewer of Op Art paintings such as *Fission* is disorienting and sometimes disturbing, and some works can even induce motion sickness. Thoroughly modernist in the insistence a painting is a two-dimensional surface covered with pigment and not a representation of any person, object, or place, the Op Art movement nonetheless embraced the Renaissance notion that the painter can create the illusion of depth through perspective.

Abstraction in Sculpture

Painters were not the only artists interested in Clement Greenberg's formalist ideas. American sculptors also strove to arrive at purity in their medium. While painters worked to emphasize flatness, sculptors, understandably, chose to focus on three-dimensionality as the unique characteristic and inherent limitation of the sculptural idiom.

DAVID SMITH After experimenting with a variety of sculptural styles and materials, Indiana-born and Ohio-raised DAVID SMITH (1906–1965) produced metal sculptures that have affinities with the Abstract Expressionist movement in painting. In the

David Smith on Outdoor Sculpture

From ancient times, sculptors have frequently created statues for display in the open air, whether a portrait of a Roman emperor in a forum or Michelangelo's *David* (FIG. 17-13) in Florence's Piazza della Signoria. But rarely have sculptors taken into consideration the effects of sunlight in the conception of their works. American sculptor David Smith was an exception.

Smith learned to weld in an automobile plant in 1925 and later applied to his art the technical expertise in handling metals he gained from that experience. In addition, working in large scale at the factories helped him visualize the possibilities for monumental metal sculpture. His works, for example, *Cubi XII* (FIG. 25-16), created for display in the open air, lose much of their character in the sterile lighting of a museum.

I like outdoor sculpture and the most practical thing for outdoor sculpture is stainless steel, and I make them and I polish them in such a way that on a dull day, they take on the dull blue, or the color of the sky in the late afternoon sun, the glow, golden like the rays, the colors of nature. And in a particular sense, I have used atmosphere in a reflective way on the surfaces. They are colored by the sky and the surroundings, the green or blue of water. Some are down by the water and some are by the mountains. They reflect the colors. They are designed for the outdoors.*

*Quoted in Cleve Gray, ed., *David Smith by David Smith* (New York: Holt, Rinehart, and Winston, 1968), 133.

25-16 DAVID SMITH, *Cubi XII*, 1963. Stainless steel, 9′ 1⅝″ high. Hirshhorn Museum and Sculpture Garden, Smithsonian Institution, Washington, D.C. (gift of the Joseph H. Hirshhorn Foundation, 1972). Art © David Smith, Licensed by VAGA, NY. Photo by Lee Stalsworth, Smithsonian Hirshhorn Museum and Sculpture Garden.

David Smith designed his abstract metal sculptures of simple geometric forms to reflect the natural light and color of their outdoor settings, not the sterile illumination of a museum gallery.

1 ft.

1960s he produced a series of monumental works called *Cubi*, designed for display in the open air (see "David Smith on Outdoor Sculpture," above). *Cubi XII* (FIG. 25-16), a characteristic example, consists of simple geometric forms—cubes and rectangular bars. Made of stainless-steel sections piled on top of one another, often at unstable angles, and then welded together, the *Cubi* sculptures make a striking visual statement. Smith added gestural elements reminiscent of Abstract Expressionism by burnishing the metal with steel wool, producing swirling random-looking patterns that draw attention to the two-dimensionality of the sculptural surface. This treatment, which captures the light hitting the artwork, activates the surface and imparts a texture to his pieces.

TONY SMITH A predominantly sculptural movement that emerged in the 1960s among artists seeking Greenbergian purity of form was *Minimalism*. One leading Minimalist was New Jersey native TONY SMITH (1912–1980), who created simple volumetric sculptures such as *Die* (FIG. 25-17). Minimalist artworks generally lack identifiable subjects, colors, surface textures, and narrative elements, and are perhaps best described simply as three-dimensional objects. By rejecting illusionism and reducing sculpture to basic geometric forms, Smith and other Minimalists emphatically emphasized their art's "objecthood" and concrete tangibility. In so doing, they reduced experience to its most fundamental level, preventing viewers from drawing on assumptions or preconceptions when dealing with the art before them.

1 ft.

25-17 TONY SMITH, *Die,* 1962. Steel, 6′ × 6′ × 6′. Museum of Modern Art, New York (gift of Jane Smith in honor of Agnes Gund).

By rejecting illusionism and symbolism and reducing sculpture to basic geometric forms, Minimalist Tony Smith emphasized the "objecthood" and concrete tangibility of his sculptures.

Donald Judd on Sculpture and Industrial Materials

In a 1965 essay entitled "Specific Objects," the Minimalist sculptor Donald Judd described the advantages of sculpture over painting and the attractions of using industrial materials for his works (FIG. 25-18).

> Three dimensions are real space. That gets rid of the problem of illusionism . . . one of the salient and most objectionable relics of European art. The several limits of painting are no longer present. A work can be as powerful as it can be thought to be. Actual space is intrinsically more powerful and specific than paint on a flat surface. . . . The use of three dimensions makes it possible to see all sorts of materials and colors. Most of [my] work involves new materials, either recent inventions or things not used before in art. Little was done until lately with the wide range of industrial products. . . . Materials vary greatly and are simply materials—formica, aluminum, cold-rolled steel, plexiglas, red and common brass, and so forth. They are specific. If they are used directly, they are more specific. Also, they are usually aggressive. There is an objectivity to the obdurate identity of a material. . . . The form of a work of art and its materials are closely related. In earlier work the structure and the imagery were executed in some neutral and homogeneous material.*

*Donald Judd, *Complete Writings 1959–1975* (New York: New York University Press, 1975), 181–189.

25-18 DONALD JUDD, *Untitled*, 1969. Brass and colored fluorescent Plexiglas on steel brackets, 10 units, $6\frac{1}{8}'' \times 2' \times 2' 3''$ each, with 6″ intervals. Hirshhorn Museum and Sculpture Garden, Smithsonian Institution, Washington, D.C. (gift of Joseph H. Hirshhorn, 1972). © Donald Judd Estate/Licensed by VAGA, New York.

Judd's Minimalist sculpture incorporates boxes fashioned from undisguised industrial materials. The artist used Plexiglas because its translucency gives the viewer access to the work's interior.

1 ft.

DONALD JUDD Another Minimalist sculptor, DONALD JUDD (1928–1994), embraced a spare, universal aesthetic corresponding to the core tenets of the movement. Born in Missouri, Judd studied philosophy and art history at Columbia University in New York City, where he produced most of his major works. Judd's determination to arrive at a visual vocabulary devoid of deception or ambiguity propelled him away from representation and toward precise and simple sculpture. For Judd, a work's power derived from its character as a whole and from the specificity of its materials (see "Donald Judd on Sculpture and Industrial Materials," above). *Untitled* (FIG. 25-18) presents basic geometric boxes constructed of brass and red Plexiglas, undisguised by paint or other materials. The artist did not intend the work to be metaphorical or symbolic. It is a straightforward declaration of sculpture's objecthood. Judd used Plexiglas because its translucency enables the viewer access to the interior, thereby rendering the sculpture both open and enclosed. This aspect of the design reflects Judd's desire to banish ambiguity or falseness from his works.

Perhaps surprisingly, despite the ostensible connections between Minimalism and Greenbergian formalism, the critic did not embrace this direction in art:

> Minimal Art remains too much a feat of ideation [the mental formation of ideas], and not enough anything else. Its idea remains an idea, something deduced instead of felt and discovered. The geometrical and modular simplicity may announce and signify the artistically furthest-out, but the fact that the signals are understood for what they want to mean betrays them artistically. There is hardly any aesthetic surprise in Minimal Art. . . . Aesthetic surprise hangs on forever—it is there in Raphael as it is in Pollock—and ideas alone cannot achieve it.[10]

LOUISE NEVELSON Although Minimalism was a dominant sculptural trend in the 1960s, many sculptors pursued other styles. Russian-born LOUISE NEVELSON (1899–1988) created sculpture combining a sense of the architectural fragment with the power of Dada and Surrealist found objects to express her personal

25-19 LOUISE NEVELSON, *Tropical Garden II,* 1957–1959. Wood painted black, 5′ 11½″ × 10′ 11¾″ × 1′. Musée National d'Art Moderne, Centre Georges Pompidou, Paris.

The monochromatic color scheme unifies the diverse sculpted forms and found objects in Nevelson's "walls" and creates a mysterious field of shapes and shadows suggesting magical environments.

1 ft.

sense of life's underlying significance. Multiplicity of meaning was important to Nevelson. She sought "the in-between place. . . . The dawns and the dusks"[11]—the transitional realm between one state of being and another.

Beginning in the late 1950s, Nevelson assembled sculptures of found wooden objects and forms, enclosing small sculptural compositions in boxes of varied sizes, and joined the boxes to one another to form "walls," which she then painted in a single hue—usually black, white, or gold. This monochromatic color scheme unifies the diverse parts of pieces such as *Tropical Garden II* (FIG. **25-19**) and creates a mysterious field of shapes and shadows. The structures suggest magical environments resembling the treasured secret hideaways dimly remembered from childhood. Yet the boxy frames and the precision of the manufactured found objects create a rough geometric structure the eye roams over freely, lingering on some details. The parts of a Nevelson sculpture and their interrelation recall the *Merz* constructions of Kurt Schwitters (FIG. 24-29). The effect is also rather like viewing the side of an apartment building from a moving elevated train or looking down on a city from the air.

LOUISE BOURGEOIS In contrast to the architectural nature of Nevelson's work, a sensuous organic quality recalling the evocative Biomorphic Surrealist forms of Joan Miró (FIG. 24-58) pervades the work of French-American artist LOUISE BOURGEOIS (1911–2010). *Cumul I* (FIG. **25-20**) is a collection of round-headed units huddled, with their heads protruding, within a collective cloak dotted with holes. The units differ in size, and their position within the group lends a distinctive personality to each. Although the shapes remain abstract, they refer strongly to human figures.

Bourgeois used a wide variety of materials in her works, including wood, plaster, latex, and plastics, in addition to alabaster, marble, and bronze. She exploited each material's qualities to suit the expressiveness of the piece.

1 ft.

25-20 LOUISE BOURGEOIS, *Cumul I,* 1969. Marble, 1′ 10⅜″ × 4′ 2″ × 4′. Musée National d'Art Moderne, Centre Georges Pompidou, Paris. © Louise Bourgeois/Licensed by VAGA, New York. ■◀

Bourgeois's sculptures are made up of sensuous organic forms that recall the Biomorphic Surrealist forms of Miró (FIG. 24-58). Although the shapes remain abstract, they refer strongly to human figures.

In *Cumul I,* the alternating high gloss and matte finish of the marble increases the sensuous distinction between the group of swelling forms and the soft folds swaddling them. As did Barbara Hepworth (FIG. 24-62), Bourgeois connected her sculpture with the body's multiple relationships to landscape: "[My pieces] are anthropomorphic and they are landscape also, since our body could be considered from a topographical point of view, as a land with mounds and valleys and caves and holes."[12] However, Bourgeois's sculptures are more personal and more openly sexual than Hepworth's. *Cumul I* represents perfectly the allusions Bourgeois sought: "There has always been sexual suggestiveness in my work. Sometimes I am totally concerned with female shapes—characters of breasts like clouds—but often I merge the activity—phallic breasts, male and female, active and passive."[13]

EVA HESSE A Minimalist in the early part of her career, EVA HESSE (1936–1970) later moved away from the severity characterizing much of Minimal art. She created sculptures that, although spare and simple, have a compelling presence. Using nontraditional sculptural materials such as fiberglass, cord, and latex, Hesse produced sculptures whose pure Minimalist forms appear to crumble, sag, and warp under the pressures of atmospheric force and gravity. Born Jewish in Hitler's Germany, the young Hesse hid with a Christian family when her parents and elder sister had to flee the Nazis.

25-21 EVA HESSE, *Hang-Up,* 1965–1966. Acrylic on cloth over wood and steel, 6′ × 7′ × 6′ 6″. Art Institute of Chicago, Chicago (gift of Arthur Keating and Mr. and Mrs. Edward Morris by exchange).

Hesse created spare and simple sculptures with parts extending into the room. She wanted her works to express the strangeness and absurdity she considered the central conditions of modern life.

She did not reunite with them until the early 1940s, just before her parents divorced. Those extraordinary circumstances helped give her a lasting sense that the central conditions of modern life are strangeness and absurdity. Struggling to express these qualities in her art, Hesse created informal sculptural arrangements with units often hung from the ceiling, propped against the walls, or spilled out along the floor. She said she wanted her pieces to be "non art, non connotative, non anthropomorphic, non geometric, non nothing, everything, but of another kind, vision, sort."[14]

Hang-Up (FIG. **25-21**) fulfills these requirements. The piece resembles a carefully made empty frame sprouting a strange feeler extending into the room and doubling back to the frame. Hesse wrote that in this work, for the first time, her "idea of absurdity or extreme feeling came through. . . . [*Hang-Up*] has a kind of depth I don't always achieve and that is the kind of depth or soul or absurdity of life or meaning or feeling or intellect that I want to get."[15] The sculpture possesses a disquieting and touching presence, suggesting the fragility and grandeur of life amid the pressures of the modern age. Hesse was herself a touching and fragile presence in the art world. She died of a brain tumor at age 34.

ISAMU NOGUCHI Another sculptor often considered a Minimalist because of pure geometric works such as *Red Cube,* which he created in 1968 for the sidewalk in front of a New York City skyscraper, is Japanese American artist ISAMU NOGUCHI (1904–1988). His work defies easy classification, however, and in sculptures such as *Shodo Shima Stone Study* (FIG. **25-21A**), Noguchi brilliantly wedded Western and Oriental themes and styles.

25-21A NOGUCHI, *Shodo Shima,* 1978.

Pop Art

Despite their differences, the Abstract Expressionists, Post-Painterly Abstractionists, Op Art painters, and Minimalist sculptors all adopted an artistic vocabulary of resolute abstraction. Other artists, however, observing that the insular and introspective attitude of the avant-garde had alienated the public, sought to harness the communicative power of art to reach a wide audience. Thus was born the Independent Group in London (FIG. 25-1) and the art movement that came to be known as Pop.

Although Pop Art originated in England, the movement found its greatest articulation and success in the United States, in large part because the more fully matured American consumer culture provided a fertile environment in which the movement flourished through the 1960s. Indeed, Independent Group members claimed their inspiration came from Hollywood, Detroit, and New York's Madison Avenue, paying homage to America's predominance in the realms of mass media, mass production, and advertising.

JASPER JOHNS One of the artists pivotal to the early development of American Pop Art was JASPER JOHNS (b. 1930), who grew up in South Carolina and moved to New York City in 1952. Johns sought to draw attention to common objects in the world—what he called things "seen but not looked at."[16] To this end, he did several series of paintings of numbers, alphabets, flags, and maps of the United States—all of which are items people view frequently but rarely scrutinize. He created his first

1 ft.

flag painting in 1954 at the height of the Cold War. Initially labeled a Neo-Dadaist because of the kinship of his works to Marcel Duchamp's readymades (FIG. 24-27), Johns also had strong ties to the Surrealists, especially René Magritte, whose painting of a pipe labeled "This is not a pipe" (FIG. 24-56) is conceptually a forerunner of Johns's flags—for example, *Three Flags* (FIG. **25-22**), which could easily carry the label "These are not flags." In fact, when asked why he chose the American flag as a subject, Johns replied he had a dream in which he saw himself painting a flag. The world of dreams was central to Surrealism (see Chapter 24).

In *Three Flags*, Johns painted a trio of overlapping American national banners of decreasing size, with the smallest closest to the viewer, reversing traditional perspective, which calls for diminution of size with distance. Johns drained meaning from the patriotic emblem by reducing it to a repetitive pattern—not the flag itself but three pictures of a flag in one. Nevertheless, the heritage of Abstract Expressionism is still apparent. Although Johns rejected the heroic, highly personalized application of pigment championed by the 1950s action painters, he painted his flags in *encaustic* (liquid wax and dissolved pigment; see "Encaustic Painting," Chapter 7, page 218) mixed with newsprint on three overlapping canvases. His flags thus retain a pronounced surface texture, emphasizing that the viewer is looking at a handmade painting, not a machine-made fabric. The painting, like the flags, is an object, not an illusion of other objects.

ROBERT RAUSCHENBERG A close friend of Johns's, ROBERT RAUSCHENBERG (1925–2008) began using mass-media images in his work in the 1950s. Rauschenberg set out to create works that would be open and indeterminate, and he began by making *combines,* which intersperse painted passages with sculptural elements. Combines are, in a sense, Rauschenberg's personal variation on *assemblages,* artworks constructed from already existing objects. At times, these combines seem to be sculptures with painting incorporated into certain sections. Others seem to be paint-

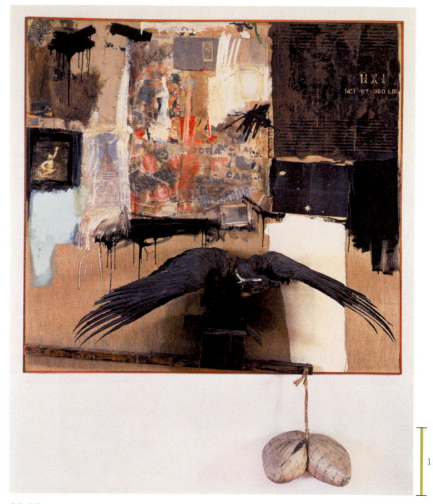

1 ft.

25-23 ROBERT RAUSCHENBERG, *Canyon*, 1959. Oil, pencil, paper, fabric, metal, cardboard box, printed paper, printed reproductions, photograph, wood, paint tube, and mirror on canvas, with oil on bald eagle, string, and pillow, 6′ 9¾″ × 5′ 10″ × 2′. Sonnabend Collection, New York. © Robert Rauschenberg/ Licensed by VAGA, New York.

Rauschenberg's "combines" intersperse painted passages with sculptural elements. *Canyon* incorporates pigment on canvas with pieces of printed paper, photographs, a pillow, and a stuffed eagle.

Roy Lichtenstein on Pop Art

In November 1963, Roy Lichtenstein was one of eight painters interviewed for a profile on Pop Art in *Art News*. Gene R. Swenson posed the questions. Some of Lichtenstein's answers follow.

[Pop Art is] the use of commercial art as a subject matter in painting . . . [Pop artists portray] what I think to be the most brazen and threatening characteristics of our culture, things we hate, but which are also so powerful in their impingement on us. . . . I paint directly . . . [without] perspective or shading. It doesn't look like a painting *of* something, it looks like the thing itself. Instead of looking like a painting *of* a billboard . . . Pop art seems to be the actual thing. It is an intensification, a stylistic intensification of the excitement which the subject matter has for me; but the style is . . . cool. One of the things a cartoon does is to express violent emotion and passion in a completely mechanized and removed style. To express this thing in a painterly style would dilute it. . . . Everybody has called Pop Art "American" painting, but it's actually industrial painting. America was hit by industrialism and capitalism harder and sooner . . . I think the meaning of my work is that it's industrial, it's what all the world will soon become. Europe will be the same way, soon, so it won't be American; it will be universal.*

25-24 ROY LICHTENSTEIN, *Hopeless*, 1963. Oil and synthetic polymer paint on canvas, 3′ 8″ × 3′ 8″. Kunstmuseum Basel, Basel. © Estate of Roy Lichtenstein.

Comic books appealed to Lichtenstein because they were a mainstay of popular culture, meant to be read and discarded. The Pop artist immortalized their images on large canvases.

*G. R. Swenson, "What Is Pop Art? Interviews with Eight Painters," *Art News* 62, no. 7 (November 1963), 25, 64.

---

ings with three-dimensional objects attached to the surface. In the 1950s, assemblages usually contained an array of art reproductions, magazine and newspaper clippings, and passages painted in an Abstract Expressionist style. In the early 1960s, Rauschenberg adopted the commercial medium of *silk-screen printing,* first in black and white and then in color, and began filling entire canvases with appropriated news images and anonymous photographs of city scenes.

Canyon (FIG. **25-23**) is typical of his combines. Pieces of printed paper and photographs cover parts of the canvas. Much of the unevenly painted surface consists of pigment roughly applied in a manner reminiscent of de Kooning's work (FIG. 25-8). A stuffed bald eagle attached to the lower part of the combine spreads its wings as if lifting off in flight toward the viewer. Completing the combine, a pillow dangles from a string attached to a wood stick below the eagle. The artist presented the work's components in a jumbled fashion. He tilted or turned some of the images sideways, and each overlays part of another image. The compositional confusion may resemble that of a Dada collage, but the parts of Rauschenberg's combines maintain their individuality more than those, for example, in a Schwitters piece (FIG. 24-29). The eye scans a Rauschenberg canvas much as it might survey the environment on a walk through a city. The various recognizable images and objects seem unrelated and defy a consistent reading, although Rauschenberg chose all the elements of his combines with specific

meanings in mind. For example, Rauschenberg based *Canyon* on a Rembrandt painting of Jupiter in the form of an eagle carrying the boy Ganymede heavenward. The photo in the combine is a reference to the Greek boy, and the hanging bag is a visual pun on his buttocks.

ROY LICHTENSTEIN As the Pop Art movement matured, the images became more concrete and tightly controlled. ROY LICHTENSTEIN (1923–1997), who was born in Manhattan not far from Madison Avenue, the center of the American advertising industry, developed an interest in art in elementary school and as a teenager took weekend painting classes at the Parsons School of Design before enrolling at Ohio State University. He served in the army during World War II and was stationed in France, where he was able to visit the Musée du Louvre and Chartres Cathedral. In the late 1950s, however, he turned his attention to commercial art and especially to the comic book as a mainstay of American popular culture (see "Roy Lichtenstein on Pop Art," above).

In paintings such as *Hopeless* (FIG. **25-24**), Lichtenstein excerpted an image from a comic book, a form of entertainment meant to be read and discarded, and immortalized the image on a large canvas. Aside from that modification, Lichtenstein remained remarkably faithful to the original comic-strip image. His subjects were typically the melodramatic scenes that were hallmarks of

25-25 ANDY WARHOL, *Green Coca-Cola Bottles,* 1962. Oil on canvas, 6′ 10½″ × 4′ 9″. Whitney Museum of American Art, New York.

Warhol was the quintessential American Pop artist. Here, he selected an icon of mass-produced, consumer culture, and then multiplied it, reflecting Coke's omnipresence in American society.

romance comic books popular at the time and included "balloons" with the words the characters speak. Lichtenstein also used the visual vocabulary of the comic strip, with its dark black outlines and unmodulated color areas, and retained the familiar square dimensions. Moreover, his printing technique, *benday dots,* called attention to the mass-produced derivation of the image. Named after its inventor, the newspaper printer Benjamin Day (1810–1889), the benday-dot system involves the modulation of colors through the placement and size of colored dots. Lichtenstein thus transferred the visual shorthand language of the comic book to the realm of monumental painting.

ANDY WARHOL
The quintessential American Pop artist was ANDY WARHOL (1928–1987). An early successful career as a commercial artist and illustrator grounded Warhol in the sensibility and

25-25A WARHOL, *Marilyn Diptych,* 1962. ◼️▪️

visual rhetoric of advertising and the mass media. This knowledge proved useful for his Pop artworks, which often depicted icons of mass-produced consumer culture, such as *Green Coca-Cola Bottles* (FIG. **25-25**), and Hollywood celebrities, such as Marilyn Monroe (1926–1962; FIG. **25-25A**). Warhol

favored reassuringly familiar objects and people. He explained his attraction to the ubiquitous curved Coke bottle:

> What's great about this country is that America started the tradition where the richest consumers buy essentially the same things as the poorest. You can be watching TV and see Coca-Cola, and you can know that the President drinks Coke, Liz Taylor drinks Coke, and just think, you can drink Coke, too. A Coke is a Coke and no amount of money can get you a better Coke.[17]

As did other Pop artists, Warhol used a visual vocabulary and a printing method that reinforced the image's connections to consumer culture. The silk-screen technique allowed Warhol to print the image endlessly (although he varied each bottle slightly). The repetition and redundancy of the Coke bottle reflect the saturation of this product in American society—in homes, at work, literally everywhere, including gas stations, as immortalized by GEORGE SEGAL (1924–2000) in 1963 (FIG. **25-25B**). So immersed was Warhol in a culture of

25-25B SEGAL, *Gas Station,* 1963.

mass production that he not only produced numerous canvases of the same image but also named his studio "the Factory."

CLAES OLDENBURG
In the 1960s, CLAES OLDENBURG (b. 1929) also produced Pop artworks that incisively commented on American consumer culture, but his medium was sculpture. The son of a Swedish diplomat who moved to the United States in 1936, Oldenburg attended school in Chicago and graduated from Yale University in 1950. His early works consisted of plaster reliefs of food and clothing items. Oldenburg constructed these sculptures of plaster layered on chicken wire and muslin, painting them with cheap commercial house enamel. In later works, focused on the same subjects, he shifted to large-scale stuffed sculptures of sewn vinyl or canvas, many of which he exhibited in a show he titled *The Store*—an appropriate comment on the function of art as a commodity in a consumer society.

Oldenburg is best known, however, for his mammoth outdoor sculptures. In 1966, a group of graduate students at the Yale School of Architecture, calling themselves the Colossal Keepsake Corporation, raised funds for materials for a giant sculpture that Oldenburg agreed to create (in secret and without a fee) as a gift to his alma mater. The work, *Lipstick (Ascending) on Caterpillar Tracks* (FIG. **25-26**), was Oldenburg's first monumental public sculpture. He installed *Lipstick* on Ascension Day, May 15, 1969, on Beineke Plaza across from the office of the university's president, the site of many raucous protests against the Vietnam War. Oldenburg's characteristic humor emerges unmistakably in the combination of phallic and militaristic imagery, especially in the double irony of the "phallus" being a woman's cosmetic item, and the Caterpillar-type endless-loop metal tracks suggesting not a tractor-earthmover for construction work but a military tank designed for destruction in warfare. *Lipstick* was to be a speaker's platform for protesters, and originally the lipstick tip was a drooping red vinyl balloon the speaker had to inflate, underscoring the sexual innuendo. (Oldenburg once remarked that art collectors preferred nudes, so he produced nude cars, nude telephones, and nude electric plugs to please them.)

Vandalism and exposure to the elements (the original tractor was plywood) caused so much damage to *Lipstick* that it had to be removed and reconstructed in metal and fiberglass. Yale formally accepted the controversial and unsolicited repaired gift in 1974,

1 ft.

Designed as a speaker's platform for antiwar protesters, *Lipstick* humorously combines phallic and militaristic imagery. Originally the lipstick tip was soft red vinyl and had to be inflated.

when the architectural historian Vincent Scully (b. 1920), then master of Yale's Morse College, offered a permanent home for *Lipstick* in the college courtyard.

Also usually classified as a Pop Art sculptor was French-born NIKI DE SAINT-PHALLE (1930–2002), because her sculptures remind many viewers of dolls and folk art. Her most famous works are the series of polyester statues of women she called *Nanas* (FIG. **25-26A**), oversized, brightly colored sculptures that are feminist commentaries on popular stereotypes of female beauty.

25-26A SAINT-PHALLE, *Black Venus*, 1965–1967.

Superrealism

Like the Pop artists, the artists associated with *Superrealism* sought a form of artistic communication more accessible to the public than the remote, unfamiliar visual language of the Abstract Expressionists, Post-Painterly Abstractionists, and Minimalists. The Superrealists expanded Pop's iconography in both painting and sculpture by making images in the late 1960s and 1970s involving scrupulous fidelity to optical fact. Because many Superrealists used photographs as sources for their imagery, art historians also refer to this postwar art movement as *Photorealism*.

AUDREY FLACK One of Superrealism's pioneers was lifelong New Yorker AUDREY FLACK (b. 1931), who studied the history of art at New York University's Institute of Fine Arts after graduating from Yale. Her paintings, such as *Marilyn* (FIG. **25-27**), were not simply technical exercises in recording objects in minute detail but were also conceptual inquiries into the nature of photography and the extent to which photography constructs an understanding of reality. Flack observed: "[Photography is] my whole life, I studied art history, it was always photographs, I never saw the paintings, they were in Europe. . . . Look at TV and at magazines and reproductions, they're all influenced by photo-vision."[18] The photograph's formal

1 ft.

25-27 AUDREY FLACK, *Marilyn*, 1977. Oil over acrylic on canvas, 8′ × 8′. University of Arizona Museum, Tucson (museum purchase with funds provided by the Edward J. Gallagher Jr. Memorial Fund).

Flack's pioneering Photorealist still lifes record objects with great optical fidelity. *Marilyn* alludes to Dutch vanitas paintings (FIG. 20-1) and incorporates multiple references to the transience of life.

Chuck Close on Photorealist Portrait Painting

In a widely read 1970 interview in the journal *Artforum*, art critic Cindy Nemser asked Photorealist painter Chuck Close about the scale of his huge portraits (FIG. 25-28) and the relationship of his canvases to the photographs that lie behind them. He answered in part:

The large scale allows me to deal with information that is overlooked in an eight-by-ten inch photograph . . . My large scale forces the viewer to focus on one area at a time. In that way he is made aware of the blurred areas that are seen with peripheral vision. Normally we never take those peripheral areas into account. When we focus on an area it is sharp. As we turn our attention to adjacent areas they sharpen up too. In my work, the blurred areas don't come into focus, but they are too large to be ignored. . . . In order to . . . make [my painted] information stack up with photographic information, I tried to purge my work of as much of the baggage of traditional portrait painting as I could. To avoid a painterly brush stroke and surface, I use some pretty devious means, such as razor blades, electric drills and airbrushes. I also work as thinly as possible and I don't use white paint as it tends to build up and become chalky and opaque. In fact, in a nine-by-seven foot picture, I only use a couple of tablespoons of black paint to cover the entire canvas.*

*Cindy Nemser, "Chuck Close: Interview with Cindy Nemser," *Artforum* 8, no. 5 (January 1970), 51–55.

25-28 CHUCK CLOSE, *Big Self-Portrait*, 1967–1968. Acrylic on canvas, 8′ 11″ × 6′ 11″. Walker Art Center, Minneapolis (Art Center Acquisition Fund, 1969). ◼◀

Close's goal was to translate photographic information into painted information. In his portraits, he deliberately avoided creative compositions, flattering lighting effects, and revealing facial expressions.

1 ft.

---

qualities also intrigued her, and she used photographic techniques by first projecting an image in slide form onto the canvas. By next using an *airbrush* (a device originally designed as a photo-retouching tool that sprays paint with compressed air), Flack could duplicate the smooth gradations of tone and color found in photographs. Most of her paintings are still lifes that present the viewer with a collection of familiar objects painted with great optical fidelity. *Marilyn* is a still life incorporating photographs of the face of famed Hollywood actress Marilyn Monroe. It is a poignant commentary on Monroe's tragic life and differs markedly from Warhol's *Marilyn Diptych* (FIG. 25-25A), which celebrates celebrity and makes no allusion to the death of the glamorous star. Flack's still life includes multiple references to death and alludes to Dutch vanitas paintings (FIG. 20-1). In addition to the black-and-white photographs of a youthful, smiling Monroe, fresh fruit, an hourglass, a burning candle, a watch, and a calendar all refer to the passage of time and the transience of life on earth.

CHUCK CLOSE Also usually considered a Superrealist is CHUCK CLOSE (b. 1940), who grew up near Seattle and attended the University of Washington and Yale University. He is best known for his large-scale portraits, such as *Big Self-Portrait* (FIG. **25-28**). However, Close felt his connection to the Photorealists was tenuous, because for him realism, rather than an end in itself, was the

result of an intellectually rigorous, systematic approach to painting. He based his paintings of the late 1960s and early 1970s on photographs, and his main goal was to translate photographic information into painted information. Because he aimed simply to record visual information about his subject's appearance, Close deliberately avoided creative compositions, flattering lighting effects, and revealing facial expressions. Not interested in providing great insight into the personalities of those portrayed, Close painted anonymous and generic people, mostly friends. By reducing the variables in his paintings (even their canvas size is a constant 9 by 7 feet), he could focus on employing his methodical presentations of faces, thereby encouraging the viewer to deal with the formal aspects of his works. Indeed, because of the large scale of Close's paintings, careful scrutiny causes the images to dissolve into abstract patterns (see "Chuck Close on Photorealist Portrait Painting," above).

LUCIAN FREUD Born in Berlin, LUCIAN FREUD (1922–2011) moved to London with his family in 1933 when Adolph Hitler became German chancellor. The grandson of Sigmund Freud, the painter is best known for his unflattering close-up views of faces in which the sitter seems almost unaware of the painter's presence, and for his portrayals of female and male nudes in foreshortened and often contorted poses. Although Freud always used living

1 in.

25-29 LUCIAN FREUD, *Naked Portrait,* 1972–1973. Oil on canvas, 2′ × 2′. Tate Modern, London.

Freud's brutally realistic portrait of an unnamed woman lying on a bed in an awkward position gives the impression the viewer is an intruder in a private space, but the setting is the artist's studio.

DUANE HANSON Not surprisingly, many sculptors also were Superrealists, including Minnesota-born DUANE HANSON (1925–1996), who spent much of his career in southern Florida. Hanson perfected a casting technique that enabled him to create life-size figurative sculptures many viewers mistake at first for real people. Hanson began by making plaster molds from live models and then filled the molds with polyester resin. After the resin hardened, he removed the outer molds and cleaned, painted with an airbrush, and decorated the sculptures with wigs, clothes, and other accessories. These works, such as *Supermarket Shopper* (FIG. **25-30**), depict stereotypical average Americans, striking chords with the public specifically because of their familiarity. Hanson explained his choice of imagery:

The subject matter that I like best deals with the familiar lower- and middle-class American types of today. To me, the resignation, emptiness and loneliness of their existence captures the true reality of life for these people. . . . I want to achieve a certain tough realism which speaks of the fascinating idiosyncrasies of our time.[21]

models whose poses he determined, his paintings convey the impression the artist and the viewer are intruders in a private realm.

In *Naked Portrait* (FIG. **25-29**), the viewer observes an unnamed woman lying in an uncomfortable, almost fetal, position at the foot of a bed. Freud depicted her from a sharp angle above and to the left. In the foreground is a small table with the painter's tools on it, revealing that this is not the woman's bedroom but the painter's studio and that the woman is the subject of intense scrutiny by the artist. Freud's models do not have perfect bodies. Some are overweight, and many are well beyond their prime. These are truly "naked portraits" of real people. They break sharply with the Western tradition from Greek antiquity to the Renaissance and into the modern era of depicting idealized Venuses, Eves, and courtesans in graceful and often erotic poses. Freud explained his interest in nudity: "I'm really interested in people as animals. Part of my liking to work from them naked is for that reason. Because I can see more."[19] Regarding the setting of his paintings, Freud observed: "I work from people that interest me, and that I care about and think about, in rooms that I live in and know."[20]

1 ft.

25-30 DUANE HANSON, *Supermarket Shopper,* 1970. Polyester resin and fiberglass polychromed in oil, with clothing, steel cart, and groceries, life-size. Nachfolgeinstitut, Neue Galerie, Sammlung Ludwig, Aachen. © Estate of Duane Hanson/Licensed by VAGA, New York.

Hanson used molds from live models to create his Superrealistic life-size painted plaster sculptures. His aim was to capture the emptiness and loneliness of average Americans in familiar settings.

Photography

Although Superrealist artists admired the ability of photography to reproduce faithfully the appearance of people, objects, and places, photographers themselves used their medium to pursue varied ends. The photographs of Edward Weston (FIGS. 24-44 and 24-44A) and Dorothea Lange (FIG. 24-76) represent the two poles of American photography between the world wars—the art photograph (Weston), which transforms the real into the abstract, and the documentary photograph (Lange), which records people and events directly, without artifice. In the postwar period both approaches to photography continued to flourish.

DIANE ARBUS During the 1960s, the most famous photographer of people—with all their blemishes, both physical and psychological—was DIANE ARBUS (1923–1971). New York–born and –educated, Diane Nemerov married Allan Arbus when she was 18 and worked with her husband as a fashion photographer. After their divorce in 1959, Diane chose as her subjects the opposite of the beautiful people with perfect makeup and trendy clothes she had photographed constantly in the 1950s. Her photographs record ordinary people living ordinary lives, people with physical deformities, and people at the margins of society, for example, transvestites—in short, people who rarely were the chosen subjects of professional photographers.

One of Arbus's most memorable photographs (FIG. 25-31) is of a boy she encountered in New York City's Central Park in 1962 carrying a toy hand grenade. She asked him to stand still and pose

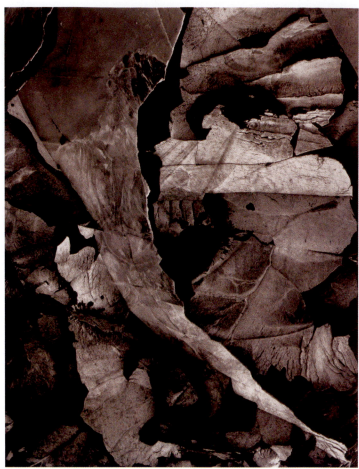

25-32 MINOR WHITE, *Moencopi Strata, Capitol Reef, Utah*, 1962. Gelatin silver print, 1′ $\frac{1}{8}$″ × 9$\frac{1}{4}$″. Museum of Modern Art, New York. © The Minor White Archive, Princeton University.

White's "straight photograph" of a natural rock formation is also an abstract composition of jagged shapes and contrasts of light and dark reminiscent of Abstract Expressionist action paintings.

for her, and as she moved around him searching for the perfect angle, he became impatient, his body tensed, and his face formed a menacing expression. She snapped the shutter and recorded his peculiar grimace and eerie clawlike left hand. The empty space all around the boy contributes to the sense he is a disturbed personality isolated from society, in contrast to the "normal" family at the top right of the photograph. Arbus's own life was not "picture perfect" either. She committed suicide in 1971.

MINOR WHITE Minneapolis native MINOR WHITE (1908–1976) moved to Portland, Oregon, in 1938 and became a photographer for the Works Progress Administration. He served in the United States Army in World War II and then settled in New York City in 1945, where he met Alfred Stieglitz, whose *Equivalent* photographs (FIG. 24-43A) he greatly admired. Deeply influenced by Zen Buddhism, White sought to incorporate a mystical element in his own work. His 1962 photograph (FIG. 25-32) of a rock formation in Utah is a characteristic example. A "straight photograph" in the tradition of Stieglitz and Weston, it is also an abstract composition of jagged shapes and contrasts of light and dark reminiscent of Abstract Expressionist action paintings (FIG. 25-8C). Viewers of *Moencopi Strata, Capitol Reef, Utah* may recognize White's nominal subject as a detail of a landscape, but in his hands nature becomes the springboard for meditation. As one of the founders and the longtime editor (1952–1975) of *Ap-*

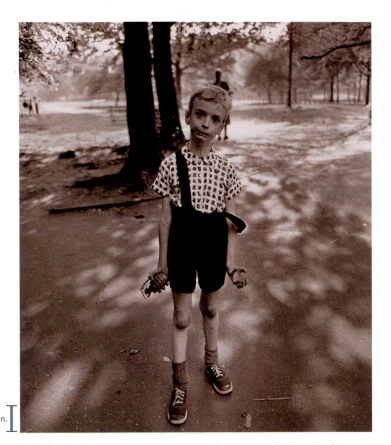

25-31 DIANE ARBUS, *Child with Toy Hand Grenade, New York, New York*, 1962. Gelatin silver print, 7$\frac{1}{4}$″ × 8$\frac{3}{8}$″. The Museum of Modern Art, New York.

Arbus specialized in photographs of people on the margins of society. Her photograph of a boy holding a toy hand grenade in New York's Central Park presents him as a menacing, isolated personality.

Judy Chicago on *The Dinner Party*

One of the acknowledged masterpieces of feminist art is Judy Chicago's *The Dinner Party* (FIG. 25-33), which required a team of nearly 400 to create and assemble. In 1979, Chicago published a book explaining the genesis and symbolism of the work.

[By 1974] I had discarded [my original] idea of painting a hundred abstract portraits on plates, each paying tribute to a different historic female figure. . . . In my research I realized over and over again that women's achievements had been left out of history . . . My new idea was to try to symbolize this. . . . [I thought] about putting the plates on a table with silver, glasses, napkins, and tablecloths, and over the next year and a half the concept of *The Dinner Party* slowly evolved. I began to think about the piece as a reinterpretation of the Last Supper from the point of view of women, who, throughout history, had prepared the meals and set the table. In my "Last Supper," however, the women would be the honored guests. Their representation in the form of plates set on the table would express the way women had been confined, and the piece would thus reflect both women's achievements and their oppression. . . . My goal with *The Dinner Party* was . . . to forge a new kind of art expressing women's experience . . . [It] seemed appropriate to relate our history through art, particularly through techniques traditionally associated with women—china-painting and needlework.*

*Judy Chicago, "The Dinner Party": *A Symbol of Our Heritage* (Garden City, N.Y.: Anchor Press, 1979), 11–12.

10 ft.

25-33 JUDY CHICAGO, *The Dinner Party*, 1979. Multimedia, including ceramics and stitchery, 48′ long on each side. The Brooklyn Museum, Brooklyn.

Chicago's *Dinner Party* honors 39 women from antiquity to 20th-century America. The triangular form and the materials—painted china and fabric—are traditionally associated with women.

erture, the leading art photography magazine of the time, White had a profound influence on the development of the medium in the postwar period.

Feminist Art

With the renewed interest in representation the Pop artists and Superrealists introduced in the 1960s and 1970s, artists once again began to embrace the persuasive powers of art to communicate with a wide audience. In the 1970s, many artists began to investigate the social dynamics of power and privilege, especially in relation to gender, although racial, ethnic, and sexual orientation issues have also figured prominently in the art of recent decades (see Chapter 26). Women artists played a significant role in the feminist movement, which sought equal rights for women in contemporary society and focused attention on the subservient place of women in societies throughout history. Spearheading the feminist art movement of the 1970s were Judy Chicago (FIG. 25-33) and Miriam Schapiro (FIG. 25-34). Chicago and a group of students at California State University,

Fresno, founded the Feminist Art Program, and Chicago and Schapiro coordinated it at the California Institute of the Arts in Valencia. In 1972, as part of this program, teachers and students joined to create projects such as Womanhouse, an abandoned house in Los Angeles they completely converted into a suite of "environments," each based on a different aspect of women's lives and fantasies.

JUDY CHICAGO A major goal of Chicago native Judy Cohen, who took the name JUDY CHICAGO (b. 1939), was to educate the public about women's role in history and the fine arts and to establish a respect for women and their art. Chicago sought to forge a new kind of art expressing women's experiences and to find a way to make that art accessible to a large audience. Inspired early in her career by the work of Barbara Hepworth (FIG. 24-62), Georgia O'Keeffe (FIGS. I-5 and 24-42), and Louise Nevelson (FIG. 25-19), Chicago developed a personal painting style that consciously included abstract organic vaginal images. In the early 1970s, Chicago began planning an ambitious piece, *The Dinner Party* (FIG. **25-33**), using craft techniques (such as china painting and needlework)

1 ft.

25-34 MIRIAM SCHAPIRO, *Anatomy of a Kimono* (detail of a 10-panel composition), 1976. Fabric and acrylic on canvas, entire work 6′ 8″ × 52′ 2½″. Collection of Bruno Bischofberger, Zurich.

Schapiro calls her huge sewn collages *femmages* to make the point that women had been doing collages of fabric long before Picasso (FIG. 24-16). This femmage incorporates patterns from Japanese kimonos.

traditionally practiced by women, to celebrate the achievements and contributions women had made throughout history (see "Judy Chicago on *The Dinner Party*," page 809). She originally conceived the work as a feminist *Last Supper* for 13 "honored guests," as in the biblical account of Christ's passion, but at Chicago's table the guests are women instead of men. The number of women in a witches' coven is also 13, and the artist intended her feminist *Dinner Party* additionally to refer to witchcraft and the worship of the Mother Goddess. But because Chicago had uncovered so many worthy women in the course of her research, she tripled the number of guests and placed table settings for 39 women around a triangular table 48 feet long on each side. The triangular form refers to the ancient symbol for both woman and the Goddess. The notion of a dinner party also alludes to women's traditional role as homemakers.

The Dinner Party rests on a triangular white tile floor inscribed with the names of 999 additional women of achievement to signify that the accomplishments of the 39 honored guests rest on a foundation other women laid. Among those with place settings at the table are American painter Georgia O'Keeffe, Egyptian pharaoh Hatshepsut (see "Hatshepsut," Chapter 3, page 69), British writer Virginia Woolf, Native American guide Sacagawea, and American suffragist Susan B. Anthony. Each woman's place has identical eating utensils and a goblet but features a unique oversized porcelain plate and a long place mat or table runner covered with imagery reflecting significant facts about that woman's life and culture. The plates range from simple concave shapes with china-painted imagery to dishes whose sculptured three-dimensional designs almost seem to struggle to free themselves. The designs on each plate incorporate both butterfly and vulval motifs—the butterfly as the ancient symbol of liberation and the vulva as the symbol of female sexuality. Each table runner combines traditional needlework techniques, including needlepoint, embroidery, crochet, beading, patchwork, and appliqué. *The Dinner Party* is more than the sum of its parts, however. Of monumental size, as so many great works of public art have been throughout the ages, Chicago's 1979 masterwork provides viewers with a powerful launching point for considering broad feminist concerns.

MIRIAM SCHAPIRO After enjoying a thriving career as a hard-edge painter in California in the late 1960s, Toronto-born MIRIAM SCHAPIRO (b. 1923) became fascinated with the hidden metaphors for womanhood she then saw in her abstract paintings. Intrigued by the materials she had used to create a doll's house for her part in Womanhouse, in the 1970s Schapiro began to make huge sewn collages, assembled from fabrics, quilts, buttons, sequins, lace trim, and rickrack collected at antique shows and fairs. She called these works *femmages* to make the point that women had been doing collages using these materials long before Pablo Picasso (FIG. 24-16) introduced them to the art world. *Anatomy of a Kimono* (FIG. **25-34**) is one of a series of monumental femmages based on the patterns of Japanese kimonos, fans, and robes. This vast 10-panel composition (more than 52 feet long and almost 7 feet high) repeats the kimono shape in a sumptuous array of fabric fragments.

CINDY SHERMAN After studying painting in Buffalo, CINDY SHERMAN (b. 1954) switched to photography as her primary means of expression. She addresses in her work the way much of Western art presents female beauty for the enjoyment of the "male gaze," a primary focus of contemporary feminist theory, which explores gender as a socially constructed concept. Since 1977, Sherman has produced a series of more than 80 black-and-white photographs called *Untitled Film Stills*. She got the idea for the series after examining soft-core pornography magazines and noting the stereotypical ways they depicted women. She decided to produce her own series of photographs, designing, acting in, directing, and photographing the works. In so doing, she took control of her own image and constructed her own identity, a primary feminist concern.

In works from the series, such as *Untitled Film Still #35* (FIG. **25-35**), Sherman appears, often in costume and wig, in a photograph that seems to be a film still. Most of the images in this series recall popular film genres but are sufficiently generic that the viewer cannot relate them to specific movies. Sherman often reveals the constructed nature of these images with the shutter release cable she holds in her hand to take the pictures. (The cord runs across

25-35 CINDY SHERMAN, *Untitled Film Still #35*, 1979. Gelatin silverprint, 10″ × 8″. Private collection. ▣◀

Sherman here assumed a role for one of 80 photographs resembling film stills in which she addressed the way women have been presented in Western art for the enjoyment of the "male gaze."

25-36 ANA MENDIETA, *Flowers on Body,* 1973. Color photograph of earth/body work with flowers, executed at El Yagul, Mexico. Courtesy of the Estate of Ana Mendieta and Galerie Lelong, New York.

In this earth/body sculpture, Mendieta appears covered with flowers in a grave- or womblike cavity to address issues of birth and death, as well as the human connection to the earth.

the floor in *#35*.) Although the artist is still the object of the viewer's gaze in these images, the identity is one she alone chose to assume.

ANA MENDIETA Cuban-born artist ANA MENDIETA (1948–1985) also used her body as a component in her artworks. Although gender issues concerned her, Mendieta's art also dealt with issues of spirituality and cultural heritage. The artist's best-known series, *Silueta* (Silhouettes), consists of approximately 200 earth/body works completed between 1973 and 1980. These works represented Mendieta's attempt to carry on, as she described, "a dialogue between the landscape and the female body (based on my own silhouette)."[22]

Flowers on Body (FIG. 25-36) is a documentary photograph of the first of the earth/body sculptures in the *Silueta* series. In this work, Mendieta appears covered with flowers in an earthen, grave- or womblike cavity. Executed at El Yagul, a Mexican archaeological site, the work speaks to the issues of birth and death, the female experience of childbirth, and the human connection to the earth. Objects and locations from nature play an important role in Mendieta's art. She explained the centrality of this connection to nature:

I believe this has been a direct result of my having been torn from my homeland during my adolescence. I am overwhelmed by the feeling of having been cast from the womb (nature). My art is the way I re-establish the bonds that unite me to the universe. It is a return to the maternal source. Through my earth/body sculptures I become one with the earth.[23]

Beyond their sensual, moving presence, Mendieta's works also generate a palpable spiritual force. In longing for her homeland, she sought the cultural understanding and acceptance of the spiritual powers inherent in nature that modern Western societies often seem to reject in favor of scientific and technological developments. Mendieta's art is lyrical and passionate and operates at the intersection of cultural, spiritual, physical, and feminist concerns.

HANNAH WILKE Another artist who used her nude body as her medium was New Yorker HANNAH WILKE (1940–1993), who studied art at Temple University. Enlarging images from her mixed media

25-37 HANNAH WILKE, *S.O.S. Starification Object Series,* 1974–1982. 10 black and white photographs and 16 chewing gum sculptures mounted on ragboard, , 3′ 5″ × 4′ 10″ framed. © Marsie, Emanuelle, Damon, and Andrew Scharlatt/Licensed by VAGA, New York, NY. Courtesy Ronald Feldman Fine Arts, New York.

In this photographic series, Wilke posed topless decorated with chewing-gum sculptures of vulvas, which allude to female pleasure, but also to pain, because they resemble scars.

installation of 35 photographs, *S.O.S. Starification Object Series, An Adult Game of Mastication* (FIG. **25-37**), 1974–1975, Wilke, in *S.O.S. Starification Object Series,* 1974–1982, presented images of herself that trigger readings simultaneously metaphorical and real, stereotypical and unique, erotic and disconcerting, and that deal with both pleasure and pain. In these 10 black-and-white photographs, Wilke appears topless. In each, pieces of chewed gum shaped into small vulvas decorate her body. While these tiny vaginal sculptures allude to female pleasure, they also appear as scars, suggesting pain. Ultimately, Wilke hoped women would "take control of and have pride in the sensuality of their own bodies and create a sexuality in their own terms, without deferring to concepts degenerated by culture."[24]

MAGDALENA ABAKANOWICZ Not strictly feminist in subject, but created using materials traditionally associated with women, are the sculptures of Polish fiber artist MAGDALENA ABAKANOWICZ (b. 1930). A leader in the exploration of the expressive powers of weaving techniques in large-scale artworks, Abakanowicz gained fame with experimental freestanding figural works expressing the stoic, everyday toughness of the human spirit. For Abakanowicz, fiber materials are deeply symbolic:

I see fiber as the basic element constructing the organic world on our planet, as the greatest mystery of our environment. It is from fiber that all living organisms are built—the tissues of plants and ourselves. . . . Fabric is our covering and our attire. Made with our hands, it is a record of our souls.[25]

Abakanowicz's sculptures are to a great degree reflections of her early life experiences as a member of an aristocratic family disturbed by the dislocations of World War II and its aftermath. Initially attracted to weaving as a medium easily adaptable to the small studio space she had available, Abakanowicz gradually developed huge abstract hangings she called Abakans that suggest organic spaces as well as giant pieces of clothing. She returned to a smaller scale with works based on human forms—*Heads, Seated Figures,* and *Backs*—multiplying each type for exhibition in groups as symbols for the individual in society lost in the crowd yet retaining some distinctiveness.

This impression is especially powerful in *80 Backs* (FIG. **25-38**). Abakanowicz made each piece by pressing layers of natural organic fibers into a plaster mold. Every sculpture depicts the slumping shoulders, back, and arms of a figure of indeterminate sex and

ARCHITECTURE AND SITE-SPECIFIC ART

Some of the most innovative architects of the first half of the 20th century, most notably Frank Lloyd Wright (FIGS. 24-45, 24-46, and 24-79), Ludwig Mies van der Rohe (FIG. 24-67), and Le Corbusier (FIG. 24-68), concluded their long and productive careers in the postwar period. At the same time, younger architects rose to international prominence, some working in the modernist idiom but others taking architectural design in new "postmodern" directions.

Modernism

In parallel with the progressive movement toward formal abstraction in painting and sculpture in the decades following World War II, modernist architects became increasingly concerned with a formalism stressing simplicity. They articulated this in buildings that retained intriguing organic sculptural qualities, as well as in buildings adhering to a more rigid geometry.

FRANK LLOYD WRIGHT The last great building Frank Lloyd Wright designed was the Solomon R. Guggenheim Museum (FIG. 25-39) in New York City. Using reinforced concrete almost as a sculptor might use resilient clay, Wright, who often described his architecture as "organic," designed a structure inspired by the spiral of a snail's shell. Wright had introduced curves and circles into some of his plans in the 1930s, and as the architectural historian Peter Blake noted, "The spiral was the next logical step; it is the circle brought into the third and fourth dimensions."[26] Inside the building (FIG. 26-44), the shape of the shell expands toward the top, and a winding interior ramp spirals to connect the gallery bays. A skylight strip embedded in the museum's outer wall provides illumination to the ramp, which visitors can stroll up (or down, if they first take an elevator to the top of the building), viewing the artworks displayed along the gently sloping pathway. Thick walls and the solid organic shape give the building, outside and inside, the sense of turning in on itself, and the long interior viewing area opening onto a 90-foot central well of space creates a sheltered environment, secure from the bustling city outside.

25-38 MAGDALENA ABAKANOWICZ, *80 Backs,* 1976–1980. Burlap and resin, each figure 2′ 3″ high. Museum of Modern Art, Dallas.

Polish fiber artist Abakanowicz explored the stoic, everyday toughness of the human spirit in this group of nearly identical sculptures that serve as symbols of distinctive individuals lost in the crowd.

1 ft.

rests legless directly on the floor. The repeated pose of the figures in *80 Backs* suggests meditation, submission, and anticipation. Although made from a single mold, the figures achieve a touching sense of individuality because each assumed a slightly different posture as the material dried and because the artist imprinted a different pattern of fiber texture on each.

25-39 FRANK LLOYD WRIGHT, Solomon R. Guggenheim Museum (looking southeast), New York, 1943–1959. ◼◀

Using reinforced concrete almost as a sculptor might use resilient clay, Wright designed a snail shell–shaped museum with a winding, gently inclined interior ramp for the display of artworks.

LE CORBUSIER Compared with his pristine geometric design for Villa Savoye (FIG. 24-68), the organic forms of Le Corbusier's Notre-Dame-du-Haut (FIG. **25-40**) come as a startling surprise. Completed in 1955 at Ronchamp, France, the chapel attests to the boundless creativity of this great architect. A fusion of architecture and sculpture, the small chapel, which replaced a building destroyed in World War II, occupies a pilgrimage site in the Vosges Mountains. The monumental impression of Notre-Dame-du-Haut seen from afar is somewhat deceptive. Although one massive exterior wall (FIG. 25-40, *top*) contains a pulpit facing a spacious outdoor area for large-scale open-air services on holy days, the interior (FIG. 25-40, *bottom*) holds at most 200 people. The intimate scale, stark and heavy walls, and mysterious illumination (jewel tones cast from the deeply recessed stained-glass windows) give this space an aura reminiscent of a sacred cave or a medieval monastery.

Notre-Dame-du-Haut's structure may look free-form to the untrained eye, but Le Corbusier based it, as did the designers of Romanesque and Gothic cathedrals, on an underlying mathematical system. The pilgrimage church has a frame of steel and metal mesh, which the builders sprayed with concrete and painted white, except for two interior private chapel niches with colored walls and the roof, which Le Corbusier wished to have darken naturally with the passage of time. The roof appears to float freely above the worshipers in their pews (FIG. 25-40, *bottom*), intensifying the quality of mystery in the interior space. In reality, a series of nearly invisible blocks holds up the roof. The mystery of the roof's means of support recalls the reaction to Hagia Sophia's miraculously floating dome (FIG. 9-8) a millennium and a half before in Byzantium. Le Corbusier's preliminary sketches for the building indicate he linked the design with the shape of praying hands, with the wings of a dove (representing both peace and the Holy Spirit), and with the prow of a ship (a reminder the term for the central aisle in a traditional basilican church is *nave*—Latin for "ship"). Le Corbusier hoped that in the mystical interior he created and in the rolling hills around the church, men and women would reflect on the sacred and the natural. No one who has visited Notre-Dame-du-Haut, whether on a bright sunlit day or in a thundering storm, has come away unmoved.

EERO SAARINEN Dramatic, sweeping, curvilinear rooflines are also characteristic features of the buildings designed by Finnish-born architect EERO SAARINEN (1910–1961). One of his signature buildings of the late 1950s is the former Trans World Airlines terminal (now the Jet Blue Airways terminal, FIG. **25-41**) at John F.

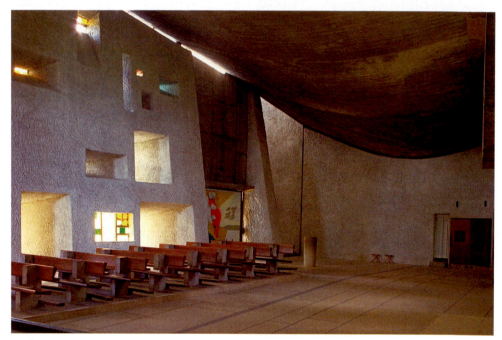

25-40 LE CORBUSIER, Notre-Dame-du-Haut, Ronchamp, France, 1950–1955. *Top:* exterior looking northwest; *bottom:* interior looking southwest. ◼◀

The organic forms of Le Corbusier's mountaintop chapel at Ronchamp present a fusion of architecture and sculpture. The heavy sprayed concrete walls enclose an intimate and mysteriously lit interior that has the aura of a sacred cave.

Kennedy International Airport in New York. The terminal, which Saarinen based on the theme of motion, consists of two immense concrete shells split down the middle and slightly rotated, giving the building a fluid curved outline that fits its corner site. The shells immediately suggest expansive wings and flight. Saarinen also designed everything on the interior, including the furniture, ventilation ducts, and signboards, with this same curvilinear vocabulary in mind.

JOERN UTZON Saarinen was responsible for selecting the Danish architect JOERN UTZON (1918–2008) to build the Sydney Opera House (FIG. **25-42**) in Australia. Utzon's design is a bold

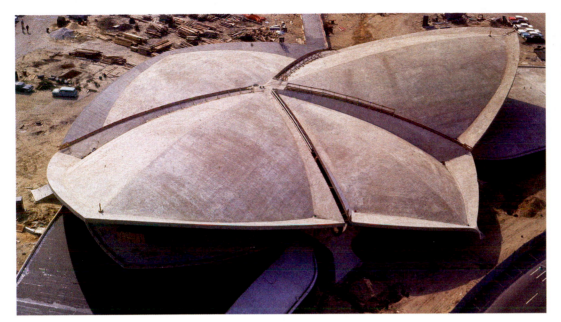

25-41 EERO SAARINEN, Terminal 5 (Jet Blue Airways terminal, formerly the Trans World Airlines terminal; looking southeast), John F. Kennedy International Airport, New York, 1956–1962.

Saarinen based the design for this airline terminal on the theme of motion. The concrete-and-glass building's dramatic, sweeping, curvilinear rooflines suggest expansive wings and flight.

composition of organic forms on a colossal scale. Utzon worked briefly with Frank Lloyd Wright at Taliesin (Wright's Wisconsin residence), and the style of the Sydney Opera House resonates distantly with the graceful curvature of New York's Guggenheim Museum (FIG. 25-39). Clusters of immense concrete shells—the largest is 200 feet tall—rise from massive platforms and soar to delicate peaks. Recalling at first the *ogival* (pointed) shapes of Gothic vaults, the shells also suggest both the buoyancy of seabird wings and the billowing sails of the tall ships of the European settlers who emigrated to Australia in the 18th and 19th centuries. These architectural metaphors are appropriate to the harbor surrounding Bennelong Point, whose bedrock foundations support the building. Utzon's matching of the structure with its site and atmosphere adds to the organic nature of the design.

Though construction of the building began in 1959, completion of the opera house had to wait until 1972, primarily because Utzon's daring design required construction technology not yet developed. Today, the opera house is Sydney's defining symbol, a monument of civic pride that functions as the city's cultural center. In addition to the opera auditorium, the complex houses auxiliary halls and rooms for concerts, the performing arts, motion pictures, lectures, art exhibitions, and conventions.

MIES VAN DER ROHE Sculpturesque building design was not the only manifestation of postwar modernist architecture. From the mid-1950s through the 1970s, other architects created massive, sleek, and geometrically rigid buildings. They designed most of these structures following Bauhaus architect Mies van der Rohe's contention

25-42 JOERN UTZON, Sydney Opera House (looking southeast), Sydney, Australia, 1959–1972.

The soaring clusters of concrete shells of Utzon's opera house on an immense platform in Sydney's harbor suggest both the buoyancy of seabird wings and the billowing sails of tall ships.

that "less is more." Many of these more Minimalist designs are powerful, heroic presences in the urban landscape that effectively symbolize the giant corporations often inhabiting them.

The purest example of these corporate skyscrapers is the mid-1950s rectilinear glass-and-bronze Seagram Building (FIG. **25-43**) in Manhattan designed by Mies van der Rohe and American architect Philip Johnson (FIG. 25-46). By this time, the concrete-steel-and-glass towers pioneered by Louis Sullivan (FIGS. 23-40, 23-40A, and 23-41) and carried further by Mies van der Rohe himself (FIG. 24-67) had become a familiar sight in cities throughout the world. Appealing in its structural logic and clarity, the style, easily imitated, quickly became the norm for postwar commercial high-rise buildings. The architects of the Seagram Building deliberately designed it as a thin shaft, leaving the front quarter of its midtown site as an open pedestrian plaza. The tower appears to rise from the pavement on stilts. Glass walls even surround the recessed lobby. The building's recessed structural elements make it appear to have a glass skin, interrupted only by the thin strips of bronze anchoring the windows. The bronze metal and the amber glass windows give the tower a richness found

in few of its neighbors. Mies van der Rohe and Johnson carefully planned every detail of the Seagram Building, inside and out, to create an elegant whole. They even designed the interior and exterior lighting to make the edifice an impressive sight both day and night.

SKIDMORE, OWINGS & MERRILL The architectural firm SKIDMORE, OWINGS & MERRILL (SOM), perhaps the purest proponent of Miesian-inspired structures, designed a number of these simple rectilinear glass-sheathed buildings, and SOM's success indicates the popularity of this building type. By 1970, the company comprised more than a thousand architects and had offices in New York, Chicago, San Francisco, Portland, and Washington, D.C. In 1974, the firm completed the Sears Tower (FIG. **25-44**), a mammoth corporate building in Chicago. Consisting of nine clustered shafts soaring vertically, this 110-floor building provides offices for more than 12,000 workers. Original plans called for 104 stories, but the architects acquiesced to Sears's insistence on making the building the tallest (measured to the structural top) in the world at the time. The tower's size, coupled with the black

25-43 LUDWIG MIES VAN DER ROHE and PHILIP JOHNSON, Seagram Building (looking northeast), New York, 1956–1958. ◼◀

Massive, sleek, and geometrically rigid, this modernist skyscraper has a bronze and glass skin masking its concrete-and-steel frame. The giant corporate tower appears to rise from the pavement on stilts.

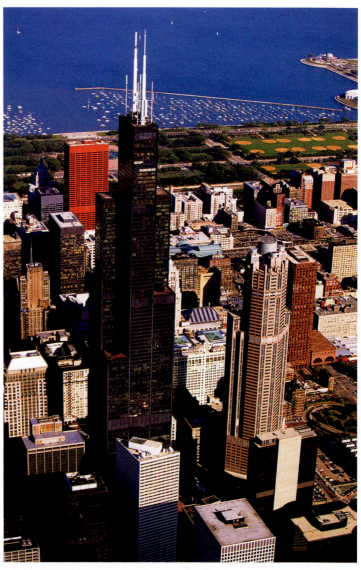

25-44 SKIDMORE, OWINGS & MERRILL, Willis Tower (formerly Sears Tower; looking east), Chicago, 1974. ◼◀

Consisting of nine black aluminum and smoked glass shafts soaring to 110 stories, the Willis (Sears) Tower dominates Chicago's skyline. It was the world's tallest building at the time of its construction.

aluminum sheathing it and the smoked glass, establish a dominant presence in a city of many corporate skyscrapers—exactly the image Sears executives wanted to project.

Postmodernism

The restrictiveness of modernist architecture and the impersonality and sterility of many modernist structures eventually led to a rejection of modernism's authority in architecture. Along with the apparent lack of responsiveness to the unique character of the cities and neighborhoods in which modernist architects built their structures, these reactions ushered in *postmodernism,* one of the most dramatic developments in later-20th-century architecture as well as in contemporary painting and sculpture (see Chapter 26). Postmodernism in architecture is not a unified style. It is a widespread cultural phenomenon far more encompassing and accepting than the more rigid confines of modernist practice. In contrast to the simplicity of modernist architecture, the terms most often invoked to describe postmodern architecture are pluralism, complexity, and eclecticism. Whereas the modernist program was reductive, the postmodern vocabulary of the 1970s and 1980s was expansive and inclusive.

Among the first to explore this new direction in architecture were Jane Jacobs (1916–2006) and Robert Venturi (FIG. 25-48). In their influential books *The Death and Life of Great American Cities* (Jacobs, 1961) and *Complexity and Contradiction in Architecture* (Venturi, 1966), Jacobs and Venturi argued that the uniformity and anonymity of modernist architecture (in particular, the corporate skyscrapers dominating many urban skylines) were unsuited to human social interaction and that diversity is the great advantage of urban life. Postmodern architects accepted, indeed embraced, the messy and chaotic nature of big-city life.

When designing these varied buildings, many postmodern architects consciously selected past architectural elements or references and juxtaposed them with contemporary elements or fashioned them of high-tech materials, thereby creating a dialogue between past and present. Postmodern architecture incorporates not only traditional architectural references but references to mass cul-

ture and popular imagery as well. This was precisely the "complexity and contradiction" Venturi referred to in the title of his book.

CHARLES MOORE A clear example of the eclecticism and the dialogue between traditional and contemporary elements found in postmodern architecture is the Piazza d'Italia (FIG. **25-45**) by American architect CHARLES MOORE (1925–1993), who was educated at the University of Michigan and Princeton University and served as dean of the Yale School of Architecture from 1965 to 1970. Designed in the late 1970s in New Orleans, the Piazza d'Italia is an open plaza dedicated to the city's Italian-American community. Appropriately, Moore selected elements relating specifically to Italian history, all the way back to ancient Roman culture.

Backed up against a contemporary high-rise building and set off from urban traffic patterns, the Piazza d'Italia is accessible to pedestrians from three sides through gateways of varied design. The approaches lead to an open circular area partially formed by short segments of colonnades arranged in staggered concentric arcs, which direct the eye to the focal point of the composition—an *exedra.* This recessed area on a raised platform serves as a *rostrum* (speaker's platform) during the annual festivities of Saint Joseph's Day. Moore inlaid the piazza's pavement with a map of Italy centered on Sicily, from which the majority of the city's Italian families originated. From there, the map's Italian "boot" moves in the direction of the steps that ascend the rostrum and correspond to the Alps.

The piazza's most immediate historical reference is to the Roman forum (FIGS. 7-12 and 7-44). However, its circular form alludes to the ideal geometric figure of the Renaissance (FIGS. 17-3A and 17-21). The irregular placement of the concentrically arranged colonnade fragments inserts a note of instability into the design reminiscent of Mannerism (FIG. 17-55). Illusionistic devices, such as the continuation of the piazza's pavement design (apparently through a building and out into the street), are Baroque in character (FIG. 19-4). Moore incorporated all of the classical orders—most with whimsical modifications. Nevertheless, challenging the piazza's historical character are modern features, such as the stainless-steel columns and capitals, neon collars around the column necks, and neon lights framing various parts of the exedra.

25-45 CHARLES MOORE, *Piazza d'Italia* (looking northeast), New Orleans, 1976–1980.

Moore's circular postmodern Italian plaza incorporates elements drawn from ancient Roman architecture with the instability of Mannerist designs and modern stainless-steel columns with neon collars.

Philip Johnson on Postmodern Architecture

Philip Johnson, who died in 2005 at age 98, had a distinguished career spanning almost the entire 20th century, during which he transformed himself from a modernist closely associated with Mies van der Rohe (FIG. 25-43) into one of the leading postmodernists, whose AT&T (now Sony) Building (FIG. 25-46) in New York City remains an early icon of postmodernism. In the following passages, Johnson commented on his early "Miesian" style and about the incorporation of various historical styles in postmodernist buildings.

> My eyes are set by the Miesian tradition . . . The continuity with my Miesian approach also shows through in my classicism. . . . [But in] 1952, about the same time that my whole generation did, I became very restless. . . . In the last decade there has been such a violent switch that it is almost embarrassing. But it isn't a switch, so much as a centrifugal splintering of architecture, to a degree that I don't think has been seen in the past few hundred years. Perfectly responsible architects build, even in one year, buildings that you cannot believe are done by the same person.*
>
> Structural honesty seems to me one of the bugaboos that we should free ourselves from very quickly. The Greeks with their marble columns imitating wood, and covering up the roofs inside! The Gothic designers with their wooden roofs above to protect their delicate vaulting. And Michelangelo, the greatest architect in history, with his Mannerist column! There is only one absolute today and this is change. There are no rules, surely no certainties in any of the arts. There is only the feeling of a wonderful freedom, of endless possibilities to investigate, of endless past years of historically great buildings to enjoy.†

*Quoted in Paul Heyer, *Architects on Architecture: New Directions in America* (New York: Van Nostrand Reinhold, 1993), 285–286.
†Ibid., 279.

25-46 PHILIP JOHNSON and JOHN BURGEE (with SIMMONS ARCHITECTS), Sony Building (formerly AT&T Building; looking southwest), New York, 1978–1984.

In a startling shift of style, modernist Johnson (FIG. 25-43) designed this postmodern skyscraper with more granite than glass and with a variation on a classical pediment as the crowning motif.

In sum, Moore designed the Piazza d'Italia as a complex conglomeration of symbolic, historical, and geographic allusions—some overt and others obscure. Although the piazza's specific purpose was to honor the Italian community of New Orleans, its more general purpose was to revitalize an urban area by becoming a focal point and an architectural setting for the social activities of neighborhood residents. Unfortunately, the piazza suffered extensive damage during Hurricane Katrina in 2005.

PHILIP JOHNSON Even architects instrumental in the proliferation of the modernist idiom embraced postmodernism. Early in his career, PHILIP JOHNSON (1906–2005), for example, had been a leading proponent of modernism and worked with Mies van der Rohe on the design of the Seagram Building (FIG. 25-43). Johnson even served as director of the Department of Architecture at New York's Museum of Modern Art, the bastion of modernism, in 1930–1934 and 1946–1954. Yet he made one of the most startling shifts of style in 20th-century architecture, eventually moving away from the severe geometric formalism exemplified by the Seagram Building to a classical transformation of it in his AT&T (American Telephone and Telegraph) Building (now the Sony Building, FIG. **25-46**) in New York City. Architect JOHN BURGEE (b. 1933) codesigned it with assistance from the firm SIMMONS ARCHITECTS. This structure was influential in turning architectural taste and practice away from modernism and toward postmodernism—from organic "concrete sculpture" and the rigid "glass box" to elaborate shapes, motifs, and silhouettes freely adapted from historical styles (see "Philip Johnson on Postmodern Architecture," above).

The 660-foot-high slab of the former AT&T Building is mostly granite. Johnson reduced the window space to some 30 percent of the structure, in contrast to modernist glass-sheathed skyscrapers. His design of its exterior elevation is classically tripartite, having an arcaded base and arched portal; a tall, shaftlike body segmented by slender *mullions* (vertical elements dividing a window); and a crowning pediment broken by an *orbiculum* (a disklike opening). The arrangement refers to the base, column, and entablature system wave of postmodernism than did his AT&T tower. The Portland Building (FIG. **25-47**) by Indianapolis-born architect MICHAEL GRAVES (b. 1934) reasserts the wall's horizontality against the verticality of the tall, window-filled shaft. Graves favored the square's solidity and stability, making it the main body of his composition (echoed in the windows), which rests upon a wider base and carries a set-back penthouse crown. Narrow vertical windows tying together seven stories open two paired facades. These support capital-like large hoods on one pair of opposite facades and a frieze of stylized Baroque roundels tied by bands on the other pair. A huge painted keystone motif joins five upper levels on one facade pair, and painted surfaces further define the building's base, body, and penthouse levels.

The modernist purist surely would not welcome the ornamental wall, color painting, or symbolic reference. These features, taken together, raised an even greater storm of criticism than greeted the Sydney Opera House or the AT&T Building. Various critics denounced Graves's Portland Building as "an enlarged jukebox," an "oversized Christmas package," a "marzipan monstrosity," a "histrionic masquerade," and a kind of "pop surrealism." Yet others approvingly noted its classical references as constituting a "symbolic temple" and praised the building as a courageous architectural adventure. Whatever history's verdict will be, the Portland Building, like the AT&T tower, is an early marker of postmodernist innovation that borrowed from the lively, if more-or-less garish, language of pop culture. The night-lit dazzle of entertainment sites such as Las Vegas, and the carnival colors, costumes, and fantasy of theme-park props, all lie behind the Portland Building design, which many critics regard as a vindication of architectural populism against the pretension of modernist elitism.

ROBERT VENTURI As coauthor of *Learning from Las Vegas* (1972), Philadelphia native ROBERT VENTURI (b. 1925) codified these ideas about populism and postmodernism. An early example of Venturi's work is the house (FIG. **25-48**) he designed in 1962 for his mother. A fundamental axiom of modernism is that a building's form must arise directly and logically from its function and structure. Against this rule, Venturi asserted form should be separate from function and structure. Thus, the Vanna Venturi house has an

25-47 MICHAEL GRAVES, Portland Building (looking northwest), Portland, 1980.

In this early example of postmodern architecture, Graves reasserted the horizontality and solidity of the wall. He drew attention to the mural surfaces through polychromy and ornamental motifs.

of classical architecture (FIG. 5-13). More specifically, the pediment, indented by the circular space, resembles the crown of a typical 18th-century Chippendale high chest of drawers. It rises among the monotonously flat-topped glass towers of the New York skyline as an ironic rebuke to the rigid uniformity of modernist architecture.

MICHAEL GRAVES Philip Johnson at first endorsed, then disapproved of, a building that rode considerably farther on the

25-48 ROBERT VENTURI, Vanna Venturi House, Chestnut Hill, Pennsylvania, 1962.

Venturi asserted form should be separate from function and structure. In this house, the facade features an oversized roof recalling a classical temple, but split open at the middle and combined with an arch over the door.

25-49 RICHARD ROGERS and RENZO PIANO, Centre Georges Pompidou (the "Beaubourg," looking northeast), Paris, France, 1977. ◼◂

The architects fully exposed the anatomy of this six-level building, as in the century-earlier Crystal Palace (FIG. 22-47), and color-coded the internal parts according to function, as in a factory.

oversized gable roof that recalls classical temple design more than domestic architecture. However, the gable has a missing central section, which reveals the house's "chimney" (a penthouse suite). Moreover, Venturi inserted an arch motif over the doorway's lintel, and the placement of the windows violates the symmetry of both classical and modernist design.

ROGERS AND PIANO During their short-lived partnership, British architect RICHARD ROGERS (b. 1933) and Italian architect RENZO PIANO (b. 1937) used motifs and techniques from ordinary industrial buildings in their design for the Georges Pompidou National Center of Art and Culture in Paris, known popularly as the "Beaubourg" (FIG. **25-49**). The architects fully exposed the anatomy of this six-level building, which is a kind of updated version of the Crystal Palace (FIG. 22-47), and made its "metabolism" visible. They color-coded pipes, ducts, tubes, and corridors according to function (red for the movement of people, green for water, blue for air-conditioning, and yellow for electricity), much as in a sophisticated factory.

Critics who deplore the Beaubourg's vernacular qualities disparagingly refer to the complex as a "cultural supermarket" and point out that its exposed entrails require excessive maintenance to protect them from the elements. Nevertheless, the building has been immensely popular with visitors since it opened. The flexible interior spaces and the colorful structural body provide a festive environment for the crowds flowing through the building and enjoying its art galleries, industrial design center, library, science and music centers, conference rooms, research and archival facilities, movie theaters, rest areas, and restaurant (which looks down and through the building), as well as dramatic panoramas of Paris from its terrace. The sloping plaza in front of the main entrance has become part of the local scene. Peddlers, street performers, Parisians, and tourists fill this square at almost all hours of the day and night. The kind of secular activity that once occurred in the open spaces in front of cathedral portals now takes place next to a center for culture and popular entertainment.

Environmental and Site-Specific Art

One of the most exciting developments in postwar art and architecture has been *Environmental Art,* sometimes called *earthworks.* Environmental Art stands at the intersection of architecture and sculpture. It emerged as a major form of artistic expression in the 1960s and includes a wide range of artworks, most of which are *site-specific* (created for a unique location) and in the open air. Many artists associated with the Environmental Art movement also used natural or organic materials, including the land itself. It is no coincidence this art form developed during a period of increased concern for the environment. The ecology movement of the 1960s and 1970s aimed to publicize and combat escalating pollution, depletion of natural resources, and the dangers of toxic waste. The problems of public aesthetics (for example, litter, urban sprawl, and compromised scenic areas) were also at issue. Widespread concern in the United States about the environment led to the passage of the National Environmental Policy Act in 1969 and the creation of the federal Environmental Protection Agency. Environmental artists used their art to call attention to the landscape and, in so doing, were part of this national dialogue.

As an innovative artistic genre challenging traditional assumptions about art making, Environmental Art clearly has an avant-garde, progressive dimension. But as Pop artists did in their time, Environmental artists insist on moving art out of the rarefied atmosphere of museums and galleries and into the public sphere. Most encourage spectator interaction with their works. Ironically, the remote locations of many earthworks have limited public access.

ROBERT SMITHSON One of the pioneering Environmental artists was New Jersey–born ROBERT SMITHSON (1938–1973), who used industrial construction equipment to manipulate vast quantities of earth and rock on isolated sites. Smithson's best-known project is *Spiral Jetty* (FIG. **25-50**), a mammoth 1,500-foot-long coil of black basalt, limestone rocks, and earth extending out into Great Salt Lake in Utah. As he was driving by the lake one

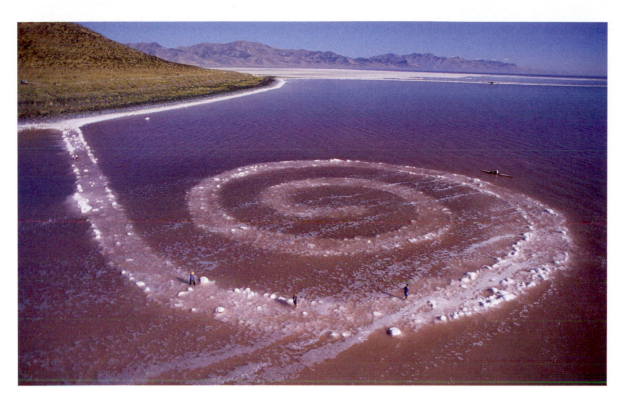

Smithson used industrial
equipment to create
environmental artworks
by manipulating earth
and rock. *Spiral Jetty* is
a mammoth coil of black
basalt, limestone, and
earth extending into Great
Salt Lake.

day, Smithson came across some abandoned mining equipment, left there by a company that had tried and failed to extract oil from the site. Smithson saw this as a testament to the enduring power of nature and the inability of humans to conquer it. He decided to create an artwork in the lake that ultimately became a monumental spiral curving out from the shoreline and running 1,500 linear feet into the water. Smithson insisted on designing his work in response to the location itself. He wanted to avoid the arrogance of an artist merely imposing an unrelated concept on the site. The spiral idea grew from Smithson's first impression of the location. Then, while researching Great Salt Lake, Smithson discovered that the molecular structure of the salt crystals coating the rocks at the water's edge is spiral in form.

> As I looked at the site, it reverberated out to the horizons only to suggest an immobile cyclone while flickering light made the entire landscape appear to quake. A dormant earthquake spread into the fluttering stillness, into a spinning sensation without movement. The site was a rotary that enclosed itself in an immense roundness. From that gyrating space emerged the possibility of the Spiral Jetty.[27]

Smithson not only recorded *Spiral Jetty* in photographs, but also filmed its construction in a movie describing the forms and life of the whole site. The photographs and film have become increasingly important, because fluctuations in Great Salt Lake's water level often place *Spiral Jetty* underwater. Smithson tragically died at age 35 in a plane crash while surveying a site for a new earthwork in Amarillo, Texas.

PERFORMANCE
AND CONCEPTUAL ART
AND NEW MEDIA

Environmental Art, although a singular artistic phenomenon, typifies postwar developments in the art world in redefining the nature of an "artwork" and expanding the range of works artists and the

public at large consider "art." Some of the new types of artworks are the result of the invention of new media, such as computers and video cameras. But the new art forms also reflect avant-garde artists' continued questioning of the status quo.

Performance Art

An important new artistic genre that emerged in the decades following World War II was *Performance Art*. Performance artists replace traditional stationary artworks with movements, gestures, and sounds performed before an audience, whose members sometimes participate in the performance. The informal and spontaneous events Performance artists staged anticipated the rebellion and youthful exuberance of the 1960s and at first pushed art outside the confines of mainstream art institutions (museums and galleries). Performance Art also served as an antidote to the pretentiousness of most traditional art objects and challenged art's function as a commodity. In the later 1960s, however, museums commissioned performances with increasing frequency, thereby neutralizing much of the subversiveness characteristic of this new art form. Unfortunately, because the earliest Performance artists created their works before the widespread availability of inexpensive handheld video cameras, the only records of their performances are the documentary photographs taken during the events. Photographs are unsatisfying, if invaluable, records because they lack the element of time integral to Performance Art.

JOHN CAGE Many of the artists instrumental in the development of Performance Art were students or associates of the charismatic American teacher and composer John Cage (1912–1992). Cage encouraged his students at both the New School for Social Research in New York and Black Mountain College in North Carolina to link their art directly with life. He brought to music composition some of the ideas of Duchamp and of Eastern philosophy. Cage used methods such as chance to avoid the closed structures marking traditional music and, in his view, separating it from the unpredictable and multilayered qualities of daily existence. For

Carolee Schneemann on Painting, Performance Art, and Art History

Born in Pennsylvania, Carolee Schneemann (FIG. 25-51) studied painting at Bard College and the University of Illinois before settling in New York City in 1962, where she became one of the pioneering Performance artists of the 1960s. In notes she wrote in 1962–1963, Schneemann reflected on the nature of art production and contrasted her kinetic works with more traditional art forms.

> Environments, happenings—concretions—are an extension of my painting-constructions which often have moving (motorized) sections. . . . [But, the] steady exploration and repeated viewing which the eye is required to make with my painting-constructions is reversed in the performance situation where the spectator is overwhelmed with changing recognitions, carried emotionally by a flux of evocative actions and led or held by the specified time sequence which marks the duration of a performance. In this way the audience is actually *visually* more *passive* than when confronting a . . . "still" work . . . With paintings, constructions and sculptures the viewers are able to carry out repeated examinations of the work, to select and vary viewing positions (to walk with the eye), to touch surfaces and to freely indulge responses to areas of color and texture at their chosen speed.*

Readers of this book will also take special interest in Schneemann's 1975 essay entitled "Woman in the Year 2000," in which she envisioned what introductory art history courses would be like at the beginning of the 21st century:

> By the year 2000 [every] young woman will study Art Istory [sic] courses enriched by the inclusion, discovery, and re-evaluation of works by women artists: works (and lives) until recently buried away, willfully destroyed, [or] ignored.†

A comparison between this 14th edition of *Art through the Ages* and editions published in the 1960s and 1970s will immediately reveal the accuracy of Schneemann's prediction.

*Quoted in Bruce McPherson, ed., *More Than "Meat Joy": Complete Performance Works and Selected Writings* (New Paltz, N.Y.: Documentext, 1979), 10–11.
†Ibid., 198.

25-51 CAROLEE SCHNEEMANN, *Meat Joy* (performance at Judson Church, New York City), 1964.

In her performances, Schneemann transformed the nature of Performance Art by introducing a feminist dimension through the use of her body (often nude) to challenge traditional gender roles.

---

example, the score for one of Cage's piano compositions instructs the performer to appear, sit down at the piano, raise the keyboard cover to mark the beginning of the piece, remain motionless at the instrument for 4 minutes and 33 seconds, and then close the keyboard cover, rise, and bow to signal the end of the work. The "music" would be the unplanned sounds and noises (such as coughs and whispers) emanating from the audience during the "performance."

ALLAN KAPROW One of Cage's students in the 1950s was ALLAN KAPROW (1927–2006). Schooled in art history as well as music composition, Kaprow sought to explore the intersection of art and life. He believed, for example, that Jackson Pollock's actions when producing a painting (FIG. 25-7) were more important than the finished painting. This led Kaprow to develop a type of event known as a *Happening*. He described a Happening as

> an assemblage of events performed or perceived in more than one time and place. Its material environments may be constructed, taken over directly from what is available, or altered slightly: just as its activities may be invented or commonplace. A Happening, unlike a stage play, may occur at a supermarket, driving along a highway, under a pile of rags, and in a friend's kitchen, either at once or sequentially. If sequentially, time may extend to more than a year. The Happening is performed according to plan but without rehearsal, audience, or repetition. It is art but seems closer to life.[28]

Happenings were often participatory. One Happening consisted of a constructed setting with partitions on which viewers wrote phrases, while another involved spectators walking on a pile of tires. One of Kaprow's first Happenings, titled *18 Happenings in Six Parts*, took place in 1959 in the Reuben Gallery in New York City. For the event, he divided the gallery space into three sections with translucent plastic sheets. Over the course of the 90-minute piece, performers, including Kaprow's artist friends, bounced balls, read from placards, extended their arms like wings, and played records as slides and lights switched on and off in programmed sequences.

FLUXUS Other Cage students interested in the composer's search to find aesthetic potential in the nontraditional and commonplace formed the *Fluxus* group. Eventually expanding to include European and Japanese artists, this group's performances were more theatrical than Happenings. To distinguish their performances from Happenings, the artists associated with Fluxus coined the term *Events* to describe their work. Events focused on single actions, such as turning a light on and off or watching falling snow—what Fluxus artist La Monte Young (b. 1935) called "the theater of the single event."[29] Events usually took place on a stage separating the performers from the audience but without costumes or added decor. Events were not spontaneous. They followed a compositional "score," which, given the restricted nature of these performances, was short.

CAROLEE SCHNEEMANN Some artists, notably Carolee Schneemann (b. 1939) in the United States and members of the Concrete Art Association in Japan, produced artworks integrating painting and performance (see "Carolee Schneemann on Painting, Performance Art, and Art History," page 822). Schneemann's self-described "kinetic theater" radically transformed the nature of Performance Art by introducing a feminist dimension through the use of her body (often nude) to challenge "the psychic territorial power lines by which women were admitted to the Art Stud Club."[30] In her 1964 performance, *Meat Joy* (FIG. **25-51**), Schneemann reveled in the taste, smell, and feel of raw sausages, chickens, and fish.

JOSEPH BEUYS The leftist politics of the Fluxus group in the early 1960s strongly influenced German artist Joseph Beuys (1921–1986). Drawing on Happenings and Fluxus, Beuys created actions aimed at illuminating the condition of modern humanity. He wanted to make a new kind of sculptural object that would include "Thinking Forms: how we mould our thoughts or Spoken Forms: how we shape our thoughts into words or Social Sculpture: how we mould and shape the world in which we live."[31]

Beuys's commitment to artworks stimulating thought about art and life derived in part from his experiences as a pilot during the war. After the enemy shot down his plane over the Crimea, nomadic Tatars nursed him back to health by swaddling his body in fat and felt to warm him. Fat and felt thus symbolized healing and regeneration to Beuys, and he incorporated these materials into many of his sculptures and actions, such as *How to Explain Pictures to a Dead Hare* (FIG. **25-52**). This one-person event consisted of stylized actions evoking a sense of mystery and sacred ritual. Beuys appeared in a room hung with his drawings, cradling a dead hare to which he spoke softly. Beuys coated his head with honey covered with gold leaf, creating a shimmering mask. In this manner, he took on the role of the shaman, an individual with special spiritual powers. As a shaman, Beuys believed he was acting to help revolutionize human thought so each human being could become a truly free and creative person.

25-52 Joseph Beuys, *How to Explain Pictures to a Dead Hare* (performance at Schmela Gallery, Düsseldorf), 1965. ◼◀

In this one-person event, Beuys coated his head with honey and gold leaf. Assuming the role of a shaman, he used stylized actions to evoke a sense of mystery and sacred ritual.

JEAN TINGUELY The paradoxical notion of destruction as an act of creation surfaces in a number of kinetic artworks, most notably in the sculpture of Jean Tinguely (1925–1991). Trained as a painter in his native Switzerland, Tinguely gravitated to motion sculpture. In the 1950s, he made a series of *metamatics*, motor-driven devices that produced instant abstract paintings. He programmed these metamatics electronically to act with an anti-mechanical unpredictability when someone inserted a felt-tipped marking pen into a pincer and pressed a button to initiate the pen's motion across a small sheet of paper clipped to an "easel." Participants in his metamatic demonstrations could use different-colored markers in succession and could stop and start the device to achieve some degree of control over the final image. These operations created a series of small works resembling Abstract Expressionist paintings.

In 1960, Tinguely expanded the scale of his work with a kinetic piece designed to "perform" and then destroy itself in the sculpture garden of the Museum of Modern Art in New York City. He created

Tinguely produced motor-driven devices programmed to make instant abstract paintings. To explore the notion of destruction as an act of creation, he designed this one to perform and then destroy itself.

Homage to New York (FIG. 25-53) with the aid of engineer Billy Klüver (1927–2004), who helped him scrounge wheels and other moving objects from a dump near Manhattan. The completed structure, painted white for visibility against the dark night sky, included a player piano modified into a metamatic painting machine, a weather balloon that inflated during the performance, vials of colored smoke, and a host of gears, pulleys, wheels, and other found machine parts.

Homage to New York premiered (and instantly self-destructed) on March 17, 1960, with the state's governor, Nelson Rockefeller (1908–1979), an array of other distinguished guests, and three television crews in attendance. Once Tinguely turned on the machine, smoke poured from its interior and the piano caught fire. Various parts of the machine broke off and rambled away, while one of the metamatics tried but failed to produce an abstract painting. Finally, Tinguely summoned a firefighter to extinguish the blaze and ensure the demise of his artwork-machine with an ax. Like Tinguely's other kinetic sculptures, *Homage to New York* recalls the satiric Dadaist spirit and the droll import of Klee's *Twittering Machine* (FIG. 24-59). But Tinguely deliberately made the wacky behavior of *Homage to New York* more playful and more endearing. Having been given a freedom of eccentric behavior unprecedented in the mechanical world, Tinguely's creations often seemed to behave with the whimsical individuality of human actors.

Conceptual Art

The relentless challenges to artistic convention fundamental to the historical avant-garde reached a logical conclusion with *Conceptual Art* in the late 1960s. Conceptual artists maintained that the "artfulness" of art lay in the artist's idea, rather than in its final expression. These artists regarded the idea, or concept, as the defining component of the artwork. Indeed, some Conceptual artists eliminated the object altogether.

JOSEPH KOSUTH Born in Toledo, Ohio, and educated at the School of Visual Arts in New York City, JOSEPH KOSUTH (b. 1945) was a major proponent of Conceptual Art.

> Like everyone else I inherited the idea of art as a set of *formal* problems. So when I began to re-think my ideas of art, I had to re-think that thinking process . . . [T]he radical shift, was in changing the idea of art itself. . . . It meant you could have an art work which was that *idea* of an art work, and its formal components weren't important. I felt I had found a way to make art without formal

components being confused for an expressionist composition. The expression was in the idea, not the form—the forms were only a device in the service of the idea.[32]

Kosuth's work operates at the intersection of language and vision, dealing with the relationship between the abstract and the concrete. For example, in *One and Three Chairs* (FIG. 25-54),

1 ft.

25-54 JOSEPH KOSUTH, *One and Three Chairs,* 1965. Wooden folding chair, photographic copy of a chair, and photographic enlargement of a dictionary definition of a chair; chair, 2' 8¾" × 1' 2⅞" × 1' 8⅞"; photograph, 3' × 2' ⅛"; text panel, 2' × 2' ⅛". Museum of Modern Art, New York (Larry Aldrich Foundation Fund).

Conceptual artists regard the concept as an artwork's defining component. To portray "chairness," Kosuth juxtaposed a chair, a photograph of the chair, and a dictionary definition of *chair*.

Kosuth juxtaposed a real chair, a full-scale photograph of the same chair, and an enlarged reproduction of a dictionary definition of the word *chair*. By so doing, the Conceptual artist asked viewers to ponder the notion of what constitutes "chairness."

25-55A NAUMAN, *Self-Portrait as Fountain*, 1966–1967.

BRUCE NAUMAN In the mid-1960s in California, Indiana native BRUCE NAUMAN (b. 1941) made his artistic presence known when he abandoned painting and turned to object-making. Since then, his work, produced since 1979 in New Mexico, has been extremely varied. In addition to sculptural pieces constructed from different materials, including neon lights (FIG. **25-55**), rubber, fiberglass, and cardboard, he has also produced photographs (FIG. **25-55A**), films, videos, books, and large room installations, as well as Performance Art. Nauman's work of the 1960s intersected with that of the Conceptual artists, especially in terms of the philosophical exploration that was the foundation of much of his art, and in his interest in language and wordplay.

The True Artist Helps the World by Revealing Mystic Truths (FIG. 25-55) was the first of Nauman's many neon sculptures. He selected neon because he wanted to find a medium that would be identified with a nonartistic function. Determined to discover a way to connect objects with words, he drew on the method outlined in *Philosophical Investigations*, in which the Austrian philosopher Ludwig Wittgenstein (1889–1951) encouraged contradictory and nonsensical arguments. Nauman's neon sculpture spins out an

emphatic assertion, which is also the work's title, but as Nauman explained, "[The statement] was kind of a test—like when you say something out loud to see if you believe it. . . . [I]t was on the one hand a totally silly idea and yet, on the other hand, I believed it."[33]

Other Conceptual artists pursued the notion that the idea is a work of art itself by creating works involving invisible materials, such as inert gases, radioactive isotopes, or radio waves. In each case, viewers must base their understanding of the artwork on what they know about the properties of these materials, rather than on any visible empirical data, and must depend on the artist's linguistic description of the work. Ultimately, the Conceptual artists challenged the very premises of artistic production, pushing art's boundaries to a point where no concrete definition of *art* is possible.

New Media

During the 1960s and 1970s, many avant-garde artists eagerly embraced technologies previously unavailable in their attempt to find new avenues of artistic expression. Among the most popular new media were video recording and computer graphics.

VIDEO Initially, only commercial television studios possessed video equipment, but in the 1960s, with the development of relatively inexpensive portable video recorders and of electronic devices allowing manipulation of recorded video material, artists began to explore in earnest the expressive possibilities of this new technology. In its basic form, video recording involves a special motion-picture camera that captures visible images and translates them into electronic data for display on a video monitor or television screen. Video pictures resemble photographs in the amount of detail they contain, but, like computer graphics, a video image consists of a series of points of light on a grid, giving the impression of soft focus. Viewers looking at television or video art are not aware of the monitor's surface. Instead, fulfilling the ideal of Renaissance artists, they concentrate on the image and look through the glass surface, as through a window, into the "space" beyond. Video images combine the optical realism of photography with the sense that the subjects move in real time in a deep space "inside" the monitor.

NAM JUNE PAIK When video introduced the possibility of manipulating subjects in real time, artists such as Korean-born NAM JUNE PAIK (1932–2006) were eager to work with the medium. Inspired by the ideas of John Cage and after studying music performance, art history, and Eastern philosophy in Korea and Japan, Paik worked with electronic music in Germany in the late 1950s. In 1965, after relocating to New York City, Paik acquired the first inexpensive video recorder sold in Manhattan (the Sony Porta-Pak) and immediately recorded everything he saw out the window of his taxi on the return trip to his studio downtown. Experience acquired as artist-in-residence at television stations WGBH in Boston and WNET in New York allowed him to experiment with the most advanced broadcast video technology.

A grant permitted Paik to collaborate with the gifted Japanese engineer-inventor Shuya Abe (b. 1932) in developing a video synthesizer. This instrument enables artists to manipulate and change the electronic video information in various ways, causing images or parts of images to stretch, shrink, change color, or break up. With the synthesizer, artists can also layer images, inset one image into another, or merge images from various cameras with those from video recorders to make a single visual kaleidoscopic "time-collage." This kind of compositional freedom permitted Paik to

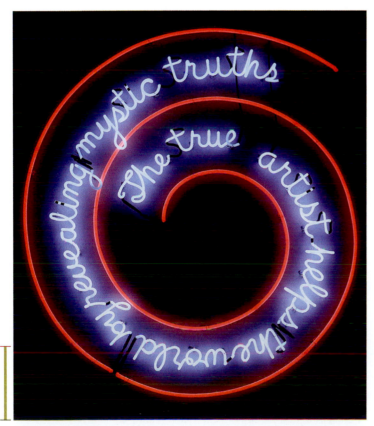

1 ft.

25-55 BRUCE NAUMAN, *The True Artist Helps the World by Revealing Mystic Truths*, 1967. Neon with glass tubing suspension frame, 4′ 11″ high. Private collection.

Nauman explores his interest in language and wordplay in his art. He described this Conceptual neon sculpture's emphatic assertion as "a totally silly idea," but an idea he believed.

25-56 NAM JUNE PAIK, Video still from *Global Groove*, 1973. ¾″ video-tape, color, sound, 30 minutes. Collection of the artist. ■◄

Korean-born video artist Paik's best-known work is a cascade of fragmented sequences of performances and commercials intended as a sample of the rich worldwide television menu of the future.

combine his interests in painting, music, Eastern philosophy, global politics for survival, humanized technology, and cybernetics. Paik called his video works "physical music" and said his musical background enabled him to understand time better than could video artists trained in painting or sculpture.

Paik's best-known video work, *Global Groove* (FIG. **25-56**), combines in quick succession fragmented sequences of female tap dancers, poet Allen Ginsberg (1926–1997) reading his work, a performance by Fluxus artist and cellist Charlotte Moorman (1933–1991) using a man's back as her instrument, Pepsi commercials from Japanese television, Korean drummers, and a shot of the Living Theatre group performing a controversial piece called *Paradise Now*. Commissioned originally for broadcast over the United Nations satellite, the cascade of imagery in *Global Groove* gives viewers a glimpse of the rich worldwide television menu Paik predicted would be available in the future—a prediction that has been fulfilled with the advent of affordable cable and satellite television service.

COMPUTER GRAPHICS Perhaps the most promising new medium for creating and manipulating illusionistic three-dimensional forms is computer graphics. This new medium uses light to make images and, like photography, can incorporate specially recorded camera images. Unlike video recording, computer graphic art enables artists to work with wholly invented forms, as painters can. Developed during the 1960s and 1970s, this technology opened up new possibilities for both abstract and figural art. It involves

electronic programs dividing the surface of the computer monitor's cathode-ray tube into a grid of tiny boxes called "picture elements," or *pixels*. Artists can electronically address pixels individually to create a design, much as knitting or weaving patterns have a grid matrix as a guide for making a design in fabric. Once created, parts of a computer graphic design can be changed quickly through an electronic program, enabling artists to revise or duplicate shapes in the design and to manipulate at will the color, texture, size, number, and position of any desired detail. Computer graphics pictures appear in luminous color on the cathode-ray tube. The effect suggests a view into a vast world existing inside the tube.

DAVID EM One of the pioneering artists working in this electronic painting mode, DAVID EM (b. 1952) uses what he terms *computer imaging* to fashion fantastic imaginary landscapes. These have an eerily believable existence within the "window" of the computer monitor. When he was artist-in-residence at the California Institute of Technology's Jet Propulsion Laboratory, Em created brilliantly colored scenes of alien worlds using the laboratory's advanced computer graphics equipment. He also had access to software programs developed to create computer graphics simulations of NASA's missions in outer space. Creating images with the computer afforded Em great flexibility in manipulating simple geometric shapes—shrinking or enlarging them, stretching or reversing them, repeating them, adding texture to their surfaces, and creating the illusion of light and shadow. In images such as *Nora* (FIG. **25-57**), Em created futuristic geometric versions of Surrealistic dreamscapes whose forms seem familiar and strange at the same time. The illusion of space in these works is immensely vivid and seductive. It almost seems possible to wander through the tubelike foreground "frame" and up the inclined foreground plane or to hop aboard the hovering globe at the lower left for a journey through the strange patterns and textures of this mysterious labyrinthine setting.

AFTER 1980 The decades following the conclusion of World War II were unparalleled in the history of western art through the ages for innovation in form and content and for the development of new media. Those exciting trends have continued unabated since 1980—and with an increasingly international dimension that will be explored in Chapter 26.

25-57 DAVID EM, *Nora*, 1979. Computer-generated color photograph, 1′ 5″ × 1′ 11″. Private collection. ■◄

Unlike video recording, computer graphic art enables the creation of wholly invented forms, as in painting. Em builds fantastic digital images of imaginary landscapes out of tiny boxes called pixels.

1 in.

MODERNISM AND POSTMODERNISM IN EUROPE AND AMERICA, 1945 TO 1980

PAINTING, SCULPTURE, AND PHOTOGRAPHY

Pollock, *Lavender Mist,* 1950

▌ The art of the decades following World War II reflects cultural upheaval—the rejection of traditional values, the civil rights and feminist movements, and the new consumer society.

▌ The first major postwar avant-garde art movement was Abstract Expressionism, which championed an artwork's formal elements rather than its subject. Gestural abstractionists, such as Pollock and de Kooning, sought expressiveness through energetically applied pigment. Chromatic abstractionists, such as Rothko, struck emotional chords through large areas of pure color.

▌ Post-Painterly Abstraction promoted a cool rationality in contrast to Abstract Expressionism's passion. Both hard-edge painters, such as Kelly and Stella, and color-field painters, such as Frankenthaler and Louis, pursued purity in art by emphasizing the flatness of pigment on canvas.

Hanson, *Supermarket Shopper,* 1970

▌ Pop artists, such as Johns, Lichtenstein, and Warhol, turned away from abstraction to the representation of subjects grounded in popular culture—flags, comic strips, Coca-Cola bottles—sometimes employing commercial printing techniques.

▌ Riley and other Op artists sought to produce optical illusions of motion and depth using only geometric forms on two-dimensional surfaces.

▌ Superrealists, such as Flack, Close, and Hanson—kindred spirits to Pop artists in many ways—created paintings and sculptures featuring scrupulous fidelity to optical fact.

▌ The leading sculptural movement of this period was Minimalism. Tony Smith and Judd created artworks consisting of simple and unadorned geometric shapes to underscore the "objecthood" of their sculptures.

Chicago, *Dinner Party,* 1979

▌ Arbus and White represent the two poles of photography in the postwar period—documentary photography and art photography.

▌ Many artists pursued social agendas in their work. Postwar feminist artists include Chicago, whose *Dinner Party* honors important women throughout history and features crafts traditionally associated with women; Sherman, who explored the "male gaze" in her photographs resembling film stills; and Mendieta and Wilke, whose bodies were their subjects.

ARCHITECTURE AND SITE-SPECIFIC ART

Utzon, Sydney Opera House, 1959–1972

▌ Some of the leading early-20th-century modernist architects remained active after 1945. Wright built the snail-shell Guggenheim Museum, Le Corbusier the sculpturesque Notre-Dame-du-Haut, and Mies van der Rohe the Minimalist Seagram skyscraper. Younger architects Saarinen and Utzon designed structures with dramatic curvilinear rooflines.

▌ In contrast to modernist architecture, postmodernist architecture is complex and eclectic and often incorporates references to historical styles. Among the best-known postmodern projects are Moore's Piazza d'Italia and Graves's Portland Building, both of which incorporate classical motifs.

▌ Site-specific art stands at the intersection of architecture and sculpture. Smithson's *Spiral Jetty* is a mammoth coil of natural materials in Utah's Great Salt Lake.

PERFORMANCE AND CONCEPTUAL ART AND NEW MEDIA

Schneemann, *Meat Joy,* 1964

▌ Among the most significant developments in the art world after World War II has been the expansion of the range of works considered "art."

▌ Performance artists, notably Schneemann and Beuys, replace traditional stationary artworks with movements and sounds performed before an audience. Performance Art often addresses the same social and political issues that contemporaneous painters and sculptors explore.

▌ Kosuth and other Conceptual artists believe the "artfulness" of art is in the artist's idea, not the work resulting from the idea.

▌ Paik and others have embraced video recording technology to produce artworks combining images and sounds.

▌ Em was a pioneer in exploring computer graphics as an art form. Unlike video recording, computer art enables artists to work with wholly invented forms, as painters can.

Smith's mixed-media canvases celebrate her Native American identity. Above the painting, as if hung from a clothesline, are cheap trinkets she proposes to trade for the return of confiscated land.

Overlapping the collage and the central motif of the canoe in Smith's anti-Columbus Quincentenary Celebration is dripping red paint, symbolic of the shedding of Native American blood.

The sports teams represented in *Trade* all have American Indian–derived names, reminding viewers of the vocal opposition to these names and to practices such as the Atlanta Braves' "tomahawk chop."

1 ft.

26-1 JAUNE QUICK-TO-SEE SMITH, *Trade* (*Gifts for Trading Land with White People*), 1992. Oil and mixed media on canvas, 5′ × 14′ 2″. Chrysler Museum of Art, Norfolk.

Newspaper clippings chronicle the conquest of Native America by Europeans and include references to the problems facing those living on reservations today—poverty, alcoholism, disease.

CONTEMPORARY ART WORLDWIDE

ART AS SOCIOPOLITICAL MESSAGE

Although televisions, cell phones, and the Internet have brought people all over the world closer together than ever before in history, national, ethnic, religious, and racial conflicts are unfortunate and unavoidable facts of contemporary life. Some of the most eloquent voices raised in protest about the major political and social issues of the day have been those of painters and sculptors, who can harness the power of art to amplify the power of the written and spoken word.

JAUNE QUICK-TO-SEE SMITH (b. 1940) is a Native American artist descended from the Shoshone, Salish, and Cree peoples. Raised on the Flatrock Reservation in Montana, she is steeped in the traditional culture of her ancestors, but she trained as an artist in the European-American tradition at Framingham State College in Massachusetts and at the University of New Mexico. Smith's ethnic heritage has always informed her art, however, and her concern about the invisibility of Native American artists has led her to organize exhibitions of their art. Her self-identity has also been the central theme of her mature work as an artist.

In 1992, Smith created what many critics consider her masterpiece: *Trade* (FIG. 26-1), subtitled *Gifts for Trading Land with White People*. A complex multimedia work of monumental size, *Trade* is Smith's response to what she called "the Quincentenary Non-Celebration," that is, White America's celebration of the 500th anniversary of Christopher Columbus's arrival in what Europeans called the New World. *Trade* combines collage elements and attached objects, reminiscent of a Rauschenberg combine (FIG. 25-23), with energetic brushwork recalling Willem de Kooning's Abstract Expressionist canvases (FIG. 25-8) and clippings from Native American newspapers. The clippings include images chronicling the conquest of Native America by Europeans and references to the problems facing those living on reservations today—poverty, alcoholism, disease. The dripping red paint overlaying the collage with the central motif of the canoe is symbolic of the shedding of Native American blood.

Above the painting, as if hung from a clothesline, is an array of objects. These include Native American artifacts, such as beaded belts and feather headdresses, plastic tomahawks and "Indian princess" dolls, and contemporary sports memorabilia from teams with American Indian–derived names—the Cleveland Indians, Atlanta Braves, and Washington Redskins. The inclusion of these objects reminds viewers of the vocal opposition to the use of these and similar names for high school and college as well as professional sports teams. All the cheap artifacts together also have a deeper significance. As the title indicates and Smith explained:

Why won't you consider trading the land we handed over to you for these silly trinkets that so honor us? Sound like a bad deal? Well, that's the deal you gave us.[1]

SOCIAL AND POLITICAL ART

Jaune Quick-to-See Smith's *Trade* (FIG. 26-1) is the unique product of the artist's heritage as a Native American who has sought to bridge native and European artistic traditions, but her work parallels that of many other innovative artists of the decades since 1980 in addressing contemporary social and political issues. This focus on the content and meaning of art represents, as did the earlier work of the Pop artists and Superrealists (see Chapter 25), a rejection of modernist formalist doctrine and a desire on the part of artists once again to embrace the persuasive powers of art to communicate with a wide audience.

POSTMODERNISM The rejection of the principles underlying modernism is a central element in the diverse phenomenon in art, as in architecture, known as postmodernism (see page 817). No simple definition of *postmodernism* is possible, but it represents the erosion of the boundaries between high culture and popular culture—a separation Clement Greenberg and the modernists had staunchly defended.

For many recent artists, postmodernism involves examining the process by which meaning is generated and the negotiation or dialogue that transpires between viewers and artworks. This kind of examination of the nature of art parallels the literary field of study known as critical theory. Critical theorists view art and architecture, as well as literature and the other humanities, as a culture's intellectual products or "constructs." These constructs unconsciously suppress or conceal the real premises informing the culture, primarily the values of those politically in control. Thus, cultural products function in an ideological capacity, obscuring, for example, racist or sexist attitudes. When revealed by analysis, the facts behind these constructs, according to critical theorists, contribute to a more substantial understanding of artworks, buildings, books, and the overall culture.

Many critical theorists use an analytical strategy called *deconstruction*, after a method developed by French intellectuals in the 1960s and 1970s. In deconstruction theory, all cultural contexts are "texts." Critical theorists who employ this approach seek to uncover—to deconstruct—the facts of power, privilege, and prejudice underlying the practices and institutions of any given culture. In so doing, scholars can reveal the precariousness of structures and systems, such as language and cultural practices, along with the assumptions underlying them.

Critical theorists do not agree upon any single philosophy or analytical method, because in principle they oppose firm definitions.

They do share a healthy suspicion of all traditional truth claims and value standards, all hierarchical authority and institutions. For them, deconstruction means destabilizing established meanings, definitions, and interpretations while encouraging subjectivity and individual differences. Indeed, if there is any common denominator in the art of the decades since 1980, it is precisely the absence of any common denominator. Diversity of style and content and the celebration of individual personalities, backgrounds, and approaches to art are central to the notion of postmodernist art. The art of the 1980s and 1990s and of the opening decades of the 21st century is worldwide in scope, encompasses both abstraction and realism, and addresses a wide range of contemporary social and political issues.

Social Art: Gender and Sexuality

Many artists who have embraced the postmodern interest in investigating the dynamics of power and privilege have focused on issues of gender and sexuality in the contemporary world.

BARBARA KRUGER In the 1970s, some feminist artists, chief among them Cindy Sherman (FIG. 25-35), explored the "male gaze" and the culturally constructed notion of gender in their art. BARBARA KRUGER (b. 1945), who studied at Syracuse University and then at the Parsons School of Design in New York under Diane Arbus (FIG. 25-31), examines similar issues in her photographs. The strategies and techniques of contemporary mass media fascinate Kruger, who was a commercial graphic designer early in her career and the art director of *Mademoiselle* magazine in the late 1960s. In *Untitled* (*Your Gaze Hits the Side of My Face*; FIG. **26-2**), Kruger incorporated the layout techniques magazines and billboards use to sell consumer goods. Although she favored the reassuringly familiar format and look of advertising, Kruger's goal was to subvert the typical use of advertising imagery. She aimed to expose the deceptiveness of the media messages the viewer complacently absorbs. Kruger wanted to undermine the myths—particularly those about women—the media constantly reinforce. Her large (often four by six feet) word-and-photograph collages challenge the cultural attitudes embedded in commercial advertising. She has often used T-shirts, postcards, matchbooks, and billboards to present her work to a wide public audience.

In *Your Gaze*, Kruger overlaid a photograph of a classically beautiful sculpted head of a woman (compare FIG. 5-62A) with a vertical row of text composed of eight words. The words cannot be taken in with a single glance. Reading them is a staccato exercise, with an overlaid cumulative quality that delays understanding and

CONTEMPORARY ART WORLDWIDE

1980	1990	2000
▌ Social and political issues—gender and sexuality; ethnic, religious, and national identity; violence, homelessness, and AIDS—figure prominently in the art of Kruger, Wojnarowicz, Wodiczko, Ringgold, Weems, and many others	▌ Artworks addressing pressing political and social issues continue to be produced in great numbers by, among others, Quick-to-See Smith, Sikander, Bester, Hammons, and Neshat	▌ Modern, postmodern, and traditional art forms coexist today in the increasingly interconnected worldwide art scene as artists on all continents work with age-old materials and also experiment with the new media of digital photography, computer graphics, and video
▌ Stirling, Pei, and other postmodern architects incorporate historical references into designs for museums and other public buildings	▌ Realistic figure painting and sculpture (Kiki Smith, Saville) as well as abstraction (Schnabel, Kiefer, Donovan) remain vital components of the contemporary art scene	
▌ Site-specific artworks by Lin and Serra and exhibitions of the work of Mapplethorpe and Ofili become lightning rods for debate over public financing of art	▌ Deconstructivism (Behnisch, Gehry, Hadid) and green architecture (Piano) emerge as major architectural movements	

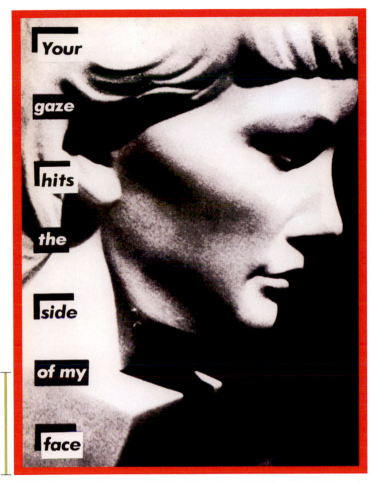

1 ft.

26-2 BARBARA KRUGER, *Untitled* (*Your Gaze Hits the Side of My Face*), 1981. Photograph, red painted frame, 4′ 7″ × 3′ 5″. Courtesy Mary Boone Gallery, New York. ◼

Kruger has explored the "male gaze" in her art. Using the layout techniques of mass media, she constructed this word-and-photograph collage to challenge culturally constructed notions of gender.

intensifies the meaning (rather like reading a series of roadside billboards from a speeding car). Kruger's use of text in her work is significant. Many cultural theorists have asserted language is one of the most powerful vehicles for internalizing stereotypes and conditioned roles. Some feminist artists, most notably the GUER-RILLA GIRLS (FIG. **26-2A**), have created powerful artworks consisting only of words—presented in a style and format reminiscent of the same kinds of magazine ads Kruger incorporates in her photo-collages.

THE ADVANTAGES OF BEING A WOMAN ARTIST:

26-2A GUERRILLA GIRLS, *Advantages of Being a Woman Artist*, 1988.

DAVID WOJNAROWICZ For many artists, their homosexuality is as important—or even more important—an element of their personal identity as their gender, ethnicity, or race. Beginning in the early 1980s, unwelcome reinforcement for their self-identification came from confronting daily the devastating effects of AIDS (acquired immune deficiency syndrome) in the gay community. Some sculptors and painters responded by producing deeply moving works of art. DAVID WOJNAROWICZ (1955–1992) dropped out of high school in his hometown of Red Bank, New Jersey, and moved to New York City, where he lived on the streets before achieving success as an artist. A gay activist, he watched his lover and many of his friends die of AIDS. He reacted by creating disturbing yet eloquent works about the tragedy of this disease, which eventually claimed his own life. In *When I Put My Hands on Your Body* (FIG. **26-3**), he overlaid a photograph of a pile of skeletal remains with evenly spaced typed commentary communicating his feelings about watching a loved one dying of AIDS. Wojnarowicz movingly describes the effects of AIDS on the human body and soul:

> When I put my hands on your body on your flesh I feel the history of that body. . . . I see the flesh unwrap from the layers of fat and disappear. . . . I see the organs gradually fade into transparency. . . . It makes me weep to feel the history of you of your flesh beneath my hands.

26-3 DAVID WOJNAROWICZ, *When I Put My Hands on Your Body*, 1990. Gelatin silver print and silk-screened text on museum board, 2′ 2″ × 3′ 2″. Private collection.

In this disturbing yet eloquent print, Wojnarowicz overlaid typed commentary on a photograph of skeletal remains. He movingly communicated his feelings about watching a loved one die of AIDS.

1 ft.

Public Funding of Controversial Art

Although art can be beautiful and uplifting, throughout history art has also challenged and offended. Since the early 1980s, a number of heated controversies about art have surfaced in the United States. There have been many calls to remove "offensive" works from public view (see "Richard Serra's *Tilted Arc*," page 855) and, in reaction, accusations of censorship. The central questions in all cases have been whether there are limits to what art can appropriately be exhibited, and whether governmental authorities have the right to monitor and pass judgment on creative endeavors. A related question is whether the acceptability of a work should be a criterion in determining the public funding of art.

Two exhibits in 1989 placed the National Endowment for the Arts (NEA), a U.S. government agency charged with distributing federal funds to support the arts, squarely in the middle of this debate. One of the exhibitions, devoted to recipients of the Awards for the Visual Arts (AVA), took place at the Southeastern Center for Contemporary Art in North Carolina. Among the award winners was Andres Serrano, whose *Piss Christ*, a photograph of a crucifix submerged in urine, sparked an uproar. Responding to this artwork, Reverend Donald Wildmon, an evangelical minister from Mississippi and head of the American Family Association, expressed outrage that this kind of work was in an exhibition funded by the NEA and the Equitable Life Assurance Society (a sponsor of the AVA). He demanded the work be removed and launched a letter-writing campaign that caused Equitable Life to cancel its sponsorship of the awards. To Wildmon and other staunch conservatives, this exhibition, along with *Robert Mapplethorpe: The Perfect Moment*, which included erotic and openly homosexual images of the artist (FIG. 26-4) and others, served as evidence of cultural depravity and immorality. These critics insisted that art of an offensive character should not be funded by government agencies such as the NEA. As a result of media furor over *The Perfect Moment*, the director of the Corcoran Museum of Art decided to cancel the scheduled exhibition of this traveling show. But Dennis Barrie, Director of the Contemporary Arts Center in Cincinnati, chose to mount the show. The government indicted Barrie on charges of obscenity, but a jury acquitted him six months later.

These controversies intensified public criticism of the NEA and its funding practices. The next year, the head of the NEA, John Frohnmayer, vetoed grants for four lesbian, gay, or feminist performance artists—Karen Finley, John Fleck, Holly Hughes, and Tim Miller—who became known as the "NEA Four." Infuriated by what they perceived as overt censorship, the artists filed suit, eventually settling the case and winning reinstatement of their grants. Congress responded by dramatically reducing the NEA's budget, and the agency no longer awards grants or fellowships to individual artists.

26-4 ROBERT MAPPLETHORPE, *Self-Portrait,* 1980. Gelatin silver print, 7¾″ × 7¾″. Robert Mapplethorpe Foundation, New York.

Mapplethorpe's *Perfect Moment* show led to a landmark court case on freedom of expression for artists. In this self-portrait, an androgynous Mapplethorpe confronts the viewer with a steady gaze.

1 in.

Controversies have also erupted on the municipal level. In 1999, Rudolph Giuliani, then mayor of New York, joined a number of individuals and groups protesting the inclusion of several artworks in the exhibition *Sensation: Young British Artists from the Saatchi Collection* at the Brooklyn Museum. Chris Ofili's *The Holy Virgin Mary* (FIG. 26-10), a collage of Mary incorporating cutouts from pornographic magazines and shellacked clumps of elephant dung, became the flashpoint for public furor. Denouncing the show as "sick stuff," the mayor threatened to cut off all city subsidies to the museum.

Art that seeks to unsettle and challenge is critical to the cultural, political, and psychological life of a society. The regularity with which this kind of art raises controversy suggests it operates at the intersection of two competing principles: free speech and artistic expression on the one hand and a reluctance to impose images upon an audience that finds them repugnant or offensive on the other. What these controversies do demonstrate, beyond doubt, is the enduring power of art.

Wojnarowicz juxtaposed text with imagery, which, like works by Barbara Kruger (FIG. 26-2) and the Guerrilla Girls (FIG. 26-2A), paralleled the use of both words and images in advertising. The public's familiarity with this format ensured greater receptivity to the artist's message.

ROBERT MAPPLETHORPE One brilliant gay artist who became the central figure in a heated debate in the halls of the U.S. Congress as well as among the public at large was ROBERT MAPPLETHORPE (1946–1989). Born in Queens, New York, Mapplethorpe studied drawing, painting, and sculpture at the Pratt

Institute in Brooklyn, but after he purchased a Polaroid camera in 1970, he became increasingly interested in photography. Mapplethorpe's *The Perfect Moment* traveling exhibition, funded in part by the National Endowment for the Arts, featured his photographs of flowers and people, many nude, some depicting children, some homoerotic and sadomasochistic in nature. The show led to a landmark court case in Cincinnati on freedom of expression for artists and prompted new legislation establishing restrictions on government funding of the arts (see "Public Funding of Controversial Art," page 832).

Never at issue was Mapplethorpe's technical mastery of the photographic medium. His gelatin silver prints have glowing textures with rich tonal gradations of black, gray, and white. In many ways, Mapplethorpe was the heir of Edward Weston, whose innovative compositions of still lifes (FIG. 24-44) and nudes (FIG. 24-44A) helped establish photography as an art form on a par with painting and sculpture. What shocked the public was not nudity per se—a traditional subject with roots in antiquity, indeed at the very birth of art during the Old Stone Age (FIGS. 1-5, 1-6, and 1-6A)—but the

openly gay character of many of Mapplethorpe's images. *The Perfect Moment* photographs included, in addition to some very graphic images of homosexual men, a series of self-portraits documenting Mapplethorpe's changing appearance almost up until he died from AIDS only months after the show opened in Philadelphia in December 1988. The self-portrait reproduced here (FIG. **26-4**) presents Mapplethorpe as an androgynous young man with long hair and makeup, confronting the viewer with a steady gaze. Mapplethorpe's photographs, like the work of David Wojnarowicz (FIG. 26-3) and other gay and lesbian artists of the time, are inextricably bound with the social upheavals in American society and the struggle for equal rights for women, homosexuals, minorities, and the disabled during the second half of the 20th century.

SHAHZIA SIKANDER The struggle for recognition and equal rights has never been confined to the United States, least of all in the present era of instant global communication. In the Muslim world, women and homosexuals face especially difficult challenges, which SHAHZIA SIKANDER (b. 1969) brilliantly addresses in her work. Born in Lahore, Pakistan, and trained at the National College of Arts in the demanding South Asian/Persian art of miniature painting, she earned an MFA from the Rhode Island School of Design and now lives in New York City. So thoroughly immersed in the methods of miniature painting that she makes her own paper, pigments, and squirrel-hair brushes, Sikander nonetheless imbues this traditional art form with contemporary meaning. In *Perilous Order* (FIG. **26-5**), she addresses homosexuality, intolerance, and hypocrisy by portraying a gay friend in the guise of the Mughal emperor Aurangzeb (r. 1658–1707), who was a strict enforcer of Islamic orthodoxy although reputed to be a homosexual. Sikander depicted him framed against a magnificent marbleized background ringed by voluptuous nude Hindu nymphs and behind the shadow of a veiled Hindu goddess. *Perilous Order* thus also incorporates a reference to the tensions between the Muslim and Hindu populations of Pakistan and India today.

Social Art: Race, Ethnicity, and National Identity

Gender and sexual-orientation issues are by no means the only societal concerns contemporary artists have addressed in their work. Race, ethnicity, and national identity are among the other pressing issues that have given rise to important artworks during the past few decades.

FAITH RINGGOLD One of the leading artists addressing issues associated with African American women is Harlem native FAITH RINGGOLD (b. 1930), who studied painting at the City College of New York and taught art education in the New York public schools for 18 years. In the 1960s, Ringgold produced numerous works that provided pointed and incisive commentary on the realities of racial prejudice. She increasingly incorporated references to gender as well and, in the 1970s, turned to fabric as the predominant material in her art. Using fabric enabled Ringgold to make more pointed reference to the domestic sphere, traditionally

1 in.

26-5 SHAHZIA SIKANDER, *Perilous Order*, 1994–1997. Vegetable color, dry pigment, watercolor, and tea on Wasli paper, 10½″ × 8″. Whitney Museum of American Art, New York (purchase, with funds from the Drawing Committee).

Imbuing miniature painting with a contemporary message about hypocrisy and intolerance, Sikander portrayed a gay friend as a homosexual Mughal emperor who enforced Muslim orthodoxy.

26-6 Faith Ringgold, *Who's Afraid of Aunt Jemima?* 1983. Acrylic on canvas with fabric borders, quilted, 7′ 6″ × 6′ 8″. Private collection.

In this quilt, a medium associated with women, Ringgold presented a tribute to her mother that also addresses African American culture and the struggles of women to overcome oppression.

26-6A SIMPSON, *Stereo Styles*, 1988.

26-6B WEEMS, *Man Smoking/ Malcolm X*, 1990.

associated with women, and to collaborate with her mother, Willi Posey, a fashion designer. After her mother's death in 1981, Ringgold created *Who's Afraid of Aunt Jemima?* (FIG. **26-6**), a quilt composed of dyed, painted, and pieced fabric. A moving tribute to her mother, this "story quilt"—Ringgold's signature art form—merges the personal and the political. Combining words with pictures, as did Barbara Kruger (FIG. 26-2) and David Wojnarowicz (FIG. 26-3), Ringgold incorporates a narrative in her quilt. *Aunt Jemima* tells the witty story of the family of the stereotypical black "mammy" in the mind of the public, but here Jemima is a successful African American businesswoman. Ringgold narrates the story using black dialect interspersed with embroidered portraits and traditional patterned squares. *Aunt Jemima,* while resonating with autobiographical references, also speaks to the larger issues of the history of African American culture and the struggles of women to overcome oppression. Other contemporary feminist artists who have addressed similar racial and social issues are LORNA SIMPSON (b. 1960; FIG. **26-6A**) and CARRIE MAE WEEMS (b. 1953; FIG. **26-6B**).

MELVIN EDWARDS In his art, Californian MELVIN EDWARDS (b. 1937) explores a very different aspect of the black experience in America—the history of collective oppression of African Americans. One of Edwards's major sculptural series focused on the metaphor of lynching to provoke thought about the legacy of racism. His *Lynch Fragments* series, produced over more than three decades beginning in 1963, encompassed more than 150 welded-steel sculptures. Lynching as an artistic theme prompts an immediate and visceral response, conjuring chilling and gruesome images from the past. Edwards sought to extend this emotional resonance further in his art. He constructed the series' relatively small sculptures, such as *Tambo* (FIG. **26-7**), from found metal objects—for example, chains, hooks, hammers, spikes, knife blades, and handcuffs. Although Edwards often intertwined or welded together the individual metal components so as to diminish immediate identification of them, the sculptures still retain a haunting connection to the overall theme. These works refer to a historical act that evokes a

26-7 Melvin Edwards, *Tambo,* 1993. Welded steel, 2′ 4⅛″ × 2′ 1¼″. Smithsonian American Art Museum, Washington, D.C.

Edwards's welded sculptures of chains, spikes, knife blades, and other found objects allude to the lynching of African Americans and the continuing struggle for civil rights and an end to racism.

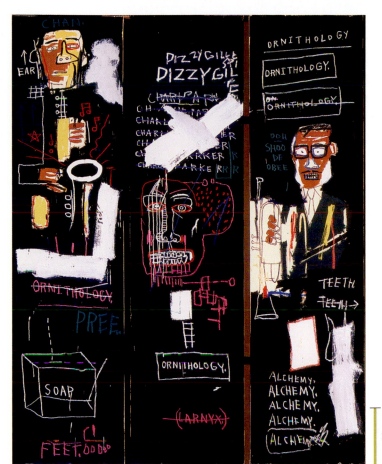

26-8 Jean-Michel Basquiat, *Horn Players,* 1983. Acrylic and oil paintstick on three canvas panels, 8′ × 6′ 3″. Broad Foundation, Santa Monica.

In this tribute to two legendary African American musicians, Basquiat combined bold colors, fractured figures, and graffiti to capture the dynamic rhythms of jazz and the excitement of New York.

collective memory of oppression, but they also speak to the continuing struggle for civil rights and an end to racism. While growing up in Los Angeles, Edwards experienced racial conflict firsthand. Among the metal objects incorporated into his *Lynch Fragments* sculptures are items he found in the streets in the aftermath of the Watts riots in 1965. The inclusion of these found objects imbues his disquieting, haunting works with an even greater intensity.

JEAN-MICHEL BASQUIAT The work of JEAN-MICHEL BASQUIAT (1960–1988) focuses on still another facet of the minority cultural experience in America. Born in Brooklyn in a comfortable home—his father was an accountant from Haiti and his mother a black Puerto Rican—Basquiat rebelled against middle-class values, dropped out of school at 17, and took to the streets. He first burst onto the New York art scene as the anonymous author of witty graffiti in Lower Manhattan signed SAMO (a dual reference to the derogatory name *Sambo* for African Americans and to "same old shit"). Basquiat first drew attention as an artist in 1980 when he participated in a group show—the "Times Square Show"—in an abandoned 42nd Street building. Eight years later, after a meteoric rise to fame, he died of a heroin overdose at age 27.

Basquiat was self-taught, both as an artist and about the history of art, but he was not a "primitive." His sophisticated style owes a debt to diverse sources, including the late paintings of Pablo Picasso, Abstract Expressionism, and the "art brut" of Jean Dubuffet (FIG. 25-4). Many of Basquiat's paintings celebrate black heroes, for example, the legendary jazz musicians Charlie "Bird" Parker and Dizzy Gillespie, whom he memorialized in *Horn Players* (FIG. **26-8**). The fractured figures, the bold colors against a black background, and the deliberately scrawled, crossed-out, and misspelled graffiti ("ornithology"—the study of birds—is a pun on Parker's nickname) create a dynamic composition suggesting the rhythms of jazz music and the excitement of the streets of New York, "the city that never sleeps."

KEHINDE WILEY Many African American artists have lamented the near-total absence of blacks in Western painting and sculpture, except as servants (compare FIG. 26-13), as well as in histories of Western art until quite recently. Los Angeles native KEHINDE WILEY (b. 1977) set out to correct that discriminatory imbalance. Wiley earned his MFA at Yale University and is currently artist-in-residence at the Studio Museum in Harlem, where he has achieved renown for his large-scale portraits of young urban African American men. Wiley's trademark paintings, however, are reworkings of historically important portraits in which he substitutes

26-9 Kehinde Wiley, *Napoleon Leading the Army over the Alps*, 2005. Oil on canvas, 9′ × 9′. Brooklyn Museum, Brooklyn (Collection of Suzi and Andrew B. Cohen).

Wiley's trademark paintings are reworkings of famous portraits (FIG. 22-1A) in which he substitutes young African American men in contemporary dress in order to situate them in "the field of power."

figures of young black men in contemporary dress in order to situate them in what he calls "the field of power." One example is *Napoleon Leading the Army over the Alps* (FIG. 26-9), based on Jacques-Louis David's painting (FIG. 22-1A) of the same subject. To evoke the era of the original, Wiley presented his portrait of an African American Napoleon on horseback in a gilt wood frame. Although in many details an accurate reproduction of David's canvas, Wiley's version is not a slavish copy. His heroic narrative unfolds against a vibrantly colored ornate wallpaper-like background instead of a dramatic sky—a distinctly modernist reminder to the viewer that this is a painting and not a window onto an Alpine landscape.

CHRIS OFILI In the global artistic community of the contemporary world, the exploration of personal social, ethnic, and national identity is a universal theme. Three artists who, like Shahzia Sikander (FIG. 26-5), incorporate their

national artistic heritages in their work are TRIGO PIULA (b. ca. 1950; FIG. 26-9A), CHRIS OFILI (b. 1968; FIG. 26-10), and Cliff Whiting (FIG. 26-11).

One theme Ofili has treated is religion, interpreted through the eyes of a British-born Catholic of Nigerian descent. Ofili's *The Holy Virgin Mary* (FIG. 26-10) depicts Mary in a manner that departs radically from conventional Renaissance representations. Ofili's work presents the Virgin in simplified form, and she appears to float in an indeterminate space. The artist employed brightly colored pigments, applied to the canvas in multiple layers of beadlike dots (inspired by images from ancient caves in Zimbabwe). Surrounding the Virgin are tiny images of genitalia and buttocks cut out from pornographic magazines, which, to the artist, parallel the putti often surrounding Mary in Renaissance paintings. Another reference to Ofili's African heritage surfaces in the clumps of elephant dung—one attached to the Virgin's breast, and two more on which the canvas rests, serving as supports. The dung enabled Ofili to incorporate Africa into his work in a literal way. Still, he wants the viewer to move beyond the cultural associations of the materials and see them in new ways.

26-9A PIULA, *Ta Tele*, 1988.

Not surprisingly, *The Holy Virgin Mary* elicited strong reactions. Its inclusion in the *Sensation* exhibition at the Brooklyn Museum in 1999 with other intentionally "sensational" works by young British artists prompted indignant (but unsuccessful) demands for cancellation of the show and countercharges of censorship (see "Public Funding of Controversial Art," page 832).

CLIFF WHITING In New Zealand today, some artists draw on their Maori heritage for formal and iconographic inspiration. The historic Maori woodcarving craft brilliantly reemerges in what CLIFF WHITING (TE WHANAU-A-APANUI, b. 1936) calls a "carved mural" (FIG. 26-11). Whiting's *Tawhiri-Matea* is a masterpiece in the venerable tradition of Oceanic wood sculpture, but it is a work designed for the very modern environment of an exhibition gallery. The artist suggested the wind turbulence with the restless curvature of the main motif and its myriad serrated edges. The 1984 mural depicts events in the Maori creation myth. The central figure, Tawhiri-Matea, god of the winds, wrestles to control the children of the four winds, seen as blue spiral forms. Ra, the sun, energizes the scene from the top left, complemented by Marama, the moon, in the opposite corner. The top right image refers to the primal separation of Ranginui, the Sky Father, and Papatuanuku, the Earth Mother. Spiral koru motifs symbolizing growth and energy flow through the composition. Blue waves and green fronds around Tawhiri suggest his brothers Tangaroa and Tane, gods of the sea and forest.

Whiting is securely at home with the native tradition of form and technique, as well as with the worldwide aesthetic of modern design. Out of the seamless fabric made by uniting both, he feels something new can develop that loses nothing of the power of the old. The artist champions not only the renewal of Maori cultural life and its continuity in art but also the education of the young in the values that made their culture great—values he asks them to perpetuate.

26-10 CHRIS OFILI, *The Holy Virgin Mary*, 1996. Paper collage, oil paint, glitter, polyester resin, map pins, elephant dung on linen, 7′ 11″ × 5′ 11 5/16″. Victoria Miro Gallery, London.

Ofili, a British-born Catholic of Nigerian descent, represented the Virgin Mary with African elephant dung on one breast and surrounded by genitalia and buttocks. The painting produced a public outcry.

26-11 CLIFF WHITING (TE WHANAU-A-APANUI), *Tawhiri-Matea (God of the Winds)*, 1984. Oil on wood and fiberboard, 6′ 4 3/8″ × 11′ 10 3/4″. Meteorological Service of New Zealand, Wellington.

In this carved wooden mural depicting the Maori creation myth, Cliff Whiting revived Oceanic formal and iconographic traditions and techniques. The abstract curvilinear design suggests wind turbulence.

26-12 WILLIE BESTER, *Homage to Steve Biko*, 1992. Mixed media, 3' 7⅚" × 3' 7⅚". Collection of the artist.

Homage to Steve Biko is a tribute to a leader of the Black Liberation movement, which protested apartheid in South Africa. References to the injustice of Biko's death fill this complex painting.

1 ft.

Political Art

Although almost all of the works discussed thus far are commentaries on contemporary society—seen through the lens of these artists' personal experiences—they do not incorporate references to specific events, nor do they address conditions affecting all people regardless of their gender, race, or national origin, for example, street violence, homelessness, and industrial pollution. Other artists, however, have confronted precisely those aspects of contemporary life in their work.

WILLIE BESTER Political oppression in South Africa figures prominently in the paintings of WILLIE BESTER (b. 1956), one of many South African artists who were vocal critics of apartheid (government-sponsored racial separation). Bester's 1992 *Homage to Steve Biko* (FIG. **26-12**) is a tribute to the gentle and heroic leader of the South African Black Liberation Movement whom the authorities killed while in detention. The exoneration of the two white doctors in charge of him sparked protests around the world. Bester packed his picture with references to death and injustice. Biko's portrait, at the center, is near another of the police minister, James Kruger, who had Biko transported 1,100 miles to Pretoria in the yellow Land Rover ambulance seen left of center and again beneath Biko's portrait. Bester portrayed Biko with his chained fists raised in the classic worldwide protest gesture. This portrait memorializes both Biko and the many other antiapartheid activists, as indicated by the white graveyard crosses above a blue sea of skulls beside Biko's head. The crosses stand out against a red background, recalling the inferno of burned townships. The stop sign (lower left) seems to mean "stop Kruger," or perhaps "stop apartheid." The tagged foot, as if in a morgue, above the ambulance (to the left) also refers to Biko's death. The red crosses on this vehicle's door and on Kruger's reflective dark glasses repeat, with sad irony, the graveyard crosses.

Blood-red and ambulance-yellow are in fact unifying colors dripped or painted on many parts of the canvas. Writing and numbers, found fragments and signs, both stenciled and painted—favorite Cubist motifs (FIGS. 24-14 and 24-16)—also appear throughout the composition. Numbers refer to dehumanized life under apartheid. Found objects—wire, sticks, cardboard, sheet metal, cans, and other discards—from which the poor construct fragile, impermanent township dwellings, remind viewers of the degraded lives of most South African people of color. The oilcan guitar (bottom center), another recurrent Bester symbol, refers both to the social harmony and joy provided by music and to the control imposed by apartheid policies. The whole composition is rich in texture and dense in its collage combinations of objects, photographs, signs, symbols, and pigment. *Homage to Steve Biko* is a radical and powerful critique of an oppressive sociopolitical system, and it exemplifies the extent to which art can be invoked in the political process.

DAVID HAMMONS Racism of all kinds is a central theme of the work of DAVID HAMMONS (b. 1943). Born in Springfield, Illinois, Hammons, an African American, moved to Los Angeles in 1962, where he studied art at the Chouinard and Otis Art Institutes before settling in Harlem in 1974. In his *installations* (artworks creating an artistic environment in a room or gallery), Hammons combines sharp social commentary with beguiling sensory elements to push viewers to confront racism in American society. He created *Public Enemy* (FIG. **26-13**) for an exhibition at the Museum of Modern Art in New York in 1991. Hammons enticed viewers to interact with the installation by scattering fragrant autumn leaves on the floor and positioning helium-filled balloons throughout the gallery. The leaves crunched underfoot, and the dangling strings of the balloons gently brushed spectators walking around the installation. Once drawn into the environment, viewers encountered the centerpiece of *Public Enemy*—large black-and-white photographs of a public monument in front of the American Museum of Natural History in New York City depicting President Theodore Roosevelt (1858–1919) triumphantly seated on a horse, flanked by an African American man and a Native American man, both men appearing in the role of servants. Around the edge of the installation, circling the photographs of the monument, were piles of sandbags with both real and toy guns propped on top, aimed at the statue. By selecting evocative found objects and presenting them in a dynamic manner, encouraging viewer interaction, Hammons attracted an audience and then revealed the racism embedded in received cultural heritage and prompted reexamination of American values and cultural emblems.

try to visualize the real products of the uses of power.[2]

Mercenaries IV (FIG. 26-14), a canvas rivaling the monumental history paintings of the 19th century in size, presents a mysterious tableau of five tough freelance military professionals willing to fight, for a price, for any political cause. The three clustering at the right side of the canvas react with tense physical gestures to something one of the two other mercenaries standing at the far left is saying. The dark uniforms and skin tones of the four black fighters flatten their figures and make them stand out against the searing dark red background. The slightly modulated background seems to push their forms forward up against the picture plane and becomes an echoing void in the space between the two groups. Golub painted the mercenaries so that the viewer's eye is level with the menacing figures' knees. He placed the men so close to the front plane of the work that the lower edge of the painting cuts off their feet, thereby trapping the viewer in the painting's compressed space. Golub emphasized both the scarred light tones of the white mercenary's skin and the weapons. Modeled with shadow and gleaming highlights, the guns contrast with the harshly scraped, flattened surfaces of the figures. The rawness of the canvas reinforces the rawness of the imagery. Golub often dissolved certain areas with solvent after applying pigment and scraped off applied paint with, among other tools, a meat cleaver. The feeling of peril confronts viewers mercilessly. They become one with all the victims caught in today's political battles.

LEON GOLUB During his long and successful career as a painter, LEON GOLUB (1922–2004) expressed a brutal vision of contemporary life. Born in Chicago and trained at the University of Chicago and the Art Institute of Chicago, he is best known for his two series of paintings titled *Assassins* and *Mercenaries*. In these large-scale works on unstretched canvases, anonymous characters inspired by newspaper and magazine photographs participate in atrocious street violence, terrorism, and torture. The paintings have a universal impact because they suggest not specific stories but a condition of being. As Golub observed:

Through media we are under constant, invasive bombardment of images—from all over—and we often have to take evasive action to avoid discomforting recognitions. . . . The work [of art] should have an edge, veering between what is visually and cognitively acceptable and what might stretch these limits as we encounter or

1 ft.

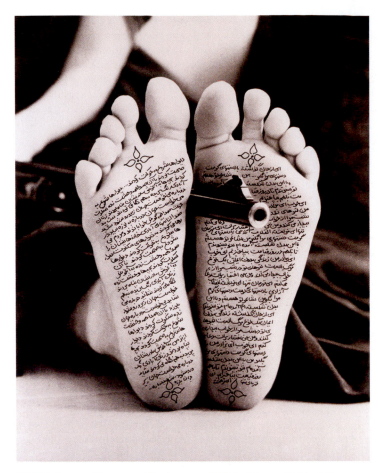

26-15 SHIRIN NESHAT, *Allegiance and Wakefulness*, 1994. Offset print. Israel Museum, Jerusalem.

Neshat's photographs address the repression of women in postrevolutionary Iran. She poses in traditional veiled garb but wields a rifle and displays militant Farsi poetry on her exposed body parts.

SHIRIN NESHAT Violence also plays a significant role in the art of SHIRIN NESHAT (b. 1957), who grew up in a Westernized Iranian home and attended a Catholic boarding school in Tehran before leaving her homeland to study art in California, where she earned undergraduate and graduate degrees from the University of California, Berkeley. Today, she lives in New York City and produces films, video, and photographs critical of the fundamentalist Islamic regime in Iran, especially in its treatment of women. Neshat often poses for her photographs wearing a veil—the symbol for her of the repression of Muslim women—and with her face and exposed parts of her body covered with Farsi (Persian) messages. A rifle often figures prominently in the photographs as an emblem of militant feminism, a notion foreign to the Muslim faith. In *Allegiance and Wakefulness* (FIG. **26-15**) from her *Women of Allah* series, the viewer sees only Neshat's feet covered with verses of militant Farsi poetry and the barrel of a rifle.

KRZYSZTOF WODICZKO Born in Poland, KRZYSZTOF WODICZKO (b. 1943) focuses on more universal concerns in his art. When working in Canada in 1980, he developed artworks involving outdoor slide images. He projected photographs on specific buildings to expose how civic buildings embody, legitimize, and perpetuate power. When Wodiczko moved to New York City in 1983, the pervasive homelessness troubled him, and he resolved to use his art to publicize this problem. In 1987, he produced *The Home-*

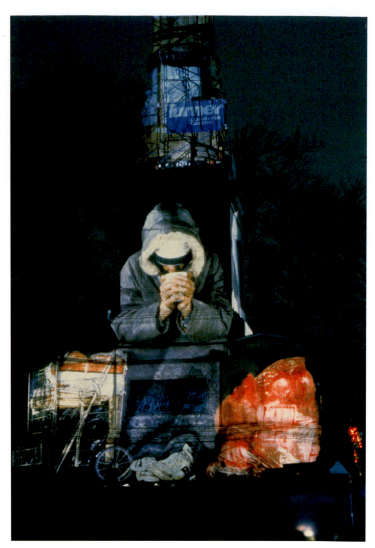

26-16 KRZYSZTOF WODICZKO, *The Homeless Projection*, 1986. Outdoor slide projection at the Civil War Soldiers and Sailors Monument, Boston. ◼◀

To publicize their plight, Wodiczko projected on the walls of a monument on Boston Common images of homeless people and their plastic bags filled with their few possessions.

less Projection (FIG. **26-16**) as part of a New Year's celebration in Boston. The artist projected images of homeless people on all four sides of the Civil War Soldiers and Sailors Monument on Boston Common. In these photos, the homeless appear flanked by plastic bags filled with their few possessions. At the top of the monument, Wodiczko projected a local condominium construction site, which helped viewers make a connection between urban development and homelessness.

HANS HAACKE Some contemporary artists have produced important works exposing the politics of the art world itself, specifically the role of museums and galleries in validating art, the discriminatory policies and politics of these cultural institutions, and the corrupting influence of corporate sponsorship of art exhibitions. German artist HANS HAACKE (b. 1936) has focused his attention on the politics of art museums and how acquisition and exhibition policies affect the public's understanding of art history. The specificity of his works, based on substantial research, makes them stinging indictments of the institutions whose practices he critiques.

26-17 HANS HAACKE, *MetroMobiltan*, 1985. Fiberglass construction, three banners, and photomural, 11′ 8″ × 20′ × 5′. Musée National d'Art Moderne, Centre Georges Pompidou, Paris.

MetroMobiltan focuses attention on the connections between political and economic conditions in South Africa and the conflicted politics of corporate patronage of art exhibitions.

In *MetroMobiltan* (FIG. **26-17**), Haacke illustrated the connection between the realm of art (more specifically, the Metropolitan Museum of Art in New York) and the world of political and economic interests. *MetroMobiltan* is a large sculptural work that includes a photomural of the funeral procession for black victims shot by the South African police at Cross Roads, near Cape Town, on March 16, 1985. This photomural serves as the backdrop for a banner for the 1980 Mobil Oil–sponsored Metropolitan Museum show *Treasures of Ancient Nigeria*. In 1980, Mobil was a principal investor in South Africa, and Haacke's work suggests one major factor in Mobil's sponsorship of this exhibition was that Nigeria is one of the richest oil-producing countries. In 1981, political activists pressured Mobil's board of directors to stop providing oil to the white South African military and police. Printed on the blue banners hanging on either side of *Metro-Mobiltan* is the official corporate response refusing to comply with this demand. Haacke set the entire tableau in a fiberglass replica of the Metropolitan Museum's entablature. By bringing together these disparate visual and textual elements referring to the museum, Mobil Oil, and Africa, the artist forced viewers to think about the connections among multinational corporations, political and economic conditions in South Africa, and the conflicted politics of corporate patronage of art exhibitions, thereby undermining the public's naive view that cultural institutions are exempt from political and economic concerns.

XU BING A different kind of political/cultural commentary has been the hallmark of XU BING (b. 1955), a Chongqing, China, native who was forced to work in the countryside with peasants during the Cultural Revolution of 1966 to 1976 under Mao Tse-tung (1893–1976). Xu later studied printmaking in Beijing at the Central Academy of Fine Arts. He moved to the United States in 1990 at the invitation of the University of Wisconsin, where two years earlier he had exhibited his most famous work, a large installation called *A Book from the Sky* (FIG. **26-18**). First exhibited in China and Japan before being installed at Wisconsin's Chazen Museum of Art, the work presents an enormous number of woodblock-printed texts in characters evocative of Chinese writing but invented by the artist.

Producing them required both an intimate knowledge of genuine Chinese characters and extensive training in block carving. Xu's work, however, is no hymn to tradition. Critics have interpreted it both as a stinging critique of the meaninglessness of contemporary political language and as a commentary on the illegibility of the past. Like many works of art, past and present, Eastern and Western, Xu's postmodern masterpiece can be read on many levels.

26-18 XU BING, *A Book from the Sky*, 1987. Installation at Chazen Museum of Art, University of Wisconsin, Madison, 1991. Moveable-type prints and books.

Xu trained as a printmaker in Beijing. *A Book from the Sky*, with its invented Chinese woodblock characters, may be a stinging critique of the meaninglessness of contemporary political language.

26-19 EDWARD BURTYNSKY, *Densified Scrap Metal #3a, Hamilton, Ontario*, 1997. Dye coupler print, 2′ 2¾″ × 2′ 10⅜″. National Gallery of Canada, Ottawa (gift of the artist, 1998).

Burtynsky's "manufactured landscapes" are commentaries on the destructive effects on the environment of industrial plants and mines, but his photographs transform ugliness into beauty.

1 ft.

EDWARD BURTYNSKY Concern with the destructive effects of industrial plants and mines on the environment has been the motivation for the photographs of "manufactured landscapes" by Canadian EDWARD BURTYNSKY (b. 1955). The son of a Ukrainian immigrant who worked in the General Motors plant in St. Catharines, Ontario, Burtynsky studied photography and graphic design at Ryerson University and Niagara College. He uses a large-format field camera to produce high-resolution negatives of industrial landscapes littered with tires, scrap metal, and industrial refuse. His choice of subjects is itself a negative commentary on modern manufacturing processes, but Burtynsky transforms ugliness into beauty in his color prints. His photograph (FIG. **26-19**) of a Toronto recycling plant from his *Urban Mines* series converts bundles of compressed scrap metal into a striking abstract composition of multicolored rectangles. Burtynsky's work thus merges documentary and fine-art photography and bears comparison with the photographs of Margaret Bourke-White (FIG. 24-76) and Minor White (FIG. 25-32).

OTHER MOVEMENTS AND THEMES

Despite the high visibility of contemporary artists whose work deals with the pressing social and political issues of the world, some critically acclaimed living artists have produced innovative modernist art during the postmodern era. Abstraction remains a valid and compelling approach to painting and sculpture in the 21st century, as does more traditional figural art.

Abstract Painting and Sculpture

Already in the 1970s, Susan Rothenberg (FIG. 25-8D) had produced monumental "Neo-Expressionist" paintings inspired by German Expressionism and American Abstract Expressionism. Today, several important contemporary artists continue to explore this dynamic style.

JULIAN SCHNABEL New Yorker JULIAN SCHNABEL (b. 1951), who wrote and directed a 1996 film about fellow artist Jean-Michel Basquiat (FIG. 26-8), has experimented widely with media and materials in his forceful restatements of the premises of Abstract Expressionism. Schnabel's Neo-Expressionist works range from paint on velvet and tarpaulin to a mixture of pigment and fragmented china plates bonded to wood. He has a special interest in the physicality of objects, and by combining broken crockery and paint, as in The Walk Home (FIG. **26-20**), he has found an extension of what paint can do. Superficially, Schnabel's paintings recall the work of the gestural abstractionists, especially the spontaneous drips of Jackson Pollock (FIG. 25-6) and the energetic brushstrokes of Willem de Kooning (FIG. 25-8), but their Abstract Expressionist works lack the thick, mosaiclike texture of Schnabel's canvases. The amalgamation of media brings together painting, mosaic, and low-relief sculpture, and considerably amplifies the expressive impact of his paintings.

ANSELM KIEFER Neo-Expressionism was by no means a solely American movement. German artist ANSELM KIEFER (b. 1945), who studied art in Düsseldorf with Joseph Beuys (FIG. 25-52) in the early 1970s, and has lived and worked in Barjac, France, since 1992, has produced some of the most lyrical and engaging works of recent decades. Like Schnabel's canvases, Kiefer's paintings, such as *Nigredo* (FIG. **26-21**), are monumental in scale, recall Abstract Expressionist works, and draw the viewer to their textured surfaces, made more complex by the addition of materials such as straw and lead. It is not merely the impressive physicality of Kiefer's paintings that accounts for the impact of his work, however. His images function on a mythological or metaphorical level as well as on a historically specific one. Kiefer's works of the 1970s and 1980s often involve a reexamination of German history, particularly the painful Nazi era of 1933–1945, and evoke the feeling of despair.

26-20 JULIAN SCHNABEL, *The Walk Home,* 1984–1985. Oil, plates, copper, bronze, fiberglass, and Bondo on wood, 9′ 3″ × 19′ 4″. Broad Art Foundation and the Pace Gallery, New York. ◼◂

Schnabel's paintings recall the work of the gestural abstractionists, but he employs an amalgamation of media, bringing together painting, mosaic, and low-relief sculpture.

1 ft.

Kiefer believes Germany's participation in World War II and the Holocaust left permanent scars on the souls of the German people and on the souls of all humanity.

Nigredo (blackening) pulls the viewer into an expansive landscape depicted using Renaissance perspective principles. This landscape, however, is far from pastoral or carefully cultivated. Rather, it appears bleak and charred. Although it does not make specific reference to the Holocaust, this incinerated landscape indirectly alludes to the horrors of that historical event. More generally, the blackness of the landscape may refer to the notion

of alchemical change or transformation, a concept of great interest to Kiefer. Black is one of the four symbolic colors of the alchemist—a color referencing both death and the molten, chaotic state of substances broken down by fire. Because the alchemist focuses on the transformation of substances, the emphasis on blackness is not absolute, but can also be perceived as part of a process of renewal and redemption. Kiefer thus imbued his work with a deep symbolic meaning that, when combined with the intriguing visual quality of his parched, congealed surfaces, results in paintings of enduring power.

26-21 ANSELM KIEFER, *Nigredo,* 1984. Oil paint on photosensitized fabric, acrylic emulsion, straw, shellac, relief paint on paper pulled from painted wood, 11′ × 18′. Philadelphia Museum of Art, Philadelphia (gift of Friends of the Philadelphia Museum of Art).

Kiefer's paintings have thickly encrusted surfaces incorporating materials such as straw. Here, the German artist used perspective to pull the viewer into an incinerated landscape alluding to the Holocaust.

1 ft.

26-22 Wu Guanzhong, *Wild Vines with Flowers Like Pearls*, 1997. Ink on paper, 2′ 11½″ × 5′ 11″. Singapore Art Museum, Singapore (donation from Wu Guanzhong).

In a brilliant fusion of traditional Chinese subject matter and technique with modern Western Abstract Expressionism, Wu depicted the wild vines of the Yangtze River valley.

1 ft.

WU GUANZHONG Abstraction is a still-vital pictorial mode in Asia, where the most innovative artists working in the Neo-Expressionist mode have merged Western and Eastern traditions in their work. WU GUANZHONG (1919–2010) attended the National Art College in Hangzhou, graduating in 1942, and then studied painting in Paris at the École Nationale Supérieure des Beaux-Arts from 1946 to 1950, when he returned to China to take up teaching positions at several prestigious art academies. His early work, reflecting his exposure to the Western tradition, was primarily oil painting on canvas, but in the 1970s he began to embrace the traditional Chinese medium of ink and color on paper, later often restricting his palette only to ink. His mature work, for example, *Wild Vines with Flowers Like Pearls* (FIG. **26-22**), painted in 1997, combines the favored medium and subject matter of the centuries-old *literati* tradition—the 17th-century paintings of Shitao were important forerunners—with an abstract style strongly influenced by Pollock. American Abstract Expressionist painting was politically impossible to pursue during the Cultural Revolution, when Wu, like Xu Bing (FIG. 26-18), was sentenced to labor on a rural farm because of his refusal to conform to official doctrine.

The inspiration for *Wild Vines*, as for so many of Wu's paintings, was the mountainous landscape and forests of the Yangtze River. The free composition and bold thick brushstrokes brilliantly balance abstract, sweeping, crisscrossing lines with the suggestive shapes of vines and flowers. His work, like that of SONG SU-NAM (b. 1938; FIG. **26-22A**) in Korea and EMILY KAME KNGWARREYE (1910–1996; FIG. **26-22B**) in Australia, represents a highly successful fusion of traditional local and modern Western style and subject matter.

26-22A SONG, *Summer Trees*, 1983.

26-22B KNGWARREYE, *Untitled*, 1992.

KIMIO TSUCHIYA In contemporary Japan, as in China, no single artistic style, medium, or subject dominates, but much of the art produced during the past few decades springs from ideas or beliefs integral to the national culture over many centuries. For example, the Shinto belief in the generative forces in nature and

in humankind's position as part of the totality of nature holds great appeal for contemporary artists such as KIMIO TSUCHIYA (b. 1955), who studied sculpture in London and Tokyo. Tsuchiya is best known for his large-scale sculptures (FIG. **26-23**) constructed of branches or driftwood. Despite their abstract nature, his works assert the life forces found in natural materials, thereby engaging viewers in a consideration of their own relationship to

1 ft.

26-23 KIMIO TSUCHIYA, *Symptom*, 1987. Branches, 13′ 1½″ × 14′ 9⅛″ × 3′ 11¼″. **Installation at the exhibition *Jeune Sculpture '87*, Paris 1987.**

Tsuchiya's sculptures consist of branches or driftwood, and despite their abstract nature, they assert the life forces found in natural materials. His approach to sculpture reflects ancient Shinto beliefs.

Donovan's sculptures consist of everyday components, such as straws, plastic cups, and wire. The abstract forms suggest rolling landscapes, clouds, fungus, and other natural forms.

nature. Tsuchiya does not specifically invoke Shinto when speaking about his art, but it is clear he has internalized Shinto principles. He identifies as his goal "to bring out and present the life of nature emanating from this energy of trees. . . . It is as though the wood is part of myself, as though the wood has the same kind of life force."[3]

TARA DONOVAN Brooklynite TARA DONOVAN (b. 1969) studied at the School of Visual Arts in New York City, the Corcoran College of Art and Design in Washington, D.C., and Virginia Commonwealth University in Richmond. She was the first recipient (in 2005) of the Alexander Calder Foundation's Calder Prize for sculpture. Donovan has won an international reputation for her installations (FIG. **26-24**) of large sculptural works composed of thousands of small everyday objects, such as toothpicks, straws, pins, paper plates, plastic cups, and electrical wire. Her abstract sculptures often suggest rolling landscapes, clouds, fungus, and other natural forms, although she seeks in her work not to mimic those forms but to capture nature's dynamic growth. Some of Donovan's installations are unstable and can change shape during the course of an exhibition.

Figural Painting and Sculpture

Recent decades have brought a revival of interest in figural art, both in painting and sculpture, a trend best exemplified in the earlier postwar period by Lucian Freud (FIG. 25-29), who remained an active and influential painter until his death in July 2011.

JENNY SAVILLE Fellow Briton JENNY SAVILLE (b. 1970) is the leading figure painter in the Freud mold of the younger generation of European and American artists. Born in Cambridge, England, and trained at the Glasgow School of Art in Scotland, Saville lives and paints in an old palace in Palermo, Italy. Her best-known works are over-life-size self-portraits in which she exaggerates the girth of her body and delights in depicting heavy folds of flesh with visible veins in minute detail and from a sharply foreshortened angle, which further distorts the body's proportions. Her nude self-portraits deserve comparison not only with those of Freud but also

of Egon Schiele (FIG. 24-10), despite the vivid contrast between Schiele's emaciated body and Saville's obesity.

Saville's paintings are a commentary on the contemporary obsession with the lithe bodies of fashion models. In *Branded* (FIG. **26-25**), she underscores the dichotomy between the popular notion of a beautiful body and the imperfect bodies of most people by "branding" her body with words inscribed in her flesh—*delicate, decorative, petite*. Art critic Michelle Meagher has described Saville's paintings as embodying a "feminist aesthetics of disgust."[4]

1 ft.

26-25 JENNY SAVILLE, *Branded*, 1992. Oil on canvas, 7′ × 6′. Charles Saatchi Collection, London.

Saville's unflattering foreshortened self-portrait "branded" with words such as *delicate* and *petite* underscores the dichotomy between the perfect bodies of fashion models and those of most people.

KIKI SMITH A distinctly unflattering approach to the representation of the human body is also the hallmark of New York–based KIKI SMITH (b. 1954), the daughter of Minimalist sculptor Tony Smith (FIG. 25-17). In her work, Smith has explored the question of who controls the human body, an interest that grew out of her training as an emergency medical service technician. Smith, however, also wants to reveal the socially constructed nature of the body, and she encourages the viewer to consider how external forces shape people's perceptions of their bodies. In works such as *Untitled* (FIG. **26-26**), the artist dramatically departed from conventional representations of the body, both in art and in the media. She suspended two life-size wax figures, one male and one female, both nude, from metal stands. Smith marked each of the sculptures with long white drips—body fluids running from the woman's breasts and down the man's leg. She commented:

> Most of the functions of the body are hidden . . . from society. . . . [W]e separate our bodies from our lives. But, when people are

dying, they are losing control of their bodies. That loss of function can seem humiliating and frightening. But, on the other hand, you can look at it as a kind of liberation of the body. It seems like a nice metaphor—a way to think about the social—that people lose control despite the many agendas of different ideologies in society, which are trying to control the body(ies) . . . medicine, religion, law, etc. Just thinking about control—who has control of the body? . . . Does the mind have control of the body? Does the social?[5]

JEFF KOONS The sculptures of JEFF KOONS (b. 1955) form a striking counterpoint to the figural art of Kiki Smith. Trained at the Maryland Institute College of Art in Baltimore, Koons worked early in his career as a commodities broker. He first became prominent in the art world for a series of works in the early 1980s involving the exhibition of everyday commercial products such as vacuum cleaners. Clearly following in the footsteps of Marcel Duchamp (FIG. 24-27), Koons made no attempt to manipulate or

1 ft.

26-26 KIKI SMITH, *Untitled*, 1990. Beeswax and microcrystalline wax figures on metal stands, female figure installed height 6′ 1½″ and male figure installed height 6′ 5″. Whitney Museum of American Art, New York (purchased with funds from the Painting and Sculpture Committee).

Asking "Who controls the body?" Kiki Smith sculpted two life-size wax figures of a nude man and woman with body fluids running from the woman's breasts and down the man's leg.

1 ft.

26-27 JEFF KOONS, *Pink Panther*, 1988. Porcelain, 3′ 5″ high. Museum of Contemporary Art, Chicago (Gerald S. Elliot Collection). ◼◀

Koons creates sculptures highlighting everything he considers wrong with contemporary American consumer culture. In this work, he intertwined a centerfold nude and a cartoon character.

alter the machine-made objects. More recently, he, like Californian ROBERT ARNESON (1930–1992; FIG. 26-27A), turned to ceramic sculpture. In *Pink Panther* (FIG. 26-27), Koons, who divides his time between his hometown of York, Pennsylvania, and New York City, intertwined a magazine centerfold nude with a famous cartoon character. He reinforced the trite and kitschy nature of this imagery by titling the exhibition of which this work was a part *The Banality Show*. Some art critics have argued Koons and his work instruct viewers because both artist and artwork serve as the most visible symbols of everything wrong with contemporary American society. Regardless of whether this is true, Koons's prominence in the art world indicates he has developed an acute understanding of the dynamics of consumer culture.

26-27A ARNESON, *California Artist*, 1982.

MARISOL ESCOBAR Known simply by her first name, MARISOL ESCOBAR (b. 1930) grew up in a wealthy, widely traveled Venezuelan family. Born in Paris and educated there, in Los Angeles, and in New York City, Marisol first studied painting and drawing, but after discovering Pre-Columbian art in 1951, she pursued a career as a sculptor. Marisol also spent time in Italy, where she developed a deep admiration for Renaissance art.

In the 1960s, Marisol was one of the inner circle of New York Pop artists, and she appeared in two of Andy Warhol's films. Some of her works at that time portrayed prominent public figures, including the Hollywood actor John Wayne and the family of U.S. president John F. Kennedy. Her subjects were always people, however, not the commercial products of consumer culture that fascinated most leading Pop artists and still are prominent in the art of Jeff Koons and others.

Marisol retained her interest in figural sculpture long after Pop Art gave way to other movements. One of her most ambitious works (FIG. 26-28) is a multimedia three-dimensional version of Leonardo da Vinci's *Last Supper* (FIG. 17-4), including the walls and windows of the dining room in order to replicate the Renaissance master's application of linear perspective. By reproducing the fresco in three dimensions, she transformed it into an object. Marisol's figures are painted wood, with the exception of Christ, whose stone body is the physical and emotional anchor of the composition. In many of her sculptures, the female figures have Marisol's features, and in this tableau she added a seated armless portrait of herself looking at the *Last Supper*. Catholic and deeply religious—as a teenager she emulated martyr saints by inflicting physical harm on herself—Marisol may have wanted to show herself as a witness to Christ's last meal. But more likely her presence here is a tribute to the 16th-century painter. (She also made a sculptural replica of Leonardo's *Madonna and Child with Saint Anne* [FIG. 17-3].)

Marisol's *Self-Portrait Looking at the Last Supper* is a commentary on the artist not only as a creator but also as a viewer of the works of earlier artists, a link in an artistic chain extending back to antiquity. One pervasive element in the work

26-28A TANSEY, *A Short History of Modernist Painting*, 1982.

of contemporary artists is a self-consciousness of the postmodern painter or sculptor's position in the continuum of art history. No one better exemplifies that aspect of contemporary art than MARK TANSEY (b. 1949; FIG. 26-28A).

KANE KWEI AND PAA JOE Painted wood sculpture remains a vital artistic medium in Africa, where it has a venerable heritage throughout the continent. Some contemporary African artists have pioneered new forms, however, often under the influence

1 ft.

26-28 MARISOL ESCOBAR, *Self-Portrait Looking at the Last Supper*, 1982–1984. Painted wood, stone, plaster, and aluminum, 10' 1½" × 29' 10" × 5' 1". Metropolitan Museum of Art, New York (gift of Mr. and Mrs. Roberto C. Polo, 1986).

In a tribute to the Renaissance master, Marisol created a sculptural replica of Leonardo's *Last Supper* (FIG. 17-4), transforming the fresco into an object. She is the seated viewer as well as the artist.

26-29 PAA JOE, running shoe, airplane, automobile and other coffins inside the artist's showroom in Teshi, Ghana, 2000. Painted wood.

The caskets of Paa Joe take many forms, including items of clothing, airplanes, and automobiles. The forms always relate to the deceased, but many collectors buy the caskets as art objects.

of modern Western art movements. Kane Kwei (1922–1992) of the Ga people in urban coastal Ghana created a new kind of wooden casket that brought him both critical acclaim and commercial success. Beginning around 1970, Kwei, trained as a carpenter, created one-of-a-kind coffins crafted to reflect the deceased's life, occupation, or major accomplishments. On commission he made such diverse shapes as a cow, a whale, a bird, a Mercedes Benz, and various local food crops, such as onions and cocoa pods, all pieced together using nails and glue rather than carved. Kwei also created coffins in traditional African leaders' symbolic forms, such as an eagle, an elephant, a leopard, and a stool.

Kwei's sons and his cousin PAA JOE (b. 1944) have carried on his legacy. In a photograph (FIG. 26-29) shot around 2000 outside Joe's showroom in Teshi, several large caskets are on display, including a running shoe, an airplane, and an automobile. Many of the coffins Kwei and Joe produced never served as burial containers. Collectors and curators purchased them for display in private homes, art galleries, and museums. The coffins' forms, derived from popular culture, strike a familiar chord in the Western world because they recall Pop Art sculptures (FIG. 25-26), which accounts in large part for the international appeal of Kwei and Joe's work.

ARCHITECTURE
AND SITE-SPECIFIC ART

The work of architects and Environmental artists today is as varied as that of contemporary painters and sculptors, but the common denominator in the diversity of contemporary architectural design and site-specific projects is the breaking down of national boundaries, with leading practitioners working in several countries and even on several continents, often simultaneously.

Architecture

In the late 20th and early 21st century, one of the by-products of the globalization of the world's economy has been that leading architects have received commissions to design buildings far from their home bases. In the rapidly developing emerging markets of Asia, the Middle East, Africa, Latin America, and elsewhere, virtually every architect with an international reputation can list a recent building in Beijing or another urban center on his or her résumé.

NORMAN FOSTER Award-winning architect NORMAN FOSTER (b. 1935) began his study of architectural design at the University of Manchester, England. After graduating, he won a fellowship to attend the master's degree program at the Yale School of Architecture, where he met Richard Rogers (FIG. 25-49). The two decided to open a joint architectural firm when they returned to London in 1962, but they established separate practices several years later. Their designs still have much in common, however,

26-30 NORMAN FOSTER, Hong Kong and Shanghai Bank (looking southwest), Hong Kong, China, 1979–1986.

Foster's High-Tech tower has an exposed steel skeleton featuring floors with uninterrupted working spaces. At the base is a 10-story atrium illuminated by computerized mirrors that reflect sunlight.

26-31 RENZO PIANO, aerial view (*top;* looking northwest) and three "huts" (*bottom;* looking southeast), Tjibaou Cultural Centre, Noumea, New Caledonia, 1998.

A pioneering example of "green architecture," Piano's complex of 10 bamboo units, based on traditional New Caledonian village huts, has adjustable skylights in the roofs for natural climate control.

each that he calls "villages," suspended from steel girders resembling bridges. Escalators connect the floors in each village—the floors are related by function—but the elevators stop at only one floor in each community of floors. At the base of the building is a plaza opening onto the neighboring streets. Visitors ascend on escalators from the plaza to a spectacular 10-story, 170-feet-tall atrium bordered by balconies with additional workspaces. What Foster calls "sun scoops"—computerized mirrors on the south side of the building—track the movement of the sun across the Hong Kong sky and reflect the sunlight into the atrium and piazza, flooding the dramatic spaces with light at all hours of the day. Not surprisingly, the roof of this High-Tech skyscraper serves as a landing pad for corporate helicopters.

because they share a similar outlook. Foster and Rogers are the leading proponents of what critics call *High-Tech* architecture, the roots of which can be traced to Joseph Paxton's mid-19th-century Crystal Palace (FIG. 22-47) in London. High-Tech architects design buildings incorporating the latest innovations in engineering and technology and exposing the structures' component parts. High-Tech architecture is distinct from other postmodern architectural movements in dispensing with all historical references.

Foster's design for the headquarters (FIG. 26-30) of the Hong Kong and Shanghai Bank Corporation (HSBC), which cost $1 billion to build, exemplifies the High-Tech approach to architecture. The banking tower is as different from Philip Johnson's postmodern AT&T Building (FIG. 25-46) as it is from the modernist glass-and-steel Seagram Building (FIG. 25-43) and Sears Tower (FIG. 25-44). The 47-story Hong Kong skyscraper has an exposed steel skeleton with the elevators and other service elements located in giant piers at the short ends of the building, a design that provides uninterrupted communal working spaces on each cantilevered floor. Foster divided the tower into five horizontal units of six to nine floors

GREEN ARCHITECTURE The harnessing of solar energy as a power source is one of the key features of what critics commonly refer to as *green architecture*—ecologically friendly buildings that use "clean energy" and sustain the natural environment. Green architecture is the most important trend in architectural design in the early 21st century. A pioneer in this field is Renzo Piano, the codesigner with Richard Rogers of the Pompidou Center (FIG. 25-49) in Paris. Piano won an international competition to design the Tjibaou Cultural Centre (FIG. 26-31, *left*) in Noumea, New Caledonia. Named in honor of the assassinated political leader Jean-Marie Tjibaou (1936–1989), the center consists of 10 beehive-shaped bamboo "huts" nestled in pine trees on a narrow island peninsula in the Pacific Ocean. Rooted in the village architecture of the Kanak people of New Caledonia, each unit of Piano's postmodern complex has an adjustable skylight as a roof (FIG. 26-31, *right*) to provide natural—sustainable—climate control. The curved profile of the Tjibaou pavilions also helps the structures withstand the pressure of the hurricane-force winds common in the South Pacific.

26-32 Günter Behnisch, Hysolar Institute (looking north), University of Stuttgart, Stuttgart, Germany, 1987.

The roof, walls, and windows of the Deconstructivist Hysolar Institute seem to explode, avoiding any suggestion of stable masses and frustrating viewers' expectations of how a building should look.

DECONSTRUCTIVISM In architecture, as in painting and sculpture, deconstruction as an analytical and design strategy emerged in the 1970s. The name given to this postmodern architectural movement is *Deconstructivism*. Deconstructivist architects attempt to disrupt the conventional categories of architecture and to rupture the viewer's expectations based on them. Destabilization plays a major role in Deconstructivist architecture. Disorder, dissonance, imbalance, asymmetry, irregularity, and unconformity replace their opposites—order, harmony, balance, symmetry, regularity, and clarity. The seemingly haphazardly presented volumes, masses, planes, borders, lighting, locations, directions, spatial relations, as well as the disguised structural facts of Deconstructivist design, challenge the viewer's assumptions about architectural form as it relates to function. According to Deconstructivist principles, the very absence of the stability of traditional categories of architecture in a structure announces a "deconstructed" building.

GÜNTER BEHNISCH Audacious in its dissolution of form is the Hysolar Institute (FIG. **26-32**) at the University of Stuttgart, Germany, by GÜNTER BEHNISCH (1922–2010). Behnisch, who gained international attention as the architect of the Olympic Park in Munich for the 1972 Olympic Games, designed the institute as part of a joint German–Saudi Arabian research project on the technology of solar energy. In the Hysolar Institute, Behnisch intended to deny the possibility of spatial enclosure altogether, and his apparently chaotic arrangement of the structural units defies easy analysis. The shapes of the roof, walls, and windows seem to explode, avoiding any suggestion of clear, stable masses. Behnisch aggressively played with the traditional concepts of architectural design. The disordered architectural elements of the Hysolar Institute seem precarious and visually threaten to collapse, frustrating the viewer's expectations of how a building should look.

FRANK GEHRY The architect most closely identified with Deconstructivist architecture is Canadian FRANK GEHRY (b. 1929). Trained in sculpture, and at different times a collaborator with Donald Judd (FIG. 25-18) and Claes Oldenburg (FIG. 25-26), Gehry works up his designs by constructing models and then cutting them up and arranging the parts until he has a satisfying composition. Among Gehry's most notable projects is the Guggenheim Museum (FIGS. **26-33** and **26-34**) in Bilbao, Spain, one

26-33 FRANK GEHRY, Guggenheim Bilbao Museo (looking south), Bilbao, Spain, 1997.

Gehry's limestone-and-titanium Bilbao museum is an immensely dramatic building. Its disorder and seeming randomness of design epitomize Deconstructivist architectural principles.

Frank Gehry on Architectural Design and Materials

Frank Gehry has been designing buildings since the 1950s, but only in the 1970s did he begin to break away from the rectilinearity of modernist architecture and develop the dramatic sculptural style seen in buildings such as the Guggenheim Museum (FIGS. 26-33 and 26-34) in Bilbao. In 1999, the Deconstructivist architect reflected on his career and his many projects in a book simply titled *Gehry Talks*.

> My early work was rectilinear because you take baby steps. I guess the work has become a kind of sculpture as architecture.... I'm a strict modernist in the sense of believing in purity, that you shouldn't decorate. And yet buildings need decoration, because they need scaling elements. They need to be human scale, in my opinion. They can't just be faceless things. That's how some modernism failed.*
>
> They teach materials and methods in architecture school, as a separate course. I'm a craftsman.... It seems to me that when you're doing architecture, you're building something out of something. There are social issues, there's context, and then there's how do you make the enclosure and what do you make it with? ... I explored metal: how it dealt with the light ... It does beautiful things with light.... Flat was a fetish, and everybody was doing that. I found out that I could use metal if I didn't worry about it being flat; I could do it cheaper. It was intuitive. I just went with it. I liked it. Then when I saw it on the building, I loved it.... Bilbao ... [is] titanium.... [I] prefer titanium because it's stronger; it's an element, a pure element, and it doesn't oxidize. It stays the same forever. They give a hundred-year guarantee!†

*Milton Friedman, ed., *Gehry Talks: Architecture + Process,* rev. ed. (New York: Universe, 2002), 47–48.
†Ibid., 44, 47.

26-34 FRANK GEHRY, atrium of the Guggenheim Bilbao Museo, Bilbao, Spain, 1997.

The glass-walled atrium of the Guggenheim Bilbao Museum soars skyward 165 feet. The asymmetrical and imbalanced screens and vaults flow into one another, creating a sense of disequilibrium.

26-34A STIRLING, Neue Staatsgalerie, Stuttgart, 1977–1983.

26-34B LIBESKIND, Denver Art Museum, 2006.

of several art museum projects of the past few decades as notable for their innovative postmodern architectural designs as for the important art collections they house. These include the Neue Staatsgalerie (FIG. **26-34A**) in Stuttgart, Germany, by British architect JAMES STIRLING (1926–1994); the Denver Art Museum (FIG. **26-34B**) by Polish-born DANIEL LIBESKIND (b. 1946); and the Grande Louvre Pyramide (FIG. 26-36) in Paris.

Gehry's Bilbao museum appears to be a collapsed or collapsing aggregate of units. Visitors approaching the building see a mass of irregular asymmetrical and imbalanced forms whose profiles change dramatically with every shift of the viewer's position. The limestone- and titanium-clad exterior lends a space-age character to the structure and highlights further the unique cluster effect of the many forms (see "Frank Gehry on Architectural Design and Materials," above). A group of organic forms Gehry refers to as a "metallic flower" tops the museum. In the center of the museum, an enormous glass-walled atrium (FIG. 26-34) soars 165 feet above the ground, serving as the focal point for the three levels of galleries radiating from it. The seemingly weightless screens, vaults, and volumes of the interior float and flow into one another, guided only by light and dark cues. The Guggenheim Museum in Bilbao is a profoundly compelling structure. Its disorder, its deceptive randomness of design, and the disequilibrium it prompts in viewers epitomize Deconstructivist principles.

have an emotional effect upon the viewer. A prime example of her work is the Vitra Fire Station (FIG. **26-35**) in Weil-am-Rhein, Germany, completed in 1993. Composed of layers of reinforced concrete slabs and unframed window panes, the building features a boldly projecting (functionless) "wing" that suggests a burst of energy shooting out from the structure. It expresses the sudden mobilization of the firefighters within the time the alarm sounds and the time they jump into their trucks to race out to extinguish a blaze.

Zaha Hadid is the first woman to win the Pritzker Architecture Prize (in 2004), the architectural equivalent of the Nobel Prize in literature. The first recipient was Philip Johnson in 1979. Other previous winners include Norman Foster, Frank Gehry, Renzo Piano, James Stirling, Joern Utzon, Robert Venturi, and Ieoh Ming Pei.

IEOH MING PEI The latest chapter in the long architectural history of the Louvre—the former French royal residence (FIGS. 15-16, 18-14, and 20-25), now one of the world's greatest art museums—is a monumental glass-and-steel pyramid erected in the palace's main courtyard in 1988. Designed by the Chinese-American architect IEOH MING PEI (b. 1917), the Grand Louvre Pyramide (FIG. **26-36**) is the dramatic postmodern entryway to the museum's priceless collections. Although initially controversial because conservative critics considered it a jarring, dissonant intrusion in a hallowed public space left untouched for centuries, Pei's pyramid, like Rogers and Piano's Pompidou Center (FIG. 25-49) a decade before, quickly captured the French public's imagination and admiration.

There are, in fact, four Louvre glass pyramids: the grand central pyramid plus the three small echoes of it bordering the large fountain-filled pool surrounding the glass entryway. Consistent with postmodern aesthetics, Pei turned to the past for inspiration, choosing the quintessential emblem of ancient Egypt (FIG. 3-7), an appropriate choice given the Louvre's rich collection of Egyptian art. But Pei transformed his ancient solid stone models (see "Building the Great Pyramids," Chapter 3, page 62) into a transparent "tent," simultaneously permitting an almost uninterrupted view of the wings of the royal palace courtyard and serving as a skylight for the new underground network of ticket booths, offices, shops, restaurants, and conference rooms he also designed.

Environmental and Site-Specific Art

When Robert Smithson created *Spiral Jetty* (FIG. 25-50) in Utah's Great Salt Lake in 1970, he was a trailblazer in the new genre of Environmental Art, or earthworks. In recent decades, earthworks

26-35 ZAHA HADID, Vitra Fire Station (looking east), Weil-am-Rhein, Germany, 1989–1993.

Inspired by Suprematism, Hadid employed dynamically arranged, unadorned planes for the Vitra Fire Station. The design suggests the burst of energy of firefighters racing out to extinguish a blaze.

ZAHA HADID One of the most innovative living architects is Iraqi Deconstructivist ZAHA HADID (b. 1950). Born in Baghdad, Hadid studied mathematics in Beirut, Lebanon, and architecture in London and has designed buildings in England, Germany, Austria, France, Italy, Spain, and the United States. Deeply influenced by the Suprematist theories and paintings of Kazimir Malevich (FIG. 24-30), who championed the use of pure colors and abstract geometric shapes to express "the supremacy of pure feeling in creative art," Hadid employs unadorned planes in dynamic arrangements that

26-36 IEOH MING PEI, Grand Louvre Pyramide (looking southwest), Musée du Louvre, Paris, France, 1988.

Egyptian stone architecture inspired Pei's postmodern entryway to the Louvre, but his glass-and-steel pyramid is a transparent tent serving as a skylight for the underground extension of the old museum.

Maya Lin's Vietnam Veterans Memorial

Maya Lin's design for the Vietnam Veterans Memorial (FIG. 26-37) is, like Minimalist sculptures (FIGS. 25-17 and 25-18), an unadorned geometric form. Yet the monument, despite its serene simplicity, actively engages viewers in a psychological dialogue, rather than standing mute. This dialogue gives visitors the opportunity to explore their feelings about the Vietnam War and perhaps arrive at some sense of closure.

The history of the Vietnam Veterans Memorial provides dramatic testimony to this monument's power. In 1981, a jury of architects, sculptors, and landscape architects selected Lin's design from among 1,400 entries in a blind competition for a memorial to be placed in Constitution Gardens in Washington, D.C. Conceivably, the jury not only found her design compelling but also thought its simplicity would be the least likely to provoke controversy. But when the jury made its selection public, heated debate ensued. Even the wall's color came under attack. One veteran charged that black is "the universal color of shame, sorrow and degradation in all races, all societies worldwide."* But the sharpest protests concerned the form and siting of the monument. Because of the stark contrast between the massive white memorials (the Washington Monument and the Lincoln Memorial) bracketing Lin's sunken wall, some people interpreted her Minimalist design as minimizing the Vietnam War and, by extension, the efforts of those who fought in the conflict. Lin herself, however, described the wall as follows:

> The Vietnam Veterans Memorial is not an object inserted into the earth but a work formed from the act of cutting open the earth and polishing the earth's surface—dematerializing the stone to pare surface, creating an interface between the world of the light and the quieter world beyond the names.†

Due to the vocal opposition, a compromise was necessary to ensure the memorial's completion. The Commission of Fine Arts, the federal group overseeing the project, commissioned an additional memorial from artist Frederick Hart (1943–1999) in 1983. This larger-than-life-size realistic bronze sculpture of three soldiers,

26-37 MAYA YING LIN, Vietnam Veterans Memorial (looking north), Washington, D.C., 1981–1983.

Like Minimalist sculpture, Lin's memorial to veterans of the Vietnam War is a simple geometric form. Its inscribed polished walls actively engage viewers in a psychological dialogue about the war.

armed and uniformed, now stands approximately 120 feet from Lin's wall. Several years later, a group of nurses, organized as the Vietnam Women's Memorial Project, received approval for a sculpture honoring women's service in the Vietnam War. The seven-foot-tall bronze statue by Glenna Goodacre (b. 1939) depicts three female figures, one cradling a wounded soldier in her arms. Unveiled in 1993, the work occupies a site about 300 feet south of the Lin memorial.

Whether celebrated or condemned, Lin's Vietnam Veterans Memorial generates dramatic responses. Commonly, visitors react very emotionally, even those who know none of the soldiers named on the monument. The polished granite surface prompts individual soul-searching—viewers see themselves reflected among the names. Many visitors leave mementos at the foot of the wall in memory of loved ones they lost in the Vietnam War or make rubbings from the incised names. It can be argued that much of this memorial's power derives from its Minimalist simplicity. Like Minimalist sculpture, it does not dictate response and therefore successfully encourages personal exploration.

*Elizabeth Hess, "A Tale of Two Memorials," *Art in America* 71, no. 4 (April 1983): 122.
†Excerpt from an unpublished 1995 lecture, quoted in Kristine Stiles and Peter Selz, *Theories and Documents of Contemporary Art: A Sourcebook of Artists' Writings* (Berkeley and Los Angeles: University of California Press, 1996), 525.

and other site-specific artworks that bridge the gap between architecture and sculpture have become an established mode of artistic expression. As is true of all other media in the postmodern era, these artworks take a dazzling variety of forms—and some of them have engendered heated controversies.

MAYA YING LIN Variously classified as either a work of Minimalist sculpture or architecture is the Vietnam Veterans Memorial (FIG. 26-37) in Washington, D.C., designed in 1981 by MAYA YING LIN

(b. 1959) when she was a 16-year-old student at the Yale School of Architecture. The austere, simple memorial, a V-shaped wall constructed of polished black granite panels, begins at ground level at each end and gradually ascends to a height of 10 feet at the center of the V. Each wing is 246 feet long. Lin set the wall into the landscape, enhancing visitors' awareness of descent as they walk along the wall toward the center. The names of the Vietnam War's 57,939 American casualties (and those missing in action) incised on the memorial's walls, in the order of their deaths, contribute to the monument's dramatic effect.

Architecture and Site-Specific Art　**853**

26-38 RACHEL WHITEREAD, *Holocaust Memorial* (looking northwest), Judenplatz, Vienna, Austria, 2000.

Whiteread's monument to the 65,000 Austrian Jews who perished in the Holocaust is a tomblike concrete block with doors that cannot be opened and library books seen from behind.

When Lin designed this pristinely simple monument, she gave a great deal of thought to the purpose of war memorials. Her conclusion was a memorial

> should be honest about the reality of war and be for the people who gave their lives. . . . [I] didn't want a static object that people would just look at, but something they could relate to as on a journey, or passage, that would bring each to his own conclusions. . . . I wanted to work with the land and not dominate it. I had an impulse to cut open the earth . . . an initial violence that in time would heal. The grass would grow back, but the cut would remain.[6]

In light of the tragedy of the war, this unpretentious memorial's allusion to a wound and long-lasting scar contributes to its communicative ability (see "Maya Lin's Vietnam Veterans Memorial," page 853).

RACHEL WHITEREAD Another controversial memorial commissioned for a specific historical setting is the Viennese Holocaust Memorial by British sculptor RACHEL WHITEREAD (b. 1963). In 1996, the city of Vienna chose Whiteread as the winner of the competition to design a commemorative monument to the 65,000 Austrian Jews who perished at the hands of the Nazis during World War II (FIG. **26-38**). The decision to focus attention on a past most Austrians wished to forget unleashed a controversy that delayed construction of the monument until 2000. Also controversial was the Minimalist severity of Whiteread's massive block of concrete planted in a Baroque square at the heart of the Austrian capital—as was, at least initially, the understated form of Lin's Vietnam monument (FIG. **26-37**) juxtaposed with the Washington and Lincoln Monuments in Washington, D.C.

Whiteread modulated the surface of the Holocaust memorial only slightly by depicting in low relief the shapes of two doors and hundreds of identical books on shelves, with the edges of the covers and the pages rather than the spines facing outward. The book motif was a reference both to Jews as the "People of the Book" and to the book burnings that accompanied Jewish persecutions throughout the centuries and under the Nazis. Around the base, Whiteread inscribed the names of Nazi concentration camps in German, Hebrew, and English. The setting for the memorial is Judenplatz (Jewish Square), the site of a synagogue destroyed in 1421. The brutality of the tomblike monument—it cannot be entered, and its shape suggests a prison block—was a visual as well as psychological shock in the beautiful Viennese square. Whiteread's purpose, however, was not to please but to create a memorial that met the jury's charge to "combine dignity with reserve and spark an aesthetic dialogue with the past in a place that is replete with history."

Whiteread had gained fame in 1992 for her monument commemorating the demolition of a working-class neighborhood in East London. *House* took the form of a concrete cast of the space inside the last standing Victorian house on the site. She had also made sculptures of "negative spaces," for example, the space beneath a chair or mattress or sink. In Vienna, she represented the space behind the shelves of a library. In drawing viewers' attention to the voids between and inside objects and buildings, Whiteread pursued in a different way the same goal as Pop Art innovator Jasper Johns (FIG. 25-22), who painted things "seen but not looked at."

RICHARD SERRA Also unleashing an emotional public debate, but for different reasons and with a decidedly different outcome, was *Tilted Arc* (FIG. **26-39**) by San Franciscan RICHARD SERRA (b. 1939), who worked in steel mills in California before studying art at Yale. He now lives in New York, where he received a commission in 1979 from the General Services Administration (GSA), the federal agency responsible for overseeing the selection and installation of artworks for government buildings, to install a 115-foot-long, 12-foot-high curved wall of Cor-Ten steel in the plaza in front of the Jacob K. Javits Federal Building in lower Manhattan. He completed the project in 1981. Serra wished *Tilted Arc* to "dislocate or alter the decorative function of the plaza and actively

Richard Serra's *Tilted Arc*

When Richard Serra installed *Tilted Arc* (FIG. 26-39) in the plaza in front of the Javits Federal Building in New York City in 1981, much of the public immediately responded with hostile criticism. Prompting the chorus of complaints was the uncompromising presence of a Minimalist sculpture bisecting the plaza. Many argued *Tilted Arc* was ugly, attracted graffiti, interfered with the view across the plaza, and prevented use of the plaza for performances or concerts. Due to the sustained barrage of protests and petitions demanding the removal of *Tilted Arc,* the General Services Administration, which had commissioned the sculpture, held a series of public hearings. Afterward, the agency decided to remove Serra's sculpture despite its prior approval of the artist's model. This, understandably, infuriated Serra, who had a legally binding contract acknowledging the site-specific nature of *Tilted Arc.* "To remove the work is to destroy the work," the artist stated.*

This episode raised intriguing issues about the nature of public art, including the public reception of experimental art, the artist's responsibilities and rights when executing public commissions, censorship in the arts, and the purpose of public art. If an artwork is on display in a public space outside the relatively private confines of a museum or gallery, do different guidelines apply? As one participant in the *Tilted Arc* saga asked, "Should an artist have the right to impose his values and taste on a public that now rejects his taste and values?"† One of the express functions of the historical avant-garde was to challenge convention by rejecting tradition and disrupting the complacency of the viewer. Will placing experimental art in a public place always cause controversy? From Serra's statements, it is clear he intended the sculpture to challenge the public.

Another issue *Tilted Arc* presented involved the rights of the artist, who in this case accused the GSA of censorship. Serra filed a lawsuit against the federal government for infringement of his First Amendment rights and insisted "the artist's work must be uncensored, respected, and tolerated, although deemed abhorrent, or perceived as challenging, or experienced as threatening."‡ Did removal of the work constitute censorship? A U.S. district court held it did not.

Ultimately, who should decide what artworks are appropriate for the public arena? One artist argued, "We cannot have public art by plebiscite [popular vote]."§ But to avoid recurrences of the *Tilted Arc* controversy, the GSA changed its procedures and now solicits input from a wide range of civic and neighborhood groups before commissioning public artworks. Despite the removal of *Tilted Arc* (now languishing in storage), the sculpture maintains a powerful presence in all discussions of the aesthetics, politics, and dynamics of public art.

*Grace Glueck, "What Part Should the Public Play in Choosing Public Art?" *New York Times,* February 3, 1985, 27.
†Calvin Tomkins, "The Art World: Tilted Arc," *New Yorker,* May 20, 1985, 98.
‡Ibid., 98–99.
§Ibid., 98.

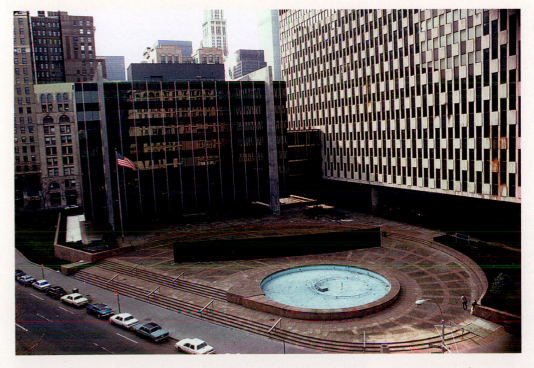

26-39 RICHARD SERRA, *Tilted Arc,* Jacob K. Javits Federal Plaza, New York City, 1981.

Serra intended his Minimalist *Tilted Arc* to alter the character of an existing public space. He succeeded but unleashed a storm of protest that caused the government to remove the work.

bring people into the sculpture's context."[7] In pursuit of that goal, Serra situated the sculpture so that it bisected and consequently significantly altered the space of the open plaza and interrupted the traffic flow across the square. By creating such a monumental presence in this large public space, Serra succeeded in forcing viewers to reconsider the plaza's physical space as a sculptural form—but only temporarily, because the public forced the sculpture to be removed (see "Richard Serra's *Tilted Arc,*" above).

26-40 CHRISTO and JEANNE-CLAUDE, *Surrounded Islands, Biscayne Bay, Miami, Florida, 1980–1983.* ◼◁

Christo and Jeanne-Claude created this Environmental artwork by surrounding 11 small islands with 6.5 million square feet of pink fabric. Characteristically, the work existed for only two weeks.

CHRISTO AND JEANNE-CLAUDE The most famous Environmental artists of the past few decades are CHRISTO (b. 1935) and his deceased spouse JEANNE-CLAUDE (1935–2009). In their works they sought to intensify the viewer's awareness of the space and features of rural and urban sites. However, rather than physically alter the land itself, as Robert Smithson (FIG. 25-50) often did, Christo and Jeanne-Claude prompted this awareness by temporarily modifying the landscape with cloth. Christo studied art in his native Bulgaria and in Austria. After moving from Vienna to Paris, he began to encase objects in clumsy wrappings, thereby appropriating bits of the real world into the mysterious world of the unopened package whose contents can be dimly seen in silhouette under the wrap.

Starting in 1961, Christo and Jeanne-Claude began to collaborate on large-scale projects normally dealing with the environment itself. For example, in 1969 the couple wrapped more than a million square feet of Australian coastline and in 1972 hung a vast curtain across a valley at Rifle Gap, Colorado. Their projects require years of preparation and research, and scores of meetings with local authorities and interested groups of local citizens. These temporary artworks are usually on view for only a few weeks.

Surrounded Islands, Biscayne Bay, Miami, Florida, 1980–1983 (FIG. **26-40**), created in Biscayne Bay for two weeks in May 1983, typifies Christo and Jeanne-Claude's work. For this project, they surrounded 11 small artificial islands in the bay (previously created from a dredging project) with 6.5 million square feet of specially fabricated pink polypropylene floating fabric. This Environmental artwork required three years of preparation to obtain the required permits and to assemble the labor force and obtain the $3.2 million needed to complete the project. The artists raised the money by selling Christo's original preparatory drawings, collages, and models of works he created in the 1950s and 1960s. Huge crowds watched as crews removed accumulated trash from the 11 islands (to assure maximum contrast between their dark colors, the pink of the cloth, and the blue of the bay) and then unfurled the fabric "cocoons" to form magical floating "skirts" around each tiny bit of land. Despite the brevity of its existence, *Surrounded Islands* lives on in the host of photographs, films, and books documenting the project.

ANDY GOLDSWORTHY The most prominent heir today to the earthworks tradition of Robert Smithson is Environmental artist and photographer ANDY GOLDSWORTHY (b. 1956). Goldsworthy's medium is nature itself—stones, tree roots, leaves, flowers, ice. Because most of his works are ephemeral, the victims of tides, rainstorms, and the changing seasons, he records them in stunning color photographs that are artworks in their own right. Golds-

26-41 ANDY GOLDSWORTHY, *Cracked Rock Spiral*, St. Abbs, Scotland, 1985.

Goldsworthy's earthworks are "collaborations with nature." At St. Abbs, he split pebbles of different sizes in two, scratched white around the cracks using another stone, and then arranged them in a spiral.

26-42 KEITH HARING, *Tuttomondo,* Sant'Antonio (looking south), Pisa, Italy, 1989.

Haring burst onto the New York art scene as a subway graffito artist and quickly gained an international reputation. His Pisa mural features his signature cartoonlike characters and is a hymn to life.

and displayed a genius for marketing himself and his work. In 1986, he parlayed his popularity into a successful business by opening The Pop Shop in the SoHo (South of Houston Street) gallery district of lower Manhattan, where he sold posters, T-shirts, hats, and buttons featuring his universally appealing schematic human and animal figures, especially his two most popular motifs—a crawling baby surrounded by rays and a barking dog.

Haring's last major work was a commission to paint a huge mural at the church of Saint Anthony in Pisa, Italy, a confirmation of his international reputation. *Tuttomondo* (*Everybody*) encapsulates Haring's style (FIG. **26-42**)—bright single-color cavorting figures with black outlines against a matte background. The motifs include a winged man, a figure with a television head, a mother cradling a baby, and a dancing dog. It is a hymn to the joy of life (compare FIG. 24-2A). Haring died of AIDS the next year. He was 31 years old.

worthy's international reputation has led to commissions in his native England, Scotland (where he now lives), France, Australia, the United States, and Japan, where his work has much in common with the sculptures of Kimio Tsuchiya (FIG. 26-23). Goldsworthy seeks not to transform the landscape in his art but, in his words, to "collaborate with nature."

One of Goldsworthy's most beautiful "collaborations" is also a tribute to Robert Smithson and *Spiral Jetty* (FIG. 25-50). *Cracked Rock Spiral* (FIG. **26-41**), which he created at St. Abbs, Scotland, on June 1, 1985, consists of pebbles Goldsworthy split in two, scratched white around the cracks using another stone, and then arranged in a spiral that grows wider as it coils from its center.

GRAFFITI AND MURAL PAINTING Although generally considered a modern phenomenon, the concept of site-specific art is as old as the history of art. Indeed, the earliest known paintings are those covering the walls and ceilings of Paleolithic caves in southern France and northern Spain (see Chapter 1). A contemporary twist on the venerable art of mural painting is the graffiti and graffiti-inspired art of, among others, Jean-Michel Basquiat (FIG. 26-8) and KEITH HARING (1958–1990). Haring grew up in Kutztown, Pennsylvania, attended the School of Visual Arts in New York, and, as did Basquiat, burst onto the New York art scene as a graffiti artist in the city's subway system. The authorities would constantly remove his chalk figures, which he drew on blank black posters awaiting advertisers, and arrested Haring whenever they spotted him at work. However, Haring quickly gained a wide and appreciative audience for his linear cartoon-inspired fantasies, and began to sell paintings to avid collectors. Haring, like Andy Warhol (FIGS. 25-25 and 25-25A), was thoroughly in tune with pop culture

NEW MEDIA

In addition to taking the ancient arts of painting and sculpture in new directions, contemporary artists have continued to explore the expressive possibilities of the various new media developed in the postwar period, especially digital photography, computer graphics, and video.

ANDREAS GURSKY German photographer ANDREAS GURSKY (b. 1955) grew up in Düsseldorf, where his father was a commercial photographer. Andreas studied photography at Düsseldorf's Kunstakademie (Academy of Art) and since the mid-1990s has used computer and digital technology to produce gigantic color prints in which he combines and manipulates photographs taken with a wide-angle lens, usually from a high vantage point. The size of his photographs, sometimes almost a dozen feet wide, intentionally rivals 19th-century history paintings. But as was true of Gustave Courbet (FIGS. 22-26 and 22-27) in his day, Gursky's subjects come from everyday life. He records the mundane world of the modern global economy—vast industrial plants, major department stores, hotel lobbies, and stock and commodity exchanges—and transforms the commonplace into striking, almost abstract, compositions. (Compare the photographs of Edward Burtynsky, FIG. 26-19.)

1 ft.

26-43 ANDREAS GURSKY, *Chicago Board of Trade II*, 1999. C-print, 6′ 9½″ × 11′ 5⅝″. Matthew Marks Gallery, New York.

Gursky manipulates digital photographs to produce vast tableaus depicting characteristic places of the modern global economy. The size of his prints rivals 19th-century history paintings.

Gursky's enormous 1999 print (FIG. **26-43**) documenting the frenzied activity on the main floor of the Chicago Board of Trade is a characteristic example of his work. He took a series of photographs from a gallery, creating a panoramic view of the traders in their brightly colored jackets. He then combined several digital images using commercial photo-editing software to produce a blurred tableau of bodies, desks, computer terminals, and strewn paper in which both mass and color are so evenly distributed as to negate the traditional Renaissance notion of perspective. In using the computer to modify the "objective truth" and spatial recession of "straight photography," Gursky blurs the distinction between painting and photography.

JENNY HOLZER Gallipolis, Ohio, native JENNY HOLZER (b. 1950) studied art at Ohio University and the Rhode Island School of Design. In 1990, she became the first woman to represent the United States at the prestigious Venice Biennale art exhibition. Holzer has won renown for several series of artworks using electronic signs, most involving light-emitting diode (LED) technology, and has created light-projection shows worldwide. In 1989, she assembled a major installation at the Solomon R. Guggenheim Museum in New York that included elements from her previous series and consisted of a large continuous LED display spiraling around the interior ramp (FIG. **26-44**) of Frank Lloyd Wright's landmark building (FIG. 25-39). Holzer believes in the communicative power of language, and her installation focused specifically on text. She invented sayings with an authoritative

10 ft.

26-44 JENNY HOLZER, *Untitled* (selections from *Truisms, Inflammatory Essays, The Living Series, The Survival Series, Under a Rock, Laments,* and *Child Text*), 1989. Extended helical tricolor LED electronic display signboard, 16′ × 162′ × 6′. Installation at the Solomon R. Guggenheim Museum, New York, December 1989–February 1990 (partial gift of the artist, 1989).

Holzer's 1989 installation consisted of electronic signs created using LED technology. The continuous display of texts wound around the Guggenheim Museum's spiral interior ramp.

tone for her LED displays—for example, "Protect me from what I want," "Abuse of power comes as no surprise," and "Romantic love was invented to manipulate women." The statements, which people could read from a distance, were intentionally vague and, in some cases, contradictory.

ADRIAN PIPER Video artists, like other artists, pursue diverse goals. ADRIAN PIPER (b. 1948) has used video art to effect social change—in particular, to combat pervasive racism. Born in New York City, she studied art at the School of Visual Arts and philosophy at the City College of New York but now lives in Berlin, Germany. Her videos, such as the installation *Cornered* (FIG. **26-45**), are provocative and confrontational. *Cornered* included a video monitor placed behind an overturned table. Piper appeared on the video monitor, literally cornered behind the table, as she spoke to viewers. Her comments sprang from her experiences as a light-skinned African American woman and from her belief that although overt racism had diminished, subtle and equally damaging forms of bigotry were still rampant. "I'm black," she announces on the 16-minute videotape. "Now let's deal with this social fact and the fact of my stating it together. . . . If you feel that my letting people know that I'm not white is making an unnecessary fuss, you must feel that the right and proper course of action for me to take is to pass for white. Now this kind of thinking presupposes a belief that it's inherently better to be identified as white," she continues. The directness of Piper's art forces viewers to examine their own behaviors and values.

BILL VIOLA For much of his artistic career, BILL VIOLA (b. 1951) has also explored the capabilities of digitized imagery, producing many video installations and single-channel works. Often focusing on sensory perception, the pieces not only heighten viewer awareness of the senses but also suggest an exploration into the spiritual realm. Viola, who majored in art and music at Syracuse University, spent years after graduating seriously studying Buddhist, Chris-

1 ft.

26-46 BILL VIOLA, *The Crossing*, 1996. Video/sound installation with two channels of color video projection onto screens 16′ high. ◼◀

Viola's video projects use extreme slow motion, contrasts in scale, shifts in focus, mirrored reflections, and staccato editing to create dramatic sensory experiences rooted in tangible reality.

26-45 ADRIAN PIPER, *Cornered*, 1988. Mixed-media installation of variable size; video monitor, table, and birth certificates. Museum of Contemporary Art, Chicago. ◼◀

In this installation, Piper, a light-skinned African American, appeared on a video monitor, "cornered" behind an overturned table, and made provocative comments about racism and bigotry.

tian, Sufi, and Zen mysticism. Because he fervently believes in art's transformative power and in a spiritual view of human nature, Viola designs works encouraging spectator introspection. His video projects have involved using techniques such as extreme slow motion, contrasts in scale, shifts in focus, mirrored reflections, staccato editing, and multiple or layered screens to achieve dramatic effects.

The power of Viola's work is evident in *The Crossing* (FIG. **26-46**), an installation piece involving two color video channels projected on 16-foot-high screens. The artist either shows the two projections on the front and back of the same screen or on two separate screens in the same installation. In these two companion videos, shown simultaneously on the two screens, a man surrounded in darkness appears, moving closer until he fills the screen. On one screen, drops of water fall from above onto the man's head, while on the other screen, a small fire breaks out at the man's feet. Over the next few minutes, the water and fire increase in intensity until the man disappears in a torrent of water on one screen (FIG. 26-46) and flames consume the man on the other screen. The deafening roar of a raging fire and a torrential downpour accompany these visual images. Eventually, everything subsides and fades into darkness. This installation's elemental nature and its presentation in a dark space immerse viewers in a pure sensory experience very much rooted in tangible reality.

1 in. ⌶

26-47 TONY OURSLER, *Mansheshe*, 1997. Ceramic, glass, video player, videocassette, CPJ-200 video projector, sound, 11″ × 7″ × 8″ each. Courtesy of the artist and Metro Pictures, New York.

Video artist Oursler projects his digital images onto sculptural objects, insinuating them into the "real" world. Here, he projected talking heads onto egg-shaped forms suspended from poles.

26-48 MATTHEW BARNEY, *Cremaster* cycle, installation at the Solomon R. Guggenheim Museum, New York, 2003.

Barney's vast multimedia installations of drawings, photographs, sculptures, and videos typify the relaxation at the opening of the 21st century of the traditional boundaries among artistic media.

TONY OURSLER Whereas Viola, Piper, and other artists present video and digital imagery to their audiences on familiar flat screens, thus reproducing the format in which we most often come into contact with electronic images, New Yorker TONY OURSLER (b. 1957), who studied art at the California Institute of the Arts, manipulates his images, projecting them onto sculptural objects. This has the effect of taking the images out of the digital world and insinuating them into the "real" world. Accompanied by sound tapes, Oursler's installations, such as *Mansheshe* (FIG. **26-47**), not only engage but often challenge the viewer. In this example, Oursler projected talking heads onto egg-shaped forms suspended from poles. Because the projected images of people look directly at the viewer, the statements they make about religious beliefs, sexual identity, and interpersonal relationships cannot be easily dismissed.

MATTHEW BARNEY A major trend in the art world today is the relaxation of the traditional boundaries between artistic media. In fact, many contemporary artists are creating vast and complex multimedia installations combining new and traditional media. One of these artists is MATTHEW BARNEY (b. 1967), who studied art at Yale University. The 2003 installation (FIG. **26-48**) of his epic *Cremaster* cycle (1994–2002) at the Solomon R. Guggenheim Museum in New York typifies the expansive scale of many contemporary works. A multimedia extravaganza involving drawings, photographs, sculptures, videos, films, and performances (presented in videos), the *Cremaster* cycle is a lengthy narrative set in a self-enclosed universe Barney created. The title of the work refers to the cremaster muscle, which controls testicular contractions in response to external stimuli. Barney uses the development of this muscle in the embryonic process of sexual differentiation as the conceptual springboard for the entire *Cremaster* project, in which he explores the notion of creation in expansive and complicated ways. The cycle's narrative, revealed in the five 35-millimeter feature-length films and the artworks, makes reference to, among other things, a musical revue in Boise, Idaho (where San Francisco–born Barney grew up), the life cycle of bees, the execution of convicted murderer Gary Gilmore, the construction of the Chrysler Building (FIG. 24-47), Celtic mythology, Masonic rituals, a motorcycle race, and a lyric opera set in late-19th-century Budapest. In the installation, Barney tied the artworks together conceptually by a five-channel video piece projected on screens hanging in the Guggenheim's rotunda. Immersion in Barney's constructed world is disorienting and overwhelming and has a force that competes with the immense scale and often frenzied pace of contemporary life.

WHAT NEXT? No one knows what the next years and decades will bring, but given the expansive scope of postmodernism, it is certain no single approach to or style of art will dominate. New technologies will undoubtedly continue to redefine what constitutes a "work of art." The universally expanding presence of computers, digital technology, and the Internet may well erode what few conceptual and geographical boundaries remain, and make art and information about art available to virtually everyone, thereby creating a truly global artistic community. As this chapter has revealed, substantial progress has already been made in that direction.

CONTEMPORARY ART WORLDWIDE

SOCIAL AND POLITICAL ART

Mapplethorpe, *Self-Portrait,* 1980

❚ Many contemporary artists use art to address pressing social and political issues and to define their personal identities.

❚ Gender and sexuality are central themes in the work of Barbara Kruger, the Guerrilla Girls, David Wojnarowicz, Robert Mapplethorpe, and Shahzia Sikander. Faith Ringgold, Lorna Simpson, Carrie Mae Weems, Melvin Edwards, Jean-Michel Basquiat, and Kehinde Wiley address issues of concern to African Americans. Jaune Quick-to-See Smith focuses on Native American heritage, Chris Ofili and Trigo Piula on their African roots, and Cliff Whiting on traditional Maori themes.

❚ Other artists have treated political and economic issues: Willie Bester, apartheid in South Africa; David Hammons, racial discrimination; Leon Golub, violence; Shirin Neshat, the challenges facing Muslim women; Krzystof Wodiczko, the plight of the homeless; and Edward Burtynsky, industrial pollution.

Basquiat, *Horn Players,* 1983

OTHER MOVEMENTS AND THEMES

❚ Contemporary art encompasses a phenomenal variety of styles ranging from abstraction to brutal realism, both in America and worldwide.

❚ Leading abstract painters and sculptors include Julian Schnabel and Tara Donovan in the United States, Anselm Kiefer in Germany, Emily Kame Kngwarreye in Australia, and Wu Guanzhong, Song Su-nam, and Kimio Tsuchiya in China, Korea, and Japan, respectively.

❚ Among today's best-known figural painters and sculptors are Kiki Smith, Jeff Koons, and Venezuelan Marisol in the United States, and expatriate Englishwoman Jenny Saville in Italy.

Smith, *Untitled,* 1990

ARCHITECTURE AND SITE-SPECIFIC ART

❚ Postmodern architecture is as diverse as contemporary painting and sculpture. Leading Hi-Tech architects include Norman Foster and Renzo Piano. Among the major champions of Deconstructivism are Günter Behnisch, Frank Gehry, Daniel Libeskind, and Zaha Hadid.

❚ The monuments designed by Maya Lin, Rachel Whiteread, and Richard Serra bridge the gap between architecture and sculpture, as do the Environmental artworks of Christo and Jean-Claude and of Andy Goldsworthy.

Hadid, Vitra Fire Station, 1989–1993

NEW MEDIA

❚ Many contemporary artists have harnessed new technologies in their artistic production: Andreas Gursky, digital photography; Jenny Holzer, LED displays; Adrian Piper, Bill Viola, and Tony Oursler, video; and Matthew Barney, complex multimedia installations.

Oursler, *Mansheshe,* 1997

NOTES

Introduction

1. Quoted in George Heard Hamilton, *Painting and Sculpture in Europe, 1880–1940,* 6th ed. (New Haven, Conn.: Yale University Press, 1993), 345.
2. Quoted in *Josef Albers: Homage to the Square* (New York: Museum of Modern Art, 1964), n.p.

Chapter 15

1. Francisco de Hollanda, *De pintura antigua* (1548), quoted in Robert Klein and Henri Zerner, *Italian Art, 1500–1600: Sources and Documents* (Englewood Cliffs, N.J.: Prentice-Hall, 1966), 33.

Chapter 16

1. Ghiberti, *I commentarii,* II. Quoted in Elizabeth Gilmore Holt, ed., *A Documentary History of Art, I: The Middle Ages and the Renaissance* (Princeton, N.J.: Princeton University Press, 1981), 157–158.
2. Translated by Catherine Enggass, in Howard Saalman, ed., *Antonio Manetti, Life of Brunelleschi* (University Park: Pennsylvania State University Press, 1970), 42.
3. Giorgio Vasari, *Life of Lorenzo Ghiberti.* Translated by Gaston du C. de Vere, ed., *Giorgio Vasari, Lives of the Painters, Sculptors, and Architects* (New York: Knopf, 1996), 1: 304.
4. Ghiberti, *I commentarii,* II. Quoted in Holt, 161.
5. Quoted in H. W. Janson, *The Sculpture of Donatello* (Princeton, N.J.: Princeton University Press, 1965), 154.
6. Vasari, *Life of Masaccio.* Translated by Gaston du C. de Vere, 1: 318.
7. Martial, *Epigrams,* 10.32.

Chapter 17

1. Plato, *Ion,* 534. Translated by Benjamin Jowett, *The Dialogues of Plato,* 4th ed., vol. 1 (Oxford: Clarendon Press, 1953), 107–108.
2. Da Vinci to Ludovico Sforza, ca. 1480–1481. In Elizabeth Gilmore Holt, ed., *A Documentary History of Art* (Princeton: Princeton University Press, 1981), I: 274–275.
3. Quoted in Anthony Blunt, *Artistic Theory in Italy,* 1450–1600 (London: Oxford University Press, 1964), 34.
4. Quoted in James M. Saslow, *The Poetry of Michelangelo: An Annotated Translation* (New Haven, Conn.: Yale University Press, 1991), 407.
5. Giorgio Vasari, *Lives of the Painters, Sculptors, and Architects.* Translated by Gaston du C. de Vere (New York: Knopf, 1996), 2: 736.
6. Quoted in A. Richard Turner, *Renaissance Florence: The Invention of a New Art* (New York: Abrams, 1997), 163.
7. Quoted in Bruce Boucher, *Andrea Palladio: The Architect in His Time* (New York: Abbeville Press, 1998), 229.
8. Quoted in Robert J. Clements, *Michelangelo's Theory of Art* (New York: New York University Press, 1961), 320.

Chapter 18

1. Translated by Erwin Panofsky, in Wolfgang Stechow, *Northern Renaissance Art 1400–1600: Sources and Documents* (Evanston, Ill.: Northwestern University Press, 1989), 123.
2. Translated by Bernhard Erling, in Stechow, 129–130.
3. Giorgio Vasari, *Lives of the Painters, Sculptors, and Architects.* Translated by Gaston du C. de Vere (New York: Knopf, 1996), 2: 863.

Chapter 19

1. Filippo Baldinucci, *Vita del Cavaliere Giovanni Lorenzo Bernini* (1681). Translated by Robert Enggass, in Enggass and Jonathan Brown, *Italian and Spanish Art 1600–1750: Sources and Documents* (Evanston, Ill.: Northwestern University Press, 1992), 116.
2. John Milton, *Il Penseroso* (1631, published 1645), 166.

Chapter 20

1. Quoted in Julie Berger Hochstrasser, *Still Life and Trade in the Dutch Golden Age* (New Haven, Conn.: Yale University Press, 2007), 16.
2. Translated by Kristin Lohse Belkin, *Rubens* (London: Phaidon, 1998), 47.
3. Albert Blankert, *Johannes Vermeer van Delft 1632–1675* (Utrecht: Spectrum, 1975), 133, no. 51. Translated by Bob Haak, *The Golden Age: Dutch Painters of the Seventeenth Century* (New York: Abrams, 1984), 450.

Chapter 21

1. Translated by Robert Goldwater and Marco Treves, eds., *Artists on Art,* 3d ed. (New York: Pantheon Books, 1958), 157.
2. Quoted in Thomas A. Bailey, *The American Pageant: A History of the Republic,* 2d ed. (Boston: Heath, 1961), 280.
3. Translated by Elfriede Heyer and Roger C. Norton, in Charles Harrison, Paul Wood, and Jason Gaiger, eds., *Art in Theory 1648–1815: An Anthology of Changing Ideas* (Oxford: Blackwell, 2000), 451–453.

Chapter 22

1. Théophile Gautier, *Histoire de Romantisme* (Paris: Charpentier, 1874), 204.
2. Quoted in Helmut Borsch-Supan, *Caspar David Friedrich* (New York: Braziller, 1974), 7.
3. Translated by Jason Gaiger, in Charles Harrison, Paul Wood, and Jason Gaiger, eds., *Art in Theory 1815–1900: An Anthology of Changing Ideas* (Oxford: Blackwell, 1998), 54.
4. Quoted by Brian Lukacher, in Stephen F. Eisenman, ed., *Nineteenth Century Art: A Critical History* (New York: Thames & Hudson, 2007), 126.
5. Quoted in John W. McCoubrey, *American Art 1700–1960: Sources and Documents* (Upper Saddle River, N.J.: Prentice Hall, 1965), 98.
6. Quoted in Thomas A. Bailey, *The American Pageant: A History of the Republic,* 2d ed. (Boston: Heath, 1961), 280.
7. Quoted in Linda Nochlin, *Realism and Tradition in Art 1848–1900* (Upper Saddle River, N.J.: Prentice Hall, 1966), 42.
8. Quoted in George Heard Hamilton, *Manet and His Critics* (New Haven, Conn.: Yale University Press, 1954), 45.
9. Quoted in Eisenman, ed., *Nineteenth Century Art,* 336.
10. *New York Weekly Tribune,* September 30, 1865.
11. Quoted in Nikolai Cikovsky Jr. and Franklin Kelly, *Winslow Homer* (Washington, D.C.: National Gallery of Art, 1995), 26.

12. Quoted in Lloyd Goodrich, *Thomas Eakins, His Life and Work* (New York: Whitney Museum of American Art, 1933), 51–52.

13. Quoted in Nicholas Pevsner, *An Outline of European Architecture* (Baltimore: Penguin, 1960), 627.

14. Letter from Delaroche to François Arao, quoted in Helmut Gernsheim, *Creative Photography* (New York: Bonanza Books, 1962), 24.

15. Quoted in Naomi Rosenblum, *A World History of Photography*, 4th ed. (New York: Abbeville Press, 2007), 69.

16. Quoted in Kenneth MacGowan, *Behind the Screen* (New York: Delta, 1965), 49.

Chapter 23

1. Quoted in Linda Nochlin, *Realism* (Harmondsworth: Penguin, 1971), 28.

2. Clement Greenberg, "Modernist Painting," *Art and Literature*, no. 4 (Spring 1965): 193–194.

3. Quoted in Linda Nochlin, *Impressionism and Post-Impressionism 1874–1904: Sources and Documents* (Englewood Cliffs, N.J.: Prentice Hall, 1966), 35.

4. Translated by Carola Hicks, in Charles Harrison, Paul Wood, and Jason Gaiger, *Art in Theory 1815–1900* (Oxford: Blackwell, 1998), 595.

5. Quoted in John McCoubrey, *American Art 1700–1960: Sources and Documents* (Englewood Cliffs, N.J.: Prentice Hall, 1965), 184.

6. Quoted in Robert Goldwater and Marco Treves, eds., *Artists on Art, from the XIV to the XX Century* (New York: Pantheon, 1945), 322.

7. Ibid., 375.

8. Vincent van Gogh to Theo van Gogh, September 1888, in J. van Gogh–Bonger and V. W. van Gogh, eds., *The Complete Letters of Vincent van Gogh* (Greenwich, Conn.: New York Graphic Society, 1979), 3: 534.

9. Vincent van Gogh to Theo van Gogh, July 16, 1888, in W. H. Auden, ed., *Van Gogh: A Self-Portrait. Letters Revealing His Life as a Painter* (New York: Dutton, 1963), 299.

10. Quoted in Sam Hunter, John Jacobus, and Daniel Wheeler, *Modern Art*, 3d ed. (Upper Saddle River, N.J.: Prentice Hall, 2004), 28.

11. Cézanne to Émile Bernard, March 1904. Quoted in Goldwater and Treves, *Artists on Art*, 363.

12. Cézanne to Émile Bernard, April 15, 1904. Ibid., 363.

13. Translated by Akane Kawakami, in Harrison, Wood, and Gaiger, *Art in Theory*, 1066.

14. Quoted in George Heard Hamilton, *Painting and Sculpture in Europe 1880–1940*, 6th ed. (New Haven, Conn.: Yale University Press, 1993), 124.

15. Quoted in V. Frisch and J. T. Shipley, *Auguste Rodin* (New York: Stokes, 1939), 203.

16. Quoted in Eileen Boris, *Art and Labor: Ruskin, Morris, and the Craftsman Ideal in America* (Philadelphia: Temple University Press, 1986), 7.

Chapter 24

1. Quoted in John Elderfield, *The "Wild Beasts": Fauvism and Its Affinities* (New York: Museum of Modern Art, 1976), 29.

2. Translated by Charles Harrison and Paul Wood, eds., *Art in Theory 1900–2000: An Anthology of Changing Ideas* (Oxford: Blackwell, 2003), 65.

3. Quoted in Frederick S. Levine, *The Apocalyptic Vision: The Art of Franz Marc as German Expressionism* (New York: Harper & Row, 1979), 57.

4. Quoted in Sam Hunter, John Jacobus, and Daniel Wheeler, *Modern Art*, rev. 3d ed. (Upper Saddle River, N.J.: Prentice Hall, 2004), 121.

5. Quoted in George Heard Hamilton, *Painting and Sculpture in Europe 1880–1940*, 6th ed. (New Haven, Conn.: Yale University Press, 1993), 246.

6. Ibid., 238.

7. Quoted in Edward Fry, ed., *Cubism* (London: Thames & Hudson, 1966), 112–113.

8. Quoted in Françoise Gilot and Carlton Lake, *Life with Picasso* (New York: McGraw-Hill, 1964), 77.

9. Pablo Picasso, "Statement to Simone Téry," in Harrison and Wood, eds., *Art in Theory 1900–2000*, 649.

10. Quoted in Roland Penrose, *Picasso: His Life and Work*, rev. ed. (New York: Harper & Row, 1971), 311.

11. Filippo Tommaso Marinetti, *The Foundation and Manifesto of Futurism* (*Le Figaro*, February 20, 1909). Translated by Joshua C. Taylor, in Herschel B. Chipp, *Theories of Modern Art: A Source Book by Artists and Critics* (Berkeley and Los Angeles: University of California Press, 1968), 284.

12. Ibid., 286.

13. Quoted in Robert Short, *Dada and Surrealism* (London: Octopus Books, 1980), 18.

14. Quoted in Robert Motherwell, ed., *The Dada Painters and Poets: An Anthology*, 2d ed. (Cambridge, Mass.: Belknap Press of Harvard University, 1989).

15. Hans Richter, *Dada: Art and Anti-Art* (London: Thames & Hudson, 1961), 64–65.

16. Ibid., 57.

17. Quoted in Arturo Schwarz, *The Complete Works of Marcel Duchamp* (London: Thames & Hudson, 1965), 466.

18. Translated by Howard Dearstyne, in Robert L. Herbert, *Modern Artists on Art*, 2d ed. (Mineola, N.Y.: Dover, 2000), 117.

19. Ibid., 124.

20. Translated by Herbert Read and Leslie Martin, quoted in Chipp, *Theories of Modern Art*, 325–330.

21. Quoted in Sam Hunter, *American Art of the 20th Century* (New York: Abrams, 1972), 30.

22. Ibid., 37.

23. Charles C. Eldredge, "The Arrival of European Modernism," *Art in America* 61 (July–August 1973): 35.

24. Quoted in Gail Stavitsky, "Reordering Reality: Precisionist Directions in American Art 1915–1941," in *Precisionism in America 1915–1941: Reordering Reality* (New York: Abrams, 1994), 12.

25. Quoted in Karen Tsujimoto, *Images of America: Precisionist Painting and Modern Photography* (Seattle: University of Washington Press, 1982), 70.

26. Dorothy Norman, *Alfred Stieglitz: An American Seer* (Millerton, N.Y.: Aperture, 1973), 9–10.

27. Ibid., 161.

28. Quoted in Vincent Scully Jr., *Frank Lloyd Wright* (New York: Braziller, 1960), 18.

29. Quoted in Edgar Kauffmann, ed., *Frank Lloyd Wright: An American Architect* (New York: Horizon, 1955), 205, 208.

30. Quoted in Matthias Eberle, *World War I and the Weimar Artists: Dix, Grosz, Beckmann, Schlemmer* (New Haven, Conn.: Yale University Press, 1985), 54.

31. Ibid., 22.

32. Ibid., 42.

33. Quoted in William S. Rubin, *Dada, Surrealism, and Their Heritage* (New York: Museum of Modern Art, 1968), 64.

34. Quoted in Hamilton, *Painting and Sculpture in Europe 1880–1940*, 6th ed. (New Haven, Conn.: Yale University Press, 1993), 392.

35. Quoted in Richter, *Dada*, 155.

36. Ibid., 159.

37. Quoted in Rubin, *Dada, Surrealism*, 111.

38. Quoted in Hunter, Jacobus, and Wheeler, *Modern Art*, 179.

39. Quoted in William S. Rubin, *Miró in the Collection of the Museum of Modern Art* (New York: Museum of Modern Art, 1973), 32.

40. Translated by Norbert Guterman, quoted in Chipp, *Theories of Modern Art*, 182–186.

41. Translated by Nicholas Bullock, quoted in Harrison and Wood, *Art in Theory 1900–2000*, 281.

42. Quoted in Kenneth Frampton, *Modern Architecture: A Critical History*, 4th ed. (New York: Thames & Hudson, 2007), 147.

43. Quoted in Michel Seuphor, *Piet Mondrian: Life and Work* (New York: Abrams, 1956), 117.

44. Piet Mondrian, *Plastic Art and Pure Plastic Art* (1937), quoted in Hamilton, *Painting and Sculpture*, 319.

45. Mondrian, *Plastic Art*, quoted in Chipp, *Theories of Modern Art*, 349.

46. Ibid., 350.

47. Quoted in H. H. Arnason and Peter Kalb, *History of Modern Art*, 5th ed. (Upper Saddle River, N.J.: Prentice Hall, 2004), 154.

48. Quoted in Herbert, *Modern Artists on Art*, 173.

49. Ibid., 177.

50. Quoted in Hans L. Jaffé, comp., *De Stijl* (New York: Abrams, 1971), 185–188.

51. Piet Mondrian, *Dialogue on the New Plastic* (1919). Translated by Harry Holzman and Martin S. James, in Harrison and Wood, *Art in Theory 1900–2000*, 285.

52. Quoted in Wayne Craven, *American Art: History and Culture* (Madison, Wis.: Brown & Benchmark, 2003), 403.

53. Quoted in Vivian Endicott Barnett, "Banned German Art: Reception and Institutional Support of Modern German Art in the United States, 1933–45," in

Stephanie Barron, *Exiles and Emigrés: The Flight of European Artists from Hitler* (Los Angeles: Los Angeles County Museum of Art, 1997), 283.

54. Quoted in Frances K. Pohl, *Ben Shahn: New Deal Artist in a Cold War Climate, 1947–1954* (Austin: University of Texas Press, 1989), 159.

55. Quoted in Henry Louis Gates Jr., "New Negroes, Migration, and Cultural Exchange," in Elizabeth Hutton Turner, ed., *Jacob Lawrence: The Migration Series* (Washington, D.C.: Phillips Collection, 1993), 20.

56. Wanda M. Corn, *Grant Wood: The Regionalist Vision* (New Haven, Conn.: Yale University Press, 1983), 131.

57. Quoted in Matthew Baigell, *A Concise History of American Painting and Sculpture* (New York: Harper & Row, 1984), 264.

58. Quoted in Milton Meltzer, *Dorothea Lange: A Photographer's Life* (New York: Farrar, Straus, Giroux, 1978), 133, 220.

59. Quoted in Philip Johnson, *Mies van der Rohe,* rev. ed. (New York: Museum of Modern Art, 1954), 200–201.

Chapter 25

1. Dawn Ades and Andrew Forge, *Francis Bacon* (London: Thames & Hudson, 1985), 8; and David Sylvester, *The Brutality of Fact: Interviews with Francis Bacon,* 3d ed. (London: Thames & Hudson, 1987), 182.

2. Clement Greenberg, "Toward a Newer *Laocoon,*" *Partisan Review* 7, no. 4 (July–August 1940): 305.

3. Clement Greenberg, "Sculpture in Our Time," *Arts Magazine* 32, no. 9 (June 1956): 22.

4. Marcus Rothko and Adolph Gottlieb, quoted in Edward Alden Jewell, "The Realm of Art: A New Platform and Other Matters: 'Globalism' Pops into View," *New York Times,* June 13, 1943, 9.

5. Reprinted in Harold Rosenberg, *The Tradition of the New* (New York: Horizon, 1959), 25.

6. Quoted in Thomas Hess, *Barnett Newman* (New York: Walker and Company, 1969), 51.

7. Quoted in John P. O'Neill, ed., *Barnett Newman: Selected Writings and Interviews* (New York: Knopf, 1990), 108.

8. Rothko and Gottlieb, "The Realm of Art," 9.

9. Quoted in Selden Rodman, *Conversations with Artists* (New York: Devin-Adair, 1957), 93–94.

10. Clement Greenberg, "Recentness of Sculpture," in Gregory Battcock, ed., *Minimal Art: A Critical Anthology* (New York: Dutton, 1968), 183–184.

11. Louise Nevelson, quoted in John Gordon, *Louise Nevelson* (New York: Praeger, 1967), 12.

12. Quoted in Deborah Wye, *Louise Bourgeois* (New York: Museum of Modern Art, 1982), 22.

13. Ibid., 25.

14. Quoted in Lucy Lippard, *Eva Hesse* (New York: New York University Press, 1976), 165.

15. Ibid., 56.

16. Quoted in Richard Francis, *Jasper Johns* (New York: Abbeville, 1984), 21.

17. Andy Warhol, *The Philosophy of Andy Warhol* (New York: Harcourt Brace Jovanovich, 1975), 100.

18. Quoted in Christine Lindey, *Superrealist Painting and Sculpture* (London: Orbis, 1980), 50.

19. Quoted in Sebastian Smee, *Lucian Freud: Beholding the Animal* (Cologne: Taschen, 2009), 61.

20. Ibid., 7

21. Lindey, *Superrealist Painting,* 130.

22. Quoted in Susanna Torruella Leval, "Recapturing History: The (Un)official Story in Contemporary Latin American Art," *Art Journal* 51, no. 4 (Winter 1992): 74.

23. Ibid.

24. Hannah Wilke, "Visual Prejudice," in *Hannah Wilke: A Retrospective* (Columbia: University of Missouri Press, 1989), 141.

25. Quoted in Mary Jane Jacob, *Magdalena Abakanowicz* (New York: Abbeville, 1982), 94.

26. Peter Blake, *Frank Lloyd Wright* (Harmondsworth: Penguin, 1960), 115.

27. Quoted in Nancy Holt, ed., *The Writings of Robert Smithson* (New York: New York University Press, 1975), 111.

28. Quoted in H. H. Arnason and Peter Kalb, *History of Modern Art,* 5th ed. (Upper Saddle River, N.J.: Prentice Hall, 2004), 489.

29. Quoted in Barbara Haskell, *Blam! The Explosion of Pop, Minimalism, and Performance 1958–1964* (New York: Whitney Museum of American Art), 53.

30. Quoted in Bruce McPherson, ed., *More Than "Meat Joy": Complete Performance Works and Selected Writings* (New Paltz, N.Y.: Documentext, 1979), 52.

31. Quoted in Caroline Tisdall, *Joseph Beuys* (New York: Thames & Hudson, 1979), 6.

32. Quoted in "Joseph Kosuth: Art as Idea as Idea," in Jeanne Siegel, ed., *Artwords: Discourse on the 60s and 70s* (Ann Arbor, Mich.: UMI Research Press, 1985), 221, 225.

33. Quoted in Brenda Richardson, *Bruce Nauman: Neons* (Baltimore: Baltimore Museum of Art, 1982), 20.

Chapter 26

1. Quoted in Arlene Hirschfelder, *Artists and Craftspeople* (New York: Facts on File, 1994), 115.

2. Quoted in Richard Marshall and Robert Mapplethorpe, *50 New York Artists* (San Francisco: Chronicle Books, 1986), 448–449.

3. Quoted in Junichi Shiota, *Kimio Tsuchiya, Sculpture 1984–1988* (Tokyo: Morris Gallery, 1988), 3.

4. Michelle Meagher, "Jenny Saville and a Feminist Aesthetics of Disgust," *Hypatia* 18.4 (Fall/Winter 2003), 23–41.

5. Quoted in Donald Hall, *Corporal Politics* (Cambridge: MIT List Visual Arts Center, 1993), 46.

6. Quoted in "Vietnam Memorial: America Remembers," *National Geographic* 167, no. 5 (May 1985): 557.

7. Quoted in Calvin Tomkins, "The Art World: *Tilted Arc,*" *New Yorker,* May 20, 1985, 100.

GLOSSARY

Note: Text page references are in parentheses. References to bonus image online essays are in *blue.*

a secco—Italian, "dried." See *fresco.* (491)

abstract—Non-representational; forms and colors arranged without reference to the depiction of an object. (5)

Abstract Expressionism—The first major American avant-garde movement, Abstract Expressionism emerged in New York City in the 1940s. The artists produced *abstract* paintings that expressed their state of mind and that they hoped would strike emotional chords in viewers. The movement developed along two lines: *gestural abstraction* and *chromatic abstraction.* (790)

action painting—Also called *gestural abstraction.* The kind of *Abstract Expressionism* practiced by Jackson Pollock, in which the emphasis was on the creation process, the artist's gesture in making art. Pollock poured liquid paint in linear webs on his canvases, which he laid out on the floor, thereby physically surrounding himself in the painting during its creation. (793)

additive light—Natural light, or sunlight, the sum of all the wavelengths of the visible *spectrum.* See also *subtractive light.* (7)

additive sculpture—A kind of sculpture *technique* in which materials (for example, clay) are built up or "added" to create form. (11)

aerial perspective—See *perspective.* (455)

airbrush—A tool that uses compressed air to spray paint onto a surface. (806)

aisle—The portion of a *basilica* flanking the *nave* and separated from it by a row of *columns* or *piers.* (xxx, 12)

alchemy—The study of seemingly magical changes, especially chemical changes. (533)

altarpiece—A panel, painted or sculpted, situated above and behind an altar. See also *retable.* (404)

ambulatory—A covered walkway, outdoors (as in a church *cloister*) or indoors; especially the passageway around the *apse* and the *choir* of a church. In Buddhist architecture, the passageway leading around the *stupa* in a *chaitya hall.* (xxx)

amphitheater—Greek, "double theater." A Roman building type resembling two Greek theaters put together. The Roman amphitheater featured a continuous elliptical *cavea* around a central *arena.* (401)

Analytic Cubism—The first phase of *Cubism,* developed jointly by Pablo Picasso and Georges Braque, in which the artists analyzed form from every possible vantage point to combine the various views into one pictorial whole. (735)

anamorphic image—A distorted image that must be viewed by some special means (such as a mirror) to be recognized. (544)

ancien régime—French, "old order." The term used to describe the political, social, and religious order in France before the Revolution at the end of the 18th century. (624)

apostle—Greek, "messenger." One of the 12 disciples of Jesus. (xxxiv)

apse—A recess, usually semicircular, in the wall of a building, commonly found at the east end of a church. (xxx, 413)

arcade—A series of *arches* supported by *piers* or *columns.* (413, 15-4A)

Arcadian (adj.)—In Renaissance and later art, depictions of an idyllic place of rural peace and simplicity. Derived from Arcadia, an ancient district of the central Peloponnesos in southern Greece. (513)

arch—A curved structural member that spans an opening and is generally composed of wedge-shaped blocks (*voussoirs*) that transmit the downward pressure laterally. See also *thrust.* (xxviii)

architrave—The *lintel* or lowest division of the *entablature;* also called the epistyle. (xxvi)

armature—The crossed, or diagonal, *arches* that form the skeletal framework of a *Gothic rib vault.* In sculpture, the framework for a clay form. (11)

arriccio—In *fresco* painting, the first layer of rough lime plaster applied to the wall. (408)

Art Deco—Descended from *Art Nouveau,* this movement of the 1920s and 1930s sought to upgrade industrial design as a "fine art" and to work new materials into decorative patterns that could be either machined or handcrafted. Characterized by streamlined, elongated, and symmetrical design. (759)

Art Nouveau—French, "new art." A late-19th- and early-20th-century art movement whose proponents tried to synthesize all the arts in an effort to create art based on natural forms that could be mass produced by technologies of the industrial age. The movement had other names in other countries: Jugendstil in Austria and Germany, Modernismo in Spain, and Floreale in Italy. (716)

assemblage—An artwork constructed from already existing objects. (802)

atmospheric perspective—See *perspective.* (455)

atrium—The central reception room of a Roman house that is partly open to the sky. Also the open, *colonnaded* court in front of and attached to a Christian *basilica.* (560)

attribute—(n.) The distinctive identifying aspect of a person, for example, an object held, an associated animal, or a mark on the body. (v.) To make an *attribution.* (5)

attribution—Assignment of a work to a maker or makers. (6)

automatism—In painting, the process of yielding oneself to instinctive motions of the hands after establishing a set of conditions (such as size of paper or medium) within which a work is to be created. (763)

avant-garde—French, "advance guard" (in a platoon). Late-19th- and 20th-century artists who emphasized innovation and challenged established convention in their work. Also used as an adjective. (724)

baldacchino—A canopy on *columns,* frequently built over an altar. The term derives from *baldacco.* (243, 561)

baldacco—Italian, "silk from Baghdad." See *baldacchino.* (561)

baldric—A sashlike belt worn over one shoulder and across the chest to support a sword. (19-28B)

Baroque—The traditional blanket designation for European art from 1600 to 1750. The stylistic term *Baroque,* which describes art that features dramatic theatricality and elaborate ornamentation in contrast to the simplicity and orderly rationality of *Renaissance* art, is most appropriately applied to Italian art of this period. The term derives from *barroco.* (558)

barrel vault—See *vault.* (xxviii, 585)

barroco—Portuguese, "irregularly shaped pearl." See *Baroque.* (558)

base—In ancient Greek architecture, the molded projecting lowest part of *Ionic* and *Corinthian* columns. (*Doric* columns do not have bases.) (xxvi)

basilica (adj. **basilican**)—In Roman architecture, a public building for legal and other civic proceedings, rectangular in plan with an entrance usually on a long side. In Christian architecture, a church somewhat resembling the Roman basilica, usually entered from one end and with an *apse* at the other. (xxx, 413, 471)

bas-relief—See *relief*. (12, 708)

batik—An Indonesian fabric-dyeing technique using melted wax to form patterns the dye cannot penetrate. (26-22B)

battlement—A low parapet at the top of a circuit wall in a fortification. (416)

Bauhaus—A *school* of architecture in Germany in the 1920s under the aegis of Walter Gropius, who emphasized the unity of art, architecture, and design. (772)

bay—The space between two columns, or one unit in the *nave arcade* of a church; also, the passageway in an *arcuated* gate. (411, 413)

Beaux-Arts—An architectural *style* of the late 19th and early 20th centuries in France. Based on ideas taught at the École des Beaux-Arts in Paris, the Beaux-Arts style incorporated *classical* principles, such as symmetry in design, and included extensive exterior ornamentation. (677)

belvedere—Italian, "beautiful view." A building or other structure with a view of a *landscape* or seascape. (511)

benday dots—Named after the newspaper printer Benjamin Day, the benday dot system involves the modulation of *colors* through the placement and size of colored dots. (804)

Biomorphic Surrealism—See *Surrealism*. (763)

bottega—An artist's studio-shop. (457)

braccia—Italian, "arm." A unit of measurement; 1 braccia equals 23 inches. (470)

breakfast piece—A *still life* that includes bread and fruit. (589)

breviary—A Christian religious book of selected daily prayers and Psalms. (312, 386, 438)

bucranium (pl. **bucrania**)—Latin, "bovine skull." A common motif in classical architectural ornament. (547, 1-16A)

buon fresco—See *fresco*. (408, 491)

burgher—A middle-class citizen. (23-32A)

burin—A pointed tool used for *engraving* or *incising*. (444)

caduceus—In ancient Greek mythology, a magical rod entwined with serpents, the attribute of Hermes (Roman, Mercury), the messenger of the gods. (447)

calotype—From the Greek *kalos*, "beautiful." A photographic process in which a positive image is made by shining light through a negative image onto a sheet of sensitized paper. (679, 680)

camera lucida—Latin, "lighted room." A device in which a small lens projects the image of an object downward onto a sheet of paper. (679)

camera obscura—Latin, "dark room." An ancestor of the modern camera in which a tiny pin-hole, acting as a lens, projects an image on a screen, the wall of a room, or the ground-glass wall of a box; used by artists in the 17th, 18th, and early 19th centuries as an aid in drawing from nature. (599)

campanile—A bell tower of a church, usually, but not always, freestanding. (416)

canon—A rule, for example, of proportion. The ancient Greeks considered beauty to be a matter of "correct" proportion and sought a canon of proportion, for the human figure and for buildings. The fifth-century BCE sculptor Polykleitos wrote the *Canon*, a treatise incorporating his formula for the perfectly proportioned statue. (10)

canonized—Declared a saint by the Catholic Church. (14-5A)

capital—The uppermost member of a *column*, serving as a transition from the *shaft* to the *lintel*. In *classical* architecture, the form of the capital varies with the *order*. (xxvi, 402)

capriccio—Italian, "originality." One of several terms used in Italian *Renaissance* literature to praise the originality and talent of artists. (492)

cartoon—In painting, a full-size preliminary drawing from which a painting is made. (408, 490)

carving—A *technique* of sculpture in which the artist cuts away material (for example, from a stone block) in order to create a *statue* or a *relief*. (11)

cassone (pl. **cassoni**)—A carved chest, often painted or gilded, popular in *Renaissance* Italy for the storing of household clothing. (519)

casting—A sculptural *technique* in which the artist pours liquid metal, plaster, clay, or another material into a *mold*. When the material dries, the sculptor removes the cast piece from the mold. (11)

cathedral—A bishop's church. The word derives from *cathedra*, referring to the bishop's chair. (412)

cella—The chamber at the center of an ancient temple; in a *classical* temple, the room (Greek, *naos*) in which the *cult statue* usually stood. (xxvi, 506)

central plan—See *plan*. (xxviii, 471)

chacmool—A *Mesoamerican* statuary type depicting a fallen warrior on his back with a receptacle on his chest for sacrificial offerings. (491, 771)

chaitya hall—A South Asian rock-cut temple hall having a votive *stupa* at one end. (429)

chancel arch—The arch separating the chancel (the *apse* or *choir*) or the *transept* from the *nave* of a basilica or church. (413)

chapter house—The meeting hall in a *monastery*. (473)

chartreuse—A Carthusian *monastery*. (425)

chasing—The engraving or embossing of metal. (561)

chasseur—French cavalry officer. (22-13A)

château (pl. **châteaux**)—French, "castle." A luxurious country residence for French royalty, developed from medieval castles. (545)

cherub—A chubby winged child angel. (440)

chiaroscuro—In drawing or painting, the treatment and use of light and dark, especially the gradations of light that produce the effect of *modeling*. (409)

chiaroscuro woodcut—A *woodcut* technique using two blocks of wood instead of one. The printmaker carves and inks one block in the usual way in order to produce a traditional black-and-white print. Then the artist cuts a second block consisting of broad highlights that can be inked in gray or color and printed over the first block's impression. (537)

choir—The space reserved for the clergy and singers in the church, usually east of the *transept* but, in some instances, extending into the *nave*. (12)

chromatic abstraction—A kind of *Abstract Expressionism* that focuses on the emotional resonance of color, as exemplified by the work of Barnett Newman and Mark Rothko. (791)

chronology—In art history, the dating of art objects and buildings. (2)

Cinquecento—Italian, "500," that is, the 1500s or 16th century. (487)

cire perdue—See *lost-wax process*. (561)

city-state—An independent, self-governing city. (406)

Classical—The art and culture of ancient Greece between 480 and 323 BCE. Lowercase *classical* refers more generally to Greco-Roman art and culture. (402)

clerestory—The *fenestrated* part of a building that rises above the roofs of the other parts. The oldest known clerestories are Egyptian. In Roman *basilicas* and medieval churches, clerestories are the windows that form the *nave*'s uppermost level below the timber ceiling or the *vaults*. (xxx, 413, 15-4A)

cloisonné—A decorative metalwork technique employing *cloisons;* also, decorative brickwork in later Byzantine architecture. (705)

cloister—A *monastery* courtyard, usually with covered walks or *ambulatories* along its sides. (464)

cluster pier—See *compound pier*. (14-12A)

collage—A composition made by combining on a flat surface various materials, such as newspaper, wallpaper, printed text and illustrations, photographs, and cloth. (8, 723, 738)

colonnade—A series or row of *columns*, usually spanned by *lintels*. (xxvi)

color—The value, or tonality, of a color is the degree of its lightness or darkness. The intensity, or saturation, of a color is its purity, its brightness or dullness. See also *primary colors, secondary colors,* and *complementary colors*. (7, 701)

color-field painting—A variant of *Post-Painterly Abstraction* in which artists sought to reduce painting to its physical essence by pouring diluted paint onto unprimed canvas and letting these pigments soak into the fabric, as exemplified by the work of Helen Frankenthaler and Morris Louis. (796)

colorito—Italian, "colored" or "painted." A term used to describe the application of paint.

Characteristic of the work of 16th-century Venetian artists who emphasized the application of paint as an important element of the creative process. Central Italian artists, in contrast, largely emphasized *disegno*—the careful design preparation based on preliminary drawing. (513)

colossal order—An architectural design in which the *columns* or *pilasters* are two or more stories tall. Also called a giant order. (482)

column—A vertical, weight-carrying architectural member, circular in cross-*section* and consisting of a *base* (sometimes omitted), a *shaft*, and a *capital*. (10, 402)

combines—The name American artist Robert Rauschenberg gave to his *assemblages* of painted passages and sculptural elements. (802)

commedia dell'arte—A traditional Italian comic play performed by actors and musicians. (24-19A)

complementary colors—Those pairs of *colors*, such as red and green, that together embrace the entire *spectrum*. The complement of one of the three *primary colors* is a mixture of the other two. (7, 701)

compline—The last prayer of the day in a *Book of Hours*. (438)

Composite capital—A capital combining *Ionic* volutes and *Corinthian* acanthus leaves, first used by the ancient Romans. (475, 16-36A)

composition—The way in which an artist organizes *forms* in an artwork, either by placing shapes on a flat surface or arranging forms in space. (7)

compound pier—A *pier* with a group, or cluster, of attached *shafts*, or *responds*, especially characteristic of *Gothic* architecture. (14-12A)

Conceptual Art—An American *avant-garde* art movement of the 1960s whose premise was that the "artfulness" of art lay in the artist's idea rather than its final expression. (824)

concrete—A building material invented by the Romans and consisting of various proportions of lime mortar, volcanic sand, water, and small stones. (xxviii)

condottiere (pl. **condottieri**)—An Italian mercenary general. (448)

confraternity—In Late Antiquity, an association of Christian families pooling funds to purchase property for burial. In late medieval Europe, an organization founded by laypersons who dedicated themselves to strict religious observances. (404)

connoisseur—An expert in *attributing* artworks to one artist rather than another. More generally, an expert on artistic *style*. (6)

Constructivism—An early-20th-century Russian art movement formulated by Naum Gabo, who built up his sculptures piece by piece in space instead of carving or *modeling* them. In this way the sculptor worked with "volume of mass" and "volume of space" as different materials. (748)

contour line—In art, a continuous line defining the outer shape of an object. (7)

contrapposto—The disposition of the human figure in which one part is turned in opposition to another part (usually hips and legs one way, shoulders and chest another), creating a counterpositioning of the body about its central axis. Sometimes called "weight shift" because the weight of the body tends to be thrown to one foot, creating tension on one side and relaxation on the other. (452)

corbel—A projecting wall member used as a support for some element in the superstructure. Also, *courses* of stone or brick in which each course projects beyond the one beneath it. Two such walls, meeting at the topmost course, create a corbeled *arch* or corbeled *vault*. (528)

Corinthian capital—A more ornate form than *Doric* or *Ionic*; it consists of a double row of acanthus leaves from which tendrils and flowers grow, wrapped around a bell-shaped *echinus*. Although this *capital* form is often cited as the distinguishing feature of the Corinthian *order*, no such order exists, in strict terms, but only this type of capital used in the *Ionic* order. (xxvi, 402, 475)

cornice—The projecting, crowning member of the *entablature* framing the *pediment*; also, any crowning projection. (xxvi, 474)

corona civica—Latin, "civic crown." A Roman honorary wreath worn on the head. (7)

covenant—In Judaism and Christianity, a binding agreement between God and humans. (449)

crossing—The space in a *cruciform* church formed by the intersection of the *nave* and the *transept*. (14-18A)

cross-hatching—See *hatching*. (443)

cross vault—See *vault*. (xxviii)

crossing square—The area in a church formed by the intersection (*crossing*) of a *nave* and a *transept* of equal width, often used as a standard *module* of interior proportion. (xxx, 471)

cruciform—Cross-shaped. (471)

Cubism—An early-20th-century art movement that rejected *naturalistic* depictions, preferring *compositions* of shapes and *forms* abstracted from the conventionally perceived world. See also *Analytic Cubism* and *Synthetic Cubism*. (735)

cupola—An exterior architectural feature composed of a *drum* with a shallow cap; a *dome*. (526)

cutaway—An architectural drawing that combines an exterior view with an interior view of part of a building. (12, 493)

Dada—An early-20th-century art movement prompted by a revulsion against the horror of World War I. Dada embraced political anarchy, the irrational, and the intuitive. A disdain for convention, often enlivened by humor or whimsy, is characteristic of the art the Dadaists produced. (723, 744)

daguerreotype—A photograph made by an early method on a plate of chemically treated metal; developed by Louis J. M. Daguerre. (679, 680)

De Stijl—Dutch, "the style." An early-20th-century art movement (and magazine), founded by Piet Mondrian and Theo van Doesburg, whose members promoted utopian ideals and developed a simplified geometric style. (768)

deconstruction—An analytical strategy developed in the late 20th century according to which all cultural "constructs" (art, architecture, literature) are "texts." People can read these texts in a variety of ways, but they cannot arrive at fixed or uniform meanings. Any interpretation can be valid, and readings differ from time to time, place to place, and person to person. For those employing this approach, deconstruction means destabilizing established meanings and interpretations while encouraging subjectivity and individual differences. (830)

Deconstructivism—An architectural *style* using *deconstruction* as an analytical strategy. Deconstructivist architects attempt to disorient the observer by disrupting the conventional categories of architecture. The haphazard presentation of *volumes, masses, planes*, lighting, and so forth challenges the viewer's assumptions about *form* as it relates to function. (850)

Der Blaue Reiter—German, "the blue rider." An early-20th-century *German Expressionist* art movement founded by Vassily Kandinsky and Franz Marc. The artists selected the whimsical name because of their mutual interest in the color blue and horses. (729)

di sotto in sù—Italian, "from below upward." A *perspective* view seen from below. (483, 525)

diagonal rib—See *rib*. (xxx)

Die Brücke—German, "the bridge." An early-20th-century *German Expressionist* art movement under the leadership of Ernst Ludwig Kirchner. The group thought of itself as the bridge between the old age and the new. (727)

diptych—A two-paneled painting or *altarpiece*; also, an ancient Roman, Early Christian, or Byzantine hinged writing tablet, often of ivory and carved on the external sides. (428)

disegno—Italian, "drawing" and "design." *Renaissance* artists considered drawing to be the external physical manifestation (*disegno esterno*) of an internal intellectual idea of design (*disegno interno*). (492, 513)

divine right—The belief in a king's absolute power as God's will. (602)

divisionism—See *pointillism*. (700)

documentary evidence—In art history, the examination of written sources in order to determine the date of an artwork, the circumstances of its creation, or the identity of the artist(s) who made it. (2)

dome—A hemispherical *vault*; theoretically, an *arch* rotated on its vertical axis. In *Mycenaean* architecture, domes are beehive-shaped. (xxviii, 14-18A)

donor portrait—A portrait of the individual(s) who commissioned (donated) a religious work, for example, an *altarpiece*, as evidence of devotion. (423)

Doric—One of the two systems (or *orders*) invented in ancient Greece for articulating the three units of the elevation of a *classical* building—the platform, the *colonnade*, and the superstructure (*entablature*). The Doric order is characterized by, among other features, *capitals* with funnel-shaped *echinuses*, *columns* without *bases,* and a *frieze* of *triglyphs* and *metopes.* See also *Ionic.* (xxvi, 475, 528)

dressed masonry—Stone blocks shaped to the exact dimensions required, with smooth faces for a perfect fit. (474)

drum—One of the stacked cylindrical stones that form the *shaft* of a *column.* Also, the cylindrical wall that supports a *dome.* (xxviii)

drypoint—An *engraving* in which the design, instead of being cut into the plate with a *burin,* is scratched into the surface with a hard steel "pencil." See also *etching, intaglio.* (444)

earthworks—See *Environmental Art.* (820)

echinus—The convex element of a *capital* directly below the *abacus.* (xxvi)

écorché—The representation of a nude body as if without skin. (470)

edition—A set of impressions taken from a single print surface. (444)

elevation—In architecture, a head-on view of an external or internal wall, showing its features and often other elements that would be visible beyond or before the wall. (12, 413)

empiricism—The search for knowledge based on observation and direct experience. (663)

encaustic—A painting *technique* in which pigment is mixed with melted wax and applied to the surface while the mixture is hot. (802)

engaged column—A half-round *column* attached to a wall. See also *pilaster.* (xxvi, 476)

engraving—The process of *incising* a design in hard material, often a metal plate (usually copper); also, the *print* or impression made from such a plate. (443, 444)

Enlightenment—The Western philosophy based on empirical evidence that dominated the 18th century. The Enlightenment was a new way of thinking critically about the world and about humankind, independently of religion, myth, or tradition. (615)

en plein air—See *plein air.* (686, 687, 689, 693, 694, 23-2A, 23-7A)

entablature—The part of a building above the *columns* and below the roof. The entablature has three parts: *architrave, frieze,* and *pediment.* (xxvi)

Environmental Art—An American art form that emerged in the 1960s. Often using the land itself as their material, Environmental artists construct monuments of great scale and minimal form. Permanent or impermanent, these works transform some section of the environment, calling attention both to the land itself and to the hand of the artist. Sometimes referred to as earthworks. (820)

escutcheon—An emblem bearing a coat of arms. (516)

etching—A kind of *engraving* in which the design is *incised* in a layer of wax or varnish on a metal plate. The parts of the plate left exposed are then etched (slightly eaten away) by the acid in which the plate is immersed after incising. See also *drypoint, intaglio.* (444)

Eucharist—In Christianity, the partaking of the bread and wine, which believers hold to be either Christ himself or symbolic of him. (241, 426)

Events—See *Fluxus.* (823)

exedra—Recessed area, usually semicircular. (817)

exemplum virtutis—Latin, "example or model of virtue." (634)

Expressionism (adj. **Expressionist**)—Twentieth-century art that is the result of the artist's unique inner or personal vision and that often has an emotional dimension. Expressionism contrasts with art focused on visually describing the empirical world. (727)

facade—Usually, the front of a building; also, the other sides when they are emphasized architecturally. (412)

fantasia—Italian, "imagination." One of several terms used in Italian *Renaissance* literature to praise the originality and talent of artists. (492)

fasces—A bundle of rods with an ax attached, representing an emblem of authority in ancient Rome. (640)

Fauves—French, "wild beasts." See *Fauvism.* (724)

Fauvism—An early-20th-century art movement led by Henri Matisse. For the Fauves, *color* became the formal element most responsible for pictorial coherence and the primary conveyor of meaning. (724)

Favrile—A type of leaded stained glass patented by Louis Comfort Tiffany in the late 19th century. (23-36B)

femmages—The name American artist Miriam Schapiro gave to her sewn *collages,* assembled from fabrics, quilts, buttons, sequins, lace trim, and rickrack collected at antique shows and fairs. (810)

femme fatale—French, "fatal woman." A destructive temptress of men. (708)

femme savante—French, "learned woman." The term used to describe the cultured hostesses of *Rococo* salons. (617)

fenestra coeli—Latin, "window to Heaven." (576)

fête galante—French, "amorous festival." A type of *Rococo* painting depicting the outdoor amusements of French upper-class society. (620, 621)

feudalism—The medieval political, social, and economic system held together by the relationship between landholding *liege lords* and the *vassals* who were granted tenure of a portion of their land and in turn swore allegiance to the liege lord. (424)

fin-de-siècle—French, "end of the century." A period in Western cultural history from the end of the 19th century until just before World War I, when decadence and indulgence masked anxiety about an uncertain future. (711)

finial—A crowning ornament. (429)

fleur-de-lis—A three-petaled iris flower; the royal flower of France. (586)

Floreale—See *Art Nouveau.* (716)

florin—The denomination of gold coin of *Renaissance* Florence that became an international currency for trade. (417)

flute or **fluting**—Vertical channeling, roughly semicircular in cross-*section* and used principally on *columns* and *pilasters.* (xxvi)

Fluxus—A group of American, European, and Japanese artists of the 1960s who created *Performance Art.* Their performances, or Events, often focused on single actions, such as turning a light on and off or watching falling snow, and were more theatrical than *Happenings.* (823)

flying buttress—See *buttress.* (xxx, 15-4A)

fons vitae—Latin, "fountain of life." A symbolic fountain of everlasting life. (426)

foreshortening—The use of *perspective* to represent in art the apparent visual contraction of an object that extends back in space at an angle to the perpendicular plane of sight. (10, 401)

form—In art, an object's shape and structure, either in two dimensions (for example, a figure painted on a surface) or in three dimensions (such as a *statue*). (7)

formal analysis—The visual analysis of artistic *form.* (7)

formalism—Strict adherence to, or dependence on, stylized shapes and methods of *composition.* An emphasis on an artwork's visual elements rather than its subject. (790)

freestanding sculpture—See *sculpture in the round.* (12)

fresco—Painting on lime plaster, either dry (dry fresco, or fresco secco) or wet (true, or buon, fresco). In the latter method, the pigments are mixed with water and become chemically bound to the freshly laid lime plaster. Also, a painting executed in either method. (408, 409)

fresco secco—See *fresco.* (408, 491)

frieze—The part of the *entablature* between the *architrave* and the *cornice;* also, any sculptured or painted band in a building. See *register.* (xxvi)

Futurism—An early-20th-century Italian art movement that championed war as a cleansing agent and that celebrated the speed and dynamism of modern technology. (741)

genius—Latin, "spirit." In art, the personified spirit of a person or place. (17-52A)

genre—A *style* or category of art; also, a kind of painting that realistically depicts scenes from everyday life. (5, 439, 548)

German Expressionism—An early-20th-century regional Expressionist movement. (727)

gesso—Plaster mixed with a binding material, used as the base coat for paintings on wood panels. (433)

gestural abstraction—Also known as *action painting.* A kind of *abstract* painting in which the gesture, or act of painting, is seen as the subject of art. Its most renowned proponent was Jackson Pollock. See also *Abstract Expressionism.* (791)

giant order—See *colossal order.* (482)

gigantomachy—In ancient Greek mythology, the battle between gods and giants. (17-54A)

giornata (pl. **giornate**)—Italian, "day." The section of plaster that a *fresco* painter expects to complete in one session. (408)

glaze—A vitreous coating applied to pottery to seal and decorate the surface; it may be colored, transparent, or opaque, and glossy or *matte.* In *oil painting,* a thin, transparent, or semitransparent layer applied over a *color* to alter it slightly. (427, 471)

Gobelin tapestry—A *tapestry* produced on a vertical loom using a weaving *technique* in which no *weft* threads extend the full width of the fabric. (24-66B)

gold leaf—Gold beaten into tissue-paper-thin sheets that then can be applied to surfaces. (405)

Gothic Revival—See *Neo-Gothic.* (676)

gouache—A painting *medium* consisting of watercolor mixed with gum. (731)

Grand Manner portraiture—A type of 18th-century portrait painting designed to communicate a person's grace and class through certain standardized conventions, such as the large scale of the figure relative to the canvas, the controlled pose, the *landscape* setting, and the low *horizon line.* (630)

graver—An *engraving* tool. See also *burin.* (444)

Greek cross—A cross with four arms of equal length. (508, 564)

green architecture—Ecologically friendly architectural design using clean energy to sustain the natural environment. (849)

grisaille—A *monochrome* painting done mainly in neutral grays to simulate sculpture. (409, 502, 13-36A, 15-8A)

groin—The edge formed by the intersection of two barrel *vaults.* (xxviii)

groin vault—See *vault.* (xxviii, 14-12A)

guild—An association of merchants, craftspersons, or scholars in medieval and *Renaissance* Europe. (410)

halberd—A combination spear and battle-ax. (514)

Happenings—A term coined by American artist Allan Kaprow in the 1960s to describe loosely structured performances, whose creators were trying to suggest the aesthetic and dynamic qualities of everyday life; as actions, rather than objects, Happenings incorporate the fourth dimension (time). (822)

hard-edge painting—A variant of *Post-Painterly Abstraction* that rigidly excluded all reference to gesture and incorporated smooth knife-edge geometric forms to express the notion that painting should be reduced to its visual components. (795)

harpies—Mythological creatures of the underworld. (17-8A)

hatching—A series of closely spaced drawn or *engraved* parallel lines. Cross-hatching employs sets of lines placed at right angles. (443)

hierarchy of scale—An artistic convention in which greater size indicates greater importance. (11, 14-16A)

high relief—See *relief.* (12)

High-Tech—A contemporary architectural *style* calling for buildings that incorporate the latest innovations in engineering and technology and expose the structures' component parts. (849)

hookah—A Moroccan water pipe. (22-17A)

horizon line—See *perspective.* (455)

hôtel—French, "town house." (616)

hue—The name of a *color.* See also *primary colors, secondary colors,* and *complementary colors.* (7, 701)

humanism—In the *Renaissance,* an emphasis on education and on expanding knowledge (especially of *classical* antiquity), the exploration of individual potential and a desire to excel,

and a commitment to civic responsibility and moral duty. (407)

icon—A portrait or image; especially in Byzantine churches, a panel with a painting of sacred personages that are objects of veneration. In the visual arts, a painting, a piece of sculpture, or even a building regarded as an object of veneration. (405)

iconoclasm—The destruction of religious or sacred images. In Byzantium, the period from 726 to 843 when there was an imperial ban on such images. The destroyers of images were known as iconoclasts. Those who opposed such a ban were known as iconophiles. (431, 540)

iconoclast—See *iconoclasm.* (431, 540)

iconography—Greek, the "writing of images." The term refers both to the content, or subject, of an artwork and to the study of content in art. It also includes the study of the symbolic, often religious, meaning of objects, persons, or events depicted in works of art. (5)

illuminated manuscript—A luxurious handmade book with painted illustrations and decorations. (405)

illusionism (adj. **illusionistic**)—The representation of the three-dimensional world on a two-dimensional surface in a manner that creates the illusion that the person, object, or place represented is three-dimensional. See also *perspective.* (8)

impasto—A layer of thickly applied pigment. (520, 790)

impost block—The uppermost block of a wall or *pier* beneath the *springing* of an *arch.* (16-31A)

Impressionism—A late-19th-century art movement that sought to capture a fleeting moment, thereby conveying the elusiveness and impermanence of images and conditions. (687)

incise—To cut into a surface with a sharp instrument; also, a method of decoration, especially on metal and pottery. (444)

incubus—A demon believed in medieval times to prey, often sexually, on sleeping women. (650)

indulgence—A religious pardon for a sin committed. (504, 540)

ingegno—Italian, "innate talent." One of several terms used in Italian *Renaissance* literature to praise the originality and talent of artists. (492)

installation—An artwork that creates an artistic environment in a room or gallery. (838, 25-25B)

intaglio—A graphic technique in which the design is *incised,* or scratched, on a metal plate, either manually (*engraving, drypoint*) or chemically (*etching*). The incised lines of the design take the ink, making this the reverse of the *woodcut* technique. (444)

intensity—See *color.* (7)

internal evidence—In art history, the examination of what an artwork represents (people, clothing, hairstyles, and so on) in order to determine its date. Also, the examination of the *style* of an artwork to identify the artist who created it. (3)

International style—A *style* of 14th- and 15th-century painting begun by Simone Martini, who adapted the French *Gothic* manner to Sienese art fused with influences from northern

Europe. This style appealed to the aristocracy because of its brilliant *color,* lavish costumes, intricate ornamentation, and themes involving splendid processions of knights and ladies. Also, a style of 20th-century architecture associated with Le Corbusier, whose elegance of design came to influence the look of modern office buildings and skyscrapers. (413, 774)

intonaco—In *fresco* painting, the last layer of smooth lime plaster applied to the wall; the painting layer. (408)

invenzione—Italian, "invention." One of several terms used in Italian *Renaissance* literature to praise the originality and talent of artists. (492)

Ionic—One of the two systems (or *orders*) invented in ancient Greece for articulating the three units of the elevation of a *classical* building: the platform, the *colonnade,* and the superstructure (*entablature*). The Ionic order is characterized by, among other features, *volutes, capitals, columns* with *bases,* and an uninterrupted *frieze.* (xxvi, 475)

jambs—In architecture, the side posts of a doorway. (xxxi)

Japonisme—The French fascination with all things Japanese. Japonisme emerged in the second half of the 19th century. (696)

Jugendstil—See *Art Nouveau.* (716)

keystone—See *voussoir.* (xxviii, 528)

lancet—In *Gothic* architecture, a tall narrow window ending in a *pointed arch.* (778, 14-5A, 22-43A)

landscape—A picture showing natural scenery, without narrative content. (5, 416)

Landschaft—German, "landscape." (550)

lateral section—See *section.* (12)

laudatio—Latin, "essay of praise." (458)

line—The extension of a point along a path, made concrete in art by drawing on or chiseling into a *plane.* (7)

linear perspective—See *perspective.* (192, 453, 455)

literati—In China, talented amateur painters and scholars from the landed gentry. (844, 26-22A)

lithograph—See *lithography.* (666)

lithography—A printmaking technique in which the artist uses an oil-based crayon to draw directly on a stone plate and then wipes water onto the stone. When ink is rolled onto the plate, it adheres only to the drawing. The *print* produced by this method is a lithograph. (666)

local color—An object's true *color* in white light. (689)

loggia—A gallery with an open *arcade* or a *colonnade* on one or both sides. (464, 14-19A)

longitudinal plan—See *plan.* (xxviii)

longitudinal section—See *section.* (12)

lost-wax (cire perdue) process—A bronze-*casting* method in which a figure is modeled in wax and covered with clay; the whole is fired, melting away the wax (French, *cire perdue*) and hardening the clay, which then becomes a *mold* for molten metal. (561)

low relief—See *relief.* (12)

lunette—A semicircular area (with the flat side down) in a wall over a door, niche, or window; also, a painting or *relief* with a semicircular frame. (439)

machicolated gallery—A gallery in a defensive tower with holes in the floor to allow stones or hot liquids to be dumped on enemies below. (416)

magus (pl. **magi**)—One of the three wise men from the East who presented gifts to the infant Jesus. (xxxiv)

maniera—Italian, "style" or "manner." See *Mannerism*. (520, 570)

maniera greca—Italian, "Greek manner." The Italo-*Byzantine* painting *style* of the 13th century. (404, 14-7A)

Mannerism—A *style* of later *Renaissance* art that emphasized "artifice," often involving contrived imagery not derived directly from nature. Such artworks showed a self-conscious stylization involving complexity, caprice, fantasy, and polish. Mannerist architecture tended to flout the *classical* rules of order, stability, and symmetry, sometimes to the point of parody. (520)

martyrium—A shrine to a Christian *martyr*. (507)

mass—The bulk, density, and weight of matter in *space*. (8)

Mass—The Catholic and Orthodox ritual in which believers understand that Christ's redeeming sacrifice on the cross is repeated when the priest consecrates the bread and wine in the *Eucharist*. (xxxv)

matins—In Christianity, early morning prayers. (438)

matte—In painting, pottery, and photography, a dull finish. (426)

maulstick—A stick used to steady the hand while painting. (549)

mausoleum—A monumental tomb. The name derives from the mid-fourth-century BCE tomb of Mausolos at Halikarnassos, one of the Seven Wonders of the ancient world. (225, 425)

medium (pl. **media**)—The material (for example, marble, bronze, clay, *fresco*) in which an artist works; also, in painting, the vehicle (usually liquid) that carries the pigment. (7)

mela medica—Italian, "medicinal apples" (oranges). The emblem of the Medici family of *Renaissance* Florence. (468)

memento mori—Latin, "reminder of death." In painting, a reminder of human mortality, usually represented by a skull. (583, 21-7A, 25-25B)

mendicants—In medieval Europe, friars belonging to the Franciscan and Dominican orders, who renounced all worldly goods, lived by contributions of laypersons (the word *mendicant* means "beggar"), and devoted themselves to preaching, teaching, and doing good works. (404)

Messiah—The savior of the Jews prophesied in Hebrew scripture. Christians believe that Jesus of Nazareth was the Messiah. (xxxiv)

metamatics—The name Swiss artist Jean Tinguely gave to the motor-driven devices he constructed to produce instant abstract paintings. (823)

metope—The square panel between the *triglyphs* in a *Doric frieze,* often sculpted in *relief*. (xxvi)

miniatures—Small individual Indian paintings intended to be held in the hand and viewed by one or two individuals at one time. (23-24A)

Minimalism—A predominantly sculptural American trend of the 1960s characterized by works featuring a severe reduction of *form,* often to single, homogeneous units. (798)

mobile—A kind of sculpture, invented by Alexander Calder, combining nonobjective organic forms and motion in balanced structures hanging from rods, wires, and colored, organically shaped plates. (783)

modernism—A movement in Western art that developed in the second half of the 19th century and sought to capture the images and sensibilities of the age. Modernist art goes beyond simply dealing with the present and involves the artist's critical examination of the premises of art itself. (689)

Modernismo—See *Art Nouveau*. (716)

module (adj. **modular**)—A basic unit of which the dimensions of the major parts of a work are multiples. The principle is used in sculpture and other art forms, but it is most often employed in architecture, where the module may be the dimensions of an important part of a building, such as the diameter of a *column*. (10, 470)

mold—A hollow form for *casting*. (11)

monastery—A group of buildings in which monks live together, set apart from the secular community of a town. (425)

monastic—Relating to life in a *monastery*. (404, 425)

monastic order—An organization of monks living according to the same rules, for example, the Benedictine, Franciscan, and Dominican orders. (404)

monochrome (adj. **monochromatic**)—One color. (593)

mosaic—Patterns or pictures made by embedding small pieces (*tesserae*) of stone or glass in cement on surfaces such as walls and floors; also, the *technique* of making such works. (23-24A)

mullion—A vertical member that divides a window or that separates one window from another. (818)

mural—A wall painting. (407, 408, 409)

mystery play—A dramatic enactment of the holy mysteries of the Christian faith performed at church portals and in city squares. (409, 426)

mystic marriage—A spiritual marriage of a woman with Christ. (437)

Nabis—Hebrew, "prophet." A group of *Symbolist* painters influenced by Paul Gauguin. (707)

naos—See *cella*. (33, 115, 506)

naturalism—The style of painted or sculptured representation based on close observation of the natural world that was at the core of the *classical* tradition. (401)

Naturalistic Surrealism—See *Surrealism*. (763)

nave—The central area of an ancient Roman *basilica* or of a church, demarcated from *aisles* by *piers* or *columns*. (xxx, 413, 15-4A)

nave arcade—In *basilica* architecture, the series of *arches* supported by *piers* or *columns* separating the *nave* from the *aisles*. (xxx)

Neoclassicism—A *style* of art and architecture that emerged in the late 18th century as part of a general revival of interest in *classical* cultures. Neoclassical artists adopted themes and styles from ancient Greece and Rome. (633)

Neo-Expressionism—An art movement that emerged in the 1970s and that reflects artists' interest in the expressive capability of art, seen earlier in *German Expressionism* and *Abstract Expressionism*. (793, 25-8D)

Neo-Gothic—The revival of the *Gothic style* in architecture, especially in the 19th century. (676)

Neoplasticism—The Dutch artist Piet Mondrian's theory of "pure plastic art," an ideal balance between the universal and the individual using an abstract formal vocabulary. (769)

Neue Sachlichkeit—German, "new objectivity." An art movement that grew directly out of the World War I experiences of a group of German artists who sought to show the horrors of the war and its effects. (760)

nipote—Italian, "nephew." (16-41A)

oculus (pl. **oculi**)—Latin, "eye." The round central opening of a *dome*. Also, a small round window in a *Gothic cathedral*. (xxviii, 14-6A, 16-31A)

odalisque—A woman in a Turkish harem. (649)

ogee arch—An *arch* composed of two double-curving lines meeting at a point. (420)

ogive (adj. **ogival**)—The diagonal *rib* of a *Gothic vault;* a pointed, or Gothic, *arch*. (402, 815, 16-31A)

oil painting—A painting *technique* using oil-based pigments that rose to prominence in northern Europe in the 15th century and is now the standard medium for painting on canvas. (426)

Op Art—An artistic movement of the 1960s in which painters sought to produce optical illusions of motion and depth using only geometric forms on two-dimensional surfaces. (796)

optical mixture—The visual effect of juxtaposed *complementary colors*. (701)

orbiculum—A disklike opening. (818)

Orphism—A form of *Cubism* developed by the French painter Robert Delaunay in which color plays an important role. (736)

orrery—A mechanical model of the solar system demonstrating how the planets revolve around the sun. (615)

orthogonal—A line imagined to be behind and perpendicular to the picture *plane;* the orthogonals in a painting appear to recede toward a *vanishing point* on the horizon. (435, 455)

palette knife—A flat tool used to scrape paint off the *palette*. Artists sometimes also use the palette knife in place of a brush to apply paint directly to the canvas. (665)

papier collé—French, "stuck paper." See *collage*. (738)

parallel hatching—See *hatching*. (443)

parapet—A low, protective wall along the edge of a balcony, roof, or bastion. (416)

parchment—Lambskin prepared as a surface for painting or writing. (492)

pastel—A powdery paste of pigment and gum used for making crayons; also, the pastel crayons themselves. (697)

patron—The person or entity that pays an artist to produce individual artworks or employs an artist on a continuing basis. (6)

pediment—In *classical* architecture, the triangular space (gable) at the end of a building, formed by the ends of the sloping roof above the *colonnade;* also, an ornamental feature having this shape. (xxvi, 470)

pendentive—A concave, triangular section of a hemisphere, four of which provide the transition from a square area to the circular base of a covering *dome.* Although pendentives appear to be hanging (pendant) from the dome, they in fact support it. (xxxii, 473, 502)

Performance Art—An American *avant-garde* art trend of the 1960s that made time an integral element of art. It produced works in which movements, gestures, and sounds of persons communicating with an audience replace physical objects. Documentary photographs are generally the only evidence remaining after these events. See also *Happenings.* (821)

period style—See *style.* (3)

peripteral—See *peristyle.* (xxvi)

peristyle—In *classical* architecture, a *colonnade* all around the *cella* and its porch(es). A peripteral colonnade consists of a single row of *columns* on all sides; a dipteral colonnade has a double row all around. (xxvi)

personal style—See *style.* (4)

personification—An *abstract* idea represented in bodily form. (5)

perspective—A method of presenting an illusion of the three-dimensional world on a two-dimensional surface. In linear perspective, the most common type, all parallel lines or surface edges converge on one, two, or three vanishing points located with reference to the eye level of the viewer (the horizon line of the picture), and associated objects are rendered smaller the farther from the viewer they are intended to seem. Atmospheric, or aerial, perspective creates the illusion of distance by the greater diminution of color intensity, the shift in color toward an almost neutral blue, and the blurring of contours as the intended distance between eye and object increases. (8, 409, 435, 453, 455)

philosophe—French, "thinker, philosopher." The term applied to French intellectuals of the *Enlightenment.* (624)

photomontage—A *composition* made by pasting together pictures or parts of pictures, especially photographs. See also *collage.* (723)

Photorealism—See *Superrealism.* (917)

physical evidence—In art history, the examination of the materials used to produce an artwork in order to determine its date. (2)

piano nobile—Italian, "noble floor." The main (second) floor of a building. (16-37A)

piazza—Italian, "plaza." (560)

Picturesque garden—An "unordered" garden designed in accord with the *Enlightenment* taste for the natural. (638)

pier—A vertical, freestanding masonry support. (12)

Pietà—A painted or sculpted representation of the Virgin Mary mourning over the body of the dead Christ. (xxxv, 432, 730)

pilaster—A flat, rectangular, vertical member projecting from a wall of which it forms a part. It usually has a *base* and a *capital* and is often *fluted.* (463)

pinnacle—In *Gothic* churches, a sharply pointed ornament capping the *piers* or flying *buttresses;*

also used on church *facades.* (xxx, 411, 413, 22-43A)

Pittura Metafisica—Italian, "metaphysical painting." An early-20th-century Italian art movement led by Giorgio de Chirico, whose work conveys an eerie mood and visionary quality. (763)

pixels—Shortened form of "picture elements." The tiny boxes that make up digital images displayed on a computer monitor. (826)

plan—The horizontal arrangement of the parts of a building or of the buildings and streets of a city or town, or a drawing or diagram showing such an arrangement. In an axial plan, the parts of a building are organized longitudinally, or along a given axis; in a central plan, the parts of the structure are of equal or almost equal dimensions around the center. (12)

plane—A flat surface. (7)

Plateresque—A style of Spanish architecture characterized by elaborate decoration based on *Gothic,* Italian *Renaissance,* and Islamic sources; derived from the Spanish word *platero,* meaning "silversmith." (552)

platero—See *Plateresque.* (552)

plein air—An approach to painting very popular among the *Impressionists,* in which an artist sketches outdoors to achieve a quick impression of light, air, and color. The artist then takes the sketches to the studio for reworking into more finished works of art. (686, 687, 689, 693, 694, 23-2A, 23-7A)

poesia—A term describing "poetic" art, notably Venetian *Renaissance* painting, which emphasizes the lyrical and sensual. (514)

pointed arch—A narrow *arch* of pointed profile, in contrast to a semicircular arch. (3, 402, 420, 12-10A, 16-31A)

pointillism—A system of painting devised by the 19th-century French painter Georges Seurat. The artist separates *color* into its component parts and then applies the component colors to the canvas in tiny dots (points). The image becomes comprehensible only from a distance, when the viewer's eyes optically blend the pigment dots. Sometimes referred to as divisionism. (700)

polyptych—An *altarpiece* composed of more than three sections. (426)

Pop Art—A term coined by British art critic Lawrence Alloway to refer to art, first appearing in the 1950s, that incorporated elements from consumer culture, the mass media, and popular culture, such as images from motion pictures and advertising. (787)

portico—A roofed *colonnade;* also an entrance porch. (464)

positivism—A Western philosophical model that promoted science as the mind's highest achievement. (663)

post-and-lintel system—A system of construction in which two posts support a *lintel.* (xxviii)

Post-Impressionism—The term used to describe the stylistically heterogeneous work of the group of late-19th-century painters in France, including van Gogh, Gauguin, Seurat, and Cézanne, who more systematically examined

the properties and expressive qualities of *line,* pattern, *form,* and *color* than the *Impressionists* did. (699)

postmodernism—A reaction against *modernist formalism,* seen as elitist. Far more encompassing and accepting than the more rigid confines of modernist practice, postmodernism offers something for everyone by accommodating a wide range of *styles,* subjects, and formats, from traditional easel painting to *installation* and from *abstraction* to *illusionistic* scenes. Postmodern art often includes irony or reveals a self-conscious awareness on the part of the artist of art-making processes or the workings of the art world. (817)

Post-Painterly Abstraction—An American art movement that emerged in the 1960s and was characterized by a cool, detached rationality emphasizing tighter pictorial control. See also *color-field painting* and *hard-edge painting.* (795)

Poussiniste—A member of the French Royal Academy of Painting and Sculpture during the early 18th century who followed Nicolas Poussin in insisting that *form* was the most important element of painting. See also *Rubéniste.* (621)

Precisionism—An American art movement of the 1920s and 1930s. The Precisionists concentrated on portraying man-made environments in a clear and concise manner to express the beauty of perfect and precise machine forms. (755)

predella—The narrow ledge on which an *altarpiece* rests on an altar. (411)

prefiguration—In Early Christian art, the depiction of Old Testament persons and events as prophetic forerunners of Christ and New Testament events. (238, 435, 449)

primary colors—Red, yellow, and blue—the colors from which all other colors may be derived. (7, 701)

primitivism—The incorporation in early-20th-century Western art of stylistic elements from the artifacts of Africa, Oceania, and the native peoples of the Americas. (733, 734)

print—An artwork on paper, usually produced in multiple impressions. (444)

Productivism—An art movement that emerged in the Soviet Union after the Russian Revolution; its members believed that artists must direct art toward creating products for the new society. (748)

proportion—The relationship in size of the parts of persons, buildings, or objects, often based on a *module.* (10)

proscenium—The part of a theatrical stage in front of the curtain. (563)

provenance—Origin or source; *findspot.* (3)

pseudoperipteral—In Roman architecture, a pseudoperipteral temple has a series of engaged *columns* all around the sides and back of the *cella* to give the appearance of a *peripteral colonnade.* (xxvi)

pulpit—A raised platform in a church or *mosque* on which a priest or *imam* stands while leading the religious service. (402)

punchwork—Tooled decorative work in *gold leaf.* (412)

Purism—An early-20th-century art movement that embraced the "machine aesthetic" and sought purity of *form* in the clean functional lines of industrial machinery. (741)

putto (pl. **putti**)—A cherubic young boy. (458)

quadrifrons—Latin, "four-fronted." An *arch* with four equal *facades* and four *arcuated bays*. (18-14A)

quadro riportato—A ceiling design in which painted scenes are arranged in panels that resemble framed pictures transferred to the surface of a shallow, curved *vault*. (568)

quatrefoil—A shape or plan in which the parts assume the form of a cloverleaf. (419)

Quattrocento—Italian, "400," that is, the 1400s or 15th century. (447)

quoins—The large, sometimes *rusticated*, usually slightly projecting stones that often form the corners of the exterior walls of masonry buildings. (509)

radiating chapels—In medieval churches, chapels for the display of *relics* that opened directly onto the *ambulatory* and the *transept*. (xxx)

Rayograph—A photograph produced without a camera by placing objects on photographic paper and then exposing the paper to light; named for the American artist Man Ray. (752)

Realism—A movement that emerged in mid-19th-century France. Realist artists represented the subject matter of everyday life (especially subjects that previously had been considered inappropriate for depiction) in a relatively *naturalistic* mode. (663)

refectory—The dining hall of a Christian *monastery*. (464)

regional style—See *style*. (3)

Regionalism—A 20th-century American art movement that portrayed American rural life in a clearly readable, *Realist* style. Major Regionalists include Grant Wood and Thomas Hart Benton. (777)

relics—The body parts, clothing, or objects associated with a holy figure, such as the Buddha or Christ or a Christian *saint*. (xxx)

relief—In sculpture, figures projecting from a background of which they are part. The degree of relief is designated high, low (bas), or sunken. In the last, the artist cuts the design into the surface so that the highest projecting parts of the image are no higher than the surface itself. See also *repoussé*. (444)

relief sculpture—See *relief*. (12)

Renaissance—French, "rebirth." The term used to describe the history, culture, and art of 14th- through 16th-century western Europe during which artists consciously revived the *classical* style. (401, 406)

renovatio—Latin, "renewal." During the *Carolingian* period, Charlemagne sought to revive the culture of ancient Rome (renovatio imperii Romani). (402)

respond—An engaged *column, pilaster,* or similar element that either projects from a *compound pier* or some other supporting device or is bonded to a wall and carries one end of an *arch*. (xxx)

retable—An architectural screen or wall above and behind an altar, usually containing painting, sculpture, or other decorations. See also *altarpiece*. (426)

revetment—In architecture, a wall covering or facing. (418)

rib—A relatively slender, molded masonry *arch* that projects from a surface. In *Gothic* architecture, the ribs form the framework of the *vaulting*. A diagonal rib is one of the ribs that form the X of a *groin vault*. A transverse rib crosses the *nave* or *aisle* at a 90° angle. (xxx, 12, 16-31A)

rib vault—A *vault* in which the diagonal and transverse *ribs* compose a structural skeleton that partially supports the masonry *web* between them. (14-5A)

Rococo—A style, primarily of interior design, that appeared in France around 1700. Rococo interiors featured lavish decoration, including small sculptures, ornamental mirrors, easel paintings, *tapestries, reliefs,* wall paintings, and elegant furniture. The term Rococo derived from the French word *rocaille* (pebble) and referred to the small stones and shells used to decorate grotto interiors. (616)

Romanesque—"Roman-like." A term used to describe the history, culture, and art of medieval western Europe from ca. 1050 to ca. 1200. (333, 413, 476)

Romanticism—A Western cultural phenomenon, beginning around 1750 and ending about 1850, that gave precedence to feeling and imagination over reason and thought. More narrowly, the art movement that flourished from about 1800 to 1840. (650)

rose window—A circular *stained-glass* window. (xxxi, 412)

rostrum—Speaker's platform. (807)

rotunda—The circular area under a *dome*; also a domed round building. (426)

roundel—See *tondo*. (473, 10-15A)

Rubéniste—A member of the French Royal Academy of Painting and Sculpture during the early 18th century who followed Peter Paul Rubens in insisting that *color* was the most important element of painting. See also *Poussiniste*. (621)

rusticate (n. rustication)—To give a rustic appearance by roughening the surfaces and beveling the edges of stone blocks to emphasize the joints between them. Rustication is a technique employed in ancient Roman architecture, and was also popular during the *Renaissance*, especially for stone *courses* at the ground-floor level. (474)

sacra conversazione—Italian, "holy conversation." A style of *altarpiece* painting popular after the middle of the 15th century, in which *saints* from different epochs are joined in a unified space and seem to be conversing either with one another or with the audience. (512)

sacra rappresentazione (pl. **sacre rappresentazioni**)—Italian, "holy representation." A more elaborate version of a *mystery play* performed for a lay audience by a *confraternity*. (409)

saint—From the Latin word *sanctus,* meaning "made holy by God." Applied to persons who suffered and died for their Christian faith or who merited reverence for their Christian devotion while alive. In the Roman Catholic Church, a worthy deceased Catholic who is canonized by the pope. (402)

Saint-Simonianism—An early-19th-century utopian movement that emphasized the education and enfranchisement of women. (667)

saltimbanque—An itinerant circus performer. (24-11A)

sarcophagus (pl. **sarcophagi**)—Greek, "consumer of flesh." A coffin, usually of stone. (402, 449)

saturation—See *color*. (7, 701)

satyr—A Greek mythological follower of Dionysos having a man's upper body, a goat's hindquarters and horns, and a horse's ears and tail. (22-33A)

school—A chronological and stylistic classification of works of art with a stipulation of place. (6)

scudi—Italian, "shields." A coin denomination in 17th-century Italy. (572)

sculpture in the round—Freestanding figures, *carved* or *modeled* in three dimensions. (12)

secco—Italian, "dry." See also *fresco*. (408, 491)

secondary colors—Orange, green, and purple, obtained by mixing pairs of *primary colors* (red, yellow, blue). (7, 701)

section—In architecture, a diagram or representation of a part of a structure or building along an imaginary *plane* that passes through it vertically. Drawings showing a theoretical slice across a structure's width are lateral sections. Those cutting through a building's length are longitudinal sections. See also *elevation* and *cutaway*. (12)

segmental pediment—A *pediment* with a curved instead of a triangular *cornice*. (509)

sfumato—Italian, "smoky." A smokelike haziness that subtly softens outlines in painting; particularly applied to the paintings of Leonardo da Vinci and Correggio. (427, 492)

sibyl—A Greco-Roman mythological prophetess. (428)

signoria—The governing body in the Republic of Florence. (451)

silk-screen printing—An industrial printing *technique* that creates a sharp-edged image by pressing ink through a design on silk or a similar tightly woven porous fabric stretched tight on a frame. (803)

silverpoint—A *stylus* made of silver, used in drawing in the 14th and 15th centuries because of the fine *line* it produced and the sharp point it maintained. (433, 492)

Simultanéisme—Robert Delaunay's version of *Cubism* in which he created spatial effects and kaleidoscopic movement solely through color contrasts; also known as *Orphism*. (736)

simultaneous contrasts—The phenomenon of juxtaposed *colors* affecting the eye's reception of each, as when a painter places dark green next to light green, making the former appear even darker and the latter even lighter. See also *successive contrasts*. (701)

sinopia—A burnt-orange pigment used in *fresco* painting to transfer a *cartoon* to the *arriccio* before the artist paints the plaster. (408)

site-specific art—Art created for a specific location. See also *Environmental Art*. (820)

space—In art history, both the actual area an object occupies or a building encloses, and the *illusionistic* representation of space in painting and sculpture. (8)

spectrum—The range or band of visible colors in natural light. (7)

springing—The lowest stone of an *arch*, resting on the *impost block*. In *Gothic* vaulting, the lowest stone of a diagonal or transverse *rib*. (340, 373)

stained glass—In *Gothic* architecture, the colored glass used for windows. (xxx, 12)

stanza (pl. **stanze**)—Italian, "room." (494)

statue—A three-dimensional sculpture. (12)

stigmata—In Christian art, the wounds Christ received at his crucifixion that miraculously appear on the body of a *saint*. (405)

still life—A picture depicting an arrangement of inanimate objects. (5, 575)

stretcher bar—One of a set of wooden bars used to stretch canvas to provide a taut surface for painting. (431)

stringcourse—A raised horizontal *molding*, or band, in masonry. Its principal use is ornamental but it usually reflects interior structure. (474)

style—A distinctive artistic manner. Period style is the characteristic style of a specific time. Regional style is the style of a particular geographical area. Personal style is an individual artist's unique manner. (3)

stylistic evidence—In art history, the examination of the *style* of an artwork in order to determine its date or the identity of the artist. (3)

stylobate—The uppermost course of the platform of a *classical* Greek temple, which supports the *columns*. (116, 506)

stylus—A needlelike tool used in *engraving* and *incising*; also, an ancient writing instrument used to inscribe clay or wax tablets. (433, 444, 492)

subtractive light—The painter's light in art; the light reflected from pigments and objects. See also *additive light*. (7)

subtractive sculpture—A kind of sculpture technique in which materials are taken away from the original mass; *carving*. (11)

successive contrasts—The phenomenon of colored afterimages. When a person looks intently at a *color* (green, for example) and then shifts to a white area, the fatigued eye momentarily perceives the *complementary color* (red). See also *simultaneous contrasts*. (701)

Superrealism—A *school* of painting and sculpture of the 1960s and 1970s that emphasized producing artworks based on scrupulous fidelity to optical fact. The Superrealist painters were also called Photorealists because many used photographs as sources for their imagery. (805)

Suprematism—A type of art formulated by Kazimir Malevich to convey his belief that the supreme reality in the world is pure feeling, which attaches to no object and thus calls for new, nonobjective forms in art—shapes not related to objects in the visible world. (747)

Surrealism—A successor to *Dada*, Surrealism incorporated the improvisational nature of its predecessor into its exploration of the ways to express in art the world of dreams and the unconscious. Biomorphic Surrealists, such as Joan Miró, produced largely *abstract compositions*. *Naturalistic* Surrealists, notably Salvador Dalí, presented recognizable scenes transformed into a dream or nightmare image. (763)

symbol—An image that stands for another image or encapsulates an idea. (5)

Symbolism—A late-19th-century movement based on the idea that the artist was not an imitator of nature but a creator who transformed the facts of nature into a *symbol* of the inner experience of that fact. (707)

Synthetic Cubism—A later phase of *Cubism*, in which paintings and drawings were constructed from objects and shapes cut from paper or other materials to represent parts of a subject, in order to engage the viewer with pictorial issues, such as figuration, realism, and abstraction. (736)

tapestry—A weaving *technique* in which the *weft* threads are packed densely over the *warp* threads so that the designs are woven directly into the fabric. (513, 618)

technique—The processes artists employ to create *form*, as well as the distinctive, personal ways in which they handle their materials and tools. (7)

tempera—A *technique* of painting using pigment mixed with egg yolk, glue, or casein; also, the *medium* itself. (404, 426, 427)

tenebrism—Painting in the "shadowy manner," using violent contrasts of light and dark, as in the work of Caravaggio. The term derives from *tenebroso*. (571)

tenebroso—Italian, "shadowy." See *tenebrism*. (571)

terminus ante quem—Latin, "point [date] before which." (2)

terminus post quem—Latin, "point [date] after which." (2)

terracotta—Hard-baked clay, used for sculpture and as a building material. It may be *glazed* or painted. (414)

texture—The quality of a surface (rough, smooth, hard, soft, shiny, dull) as revealed by light. In represented texture, a painter depicts an object as having a certain texture even though the pigment is the real texture. (8)

tholos (pl. **tholoi**)—A temple with a circular plan. Also, the burial chamber of a *tholos tomb*. (xxvi, 506)

thrust—The outward force exerted by an *arch* or a *vault* that must be counterbalanced by a *buttress*. (16-31A)

tonality—See *color*. (7)

tondo (pl. **tondi**)—A circular painting or *relief* sculpture. (473)

tracery—Ornamental stonework for holding *stained glass* in place, characteristic of *Gothic cathedrals*. In plate tracery, the glass fills only the "punched holes" in the heavy ornamental stonework. In bar tracery, the stained-glass windows fill almost the entire opening, and the stonework is unobtrusive. (xxxi, 414)

tramezzo—A screen placed across the *nave* of a church to separate the clergy from the lay audience. (14-6A)

transept—The part of a church with an axis that crosses the *nave* at a right angle. (xxx, 452, 14-5A)

transubstantiation—The transformation of the Eucharistic bread and wine into the body and blood of Christ. (19-18A)

transverse rib—See *rib*. (xxx)

trefoil arch—A triple-lobed arch. (402)

triforium—In a *Gothic cathedral*, the *blind arcaded* gallery below the *clerestory*; occasionally, the *arcades* are filled with *stained glass*. (15-4A)

triglyph—A triple projecting, grooved member of a *Doric frieze* that alternates with *metopes*. (xxvi, 528)

triptych—A three-paneled painting, ivory plaque, or *altarpiece*. Also, a small, portable shrine with hinged wings used for private devotion. (415)

triumphal arch—In Roman architecture, a freestanding *arch* commemorating an important event, such as a military victory or the opening of a new road. (463)

trompe l'oeil—French, "fools the eye." A form of *illusionistic* painting that aims to deceive viewers into believing they are seeing real objects rather than a representation of those objects. (483, 19-14A)

true fresco—See *fresco*. (408, 409)

trumeau—In church architecture, the *pillar* or center post supporting the *lintel* in the middle of the doorway. (xxxi, 15-2A)

tunnel vault—See *vault*. (xxviii, 12, 473)

Tuscan column—The standard type of Etruscan *column*. It resembles ancient Greek *Doric* columns but is made of wood, is unfluted, and has a *base*. Also a popular motif in *Renaissance* and *Baroque* architecture. (475, 506)

tympanum (pl. **tympana**)—The space enclosed by a *lintel* and an *arch* over a doorway. (xxxi, 426, 478, 14-12A)

ukiyo-e—Japanese, "pictures of the floating world." During the Edo period, *woodcut prints* depicting brothels, popular entertainment, and beautiful women. (23-16B)

Usonian—Frank Lloyd Wright's term for the inexpensive houses he designed for ordinary people. *Usonian* derives from "United States of North America." (784)

value—See *color*. (7, 701)

vanishing point—See *perspective*. (435, 455)

vanitas—Latin, "vanity." A term describing paintings (particularly 17th-century Dutch *still lifes*) that include references to death. (583, 18-3A, 21-7A)

vault (adj. **vaulted**)—A masonry roof or ceiling constructed on the *arch* principle, or a concrete roof of the same shape. A barrel (or tunnel) vault, semicylindrical in cross-*section*, is in effect a deep arch or an uninterrupted series of arches, one behind the other, over an oblong space. A quadrant vault is a half-barrel vault. A groin (or cross) vault is formed at the point at which two barrel vaults intersect at right angles. In a ribbed vault, there is a framework of *ribs* or arches under the intersections of the vaulting sections. A sexpartite vault is one whose ribs divide the vault into six compartments. A fan vault is a vault characteristic of

English *Perpendicular Gothic* architecture, in which radiating ribs form a fanlike pattern. (xxviii, 12)

vaulting web—See *web*. (xxx)

veduta (pl. **vedute**)—Italian, "scenic view." (632)

vellum—Calfskin prepared as a surface for writing or painting. (492)

vita—Italian, "life." Also, the title of a biography. (570)

volume—The *space* that *mass* organizes, divides, or encloses. (8)

volute—A spiral, scroll-like form characteristic of the ancient Greek *Ionic* and the Roman *Composite capital*. (xxvi)

voussoir—A wedge-shaped stone block used in the construction of a true *arch*. The central voussoir, which sets the arch, is called the keystone. (xxviii, 528)

wainscoting—Paneling on the lower part of interior walls. (705)

web—The masonry blocks that fill the area between the *ribs* of a *groin vault*. Also called vaulting web. (xxx)

weld—To join metal parts by heating, as in assembling the separate parts of a *statue* made by *casting*. (11)

wet-plate photography—An early photographic process in which the photographic plate is exposed, developed, and fixed while wet. (680)

woodcut—A wooden block on the surface of which those parts not intended to *print* are cut away to a slight depth, leaving the design raised; also, the printed impression made with such a block. (442, 444)

zoopraxiscope—A device invented by Eadweard Muybridge in the 19th century to project sequences of still photographic images; a predecessor of the modern motion-picture projector. (684)

BIBLIOGRAPHY

This list of books is very selective but comprehensive enough to satisfy the reading interests of the beginning art history student and general reader. Significantly expanded from the previous edition, the 14th edition bibliography can also serve as the basis for undergraduate research papers. The resources listed range from works that are valuable primarily for their reproductions to those that are scholarly surveys of schools and periods or monographs on individual artists. The emphasis is on recent in-print books and on books likely to be found in college and municipal libraries. No entries for periodical articles appear, but the bibliography begins with a list of some of the major journals that publish art historical scholarship in English.

Selected Periodicals

American Art
American Journal of Archaeology
Antiquity
Archaeology
Archives of American Art
Art Bulletin
Art History
Art in America
Art Journal
Artforum International
Artnews
Burlington Magazine
Gesta
History of Photography
Journal of Egyptian Archaeology
Journal of Roman Archaeology
Journal of the Society of Architectural Historians
Journal of the Warburg and Courtauld Institutes
Latin American Antiquity
October
Oxford Art Journal
Women's Art Journal

General Studies

Baxandall, Michael. *Patterns of Intention: On the Historical Explanation of Pictures.* New Haven, Conn.: Yale University Press, 1985.

Bindman, David, ed. *The Thames & Hudson Encyclopedia of British Art.* London: Thames & Hudson, 1988.

Boström, Antonia. *The Encyclopedia of Sculpture.* 3 vols. London: Routledge, 2003.

Broude, Norma, and Mary D. Garrard, eds. *The Expanding Discourse: Feminism and Art History.* New York: Harper Collins, 1992.

Bryson, Norman. *Vision and Painting: The Logic of the Gaze.* New Haven, Conn.: Yale University Press, 1983.

Bryson, Norman, Michael Ann Holly, and Keith Moxey. *Visual Theory: Painting and Interpretation.* New York: Cambridge University Press, 1991.

Burden, Ernest. *Illustrated Dictionary of Architecture.* 2d ed. New York: McGraw-Hill, 2002.

Büttner, Nils. *Landscape Painting: A History.* New York: Abbeville, 2006.

Carrier, David. *A World Art History and Its Objects.* University Park: Pennsylvania State University Press, 2009.

Chadwick, Whitney. *Women, Art, and Society.* 4th ed. New York: Thames & Hudson, 2007.

Cheetham, Mark A., Michael Ann Holly, and Keith Moxey, eds. *The Subjects of Art History: Historical Objects in Contemporary Perspective.* New York: Cambridge University Press, 1998.

Chilvers, Ian, and Harold Osborne, eds. *The Oxford Dictionary of Art.* 3d ed. New York: Oxford University Press, 2004.

Corbin, George A. *Native Arts of North America, Africa, and the South Pacific: An Introduction.* New York: Harper Collins, 1988.

Crouch, Dora P., and June G. Johnson. *Traditions in Architecture: Africa, America, Asia, and Oceania.* New York: Oxford University Press, 2000.

Curl, James Stevens. *Oxford Dictionary of Architecture and Landscape Architecture.* 2d ed. New York: Oxford University Press, 2006.

Duby, Georges, ed. *Sculpture: From Antiquity to the Present.* 2 vols. Cologne: Taschen, 1999.

Encyclopedia of World Art. 17 vols. New York: McGraw-Hill, 1959–1987.

Fielding, Mantle. *Dictionary of American Painters, Sculptors, and Engravers.* 2d ed. Poughkeepsie, N.Y.: Apollo, 1986.

Fine, Sylvia Honig. *Women and Art: A History of Women Painters and Sculptors from the Renaissance to the 20th Century.* Rev. ed. Montclair, N.J.: Alanheld & Schram, 1978.

Fleming, John, Hugh Honour, and Nikolaus Pevsner. *The Penguin Dictionary of Architecture and Landscape Architecture.* 5th ed. New York: Penguin, 2000.

Frazier, Nancy. *The Penguin Concise Dictionary of Art History.* New York: Penguin, 2000.

Freedberg, David. *The Power of Images: Studies in the History and Theory of Response.* Chicago: University of Chicago Press, 1989.

Gaze, Delia., ed. *Dictionary of Women Artists.* 2 vols. London: Routledge, 1997.

Hall, James. *Dictionary of Subjects and Symbols in Art.* 2d ed. Boulder, Colo.: Westview, 2008.

Harris, Anne Sutherland, and Linda Nochlin. *Women Artists: 1550–1950.* Los Angeles: Los Angeles County Museum of Art; New York: Knopf, 1977.

Hauser, Arnold. *The Sociology of Art.* Chicago: University of Chicago Press, 1982.

Hults, Linda C. *The Print in the Western World: An Introductory History.* Madison: University of Wisconsin Press, 1996.

Kemp, Martin. *The Science of Art: Optical Themes in Western Art from Brunelleschi to Seurat.* New Haven, Conn.: Yale University Press, 1990.

Kostof, Spiro, and Gregory Castillo. *A History of Architecture: Settings and Rituals.* 2d ed. Oxford: Oxford University Press, 1995.

Kultermann, Udo. *The History of Art History.* New York: Abaris, 1993.

Lucie-Smith, Edward. *The Thames & Hudson Dictionary of Art Terms.* 2d ed. New York: Thames & Hudson, 2004.

Moffett, Marian, Michael Fazio, and Lawrence Wadehouse. *A World History of Architecture.* Boston: McGraw-Hill, 2004.

Morgan, Anne Lee. *Oxford Dictionary of American Art and Artists.* New York: Oxford University Press, 2008.

Murray, Peter, and Linda Murray. *A Dictionary of Art and Artists.* 7th ed. New York: Penguin, 1998.

Nelson, Robert S., and Richard Shiff, eds. *Critical Terms for Art History.* Chicago: University of Chicago Press, 1996.

Pazanelli, Roberta, ed. *The Color of Life: Polychromy in Sculpture from Antiquity to the Present.* Los Angeles: J. Paul Getty Museum, 2008.

Penny, Nicholas. *The Materials of Sculpture.* New Haven, Conn.: Yale University Press, 1993.

Pevsner, Nikolaus. *A History of Building Types.* London: Thames & Hudson, 1987. Reprint of 1979 ed.

———. *An Outline of European Architecture.* 8th ed. Baltimore: Penguin, 1974.

Pierce, James Smith. *From Abacus to Zeus: A Handbook of Art History.* 7th ed. Upper Saddle River, N.J.: Pearson Prentice Hall, 1998.

Placzek, Adolf K., ed. *Macmillan Encyclopedia of Architects.* 4 vols. New York: Macmillan, 1982.

Podro, Michael. *The Critical Historians of Art.* New Haven, Conn.: Yale University Press, 1982.

Pollock, Griselda. *Vision and Difference: Femininity, Feminism, and Histories of Art.* London: Routledge, 1988.

Pregill, Philip, and Nancy Volkman. *Landscapes in History Design and Planning in the Eastern and Western Traditions.* 2d ed. Hoboken, N.J.: Wiley, 1999.

Preziosi, Donald, ed. *The Art of Art History: A Critical Anthology.* New York: Oxford University Press, 1998.

Read, Herbert. *The Thames & Hudson Dictionary of Art and Artists.* Rev. ed. New York: Thames & Hudson, 1994.

Reid, Jane D. *The Oxford Guide to Classical Mythology in the Arts 1300–1990s.* 2 vols. New York: Oxford University Press, 1993.

Rogers, Elizabeth Barlow. *Landscape Design: A Cultural and Architectural History.* New York: Abrams, 2001.

Roth, Leland M. *Understanding Architecture: Its Elements, History, and Meaning.* 2d ed. Boulder, Colo.: Westview, 2006.

Schama, Simon. *The Power of Art.* New York: Ecco, 2006.

Slatkin, Wendy. *Women Artists in History: From Antiquity to the 20th Century.* 4th ed. Upper Saddle River, N.J.: Prentice Hall, 2000.

Steer, John, and Antony White. *Atlas of Western Art History: Artists, Sites, and Monuments from Ancient Greece to the Modern Age.* New York: Facts on File, 1994.

Stratton, Arthur. *The Orders of Architecture: Greek, Roman, and Renaissance.* London: Studio, 1986.

Summers, David. *Real Spaces: World Art History and the Rise of Western Modernism.* London: Phaidon, 2003.

Sutton, Ian. *Western Architecture: From Ancient Greece to the Present.* New York: Thames & Hudson, 1999.

Trachtenberg, Marvin, and Isabelle Hyman. *Architecture, from Prehistory to Post-Modernism.* 2d ed. Upper Saddle River, N.J.: Prentice Hall, 2003.

Turner, Jane, ed. *The Dictionary of Art.* 34 vols. New ed. New York: Oxford University Press, 2003.

Watkin, David. *A History of Western Architecture.* 4th ed. London: Laurence King, 2010.

West, Shearer. *Portraiture.* New York: Oxford University Press, 2004.

Wittkower, Rudolf. *Sculpture Processes and Principles.* New York: Harper & Row, 1977.

Wren, Linnea H., and Janine M. Carter, eds. *Perspectives on Western Art: Source Documents and Readings from the Ancient Near East through the Middle Ages.* New York: Harper & Row, 1987.

Zijlmans, Kitty, and Wilfried van Damme, eds. *World Art Studies: Exploring Concepts and Approaches.* Amsterdam: Valiz, 2008.

Chapter 14: Late Medieval Italy

Bomford, David. *Art in the Making: Italian Painting before 1400.* London: National Gallery, 1989.

Borsook, Eve, and Fiorelli Superbi Gioffredi. *Italian Altarpieces 1250–1550: Function and Design.* Oxford: Clarendon, 1994.

Bourdua, Louise. *The Franciscans and Art Patronage in Late Medieval Italy.* New York: Cambridge University Press, 2004.

Cole, Bruce. *Sienese Painting: From Its Origins to the Fifteenth Century.* New York: Harper Collins, 1987.

Derbes, Anne. *Picturing the Passion in Late Medieval Italy: Narrative Painting, Franciscan Ideologies, and the Levant.* New York: Cambridge University Press, 1996.

Derbes, Anne, and Mark Sandona, eds. *The Cambridge Companion to Giotto.* New York: Cambridge University Press, 2004.

Hills, Paul. *The Light of Early Italian Painting.* New Haven, Conn.: Yale University Press, 1987.

Maginnis, Hayden B. J. *Painting in the Age of Giotto: A Historical Reevaluation.* University Park: Pennsylvania State University Press, 1997.

———. *The World of the Early Sienese Painter.* University Park: Pennsylvania State University Press, 2001.

Meiss, Millard. *Painting in Florence and Siena after the Black Death.* Princeton, N.J.: Princeton University Press, 1976.

Moskowitz, Anita Fiderer. *Italian Gothic Sculpture, c. 1250–c. 1400.* New York: Cambridge University Press, 2001.

———. *Nicola & Giovanni Pisano: The Pulpits: Pious Devotion, Pious Diversion.* London: Harvey Miller, 2005.

Norman, Diana, ed. *Siena, Florence, and Padua: Art, Society, and Religion 1280–1400.* New Haven, Conn.: Yale University Press, 1995.

Poeschke, Joachim. *Italian Frescoes: The Age of Giotto, 1280–1400.* New York: Abbeville, 2005.

Pope-Hennessy, John. *Italian Gothic Sculpture.* 3d ed. Oxford: Phaidon, 1986.

Stubblebine, James H. *Duccio di Buoninsegna and His School.* Princeton, N.J.: Princeton University Press, 1979.

White, John. *Art and Architecture in Italy: 1250–1400.* 3d ed. New Haven, Conn.: Yale University Press, 1993.

———. *Duccio: Tuscan Art and the Medieval Workshop.* London: Thames & Hudson, 1979.

Renaissance Art, General

Adams, Laurie Schneider. *Italian Renaissance Art.* Boulder, Colo.: Westview, 2001.

Andrés, Glenn M., John M. Hunisak, and Richard Turner. *The Art of Florence.* 2 vols. New York: Abbeville, 1988.

Campbell, Gordon. *The Grove Encyclopedia of Northern Renaissance Art.* New York: Oxford University Press, 2009.

———. *Renaissance Art and Architecture.* New York: Oxford University Press, 2005.

Campbell, Lorne. *Renaissance Portraits: European Portrait-Painting in the Fourteenth, Fifteenth, and Sixteenth Centuries.* New Haven, Conn.: Yale University Press, 1990.

Christian, Kathleen, and David J. Drogin, eds. *Patronage and Italian Renaissance Sculpture.* Burlington, Vt.: Ashgate, 2010.

Cole, Bruce. *Italian Art, 1250–1550: The Relation of Renaissance Art to Life and Society.* New York: Harper & Row, 1987.

———. *The Renaissance Artist at Work: From Pisano to Titian.* New York: Harper Collins, 1983.

Cranston, Jodi. *The Poetics of Portraiture in the Italian Renaissance.* New York: Cambridge University Press, 2000.

Frommel, Christoph Luitpold. *The Architecture of the Italian Renaissance.* London: Thames & Hudson, 2007.

Furlotti, Barbara, and Guido Rebecchini. *The Art of Mantua: Power and Patronage in the Renaissance.* Los Angeles: J. Paul Getty Museum, 2008.

Hall, Marcia B. *Color and Meaning: Practice and Theory in Renaissance Painting.* Cambridge: Cambridge University Press, 1992.

Hartt, Frederick, and David G. Wilkins. *History of Italian Renaissance Art.* 7th ed. Upper Saddle River, N.J.: Prentice Hall, 2010.

Haskell, Francis, and Nicholas Penny. *Taste and the Antique: The Lure of Classical Sculpture 1500–1900.* New Haven, Conn.: Yale University Press, 1981.

Kent, F. W., and Patricia Simons, eds. *Patronage, Art, and Society in Renaissance Italy.* Canberra: Humanities Research Centre and Clarendon Press, 1987.

King, Catherine E. *Renaissance Women Patrons: Wives and Widows in Italy, c. 1300–1550.* Manchester: Manchester University Press, 1998.

Levey, Michael. *Florence: A Portrait.* Cambridge, Mass.: Harvard University Press, 1998.

Lubbock, Jules. *Storytelling in Christian Art from Giotto to Donatello.* New Haven, Conn.: Yale University Press, 2006.

Paoletti, John T., and Gary M. Radke. *Art, Power, and Patronage in Renaissance Italy.* Upper Saddle River, N.J.: Prentice Hall, 2005.

Partridge, Loren. *Art of Renaissance Florence, 1400–1600.* Berkeley and Los Angeles: University of California Press, 2009.

Pope-Hennessy, John. *Introduction to Italian Sculpture.* 3d ed. 3 vols. New York: Phaidon, 1986.

Richardson, Carol M., Kim W. Woods, and Michael W. Franklin, eds. *Renaissance Art Reconsidered: An Anthology of Primary Sources.* Malden, Mass.: Blackwell, 2007.

Smith, Jeffrey Chipps. *The Northern Renaissance.* New York: Phaidon, 2004.

Snyder, James, Larry Silver, and Henry Luttikhuizen. *Northern Renaissance Art: Painting, Sculpture, the Graphic Arts from 1350 to 1575.* 2nd ed. Upper Saddle River, N.J.: Prentice Hall, 2005.

Strinati, Claudio, and Pomeroy, Jordana. *Italian Women Artists from Renaissance to Baroque.* Milan: Skira, 2007.

Thomson, David. *Renaissance Architecture: Critics, Patrons, and Luxury.* Manchester: Manchester University Press, 1993.

Tinagli, Paola. *Women in Italian Renaissance Art: Gender, Representation, Identity.* Manchester: Manchester University Press, 1997.

Wittkower, Rudolf. *Architectural Principles in the Age of Humanism.* 4th ed. London: Academy, 1988.

Woods, Kim W. *Making Renaissance Art.* New Haven, Conn.: Yale University Press, 2007.

———. *Viewing Renaissance Art.* New Haven, Conn.: Yale University Press, 2007.

Woods-Marsden, Joanna. *Renaissance Self-Portraiture: The Visual Construction of Identity and the Social Status of the Artist.* New Haven, Conn.: Yale University Press, 1998.

Chapter 15: Late Medieval and Early Renaissance Art in Northern Europe

Ainsworth, Maryan W., and Maximiliaan P. J. Martens. *Petrus Christus, Renaissance Master of Bruges.* New York: Metropolitan Museum of Art, 1994.

Art from the Court of Burgundy: The Patronage of Philip the Bold and John the Fearless 1364–1419. Cleveland: Cleveland Museum of Art, 2004.

Baxandall, Michael. *The Limewood Sculptors of Renaissance Germany.* New Haven, Conn.: Yale University Press, 1980.

Borchert, Till-Holger. *Age of Van Eyck: The Mediterranean World and Early Netherlandish Painting, 1430–1530.* New York: Thames & Hudson, 2002.

Brinkmann, Bodo. *Konrad Witz.* Ostfildern: Hatje Cantz, 2011.

Campbell, Lorne. *The Fifteenth-Century Netherlandish Schools.* London: National Gallery Publications, 1998.

———. *Van der Weyden.* London: Chaucer, 2004.

Châtelet, Albert. *Early Dutch Painting.* New York: Konecky, 1988.

Friedländer, Max J. *Early Netherlandish Painting.* 14 vols. New York: Praeger/Phaidon, 1967–1976.

———. *From Van Eyck to Bruegel.* 3d ed. Ithaca, N.Y.: Cornell University Press, 1981.

Harbison, Craig. *The Mirror of the Artist: Northern Renaissance Art in Its Historical Context.* New York: Abrams, 1995.

Jacobs, Lynn F. *Early Netherlandish Carved Altarpieces, 1380–1550: Medieval Tastes and Mass Marketing.* Cambridge: Cambridge University Press, 1998.

Kemperdick, Stephan. *Rogier van der Weyden.* Cologne: H. F. Ullmann, 2007.

Kemperdick, Stephan, and Jocen Sander, eds. *The Master of Flémalle and Rogier van der Weyden.* Ostfildern: Hatje Cantz, 2009.

Lane, Barbara G. *The Altar and the Altarpiece: Sacramental Themes in Early Netherlandish Painting.* New York: Harper & Row, 1984.

Meiss, Millard. *French Painting in the Time of Jean de Berry: The Limbourgs and Their Contemporaries.* New York: Braziller, 1974.

Michiels, Alfred. *Hans Memling*. London: Parkstone, 2008.

Müller, Theodor. *Sculpture in the Netherlands, Germany, France, and Spain: 1400–1500*. New Haven, Conn.: Yale University Press, 1986.

Nash, Susie. *Northern Renaissance Art*. New York: Oxford University Press, 2008.

Pächt, Otto. *Early Netherlandish Painting from Rogier van der Weyden to Gerard David*. New York: Harvey Miller, 1997.

Panofsky, Erwin. *Early Netherlandish Painting: Its Origins and Character*. 2 vols. Cambridge, Mass.: Harvard University Press, 1966.

Parshall, Peter, ed. *The Woodcut in Fifteenth-Century Europe*. New Haven, Conn.: Yale University Press, 2009.

Parshall, Peter, and Rainer Schoch. *Origins of European Printmaking: Fifteenth-Century Woodcuts and Their Public*. New Haven, Conn.: Yale University Press, 2005.

Prevenier, Walter, and Wim Blockmans. *The Burgundian Netherlands*. Cambridge: Cambridge University Press, 1986.

Tomlinson, Amanda. *Van Eyck*. London: Chaucer, 2007.

Wolfthal, Diane. *The Beginnings of Netherlandish Canvas Painting, 1400–1530*. New York: Cambridge University Press, 1989.

Chapter 16: The Renaissance in Quattrocento Italy

Ahl, Diane Cole. *Fra Angelico*. New York: Phaidon, 2008.
———, ed. *The Cambridge Companion to Masaccio*. New York: Cambridge University Press, 2002.

Ames-Lewis, Francis. *Drawing in Early Renaissance Italy*. 2d ed. New Haven, Conn.: Yale University Press, 2000.
———. *The Intellectual Life of the Early Renaissance Artist*. New Haven, Conn.: Yale University Press, 2000.

Baxandall, Michael. *Painting and Experience in Fifteenth-Century Italy: A Primer in the Social History of Pictorial Style*. 2d ed. New York: Oxford University Press, 1988.

Bober, Phyllis Pray, and Ruth Rubinstein. *Renaissance Artists and Antique Sculpture: A Handbook of Sources*. Oxford: Oxford University Press, 1986.

Borsook, Eve. *The Mural Painters of Tuscany*. New York: Oxford University Press, 1981.

Cole, Alison. *Virtue and Magnificence: Art of the Italian Renaissance Courts*. New York: Abrams, 1995.

Cole, Bruce. *Masaccio and the Art of Early Renaissance Florence*. Bloomington: Indiana University Press, 1980.

Dempsey, Charles. *The Portrayal of Love: Botticelli's* Primavera *and Humanist Culture at the Time of Lorenzo the Magnificent*. Princeton, N.J.: Princeton University Press, 1992.

Edgerton, Samuel Y., Jr. *The Heritage of Giotto's Geometry: Art and Science on the Eve of the Scientific Revolution*. Ithaca, N.Y.: Cornell University Press, 1991.
———. *The Renaissance Rediscovery of Linear Perspective*. New York: Harper & Row, 1976.

Gilbert, Creighton, ed. *Italian Art 1400–1500: Sources and Documents*. Evanston, Ill.: Northwestern University Press, 1992.

Goldthwaite, Richard A. *The Building of Renaissance Florence: An Economic and Social History*. Baltimore: Johns Hopkins University Press, 1980.

Goy, Richard J. *Building Renaissance Venice: Patrons, Architects, and Builders c. 1430–1500*. New Haven, Conn.: Yale University Press, 2006.

Heydenreich, Ludwig H. *Architecture in Italy, 1400–1500*. 2d ed. New Haven, Conn.: Yale University Press, 1996.

Hollingsworth, Mary. *Patronage in Renaissance Italy: From 1400 to the Early Sixteenth Century*. Baltimore: Johns Hopkins University Press, 1994.

Holmes, Megan. *Fra Filippo Lippi: The Carmelite Painter*. New Haven, Conn.: Yale University Press, 1999.

Kemp, Martin. *Behind the Picture: Art and Evidence in the Italian Renaissance*. New Haven, Conn.: Yale University Press, 1997.

Kempers, Bram. *Painting, Power, and Patronage: The Rise of the Professional Artist in the Italian Renaissance*. London: Penguin, 1992.

Kent, Dale. *Cosimo de' Medici and the Florentine Renaissance: The Patron's Oeuvre*. New Haven, Conn.: Yale University Press, 2000.

Lieberman, Ralph. *Renaissance Architecture in Venice*. New York: Abbeville, 1982.

Lindow, James R. *The Renaissance Palace in Florence: Magnificence and Splendour in Fifteenth-Century Italy*. Burlington Vt.: Ashgate, 2007.

Manca, Joseph. *Andrea Mantegna and the Italian Renaissance*. New York: Parkstone, 2006.

McAndrew, John. *Venetian Architecture of the Early Renaissance*. Cambridge, Mass.: MIT Press, 1980.

Murray, Peter. *Renaissance Architecture*. New York: Electa/Rizzoli, 1985.

Olson, Roberta J. M. *Italian Renaissance Sculpture*. London: Thames & Hudson, 1992.

Osborne, June. *Urbino: The Story of a Renaissance City*. Chicago: University of Chicago Press, 2003.

Poeschke, Joachim. *Donatello and His World: Sculpture of the Italian Renaissance*. New York: Abrams, 1993.

Radke, Gary M., ed. *The Gates of Paradise: Lorenzo Ghiberti's Renaissance Masterpiece*. New Haven, Conn.: Yale University Press, 2007.

Seymour, Charles. *Sculpture in Italy: 1400–1500*. New Haven, Conn.: Yale University Press, 1992.

Turner, A. Richard. *Renaissance Florence: The Invention of a New Art*. New York: Abrams, 1997.

Wackernagel, Martin. *The World of the Florentine Renaissance Artist: Projects and Patrons, Workshops and Art Market*. Princeton, N.J.: Princeton University Press, 1981.

Welch, Evelyn. *Art and Society in Italy 1350–1500*. Oxford: Oxford University Press, 1997.

White, John. *The Birth and Rebirth of Pictorial Space*. 3d ed. Boston: Faber & Faber, 1987.

Wright, Alison. *The Pollaiuolo Brothers: The Arts of Florence and Rome*. New Haven, Conn.: Yale University Press, 2005.

Zöllner, Frank. *Sandro Botticelli*. New ed. New York: Prestel, 2009.

Chapter 17: Renaissance and Mannerism in Cinquecento Italy

Beltramini, Guido, and Howard Burns. *Palladio*. London: Royal Academy, 2008.

Blunt, Anthony. *Artistic Theory in Italy, 1450–1600*. London: Oxford University Press, 1975.

Brambilla Barcilon, Pinnin. *Leonardo: The Last Supper*. Chicago: University of Chicago Press, 2001.

Brock, Maurice. *Bronzino*. Paris: Flammarion, 2002.

Brown, David Alan, and Sylvia Ferino-Pagden, eds. *Bellini, Giorgione, Titian, and the Renaissance of Venetian Painting*. New Haven, Conn.: Yale University Press, 2006.

Brown, Patricia Fortini. *Art and Life in Renaissance Venice*. New York: Abrams, 1997.

Cole, Bruce. *Titian and Venetian Painting, 1450–1590*. Boulder, Colo.: Westview, 2000.

Cooper, Tracy E. *Palladio's Venice: Architecture and Society in a Renaissance Republic*. New Haven, Conn.: Yale University Press, 2005.

Cranston, Jodi. *The Muddled Mirror: Materiality and Figuration in Titian's Later Paintings*. University Park, Pa.: Pennsylvania State University Press, 2010.

Dal Pozzolo, Enrico. *Giorgione*. Milan: Motta, 2010.

De Vecchi, Pierluigi. *Raphael*. New York: Abbeville, 2002.

Ekserdjian, David. *Correggio*. New Haven, Conn.: Yale University Press, 1997.
———. *Parmigianino*. New Haven, Conn.: Yale University Press, 2006.

Falomir, Miguel, ed. *Tintoretto*. Madrid: Museo Nacional del Prado, 2007.

Ferino-Pagden, Sylvia, and Giovanna Nepi Scirè. *Giorgione: Myth and Enigma*. Milan: Skira, 2004.

Franklin, David. *Painting in Renaissance Florence, 1500–1550*. New Haven, Conn.: Yale University Press, 2001.

Freedberg, Sydney J. *Painting in Italy: 1500–1600*. 3d ed. New Haven, Conn.: Yale University Press, 1993.

Goffen, Rona. *Piety and Patronage in Renaissance Venice: Bellini, Titian, and the Franciscans*. New Haven, Conn.: Yale University Press, 1986.
———. *Renaissance Rivals: Michelangelo, Leonardo, Raphael, Titian*. New Haven, Conn.: Yale University Press, 2002.

Hall, Marcia B. *After Raphael: Painting in Central Italy in the Sixteenth Century*. New York: Cambridge University Press, 1999.
———. *Rome*. Artistic Centers of the Italian Renaissance. New York: Cambridge University Press, 2005.
———. *The Sacred Image in the Age of Art: Titian, Tintoretto, Barocci, El Greco, Caravaggio*. New Haven, Conn.: Yale University Press, 2011.
———, ed. *The Cambridge Companion to Raphael*. New York: Cambridge University Press, 2005.

Hollingsworth, Mary. *Patronage in Sixteenth Century Italy*. London: John Murray, 1996.

Holt, Elizabeth Gilmore, ed. *A Documentary History of Art. Vol. 2, Michelangelo and the Mannerists*. Rev. ed. Princeton, N.J.: Princeton University Press, 1982.

Humfrey, Peter. *Painting in Renaissance Venice*. New Haven, Conn.: Yale University Press, 1995.
———. *Titian*. London: Phaidon, 2007.

Huse, Norbert, and Wolfgang Wolters. *The Art of Renaissance Venice: Architecture, Sculpture, and Painting*. Chicago: University of Chicago Press, 1990.

Ilchman, Frederick, ed. *Titian, Tintoretto, Veronese: Rivals in Renaissance Venice*. Boston: Museum of Fine Arts, 2009.

Kliemann, Julian-Matthias, and Michael Rohlmann. *Italian Frescoes: High Renaissance and Mannerism, 1510–1600*. New York: Abbeville, 2004.

Levey, Michael. *High Renaissance*. New York: Viking Penguin, 1978.

Lotz, Wolfgang. *Architecture in Italy, 1500–1600*. 2d ed. New Haven, Conn.: Yale University Press, 1995.

Meilman, Patricia, ed. *The Cambridge Companion to Titian*. New York: Cambridge University Press, 2004.

Nichols, Tom. *Tintoretto: Tradition and Identity*. London: Reaktion, 2004.

Partridge, Loren. *The Art of Renaissance Rome*. New York: Abrams, 1996.

Pietrangeli, Carlo, André Chastel, John Shearman, John O'Malley, S.J., Pierluigi de Vecchi, Michael Hirst, Fabrizio Mancinelli, Gianluigi Colalucci, and Franco Bernbei. *The Sistine Chapel: The Art, the History, and the Restoration*. New York: Harmony, 1986.

Pilliod, Elizabeth. *Pontormo, Bronzino, Allori: A Genealogy of Florentine Art*. New Haven, Conn.: Yale University Press, 2001.

Pope-Hennessy, John. *Italian High Renaissance and Baroque Sculpture*. 3d ed. 3 vols. Oxford: Phaidon, 1986.

Rosand, David. *Painting in Cinquecento Venice: Titian, Veronese, Tintoretto*. New Haven, Conn.: Yale University Press, 1982.

Rowe, Colin, and Leon Satkowski. *Italian Architecture of the 16th Century*. New York: Princeton Architectural Press, 2002.

Shearman, John K. G. *Mannerism*. Baltimore: Penguin, 1978.

———. *Only Connect . . . Art and the Spectator in the Italian Renaissance*. Princeton, N.J.: Princeton University Press, 1990.

Summers, David. *Michelangelo and the Language of Art*. Princeton, N.J.: Princeton University Press, 1981.

Talvacchia, Bette. *Raphael*. London: Phaidon, 2007.

Tronzo, William, ed. *St. Peter's in the Vatican*. New York: Cambridge University Press, 2005.

Wilde, Johannes. *Venetian Art from Bellini to Titian*. Oxford: Clarendon, 1981.

Williams, Robert. *Art, Theory, and Culture in Sixteenth-Century Italy: From Techne to Metatechne*. New York: Cambridge University Press, 1997.

Zöllner, Frank. *Leonardo da Vinci: The Complete Paintings and Drawings*. Cologne: Taschen, 2007.

Chapter 18: High Renaissance and Mannerism in Northern Europe and Spain

Ainsworth, Maryan W. *Man, Myth, and Sensual Pleasures: Jan Gossart's Renaissance. The Complete Works*. New York: Metropolitan Museum of Art, 2010.

Bartrum, Giulia, ed. *Albrecht Dürer and His Legacy: The Graphic Work of a Renaissance Artist*. Princeton, N. J.: Princeton University Press, 2003.

Bätschmann, Oskar, and Pascal Griener. *Hans Holbein*. Princeton, N. J.: Princeton University Press, 1997.

Blunt, Anthony. *Art and Architecture in France, 1500–1700*. Rev. ed. New Haven, Conn.: Yale University Press, 1999.

Brinkmann, Bodo, ed. *Cranach*. London: Royal Academy of Arts, 2008.

Buck, Stephanie, and Jochen Sander. *Hans Holbein the Younger: Painter at the Court of Henry VIII*. New York: Thames & Hudson, 2004.

Chapius, Julien. *Tilman Riemenschneider: Master Sculptor of the Late Middle Ages*. Washington, D.C.: National Gallery of Art, 1999.

Chastel, André. *French Art: The Renaissance, 1430–1620*. Paris: Flammarion, 1995.

Davies, David, and John H. Elliott. *El Greco*. London: National Gallery, 2003.

Dixon, Laurinda. *Bosch*. New York: Phaidon, 2003.

Farago, Claire, ed. *Reframing the Renaissance: Visual Culture in Europe and Latin America, 1450–1650*. New Haven, Conn.: Yale University Press, 1995.

Foister, Susan. *Holbein and England*. New Haven, Conn.: Paul Mellon Centre for British Art, 2005.

Gibson, W. S. *"Mirror of the Earth": The World Landscape in Sixteenth-Century Flemish Painting*. Princeton, N.J.: Princeton University Press, 1989.

Harbison, Craig. *The Mirror of the Artist: Northern Renaissance Art in Its Historical Context*. New York: Abrams, 1995.

Koerner, Joseph Leo. *The Reformation of the Image*. Chicago: University of Chicago Press, 2004.

Landau, David, and Peter Parshall. *The Renaissance Print: 1470–1550*. New Haven, Conn.: Yale University Press, 1994.

Price, David Hotchkiss. *Albrecht Dürer's Renaissance: Humanism, Reformation, and the Art of Faith*. Ann Arbor: University of Michigan Press, 2003.

Roberts-Jones, Philippe, and Françoise Roberts-Jones. *Pieter Bruegel*. New York: Abrams, 2002.

Silver, Larry. *Hieronymous Bosch*. New York: Abbeville, 2006.

Smith, Jeffrey C. *German Sculpture of the Later Renaissance, c. 1520–1580: Art in an Age of Uncertainty*. Princeton, N.J.: Princeton University Press, 1993.

Stechow, Wolfgang. *Northern Renaissance Art, 1400–1600: Sources and Documents*. Evanston, Ill.: Northwestern University Press, 1989.

Zerner, Henri. *Renaissance Art in France: The Invention of Classicism*. Paris: Flammarion, 2003.

Baroque Art, General

Blunt, Anthony, ed. *Baroque and Rococo: Architecture and Decoration*. Cambridge: Harper & Row, 1982.

Harris, Ann Sutherland. *Seventeenth-Century Art & Architecture*. Upper Saddle River, N.J.: Prentice Hall, 2005.

Harrison, Charles, Paul Wood, and Jason Gaiger, eds. *Art in Theory, 1648–1815: An Anthology of Changing Ideas*. Oxford: Blackwell, 2000.

Held, Julius, and Donald Posner. *17th- and 18th-Century Art: Baroque Painting, Sculpture, Architecture*. New York: Abrams, 1971.

Lagerlöf, Margaretha R. *Ideal Landscape: Annibale Carracci, Nicolas Poussin, and Claude Lorrain*. New Haven, Conn.: Yale University Press, 1990.

Lawrence, Cynthia, ed. *Women and Art in Early Modern Europe: Patrons, Collectors, and Connoisseurs*. University Park: Pennsylvania State University Press, 1997.

Lemerle, Frédérique, and Yves Pauwels. *Baroque Architecture, 1600–1750*. Paris: Flammarion, 2008.

Minor, Vernon Hyde. *Baroque & Rococo: Art & Culture*. New York, Abrams, 1999.

Norberg-Schulz, Christian. *Baroque Architecture*. New York: Rizzoli, 1986.

———. *Late Baroque and Rococo Architecture*. New York: Electa/Rizzoli, 1985.

Toman, Rolf. *Baroque: Architecture, Sculpture, Painting*. Cologne: Könemann, 1998.

Chapter 19: The Baroque in Italy and Spain

Bissel, R. Ward. *Artemisia Gentileschi and the Authority of Art*. University Park: Pennsylvania State University Press, 1999.

Brown, Jonathan. *The Golden Age of Painting in Spain*. New Haven, Conn.: Yale University Press, 1991.

———. *Velázquez: Painter and Courtier*. New Haven, Conn.: Yale University Press, 1988.

Christiansen, Keith, and Judith W. Mann. *Orazio and Artemisia Gentileschi*. New York: Metropolitan Museum of Art, 2001.

Enggass, Robert, and Jonathan Brown. *Italy and Spain, 1600–1750: Sources and Documents*. Upper Saddle River, N.J.: Prentice Hall, 1970.

Freedberg, Sydney J. *Circa 1600: A Revolution of Style in Italian Painting*. Cambridge, Mass.: Harvard University Press, 1983.

Fried, Michael. *The Moment of Caravaggio*. Princeton, N.J.: Princeton University Press, 2010.

Haskell, Francis. *Patrons and Painters: A Study in the Relations between Italian Art and Society in the Age of the Baroque*. Rev. ed. New Haven, Conn.: Yale University Press, 1980.

Krautheimer, Richard. *The Rome of Alexander VII, 1655–1677*. Princeton, N.J.: Princeton University Press, 1985.

Montagu, Jennifer. *Roman Baroque Sculpture: The Industry of Art*. New Haven, Conn.: Yale University Press, 1989.

Puglisi, Catherine. *Caravaggio*. London: Phaidon, 2000.

Schroth, Sarah, and Ronni Baer. *El Greco to Velazquez: Art during the Reign of Philip III*. Boston: Museum of Fine Arts, 2008.

Strinati, Claudio, and Pomeroy, Jordana. *Italian Women Artists from Renaissance to Baroque*. Milan: Skira, 2007.

Tomlinson, Janis. *From El Greco to Goya: Painting in Spain 1561–1828*. Upper Saddle Ridge, N.J.: Prentice Hall, 1997.

Tronzo, William, ed. *St. Peter's in the Vatican*. New York: Cambridge University Press, 2005.

Varriano, John. *Caravaggio: The Art of Realism*. University Park: Pennsylvania University Press, 2006.

———. *Italian Baroque and Rococo Architecture*. New York: Oxford University Press, 1986.

Wittkower, Rudolf. *Art and Architecture in Italy 1600–1750*. 6th ed. 3 vols. Revised by Joseph Connors and Jennifer Montagu. New Haven, Conn.: Yale University Press, 1999.

Chapter 20: The Baroque in Northern Europe

Alpers, Svetlana. *The Art of Describing: Dutch Art in the Seventeenth Century*. Chicago: University of Chicago Press, 1984.

———. *The Making of Rubens*. New Haven, Conn.: Yale University Press, 1995.

———. *Rembrandt's Enterprise: The Studio and the Market*. Chicago: University of Chicago Press, 1988.

Belkin, Kristin Lohse. *Rubens*. London: Phaidon, 1998.

Biesboer, Pieter, Martina Brunner-Bulst, Henry D. Gregory, and Christian Klemm. *Pieter Claesz: Master of Haarlem Still Life*. Zwolle: Waanders, 2005.

Blunt, Anthony. *Art and Architecture in France, 1500–1700*. Rev. ed. New Haven, Conn.: Yale University Press, 1999.

Brown, Christopher. *Scenes of Everyday Life: Dutch Genre Painting of the Seventeenth Century*. London: Faber & Faber, 1984.

Bryson, Norman. *Word and Image: French Painting of the Ancien Régime*. Cambridge: Cambridge University Press, 1981.

Carr, Dawson W., ed. *Velázquez*. London: National Gallery, 2006.

Chapman, Perry. *Rembrandt's Self-Portraits: A Study in 17th-Century Identity*. Princeton, N.J.: Princeton University Press, 1990.

Chastel, André. *French Art: The Ancien Régime, 1620–1775*. New York: Flammarion, 1996.

Chong, Alan, and Wouter Kloek. *Still-Life Paintings from the Netherlands, 1550–1720*. Zwolle: Waanders, 1999.

Franits, Wayne. *Dutch Seventeenth-Century Genre Painting: Its Stylistic and Thematic Evolution*. New Haven, Conn.: Yale University Press, 2008.

———. *Looking at Seventeenth-Century Dutch Art: Realism Reconsidered*. Cambridge: Cambridge University Press, 1997.

———, ed. *The Cambridge Companion to Vermeer*. New York: Cambridge University Press, 2001.

Haak, Bob. *The Golden Age: Dutch Painters of the Seventeenth Century*. New York: Abrams, 1984.

Hochstrasser, Julie Berger. *Still Life and Trade in the Dutch Golden Age*. New Haven, Conn.: Yale University Press, 2007.

Keazor, Henry. *Nicholas Poussin, 1594–1665*. Cologne: Taschen, 2007.

Kiers, Judikje, and Fieke Tissink. *Golden Age of Dutch Art: Painting, Sculpture, Decorative Art*. New York: Thames & Hudson, 2000.

Liedtke, Walter. *Vermeer: The Complete Paintings*. Antwerp: Ludion, 2008.

———. *A View of Delft: Vermeer and His Contemporaries*. Zwolle: Wanders, 2000.

Mérot, Alain. *French Painting in the Seventeenth Century*. New Haven, Conn.: Yale University Press, 1995.

Muller, Sheila D., ed. *Dutch Art: An Encyclopedia.* New York: Garland, 1997.

North, Michael. *Art and Commerce in the Dutch Golden Age.* New Haven, Conn.: Yale University Press, 1997.

Olson, Todd P. *Poussin and France.* New Haven, Conn.: Yale University Press, 2000.

Rosenberg, Jakob, Seymour Slive, and E. H. ter Kuile. *Dutch Art and Architecture, 1600–1800.* New Haven, Conn.: Yale University Press, 1979.

Schama, Simon. *The Embarrassment of Riches: An Interpretation of Dutch Culture in the Golden Age.* Berkeley: University of California Press, 1988.

Schroth, Sarah, and Ronni Baer, eds. *El Greco to Velázquez: Art during the Reign of Philip III.* Boston: Museum of Fine Arts, 2008.

Slatkes, Leonard J., and Wayne Franits. *The Paintings of Hendrick ter Brugghen 1588–1629: Catalogue Raisonné.* Philadelphia: John Benjamins, 2007.

Stechow, Wolfgang. *Dutch Landscape Painting of the 17th Century.* 3d ed. Oxford: Phaidon, 1981.

Summerson, John. *Inigo Jones.* New Haven, Conn.: Yale University Press, 2000.

Vlieghe, Hans. *Flemish Art and Architecture, 1585–1700.* New Haven, Conn.: Yale University Press, 1998.

Westermann, Mariët. *Rembrandt.* London: Phaidon, 2000.

———. *A Worldly Art: The Dutch Republic 1585–1718.* New Haven, Conn.: Yale University Press, 1996.

Zega, Andres, and Bernd H. Dams. *Palaces of the Sun King: Versailles, Trianon, Marly: The Châteaux of Louis XIV.* New York: Rizzoli, 2002.

Zell, Michael. *Reframing Rembrandt: Jews and the Christian Image in Seventeenth-Century Amsterdam.* Berkeley: University of California Press, 2002.

Chapter 21: Rococo to Neoclassicism: The 18th Century in Europe and America

Beddington, Charles. *Venice: Canaletto and His Rivals.* London: National Gallery, 2010.

Bermingham, Ann. *Landscape and Ideology: The English Rustic Tradition, 1740–1850.* Berkeley: University of California Press, 1986.

Boime, Albert. *Art in the Age of Revolution, 1750–1800.* Chicago: University of Chicago Press, 1987.

Bowron, Edgar Peters, and Joseph J. Rishel, eds. *Art in Rome in the Eighteenth Century.* Philadelphia: Philadelphia Museum of Art, 2000

Braham, Allan. *The Architecture of the French Enlightenment.* Berkeley: University of California Press, 1980.

Brion, Marcel. *Art of the Romantic Era: Romanticism, Classicism, Realism.* New York: Praeger, 1966.

Conisbee, Philip. *Painting in Eighteenth-Century France.* Ithaca, N.Y.: Phaidon/Cornell University Press, 1981.

Craske, Matthew. *Art in Europe, 1700–1830: A History of the Visual Arts in an Era of Unprecedented Urban Economic Growth.* New York: Oxford University Press, 1997.

Crow, Thomas E. *Painters and Public Life in Eighteenth-Century Paris.* New Haven, Conn.: Yale University Press, 1985.

Gaunt, W. *The Great Century of British Painting: Hogarth to Turner.* New York: Phaidon, 1971.

Goodman, Elise, ed. *Art and Culture in the Eighteenth Century: New Dimensions and Multiple Perspectives.* Newark: University of Delaware Press, 2001.

Harrison, Charles, Paul Wood, and Jason Gaiger, eds. *Art in Theory, 1648–1815: An Anthology of Changing Ideas.* Oxford: Blackwell, 2000.

Hedley, Jo. *François Boucher: Seductive Visions.* London: Wallace Collection, 2004.

Herrmann, Luke. *British Landscape Painting of the Eighteenth Century.* New York: Oxford University Press, 1974.

Honour, Hugh. *Neo-Classicism.* Harmondsworth: Penguin, 1968.

Irwin, David. *Neoclassicism.* London: Phaidon, 1997.

Jarrassé, Dominique. *18th-Century French Painting.* Paris: Terrail, 1999.

Kalnein, Wend Graf, and Michael Levey. *Art and Architecture of the Eighteenth Century in France.* New York: Viking/Pelican, 1973.

Lee, Simon. *David.* London: Phaidon, 1999.

Levey, Michael. *Rococo to Revolution: Major Trends in Eighteenth-Century Painting.* London: Thames & Hudson, 1966.

Rosenblum, Robert. *Transformations in Late Eighteenth-Century Art.* Princeton, N.J.: Princeton University Press, 1970.

Roston, Murray. *Changing Perspectives in Literature and the Visual Arts, 1650–1820.* Princeton, N.J.: Princeton University Press, 1990.

Rykwert, Joseph. *The First Moderns: Architects of the Eighteenth Century.* Cambridge, Mass.: MIT Press, 1983.

Stillman, Damie. *English Neo-Classical Architecture.* 2 vols. London: Zwemmer, 1988.

Waterhouse, Ellis Kirkham. *Painting in Britain: 1530–1790.* 4th ed. New Haven, Conn.: Yale University Press, 1979.

Wilton, Andrew. *The Swagger Portrait: Grand Manner Portraiture in Britain from Van Dyck to Augustus John, 1630–1930.* London: Tate Gallery, 1992.

19th and 20th Centuries, General

Arnason, H. H., and Peter Kalb. *History of Modern Art: Painting, Sculpture, Architecture, Photography.* 6th ed. Upper Saddle River, N.J.: Prentice Hall, 2009.

Ashton, Dore. *Twentieth-Century Artists on Art.* New York: Pantheon Books, 1985.

Barnitz, Jacueline. *Twentieth-Century Art of Latin America.* Austin: University of Texas Press, 2001.

Brettell, Richard R. *Modern Art, 1851–1929: Capitalism and Representation.* New York: Oxford University Press, 1999.

Brown, Milton, Sam Hunter, and John Jacobus. *American Art: Painting, Sculpture, Architecture, Decorative Arts, Photography.* New York: Abrams, 1979.

Burnham, Jack. *Beyond Modern Sculpture: The Effects of Science and Technology on the Sculpture of This Century.* New York: Braziller, 1968.

Butler, Cornelia, and Alexandra Schwartz, eds. *Modern Women: Women Artists at the Museum of Modern Art.* New York: Museum of Modern Art, 2010.

Chipp, Herschel B. *Theories of Modern Art.* Berkeley: University of California Press, 1968.

Chu, Petra ten-Doesschate. *Nineteenth-Century European Art.* 2d ed. Upper Saddle River, N.J.: Prentice Hall, 2006.

Coke, Van Deren. *The Painter and the Photograph from Delacroix to Warhol.* Rev. ed. Albuquerque: University of New Mexico Press, 1972.

Colquhoun, Alan. *Modern Architecture.* New York: Oxford University Press, 2002.

Craven, Wayne. *American Art: History and Culture.* Rev. ed. New York: McGraw-Hill, 2002.

Dennis, Rafael Cardoso, and Colin Trodd, eds. *Art and the Academy in the Nineteenth Century.* New Brunswick, N.J.: Rutgers University Press, 2000.

Doordan, Dennis P. *Twentieth-Century Architecture.* New York: Abrams, 2002.

Doss, Erika. *Twentieth-Century American Art.* New York: Oxford University Press, 2002.

Driskell, David C. *Two Centuries of Black American Art.* Los Angeles: Los Angeles County Museum of Art; New York: Knopf, 1976.

Eisenmann, Stephen F., ed. *Nineteenth-Century Art: A Critical History.* 4th ed. New York: Thames & Hudson, 2011.

Elsen, Albert. *Origins of Modern Sculpture.* New York: Braziller, 1974.

Facos, Michelle. *An Introduction to Nineteenth-Century Art.* New York: Routledge, 2011.

Foster, Hal, Rosalind Krauss, Yve-Alain Bois, and Benjamin H. D. Buchloh. *Art since 1900: Modernism, Antimodernism, Postmodernism.* New York: Thames & Hudson, 2004.

Frampton, Kenneth. *Modern Architecture: A Critical History.* 4th ed. New York: Thames & Hudson, 2007.

Frascina, Francis, and Charles Harrison, eds. *Modern Art and Modernism: A Critical Anthology.* New York: Harper & Row, 1982.

Giedion, Siegfried. *Space, Time, and Architecture: The Growth of a New Tradition.* 4th ed. Cambridge, Mass.: Harvard University Press, 1965.

Goldwater, Robert, and Marco Treves, eds. *Artists on Art.* 3d ed. New York: Pantheon, 1958.

Greenough, Sarah, Joel Snyder, David Travis, and Colin Westerbeck. *On the Art of Fixing a Shadow: One Hundred and Fifty Years of Photography.* Washington, D.C.: National Gallery of Art; Chicago: Art Institute of Chicago, 1989.

Hamilton, George H. *Painting and Sculpture in Europe, 1880–1940.* 6th ed. New Haven, Conn.: Yale University Press, 1993.

Harrison, Charles, and Paul Wood. *Art in Theory, 1900–2000: An Anthology of Changing Ideas.* Oxford: Blackwell, 2003.

Herbert, Robert L., ed. *Modern Artists on Art.* Upper Saddle River, N.J.: Prentice Hall, 1971.

Hertz, Richard, and Norman M. Klein, eds. *Twentieth-Century Art Theory: Urbanism, Politics, and Mass Culture.* Englewood Cliffs, N.J.: Prentice Hall, 1990.

Heyer, Paul. *Architects on Architecture: New Directions in America.* New York: Van Nostrand Reinhold, 1993.

Hills, Patricia. *Modern Art in the USA: Issues and Controversies of the 20th Century.* Upper Saddle River, N.J.: Prentice Hall, 2000.

Hitchcock, Henry-Russell. *Architecture: Nineteenth and Twentieth Centuries.* 4th ed. New Haven, Conn.: Yale University Press, 1977.

Hunter, Sam, John Jacobus, and Daniel Wheeler. *Modern Art: Painting, Sculpture, Architecture, Photography.* Rev. 3d ed. Upper Saddle River, N.J.: Prentice Hall, 2004.

Janson, Horst W. *19th-Century Sculpture.* New York: Abrams, 1985.

Jencks, Charles. *Modern Movements in Architecture.* Garden City, N.Y.: Anchor; Doubleday, 1973.

Kaufmann, Edgar, Jr., ed. *The Rise of an American Architecture.* New York: Metropolitan Museum of Art; Praeger, 1970.

Krauss, Rosalind E. *The Originality of the Avant-Garde and Other Modernist Myths.* Cambridge, Mass.: MIT Press, 1985.

———. *Passages in Modern Sculpture.* Cambridge, Mass.: MIT Press, 1981.

Lewis, Samella S. *African American Art and Artists.* Rev. ed. Berkeley: University of California Press, 1994.

Licht, Fred. *Sculpture, Nineteenth and Twentieth Centuries.* Greenwich, Conn.: New York Graphic Society, 1967.

Marien, Mary Warner. *Photography: A Cultural History.* 3d ed. Upper Saddle River, N.J.: Prentice Hall, 2011.

Mason, Jerry, ed. *International Center of Photography Encyclopedia of Photography.* New York: Crown, 1984.

McCoubrey, John W. *American Art, 1700–1960: Sources and Documents.* Englewood Cliffs, N.J.: Prentice Hall, 1965.

Newhall, Beaumont. *The History of Photography.* New York: Museum of Modern Art, 1982.

Osborne, Harold. *The Oxford Companion to Twentieth-Century Art.* New York: Oxford University Press, 1981.

Pohl, Frances K. *Framing America: A Social History of American Art.* 2d ed. New York: Thames & Hudson, 2008.

Rose, Barbara. *American Art since 1900.* Rev. ed. New York: Praeger, 1975.

Rosenblum, Naomi. *A World History of Photography.* 4th ed. New York: Abbeville, 2007.

Rosenblum, Robert. *Modern Painting and the Northern Romantic Tradition: Friedrich to Rothko.* New York: Harper & Row, 1975.

Rosenblum, Robert, and Horst W. Janson. *19th-Century Art.* Rev. ed. Upper Saddle River, N.J.: Prentice Hall, 2005.

Ross, Stephen David, ed. *Art and Its Significance: An Anthology of Aesthetic Theory.* Albany: State University of New York Press, 1987.

Russell, John. *The Meanings of Modern Art.* New York: Museum of Modern Art; Thames & Hudson, 1981.

Scully, Vincent. *Modern Architecture.* Rev. ed. New York: Braziller, 1974.

Spalding, Francis. *British Art since 1900.* London: Thames & Hudson, 1986.

Spencer, Harold. *American Art: Readings from the Colonial Era to the Present.* New York: Scribner, 1980.

Steinberg, Leo. *Other Criteria: Confrontations with 20th-Century Art.* New York: Oxford University Press, 1972.

Szarkowski, John. *Photography until Now.* New York: Museum of Modern Art, 1989.

Upton, Dell. *Architecture in the United States.* Oxford: Oxford University Press, 1998.

Weaver, Mike. *The Art of Photography: 1839–1989.* New Haven, Conn.: Yale University Press, 1989.

Whiffen, Marcus, and Frederick Koeper. *American Architecture, 1607–1976.* Cambridge, Mass.: MIT Press, 1983.

Wilmerding, John. *American Art.* Harmondsworth: Penguin, 1976.

Wilson, Simon. *Holbein to Hockney: A History of British Art.* London: Tate Gallery & Bodley Head, 1979.

Chapter 22: Romanticism, Realism, Photography: Europe and America, 1800 to 1870

Amic, Sylvain, et al. *Gustave Courbet.* Ostfildern: Hatje Cantz, 2008.

Bartoli, Damien, and Frederick C. Ross. *William Bouguereau.* 2 vols. New York: Antique Collectors' Club, 2010.

Bellenger, Sylvain. *Girodet, 1767–1824.* Paris: Gallimard, 2005.

Bergdoll, Barry. *European Architecture 1750–1890.* New York: Oxford University Press, 2000.

Boime, Albert. *The Academy and French Painting in the 19th Century.* London: Phaidon, 1971.

———. *Art in the Age of Bonapartism, 1800–1815.* Chicago: University of Chicago Press, 1990.

Bordes, Philippe. *Jacques-Louis David: Empire to Exile.* New Haven, Conn.: Yale University Press, 2007.

Brown, David Blayney. *Romanticism.* New York: Phaidon, 2001.

Bryson, Norman. *Tradition and Desire: From David to Delacroix.* New York: Cambridge University Press, 1984.

Burns, Sarah, and John Davis. *American Art to 1900: A Documentary History.* Berkeley and Los Angeles: University of California Press, 2009.

Clark, T. J. *The Absolute Bourgeois: Artists and Politics in France, 1848–1851.* London: Thames & Hudson, 1973.

———. *Image of the People: Gustave Courbet and the 1848 Revolution.* London: Thames & Hudson, 1973.

———. *The Painting of Modern Life: Paris in the Art of Manet and His Followers.* Princeton, N.J.: Princeton University Press, 1984.

Clay, Jean. *Romanticism.* New York: Phaidon, 1981.

Eitner, Lorenz. *Neoclassicism and Romanticism, 1750–1850: An Anthology of Sources and Documents.* New York: Harper & Row, 1989.

Fried, Michael. *Courbet's Realism.* Chicago: University of Chicago Press, 1982.

———. *Manet's Modernism, or, The Face of Painting in the 1860s.* Chicago: University of Chicago Press, 1996.

Hilton, Timothy. *The Pre-Raphaelites.* New York: Oxford University Press, 1970.

Hofmann, Werner. *Caspar David Friedrich.* New York: Thames & Hudson, 2001.

———. *Goya.* New York: Thames & Hudson, 2003.

Holt, Elizabeth Gilmore, ed. *From the Classicists to the Impressionists: A Documentary History of Art and Architecture in the Nineteenth Century.* Garden City, N.J.: Anchor Books; Doubleday, 1966.

Honour, Hugh. *Romanticism.* New York: Harper & Row, 1979.

Koerner, Joseph Leo. *Caspar David Friedrich and the Subject of Landscape.* 2d ed. London: Reaktion, 2009.

Krell, Alain. *Manet and the Painters of Contemporary Life.* London: Thames & Hudson, 1996.

Kroeber, Karl. *British Romantic Art.* Berkeley: University of California Press, 1986.

Le Men, Ségolène. *Courbet.* New York: Abbeville, 2008.

Lewis, Michael J. *The Gothic Revival.* New York: Thames & Hudson, 2002.

Licht, Fred. *Goya.* New York: Abbeville, 2001.

Mainardi, Patricia. *Art and Politics of the Second Empire: The Universal Expositions of 1855 and 1867.* New Haven, Conn.: Yale University Press, 1987.

———. *The End of the Salon: Art and the State in the Early Third Republic.* Cambridge: Cambridge University Press, 1993.

Middleton, Robin. *Architecture of the Nineteenth Century.* London: Phaidon, 2003.

Middleton, Robin, and David Watkin. *Neoclassical and 19th-Century Architecture.* 2 vols. New York: Electa/Rizzoli, 1987.

Needham, Gerald. *19th-Century Realist Art.* New York: Harper & Row, 1988.

Nochlin, Linda. *Realism and Tradition in Art, 1848–1900: Sources and Documents.* Upper Saddle River, N.J.: Prentice Hall, 1966.

Novak, Barbara. *American Painting of the Nineteenth Century: Realism and the American Experience.* New York: Harper & Row, 1979.

Novak, Barbara. *Nature and Culture: American Landscape and Painting, 1825–1875.* 3d ed. New York: Oxford University Press, 2007.

Nature and Culture: American Landscape and Painting, 1825–1875. 3d ed. New York: Oxford University Press, 2007.

Novotny, Fritz. *Painting and Sculpture in Europe, 1780–1880.* 3d ed. New Haven, Conn.: Yale University Press, 1988.

Porterfield, Todd. *The Allure of Empire: Art in the Service of French Imperialism 1798–1836.* Princeton, N.J.: Princeton University Press, 1998.

Rosen, Charles, and Henri Zerner. *Romanticism and Realism: The Mythology of Nineteenth-Century Art.* New York: Viking, 1984.

Rubin, James Henry. *Courbet.* London: Phaidon, 1997.

———. *Manet: Initial M, Hand and Eye.* Paris: Flammarion, 2010.

Shelton, Andrew Carrington. *Ingres.* London: Phaidon, 2008.

Sloane, Joseph C. *French Painting between the Past and the Present: Artists, Critics, and Traditions from 1848 to 1870.* Princeton, N.J.: Princeton University Press, 1973.

Symmons, Sarah. *Goya.* London: Phaidon, 1998.

Taylor, Joshua, ed. *Nineteenth-Century Theories of Art.* Berkeley: University of California Press, 1987.

Tillier, Betrand, et al. *Gustave Courbet.* New York: Metropolitan Museum of Art, 2008.

Toman, Rolf, ed. *Neoclassicism and Romanticism: Architecture, Sculpture, Painting, Drawings, 1750–1848.* Cologne: Könemann, 2006.

Vaughn, William. *German Romantic Painting.* New Haven, Conn.: Yale University Press, 1980.

Wolf, Bryan Jay. *Romantic Revision: Culture and Consciousness in Nineteenth-Century American Painting and Literature.* Chicago: University of Chicago Press, 1986.

Wood, Christopher. *The Pre-Raphaelites.* New York: Viking, 1981.

Chapter 23: Impressionism, Post-Impressionism, Symbolism: Europe and America, 1870 to 1900

Baal-Teshuva, Jacob. *Louis Comfort Tiffany.* Cologne: Taschen, 2008.

Bergdoll, Barry. *European Architecture 1750–1890.* New York: Oxford University Press, 2000.

Bryson, Norman. *Tradition and Desire: From David to Delacroix.* New York: Cambridge University Press, 1984.

Calloway, Stephen. *Aubrey Beardsley.* New York: Harry N. Abrams, 1998.

Clark, T. J. *The Painting of Modern Life: Paris in the Art of Manet and His Followers.* Princeton, N.J.: Princeton University Press, 1984.

Cogeval, Guy, ed. *Claude Monet, 1840–1926.* Paris: Réunion des Musées Nationaux, 2010.

Distel, Anne. *Renoir.* New York: Abbeville, 2010.

Eitner, Lorenz. *Neoclassicism and Romanticism, 1750–1850: An Anthology of Sources and Documents.* New York: Harper & Row, 1989.

Facos, Michelle. *Symbolism in Context.* Berkeley: University of California Press, 2009.

Hauptmann, Jodi. *Beyond the Visible: The Art of Odilon Redon.* New York: Museum of Modern Art, 2005.

Loyrette, Henri, Sebastien Allard, and Laurence Des Cars. *Nineteenth Century French Art: From Romanticism to Impressionism, Post-Impressionism, and Art Nouveau.* Paris: Flammarion, 2007.

Masson, Raphaël, and Véronique Mattiussi. *Rodin.* Paris: Flammarion, 2004.

McShine, Kynaston, ed. *Edvard Munch: The Modern Life of the Soul.* New York: Museum of Modern Art, 2006.

Middleton, Robin. *Architecture of the Nineteenth Century.* London: Phaidon, 2003.

Middleton, Robin, and David Watkin. *Neoclassical and 19th-Century Architecture.* 2 vols. New York: Electa/Rizzoli, 1987.

Pfeiffer, Ingrid, et al. *Women Impressionists.* Ostfildern: Hatje Cantz, 2008.

Swinbourne, Anna. *James Ensor.* New York: Museum of Modern Art, 2009.

Thomson, Belinda, ed. *Gauguin: Maker of Myth.* London: Tate, 2010.

Zerbst, Rainer. *Gaudí: The Complete Buildings.* Cologne: Taschen, 2005.

Chapter 24: Modernism in Europe and America, 1900 to 1945

Antliff, Mark. *Cultural Politics and the Parisian Avant-Garde*. Princeton, N.J.: Princeton University Press, 1993.

Antliff, Mark, and Patricia Leighten. *Cubism and Culture*. New York: Thames & Hudson, 2001.

Arnaldo, Javier, and Max Hollein. *Kirchner*. Ostfildern: Hatje Cantz, 2010.

Baigell, Matthew. *The American Scene: American Painting of the 1930s*. New York: Praeger, 1974.

Barr, Alfred H., Jr. *Cubism and Abstract Art: Painting, Sculpture, Constructions, Photography, Architecture, Industrial Arts, Theatre, Films, Posters, Typography*. Cambridge, Mass.: Belknap, 1986.

Barron, Stephanie. *Exiles and Emigrés: The Flight of European Artists from Hitler*. Los Angeles: Los Angeles County Museum of Art, 1997.

————, ed. *Degenerate Art: The Fate of the Avant-Garde in Nazi Germany*. Los Angeles: Los Angeles County Museum of Art, 1991.

Bayer, Herbert, Walter Gropius, and Ise Gropius. *Bauhaus, 1919–1928*. New York: Museum of Modern Art, 1975.

Bearden, Romare, and Harry Henderson. *A History of African-American Artists from 1792 to the Present*. New York: Pantheon, 1993.

Bergdoll, Barry. *Bauhaus 1919–1933*. New York: Museum of Modern Art, 2009.

Bouvet, Vincent, and Gérard Durozoi. *Paris between the Wars 1919–1939: Art, Life & Culture*. New York: Vendome, 2010.

Breton, André. *Surrealism and Painting*. New York: Harper & Row, 1972.

Brown, Milton. *Story of the Armory Show: The 1913 Exhibition That Changed American Art*. 2d ed. New York: Abbeville, 1988.

Campbell, Mary Schmidt, David C. Driskell, David Lewis Levering, and Deborah Willis Ryan. *Harlem Renaissance: Art of Black America*. New York: Studio Museum in Harlem; Abrams, 1987.

Cowling, Elizabeth, ed. *Picasso: Challenging the Past*. London: National Gallery, 2011.

Cox, Neil. *Cubism*. London: Phaidon, 2000.

Curtis, Penelope. *Sculpture 1900–1945*. New York: Oxford University Press, 1999.

Curtis, William J. R. *Modern Architecture since 1900*. Upper Saddle River, N.J.: Prentice Hall, 1996.

Davidson, Abraham A. *Early American Modernist Painting, 1910–1935*. New York: Harper & Row, 1981.

Dietrich, Dorothea, ed. *Dada: Zurich, Berlin, Hannover, Cologne, New York, Paris*. Washington, D.C.: National Gallery, 2008.

Du Pont, Diana C. *Tamayo: A Modern Icon Reinterpreted*. Santa Barbara, Calif.: Santa Barbara Museum of Art, 2007.

Eberle, Matthias. *World War I and the Weimar Artists: Dix, Grosz, Beckmann, Schlemmer*. New Haven, Conn.: Yale University Press, 1985.

Edwards, Steve, and Paul Wood, eds. *Art of the Avant-Gardes*. New Haven, Conn.: Yale University Press, 2004.

Elderfield, John. *The "Wild Beasts": Fauvism and Its Affinities*. New York: Museum of Modern Art, 1976.

Fer, Briony, David Batchelor, and Paul Wood. *Realism, Rationalism, Surrealism: Art between the Wars*. New Haven, Conn.: Yale University Press, 1993.

Friedman, Mildred, ed. *De Stijl, 1917–1931: Visions of Utopia*. Minneapolis: Walker Art Center; New York: Abbeville, 1982.

Gale, Matthew. *Dada and Surrealism*. London: Phaidon, 1997.

Goldberg, Rose Lee. *Performance: Live Art 1909 to the Present*. New York: Abrams, 1979.

Golding, John. *Cubism: A History and an Analysis, 1907–1914*. Cambridge, Mass.: Belknap, 1988.

Gordon, Donald E. *Expressionism: Art and Idea*. New Haven, Conn.: Yale University Press, 1987.

Harrison, Charles, Francis Frascina, and Gil Perry. *Primitivism, Cubism, Abstraction: The Early Twentieth Century*. New Haven, Conn.: Yale University Press, 1993.

Herbert, James D. *Fauve Painting: The Making of Cultural Politics*. New Haven, Conn.: Yale University Press, 1992.

Herrera, Hayden, ed. *Frida Kahlo*. Minneapolis: Walker Art Center, 2007.

Hills, Patricia. *Painting Harlem Modern: The Art of Jacob Lawrence*. Berkeley and Los Angeles: University of California Press, 2009.

Hitchcock, Henry-Russell, and Philip Johnson. *The International Style*. New York: Norton, 1995.

Hurlburt, Laurance P. *The Mexican Muralists in the United States*. Albuquerque: University of New Mexico Press, 1989.

Jaffé, Hans L. C. *De Stijl, 1917–1931: The Dutch Contribution to Modern Art*. Cambridge, Mass.: Belknap, 1986.

Krauss, Rosalind. *The Originality of the Avant-Garde and Other Modernist Myths*. Cambridge, Mass.: MIT Press, 1986.

Kuspit, Donald. *The Cult of the Avant-Garde Artist*. Cambridge: Cambridge University Press, 1993.

Lloyd, Jill. *German Expressionism: Primitivism and Modernity*. New Haven, Conn.: Yale University Press, 1991.

Lodder, Christina. *Russian Constructivism*. New Haven, Conn.: Yale University Press, 1983.

Lozano, Luis Martin, and Juan Coronel Rivera. *Diego Rivera: The Complete Murals*. Cologne: Taschen, 2008.

Martin, Marianne W. *Futurist Art and Theory*. Oxford: Clarendon, 1968.

Motherwell, Robert, ed. *The Dada Painters and Poets: An Anthology*. 2d ed. Boston: Hall, 1981.

Mundy, Jennifer. *Duchamp, Man Ray, Picabia*. London: Tate, 2008.

Orvell, Miles. *American Photography*. New York: Oxford University Press, 2003.

Peters, Olaf. *Otto Dix*. New York: Prestel, 2010.

Rhodes, Colin. *Primitivism and Modern Art*. New York: Thames & Hudson, 1994.

Richter, Hans. *Dada: Art and Anti-Art*. London: Thames & Hudson, 1961.

Rochfort, Desmond. *Mexican Muralists: Orozco, Rivera, Siqueiros*. San Francisco: Chronicle, 1998.

Rosenblum, Robert. *Cubism and Twentieth-Century Art*. Rev. ed. New York: Abrams, 1984.

Rubin, William S. *Dada and Surrealist Art*. New York: Abrams, 1968.

————, ed. *Pablo Picasso: A Retrospective*. New York: Museum of Modern Art; Boston: New York Graphic Society, 1980.

————. *"Primitivism" in 20th-Century Art: Affinity of the Tribal and the Modern*. 2 vols. New York: Museum of Modern Art, 1984.

Selz, Peter. *German Expressionist Painting*. Berkeley: University of California Press, 1974. Reprint of 1957 edition.

Silver, Kenneth E. *Esprit de Corps: The Art of the Parisian Avant-Garde and the First World War, 1914–1925*. Princeton, N.J.: Princeton University Press, 1989.

Smith, Terry. *Making the Modern: Industry, Art, and Design in America*. Chicago: University of Chicago Press, 1993.

Stott, William. *Documentary Expression and Thirties America*. New York: Oxford University Press, 1973.

Taylor, Joshua C. *Futurism*. New York: Museum of Modern Art, 1961.

Taylor, Michael R., ed. *Arshile Gorky: A Retrospective*. New Haven, Conn.: Yale University Press, 2009.

Terraroli, Valerio, ed. *Art of the Twentieth Century, 1900–1919: The Avant-Garde Movements*. Milan: Skira, 2006.

————. *Art of the Twentieth Century, 1920–1945: The Artistic Culture between the Wars*. Milan: Skira, 2006.

Tisdall, Caroline, and Angelo Bozzolla. *Futurism*. New York: Oxford University Press, 1978.

Trachtenberg, Alan. *Reading American Photographs: Images as History—Mathew Brady to Walker Evans*. New York: Hill and Wang, 1989.

Troyen, Carol, ed. *Edward Hopper*. Boston: Museum of Fine Arts, 2007.

Tsujimoto, Karen. *Images of America: Precisionist Painting and Modern Photography*. Seattle: University of Washington Press, 1982.

Tucker, William. *Early Modern Sculpture*. New York: Oxford University Press, 1974.

Vogt, Paul. *Expressionism: German Painting, 1905–1920*. New York: Abrams, 1980.

Weiss, Jeffrey S. *The Popular Culture of Modern Art: Picasso, Duchamp, and Avant-Gardism*. New Haven, Conn.: Yale University Press, 1994.

Whitford, Frank. *Bauhaus*. New York: Thames & Hudson, 1984.

Chapter 25: Modernism and Postmodernism in Europe and America, 1945 to 1980

Alloway, Lawrence. *American Pop Art*. New York: Whitney Museum of American Art; Macmillan, 1974.

————. *Topics in American Art since 1945*. New York: Norton, 1975.

Altshuler, Bruce. *Isamu Noguchi*. New York: Abbeville, 1994.

Anfam, David. *Abstract Expressionism*. New York: Thames & Hudson, 1990.

Archer, Michael. *Art since 1960*. New ed. New York: Thames & Hudson, 2002.

Ashton, Dore. *American Art since 1945*. New York: Oxford University Press, 1983.

————. *The New York School: A Cultural Reckoning*. Harmondsworth: Penguin, 1979.

Ballantyne, Andrew, ed. *Architectures: Modernism and After*. Malden, Mass: Blackwell, 2004.

Battcock, Gregory, ed. *Idea Art: A Critical Anthology*. New York: Dutton, 1973.

————. *Minimal Art: A Critical Anthology*. New York: Studio Vista, 1969.

————. *The New Art: A Critical Anthology*. New York: Dutton, 1973.

————. *New Artists Video: A Critical Anthology*. New York: Dutton, 1978.

Battcock, Gregory, and Robert Nickas, eds. *The Art of Performance: A Critical Anthology*. New York: Dutton, 1984.

Beardsley, John, and Jane Livingston. *Hispanic Art in the United States: Thirty Contemporary Painters and Sculptors*. Houston: Museum of Fine Arts; New York: Abbeville, 1987.

Beardsley, Richard. *Earthworks and Beyond: Contemporary Art in the Landscape*. New York: Abbeville, 1984.

Broude, Norma, and Mary D. Garrard. *The Power of Feminist Art: The American Movement of the 1970s, History and Impact*. New York: Abrams, 1994.

Bürger, Peter. *Theory of the Avant-Garde*. Minneapolis: University of Minnesota Press, 1984.

Butler, Cornelia H., ed. *WACK! Art and the Feminist Revolution*. Cambridge, Mass.: MIT Press, 2007.

Causey, Andrew. *Sculpture since 1945*. New York: Oxford University Press, 1998.

Caws, Mary Ann. *Robert Motherwell*. New York: Columbia University Press, 1996.

Cockcroft, Eva, John Weber, and James Cockcroft. *Toward a People's Art*. New York: Dutton, 1977.

Cohn, Marjorie, and Eliza Rathbone. *Mark Rothko*. Ostfildern: Hatje Cantz, 2001.

Crow, Thomas. *The Rise of the Sixties: American and European Art in the Era of Dissent*. New Haven, Conn.: Yale University Press, 2005.

Finch, Christopher. *Chuck Close: Work*. New York: Prestel, 2010.

Frascina, Francis, ed. *Pollock and After: The Critical Debate*. New York: Harper & Row, 1985.

Gale, Matthew, ed. *Francis Bacon*. New York: Rizzoli, 2009.

Gaugh, Harry F. *Franz Kline*. New York: Abbeville, 1994.

Geldzahler, Henry. *New York Painting and Sculpture, 1940–1970*. New York: Dutton, 1969.

Godfrey, Tony. *Conceptual Art*. London: Phaidon, 1998.

Goldberg, Rose Lee. *Performance Art: From Futurism to the Present*. Rev. ed. New York: Abrams, 1988.

Goldhagen, Sarah Williams, and Réjean Legault. *Anxious Modernisms: Experimentation in Postwar Architectural Culture*. Cambridge, Mass.: MIT Press, 2002.

Goodman, Cynthia. *Digital Visions: Computers and Art*. New York: Abrams, 1987.

Goodyear, Frank H., Jr. *Contemporary American Realism since 1960*. Boston: New York Graphic Society, 1981.

Gouma-Peterson, Thalia. *Miriam Schapiro: Shaping the Fragments of Art and Life*. New York: Abrams, 2000.

Green, Jonathan. *American Photography: A Critical History 1945 to the Present*. New York: Abrams, 1984.

Greenberg, Clement. *Clement Greenberg: The Collected Essays and Criticism*. Edited by J. O'Brien. 4 vols. Chicago: University of Chicago Press, 1986–1993.

Grundberg, Andy. *Photography and Art: Interactions since 1945*. New York: Abbeville, 1987.

Guilbaut, Serge. *How New York Stole the Idea of Modern Art*. Chicago: University of Chicago Press, 1983.

Hays, K. Michael, and Carol Burns, eds. *Thinking the Present: Recent American Architecture*. New York: Princeton Architectural, 1990.

Henri, Adrian. *Total Art: Environments, Happenings, and Performance*. New York: Oxford University Press, 1974.

Hobbs, Robert. *Lee Krasner*. New York: Abbeville, 1993.

Hoffman, Katherine. *Explorations: The Visual Arts since 1945*. New York: Harper Collins, 1991.

Hopkins, David. *After Modern Art, 1945–2000*. New York: Oxford University Press, 2000.

Hughes, Robert. *The Shock of the New*. New York: Knopf, 1981.

Hunter, Sam. *An American Renaissance: Painting and Sculpture since 1940*. New York: Abbeville, 1986.

Jacobs, Jane. *The Death and Life of Great American Cities*. New York: Random House, 1961.

Jacobus, John. *Twentieth-Century Architecture: The Middle Years, 1940–1964*. New York: Praeger, 1966.

Jencks, Charles. *The Language of Post-Modern Architecture*. 6th ed. New York: Rizzoli, 1991.

———. *What Is Post-Modernism?* 3d ed. London: Academy Editions, 1989.

Johnson, Ellen H., ed. *American Artists on Art from 1940 to 1980*. Boulder, Colo.: Westview, 1982.

Joselit, David. *American Art since 1945*. New York: Thames & Hudson, 2003.

Kaprow, Allan. *Assemblage, Environments, and Happenings*. New York: Abrams, 1966.

Kirby, Michael. *Happenings*. New York: Dutton, 1966.

Kotz, Mary Lynn. *Rauschenberg: Art and Life*. New York: Abrams, 2004.

Kramer, Hilton. *The Age of the Avant-Garde: An Art Chronicle of 1956–1972*. New York: Farrar, Straus & Giroux, 1973.

Leja, Michael. *Reframing Abstract Expressionism: Subjectivity and Painting in the 1940s*. New Haven, Conn.: Yale University Press, 1993.

Lippard, Lucy R. *Mixed Blessings: New Art in a Multicultural America*. New York: Pantheon, 1990.

———. *Pop Art*. New York: Praeger, 1966.

———, ed. *From the Center: Feminist Essays on Women's Art*. New York: Dutton, 1976.

———. *Six Years: The Dematerialization of the Art Object from 1966 to 1972*. New York: Praeger, 1973.

Livingston, Jane, ed. *The Paintings of Joan Mitchell*. New York: Whitney Museum of American Art, 2002.

Lovejoy, Margot. *Postmodern Currents: Art and Artists in the Age of the Electronic Media*. Ann Arbor, Mich.: UMI Research Press, 1989.

Lucie-Smith, Edward. *Art Now*. Edison, N.J.: Wellfleet, 1989.

———. *Movements in Art since 1945*. New ed. New York: Thames & Hudson, 2001.

Mamiya, Christin J. *Pop Art and Consumer Culture: American Super Market*. Austin: University of Texas Press, 1992.

Marder, Tod A. *The Critical Edge: Controversy in Recent American Architecture*. New Brunswick, N.J.: Rutgers University Press, 1980.

———. *An International Survey of Recent Painting and Sculpture*. New York: Museum of Modern Art, 1984.

Mercurio, Gianni. *Lichtenstein: Meditations on Art*. Milan: Skira, 2010.

Meyer, Ursula. *Conceptual Art*. New York: Dutton, 1972.

Mitchell, William J. *The Reconfigured Eye: Visual Truth in the Post-Photographic Era*. Cambridge, Mass.: MIT Press, 1992.

Morris, Francis, ed. *Louise Bourgeois*. New York: Rizzoli, 2008.

Polcari, Stephen. *Abstract Expressionism and the Modern Experience*. Cambridge: Cambridge University Press, 1991.

Popper, Frank. *Origins and Development of Kinetic Art*. Translated by Stephen Bann. Greenwich, Conn.: New York Graphic Society, 1968.

Price, Jonathan. *Video Visions: A Medium Discovers Itself*. New York: New American Library, 1977.

Reichardt, Jasia, ed. *Cybernetics, Art, and Ideas*. Greenwich, Conn.: New York Graphics Society, 1971.

Robbins, Corinne. *The Pluralist Era: American Art, 1968–1981*. New York: Harper & Row, 1984.

Rorimer, Anne. *New Art in the 60s and 70s: Redefining Reality*. New York: Thames & Hudson, 2001.

Rosen, Randy, and Catherine C. Brawer, eds. *Making Their Mark: Women Artists Move into the Mainstream, 1970–1985*. New York: Abbeville, 1989.

Rosenberg, Harold. *The Tradition of the New*. New York: Horizon, 1959.

Rush, Michael. *New Media in Art*. 2d ed. New York: Thames & Hudson, 2005.

Russell, John, and Suzi Gablik. *Pop Art Redefined*. New York: Praeger, 1969.

Sandford, Mariellen R., ed. *Happenings and Other Acts*. New York: Routledge, 1995.

Sandler, Irving. *Art of the Postmodern Era*. New York: Harper Collins, 1996.

———. *The Triumph of American Painting: A History of Abstract Expressionism*. New York: Praeger, 1970.

Sayre, Henry M. *The Object of Performance: The American Avant-Garde since 1970*. Chicago: University of Chicago Press, 1989.

Schneider, Ira, and Beryl Korot. *Video Art: An Anthology*. New York: Harcourt Brace Jovanovich, 1976.

Shapiro, David, and Cecile Shapiro. *Abstract Expressionism: A Critical Record*. New York: Cambridge University Press, 1990.

Shiff, Richard. *Barnett Newman: A Catalogue Raisonné*. New Haven, Conn.: Yale University Press, 2004.

Sims, Lowery Stokes. *Wifredo Lam and the International Avant-Garde, 1923–1982*. Austin, Tex.: University of Texas Press, 2002.

Smagula, Howard. *Currents: Contemporary Directions in the Visual Arts*. 2d ed. Upper Saddle River, N.J.: Prentice Hall, 1989.

Smee, Sebastian. *Lucian Freud: Beholding the Animal*. Cologne: Taschen, 2009.

Sonfist, Alan, ed. *Art in the Landscape: A Critical Anthology of Environmental Art*. New York: Dutton, 1983.

Sontag, Susan. *On Photography*. New York: Farrar, Straus & Giroux, 1973.

Stiles, Kristine, and Peter Selz. *Theories and Documents of Contemporary Art: A Sourcebook of Artists' Writings*. Berkeley and Los Angeles: University of California Press, 1996.

Taylor, Brendon. *Contemporary Art: Art since 1970*. Upper Saddle River, N.J.: Prentice Hall, 2005.

Terraroli, Valerio, ed. *Art of the Twentieth Century, 1946–1968: The Birth of Contemporary Art*. Milan: Skira, 2007.

Tuchman, Maurice. *American Sculpture of the Sixties*. Los Angeles: Los Angeles County Museum of Art, 1967.

Varnedoe, Kirk. *Pictures of Nothing: Abstract Art since Pollock*. Princeton: Princeton University Press, 2006.

Venturi, Robert. *Complexity and Contradiction in Architecture*. New York: Museum of Modern Art, 1966.

Venturi, Robert, Denise Scott-Brown, and Steven Isehour. *Learning from Las Vegas*. Cambridge, Mass.: MIT Press, 1972.

Waldman, Diane. *Collage, Assemblage, and the Found Object*. New York: Abrams, 1992.

Wallis, Brian, ed. *Art after Modernism: Rethinking Representation*. New York: New Museum of Contemporary Art in association with David R. Godine, 1984.

Wheeler, Daniel. *Art since Mid-Century: 1945 to the Present*. Upper Saddle River, N.J.: Prentice Hall, 1991.

Wood, Paul. *Modernism in Dispute: Art since the Forties*. New Haven, Conn.: Yale University Press, 1993.

Chapter 26: Contemporary Art Worldwide

Buchhart, Dieter, et al., *Jean-Michel Basquiat*. Ostfildern: Hatje Cantz, 2010.

Butler, Cornelia H., and Lisa Gabrielle Mark. *WACK!: Art and the Feminist Revolution*. Cambridge, Mass.: MIT Press, 2007.

Celent, Germano. *Anselm Kiefer*. Milan: Skira, 2007.

Chilvers, Ian, and John Glaves-Smith. *Oxford Dictionary of Modern and Contemporary Art*. 2d ed. New York: Oxford University Press, 2009.

Cook, Peter. *New Spirit in Architecture*. New York: Rizzoli, 1990.

Cummings, P. *Dictionary of Contemporary American Artists*. 6th ed. New York: St. Martin's, 1994.

Deepwell, K., ed. *New Feminist Art*. Manchester: Manchester University Press, 1994.

Enwezor, Okwui, and Chika Okeke-Agulu. *Contemporary African Art since 1980*. Bologna: Damiani, 2009.

Ferguson, Russell, ed. *Discourses: Conversations in Postmodern Art and Culture*. Cambridge, Mass.: MIT Press, 1990.

Fineberg, Jonathan. *Art since 1940: Strategies of Being.* 2d ed. Upper Saddle River, N.J.: Prentice Hall, 2000.

Galassi, Peter. *Andreas Gursky.* New York: Museum of Modern Art, 2001.

Ghirardo, Diane. *Architecture after Modernism.* New York: Thames & Hudson, 1996.

Goldsworthy, Andy. *Andy Goldsworthy: A Collaboration with Nature.* New York: Abrams, 1990.

Heartney, Eleanor, Helaine Posner, Nancy Princenthal, and Sue Scott. *After the Revolution: Women Who Transformed Contemporary Art.* New York: Prestel, 2007.

Hertz, Richard, ed. *Theories of Contemporary Art.* 2d ed. Upper Saddle River, N.J.: Prentice Hall, 1993.

Hopkins, David. *After Modern Art, 1945–2000.* New York: Oxford University Press, 2000.

Jencks, Charles. *The New Paradigm in Architecture: The Language of Post-Modernism.* New Haven, Conn.: Yale University Press, 2002.

Jodidio, Philip. *100 Contemporary Architects.* Cologne: Taschen, 2008.

Kasfir, Sidney Littlefield. *Contemporary African Art.* New York: Thames & Hudson, 1999.

Kolossa, Alexandra. *Keith Haring 1958–1990: A Life for Art.* Cologne: Taschen, 2009.

Kotz, Mary Lunn. *Rauschenberg: Art and Life.* New York: Abrams, 2004.

Lippard, Lucy R. *Mixed Blessings: New Art in a Multicultural America.* New York: Pantheon, 1990.

Mullins, Charlotte. *Painting People: Figure Painting Today.* New York: Thames & Hudson, 2008.

Nesbitt, Judith, ed. *Chris Ofili.* London: Tate, 2010.

Norris, Christopher, and Andrew Benjamin. *What Is Deconstruction?* New York: St. Martin's, 1988.

Paul, Christiane. *Digital Art.* 2d ed. New York: Thames & Hudson, 2008.

Pauli, Lori, ed. *Manufactured Landscapes: The Photographs of Edward Burtynsky.* New Haven, Conn.: Yale University Press, 2003.

Perry, Gill, and Paul Wood. *Themes in Contemporary Art.* New Haven, Conn.: Yale University Press, 2004.

Raskin, David. *Donald Judd.* New Haven, Conn.: Yale University Press, 2010.

Risatti, Howard, ed. *Postmodern Perspectives: Issues in Contemporary Art.* Upper Saddle River, N.J.: Prentice Hall, 1990.

Sandler, Irving. *Art of the Postmodern Era.* New York: Harper Collins, 1996.

Smith, Terry. *What Is Contemporary Art?* Chicago: University of Chicago Press, 2009.

Sollins, Susan, ed. *Art: 21 (Art in the Twenty-first Century).* 5 vols. New York: Abrams, 2001–2009.

Stiles, Kristine, and Peter Selz. *Theories and Documents of Contemporary Art: A Sourcebook of Artists' Writings.* Berkeley and Los Angeles: University of California Press, 1996.

Taylor, Brendon. *Contemporary Art: Art since 1970.* Upper Saddle River, N.J.: Prentice Hall, 2005.

Terraroli, Valerio, ed. *Art of the Twentieth Century, 1969–1999: Neo-avant-gardes, Postmodern and Global Art.* Milan: Skira, 2009.

Wands, Bruce. *Art of the Digital Age.* New York: Thames & Hudson, 2007.

Warren, Lynne. *Jeff Koons.* New Haven, Conn.: Yale University Press, 2008.

Wines, James. *Green Architecture.* Cologne: Taschen, 2008.

CREDITS

Vatican Museums; **17-18A:** Vatican Museums and Galleries, Vatican City, Italy/The Bridgeman Art Library International; **17-18B_1:** Vatican Museums and Galleries, Vatican City, Italy/The Bridgeman Art Library International; **17-19:** akg-images/Electa; **17-20:** © Erich Lessing/Art Resource, NY; **17-21:** © Scala/Art Resource, NY; **17-22:** © Cengage Learning; **17-23:** © The Trustees of the British Museum/Art Resource, NY; **17-24:** © Cengage Learning; **17-25:** © Guido Alberto Rossi/Photolibrary; **17-26:** © Alinari Archives/Corbis; **17-26A:** © Guido Alberto Rossi/Photolibrary; **17-27:** © Alinari Archives/Corbis; **17-28:** © Mark Edward Smith/Photolibrary; **17-29:** © Cengage Learning; **17-30:** © 2010 Fred Kleiner; **17-30A:** © Scala/Art Resource, NY; **17-31:** © John Heseltine/Corbis; **17-31A:** © The Frick Collection, NY. 1915.1.3; **17-32:** © Scala/Art Resource, NY; **17-33:** © 1999 Board of Trustees, National Gallery of Art, Washington, D.C.; **17-34:** © Cameraphoto Arte, Venice/Art Resource, NY; **17-35:** © Erich Lessing/Art Resource, NY; **17-36:** © Scala/Art Resource, NY; **17-37:** © Scala/Art Resource, NY; **17-38:** © Erich Lessing/Art Resource, NY; **17-39:** © Scala/Ministero per i Beni e le Attività culturali/Art Resource, NY; **17-40:** © Erich Lessing/Art Resource, NY; **17-40A:** Photograph © 2011 National Museum of Women in the Arts; **17-41:** © Scala/Art Resource, NY; **17-42:** © Scala/Art Resource, NY; **17-42A:** The Art Archive/Pinacoteca Nazionale di Siena/Alfredo Dagli Orti/Picture Desk; **17-43:** © Erich Lessing/Art Resource, NY; **17-44:** © Scala/Art Resource, NY; **17-45:** Nå-tional Gallery, London; **17-46A:** Image copyright © The Metropolitan Museum of Art/Art Resource, NY; **17-46:** The Bridgeman Art Library International; **17-47:** The Bridgeman Art Library International; **17-48:** © Scala/Art Resource, NY; **17-49:** © Scala/Art Resource, NY; **17-50:** Canali Photobank, Italy; **17-51:** © Alinari/Art Resource, NY; **17-52:** © Erich Lessing/Art Resource, NY; **17-52A:** © Lauros/Giraudon/The Bridgeman Art Library; **17-53:** © 206 Fred S. Kleiner; **17-54:** Superstock/Photolibrary; **17-54A:** © Scala/Art Resource, NY; **17-55:** © Jonathan Poore/Cengage Learning; **17-56:** The Art Archive/Gianni Dagli Orti/Picture Desk; **17-57:** © Cengage Learning; **UNF 17-01:** © Arte & Immagini srl/Corbis; **UNF 17-2:** © Scala/Art Resource, NY; **UNF 17-3:** © Erich Lessing/Art Resource, NY; **UNF 17-4:** © Scala/Art Resource, NY; **UNF 17-5:** © Erich Lessing/Art Resource, NY.

Chapter 18—Opener: © Institut Amatller D'art Hispànic; (all details) akg-images/Electa; **timeline:** © Institut Amatller D'art Hispànic; **18-2:** © Musée Unterlinden, Colmar Musée Unterlinden, Colmar Inv. 88.RP.139; **18-3:** © The Trustees of the British Museum/Art Resource, NY; **18-3A:** © Erich Lessing/Art Resource, NY; **18-4:** akg-images; **18-4A:** © Graphische Sammlung Albertina, Vienna, Austria/The Bridgeman Art Library; **18-5:** Photograph © 2011 Museum of Fine Arts, Boston; **18-5A:** © The Trustees of The British Museum/Art Resource, NY; **18-6:** © Victoria & Albert Museum, London/Art Resource, NY; **18-7a:** Bildarchiv Preussischer Kulturbesitz/Art Resource, NY; **18-7b:** Bildarchiv Preussischer Kulturbesitz/Art Resource, NY; **18-8:** © The Trustees of The British Museum; **18-9:** Staatliche Kunsthalle, Karlsruhe.; **18-10:** © Bildarchiv Preussischer Kulturbesitz/Art Resource, NY; **18-11:** © National Gallery, London/Art Resource, NY; **18-11A:** © Scala/Art Resource, NY; **18-12:** © Réunion des Musées Nationaux/Art Resource, NY; **18-13:** © Jonathan Poore/Cengage Learning; **18-14:** © Jonathan Poore/Cengage Learning; **18-14A:** © 209 Fred. S. Kleiner; **18-15:** © Bildarchiv Preussischer Kulturbesitz/Art Resource, NY; **18-15A:** © Erich Lessing/Art Resource, NY; **18-16:** © Réunion des Musées Nationaux/Art Resource, NY; **18-17:** Uppsala University Art Collection; **18-18:** Oeffentliche Kunstsammlung Basel, photo Martin Bühler; **18-19:** The Royal Collection © 2011 Her Majesty Queen Elizabeth II; **18-20:** © Erich Lessing/Art Resource, NY; **18-21:** © Bildarchiv Preussischer Kulturbesitz/Art Resource, NY; **18-22:** Kunsthistorisches Museum, Vienna; **18-22A:** © Scala/Art Resource, NY; **18-23:** © Institut Amatller D'art Hispànic; **18-23A:** © John Elk III; **18-24:** © Adam Woolfitt/Photolibrary; **18-25:** © Scala/Art Resource, NY; **18-26:** © The Metropolitan Museum of Art/Art Resource, NY; **UNF 18-01:** Photograph © 2011 Museum of Fine Arts, Boston; **UNF 18-2:** © National Gallery, London/Art Resource, Ny; **UNF 18-3:** © Réunion des Musées Nationaux/Art Resource, NY; **UNF 18-4:** Kunsthistorisches Museum, Vienna; **UNF 18-5:** © Institut Amatller D'art Hispànic.

Chapter 19—Opener: The Art Archive/Gianni Dagli Orti/Picture Desk; **(detail 1):** © Massimo Listri/Corbis; **(detail 2):** © 2011 Fred Kleiner; **(detail 3):** © Vanni/Art Resource, NY; **(detail 4):** akg-images/Gerard Degeorge; **timeline** © Vanni/Art Resource, NY; **19-2:** akg-images/Pirozzi; **19-3:** © Andrea Jemolo/Corbis; **19-4:** © Cuboimages/Photolibrary; **19-4A:** Canali Photobank, Italy; **19-5:** akg-images/Joseph Martin; **Map 19-1:** © Cengage Learning; **19-6:** © Scala/Art Resource, NY; **19-6A:** © Araldo de Luca/Corbis; **19-7:** © Araldo de Luca; **19-8:** akg-images/Pirozzi; **19-9:** © Scala/Art Resource, NY; **19-9A:** © Scala/Art Resource, NY; **19-11:** © Bednorz-Images; **19-12:** © Raimund Kutter/Photolibrary; **19-13:** © Cengage Learning; **19-14A:** © Alinari/The Bridgeman Art Library; **19-14:** © Scala/Ministero per i Beni e le Attività culturali/Art Resource, NY; **19-15:** © Alinari/Art Resource, NY; **19-16:** © Scala/Art Resource, NY; **19-17:** © Scala/Art Resource, NY; **19-17A:** Image copyright © The Metropolitan Museum of Art/Art Resource, NY; **19-18A:** © Scala/Art Resource, NY; **19-18:** © Scala/Art Resource, NY; **19-19:** © Alinari/Art Resource, NY; **19-20:** The Royal Collection © 2011 Her Majesty Queen Elizabeth II; **19-21:** Nimatallah/Art Resource, NY; **19-22:** © The Bridgeman Art Library International; **19-23:** © Scala/Art Resource, NY; **19-24:** Summerfield Press Ltd.; **19-25:** © Erich Lessing/Art Resource, NY; **19-25A:** © Erich Lessing/Art Resource, NY; **19-26:** © Erich Lessing/Art Resource, NY; **19-27:** © Wadsworth Atheneum Museum of Art/Art Resource, NY; **19-28:** © Victoria & Albert Museum, London/Art Resource, NY; **19-28A:** © Scala/Art Resource, NY; **19-28B:** © 2011 The Frick Collection, NY; **19-29:** © Scala/Art Resource, NY; **19-30:** © Erich Lessing/Art Resource, NY; **UNF 19-01:** © Bednorz-Images; **UNF 19-2:** © Araldo de Luca; **UNF 19-3:** © Jonathan Poore/Cengage Learning; **UNF 19-4:** Summerfield Press Ltd.; **UNF 19-5:** © Erich Lessing/Art Resource, NY.

Chapter 20—Opener: akg-images; **timeline:** akg-images; **20-01A:** © Erich Lessing/Art Resource, NY; **20-2:** IRPA-KIK, Brussels, www.kikirpa.be; **20-2A:** © Erich Lessing/Art Resource, NY; **20-3:** © Erich Lessing/Art Resource, NY; **20-4:** © Scala/Art Resource, NY; **20-5:** © Réunion des Musées Nationaux/Art Resource, NY; **20-6:** © Scala/Art Resource, NY; **20-7:** Centraal Museum, Utrecht, photo Ernst Moritz, The Hague; **20-8:** © Alinari/The Bridgeman Art Library; **20-9:** Frans Halsmuseum, Haarlem; **20-10:** Frans Halsmuseum, Haarlem; **20-11:** National Gallery of Art; **20-12:** © Erich Lessing/Art Resource, NY; **20-13:** © The Bridgeman Art Library; **20-13A:** akg-images; **20-14:** © The Bridgeman Art Library; **20-15:** © English Heritage Photo Library/The Bridgeman Art Library International; **20-15A:** © 2011 The Frick Collection, NY. 196.1.97; **20-16:** © The Pierpont Morgan Library/Art Resource, NY; **20-17:** © National Gallery, London/Art Resource, NY; **20-18:** Mauritshuis, The Hague; **20-18A:** © Erich Lessing/Art Resource, NY; **20-18B:** © Giraudon/The Bridgeman Art Library; **20-19:** National Gallery of Art; **20-20:** © Erich Lessing/Art Resource, NY; **20-20A:** akg-images; **20-21:** Rijksmuseum, Amsterdam; **20-22:** The Bridgeman Art Library International; **20-23:** The Toledo Museum of Art, OH. Purchased with funds from the Libbey Endowment, Gift of Edward Drummond Libbey, 1956.57; **20-24:** © Réunion des Musées Nationaux/Art Resource, NY; **20-25:** © Jonathan Poore/Cengage Learning; **20-26:** © Yann Arthus-Bertrand/Altitude; **20-27:** © Massimo Listri/Corbis; **20-28:** g Bernard Annebicque/CORBIS SYGMA; **20-29:** akg-images/Paul M. R. Maeyaert; **20-30:** © Jonathan Poore/Cengage Learning; **20-31:** © Erich Lessing/Art Resource, NY; **20-32:** Photograph: The Art Institute of Chicago.; **20-32A:** © Scala/Art Resource, NY; **20-33:** Photo copyright © Philadelphia Museum of Art, E1950-2-1; **20-34:** © Réunion des Musées Nationaux/Art Resource, NY; **20-35:** © Erich Lessing/Art Resource, NY; **20-36:** © Erich Lessing/Art Resource, NY; **20-37:** © Angelo Hornak/CORBIS; **20-38:** © Angelo Hornak/CORBIS; **UNF 20-01:** © Scala/Art Resource, NY; **UNF 20-2:** © The Pierpont Morgan Library/Art Resource, NY; **UNF 20-3:** National Gallery of Art; **UNF 20-4:** © Erich Lessing/Art Resource, NY; **UNF 20-5:** © Angelo Hornak/CORBIS.

Chapter 21—Opener: © Bridgeman-Giraudon/Art Resource, NY; **21-01A:** © Jason Hawkes/Terra/Corbis; **Map 21-1:** © Cengage Learning; **timeline:** © Bridgeman-Giraudon/Art Resource, NY; **21-2:** akg-images/Bildarchiv Monheim; **21-3:** © Erich Lessing/Art Resource, NY; **21-3A:** Hervé Champollion/akg-images; **21-4:** © Erich Lessing/Art Resource, NY; **21-5A:** akg-images/Bildarchiv Monheim; **21-5B:** © Erich Lessing/Art Resource, NY; **21-6:** The Art Archive/Musée du Louvre Paris/Gianni Dagli Orti; **21-7:** © Scala/Art Resource, NY; **21-7A:** © Bildarchiv Preussischer Kulturbesitz/Art Resource, NY; **21-8:** By kind permission of the Trustees of the Wallace Collection, London.; **21-9:** © Wallace Collection, London, UK/The Bridgeman Art Library; **21-10:** © Scala/Ministero per i Beni e le Attività culturali/Art Resource, NY; **21-11:** Image copyright © The Metropolitan Museum of Art/Art Resource, NY; **21-11A:** © National Gallery, London/Art Resource, NY; **21-12:** The Art Archive/John Meek/Picture Desk; **21-13:** © Réunion des Musées Nationaux/Art Resource, NY; **21-14:** The Art Archive/Musée du Louvre Paris/Gianni Dagli Orti; **21-15:** Summerfield Press, Ltd; **21-15A:** © Erich Lessing/Art Resource, NY; **21-16:** Image copyright © The Metropolitan Museum of Art/Art Resource, NY; **21-17:** National Gallery, London; **21-18:** The National Gallery of Art; **21-19:** © National Gallery, London, UK/The Bridgeman Art Library; **21-20:** National Gallery of Canada; **21-21:** Photograph © 2011 Museum of Fine Arts, Boston, 30.781; **21-22:** © Scala/Art Resource, NY; **21-23:** © Peter Aprahamian/CORBIS; **21-23A:** Electa/akg-images; **21-24:** Photo: Katherine Wetzel © Virginia Museum of Fine Arts; **21-25:** © Réunion des Musées Nationaux/Art Resource, NY; **21-26:** © Scala/Art Resource, NY; **21-27:** © Jonathan Poore/Cengage Learning; **21-27A:** akg-images/Bildarchiv Monheim; **21-28:** © Eric Crichton/Encyclopedia/Corbis; **21-28A:** akg/Bildarchiv Monheim; **21-29:** © ART on FILE/Corbis Art/Corbis; **21-30:** Thomas Jefferson Foundation; **21-31:** © Michael Freeman/Value Art/Corbis; **21-32:** Photo © The Library of Virginia; **21-33:** © Smithsonian American Art Museum, Washington, DC/Art Resource, NY; **UNF 21-01:** akg-images/Bildarchiv Monheim; **UNF 21-2:** © Bridgeman-Giraudon/Art Resource, NY; **UNF 21-3:** © Scala/Art Resource, NY; **UNF 21-4:** Photo: Katherine Wetzel © Virginia Museum of Fine Arts; **UNF 21-5:** © Jonathan Poore/Cengage Learning.

Chapter 22—Opener: © Réunion des Musées Nationaux/Art Resource, NY; **timeline:** © Réunion des Musées Nationaux/Art Resource, NY; **22-01A:** © Erich Lessing/Art Resource, NY; **22-2:** © Réunion des Musées Nationaux/Art Resource, NY; **22-2A:** © Erich Lessing/Art Resource, NY; **22-3:** © Jonathan Poore/Cengage Learning; **22-4:** © Scala/Ministero per i Beni e le Attività culturali/Art Resource, NY; **22-4A:** © Réunion des Musées Nationaux/Art Resource, NY; **22-5:** © Réunion des Musées Nationaux/Art Resource, NY; **22-5A:** © Réunion des Musées Nationaux/Art Resource, NY; **22-6:** © Réunion des Musées Nationaux/Art Resource, NY; **22-7:** © Réunion des Musées Nationaux/Art Resource, NY; **22-8:** © The Bridgeman Art Library International; **22-9:** © The Pierpont Morgan Library/Art Resource, NY; **22-10:** Image copyright © The Metropolitan Museum of Art/Art Resource, NY; **22-10A:** © Erich Lessing/Art Resource, NY; **22-11:** The Art Archive/Museo del Prado Madrid/Gianni Dagli Orti/Picture Desk; **22-12:** © Erich Lessing/Art Resource, NY; **22-13:** © Erich Lessing/Art Resource, NY; **22-13A:** © Réunion des Musées Nationaux/Art Resource, NY; **22-14:** © Giraudon/Art Resource, NY; **22-15:** © Réunion des Musées Nationaux/Art Resource, NY; **22-15A:** © Erich Lessing/Art Resource, NY; **22-16:** © Réunion des Musées Nationaux/Art Resource, NY; **22-17A:** © Erich Lessing/Art Resource, NY; **22-17:** The Art Archive/Musée d'Orsay Paris/Gianni Dagli Orti/Picture Desk; **22-18:** © Jonathan Poore/Cengage Learning; **22-19:** © Bildarchiv Preussischer Kulturbesitz/Art Resource, NY; **22-20:** © Bildarchiv Preussischer Kulturbesitz/Art Resource, NY; **22-21:** © National Gallery, London/Art Resource, NY; **22-22:** Photograph © 2011 Museum of Fine Arts, Boston, 99.22; **22-23:** Image copyright © The Metropolitan Museum of Art/Art Resource, NY; **22-24:** © Smithsonian American Art Museum, Washington, DC/Art Resource, NY; **22-25:** Photo copyright © The Cleveland Museum of Art; **22-26:** © Staatliche Kunstsammlungen Dresden/The Bridgeman Art Library; **22-27:** © Erich

MUSEUM INDEX

Note: *Figure numbers in* blue *indicate bonus images.*

SUBJECT INDEX

In Praise of Folly (Erasmus), 535
incising, 444
incubus, 650
Independent Group, 787, 801
India. See South Asian art
L'Indifférent (Watteau), 620–621, 620
indulgences, 504, 540
Industrial Revolution, 616
    and Art Nouveau, 23.36A
    and Arts and Crafts movement, 715
    and the Enlightenment, 615, 624–625
    and German Expressionism, 727
    and Impressionist art, 687, 694
    and late 19th century art European and
        American art, 687, 688, 694, 715
    and Napoleonic era art, 645
    and Neo-Gothic architecture, 676
    and Pre-Raphaelite art, 674
    and Realism, 667
    and Romanticism, 659–660
    and social Darwinism, 689
Inferno (Dante), 712
ingegno, 492
Inghelbrecht, Peter, 422, 423
Ingram Street Tea Room, Glasgow, 716, 716
Ingres, Jean-Auguste-Dominique, 654, 679,
    23.26A, 24.2A, 24.22A
    Apotheosis of Homer, 648, 649
    Grande Odalisque, 649, 649
    Napoleon on His Imperial Throne, 646,
        22.2A
Innocent III (Pope), 472
Innocent X (Pope), 557, 558
Insane Woman (Géricault), 654, 654
installations, 838–839, 841, 844–845,
    858–859, 860, 25.25B
intaglio, 444
intensity, 7
internal evidence, 3
International Style (medieval Europe),
    413–414, 460, 461, 469
International style (Modernist architecture),
    774–775
The Interpretation of Dreams (Freud), 707,
    744
intonaco, 408
invenzione, 492
investiture of Zimri-Lim, palace, Mari
    (mural), 43
Ionic order, xxvi, xxvi, 475, 17.30A
iron. See cast iron; wrought iron
iron bridge, Coalbrookdale (Darby and
    Pritchard), 625, 625
Isaac. See Abraham and Isaac
Isaac and His Sons, Gates of Paradise,
    Baptistery of San Giovanni, Florence
    (Ghiberti), 454–455, 455
Isabella (queen of Castile), 506
Isabella d'Este (Titian), 518, 518, 519, 17.40A
Isabella Stewart Gardner Museum, Boston,
    753
Isenheim (Germany), Hospital of Saint
    Anthony, 535, 536
Isenheim Altarpiece (Grünewald), 535, 536,
    762
Isidorus of Miletus, Hagia Sophia
    (Constantinople), xxxii, 814
Islam. See Islamic art; Ottoman Empire
Islamic art, 552, 677, 717
Istanbul. See Constantinople
Italian 13th century art, 3–4, 402–406, 421,
    14.6A
Italian 14th century art, 406–420, 421,
    14.7A, 14.8A, 14.8B, 14.10A, 14.12A,
    14.16A, 14.18A, 14.18B, 14.19A
Italian Baroque art, 558–574, 561map, 581
    architecture, 556, 557, 558–561, 564–566,
        19.4A, 19.9A, 19.14A
    and late 19th century art European and
        American sculpture, 23.31A
    painting. See Italian Baroque painting
    Rembrandt and, 20.13A
    sculpture, 561, 562–563, 19.6A
    timeline, 558
Italian Baroque painting
    Caravaggio, 569–571, 19.17A, 19.18A
    Carracci, 567–569, 570
    Gaulli, 574

Gentileschi, 571–572
    Pietro da Cortona, 573–574
    Pozzo, 574, 575
    Reni, 572–573
Italian Cinquecento Renaissance art,
    488–520, 488map, 531
    Andrea del Sarto, 17.8A
    architecture, 493, 506–512, 17.6A,
        17.26A, 17.30A
    and David, 635
    and Dürer, 537, 18.5A
    and Flemish Baroque art, 586
    Leonardo da Vinci, 489–493, 17.3A, 17.6A
    Michelangelo Buonarroti, 11, 486, 487,
        497–506, 507–509, 636, 643, 17.18A,
        17.18B, 17.26A
    painting. See Italian Cinquecento
        Renaissance painting
    Raphael, 493–497, 17.10A
    and Rococo architecture, 21.1A
    societal contexts, 488, 510
    timeline, 488
Italian Cinquecento Renaissance painting
    Andrea del Sarto, 17.8A
    Bellini, 512–513, 17.32A
    Giorgione, 514–515
    Leonardo da Vinci, 489–490, 491–492
    Michelangelo Buonarroti, 486, 487,
        502–504, 642, 643, 17.18A, 17.18B
    Raphael, 493–497, 17.10A
    Titian, 515–517, 518, 519–520
Italian late medieval art, 400–421, 405map
    13th century, 402–406, 421, 14.6A
    14th century. See Italian 14th century art
    societal contexts, 404, 406–407
    timeline, 402
    See also Renaissance
Italian Mannerism, 488map, 520–530, 531
    architecture, 528–530
    and El Greco, 553
    and Francis I, 545
    and Goujon, 18.14A
    and Napoleonic era art, 649
    painting, 520–526, 16.42A, 16.46A,
        16.54A
    sculpture, 526–527, 16.52A
    timeline, 488
Italian Quattrocento Renaissance art,
    446–485
    Florence, 448–476, 449map, 485
        architecture, 470–476, 481–482,
            16.31A, 16.32A, 16.37A
        engraving, 469–470
        painting. See Florentine Quattrocento
            Renaissance painting
        sculpture. See Florentine
            Quattrocento Renaissance sculpture
    princely courts, 477–484, 485, 16.41A,
        16.43A, 16.49A
    societal contextss, 448, 449, 451, 472, 476
    timeline, 448
    Venice, 16.37A

J

Jack in the Pulpit No. 4 (O'Keeffe), 4, 4, 757,
    758
Jackson Pollock painting in his studio in
    Springs, Long Island, New York
    (Namuth), 792
Jacob, Max, 24.19A
Jacob Wrestling with the Angel (Vision after
    the Sermon) (Gauguin), 703–705, 703
Jacobs, Jane, 817
Jacobus de Voragine, 16.12A, 16.24A
Jacopo della Quercia, 498
jambs, xxxi, 20.2A
James I (king of England), 611
James, Saint, 16.49A
Jan van Haeght, 15.11A
Jane Avril (Toulouse-Lautrec), 23.15A
Janis, Sidney, 793
Japanese art, 8–9, 696, 697, 699, 705, 717,
    801, 844–845, 23.15A, 23.16B, 23.27A,
    25.21A
Japonaiserie: Flowering Plum Tree (van
    Gogh), 23.16B
Japonisme, 696, 697, 23.16B
jazz, 755, 835

Jean d'Orbais, Reims Cathedral, 402, 418,
    451
Jean de Boulogne. See Giovanni da Bologna
Jean de Loup, Reims Cathedral, 402, 418,
    451
Jean-Baptiste Belley (Girodet-Trioson), 648,
    22.5A
Jeanne-Claude, Surrounded Islands,
    Biscayne Bay, Miami, Florida,
    1980–1983, 856, 856
Jeanneret, Charles-Edouard. See Le
    Corbusier
Jefferson City (Missouri), State Capitol, 778,
    779
Jefferson, Thomas, 624
    Monticello, near Charlottesville, 638, 639
    Rotunda, University of Virginia, 639, 639
    U.S. Capitol, Washington, D.C., 638–639
Jerome, Saint, 512, 520, 550
Jerusalem, 14.10A
Jesuit order (Society of Jesus), 529–530, 574
Jesus, life of, xxxiv–xxxv, 411
    See also Christ; Passion of Christ; specific
        events
jewelry. See luxury arts; metalwork
Jewish Cemetery (Ruisdael), 598, 20.18A
Joe, Paa, airplane and cow coffins, 848, 848
John the Baptist, Saint, xxxiv, 428, 489–490,
    708, 15.8A, 16.43A
John the Evangelist, Saint, xxxv, 409, 428,
    432, 540, 608, 16.43A
Johns, Jasper, 801–802, 854
    Three Flags, 802, 802
Johnson, Charles Spurgeon, 755
Johnson, James Weldon, 755
Johnson, Philip, 818
    Seagram Building, New York, 718, 816,
        816, 849
    Sony Building (AT&T Building), New
        York, 818–819, 818, 849
Jones, Inigo, Banqueting House, Whitehall,
    London, 611–612, 611
Joseph I (emperor of Austria), 21.3A
Joseph of Arimathea, xxxv, 432
Joseph, Saint, 520, 493
Josephine (empress of France), 645
The Joy of Life (Le Bonheur de Vivre)
    (Matisse), 732, 24.2A, 24.4A
The Joyous Science (Nietzsche), 761
Judas Iscariot. See Betrayal of Jesus
Judd, Donald, 799, 850
    Untitled, 799, 799
Judgment Day. See Last Judgment
Judgment of Paris (Cranach), 542, 542
Judith Slaying Holofernes (Gentileschi), 571,
    571, 20.13A
Jugendstil. See Art Nouveau
Julius II (Pope), 487, 493, 499–500, 502, 507,
    510, 17.18A
Jung, Carl, 744, 763, 768
The Jungle (Lam), 24.59A
Junius Bassus sarcophagus, xxxv
Juno. See Hera
Juno (Rembrandt), 20.15A
Jupiter. See Zeus
Jupiter and Semele (Moreau), 23.24A
Just What Is It That Makes Today's Homes
    So Different, So Appealing? (Hamilton),
    786, 787
Justice of Otto III (Bouts), 435, 15.11A
Juvara, Filippo, dome, Sant'Andrea, 482

K

Kahlo, Frida, The Two Fridas, 781, 781
Kahnweiler, Daniel, 732
Kaisersaal (Imperial Hall), Residenz
    (Episcopal Palace), Würzburg
    (Neumann, Bossi, and Tiepolo), 619,
    21.5A
Kalf, Willem, 589
    Still Life with a Late Ming Ginger Jar, 601,
    601
Kallikrates
    Parthenon, Athens, 476, 490–491, 668
Kandinsky, Vassily, 751, 765, 768, 792,
    24.66A
    Concerning the Spiritual in Art, 729
    Improvisation 28, 729–730, 729

Kaprow, Allan, 25.25B
    18 Happenings in Six Parts, 823
Karlskirche (Church of Saint Charles
    Borromaeus), Vienna (Fischer von
    Erlach), 619, 21.3A
Käsebier, Gertrude, Blessed Art Thou among
    Women, 712, 712
Kauffmann, Angelica, Cornelia Presenting
    Her Children as Her Treasures (Mother
    of the Gracchi), 634–635, 634
Kaufmann House (Fallingwater), Bear Run
    (Wright), 784, 784
Keats, John, 655
Kedleston House, Derbyshire (Adam), 633
Kelly, Ellsworth, 797
    Red Blue Green, 795, 795
Kent, William, Chiswick House, near
    London, 637, 637, 638
keystones, xxviii
Kiefer, Anselm, Nigredo, 842–843, 843
Kierkegaard, Søren, 789
kinetic sculpture, 743
king on horseback with attendants, Benin
    (bronze sculpture), xxxvi, 11, 12
King Philip IV of Spain (Fraga Philip)
    (Velázquez), 577, 19.28B
Kirchner, Ernst Ludwig, 751, 765
    Chronik der Brücke, 727
    Street, Dresden, 728, 728
The Kiss (Klimt), 711, 711
Kitchen Table series (Weems), 26.6B
Kiyonaga, Torii, Two Women at the Bath,
    696, 696
Klee, Paul, 765
    Twittering Machine, 768, 768, 824
Klimt, Gustav, 731
    The Kiss, 711, 711
Kline, Franz, 793, 25.8C
    Mahoning, 25.8A
Klüver, Billy, 824
Kngwarreye, Emily Kame, 844
    Untitled, 26.22B
Knidos (Greece), Aphrodite of Knidos
    (Praxiteles), 469
Knight, Death, and the Devil (Dürer),
    18.5A
Koberger, Anton, Nuremberg Chronicle,
    442–443, 443
Kollwitz, Käthe, 722
    Woman with Dead Child, 730, 731
Koons, Jeff, 846–847
    Pink Panther, 846, 847
Korean art, 26.22A
Korin, Waves at Matsushima, 8–9, 9
Kosuth, Joseph, One and Three Chairs,
    824–825, 824
Kouros (Noguchi), 25.21A
Krafft-Ebing, Richard von, 765
Kraków (Poland), Saint Mary, 442, 442
Kramer, Hilton, 26.27A
Krasner, Lee, 792, 25.8C
    The Seasons, 25.7A
Der Krieg (Dix), 762, 762
Kritios Boy, Athens (sculpture), 452
Kronos (Saturn) (Greek/Roman deity), 652,
    653
Kruger, Barbara, 832, 834, 26.6A
    Untitled (Your Gaze Hits the Side of My
        Face), 830–831, 831
Krul, Jan Harmensz, 20.20A
Kuhn, Walt, 751
Kwei, Kane, 847–848

L

L.H.O.O.Q. (Duchamp), 744, 745, 24.27A
La Fosse, Charles de, dome, Église du Dôme
    (Church of the Invalides), Paris
    (Hardouin-Mansart), 606
La Madeleine, Paris (Vignon), 646, 647
La Tour, Georges de, Adoration of the
    Shepherds, 610–611, 611
La Zecca. See Mint, Piazza San Marco,
    Venice
Labille-Guiard, Adélaïde, Self-Portrait with
    Two Pupils, 628, 628
Labrouste, Henri, 718
    Bibliothèque Sainte-Geneviève, Paris,
        678–679, 678